Handbook of

SEVENTH-DAY ADVENTIST

THEOLOGY

COMMENTARY
REFERENCE
SERIES

Volume 12

Handbook of

SEVENTH-DAY ADVENTIST

THEOLOGY

REVIEW AND HERALD® PUBLISHING ASSOCIATION
HAGERSTOWN, MD 21740

Editors

Editor
RAOUL DEDEREN

Editorial Assistant
NANCY J. VYHMEISTER

General Editor
GEORGE W. REID

Associate Editors
FRANK B. HOLBROOK

HERBERT KIESLER

EKKEHARDT MÜLLER

GERHARD PFANDL

WILLIAM H. SHEA

ANGEL MANUEL RODRÍGUEZ

Biblical Research Institute Committee

v

Contributors

Niels-Erik Andreasen	Professor of Old Testament, President of Andrews University
Ivan T. Blazen	Professor of New Testament, Loma Linda University
Charles E. Bradford	Former President of the North American Division
John Brunt	Professor of New Testament, Vice President for Academic Administration, Walla Walla College
Aecio Cairus	Professor of Old Testament, Adventist International Institute of Advanced Studies
Fernando L. Canale	Professor of Theology and Philosophy, Andrews University
Richard M. Davidson	Professor of Old Testament, Andrews University
Raoul Dederen	Professor Emeritus of Systematic Theology, Andrews University
John M. Fowler	Associate Director, Department of Education, General Conference
The late Gerhard F. Hasel	Former Professor of Old Testament, Andrews University
Frank B. Holbrook	Associate Director, Biblical Research Institute
William H. Johnsson	Editor, *Adventist Review,* General Conference
Herbert Kiesler	Associate Director, Biblical Research Institute
Miroslav M. Kiš	Professor of Ethics, Andrews University
Hans K. LaRondelle	Professor Emeritus of Theology, Andrews University
Richard Lehmann	President, Franco-Belgian Union Conference
Daegeuk Nam	Professor of Theology, Korean Sahmyook University
George W. Reid	Director, Biblical Research Institute
George E. Rice	Pastor, Chesapeake Conference, North American Division
Calvin B. Rock	Vice President, General Conference
Angel Manuel Rodríguez	Associate Director, Biblical Research Institute
William H. Shea	Associate Director, Biblical Research Institute
The late Kenneth A. Strand	Professor of Church History, Andrews University
Peter M. van Bemmelen	Professor of Theology, Andrews University
Mario Veloso	Associate Secretary, General Conference
Nancy J. Vyhmeister	Professor of Missions, Andrews University
Eric Claude Webster	Editor, *Signs of the Times,* South Africa

Table of Contents

Foreword

With delegates from all parts of the world assembled in Nairobi's Kenyatta Center for their 1988 Annual Council, leaders of the Seventh-day Adventist Church wrestled with the challenge of how to strengthen unity among a body of believers diffused through more than 220 countries and in widely diverse cultural settings. The same commonality of faith and practice so important to the expanding apostolic church they recognized as equally important for the body of Christ's believers in the end-time.

The council authorized preparation of a volume to review carefully the biblical teachings undergirding the dynamic Adventist movement. This is that volume. Under the direction of the Biblical Research Institute, the project has been more than 10 years in the making. As the editor notes in his preface, its purpose is to provide for both believers and inquirers a faith-centered, reasoned exploration of these truths as seen by Seventh-day Adventists.

This occasion offers opportunity for the Institute to express its enduring appreciation to Raoul Dederen, who with his unique blend of Christian commitment, theological skills, sage judgment, tact, and tenacity toiled to bring this work to completion.

—George W. Reid, Director
Biblical Research Institute
January 2000

Preface

In a time of fast, pluralistic change in all areas of human theory and practice, when believing Seventh-day Adventists have to face the rest of the world with a well-founded understanding of their faith, the leadership of the church decided to make available to church members and the general public a basic handbook setting forth the main doctrines and practices of Seventh-day Adventists. With the rapid spread of the Adventist movement into virtually every country and culture a work of this kind would reinforce the unity called for in Christ's mandate to His followers. More than 20 years ago the need was recognized, leading to early planning and some effort to prepare such a volume.

However, the preparation of this work itself was mandated by an action of the 1988 Annual Council meeting of the General Conference Executive Committee in Nairobi, Kenya. It made the Biblical Research Institute (BRI) responsible for its preparation and overall content. Raoul Dederen was appointed to serve, under the auspices of BRI, as project director and editor of the volume.

After careful consideration of the nature of the target and limitations of the projected handbook, authors were selected from around the world, not only on the basis of their own scholarly and pastoral expertise but also because of their ability to translate their scholarship into accessible language and concepts for the sake of nonspecialist readers. A set of guidelines was sent to each of them, dealing essentially with content, format, length, and writing style.

The book has a plot, one that tries to do some justice to three general ways of talking about God and the world, i.e., the Scriptures, history, and the testimony of Ellen G. White. Authors were requested to devote the bulk of their articles to the biblical data, abstaining as much as possible from referring to nonscriptural sources. This was an occasion to let the *Scriptures* speak. A brief historical overview of the doctrine under review should follow, preceding a compilation of representative statements from Ellen G. White in whatever fashion deemed most helpful. A "literature" section would come last, namely, a short list of works used by the author and regarded as helpful for further investigation of the topic. The scriptural part of an article would conclude with a few remarks regarding practical implications for daily Christian life, except when the topic itself focused already on Christian living, as in the case of Christian lifestyle and behavior. The Revised Standard Version was to be used as the standard text in citations of biblical passages. All Hebrew and Greek words were to be transliterated into English characters. There would be no footnotes or endnotes. Although in parts of the world the current trend is toward gender-inclusive language, the fact that more than nine tenths of Adventists live where English is a second language did lead us in some cases to favor longstanding practice and be less exacting on this point. Cross-references, a glossary, and a general index would add to the usefulness of this resource.

The 28 articles that make up this volume have been in process for some 10 years. Whoever has pursued two dozen theologians around the world through their academic schedules, their researches, their sabbaticals, will understand that a work of this kind cannot be produced overnight. Although each article is signed, it was agreed from the start that all contributions would be subject to review and suggestions from the Biblical Research Institute Committee (BRICOM), a group of 40 persons predominantly scholars but including a few administrators. With its international composition BRICOM was called to function as an efficient sounding board.

In other words, many shared in the task of planning and writing this book, from consultation on the outline through the writing and revision of successive drafts. This book is not simply a collection of parts written separately by individual contributors. In fact, no part of it is the work of a single author. As the text proceeded through editing and consultation, all parts of the book and the book as a whole profited from this cooperative approach.

The whole working team, i.e., authors and BRICOM members—many of whom were authors—could claim to be genuinely international. They represented countries from all around the globe: Argentina, Australia, Austria, Barbados, Belgium, Brazil, Canada, Chile, Colombia, Denmark, France, Germany, Ghana, India, Jamaica, Korea, the Netherlands, Norway, Puerto Rico, Russia, South Africa, the United Kingdom, Uruguay, as well as the United States. They wrote this work for a worldwide readership.

The aim of the editorial staff and contributors has been to produce a work of reference written in a spirit of unqualified loyalty to the Scriptures as the written Word of God, in the hope that these pages will be fruitful for personal reflection in faith and practice. It is not intended as an exercise in *speculative* theology. We are not arguing a point of view peculiar to a small avant-garde school of Adventist thinking. What is presented here is broadly representative of mainstream Adventist theology and biblical scholarship as they are practiced throughout the worldwide Adventist Church. It is a work of *constructive* theology, biblically based and Christ-centered, one that tries to see the whole in terms of the interrelationship of all its parts, and the parts always in terms of their relationship to one another and to the whole. Nor is it designed with the scholar or the specialist in mind (though hopefully such will find it useful), but rather for the general reader seeking a comprehensible exposition of the pertinent facts concerning the main tenets of Adventist theology, supplying the information such a reader might reasonably expect in comprehensive compass.

Since the Christian faith is so rich and because those to whom it is announced are so varied, some readers will look for a fuller or different treatment of either section; and reasonably so. Some will deplore that something was left out, something was given too much attention, or something was given the wrong emphasis. More than once we wished that more discussion could be given to important scriptural, historical, or Ellen G. White statements. But it proved to be impossible to give any further treatment of either area without making disproportionate demands on space. A reference work, even of this size, has its limitations.

This volume is sent forth, not with any idea of finality, but rather in the hope that it will be of use in Adventist and non-Adventist homes, classrooms, and libraries, as well as in pastoral offices as a handy and valued reference tool for information on various aspects of Adventist understanding and practice.

There remains the happy task of expressing thanks to the large company of those who in many ways have contributed to the making of this book. It is possible to mention by name only a few of them. There are, first, my immediate associates: Nancy Vyhmeister and the BRI staff under the leadership of George W. Reid. Next, the debt owed to the 27 authors who have so generously given of their time and learning should be obvious. I should also pay a special word of tribute to the members of the General Conference Executive Committee who originated this project. Without their inspiration and constant support there would have been no *Handbook of Seventh-day Adventist Theology*.

Finally a word of thanks is due for help of another kind. It is needless to say that the production of a work of this magnitude has involved a great deal of typing and other auxiliary work. Each article needed to be drafted many times before it went to the printer. In this connection special thanks are due to a battery of faithful secretaries and more particularly to our desktop specialist and designer, Martha Lunt. Special thanks are due Robert J. Kinney and Ted N. C. Wilson, presidents of the Review and Herald Publishing Association, for their constant interest in the work. We are also indebted to Nancy Vyhmeister and the editorial staff of the Review and Herald, more particularly Richard W. Coffen, vice president, and James Cavil and his associates, who managed so expertly the long and laborious copyediting process.

—Raoul Dederen
Andrews University

List of Abbreviations for Volume 12

ELLEN G. WHITE WORKS

A A	*The Acts of the Apostles*
AG	*God's Amazing Grace*
AH	*The Adventist Home*
CD	*Counsels on Diet and Foods*
CG	*Child Guidance*
CH	*Counsels on Health*
ChS	*Christian Service*
CL	*Country Living*
CM	*Colporteur Ministry*
COL	*Christ's Object Lessons*
CS	*Counsels on Stewardship*
CSW	*Counsels on Sabbath School Work*
CT	*Counsels to Parents, Teachers, and Students*
CW	*Counsels to Writers and Editors*
DA	*The Desire of Ages*
Ed	*Education*
1888 Materials	*Ellen G. White 1888 General Conference Materials*
Ev	*Evangelism*
EW	*Early Writings*
FE	*Fundamentals of Christian Education*
FLB	*The Faith I Live By*
FW	*Faith and Works*
GC	*The Great Controversy*
GW	*Gospel Workers*
HL	*Healthful Living*
HP	*In Heavenly Places*
LDE	*Last Day Events*
LS	*Life Sketches of Ellen G. White*
Mar	*Maranatha*
MB	*Thoughts From the Mount of Blessing*
MCP	*Mind, Character, and Personality* (2 vols.)
MH	*The Ministry of Healing*
ML	*My Life Today*
MM	*Medical Ministry*
MR	*Manuscript Release*
MYP	*Messages to Young People*
OHC	*Our High Calling*
PK	*Prophets and Kings*
PP	*Patriarchs and Prophets*
SAT	*Sermons and Talks*
SC	*Steps to Christ*
SD	*Sons and Daughters of God*
SG	*Spiritual Gifts* (4 vols.)

SL	*The Sanctified Life*
SLP	*Sketches From the Life of Paul*
SM	*Selected Messages* (3 vols.)
SP	*The Spirit of Prophecy* (4 vols.)
SR	*The Story of Redemption*
SW	*The Southern Work*
T	*Testimonies for the Church* (9 vols.)
TT	*Testimony Treasures*
TDG	*This Day With God*
Te	*Temperance*
TM	*Testimonies to Ministers and Gospel Workers*
TMK	*That I May Know Him*
TSB	*Testimonies on Sexual Behavior, Adultery, and Divorce*
UL	*The Upward Look*
WM	*Welfare Ministry*

OTHER REFERENCES

ANET	Pritchard, James B., ed. *Ancient Near Eastern Texts Relating to the Old Testament.* Princeton: Princeton University Press, 1969.
ANF	*The Anti-Nicene Fathers,* Ed. Alexander Roberts and James Donaldson. 10 vols. New York: Christian Literature Co., 1885-1887.
AR	*Adventist Review*
AUCR	*Australasian Union Conference Record*
BC	Nichol, Francis D., ed. *The Seventh-day Adventist Bible Commentary.* 7 vols. Rev. ed. Washington, D.C.: Review and Herald, 1978.
BE	*Bible Echo*
BTS	*Bible Training School*
CFOF	Froom, LeRoy E. *The Conditionalist Faith of Our Fathers.* 2 vols. Washington, D.C.: Review and Herald, 1965, 1966.
GCB	*General Conference Bulletin*
GH	*Gospel Herald*
NPNF-1	*The Nicene and Post-Nicene Fathers.* First series. Ed. Philip Schaff. 14 vols. New York: Christian Literature Co., 1886-1889.
NPNF-2	*The Nicene and Post-Nicene Fathers.* Second Series. Ed. Philip Schaff and Henry Wace. 14 vols. New York: Christian Literature Co., 1890-1899.
PFOF	Froom, LeRoy E. *The Prophetic Faith of Our Fathers.* 4 vols. Washington, D.C.: Review and Herald, 1946-1954.
PUR	*Pacific Union Recorder*
QOD	*Seventh-day Adventists Answer Questions on Doctrine.* Washington, D.C.: Review and Herald, 1957.
RH	*Review and Herald*
ST	*Signs of the Times*
TDNT	Kittel, Gerhard, and Gerhard Friedrich, eds. 10 vols. *Theological Dictionary of the New Testament.* Grand Rapids: Eerdmans, 1964-1976.
YI	*Youth's Instructor*

OTHER ABBREVIATIONS

ADRA	Adventist Development and Relief Agency
b	born
c	circa
d	died
Gr.	Greek
Heb.	Hebrew

MS(S)	Manuscript(s)
NAD	North American Division
NT	New Testament
OT	Old Testament
SDA	Seventh-day Adventist

1. Hebrew Alphabet

א = '	ד = $\underline{d}$	י = y	ס = s	ר = r
בּ = b	ה = h	כּ = k	ע = '	שׂ = $\acute{s}$
ב = $\underline{b}$	ו = w	כ = $\underline{k}$	שׁ = $\check{s}$
גּ = g	ז = z	ל = l	פּ = p	תּ = t
ג = $\underline{g}$	ח = h	מ = m	פ = $\underline{p}$	ת = $\underline{t}$
ד = d	ט = t	נ = n	צ = s	
			ק = q	

Masoretic Vowel Pointings

ַ = a	ְ (vocal shewa) = ^{e}	ֹ = $\bar{o}$
ָ = $\bar{a}$	ֱ = $\hat{e}$	ֳ = ^{o}
ֳ = ^{a}	ִ = i	וֹ = $\hat{o}$
ֶ = e	ִי = $\hat{i}$	ֻ = u
ֵ = $\bar{e}$	ָ = o	וּ = $\hat{u}$

2. Greek Alphabet

α = a	ζ = z	λ = l	π = p	φ = ph
β = b	η = $\bar{e}$	μ = m	ρ = r	χ = ch
γ = g	θ = th	ν = n	σ, ς = s	ψ = ps
δ = d	ι = i	ξ = x	τ = t	ω = $\bar{o}$
ε = e	κ = k	ο = o	υ = y	' = h

Glossary

This glossary is not intended to provide new information or greater precision. Since most terms have already been explained in the text itself, the glossary is mainly provided as a convenience to the reader and a quick memory refresher. The definitions reflect the meanings of these terms as used in the pages of the present volume.

Anthropology
From the Gr. *anthropos,* "man," and *logos,* "discourse." In theology the study of the origin, nature, and destiny of man as contrasted with the study of God or of angels.

Apocrypha
A collection of books and sections of books not contained in the Jewish and Protestant canons but received by the Roman Catholic church under the name of deuterocanonicals.

Aramaic
A Semitic language used extensively in the Near East since the rise to power of the Assyrians and Babylonians. Spoken by the Jews during and after the Babylonian exile, Aramaic was the vernacular in Palestine in the days of Christ.

Atonement
An Anglo-Saxon term that has the force of "at-one-ment," or "making at one." It speaks of a process of healing the breach between God and humankind opened by sin and is associated with the life and death of Jesus Christ.

Biblical criticism
The scientific study and analysis of the human elements that have entered into the composition of the Scriptures.

Binitarianism
The belief that there are only two persons in the Godhead, i.e., the Father and the Son.

Canon
From the Gr. *kanōn,* "measuring rod." A list that serves as a rule or measuring rod. In Christian language the term denotes the list of inspired books accepted as inspired composing the Old Testament and New Testament Scriptures.

Chiasm
The use of inverted parallelism in Heb. literature or poetry. Regular parallelism follows the order of A, B, A^1, B^1. Chiasm inverts the order to A, B, B^1, A^1. The word derives from the Gr. letter *chi* (X).

Deism	The system of thought that advocates natural religion and the existence of God on the basis of human reason and the laws of nature rather than revelation and the teachings of a church.
Demythologization	A method of New Testament interpretation originated by Rudolf Bultmann (1884-1976). It insists on the need to strip the New Testament, especially the Gospels, from their mythological forms and stories such as belief in Jesus' divine power, His preexistence and virgin birth, His comings and goings between heaven and earth, and His resurrection from the dead as "utterly inconceivable" as historical faith. Such mythological language is then to be reinterpreted in anthropological (human-oriented) or, better, existential (personal) categories.
Determinism	The theory according to which human acts of the will, historical events, or occurrences in nature are determined, i.e., decided, by external and antecedent causes, such as the environment, the human genetic makeup, or God. Thus nothing occurs in human behavior, for instance, as the result of free will.
Dispensationalism	While they differ in their opinions as to the number of dispensations, dispensational theologians hold that God has unfolded His plan of salvation or covenant of grace in successive dispensations or periods of time throughout human history.
Docetism	(Gr. *dokeō,* "I seem"). A system of thought that held that Christ only "seemed" to have a human body, to have suffered on the cross, and to have risen from the dead.
Dualism	(Lat. *dualis,* from *duo,* "two"). A view that holds that all reality is composed of two distinct, antagonistic, and coequal fundamental principles. Thus, good and evil, spirit and matter, truth and error, body and soul are typical expressions of dualism.
Ebionites	An early-centuries group of Jewish Christians who regarded Jesus as the human son of Joseph and Mary, who was made the Anointed One at baptism. They also insisted on the binding character of the whole Mosaic Law.
Economy, divine	God's saving plan revealed through redemption in Jesus Christ.
Empiricism	The philosophical system of thought that claims that experience is the only valid source of knowledge.
Endogamy	Marriage within one's own group.
Enlightenment	The eighteenth-century philosophical movement that held that truth

can be obtained only through reason, observation, and experiment. It has since then influenced much of the Western world.

Epistemology   (Gr. *epistēmē,* "knowledge," and *logos,* "discourse"). An inquiry into the principles underlying the nature and source of knowledge, its limits, and the validity of its claims.

Eschatology   From the Gr. *eschatos,* "last," and *logos,* "discourse." The doctrine concerned with the final events in the history of the world.

Ethical   That which conforms to accepted standards of conduct.

Ethics   The science dealing with what is good and bad, and with moral duty, thus determining behavior and lifestyle.

Etiology   From the Gr. *aitiologia,* "a statement of causes." The science of inquiring into the causes or reasons for things.

Evangelicalism   A modern Protestant movement that transcends denominational boundaries and promotes the interests of scriptural Christianity. The authority of the Scriptures, the word of God written and therefore inerrant in its original autographs, is the foundational tenet of the movement.

Expiation   From the Lat. *expiare,* "to atone for." The reparation for a wrong, the satisfaction of the demands of justice through paying a penalty. In God's plan of salvation Christ's sacrificial death relieves its beneficiaries from the penal consequences otherwise involved in breaking the law of God.

Filioque   Meaning "and from the Son," the term was inserted in the Nicene Creed (A.D. 325) by Western Catholicism to state that the Holy Spirit proceeds from the Father *and the Son.*

Forensic   That which belongs to courts of justice or to public debate.

Form criticism   A method of biblical study employed to uncover the assumed preliterary (oral) development behind the various literary forms of the biblical writings.

Gnosticism   (Gr. *gnōsis,* "knowledge"). A system that emphasizes dualism, holding that matter is evil and that emancipation—in Christianity salvation—comes through knowledge.

Hellenism   A body of humanistic and classical ideals associated with the culture, language, and philosophy of life prevalent in the Graeco-Roman world during the time of Christ.

Hermeneutics

(Gr. *hermēneus,* "interpreter"). The art and science of interpretation, as of the Bible.

Higher criticism

In the case of the Scriptures, a term applied to the historical and literary criticism of the Bible. This criticism is basically concerned with the literary sources and genres of the Scriptures, and matters of authorship.

Historical criticism

An attempt to verify the truthfulness and to understand the meaning of the Scriptures on the basis of the principles and procedures of secular-historical science.

Historicism

A hermeneutical system that sees a sequential development, a historical continuum in the biblical apocalyptic visions, over against a fulfillment entirely in the past or totally in the future.

Homoousios

Literally "of the same substance." A term used in the early Christian councils, especially Nicea (325), to affirm that the Father and the Son are of the same divine substance or nature.

Idealism

A theory that holds that the essential nature of reality lies in a realm transcending phenomena, as, for instance, in consciousness or reason. The visible things of this world are merely copies of the perfect realities of another, supersensible world.

Imago Dei

(Lat. "image of God") in which, as stated in Genesis 1:26, 27, man and woman were created.

Imputation

From the Lat. *imputare,* "to reckon," "to charge to one's account." In Christian theology the ascription, by substitution, of God's righteousness to the believer in Christ. In the opposite sense the term is also applied to Christ who, though He was innocent, allowed Himself to be counted guilty and a sinner by (when?) dying a substitutionary death on the cross, taking the sinner's place.

Intertestamental

Relating to the period separating the Old and New Testaments.

Kenoticism

A system of thought that holds that in order to become man the Son of God emptied Himself temporarily of some of His divine attributes, more particularly His omnipotence, omniscience, and omnipresence.

Liberalism

Though used with a variety of shades of meaning, the term describes a movement in modern Protestant theology emphasizing intellectual freedom and a secular humanism inconsistent with biblical orthodoxy.

Lower criticism	Another name for textual criticism of the Bible, i.e., the study of the text of the Scriptures to determine, as far as possible, what was actually written by the inspired authors.
Marcionism	A second- and third-century-A.D. doctrinal system that attracted a wide following. It rejected the Old Testament and its Creator-God as well as part of the New Testament, denying Christ's corporality and full humanity.
Mas(s)oretes	Jewish scribes who worked on the Hebrew text of the Old Testament during the first millennium A.D.
Middle Ages, Medieval	The period of European history from about A.D. 500 to about A.D. 1500. More recent writers hold it to begin about 1100.
Millennium	Derived from the Lat. *mille,* "thousand," and *annum,* "year." The word is a theological term used to describe the thousand years of Revelation 20:1-10.
Mishnah	A collection, compiled toward the end of the second century A.D., of the oral traditions that the Jews had developed regarding Scripture.
Monarchianism	In an attempt to safeguard monotheism and the unity ("monarchy") of God, some second- and third-century theologians maintained that Jesus was a mere man taken up into the Godhead. Others saw Jesus and the Spirit as mere modes or functions of the one God.
Monism	(Gr. *monos,* "alone," "single"). A system of philosophy that appeals to a single unifying substance or principle to explain the diversity of all that is.
Montanism	A second-century apocalyptic movement which emphasized the continuance of the Spirit's prophetic gifts and a strict ascetic discipline.
Mystery	(Gr. *mustērion,* "something closed," "a secret"). In the New Testament the word refers to a divine plan or a truth previously hidden but presently revealed, the inner essence of which cannot be fully understood by the finite mind.
Neoorthodoxy	The twentieth-century Protestant movement characterized by a reaction against theological liberalism and claiming to return to the basic principles of Reformation theology.
Ontology	The "science of being," dealing with the nature and essence of being.

Ordinance

The term is used in the Scriptures in reference to decrees or regulations ordained by God or by a government. In English it is commonly used in reference to institutions of divine origin such as foot washing and the Lord's Supper.

Orthodoxy

From the Gr. *orthos doxa,* "right praise," "right opinion." Describes a pattern of belief consistent with the fundamental teachings of a church as compared with heterodoxy or heresy. The term, with a capital letter, is also used to identify the independent churches, situated mainly in Eastern Europe, that acknowledge the honorary primacy of the patriarch of Constantinople.

Panentheism

From the Gr. *pan,* "all," *en,* "in," and *theos,* "God." The belief that while the Being of God penetrates the whole universe, His Being is more than the universe.

Pantheism

From the Gr. *pan,* "all," and *theos,* "God." The system that identifies God with the world and the world with God. Here all things are divine and no real distinction exists between God and the forces and laws of the universe.

Parousia

From the Gr. *parousia,* "presence" or "arrival." A term used in the New Testament to denote the second coming of Christ in glory and power.

Penal

From the Lat. *poena,* "punishment." Related to or involving punishment. In Christological language a term used to affirm that Christ bore the punishment sinners deserve.

Pericope

(Gr. *perikopē,* "section"). A selection from a writing, hence a passage from the Scriptures.

Pietism

A religious movement that originated in seventeenth-century Germany in reaction to formalism and intellectualism. It stressed Bible study and personal religious experience.

Pluralism

The view that contradictory doctrines in faith and morals could be professed by different persons, all equally in good standing in the same church. These positions usually vary according to the premises or postulates used in reflecting on the source of revelation, according to the methodology employed, or according to the cultural context within which theology operates.

Polytheism

The belief in or worship of many gods.

Positivism

A philosophy that confines intellectual inquiry and knowledge to observable ("positive") and experimental facts, hence shunning all philosophical and metaphysical speculation.

Postcanonical   Relating to a person, an event, or a writing following the formation of the canon of Scripture.

Preterism   A mode of prophetic interpretation that places the fulfillment of biblical apocalyptic prophecies, notably those found in the book of Daniel and in the Apocalypse, entirely in the past.

Propensity   An intense and often urgent inclination, a decisive tendency.

Propitiation   From Lat. *propitiare,* "to render favorable." Propitiation carries the idea of appeasing the offended person, of regaining the favor of a high individual. However, contrary to the Greek notion of appeasing an angry deity, the New Testament writers see no irreconcilable contrast in God between love and wrath, a wrath purged of all admixture of human limitation and sinful vindictiveness. Here the divine mystery of love is perceived in the midst of the reality of wrath.

Pseudepigrapha   Pseudonymous or anonymous Jewish writings dating from the centuries immediately before and after the time of Christ.

Rationalism   From the Lat. *ratio,* "reason." A system of thought that holds that human reason is self-sufficient in the pursuit of truth, even religious truth.

Redaction criticism   A method of biblical study employed to uncover the assumed latest layer of tradition used by the redactor in the composition, for instance, of the Gospels.

Reincarnation   The theory that souls migrate from one body to another, whether human or animal.

Roman Catholicism   The faith, worship, and practice of the Christians in communion with the bishop of Rome.

Sacrament   A religious rite instituted by Jesus Christ, such as baptism, foot washing, and the Lord's Supper. The scope of what the term comprises varies widely. Some Protestants favor the "ordinance."

Scholasticism   A philosophical and theological system first developed in the medieval schools of Roman Catholic Europe. It aimed at defining and systematizing religious dogma with the help of philosophical concepts and the tradition of patristic theology, especially Augustine of Hippo and later with Aristotelianism.

Soteriology   From the Gr. *sōtēria,* "deliverance," and *logos,* "discourse." It is that area of Christian theology that deals with God's plan of redemption, more particularly Christ's work of salvation.

Source criticism	A method of biblical study employed to uncover the assumed sources underlying the scriptural text.
Synoptics	The first three Gospels, according to Matthew, Mark, and Luke. So-called because when read side by side (synoptically) they present certain parallels in structure and content.
Talmud	The Jewish compilations comprising the Mishnah, or oral teachings of the Jews, and the Gemara, a collection of discussions on the Mishnah.
Theodicy	(Gr. *theos*, "God," and *dikē*, "justice"). The study and defense of God's goodness and omnipotence in view of the existence of evil.
Theology	From Gr. *theos*, "God," and *logos*, "discourse." The ordered study of God and of His relation to the world, especially by analysis of the teachings of the Old and New Testament Scriptures.
Tradition	From the Lat. *traditio*, "something handed over." That which is handed over, particularly teachings handed over from a teacher to a disciple. Hence in Christian theology a body of doctrines, practices, and experiences revealed by God and delivered by Him to His people through the mouth or writings of His prophets and apostles, identified with the Scriptures. The Roman Catholic account of tradition claims that written and unwritten traditions, originating with Christ and the apostles, form an original and authentic source of doctrine alongside Scripture.
Universalism	A doctrine that affirms that all human beings will be saved ultimately because all are by nature children of God.
Wholistic	Denoting completeness, as for instance a wholistic understanding of the human nature. A human being is a single whole and must be treated as such. The word is sometimes spelled "holistic," as derived from the Gr. *holos*, "whole" or "all."

Who Are Seventh-day Adventists?

Nancy J. Vyhmeister

Introduction

A simple answer to the question "Who are Seventh-day Adventists?" can be stated briefly: the Seventh-day Adventist Church is a worldwide body of more than 10 million Christians who observe Saturday as the Sabbath and expect Jesus' second coming soon. In more detail, one might say that Seventh-day Adventists are a conservative Protestant body of evangelical Christians whose faith is grounded in the Bible and centered on Jesus, with stress on His atoning death on the cross, ministry in the heavenly sanctuary, and soon return to redeem His people. They are known for their Sabbath observance, for their empha-sis on maintaining health as part of religious duty, and for their mission activities around the world.

This introductory chapter seeks first to nar-rate the history of the church, from its fore-runners until the early twentieth century. A second section contains an overview of the church as it operates today, as well as glimpses of important issues affecting the Sev-enth-day Adventist Church. The bibliography of this article contains a list of sources used, as well as books for further reading on the history and operation of the Seventh-day Adventist Church.

I. Antecedents and Nineteenth-Century Adventism

The name "Seventh-day Adventist" was adopted in 1860. Those who chose this name decided to explain themselves in terms of their distinctive beliefs—the observance of God's holy day on the seventh day of the week and confidence in Jesus' imminent second advent. The Seventh-day Adventist Publishing Asso-ciation was incorporated in 1861. Formal or-ganization of the General Conference of Seventh-day Adventists came in 1863.

1

The birth of the official church dates to the early 1860s. Its gestation period covers decades. Its roots reach back to apostolic times, since the pioneers saw themselves as continuing the New Testament tradition.

A. Forerunners
of the Seventh-day Adventist
Church

Early in the nineteenth century, Bible interpreters around the world wrote and spoke of the nearness of the second coming of Jesus. Intense study of the prophecies of Daniel and Revelation led many to the conclusion that the prophetic time periods were about to end. Manuel de Lacunza, a Jesuit born in Chile, studied the Bible for 20 years before writing *La venida del Mesías en gloria y magestad* (The Coming of the Messiah in Glory and Majesty). Lacunza's work was translated into English by the London preacher Edward Irving, who appended to it a report of the first Albury Prophetic Conference. To the Albury Conferences, held yearly from 1826 to 1830, came clergy from different churches and communions to study the nearness of the Second Advent, the prophecies of Daniel and Revelation, and "the duties of the church arising from these questions" (PFOF 3:276). Joseph Wolff, one of the 20 who attended the 1826 conference, traveled extensively throughout Western and Central Asia, teaching that Christ would come about 1847 to establish a millennial rule in Jerusalem. In Switzerland, François Gaussen presented, beginning in 1837, a series of Sunday school lectures on the prophecies of Daniel; in these he showed that Daniel and Revelation portrayed the history of the world, which would soon come to a close.

In North America, the early nineteenth century was a time of great religious fervor. From this period of the "Great Revival" came a strong foreign missionary movement, the camp meeting with its unique hymnody, the Sunday school movement, and the American Bible Society. "Prophecy was the motivating force in much of the religious thought and activity"

of the period (PFOF 4:85). Sermons, pamphlets, and books proclaimed that events occurring in the world could only be a prelude to the millennium. The prophetic periods of Daniel and Revelation were seen as coming to a close. Within this setting, the precursors of the Seventh-day Adventist Church arose.

On the other hand, Adventist roots go back much farther. In the sixteenth century Martin Luther had written that he was convinced the day of judgment would not delay more than 300 years. The original "Adventists," or believers in the second coming of Christ, were the apostles themselves. Paul looked forward to Jesus' return with great expectation (1 Thess. 4:16). All of these expressions of faith were ultimately based on Jesus' own promise: "I will come again" (John 14:3).

B. The Millerite Movement

In Low Hampton, New York, farmer William Miller began a careful study of his Bible at the time of his conversion in 1816. After two years of investigation he came to the conclusion that, according to the prophecy of Daniel 8:14, "in about twenty-five years . . . all the affairs of our present state would be wound up" (Miller 12). Miller spent another five years examining and reexamining the arguments for and against his beliefs. By then he was convinced, not only of the nearness of Christ's coming, but also of his obligation to share what he believed. Being self-educated and shy by nature, Miller was afraid to stand up and proclaim what he had found from his study of prophecy.

In 1831 William Miller covenanted with God that if he were asked to preach he would "go and tell them what I find in the Bible about the Lord's coming" (*ibid.* 17). Even as Miller prayed, a young man was on his way to invite the Bible-studying farmer to lead out in a revival. Surprised at the rapid answer, Miller struggled in prayer for an hour until he was ready to accept the invitation to speak in nearby Dresden.

In 1832 Miller published a series of eight

2

articles in a Vermont newspaper. By 1834 he was devoting all his time to preaching and writing. In 1836 he brought out a book, later enlarged to contain a chronology and prophetic charts. From October 1834 to June 1839 Miller's log records 800 lectures given in response to direct invitations.

As preachers from other denominations joined Miller, the number of believers grew. Those who participated in the movement were called "Millerites" or "Adventists." In 1840 Joshua Himes launched the *Signs of the Times,* the first of a large corpus of Millerite publications. That same year a call was issued to attend the first "General Conference of Christians Expecting the Advent" in Boston. This meeting was followed by a second in 1841. The 200 persons present laid down a strategy for the distribution of literature and the preaching of the Advent message among the various denominations they represented.

Beginning in 1842 Millerite camp meetings were held "to awake sinners and purify Christians by giving the Midnight Cry, namely, to hold up the immediate coming of Christ to judge the world" (Hale, Plumer, and Cole 88). Miller later estimated that 200 ministers, 500 public lecturers, and 50,000 believers from many different churches and communions were involved in the movement. With their charts, books, periodicals, and large tent meetings, the Millerites made a great impression on their contemporaries in the northeastern states. They also began to arouse opposition from the mainstream churches.

Rumors about the fanatical beliefs of the Millerites were rife. Newspapers carried articles containing more fancy than truth: one stated that the Adventists were preparing ascension robes. The public ridicule to which Millerites were subjected led most of them to separate in 1843 from the churches to which they had belonged.

C. The Great Disappointment

Miller had taught that the world would end sometime in 1843. By the summer of that year he expressed disappointment that Christ had not yet come, but urged believers to continue watching for the soon coming of the Lord. In February of 1844 a group of Adventist preachers, which did not include Miller, came to the understanding that the 2300-day prophecy of Daniel 8:14 would not end until the autumn of 1844. The specific day, October 22, was determined shortly afterward.

The new date for the Second Coming was calculated on the basis of the date for the Jewish Day of Atonement in the seventh month of the Karaite Jewish calendar. Since Christ our Passover was crucified on the day the Passover lamb was slain and came to life on the day of the wave sheaf, it was logical to expect that He would come from the heavenly Holy of Holies to announce the beginning of the year of jubilee on the Day of Atonement.

The October 22 date was slow to be accepted. But as the time approached, enthusiasm mounted. However, not everyone joined the "seventh-month movement." Miller himself decided that October 22, 1844, was the correct date a mere two weeks before the fateful day.

With solemn joy and great expectation the Millerites met in homes and churches on October 22, 1844, to await the returning Christ. Alas! Their hopes were dashed. To their disappointment was added the ridicule of scoffers, joined by some who, out of fear, had claimed faith in the Advent. The faithful, sure that their movement had been led by God, tried to understand where they had gone wrong.

After the Great Disappointment those who had expected the Advent split into groups differing in their opinions on why Christ had not come. The majority were sure they had been right in applying the 2300-day prophecy to the Second Coming; since Christ had not come, they must have been wrong in their chronology. A minority group affirmed they had been right about the event and the chronology; Christ's coming had been a "spiritual" event in the life of the believers. They became known as "spiritualizers" and many of them went over to the Shakers. Some set further dates for the Second Coming, only to be disappointed again. Another group maintained that the chronology was correct but that they had expected the wrong event; among these were the founders of the Seventh-day Adventist Church.

William Miller continued to expect the return of Jesus, though admitting that the historical and chronological sources on which the calculations had been based might have been in error. In his expectation of the soon coming of Jesus he disassociated himself from those who believed that the error had been in the event expected rather than the time, all the while treating them as Christian brethren. He did not accept the new understanding of the heavenly sanctuary, death sleep, or Sabbath observance, along with the pioneers of the Seventh-day Adventist Church. In 1849 Miller died in the hope of a soon-coming Saviour.

On October 23, 1844, Hiram Edson and a Millerite friend set out to encourage those who, with them, had suffered disappointment. As they crossed Edson's cornfield after praying together, Edson had a sudden flash of insight. Millerites had thought that the sanctuary to be cleansed (Dan. 8:14) was the church on earth, to be purified from sin at Christ's second coming. Edson comprehended that the sanctuary to be cleansed was not on earth but in heaven; October 22 marked the beginning, not the end, of the antitypical day of atonement. Jesus had entered the Most Holy Place of the heavenly sanctuary to perform a special work before coming to this earth.

Edson and his Millerite friends reexamined the Scriptures in this light. In 1845 Owen R. L. Crosier elaborated Edson's view, articulating the position later adopted by Seventh-day Adventists. October 22, 1844, marked the beginning of the cleansing of the heavenly sanctuary and the opening of the investigative, pre-Advent judgment; the second coming of Christ to earth was future. No date was fixed, but the agreement was that the visible return of Jesus would be soon. After it would fol-

low the millennium, during which Christ and the saints would reign in heaven. At the end of the 1,000 years the renewal of the earth and the establishment of the kingdom would take place.

D. Early Seventh-day Adventist Teachings

Already before 1844 the continuing validity of the seventh-day Sabbath (Saturday) as the day of worship was a concern for certain Millerites. At the same time, Rachel Oakes Preston, a Seventh Day Baptist, shared some of her church's publications with Christians in Washington, New Hampshire, who were expecting "their redemption" along with other Adventists. Their preacher, Frederick Wheeler, soon began to observe the Sabbath and some time late in 1844 that congregation became the first group of Adventist Sabbathkeepers. The Sabbath, along with the heavenly sanctuary, became "present truth" for these believers.

Although most Millerites believed in the conscious state of the dead, a number espoused the teaching that the dead are unconscious and know nothing. In 1842, after studying what the Bible says about the condition of the dead, George Storrs, a former Methodist preacher, wrote a book popularly known as Storrs' *Six Sermons.* In it he affirmed that the Bible teaches that the dead—good or bad—know nothing and figuratively sleep until the resurrection. William Miller and other leaders opposed this teaching but were not able to convince their followers that their own view was right. Unable to agree in 1845 on the state of the dead or the eternal punishment of the wicked, the Millerites in attendance at the 1845 Albany Conference limited themselves to stating that the righteous receive their reward at the time of the Second Coming. Meanwhile, early Adventist leaders such as Joseph Bates, Ellen Harmon, and James White accepted—in consonance with their belief in the soon-coming resurrection—the biblical teaching of conditional immortality and death sleep.

Beginning in 1845, the early Adventists

published their views in pamphlets, in their own periodicals, and in friendly newspapers. Tracts and broadsides proclaiming the new understanding of the heavenly sanctuary and the Sabbath flowed from the pen of Adventist leaders. The first issue of *Present Truth* appeared in 1849.

From 1848 through 1850 "Sabbath Conferences" were held in different places in New England. These meetings clarified the Sabbath teaching and served to unite "the brethren on the great truths connected with the message of the third angel" (J. White 5). In these conferences believers studied Scripture and prayed for a clear understanding of correct doctrine. During these years representatives of several religious groups came to a unified understanding of pillars of Adventist faith, such as the Sabbath, the Second Coming, and the state of the dead. Their common theology formed the basis for the later development of the church.

E. Early Adventist Leaders

Most prominent among those individuals who came out of the Millerite movement and led in founding the Seventh-day Adventist Church were Joseph Bates and James and Ellen White. Yet these, as well as other pioneers, would not have thought of themselves as founders of a new religious movement. They rather considered themselves to be spiritual heirs of truth and repairers of the breach; not innovators but reformers. They were not inventing doctrine; they were finding it in the Bible. Thus they traced their roots ultimately to the Old and New Testaments.

1. Joseph Bates (1792-1872)

An important member of the founding trio, Joseph Bates—mariner, reformer, and preacher—was born in New England in 1792. Bates went to sea at 15, working his way up to ship captain in 1820. His autobiography describes his sailing adventures and ports of call around the world. After his conversion, around 1824, he commanded a ship on which he allowed no

alcoholic beverages, no swearing and "no washing and mending of clothes on Sunday." His life at sea ended in 1827, soon after he was baptized into the Fairhaven, Massachusetts, Christian Church, where his wife, Prudence, was already a member. A moderately wealthy man, Bates settled down as a businessman with great interest in civic matters, including temperance, antislavery, and education.

In 1839 Bates accepted Miller's views on the Second Coming. From then on he devoted his whole attention to the Millerite movement. In 1844 he sold his home, settled his accounts, and became a preacher. In early 1845 Bates read T. M. Preble's article on the Sabbath, recently published in *The Hope of Israel*. He then traveled to Washington, New Hampshire, where he studied a whole night through with Frederick Wheeler before deciding to keep Saturday. The following year Bates wrote a 48-page tract entitled "The Seventh-day Sabbath, a Perpetual Sign." In it he presented the Sabbath on the basis of the Ten Commandments as the moral guide and rule for Christians. In the second edition, the following year, Bates placed the Sabbath in the context of the third angel's message in Revelation 14. Accepting the identification of the beast with the Papacy, Bates believed that the change of the weekly day of worship from Saturday to Sunday was the badge of papal authority.

Preaching the Second Coming, the Sabbath, the heavenly sanctuary, and death sleep, Bates traveled west to Michigan in 1849. After gathering a group of converts in Jackson, he moved on to Battle Creek in 1852. From 1855 onward, Adventist work centered in Battle Creek, Michigan. During the church's formative years, Bates was usually asked to assume the chairmanship of its conferences. He presided at the 1860 meeting that adopted the name Seventh-day Adventist for the fledgling publishing house. He also chaired the organization of the Michigan Conference in 1861.

Bates advocated and practiced healthful living. As a result, his was a long and healthy life. At age 76, Bates was one of the featured speakers at the first Adventist camp meeting, held in Wright, Michigan, in 1868. During 1871, already 79 years old, Bates held at least 100 meetings, besides the services of his local church. He died at the Health Institute in Battle Creek in March of 1872.

2. James Springer White (1821-1881)

Born in Palmyra, Maine, in 1821, James White suffered as a lad from physical ailments. His poor health kept him from attending school until he was 19. Then, to make up for lost time, he studied 18 hours a day for 12 weeks to earn his teaching certificate. After teaching one year White attended school for another 17 weeks. This constituted the whole of his formal education.

James was baptized into the Christian Connection at 15. After his second year of teaching he learned the Millerite teachings from his mother. In 1842 White first heard Miller preach. Soon after he acquired his own prophetic charts, borrowed a horse, and ventured out to proclaim the Advent message. He was ordained to the ministry of the Christian Connection in 1843.

Even before the Disappointment, White met Ellen Harmon. Their relationship, however, developed later, after they had worked together combating fanaticism in eastern Maine in 1845. The two were married by the justice of the peace in Portland, Maine, on August 30, 1846. Shortly afterward they began to observe the Sabbath.

From 1848 onward, James gave himself entirely to ministry. During the Dorchester, Massachusetts, conference late in 1848, Ellen saw in vision that James should publish a paper explaining the truths held by the poor and widely scattered group of Sabbathkeepers. In response James began to publish the *Present Truth* in July 1849. The main emphases of the paper were the Sabbath message and the Adventist view of the sanctuary. In 1850 the Adventists first published the *Advent Review* "to cheer and refresh the true believer, by showing the fulfillment of prophecy in the past

wonderful work of God" (Himes, Bliss, and Hale 1). James White was editor of both papers. In November of that year, the two publications were combined into one: *Second Advent Review and Sabbath Herald,* the precursor of today's *Adventist Review.*

The Whites moved to Battle Creek, Michigan, in 1855. In 1860 James participated in the choosing of the denomination's name. When the newly formed Seventh-day Adventist Publishing Association of Battle Creek was incorporated under Michigan laws in May of 1861, James White was its president, as well as editor of the *Review and Herald.*

James White was president of the General Conference from 1865 to 1867, from 1869 to 1871, and again from 1874 to 1880. In June of 1874 he began the journal *Signs of the Times* in Oakland, California.

Constant involvement in leadership and administration, as well as editorial work and travel, sapped White's energy. A malaria attack in August of 1881 put him in the Battle Creek Sanitarium, where he died on August 6. He was buried in the White family plot at Oak Hill Cemetery in Battle Creek.

3. Ellen Gould (Harmon) White (1827-1915)

For 35 years the life of Ellen Harmon was entwined with that of James White. Together they built a family and a church. The Seventh-day Adventist Church recognizes Ellen White as a messenger of the Lord, the recipient of a unique and fruitful gift of prophecy.

Ellen was born in a farm home north of Gorham, Maine. She and her twin, Elizabeth, were the youngest of eight children. During her childhood the family moved to Portland, Maine, where her father was a hatmaker.

At the age of 9, when returning from school one afternoon, Ellen was hit in the face by a stone thrown by a classmate. She lay unconscious for three weeks. Her broken nose and probable concussion made breathing difficult. By the age of 12 she felt sufficiently strong to return to school, but was not long able to endure the stress; her formal schooling thus came to an end. Ellen's parents taught her practical skills at home. Her later education came largely from reading.

Ellen's family took religion seriously. Her father was a deacon at the local Methodist church. In 1840 Ellen and other members of her family heard William Miller lecture and accepted the belief that Jesus would return to earth about the year 1843. Ellen was baptized by immersion on June 26, 1842, and received into the Methodist Church.

In December of 1844, at a time when many disappointed Millerites were faltering in their faith, Ellen met in worship with four other women at the home of a friend. While they were praying, 17-year-old Ellen experienced her first vision, in which she saw a representation of the journey of the Adventist people to heaven: they walked a narrow path toward the heavenly city, high above the world, their eyes fixed on Jesus. Ellen also saw the Second Advent and the glories of the New Jerusalem (EW 13-20).

As Ellen told other believers her vision, the Adventist group felt encouraged. They urged her to tell what she had seen in that first vision as well as subsequent ones. Reluctantly she began to go from place to place, giving her testimony. On one of these trips she worked with a young Adventist preacher, James White. They were married on August 30, 1846.

Henry Nichols White, born August 26, 1847, initiated Ellen into the joys and sorrows of motherhood. Her second son, James Edson, was born at Rocky Hill, Connecticut, in July 1849. William Clarence joined the family in 1854. John Herbert, born in 1860, lived only a few months. Their firstborn died of pneumonia in 1863. Ellen's greatest concern was to have to leave her boys with others while she traveled with her husband. Extant letters to her sons show a rare mixture of motherly concern and pastoral care.

In the late 1840s Ellen and James White attended several Bible conferences. At these meetings doctrinal conclusions reached by studying the Bible were corroborated by Ellen's visions, leading to confidence in the positions taken.

In 1848 Ellen had a vision instructing her husband to begin to print a little paper. The first issue of the *Present Truth* followed. From then on, the Whites spent much time and effort in the preparation and publication of pamphlets and papers.

Shortly after the Whites moved to Battle Creek in 1855, Ellen had a vision in which she was shown matters important to the Battle Creek church. She wrote out what she had seen and read it in church the following Sabbath. The members decided that the testimony would benefit other believers. Then and there they voted to publish the first of the *Testimonies for the Church,* a 16-page pamphlet of what would eventually become a nine-volume set.

On March 14, 1858, Ellen had a two-hour vision of events in the great conflict between good and evil, spanning the centuries from the Fall to the new earth. This vision was the basis for the first volume of *Spiritual Gifts,* precursor of *The Great Controversy.* The frame house in Battle Creek where she did much of the writing for this book stands today to remind this generation of the God-given work of Ellen White.

Not all of Ellen White's time was devoted to writing, preaching, or traveling. Her diaries and letters of the early Battle Creek period show her as mother and homemaker, making a garden, sewing clothes, or visiting neighbors. Her home was a haven to traveling preachers, young people desirous of obtaining an education, and persons in distress.

After the Otsego health vision in 1863, Ellen White understood the important relation between healthful living and spiritual health. Later she was shown that the church should begin an institution to care for the sick and teach healthful living. This led to the 1866 opening of the Western Health Reform Institute, later known as Battle Creek Sanitarium.

During the 1870s Ellen traveled with her husband, both in search of health for him and to further the work of the church. At camp meetings she would address large audiences in a clear voice that could be heard by thousands. Her talks on Christian temperance were in great demand among Christians of all persuasions. When James passed away in 1881, Ellen largely retired from the public scene until 1883. When her health returned, she vowed to press on with the work they had both loved.

In 1885 Ellen White and her son William traveled to Europe. From Basel, Switzerland, Ellen made trips to Scandinavia, Germany, France, and Italy encouraging others to evangelize Europe and attempting to unify the Adventists in these countries. Even as she traveled, she continued writing.

After returning to the United States, Ellen settled in California to continue her writing. In 1891 she was asked by church leaders to go to Australia. Here she worked with the founders of Avondale College to open a school that was to be a pattern in Adventist education.

In 1900 Mrs. White returned to California, where she continued writing whenever she was not traveling and speaking at church meetings. In the early years of the new century she wrote extensively about the need for evangelizing cities and reaching the African-Americans in the South. At the age of 81 she attended the 1909 General Conference session in Washington, D.C. On this five-month trip Ellen White spoke 72 times in 27 places before returning to her home at Elmshaven, near St. Helena.

Her death came in 1915, five months after she fell and broke her hip. The funeral was held in the Battle Creek Tabernacle. She was buried beside her husband in the Oak Hill Cemetery.

F. Early Adventist History

The pioneers who met at the Sabbath or Bible conferences in the late 1840s studied their Bibles long and prayerfully to determine correct doctrines. They felt they had to be in harmony with Scripture. At the same time, they were afraid to urge others to join them, considering that the door to salvation was shut. The pioneers' attitude on the possibility of others' being saved changed, however, because of their careful study of the Bible, Ellen White's visions of a message going around the world, and the conversion of people who had not been part of the 1844 movement. By 1852 the "shut door" had become the "open door" and the missionary zeal of the little band led them to preach and teach throughout the Eastern states.

1. The 1850s: Publishing

The publishing work, first in Rochester, New York, and later in Battle Creek, Michigan, occupied a prominent place in Adventist endeavors in the 1850s. The precursor of today's weekly *Adventist Review* began to be published in 1850. The *Youth's Instructor* came out in 1852. From 1849 to 1854, Adventist periodicals announced the publication of 39 pamphlets. From 1852 to 1860, 26 books were announced.

The first literature in a language other than English appeared late in the decade. Translations of tracts into German, French, and Dutch were made to reach the non-English-speaking immigrants. It was hoped that they might also send these materials to their relatives in the homelands from which they had come to America.

From 1855 until his death in 1903, the name of Uriah Smith was synonymous with Seventh-day Adventist publishing. With the exception of a few years during that period, Smith was editor of the *Review*. At times he was also proofreader, business manager, and bookkeeper. Talented in writing, Smith was also gifted with mechanical aptitude; he invented and patented an artificial leg with flexible knee and ankle joints and a school desk with a folding seat. His books on Revelation (1867) and Daniel (1873) were combined into one volume, *The Prophecies of Daniel and the Revelation,* the first doctrinal book sold by Adventist colporteurs.

2. The 1860s: Organization

The church adopted its name in 1860, organized local conferences in 1861, and finally established the General Conference in 1863. Several of the leading brethren had opposed such a move, affirming that organization was "Babylon." The more pragmatic, who saw that it was indispensable to have a legal body to own the press and the church buildings, won the day.

In the 1860s the health message was emphasized. After Ellen White had her Otsego, Michigan, health vision, she wrote extensively on the subject. Her husband joined her in putting out materials to teach people how to live in harmony with the laws of health. In 1866 the first Adventist health institution began in Battle Creek. At the Western Health Reform Institute patients could learn the principles of healthful living, even as they recovered from illness. Financial struggles marked the first few years, as the physicians were not graduates of well-known medical schools. When John Harvey Kellogg completed his medical course at Bellevue Hospital Medical College in New York and joined the staff in 1875, the situation changed. In 1877 the first of several additions was put up. By the turn of the century the Battle Creek Sanitarium had more than 900 staff members.

3. The 1870s: Education and Mission

Two landmark events occurred in the 1870s. Battle Creek College was founded in 1874. In the same year, the first official Seventh-day Adventist missionary left the United States for service in Europe.

When in 1872 the church took responsibility for G. H. Bell's "Select School" in Battle Creek, the Adventist school system was born. In 1874 Battle Creek College opened with 100 students. At first the curriculum closely followed the classical model current at that time,

in spite of Ellen White's insistence on practical and industrial training. By the end of the century, the classical course and the granting of degrees were abolished. Battle Creek College closed in 1901 to reopen as Emmanuel Missionary College in Berrien Springs, Michigan. The new school specialized in the training of teachers and ministers.

John Nevins Andrews (1829-1883) was the first missionary officially sent overseas by the Seventh-day Adventist Church. In 1874 Andrews and his two motherless children embarked for Liverpool, en route to Switzerland. There he visited Adventist believers and carried out public evangelism. However, his greatest devotion was to writing, since, by his own admission, he was a scholar with a weak physical constitution. In 1876 a publishing house was founded in Basel, Switzerland. Andrews wrote extensively on Adventist doctrines, in English as well as in German and French.

In the 1860s, during the U.S. Civil War, Andrews had represented the church in Washington, D.C., to explain why Seventh-day Adventists believed in noncombatancy. He also wrote the *History of the Sabbath and the First Day of the Week,* which in its last edition contained more than 800 pages.

Another development of the 1870s was important to the Seventh-day Adventist Church: the tithing system was instituted, with each member urged to return one tenth of his or her income. In the 1850s the pioneers had struggled to finance the work they felt God had given them to do. In 1863 James White had written in the *Review and Herald* that God could hardly demand less than the tenth of the increase, just as He had asked of the Israelites. From then on the idea of tithing income became more and more common. The General Conference session of 1876 voted that all church members should "devote one tenth of their income from whatever source, to the cause of God." Furthermore, ministers were to instruct their congregations in this practice. In 1879 at the General Conference session, April 17, the following resolution was passed: "*Resolved,* That we earnestly request our brethren everywhere to take their stand fully and heartily upon this system [tithing], believing that it will not only improve the financial condition of the cause, but bring a great blessing to themselves personally" ("Business Proceedings" 1879, 133). The tithe was the Lord's (Lev. 27:30), to be used for the support of the ministry. Thus a solid financial basis was created for the overseas expansion of the church.

G. The End of the Century

In the 1880s foreign missions—directed mainly to those who were already Christians—were stimulated by Ellen White's presence in Europe and her writings about Europe in the homeland church papers. At the same time, other continents were entered, usually by literature evangelists. A group of missionaries, led by S. N. Haskell, sailed to Australia in 1885; in 1886 the first Seventh-day Adventist church in the Southern Hemisphere was organized in Melbourne. The first Seventh-day Adventist tracts arrived in Brazil in 1879, addressed to German immigrants. Within 10 years several families were keeping the Sabbath. In 1888 Abram La Rue, a self-supporting former seaman, retired from sheepherding in California, began to work among English-speaking sailors in the port of Hong Kong. A miner from Nevada took Seventh-day Adventist publications with him to South Africa where he went to seek diamonds. About 1885, the first convert began to keep the Sabbath. He was shortly joined by another South African, Pieter Wessels, who had become convinced from the Bible that the seventh-day Sabbath was the right day to observe.

The 1880s saw the doubling of church membership (15,570 to 29,711). However, the outstanding event of the decade was probably the 1888 Minneapolis General Conference session. At that meeting, young editors Alonzo T. Jones and Ellet J. Waggoner presented a series of messages on righteousness by faith. Ellen White approved their emphasis on Christ's righteousness. Some church leaders feared that the teaching of Jones and Waggoner might detract from what they perceived as the church's task, to preach the Sabbath and exalt God's law. Misunderstanding and division clouded the meeting. After the session Ellen White and the two young preachers traveled from coast to coast, preaching the message of righteousness by faith. Many members welcomed the new emphasis; others insisted on retaining a legalistic stance that viewed the law, rather than the cross, as the center of Adventism. Ellen White's writings after that conference show an even stronger emphasis on the gospel in Christ. For example, "Our only ground of hope is in the righteousness of Christ imputed to us, and in that wrought by His Spirit working in and through us" (SC 63). Minneapolis marked a renewed emphasis on a message centered on Jesus Christ.

Late in 1890 the missionary ship *Pitcairn,* built with Sabbath School offerings from the Adventist churches in the United States, arrived at Pitcairn Island in the Pacific Ocean. Attracted by the report of the mutiny of the *Bounty,* James White had sent literature there in 1876. An Adventist ship's carpenter, John Tay, spent five weeks on Pitcairn in 1886 and led the inhabitants to accept the Bible teachings on the Sabbath.

With the *Pitcairn* Adventist missions came of age. Supported by church members worldwide, mission projects multiplied. Two colporteurs began selling books in Madras, India, in 1893. Georgia Burrus, the first missionary officially sent by the church to India, arrived in Calcutta in 1895; the following year she established a school for girls. The publishing work was well established by the end of the decade. A 1894 land grant from Cecil Rhodes, prime minister of the Cape Colony, provided 12,000 acres near Bulawayo, Zimbabwe. Thus began the Solusi Mission, now Solusi College. Avondale College in Australia, River Plate College in Argentina, and Friedensau Seminary in Germany were established before the turn of the century.

H. Church Reorganization

By 1900 the Seventh-day Adventist Church had 1,500 workers and a membership of 75,767. Its administration was vastly different from what it had been when the church was organized in 1863. The headquarters remained in Battle Creek, Michigan, along with the publishing house, the college, and the sanitarium. Decision makers in Battle Creek often had little information about situations in the places affected by their decisions. Communications were slow and difficult. Power was centered in the General Conference president. To add to this difficult administrative situation, foreign missionaries were sent out by three different entities: the Foreign Mission Board, the General Conference, and the Medical Missionary and Benevolent Association.

Before 1901 some steps had already been taken to facilitate church operations. From 1882 onward the church in Europe took various measures to allow for local initiative. The 1888 General Conference session proposed that North America be divided into several sections, following the European model. In 1894 the conferences of Australia and New Zealand organized themselves into the Australasian Union Conference.

Ellen White was increasingly vocal in urging decentralization: "New conferences must be formed. . . . The Lord God of Israel will link us all together. The organizing of new conferences is not to separate us. It is to bind us together" (GCB 1901, 69). At the same time she proposed a thorough reorganization, with a General Conference Committee representing all phases of the work.

Six major changes were set in operation as a result of the 1901 meeting: (1) organization of union conferences; (2) the transfer of ownership and management of all institutions to the organizations where they were located; (3) creation of departments—such as Sabbath School, education, and publishing—in the General Conference; (4) strengthening of committees by placing on them representatives of the different areas; (5) placing of responsibility for the details of church work on those located where the work was done; (6) creation of a representative General Conference Committee.

After the 1901 reorganization, the General Conference Committee consisted of 25 members. These included six union presidents from North America, one president from Europe, and one from Australia. In addition, the chairmen of the departments—later called secretaries and more recently, directors—were members of the committee. Greater authority was invested in this body, which represented the church around the world. The chairman of this committee was to be elected annually from among the officers.

Arthur G. Daniells became the first chairman; he remained as president until 1922. Daniells deserves mention for more than his long tenure. In 1902 he oversaw the transfer of church headquarters from Battle Creek to Washington, D.C. He carried out the reorganization begun in 1901. He traveled extensively, convinced that to lead the church he needed firsthand information from the mission fields. The number of missionaries sent abroad soared during Daniells' presidency. In addition he led in the formation of the ministerial association and the launching of the journal *The Ministry.* Among his writings, two books stand out: *Christ Our Righteousness* and *The Abiding Gift of Prophecy,* on the work and person of Ellen G. White.

A further development in Seventh-day Adventist Church organization was the formation of "divisions." At first the work in the different sections of the world field was under the supervision of a vice president of the General Conference. In 1913 the constitution and bylaws for a European Division Conference were approved. Other divisions were added. By 1922 the current pattern of divisions as sections of the General Conference Executive Committee had evolved (see II. F).

I. Conflict With Kellogg

The first decade of the twentieth century was particularly difficult for the Adventist Church. Ellen White repeatedly advised against the concentration of church institutions in Battle Creek. The burning of the sanitarium and the publishing house in 1902 were seen by some as retribution for disregarding her advice. Perhaps more difficult than the fires that pushed the General Conference and the Review and Herald to Washington, D.C., was the conflict between church leaders and Dr. John H. Kellogg.

An able physician and famous surgeon, John Harvey Kellogg wrote more than 50 books, mostly on medical topics. He directed the Battle Creek Sanitarium from 1876 until his death in 1943. As an ardent proponent of health reform, Kellogg advocated hydrotherapy, exercise, and a vegetarian diet. As an inventor, he devised machines for physical therapy, formulated early meat analogs, and concocted the first corn flakes, which his brother W. K. Kellogg later commercialized. From 1895 to 1910 he directed the American Medical Missionary College in Chicago. His medical mission in Chicago included a workingmen's home, with inexpensive food and lodging; a home for unwed or destitute mothers; various clinics; an employment agency for released prisoners; and a mail-order catalog store.

In 1894 Battle Creek personnel opened the Guadalajara Clinic in Mexico, the first of Adventist medical ventures outside the United States. The early endeavors grew into a mission school and sanitarium. This institution, as well as those in Battle Creek and Chicago belonged to Kellogg's International Medical Missionary and Benevolent Society and not to the Seventh-day Adventist Church.

Kellogg acted independently of the advice of church leaders. Repeatedly, Ellen White implored him to follow instructions. When the Battle Creek Sanitarium burned, church leaders urged him to rebuild only one building, not to exceed five stories in height and 450 feet in length. When the construction commenced, it became evident that Kellogg had followed his own plan for a much larger, more ornate structure than the one agreed upon. Kellogg's book, *The Living Temple,* published in 1903, contained elements of pantheism. When reprimanded by Ellen White for his unorthodox writing, Kellogg separated from the church. The institutions under his International Medical Missionary and Benevolent Society went with him.

II. The Twentieth-Century Seventh-day Adventist Church

By the time of Ellen White's death in 1915, the organization of the Seventh-day Adventist Church was in place. Schools and colleges were operational around the world. Hospitals and clinics brought healing as well as health education to multitudes. Baptisms in faraway places were numerous. The church was entering its adult phase. There were, however, challenges to be faced, from outside the church as well as within.

Wars caused disruption to the Adventist Church. World War I was especially hard on European Adventists and the missions they sustained in Africa and South America. Reconstruction and reorganization came slowly. No sooner, it seemed, had the church fully recovered from war than war clouds were again brewing over Europe. World War II forced the closing of many missions and required an enormous outlay of funds for relief and reconstruction in Europe. In spite of it all, the Adventist Church grew throughout the world.

A. The Growth of the Church

Growth, together with growing pains, has marked the process of maturation. The membership of the Seventh-day Adventist Church grew from 5,440 members in 1870 to 10,163,414 in 1998. In 1900, only 17 percent of the membership of the church lived outside of North America. As of 1998, 91.23 percent of the total membership lived in countries outside of

North America. At the same time, 81.82 percent of all Seventh-day Adventist evangelistic workers were laboring in divisions other than North America.

The Seventh-day Adventist mission program, begun in 1874 with the sending of J. N. Andrews to Switzerland, received a great impetus under the presidency of A. G. Daniells (1901-1922), who believed that in North America laypersons, well supplied with literature, could accomplish their missionary task in the homeland. Ministers and tithe to support them should be sent overseas. In 1902 alone—when there were fewer than 60,000 members in the United States—60 missionaries and their families left the country. Efforts were concentrated first on England, Germany, and Australia, countries which could, in turn, send out missionaries. Through the Sabbath School mission reports, the church kept abreast of advances in far-flung lands.

Mission today flows in many directions. No longer are all the missionaries sent from North America, Europe, and Australia. For example, in 1960, 156 new missionaries were sent from North America, while 114 left their homes in divisions other than the North American. In 1998 1,071 workers served the church in divisions other than their own. Seventh-day Adventist missionaries go from everywhere to everywhere. Filipinos administer church institutions or nurse the sick in Africa; Argentinians practice missionary medicine in Nepal; an Indian edits a Seventh-day Adventist journal in the United States; a Ghanaian serves at the General Conference; professors from nearly 20 nations teach at the Theological Seminary at Andrews University. In addition to these interdivision workers, many others serve in neighboring nations or even in different parts of their own country.

The church uses many and varied methods to reach people with the gospel message. These may be as quiet as a neighborly visit or as public as an evangelistic crusade with thousands attending. Some of the more spectacular methods or movements are described below.

1. Publishing

The importance of the publishing work of early Adventists has already been noted. Tracts, pamphlets, and periodicals were the vehicle of "present truth" as discovered by the pioneers (see I. F. 1).

The significance of the printed page in the spread of Adventism around the world must likewise be noted. The first overseas publication was the French *Les Signes des Temps,* which came off the press in Basel, Switzerland, in 1876. In many lands books or periodicals brought the first news of Adventism. Some of these were simply given by believers to a friendly sea captain to deliver in a faraway port; others were mailed to specific persons. For example, in 1879 the message came to the German settlers of Santa Catarina, Brazil, in copies of *Die Stimme der Wahrheit* mailed from Battle Creek. Colporteurs took books and periodicals around the world; for example: La Rue to Hong Kong (1888); Arnold to Antigua (1889 or 1890); Lenker and Stroup to Madras, India (1893); Davis and Bishop to Chile (1894); Caldwell to the Philippines (1905).

As of 1998 Seventh-day Adventist publications—including books, magazines, and pamphlets both for church members and for evangelism—were printed in 272 languages and dialects. That same year 57 publishing houses around the world produced 285 periodicals, and the total sale of literature was nearly US$114 million. Of the more than 24,400 literature evangelists selling Adventist literature at the end of 1998, 4,680 were students earning their way through school.

2. Radio and Television

In 1926 Adventist evangelist H.M.S. Richards made his debut on radio, broadcasting occasionally on local radio stations in central California. Convinced that he could reach millions by radio, Richards began in 1930 a weekly broadcast in Los Angeles. In 1936 a male quartet joined him. In 1937 they were called the King's Heralds; the program became the *Voice of Prophecy.* On January 4, 1942, the program was first heard coast to coast. That same year the Voice of Prophecy Bible Correspondence School opened, enrolling more than 2,000 listeners in the first month.

Even during World War II Adventist radio programs were launched in other countries (Australia, 1943) and in other languages (Spanish and Portuguese, 1943). Native speakers conveyed the gospel message in their own tongues. Some broadcasts chose the name Voice of Hope. In some places, local musicians added their talents to the programming. The King's Heralds sang in some 20 languages. New correspondence courses were prepared in English and other languages.

In 1992, on the fiftieth anniversary of the first coast-to-coast *Voice of Prophecy* broadcast, 133 Bible schools around the world offered courses in 66 different languages and dialects. Some 2,000 radio stations aired programs in 36 languages.

Adventist World Radio first went on the air in 1971, using facilities leased in Portugal. Twenty-two weekly broadcasts used 13 languages in the first week of broadcasting. Other stations were added: Malta, 1975; Sri Lanka, 1976; Andorra, 1980; Gabon, Africa, 1983. Since 1987 Adventist World Radio's KSDA on Guam has been broadcasting to Asia and the Pacific. The programming includes much more than the *Voice of Prophecy.* Responses from different parts of China indicate that the gospel is being heard, regardless of national barriers.

In 1950 William Fagal and his team put *Faith for Today,* the first truly national religious telecast in the United States, live, on one New York Station. In 1963 *Faith for Today* was the first religious television program to be broadcast in color. In 1985 the program became *Lifestyle Magazine,* with host Dan Matthews. Through the years *Faith for Today* has offered its viewers Bible courses, reading materials, and contact with local church pastors.

Two later Seventh-day Adventist telecasts deserve mention. George Vandeman began his telecast, *It Is Written,* in 1956. Vandeman and his team have offered hundreds of seminars, especially on the book of Revelation, to viewers who wish further study. In 1973 C. D. Brooks initiated the program *Breath of Life,* a telecast especially directed toward African-Americans. Music and preaching characterize this program.

3. Missionary Ships and Airplanes

In 1921 Leo and Jessie Halliwell were asked to serve as missionaries in Brazil. On a boat trip on the Amazon, Halliwell was amazed at the isolation, the poverty, and the illness along the river. He became convinced that a small ship or launch would be the most effective means of reaching people along the 40,000 miles of navigable rivers in the Amazon basin. The Adventist young people of North and South America responded with funds for the mission launch. On his furlough in 1930 Halliwell took a course in tropical medicine. When he returned to Brazil he sketched the design for his boat; he also helped to build it. For the next 28 years the Halliwells traveled the Amazon and its tributaries, covering some 12,000 miles each year in the *Luzeiro* (Lightbearer), bringing hope and healing to riverbank dwellers. As many as seven boats plied rivers in the Amazon basin at one time. Through the years, the boats have kept the same name. By 1992 the count was up to 23: *Luzeiro XXIII* was operating out of Manaus.

Missionary airplanes, covering miles of inhospitable terrain in minutes, came on the scene after World War II. Borneo and Africa were the first areas to benefit from this service. The General Conference voted an aviation policy in 1960. The first official denominational plane, the *Fernando Stahl,* went into service in 1963 in the Amazon region of Peru. Other planes were added to the fleet, in South America, Africa, and Australasia. Ferrying personnel and supplies, these small planes, piloted by courageous and adventuresome missionaries, land on tiny airstrips, days by foot from cities or towns.

The missionary aviation program peaked in 1981, with 32 airplanes reported in use. By 1998 the program had declined noticeably, mainly because of the development of roads into isolated regions, increases in operation costs, and the placing of financial responsibility for operation in the hands of the local fields—which have access to fewer financial resources than overseas missionaries.

4. Intentional Mission

With the 1901 reorganization, mission to the whole world, Christian as well as non-Christian, became a priority. Since 1950, the church has taken definite steps toward systematic mission to all parts of the world. Special attention has been given to non-Christian religions. To reach the unreached, intentional strategies of mission have been developed.

Study and research on ways to reach Muslims with the gospel began with Erich Bethman's *Bridge to Islam,* published in 1950. In the 1960s several conferences on Islam were held. The SDA Global Centre for Islamic Studies, at Newbold College in England, was opened in 1989 to study appropriate methods for reaching Muslims with Christ, training workers in these methods, and serving as an international resource center. The Center for Religious Studies of the Far Eastern Division began functioning at the Adventist International Institute of Advanced Studies in the Philippines in the early 1990s.

A special institute to study ways of reaching Hindus was established in India in 1992. A similar organization, dedicated to the study of Buddhism and evangelism of Buddhists, began to function in Thailand in 1992.

The Hebrew Scripture Association was created in 1955. Its purpose was to present the gospel in ways that would be attractive to Jews. In 1959 an evangelistic center for Jews opened in New York City. The journal *Shabbat Shalom* is published regularly for Jewish readers.

In 1966 the Department of World Mission became the sixth department of the SDA Theo-logical Seminary at Andrews University (Berrien Springs, Michigan). Its purpose was not only to offer mission classes to seminary students but also to conduct intensive courses for missionaries about to leave on assignment. This second task was later taken over by the Institute of World Mission, operated by the General Conference on the campus of Andrews University.

The first student missionary left Columbia Union College, in Washington, D.C., to Mexico in 1959. In 1998, 317 North American young people served as volunteers in 10 world divisions; worldwide, the figure was more than 1,200. In exchange for a small stipend and great satisfaction, student missionaries delay their college education for as much as one year to participate in some form of mission away from their country. Many have been involved in teaching conversational English in cities of Asia. Their reports have awakened the interest of other laypersons in mission. Many former student missionaries have later gone overseas as full-time missionaries.

In keeping with the intentional mission thrust, church leaders began devising organized quinquennial programs for evangelism and church growth. The One Thousand Days of Reaping resulted in a grand total of 1,171,390 baptisms, reported in a mission pageant at the 1985 session of the General Conference. At that same meeting Harvest 90 was launched. Its goals were to double the number of accessions reached during the One Thousand Days of Reaping and "double the number of members equipped for soul-winning activities according to their spiritual gifts, making every Seventh-day Adventist church a center of training for service" ("Harvest 90 Objectives" 18). At the end of the quinquennium, 2,490,105 accessions were reported. In areas of the world where figures were kept, the number of church members involved in soul-winning activities had risen by 76.4 percent.

At the 1990 General Conference session the Global Mission strategy was launched in order to create an awareness of the enormity of the task still remaining. Global Mission divided the world's population into 5,000 geographical units of approximately 1 million inhabitants. At the time, there were some 2,300 people groups without any Adventist presence. As of August 1999 the number of unentered people groups has decreased to 1,700, most of them in Asia. At the same time the Global Mission reported that each day 4.5 new Adventist congregations were being established.

B. Lay Involvement in Mission

Parallel to official church mission efforts, significant lay initiatives have provided services and evangelism. Many of these function today under the umbrella of the Adventist-Laymen's Services and Industries, working in close harmony with the church administration.

The earliest major self-supporting institution was founded near Nashville, Tennessee, in 1904. The Madison institutions included a school, a farm, a health care facility, a health food factory, and a printing press. Workers trained at Madison often set up their own schools in rural areas or treatment rooms in towns or cities. Several self-supporting medical institutions, located throughout the South, grew out of the Madison enterprise. In other countries Adventist laypersons opened treatment rooms for hydrotherapy and massage. Today several self-supporting secondary schools and colleges train young people in practical and academic disciplines. The emphasis, however, is on practical training for ministering to others.

Another avenue for service is provided by self-supporting vegetarian restaurants. Here wholesome food is accompanied by the sharing of the Bread of Life. These restaurants, operated by Adventist laypersons, are to be found across North America, in Europe, South America, Australia, and Asia.

Elder J. L. Tucker initiated the *Quiet Hour* broadcast in Portland, Oregon, in 1937. Besides radio programming, the Quiet Hour now presents *Search,* a television series on health. In addition, Quiet Hour speakers preach in evangelistic meetings around the globe. Funds gathered by the Quiet Hour have gone to pay for missionary airplanes, vans, and jeeps; Bibles; jungle chapels; and scholarships for worthy students.

In 1986 the Three Angels Broadcasting Network became the first lay-operated Seventh-day Adventist television uplink station. Since 1987, 3ABN has been broadcasting 24 hours a day to a satellite 22,300 miles from earth, from which the signal is reflected back to satellite dishes. The programming is basically religious and includes some non-Seventh-day Adventist materials.

Another manifestation of lay interest in mission is Maranatha Volunteers International. Maranatha began with a group of private pilots who would fly wherever a building needed to be put up. Today volunteers arrive by various modes of travel, but always to construct a facility for the church. Since 1969 Maranatha has completed 1,782 building projects in 59 countries, valued at more than $99 million. In 1998 alone nearly 3,000 volunteers joined Maranatha projects. The buildings put up by volunteers include churches, hospitals, clinics, orphanages, schools, and housing for church workers. All those who are willing to pay their own transportation to the building site are welcome. Volunteers need not have any previous experience in construction.

In 1985 Adventist Frontier Missions was formed to send American lay missionaries to plant Seventh-day Adventist churches in remote areas. In so doing, Adventist Frontier Missions wanted to bring American Adventists into closer contact with worldwide mission. In 1998 18 families were serving in 15 different projects on several continents.

C. Educational System

Battle Creek College, founded in 1874, was the first Seventh-day Adventist tertiary level institution. Its successor, Emmanuel Missionary College, was developed, beginning in 1901,

16

as a missionary training school in Berrien Springs, Michigan. Because of the nature of the work-study programs conducted there, no degrees were granted until 1910.

Adventists were wary of accreditation, which they felt might deprive educational institutions of their Adventist orientation. Doctoral degrees were considered unnecessary or even dangerous. Thus, for example, Pacific Union College in California received its first Ph.D. on campus only in 1928. It was the first Adventist college to qualify for accreditation. Other Adventist colleges in the United States followed suit over the next decade. Educational institutions in countries other than the United States have more readily sought and received recognition, mostly from their respective governments.

The first graduate courses—for ministers—were organized by Pacific Union College in the summer of 1933. The Advanced Bible School functioned for three summers before being transferred to Washington, D.C., as the very early beginning of the SDA Theological Seminary.

Flagship institutions of the Adventist tertiary system in North America are Andrews University (Berrien Springs, Michigah), with emphasis on education, liberal arts, and theology, and Loma Linda University (Loma Linda, California), with emphasis on health sciences. In 1998 15 tertiary level Adventist institutions functioned in North America. The combined enrollment of these institutions was 20,939.

As of 1998 Seventh-day Adventist higher education outside of North America was carried out in 75 tertiary institutions. At least a score of these have achieved university status. Doctoral programs are offered in three institutions in the United States, one in Asia, one in Inter-America, and three in South America.

At the other end of the educational spectrum, in 1998 the church operated 4,450 elementary schools with 723,473 pupils and 1,014 secondary schools with 208,486 pupils. A large percentage of these students are not children of church members; they attend Adventist schools because of the good reputation of Seventh-day Adventist education.

D. Medical Work

Since the founding in 1866 of the Western Health Institute, precursor of Battle Creek Sanitarium, health work has been prominent among Seventh-day Adventists. The theological background to this emphasis is the recognition of God as Creator and the human person as the temple of the Holy Spirit (1 Cor. 6:19). Health is closely related to spirituality; a healthy body facilitates spiritual growth. Hence, the maintenance of health, as well as health education and prevention, are part of religion. In addition, Adventists offer health care as a service to the church and the community.

The "sanitarium" idea began in Battle Creek, under the tutelage of Ellen White and Dr. J. H. Kellogg. Patients stayed long enough to profit from diet, exercise, massage, and hydrotherapy. They also participated in the spiritual activities of the institution. The sanitarium concept was transported in 1897 to Sydney, Australia, and in 1898 to the Skodsborg Sanitarium in Denmark. Early "medical missionaries" carried their equipment for hot fomentations along with their Bibles.

Clinics and hospitals were often set up as an entering wedge in non-Christian lands. For example, in Hindu Nepal, where no evangelism of any kind was permitted, the Scheer Memorial Hospital has operated since 1957 with full government approval. Since restrictions on church activities have been lessened, Adventist congregations function in Nepal.

Ellen White was herself involved in the purchase of the Loma Linda health resort. The College of Medical Evangelists was founded on that estate to prepare medical missionaries. The nursing course began first; the medical course followed. Today the institution is known as Loma Linda University. The Loma Linda University Medical Center is well known for its pioneering work in heart transplants in infants. Its proton accelerator, which began to function in 1991, is one of the first of its kind to combat the growth of cancerous tumors. Its open-heart surgery team has visited many countries to perform operations and train local staff.

Preventive medicine and health education are also important facets of the Seventh-day Adventist medical system. Degrees in public health are offered by Loma Linda University, on campus as well as by extension; master's degrees in health are also available in the Philippines and in Chile. Health professionals as well as pastors take an active role in teaching ways to maintain or improve health. Adventist smoking cessation, weight control, and stress reduction programs are part of this worldwide educational thrust.

Throughout the world in 1998 the Seventh-day Adventist Church operated 162 sanitariums and hospitals with 19,700 beds. In addition, there were 102 nursing homes or retirement centers, 361 clinics, and dispensaries. and 25 orphanages and children's homes. A total of 75,586 employees served these institutions.

E. Welfare and Development

Closely related to the assistance provided by Seventh-day Adventist medical services is welfare and development work. Help is rendered to the needy both at the local church level and as part of a General Conference plan.

In 1874 women of the Battle Creek church formed the "Dorcas and Benevolent Association." Their name remembered the Christian woman in Joppa who made garments for the poor (Acts 9:36-39). The Battle Creek women made clothes and supplied food for needy families, cared for orphans, and ministered to the sick. The idea spread and many Dorcas societies were established around the world. The first federation of Dorcas societies was formed in 1934 by churches in the Chicago area. Their objective was—and remains—to help people in need, regardless of creed, class, or ethnic origin.

Many local churches maintain Community Services centers, from which they serve the indigent and victims of disasters. Assistance takes the form of clothing, bedding, food, furniture, and cash. The services also may include adult education classes in family, health, and coping skills. Some churches or federations maintain vans, filled with clothes and food, ready to meet emergencies.

The Adventist Development and Relief Agency(ADRA) operates from General Conference headquarters, with representatives at division and union levels. ADRA coordinates relief for victims of large-scale disasters, such as earthquakes or floods. The agency also works in a variety of development projects. These include the development of water resources; construction of schools, hospitals, and dams; development of primary health care; and self-help programs, such as gardening or crafts. The major part of ADRA funds comes from foundations and governments, rather than from church monies. Services are rendered primarily to those outside the Seventh-day Adventist Church and largely in needy countries.

F. Church Organization

The Seventh-day Adventist Church functions as a worldwide body. Local churches are grouped into conferences or missions—so-called because they are financially dependent on the higher level of organization. In turn, the conferences and missions form unions, usually created along national, ethnic, or linguistic lines. The unions are grouped into divisions, which function as branches of the General Conference of Seventh-day Adventists, with headquarters in Silver Spring, Maryland, U.S.A. The 12 divisions are the Africa-Indian Ocean, Eastern Africa, Euro-Africa, Euro-Asia, Inter-American, North American, Northern Asia-Pacific, South American, Southern Asia-Pacific, South Pacific, Southern Asia, and the Trans-European.

At each level government is representative. The local churches send representatives to the conference or mission sessions. Confer-

of this volume contains a brief history of the unfolding of the Seventh-day Adventist position considered. Further information on theological development will be found there.

III. Literature

Adventist Review. General weekly paper of the Seventh-day Adventist Church, the magazine has been published continuously, under varying names, since 1850.

"Business Proceedings of the Fourth Special Session of the General Conference of S. D. Adventists." *Review and Herald,* Apr. 24, 1879.

Dabrowski, Rajmund L., ed. *Michael Belina Czechowski: 1818-1876.* Warsaw: Znaki Czasu Publishing House, 1979.

Delafield, D. A. *Ellen G. White in Europe.* Washington, D.C.: Review and Herald, 1975.

Fernandez, Gil, ed. *Light Dawns Over Asia: Adventism's Story in the Far Eastern Division, 1888-1988.* Silang, Cavite, Philippines: AIIAS Publications, 1990.

Froom, LeRoy. *The Prophetic Faith of Our Fathers.* 4 vols. Washington, D.C.: Review and Herald, 1950-1954.

General Conference of Seventh-day Adventists. *Annual Statistical Report.*

"General Conference Proceedings." *General Conference Bulletin,* Apr. 5, 1901.

Gordon, Paul A. *The Sanctuary, 1844, and the Pioneers.* Hagerstown, Md.: Review and Herald, 1983.

Graybill, Ronald. *Ellen G. White and Church Race Relations.* Washington, D.C.: Review and Herald, 1970.

———. *Mission to Black America.* Mountain View, Calif.: Pacific Press, 1971.

Hale, E., Jr., Henry Plumer, and Timothy Cole. "Second Advent Conference and Camp-meeting." *Signs of the Times,* June 15, 1842.

"Harvest 90 Objectives." *Ministry,* December 1985.

Himes, Joshua V., S. Bliss, and A. Hale. Editorial. *Advent Review,* August 1850.

Knight, George. *From 1888 to Apostasy: The Case of A. T. Jones.* Hagerstown, Md.: Review and Herald, 1987.

———, ed. *The Early Adventist Educators.* Berrien Springs, Mich.: Andrews University Press, 1983.

Martin, Walter. *The Truth About Seventh-day Adventism.* Grand Rapids: Zondervan Publishing House, 1960.

Maxwell, C. Mervyn. *Tell It to the World.* Mountain View, Calif.: Pacific Press, 1976.

Miller, William. *Apology and Defence.* Boston: J. V. Himes, 1845.

Mitchell, David. *Seventh-day Adventists: Faith in Action.* New York: Vantage Press, 1958.

Neufeld, Don F., ed. *Seventh-day Adventist Encyclopedia.* 2 vols. 2nd rev. ed. Commentary Reference Series. Hagerstown, Md.: Review and Herald, 1996.

Olsen, V. Norskov, ed. *The Advent Hope in Scripture and History.* Hagerstown, Md.: Review and Herald, 1987.

Robinson, Dores E. *The Story of Our Health Message.* Nashville: Southern Pub. Assn., 1943.

Schwarz, Richard W. *John Harvey Kellogg, M.D.* Nashville: Southern Pub. Assn., 1970.

———. *Light Bearers to the Remnant.* Mountain View, Calif.: Pacific Press, 1979.

Seventh-day Adventist Encyclopedia. Ed. Don Neufeld. 2nd. rev. ed. Hagerstown, Md.: Review and Herald, 1996.

Spalding, Arthur. *Origin and History of Seventh-day Adventists.* 4 vols. Washington, D.C.: Review and Herald, 1961, 1962. (This history of the Adventist Church goes from 1843 to 1947.)

Spicer, William A. *Our Story of Missions.* Mountain View, Calif.: Pacific Press, 1921.

Strand, Kenneth A., ed. *The Sabbath in Scripture and History.* Washington, D.C.: Review and Herald, 1982.

Utt, Richard. *A Century of Miracles.* Mountain View, Calif.: Pacific Press, 1963.

Vyhmeister, Werner K. *Mision de la iglesia adventista.* Brasilia: Seminario Adventista Latinoamericano de Teologia, 1980.

White, Arthur. *Ellen G. White.* 6 vols. Washington, D.C.: Review and Herald, 1981-1986.

White, James. "The Work of the Lord." *Review and Herald,* May 6, 1852.

Revelation and Inspiration

Peter M. van Bemmelen

Introduction

That the living God has revealed Himself and continues to reveal Himself to the human family is foundational to Christian faith. The Scriptures, both OT and NT, present a record of the way God manifested Himself in human history—especially the history of Israel, and supremely in the person of Jesus Christ. Without this divine revelation, humanity would perish, ignorant of God's true character and will and estranged from Him through sin and guilt.

In Scripture the creation of the world and the majesty, beauty, and bounteous provisions of nature are perceived as manifestations of God's glory, wisdom, and loving care for His creatures. Such manifestations are referred to in theology as general revelation. However, the present condition of humanity and this world, filled with sin, disruption, disaster, and death, raises serious questions about the possibility of a true knowledge of God through the natural world or through human experience. Scriptural evidence suggests that such wisdom and knowledge as can be gained from

these sources by themselves is inadequate to give us a true understanding of God's character of love and His intention to save us from sin and death.

God has met this predicament by making Himself known to human beings on a personal level. In theological language this is called special revelation, particularly as it is revealed and recorded in the Scriptures. Fully aware of the various criticisms of the Bible—ethical, historical, linguistic, scientific, philosophical, and theological—we have chosen to focus on the claims made by the biblical writers regarding their own and each other's writings, and especially on Jesus' attitude toward and use of the Scriptures. The prophets, apostles, and supremely Jesus Himself accepted the Scriptures as the trustworthy and authoritative Word of God, given by the Holy Spirit in human language. Revelation and inspiration are ultimately acknowledged as divine mysteries; however, even our limited human understanding of these subjects is of crucial importance for a mature, intelligent Christian faith.

I. Revelation
  A. Definition
  B. Biblical Terminology
    1. The OT
    2. The NT
II. General Revelation
  A. Introduction and Definition
  B. Modalities of General Revelation
    1. Nature
    2. Human Beings
    3. History
  C. Natural Theology and the Salvation of the Gentiles

III. Special Revelation
  A. Introduction and Definition
  B. Characteristics of Special Revelation
    1. Special Revelation as Selective
    2. Special Revelation as Redemptive
    3. Special Revelation as Accommodative
IV. Biblical Inspiration
  A. Introduction: The Problem of Definition
  B. A Biblical View of Inspiration
    1. Inspiration: Word or Concept?
    2. The Human Shape of Scripture
    3. The God-breathed Character of Scripture

I. Revelation

A. Definition

The noun "revelation" and the verb "to reveal" are used in theological as well as in secular language. The basic meaning of the verb, which is derived from the Latin *revelare,* is to take away a covering, to uncover or unveil something that is hidden; therefore, to make known what is secret or unknown. The noun can refer to the act of revealing but also to that which has been revealed. In common language many other words—such as "tell," "make known," "bring out into the open," "bring to light"—are used to express the same idea.

In reference to God's act of revealing Himself and His will and purpose for the human family, these words acquire a new depth of meaning. The essence of divine revelation can be summed up by saying that God reveals Himself in words and acts, through many different channels, but most fully in the person of Jesus Christ. God's explicit intention is that through this revelation human beings may come to know Him and enter into a saving relationship, which will result in eternal fellowship with Him (John 17:3).

B. Biblical Terminology

1. The OT

English translations of the Bible use the words "reveal" and "revelation," but not as frequently as one might expect. In the RSV the verb "reveal" occurs 65 times, of which 28 are in the OT as a translation of the Hebrew or Aramaic verb *gālāh* (except in Genesis 41:25, where it is translated from the Hebrew verb *nāgad*). The verb *gālāh,* like the Latin *revelare,* expresses the idea of uncovering something that was covered or hidden. It occurs frequently with a merely secular meaning (Ruth uncovers the feet of Boaz, Ruth 3:4), as well as in reference to divine revelations (God reveals Nebuchadnezzar's dream in Daniel 2:19). The noun "revelation" occurs twice in the RSV OT as a translation of forms of the verbs *yārāh* and *gālāh* (Hab. 2:19; 2 Sam. 7:27).

Other words and phrases are used in the OT to describe divine revelations. Some expressions focus on their auditory aspect: "The word of the Lord that came to Jeremiah" (Jer. 47:1); "And the Lord said to Moses" (Lev. 19:1); or the oft-repeated "Thus says the Lord" (Amos 1:3). Such phrases occur hundreds of times and highlight the auditive aspect of revelation.

The visual also is essential in the process of God's self-revelation. Verbs such as *rā'āh* (see, be seen, appear, cause to see, show) and *ḥāzāh* (see, see in vision or dream, behold), and the nouns *rō'eh* (seer), *mar'eh* (sight, appearance, vision), *ḥōzeh* (seer), *ḥāzôn* (vision) are also used. Other more general cognitive words used are *ḥāwāh* (to make known, to inform), *yāda'* (to know, to make known, to publish), and *nāgad* (to make known, to report, to tell). This list is by no means exhaustive but shows the variety of words used to describe the different ways in which God communicates with people on earth.

A study of all the revelatory expressions in

the Bible shows the conviction of the biblical writers that they were the recipients and messengers of divine revelation. In the OT this consciousness is especially prominent in the writings of the prophets, but it is also found elsewhere. King David, who is referred to as "the anointed of the God of Jacob, the sweet psalmist of Israel," expresses this conviction: "The Spirit of the Lord speaks by me, his word is upon my tongue" (2 Sam. 23:1, 2). Solomon's wisdom comes as a gift promised by divine revelation and is itself a manifestation of God's wisdom (1 Kings 3:5-14).

Terms that indicate God's revelation are also used in reference to specific events attributed to God's action or intervention. To Noah God announced, "Behold, I will bring a flood of waters upon the earth" (Gen. 6:17) and instructed him to build an ark, so that he and his family might be saved. God gave Moses and Aaron power to perform signs so that Israel might believe that God had appeared to Moses and instructed him to lead them out of Egypt (Ex. 4:1-9, 27-31). On another occasion God employed a violent storm and the belly of a giant fish to nudge a runaway prophet into fulfilling his God-appointed task (Jonah 1:4–3:3). Such divine actions or interventions were usually preceded or accompanied by explanatory revelations. Amos states, "Surely the Lord God does nothing, without revealing his secret to his servants the prophets" (Amos 3:7). According to the OT, words and acts belong together in God's dealings with human beings.

Frequent OT references to prophets, visions, dreams, signs, and wonders provide evidence of the persistent desire of God to reveal Himself through channels of His choice. The personal manifestations of God to Abraham, Isaac, Jacob, Moses—so-called theophanies, or appearances of God—and His cloud-concealed presence during the Exodus were intended to show His loving purpose to enter into a special covenant relationship with Abraham and his descendants, so that through Israel God might make Himself, His will, His salvation, and His gracious character known to all peoples (Gen. 12:1-3; 22:15-18; 26:1-5; 28:10-15; Ex. 19:1-6).

In the letter to the Hebrews the entire process of divine revelation in the OT is summed up in these words: "In many and various ways God spoke of old to our fathers by the prophets" (Heb. 1:1). This statement stresses the preeminence of God's speaking through the prophets. It does not, however, limit the divine revelation to the prophetic witness.

The common OT word for prophet is *nābî'*, which occurs more than 300 times. Its derivation is uncertain, but it is widely held to have a passive sense, "one who is called," and an active sense, "caller, speaker." The first stresses the divine origin of the prophetic ministry, while the second focuses on the task of the prophet as a spokesperson or mouth for God. The latter meaning is illustrated by the appointment of Aaron as spokesman on behalf of Moses to Israel and to Pharaoh. God told Moses, "See, I make you as God to Pharaoh; and Aaron your brother shall be your prophet. You shall speak all that I command you; and Aaron your brother shall tell Pharaoh to let the people of Israel go out of his land" (Ex. 7:1, 2; cf. 4:10-16).

Other terms were used to refer to prophets. When Saul was seeking the lost asses of his father, his servant suggested that they consult "a man of God" in the nearby city. This man of God is also referred to as "the seer" *(ro'eh),* with the note that this word is equivalent to "prophet" (1 Sam. 9:9). This same parallelism appears elsewhere with the word *ḥozeh* (seer) in 2 Samuel 24:11; 2 Kings 17:13; Isaiah 29:10; for all practical purposes these two Hebrew words and *nābî'* are synonyms.

Not only did the prophets proclaim the word of the Lord by mouth, but they also wrote many of the things that had been revealed to them, either by divine command or by the prompting of God's Spirit. The first known writing prophet was Moses, who wrote what came to be known as the Torah, or the law (Joshua 8:31; Luke 24:44). Later prophets also were moved by the Spirit to put their messages into writing. The Lord told Jeremiah, "Take a scroll and write on it all the words that I have spoken to you" (Jer. 36:2). Daniel referred to these as "the word of the Lord to Jeremiah the prophet" (Dan. 9:2).

The word of the Lord written down by Moses and the prophets became a prominent means by which God revealed Himself and His purposes for Israel and the nations. It was the divine intention that these books should be read and heard by future generations so that the people might know God as their Saviour and King. By obeying His word they would experience His blessings (Deut. 4:5-8; Josh. 1:8; Ps. 1:1-3) and be warned of the terrible consequences of turning away from God (Deut. 31:26-29; Isa. 30:8-14).

Long after the dynamic voice of the prophets had fallen silent, the living voice of God still spoke through their writings. Undoubtedly to these writings could be applied the words written earlier: "The secret things belong to the Lord our God; but the things that are revealed belong to us and to our children for ever, that we may do all the words of this law" (Deut. 29:29; see also *Spiritual Gifts* IV).

2. The NT

The NT also uses various words to convey the idea of divine revelation. The verb *apokalyptō* (to reveal) and the noun *apokalypsis* are the most prevalent. These words are generally used in a religious context and refer to such revelations as that of the righteousness and wrath of God (Rom. 1:17, 18), the second coming of Jesus (1 Cor. 1:7; 1 Peter 1:13), the coming of antichrist (2 Thess. 2:3), the knowledge of human thoughts (Luke 12:2), or the Revelation of Jesus to John (Rev. 1:1). The word *phaneroō*, "to disclose or reveal," is also used (Rom. 16:26). Other words used in the context of divine revelation are *gnōrizō* (to make known, Eph. 1:9), *deiknymi* (to point out, John 5:20), *epiphainō* (to appear, show itself, Luke 1:79), and *chrēmatizō*

(to impart a revelation, Matt. 2:12, 22).

While significant OT phrases such as "the word of the Lord came" or "thus says the Lord" do not appear in the NT, the NT does not negate various types of divine revelation to human beings. God communicated with Joseph through dreams (Matt. 1:20; 2:12, 13, 19, 22). Zechariah the priest (Luke 1:22), Ananias of Damascus (Acts 9:10), the centurion Cornelius (Acts 10:3), and the apostle Peter (Acts 11:5) received visions. Paul could speak of the danger of "being too elated by the abundance of revelations" (2 Cor. 12:7), which he apparently received on many occasions during his ministry (Acts 16:9, 10; 18:9, 10; 26:19; 27:23, 24; 2 Cor. 12:1-4; Gal. 2:1, 2).

The revelational terminology of the NT focuses on Jesus Christ. John the Baptist testified, "I came baptizing with water, that he [the Christ] might be revealed to Israel" (John 1:31). John the apostle presents Jesus as "the Word," the only Son from the Father, who "became flesh," and who "has made him known" (John 1:1, 14, 18). Matthew tells us that "no one knows the Father except the Son and any one to whom the Son chooses to reveal him" (Matt. 11:27). The revelation of God in theophanies, visions, dreams, and prophetic utterances has now found its culmination and fulfillment in the incarnation of the Son. For this reason the Epistle to the Hebrews begins with a majestic summary: "In many and various ways God spoke of old to our fathers by the prophets; but in these last days He has spoken to us by a Son. . . . He reflects the glory of God and bears the very stamp of his nature" (Heb. 1:1-3). Christ is God revealed in human form; thus He could say in words that would fit no other human lips: "He who has seen me has seen the Father" (John 14:9).

Paul also uses a wide range of revelational terms and he, perhaps more than any other, presents Christ as the fullest revelation of God. Paul received the gospel which he preaches not from man but "through a revelation of Jesus Christ" (Gal. 1:12). The crucified and risen Lord appeared to him on the road to Damascus while he was persecuting the Christians (Acts 9:1-9). The mystery of Christ was made known to him by revelation; this mystery "was not made known to the sons of men in other generations as it has now been revealed to his holy apostles and prophets by the Spirit" (Eph. 3:5). The role of the Holy Spirit is crucial to the revelation of Jesus Christ; in this Paul is in full agreement with the rest of the NT (John 14:26; 15:26; 16:13, 14; 1 Peter 1:10-12).

While Paul proclaims the gospel of the incarnation, death, and resurrection of Christ as a mystery, he also closely ties both the revelation and its proclamation to the OT (Rom. 1:1-3; 16:25, 26; 1 Cor. 15:3, 4; 2 Tim. 3:14, 15). This again is in full harmony with Jesus' own understanding and use of the Scriptures, both before and after His resurrection (Luke 22:37; 24:25-27, 44-47; John 5:39-47).

The Scriptures play an essential role in divine self-disclosure: Christ is revealed in and through the Scriptures. The dynamic voice of the apostles, like that of the ancient prophets may fall silent, but the Holy Spirit will still speak through their writings and unfold the mystery of Jesus Christ to all nations and all generations until He comes again.

II. General Revelation

A. Introduction and Definition

Revelational language is mostly used in connection with people. But the Bible also uses such language in regard to phenomena of the natural world. Phrases such as "the heavens are telling the glory of God" (Ps. 19:1) show that God reveals Himself through His created works. Different terms have been used to refer to this concept; however, "general revelation" is probably the most common.

Not only does the Bible speak about a revelation in nature (Ps. 19:1-4; Rom. 1:19-23), but it points to an inner awareness of God in the human consciousness. The author of Ecclesiastes asserts that God "has put eternity into man's mind" (Eccl. 3:11), while the apostle Paul speaks of Gentiles who "show that what the law requires is written on their hearts, while their conscience also bears witness" (Rom. 2:15). The moral responsibility, the universal awareness of a distinction between good and evil, right and wrong, has been seen as a manifestation of God in the human consciousness.

General revelation can be defined as that revelation of God that is universal, accessible to all human beings everywhere, by which God is known as Creator, Sustainer, and Lord of the entire universe. As far as humanity is concerned, this general revelation is both external and internal; it is also inescapable. No matter where we turn we are confronted with God's handiwork and ultimately with the presence of God, for as Paul proclaimed to the Athenian philosophers, "In him we live and move and have our being" (Acts 17:28).

Various questions have been raised in regard to general revelation. A crucial issue is whether general revelation provides the necessary elements for a rational knowledge of God, a natural theology. What concept of God will be deduced from the pervasive presence of evil, suffering, deterioration, destruction, and death? Another vital question, especially in the context of an increasingly articulate religious pluralism, is whether general revelation provides a saving knowledge of God. Is God known by followers of any or all religions or worldviews apart from the Judaeo-Christian tradition and, if so, are Christian missions necessary? Has God revealed Himself universally, so that every religion leads to a saving knowledge of God?

In order to address these questions, one must recognize the situation in which the human family finds itself. According to the Bible, at the end of Creation, "God saw everything that he had made, and behold, it was very good" (Gen. 1:31). This "very good" included the first human pair, whom God had created in His own image and likeness. In them was no imperfection—spiritual, moral, mental, or physical. In the words of Ecclesiastes 7:29, "God made man upright." This perfection, unfortunately, did not last long. According to Genesis 3, Adam and Eve distrusted and disobeyed. The consequences were radical. Shame and fear replaced love and respect. Guilt-ridden, the pair hid at the approach of the Creator. Since then, evil, suffering, and death among human beings are stark realities that cannot be denied or escaped. The world is no longer "very good." According to Paul, "the whole creation has been groaning" (Rom. 8:22). Human beings are "subject to lifelong bondage" (Heb. 2:15). In their alienation from God, human beings find it difficult to receive and interpret God's revelation. They find it even harder to respond in love and faith to that revelation. (See Sin III. B. 1-3; Man II. A, B.)

B. Modalities of General Revelation

Generally speaking, three main modalities of general revelation have been distinguished: nature, human beings, and history. While Scriptures warrant this distinction, Christians disagree on the extent to which revelation is mediated through each.

1. Nature

Biblical writers often refer to the phenomena of nature as a revelation of God and His attributes. All aspects of the universe in which we live are manifestations of divine glory and wisdom. Several psalms ascribe praise to God as the Creator of heaven and earth, who constantly upholds all His works and provides for the needs of all living creatures, including His human children (Ps. 8:1-4; 19:1-6; 33:1-9; 104:1-35; 136:1-9). These psalms of praise for the community of faith show that the works of creation are a revelation of God's majesty and loving care. Many other portions of the OT, especially in Job and Isaiah, convey the same message. The challenging questions of Isaiah 40:12-31 point to an omnipotent, yet tender-hearted, Creator and Lord.

Jesus frequently directed the attention of His hearers to the things of nature to illustrate spiritual truths. The birds of the air and the lilies of the field show God's care for the humblest creatures, and Jesus asks, "Are you not of more value than they?" (Matt. 6:26). God causes the sun to "rise on the evil and on the good, and sends rain on the just and on the unjust" (Matt. 5:44, 45). Other lessons from nature include the good tree that bears good fruit and the bad tree that bears evil fruit—the false prophets (Matt. 7:15-20). In harmony with Genesis 3, Jesus teaches that nature reveals the knowledge of good and evil.

The phenomena of nature, however, give us an ambivalent picture of good and evil. Further, as a consequence of evil, nature at times becomes the instrument of divine judgment. The greatest "natural disaster" to hit this world was the worldwide flood of Noah's time. According to Genesis 6-8, it was God's response to the determined wickedness of the antediluvians. The Bible frequently presents destructive forces in the natural world as manifestations of divine wrath upon human sin (the 10 plagues upon Egypt, Exodus 7:1–12:32; the devastating drought in the time of Ahab and Jezebel, 1 Kings 17:1; or the storm that threatened the ship in which Jonah tried to flee, Jonah 1:1-16). All are set forth as divine responses to human rebellion, apostasy, and disobedience. And although Scripture shows us in Job 1 and 2 that natural disasters may be the result of satanic activity, their ultimate control is always attributed to God. Concerning the disasters that befall Job, God said to Satan, "you moved me against him, to destroy him without cause" (Job 2:3).

Paul affirms nature as a modality of divine revelation. God, he said, is "clearly perceived in the things that have been made" (Rom. 1:20). According to Scripture, nature shows divine glory, wisdom, and care. However, in the decay, disease, disaster, and death so prevalent in this world of sin, nature also displays the consequences of the Fall. God's care is daily manifested, but God's judgment upon human sin is also clearly exhibited. Both aspects need to be kept in mind to understand the matter of natural theology.

2. Human Beings

Human beings constitute another modality of general revelation. Even in their fallen condition they bear the marks of their divine origin (Gen. 1:26, 27). When David beheld God's mighty works, he cried out, "What is man that thou art mindful of him?" He answered his own question with the affirmation that God had crowned him with glory and honor (Ps. 8:4, 5).

The Scriptures strongly suggest that human beings have an intuitive knowledge of God. From the outset a knowledge of His existence is assumed: "In the beginning God created the heavens and the earth" (Gen. 1:1). At Athens the apostle Paul asserted that God "is not far from each one of us" and corroborated that assertion with a quotation from the Cretan poet Epimenides (sixth century B.C.): "In him we live and move and have our being" (Acts 17:27, 28). Still, despite this intuitive awareness, to these wise men "the God who made the world and everything in it," was an unknown God (verses 23, 24).

The Bible also points to the voice of conscience as a manifestation of God. The main task of conscience is to encourage us to do the right and to avoid the wrong. It also pronounces judgment. This faculty is a universal phenomenon, even though its operation differs from person to person. According to the NT, the voice of conscience can be resisted and even suppressed (1 Tim. 4:2; Titus 1:15).

Human reason has been presented as a means by which a true knowledge of God can be attained. Some, especially among rationalists and deists, went so far as to claim that the light of reason was fully adequate to know God, His attributes, and His will, and that supernatural revelation was not indispensable. Reason plays a crucial role in receiving and understanding revelation and in grasping divine truth, but it does not generate them. This fact was expressed long ago in Zophar's question to Job: "Can you find out the deep things of God? Can you find out the limit of the Almighty? It is higher than heaven—what can you do?" (Job 11:7). Paul noted that through reason and wisdom the world did not know God (1 Cor. 1:21). The Bible does not present autonomous human reason as a source of a true knowledge of God.

3. History

History is also considered by many as a modality of general revelation. The Scriptures present God as the Lord of history as well as the Lord of nature. In the words of the prophet Daniel, "He changes times and seasons; he removes kings and sets up kings" (Dan. 2:21). The prophetic and historical accounts of the Bible consistently portray God as directing the affairs of nations and judging them and their rulers (Gen. 6:6, 7; 11:7-9; 18:16–19:25; Jer. 18:7-11; Amos 1:3–2:16). Paul declared to the wise men on the Areopagus that God "made from one every nation of men to live on all the face of the earth, having determined allotted periods and the boundaries of their habitation" (Acts 17:26).

Yet, without specific divine enlightenment to interpret the ever-changing flow of history, it is difficult for short-lived human beings to perceive the divine hand in the confusing panorama of historical events. Only in the light of the Scriptures are we able to trace the outworking of God's purpose for the salvation of sinners, first in the history of Israel; in the life, death, and resurrection of Jesus Christ; and in the proclamation of the gospel through the apostolic church (Matt. 24:1-14; Acts 7:1-53; 10:34-43; 13:16-41; 17:22-31; Eph. 1:3–3:13). The Bible gives meaning and purpose to the whole of human history, but that meaning and purpose cannot be detected apart from Scriptures. While history is a modality of divine revelation, that revelation can be recognized only when God Himself provides a divine interpretation of its events.

The evidence presented in the preceding survey of nature, human beings, and history

28

strongly suggests that each constitutes a channel of divine revelation. But this revelation alone is not an adequate source for a natural theology. It does not give a knowledge of God that can bring assurance, peace, and reconciliation with God. (See God I. B.)

C. Natural Theology and the Salvation of the Gentiles

For centuries students of the Scriptures have debated whether a true knowledge of God can be derived from the natural world and through logical reasoning. Through rational reflection the ancient Greek philosophers came to the conclusion that there was a universal reason (Gr. *logos*) which they called God (Gr. *theos*). This philosophical knowledge about God was called "theology" (Gr. *theologia*), a reasoned knowledge concerning God. It also was called natural theology to distinguish it from mythical theology, the knowledge of the gods. Although this natural theology made the Greek philosophers critical of their ancient mythology, it did not turn them from worshiping many gods to worship the one true God.

The apostle Paul never uses the word "theology." However, his writings give evidence not only that he was acquainted with the natural theology of the Greeks, but that he was convinced of its inadequacy to lead people to a saving knowledge of God. Paul states that "Greeks seek wisdom," but asserts the ineffectiveness of their wisdom, for "the world did not know God through wisdom" (1 Cor. 1:22, 21).

Paul believed that creation reveals God but also that the knowledge of God it manifests is suppressed by human minds darkened by unbelief, distrust, guilt, and ignorance (Rom. 1:19-21). The wisdom gained from God's works by those who are unenlightened by the Spirit of God leads to idolatry rather than to the worship of the true God. The apostle pointed out that human beings "exchanged the truth about God for a lie and worshiped and served the creature rather than the Creator" (verse 25). The final result was base idolatry, gross immorality, and hideous criminality (verses 22-32; cf. Eph. 4:17-19).

Another much-debated question is whether Gentiles can be saved through the revelation of God in nature, in conscience, and in history. The biblical evidence suggests that a true knowledge of God can be gained only from creation and providence when, in response to the gracious working of the Holy Spirit, human minds and hearts are transformed and the spiritual perceptions are aroused. Scripture closely connects the transforming action of the Spirit with the proclamation of the Word of God, the gospel of salvation through Jesus Christ (Acts 2:38, 39; 10:42-44; 11:15-18; Gal. 3:1-5; 1 Peter 1:10-12). Salvation comes through Christ alone, as Jesus Himself witnessed: "I am the way, and the truth, and the life; no one comes to the Father, but by me" (John 14:6). For this reason Jesus told His disciples, "Go into all the world and preach the gospel to the whole creation. He who believes and is baptized will be saved; but he who does not believe will be condemned" (Mark 16:15, 16; cf. Matt. 28:18-20; Rom. 10:9-17; 1 Tim. 2:3-7).

Certainly "the true light that enlightens every man" (John 1:9) can penetrate even where Scripture is not known. Further, Paul speaks of "Gentiles who have not the law" yet "do by nature what the law requires," so that "they show that what the law requires is written on their hearts" (Rom. 2:14, 15). These statements indicate that the Holy Spirit can work transformation even where the word of the gospel is not preached by the human voice, but they do not suggest that there is salvation apart from Jesus Christ. Neither do they imply that non-Christian religions are alternative ways to a saving knowledge of God. (See God VII. C. 5.)

III. Special Revelation

A. Introduction and Definition

Turning away from God has always brought tragic consequences. Human beings, estranged from God by sin, guilt, shame, and fear have distorted and suppressed the knowledge of God as manifested in nature and in human consciousness. The whole earth, and especially all living beings—plants, animals, and humans—have become subject to decay, disease, and finally death. In this condition, humanity desperately needed a new revelation of God, a revelation that would not only restore the broken relationship between God and humanity but would ultimately bring the entire universe back into harmony with God. Christians hold that God has given such a revelation, that "he has made known to us in all wisdom and insight the mystery of his will, according to his purpose which he set forth in Christ" (Eph. 1:9, 10).

This revelation is often referred to as special revelation in contrast with general revelation. Whereas general revelation is universal, accessible to all human beings everywhere, special revelation is addressed to specific human beings and is not immediately accessible to all. Whereas through general revelation God is known as Creator, Sustainer, and Lord of the universe, in special revelation He reveals Himself in a personal way to redeem humanity from sin and reconcile the world to Himself.

The center and substance of special revelation is the person of Jesus Christ, God in human flesh (1 Tim. 3:16; John 1:14, 18). In His manifestation in human form on earth, the Son of God submitted Himself to the limitations of human nature: He was "born of woman, born under the law" (Gal. 4:4). He became flesh, Jesus, the carpenter of Nazareth, a Jew who lived for about thirty-three years in Palestine, who died on a cross outside Jerusalem under the governor Pontius Pilate, and who rose from the tomb and ascended to His Father.

God never intended that this revelation would come to humanity as a thunderbolt from a blue sky. On the contrary, from the moment that our first ancestors fell into sin God began to reveal His purpose to save us through a promised seed or descendant of the woman. For thousands of years God revealed Himself through channels of His choice, especially through patriarchs and prophets, to prepare the human family for the supreme revelation, the incarnation of the Son of God. The entire history of preparatory revelations belongs to the realm of special revelation. (See Christ I-III.)

God provided not only anticipatory revelations but also confirmatory testimonies. From among His disciples Jesus chose 12 apostles to witness His life, death, and resurrection, to be eyewitnesses of the supreme revelation of God (Acts 1:21, 22; 1 John 1:1-3). In view of their unique calling and authority as heralds of divine revelation, Paul could say that the church was "built upon the foundation of the apostles and prophets, Christ Jesus himself being the cornerstone" (Eph. 2:20).

This complex dynamic process of divine revelation—in the history of Israel; in the life, death, and resurrection of Jesus Christ; and in the apostolic witness of that supreme event—would be of no use to later generations unless it were preserved and conveyed to them in a trustworthy, authoritative, and persuasive way. Under the impulse and guidance of the Holy Spirit, prophets and apostles not only proclaimed but also recorded what God revealed to them. Under the guiding hand of divine providence, their writings were eventually put together to form the OT and NT.

The Scriptures as the record of special revelation have become an essential factor in the process of divine revelation. While an equation of special revelation with the Scriptures fails to do justice to the complexity of the process of revelation, the Scriptures do fulfill a crucial role in that process. According to the biblical writers the Scriptures come to us as the word of God. That was the conviction of prophets and apostles and of the Lord Jesus Himself (see Dan. 9:2; Matt. 4:4; Mark 7:13; Heb. 4:12). The knowledge of the only true God as revealed in Jesus Christ is conveyed through the Scriptures, under the illumination of the Holy Spirit.

Special revelation is the entire process by which God has revealed Himself and His redemptive purpose for the human race to and through Israel, the prophets, apostles, but supremely in Jesus Christ. It is also the means by which He continues to reveal Himself through the Scriptures under the illuminating and convicting power of the Holy Spirit, and through the proclamation of the church to all nations on earth. At the heart of this process is the great redemptive act of the incarnation of the Son of God, who through His life, death, resurrection, and intercession, redeems from sin all who believe in Him and restores in them the true knowledge of God.

In the deepest sense the process of revelation and redemption are one, for both center in the person of Jesus Christ. Both will come to final fruition when Christ returns to reveal Himself in the fullness of His glory to bestow immortality upon His people and to take them into the presence of the Father. Even then the mysteries of redemptive revelation will continue to arouse the deepest gratitude and the keenest study on the part of the redeemed. As Paul says, "For now we see in a mirror dimly, but then face to face. Now I know in part; then I shall understand fully, even as I have been fully understood" (1 Cor. 13:12).

B. Characteristics
of Special Revelation

Special revelation is distinguished by its specific characteristics: 1. Special revelation is selective: God communicates with specific human beings on a Person-to-person basis with all that is involved in such communication. 2. Special revelation is redemptive: the primary focus of special revelation is the sin-

ner, whom God wants to save and restore. 3. Special revelation is accommodative: it is marked by divine condescension, or accommodation, to the level of humanity. This characteristic is inextricably intertwined with the previous ones and culminates in the incarnation of the Son of God.

1. Special Revelation as Selection

In revealing Himself to humanity God chose specific persons to whom and through whom to make known His character and His will. He chose Abraham and made a covenant with him, promising him descendants and blessings (Gen. 12:1-3; 22:15-18). The covenant promise began to be fulfilled with the birth of Isaac. To him and to Jacob, his son, the initial promise was repeated and confirmed by God (Gen. 26:1-5; 28:12-15).

God appeared to these patriarchs in so-called theophanies. We learn from the Genesis narratives that "the Lord appeared to Abram" (Gen. 12:7; 17:1) and to his descendants (Gen. 26:2; 35:9). God also revealed Himself to them in visions and dreams (see Gen. 15:1; 28:12; 31:10, 11; 46:2). In a very special theophany, Jacob, the father of the 12 tribes, struggled with God and received the divine blessing (Gen. 32:24-28).

God's election of Israel as the recipient and channel of His special revelation continued in succeeding generations. A high point of God's self-revelation occurred at the Exodus, when God revealed Himself through mighty acts of redemption, and proclaimed His glory or character as a compassionate and forgiving God. The revelations of Yahweh as the merciful Redeemer and the supreme lawgiver (Ex. 3, 20, 24) were deeply engraved on the consciousness of Israel and provided a firm foundation for all subsequent revelations.

The Lord continued to reveal Himself to the chosen nation in a special way, primarily through men and women on whom He bestowed the gift of prophecy. Among these were: Samuel (1 Sam. 3:21), Isaiah (Isa. 6), Huldah (2 Kings 22:14-16), and many others.

God Himself called to the prophetic office; never was anybody endowed with this gift as a result of human initiative or effort. As Peter states it, "no prophecy ever came by the impulse of man, but men moved by the Holy Spirit spoke from God" (2 Peter 1:21).

God's relationship and providential dealing with the chosen nation were unique. To no other nation on earth did He reveal Himself as He did to Israel. One of the psalmists stated that God "has not dealt thus with any other nation; they do not know his ordinances" (Ps. 147:20). Centuries later Paul affirmed that the advantage of the Jews was "much in every way"; they had been "entrusted with the oracles of God" (Rom. 3:1, 2). The results of God's special revelation to Israel were unparalleled. They alone worshiped the one true God. No other nation had a law like the Ten Commandments. The Sabbath as a weekly day of rest commemorating Creation was peculiar to Israel. And no nation could claim to have a body of sacred Scripture produced by inspired writers over a period of more than a thousand years. A prominent feature of Yahweh's special revelation to Israel was the oft-repeated promise of a royal Son, the son of David, who would bring redemption and everlasting peace, not only to Israel but to the ends of the earth (Gen. 49:8-10; 2 Sam. 7:8-16; Ps. 2:1-11; Isa. 9: 6, 7; 11:1-10; 49:1-6; Jer. 23:5, 6; Micah 5:2-4; Zech. 9:9, 10).

Although the revelations made by Yahweh to Israel and His providential dealing with the chosen nation were unparalleled, the Lord made it clear from the beginning that the revelation given to Israel was for the benefit of all nations on earth. God had said to Abraham that in him and his descendants all the families of the earth would be blessed (Gen. 12:3; 22:18). At Mount Sinai the Lord reminded Israel how He had redeemed them from Egypt and told them, "If you will obey my voice and keep my covenant, you shall be my own possession among all peoples" (Ex. 19:5). This revelation was certainly selective. But imme-diately the Lord added, "for all the earth is mine, and you shall be to me a kingdom of priests and a holy nation" (verses 5, 6). God chose Israel to reveal Himself and His redemptive purpose to the whole earth, to be His witnesses among the nations (Isa. 43:9-12).

2. Special Revelation as Redemption

The supreme purpose of all forms or modalities of special revelation is to bring redemption to sinful human beings. The revelations given to Moses and the prophets, and through them to Israel, were intended to bring a knowledge of "the Lord, a God merciful and gracious, slow to anger, and abounding in steadfast love and faithfulness, keeping steadfast love for thousands, forgiving iniquity and transgression and sin" (Ex. 34:6, 7).

Redemption centers in Jesus Christ; therefore, so does special revelation. However, the revelations given of old were partial and progressive; they came "in many and various ways," until at last God revealed Himself in His Son, who fully reflected "the glory of God" and bore "the very stamp of his nature" (Heb. 1:1, 4). It is not surprising, therefore, that the prophets "searched and inquired about this salvation," and "inquired what person or time was indicated by the Spirit of Christ within them when predicting the sufferings of Christ and the subsequent glory" (1 Peter 1:10, 11). Jesus affirmed the privilege of His disciples: "Truly, I say to you, many prophets and righteous men longed to see what you see, and did not see it, and to hear what you hear, and did not hear it" (Matt. 13:17). From these and many other passages it is evident that special revelation is progressive as is the believer's understanding of that revelation (Prov. 4:18; John 16:12, 13; 1 Cor. 13:9-12).

Because special revelation is redemptive, the Bible as the written record of special revelation in all its diversity finds its common focal point in Christ and His salvation. The aged apostle Paul pointed Timothy to the Holy Scriptures as the God-given means to instruct him, "for salvation through faith in Christ Jesus" (2 Tim. 3:15). This saving knowledge is specific, yet universal in its intent. Because in Christ "are hid all the treasures of wisdom and knowledge" (Col. 2:3), He can bring all people to Himself and to the Father.

3. Special Revelation as Accommodation

No revelation would accomplish its divinely intended purpose if it were beyond the possibility of humans to receive and grasp it. In order to reach us in our fallen condition, God accommodates His revelation to human capacity. The Lord condescends to our level of understanding, using human language, employing figures and symbols known to human beings to reveal Himself so that we may know Him and understand His character and His dealings with us. This accommodation, or condescension, is found in all His dealings with the human race, yet it reached its climax in the incarnation of the Son of God, who became a human being, Jesus of Nazareth.

The very fact that God selects fallen beings to convey the revelation of Himself to other fallen beings, in human language, with all its foibles and imperfections, is by itself an unfathomable act of condescension. While we do recognize divine accommodation in the Scriptures, we must guard against pressing the concept of accommodation so far as to deny or distort the true meaning of Scripture.

Of the many different forms or manifestations of divine accommodation, we can only provide some samples. One prominent form is the use of anthropomorphic language in reference to God's person and His attitude toward human beings. God is represented in the Bible as having a bodily form; He has a face (Ex. 33:20), eyes (Ps. 11:4), ears (Ps. 18:6), nostrils and mouth (verse 8), arms and hands (Isa. 62:8), and feet (Ex. 24:10).

Scripture also ascribes human feelings and attitudes to God. He remembers (Ex. 2:24), hates (Ps. 5:5; Isa. 61:8), abhors (Ps. 106:40), laughs (Ps. 2:4), is angry (1 Kings 11:9), and is pleased (Matt. 3:17; Col. 3:20). If such expressions are understood in an extreme literal sense, we may have a distorted picture of God. The Bible itself contains corrective cautions against misinterpreting the human expressions used in reference to God. While 1 Samuel 15:11 reports God as saying "I repent that I have made Saul king," the same chapter affirms that God "is not a man, that he should repent" (verse 29). In Genesis 15 we find God condescending to ratify His covenant, as was the custom of the day. In many other passages, He speaks in human language so that He might be understood.

IV. Biblical Inspiration

A. Introduction: The Problem of Definition

Christians commonly refer to the Bible as an inspired Book, a holy Book, a divine Book, or simply as Scripture. Jesus often appealed to or quoted from the Scriptures, and there can be no question that He considered the Hebrew Scriptures as carrying divine authority (Matt. 4:4; John 10:35). The apostle Paul, likewise, accepted the Scriptures as being of divine origin (2 Tim. 3:16). He referred to them as "the holy scriptures" (Rom. 1:2), "the oracles of God" (Rom. 3:2), and "the sacred writings" (2 Tim. 3:15).

Belief that the Hebrew Scriptures came into being as the result of divine inspiration has been widespread and persistent among Jews and Christians. However, there is no agreement as to exactly what "inspiration" means. Concepts on biblical inspiration range from verbal dictation by the Holy Spirit to merely human inspiration. Some think the concept of inspiration should be discarded altogether.

A number of factors have contributed to the diversity of opinions concerning biblical inspiration. While the concept is biblical, the word "inspiration" is not. In addition, those who study the issue of inspiration do not all start from the same presuppositions. Finally,

33

no biblical author presents a detailed discussion of the topic. Because of these factors, a detailed study of the biblical evidence for inspiration is necessary.

B. A Biblical View of Inspiration

1. Inspiration: Word or Concept?

The words "inspiration" and "inspired" do not appear as such in the original languages of the Bible. They are derived from the Latin and appeared in the Vulgate translation of 2 Timothy 3:16 and 2 Peter 1:21. Their basic meaning is to "breathe in."

In 2 Timothy 3:16 Paul affirms that all Scripture is *theopneustos,* or "breathed by God." Benjamin Warfield concludes that "Scripture is called *theopneustos* in order to designate it as 'God-breathed,' the product of divine inspiration"; thus "the Scriptures owe their origin to an activity of God the Holy Ghost and are in the highest and truest sense His creation" (296).

Peter points out that "men . . . spoke from God," *pheromenoi* (carried, blown, or impulsed) "by the Holy Spirit" (2 Peter 1:21). Following the Vulgate, some translations have used the word "inspired" here, but most have used the phrase "moved by the Holy Spirit." In any case, the sense of the text is that biblical prophecy has its origin in the Holy Spirit.

Thus, while the word "inspiration" is not a precise translation of any Greek word used in the Bible to describe the process by which Scripture comes to the human mind, it may be appropriately used to represent a process in which the Holy Spirit works on selected human beings, to move them to proclaim messages received from God. Some spoke the word; some wrote it. The written form constitutes the God-breathed Scriptures (2 Tim. 3:16). "Inspiration" refers to the Holy Spirit's work on these messengers or prophets, whether they spoke or wrote. Because these people were "inspired" or "moved by the Holy Spirit" (2 Peter 1:21), their utterances and writings may be considered inspired as well (2 Tim. 3:16).

While the word "inspiration" focuses primarily on the activity of the Holy Spirit, a careful study of the biblical data makes it clear that both human and divine activity are involved in the process by which the Scriptures came to be written.

2. The Human Shape of Scripture

At face value the Scripture is a human book, or rather a collection of human books. Many of these have a human name attached to them; all bear the marks of human authorship. This authorship shows in their opening words: "the words of Jeremiah" (Jer. 1:1), "the proverbs of Solomon" (Prov. 1:1), "the elder to the beloved Gaius" (3 John 1), "Paul . . . and our brother Sosthenes, to the church of God which is at Corinth" (1 Cor. 1:1, 2). The first five books of the OT are attributed to Moses, many of the Psalms to David and Asaph. The prophetic books each bear the name of a prophet, the Gospels the name of an apostle or of a close associate of the apostles. Thirteen letters explicitly mention Paul as their author, and the book of Revelation was written by John, traditionally understood to be the apostle John.

Authors frequently refer to themselves with personal pronouns; they also record their own experiences (Ezra 8:15-30; Neh. 1:1-11; Isa. 6:1-8; Jer. 1:1-19; Dan. 7:1-28; Gal. 1:12–2:10; Rev. 1:9-19). Peculiar characteristics of style and language point to the distinct individuality of each writer.

Numerous historical references and literary forms link the biblical writings with their times and backgrounds. Many of the laws of Moses show remarkable parallels with other ancient laws, such as those of Hammurabi. Patriarchal customs and social conditions in Genesis reflect in a notable way the conditions in Mesopotamia and Egypt in the second millennium B.C. Significant parallels exist between some psalms and Canaanite religious literature, and between some biblical proverbs and their contemporary Egyptian proverbs.

These and other parallels between biblical and nonbiblical literature give the Bible a very human face.

Some books of the Bible belong to the world's classics, as expressions of the deepest human emotions. Human drama is portrayed in Job and in Ruth, passionate yet delicate love in the Song of Solomon, gripping suspense in Esther, and supreme distress in Lamentations. And one cannot remain untouched by Paul's plea for a wayward slave in the Epistle to Philemon.

The historical books of the Bible provide evidence of historical research (Luke 1:1-4). The apostle Paul quotes pagan authors (Acts 17:28; 1 Cor. 15:32, 33; Titus 1:12). Jude cites the pseudepigraphical book of Enoch (Jude 14, 15).

The human shape of Scripture is unmistakable. Human authors—using human language, quoting human sources, operating in specific human contexts, describing human emotions—are subject to all the weaknesses and failures of humanity. Prophets and apostles were not free from sin. They doubted, they were afraid, at times they succumbed to temptation (Ex. 4:10-14; Num. 20:10-12; 2 Sam. 11:1-27; 1 Kings 19:1-3; Luke 22:54-62). Neither were they free from pride and prejudice, as is quite evident from Jonah and the Gospel narratives (Matt. 20:20-28).

One may well wonder how some forty writers from divergent historical and cultural backgrounds, who differed widely in status and occupation, as well as in intellectual and spiritual endowments, produced a collection of books that manifests a remarkable unity and that from beginning to end reveals one God, Creator of heaven and earth, whose love embraces all things. Beyond this, one may wonder how such writers portrayed a person like Jesus of Nazareth, so truly human and yet so completely free from all the weakness and imperfection of the biblical writers themselves. The answer to these questions, as Christians through the ages have believed, lies in the fact that the Scriptures have not

merely a distinct human character but also a divine origin.

3. The God-breathed Character of Scripture

Just as plain as the idea of the human shape of Scripture is the conviction of its human authors that their writings owe their origin to God. In the words of 2 Timothy 3:16, they are God-breathed. That conviction comes to expression in many different ways.

Innumerable places in the Scriptures show single sentences, large paragraphs, or even entire chapters directly attributed to God as speaker. The very first chapter of the Bible, for instance, presents God as a speaking God. The different acts of Creation are introduced and initiated by the phrase "And God said" (Gen. 1:3, 6, 9, 11, 14, 20, 24, 26). As soon as God had created the first human beings He spoke to them (verses 28, 29). Throughout Genesis we find God speaking to human beings, usually to those who believe in Him, but at times also to those who do not acknowledge Him (Gen. 4:6-16). From Exodus 3:4, where God calls Moses, through the Pentateuch, we find the ever-recurring phrase "And the Lord said to Moses," or words of similar intent (Ex. 20:22; 25:1; 34:1, 6; Lev. 1:1; Num. 1:1; Deut. 32:48).

Moses announced that the Lord would communicate in future times with His chosen people through prophets (Deut. 13:1-5; 18:15-19). In fulfillment of promises such as verse 18, many prophets arose through the centuries. They spoke and wrote the words that God put in their mouths and in their hearts and minds. Ezekiel received this command, "Son of man, all my words that I shall speak to you receive in your heart, and hear with your ears. And go . . . to your people, and say to them, 'Thus says the Lord God' " (Eze. 3:10, 11). To Jeremiah the Lord declared, "Before I formed you in the womb I knew you, and before you were born I consecrated you; I appointed you a prophet to the nations" (Jer. 1:5). "Behold, I have put my words in your mouth" (verse 9).

There is every reason to assume that such commands apply to all the prophets appointed by God. They spoke and wrote the word of the Lord.

The spoken word became the Written Word by divine impulse and command. There is sufficient evidence in the books of Moses and the prophets to show that God called them to speak and to write the words He had entrusted to them (Ex. 17:14; Deut. 31:19, 24; Jer. 36:2; Hab. 2:2). Through the Written Word God would speak to later generations, long after its human authors had passed away (Deut. 29:29; Isa. 30:8). The book of the law of Moses was to be studied, believed, and obeyed by successive generations in Israel, for it was the law of the Lord. Israel's prosperity and relationship with God as His covenant people depended on their wholehearted acceptance of His law. When they rejected the law, they actually rejected the Lord, and the results were disastrous (Joshua 1:7, 8; 8:34, 35; 1 Kings 2:1-3; Isa. 5:24, 25; Dan. 9:11-13).

Books by prophets, wise men, and psalmists were added to the law of Moses in subsequent centuries. In some of these we find statements by the human authors that point to God as the source of what they wrote. Of the young prophet Samuel it is written, "And Samuel grew, and the Lord was with him and let none of his words fall to the ground." "The Lord appeared again at Shiloh, for the Lord revealed himself to Samuel at Shiloh by the word of the Lord. And the word of Samuel came to all Israel" (1 Sam. 3:19, 21; 4:1). David testified about himself, "The Spirit of the Lord speaks by me, his word is upon my tongue" (2 Sam. 23:2). Solomon, "the Preacher, the son of David, king in Jerusalem" (Eccl. 1:1), "taught the people knowledge, weighing and studying and arranging proverbs with great care" (Eccl. 12:9). That is the human aspect of his writings. Yet, immediately he adds that "the sayings of the wise . . . are given by one Shepherd" (verse 11), the Lord, the God of Israel.

Though written by human authors, law, history, prophecy, psalms, and proverbs were all attributed to God. He was the One who called human beings to be His messengers, revealed Himself to them, instructed them through His Spirit, endowed them with wisdom, guided them in their research, and moved them to speak and write. True, the evidence for this attribution of the OT writings to God is much more prominent in some parts of them than in others; it is especially limited in the historical parts. Still, that all of the OT was regarded as of divine origin becomes explicit in the NT.

The four Gospels show us that Jesus constantly appealed to the Scriptures of the OT as having ultimate authority. Underlying these appeals was the fundamental conviction of the divine origin of Scriptures. When tempted by the devil to relieve His hunger, Jesus resisted by quoting Deuteronomy 8:3: "Man shall not live by bread alone, but by every word that proceeds from the mouth of God" (Matt. 4:4). Three times He refuted Satan's temptations with the answer "It is written," clearly implying that all Scripture proceeds from God.

On another occasion Jesus introduced the quotation of Psalm 110:1 with the words "David himself, inspired by the Holy Spirit, declared" (Mark 12:36). He quoted the words of Genesis 2:24 as if spoken by God, in spite of the fact that in the original they appear to be a comment by Moses (Matt. 19: 4, 5). When Jesus introduced statements from the OT with expressions such as "It is written," (Matt. 21:13) "have you never read" (verse 16), or "this scripture must be fulfilled in me" (Luke 22:37), He attributed to Scripture divine inspiration and authority. (See Christ I. B. 1. b.)

In a confrontation with the Pharisees and scribes, our Lord drew a sharp distinction between human tradition and "the Word of God" (Matt. 15:6), a phrase used by Jesus in reference to the OT (see John 10:35; 17:17). In referring to the word He preached as the word of God (Luke 8:21; 11:28), He did so in the awareness that He spoke the words which the Father had given Him to speak (John 14:24; 17:8). He also knew that the Holy Spirit would bring these words to the remembrance of His disciples who would proclaim the same words in oral and written form (John 14:25, 26; 16:13-15).

The apostles accepted the OT as divinely inspired. They attributed words written by prophets and psalmists to the Holy Spirit. Peter introduced Psalms 69:25 and 109:8 to his fellow believers in the upper room by saying, "The scripture had to be fulfilled, which the Holy Spirit spoke beforehand by the mouth of David" (Acts 1:16, 20). Similar statements crediting the Holy Spirit as the source of words from the OT can be found in several places in Acts and in the Epistles (Acts 4:25; 28:25; Heb. 3:7; 10:15). God was the One who spoke through the mouth of His chosen servants (Acts 3:18, 21; Rom. 1:2; Heb. 1:1; Rev. 10:7).

This conviction that the prophetic writings originated with God is summed up in the words of Peter: "No prophecy ever came by the impulse of man, but men moved by the Holy Spirit spoke from God" (2 Peter 1:21). Paul, with obvious reference to "the sacred writings," with which Timothy had been acquainted from childhood, declared, "All Scripture is inspired by God" (2 Tim. 3:16). For the Lord Jesus and for the apostles, all Scripture, all of the OT, originated with God and was truly God-breathed.

The NT suggests that the apostolic writings were accepted as being part of Holy Scripture, together with the OT. As one would expect, such indications are especially found in the later books of the NT (Luke 10:7; cf. 1 Tim. 5:18). In 1 Timothy 5:18 Paul juxtaposes a statement of Jesus, "The laborer deserves his wages" with a quotation from the OT (Deut. 25:4) and introduces both with the phrase "for the Scripture says." The introductory phrase suggests that the apostle Paul was acquainted with the Gospel of Luke and recognized it as Scripture. In a similar manner, Peter appears to recognize Paul's letters as Scripture, "according to the wisdom given him" (2 Peter 3:15, 16).

Paul, Peter, and John use expressions that clearly exhibit their consciousness of being moved, like the prophets of old, by the Holy Spirit (Eph. 3:4, 5; 1 Peter 1:12; Rev. 1:10, 11). They are conscious of speaking and writing with divine authority.

The application of 2 Timothy 3:16, that all Scripture is God-breathed, should be made not only to the books of the OT but to those of the NT as well. That their writings were already recognized as inspired Scripture by Christian authors of the second century A.D. provides additional justification for such an application.

C. Mode, Locus, and Extent of Inspiration

Given the human and divine aspects of Scripture, one must ask how these two aspects relate to each other. Unfortunately, biblical writers do not directly address the question. However, scattered throughout the books of the Bible one finds indications and suggestions concerning the process of inspiration and its results. On the basis of these biblical data we will try to reach some conclusions. The subject will be discussed here in terms of the mode, the locus, and the extent of inspiration.

1. The Mode of Inspiration

Biblical authors agree on the crucial role of the Holy Spirit in moving them to write. The initiative is wholly with the Spirit: He calls, gives revelations, moves, or inspires. Peter states it succinctly: "No prophecy ever came by the impulse of man" (2 Peter 1:21). Even the unwilling prophet Balaam could utter only what the Lord allowed him to say (Num. 24:2-9, 13).

While recognizing the fact of inspiration, we must examine the mode in which it occurs. This entails studying the process by which biblical authors received revelations and wrote them down.

God commonly revealed Himself to prophets in visions and dreams (Num. 12:6). They then wrote down what they had seen and heard, either immediately or later. We ask, Did the prophets do the writing of themselves, or was it always under God's guidance? This question must be answered indirectly, for the prophets say little about the matter.

Jeremiah's experience helps answer our question. The Lord tells the prophet, "Take a scroll and write on it all the words that I have spoken to you against Israel and Judah and all the nations" (Jer. 36:2). It is hard to believe that Jeremiah, unaided by the Spirit of God, could have remembered and written down what God had revealed to him over a period of many years. The story continues: Jeremiah called Baruch, who "wrote upon a scroll at the dictation of Jeremiah all the words of the Lord which he had spoken to him" (verse 4). Then "Baruch read the words of Jeremiah from the scroll" (verse 10), but these words were "the words of the Lord" (verses 8, 11).

This identification of the words of the prophet as the words of the Lord suggests strongly that the prophet was inspired, i.e., was moved and directed by the Spirit of God, in putting the words of the Lord in written form. Likewise, when the prophet Micah, contrasting his message with that of false prophets, exclaimed, "But as for me, I am filled with power, with the Spirit of the Lord, . . . to declare to Jacob his transgression and to Israel his sin" (Micah 3:8), he included written as well as spoken words.

When King Jehoiakim defiantly burned the scroll, "Jeremiah took another scroll and gave it to Baruch the scribe, . . . who wrote on it at the dictation of Jeremiah all the words of the scroll which Jehoiakim king of Judah had burned in the fire; and many similar words were added to them" (Jer. 36:32). This was a second, enlarged edition of the book of Jeremiah.

The experience of Jeremiah indicates that the prophets did not write their books as if they were mere copyists. They were fully involved, while moved and guided by the Spirit, in their writing. The same can be said of biblical writers who are not specifically referred to as prophets. Solomon, the author of many proverbs and songs, tells us that he "taught the people knowledge, weighing and studying and arranging proverbs with great care." He also "sought to find pleasing words, and uprightly he wrote words of truth" (Eccl. 12:9, 10). Luke, author of the Gospel and of Acts, tells us that it seemed good to him, "having followed all things closely [or accurately] for some time past, to write an orderly account" (Luke 1:3). Thus, careful historical research and literary assessment were important to the composition of the books written by Solomon and Luke. There is good reason to believe that a similar process was involved in the composition of other biblical books, even when that fact is not explicitly stated.

Whether the human messengers in the process of speaking or writing were always conscious of the moving of the Holy Spirit is not entirely clear. However, indications of such consciousness are found frequently in connection with the names of prophets and apostles. A careful study of the biblical data suggests that both the inspired persons themselves as well as others who heard them or read their writings recognized this special moving of the divine Spirit in their communications (Moses, Num. 12:7, 8; Joshua, Deut. 34:9; Samuel, 1 Sam. 3:19; David, 2 Sam. 23:2; Ezekiel, Eze. 2:2; Daniel, Dan. 9:22; 10:9-11; Micah, Micah 3:8; Peter, Acts 11:12; Paul, 1 Cor. 7:40; John, Rev. 1:10).

Remarks by Paul in 1 Corinthians 7 have led some to conclude that Paul distinguishes between things he said under inspiration and other things which were merely his personal opinion. He writes in verse 10, "To the married I give charge, not I but the Lord"; in verse 12 he adds, "To the rest I say, not the Lord." Again in verse 25 he states, "Now concerning the unmarried, I have no command of the Lord, but I give my opinion as one who by the Lord's mercy is trustworthy." These texts do not, in fact, deal with the issue of inspiration. The contrast Paul draws in verses 10 and 12 is that in one case he can refer to an explicit command of the Lord (Matt. 5:32; 19:1-6), whereas in the other he cannot. Yet the advice in verse 12 and elsewhere is given under inspiration, for Paul concludes this discourse on questions regarding marriage with the emphatic assertion, "I think that I have the Spirit of God" (1 Cor. 7:40). The Bible may not explain distinctly the process by which the Holy Spirit moved and guided the writers of the different books of Scripture, but one fact is clear: These writers functioned fully as human beings with the involvement of their total personality.

2. The Locus of Inspiration

The locus of inspiration concerns the question Who or what is inspired? Does inspiration pertain to specific individuals chosen by God, such as prophets and apostles, or to the messages they delivered in oral or written form—particularly to the Scriptures, or to the community of faith in which the Scriptures originated? The first two options have long been a matter of debate; the third option has especially come to the fore in recent years.

The biblical evidence presented earlier in this article points to specific individuals, chosen by God, as the primary locus of the working of the Holy Spirit. Scripture says "Men moved by the Holy Spirit spoke from God" (2 Peter 1:21); "The Spirit of the Lord speaks by me, his word is upon my tongue" (2 Sam. 23:2); "As for me, I am filled with power, with the Spirit of the Lord" (Micah 3:8).

Whether inspiration should be attributed to the inspired writers or to the Scriptures written by them is to a large extent a needless dilemma. It is clear that the primary locus of inspiration is in people. The Holy Spirit moved upon people to speak or write; yet what they spoke or wrote was the inspired word of God. In the words of Paul to Timothy, "All Scripture is God-breathed" (2 Tim. 3:16, NIV). Peter recognized the letters of Paul as part of the Scriptures, written according to "the wisdom that God gave him" (2 Peter 3:15, NIV). In writing his Epistles, Paul was inspired or moved by the Holy Spirit, and the letters he produced became part of the God-breathed Scriptures.

Inspiration worked on Paul, and under inspiration Paul wrote inspired letters. The primary locus of inspiration is the apostle; the result of that inspiration is Holy Scriptures.

The third option for the locus of inspiration, the community of faith where Scripture had its origin, hardly deserves mention as a viable alternative. The concept is based, to a great extent, on a specific method of Bible study. By a literary-historico-critical study of the Bible, scholars have come to the conclusion that many biblical books are the end product of a long process, in which unknown writers, editors, and redactors were involved. On the basis of such phenomena, the understanding that books of the Bible had specific authors—who lived in well-defined historical contexts, and wrote under inspiration—is denied. Instead of these authors being inspired, the community among which the writing reached its final form is inspired to recognize the validity and authority of the Bible message. (See Interpretation IV. F, G.)

While there is evidence of redaction and editing, much of this can be attributed to the inspired authors themselves, to their immediate associates, or possibly even to later inspired writers. Joshua, for instance, may well have—under divine inspiration—edited the books of Moses and made additions to them, such as, for example, the last verses of Deuteronomy. In any case, given the absence of evidence for the locus of inspiration in a community rather than in a biblical author, the statements of Scripture must stand. The locus of inspiration is in the inspired author.

3. The Extent of Inspiration

The "extent of inspiration" refers to the matter of how much of the Bible is inspired. Are the words of the Bible themselves inspired? Or are only the thoughts behind the words inspired? Are some parts of the Bible more inspired than others? Are some parts not inspired at all? Is the Bible inspired in its totality or is it inspired only in degrees?

From discussion of special revelation and

inspiration (III. B and IV. B) it is evident that the revelation-inspiration process has many aspects and that available information does not answer all our questions. However, there is little doubt that thoughts as well as words are involved in this process. In visions and dreams or by impressions of the Holy Spirit, inspired persons received thoughts in visual or verbal form. These they then conveyed faithfully and truthfully as they had received. At times they seem to express their messages in precisely the words given to them by the Spirit.

Regardless of the way the thoughts were received, the biblical writers emphasize that their words are words from God. Moses quotes God as saying that He will put His words in the mouth of the prophets (Deut. 18:18; cf. Jer. 1:9). Referring to Scripture, Jesus declared, quoting from Deuteronomy 8:3, that "man shall not live by bread alone, but by every word that proceeds from the mouth of God" (Matt. 4:4).

The words written by the biblical authors are distinctly human words. For that reason they can introduce their books with such expressions as "the words of Jeremiah" (Jer. 1:1) or "the proverbs of Solomon" (Prov. 1:1). The thoughts, and at times the words, are given by revelation of God to be expressed by the human authors in words familiar to them and their immediate readers.

Truly the Scriptures are fully human and fully divine. Any idea that some parts of the Bible are merely human while other parts are divinely inspired contradicts the way the biblical writers present the matter. Paul's words, that "all Scripture is God-breathed," do not allow for any concept of partial inspiration. Neither are there any hints in Scripture suggesting degrees of inspiration. Some portions of Scripture may be more important than other portions (Jesus speaks in Matthew 23:23 about "the weightier matters of the law"), but that does not mean that they are more inspired. Every Christian would do well to receive the words of Holy Scripture in the

manner in which the believers in Thessalonica accepted the words of Paul, "not as the word of men but as what it really is, the word of God" (1 Thess. 2:13).

D. Effects of Inspiration

What does inspiration accomplish? What are the effects of the special influence exercised by the Holy Spirit on the inspired writers? Does the moving of the Spirit give to their writings qualities that make the Bible different from any other book in the world? The majority of Christians throughout the centuries have answered the last question in the affirmative, though they have differed as to the unique qualities, attributes, or effects of inspiration. Some of these differences and the conflicts engendered by them will be discussed in the historical survey at the end of this article.

The primary purpose here is to consider four qualities of Scripture: Scripture is the living voice of God, the authority of Scripture, the truthfulness of Scripture, and the sufficiency of Scripture. While it is appropriate to look at each of these effects of inspiration separately, qualities of Scripture should never be seen in isolation from each other. They constitute the different hues of a spectrum of colors formed by the bright light of the Word of God.

1. Scripture: The Living Voice of God

In diverse ways the biblical writers stress that the words of Scripture are God's voice speaking to human beings as an ever-present dynamic reality. The "thus says the Lord" of the prophets speaks as directly to human beings in the twentieth century A.D. as in the eighth or fifteenth century B.C. When the Sadducees tried to trap Jesus with a question about the resurrection, He straightforwardly told them, "You are wrong, because you know neither the scriptures nor the power of God." He asked them, "Have you not read what was said to you by God, 'I am the God of Abraham, and the God of Isaac, and the God of Jacob'? He is not God of the dead, but of the living"

(Matt. 22:29, 31, 32). Jesus quoted here words spoken by God to Moses and recorded more than 1,000 years earlier as applicable to his questioners: "What was said to you by God."

In Scripture God speaks to all generations. Referring to certain judgments that came upon Israel of old because of their unbelief, Paul reminds the Christian believers in Corinth that "these things happened to them as a warning, but they were written down for our instruction, upon whom the end of the ages has come" (1 Cor. 10:11). Peter, speaking about the revelations regarding the sufferings and the glory of Christ given by the Spirit to the prophets, told his fellow Christians that those prophets "were serving not themselves but you" (1 Peter 1:12). The word of God given through prophets, psalmists, sacred historians, and apostles is a living word that speaks directly to those who read or hear that word. This is forcefully expressed in Hebrews 4:12: "For the word of God is living and active, sharper than any two-edged sword, piercing to the division of soul and spirit, of joints and marrow, and discerning the thoughts and intentions of the heart."

The Spirit of God who moved the human authors of the Bible to write is the same Spirit who addresses each generation in and through the words they wrote. For this reason NT writers quote words from the OT as being spoken by the Holy Spirit (Heb. 3:7-11; 10:15-17). Because of this, John the revelator concludes each of his letters to the seven churches with the urgent admonition: "He who has an ear, let him hear what the Spirit says to the churches" (Rev. 2:7, 11, 17, 29; 3:6, 13, 22). Thus "word" and "Spirit" belong together. The apostle Paul refers to the Word of God as "the sword of the Spirit" (Eph. 6:17). The Spirit of God gives efficacy and power to the Word of God. The new birth or regeneration is attributed both to the Spirit and to the Word. Jesus told Nicodemus that it was necessary to be born anew of the Spirit (John 3:5-7) while Peter wrote to the scattered believers, that they were "born anew, . . . through the living and abiding word of God" (1 Peter 1:23).

2. Scripture: Its Authority

From Genesis to Revelation supreme authority is ascribed to God, the Creator of heaven and earth. As such, He revealed Himself to the patriarchs (Gen. 17:1; 35:11; 48:3) and to Moses (Ex. 3:13-15; 6:2, 3). David acknowledged the Lord as ruler above all, to whom belong greatness, power, and majesty (1 Chron. 29:10-13). Daniel, as well as Nebuchadnezzar and Darius, ascribe supreme wisdom and everlasting dominion to the God of heaven (Dan. 2:20-22; 4:34, 35; 6:26, 27).

The authority of God is, however, primarily based not on His infinite power and knowledge but on His character. To Moses God revealed Himself as "the Lord, a God merciful and gracious, slow to anger, and abounding in steadfast love and faithfulness" (Ex. 34:6). Consequently the authority of the Lord is not exercised as it is by human rulers. God's absolute authority is an authority of love and peace, expressed in humility, service, and self-sacrifice. This authority is supremely manifested in the incarnation, death, and resurrection of Jesus Christ, "who is the head of all rule and authority" (Col. 2:10), yet who laid down His life by His own power and authority (John 10:17, 18).

The authority of Scripture as the Written Word of God manifests all the characteristics of the authority of God. Its authority is expressed in absolute demands of obedience (Ex. 20:1-17), in compassionate pleas of love (Isa. 1:18; Matt. 11:28), in promises of forgiveness and blessing (Matt. 5:3-12; 1 John 1:9), and in earnest warnings of judgment (Jer. 6:1-8).

God endowed His chosen messengers with His own authority when they spoke or wrote under the impulse of the Holy Spirit. Therefore the writings of prophets and apostles speak with divine authority to every generation, even though the human authors of those writings have long since passed away. Thus Paul can say that the church is "built upon the foundation of the apostles and prophets, Christ Jesus himself being the cornerstone"

(Eph. 2:20). Thus Peter admonishes believers to "remember the predictions of the holy prophets and the commandment of the Lord and Savior through your apostles" (2 Peter 3:2). The authority of prophets and apostles was based on God's calling them and making them recipients and witnesses of divine revelation (John 15:16; Acts 9:15, 16; 2 Peter 1:18; 1 John 1:1-4).

Jesus repeatedly confirmed the authority of the Scriptures. He resisted the temptations of the devil with a decisive "It is written" (Matt. 4:4, 7, 10). He refuted accusations of His opponents by quoting to them specific Scriptures which exposed their misunderstanding and misinterpretation of the word of God (Matt. 12:1-7). When the Jews accused Jesus of blasphemy, He quoted Psalm 82:6 and affirmed the authority of the word of God with the categorical assertion that "Scripture cannot be broken" (John 10:33-35). He finally silenced His questioners by asking how the Messiah could be both the son and Lord of David, according to the Scriptures (Matt. 22:41-46).

Jesus and the apostles appealed to Scripture to show that in Him its types and prophecies had met their fulfillment. His conception and birth fulfilled "what the Lord had spoken by the prophet" (Matt. 1:22, 23); the place of His birth had been "written by the prophet" (Matt. 2:5). After reading a messianic prophecy from Isaiah 61:1, 2, Jesus solemnly declared to His audience, "Today this scripture has been fulfilled in your hearing" (Luke 4:21). Announcing His impending death, Jesus told His own that Isaiah 53:12 "must be fulfilled" (Luke 22:37). After His resurrection He showed them "that everything written about me in the law of Moses and the prophets and the psalms must be fulfilled" (Luke 24:44).

The apostle Paul refers to the OT as "the holy scriptures" (Rom. 1:2), "the oracles of God" (Rom. 3:2), and "the sacred writings" (2 Tim. 3:15), titles that express their divine origin and authority.

Jesus and the apostles used the word "Scripture" or "Scriptures" only in reference to a well-known and firmly established body of writings. When Jesus said to the Jewish leaders, "You search the scriptures" (John 5:39), or when Paul argued with the Jews in Thessolonica "from the scriptures" (Acts 17:2), they appealed to the Hebrew Scriptures—the law, the prophets, and the writings.

The same authority came to be attached to the 27 books of the NT. The apostle Peter already placed the letters of Paul on a level with "the other scriptures" (2 Peter 3:16), by which he undoubtedly meant the OT. Together, OT and NT form the canon, or rule, of faith and doctrine. There is wide agreement among Christians that the canon of the NT consists of 27 books. The Roman Catholic and Orthodox churches have included in the OT canon the so-called Apocrypha, or deuterocanonical books, but Protestants have adhered to the 39 books of the Hebrew Scriptures. There is no evidence that the Jews in Palestine, or Jesus, or the apostles considered the Apocrypha to be a part of the Scriptures.

The principle of the supreme authority of the Scriptures is often expressed in the Latin phrase *sola scriptura,* "by Scripture alone." In other words, only in the Scriptures has God committed to the human race in written form the supreme and authoritative revelation of Himself and His will, by which everything else is to be tested. No other holy books, sacred histories, ancient traditions, ecclesiastical pronouncements, or creedal statements may be accorded authority equal to that of the Bible.

This also means that conscience, reason, feelings, and religious or mystical experiences are subordinate to the authority of Scripture. These may have a legitimate sphere, but they should constantly be brought under the scrutiny of the Word of God (Heb. 4:12).

The Bible warns repeatedly against anything or anybody that would undermine or usurp the authority of the Word of God. It warns against false prophets who pretend to speak words from God (Deut. 18:20-22; Jer. 27:14, 15; Matt. 7:15), against false apostles claiming to be true apostles (2 Cor. 11:12, 13), and false christs who will deceive many (Matt. 24:24), all of them substituting their own authority for that of God.

The authority of the Scriptures has been the target of blatant opposition or subtle substitution for thousands of years. In Jesus' days the Jews had "made void the word of God" through their tradition; Jesus accused them of worshiping God in vain, "teaching as doctrines the precepts of men" (Matt. 15:6, 9). Other means by which biblical authority has been undermined are worldly wisdom, science, and philosophy (1 Cor. 1:20-25; Col. 2:8), adding to or taking away from the Word of God (Deut. 4:2; 12:32; Rev. 22:18, 19), or twisting the meaning of the Scriptures (2 Peter 3:16).

The *sola scriptura* principle is as much in danger of opposition now as at any time in the past. Through exalting the authority of human reason, tradition, and science, many have come to deny or to limit the authority of Scripture. Christians who still submit in humility and faith to the authority of Scripture as the living and supreme Word of God must be prepared to give account of their faith and to say with the apostles, "We must obey God rather than men" (Acts 5:29).

3. Scripture: Its Truthfulness

One of the attributes of God is His truthfulness. Throughout the Scriptures this characteristic is constantly proclaimed. He is called "the God of truth" (Isa. 65:16), who speaks the truth (Isa. 45:19). All His words are true—promises (2 Sam. 7:28), laws (Neh. 9:13), ordinances (Ps. 19:9), commandments (Ps. 119:151), judgments (Rev. 16:7; 19:2). Whatever God says is true and trustworthy (chap. 19:9; 21:5; 22:6). The attribute of truthfulness also belongs to the Son, who was "full of . . . truth" (John 1:14), and to the "Spirit of truth" (chap. 14:17; 1 John 5:7).

When God chose human beings as messengers, He not only endowed them with His authority but also clothed their words with His truthfulness when they spoke or wrote under inspiration. Numerous assertions on the part of the inspired messengers affirm that they speak the truth. At other times this fact is acknowledged by others. Solomon, the Preacher, uprightly "wrote words of truth" (Eccl. 12:10). Jeremiah testified, "In truth the Lord sent me to you to speak all these words" (Jer. 26:15). John affirms that "his testimony is true" and that he "tells the truth" (John 19:35; cf. 21:24). Paul repeatedly asserts the truth of what he writes (Rom. 9:1; 2 Cor. 11:10); he states that he has been appointed a "teacher of the Gentiles in faith and truth" (1 Tim. 2:7).

There are also general declarations of the truth of God's Word. The psalmist declares, "The sum of thy word is truth" (Ps. 119:160). The gospel preached by the apostles is "the word of truth" (Eph. 1:13; see also Col. 1:5). Jesus emphatically affirms, "Thy word is truth" (John 17:17).

Because all of Scripture is God's word and every word that comes from God is true, it seems difficult to avoid the conclusion that all of Scripture is truth. That is evidently what the biblical authors claimed for their writings. This is what our Lord affirmed and what the majority of Christians through the centuries held and confessed.

The implications of the complete veracity of Scripture are clear. Not only do its authors tell the truth in what they say about God and salvation but also in regard to other matters. The historical narratives of the Bible are to be accepted as reliable and true. Among these authentic accounts of real events are the creation of the world and the first human beings in six days, the fall of Adam and Eve, the universal flood, the lives of the patriarchs, the history of Israel, the Gospel narratives, and the story of the Spirit-led origin and development of the apostolic church.

The claim that Scripture is true in everything it says has never gone unchallenged. Already during the first Christian centuries the historicity of many biblical narratives was questioned by pagan philosophers opposed to Christianity. But especially in modern times the assertion of the autonomy of human reason has led to a denial not only of the inspiration, authority, and truthfulness of Scripture, but of the intrusion of the supernatural in the natural world, especially in the incarnation and bodily resurrection of the Son of God. As a consequence the biblical narratives have been reinterpreted as myths or legends. Such assertions, however, run counter to explicit assertions of prophets and apostles that their words are truth because they transmit the Word of God.

Many today claim that there are numerous errors, contradictions, historical inaccuracies, anachronisms, and other flaws in the Scriptures. Worse still, it is alleged, the Bible contains deliberate distortions of historical events (e.g., the Exodus), narratives colored by national pride and prejudice (e.g., the story of Esther), and pseudonymous authorship (e.g., that the book of Daniel was not written by a sixth-century prophet). Such claims and allegations constitute a serious indictment against the truthfulness of Holy Scripture. (See Interpretation IV. F, G.)

Although it may not be possible to find satisfactory answers to all the criticisms leveled against the Bible, much recently discovered historical and archaeological evidence has corroborated the historical reliability and accuracy of the scriptural narratives. The precise fulfillment of biblical prophecies in the history of ancient Israel, in the life and death of Jesus of Nazareth, in the unfolding drama of the Christian Church, as well as in the climactic events of our own age have provided abundant confirmation of the veracity of Scripture. But more important still, the recognition of the uniqueness, graciousness, and majesty of the God who reveals Himself in Scripture, and above all the experience of salvation through faith in the living Christ to which the Scriptures testify, has, under the prompting of the Holy Spirit, convinced millions in past and present that Scripture is all it claims to be: the Word of God, the Word of truth.

4. Scripture: Its Clarity and Sufficiency

Some claim that the Bible is an obscure book, much of which is difficult, if not impossible, to understand. On the other hand, to countless others, Scripture is full of light and comfort. The Bible strikes them as clear and easy to grasp. Why this difference?

According to the biblical writers the problem is not in the Scriptures. They affirm in a variety of ways that God's Word is a source of light and understanding. The psalmist wrote, "Thy word is a lamp to my feet and a light to my path" and, "The unfolding of thy words gives light; it imparts understanding to the simple" (Ps. 119:105, 130). The apostle Peter refers to the prophetic word as "a lamp shining in a dark place" (2 Peter 1:19). The sacred writings, according to Paul, "are able to instruct you for salvation through faith in Christ Jesus" (2 Tim. 3:15).

Paul touches here on a serious problem, namely our attitude toward Scriptures or, more precisely, our attitude toward God, who reveals Himself in the Scriptures. Faith in God and in Christ is essential. We may study the Scriptures and yet never understand them because we do not believe their message. The Jewish teachers and leaders in the days of Jesus searched the Scriptures diligently but did not understand their true meaning. According to Jesus, their problem was unbelief (John 5:39, 40, 46, 47).

No serious student of the Bible will deny that there are difficulties in Scripture. Peter admits that Paul's letters contain "some things in them hard to understand" (2 Peter 3:16); he does not say that they are impossible to understand. However, these difficulties do not affect the clarity of Scripture, much of which can be understood by young children. The message of salvation is presented in such a plain manner that even people of limited intelligence can grasp it. "The testimony of the Lord is sure, making wise the simple" (Ps. 19:7), says the psalmist. Jesus went a step further and thanked His Father that the truth concerning His person and His works was hidden from the wise and understanding but revealed to babes (Matt. 11:25).

Not only are the Scriptures clear in what they teach; they are also sufficient for the purpose for which God gave them. When Paul writes that the Scriptures are able to instruct us for salvation through faith in Christ Jesus, he further explains that all Scripture, being God-breathed, is "profitable for teaching, for reproof, for correction, and for training in righteousness," so that every believer "may be complete, equipped for every good work" (2 Tim. 3:16, 17). No other writing, tradition, human wisdom, or experience is to be put on the same level as the Scriptures. Scripture itself repeatedly warns neither to add to nor to take away from what God has revealed in His Word (Deut. 4:2; 12:32; Rev. 22:18).

The Bible should be read and studied by every human being endowed with intelligence. The eternal gospel, as recorded in the Scriptures, is intended for "every nation and tribe and tongue and people" (Rev. 14:6). The Bible can benefit poor and wealthy, unlearned and educated, young and old. Although the Scriptures were originally written in Hebrew, Aramaic, and Greek, God intended them to speak to all the members of the human family in their own tongues. That intention is fast becoming a reality now that the Bible has been translated into thousands of languages. The Word of God will accomplish the purpose for which He sent it into the world (Isa. 55:10, 11). It will not fail. To those who believe and accept that Word, it means eternal life; to those who reject it or twist its meaning, it means perdition and eternal death (Matt. 7:24-27; 2 Peter 3:16).

The Scriptures were given to humanity not to be subjected to criticism, but to reveal God and the salvation He offers in Jesus Christ. Though written by human beings in human language, they speak as the living voice of God in order that we may know Him and believe in Him. As the Word of God, they are the Word of truth, which does not deceive. The history given in the Bible is completely reliable and trustworthy. The promises of Scripture are to be received by faith, its commands to be obeyed by the grace of God. Above all the Holy Scriptures "are able to instruct you for salvation through faith in Christ Jesus" (2 Tim. 3:15).

V. Practical Applications

When we study the Bible, a realization of its divine origin and authority as well as of its human character is of crucial importance. If we a priori reject the possibility of supernatural revelation, the Bible will be seen as a purely human product, and our interpretation will be biased from the outset. If, on the other hand, we lose sight of its human shape, we are in danger of interpreting its statements in an uncritical, dogmatic manner. In view of their divine-human character, our study of the Scriptures should be conducted in a spirit of humility as well as honest inquiry, with earnest prayers that the Holy Spirit, the Spirit of truth, may guide us "into all the truth" (John 16:13). Some practical guidelines in our search for a personal knowledge of God through the Scriptures are here suggested:

1. We should study the Scriptures with the deep conviction of faith that they are as the living voice of God speaking to us personally. It is through "the living and abiding word of God" that we "have been born anew" (1 Peter 1:23). A true knowledge of God can grow and mature only by an obedient listening to His Word (Rom. 10:14-17; 16:25-27).

2. The foremost purpose of the Bible is to strengthen our faith in Jesus Christ as our Saviour from sin and as Lord of our life. "The sacred writings," wrote Paul, ". . . are able to instruct you for salvation through faith in Christ Jesus" (2 Tim. 3:15). One should always read and study the Bible with the definite aim to "grow in the grace and knowledge of our Lord and Savior Jesus Christ" (2 Peter 3:18).

3. In reading the Bible we should pay

special attention to its numerous promises. Through them God intends that we find the assurance of forgiveness, peace of heart and mind, comfort in times of suffering, hope for this life as well as for the life to come, and an abiding joy in the knowledge that God in His love and mercy has adopted us as His sons and daughters through faith in Christ (Rom. 15:4; 2 Peter 1:3, 4).

4. The Scriptures also function as a guide for practical Christian living. The biblical principle of love for God and for our fellow humans lies at the foundation of the well-being of all our spiritual and social relationships. Those who, with God's help, study and practice the Ten Commandments and the many Scripture principles for practical living derived from them will become truly balanced persons, sound in body, mind, and spirit. "Blessed [or happy] are those whose way is blameless, who walk in the law of the Lord" (Ps. 119:1).

5. Because the Scriptures are the very words of God in human language, we may have confidence that they always speak the truth. Jesus prayed to the Father for His disciples in all ages, "Sanctify them in the truth; thy word is truth" (John 17:17). We should trust in God's Word as a reliable word. This is true not only of its spiritual teachings but also of its records of the origin and early history of our world, the narratives of the Flood, the patriarchs, the Exodus, the history of Israel, as well as the Gospel records of Christ's birth, ministry, death, and resurrection, and the history of the early church. These narratives are not myths but authentic historical records and should be accepted as such (Luke 1:1-4; 2 Peter 1:16-21). A denial of their historicity sooner or later will lead to a rejection of the spiritual and moral teachings of Scripture as well. The historical, spiritual, and moral teachings of the Bible are inextricably intertwined and cannot be separated from each other.

6. Because the Scriptures are subject to the limitations, imperfections, and historical conditioning of human existence, it is useful and necessary to study the languages in which they were written, the historical background in which they originated, and the human conditions which they addressed. We should beware, however, of exaggerating the differences, the distances in time and space, between conditions in biblical times and in our own time. Neither human nature nor biblical principles of truth change (cf. Eccl. 1:9, 10). God's Word is intended for all people in all ages everywhere (Matt. 24:14; 28:18-20; Acts 1:6-8; Rev. 14:6).

To sum it all up in the words of Paul, let us receive the Scriptures, "not as the word of men but as what it really is, the word of God, which is at work in you believers" (1 Thess. 2:13). That Word will give us hope, comfort, faith, wisdom, love, and at last life eternal in the wonderful presence of our Lord.

VI. Historical Overview

A. The Early and Medieval Church

While early Christian writers did not discuss revelation-inspiration as a distinct issue, the Church Fathers had much to say on the subject. During the early period there was general agreement that in Jesus Christ a new and full revelation had been given. Using the NT terminology, Christ is referred to as the Word of God, the image of the Father, the Master, the Teacher, the Way, the Light of the world. Irenaeus (c. 130-c. 200) calls Christ "the only true and steadfast Teacher, the Word of God, our Lord Jesus Christ" (*Against Heresies,* pref. 5) and asserts that "in no other way could we have learned the things of God, unless our Master, existing as the Word, had become man. For no other being had the power of revealing to us the things of the Father, except His own proper Word" (*Against Heresies* 5. 1. 1). Clement of Alexandria (c. 150-c. 215) affirms that "our Instructor is the holy God Jesus, the Word, who is the guide of all humanity. The loving God Himself is our Instructor" (*The Instructor* 1. 7).

This emphasis on Christ as the supreme divine teacher and Word of God did not mean, however, a denial or disparagement of the revelations given in the pre-Christian Era. According to the same Clement, the Word "has appeared as our Teacher." He is "the Lord, who from the beginning gave revelations by prophecy, but now plainly calls to salvation" (*Exhortation to the Heathen* 1). In opposition to Gnostic heresies, Irenaeus stressed the unity and the progress of revelation through the Word from Creation until its culmination in Christ's incarnation and the subsequent witness of the apostles to the Word.

René Latourelle summarizes, "Irenaeus is aware of the dynamic and historical aspect of revelation. He stresses the movement, the progress, the profound unity. He sees the Word of God at work from the very beginning . . . the apostles, the church—these are all distinct moments in the activity of the Word, in the economy of the progressive manifestation of the Father through the Word. . . . Hence, the indivisible unity of the two Testaments" (105). Such views represent the general understanding of early Christians.

Already in the NT, and abundantly in Christian writers of the second century, the acceptance of the NT writings as Scripture is evident. Irenaeus refers to the Scriptures as "the good words of revelation" (*Against Heresies* 1. 3. 6). Similar sentiments were expressed by other early Christian writers.

In their confrontation with heresies such as Montanism, Gnosticism, or Marcionism, the Church Fathers defended the Christian faith on the basis of the entire Scriptures with an appeal to the true apostolic tradition. There can be little doubt that "in the early Christian Fathers, tradition *(paradosis, traditio)* means the revelation made by God and delivered by Him to His faithful people through the mouth of His prophets and apostles" (*Oxford Dictionary of the Christian Church* 1983, 1388). However, with the passing of time some de-

velopments tended to weaken the supreme authority of the Scriptures.

The appeal to tradition, as maintained in the churches of apostolic origin—especially that of Rome—was gradually changed into the claim that the Bible was to be accepted on the authority of the church. The church, it was claimed, determined which books belonged to the canon of the Bible. Furthermore, through the influence of Basil the Great (c. 330-379) it came to be held that unwritten traditions of apostolic origin, not found in the Scriptures but preserved in the church, could be accepted as having divine authority. Another tendency was to attribute special authority to the writings of the Church Fathers. These developments did not happen suddenly, but took place gradually, and in the West they were reinforced by the growth of papal authority over the centuries.

During the Middle Ages Scholasticism brought the question of the relationship between reason and revelation to the forefront. The first question addressed by Thomas Aquinas (1225-1274) in his *Summa Theologica* asks whether we need any knowledge besides philosophical science. He answers in the affirmative, explaining that "it was necessary for the salvation of man that certain truths which exceed human reason should be made known to him by divine revelation." He adds that even those truths about God that human reason could have discovered needed to be taught by divine revelation, because "the rational truth about God would have appeared to only a few, and even so after a time and mixed with many mistakes" (*Summa Theologica* 1ᵃ. 1. 1). Aquinas makes a clear distinction between truths of reason and truths of revelation. The faith of the Christian "rests on the revelation made to the Prophets and Apostles, who wrote the canonical books, not on a revelation, if such there be, made to any other teacher" (*ibid.* 1ᵃ. 1. 8). However, the believer needs to adhere to the teaching of the church, which proceeds from the truth as revealed in Holy

Scripture, as an infallible and divine rule (*ibid.* 2ª: 2ᵃᶜ. 3). Although Aquinas clearly accepts Scripture as the primary source of revealed truth, his teaching nevertheless tended to dilute its authority through his rationalistic approach to theology on the one hand, and through his emphasis on the infallibility of the teaching of the church on the other.

In the late Middle Ages the question of the relation between Scripture and tradition as sources of revelation became more acute. On one hand, some scholars held that Scripture and tradition were essentially identical, the tradition being a faithful interpretation of the revelation given through prophets and apostles; both came from the same divine source and were preserved in the unity of faith within the church. Others held that there were two distinct sources of revelation: the written tradition of the Scriptures and unwritten traditions transmitted by the apostles to their successors; both were to be accepted as a divine authority.

B. Reformation and Counter-Reformation

Martin Luther (1483-1546) affirmed that in their sinful, corrupt condition, human beings do not and cannot know God. To meet their need, God has revealed Himself in certain specific ways. God is not a vague entity, rather "He is a God revealed and, so to speak sealed. He has circumscribed Himself with a certain place, Word, and signs, so that He might be acknowledged and grasped" (*Commentary on Psalm 51:6*). Supremely God has revealed Himself in Jesus Christ, the Word made flesh, and Christ is revealed in Scripture, the written Word, and in the proclamation of the gospel. The proper knowledge of God, as Luther called it, is uniquely given to us in Scripture.

Early in his career Luther became critical of the rationalistic approach of Scholastic philosophy and theology as is evident from his *Disputation Against Scholastic Theology* written in 1517. Luther became convinced that the ultimate standard for faith and doctrine

should be Scripture alone (*sola scriptura*): "Scripture alone is the true lord and master of all writings and doctrine on earth" (*Luther's Works* 32:11, 12). All truth and doctrine essential for our knowledge of God and salvation is revealed to us in the Word.

In contrast with scholastic theologians, Luther was not willing to acknowledge that the authority of the church was needed to affirm what is God's Word or to provide the right interpretation of the Scriptures. Rather, it was the work of the Holy Spirit to bring the external word of Scripture into the heart and to convince the human spirit that this is the Word of God.

The views of John Calvin (1509-1564) on revelation and the authority of Scripture were similar to those of Luther. In his influential work *Institutes of the Christian Religion,* he took the position that a man blinded by sin cannot benefit from the revelation of God's "everlasting Kingdom in the mirror of his works with very great clarity" (*ibid.* 1. 5. 11). In His goodness and mercy, God "added the light of his Word by which to become known unto salvation" (*ibid.* 1. 6. 1). Like Luther before him, Calvin repudiated as a malicious falsehood the claim that the credibility of Scripture should depend on the judgment of the church. Rather the church should be itself rooted in and dependent on Scripture. The Reformer stated emphatically, "Let this point therefore stand: that those whom the Holy Spirit has inwardly taught truly rest upon Scripture, and that Scripture indeed is self-authenticated" (*ibid.* 1. 7. 5).

The essence of revelation, according to Calvin, is the gospel, which is "the clear manifestation of the mystery of Christ." This would include the OT promises and testimonies which God gave to the patriarchs of old, but in a higher sense the word refers to "the proclamation of the grace manifested in Christ" (*ibid.* 2. 9. 2). Calvin pointed out that "where the whole law is concerned, the gospel differs from it only in clarity of manifestation" (*ibid.* 2. 9. 4). In essence, therefore, the

OT and NT constitute a unity, both being a revelation of the gospel of Jesus Christ. The New, however, gives clearer proclamation of Christ than the Old.

In reaction to the Protestant reformation the Roman Catholic Church redefined its position in the Council of Trent (1545-1563), claiming that the apostolic tradition included both Scripture and tradition handed down by the church. The Council promulgated in 1546 the "Decree Concerning the Canonical Scriptures," which affirmed that the gospel of old promised through the prophets in the Holy Scriptures, was promulgated by the Lord Jesus Christ and by His command preached by His apostles to every creature "as the source of every saving truth and of instruction in morals." However, "this truth and instruction is contained in the written books and in the unwritten traditions." Therefore the OT and NT, as well as the traditions relating to faith and morals, are to be received and venerated with equal feelings of piety and reverence, "as having been dictated either by Christ's own word of mouth, or by the Holy Spirit, and preserved in the Catholic Church by a continuous succession" (Denzinger 244). The council inserted in the decree a list of sacred and canonical books, which included the so-called Apocrypha, and pronounced an anathema on anyone who would not accept this list in its entirety.

Although the Tridentine Council rejected a proposal that the apostolic tradition be considered as partly contained in the Scriptures and partly in the unwritten traditions, a long debate ensued. The issue was whether there were two sources of revelation—Scripture and tradition—or whether the two should be considered as two streams of one tradition, one written and one unwritten.

C. The Age of Reason and the Enlightenment

The modern debate about revelation and inspiration originated in the Age of Reason, with the rise of rationalism, modern science, and biblical criticism. These and intellectual movements such as deism and the Enlightenment led many to question the necessity or even the existence of divine revelation. Such questioning challenged the very essentials of the Christian faith and especially manifested itself in incisive criticism or even wholesale denial of the Bible as an inspired source and record of revelation. This in turn called for deeper reflection on the reality and nature of revelation by those who maintained fundamental Christian convictions.

The discoveries of Nicolaus Copernicus (1473-1543), Galileo Galilei (1564-1642), and Johannes Kepler (1571-1630) brought about the definitive change from a geocentric to a heliocentric view of the solar system. When eventually the scientific evidence for the heliocentric view proved to be irrefutable, the divine revelation and infallibility of the Bible—which was understood to teach a geocentric view—were questioned. Other scientific discoveries made during the seventeenth and eighteenth centuries, especially Isaac Newton's (1642-1727) laws of gravity, enhanced a mechanistic concept of the universe. From such a perspective, a supernatural revelation was perceived as unnecessary or even misleading, as a myth or deceptive concoction of religionists.

The dawn of modern science was matched by the rise of rationalism, making human reason the criterion for truth. René Descartes (1596-1650) initiated a philosophical revolution when in 1637 he enunciated his axiom *"Cogito, ergo sum"* ("I think; therefore I am") as the basic principle for attaining true knowledge. Descartes, a faithful Roman Catholic, never intended to deny the need for divine revelation, but his philosophy could not but bring into question the relationship between reason and revelation. His younger contemporary and admirer Baruch Benedict de Spinoza (1632-1677) went beyond Descartes by making a sharp distinction between the sphere of reason and the sphere of revelation (by which he clearly meant Scripture), making reason the ultimate arbiter of what could be accepted as truth in Scripture. Spinoza considered many things in Scripture to be repugnant to reason and pointed out what to him seemed to be undeniable contradictions.

The rise of modern biblical criticism was frequently, as in the case of Spinoza, correlated with a rationalistic approach to the Bible and a reduced view of the role of divine revelation. Other factors contributed to this development. Probably the first full-scale modern work on biblical criticism, *Histoire critique du Vieux Testament,* was published in 1678 and earned for its author, the French priest Richard Simon (1638-1712), the designation of "father of biblical criticism." Simon wanted to demonstrate the insufficiency of Scripture and consequently the need for ecclesiastical authority and tradition for its correct interpretation. But at that time neither Protestants nor Roman Catholics could accept his critical handling of the Bible.

In England the criticism of the deists focused strongly on what were considered to be the moral imperfections of the Bible, especially in the OT. In 1693 Charles Blount (1654-1693) published a collection of papers and letters, *The Oracles of Reason.* Here Blount denied any need for a specially revealed religion. Deists generally agreed that reason was adequate for natural religion and that true Christianity was nothing but the religion of reason. The mysteries of the Christian religion, such as the Trinity and the atoning death of Christ, were considered later accretions, not part of the simple original Christian faith. Many of the famous Boyle Lectures, which started in 1692, treated the topic of revelation. Joseph Butler's (1692-1752) *The Analogy of Religion, Natural and Revealed, to the Constitution and Course of Nature,* which appeared in 1736, argued incisively that many of the objections to supernatural revelation were equally valid against natural religion, as both presented unexplainable mysteries. Butler stressed an inductive approach to the question of divine revelation and, unlike Blount and other deists, rejected the imposition of any a priori conditions to which a divine revelation should conform.

To circumvent moral and historical criticism of Scripture, a number of scholars in Britain suggested that the inspiration of the Bible was either partial or graded. The theory of degrees of inspiration was considered to allow for historical errors and moral imperfections in Scripture while maintaining its inspiration and authority in matters of faith and practice. Others, however, such as John Wesley (1703-1791) and Charles Simeon (1759-1836) rejected such a compromise with rationalistic theology and upheld the plenary inspiration and infallibility of the Bible.

During the eighteenth century, the era of Enlightenment, the controversy over the necessity and nature of divine revelation and the authority and inspiration of the Bible, sparked by Deist literature in England, also affected other countries. François-Marie Voltaire (1694-1778), thoroughly acquainted with English deists and their writings, never denied God's existence but was highly critical of any revealed religion. In Germany the works of English Deists played a significant role in the rise of higher criticism in the second half of the century. Gotthold Ephraim Lessing (1729-1781), German writer and dramatist, published between 1774 and 1778 seven fragments from the previously unpublished *Apology for or Defense of the Rational Worshippers of God,* by Herman Samuel Reimarus (1694-1768). The fragments presented familiar Deist arguments against a supernatural revelation. Lessing argued that historical records, including biblical records of miracles, could have only relative certainty and that truths of reason could not be proved by history. Lessing himself did not completely deny revelation, but in his work, *The Education of the Human Race,* published in 1780, compared revelation to education. As education helps us to grasp things faster than we would on our own, revelation teaches us truths which we could discover by our reason. When reason has been perfected, revelation will become superfluous.

D. Contemporary Development

The doctrine of revelation and inspiration has emerged as a crucial issue in the theological debate in the last two centuries. A never-ending stream of literature on these subjects, sometimes calm, sometimes turbulent, challenges Christians. It is evident that faith in divine revelation and in the inspiration, as well as in the trustworthiness and authority of Scripture, is being eroded in a variety of ways.

In reaction to the rationalistic approach of the eighteenth century, Friedrich Schleiermacher (1768-1834) postulated the feeling of absolute dependence on God as the basis of Christian faith. He defined the idea of revelation as "the originality of the fact which lies at the foundation of a religious communion" but was unwilling to accept its cognitive operation, for "that would make the revelation to be originally and essentially doctrine" (Schleiermacher 50). For him, inspiration had only a subordinate significance. He distinctly limited to the NT the authority of Scripture to formulate doctrine. Religious experience, rather than Scripture, became the criterion for judging spiritual truth and values. The focus of theology shifted increasingly from the transcendent to the immanent.

Nineteenth-century liberal or modern theology, with its anthropocentric emphasis, often combined a strong belief in human progress with an attitude critical of so-called dogmatism and bibliolatry. According to this theology the Bible cannot be equated with the Word of God; it merely contains words of God. Scripture is not so much the revealed Word of God as a unique record of religious experiences with Jesus Christ as the supreme manifestation of God-consciousness or the highest moral example.

Belief in human progress was reinforced by rapid advances in science and technology. As a result of the writings of Charles Lyell (1797-1875) and Charles Darwin (1809-1882) the theories of geological uniformitarianism and biological evolution undermined the faith of many in the facticity of the Genesis accounts of Creation, the Fall, and a worldwide flood. Confidence in the reliability of the history of Scripture, the accuracy of its text, and the genuineness of the authorship of many of its books was further reduced by what were claimed to be the assured results of historical and literary criticism. Proponents of critical methodology, whose presuppositions excluded supernatural revelations or interventions such as predictive prophecies or miracles, studied the Bible as they would any other book, placing it on a par with other ancient literature.

Concepts of revelation and inspiration were reinterpreted to fit the new theology. Albrecht Ritschl (1822-1889) in Germany defined revelation as the manifestation of the divine ideal for man in the person of Jesus of Nazareth. J. Frederick Denison Maurice (1805-1872), in England, saw it as an immediate unveiling of God to the soul. To Ernest Troeltsch (1865-1923), leading representative of the history of religions school and the historical-critical method, no divine revelation could be considered absolute, because of the historical relativity of all events. Troeltsch stressed that historical data, including biblical data, must be evaluated by the principle of analogy which means that past events can be accepted as probable only if they are analogous to present events. Measured by this principle of historical criticism, many biblical events, such as the Incarnation, virgin birth, and resurrection of Christ could not be considered historical.

Two world wars in the first half of the twentieth century shattered all dreams of human progress and exposed the inadequacy of the prevailing theology with its emphasis on divine immanence. Karl Barth (1886-1968) initiated a revolt against this theology. He and other theologians, such as Rudolf Bultmann (1884-1976) and Emil Brunner (1889-1966), stressed the transcendent God as the wholly other. Barth developed a theology of the Word, according to which God speaks His decisive word in Jesus Christ, who alone is revelation in the true sense. Scripture and the preached word are only witnesses to revelation, but God in His grace addresses us through them.

Although the neoorthodox theologians made revelation central to their theology, they considered Scripture as only a fallible human witness to that revelation. Like their liberal predecessors, they upheld the historical-critical method as essential to the study and interpretation of Scripture and rejected or reinterpreted such concepts as biblical authority, inspiration, and truth. Brunner taught that truth consists in an I-Thou encounter, not in propositional statements.

In the face of calls for radical renewal and change in the understanding of revelation and inspiration, many scholars in different denominations have appealed to Scripture's own teaching, maintaining that the concept of revelation includes all forms of supernatural manifestation and communication found in the Bible, even divine acts and words. This view has been set forth extensively by Carl F. H. Henry (1913-) in his comprehensive work *God, Revelation, and Authority* (six volumes, 1976-1983). Twentieth-century evangelical theologians generally have maintained the plenary, verbal inspiration and inerrancy of the Bible, though there is no unanimity among them about the precise meaning of these terms. However, a number of evangelical scholars, such as Clark H. Pinnock (1937-), have become uneasy with these concepts.

Despite the influence of modern liberal theology, biblical criticism, and evolutionary theories the Roman Catholic Church in the nineteenth century took a very conservative position in regard to the doctrine of revelation and inspiration. Papal encyclicals rejected the modernist position and upheld the traditional Catholic views as set forth by the Council of Trent. However, this position has changed dramatically over the last half century. Since Pius XII published the encyclical *Divino Afflante Spiritu* in 1943, Catholic scholars have moved rapidly into the vanguard of critical-biblical scholarship. This has led to a great diversity of theories in regard to

revelation and inspiration, as is evidenced in the work of Avery Dulles, *Models of Revelation* (1983). During its fourth and final session Vatican Council II promulgated the "Dogmatic Constitution on Divine Revelation," stressing that God Himself is to be considered the object of revelation in His deeds and words, which are intrinsically bound up with each other. "The most intimate truth which this revelation gives us about God and the salvation of man shines forth in Christ, who is himself both the mediator and the sum total of Revelation" (Flannery 751). The Constitution maintained the position taken at the Council of Trent that "both Scripture and Tradition must be accepted and honored with equal feelings of devotion and reverence" (*ibid.* 755).

Some Protestants are moving closer to the Catholic position. Even evangelical scholars have begun to put greater emphasis on the consensus and authority of Christian tradition. It seems that this inevitably must lead to a curtailment of the *sola scriptura* principle, which for many centuries was held to be a fundamental principle of Protestantism.

E. Adventist Understanding

From their earliest publications, Seventh-day Adventists affirmed their acceptance of the Bible as the inspired Word of God. In a small pamphlet entitled *A Word to the "Little Flock,"* published in 1847, James White stated succinctly, "The Bible is a perfect and complete revelation. It is our only rule of faith and practice" (p. 13). However, for many years there was hardly any extended discussion of revelation and inspiration in denominational publications.

In 1874 George Ide Butler (1834-1918), then serving as General Conference president, proposed in a series of articles in the *Advent Review and Sabbath Herald* a theory of degrees of inspiration. This concept, though for a short time enjoying some popularity, did not find permanent acceptance among Seventh-day Adventists. Neither did the concept of verbal or mechanical inspiration. While concepts of plenary and thought inspiration have been widely favored, the church has never formulated a precise doctrine of inspiration nor of revelation. Through more than 100 years, however, Adventists have reiterated and elaborated the convictions held by their pioneers in various statements of fundamental beliefs.

The latest statement of fundamental beliefs, adopted by the General Conference of Seventh-day Adventists during its quinquennial session at Dallas, Texas, in 1980, declares that the one God—Father, Son, and Holy Spirit—"is infinite and beyond human comprehension, yet known through His self-revelation" (No. 2). This self-revelation of the Godhead found its fullest expression in the incarnation of the Son, the Word made flesh. "Through Him all things were created, the character of God is revealed, the salvation of humanity is accomplished, and the world is judged" (No. 4).

It is through the Scriptures, however, under the illumination of the Holy Spirit and by the proclamation of the church, that the revelation of God is communicated to the world. The first of the fundamental beliefs sums it up in these words. "The Holy Scriptures, Old and New Testaments, are the written Word of God, given by divine inspiration through holy men of God who spoke and wrote as they were moved by the Holy Spirit. In this Word, God has committed to man the knowledge necessary for salvation. The Holy Scriptures are the infallible revelation of His will. They are the standard of character, the test of experience, the authoritative revealer of doctrines, and the trustworthy record of God's acts in history."

VII. Ellen G. White Comments

A. Introduction

Although Ellen White does not claim to be a theologian, her writings give evidence of deep theological insight. This is very much the case in regard to the subjects of revelation, inspiration, and Scripture. She teaches on these subjects all through her writings, but her most extensive discussions are found in the latter half of them, from about 1880 till 1915. Her greatest and persistent concern is to uplift Christ as the supreme revelation of God and to urge her readers to accept the Scriptures as the inspired, infallible, and authoritative Word of God. She upholds the Bible as the revelation of God's character, the reliable record of God's dealings with humanity, and the unerring standard of faith and doctrine.

B. Revelation

According to Ellen White a true knowledge of God is essential as "the foundation of all true education and of all true service," "both for this life and for the life to come"; therefore "we must know Him as He reveals Himself" (MH 409). She recognizes that God has revealed Himself in a variety of ways. She speaks of "the living God, as He is revealed in His word, in Christ, and in the works of creation" (GC 583). This does not mean that she considers the different revelations to be of equal clarity or sufficiency.

Frequently Ellen White writes about the revelation of God in His created works. She starts a chapter entitled "God in Nature" with this affirmation: "Upon all created things is seen the impress of the Deity. Nature testifies of God. The susceptible mind, brought in contact with the miracle and mystery of the universe, can not but recognize the working of infinite power" (Ed 99). In a similar vein she elaborates that "God has bound our hearts to Him by unnumbered tokens in heaven and in earth. Through the things of nature, and the deepest and tenderest earthly ties that human hearts can know, He has sought to reveal Himself to us." But she adds the sobering thought "Yet these but imperfectly represent His love" (SC 10).

Although she often speaks in a lofty manner about the revelation of God's love, wisdom, and power in nature, Ellen White points out that this revelation by itself tends to lead human beings to idolatry or skepticism rather than to the knowledge and worship of the only true God. She attributes this to the fact that sin caused two major changes, one in humanity's relationship to God, the other in nature. On the one hand, human beings separated from God through sin can "no longer discern the character of God in the works of His hand"; on the other hand, nature, marred by the curse of sin, "can bear but an imperfect testimony regarding the Creator. It cannot reveal His character in its perfection" (8T 256). Consequently in their human wisdom "men gather an imperfect knowledge of Him from His created works; but this knowledge, . . . tends to make men idolaters. In their blindness they exalt nature and the laws of nature above nature's God" (*ibid.* 257).

Human beings with minds darkened by sin and hearts estranged from God are in need of a personal revelation of God's character. That need God has met in Jesus Christ. "As a personal being, God has revealed Himself in His Son," for "God saw that a clearer revelation than nature was needed to portray both His personality and His character" (*ibid.* 265). This revelation is sufficient, for "all that man needs to know or can know of God has been revealed in the life and character of His Son" (*ibid.* 286), maintains Ellen White, quoting John 1:18. The emphasis on Christ as the all-sufficient revelation of God's character and personality is consistent throughout her writings. This revelation of God's love to man in Jesus Christ "centers in the cross. Its full significance tongue cannot utter; pen cannot portray; the mind of man cannot comprehend" (*ibid.* 287; MH 423).

While Ellen White's writings strongly emphasize Christ as the supreme revelation of God, at the same time she upholds revelations given to and through patriarchs, prophets, and apostles. She clearly recognizes the Scriptures as an essential part of divine revelation. In an article entitled "Christ Revealed the Father" she writes, "Jesus had imparted a knowledge of God to patriarchs, prophets, and apostles. The revelations of the Old Testament were emphatically the unfolding of the gospel, the unveiling of the purpose and will of the infinite Father" (RH Jan. 7, 1890). To Ellen White, divine revelation is a very comprehensive concept as is evident, for instance, from the following paragraph:

"The Old Testament sheds light upon the New, and the New upon the Old. Each is a revelation of the glory of God in Christ. Christ as manifested to the patriarchs, as symbolized in the sacrificial service, as portrayed in the law, and as revealed by the prophets, is the riches of the Old Testament. Christ in His life, His death, and His resurrection; Christ as He is manifested by the Holy Spirit, is the treasure of the New. Both Old and New present truths that will continually reveal new depths of meaning to the earnest seeker" (CT 462).

Appealing to the biblical record, Ellen White closely associated the prophetic gift bestowed upon patriarchs and prophets with visions and dreams. Commenting on the defiant confrontation of Moses by Miriam and Aaron, she wrote, "Their claim to the prophetic gift was not denied; God might have spoken to them in visions and dreams. But to Moses, whom the Lord Himself declared 'faithful in all mine house,' a nearer communion had been granted" (PP 385). She did not attempt to give a detailed explanation of the process of divine revelation through dreams and visions but stressed the fact that prophetic dreams were distinct from ordinary dreams as well as from Satan-inspired dreams and visions. She wrote that "dreams from the Lord are classed in the word of God with visions and are as truly the fruits of the spirit of prophecy as are visions. Such dreams, taking into the account the persons who have them and the circumstances under which they are given, contain their own proofs of their genuineness" (1T 569, 570).

C. Scripture and Inspiration

Her emphasis on the fact that Christ is the Author and culmination of divine revelation does not lead Ellen White to deny or downplay the crucial role of the Holy Scriptures as a revelation from God. To her "the whole Bible is a revelation of the glory of God in Christ" (8T 319). Those who through their own experience have seen and heard and felt the power of Christ can testify: "I needed help, and I found it in Jesus. Every want was supplied, the hunger of my soul was satisfied; the Bible is to me the revelation of Christ. . . . I believe the Bible because I have found it to be the voice of God to my soul" (*ibid.* 321; cf. SC 112).

She sees a significant analogy between the incarnation of Christ, the eternal Word, and the inscripturation of the Word of God in the Bible. In the very informative introduction to her book *The Great Controversy Between Christ and Satan* she states, "The Bible, with its God-given truths expressed in the language of men, presents a union of the divine and the human. Such a union existed in the nature of Christ, who was the Son of God and the Son of man. Thus it is true of the Bible, as it was of Christ, that 'the Word was made flesh, and dwelt among us' (John 1:14)" (GC vi; cf. "The Word Made Flesh" in 5T 746-749).

While she thus recognizes that the Scriptures are both human and divine, she firmly rejects any theory of partial inspiration or degrees of inspiration. Some denominational leaders in the 1880s suggested that parts of the Bible were divinely inspired, while others presented merely human thoughts. Ellen White responded to these ideas both in personal letters and in publications. In a penetrating chapter, "The Mysteries of the Bible a Proof of Its Inspiration" (5T 698-711), she discusses at length the difficulties and mysteries in Scripture that cannot be fully resolved or comprehended by human reason. She is aware that "the difficulties of Scripture have been urged by skeptics as an argument against the Bible," but argues that, to the contrary, "they consti-

tute a strong evidence of its divine inspiration." While on the one hand the Bible "unfolds truth with a simplicity and perfect adaptation to the needs and longings of the human heart," on the other hand "beneath these truths, so easily understood, lie mysteries which are the hiding of His glory—mysteries which overpower the mind in its research, yet inspire the sincere seeker for truth with reverence and faith. The more he searches the Bible, the deeper is his conviction that it is the word of the living God, and human reason bows before the majesty of divine revelation" (*ibid.* 700).

In the last pages of the same chapter she warns against "views in regard to the inspiration of the Bible which have not the sanction of the Spirit or the word of God." She asserts that "when men, compassed with human infirmities, . . . undertake to arraign the word of God, and to pass judgment upon what is divine and what is human, they are working without the counsel of God" (*ibid.* 709). She urges believers to "let the word of God stand just as it is. Let not human wisdom presume to lessen the force of one statement of the Scriptures" (*ibid.* 711).

The union of the divine and the human in the Scriptures is the result of the working of the Holy Spirit upon chosen human beings. According to Ellen White, "The Infinite One by His Holy Spirit has shed light into the minds and hearts of His servants. He has given dreams and visions, symbols and figures; and those to whom the truth was thus revealed have themselves embodied the thought in human language" (GC v). Elsewhere she explains more fully, "It is not the words of the Bible that are inspired, but the men that were inspired. Inspiration acts not on the man's words or his expressions but on the man himself, who, under the influence of the Holy Ghost, is imbued with thoughts. But the words receive the impress of the individual mind. The divine mind is diffused. The divine mind and will is combined with the human mind and will; thus the utterances of the man are the word of God" (1SM 21). The Holy Spirit did not override the individuality of the different writers. Rather, "the books of the Bible present a wide contrast in style, as well as a diversity in the nature of the subjects unfolded. Different forms of expression are employed by different writers; often the same truth is more strikingly presented by one than by another" (GC vi). Because "the Bible is not given to us in grand superhuman language," but "in the language of men," its language is subject to human imperfection. Emphatically she states that "the Bible was given for practical purposes" and that "God has not put Himself in words, in logic, in rhetoric, on trial in the Bible" (1SM 20, 21). She even admits the possibility or probability that some mistakes might have resulted from copying and translating the Bible (ibid. 16).

But all these things provide no pretext for anybody to sit in judgment on the Scriptures. Repeatedly Ellen White uttered strong warnings against the disastrous effects of criticism of the Bible such as this one: "The work of 'higher criticism,' in dissecting, conjecturing, reconstructing, is destroying faith in the Bible as a divine revelation. It is robbing God's Word of power to control, uplift, and inspire human lives" (AA 474).

As she sees it, one of the most significant effects of inspiration is the fact that the inspired writers were completely truthful in what they wrote. This point was stressed by Ellen White in an article "Bible Biographies," originally published in 1876 (ST Feb. 24) and later in a more permanent form (4T 9-15). While critics of the Bible asserted that many historical narratives in Scripture could not be accepted as literal history, Ellen White affirmed in emphatic terms: "The lives recorded in the Bible are authentic histories of actual individuals. From Adam down through successive generations to the times of the apostles we have a plain, unvarnished account of what actually occurred and the genuine experience of real characters." Commenting on the fact that the pages of sacred history were clouded by the record of human frailties and faults, she explained, "The scribes of God wrote as they were dictated by the Holy Spirit, having no control of the work themselves. They penned the literal truth, and stern, forbidding facts are revealed for reasons that our finite minds cannot fully comprehend." To her this truthfulness "is one of the best evidences of the authenticity of the Scriptures" (ibid. 9).

But the inspiration of Scripture is not only manifested in the truthful record of human sin and rebellion, but also in the marvelous revelations of divine mercy and forgiveness. "Bible history stays the fainting heart with the hope of God's mercy. . . . The words of inspiration comfort and cheer the erring soul" (ibid. 15). "The highest evidence of the divine authorship of the Bible," according to Ellen White, is its life-transforming power in mind and heart when "we contemplate the great things of God's Word." "This change is itself the miracle of miracles. A change wrought by the word, it is one of the deepest mysteries of the word. We cannot understand it; we can only believe, as declared by the Scriptures, it is 'Christ in you, the hope of glory.' Colossians 1:27" (Ed 171, 172).

Throughout all her writings Ellen White stressed the importance of personal Bible study. "The Bible is God's voice speaking to us, just as surely as if we could hear it with our ears," and consequently the reading and contemplation of the Scriptures should "be regarded as an audience with the Infinite One" (ST Apr. 4, 1906). In a chapter entitled "The Scriptures a Safeguard" (GC 593-602) she enunciated that "it is the first and highest duty of every rational being to learn from the Scriptures what is truth" (ibid. 598). She was deeply concerned that Christians should not be deceived by erroneous doctrines undermining their confidence in the Scriptures. She urged that the study of the Scriptures "should be critical and thorough, and should be pursued with meekness, and with sincerity of purpose, to know the truth as it is in Jesus" (RH Apr. 24, 1888). Like the Protestant Reformers, she held that it was the privilege and duty of all believers, whether learned or unlearned, to study the

Bible for themselves. In an article "The Bible to Be Understood by All" she asserted that "the Bible and the soul were made one for the other, and through the agency of the word and the Holy Spirit, God moves upon the heart," adding that "the Bible has been addressed to everyone, to every class of society, to those of every clime and age" (ST Aug. 20, 1894). All should know for themselves the conditions upon which salvation is provided.

VIII. Literature

Berkouwer, G. C. *Holy Scripture.* Studies in Dogmatics. Grand Rapids: Eerdmans, 1975.

Burtchaell, James T. *Catholic Theories of Biblical Inspiration Since 1810: A Review and Critique.* Cambridge: Cambridge University Press, 1969.

Carson, D. A., and John D. Woodbridge, eds. *Scripture and Truth.* Grand Rapids: Zondervan, 1983.

Demarest, Bruce A. *General Revelation: Historical Views and Contemporary Issues.* Grand Rapids: Zondervan, 1982.

Denzinger, Henry. *The Sources of Catholic Dogma.* London: Harder, 1957.

Dulles, Avery. *Models of Revelation.* Maryknoll, N.Y.: Orbis Books, 1992.

————. *Revelation Theology: A History.* A Crossroad Book. New York: Seabury Press, 1969.

Flannery, Austin P., ed. *Documents of Vatican II.* Grand Rapids: Eerdmans, 1975.

Forstman, H. Jackson. *Word and Spirit: Calvin's Doctrine of Biblical Authority.* Stanford, Calif.: Stanford University Press, 1962.

Greenslade, S. L., ed. *The Cambridge History of the Bible: The West From the Reformation to the Present Day.* Cambridge: Cambridge University Press, 1963.

Henry, Carl F. H. *God, Revelation, and Authority.* 6 vols. Waco, Tex.: Word, 1976-1983.

————, ed. *Revelation and the Bible: Contemporary Evangelical Thought.* Grand Rapids: Baker, 1959.

Holbrook, Frank, and Leo Van Dolson, eds. *Issues in Revelation and Inspiration.* Adventist Theological Society Occasional Papers. Vol. 1. Berrien Springs, Mich.: Adventist Theological Society Publications, 1992.

Latourelle, René. *Theology of Revelation.* New York: Alba House, 1966.

Marshall, I. Howard. *Biblical Inspiration.* Grand Rapids: Eerdmans, 1982.

McDonald, H. D. *Ideas of Revelation: An Historical Study 1700 to 1860.* London: Macmillan, 1959.

————. *Theories of Revelation: An Historical Study 1860-1960.* London: George Allen and Unwin, 1963.

Pache, René. *The Inspiration and Authority of Scripture.* Chicago: Moody, 1969.

Polman, A.D.R. *The Word of God According to St. Augustine.* Trans. A. J. Pomerans. Grand Rapids: Eerdmans, 1961.

Ramm, Bernard. *Special Revelation and the Word of God.* Grand Rapids: Eerdmans, 1961.

Sanday, William. *Inspiration.* Bampton Lectures for 1893. London: Longmans, Green, and Co., 1893.

Schleiermacher, Friedrich. *The Christian Faith.* Ed. H. R. Mackintosh and J. S. Stewart. Edinburgh: T. & T. Clark, 1928.

Thompson, Alden. *Inspiration: Hard Questions, Honest Answers.* Hagerstown, Md.: Review and Herald, 1991.

Trembath, Kern R. *Evangelical Theories of Biblical Inspiration: A Review and Proposal.* New York: Oxford University Press, 1987.

Van Bemmelen, Peter M. *Issues in Biblical Inspiration: Sanday and Warfield.* Berrien Springs, Mich.: Andrews University Press, 1988.

Warfield, Benjamin B. *The Inspiration and Authority of the Bible.* Philadelphia: Presbyterian and Reformed Pub. Co., 1948.

Weeks, Noel. *The Sufficiency of Scripture.* Edinburgh: Banner of Truth Trust, 1988.

Wenham, John. *Christ and the Bible.* London: Tyndale, 1972; Downers Grove, Ill.: InterVarsity, 1973.

Whitaker, William. *A Disputation on Holy Scripture.* Parker Society. Cambridge: Cambridge University Press, 1849.

Biblical Interpretation

Richard M. Davidson

Introduction

God has revealed Himself and His will to His prophets in specific statements of truth, and through His Spirit He has inspired the biblical writers to record the divine revelation as the trustworthy and authoritative Word of God. The Spirit also illuminates the minds of those who seek to understand and interpret the divine revelation.

The need for interpreting Scripture arises because of the finite human mind in contrast with the infinite God who reveals Himself, and because of the darkening of the human mind through sin. The necessity for the interpretative process is further mandated by our separation in time, distance, language, and culture from the scriptural autographs.

The study of the basic principles and procedures for faithfully and accurately interpreting Scripture is called biblical hermeneutics. The task of this discipline is to understand what the human writers and the divine Author of Scripture intended to communicate and also how to communicate and apply the biblical message to modern humanity.

The final goal of interpreting Scripture is to make practical application of each passage to one's individual life. The interpreter must seek to understand how each passage applies personally. The Scriptures should ultimately be read and accepted as if personally addressed to the interpreter. They are God's living and active Word for the soul.

This chapter first presents foundational principles and specific guidelines for biblical interpretation, followed by a brief history of biblical hermeneutics.

I. Interpreting the Word of God

A. Revelation-Inspiration-Illumination

The doctrine of revelation-inspiration is foundational to the whole enterprise of biblical interpretation (see Revelation/Inspiration, especially IV and V). According to the biblical record God has revealed Himself and His will in specific statements of truth to His prophets (Heb. 1:1). Through the inspiration of the Spirit He has enabled His prophets to communicate the divine revelation as the trustworthy and authoritative Word of God (2 Tim. 3:15, 16; 2 Peter 1:19-21). The same Spirit who has inspired the prophets has been promised to illumine the minds of those who seek to understand the meaning of the divine revelation (John 14:26; 1 Cor. 2:10-14).

B. The Need for Interpretation

The Bible's message is not hidden or obscure, requiring some esoteric external key to unlock its mysteries. Scripture was given by God as a revelation for all humankind. How-ever, finite human beings are unable on their own to comprehend the mind of the Infinite One (Job 11:7-9; Isa. 55:8, 9; Eccl. 3:11; Rom. 11:33, 34). Furthermore, sin has darkened and even blinded the minds of human beings (Rom. 1:21; Eph. 4:18; John 9:39-41) so that they of themselves are not capable on their own to interpret God's Word rightly. Because of the human problem of comprehension, God has provided in Scripture the keys to explain its meaning, and the Holy Spirit to guide into biblical truth (John 16:13). After His resurrection, on the road to Emmaus, Jesus Himself "interpreted [diermēneuō] to them in all the scriptures the things concerning himself" (Luke 24:27).

Already in the Old Testament the priests and Levites had the responsibility of teaching God's Word to the people (Lev. 10:11; Deut. 33:10; Mal. 2:7) and interpreting the law of God in different situations (Deut. 17:8-11; Eze. 44:23, 24). In the days of Ezra and Nehemiah, the Levites "read from the book,

59

from the law of God, clearly; and they gave the sense, so that the people understood the reading" (Neh. 8:8). This involved translating from Hebrew to the more familiar Aramaic and explaining the meaning to the recently returned exiles.

The NT witness is clear that the interpretation of Scripture is the task of the entire church, not restricted to a few specialists (see Acts 17:11; Eph. 3:18, 19; 5:10, 17). Philip interprets the meaning of Isaiah 53 to the Ethiopian eunuch (Acts 8:30, 31). The apostle Paul instructs Timothy to be sure he is "rightly handling" (orthotomeō, "to cut straight") or "handling accurately" (NASB) the Word of God (2 Tim. 2:15). In 2 Corinthians 2:17 Paul affirms that he is not like many who "adulterate" God's word. The Greek word here is kapēleuō, "to peddle," alluding to the peddlers who used such deceptive tricks that the term came to signify "adulterate." The presence of those who adulterate or corrupt the Word implies the need for careful interpretation.

The necessity for interpretation of the Scriptures today is further indicated by the separation in time, distance, and culture from the scriptural autographs. The biblical canon closed almost 2,000 years ago. Most of us are also separated geographically from the place where Scripture was written. Even the present inhabitants of the Middle East live in a very different culture from that of biblical times.

Different languages—biblical Hebrew, Aramaic, and Greek—require translation and interpretation. Different social customs; different civil, military, and political institutions; different economic and technological conditions; different patterns of thought—all these and more mandate the hermeneutical process.

C. Hermeneutics: Definition and Scope

The Greek word translated "interpret" in Luke 24:27 is diermēneuō (dia + hermēneuō), related to the English "hermeneutics." Hermeneutics is the science of interpretation. Biblical hermeneutics is the study of the basic principles and procedures for faithfully and accurately interpreting God's Word. From the biblical data we may deduce three major tasks of biblical hermeneutics: (1) to understand what the human writers of Scripture intended to convey to their hearers or readers (see Acts 2:25-31); (2) to grasp what the divine Author intends to communicate through the words of Scripture, which may not always have been fully understood by the human writer or his contemporaries (1 Peter 1:10-12); and (3) to learn how to communicate and apply both form and content of the biblical message to human beings today (see Matt. 5:17-48; 1 Peter 1:15, 16).

II. Foundational Principles for Biblical Interpretation

A. The Bible and the Bible Only

A fundamental principle set forth by Scripture concerning itself is that the Bible alone (sola scriptura) is the final norm of truth. The classical text expressing this basic premise is Isaiah 8:20: "To the law and to the testimony! If they do not speak according to this word, they have no light of dawn" (NIV). The two Hebrew words tôrāh (law) and tecûdāh (testimony) point to the two loci of authority in Isaiah's day. These now constitute holy Scripture: the Pentateuch and the testimony of the prophets to the previously revealed will of God in the Torah. Jesus summarized the two divisions of OT Scripture similarly when He referred to the "law and the prophets" (Matt. 5:17). The NT adds the authoritative revelation given by Jesus and His apostolic witnesses (see Eph. 2:20; 3:5).

1. The Primacy of Scripture

Isaiah warned apostate Israel against turning from the authority of the law and the prophets to seek counsel from spiritist mediums (Isa. 8:19). In NT times other sources of authority were threatening to usurp the final authority of the biblical revelation. One of these was tradition. But Jesus clearly indicated that Scripture is over tradition (Matt. 15:3, 6). Paul emphatically rejected tradition and human philosophy as final norms of truth for the Christian (Col. 2:8). Likewise he rejected human "knowledge" (Gr. *gnōsis*) as the final authority (1 Tim. 6:20).

Nature, rightly understood, is in harmony with God's written revelation in Scripture (see Ps. 19:1-6, revelation of God in nature; and verses 7-11, revelation of the Lord in Scripture); but as a limited and broken source of knowledge about God and reality, it must be held subservient to, and interpreted by, the final authority of Scripture (Rom. 2:14-16). Both OT and NT writers point out that since the Fall nature has become depraved (Gen. 3:17, 18; Rom. 8:20, 21) and no longer perfectly reflects truth.

The mental and emotional faculties of human beings have also become depraved since the Fall; but even before the Fall, neither human reason nor experience could safely be trusted apart from God's Word. Eve fell because she trusted her own reason and emotions above the word of God (Gen. 3:1-6). The wisest man in history perceptively observed, "There is a way which seems right to a man, but its end is the way to death" (Prov. 14:12; see Sin V. A).

2. The Sufficiency of Scripture

The principle of *sola scriptura* implies the corollary of the sufficiency of Scripture. The Bible stands alone as the unerring guide to truth; it is sufficient to make one wise unto salvation (2 Tim. 3:15). It is the standard by which all doctrine and experience must be tested (Isa. 8:20; John 17:17; 2 Tim. 3:16, 17; Heb. 4:12). Scripture thus provides the framework, the divine perspective, the foundational principles, for every branch of knowledge and experience. All additional knowledge, experience, or revelation must build upon and remain faithful to the all-sufficient foundation of Scripture.

Thus is confirmed the battle cry of the Reformation, *sola scriptura*—the Bible and the Bible only as the final norm for truth. All other sources of knowledge must be tested by this unerring standard. The appropriate human response must be one of total surrender to the ultimate authority of the Word of God (Isa. 66:2).

B. The Totality of Scripture

A second general principle of biblical interpretation is the totality of Scripture *(tota scriptura)*. It is not enough to affirm the primacy of Scripture. Those who, like Martin Luther, called for *sola scriptura* but failed to accept the Scriptures fully in their totality have ended up with a "canon within the canon." For Luther this meant depreciating the book of James (as an "epistle of straw") and despising other portions of Scripture (as presenting the way of law and not the gospel).

The self-testimony of Scripture is clear in 2 Timothy 3:16, 17: "All scripture is inspired by God and profitable for teaching, for reproof, for correction, and for training in righteousness, that the man of God may be complete, equipped for every good work."

All Scripture—not just part—is inspired by God. This certainly includes the whole OT, the canonical Scriptures of the apostolic church (see Luke 24:44, 45; John 5:39; Rom. 1:2; 3:2; 2 Peter 1:21). But for Paul it also includes the NT sacred writings as well. Paul's use of the word "scripture" (*graphē*, "writing") in 1 Timothy 5:18 points in this direction. He introduces two quotations with the words "scripture says": one from Deuteronomy 25:4 and one from the words of Jesus in Luke 10:7. The word "scripture" thus is used to refer to both the OT and the Gospel of Luke. Peter, by noting that some ignorant people "twist" Paul's writings "as they do the other Scriptures" (2 Peter 3:15, 16), puts the apostle's writings into the category of Scripture. Thus the Gospels and the Epistles of Paul are understood as "Scripture" already in NT times.

The NT is the apostolic witness to Jesus

and to His fulfillment of the OT types and prophecies. Jesus promised to send the Holy Spirit to bring to remembrance what He had taught (John 14:26). Paul states that "the mystery of Christ" was "revealed to his holy apostles and prophets by the Spirit" (Eph. 3:4, 5). Paul calls himself an apostle (Rom. 1:1; 1 Cor. 1:1). He also claims to "have the Spirit of God" (1 Cor. 7:40), to write "[commands] of the Lord" (1 Cor. 14:37), and to preach a gospel that is not human but was revealed to him by Jesus Christ Himself (Gal. 1:11, 12). The NT thus embodies the witness of the apostles, either directly (2 Peter 1:16; 1 John 1:1-3) or indirectly, through their close associates, such as Mark or Luke (Acts 12:12, 25; 15:37; Luke 1:1-3; 2 Tim. 4:11; Philemon 24), to the life and ministry of Jesus.

All Scripture, both OT and NT, is "inspired by God," literally "God-breathed" (2 Tim. 3:16). The picture is of the divine "wind," or Spirit, coming upon the prophet, so that Scripture is a product of the divine creative breath. Thus it is fully authoritative, "profitable for teaching, for reproof, for correction, and for training in righteousness."

1. Inseparable Union of the Divine and Human

A corollary of the *tota scriptura* principle is that all Scripture is an indivisible, indistinguishable union of the divine and the human. A key biblical passage that clarifies the divine nature of Scripture in relation to the human dimensions of the biblical writers is 2 Peter 1:19-21: "And we have the word of the prophets made more certain, and you will do well to pay attention to it, as to a light shining in a dark place, until the day dawns and the morning star rises in your hearts. Above all, you must understand that no prophecy of Scripture came about by the prophet's own interpretation. For prophecy never had its origin in the will *[thelēma]* of man, but men spoke from God as they were carried along *[pherō]* by the Holy Spirit" (NIV).

Several related points are developed in these verses. Verse 19 underscores the trustworthiness of Scripture: It is "the prophetic word made more sure." In verse 20 we learn why this is so: Prophecy is not a matter of the prophet's own interpretation. The context primarily points to the prophet giving the message, who does not intrude his own ideas into the message, although the statement may also be heeded by the noninspired interpreter of Scripture. Verse 21 elaborates on this point: Prophecy does not come by the *thelēma*—the initiative, the impulse, the will—of the human agent; the prophets are not communicating on their own. Rather, the Bible writers were prophets who spoke as they were moved, carried along, even driven *[pherō]* by the Holy Spirit.

This passage makes clear that the Scriptures did not come directly from heaven, but that God utilized human instrumentalities. The Holy Spirit did not abridge the freedom of the biblical writers, did not suppress their unique personalities, did not destroy their individuality. Their writings sometimes involved human research (Luke 1:1-3); the writers sometimes gave their own experiences (Moses in Deuteronomy, Luke in Acts, the psalmists); they present differences in style (contrast Isaiah and Ezekiel, John and Paul); they offer different perspectives on the same truth or event (e.g., the four Gospels). And yet, through all this thought-inspiration, the Holy Spirit is carrying along the biblical writers, guiding their minds in selecting what to speak and write, so that what they present is not merely their own interpretation, but the utterly reliable word of God, the prophetic word made more certain. The Holy Spirit imbued human instruments with divine truth in thoughts and assisted them in writing so that they faithfully committed to apt words the things divinely revealed to them (1 Cor. 2:10-13).

This first corollary of the *tota scriptura* principle, that the human and divine elements in Scripture are inextricably bound together, is reinforced by comparing the written and incarnate Word of God. Since both Jesus and Scripture are called the "Word of God" (Heb. 4:12; Rev. 19:13), it is appropriate to compare their divine-human natures. Just as Jesus, the incarnate Word of God, was fully God and fully man (John 1:1-3, 14), so the written Word is an inseparable union of the human and the divine.

2. The Bible Equals, Not Just Contains, the Word of God

A second corollary of the *totality of Scripture* principle is that the Bible *equals,* not merely *contains,* the Word of God. The testimony of Scripture is overwhelming. In the OT alone there are about 1,600 occurrences of four Hebrew words (in four different phrases with slight variations) that explicitly indicate that God has spoken: (1) "the utterance *[n^e'um]* of Yahweh," some 360 times; (2) "thus says *['āmar]* the Lord," some 425 times; (3) "and God spoke *[dibber],* some 420 times, and (4) the "word *[dābār]* of the Lord," some 395 times. Numerous times the equivalency between the prophet's message and the divine message is recorded: the prophet speaks for God (Ex. 7:1, 2; cf. Ex. 4:15, 16); God puts His words in the prophet's mouth (Deut. 18:18; Jer. 1:9); the hand of the Lord is strong upon the prophet (Isa. 8:11; Jer. 15:17; Eze. 1:3); or the word of the Lord comes to him (Hosea 1:1; Joel 1:1; Micah 1:1). Jeremiah rebukes his audience for not listening to the prophets (Jer. 25:4), which is equated with not listening to the Lord (verse 7).

The sending of prophetic messages to Israel is summarized in 2 Kings 21:10: "And the Lord said by his servants the prophets." In 2 Chronicles 36:15, 16 we read, "The Lord, the God of their fathers, sent persistently to them by his messengers . . . ; but they kept mocking the messengers of God, despising his words, and scoffing at his prophets." The prophets' message was God's message. For this reason the prophets often naturally switched from a third-person reference to God ("He") to the first person ("I") of divine speech, without any "thus saith the Lord" (see Isa. 3:1-4; Jer.

5:3, 4; Hosea 6:3, 4; Joel 2:23, 25; Zech. 9:4, 7).

Numerous times in the NT "it is written" is equivalent to "God says." For example, in Hebrews 1:5-13, seven OT citations are said to have been spoken by God, but the OT passages cited do not always specifically ascribe the statement to God (see Ps. 45:6, 7; 102:25-27; 104:4). Again, Romans 9:17 and Galatians 3:8 (citing Ex. 9:16 and Gen. 22:18, respectively) reveal a close identification between Scripture and the Word of God: the NT passages introduce the citations with "scripture says," while the OT passages have God as the speaker. The OT Scriptures as a whole are viewed as the "oracles of God" (Rom. 3:2).

Though the Bible was not verbally dictated by God so as to bypass the individuality of the human author, and thus the specific words are words chosen by the human writer, yet the human and divine elements are so inseparable, the human messenger so divinely guided in his selection of apt words to express the divine thoughts, that the words of the prophet are called the Word of God. The individual words of Scripture are regarded as trustworthy, accurately representing the divine message.

This is illustrated by a number of NT references. Jesus says, quoting Deuteronomy 8:3, "Man shall not live by bread alone, but by every word [Gr. *panti rhēmati,* "every word," translating the Heb. *qōl,* "everything"] that proceeds from the mouth of God" (Matt. 4:4). Paul says of his own inspired message, "And we impart this in words not taught by human wisdom but taught by the Spirit, interpreting spiritual truths to those who possess the Spirit" (1 Cor. 2:13). The same apostle writes, "And we also thank God constantly for this, that when you received the word of God which you heard from us, you accepted it not as the word of men but as what it really is, the word of God, which is at work in you believers" (1 Thess. 2:13).

What is stated explicitly in the NT is also indicated by the instances when Jesus and the apostles based an entire theological argument upon a crucial word or even grammatical form in the OT. So in John 10:34 Jesus appeals to Psalm 82:6 and the specific word "gods" to substantiate His divinity. Accompanying His usage is the telling remark, "And scripture cannot be broken *[luō]*" (verse 35). It cannot be *luō*—loosed, broken, repealed, annulled, or abolished—even to the specific words. In Matthew 22:41-46 He grounds His final, unanswerable argument to the Pharisees upon the reliability of the single word "Lord" in Psalm 110:1. The apostle Paul (Gal. 3:16) likewise bases his Messianic argument upon the singular number of the word "seed" (KJV) in Genesis 22:17, 18. Paul is recognizing the larger Messianic context of this passage, as it moves from a collective plural seed to a singular Seed. Jesus shows His ultimate respect for the full authority of the OT Torah when He affirms its totality: "For truly, I say to you, till heaven and earth pass away, not an iota, not a dot, will pass from the law until all is accomplished" (Matt. 5:18).

C. The Analogy of Scripture

A third general foundational principle of biblical interpretation may be termed "the analogy (or harmony) of Scripture" (*analogia scripturae*). Since all Scripture is inspired by the same Spirit and all of it is the Word of God, there is a fundamental unity and harmony among its various parts. The various parts of OT Scripture are considered by the NT writers as harmonious and of equal divine authority. NT writers may thus support their point by citing several OT sources as of equal and harmonious weight. For example, in Romans 3:10-18 we have scriptural citations from Ecclesiastes (7:20), Psalms (14:2, 3; 5:10; 10:7), and Isaiah (59:7, 8). Scripture is regarded as an inseparable, coherent whole. Major OT themes are assumed by the NT writers and further developed (see III. E. 1).

The two Testaments have a reciprocal relationship in which they mutually illuminate each other. Jesus described how the OT illuminates the NT (and Himself in particular) in John 5:39:

"You search the scriptures, because you think that in them you have eternal life; and it is they that bear witness to me." Elsewhere Jesus describes how He is the illuminator, even the fulfillment, of the OT: "Think not that I have come to abolish the law and the prophets; I have come not to abolish them but to fulfil them" (Matt. 5:17).

Neither Testament is superseded by the other, although the later revelation is tested by the former, as illustrated by the example of the Bereans, who "were more noble than those in Thessalonica, for they received the word with all eagerness, examining the scriptures daily to see if these things were so" (Acts 17:11). Even Jesus insisted that the conviction of His disciples not be based primarily upon sensory phenomena alone, but that they believe in Him because of the testimony of OT Scripture (Luke 24:25-27).

The "analogy of Scripture" principle has three main aspects: (1) Scripture as its own expositor (*scriptura sui ipsius interpres*), (2) the consistency of Scripture, and (3) the clarity of Scripture.

1. "Scripture Is Its Own Interpreter"

As Martin Luther put it, "Scripture is its own light." Because there is an underlying unity among the various parts of Scripture, one portion of Scripture interprets another, becoming the key for understanding related passages.

Jesus demonstrated this principle on the way to Emmaus when, "beginning with Moses and all the prophets, he interpreted to them in all the scriptures the things concerning himself" (Luke 24:27). Later that night in the upper room, He pointed out " 'that everything written about me in the law of Moses and the prophets and the psalms must be fulfilled.' Then he opened their minds to understand the scriptures" (verses 44, 45).

Paul expresses this same principle in 1 Corinthians 2:13: "These things we also speak, not in words which man's wisdom teaches but which the Holy Spirit teaches, comparing spiritual things with spiritual" (NKJV). This text has been translated in different ways, but certainly the apostle's own use of Scripture indicates his adoption of the principle. We have already noted the whole catena of OT quotations cited in Romans 3:10-18. The same phenomenon may be observed in Hebrews 1:5-13; 2:6, 8, 12, 13.

Applying this principle that the Bible is its own expositor, Jesus, on the way to Emmaus, showed how all that Scripture says about a given topic should be brought to bear upon the interpretation of the subject (Luke 24:27, 44, 45). This does not mean the indiscriminate stringing together of passages in "proof-text" fashion without regard for the context of each text. But since the Scriptures ultimately have a single divine Author, it is crucial to gather all that is written on a particular topic in order to be able to consider all the contours of the topic.

2. The Consistency of Scripture

Jesus succinctly stated this aspect of the analogy of Scripture: "Scripture cannot be broken" (John 10:35). Since Scripture has a single divine Author, the various parts of Scripture are consistent with each other. Thus scripture cannot be set against scripture. All the doctrines of the Bible will cohere with each other; interpretations of individual passages will harmonize with the totality of what Scripture teaches on a given subject.

While the different Bible writers may provide different emphases on the same event or topic, this will be without contradiction or misinterpretation. This is evidenced especially with parallel passages such as in the four Gospels. Each writer recorded what impressed him most under the inspiration of the Spirit, and each facet of the whole is needed to obtain the full and balanced picture.

3. The Clarity of Scripture

The principle of the analogy of Scripture also involves the clarity of Scripture. The biblical principle is that the Bible is perspicuous and does not require any ecclesiological magisterium to clarify its meaning. The biblical testimony encourages readers to study the Bible for themselves in order to understand God's message to them (e.g., Deut. 30:11-14; Luke 1:3, 4; John 20:30, 31; Acts 17:11; Rom. 10:17; Rev. 1:3).

The meaning of Scripture is clear and straightforward, able to be grasped by the diligent student. Jesus illustrates this in His dealing with the lawyer, whom He asked, "What is written in the law? How do you read?" (Luke 10:26). In other words, He expected that the Bible could be understood. When the lawyer cited Deuteronomy 6:5 and Leviticus 19:18, Jesus commended him for having answered correctly (Luke 10:28). Numerous times Jesus made the same point: "Have you never read in the scriptures?" (Matt. 21:42); "Have you not read?" (Matt. 12:3, 5; 19:4; 22:31; Mark 12:10, 26; Luke 6:3); "Let the reader understand" (Matt. 24:15; Mark 13:14).

The consistent example of the Bible writers shows that the Scriptures are to be taken in their plain, literal sense, unless a clear and obvious figure is intended. Note especially Jesus' own distinction, and the disciples' recognition, of the difference between literal and figurative language (John 16:25, 29). There is no stripping away of the "husk" of the literal sense in order to arrive at the "kernel" of a mystical, hidden, allegorical meaning, that only the initiated can uncover.

Scripture also maintains that there is a definite truth-intention of the biblical writers, and not a subjective, uncontrolled multiplicity of meanings. Jesus and the apostles spoke with authority, not giving one of many possible interpretations of a passage, but its true meaning as intended by the human writer and the divine Author (see, e.g., Acts 3:17, 18, 22-24). At the same time, the NT interpretation does not claim to exhaust the meaning of a given OT passage; there is still room for careful exegesis. There are also instances in which the biblical writer intentionally used terminology or phraseology with a breadth of meaning that encompasses several different nuances indicated by the immediate context of the passage (see John 3:3).

The specific truth-intention is vividly illustrated with regard to apocalyptic prophecy: the angel interpreter consistently gives a definite interpretation of each symbol (see Dan. 7:16-27; 8:15-26; Apocalyptic II. E). Another illustration involves those of Jesus' parables in which Jesus Himself interpreted the meaning of each part (see Matt. 13:18-23, 36-43).

This is not to deny that some parts of Scripture point beyond themselves (e.g., typology, predictive prophecy, symbols, and parables) to an extended meaning or future fulfillment. Even in these cases the extended meaning or fulfillment arises from, is consistent with, and in fact is an integral part of the specific truth-intention of the text; Scripture itself indicates the presence of such extended meaning or fulfillment (see III. E. 3).

It is also true that not every portion of Scripture was fully understood by the original hearers or even by the inspired writers. In 1 Peter 1:10-12 the apostle indicates that the OT prophets may not have always clearly understood all the Messianic implications of their prophecies. Thus Peter suggests another facet of the principle of the clarity of Scripture, i.e., that additional clearer revelation becomes a key to fuller understanding of the less clear passages. This same point seems implied also in 2 Peter 3:16, where Peter writes that some of the things Paul has written are "hard to understand." These difficult passages are not to be the starting point, which "the ignorant and unstable twist to their own destruction," but are to be viewed in the larger context of clearer scriptural statements of truth (verse 18; cf. verse 2).

The clarity of Scripture corollary also involves the concept of "progressive revelation." Hebrews 1:1-3 indicates this progress in revelation from OT prophets to God's own Son (see also John 1:16-18; Col. 1:25, 26; etc.). This is not progressive revelation in the sense that later Scripture contradicts or nullifies previous revelation, but in the sense that later revelation illuminates, clarifies, or amplifies the truths presented previously. So Jesus, in the Sermon on the Mount (Matt. 5), does not nullify the precepts of the Decalogue, but strips away from them the accretions of erroneous tradition and reveals their true depth of meaning and application. The basic insights into this fuller import of the law were already in the OT, and Jesus enables these gems of truth to shine with even greater brilliance as they are freed from the distorted interpretations of some of the scribes and Pharisees. Progressive revelation also occurs in the sense that Jesus is the fulfillment of the various types and prophecies of the OT.

A final practical application of this principle of clarity is to recognize the increasing spiral of understanding as one passage illuminates another. On one hand, later biblical authors write with conscious awareness of what has been written before and often assume and build upon what comes earlier (sometimes called the epigenetic principle or analogy of antecedent Scripture). A close reading of a later passage may indicate echoes of, or allusions to, earlier passages, which thus become the key to interpreting the fuller meaning of the later. This is especially evident in the book of Revelation. On the other hand, earlier passages may not be fully understood until seen in the light of the later revelation. This is true in particular with typology and prophecy (see Matt. 12:6, 42, 43; 1 Peter 1:10-12). Thus the spiral of understanding grows as later illuminates earlier, and earlier illuminates later.

D. "Spiritual Things Spiritually Discerned"

A fourth general principle of biblical interpretation concerns the issue of pre-understanding or objectivity. In modern hermeneutical approaches to the Bible, it is often assumed that the original intent of the Bible writer can be ascertained by the rigorous application of hermeneutical principles and exegetical tools, quite apart from any supernatural spiritual assistance. Thus non-Christians can determine the meaning of Scripture as well as Christians, if they use the tools and apply the principles correctly.

However, scriptural data leads to a different conclusion. We note in particular 1 Corinthians 2:11, 14: "For what person knows a man's thoughts except the spirit of the man which is in him? So also no one comprehends the thoughts of God except the Spirit of God." "The unspiritual man does not receive the gifts of the Spirit of God, for they are folly to him, and he is not able to understand them because they are spiritually discerned."

1. The Role of the Holy Spirit

Since the Bible ultimately is not the product of the human writer's mind but of the mind of God revealed through the Spirit (see 1 Cor. 2:12, 13), both the original meaning and its present application involve the thoughts of God, which according to Paul can be adequately comprehended only if we have the aid of the Spirit of God (1 Cor. 2:13, 14; 2 Cor. 3:14-18; cf. John 6:45; 16:13).

Some have resisted letting the Spirit have a place in the hermeneutical spiral because it seems to allow the subjective element to overcome solid exegetical/hermeneutical research. It is true that "spiritual exegesis" *alone,* attempting to rely totally on the Spirit without conscientiously applying principles of exegesis and hermeneutics arising from Scripture, is likely to lead to subjectivism. But the proper combination of dependence upon the Spirit with rigorous exegesis based upon sound hermeneutical procedures, far from leading to subjectivity, constitutes the only way of escape.

Increasingly, modern scholars concede that all come to the Scriptures with their own preunderstandings, presuppositions, and biases. This cannot be remedied by approaching the text "scientifically," without a "faith bias." In fact, since the Scriptures call for a response of faith, an attempted "neutral" stance is already at crosscurrents with the in-tent of Scripture (cf. Matt. 13:11-17; John 6:69).

Believing and Spirit-led interpreters also come with their own biases and preunderstandings and are not impervious to error (cf. Acts 11:2-18). But Christians who believe the promises of Scripture can ask God to transform their minds so that they increasingly adopt and incorporate the presuppositions of Scripture and not their own (see Rom. 12:1, 2). The Spirit of truth was promised to the disciples and to us: "When the Spirit of truth comes, he will guide you into all the truth" (John 16:13). It must be noted that the "you" here is plural; the Spirit directs interpreters together within the fellowship of the church body (Ps. 119:63; Acts 2:42; 4:32; Rom. 12:4-8; 1 Cor. 12; Eph. 4:3-6), where they may be benefited by exchange with and the correction of other believers.

Interpreters must make a decision that their preunderstandings will derive from and be under the control of the Bible, constantly open to modification and enlargement of their ideas on the basis of Scripture. They must consciously reject any external keys or systems to impose on Scripture from without, whether naturalistic (closed system of cause and effect without any room for the supernatural), evolutionary (the developmental axiom), humanistic (human beings the final norm), or relativistic (rejection of absolutes). Bible interpreters must ask the Spirit, who inspired the Word, to illuminate, shape, and modify their preunderstandings according to the Word, and to keep their understandings faithful to the Word.

2. The Spiritual Life of the Interpreter

"Spiritual things are spiritually discerned" implies not only the need of the Spirit to aid in understanding, but also that the interpreter be spiritual. The Spirit must not only illumine the mind, but also must have transformed the interpreter's heart. The approach of the interpreter must be that called for by Scripture, an attitude of consent or willingness to follow what Scripture says. Jesus stated, "If any man's will is to do his [God's] will, he shall know whether the teaching is from God or whether I am speaking on my own authority" (John 7:17).

There must be diligent, earnest prayer for understanding, after the example of David: "Teach me, O Lord, the way of thy statutes; and I will keep it to the end" (Ps. 119:33; cf. verses 34-40; Prov. 2:3-7). There must be an acceptance by faith of what the prophets say (2 Chron. 20:20; cf. John 5:46, 47).

In summary, the Bible cannot be studied as any other book, with sharpened tools of exegesis and honed principles of interpretation. At every stage of the interpretative process, the book inspired by the Spirit can be correctly understood only "from above," by the illumination and transformation of the Spirit. God's Word must be approached with reverence. Perhaps the best encapsulation of the interpreter's appropriate stance before Scripture is recorded by Isaiah: "But this is the man to whom I will look, he that is humble and contrite in spirit, and trembles at my word" (Isa. 66:2).

III. Specific Guidelines for the Interpretation of Scripture

The specific guidelines for interpreting biblical passages arise from and build upon the foundational principles thus far described. These guidelines encompass essentially the grammatico-historical method that is dictated by common sense and the laws of language to ascertain the meaning of any writing. But more than from the common interpretative sense, all these guidelines also either explicitly or implicitly arise from Scripture itself. Thus for each guideline discussed below, we will first note how it arises from Scripture. We will also provide one or more biblical examples illustrating its application in biblical interpretation.

A. Text and Translation

The first and most basic task in interpreting Scripture is to ensure that one has access to what is indeed the Holy Scriptures—both in the original languages and in modern translation. This requires attention to textual studies and to principles of translation.

1. Textual Studies

a. The preservation of the biblical text. Since the hermeneutical enterprise focuses on the written Word, the original text of the Bible must be ascertained as far as possible. The Bible itself underscores the necessity of preserving the words of sacred Scripture. Moses wrote with regard to the Torah, "You shall not add to the word which I command you, nor take from it" (Deut. 4:2; cf. 12:32). The book of Proverbs expands this principle to the whole Word of God: "Every word of God proves true. . . . Do not add to his words, lest he rebuke you, and you be found a liar" (Prov. 30:5, 6). At the close of the biblical canon, a similar warning is found: "If anyone adds to them, God will add to him the plagues described in this book, and if any one takes away from the words of the book of this prophecy, God will take away his share in the tree of life and in the holy city" (Rev. 22:18, 19).

In OT Israel, provision was made for preserving the Torah by depositing "the book of the law" in the Most Holy Place of the sanctuary beside the ark of the covenant (Deut. 31:26). There was to be public reading of the Torah every seven years at the Feast of Tabernacles (verses 9-13).

Unfortunately, no autograph copies of either OT or NT Scriptures remain. But the history of textual transmission reveals how carefully and painstakingly the biblical text has been preserved down through the centuries to the present day. Before the end of World War II critical scholars had a very low estimate of the accuracy of the received (Masoretic) Hebrew text, since its earliest manuscript dated back only to about A.D. 900 and critical editions of the Hebrew Bible proposed thousands of conjectural emendments to the text. But since 1947 and the discovery of the Dead Sea scrolls, which contained manuscripts or fragments of every OT book except Esther, scholars have been amazed to discover how the Masoretes had handed down virtually without change the textual tradition from a thousand years earlier.

The amount of MS evidence for the Greek text of the NT is far more abundant than for any other document of the ancient world. There are more than 3,000 Greek MSS of part or all of the NT text, in addition some 2,000 ancient Greek lectionaries (NT readings arranged in order of liturgical usage), about 8,000 Latin MSS, more than 2,000 MSS in other ancient versions such as Syriac and Coptic, and thousands of quotations—virtually the whole NT—in citations by the various early Church Fathers (Greenlee 697, 707). The actual amount of substantive variation among these many manuscripts is very small. F. F. Bruce affirms, "The variant readings about which any doubt remains among textual critics of the New Testament affect no material question of historic fact or of Christian faith and practice" (19, 20).

b. The need for textual studies. Although the past 150 years of diligent textual study assure us that the Scriptures have come down to us substantially as they were written, there are small variations among the many ancient biblical MSS. The science (or art) of coming as close as possible to the original text of the Old and New Testaments is textual study, often called "textual criticism." This study, as practiced by one who accepts the full authority of Scripture, rejects the presuppositions of the historical-critical method (see IV. F, G) and insists that the final norm for determining the authentic text of Scripture is found within Scripture itself.

Basic articles on textual study are found in *The Seventh-day Adventist Bible Commentary* and need not be reproduced here. The standard Hebrew and Greek Bibles give detailed information on major textual variants in the apparatus at the bottom of each page of text.

2. Translations and Versions

The Scriptures themselves give numerous examples of translation to make meaning clear. Among these are Nehemiah 8:8; Matthew 1:23; Mark 5:41; 15:22, 34; John 1:42; 9:7; Acts 9:36; 13:8; Hebrews 7:2. The emphasis given to the need for understanding Scripture (see Acts 8:30-35) suggests the importance of faithful translation.

a. The challenges involved in translation. It is difficult to represent accurately the form and content of the original languages of the Bible in the modern target languages because in the process the translator must seek to bridge various barriers, such as gaps of time, culture, and geography; changed socioeconomic-political situations; and different thought patterns.

The most significant challenge to the translation process lies in the differences in the languages themselves. The range of meaning of a word in the original language may be larger or smaller than its equivalent in the target language. Thereby the connotations of the original word are distorted by the unrelated meanings associated with the closest modern equivalent.

Grammatical and syntactical features of the original languages are not always possible to adequately represent in the modern translation. For example, the Hebrew verb stresses state, the Greek verb stresses kind of action, while the English verb emphasizes time.

At times the meaning of the original is ambiguous. The translator must decide whether to leave the translation ambiguous or attempt to remove the ambiguity—which could be potentially misleading if the incorrect meaning is chosen.

b. Translation types. Three major philosophies or theories concerning what makes the best translation result in three very different kinds of translations. *Formal translations* emphasize word-for-word equivalency in the translation process. This process gives a more exact and literal rendering of the original Hebrew/Aramaic and Greek. The result is an excellent study Bible. However, its readings are often rather wooden and stilted, and the aesthetic quality and cadences of the original may be lost. *Dynamic translations* emphasize meaning-for-meaning instead of word-for-word equivalence. The translator restructures the translation into idiomatic usage that represents the equivalent thought or meaning. The advantage of the dynamic translation is its idiomatic contemporaneity, its readability and clarity. Its drawback is that the interpretation may be misleading or erroneous—depending upon the correctness or incorrectness of the translator's interpretation. A *paraphrase* is far more free with the original than the dynamic translations. It is often intended more for devotional use than serious doctrinal study. Because a paraphrase is often more interpretation than translation, readers need to be careful how they use it.

Given the difficulties in translation and the different ways translation can be done, Bible students should be cautious in their choice of translations. A Bible translation prepared by a single denomination may be slanted or even skewed to support certain doctrines. A similar weakness also exists in a one-translator Bible, without the balance and input of many minds. Caution is also in order with regard to Bibles with systems of notes or interpretation. Likewise, translations into simplified modern language for children run the risk of distorting crucial biblical themes. The more interpretative versions should be diligently compared with a formal word-for-word translation, if not with the original Hebrew/Aramaic and Greek.

B. Historical Context

In order to understand the Scriptures, we must first seek to determine what they meant in their original setting. We must see in what situation each teaching was launched—the historical background; who said what, to whom, and under what circumstances. When we grasp these things, it will be easier to apply the Bible message to current situations.

1. The Bible as Reliable History

All the persons, events, and institutions in the flow of the OT and NT are presented as part of a record of authentic and reliable history. The later OT prophets, Jesus, and the NT writers repeatedly refer back to the accounts of Creation and the Flood. In fact, *every* NT writer explicitly or implicitly affirms the historicity of Genesis 1-11 (see Matt. 19:4, 5; 24:37-39; Mark 10:6; Luke 3:38; 17:26, 27; Rom. 5:12; 1 Cor. 6:16; 2 Cor. 11:3; Eph. 5:31; 1 Tim. 2:13, 14; Heb. 11:7; 1 Peter 3:20; 2 Peter 2:5; James 3:9; 1 John 3:12; Jude 11, 14; Rev. 14:7). Later biblical writers also refer to the time of the patriarchs, the Exodus, and other events of OT and NT history, interpreting these as reliable descriptions of God's real space-time interrelationships with His people.

The historical context of biblical accounts is accepted as true, with no attempt to reconstruct history in a different way from that presented in the biblical record. The NT writers, in their interpretation of the OT, show a remarkably clear acquaintance with the general flow and specific details of OT history (see Acts 7; 1 Cor. 10). The typological arguments of the NT writers assume the historical veracity of the persons, events, and institutions that were types of these historical realities (see 1 Cor. 10:1-11; Rom. 5:12-21; 1 Peter 3:18-22).

Likewise, in contrast with most current critical scholarship, but in harmony with the precedent of the NT writers in their interpretation of the OT, a Bible-based hermeneutic accepts at face value the biblical accounts of the creation of this world occurring in six literal, consecutive, 24-hour days (Gen. 1, 2), and a literal, worldwide Flood (Gen. 6-9). It accepts also the historicity of the patriarchal narratives (Gen. 12-50), the fifteenth-century B.C. Exodus from Egypt (Exodus-Deuteronomy; 1 Kings 6:1), the conquest of Canaan (Joshua 1-12), and the other historical assertions of Scripture, including the supernatural, miraculous events of both OT and NT.

2. Questions of Introduction

In the inner-scriptural hermeneutic of biblical writers, attention is drawn to various "questions of introduction" (date, authorship, and life setting of biblical books), and these questions sometimes become crucial to the inspired writer's argument. Where given, the declaration of the text is accepted as accurately portraying the authorship, chronology, and life setting for the text. For example, the Davidic authorship of Psalm 110 (as stated in the superscription of the psalm) is crucial to Jesus' argument concerning His Messiahship (Matt. 22:41-46). Davidic authorship is also crucial to Peter's Pentecost sermon to convince the Jews of the predicted resurrection of the Messiah (Acts 2:25-35). The "life setting" of Abraham's justification by faith in the Genesis account is significant in Paul's argument to the Romans, to show that this had happened before Abraham had been circumcised (Rom. 4:1-12).

Contrary to the assertions of much of modern critical scholarship, a Bible-based hermeneutic accepts the Pentateuch as written by Moses, not a late redaction of various source documents (see Ex. 24:4, 7; 34:27; Deut. 31:9-11; Joshua 1:7, 8; 1 Kings 2:3). Isaiah is accepted as the writer of the entire book (Isa. 1:1; see Matt. 3:3; 8:17; 12:17-21). David is the writer of the psalms that are attributed to him in their superscriptions or referred to as Davidic by NT writers (73 psalms; Matt. 22:41-46; Acts 2:25-35; etc.). Solomon is the writer of the majority of the Proverbs, of the Song of Solomon, and Ecclesiastes (Prov. 1:1; 10:1; 25:1; S. of Sol. 1:1; Eccl. 1:1, 12, 13). Daniel, the sixth-century captive and statesman in Babylon, authored the book that bears his name (Dan. 8:1; 9:2; see Matt. 24:15). Zechariah wrote the entire book that bears his name (Zech. 1:1). Peter the apostle was the writer of 2 Peter (2 Peter 1:1), and John the Gospel writer authored the Apocalypse (Rev. 1:1-4).

It must be recognized that some of the books of the Bible do not explicitly indicate the writer, time, or historical circumstances of writing. The best solutions to the questions of introduction for these books must be based upon, and in harmony with, all relevant biblical data, seen in the light of available extrabiblical evidence.

3. Historical Backgrounds

The historical background for any given passage is given by the data presented by Scripture and the illumination provided by extrabiblical sources. Thus, an acquaintance with the whole of sacred history, as well as the setting of each individual event, is crucial to unfolding the historical setting of Scriptures. This knowledge is vital to understanding later allusions to prior events. For example, when Jesus speaks of Moses' lifting "up the serpent in the wilderness" (John 3:14) He was clearly referring to Numbers 21:4-9. Likewise, the drying up of the Euphrates River (Rev. 16:12) must be seen in the light of the fall of Babylon, predicted in Jeremiah 51 and accomplished by diverting the river Euphrates to make way for the Medo-Persians.

The historical background material in Scripture is augmented by the wealth of literature from antiquity. Especially useful are the Apocrypha and Pseudepigrapha, as well as the Targums and later rabbinic materials. Individual authors, such as Philo and Josephus, also contribute to a better understanding of Scripture.

In the past 200 years, archaeological discoveries throughout the Near East have shed light on persons, events, and lifestyles of Bible times. Various customs of the patriarchal period are illuminated by texts found at Mari, Nuzi, and Ebla. While the high standard of morality and the grounding of law in the character of the divine lawgiver in the laws of Moses are different from other codes of the time, the laws of Moses show some similarities with second-millennium-B.C. codes such as that of Hammurabi. Even though their content is unique, the structure of the covenants of Scripture between God and human beings resembles that of second-millennium-B.C. suzerain treaties between Hittite overlords and their vassal kings. Babylonian cuneiform documents show why "king" Belshazzar could offer Daniel only the third place in the kingdom (Dan. 5:29): his father, Nabonidus, was still the legitimate, though absent, king of Babylon.

Likewise, the understanding of the NT is greatly aided by a knowledge of the religio-sociopolitical matrix of first-century Judaism and of the Roman world in which the NT was written. For example, the disputes between Jesus and the Pharisees are illuminated by the study of the Jewish factions. The athletic games of 2 Timothy 4:6-8 and the triumphal entry of the emperor in 2 Corinthians 2:14 make sense when seen against the background of period customs.

Many other factors must be included in the historical background. Chronology—when things happened—and geography—where events took place—contribute to an understanding of Scripture. In addition, weights, measures, and monetary systems deserve attention. Among others, the following should be taken into account: the Hebrew calendar and cycle of festivals; plant and animal life; urbanization, military tactics, climate, and agriculture.

4. Seeming Discrepancies With the Findings of Secular History

For centuries some biblical scholars have questioned the accuracy or veracity of numerous historical details in the biblical record, such as the historicity of the Exodus and conquest of Canaan, and the existence of Darius the Mede mentioned in Daniel. It is important to recognize, first of all, that many of these supposed historical inaccuracies of Scripture have evaporated in the light of further study. For example, until late in the nineteenth-century scholars pointed out that the Hittites mentioned in the Bible (Gen. 15:20, etc.) never existed. Then in the early decades of the-twentieth-century excavations uncovered evidence for an entire Hittite civilization. Again, many nineteenth-century scholars insisted that the customs of the patriarchal period were anachronistic; but discoveries at Nuzi, Mari, Ebla, and elsewhere from the patriarchal times have provided parallels to virtually all the customs portrayed in the patriarchal narratives.

It has now been shown that the Exodus narrative can fit well within the history of the eighteenth Egyptian dynasty. Recent reanalysis of the excavation data from ancient Jericho has shown that (contrary to earlier conclusions and the modern scholarly consensus built on that work) the city was destroyed about 1410 B.C., and the details involved in the destruction fit precisely the biblical account. Likewise, the analysis of Medo-Persian records has shown room for Darius the Mede in the historical record.

Not all the apparent discrepancies between the biblical record and the findings of secular history have yet been resolved. A Bible-based hermeneutic involves faith in the historical reliability of Scripture and confidence that in these points, as in so many others, additional archaeological or historical study may reconcile these tensions. At the same time, it is important that Scripture not be held hostage to the findings of secular science. Many accounts in Scripture will never be corroborated by secular history—especially the miraculous events that have left no prints. The events of Scripture ultimately are accepted not because secular historical science confirms them, but because they are recorded in the trustworthy Word of God.

5. Seeming Discrepancies in Parallel Biblical Accounts

In the historical material of Scripture, especially the OT books of Samuel/Kings and Chronicles and the NT Gospels, parallel accounts at times provide differences in details or emphases (e.g., Matt. 21:33-44; Mark 12:1-11; and Luke 20:9-18). Several principles help us with these apparent discrepancies.

a. Recognize the different purposes in the different writers. The four Gospels were written with slightly different overall purposes and plan. Matthew often arranges his material in topical, not chronological, order. Mark gives an almost breathless account of the activities of Jesus. Luke seems to be introducing Jesus to the Gentiles. And John's Gospel is unique— written, he admits, to foster faith.

b. Recognize that each writer may be relating the parts of the incident that must be combined with other accounts to form a whole. The parallel accounts of David's purchase of the threshing floor on Mount Moriah (2 Sam. 24:24; 1 Chron. 21:25) give different amounts of money paid and a different name for the owner. But the two descriptions are not necessarily in contradiction. The 50 shekels of silver were paid for the two oxen and the wooden threshing cart (and possibly the small plot of the actual threshing floor), while the 600 shekels of gold were the payment "for the place," which involved the entire site. Araunah and Ornan are simply alternative spellings of the same name.

Again, the parallel introductions to Jesus' sermon on the mount as recorded by Matthew and Luke seem on the surface to be in contradiction: Matthew says Jesus "went up on the mountain" (Matt. 5:1), while Luke says "he came down with them and stood on a level place" (Luke 6:17). Ellen White combines both of these perspectives and also the insight of Mark, as part of a larger scene: "After the ordination of the apostles [on a mountain, Mark 3:13], Jesus went with them to the seaside. Here in the early morning the people had begun to assemble. . . . The narrow beach did not afford even standing room within reach of His voice for all who desired to hear Him, and Jesus led the way back to the mountainside. Reaching a level space that offered a pleasant gathering place for the vast assembly, He seated Himself on the grass, and the disciples and the multitude followed His example" (DA 298). Other examples of appropriate and plausible harmonization of the Gospel narratives include the parallel accounts of the rich young ruler (Matt. 19:16-30; Mark 10:17-31; Luke 18:18-30), the blind beggar (Matt. 20:29-34; Mark 10:46-52; Luke 18:35-43), and the surrounding Resurrection (Matt. 28:1-15; Mark 16:1-8; Luke 24:1-11; John 20:1-10).

c. Recognize that historical reliability does not require that the different reports be identical. That we find different language used by the Gospel writers is evidence of their independent authenticity and integrity. Matthew cites the first two prayers of Jesus in the Garden of Gethsemane, which contained the same thought but slightly different words, and then in Matthew 26:44 records that Jesus "prayed for the third time, saying the same words."

d. Recognize that the accepted conventions for writing history were different in the first century. There was often a use of "phenomenological" or "observational" language, illustrated by such terms of ordinary language as "the sun set," or "the four corners" or "the ends" of the earth, without implying a geocentric cosmology or a flat earth. Often approximate numbers were used, such as the number who died at Mount Sinai (1 Cor. 10:8; cf. Num. 25:1-18). We must not expect greater levels of precision for measuring than were customary in biblical times.

e. Recognize that some similar miracles and sayings of Jesus recorded in the parallel Gospels may have occurred at different times. Jesus' ministry of three and one-half years no doubt involved repetition of teachings and duplication of miracles. One example is the feeding of the 5,000 and of the 4,000. One would be tempted to say that these are divergent accounts of the same event had not Jesus Himself referred to them as two separate occasions (Matt. 16:9, 10).

f. Recognize that there are some minor transcriptional errors in Scripture. This is particularly evident in the transcription of numbers in the parallel accounts of Samuel/ Kings and Chronicles. Textual study can assist in determining the best reading.

g. Acknowledge that it may sometimes be necessary to suspend judgment on some seeming discrepancies until more information is available. An example is the chronological data regarding the kings of Israel and Judah in Kings and Chronicles. There seemed to be hopeless confusion until Edwin Thiele's doctoral dissertation, published as *The Mysterious Numbers of the Hebrew Kings* (1951; revised 1983), showed how the application of four basic principles of chronological reckoning completely synchronizes biblical figures and extrabiblical data.

The Seventh-day Adventist Bible Commentary is an invaluable resource when dealing with issues concerning the questions of introduction and historical backgrounds. In the introductory historical articles to each volume and in the introduction to each biblical book, there are excellent treatments of evidence for authorship, date, and life setting of the biblical material, consistently accepting at face value the Scripture's own claims and data about these issues, while at the same time providing archaeological, geographical, chronological, and cultural backgrounds to illuminate the biblical record.

C. Literary Analysis

To interpret the Bible properly, one must recognize that the literary context of the Scriptures is no less important than the historical context. Scripture is not only a history book, but a literary work of art. Recent study among biblical scholars has given increasing attention to the literary characteristics and conventions of Scripture.

Scripture itself gives us numerous explicit and implicit indicators of its literary qualities and the importance of recognizing these as part of the hermeneutical task.

1. Limits of the Passage

One of the first tasks in interpreting a given passage in its immediate literary context is to recognize the limits of the passage. This is important in order to grasp the total thought unit of which the passage is a part. One can then determine what comes before and what comes after, and better understand how this segment fits into the flow of the inspired document.

While the verse and chapter divisions of the Bible do not come from biblical times, the Bible writers often provided indicators of passage limits and in their interpretation of antecedent scripture show awareness of the discrete units of Scripture. In the book of Genesis, for example, the book is divided neatly into 10 sections, each identified by the phrase "the generations of . . ." In the Psalms, along with the division into individual psalms, a number of psalms contain indicators of section divisions: (a) stanzas with refrains (Ps. 42:5, 11; 43:5), or (b) the word *selah* (71 times in Psalms; Ps. 46:3, 7, 11), or (c) an acrostic (such as Psalm 119, with succeeding verses starting with the next letter of the Hebrew alphabet).

By NT times the Pentateuch (and probably also the Prophets) was divided into small sections to be read in the synagogue every Sabbath (cf. Acts 13:15, 27; 15:21). Jesus recognized these divisions of the Torah by referring to "the passage about the bush" (Luke 20:37; cf. Ex. 3:3-6).

Following the explicit references of biblical writers, and carefully examining their writings, we may establish the literary and logical limits of the passage under consideration. For example, the narration of Jesus' sayings and activities naturally separates into sections or pericopae. Recent works provide help for "charting" a book or portion of the Bible into natural divisions, and then delimiting and analyzing the individual paragraphs.

2. Literary Types

In studying any sample of written work—and this is no less true regarding the Bible—it is crucial to understand what type of literature is being examined. This involves the more general categories of poetry and prose, and specific literary types (or genres) such as legal documents, letters, hymns, love poems, biographies, and the like. Various literary forms serve different functions, and certain basic conventions are commonly used in each of these forms of literature. Comparison of different examples of the same genre of literature reveals the common conventions and also the unique features and emphases of each. Proper interpretation is thus enhanced by the recognition of the literary form being employed.

The Bible writers frequently explicitly identify their written materials in terms of specific literary types or genres. Major literary types identified in Scripture include: "generation"/ "genealogy"/"history"/"account" (Heb. *tôlēdôt,* Gen. 2:4, plus 14 times throughout Genesis), deathbed blessings (Gen. 49; Deut. 33), laws (statutes, ordinances, judgments; Ex. 21:1; Deut. 4:44, 45), legal contracts (Gen. 21:22-32; 26:26-31; Joshua 9:15; 1 Kings 5:6-12), covenantmaking and renewal (e.g., Ex. 24; the whole book of Deuteronomy; see Deut. 29:1, 14, 15; Joshua 24), riddles (Judges 14:10-18), royal decrees (Ezra 6:3-12; 7:11-26), letters (2 Sam. 11:15; 1 Kings 21:8-10; 2 Kings 5:5, 6; 10:1-3), psalms (with various psalm types, indicated in the superscriptions) or songs (S. of Sol. 1:1), prayers (Ps. 72:20; Dan. 9:4-19), proverbs (Prov. 1:1; 10:1; 25:1), prophetic oracles or "burdens" (Heb. *massā',* Nahum 1:1; Hab. 1:1; Mal. 1:1), visions (Dan. 8:1, 2; Obadiah 1), covenant lawsuits (Heb. *rîb,* Isa. 3:13; Hosea 4:1; Micah 6:1), lamentation or funeral dirge (Heb. *qînāh,* Eze. 27:32; Amos 5:1; Lamentations), gospels (Mark 1:1), parables (Mark 4:2), "figures" (Gr. *paroimia;* John 10:6; 16:25), epistles (Rom. 16:22; 1 Cor. 5:9; 2 Peter 3:1, 16), and apocalyptic (the *apokalypsis* or Revelation of John; Rev. 1:1).

a. Prose. Many of the prose literary types have been explicitly identified and labeled by the biblical writers, as listed above. Others analyzed in modern study include such forms as speeches or sermons (Joshua 23, 24; 1 Sam. 12; 1 Kings 2:1-9; Jer. 7), lists (Gen. 10; Joshua 15-19; Num. 33; 1 Kings 4:7-19), and cultic ordinances (Lev. 1-7). Of special significance is biblical narrative, which includes such genres as history (Joshua through 2 Chronicles, Acts), reports or annals (1 Kings 11:41; 14:19, 20), autobiography (Ezra and Nehemiah), accounts of dreams and visions (Gen. 37:5-10; 40:9-19; 41:1-7; Zech. 1-6), and prophetic autobiography (Isa. 8:1-3; Jer. 36; Dan. 1-6).

Recent study has focused particularly upon the narrative as a literary type involving intricate artistry. While much of modern critical study tends to regard the narrative as fictional, the Bible student who accepts the account as factual history can benefit by examining carefully how the inspired writer has set forth the narrative to emphasize crucial points. Basic elements of narrative required to understand the "flow" of the account include: the implied author (or invisible speaker) and the implied reader, the overall point of view or perspective, the order of events and their interrelationship ("story time"), the plot, the characters and their characterization, the setting, and the implicit commentary or rhetorical techniques used in relating the narrative.

b. Poetry. The poetic sections of Scripture (approximately 40 percent of the OT and scattered sections of the NT) are arranged in verse in many modern Bible versions. Biblical poetry has special features that call for brief attention here.

The main characterizing element of Hebrew poetry is called "parallelism," or "thought rhyme" (as opposed to "sound rhyme"). Poetic parallelism traditionally has been subdivided into three major kinds: (a) synonymous, in which two succeeding lines of poetry repeat a similar thought (Ps. 1:2, 5; 103:10); (b) antithetical, in which two succeeding poetic lines present contrasting ideas (Ps. 1:6; 37:21; and many proverbs); and (c) synthetic, in which the second poetic line adds to the first by completion, enlargement, or intensification (Ps. 2:6; 103:11). This fundamental aspect of Hebrew poetry is readily apparent in modern translations as well as in the original language.

Hebrew poetry also contains meter ("measured lines"), although these are not as rigidly defined as in Greek poetry. The meter is defined by stress accents: each accented Hebrew word gets one count. One special type of meter is the *qînāh,* or "lament," which has a line of three stress accents followed by a line with two (3:2). Many of the "lament" psalms, where the writer agonizingly petitions

God for help, and virtually the whole book of Lamentations, have this "long-short" meter, which some see as approximating the "long-breath-in and short-breath-out" in the sighing of the lamenter. The metrical element of poetry is not so apparent in translation, although the long-short meter often translates into long and short lines of verse.

Many other literary devices and stylistic elements are utilized by the biblical writers, especially in poetic sections of Scripture. We find the employment of *inclusio* or "envelope construction" (the same expression at the beginning and at the end: Psalms 8, 103), acrostic (verses or groups of verses start with successive letters of the alphabet: Psalms 9, 10, 25, 34, 37, 119, 145), simile (comparison using like or as: Hosea 7:11), metaphor (one reality standing for another: Ps. 23:1; Hosea 10:1; John 10:7, 9, 11), synecdoche (the part standing for the whole: Isa. 52:1, 2), onomatopoeia (words sounding like what they describe: Jer. 19:1,10; Isa. 17:12, 13; Ps. 93:4), assonance (repetition of vowels: Isa. 5:7), paronomasia (pun/play on words: Amos 8:2, 3; Micah 1), and personification (Prov. 8). All of these literary elements contribute to the framing and forming of the message.

Each of these specific literary types has special characteristics, which are often significant in interpreting the message transmitted. Literary form and theological interpretation go hand in hand: identifying and understanding the literary type will make it possible to clarify the intended theological significance.

Several literary forms (parable, prophecy, and apocalyptic) involve an extended meaning or fulfillment that will be discussed below in the section on theological context and analysis (see III. E. 3).

3. Literary Structure

The literary structure, both of the passage and its larger literary frame, is important to the analysis. It often provides a key to the flow of thought or central theological themes.

In prose portions of Scripture, such as the NT Epistles, it is helpful to outline the passage, organizing the major units of information under topics and subtopics. From this outline meaningful thought patterns emerge. Many of the same steps employed to establish the limits of the passage (see III. C. 1) are also useful in identifying smaller patterns within the paragraph.

Close analysis of the biblical material reveals that biblical writers often carefully structured verses, chapters, books, or even blocks of books into an artistic literary pattern. Often the literary structure follows the basic elements of the literary form of the passage. So, for example, the prophetic covenant lawsuit (Heb. *rîb*) typically contains certain elements; the literary structure of Micah 6 (which the prophet specifically identifies as a *rîb,* Micah 6:1, 2) follows this basic lawsuit pattern.

Two kinds of literary structure that build upon poetic parallelism call for special attention. One common literary structuring device is "block parallelism" or "panel writing," which follows the pattern of synonymous parallelism in individual verses of poetry. We find "block parallelism" or "panel writing" as the structuring technique for such biblical books as Joshua and Jonah: the order of the first half of the book is repeated in the second half. Another common literary structuring device in Scripture is reverse parallelism (or chiasm, named after the Greek letter *chi,* which is shaped like an X), which follows the pattern of antithetical parallelism in the smaller unit of two succeeding lines of poetry. An example of the ABCB^{1}A^1 pattern of chiasm in an individual verse is evident in the "mirror image" reference to cities in Amos 5:5:

   A. Do not seek *Bethel;*
      B. and do not enter *Gilgal*
         C. or cross over to *Beersheba;*
      B^1. for *Gilgal* shall surely go into exile,
   A^1. and *Bethel* shall come to nought.

This verse has been analyzed as part of a larger chiastic structure including Amos 5:1-17, which in turn is part of an even larger chiasm, the whole book of Amos. Chiastic structures have been pointed out in more than 50 individual psalms, as well as in sections of Scripture involving several chapters (the Flood narrative of Gen. 6-9; the Sermon on the Mount, Matt. 5-7, and Heb. 6-10). Recent studies have also recognized the chiastic arrangement of various entire biblical books and blocks of books.

A biblical writer's use of a chiastic arrangement often shows the major emphasis of the inspired writer, since frequently this climactic emphasis is placed at the midpoint or heart of the chiasm. For example, in Psalm 92, the Song for the Sabbath, there are seven verses on either side of the central verse, each containing a pair of lines in poetic parallelism; but the central affirmation of the psalm, "But thou, O Lord, art on high forever" (verse 8), is placed alone at the heart of the chiasm with no matching parallel line of poetry. Thus is highlighted the climax of the psalm, both in literary structure and theological meaning.

Parallel structures in Scripture are also often illuminating because of the matching or repeating parts of the structure. What is clear in the first half of the structure may help to illuminate the matching structural element in the second half. So, for example, the chiastic arrangement in Zechariah makes it possible to affirm the Messianic character of crucial passages because their matching structural elements are clearly Messianic. Again, in Hebrews 6:17-20 the reference to Jesus' entry "behind the curtain" is clarified by comparing it with the matching structural element of Jesus' entry "through the curtain" in Hebrews 10:19, 20, which clearly shows the setting of both passages to be the inauguration of the heavenly sanctuary.

The interpreter must not import structures into the text that are not really present. There must be rigorous controls from within the text to ensure that the Bible student is not artificially imposing an outline or structure upon the biblical material. These internal controls include similar matching *themes*, concepts, or motifs, and more important, matching *key words* and clusters of words. The more explicit the verbal and structural parallels, the more certain we can be that the structure is inherent within the passage. It is not always possible, however, to determine whether the human writer was consciously crafting the structure, or whether it was so much a part of their literary approach that the structure emerged spontaneously, or whether it came by direct inspiration of God.

D. Verse-by-Verse Analysis

The ultimate goal of the Bible student is to arrive at the plain, straightforward meaning of Scripture. Based on the principle of the clarity of Scripture (see II. C. 3) one should take the text in its natural sense unless there is clear evidence that figurative language is employed by the biblical writer. For example, in Revelation 1:7, where John writes that Jesus is "coming with the clouds, and every eye will see him," the context indicates literal clouds, not figurative representations of "trouble" or some other symbolic meaning. (On recognizing and interpreting symbols, see III. E. 3. a.)

In seeking to grasp the natural sense of a biblical passage, the interpreter must carefully analyze each verse, giving attention to important points of grammar and syntax (sentence construction), and to the meaning of key words in context.

1. Grammar and Syntax

The NT writers give examples of their concern to represent faithfully the grammatical-syntactical constructions of the OT original and thus set forth the plain meaning of the OT texts for the NT readers. A vivid example of grammatical-syntactical sensitivity on the part of a NT writer is the citation of Psalm 45:6, 7 in Hebrews 1:8, 9. The apostle recognizes that the Hebrew original points to One who is God and at the same time is anointed by God, thus implying the relationship between the Father and the Son in the Godhead ("Thy throne, O God. . . . Therefore God, thy

God, has anointed thee"). Another example is the citation of Psalm 110:1 by Jesus and NT writers (Matt. 22:44 and Synoptic parallels; Acts 2:34, 35; Heb. 1:13). The inspired interpreters clearly grasped the Messianic implications from the syntax of David's words, "The Lord [the Father] said unto my Lord [the Messiah], Sit thou at my right hand" (KJV).

Following scriptural precedent, the modern interpreter should pay close attention to the grammar and syntax of the passage under consideration in order to grasp the intended meaning. For this it is helpful to consult formal (word-for-word) translations of the passage to get a feel for the sentence construction and note any unusual or difficult elements of grammar or syntax.

A thorough acquaintance with Hebrew/Aramaic and Greek grammar and syntax is, of course, ideal, but a number of study tools now available introduce the interpreter to the basic features of the Hebrew and Greek verbal system and other unique grammatical features of each language and provide an analytical key for the whole OT and NT with word-for-word grammatical and lexical information and English translation. Preparing a grammatical diagram or syntactical display based on the original language or modern versions is helpful in order to grasp the flow of thought in the passage. Such mechanical layouts may be especially beneficial for the NT Epistles, for example, where the sentence constructions are often quite complex.

2. Word Studies

Numerous examples in Scripture give evidence of the NT writers' care to represent faithfully the meaning of crucial words in an OT passage. See Paul's use of "the just shall live by *faith*" (Rom. 1:17 [KJV], citing Hab. 2:4); Matthew's selection of the LXX *parthenos*, "virgin" (Matt. 1:23), to best represent the Heb. *'almāh* of Isa. 7:14 and Christ's use of the word "gods" (John 10:34, citing Ps. 82:6).

Following NT precedent, the modern interpreter must engage in careful study of crucial words in the passage under consideration. The word-study process today is more involved, yet even more crucial, for biblical Hebrew, Aramaic, and Koine Greek are no longer living languages. A thorough study of a given word in a passage involves examining its etymology, root meaning, number and distribution of occurrences throughout Scripture, its semantic range, basic meanings, derivatives, and extrabiblical usage. The word must be studied in its multifaceted context: cultural, linguistic, thematic, canonical setting.

Fortunately, much of this research material is summarized in theological dictionaries and wordbooks that cover the basic vocabulary of the OT and NT. An analytical concordance makes it possible to look up all the occurrences of a word in the original language and thereby to study its varied uses.

At the same time, it is crucial to remember that the final determiner of the meaning of a word is the immediate context in which the word or phrase is found. For example, the term "angel of the Lord" in the OT can sometimes refer to a created angelic being, but in numerous instances the immediate context indicates that the reference must be to a divine being, i.e., the preincarnate Son of God (Gen. 16:7-13; 22:11-18; Ex. 3:2, 4, 6; Judges 13:3-22). Again, the Hebrew term *'elep* can mean "thousand" or "clan." Some have suggested that Exodus 12:37 means that 600 clans rather than 600,000 Israelites left Egypt. Even though this is theoretically a possible translation, Exodus 38:25, 26 reports the total amount of silver collected from 603,550 Israelites for building the tabernacle, a half shekel from each man; the calculation works only if *'elep* means thousand, not clan.

Some examples of word studies that make a crucial difference in biblical doctrine include such words as "forever" (Heb. *'ôlām*, Gr. *aiōnios*), which does not mean "without end" in the context of the suffering of the wicked in hellfire; "repentance" on the part of God (*nāḥam* "to be sorry, moved to pity, relent"), which is different from man's "repentance" (*šûb*, "to turn about, repent") and *ta hagia,* "the holies" in Hebrews 9:8, following the regular usage of the LXX and referring to the *whole* sanctuary, not just the Most Holy Place. Finally, the verb *enkainizo¯* in Hebrews 10:20, which is the LXX technical term for the "inauguration" of the sanctuary (Num. 7:10, 11, 84, 88), implies that Christ at His ascension entered the heavenly sanctuary to inaugurate its services, not to commence His day of atonement ministry.

E. Theological Analysis

The biblical writers provide abundant evidence for the need to ascertain the theological message of a passage as part of the hermeneutical enterprise. For example, Jesus lays bare the far-reaching theological implications of the Decalogue in His sermon on the mount (Matt. 5:17-28). The Jerusalem Council sets forth the theological import of Amos 9:11, 12—that Gentiles need not become Jews in order to become Christians (Acts 15:13-21). Paul captures the theological essence of sin in various OT passages (Rom. 3:8-20) and of righteousness by faith in his exposition of Genesis 15:6 and Psalm 32:1, 2 (Rom. 4). Peter's sermon at Pentecost (Acts 2) delineates the theology of inaugurated eschatology found in Joel 2, and his Epistle explores the theological dimensions of the Messiah's atoning work as set forth in Isaiah 53 (1 Peter 2:21-25).

1. Methods of Theological Study

In harmony with what Jesus and NT writers did in their interpretation of OT Scripture, a number of fruitful methods are available for apprehending the theological message of Scripture.

a. The book-by-book approach. Such inspired writers as John the revelator call for readers to study a complete biblical book (Rev. 22:18, 19). Each biblical writer has provided a unique perspective within the overall harmony of scriptural truth. Therefore, to grapple with an entire book and grasp its essential theological thrust is extremely rewarding. It is often

necessary to read and reread the book until the message of the writer grips the researcher and the various themes, concepts, and motifs emerge clearly. Sometimes the message will be a single overriding theme, with various subthemes and motifs; other times there will be several parallel themes. It is helpful to outline the book, charting the flow of thought by the biblical writer. Often a grasp of the literary structure of the book will aid in this process (see III. E. 1. e).

b. Verse-by-verse exposition. The sermons of Peter and Paul (Acts 2; 3; 13) illustrate the method of verse-by-verse exposition of biblical passages. The emphasis in this study is on the basic theological principles and truths that emerge from the passage and that have practical application today. It is important to focus on one verse of Scripture at a time, until diligent study and reflection, under the guidance of the Holy Spirit, have made the meaning clear.

c. Thematic/topical study. The thematic approach is clearly illustrated in Jesus' own preaching (Luke 24:25-27). This approach takes explicit biblical themes and lets Scripture interpret Scripture (see II. C), as all the biblical data setting forth a given theme are assembled and compared. The use of concordance and cross-references to trace key words and concepts is crucial. Examples of major biblical themes to be researched are Sabbath, Second Coming, death and resurrection, salvation, sanctuary, repentance, and judgment.

Sometimes this approach may take some contemporary life problem, some specific present need, some contemporary question, and seek to bring to bear all that Scripture has to say about that topic or issue. This kind of study may involve word study, use of cross-references in the Bible margins, or close examination of a single passage.

In any thematic or topical study, the four principles previously presented (II. A-D) must be respected. It is crucial to bring together *all* that Scriptures say about a given topic, in order not to distort their message. One passage cannot be used to set aside another, since the principle of the consistency of Scripture views all parts of Scripture as coherent and harmonious. Likewise, the principle of clarity of Scripture is to be followed. When these principles undergird the thematic study, there is no place for the illegitimate "proof-texting" method that assembles passages from various parts of Scripture without regard for their original context, and uses them to "prove" what they do not teach.

d. The "grand central theme" perspective. The NT writers place their theological analyses of specific passages within the larger context of the multifaceted "grand central theme" of Scripture, as set forth in the opening and closing pages of the Bible (Gen. 1-3; Rev. 20-22). These include: Creation and the original divine design for this world, the character of God, the rise of the cosmic moral conflict, the plan of redemption-restoration centering in Christ and His atoning work, and the eschatological judgment and end of sin at the climax of history.

Various NT passages point to these themes as central. Jesus sees the OT Scriptures as testifying of Him (John 5:39-47). Paul likewise understands the Christological focus of Scripture, as he determines to preach only "Jesus Christ and him crucified" (1 Cor. 2:2) and the soteriological focus of the Scriptures: they "are able to instruct you for salvation" (2 Tim. 3:15). He further recognizes the cosmic scope and implications of the gospel of salvation that he expounds from Scripture (Col. 3:11). His single-minded life quest, formed from Scripture, has a decided eschatological focus (Phil. 3:13, 14).

A powerful way to observe the beauty and unity of Scripture is to ask about every passage that one studies, What does this passage contribute to the understanding of the grand central theme of Scripture? The "grand central theme" is thus an orientation point that gives underlying unity and harmony and ultimate meaning to the various other themes of Scripture.

e. Literary structural analysis. The literary structure of a book often becomes a key to understanding its theological message more clearly or determining the central theological thrust of a book (see III. C. 3). For example, the book of Deuteronomy has been analyzed by many OT scholars as structured after the pattern of the international suzerainty treaties of the day: (a) preamble or introduction of suzerain (Deut. 1:1-5); (b) historical prologue or statement of past benefactions of the suzerain to the vassal (Deut. 1:6–4:49); (c) general stipulations (Deut. 5-11); (d) specific stipulations (Deut. 12-26); (e) blessings and curses (Deut. 27; 28); (f) witnesses (Deut. 30:19; 31:19; 32:1-43).

Recognizing a literary covenant structure for this book highlights essential theological points about the divine-human covenant relationship. Just as in the Hittite covenants the call to obedience was based upon a motive of gratitude for what the suzerain had already done for the vassal, God's commandments are set forth after reviewing how He had redeemed Israel at the Exodus. Thus the people are called to obey God, not in order to be redeemed, but because they are *already* redeemed and now can respond in gratitude for what God has already done. Deuteronomy thus rejects righteousness by works and upholds the priority of divine redeeming grace.

As a second example, the chiastic structure of the Pentateuch points to Leviticus as the apex of God's revelation. Within Leviticus, the Day of Atonement described in Leviticus 16 is the apex of the chiastic structure. The holiest day of the Jewish year, in which the holiest person on earth (the high priest) goes into the holiest place on earth (the Most Holy Place) to perform the holiest work of all the year—this is reserved for the central chapter of the Torah. Its placement within Leviticus—flanked on one side (Lev. 1–15) by constant mention of blood and sacrifice and flanked on the opposite side (Lev. 17–23) by repeated calls to holiness—provides a balanced theological perspective on the Day of Atonement.

2. Problematic Theological Passages

In dealing with apparently problematic theological passages, particularly in regard to questions about the character of God or seeming distortions of the truth, the following questions may prove helpful:

a. What is the overall picture of the character of God in Scripture, especially as it is revealed at Calvary? It must be remembered that the Father and the Son have the same character (John 14:9) and the God of the OT is the same God as in the NT (John 8:58). Rightly understood in the overarching context of the great controversy, all passages of Scripture will present a coherent and consistent portrayal of God's character. (See Great Controversy I-V.)

b. What additional specific information relevant to the problematic passage is available elsewhere in Scripture or in extrabiblical material? Often a seeming difficulty in Scripture is clarified when all the biblical facts are taken into account. An example is the slaying of Uzzah. At first glance it seems that he innocently reached out to steady the ark from falling (2 Sam. 6:3-7), but the picture becomes clearer as one realizes that the ark had been in Uzzah's own house in Kiriathjearim for about 20 years under the care of his father, Abinadab (1 Sam. 7:1, 2; 2 Sam. 6:3). During this time Uzzah had apparently lost his sense of the sacredness of the holy ark: familiarity had bred irreverence. This disrespect for the sacred is further revealed in the violation of specific divine commands concerning the transport of the ark: only the priests were to touch the ark (Num. 4:15) and the Levites were to carry the ark on their shoulders, not upon a cart (Num. 7:9). Throughout Scripture God takes the sin of irreverence seriously (cf. 2 Kings 2:23, 24; Lev. 10:1-3), because respect for God is basic to the relation between human beings and God.

Another example of further biblical data illuminating a theological problem is seen in the imprecatory (or "cursing") psalms (Ps. 35; 58; 69; 109; 139). David, the anointed representative of God, is not merely exhibiting a human outburst of anger, but specifically and consistently invoking the covenant curses of Deuteronomy 28 and Leviticus 26. He is praying for God to be faithful to His covenant by bringing the promised curses upon those who have rebelled against Him.

As an example of extrabiblical material illuminating a theological problem, we note the contemporary evidence for the wickedness of the Amorites at the time of the conquest (Gen. 15:16; Ex. 13:5). The Ras Shamra (Ugaritic) Tablets give us insight into the gross licentiousness and unbridled violence of the Canaanite religious ritual. Their debauchery had left the Canaanites incapable of responding to the Spirit of God. God in His mercy, as much as His justice, declared that there was nothing left but to execute judgment.

c. Is God acting as a divine surgeon, cutting out the infected part to save the whole body? God specifically gives this principle as the reason for the death penalty when children are totally given over to irreverence and rebellion: "And all Israel shall hear, and fear" (Deut. 21:21). The same was true with the rebellion of Korah, Dathan, and Abiram (Num. 16). This principle also further explains God's actions against those mentioned under the previous principle and others such as Achan (Joshua 7) and Ananias and Sapphira (Acts 5). The judgment upon one or a few led others to repentance and respect for God and prevented the necessity of punishing the many.

d. Does an understanding of Hebrew thought resolve the difficulty in interpretation? OT writers do not accept—and often explicitly counteract—the mythological, polytheistic theology held by their Near Eastern neighbors. Likewise, the theological thought patterns of NT writers, though expressed in Greek, stay within the trajectory of biblical Hebrew thought and do not imbibe alien thought forms of the prevailing surrounding culture such as gnosticism and platonic dualism. It must be the studied aim of the interpreter not to read ancient Near Eastern, Greek, or modern thinking into the Hebrew thought of Scripture. Recognizing the patterns of Hebrew thought resolves many apparent problems in the text. For example, Hebrew thought often does not separate causality and function. In the strong affirmation of the sovereignty of God, biblical writers at times attribute responsibility to God for acts He does not directly perform but permits to happen. Thus the passages that state that God "hardened the heart of Pharaoh" (Ex. 9:12) must be seen in light of passages in the same context that state that "Pharaoh hardened his [own] heart" (Ex. 8:15, 32; 9:34). God "caused" Pharaoh to harden his heart because Pharaoh refused to respond to repeated appeals to allow Israel to go free. God initiated the circumstances (appeals and plagues) that brought Pharaoh to a decision (hardening his heart). As another example, 2 Samuel 24:1 indicates that the Lord incited David to number Israel; 1 Chronicles 21:1 states that Satan did the inciting. God clearly does not directly cause Job's misfortunes and affliction, but rather allows Satan to act within certain bounds (Job 1:6-12; 2:6); yet the Lord Himself said to Satan, "You moved me against him, to destroy him without cause" (Job 2:3). There is no conflict in Hebrew thinking: God is said to cause that which in His sovereignty He allows.

e. What is God's ideal in the situation being described? God had given the Canaanites 400 years of probation to come to repentance (Gen. 15:16). Furthermore, He had intended to drive them out by the hornet and the Angel so that Israel need not destroy them by their own hands (Ex. 23:23, 28). But God condescended to Israel's lack of faith and worked under less than ideal conditions, all the while seeking to bring them back to the ideal (see Ex. 14; 15; 2 Kings 19; 2 Chron. 32; Isa. 37, for glimpses of God's ideal way of working).

The same principle helps to explain the divine permission for divorce in the Mosaic law. Jesus pointed out that God allowed divorce because of the hardness of their hearts, but "from the beginning it was not so" (Matt. 19:8; Gen. 2:24).

f. Is God's activity an attention-getting device, to wake up His people so that they will listen to Him? Sometimes God has to take what seem to be extreme measures to arouse His people from their lethargy and sins. Such were the various sign-actions of Ezekiel in the final days before the Babylonian captivity (Eze. 4; 5), and God's command to Hosea to marry a "wife of harlotry" in the final days of the northern kingdom's probation (Hosea 1:2).

This principle is perhaps a partial explanation of the dramatic display at Mount Sinai that caused all the people to tremble in terror (Ex. 19:16-19). In Exodus 20:20 Moses plays upon the Hebrew word for fear, which has a double connotation: "Do not fear [be in terror]; for God has come to prove you, and that the fear [reverence] of him may be before your eyes, that you may not sin." At the same time, the power and majesty displayed on Sinai are not out of character for God. He *is* a consuming fire (Deut. 4:24; Heb. 12:29) and the theophany at Sinai was only a faint reflection of His awesome holiness.

g. Are there still some points that are not fully explainable or understandable? It will not always be possible in this life to understand why God did certain things the way He did. Some issues, such as the innocent suffering and death of children and martyrs, and the unpunished cruelty of the wicked in this life, will remain unresolved until Christ comes and makes all things right. Some issues and divine actions will be understood fully only when in the hereafter God Himself reveals why He had to act, or refrain from acting, as He did in the light of the great controversy. But enough evidence and answers are given in Scripture so that the Bible student can echo the Song of Moses and the Lamb: "Just and true are thy ways, O King of the ages!" (Rev. 15:3).

3. Scriptures Pointing Beyond Themselves

In this section we have in view those parts of Scripture that inherently point to a fulfillment beyond themselves, as in prophecy and typology, or to an extended meaning beyond themselves, as in symbolism and parables.

a. Prophecy. Several general observations arising from the biblical self-testimony are foundational to the prophetic material. First, the Bible specifically claims that God is able to predict the near and distant future (Isa. 46:10; Dan. 2:45; 8:17-19; Rev. 1:19); the interpreter must not be influenced by modern rejection of future prediction and divine foreknowledge. Second, predictive prophecy was not given simply to satisfy curiosity about future events, but for moral purposes such as the establishment of faith (John 14:29) and the promotion of personal holiness in preparation for Christ's coming (Matt. 24:44; Rev. 22:7, 10, 11). Third, the controls for the interpretation of predictive prophecy must be found within Scripture itself; the fulfillment of prophecy must find complete correspondence with the prophetic data in order to be considered correct.

Fourth, understanding the literary structure of a prophetic book provides helpful corroborating support for the correct interpretation. For example, the chiastic arrangement of Revelation contains two halves that portray respectively the historical and eschatological unfolding of the great controversy. Furthermore, the introductory sanctuary scenes that structure the whole book of Revelation reveal where in the flow of history each section begins. As another example, in the literary structure of Amos, the apex of the chiasm is chapter 5, where the prophet presents his impassioned calls for Israel's repentance, showing the clear conditional nature of Amos' prophecy.

Fifth, one should be especially cautious with regard to *unfulfilled* prophecy. Jesus' counsel regarding a primary moral purpose of all prophecy is pertinent: it is given so that *when it comes to pass, we may believe* (John 14:29). Before it comes to pass, we may not understand every detail of the predictions, even though the basic outline of events and issues is clear.

Within Scripture there are two different genres of prophecy: "classical" and "apocalyptic." The hermeneutical rules for these genres are different; therefore, it is important to distinguish one from the other. The distinctions are discussed in the article on biblical apocalyptic. (See Apocalyptic II. A-F.)

b. Typology. The basic characteristics of biblical typology emerge from within Scripture in passages where the NT writers explicitly label their interpretation of the OT with the word *typos,* "type," or the NT fulfillment as *antitypos,* "antitype" (see Rom. 5:14; 1 Cor. 10:6, 11; Heb. 8:5; 9:24; 1 Peter 3:21). Typology can be defined as the study of persons, events, or institutions in salvation history that God specifically designed to predictively prefigure their antitypical eschatological fulfillment in Christ and the gospel realities brought about by Christ.

Biblical typology may be clarified by contrasting it with other approaches to Scripture. Five distinguishing characteristics of typology are the following:

(1) Typology is rooted in history. It does not lose sight of the actual historical character of the persons, events, or institutions with which it deals. This is in contradistinction to allegory, which assigns meaning that denigrates or even rejects the plain historical sense.

(2) A type points forward or predictively prefigures. This is in contrast with a symbol, which is in itself a timeless representation of truth. Symbols may, however, also become types if used in a specific typological context. For example, a lamb in Scripture symbolizes gentleness and innocence; connected with the sanctuary, the lamb becomes a symbolic type of the Lamb of God, the Messiah.

(3) A type prefigures, but not explicitly or verbally. This is in distinction to predictive prophecy. Both typology and predictive prophecy refer to the future: a type, mutely (as a person, event, or institution) and a prediction, verbally. Typology and verbal prediction go hand in hand, since each type is identified as such by some verbal indicator in Scripture.

(4) Typology involves a heightened correspondence—the antitype is greater than the type (see Jesus' announcing of Himself as "something greater than" the temple, the prophet, and the king [Matt. 12:6, 41, 42]). This is to be distinguished from a spiritual illustration or comparison, such as Peter's exhortation for women to be sober and modest as was Sarah (1 Peter 3:1-6). Sarah is an example, a model of behavior, but not a type.

(5) A type is divinely ordained to function as a prefiguration of the antitype. This is in contradistinction to a natural analogy, which many modern critical scholars have called typology. There are many analogous or similar situations in Scripture, but the NT writers reserve the word "type" for historical realities that God has divinely designed to foreshadow their antitypical fulfillment.

In their exploration of the typological fulfillment of OT persons, events, and institutions, the NT writers do not read back into the OT what is not there. Rather they remain faithful to the OT Scriptures, which have already indicated which persons, events, and institutions God has divinely designed to serve as types. The NT writers simply announce the antitypical fulfillment of what has already been indicated by the OT prophets. For example, John announces that Jesus is the antitypical Moses and refers to Deuteronomy 18:15-19, which predicts that the Messiah would be a new Moses (see John 1:21; 6:14). Again, Hebrews 8:5 announces the typological relationship between the earthly and heavenly sanctuaries, and substantiates the point by citing the OT indicator of sanctuary typology, Exodus 25:40.

The NT writers do not give an exhaustive list of OT types, but show the hermeneutical procedure, controlled by the OT indicators, of identifying biblical types. Furthermore, Jesus and the NT writers under inspiration point out NT events that God has divinely designed to be types of later events in the plan of salvation (for example, the destruction of Jerusalem as a type of the end of the world [Matt. 24]).

The NT writers all work within the same eschatological framework in announcing the nature of typological fulfillment. There are three aspects of the one eschatological fulfillment of the OT types: (1) a basic fulfillment in Christ at His first advent; (2) the derived spiritual aspect of fulfillment in the church, both individually and corporately; and (3) the final, glorious fulfillment at the second coming of Christ and beyond. So, for example, Jesus is the antitypical Israel (Matt. 2:15); the church as Christ's body is the "Israel of God" (Gal. 6:16); and the apocalyptic 144,000 at the end of time are the antitypical 12 tribes of Israel (Rev. 7; 14:1-5; 15:1-4).

What is true of historical (or horizontal) typology is also true of typology involving a vertical dimension, namely, sanctuary typology: there are three aspects of the one eschatological fulfillment. Thus Jesus is the antitypical temple (John 1:14; 2:21; Matt. 12:6); the church as His body is the temple of God, both individually and corporately (1 Cor. 3:16, 17; 2 Cor. 6:16); and Revelation portrays the apocalyptic "dwelling of God" that is with men (Rev. 21:3). But there is an *additional* aspect in sanctuary typology: the heavenly sanctuary existed even before the earthly sanctuary (Ex. 25:40; Heb. 8:5), and thus there is the overarching vertical dimension throughout both OT and NT history. The OT earthly sanctuary pointed upward to the heavenly original, as well as forward to Christ, to the church, and to the apocalyptic temple.

Not every minute detail of the type is significant. For example, there are descriptions of three different earthly sanctuaries/temples in the OT that corresponded typologically to the heavenly temple (the tabernacle of Moses, Solomon's Temple, and the eschatological temple of Ezekiel 40–48). Each was different (materials used, number of articles of furniture, dimensions, etc.), but certain basic contours were constant (number of apartments, kinds of furniture, spatial proportions, rituals and participants, sacred times, etc.). These common elements point up the basic contours of sanctuary typology, which are summarized in Hebrews 9:1-7.

c. Symbolism. A symbol is in itself a timeless representation of truth. Thus a lamb symbolizes innocence; a horn, strength. But symbols in Scripture often become the building blocks of prophecy and typology. Thus the sanctuary lamb symbolizes Christ the Lamb of God (John 1:29); the four horns and the little horn of Daniel represent specific political or religiopolitical powers. (See Apocalyptic II. E.)

In interpreting the symbols of Scripture, basic principles may be derived from Scripture's own use of symbolism.

d. Parables. Fully one third of Jesus' teachings, as recorded in Matthew, Mark, and Luke, are in parable form (some 40 different parables). We also find parables in the OT, such as Nathan's parable of the ewe lamb (2 Sam. 12:1-4) and Isaiah's parable of the vineyard (Isa. 5:1-7). The OT word for "parable," *māšal,* is also a common word for "proverb" in the book of Proverbs, thus revealing the Wisdom background of Jesus' parables. The NT word for "parable" is *parabolē,* with an etymological meaning of "placing alongside of " for the purpose of comparison.

The parable genre has a number of different forms: proverbs ("Physician, heal yourself " [Luke 4:23]), metaphors (uprooting the plant [Matt. 15:13]), figurative sayings (parable of the wineskins [Luke 5:36-38]), similitudes or similes (the parable of the mustard seed [Mark 4:30-32]), story parables (the ten virgins [Matt. 25:1-13]; the good Samaritan [Luke 10:29-37]), and allegorical parables (the parable of the sower [Mark 4:1-9, 13-20]). All the forms used by Jesus have one common element: the use of everyday experiences to draw comparisons with the truths of His kingdom.

Many of Jesus' parables have only one main point, stated by Jesus or reiterated by the Gospel writers (Matt. 18:35; 20:16; Luke 15:7, 10; 16:31). But there are also those that have several points (e.g., the parable of the sower, Matt. 13:1-23). The assigning of meaning to the parts of the story obviously is justified in these instances, because Jesus intended the deeper level of meaning and indicated its interpretation. This is different from allegorizing, in which the later interpreter reads into the text a deeper level of meaning that was never intended or indicated by the original writer.

F. Contemporary Application

1. Scripture as Transcultural and Transtemporal

For Jesus and the NT biblical writers, the contemporary application arose naturally out of their theological interpretation of OT passages.

The biblical writers insist that the theological message of Scripture is not culture-bound, applicable for only a certain people and a certain time, but permanent and universally applicable. Peter, citing Isaiah 40:6-8, forcefully states this truth: "You have been born anew, not of perishable seed but of imperishable, through the living and abiding word of God; for 'All flesh is like grass and all its glory like the flower of grass. The grass withers, and the flower falls, but the word of the Lord abides for ever.' That is the good news which was preached to you" (1 Peter 1:23-25).

Most of the ethical instruction in the NT Gospels and Epistles may be seen as the practical application of OT passages: for example, Jesus' sermon on the mount applying the principles of the Decalogue; James' application of the principles of Leviticus 19; Peter's ethical instruction building on "Be holy, for I am holy" (1 Peter 1:16, citing Lev. 11:44, 45; 19:2; 20:7).

2. Scriptural Controls for Determining Permanence

Certain parts of the OT, in particular the ceremonial and ritual laws and the enforcement of Israel's civil and theocratic laws, are no longer binding upon Christians. However, the NT writers do not arbitrarily decide what laws are still relevant, but consistently recognize the criteria within the OT itself that indicate which laws are universally binding and which have a built-in "statute of limitations."

The OT *mišpāṭîm,* or civil laws, as applications of the Decalogue, are permanent in what they affirm, but the enforcement of these principles is tied to the theocratic government, and thus a built-in "statute of limitations" is involved. When the theocracy ended in A.D. 34 (in fulfillment of Daniel 9:24, and announced in the covenant lawsuit of Stephen in Acts 7), the end of the civil enforcement of these laws also arrived.

Likewise, the sacrificial/ceremonial laws were part of the typical system that reached its fulfillment in the antitype Jesus, who carried out in reality on Calvary and is carrying out in the heavenly sanctuary what was typified in the OT rituals. The built-in "statute of limitations" of these laws was also indicated in the OT (Ex. 25:9, 40 [cf. Heb. 8:5]; Ps. 40:6-8 [cf. Heb. 10:1-10]; and Dan. 9:27).

In other cases in which God condescended to bear with Israel's hardness of heart—such as allowing slavery and divorce—and did not immediately abolish these practices, Scripture clearly indicates the divine ideal in the beginning (Gen. 1-3). The Mosaic legislation, which was revolutionary for its times, leads back toward the Edenic ideal. The NT recognizes and applies this "from the beginning" hermeneutical criterion of permanence (see Matt. 19:8).

In some instances where it might not be clear whether a particular divine command is transtemporal and transcultural, the Bible gives clear indicators of the universal and permanent nature of the material. So, for example, the law of clean and unclean foods (Lev. 11) must be seen in the context of numerous lexical, structural, and theological indicators (both in OT and NT) to make plain that this is part of a universally binding legislation; the

same is true for the laws enjoined upon the Gentiles in Acts 15.

The general principle, then, articulated and illustrated by the NT writers in their application of Scripture, is to assume the transcultural and transtemporal relevancy of biblical instruction unless Scripture itself gives criteria limiting this relevancy. However, not all biblical *practice* is necessarily biblical *instruction.* The lives of God's OT and NT saints, exemplary in many ways, were also faulty and sinful: the Bible gives an accurate picture of their lives and characters for our encouragement and also for our admonition.

Although the biblical instruction is relevant to all cultures and times, it was given to a particular culture and time. Time and place must be taken into account in application. Certain forms or practices expressing a given meaning or principle in the first century may require a different form to express the same meaning today (e.g., greeting with a holy kiss [Rom. 16:16]).

Often in the context of a passage, the Bible provides controls for us to know when it is appropriate to seek for a principle and substitute another way of working out that same principle. For example, instructions for slaves and their owners (Eph. 6:5-9) are no longer specifically valid where slavery does not exist. Circumcision as a sign of belonging to the Jewish community has been replaced with baptism in the Christian church. In these cases the form, rather than the meaning, is modified.

Moreover, Scripture makes clear that certain forms are integrally bound up with their meaning and cannot be substituted by a compatible contemporary form. For example, the seventh-day Sabbath, rooted in Creation, cannot be replaced with Sunday; the ordinance of foot washing, rooted in Jesus' explicit example and command, cannot be replaced with another expression of humility.

3. Personalizing Scripture

The final goal of interpreting Scripture is to make practical application of each passage to the individual life. Christ and the NT apostles repeatedly drove home the message of the gospel contained in the Scriptures in order to bring the hearers or readers to salvation and an ever-closer personal relationship with God.

It is essential for the interpreter to ask of the passage: What are the message and purpose of the passage that God wants me to apply personally? How does this passage impact upon my own spiritual life? What promises does it have for me to claim? What portrait of Jesus to praise Him for? What victory to experience? What sin or failure to avoid? What practical steps to take? What command to perform out of gratitude? In the description

of local situations, what timeless principles are applicable to me today?

At the Exodus God established that each succeeding generation of Israelites should consider itself to have personally come out of Egypt (Ex. 13:8, 9). This principle of personalization was repeated many times, both to OT Israel (Deut. 5:2-4; 6:20, 21) and to spiritual Israel (Gal. 3:29; Rev. 15:1, 2; 2 Cor. 5:14, 15, 21; Rom. 6:3-6; Eph. 1:20; 2:6; Heb. 4:3, 16; 6:19; 10:19, 20; 12:22-24). I should ultimately read and accept the Scriptures as if I were a participant in the mighty saving acts of God, as if God's messages were personally addressed to me—God's living and active Word to my soul.

IV. The History of Biblical Hermeneutics

A. The Inner-Biblical Hermeneutic

The history of biblical hermeneutics must begin with the way the Bible writers themselves interpreted antecedent Scripture. We have seen that the later OT writers called the people of Israel back to obedience to the standard of God's revelation in the Torah. The NT writers did not take the OT out of context in their hermeneutic, but following the example of Jesus, saw OT passages in the light of their larger canonical context. They presented a sound hermeneutical pattern to emulate.

B. Early Jewish Biblical Hermeneutics

1. Scribal Exegesis Before A.D. 70

In his dissertation David Instone Brewer analyzed all the extant writings of the scribes who preceded the Rabbinic period (A.D. 70). He concludes, "The predecessors of the rabbis before 70 C.E. did not interpret Scripture out of context, did not look for any meaning in Scripture other than the plain sense, and did not change the text to fit their interpretation, though the later rabbis did all these things" (Brewer 1). The attitude of these early scribes toward Scripture may be summarized under

five points: (a) Scripture is entirely consistent with itself, (b) every detail is significant, (c) Scripture must be interpreted according to its context, (d) there are no secondary meanings in Scripture, and (e) there is only one valid form of the Hebrew text of Scripture.

In order to interpret Scripture faithfully, the early scribal tradition developed rules of interpretation, which are neatly formulated in the seven hermeneutical rules of Hillel (d. c. A.D. 10). A number of these rules are utilized in the NT.

2. Later Rabbinic Interpretation

The later rabbis, after A.D. 70, continued the *pešat* or "plain, literal" interpretation of Scripture, but also began to mix this with a *šôd* or "secret, allegorical" approach. The 13 rules of Rabbi Ishmael ben Elisha (first half of second century A.D.) gave impetus to the development of the Midrashic method (from *derûš,* "searched") to expound the Jewish Halakah (civil and religious law). This method included embellishments of the text that departed from its plain sense. The 32 rules of Rabbi Eliezer ben Yose (second century A.D.) were employed in the interpretation of Haggadah (popular homilies). These later rules included techniques of interpretation that involved embellishing the biblical text and departure from its plain sense. Later rabbis found multiple meanings in a single text: the plain meaning, the hint that points to a hidden meaning, the secondary or allegorical meaning, and a mystical meaning hidden in the letters.

3. Nonscribal Traditions: Qumran

Not all pre-A.D. 70 Jewish exegesis stayed with the plain meaning of the text. In the Essene community of Qumran, the community leader, the Teacher of Righteousness, was considered to be the inspired interpreter of the prophets; he explained the "mysteries" of the prophetic passages as they applied to his eschatological community. The characteristic hermeneutic developed was known as *rāz pēšer,* "mystery interpretation." In the surviving samples of Qumran *rāz pēšer,* a typical approach would be to quote a biblical passage followed by the words "This means" or "Its *pēšer* is," and a strict identification of the Essene community with the text of Scripture.

By means of an atomistic interpretation of each phrase, word, and even part of a word in the prophetic writings, all was made to refer to the Qumran community. The prophets were seen as having written riddles or cryptograms for the time of the eschatological fulfillment that the Qumran people thought was already in process.

4. Nonscribal Traditions: Philo of Alexandria

The Jewish scholar Philo (first century A.D.) popularized the allegorical approach to Scripture. His work was based upon a Platonic model of reality in which the inferior, transitory world of the senses was a reflection of the superior world of eternal ideas. In his allegorical approach to Scripture, wherever there were difficulties in the biblical text, he gave up the literal sense for an allegorical interpretation. The literal sense was the historical husk which must be stripped away in order to arrive at the kernel, the hidden spiritual meaning.

The basic hermeneutical assumption of Philo was that the *interpreter* is as inspired as the biblical author. Thus, the interpreter is the final arbiter of the allegorical meaning of the text. If the text does not conform to the prevailing worldview, it is the interpreter's responsibility to reinterpret the text. The final authority is not Scripture, but the interpreter's subjective and inspired imagination.

C. Early Christian Hermeneutics

1. Early Church Fathers

A few of the early Church Fathers are noted for introducing or propounding specific hermeneutical approaches. Marcion the heretic caused a hermeneutic to be developed during the early second century, when he rejected the OT as binding Scripture for Christians. He developed the law-grace dualism, in which the OT presented a picture of law, vengeance, hate, and wrath, while the NT represented grace and love. This concept was even applied to the NT: only Luke was regarded as a true Gospel, while other portions of the NT were rejected. Many of the early Church Fathers wrote against Marcion's heresy.

Irenaeus, bishop of Lyons (c. 130-c. 200) utilized the principle of "rule of faith" to defend orthodox Christian doctrine. His rule of faith was the tradition preserved in the churches. Thus he became the father of authoritative exegesis. The final norm was not Scripture alone, but Scripture as interpreted by the authority of the church. About the same time Tertullian (c. 160-c. 240) used typology to defend the unity of Scripture, although at times his typological correspondences were mere allegory.

2. Alexandrian Hermeneutics

In the hermeneutical school of Alexandria, beginning with Clement (d. 215), the allegorism of Philo "was baptized into Christ." Clement developed five senses of Scripture: the historical, the doctrinal, the prophetic, the philosophical, and the mystical. Origen of Alexandria (185-254) claimed that the text of Scripture has three meanings patterned after the analogy with the threefold nature of man: (a) the bodily or literal meaning, which is least important; (b) the psychic or the moral (ethical) meaning; and (c) the spiritual or allegorical/mystical, which is most important and accessible to only the most mature interpreters. This threefold sense, building upon Platonic/Philonic dualism, tended to strip away the historical husk to arrive at the allegorical kernel.

3. Antiochene Hermeneutics

In contrast with the Alexandrian allegorical school, the interpreters at Antioch sought to uphold the plain, literal-historical sense of Scripture. Represented by such exegetes as Theodore of Mopsuestia (d. 428) and popularized by the preacher Chrysostom (347-407), the Antiochene hermeneutic was founded upon the same basic presuppositions set forth in this article. Its exegesis followed essentially the same guidelines as those utilized by the biblical writers in their interpretation of antecedent Scripture.

D. Medieval Hermeneutics

Unfortunately, the Antiochene hermeneutic was overshadowed and finally officially eliminated by the allegorical approach popularized by the Alexandrian school. John Cassian (c. 425) expanded Origen's threefold sense of Scripture to four: (a) historical (the literal meaning), (b) tropological (the moral meaning, from *tropos* [way of life]), (c) allegorical (mystical or Christological), and (d) anagogical (eschatological or heavenly, from *anagō*, "to lead up"). For 1,000 years the *quadriga* (the "four-horse chariot" of the allegorical method) held sway in the Roman Catholic Church. However, there were always a few who, despite persecution, accepted the full and sole authority of the Scriptures in their plain and literal sense.

E. Reformation Hermeneutics and the Historical-Grammatical Method

The Reformation interpreters of the six-

teenth century broke with the allegorical interpretation of Scripture. Gradually Martin Luther gave up "driving" the *quadriga* through the Bible and called for understanding its plain sense. In his *Table Talk* 5285 he recalled that he had been an expert at allegorizing Scripture, but now his best skill was "to give the literal, simple sense of Scripture, from which come power, life, comfort and instruction."

Luther developed four principles of interpreting Scripture. The first was *sola scriptura*, "the Bible only," as the final authority over tradition and human philosophy. Luther, of course, did not invent this biblical principle but powerfully applied it. *Sola scriptura*, along with *sola fide* (by faith alone) and *sola gratia* (by grace alone), became the battle cry of the Reformation.

Luther's second hermeneutical principle was "Scripture is its own interpreter" *(scriptura sui ipsius interpres)*, which also has solid biblical foundations. Luther rejected philosophy, as well as patristic interpretation and ecclesiastical teaching authority, as keys to interpret Scripture.

Third, Luther also applied what became known as the Christocentric principle. His key phrase was "what manifest Christ" *(was Christum treibet)*. What began as a laudable enterprise to see how Scripture points, urges, drives to Christ became dangerous as Luther came to the conclusion that not all Scripture did drive to Christ. This led him to consider some parts of Scripture as less important than others. Accompanying the Christocentric principle was a fourth: dualism between letter and spirit (law and gospel, works and grace). Much of the OT was seen as letter and much of the NT as spirit, although not all in the NT was gospel nor all in the OT was law. Both of these last two principles deny the principle of the totality of Scripture *(tota scriptura)* and lead to subjectivism. The interpreter's own experience ultimately becomes the norm.

All the other Reformers accepted the first two principles of Luther, including Zwingli,

Calvin, and the Anabaptists. These Reformers consistently upheld the Bible and the Bible alone as the standard of truth and sought to utilize Scripture, instead of tradition or scholastic philosophy, to interpret Scripture.

The biblical principles of interpretation recovered by the Reformers, coupled with the advances in textual and historical-grammatical analysis of the Renaissance (Erasmus and others), led to a robust Protestant hermeneutic that has carried on until now and has become known as the historical-grammatical-literary-theological approach or (for short) the grammatico-historical method or historical-biblical method. This method has had able proponents since Reformation times, including nineteenth-century exegetical giants such as Ernst Hengstenberg and Franz Delitzsch. It is currently the approach utilized by conservative evangelical scholarship.

F. The Enlightenment Hermeneutic and the Historical-Critical Method

1. Historical Development

In the seventeenth century Protestant interpretation fossilized into a rigid orthodoxy, with emphasis upon the precise formulations of right doctrine in creeds. This drove many to seek freedom from the stifling authoritarianism of the church. Some followed the path of pietism with its emphasis upon the individual spiritual life, but many others, in the wake of the Copernican revolution and the struggle between science and religion, decided to throw off all external authority. Thus empiricism, deism, and rationalism gained ground.

Richard Simon (1638-1712), a Protestant who became a Catholic priest, was the founder of biblical criticism. In his attempt to refute Protestantism, he raised issues that destroyed confidence in the authority of the Bible. Applying the principles of the Dutch philosopher Spinoza, Simon rejected the Mosaic authorship of the Pentateuch in favor of a long process of redaction and compilation. His 1678

book was so radical that the Catholic Church placed it on the index of forbidden works.

Within a few years, in the wake of the rise of rationalism, a number of scholars began to view Scripture in the same way as any other book. The watershed of the Enlightenment came with Johann Semler (1725-1791) and his four-volume *Treatise on the Free Investigation of the Canon* (1771-1775). He argued that the Bible was not entirely inspired and challenged the divine authority of the canon. The Bible was viewed from a purely historical perspective, to be studied like any other ancient document.

In the decades that followed, German scholars developed an approach to Scripture "from below," without reference to its divine element. This approach steadily gained ground throughout the eighteenth and nineteenth centuries and became known as higher criticism or the historical-critical method. The goal of this method was to verify the truthfulness of the biblical data using the principles and procedures of secular historical science.

2. Presuppositions of Historical Criticism

The basic presuppositions of the historical-critical method—the principles of criticism, analogy, and correlation—were articulated by Ernst Troeltsch in 1913. The principle most characteristic of the method is the principle of criticism. The word "criticism" is used here in the technical sense of Descartes' "methodological doubt" and refers to the autonomy of the investigator to interrogate and evaluate the scriptural witness, to judge the truthfulness, adequacy, and intelligibility of the specific declarations of the text.

In close relation to the principle of criticism is the principle of analogy, which assumes that present experience is the criterion for evaluating events narrated in Scripture, inasmuch as all events are, in principle, similar. In other words, the interpreter is to judge what happened in biblical times by what is happening today; if one does not see a given phenomenon happening today, in all probability it did not happen then. Since no special creation or worldwide flood occurs now, most probably neither happened then. The same is true with miracles and resurrection from the dead: these must be explained away as nonhistorical.

The principle of correlation states that history is a closed system of cause and effect with no room for supernatural intervention. Events are so correlated and interrelated that a change in any given phenomenon necessitates a change in its cause and effect. Historical explanations therefore rest on a chain of natural causes and effects. This is not to say that all historical critics deny the existence of God or the supernatural. But *methodologically,* historical criticism has no room for the supernatural; scholars using it bracket out the supernatural and look for natural causes and effects.

3. Procedures of Historical Criticism

The triumph of historical criticism was assured at the end of the nineteenth century in the influential works of Julius Wellhausen (1844-1918), who popularized an approach of the historical-critical method known as source criticism. In the twentieth century additional procedures were developed: form criticism, redaction criticism, tradition history, and most recently, canon criticism. Each of these procedures calls for brief attention.

Source criticism attempts to reconstruct and analyze the hypothetical literary sources that underlie the biblical text. Wellhausen popularized this approach to the Pentateuch, known as the new documentary hypothesis. The Pentateuch was not viewed as written by Moses, as Scripture claims (John 1:45), but rather was seen as a composite of four later documents or sources: (1) the Jahwist (J), using the divine name Yahweh, written in the southern kingdom of Judah about 880 B.C.; (2) the Elohist (E), using the divine name Elohim, written in the northern kingdom of Israel about 770 B.C.; (3) the Deuteronomist (D), written in the time of Josiah, 621 B.C.; and

(4) the Priestly (P), which began to be drafted in the time of the Babylonian exile, and continued until the time of the final redaction (compiling and editing) about 450 B.C. This hypothesis brought about a totally reconstructed picture of Israel's history.

Source criticism of the Pentateuch was undergirded by several specific presuppositions: skepticism of the historicity of the recorded narratives, an evolutionary model of Israel's development from primitive to advanced forms, the rejection of supernatural activity in this evolutionary development, and the assumption that the sources were human products of the life setting (*Sitz im Leben*) of the communities that produced them.

Various internal arguments for composite sources in the Pentateuch were employed by source critics: the use of different divine names, variations in language and style, alleged contradictions and anachronisms, and supposed doublets and repetitions. All of these arguments have been analyzed in detail by conservative scholars and found to be unconvincing. Even critical scholars today are in disarray over many aspects of the documentary hypothesis, which despite the shaking of its foundations, still has not been abandoned.

The same presuppositions undergirding Pentateuchal source criticism—plus the additional negation of predictive prophecy—have led to the hypothetical reconstruction of sources elsewhere in Scripture. For example, Isaiah has been divided into three major sources (Isaiah of Jerusalem [1–39], Deutero-Isaiah [40–55], and Trito-Isaiah [56–66]), and the book of Zechariah into two sections (1–8 and 9–14). Again, studies from those accepting the Scripture's own claims for the authorship of these books have shown the arguments of source critics to be ill-founded.

NT source criticism has focused largely on the "Synoptic problem"—the question of possible sources underlying the first three Gospels and the interrelationships among these. Several modern solutions have been suggested for the Synoptic problem. Developed in the late eighteenth century, the Griesbach hypothesis presupposed the priority of Matthew, with Luke utilizing Matthew as a source and Mark utilizing both Matthew and Luke. The Lachmann hypothesis, developed in 1835, argued for the priority of Mark, followed by Matthew and then Luke. This hypothesis was modified a few years later to include two primitive, apostolic sources: Mark and the Logia (also called "Q" for *Quelle*).

The two-source hypothesis, with various modifications, is still the most widely accepted source-critical theory, although there have been numerous reactions against it in the latter part of the twentieth century. Further developments include a four-source hypothesis (B. H. Streeter, 1924, who adds to Mark and Q an L source [material unique to Luke] and the M source [material unique to Matthew]), various multiple-source hypotheses, and the Aramaic source hypotheses.

Recently Eta Linnemann, eminent Bultmannian scholar turned evangelical, has forcefully rejected the entire source-critical endeavor on the Gospels. She has argued that there is no Synoptic problem after all, that none of the Gospels is dependent on another, but all go back directly to the ear- and eyewitnesses of the words and deeds of Jesus (185, 186).

In the 1920s another approach of the historical-critical method was developed: form criticism (German *Formgeschichte,* literally "form history"). This critical procedure, pioneered by Hermann Gunkel (1862-1932) in the OT and Rudolf Bultmann in the NT, retained many of the same naturalistic presuppositions used in source criticism, but focused upon the preliterary stage of oral traditions behind the written sources. Form critics assumed that the biblical material came into existence in much the same way as conventional folk literature of modern times and so adopted the basic principles of secular form critics like the Grimm brothers, who were studying German fairy tales.

Building upon the presuppositions of source criticism, form critics assumed that the sociological forces of the community (in its life setting) shaped the form and content of the Christian traditions, and that this material developed from short and simple units to longer and more complex traditions. The specific form-critical task was to analyze the different forms or genres of biblical literature (e.g., the different literary forms in the Psalms), to divide them into their conjectured original smaller oral units, and then hypothetically reconstruct the life setting that brought forth these forms.

In this process of reconstruction, the form critics often took little notice of the plain statements of Scripture regarding the life setting behind the material. For example, the superscriptions of the Psalms were seen as added much later and therefore not historically reliable.

Neither early source critics nor form critics of the early twentieth century paid much attention to the role of the redactors or editors who put the preexisting material together into the final canonical form: these were viewed as compilers who left little or nothing of their own stamp upon the material. But this was to change by the mid-twentieth century, with the rise of a new procedure in historical criticism: redaction criticism (German *Redaktionsgeschichte,* literally "redaction history").

Three NT scholars pioneered the approach of redaction criticism in their examination of the Synoptic Gospels: G. Bornkamm (1948, Matthew), Hans Conzelmann (1954, Luke), and W. Marxsen (1956, Mark). They began to focus upon the evangelists as full-fledged theologians. The aim of the redaction critic was to discover and describe the unique life settings (the sociological and theological motivations) of the biblical redactors/writers that caused them to shape, modify, or even create material for the final product that they wrote. The basic assumption underlying this approach is that each biblical writer has a unique theology and life setting that differs from, and may contradict, his sources as well as other redactors. This procedure tends to fracture the unity of Scripture, which is seen to contain not one but many differing, often contradictory, theologies.

A fourth procedure in historical criticism is

called tradition history (German *Traditions-geschichte*). Pioneered by Gerhard von Rad in the 1930s for the OT, it built upon source and form criticism, attempting to trace the precompositional history of traditions from stage to stage, as passed down by word of mouth from generation to generation, to the final written form. As redaction criticism became popular, tradition history came to encompass the entire history of the tradition, from oral traditions, to written sources, to final shaping by the creative redactor. The underlying assumption in this approach is that each new generation interpretively reshaped the material.

A recent procedure of the historical-critical method, called canon criticism, represents the logical conclusion to the attempt to hypothetically reconstruct the historical development of the biblical text. Pioneered by James Sanders in the 1970s and 1980s, this approach builds upon those that preceded it but focuses particularly upon the life setting (sociological and theological forces) in the synagogue and church that determined which documents were selected as canonical. As with the other historical-critical procedures, the assumption in this approach is that human, this-worldly forces can explain the process—in this case, that of canonization—without recourse to guidance by a supernatural Being.

4. Other Critical Approaches

Recently there has been a shift in critical biblical studies toward various new literary-critical hermeneutical approaches. These procedures usually do not deny the results of historical-criticism, nor do they abandon the central principle of criticism. Rather, they bracket out the historical questions concerning the historical development of the biblical text and concentrate on its final canonical shape.

Many of these literary-critical hermeneutical approaches focus upon the final form of the biblical text as a literary work of art. These include such overlapping procedures as rhetorical criticism (James Muilenberg), new literary criticism (Robert Alter), close reading

(Meir Weiss), and narrative criticism. Common to all of these is the concern for the text as a finished work of art. The literary productions of the Bible are usually divorced from history and regarded as works of fiction or myth, with their own "autonomous imaginative universe" and "imitation of reality." Emphasis is placed upon the various literary conventions utilized consciously or unconsciously by the writer as he or she crafts the biblical story into a literary work of art.

Another recent synchronic approach (i.e., an approach that deals with the final form of the text) is structuralism. Biblical structuralism builds upon modern linguistic theory of Claude Levi-Strauss and has been developed in the United States by such scholars as Daniel Patte. Its main purpose is to "decode" the text in order to uncover the subconscious "deep structures" universally inherent in language. In this method the divine absolute is replaced by an absolute from below, the deep structures of language. A related literary approach is semiotics, or "sign theory," fathered by Ferdinand de Saussure and Charles S. Pierce, which focuses upon the linguistic codes that form the framework within which the message of the text is given (much like the musical staff on which the specific notes may be placed). The major concerns of these approaches are with layers of linguistic structures or sign systems underlying the message.

A number of other approaches to Scripture retain the critical presuppositions of the historical-critical method but focus upon goals other than hypothetically reconstructing the historical development of the biblical text. Some of these approaches build upon the new trends mentioned in previous paragraphs. Major examples include philosophical hermeneutics (the metacritical hermeneutical theory of Gadamer and the hermeneutic of suspicion and retrieval of Ricoeur); hermeneutics of sociocritical theory, including sociological criticism (Gottwald), liberation (Gutierrez), and feminist hermeneutic (Trible); reader-response criticism (McKnight); and deconstructionism (Derrida).

All of these approaches tend to have some external norm—be it philosophy, sociology, Marxist political theory, feminism, postmodern pluralism, or the subjectivism of the reader—which replaces the *sola scriptura* principle and relativizes Scripture. No longer is there an objective, normative meaning of Scripture; rather there is a feminist reading, a Black reading, an Asian reading, a Lutheran reading. All are seen to have their own validity as the reader's horizon merges with the horizon of the biblical text.

G. Two Hermeneutical Methods Compared

The two major hermeneutical methods—the historical-critical method and the historico-grammatical or the historical-biblical—may be schematically compared by means of the following table. Admittedly, some scholars, who are dissatisfied with both methods, attempt to work somewhere between the two methodologies.

Historical-Critical Method

A. Definition: The attempt to verify the truthfulness and understand the meaning of biblical data on the basis of the principles and procedures of secular historical science.

B. Objective: To arrive at the correct meaning of Scripture, which is the human author's intention as understood by his contemporaries.

C. Basic Presuppositions

1. Secular norm: The principles and procedures of secular historical science constitute the external norm and proper method for evaluating the truthfulness and interpreting the meaning of biblical data.

2. Principle of criticism (methodological doubt): The autonomous human investigator may interrogate and evaluate apart from the specific declarations of the biblical text.

3. Principle of analogy: Present experience is the criterion for evaluating the probability of biblical events having occurred, since all events are similar in principle.

4. Principle of correlation (or causation): A closed system of cause and effect leaves no room for the supernatural intervention of God in history.

5. Disunity of Scripture: Since its preduction involved many human authors or redactors, Scripture cannot be compared with Scripture to arrive at a unified biblical teaching.

6. "Time-conditioned" or "culturally conditioned" nature of Scripture: The historical context is *responsible* for the production of Scripture.

7. The Bible *contains* but does not equal the Word of God: The human and divine elements of Scripture must be distinguished and separated.

Historical-Biblical Method

A. Definition: The attempt to understand the meaning of biblical data using methodological considerations arising from Scripture alone.

B. Objective: To arrive at the correct meaning of Scripture, which is what God intended to communicate, whether or not it is fully known by the human author or his contemporaries (1 Peter 1:10-12).

C. Basic Presuppositions

1. *Sola scriptura:* The authority and unity of Scripture are such that Scripture is the final norm with regard to content and method of interpretation (Isa. 8:20).

2. The Bible is the ultimate authority and is not amenable to criticism: biblical data are accepted at face value and not subjected to an external norm to determine truthfulness, adequacy, validity, intelligibility (Isa. 66:2).

3. Suspension of the compelling principle of analogy to allow for the unique activity of God as described in Scripture and in the process of the formation of Scripture (2 Peter 1:19-21).

4. Supension of the principle of correlation (or natural cause and effect) to allow for the divine intervention in history as described in Scripture (Heb. 1:1, 2).

5. Unity of Scripture: Since the many human writers are superintended by one divine Author, Scripture can be compared with Scripture to arrive at biblical doctrine (Luke 24:27; 1 Cor. 2:13).

6. Timeless nature of Scripture: God speaks through the prophet to a specific culture, yet the message transcends cultural settings as timeless truth (John 10:35).

7. The Bible *equals* the Word of God; the divine and human elements in Scripture cannot be distinguished and separated (2 Tim. 3:16, 17).

D. Basic Hermeneutical Procedures

1. Literary (source) criticism: The attempt to hypothetically reconstruct and understand the process of literary development leading to the present form of the text, based on the assumption that Scriptures are a product of the life setting of the community that produced them (often in opposition to specific scriptural statements regarding the origin and nature of the sources).

2. Form criticism: The attempt to hypothetically reconstruct the preliterary (oral) development behind the various literary forms, based on the assumption that the biblical material has an oral prehistory like conventional folk literature and arises from traditions that are formed according to the laws that govern the development of folk traditions.

3. Redaction criticism: The attempt to discover and describe the life setting, sociological and theological motivations that determined the basis upon which the redactor selected, modified, reconstructed, edited, altered, or added to traditional materials in order to make them say what was appropriate within his own life setting, according to his own theological concerns; each redactor had a unique theology and life setting differing from (and often contradicting) his sources and other redactors.

4. Tradition history: The attempt to trace the precompositional history of traditions from stage to stage as passed down by word of mouth from generation to generation to the final written form; based upon the assumption that each generation interpretively reshaped the material.

5. Canon criticism: The attempt to reconstruct the life setting (sociological and theological forces) in the synagogue and the early church that determined the present shape and contents of the biblical canon; assumes that human forces explain the canonization process.

D. Basic Hermeneutical Procedures

1. Literary analysis: Examination of the literary characteristics of the biblical materials in their canonical form, accepting as a unity those parts of Scripture that are presented as such, and accepting at face value the specific scriptural statements regarding the origins and nature of the biblical materials.

2. Form analysis: An attempt to describe and classify the various types of literature found in the canonical form of Scripture, accepting at face value the life setting for each form as indicated by the biblical data.

3. Theological analysis of biblical books: A study of the particular theological emphasis of each Bible writer (according to his own mind-set and capacity to understand), seen within the larger context of the unity of the whole Scripture, that allows the Bible to be its own interpreter and the various theological emphases to be in harmony with each other.

4. Diachronic (thematic) analysis: The attempt to trace the development of various themes and motifs chronologically through the Bible in its canonical form; based on the scriptural position that God gives added (progressive) revelation to later generations, which, however, is in full harmony with all previous revelation.

5. History of the canon: Examination of the process of canonization of Scripture, assuming that the criteria for canonicity are inherent in the biblical materials as inspired by God, and that the Holy Spirit guided the Jewish and Christian communities to recognize these canonical books, which preserved the witness of the Bible writers.

Notice the differences in definition, objective, and basic presuppositions. The first presupposition of the historical-critical method ("secular norm") represents the basic orientation of the method: human reason is the ultimate criterion for truth. Presuppositions 2-4 indicate the crucial underlying principles of the method (see the classic formulation of these by Troeltsch). The last three indicate that the method leads to the diminution of the unity, timeless relevance, and full authority of Scripture.

Based upon biblical evidence, the historical-biblical approach to hermeneutics rejects each of these presuppositions. With regard to the principle of criticism in particular, Gerhard Maier, a noted German scholar who broke with the historical-critical method, wrote, "A *critical* method must fail, because it represents an inner impossibility. For the correlative or counterpoint to revelation is not critique but obedience; it is not correction—not even on the basis of a partially recognized and applied revelation—but it is willingness to say, "let-me-be-corrected."

Both methods analyze historical context, literary features, genre or literary type, theology of the writer, the development of themes, and the process of canonization. But the historical-biblical approach rejects the principle of criticism; it *analyzes* but refuses to *critique* the Bible; it accepts the text of Scripture at face value as true and refuses to engage in the threefold process of dissection, conjecture, and hypothetical reconstruction that is basic to historical-critical analysis.

Some evangelical scholars in recent decades have attempted to make the historical-critical method acceptable by removing its antisupernatural bias while retaining the method. However, this is not really possible, because presuppositions and method are inextricably interwoven. The basis of the historical-critical method is secular historical science, which by its very nature *methodologically* excludes the supernatural and instead seeks natural causes for historical events.

Central to the historical-critical method is the principle of criticism, according to which nothing is accepted at face value, but everything must be verified or corrected by reexamining the evidence. Thus regarding the Bible, the human interpreter is the final determiner of truth; reason or experience is the final test of the authenticity of a passage. As long as this basic principle is retained, the danger of the historical-critical method has not been averted, even though the supernatural element may be accepted. If the principle of criticism is removed, the historical-*critical* method ceases to be. The presence or absence of the fundamental principle of criticism is the litmus test of whether or not critical methodology is being employed.

Those who follow the historical-biblical method apply similar study *tools* utilized in historical criticism. Careful attention is given to historical, literary and linguistic, grammatical-syntactical, and theological details, as outlined throughout this article. But while utilizing the gains brought about by the historical-critical method in sharpening various study tools for *analysis* of the biblical text, there is a consistent intent to eliminate the element of *criticism* that stands as judge upon the Word.

H. Bible-based Hermeneutics in the Advent Movement

William Miller developed a simple set of rules for interpreting the Bible. These appeared in the introduction to his *Evidence From Scripture and History of the Second Coming of Christ, About the Year 1843* (see Damsteegt 299; Hyde 112). These may be summarized as follows:

1. All Scripture is necessary and may be understood by diligent study by one who has faith.

2. Scripture must be its own expositor.

3. To understand doctrine, all the Scripture passages on the topic must be brought together.

4. God has revealed things to come by visions, in figures, and in parables; these must be studied together since one prophecy complements another. A word should be understood literally if it makes good sense; otherwise, one must discover from other passages its figurative sense.

5. A historical event is the fulfillment of prophecy only when it matches the prophecy in all details.

These hermeneutical principles all built upon the historico-grammatical method of interpretation espoused by the Reformers. Early Adventist pioneers used these principles. In 1884 Ellen White wrote, "Those who are engaged in proclaiming the third angel's message are searching the Scriptures upon the same plan that Father Miller adopted" (RH Nov. 25, 1884). After quoting five of Miller's rules, she added, "In our study of the Bible we shall all do well to heed the principles set forth."

Ellen White's writings strongly uphold all the basic presuppositions and specific guidelines for interpreting Scripture as advocated by the historico-grammatical (historical-biblical) method and as set forth in this article. (See the selected quotations in section V.)

She also demonstrated a keen sensitivity to the essential constitutive elements and the dangers involved in the use of the historical-critical method then known as "higher criticism": "The work of higher criticism, in dissecting, conjecturing, reconstructing, is destroying faith in the Bible as a divine revelation. It is robbing God's word of power to control, uplift, and inspire human lives" (AA 474).

Although most Adventist scholars have adhered to the historico-grammatical (historical-biblical) method, since 1950 some voices within Adventism have advocated a shift toward a modified historical-critical method that accepts the supernatural but also retains the principle of criticism. In 1986 the Annual Council of SDAs voted to accept the report of the Methods of Bible Study Committee, which rejected the use of the historical-critical method.

According to the report, "Even a modified use of this method that retains the principle of criticism which subordinates the Bible to human reason is unacceptable to Adventists" (AR Jan. 22, 1987).

The Seventh-day Adventist Church affirms the hermeneutic of the biblical writers, of Antioch, and of the Reformation. It rejects the allegorical method of Alexandria and medieval Catholicism, and the historical-critical method of the rationalistic Enlightment and its later developments.

In so doing, Adventists maintain the Reformers' historicist hermeneutic of prophecy, which has been abandoned by virtually all of Christendom today.

Seventh-day Adventists are the hermeneutical heirs of the Reformation. And as did the radical reformers of the sixteenth century, they continually seek to go "back to the roots," to base all their presuppositions, their principles of interpretation, their faith, and their practice upon the absolute authority of God's infallible Word.

V. Ellen G. White Comments

A. Biblical Interpretation

"In our time there is a wide departure from their [the Scriptures'] doctrines and precepts, and there is need of a return to the great Protestant principle—the Bible, and the Bible only, as the rule of faith and duty" (GC 204, 205; see also 1SM 416).

"The Holy Scriptures are to be accepted as an authoritative, infallible revelation of His will. They are the standard of character, the revealer of doctrines, and the test of experience. . . .

"The Spirit was not given—nor can it ever be bestowed—to supersede the Bible; for the Scriptures explicitly state that the word of God is the standard by which all teaching and experience must be tested" (GC vii).

"But God will have a people upon the earth to maintain the Bible, and the Bible only, as the standard of all doctrines and the basis of all reforms. The opinions of learned men, the deductions of science, the creeds or decisions of ecclesiastical councils, as numerous and discordant as are the churches which they represent, the voice of the majority—not one nor all of these should be regarded as evidence for or against any point of religious faith. Before accepting any doctrine or precept, we should demand a plain 'Thus saith the Lord' in its support" (ibid. 595; see also Ev 256; EW 78; COL 39; 5T 700; MH 462; COL 110, 111).

"The word of God is sufficient to enlighten the most beclouded mind and may be understood by those who have any desire to understand it" (5T 663; see also GC vii).

"But the Bible, with its God-given truths expressed in the language of men, presents a union of the divine and the human. Such a union existed in the nature of Christ, who was the Son of God and the Son of man. Thus it is true of the Bible, as it was of Christ, that 'the Word was made flesh, and dwelt among us' (John 1:14)" (GC vi).

"The Bible is God's voice speaking to us, just as surely as though we could hear it with our ears. If we realized this, with what awe would we open God's Word, and with what earnestness would we search its precepts! The reading and contemplation of the Scriptures would be regarded as an audience with the Infinite One" (6T 393).

"There are some that may think they are fully capable with their finite judgment to take the Word of God, and to state what are the words of inspiration, and what are not the words of inspiration. I want to warn you off that ground, my brethren in the ministry. 'Put off thy shoes from off thy feet, for the place whereon thou standest is holy ground.' There is no finite man that lives, I care not who he is or whatever his position, that God has authorized to pick and choose in His Word. . . .

"Do not let any living man come to you and begin to dissect God's Word, telling what is revelation, what is inspiration and what is not, without a rebuke. . . . We want no one to say, 'This I will reject, and this will I receive,' but we want to have implicit faith in the Bible as a whole and as it is" (7BC 919; see also COL 39).

"The Bible is its own expositor. One passage will prove to be a key that will unlock other passages, and in this way light will be shed upon the hidden meaning of the Word" (FE 187).

"The Bible is its own interpreter. With beautiful simplicity one portion connects itself with the truth of another portion, until the whole Bible is blended in one harmonious whole. Light flashes forth from one text to illuminate some portion of the Word that has seemed more obscure" (OHC 207; see also Ed 190; COL 128; TM 106).

"There should be a settled belief in the divine authority of God's holy Word. The Bible is not to be tested by men's ideas of science. Human knowledge is an unreliable guide. . . . All truth, whether in nature or in revelation, is consistent with itself in all its manifestations" (PP 114; see also Ed 123, 124).

"The Bible was not written for the scholar alone; on the contrary, it was designed for the common people. The great truths necessary for salvation are made as clear as noonday; and none will mistake and lose their way except those who follow their own judgment instead of the plainly revealed will of God" (SC 89).

"Even the prophets who were favored with the special illumination of the Spirit did not fully comprehend the import of the revelations committed to them. The meaning was to be unfolded from age to age, as the people of God should need the instruction therein contained" (GC 344; see also GC 598, 599; 7BC 920).

B. The Role of the Holy Spirit in Biblical Interpretation

"A true knowledge of the Bible can be gained only through the aid of that Spirit by whom the Word was given" (Ed 189; see also 5T 704; COL 408).

"Whenever the study of the Scriptures is entered upon without a prayerful, humble, teachable spirit, the plainest and simplest as well as the most difficult passages will be wrested from their true meaning" (GC 521).

"When the word of God is opened without reverence and without prayer; when the thoughts and affections are not fixed upon God, or in harmony with His will, the mind is clouded with doubts; and in the very study of the Bible, skepticism strengthens. The enemy takes control of the thoughts, and he suggests interpretations that are not correct. Whenever men are not in word and deed seeking to be in harmony with God, then, however learned they may be, they are liable to err in their understanding of Scripture, and it is not safe to trust to their explanations. Those who look to the Scriptures to find discrepancies have not spiritual insight. With distorted vision they will see many causes for doubt and unbelief in things that are really plain and simple" (SC 110, 111).

"The Bible student must empty himself of

every prejudice, lay his own ideas at the door of investigation, and with humble, subdued heart, with self hid in Christ, with earnest prayer, he should seek wisdom from God" (CT 463; see also GC 599, 600; TM 108; CT 463; 2SM 114).

C. Specific Guidelines for Biblical Interpretation

1. Text and Translation

"I saw that God had especially guarded the Bible; yet when copies of it were few, learned men had in some instances changed the words, thinking that they were making it more plain, when in reality they were mystifying that which was plain, by causing it to lean to their established views, which were governed by tradition" (EW 220, 221).

"Some look to us gravely and say, 'Don't you think there might have been some mistake in the copyist or in the translators?' This is all probable, and the mind that is so narrow that it will hesitate and stumble over this possibility or probability would be just as ready to stumble over the mysteries of the Inspired Word, because their feeble minds cannot see through the purposes of God. . . . All the mistakes will not cause trouble to one soul, or cause any feet to stumble, that would not manufacture difficulties from the plainest revealed truth" (1SM 16).

2. Historical Context

"The lives recorded in the Bible are authentic histories of actual individuals. From Adam down through successive generations to the times of the apostles we have a plain, unvarnished account of what actually occurred and the genuine experience of real characters" (4T 9).

"An understanding of the customs of those who lived in Bible times, of the location and time of events, is practical knowledge; for it aids in making clear the figures of the Bible and in bringing out the force of Christ's lessons" (CT 518).

3. Literary Analysis

"Written in different ages, by men who differed widely in rank and occupation, and in mental and spiritual endowments, the books of the Bible present a wide contrast in style, as well as a diversity in the nature of the subjects unfolded. Different forms of expression are employed by different writers" (GC vi).

"The Lord gave His Word in just the way He wanted it to come. He gave it through different writers, each having his own individuality, though going over the same history. Their testimonies are brought together in one Book, and are like the testimonies in a social meeting. They do not represent things in just the same style. Each has an experience of his own, and this diversity broadens and deepens the knowledge that is brought out to meet the necessities of varied minds. The thoughts expressed have not a set uniformity, as if cast in an iron mold, making the very hearing monotonous. In such uniformity there would be a loss of grace and distinctive beauty" (1SM 21, 22).

"The outward beauty of the Bible, the beauty of imagery and expression, is but the setting, as it were, for its real treasure—the beauty of holiness" (Ed 192).

4. Verse-by-Verse Analysis

"In daily study the verse-by-verse method is often most helpful. Let the student take one verse, and concentrate the mind on ascertaining the thought that God has put into that verse for him, and then dwell upon the thought until it becomes his own. One passage thus studied until its significance is clear is of more value than the perusal of many chapters with no definite purpose in view and no positive instruction gained" (ibid. 189).

"We must be careful lest we misinterpret the Scriptures. The plain teachings of the Word of God are not to be so spiritualized that the reality is lost sight of. Do not overstrain the meaning of sentences in the Bible in an effort to bring forth something odd in order to please the fancy. Take the Scriptures as they read" (1SM 170).

"The Bible is not given to us in grand superhuman language. Jesus, in order to reach man where he is, took humanity. The Bible must be given in the language of men. Everything that is human is imperfect. Different meanings are expressed by the same word; there is not one word for each distinct idea. The Bible was given for practical purposes" (*ibid.* 20).

5. Theological Analysis

"The Bible is its own expositor. Scripture is to be compared with scripture. The student should learn to view the Word as a whole, and to see the relation of its parts. He should gain a knowledge of its grand central theme, of God's original purpose for the world, of the rise of the great controversy, and of the work of redemption. He should understand the nature of the two principles that are contending for supremacy, and should learn to trace their working through the records of history and prophecy, to the great consummation" (Ed 190).

"The central theme of the Bible, the theme about which every other in the whole book clusters, is the redemption plan, the restoration in the human soul of the image of God. From the first intimation of hope in the sentence pronounced in Eden to that last glorious promise of the Revelation, . . . the burden of every book and every passage of the Bible is the unfolding of this wondrous theme— man's uplifting" (*ibid.* 125).

"Some portions of Scripture are indeed too plain to be misunderstood, but there are others whose meaning does not lie on the surface to be seen at a glance. Scripture must be compared with scripture. There must be careful research and prayerful reflection" (SC 90, 91; see also Ed 125, 126; CG 511; FE 187).

"Scriptural difficulties can never be mastered by the same methods that are employed in grappling with philosophical problems. We should not engage in the study of the Bible with that self-reliance with which so many enter the domains of science, but with a prayerful dependence upon God, and a sincere desire to learn His will. We must come with a humble and teachable spirit to obtain knowledge from the great I AM. Otherwise, evil angels will so blind our minds and harden our hearts that we shall not be impressed by the truth" (GC 599).

"Both in divine revelation and in nature, God has given to men mysteries to command their faith. This must be so. We may be ever searching, ever inquiring, ever learning, and yet there is an infinity beyond" (8T 261).

"Men of ability have devoted a lifetime of study and prayer to the searching of the Scriptures, and yet there are many portions of the Bible that have not been fully explored. Some passages of Scripture will never be perfectly comprehended until in the future life Christ shall explain them. There are mysteries to be unraveled, statements that human minds cannot harmonize" (GW 312; see also 5T 533; 1SM 20).

6. Typology, Symbolism, and Parables

"The ceremonial system was made up of symbols pointing to Christ, to His sacrifice and His priesthood. This ritual law, with its sacrifices and ordinances, was to be performed by the Hebrews until type met antitype in the death of Christ, the Lamb of God that taketh away the sin of the world" (PP 365; see also 6BC 1095; 7BC 933).

"The language of the Bible should be explained according to its obvious meaning, unless a symbol or figure is employed" (GC 599).

"Jesus taught by illustrations and parables drawn from nature and from the familiar events of everyday life. . . . In this way He associated natural things with spiritual, linking the things of nature and the life experience of His hearers with the sublime truths of the written Word. And whenever afterward their eyes rested on the objects with which He has associated eternal truth, His lessons were repeated" (CT 140).

"Natural things were the medium for the spiritual; the things of nature and the life-experience of His hearers were connected with the truths of the written Word. Leading thus from the natural to the spiritual kingdom, Christ's parables are links in the chain of truth that unites man with God, and earth with heaven" (COL 17, 18; see also 21).

7. Contemporary Application

"In order to be benefited by the reading of the words of Christ, we must make a right application of them to our individual cases" (MM 37).

"In His promises and warnings, Jesus means me. God so loved the world, that He gave His only-begotten Son, that *I* by believing in Him, might not perish, but have everlasting life. The experiences related in God's Word are to be *my* experiences. Prayer and promise, precept and warning, are mine. . . . As faith thus receives and assimilates the principles of truth, they become a part of the being and the motive power of the life. The Word of God, received into the soul, molds the thoughts, and enters into the development of character" (DA 390, 391).

"Merely to read the instruction given in the Word of God is not enough. We are to read with meditation and prayer, filled with an earnest desire to be helped and blessed. And the truth we learn must be applied to the daily experience" (2MR 95; see also 2MCP 784; 1888 Materials 1680).

D. The History of Biblical Interpretation

1. Rabbinical Hermeneutics

"The rabbis spoke with doubt and hesitancy, as if the Scriptures might be interpreted to mean one thing or exactly the opposite. The hearers were daily involved in greater uncertainty. But Jesus taught the Scriptures as of unquestionable authority" (DA 253).

"They [the leaders in Israel at the time of Jesus] studied the Scriptures only to sustain their traditions and enforce their man-made observances. By their interpretation they made them express sentiments that God had never given. Their mystical construction made indistinct that which He had made plain. They disputed over technicalities and practically denied the most essential truths. God's Word was robbed of its power, and evil spirits worked their will" (CT 438, 439).

2. Medieval Hermeneutics

"Almost imperceptibly the customs of heathenism found their way into the Christian church. The spirit of compromise and conformity was restrained for a time by the fierce persecutions which the church endured under paganism. But as persecution ceased, and Christianity entered the courts and palaces of kings, she laid aside the humble simplicity of Christ and His apostles for the pomp and pride of pagan priests and rulers; and in place of the requirements of God, she substituted human theories and traditions" (GC 49).

"For hundreds of years the circulation of the Bible was prohibited. The people were forbidden to read it or to have it in their houses, and unprincipled priests and prelates interpreted its teachings to sustain their pretensions" (GC 51).

"In lands beyond the jurisdiction of Rome there existed for many centuries bodies of Christians who remained almost wholly free from papal corruption. They were surrounded by heathenism and in the lapse of ages were affected by its errors; but they continued to regard the Bible as the only rule of faith and adhered to many of its truths" (*ibid.* 63; see also 68).

3. Reformation Hermeneutics

"The great movement that Wycliffe inaugurated, which was to liberate the conscience and the intellect, and set free the nations so long bound to the triumphal car of Rome, had its spring in the Bible. . . . Wycliffe accepted the Holy Scriptures with implicit faith as the inspired revelation of God's will, a sufficient rule of faith and practice" (*ibid.* 93).

"He [Zwingli] submitted himself to the Bible as the Word of God, the only sufficient, infallible rule. He saw that it must be its own interpreter. He dared not attempt to explain Scripture to sustain a preconceived theory or doctrine, but held it his duty to learn what is its direct and obvious teaching" (*ibid.* 173).

"The grand principle maintained by these [later English] Reformers—the same that had been held by the Waldenses, by Wycliffe, by John Huss, by Luther, Zwingli, and those who united with them—was the infallible authority of the Holy Scriptures as a rule of faith and practice.... The Bible was their authority, and by its teaching they tested all doctrines and all claims" (*ibid.* 249; see also 132).

4. Higher Criticism

"When men talk of higher criticism; when they pass their judgment upon the Word of God, call their attention to the fact that they have forgotten who was the first and wisest critic. He has had thousands of years of practical experience. He it is who teaches the so-called higher critics of the world today. God will punish all those who, as higher critics, exalt themselves, and criticise God's Holy Word" (BE Feb. 1, 1897).

"As in the days of the apostles men tried by tradition and philosophy to destroy faith in the Scriptures, so today, by the pleasing sentiments of higher criticism, evolution, spiritualism, theosophy, and pantheism, the enemy of righteousness is seeking to lead souls into forbidden paths. To many the Bible is as a lamp without oil, because they have turned their minds into channels of speculative belief that bring misunderstanding and confusion. The work of higher criticism, in dissecting, conjecturing, reconstructing, is destroying faith in the Bible as a divine revelation. It is robbing God's Word of power to control, uplift, and inspire human lives" (AA 474; see also Ed 227; MH 142; GC 522).

5. Millerite Hermeneutics

"Endeavoring to lay aside all preconceived opinions, and dispensing with commentaries, he [Miller] compared scripture with scripture by the aid of the marginal references and the concordance. He pursued his study in a regular and methodical manner; beginning with Genesis, and reading verse by verse, he proceeded no faster than the meaning of the several passages so unfolded as to leave him free from all embarrassment. When he found anything obscure, it was his custom to compare it with every other text which seemed to have any reference to the matter under consideration. Every word was permitted to have its proper bearing upon the subject of the text, and if his view of it harmonized with every collateral passage, it ceased to be a difficulty. Thus whenever he met with a passage hard to be understood he found an explanation in some other portion of the Scriptures. As he studied with earnest prayer for divine enlightenment, that which had before appeared dark to his understanding was made clear. He experienced the truth of the psalmist's words: 'The entrance of Thy words giveth light; it giveth understanding unto the simple' (Ps. 119:130)" (GC 320).

"Those who are engaged in proclaiming the third angel's message are searching the Scriptures upon the same plan that Father Miller adopted" (RH Nov. 25, 1884; see also GC 320, 321, 354).

VI. Literature

Alter, Robert. *The Art of Biblical Narrative.* New York: Basic, 1981.

———. *The Art of Biblical Poetry.* New York: Basic, 1985.

Bailey, James L. *Literary Forms in the New Testament.* Louisville: Westminster/John Knox, 1992.

Barrett, C. K., ed. *The New Testament Background: Selected Documents.* Rev. ed. San Francisco: Harper and Row, 1995.

Brewer, David I. *Techniques and Assumptions in Jewish Exegesis Before 70 CE*. Tübingen: J.C.B. Mohr, 1992.

Brown, Colin, ed. *New International Dictionary of New Testament Theology*. 4 vols. Grand Rapids: Zondervan, 1975-1978.

Bruce, F. F. *The New Testament Documents: Are They Reliable?* Rev. ed. Grand Rapids: Eerdmans, 1960.

Damsteegt, P. Gerard. *Foundations of the Seventh-day Adventist Message and Mission*. Berrien Springs: Andrews University Press, 1988.

Davidson, Richard M. "Sanctuary Typology." In *Symposium on Revelation—Book I*. Ed. Frank B. Holbrook. Daniel and Revelation Committee Series. Vol. 6. Silver Spring, Md.: Biblical Research Institute, 1992. Pp. 99-130.

Dyrness, William. *Themes in Old Testament Theology*. Downers Grove, Ill.: InterVarsity, 1979.

Fee, Gordon D. *New Testament Exegesis: A Handbook for Students and Pastors*. Philadelphia: Westminster, 1983.

Ferguson, Everett. *Backgrounds of Early Christianity*. Grand Rapids: Eerdmans, 1987.

Grant, R. M. *A Short History of the Interpretation of the Bible*. 2nd. ed. Philadelphia: Fortress, 1984.

Greenlee, J. H. "Text and Manuscripts of the New Testament," *The Zondervan Pictorial Encyclopedia of the Bible*. Ed. Merrill C. Tenney. Grand Rapids: Zondervan, 1975. Vol. 4, pp. 697-713.

Gugliotto, Lee. *Handbook for Bible Study*. Hagerstown, Md.: Review and Herald, 1995.

Guthrie, Donald. *New Testament Theology*. Downers Grove, Ill: InterVarsity Press, 1981.

Harris, R. Laird, Gleason L. Archer, and Bruce K. Waltke, eds. *Theological Wordbook of the Old Testament*. 2 vols. Chicago: Moody, 1981.

Hasel, Gerhard F. *Biblical Interpretation Today*. Washington, D.C.: Biblical Research Institute, 1985.

———. *Old Testament Theology: Basic Issues in the Current Debate*. 3rd ed. Grand Rapids: Eerdmans, 1982.

Holbrook, Frank B., ed. *The Seventy Weeks, Leviticus, and the Nature of Prophecy*. Daniel and Revelation Committee Series.

Vol. 3. Washington, D.C.: Biblical Research Institute, 1986.

———. *Symposium on Daniel*. Daniel and Revelation Committee Series. Vol. 2. Washington, D.C.: Biblical Research Institute, 1986.

———. *Symposium on Revelation—Book I*. Daniel and Revelation Committee Series. Vol. 6. Silver Spring, Md.: Biblical Research Institute, 1992.

———. *Symposium on Revelation: Exegetical and General Studies—Book II*. Daniel and Revelation Committee Series. Vol. 7. Silver Spring, Md.: Biblical Research Institute, 1992.

Hyde, Gordon M., ed. *A Symposium on Biblical Hermeneutics*. Washington, D.C.: Biblical Research Institute, 1974.

Horn, Siegfried H., ed. *Seventh-day Adventist Bible Dictionary*. Rev. ed. Washington, D.C.: Review and Herald, 1979.

Kaiser, Walter C., Jr. *Toward an Exegetical Theology*. Grand Rapids: Baker, 1981.

———. *The Uses of the Old Testament in the New*. Chicago: Moody, 1985.

Ladd, George Eldon. *A Theology of the New Testament*. Rev. ed. Grand Rapids: Eerdmans, 1993.

LaRondelle, Hans K. *The Israel of God in Prophecy: Principles of Prophetic Interpretation*. Andrews University Monographs. Berrien Springs: Andrews University Press, 1983.

Linnemann, Eta. *Historical Criticism of the Bible: Methodology or Ideology? Reflections of a Bultmannian Turned Evangelical*. Trans. Robert W. Yarbrough. Grand Rapids: Baker, 1990.

Maier, Gerhard. *Biblical Hermeneutics*. Wheaton: Crossway, 1994.

———. *The End of the Historical-Critical Method*. Trans. Edwin W. Leverenz and Rudolph F. Norden. St. Louis: Concordia, 1977.

Nichol, F. D., ed. *The Seventh-day Adventist Bible Commentary*. 7 vols. Washington, D.C.: Review and Herald, 1953-1957; revised 1976-1980.

Osborne, Grant R. *The Hermeneutical Spiral: A Comprehensive Introduction to Biblical Interpretation*. Downers Grove: InterVarsity, 1991.

Paulien, Jon. "Interpreting Revelation's Symbols," in *Symposium on Revelation—Book I*. Ed. Frank B. Holbrook. Daniel and Revelation Committee Series. Vol. 6. Silver Spring, Md.: Biblical Research Institute, 1992. Pp. 73-97.

Petersen, D. L., and K. H. Richards. *Interpreting Hebrew Poetry*. Philadelphia: Fortress, 1992.

Pritchard, J. B., ed. *Ancient Near Eastern Texts Relating to the Old Testament*. 3rd ed. Princeton University Press, 1969.

Reid, George. "Another Look at Adventist Hermeneutics." *Journal of the Adventist Theological Society* 2 (Spring 1991): 69-76.

Ryken, L. *Words of Delight: A Literary Introduction to the Bible*. 2nd ed. Grand Rapids: Baker, 1992.

———. *Words of Life: A Literary Introduction to the New Testament*. Grand Rapids: Baker, 1987.

Shea, William H. *Selected Studies on Prophetic Interpretation*. Daniel and Revelation Committee Series. Vol. 1. Washington, D.C.: Biblical Research Institute, 1982.

Stuart, Douglas. *Old Testament Exegesis: A Primer for Students and Pastors*. 2nd ed., rev. and enl. Philadelphia: Westminster, 1984.

Thiele, Edwin R. *A Chronology of the Hebrew Kings*. 3rd ed. Grand Rapids: Zondervan, 1983.

Doctrine of God

Fernando L. Canale

Introduction

The doctrine of God is foundational to Christian theology, since God relates to everything and everything is related to Him. The doctrine determines the way theologians understand and formulate the entire corpus of Christian beliefs. Philosophical ideas have commonly framed the Christian concept of God. Biblical statements have hardly shaped such formulations. Consequently, classical, modern, and postmodern interpretations of the Christian doctrine of God have been created under the influence of human philosophical concepts. Aware of this situation, careful students of the Scriptures pursue their search for understanding, determined to submit to the Bible all forms of human reasoning. Because human philosophy is called to be subject to the Bible, and since divine philosophy is already available in the Scriptures, our understanding of God must stand free from human speculations. What we can know about God must be revealed from the Scriptures.

I. Sources for the Knowledge of God

A. The Bible

The Christian doctrine of God has been interpreted in various ways. One reason for divergence in approach and content is found in the various sources from which a knowledge of God has been sought. According to the Bible, however, the source of data for the doctrine of God is His own personal revelation (Heb. 1:1-3) as faithfully recorded in Scriptures (Rom. 16:26). Nature, in its various forms, has also been considered as a source for the doctrine of God. Theology has traditionally identified the biblical teaching regarding God's revelation through nature (Ps. 19:1-6; Rom. 1:19, 20) with the human philosophical interpretation of God built on the sole basis of natural data. The doctrines of God that result from the study of nature are philosophical interpretations of God, known in theological circles as natural theology.

A study of the biblical teaching on general revelation suggests that the fact of God's general revelation should not be used to construct a natural theology. Nevertheless, the allegedly minor results produced by philosophical speculations on the being of God are utilized as presuppositions for the understanding not only of the Christian doctrine of God but also of the whole theological enterprise. However, a correct understanding of nature requires as its necessary presupposition the knowledge of God provided by revelation and not vice versa. In short, true knowledge about God can be attained only on the basis of biblical revelation. Since the Christian doctrine of God has generally been developed by assuming the speculative conclusions of natural theology as a working presupposition, the enterprise of searching for an understanding of God on the basis of the Bible alone is bound to challenge traditional ideas and render a different view of God.

B. General Revelation

According to Scripture, God's creation, even after the entrance of sin in the world, was

106

an objective tool that God utilized to reveal Himself to men and women. In order to distinguish this means from the "special revelation" of Scripture, the designation "general revelation" is broadly utilized. Paul, addressing the men of Athens on the Areopagus, clearly referred to this when he explained that God "gives to all men life and breath and everything," "that they should seek God, in the hope that they might feel after him and find him" (Acts 17:25, 26). The passage is not explicit on how this takes place but seems to suggest that general revelation has salvific intentions.

Psalm 19 presents God's creation as an objective instrument that God employs to reveal Himself to all people (cf. Ps. 65:6-13). This passage plainly states that "the heavens are telling the glory of God; and the firmament proclaims his handiwork" (Ps. 19:1), thus singling out the different aspects of the created physical world through which the glory of God can be revealed universally to all human beings throughout history (cf. Ex. 33:18, 19; 34:6, 7). The following verses explain the cognitive mode of these instruments of revelation. They share knowledge (Ps. 19:2) without words or audible voice (verse 3). In this way a foundational difference between special revelation (Scripture) and general revelation in Creation is explicitly drawn. In special revelation the cognitive content is given through human words, while in general revelation the cognitive content is given through the mode of divine works or historical events accessible to all. In special revelation God talks by way of human words; in general revelation the same God speaks by way of physical and historical facts. Finally David states the universal reach of these means of divine revelation as he underlines that "their voice goes out through all the earth, and their words to the end of the world" (verse 4).

In Romans 1:18-21 Paul takes over the OT concept of general revelation, clarifying and further developing it. In so doing he broadens the concept in three very important areas: the role of God, its content, and its final goal. Regarding the role of God in general revelation, Paul underlines that what can be known about God is plain to human beings "because God has shown it to them" (verse 19). In general revelation, as well as in special revelation, God is personally involved in the actual process of revelation. In the introduction to his Gospel John explains that the second person of the Trinity, the Word, is "the true light that enlightens every man" (1:9). General revelation is the good news that God manages to reach not only those who have access to the Scripture but also the full range of humankind. Paul identifies the content of general revelation as "the things that have been made [tois poiē masin]" (Rom. 1:20). This expression seems to point to the fact that the contents of general revelation include not only Creation (our physical world) but also God's providence, which embraces the whole range of historical events (cf. Acts 14:17).

God's invisible qualities, His personal power and divine nature, adds Paul, have been clearly visible (Rom. 1:19, 20). Although imperfect because of the darkening effects of sin, this acquired knowledge is not insignificant. Yet sinful humans consistently repudiate and pervert it (verses 18, 21-23). Hence in His mercy, God broke into man's sin-darkened existence by means of a special, supernatural revelation culminating in Christ Jesus (Heb. 1:2). (See Revelation/Inspiration II.)

II. The Reality of God

A. The Existence of God

The discussion of the rational proofs of God's existence has become a classical locus in the Christian doctrine of God. Since God does not reveal Himself continually in a direct and visible way, the question logically arises about whether there is in reality a Being that corresponds to our word "God." The biblical record does not address the issue of the existence of God by developing or suggesting rational proofs. Instead Scripture holds that "whoever would draw near to God must believe that he exists" (Heb. 11:6). Knowledge about God is necessary for faith to arise in human minds and hearts (Rom. 10:17). It is from the combined reception of God's self-revelation in history, as recorded in the Bible, and the promptings of the Holy Spirit in the mind that faith as conviction of God's existence becomes an established fact in the experience of the Christian. Rational proofs of God's existence given to us in nature do not produce such a radical conviction. The conviction of the existence of God is not produced by rational arguments but by a personal relationship with God. This relationship is initiated by God, who through the personal action of the Holy Spirit uses Scripture, nature, and history to reveal Himself to the minds and hearts of human beings. We are aware of the existence of God, then, on the basis of His personal revelation in Scripture rather than on the basis of rational arguments (cf. Matt. 16:15-17). Within this context the existence of God is usually perceived as mystery.

B. God as Mystery

Another basic aspect of the doctrine of God relates to His nature. In this regard the biblical record submits an almost overwhelming amount of information. However, before we consider some basic aspects of the manifold revelation of God being presented in the Bible, we must recognize that as we approach the study of God we enter "holy ground," on which silence is golden. In other words, we should recognize the limitations of human thinking processes when dealing with the understanding of God's self-revelation. The deficiency of our thinking process as it relates to God as subject matter of study manifests itself not only when we dis-

cover that it is impossible for us to know God by ourselves apart from His self-revelation (Job 11:7), but also when we realize the limitations in our understanding of that which is revealed. Such limitations are due not only to our sinful natures but mainly to the very nature of God, whose "greatness is unsearchable" (Ps. 145:3). We cannot fully understand the reality of God within the range of our human, finite, and limited reason. Even when grounded in biblical ideas, any human claim to perfect understanding of God tends to correspond, in the final analysis, not to the living, infinite God but rather to a god created by our own imagination. The biblical revelation about God falls within the category of mystery, understood not in its traditional meaning but rather in its biblical sense.

In its traditional sense a mystery is something that, by its very nature, cannot be known or put into words. On the contrary, the Bible closely associates mystery with revelation (Dan. 2:30, 47; Rom. 16:25; 1 Cor. 15:51; Eph. 1:9; Col. 2:2). A mystery is something that, even when hidden from human knowledge, can be made known through revelation. Furthermore, even when the mystery involves a direct revelation accessible to human knowledge, it surpasses its own revealed aspects so as to avoid any possible identification of the revealed reality with the mystery itself. Thus Paul can pray that the Ephesians may "know the love of Christ which surpasses knowledge" (Eph. 3:19). This love-surpassing knowledge belongs to the category of mystery manifest in the manifold ways in which God has chosen to reveal Himself as recorded in the Bible. Care must be taken to avoid crossing the limit between the revealed and hidden (Deut. 29:29) facets of the mystery, particularly in discussing issues like the Trinity, foreknowledge, and eternity.

III. Divine Attributes

A. Eternity

Christianity always has understood God to

be eternal (Rom. 16:26). Eternity, as a characteristic of God's being, deals with God's relationship with time. There is a deep and fateful disagreement between the traditional and the biblical understandings of eternity. The traditional understanding of eternity maintained by Christians in general is unduly influenced by Greek philosophy. It conceives that between eternity and time there exists an unbridgeable qualitative difference. Eternity is the total absence of time and anything related to time. Consequently, the eternity of God is taken to mean that God's being is totally and completely unrelated and alien to anything temporal and historical. The consequences of such an idea permeate and condition the whole classical conception of God's nature and acts.

When the idea of eternity is searched in the biblical record, however, the first facet that comes into view is that the words usually translated "eternity" have a clear, temporal meaning. In the OT 'ôlām and in the NT aiōn basically mean "a long time or duration," referring to a limited or unlimited period of time. That eternity is conceived in a temporal mode does not mean that the Bible identifies eternity with the created time we experience as a limit of our finite beings, but simply that the eternity of God is not alien to our time. God's time is, however, qualitatively different from our time, not in that it denies time but in that it both integrates and surpasses it (see II. B). For instance, we experience time as a measure of our transientness, while the eternity of God experiences time without such transitoriness, (Ps. 103:15-17; Job 36:26).

Unlike the classical Christian tradition influenced by Greek philosophy, the Bible conceives the temporal, historical mode of God's eternity as compatible with His immutability (Ps. 102:24-27; Heb. 1:10-12). Paul tells us that the plan of salvation was decided "before the foundation of the world" (Eph. 1:4). "Before" clearly assumes time previous to Creation. Paul's statement that the plan of salvation was "hidden for ages in God who created all things" (Eph. 3:9) points to past eternity as involving time as a characteristic of God's eternity. Our time had a beginning (cf. 1 Cor. 2:7) when our finite universe and its inhabitants were cre-

ated. The Creator transcends such limitations in His being and in His experience of time and history. Our time is a very limited, finite sharing in life, which is the full possession of God in ways that completely surpass even our best rational and imaginative efforts. To try to define God's time would clearly be a speculative attempt in which we would be penetrating the mystery of His being. Here silence is eloquence.

We have understood, however, something important, namely, that according to the Bible, the eternal and immutable (see III. B). God can relate directly and personally with men and women within the plane of human history in such a way that both God and human beings share the same history. God's eternity refers to the dynamic, unending life and history of God, which at the same time includes and totally surpasses the realm of our created history. According to the Bible, the distance between God and His creation that presently obstructs direct, historical communion with Him is not the consequence of the difference between a timeless, immutable God and a historical man, but rather of the difference between a holy God and a sinful humanity (Gen. 3:22-24; Isa. 59:2).

B. Immutability

Immutability is another characteristic of God's being that has been an important component of the Christian doctrine of God through the centuries. Immutability refers to the absence of change in God. The Bible straightforwardly declares that God does not change (Mal. 3:6; James 1:17). Unfortunately, however, traditional theology identified immutability with impassibility. Such an identification was required by the timeless understanding of eternity (see III. A). When immutability is understood as impassibility, God is said to possess a static life in which relations, emotions, new experiences, and changes in His inner life are totally excluded, lest the perfection of God should be tainted. In other words, immutability would describe the life of God as unrelated to human experiences and history. Such a conception has hardly any place for either a historical understanding of the great controversy between God and Satan (see Great Controversy II-V), or a real historical incarnation of Jesus Christ (see Christ I. A. 2). In so teaching, classical theology has followed Greek philosophy in total forgetfulness of the biblical concept of immutability.

On the other hand, while the Bible has no word to express "immutability," it clearly affirms that in God "there is no variation or shadow due to change" (James 1:17). The biblical understanding of God's eternity (see III. A) allows for an undergirding compatibility between God's perfection and a conception of His life that includes dynamic changes such as real newness (Isa. 43:19; Jer. 31:31; Rev. 21:5), emotions (Ex. 34:14; Num. 11:33; Deut. 4:24; 6:15), relations (Lev. 26:12; Zech. 13:9; Rev. 21:3), and even God's repentance (Ex. 32:14; Jer. 18:8; 42:10). It seems clear that the immutability of the biblical God, who is capable of changing His decision to destroy Nineveh (Jonah 3:4) on account of the Ninevites' positive response to Jonah's preaching (verse 10), cannot be understood as impassibility. However, God's change of mind, as His repenting, does not involve a change in His divine purpose for human beings, but rather an adjustment to human change of mind and purpose. In addition, the Bible conceives divine change in relation to God's dynamic life, not in relation to the constitution of His being. In other words, the reality of God does not vary, nor does He change from a less perfect into a more perfect being. God is always the same (Ps. 102:26, 27; Heb. 13:8).

According to the biblical doctrine of God, movement and change in the divine life, which according to classical theology are impossible, play a central role in the perfect nature of divine life and activity. Moreover, the Incarnation assumes that God has the capability not only of relating and living within the limits of created time but also of personally experiencing new, real historical events. The Incarnation involves a real historical movement within God's own divine life without requiring change

or development in the structure of the divine being (Phil. 2:6-8). Within this context God's immutability is consistently shown through the Bible as His "faithfulness," or constancy, in His historical acts. God is able to do things in history and to change His mind (Jer. 18:8; 42:10; Jonah 3:9, 10) without infringing upon the perfection of His being or going through a process of inner development from a lower to a higher level of being. At the same time, His eternal faithfulness (Ps. 100:5; 117:2) warrants that He will never change His mind but rather will always fulfill His plans (Isa. 25:1), oaths (Heb. 7:21), and promises of reward (Isa. 61:8), protection (Ps. 91:14), or, punishment (Ps. 119:75) in relation to human choices. Historical faithfulness is, therefore, a divine characteristic that distinguishes God from humans (Num. 23:19; 1 Sam. 15:29). The immutability of God—understood not as an impassibility but as the eternal identity of God's being with itself and the historical faithfulness, constancy, and consistency of His relation, purposes, and actions toward us—is the necessary presupposition for theological ideas such as typology, incarnation, cross, and great controversy between God and Satan as presented throughout the Bible.

C. Love and Wrath

In various ways predestination (IV. B), creation (IV. C), general revelation (I. B), historical presence (IV. D), and providence (IV. E) reveal God as a relational being, whose essence is love (1 John 4:8). Precisely because of this, His wrath is alien to His nature (Isa. 28:21). In order properly to understand the biblical concepts of divine love and wrath, it is necessary to recognize that both belong to God without contradiction. Revealing His glory to Moses, God explained that He is "a God merciful and gracious, slow to anger, and abounding in steadfast love and faithfulness, keeping steadfast love for thousands, forgiving iniquity and transgression and sin, but who will by no means clear the guilty, visiting the iniquity of the fathers upon the children and the children's children, to the third and the fourth generation" (Ex. 34:6, 7).

1. God's Love

The Scriptures state that "God is love" (1 John 4:8, 16). They reveal a "God of love" (2 Cor. 13:11) and the "love of God" (2 Cor. 13:14; cf. Eph. 2:4) for His creation. The Father (1 John 3:1), the Son (Eph. 3:19), and the Holy Spirit (Rom. 15:30) engage in expressing their inner loving nature not only in the acts of creating the universe and communing with it, but most notably by devising and implementing an amazingly wise and complex plan of salvation. The definition of God's love cannot be derived analogically from human conceptions or experiences. The meaning of love can be defined only by God through an act of direct revelation. Love is a relational reality. John clearly uncovers the relational nature of love when he remarks that "we know and believe the love God has for us. God is love, and he who abides in love abides in God, and God abides in him" (1 John 4:16).

However, there is more to divine love than its relational structure might suggest. Divine love is spelled out when, according to the eternal predestination of God, "the goodness and loving kindness of God our Savior appeared" (Titus 3:4) and the Father and Jesus Christ "gave us eternal comfort and good hope through grace" (2 Thess. 2:16). The love of God receives its most astonishing and unexpected manifestation in the life and death of Jesus Christ (Rom. 8:39; 1 John 4:10; Rom. 5:8). God's love is not only at the basis of Creation (IV. C) but also of salvation. The incarnation and cross of Christ actually reveal that divine love is an act of self-denial for the sake and benefit of another, even the lowly, despised, and undeserving. Scripture describes the essence of divine love as the Father is giving up the Son (John 3:16; Rom. 8:32; cf. 2 Cor. 5:21) and, simultaneously, the Son's giving Himself up (Gal. 2:20; Eph. 5:2; Heb. 9:14). Paul explains the self-surrender of the Son's love for the world by pointing out that Christ Jesus "did

not count equality with God a thing to be grasped, but emptied himself, taking the form of a servant, being born in the likeness of men. And being found in human form he humbled himself and became obedient unto death, even death on a cross" (Phil. 2:6-8). On this basis, it is not surprising to hear Paul affirming that Christ's affirming love "surpasses knowledge" (Eph. 3:19). It follows that divine love is the source (1 John 4:7) and model (1 Cor. 13) of human love.

2. God's Wrath

That the biblical God experiences and acts out His anger on sinners, destroying them by eternal fire appears to be foreign to His nature (Isa. 28:21). However, the biblical conception of God's wrath is not contradictory to or incompatible with His loving nature. Because God is love, His purpose is to save all human beings. Paul formulated this basic fact of Christian theology in a concise statement: "God has not destined us for wrath, but to obtain salvation through our Lord Jesus Christ" (1 Thess. 5:9). God's answer to man's sin is the offer of salvation in Jesus Christ (Gen. 3:15). If God is love and His explicit purpose is to save sinners, the question arises as to what may cause His wrath. According to Scripture, divine wrath is caused when persistent sin (Deut. 9:7; 2 Chron. 36:16; Jer. 7:20-34; 32:31-33; Hosea 12:14; Rom. 2:5; Col. 3:5, 6) leads men and women to an unchangeable rejection of His loving offering of salvation in Jesus Christ (John 3:36; Heb. 6:4-6). Because God is love, He does not wish "that any should perish, but that all should reach repentance" (1 Kings 8:46-51; 2 Peter 3:9). God's wrath can be averted by repentance (1 Kings 8:46-51; Joel 2:12-14), confession (Dan. 9:16-19), restitution (Lev. 5:16; Num. 5:7, 8), and intercession (Ex. 32:9-14).

In short, the wrath of God can be deflected if humans accept the will of God (His law) and forgiveness, freely offered to all in Jesus Christ. However, by willfully and persistently rejecting God's will and His loving gift of salvation in Jesus Christ, sinners grow stubborn in their opposition to God, thereby becoming God's enemies. Nahum explains that the wrath of God is consummated on His enemies: "The Lord is a jealous God and avenging, the Lord is avenging and wrathful; the Lord takes vengeance on his adversaries and keeps wrath for his enemies" (Nahum 1:2). During salvation history God's wrath has been consummated only occasionally and partially (Lam. 2:1-3; cf. Acts 17:30). The wrath of God will receive eschatological consummation in the last day, when "all evildoers will be stubble; the day that comes shall burn them up, says the Lord of hosts, so that it will leave them neither root nor branch" (Mal. 4:1; cf. Rev. 14:10, 19; 19:15-21; see Judgment II. E.; III. B. 3).

D. Transcendence

Transcendence is another theological concept that appears in the Bible without a specific word to express it. Transcendence basically means "independence" from, referring in the study of God's nature to His independence from His relationships with the universe.

The sense in which God is different from Creation has been understood traditionally on the basis of His timeless eternity and impassible immutability. In other words, God is different from Creation because He is timeless and nonhistorical, while Creation is temporal and historical. Working on this basis, classical theology finds a basic similitude, or analogy, between God's transcendent reality and created reality. Such a similitude is the foundation that allows human reason to talk about God and to build a natural theology. Others have suggested that between God and Creation there is an absolute and total difference, designated as "absolute transcendence." Absolute transcendence recognizes no similitude between God's eternal being and His historical creation.

The Bible conceives God as different from the world, both in terms of His reality (God is not the world, neither is the world included in His being) and in terms of His nature. It is obvious, however, that when the difference is understood as "absolute transcendence," God becomes the great unknown stranger. The consequences of traditional and modern approaches to the interpretation of God's transcendence have been, in the final analysis, responsible for the turn to panentheistic conceptions of God's immanence in the past three centuries. According to this conception, God is no longer a person independent from the world but rather the world itself, with its deep ontological cause or power to be.

The Holy Scriptures present a different picture of God's transcendence. From the onset, the doctrine of Creation sets the stage for both transcendence and similitude between God and His creation. God's creation establishes the independence of God's reality from the reality of the universe (Gen. 1:1; Heb. 11:3), and consequently, the dependence of the universe on God (Isa. 42:5).

Thus Scripture speaks clearly of the transcendence of God from the starting point of His immanence in the sanctuary. The account of the dedication ceremony of Solomon's Temple (2 Chron. 5-7) points out the transcendence of God's being beyond the realm of Creation. Starting from the affirmation of God's personal, historical immanence (IV. D) the narrative identifies the dwelling place of God in two locations: first, the dwelling of His personal glory in the earthly sanctuary-temple (2 Chron. 5:13–6:2; 6:41; 7:1-3; cf. Ex. 40:34-38), and second, His heavenly abode (2 Chron. 6:21, 25, 27, 30, 33, 39; cf. Heb. 8:1, 2; Rev. 7:15). God's heavenly abode is not yet the realm of His transcendence, since "heaven" is part of God's creation. God's dwelling in heaven, then, is to be understood as belonging to His historical immanence, that is, to his relation with other creatures not affected by sin. The demand for two abodes is owing, not to God's transcendence, but rather to the introduction of sin on earth and the need for God's personal presence with His people.

The dimension of God's transcendence comes into focus again when Solomon asks, "But will God dwell indeed with man on the earth? Behold, heaven and the highest heaven cannot contain thee; how much less this house which I have built" (2 Chron. 6:18; 1 Kings 8:27). The mystery of God's reality is perceived and expressed here. God does live on earth, even in a temple, and in heaven (immanence), yet His being completely surpasses Creation (transcendence). Only when the mystery of God's being—as totally independent from and completely surpassing, yet at the same time able and willing to enter into an intimate, dwelling relationship with His creation—is revealed are we able to recognize and worship God in His divine majesty. No effort by human reason or imagination can pierce beyond God's revelation into His divine being.

However, the Bible does not adopt the idea of an "absolute" transcendence that rules out similitudes between God and Creation. On the contrary, according to the biblical account of Creation, man and woman are created "in the image of God" (Gen. 1:27), clearly asserting a similitude between God and humanity. Yet the existence of such a similitude does not justify the speculative use of reason alone to understand God. Only God, who perfectly knows both sides of the analogy between Himself and Creation can draw cognitive analogies or comparisons about His own being in our created order. Human beings, who know only their own side of Creation, cannot properly draw an analogical picture of God's reality.

On this basis no analogy drawn from Creation can provide a foundation for attributing any physical or conceptual form to God. In other words, the analogy that exists between God and Creation does not ground the possibility of developing a natural theology. Not surprisingly, the second commandment instructs us not to make "a graven image or any

likeness of anything that is in heaven above, or that is in the earth beneath, or that is in the water under the earth" (Ex. 20:4). Only God can use analogy to reveal Himself without involving vain speculations. Some of the analogies God draws are called anthropomorphisms, that is, they attribute to God characteristics belonging to human beings. In biblical anthropomorphisms, God reveals what He is and what He can do in terms of human realities. For instance, when God says that He has an arm (Ex. 15:16; Ps. 89:13), He does not mean that He has exactly or univocally what we call an arm. The expression signifies that God's reality is capable of performing all that can be performed by a human arm, and infinitely more. We cannot conceive or imagine the actual structure of God's reality that allows Him to perform these acts. Yet the analogical language reveals to us aspects of God's being and divine capabilities, while at the same time guarding the mystery of His divine nature.

In Himself He is real and has a form, yet that divine reality and form completely surpass the reality and capability of comprehension of the highest created intelligences. Beyond the revelation of His being, silence is and always will be eloquence. Revelation is given as God Himself directly relates to our human history. From the starting point of His revelation the mystery of His transcendent being appears as that which cannot be pierced by our limited intelligence.

God's transcendence shows itself in connection with several of His attributes as revealed in the Bible: for instance, the attributes of foreknowledge, omniscience, and omnipotence. However, the transcendence of God is revealed at its deepest level in the doctrine of the Trinity.

IV. Divine Activities

A. Foreknowledge

The eternal immutable God of the Bible is capable of knowledge (Joshua 22:22): "The Lord is a God of knowledge" (1 Sam. 2:3). God not only knows Himself but He also knows the created universe. God's knowledge of Himself is described in clear trinitarian terms. Paul states that "no one comprehends the thoughts of God except the Spirit of God" (1 Cor. 2:11).

Christ Himself remarked that "no one knows the Son except the Father, and no one knows the Father except the Son and any one to whom the Son chooses to reveal him" (Matt. 11:27; cf. Luke 10:22). This knowledge belongs to the nature of God and is at the source of all divine activity, both in creation and redemption. Isaiah's recognition that the Lord's "understanding is unsearchable" (Isa. 40:28) applies to this level of divine knowledge. Since this knowledge belongs to the inner essence of the Godhead, created beings cannot achieve it now, nor will the redeemed have access to it throughout eternity.

According to Scripture, God's knowledge is perfect (Job 37:16). However, divine knowledge is not to be identified with God's omnipotence. When Scripture speaks of divine knowledge, including omniscience and foreknowledge, the passive characteristic of knowledge is not eliminated by God's divine sovereignty. If receptivity is eliminated, so is knowledge. When biblical authors depict God as one who knows the created universe, the divine capability to be affected by a created reality different from Himself is implied. However, God's knowledge of Creation surpasses human knowledge, which can reach only partial and limited knowledge of reality, while God's experiences no limitation or partiality whatsoever. The limitless characteristic of God's knowledge is presented by Scripture as both omniscience and foreknowledge. Omniscience refers to God's embracing everything in His knowledge; foreknowledge refers to God's capability of including in His omniscience not only past and present realities but also future realities, even the free actions of men and women.

The omniscience of God is clearly proclaimed by John, who specifically states that God "knows everything" (1 John 3:20). Paul articulates the same concept as he explains that before God "no creature is hidden, but all are open and laid bare to the eyes of him with whom we have to do" (Heb. 4:13). God's omniscience obviously includes the world (Job 38:33; Gen.

1:31) and human beings and their free actions (Ps. 44:21; 139:1-5; Matt. 6:8, 32; Luke 16:15; Acts 15:8).

The foreknowledge of God is clearly asserted by both Peter and Paul (Acts 2:23; Rom. 8:29; 11:2). Long before, God Himself, through the writing of Isaiah the prophet, explicitly revealed the theological meaning of foreknowledge as He proclaimed, "I am God, and there is no other; I am God, and there is none like me, declaring the end from the beginning and from ancient times things not yet done" (Isa. 46:9, 10; cf. 41:21-24; 44:6-8). Foreknowledge, then, is the affirmation that God's omniscience includes not only past and present but also future realities. Moreover, in Scripture, foreknowledge mainly refers to future historical events performed by God (Acts 15:16-18; Rom. 8:29, 30), human beings (Ps. 139:16), or both (Acts 2:23).

Scripture teaches that God knows and that His knowledge includes everything, even future free decisions of human beings who do not yet exist. The way in which He knows, however, belongs to the concealed level of the divine nature. The affirmation of God's foreknowledge is neither contradictory nor logically incompatible with human free will. Those who perceive an insurmountable contradiction implicitly assume that God's way of knowing works exactly as does our limited human way of knowing. If divine foreknowledge as presented in Scripture is taken seriously, it becomes obvious that God's knowledge works in ways we cannot figure out by analogy or imagination. This brings us back to the mystery of God.

David's reaction to the realization of God's omniscience should not be forgotten. After describing the all-encompassing knowledge of God, he simply concluded, "Such knowledge is too wonderful for me; it is high, I cannot attain it" (Ps. 139:6). God's nature as mystery (see II. B) is also present as we deal with His omniscience and foreknowledge. On one hand, through the revealed aspect of the mystery, we are able to grasp the fact of God's omniscience and foreknowledge. On the other hand, because of the concealed side of the divine nature, it is impossible for human beings to comprehend the way in which God is able to perform His cognitive activities within the realms of omniscience and foreknowledge. For this reason it is not possible to develop a theological interpretation of God's cognitive capabilities.

The revelation of God's omniscience and foreknowledge, therefore, does not provide a starting point for a theology of divine cognition. On the contrary, it shows that no human mind can comprehend the way God knows. Any attempt to interpret the structure of divine cognition aside from the revealed data is not only nonbiblical but the product of human imagination. Another purpose for the revelation of divine omniscience and foreknowledge, as seen in the Bible, is to provide the necessary framework for a clear understanding of redemptive activities such as predestination (Rom. 8:29), election (Rom. 11:28), and the cross (Acts 2:23).

B. Predestination

Omniscience and foreknowledge refer to God's cognitive activity regarding the world in general and free human actions in particular. Within this general context, predestination refers to God's volitive activity (Eph. 1:5, 9, 11) in deciding the basic components and structure required to accomplish the redemption of humankind (1 Cor. 2:7). In a general sense any divine decision that determines the nature and structure of created reality could be regarded as belonging to predestination. Thus, the creation of the world is the actualization of God's blueprint for nature. In the biblical sense predestination refers specifically to the divine plan for salvation. As Creation was the actualization of God's blueprint for created realities, predestination was His plan for the salvation of sinners.

Scripture refers to the divine blueprint for the salvation of humankind with words such as "purpose" (*prothesis,* a "plan drawn in advance" [Rom. 8:28; 9:11; Eph. 1:11; 3:11; 2 Tim.

1:9]), "mystery" (Eph. 3:9), and "hidden wisdom of God" (1 Cor. 2:7). The word "predestination," which occurs in the Bible as the verb *proōrizō* ("to decide beforehand"), is also utilized by biblical writers to refer to God's prior, eternal decision regarding His plan of salvation (Acts 4:28; Rom. 8:29, 30; 1 Cor. 2:7; Eph. 1:5, 11).

God conceived and determined the plan of salvation "before the foundation of the world" (Eph. 1:4; 1 Peter 1:20), prior to the existence of the "ages" (1 Cor. 2:7), "from the beginning" (2 Thess. 2:13; cf. John 1:1). This is the reason for the particle *pre* in "predestination." Prior to the Fall (Gen. 3), before the creation of the world (Gen. 1; 2), even prior to the ages of created time, in eternity, God devised and decided in Himself the structure of the plan for the salvation of humanity (Eph. 1:9; see Great Controversy I. A. 1-5).

God's predestination does not determine the eternal salvation or damnation of human beings, as some would have us believe. The biblical teaching does not identify of predestination with foreknowledge, whereby God is said to predestine everything He foreknows. It is true that the biblical idea of foreknowledge includes God's knowledge of our eternal destiny. However, Scripture denies on two accounts the claim that God predetermines human destinies. First, Paul clearly differentiates between foreknowledge and predestination (Rom. 8:29). Thus the two notions should not be confused. Second, according to Scripture, the salvation of human beings involves not only God's predestination plan and works of salvation but also the free response of faith to the call and prompting of the Holy Spirit. The role of free choice in the determination of our eternal destiny is implicitly present in the teaching of final judgment included in divine predestination (Acts 17:31), which entails, among other things, the incarnation and death of Jesus Christ, the free human response to the call to accept all the provisions of God's plan, and God's judgment of our response.

C. Creation

In the general context of divine omniscience, foreknowledge, predestination, and election, God's creation refers to His concrete activity that generated the existence of a new reality other than Himself, namely, the universe. Creation, then, on one hand makes real God's theoretical blueprint for the world (see Prov. 8:22-31; cf. Jer. 10:12) and, on the other, makes history possible and divine providence necessary (see IV. E).

From beginning (Gen. 1; 2) to end (Rev. 14:7) Scripture teaches that God is Creator of heavens and earth. We are told that "by the word of the Lord the heavens were made, and all their host by the breath of his mouth" (Ps. 33:6). By direct command of the Lord the universe came into existence (Ps. 148:5, 6; Heb. 3:4). Scripture specifically presents the Godhead—Father, Son, and Holy Spirit—as performing the act of Creation (1 Cor. 8:6; Heb. 1:2; Isa. 37:16; John 1:3; Gen. 1:2; Job 33:4).

Creation rests totally on God's wisdom and activity. In other words, according to Scripture, Creation does not require or assume the existence of any principle outside of God, such as matter or physical energy. Paul explains that God "calls into existence the things that do not exist" (Rom. 4:17); in a more explicit and technical way he makes plain "that the world was created by the word of God, so that what is seen was made out of things which do not appear" (Heb. 11:3). Creation is not to be understood in analogy to human creativity, for human creativity is the process of ordering a preexistent material reality. The scriptural conception, that God's creation rests totally on His power (Jer. 10:12) and does not require preexistent independent matter or an extension of His own being, is properly captured in the traditional ex nihilo (out of nothingness) formulation. Consequently, notions such as platonic dualism, neoplatonic emanationism, pantheism, panentheism, and modern evolutionism do not find support in the biblical account of the origins of reality.

Because God's eternal (see III. A), immutable (see III. B) nature is not timeless but rather compatible with created time as we know it, Genesis 1 and 2 describe the historical process of seven literal days within which God, by a series of successive and complementary creative acts, brought our world into existence. The climax of God's work of creating the world occurred on the seventh day (Gen. 2:2; cf. Mark 2:27). God's rest from creating the physical reality of heavens and earth allows the purpose of Creation to be fulfilled—the personal direct communion of God with human beings (see IV. D). In a very real sense it can be argued that such communion is constitutive of the being of humankind.

Creation brought the world from nonexistence into existence. The world is the "other" than God, a reality apart from God. This implies that God is not the sum total of reality. The idea of Creation as the "other" than God explicitly contradicts the pantheistic-panentheistic argument that because God is to be conceived as "infinite" and limitless, there can be no "other" outside of Him. In the biblical sense, creation as the manifestation of the wisdom and love of God clearly shows God's love for Creation in allowing the other over against Him. In a relational sense, God's creation limits God in order to allow "space" for the creature. In His eternal being, however, God is not limited by space and time as the creatures are. Creation, thus, becomes the necessary condition for God's relationship with creatures and, therefore, the necessary condition for history.

The reach of God's work of Creation is universal and includes everything in the universe other than God (Gen. 1:1; Isa. 40:26; John 1:1-3; Col. 1:16; Rev. 4:11; 10:6). As work designed and performed by God, Creation is not to be conceived as inherently evil or a step that God designed to attain a subsequent goal. Scripture's account of Creation clearly states that "God saw everything that he had made, and behold, it was very good" (Gen. 1:31). The divine power involved in Creation continued to operate after Creation week. The creation of

116

the physical world was completed in six days. Yet, even the physical reality of the world cannot exist without God's ceaseless work of preservation, which is continuously brought about by God's power. Ezra enunciated this basic idea: "Thou art the Lord, thou alone; thou hast made heaven, the heaven of heavens, with all their host, the earth and all that is on it, the seas and all that is in them; and thou preservest all of them; and the host of heaven worships thee" (Neh. 9:6). Paul put it briefly: "He [Christ] is before all things, and in him all things hold together" (Col. 1:17; cf. Heb. 1:3; see Creation I. A, B; II. C).

After the entrance of sin another dimension of God's creative power was revealed in the work of transforming sinners and restoring in them the image of God in which they were created (2 Cor. 5:17; Gal. 6:15; Eph. 4:24). The work of redemption requires God's creative power in order to bring into existence salvation, not only ex nihilo but from that which explicitly opposes the will and power of God. God's creative power in salvation does not behave in the same way in which His power operated in the original creation of the physical world. Such an identification would rule out two related biblical ideas: the historical conception of God's governance of human affairs (see IV. E) and the free will of the individual from the process of salvation (see IV. A). Not following the biblical understanding of God's governance and human free will would necessarily entail distortion in the interpretation of the doctrines of justification and sanctification.

The history of the world and salvation not only begins and continues on the basis of God's creation, but it also concludes with God's creation of "new heavens and a new earth" (Isa. 65:17; cf. Rev. 21:1-5).

D. Historical Presence

The Bible conceives God's presence in the world as His historical dwelling with His people. Isaiah noted that the Lord not only dwells in a "high and holy place" but also "with him who is of a contrite and humble spirit" (Isa. 57:15). The historical presence of God about which the Bible speaks becomes divine "immanence" in theology. The word "immanent" basically means something that is inherent, indwells, or exists within some other subject or substance. To affirm the immanence of God, then, means to believe that somehow God exists within the world. Some have interpreted God's immanence in the world as "pantheism," meaning that everything is God, or the more fashionable panentheism, that everything is "in" God. Both pantheism and panentheism bypass the biblical doctrine of Creation, which establishes a total difference between God's being and the reality of His creation. Usually, the Christian teaching about the immanence of God is understood to mean that God Himself is present within nature.

According to the Bible, God relates to the world in various ways. For instance, by His wisdom and power God is the Creator (Gen. 1:1–2:25; Rev. 14:7) and sustainer (Acts 17:25; Heb. 1:3) of nature and human beings, thus making human history possible. In this context, "in him we live and move and have our being" (Acts 17:28). But the works of Creation and sustenance of Creation are works of God's mighty power, which must not be confused with His personal dwelling presence in the world, which is the biblical concept of immanence. Creation and sustenance are only the conditions that make God's immanence possible. God's historical dwelling points to His relation to the world as other than Himself.

In three key historical events recorded in Scripture, the structure of God's immanence under the category of communion, in the specific sense of "dwelling with," is unveiled. The three historical events are: the first Sabbath at the end of Creation week (Gen. 2:1-3), the sanctuary (Ex. 25:8), and the incarnation of the eternal Son (John 1:14). In each event the same relational structure is maintained. The biblical conception of God sees Him entering into relation with the world He has created and continuously sustains, not as a hidden force within the depths of nature but rather as a

Person who relates with men and women as He dwells with them throughout and within the flow of human history.

When God's immanence is understood as "dwelling with"—as seen in the Sabbath, the sanctuary, and the Incarnation—the meaning of the "in Christ" (Rom. 8:1; Phil. 4:7; 2 Tim. 3:12; Philemon 6) or "Christ-in-you" relation (Rom. 8:10; Eph. 3:17; Col. 1:27) becomes clear. In both aspects, the relation is equivalent to the indwelling of the Holy Spirit (1 Cor. 6:19; 2 Tim. 1:14; Heb. 6:4). In other words, the biblical conception of what traditional theology calls God's immanence does not refer to His being and power but to His person and love. The biblical understanding of God's immanence as His "dwelling with" His people is of paramount importance for a correct understanding of God's acts and their unfolding in the great controversy between Christ and Satan, from Lucifer's rebellion against God and His law in heaven (Rev. 12:7, 8) until the eschatological restoration (Rev. 21:1-4).

Scripture understands God's immanence as His historical presence with nature (Ps. 68:8; 114:7), believers (Ps. 16:11), unbelievers (Gen. 4:16; Rev. 14:10), angels in heaven (Luke 1:19), Israel (Ex. 33:13-23), and the church (Matt. 28:20). Moreover, the Bible describes God's historical, personal presence as pervasive and ubiquitous (Jer. 23:23, 24; Ps. 139:7-12). The biblical God is able to relate to space in a way that is impossible for limited human beings. God's historical, personal, direct presence is real and simultaneous in all places of His vast universe. This capability of God's being is known in theological language as God's omnipresence.

Traditionally, Christian theology has addressed the understanding of God's immanence only after the concept of God's transcendence (see III. D) is determined on the basis of the timeless interpretation of His eternity (see III. A) and immutability (see III. B). This position, having no room for the biblical concept of God's historical presence, must go into lengthy arguments to avoid being understood as entailing pantheism or panentheism. The Bible follows the opposite route: Within the context provided by a historical interpretation of eternity and the immutable faithfulness of God's actions in history, God reveals Himself first through His historical presence as He "dwells with" His people. Even the idea of transcendence is addressed from the starting point provided by the historical understanding of God's presence.

E. Providence

The word "providence" comes from the Latin *providere,* which means to foresee. Although the word is not biblical, the concept of providence is central to Scripture and refers to the revelation regarding God's government of the world and the universe. Thus, the word is here used as a synonym for God's government.

Providence involves a multiplicity of divine actions, all of them related to the development of human and universal history. Paul distinguishes providence (Rom. 8:28) from foreknowledge and predestination (verses 29, 30). In biblical thinking, foreknowledge, predestination, and creation are the necessary conditions for God's government of human and universal history. The biblical record refers to God's providence in the context of the origin and existence of sin in heaven (Job 1:6-12; 2:1-6; Isa. 14:12-20; Eze. 28:11-19; Rev. 12:4, 7, 8) and its spread to earth with the historical fall of Adam and Eve (Gen. 3:1-7). Providence, as divine government, deals with the enactment of God's eternal plan of salvation in the contingencies and limitations proper to human nature and history. Providence, biblically conceived, belongs to the essence of God's salvific activities. According to Scripture, salvation is not the result of a single divine activity, namely, Christ's death and resurrection. Christ's death and resurrection are the grounds for all other divine salvific actions, but they alone cannot bring about the accomplishment of God's plan of salvation (predestination). God's providence, with its manifold complexities, plays an essential role in the salvation of humankind and the universe (cf. Col. 1:20).

Believers and theologians need to understand the biblical view of the way God governs history. Broadly speaking, God governs history historically. This means that God does not govern by eternal decrees that determine the course of human history. On the contrary, the biblical picture of God's providence presents God as working out His plans from within the limitations and complexities of human history. Two major types of divine providential activity are in view: indirect and direct.

1. Indirect Providential Activity

As presented in Scripture, God's indirect mode of providential activity includes the following patterns: (1) The divine decision to allow sin to follow its natural course in the general level of human history (Gen. 3:8-15) and also regarding more specific historical situations (Ps. 81:12, 13; Matt. 19:8; Acts 14:16; Rom. 1:24, 26, 28) is basic; (2) in any given situation God concretely limits evil's actual reach (Job 1:12; Ps. 124:1-3; 1 Cor. 10:13; cf. Acts 17:26); (3) God is able to use situations caused by evil human acts to bring about His purpose of salvation (Gen. 50:20; Acts 2:36); (4) at times God intervenes in order to prevent a human being from sinning (Gen. 20:6; Ps. 19:13; Jude 24). In theological language these patterns of God's providential activity are known, respectively, as the permissive, limitative, directive, and preventive wills of God.

According to Scripture, God does not control human history in the sense that He wills and executes everything that happens. God is, rather, personally involved in guiding human history to its God-appointed (predestined) goal: "to unite all things in him, things in heaven and things on earth" (Eph. 1:10). Because human nature as designed by God involves the essential characteristic of freedom or self-determination, God does not force or control human beings, much less the whole range of history. Since force is incompatible not only with freedom but also with love, God's

aim in history, which is to attract to Himself all willing human beings, cannot be accomplished by forcing or bypassing human freedom. In His involvement in human history, God is working out salvation at various levels: the individual, social, and cosmic. The results are not predetermined. Yet we are not left in uncertainty about the outcome of the future end of history.

God's foreknowledge is the ground for certainty about the future. Yet this does not take the work, risk, involvement, and even suffering out of the divine task of providence. The future is not already accomplished in God's foreknowledge; it is only anticipated. Without the biblical teaching about the reality of God's foreknowledge, both God and believers would live in uncertainty about the future. On the other hand, the contents of God's true and certain foreknowledge will become a reality by way of God's personal involvement and guidance in human history (cf. John 1:17). According to Scripture, God guides human history personally from within the flow and complexities of human realities and not from heaven by means of eternal and irresistible decrees.

2. Direct Providential Activity

God's direct providential guidance is clearly shown in Scripture by God's choice to dwell among His people, to live with them and direct them (Ex. 3:1-14; 25:8; 40:34-38). The Incarnation is clearly presented as a continuation of God's direct pattern of providential guidance of human history (John 1:14). After Christ's ascension this pattern of divine providence centered around the presence and work of Christ's representative, namely, the Holy Spirit. God's direct interventions in guiding human history also include the revelation of His will through the prophets, miraculous acts, and the mission of the church. Finally God's direct providential intervention includes His "alien work," divine wrath, both throughout the entire span of human history and in the eschatological eradication of sin from the universe (see III. C).

Divine providence utilizes all known indirect and direct manners of divine activity, those revealed in Scripture and probably many more, about which we have no idea. The guiding dynamics of God's providence is a process of education where the contents are the revelation of God's will in Scripture, the teacher is Christ through the Holy Spirit, and the students are all human beings. The purpose of this process is to change the mind of free human beings by allowing them to understand and freely choose God's revealed will. In this way believers "have the mind of Christ" (1 Cor. 2:16; cf. Phil. 2:5; 1 Peter 4:1; 2 Peter 1:4). When this transformation, directly involving divine justification and sanctification, takes place, human history develops freely according to the will of God. No control is necessary because of the intelligent and willful surrender of the believer to the law and will of God. As this community of disciples is formed (Israel in OT times and the church in NT times), it becomes an instrument in the same process that brought it into existence. The accomplishment of that purpose is the mission of the church and the reason for its existence as a corporate entity.

The achievement of God's purposes involves more than this central, universal, persuasive-educational direct and indirect activity. It involves also a work of judgment (see Judgment II-IV) and the final manifestation of divine wrath. Judgment is a strange work for a God of love and mercy (Isa. 28:21), yet an integral part of God's government, enacted only on those who knowingly and willfully reject God's blueprint for human life and history. The final achievement of God's purpose, then, requires "destroying the destroyers of the earth" (Rev. 11:18). This is not a work of control but only of retribution for the destruction and suffering caused by those who willfully reject God's law and the provisions of salvation in Jesus Christ. This retribution, which also includes the destruction of the originator of sin (Mal. 4:1; Rev. 20:10), is necessary for the creation of "a new heaven and a new earth" (Rev. 21:1), and the final eradication of evil from the universe (Nahum 1:9).

Through history and prophecy Scripture presents detailed reflection on the manifold ways in which God has been, continues to be, and will yet be involved in the providential salvific work, personally guiding every receptive human being to the achievement of present and future salvation in Jesus Christ.

V. Oneness of God

There is no specific place where the Bible discusses the whole doctrine of God. The biblical doctrine of God is developed in following the historical account of God's personal interventions and revelations in the sacred text. The doctrine of the Trinity, at the very center of the doctrine of God in particular and of Christian theology in general, is no exception. When God revealed Himself in Jesus Christ, however, a knowledge of the trinitarian nature of God became necessary for the Christian church. The incarnation of Jesus Christ involved more than the dwelling of God with humanity; it brought with it knowledge about the Father and the Holy Spirit as a necessary context for a proper understanding of Jesus Christ's incarnation, cross, resurrection, and heavenly ministry. That the Trinitarian nature of the Godhead became known through the Incarnation does not mean that it had not existed before or was not directly involved in the work of salvation. Since God is eternal and immutable, His trinitarian nature has never changed or come into being. We shall now turn our attention to the biblical teaching about the Trinity. Theological theories and doctrines about the Trinity generated by the fateful combination of biblical data and philosophical ideas will be considered in the historical section. Before the specific data revealed with the Incarnation are examined, it is necessary to consider the biblical concept of the oneness of God and OT hints regarding plurality in the divine being (see VI).

A. *Evidence From the OT*

The "oneness" of God refers to the singleness of His being. In other words, the "oneness" of God refers to the fact that according to the Bible there is only one God, as opposed to more than one. The classical OT statement about the oneness of God, which is also followed by some in the NT, pronounces God to be one: "Hear, O Israel: The Lord our God is one Lord" (Deut. 6:4). Moses, however, had already explained that "the Lord is God" and that "there is no other" (Deut. 4:39). As David heard God's covenant promise renewed to Him, he praised God and recognized that "there is no God besides thee" (2 Sam. 7:22; 1 Chron. 17:20). Through the prophet Isaiah, Yahweh Himself called Israel to recognize that "I am He. Before me no god was formed, nor shall there be any after me" (Isa. 43:10; cf. 42:8). From these texts it clearly follows that according to the OT there is only one absolute God for Israel as well as for the whole Creation. These statements say nothing, however, about the inner nature of the one absolute God.

B. *Evidence From the NT*

In spite of the fact that God revealed the inner complexity of His being in a surprising way through Jesus Christ, the basic understanding of the oneness of God, already expressed in Old Testament times, is maintained throughout the NT. Jesus Himself, when asked which commandment was the first answered by referring to Deut. 6:4: "The first is, 'Hear, O Israel: The Lord our God, the Lord is one' " (Mark 12:29). Discussing the function of the law in his letter to the Galatians, Paul categorically stated that "God is one" (Gal. 3:20). Finally, James also stated that "God is one" (James 2:19). The OT idea of God's oneness remains unchanged in the NT. Yahweh, the God of Israel, is the God of Christianity. He is the only God. There is no other. At times "oneness" can involve the meaning of unity (i.e., John 10:30; 17:21, 23). However, if the "oneness" expressed in these texts is conceived only as a gathering of independent "onenesses" that come together in order to form a unity, the specific singleness characteristic of the one Godhead to which they testify is dissolved into a plurality of gods. The oneness of God plays a decisive, systematic role in determining the referent for the biblical revelations about God. In other words, since the God of the Bible is one and not many, all the various revelations about Him presented throughout the Bible refer to the same, one divine reality and not to a plurality of divine beings.

VI. The Godhead in the OT

In the Bible the radical affirmation of God's oneness does not settle the content of His nature. By associating the oneness of God with the timeless interpretation of His eternity, classical theology concluded that God's nature must be simple; that is, one cannot think of God as having parts or components. Simplicity would rule out any form of plurality or composition. On the basis of its strong affirmations of the oneness of God, however, biblical thinking conceives His nature not in terms of simplicity but rather in terms of complex plurality. The personal complexity of the one divine being that is clearly articulated in the NT is already expressed by the OT in a less specific way. Let us consider some of the OT hints regarding the personal plurality of the one Godhead that receive further and definitive expression in the NT.

A. *The Plural of Fullness and the Godhead*

In the Creation account God refers to Himself in the plural form. "Then God said, 'Let us make man in our image, after our likeness' " (Gen. 1:26). Other instances occur elsewhere in Genesis: "Behold, the man has become like one of us" (Gen. 3:22); "Come, let us go down and there confuse their language" (Gen. 11:7). Finally, "the Lord sitting upon a throne, high and lifted up" (Isa. 6:1) in the heavenly temple (verses 1-4), revealed Himself to Isaiah and disclosed His mission by asking, "Whom shall I send, and who will go for us?" (verse 8). Though other interpretations have been suggested, when these references to God's actions in the plural are understood as "plural of fullness," it is possible to see that "a distinction in the divine Being with regard to a plurality of persons is here represented as a germinal idea" (Hasel 65). Of itself, then, the usage of the plural form in relation to God points to a concept of the divinity in which the simplicity adopted by classical theology is replaced by a concept of the one Godhead that involves plurality and complexity.

B. The Angel of Yahweh

A most interesting line of evidence that moves toward clarifying the OT concept of plurality in relation to God's essence is found in several passages that deal with the Angel of the Lord. The concept of *mal'ak YHWH* integrates the mission-oriented role of angels with God's capability to reveal Himself in a personal, direct, visible, way by adopting a created form. For instance, He took on the form of a man when He revealed Himself to Abraham (Gen. 18:1-5) and Jacob (Gen. 32:24-30). Throughout the Bible angels are created beings, not to be worshiped (Col. 2:18; Rev. 19:10). Angelic beings have the specific task of carrying out God's specific purposes relating to human history (Heb. 1:14).

The designation "angel of the Lord" or "Angel of God" is frequently used in relation to angelic beings (cf. 2 Sam. 14:17; 24:16; 1 Kings 19:7; 2 Kings 1:3, 15; 1 Chron. 21:12, 15, 16). On some specific occasions, however, the Angel of the Lord is identified with Yahweh. In Judges 2:1-5 the Angel of the Lord appears as the One who brought Israel out of Egypt and entered into covenant with their fathers, while other texts identify Yahweh as the agent of these very events (Ex. 6:6; 13:3; Deut. 5:12; 7:19; Joshua 2:10; 1 Kings 8:9). In the burning bush God appeared personally to Moses. In

this momentous theophany (Ex. 3:2-15) the Angel of the Lord appeared to Moses "in a flame of fire out of the midst of a bush" (verse 2), but immediately Yahweh is the One revealing Himself to Moses (verses 4, 6). The same direct identification of the Angel of the Lord with Yahweh occurs elsewhere (Gen. 16:7-14; 22:9-18; Judges 6:11-24). When the specific identification of the Angel of the Lord with Yahweh is understood on the basis of the biblical concepts of eternity (see III. A), immutability (see III. B), and historical presence (see IV. D), God's ability to present Himself and act directly within the realm of the temporal order of human history is underlined. Even though the identification of the Angel of the Lord with Yahweh does not prove the plurality of God's essence, in an indirect way it sets the necessary stage for discerning the dual revelation of Yahweh.

C. The Dual Revelation of Yahweh

In Genesis 16 the Angel of the Lord is not only identified by Hagar as Yahweh (verse 13) but the same Angel of the Lord, who is Yahweh, is presented as referring to Yahweh in the third person (verse 11), thus hinting the existence of a possible difference between the Angel of the Lord that is Yahweh, and Yahweh. In Exodus 23 Yahweh promises the Israelites to "send an angel before" them (verse 20). The relation of Israel with this angel is very special. Israel is required to obey the Angel of the Lord, who is portrayed not as an intermediary between Yahweh and the people but rather as the originator of revelation and forgiveness (verse 21). Finally, Yahweh declares that His "name is in him" (verse 21). The "name" refers to the nature of God, which is connected directly with His covenant name Yahweh (Ex. 3:14, 15). It is possible to see that in this passage Yahweh speaks of another Yahweh, who is the Angel sent by the Lord.

Speaking about the Messiah's dominion, in Psalm 110:1 David presents Yahweh as addressing the Messiah as "my Lord." Jesus, trying to lead the Pharisees to the OT evidence of the divine origin of the Messiah, quoted from this passage, referring to the Lord addressing the Messiah as "my Lord" (Matt. 22:44). It seems, then, that Psalm 110 not only hints the divine nature of the Messiah, but in so doing also discloses the existence of a duality of "Lords." This duality is developed further years later when Zechariah, in a vision of the Lord, sees "Joshua the high priest standing before the angel of the Lord, and Satan standing at his right hand to accuse him" (Zech. 3:1). Next, the Angel of the Lord identified with the "Lord," addresses Satan: "The Lord rebuke you, O Satan!" (verse 2). Thus the text seems to suggest the existence of two personal Yahwehs, one identified with the angel of the Lord who carries on specific redemptive activities in relation to the people (see IV. D), the other identified with the transcendent God (see III. D). The plurality regarding God—suggested by the plural form of the OT word for God (Elohim), as well as the specific idea of a personal duality between the Angel of the Lord who is Yahweh and Yahweh—does not dissolve the concept of God's oneness into polytheism. On the contrary, the incipient revelation of the presence of plurality in the biblical idea of God is to be understood on the foundation provided by the idea of oneness.

From the very outset biblical thinking does not agree with the Greek identification of oneness with simplicity as required by the timeless interpretation of God's being. On the basis of the historical interpretation of immanence (see IV. D) as personal communion, OT thinking is able to understand God's oneness as not contradictory to, but rather compatible with, a dynamic personal plurality in the Godhead.

In the OT the trinitarian nature of God is not expressly revealed in the specificity and depth that are present in the NT record. From the vantage point gained from the NT revelation of God in Christ, it is possible to interpret the overlapping concepts of oneness and plurality as OT hints of the trinitarian doctrine of God. In any case, the two lines of revelation, that which discloses the oneness of God and that which discloses plurality as related to God's oneness, do not cancel out each other but rather provide the appropriate background for the surprising revelation regarding God brought by the Incarnation.

VII. The Godhead in the NT

God's self-revelation in Jesus as concrete, historical reality brought new light for understanding God. The revelation of God in Jesus Christ did not modify the basic OT approach to the understanding of the Godhead, which includes both the idea of oneness (see V) and of personal distinctions (see VI), but simply assumed it. On the contrary, the NT deepens the dynamic concept of divine plurality already present in the OT while at the same time affirming the oneness of God. The result is the revelation of God as Trinity. The NT assumes the idea of God's oneness without further elaborating on it, while at the same time expanding the area of God's plurality. The concrete revelation of the eternal person of God the Son in Jesus Christ opened the door for a more specific revelation of a divine "Other." Christ's ascension to heaven prompted an explanation of the continuation of God's historical, personal presence, continuously manifested through the OT sanctuary and the NT Incarnation. The specific revelation and sending of the eternal person of God the Holy Spirit was necessary in order to explain the historical continuity of God's personal, historical immanence.

A. God the Son

Jesus Christ was a man born of Mary (Matt. 1:16). Those who knew Him as a child and a young adult found it difficult to accept Jesus even as a prophet (Mark 6:3-5). According to the NT, however, Jesus the man was the most direct and clear revelation of God given to humankind (John 1:18; 14:8, 9; Heb. 1:2, 3). He is God incarnate. In a very real sense, our understanding of God's Trinity arises out of Christology. When the divinity of the person of Christ is seen within the context of the OT revelation about God's plurality in oneness, the stage is set for the further revelation about the person of the Father and the person of the Holy Spirit. Without the OT background and the specific historical revelation of the eternal Son in Jesus Christ as presented by the NT writers, talk about the Father and the Holy Spirit would not have been enough to reveal the inner trinitarian being of God. These two steps were necessary if human beings were to be introduced to a deeper understanding of God's being.

1. Divinity

Several NT passages refer to Christ as God (John 1:1, 18; 20:28; Heb. 1:8, 9; 2 Peter 1:1; 1 John 5:20). John not only teaches the preexistence of Christ (John 17:5), but also expresses it in an absolute way that belongs only to God (John 1:1, 2; 8:58; cf. Col. 1:17). Divine characteristics are attributed to Christ: eternity (Heb. 1:11, 12), possession of underived life in Himself (John 1:4; 14:6), and the divine power to create (John 1:3; Heb. 1:2, 10; Col. 1:16). The introduction to the letter to the Hebrews states that the Son "reflects the glory of God and bears the very stamp of his nature" (Heb. 1:3). Paul describes Christ as being "in the form of God" (Phil. 2:6).

The "I AM" statements appear to be another way Christ Himself pointed out His divine nature. By claiming for Himself the "I AM" designation, Christ used the same name that Yahweh, revealing Himself to Moses in a theophany, declared to be His own personal name: "I AM WHO I AM" ('ehyeh 'ăšer 'ehyeh) (Ex. 3:14). This usage applies to pronouncements that underline divine attributes, such as omnipotence (John 6:20, 21), eternity (John 8:58), foreknowledge (John 13:19), the manifestation of divine glory and power (John 18:5, 6, 8), and Jesus as the source of salvation (John 8:24). Finally, the NT affirms Christ's divinity by identifying Him with the OT Yahweh. The

song of praise that heaven sings to Yahweh for His redemption (Isa. 44:23) is applied to the worship of Christ in Philippians 2:10. The statement about Yahweh's creative power and eternity recorded in Psalm 102:25-27 is quoted in Hebrews 1:10-12, where it is applied to Christ. To reinforce this line of argument, Hebrews 1:8, 9 identifies Christ with God ('elohîm) by quoting from Psalm 45:6, 7.

Paul summarizes the NT testimony to Christ's divinity by plainly stating the mystery of God's incarnation in Jesus Christ: "In him the whole fulness of deity dwells bodily" (Col. 2:9). From the starting point, "God with us" (Matt. 1:23; cf. Isa. 7:14) as Jesus of Nazareth (John 1:14), the incipient OT conception of divine plurality grows in specificity and complexity, unfolding the trinitarian nature of God's being.

2. Sonship

The historical concept of God's immanence (see IV. D) is the necessary background to understand the astonishing NT revelation of God in Jesus of Nazareth. A strict understanding of God's oneness could lead to the conclusion that Yahweh, the only God, is now in Jesus Christ; the Incarnation would, thus, encompass the whole being of God. The NT, however, abundantly shows that the fullness of divinity dwells in Jesus of Nazareth but that it is not to be understood as encompassing the whole being of God. The divinity of Jesus of Nazareth brings the OT idea of plurality in the one God to further specificity, leading to the revelation of the trinitarian nature of God's reality.

The prologues to the Gospel of John and to the Epistle to the Hebrews present Jesus of Nazareth as the incarnation of God. Both disclose a divine duality, that the Godhead includes at least two divine persons, the Father and the Son. John presents the divine nature of Jesus of Nazareth not only as the Word that "was God," but also as the Word that "was with God" (John 1:1). The divine "Other" is the "Logos." The introduction to the Epistle to the Hebrews presents the divine "Other" not as Logos but as the "Son" (Heb. 1:2) who "reflects the glory of God and bears the very stamp of his nature" (verse 3). The "Son" is incarnated in Jesus of Nazareth (Heb. 2:9). Since the divine "Other," as "Logos" or "Son," is incarnated in Jesus of Nazareth, the "fulness of the divinity" (Col. 2:9) that dwells in Him does not encompass the whole divine being.

The Incarnation brings us a deeper revelation of God's plural nature. John testifies: "We have beheld his glory, glory as of the only Son from the Father" (John 1:14). The father-son relationship is chosen not only to name the two divine persons involved but particularly to characterize the special relationship between them.

John 1:18 presents the same father-son relationship as independent from the Incarnation: "No one has ever seen God; the only Son, who is in the bosom of the Father, he has made him known." Matthew also notes a father-son relationship that is prior to and independent of God's revelatory relation to His creation: "No one knows the Son except the Father, and no one knows the Father except the Son and any one to whom the Son chooses to reveal him" (Matt. 11:27; cf. Luke 10:22).

These statements place the plurality revealed by the father-son designation in the very nature of the one God. They move beyond the level of God's immanence to His transcendence. Furthermore, these texts reveal that within the level of God's transcendence, plurality involves two centers of consciousness that are able to know each other in a unique way. Even though the father-son language chosen to express the plurality of the Godhead is taken from the human level of existence, its referent is God Himself. This language discloses the existence of a duality of the kind of reality we call person and an ongoing relationship between them as constitutive of the very nature of God. The relationship between the Father and Son exists both at the level of transcendence and immanence. Throughout the NT Fatherhood and Sonship become designations

of the one God. Thus, the title "Son of God" refers to the divine person incarnated in Jesus of Nazareth (see Matt. 14:33; Mark 3:11; Luke 4:41; 1 Cor. 1:9; Heb. 4:14).

The way the NT expresses the plurality in the Godhead on the basis of the Incarnation raises questions about the proper understanding and mutual distinction between the person of the Father (see VII. B) and the person of the Son (see Christ I). It raises questions also about the way the two divine persons relate to each other. The biblical idea of plurality in God's being entails the reality of mutual, divine relationships. The analogical meaning of the words "Father" and "Son" seems to suggest that there is a preeminence of the Father over the Son. The preeminence of God the Father over God the Son suggested by the analogy to the human father-son relationship seems to be sustained by some passages that appear to teach that the Son is generated by the Father, and that the Son is subordinated to the Father.

3. Born of the Father

Within the human context the father-son relationship involves the generation of the son from the father and mother. Arius (see IX. B. 4) affirmed the creation of the Son by the Father. Even though this position was rejected as heretical, orthodox Christian teaching kept a subordinationist emphasis built into its concept about the eternal generation of the Son (see VII. B. 4, 5). The generation of the Son from the Father cannot be analogically deduced from the process of human generation. Such a deduction would produce a speculative theory without any ground in revelation. However, some biblical expressions seem to suggest some kind of generation; for instance, when God the Son is called the "first-born" (*prōtotokos*, Col. 1:15; Rom. 8:29; Heb. 1:6; Rev. 1:5) and "only begotten" (*monogenēs*, John 1:14, 18; 3:16, 18; 1 John 4:9 [KJV]). However, *prōtotokos* is also used in a metaphorical sense (LXX of Ex. 4:22; Ps. 89:27) and when applied to Christ expresses superiority and preeminence. In a similar vein, *monogenēs* does not contain the idea of begetting but rather of uniqueness and, when applied to Christ, emphasizes His unique relationship with the Father. On the other hand, Hebrews 1:5 gives no idea of physical or spiritual generation. There is, therefore, no ground within the biblical understanding of the Godhead for the idea of a generation of the Son from the Father.

4. The Nature of the Son's Subordination

Several passages show the Son in explicit subordination to the Father. Thus, Jesus Himself declares that "the Son can do nothing of his own accord, but only what he sees the Father doing" (John 5:19; cf. verse 36). Jesus affirmed that He did nothing of His own authority but spoke only what the Father had taught Him (John 8:28; cf. 12:50; 15:15). Jesus did what the Father commanded Him (John 14:31; cf. 10:18; 12:49, 50) and prayed to Him (John 17:1). Jesus boldly stated that "the Father is greater than I" (John 14:28). These statements clearly testify to the existence of a relation of subordination between God the Son and God the Father. The subordination expressed in these texts must not be understood in an ontological sense, as if the reality of God the Son were dependent on the reality of God the Father. The biblical idea of the subordination of God the Son to God the Father belongs, not to the inner structure of divine reality, but rather to the sphere of the accomplishment of the plan of salvation.

The plan of salvation called for God the Son to take human form, becoming "obedient unto death, even death on a cross" (Phil. 2:8). "Although he was a Son, he learned obedience through what he suffered; and being made perfect he became the source of eternal salvation" (Heb. 5:8). Thus, statements that imply the subordination of God the Son to God the Father are to be understood as a result of His incarnation, the expression of His obedience to the Father. Without this subordination the Incarnation itself would not have reached its salvific purpose.

The subordination of the Son to the Father seems to go beyond the Incarnation. Paul explains that at the end Christ "delivers the kingdom to God the Father after destroying every rule and every authority and power" (1 Cor. 15:24). This subordination occurs within the level of God's immanence, where both Father and Son administer their providential rule within created history. The functional subordination of the Son does not entail, however, an ontological dependence or inferiority of the Son. In a broad sense, the subordination of the Son to the Father can be seen as expressing the unity of the inner trinitarian life as the Godhead works out salvation in and throughout the history of the great controversy. In the Bible, therefore, no ground is found for the idea that there is an ontological subordination of the Son to the Father or that the divine reality of the Father has in any way a primacy of origin over the divine reality of the Son (see IX. B. 6, 7).

B. God the Father

If "the whole fulness of deity" dwelt "bodily" in Jesus Christ (Col. 2:9), what are we to think about the Father? Is He God? What is His relationship with God the Son?

1. The Fatherhood of God in the OT

The idea of God as Father is not alien to the OT. When God is called Father in the OT, His tender care toward His chosen people is emphasized. In the wilderness God bore Israel "as a man bears his son" (Deut. 1:31). Moses called Israel's attention to God's tender providential care by asking, "Is not he your father, who created you, who made you and established you?" (Deut. 32:6). As a father, God pities (Ps. 103:13) and disciplines (Prov. 3:12) His children. God Himself uncovered His deep personal involvement by addressing Israel as "my son" (Hosea 11:1, 8). In turn, the people recognized Yahweh as their Father (Isa. 63:16; 64:8; Mal. 2:10). Yahweh is said to be the Father of the King (2 Sam. 7:14; Ps. 2:7); the close relationship between God—the source of strength, wisdom, and authority—and the King, His representative, is underlined. Even though glimpses of the plural nature of the one God are present in the OT, the presence of specific persons is not as obvious. In the OT, therefore, the Father appellation is not used to designate a person of the divine Trinity. Such distinctive usage is proper to the NT revelation in Christ.

2. The God of Jesus Christ

Jesus of Nazareth, in whom dwelt "the whole fulness of deity" (Col. 2:9; see VII. A. 1; Christ I) presented God as His Father. In His prayers, God was "my Father" (Matt. 26:39, 42; Luke 10:22) or simply "Father" (Mark 14:36; Luke 10:21; John 11:41). In the discourse on the bread of life, Jesus called God Father (John 6:27). The NT further bears witness to God as the Father of Jesus Christ. Paul spoke of God as "the Father of our Lord Jesus Christ" (Col. 1:3; cf. Eph. 1:17); Jesus, God incarnated, used the word "father" to address God; thus, the father-son image reveals the personal and relational features of the divine plurality of God's one being.

3. The Sending of the Son

Jesus taught that the Father had sent Him to the world (John 5:36, 37; 6:44, 57; 8:16, 18). The Father sent Christ to the world to fulfill a specific mission in time and space—to save the world (1 John 4:14). More specifically, He was to become the "source of eternal salvation" (Heb. 5:9). Christ described Himself as coming from heaven (John 6:38), thus emphasizing the origin of Christ's mission at the level of historical immanence.

Jesus affirmed that "he who sent me is true, and him you do not know. I know him, for I come from him, and he sent me" (John 7:28, 29). The sending of the Son is a divine act that belongs to the level of God's immanent relationship with Creation; it stems from the transcendent being of God. The sending of the Son as a historical act is a witness to an important aspect of God's dynamic life. It helps us understand the divine reality of the one God's

real and ultimate "giving up." Paul states that God "did not spare his own Son but gave him up for us all" (Rom. 8:32). Jesus declares that "God [the Father] so loved the world that he gave his only Son" (John 3:16). This divine giving up is an act as much of the Son as of the Father; it is a relational act performed by divinity itself. The proper understanding of the cross as a divine redemptive act stands on the basis of the forsakenness of God (Father and Son). The reality of divine forsakenness is possible only when the one God is understood in His biblical, trinitarian structure, which involves Father, Son, and Holy Spirit as divine, personal, conscious beings, mutually interacting among themselves and with the created universe.

The divine experience of separation that occurs at the Incarnation finds its dramatic climax at the cross. There Jesus exclaims, "My God, my God, why hast thou forsaken me?" (Mark 15:34). Both Father and Son suffer at the cross. The doctrine of the trinitarian being of God is the necessary presupposition for the proper understanding of the Incarnation and of the cross. On the other hand, these historical realities made possible a more explicit revelation of the plurality of the Godhead in the NT.

4. The Delegation to the Son

Jesus disclosed that "the Father loves the Son, and has given all things into his hand" (John 3:35; cf. 13:3), even judgment (John 5:22). Consequently, Jesus could say that "all that the Father has is mine" (John 16:15). The delegation of the Father to the Son and its counterpart, the subordination of the Son to the Father, shows the involvement of the Godhead in accomplishing the work of salvation. As the Father sends the Son on His redemptive mission, the Father surrenders everything into the hands of the Son who in turn, in His incarnate state has to learn obedience and subordination to His Father (Heb. 5:8).

In delegating the task of redemption to the Son, the Father is stressing the decisive nature of Christ's task. In delegating everything to the Son, the Father is binding Himself to the results of Christ's salvific mission. Even when the Father is personally involved in the plan of salvation (see VII. B. 5), He does not use His divine powers to predetermine the outcome of Christ's mission so as to eliminate the risk involved in a life of obedience by faith.

Christ's ascension to heaven did not end His subordination to the Father. The correlative and complementary delegation of the Father to the Son continued after Christ's ascension to heaven. After His Resurrection Christ declared that "all authority in heaven and on earth has been given to me" (Matt. 28:18). Peter wrote that after the resurrection Jesus Christ had "gone into heaven and is at the right hand of God, with angels, authorities, and powers subject to him" (1 Peter 3:22). Christ's sitting at the right hand of God the Father is described as a transitional period which will last "until his enemies should be made a stool for his feet" (Heb. 10:13). Paul even points out that in this transitional period between the ascension and the Second Coming, Christ is not merely waiting in a passive mood for time to elapse. On the contrary, in the transitional period Christ "must reign until he has put all his enemies under his feet" (1 Cor. 15:25). "When all things are subjected to him, then the Son himself will also be subjected to him who put all things under him, that God may be everything to every one" (verse 28).

When the task of redemption entrusted to Christ is achieved, the delegation of the Father to the Son as the counterpart to the Son's total subordination to the Father will end. As interrelated aspects of the intratrinitarian life, the delegation of the Father to the Son and the subordination of the Son to the Father (see VII. A. 4) do not constitute the trinitarian nature of God but rather assume it.

5. Salvific Work

In spite of the Father's delegation to the Son of all authority for the accomplishing of redemption, the NT clearly teaches the Father's direct, personal involvement in the work of salvation. The Father is said to possess foreknowledge (Matt. 24:36; Mark 13:32) and omniscience (Matt. 6:32; Luke 12:30). The Father loves His children, and His love is in them (1 John 2:15; 3:1). He reveals salvific truths (Matt. 11:25; 16:17), takes providential care of His children (Matt. 6:26; 10:29), leads the development of history (Matt. 20:23), draws people to Christ (John 6:45) for them to find salvation, qualifies His children "to share in the inheritance of the saints in light" (Col. 1:12), forgives sins (Matt. 6:15; Mark 11:25), answers prayer (Matt. 6:6, 18; 7:11; 18:19; John 15:16; 16:23), and "judges each one impartially according to his deeds" (1 Peter 1:17; cf. Matt. 10:32, 33). All these activities are to be understood within the framework of the Father's delegation to the Son.

6. Binitarian Formulas

The incarnation of God in Jesus of Nazareth dramatically clarified the OT hints regarding the plural nature of the one eternal God. The Incarnation revealed not only the fact that Jesus of Nazareth was God dwelling among us (Immanuel), but also that the plurality involved in the one eternal Godhead specifically included the reality of two divine persons, the Son and the Father. On this basis many have suggested that the Christian Godhead is to be understood as binitarian rather than trinitarian. Hence we need to consider Bible references to the Father and the Son that do not explicitly include the Holy Spirit.

It is important to bear in mind that our knowledge of God sprang from God's immanent dwelling with His people. The historical presence of the Son among us makes both possible and necessary the revelation of God the Father as a person to be distinguished from God the Son as a person. Throughout the NT this truth is expressed and integrated in different ways; one is the recurrent binitarian formula: "God the Father and the Lord Jesus Christ."

The binitarian formula is given its classical

128

expression in 1 Corinthians 8:6: "Yet for us there is one God, the Father, from whom are all things and for whom we exist, and one Lord, Jesus Christ, through whom are all things and through whom we exist." At first glance the formula appears to recognize only the divinity of the Father, who is called God, while seemingly placing the Son in a subordinate position. However, when the NT teaching on the divinity of Jesus Christ (VII. A. 1) is associated with the fact that the title "Lord" in the NT parallels the OT "Yahweh," one realizes that the formula is actually setting side by side two equally divine persons. The choice of the title "Lord" for naming the person of God the Son is clearly designated to underline the Father's delegation of His authority to the Son in matters pertaining to the direct, historical accomplishment of the plan of salvation (see VII. B. 4). This text draws a working parallelism between the way God the Father and the Lord Jesus relate to Creation. The Father is presented as the origin and ultimate end, while the Lord Jesus Christ is presented as the executor of Creation and our own existence. The parallelism discloses a mutual complementation of activities between the Father and the Son which accentuates their equal, divine standing. The formula, then, names the Christian God in a binitarian mode, which includes the personal plurality and specific relation of two equally divine persons.

With minor variations this formula is used in the introduction to several NT Epistles (Rom. 1:7; 1 Cor. 1:3; 2 Cor. 1:2, 3; Gal. 1:3; Eph. 1:2, 3; Phil. 1:2; 1 Thess. 1:1, 3; 2 Thess. 1:2; 1 Tim. 1:2; 2 Tim. 1:2; Philemon 3; 1 Peter 1:3). When so used the formula seems to summarize the basic concept of God generated by the incarnation of God in Jesus of Nazareth and Jesus' own testimony about God the Father in heaven. At times, however, the formula is integrated into its theological context. For example, Paul's closing remarks to the Ephesians underline the unity of action by saying that love and faith are given to the believers by both God the Father and the Lord Jesus Christ (Eph. 6:23; cf. 1 Thess. 3:11; 2 Thess. 2:16), thus highlighting the commonality of action (see also 1 John 1:3; 2:24; 2 John 9) in which both divine persons execute the work of redemption. At other times the formula is used to express and integrate the different salvific roles of the Father and the Son (Phil. 2:11; Col. 3:17; 1 Thess. 1:3; 3:13; 1 Peter 1:3).

One may enquire why a binitarian formula was used rather than a trinitarian one, since NT writers were aware of the existence of the third person of the Trinity. To begin, between the binitarian and trinitarian formulas is a quantitative rather than qualitative difference. In other words, the newness of the biblical conception of God occurs when plurality and oneness are said to coexist in the divine being. Once such coexistence has been discovered, the difference between a binitarian and trinitarian concept amounts only to the exclusion or inclusion of a third divine person as constitutive of the personal plurality of the one God. Besides, the binitarian formula does not deny either the existence or activity of the third divine person but rather emphasizes the specific framework needed for grasping the meaning of the Incarnation. In other words, the NT deals first of all with the understanding of God's self-revelation in Jesus of Nazareth.

The binitarian formula is the necessary presupposition for the Incarnation. Since the main task that NT writers undertake is the clarification of the incarnation of God in Christ and its implications for the whole of theology, it is not surprising to find the binitarian formula used throughout. On the other hand, the trinitarian concept and formula appear as necessary presuppositions for properly grasping the meaning of Christ's postresurrection activity through His representative, the Holy Spirit. The specific, practical concern of NT writers may explain why the trinitarian formula is less frequently utilized. A full revelation of God's being was accessible only after Jesus Christ Himself introduced the divine person of the Holy Spirit.

C. God the Holy Spirit

The trinitarian nature of the one biblical God is not complete without God the Holy Spirit. That the revelation of the Holy Spirit as the third divine person of the Godhead comes after the revelation of the Son and the Father does not mean that He is either less important or that He has been involved in salvific activities only since the time of His revelation. A proper understanding of the one Christian God and His personal plurality requires, therefore, a careful consideration of the biblical witness to God the Holy Spirit.

1. Christ's Announcement

Even though God the Spirit appears from Genesis (1:2; 6:3) onward, the explicit concept that God's plurality involves not only the persons of the Father and the Son but also a third person, the Holy Spirit, originates in Jesus Christ Himself. The revelation of the existence and specific salvific role of a third person of the one God was given by Jesus Christ as He tried to prepare the disciples for His departure from earth (John 7:33; 14:1-3). According to John, Christ hinted at the personhood and historical coming of the Holy Spirit at the Feast of Tabernacles before His death, when He promised "rivers of living water" flowing out of the believers' hearts, to explain "the Spirit, which those who believe in him were to receive" (John 7:38, 39). However, Christ clearly announced the coming of the Holy Spirit only a few hours before His crucifixion: "I will pray the Father, and he will give you another Counselor, to be with you for ever, even the Spirit of truth" (John 14:16, 17; cf. 16:4-7, 13).

After His resurrection Jesus again brought to the attention of the disciples the coming of the Holy Spirit (Luke 24:49; Acts 1:4, 5, 8). The existence of the Holy Spirit as a divine person was revealed at this time, because the Holy Spirit had to be revealed as a divine person to explain how the redemptive work of Christ would continue after His ascension, simultaneously on earth and in the heavenly sanctu-ary (Heb. 8:1, 2). The revelation of God's trinitarian nature is disclosed not with the speculative purpose of revealing the nature of God but rather so that human beings may understand God's redemptive acts in history.

2. Pentecostal Coming

As there was a historical coming of the Son to the world, there was a historical coming of the Holy Spirit to the church. The mode of historical presence of the Spirit is different from the mode in which the Son was present. The Holy Spirit's coming does not involve the taking on of human nature as did Jesus' incarnation. The mode in which God the Holy Spirit is present is such that makes Him accessible to all, while the incarnated mode of God the Son in Jesus limited His divine presence to a few human beings. This remarkable difference may have been one of the reasons why Jesus said it would be to the disciples' advantage that He should go away so that the Spirit could come to them (John 16:7).

The historical coming of the Holy Spirit to the church occurred at Pentecost, following the Resurrection. That the coming of the Holy Spirit to the church occurred on the day of Pentecost could be seen as a mere coincidence bearing little theological significance; however, the specific timing deserves special study.

a. Typological setting. In the OT, Passover and Pentecost were closely related festivals. Both were memorials and prefigurations of important aspects of God's acts of salvation. Passover (Lev. 23:5; Num. 28:16; Deut. 16:1-8) was a memorial of God as a source of freedom in connection with Israel's liberation from under Egyptian bondage (Deut. 16:1, 3, 6). Pentecost, or the Feast of Weeks (Ex. 23:16; 34:22; Lev. 23:15-22; Num. 28:26-31; Deut. 16:9-12), was a memorial of God as the source of all good gifts. The very name, Feast of Weeks, or Pentecost, pointed to the close connection between the Passover and Pentecost by making explicit reference to the 50 days between them (Lev. 23:15, 16; cf. 6BC 133, 134). As the Passover and the deliverance from Egypt were types of Jesus' mission (Matt. 2:15; cf. Hosea 11:1) and death at the cross (1 Cor. 5:7), it is possible to see Pentecost and the covenant at Sinai as types of the historical coming of the Holy Spirit. The historical coming of the Holy Spirit at Pentecost, then, would be the antitype of the Sinaitic covenant understood as the good gift of God to His people. As a distinctive function of the Sinaitic covenant was to lead Israel to redemption through a concrete understanding of God's will for man, the coming of the Holy Spirit appears designed to bring that purpose to new, surprising levels of specificity and closeness. When Jesus talked to the disciples about the historical coming of the Holy Spirit, He underscored that "the Counselor, the Holy Spirit, whom the Father will send in my name, he will teach you all things, and bring to your remembrance all that I have said to you" (John 14:26). Between God's redemptive work at Sinai and the revelation and historical coming of the Holy Spirit there is no discontinuity but rather a clear typologically conceived continuity. This does not mean, however, repetition of the same but rather the disclosure of new aspects of truth not present in past revelations. These bring our knowledge and experience of God's salvific will and acts to deeper levels.

b. The Spirit of God in the OT. The fact that the Holy Spirit is not explicitly revealed as a divine person in the OT (Gen. 1:2) does not mean that He did not exist or act as a person before His historical introduction at Pentecost. The revelation of the Holy Spirit as a person of the Godhead became possible and necessary after the historical revelation of Jesus Christ as God the Son. The OT, consequently, does not refer to the Holy Spirit as a person different from other divine persons. However, at times it is possible to understand some OT references to the rather general designation "Spirit of God" as allusions to divine activities that properly belong to the Holy Spirit. The giving of spiritual gifts to special individuals for the execution of definite tasks is the activity most commonly associated in the OT with the Spirit of God (Ex. 31:3; 35:31; Num. 11:25, 29; 24:2; 27:18; Judges 3:10; 6:34; 11:29; 13:25; 14:6, 19; 15:14; 1 Sam. 10:6, 10; 16:13; 19:20, 23; 2 Chron. 15:1; 20:14; 24:20). The Spirit of God is not so frequently presented as indwelling the heart of the believer, although the idea is, nonetheless, present in the OT. According to the Sinaitic covenant, religion was to be a deep experience of love to God: "And now, Israel, what does the Lord your God require of you, but to hear the Lord your God, to walk in all his ways, to love him, to serve the Lord your God with all your heart and with all your soul?" (Deut. 10:12). Thus Paul can describe a "real Jew" as one who is so, not by adhering to external rituals, but rather, according to Deuteronomy 10:16, he who has the real circumcision of the heart (Rom. 2:28, 29). David knew that the inner change of the heart amounts to a new creation that can be accomplished only by God Himself (Ps. 51:10). Saul not only received gifts from the Spirit, but the Spirit of the Lord changed him into another man (1 Sam. 10:6, 9). Israel in exile anticipated a spiritual revival as a result of God's putting His Spirit in them (Eze. 36:26, 27; 37:1-14).

The Spirit of God, then, is also associated in the OT with the divine indwelling in the inner being of man (cf. Isa. 57:15; Eze. 11:19; 18:31). On this basis, Jesus Christ could speak to the disciples as if they already knew the Holy Spirit before His historical personal coming at Pentecost (John 14:17). If the Holy Spirit was already acting, giving gifts, and indwelling the hearts of the believers, the newness of the NT ministry of the Spirit needs examination.

c. The newness of the Spirit in the NT. One obviously new aspect of NT revelation on the Spirit of God is that now He is clearly presented as a divine person, distinct from Father and Son (see VII. C. 4). This change, however, affects only our understanding of His personhood and not His redemptive activity. The work of the Holy Spirit in the NT appears to involve the same areas covered either by God or the Spirit of God in the OT. The newness of the

Holy Spirit in the NT has to be found in His new role as representative of Christ. According to John's interpretation of Jesus' typological reference to the Spirit (John 7:37-39), the revelation, historical coming, and redemptive task of God the Holy Spirit is essentially connected to the cross and ascension of Jesus Christ. John interprets Jesus' typology by remarking that He spoke "about the Spirit, which those who believed in him were to receive; for as yet the Spirit had not been given, because Jesus was not yet glorified" (John 7:39). Consequently, according to John, the death and glorification of the Son were necessary conditions for the historical outpouring of the Holy Spirit.

When the Holy Spirit came on the day of Pentecost, His coming was witnessed by all because of the external manifestation of supernatural gifts poured out on the believers (Acts 2:2-11). In response to questions on the theological meaning of the event, a very superficial and inadequate explanation was forwarded: "They are filled with new wine" (verse 13). In defense of the apostles, Peter addressed the multitude (verses 14-36). After identifying the seemingly strange event as a miraculous manifestation of the outpouring of the Holy Spirit (verses 15-21), Peter explained the event as a necessary step in the historical achievement of God's plan of salvation (verses 23, 24). Peter affirmed that "this Jesus God raised up, and of that we all are witnesses. Being therefore exalted at the right hand of God, and having received from the Father the promise of the Holy Spirit, he has poured out this which you see and hear" (verses 32, 33). Peter referred to Christ's heavenly enthronement (see VII. B. 4), which followed His victory at the cross and conferred on Christ "all authority in heaven and on earth" (Matt. 28:18; cf. 1 Peter 3:22).

Since Jesus Christ was to be personally involved in the task of intercession in the heavenly sanctuary (Heb. 8:1, 2; see Sanctuary II, III) the necessary, continuous, personal presence of God on earth required the revelation of the third person of the Godhead, God the Holy Spirit. The specific newness brought about by the historical coming of the Holy Spirit in the NT, then, is not to be seen in relation to the specific salvific tasks which the Spirit continues to perform as He did in OT times, but rather it is related to the new status of the Spirit as representative of Jesus Christ's triumph on the cross and His work of intercession and lordship in heaven. Jesus Christ Himself underlined the characteristic harmony and unity in which the Trinity performs the activities pertaining to salvation by pointing out that the Holy Spirit not only was His representative (John 16:13, 14) but also, because of the delegation of the Father to the Son (see VII. B. 4), the representative of the Father (John 14:16, 17). For this reason the technical expressions "in Christ" (Rom. 6:11, 23; 8:1, 39; 9:1; 1 Cor. 1:4; 3:1; 2 Cor. 2:17) and "in the Holy Spirit" (Rom. 9:1; 14:17; cf. Col. 1:8) are, in fact, equivalent.

d. Procession from the Father and the Son. The procession of the Spirit from the Father and the Son (John 15:26; 14:16, 26; Acts 2:33) is to be understood not in an ontological sense, but rather, in a historical sense as the inner divine activity involved in sending the Holy Spirit at Pentecost as the representative of Christ's presence, sacrifice, and ministry. In other words, the procession of the Spirit does not refer to an inner process in the makeup of the trinitarian being, as classical theology came to believe. The question regarding whether the Holy Spirit proceeds from the Father, from the Father and the Son, or from the Father through the Son became relevant as the "born-of-the-Father" and "procession" language we find in the Bible was misunderstood as referring to an inner, divine process that constitutes the very being of the Godhead. Biblically, however, the procession of the Holy Spirit belongs not to the constitution of the Trinity but rather to its life as the work of salvation is carried out by the historical activity of the three divine persons.

The distinction between the historical coming of the Spirit at Pentecost, as the Father's and Son's gift to the church, and the personal coming of the Spirit to the hearts of men and women is important. The book of Acts particularly underlines the historical coming of the Spirit to the church at a specific time, the day of Pentecost. Signs and miracles accompanied the outpouring of the Holy Spirit on that day and at other specific times when the Spirit came to special segments of the church. However, the Holy Spirit need not always come to the church in the same way; Pentecost was unique. At Pentecost, Christ's promise to send the Holy Spirit to the church was fulfilled; since then, the third person of the divine Trinity is present in the Christian church as the gift (Acts 2:38) of God in Christ. Therefore, the church does not need to pray for the historical coming of the Spirit as did the disciples in the upper room (Acts 1:13, 14), but rather for surrender and openness of heart to the promptings of the Spirit so that His promised presence and power (see VII. C. 6) might be manifested in the life and mission of the church.

3. Divinity

The divinity of the Holy Spirit is attested in various contexts. The Holy Spirit is described as possessing divine characteristics; He is called "Holy" (Matt. 1:20), "the Spirit of our God" (1 Cor. 6:11), and "Spirit of Jesus" (Acts 16:7). When confronting Ananias and Sapphira, Peter pointed to the divinity and personality of the Spirit. Ananias had lied to the Holy Spirit (Acts 5:3) and at the same time to God. Jesus introduced the Spirit to the disciples as "another Counselor" (John 14:16). Since the Greek *allos* means "another of the same kind," it follows that the Holy Spirit was of the same kind as Christ, namely, a divine person.

The divinity of the Holy Spirit as third person of the Trinity is further affirmed as He is described as possessing other divine attributes: omniscience (1 Cor. 2:10, 11), truth (1 John 5:7), life (Rom. 8:2), wisdom (1 Cor. 2:11), power (Luke 1:35; Rom. 15:19), and eternity (Heb. 9:14). The NT underlines the divinity of the Holy Spirit by referring to Him as performing specific divine actions, such as speaking to the fathers through the prophets (Acts 28:25), inspiration of Scriptures (2 Peter 1:21; cf. VII. C. 5. a), illumination (John 15:26; cf. VII. C. 5. b), regeneration (John 3:7, 8; Rom. 8:11; Titus 3:5), and sanctification (2 Thess. 2:13; 1 Peter 1:2). Furthermore, the divinity of the Holy Spirit is strongly affirmed as He is identified with the OT Yahweh as is Christ. Acts 28:25-27 and Hebrews 3:7-9 attribute to the direct activity of the Holy Spirit statements that in the OT are explicitly reported as Yahweh's utterances (Isa. 6:8-10 and Ps. 95:7-11; cf. Ex. 16:1-8; Deut. 1:34-36). In the NT Paul affirms the same identification: "The Lord is the Spirit" (2 Cor. 3:17). There seems to be no doubt that the NT writers understood the Holy Spirit to be God.

4. Personality

Christian theology has often neglected the study of biblical information regarding the nature and salvific activities of the Holy Spirit. Within this context the Spirit has been understood in terms of divine energy and power belonging properly to the Father's person. Thus, the Holy Spirit is understood as divested of both individuality and personality. This interpretation seems to find support in some biblical passages. For instance, while the names Father and Son evoke personal realities, the name Spirit does not necessarily do so. The gender of the Greek *pneuma* (spirit) is neuter, seemingly suggesting a nonpersonal reality. Besides, the fact that Scripture talks about the Holy Spirit as taking the bodily "form" of a "dove" (Luke 3:22), and likens Him to wind (John 3:8), water (John 7:37-39), and fire (Acts 2:3) also contributes to the superficial and mistaken idea that the Holy Spirit is not a personal being like the Father and the Son. Finally, overemphasis on the biblical description of the Holy Spirit as a gift (Acts 2:38; 10:45) that grants gifts (1 Cor. 12:4-11; Eph. 4:11; cf. VII. C. 4. e) to men and women may also be responsible for incorrectly thinking of the Holy Spirit as a "divine energy" rather than as a divine person. These biblical passages do not teach that the Holy Spirit is a nonpersonal being; they merely leave open the possibility that the Holy Spirit may be understood as a nonpersonal divine energy. Further explicit evidence is necessary to decide whether the Holy Spirit is a personal or nonpersonal being.

The NT uncovers the personal nature of the Holy Spirit in a variety of ways. While the NT writers could not change the gender of the Greek word for "spirit," when speaking of the Holy Spirit they sometimes utilized masculine pronouns to replace the neuter form Spirit (John 14:26; 15:26; 16:13), even at the cost of syntactical inconsistency. Additionally, the NT adjudicates to the Holy Spirit a variety of characteristics that explicitly reveal His personal nature. Among these the following can be mentioned: intelligence and knowledge (John 14:26; 1 Cor. 12:11), emotions (Eph. 4:30), and judgment (Acts 15:28). Also, the Spirit can be lied to (Acts 5:3, 4), resisted (Acts 7:51), and sinned against (Matt. 12:31; Mark 3:29). Furthermore, the NT presents the Holy Spirit as doing what can be done by a personal being: He speaks (Acts 8:29), teaches (Luke 12:12), reveals (Luke 2:26), testifies (Acts 20:23), searches (1 Cor. 2:10, 11), sends (Acts 13:2), guides (Acts 8:29; 11:12), declares things to come (John 16:13), and bears witness with our spirit (Rom. 8:15, 16). Moreover, the Greek expression "another Counselor" that Jesus used regarding the Holy Spirit (John 14:16) suggests not only that the Holy Spirit is a divine being but also that He is a personal being in the same way as the Father and the Son are personal beings. Likewise, the intercessory role (Rom. 8:26) that the Holy Spirit plays in the salvation of the believers can be performed only by a personal being. Finally, the glorification of the Son by the Holy Spirit (John 16:14) cannot be accomplished by a power or energy, but only by a person. Without doubt the NT writers understood the Holy Spirit as a divine personal being.

Only when we clearly grasp the biblical understanding of the Holy Spirit as a divine person does the NT specification about the OT concept of the plurality of the one God come into full view. On the basis of the biblical evidence presented above, a doctrine of the Trinity becomes both unavoidable and necessary for Christian theology. Before the biblical approach to the Trinity is considered, it is necessary, however, to examine the work of the third person of the Trinity.

5. Salvific Work

The NT presents a wealth of additional information regarding the third person of the eternal Trinity. The understanding of the Holy Spirit as a representative of the person and work of Christ on the cross and in the heavenly sanctuary is set forth and integrated, not as speculative insights into His divine nature but rather from the perspective of His salvific task.

a. Revelation-inspiration. Since the Bible is said to be the "sword of the Spirit" (Eph. 6:17), it is not surprising to find that the Holy Spirit is closely related to the processes through which the Holy Scriptures originated. The Spirit was actively involved in revelation, the process through which the truths, concepts, and information found in the Bible originated (Eze. 8:3; 11:1, 24; 37:1; 43:5; Mark 12:36; 1 Cor. 2:11; Rev. 21:10). He also took part in inspiration, the process through which these communications were shared by the prophets (2 Sam. 23:2; 2 Chron. 24:20; Eze. 11:5; Zech. 7:12; Matt. 22:43; 2 Peter 1:21). After Pentecost the revelatory-inspirational task of the Holy Spirit concentrated on guiding the disciples to a proper understanding of the truth as revealed in the historical person and work of Jesus Christ (John 16:12-15), which, when put into writing, became the NT. The reception of the Holy Spirit into the heart of the Christian believer (see VII. C. 5. c) cannot be conceived in independence from or contradiction with the truths revealed in Scriptures as a whole (see Revelation/Inspiration III, IV).

b. Illumination. According to Jesus the Holy Spirit not only takes part in the task of revealing and inspiring Scriptures, but He is also involved in convincing "the world concerning sin and righteousness and judgment" (John 16:8). It is not enough that truth be theoretically expressed in words, oral or written; it is necessary that it be written in the mind and heart of men and women (Jer. 31:33; Heb. 8:10). The writing of truth in the human mind is the work of the Holy Spirit (2 Cor. 3:3), which involves revelation-inspiration (see VII. C. 5. a), illumination, and indwelling (VII. C. 5. c). God originated Scripture through the agency of the Holy Spirit in order that divine light (knowledge), necessary for the salvation of sinners and the redemption of the world, would be available to the human race (Ps. 119:105). Yet, for the Bible to be a light and not merely a dead letter, men and women must understand it (verse 130). However, understanding the light presupposes the possessing of light: "In thy light do we see light" (Ps. 36:9). Unless God is recognized as the author of the words, a veil (2 Cor. 3:13, 14; cf. Isa. 6:9, 10; Acts 28:26, 27) hinders both mind and heart from seeing God and understanding His Word (Luke 11:34, 35). Since the Fall men and women have no light in themselves (Acts 26:18; 2 Cor. 4:3, 4; cf. John 1:5). The Spirit must remove the veil of darkness (2 Cor. 3:17, 18) from the mind so that the light may be seen. The Spirit of understanding and knowledge, given in a special way to the Messiah (Isa. 11:2), also leads human beings in the process of reading and understanding Scriptures (Eph. 1:17-23) and is one of "the gifts bestowed on us by God" (1 Cor. 2:12). The writing of the law in the heart assumes illumination but goes beyond it, requiring the indwelling of the Holy Spirit in the mind and heart of believers.

c. Indwelling. When the promptings of the Holy Spirit are accepted and sinners open themselves to God in faith, confession, and repentance, a divine-human relationship begins (Rev. 3:20). The initial act by which God is accepted into the mind and heart, thereby turning the believer into a new person, is so dramatic that Jesus refers to it as a new birth from the Holy Spirit (John 3:3-8). The divine-human relationship established through the new-birth experience is known as divine indwelling, filling (Luke 1:67; Acts 2:4; 4:31; 9:17; 13:52), or baptism of the Holy Spirit (Matt. 3:11; Mark 1:8; Luke 3:16; Acts 1:5; 11:16). Paul describes this intimate divine-human relationship not only as the circumcision of the heart (Rom. 2:29) but more specifically, as the Spirit of God dwelling "in you" (Rom. 8:9; cf. Eph. 2:22). Consequently, the body is "a temple of the Holy Spirit" (1 Cor. 6:19). The biblical view of divine indwelling in human beings can be perceived only when it is seen within the context provided by (1) the historical (see IV. D and VII. C. 2) and personal nature (see VII. C. 4) of the Holy Spirit as Christ's representative (see VII. C. 2. c and VII. C. 5. d); and (2) when one realizes that the biblical understanding of man and woman does not recognize the existence of a timeless eternal soul in the human person (see Man I. E). Consequently, the Holy Spirit cannot be conceived as a "divine energy" that penetrates the eternal substance of the soul and divinizes human nature. On the contrary, the indwelling is to be conceived within the mode of personal, historical relations (1 John 4:13). Within the relational mode the Holy Spirit dwells "in" human beings. Thus, human nature is not divinized by the Spirit's indwelling but is rather transformed into the likeness of Jesus Christ (Rom. 8:29). Since the Holy Spirit as a divine person is the representative of Christ, the indwelling brings Christ's presence to the mind and heart of the believer. Hence, the indwelling of the Spirit in the believer is the indwelling of Christ.

Because the Holy Spirit represents the victorious Christ His presence in the heart of the believer becomes a down payment of God's redemption and the guarantee of His promises (2 Cor. 1:20-22), notably of Christ's glorious second coming (2 Cor. 5:4, 5; Eph. 1:13, 14; cf. Rom. 8:11). The indwelling of the Spirit occurs "in the inner man" (Eph. 3:16), which involves heart (Rom. 5:5), mind (Rom. 8:6, 7), and spirit (verse 16). The indwelling of the Spirit that commences with the new-birth experience brings Christ to the inner man, establishing an ongoing divine-human relation that changes believers into the likeness of Jesus Christ (verses 4-17; cf. verse 29). In Romans 8 Paul specifically explains the submission of the believer to the law of God (verses 4-7), the results of the Spirit's indwelling: victory over sinful acts (verse 13), God's providential care for the believer (verse 14), sonship (verse 15), assurance of acceptance as children of God (verse 16), cosuffering with Christ (verse 17), and the future resurrection from death. Obedience to God's will is also a concrete result of the Spirit's indwelling, by which the eternal principles of the law of God are written in the heart and mind of believers (Jer. 31:33; Eze. 36:27; Rom. 2:15; Heb. 8:10; 10:16; cf. Ps. 37:31; 40:8; 119:34; Isa. 51:7). On the basis of the relational reality of Christ's indwelling the believers through the Spirit, they are said to possess "the mind of Christ" (1 Cor. 2:16; cf. 12:3) and, to "become partakers of the divine nature" (2 Peter 1:4). Hence in their daily lives the "fruit of the Spirit" (Gal. 5:22, 23) is produced.

Since the Holy Spirit does not indwell the believer as an energy that penetrates the soul, but rather as a person, the question about how He indwells human beings arises. Paul, in full agreement with the relational structure of the Spirit's indwelling, explains that "we all, with unveiled face, beholding the glory of the Lord, are being changed into his likeness from one degree of glory to another, for this comes from the Lord who is the Spirit" (2 Cor. 3:17, 18). Paul declares that sinful human beings can behold the glory of the Lord through the preaching and teaching of the gospel (2 Cor. 4:4, 5), "for it is the God who said, 'Let light shine out of darkness,' who has shone in our hearts to give the light of the knowledge of the glory of God in the face of Christ" (verse 6). The indwelling, then, occurs as a result of the specific work of the Holy Spirit. Through the inspiration of the Bible and the illumination of its contents, the Holy Spirit brings the presence of Christ to the consciousness of believers who thus are able to behold "the glory of God in the face of Christ."

When, as a response to the divine initiative of God in the Spirit, the human heart surrenders in total openness to Christ for the first time, the new birth occurs simultaneously with the baptism of the Holy Spirit as the gift of God's personal presence (Acts 2:38). The continuous process of indwelling follows. The indwelling of the Holy Spirit in the Christian is not a permanent possession, acquired once and for all at the time of the new birth. On the contrary, it must be a permanent process, daily renewed (1 Cor. 9:27) in further and deeper surrender to the Spirit's promptings, lest the believer fall into apostasy at the risk of eternal loss (Heb. 6:4-8).

d. Intercession. As a representative of Christ, the Holy Spirit performs intercessory functions that complement Christ's intercession in the heavenly sanctuary (Heb. 8:1, 2). To the clear mediatorial functions of revelation-inspiration (see VII. C. 5. a), illumination (see VII. C. 5. b), and indwelling (see VII. C. 5. c), performed by the Holy Spirit, Paul specifically adds the Holy Spirit's intercessory activity in favor of the saints' prayers (Rom. 8:26, 27).

e. Gifts. The Holy Spirit is instrumental not only in the constitution of the new creature through His work of indwelling, but also in the mission of the church through the conferral of spiritual gifts (see Spiritual Gifts II). The notion that the Spirit of God endows believers for the fulfillment of special tasks is present in the OT (Num. 11:25; 27:18; Deut. 34:9; Judges 3:10; 1 Sam. 10:6; Micah 3:8; Zech. 4:6). However, in the OT the spiritual gifts generally seem to be given to special persons rather than to the whole community of faith. This restriction is lifted in the NT, when Joel's prophecy (2:28, 29) is partially fulfilled at Pentecost with the coming of the Holy Spirit and the granting of spiritual gifts to the whole church (Acts 2:15-21, 32, 33; Eph. 4:8). Gifts are given to believers in whom Christ dwells through the Spirit. In other words, the believer receives spiritual gifts on the basis of a reception of the person of the Holy Spirit (the Gift) in total surrender (Acts 2:38) and continuous obedience to God's will (Acts 5:32). The gifts are given with the purpose of accomplishing the unity of the church (Eph. 4:13) and "to equip the saints for the work of ministry" (verse 12). They are given not as supernatural signs of God's existence or divine forgiveness but rather as necessary skills for the accomplishment of the Christian mission of representing Christ and preaching His gospel as revealed in the OT and NT Scriptures.

6. Eschatological Endowments

The OT presents the eschatological times preceding the end of redemptive history as involving a universal spreading of the knowledge of God's will as revealed in Scriptures. Such a universal, eschatological expansion is to be brought about by God through the instrumentality of His people (Ps. 72:8-11; Isa. 14:1; 45:14; 56:6, 7; 60:5, 11; Jer. 3:17; Haggai 2:7; Zech. 2:11; 8:21-23). Joel's prophecy about the universal outpouring of the Spirit on all flesh (2:28, 29) brings the instrumental component, assumed in the OT vision, regarding an eschatological universal spreading of God's kingdom, to explicit formulation.

Even though Joel's prophecy began to be fulfilled with the historical coming of the Spirit at Pentecost (Acts 2:16-21; see VII. C. 2), it is clear that its complete universal fulfillment is still future (verses 19-21). The vision of a universal spreading of the gospel message, before the end of the history of redemption is continued in NT eschatological thinking (Rev. 14:6, 7; 18:1). God's immutability expresses itself in the constancy and consistency of His historical salvific actions (III. B). Consequently, it is to be expected that in bringing the plan of redemption to its historical climax and consummation by means of the eschatological universal spreading of the gospel message God will utilize the same instrumentality He used at Pentecost, namely, the unlimited outpouring of spiritual gifts on His church. Such an eschato-logical outpouring of the Holy Spirit, which is implicitly assumed in the enlightening of the earth by the angel in Revelation 18:1, will complete the fulfillment of Joel's prophecy initiated at Pentecost.

Thus, as the coming of the Holy Spirit and His gifts empowered the emerging church in a special way, so at the end of time the Holy Spirit will bestow His gifts to the church for the finishing of the work. On both the personal and historical levels, God bestows the gifts of the Spirit as the early and latter rains (Joel 2:23; cf. Hosea 6:3). The eschatological bestowal of spiritual gifts by the Holy Spirit has the same purpose: the preaching of the gospel truths (Rev. 18:2, 4) preparing the way for Jesus Christ's second coming (Matt. 24:14; 2 Peter 3:9, 12; Rev. 14:6-12). However, as the indwelling of the Spirit in the believer is the condition for the reception of the gifts (VII. C. 5. e), the eschatological manifestation of the Holy Spirit will occur on the basis of the total surrender and openness of the church to the Spirit's illumination and indwelling.

D. Trinitarian Patterns in the NT

The specific revelation of the Holy Spirit as a divine person distinct from the Father and the Son completes the NT expansion of the biblical picture of the plurality of the one God. There are three different divine persons in the one Christian Godhead. The NT expresses the Trinitarian nature of the Godhead not only by means of a clear presentation of the different, divine persons, but also by means of short Trinitarian formulas. Binitarian (see VII. B. 6) and Trinitarian formulas are concise statements that express the Trinitarian nature of the Godhead rather than extended inquiries into its theological meaning. The following are the main instances in which Trinitarian formulas are alluded to or directly presented in the NT.

The event of Jesus' baptism brought about the clearest historical revelation of the Trinity available to us. The Son appeared in His human incarnated existence, the Holy Spirit was present in the form of a dove, and the Father revealed Himself (Matt. 3:16, 17; Mark 1:10, 11; Luke 3:21, 22; cf. 2 Peter 1:17).

The concept of Trinity, namely the idea that the three are one, is not explicitly stated but only assumed. Consequently, these passages cannot be taken as Trinitarian formulas but rather as references to the doctrine of the Trinity. Moreover, the three persons of the divinity are brought together and identified by pointing to some of the specific activities in which each has been involved in the history of salvation. Thus, Peter clearly emphasizes that the believers were "chosen and destined by God the Father and sanctified by the Spirit for obedience to Jesus Christ and for sprinkling with his blood" (1 Peter 1:2). Likewise, Paul closes his second letter to the Corinthians by wishing that "the grace of the Lord Jesus Christ and the love of God and the fellowship of the Holy Spirit be with you all" (2 Cor. 13:14). Still, these two statements only assume the divinity of Spirit and Christ, and the oneness of the three. Not a Trinitarian formula, but rather a reference to the Trinity is present here. The Pauline setting for the divine bestowal of the spiritual gifts to the church (VII. C. 5. e) in his first letter to the believers at Corinth (12:4-6) may refer also to the Trinity: Spirit, Lord, and God refer to the Holy Spirit, the Son, and the Father, respectively, thus expressing the unity of the Trinity in God's salvific action in history. However, the oneness of the Godhead cannot be reduced to a concept of unity of life or redemptive action in history.

The Trinitarian formula seems to be clearly expressed in Jesus' great missionary commission: "Go therefore and make disciples of all nations, baptizing them in the name [onoma] of the Father and of the Son and of the Holy Spirit" (Matt. 28:19). The direct reference to the Father, Son, and Holy Spirit clearly sets forth the threefold plurality of Divine Persons, while the designations of them all as the "name" of God (in singular) clearly sets forth the oneness of the Divine Being. Hence a clear Trinitarian formula, where the threeness and oneness belong together in the Divine Being is expressed.

In conclusion, the NT has not given extensive consideration to the doctrine of the Trinity as a theological locus. On the other hand, there is extensive evidence that the reality of the Trinitarian nature of the one Christian God is a biblical teaching. In Scripture God has revealed His transcendent nature as Trinity, namely three distinct divine Persons who act directly and historically in history and constitute the one divine Trinitarian being.

VIII. Impact of the Doctrine of the Godhead

The biblical doctrine of God affects at least three major domains of Christian thinking: the methodological, soteriological, and ecclesiological areas, and it permeates the entire field of Christian theology. It influences our interpretation of Scripture by determining the way we view some foundational matters that have a decisive role in our process of understanding. Among these matters we find certain disciplinary, procedural, and doctrinal issues. Within the disciplinary realm, the philosophy-theology relation has always deserved special attention. Much of Christian theology has developed under the conviction that philosophy occupies an essential role in setting the intellectual framework that the task of theology requires. Since the Reformation some theologians have challenged this conviction. The biblical doctrine of God requires the reversal of this traditional disciplinary view. If we take the biblical doctrine of God seriously, we cannot replace it with a philosophical teaching about God. Besides, disregard of biblical revelation on God leads to a distorted understanding of Christian doctrines and the capitulation of biblical authority to philosophy and tradition.

Within the procedural area, the Trinitarian Godhead of Scripture functions as the center of theology. The Trinitarian Godhead of Scripture links together the manifold aspects of life, biblical truths, and Christian teachings. As center of life, God is not the whole, but the

One who brings the whole into existence and harmony. Moreover, the biblical doctrine of God calls for a historical interpretation and understanding of Christian teachings and doctrines. Within the doctrinal field, the relational nature of the biblical Godhead grounds the relational nature of human beings which, in turn, influences the ecclesiological and missiological areas.

The biblical doctrine of God also exercises a dominant influence on the practical level, where the experience of salvation takes place. Christian experience or spirituality takes place as God and human beings relate to each other. Both God and human beings are relational by nature. Consequently, biblical spirituality can take place only within the parameters of divine and human relationality. Moreover, the biblical conception of God's historical presence (IV. D) places the salvific relationship of Christian experience not within a divine otherworldly level but within the flow of historical space and time where human beings exist and operate.

Because Christian experience is relational and historical, we must abandon classical and contemporary conceptions according to which the human experience of the salvific event occurs in the eternal "now." When Christian believers assume that the experience of salvation takes place in the otherworldly level of the eternal instant, they become convinced that most aspects of everyday life are irrelevant and therefore excluded from Christian spirituality. As Christian spirituality is viewed as a matter of interiority, individuality, withdrawal from this world, and connection with another reality, it becomes dissociated from everyday life. The fact is that an otherwordly encounter does not involve challenges or require changes in everyday life and culture. One concrete outcome of this conception is the secularization of Christian life. The biblical doctrine of God requires a much different understanding of Christian experience and spirituality. When, following Scripture, we attempt to envision Christian experience and spiritual-

ity within the historical and relational understanding of God and human nature, an inclusive rather than exclusive notion takes place. Encompassing all aspects and dimensions of human life and action, Christian experience becomes all-inclusive and entails revolutionary changes in all aspects of everyday life. Spirituality is no longer the contact with the other side in the eternal instant but the ongoing historical relationship with the God who dwells with His people within historical time and space. This view of Christian spirituality, grounded on the biblical doctrine of God, makes no room for secularization and presents a divinely originated alternative to contemporary secularism.

The biblical doctrine of God also affects the way we conceive the nature of the church. The relational nature of the biblical Godhead suggests a relational interpretation of the nature of the church. Traditional teachings claiming that the church is an institution or sacrament of God's presence in the world become groundless when one accepts the relational nature of the biblical God. A full development of the biblical doctrine of God shows the Trinitarian Godhead involved in mission. The self-appointed mission of the Godhead (IV. B) aims at the salvation of fallen human beings and the establishment of permanent harmony within the created universe. According to biblical revelation, God carries out the various tasks entailed in the mission of salvation within the historical mode of existence of His Creation. Within His master missionary plan God has called the church to play an indispensable role. The missionary calling the Christian church has received from God is not incidental; it is an essential aspect that, permeating everything, gives ultimate direction and purpose to church life and activities. (See Church IV.)

The impact of the doctrine of God on the Christian believer was summarized by Jesus Himself. Praying to His Father, Christ stated that eternal life was for their disciples to "know you, the only true God, and Jesus Christ, whom you have sent" (John 17:3, NIV). The biblical doctrine of God has been called to occupy grounding and central roles in the thinking and life of Christ's disciples.

IX. Historical Overview

From the first the NT revelation about the Father, the Son, and the Holy Spirit inspired a broad range of theological reflection that still goes on unabated. From this wealth of data only a very brief outline of salient points dealing with the understanding of God's nature and activity will be addressed in this section. The succinct survey that ensues is organized following the main historical periods of Christian theology: the patristic, medieval, reformation, and modern periods.

From the very beginning, the Christian interpretation of God was heavily influenced by extrabiblical philosophy. Because the Christian doctrine of God has become a synthesis between philosophical and biblical ideas, we need to briefly sketch the main philosophical trends that have conditioned the formulation of the Christian doctrine of God.

A. Philosophical Antecedents

The intellectual background for the Christian doctrine of God was provided by Greek philosophy, notably the Platonic and Aristotelic systems, together with some Stoic influences. Plato, by way of Neoplatonic reinterpretations of his thought, became a major influence in patristic thought. Aristotelianism played a decisive role in medieval theology. Indeed, until the end of the twentieth century, the methodological conviction that the understanding of Christian theology requires the foundation of extrabiblical philosophies has been broadly accepted.

1. Neoplatonism

As a philosophical trend, Neoplatonism refers to a synchretistic movement with strong religious overtones. It brings together, not always successfully, elements of Platonism, Pythagoreanism, Aristotelianism, and Stoicism. Influential in patristic thought were Philo (c. 20 B.C.-c. A.D. 50), the great Alexandrian Jewish philosopher, and Plutarch (c. A.D. 46-c. 120), representative of middle Platonism. They may be considered as precursors of Neoplatonism, which received systematic formulation in Plotinus (c. A.D. 205-270). These authors embraced Plato's two-world theory, yet modified it in substantial ways. For them the heavenly realm was not merely a world of timeless entities but the transcendent domain of the timeless One. Philo conceived God as timeless, one, transcendent, personal, self-sufficient spaceless, and ineffable, sharing all the perfection of being in an ineffable mode. He considered God so different from the world that a series of intermediary realities belonging to the intelligible world were necessary. God created not only the intelligible world but also our temporal world in which, by means of divine foreknowledge, He acts providentially, allowing for a certain degree of human freedom. Middle Platonism, as expressed by Plutarch, departed from Philo in that he conceived God after Plato's Demiurge, who orders the world only according to the heavenly ideas. Plotinus, sharing the same basic schema, articulated the relation between the One, the intermediary beings, and our world by way of an all-embracing emanative pantheism.

2. Aristotelianism

Aristotle's philosophy simultaneously built on and criticized Plato's system. Aristotle's system is not contradictory to Platonism or Neoplatonism, but a critical outcome of Platonism. Between them are clear differences but also basic similarities. For this reason, in a general sense, Aristotelianism has always been a contributing factor in the development of Greek philosophy even in the Neoplatonic trend noted above. Yet, as an overall systematic approach, Neoplatonism had the upper hand in influencing the patristic and early medieval periods of Christian theology. In a more specific sense Aristotelianism traces its deep influence to the twelfth-century discovery and translation of Aristotle's writings produced in Toledo, Spain, by various Arab and Jewish thinkers. It also developed as Aristotle's works were discussed and explained in Oxford and Paris. This rediscovery of Aristotle's ideas provided grounds for the scholastic synthesis of Christian theology in the medieval period.

Neoplatonism basically agrees with Aristotle on the nature of God. Differences appear in relation to God's activities. Aristotle's view did not make room for divine activity *ad extra*. God does not know the world; He did not create ex nihilo or even organize the world, which is everlasting in its temporal spacial realm. God has no dealings with human history, nor can He produce miracles. The only activity proper to the perfection, self-sufficiency, immutability, and timelessness of God is conceived in analogy to the theoretical contemplative life of the philosopher. The action proper to God is to know Himself. In not requiring an object other than Himself, God's activity is self-sufficient. Because it occurs in timelessness, it is immutable. Because the "goal" of the action is the perfect being that God is, His action is absolutely perfect.

B. Patristic Period

During the patristic period the Christian doctrine of God developed under the working assumption that the Greek Neoplatonic conception of God was, in a broad sense, compatible with biblical revelation. An ever-increasing, though not always uniform, synthesis between Greek philosophy and biblical ideas took place. Inner contradictions in the theological constructions ensued, resulting in an understanding of God cast in the matrix of Greek philosophy rather than biblical thought.

1. Justin Martyr (c. 100-c. 165)

By adopting the Platonic-Aristotelic conception of an eternal, unchangeable, impassible, incorporeal God (*First Apology* 13, 61;

Second Apology 6 [ANF 1:166, 183, 190]), Justin and the apologists set the blueprint for classical theology. Yet Justin also spoke of God in biblical, personal terms which, as they stand in Scripture, are incompatible with the philosophical ideas of eternity, immutability, and impassibility of God that Justin had implicitly adopted. This description of God corresponds to Christ's Father. Since such a being cannot act in history, a mediator is required. Drawing from later Judaism, Stoicism, and Philo, Justin speaks about the divine Logos. This Logos preexisted in God as His reason and is contained in His essence (*Dialogue With Trypho* 128, 129 [ANF 1:264]). By emanation-generation the Logos was born of the Father's will, becoming a person shortly before Creation (*Dialogue With Trypho* 61, 62 [ANF 1:227, 228]). Being Word and first-begotten of God, the Logos was also divine (*First Apology* 63 [ANF 1:184]). The Logos, and not the Father, was incarnated in Jesus Christ (*First Apology* 5; *Second Apology* 10 [ANF 1:164, 191]). The stage for the doctrine of the immanent Trinity is set, together with a certain subordinationism clearly present in the Logos doctrine.

2. Irenaeus (c. 115-c. 202)

Irenaeus approached the doctrine of God from within his apologetical concern against Gnostic heresies. He purposely followed Scripture, while Neoplatonic categories seemed to play little role in his theology. Thus, Irenaeus approached the doctrine of God from the perspective of His works rather than His nature. Two main ideas were central to Irenaeus' view of God: Creation and Trinity. According to Irenaeus, God is Creator of the world ex nihilo (*Against Heresies* 2. 1. 1; 2. 10. 4 [ANF 1:359, 370]). The Trinity moves within the historical realm, where Scripture presents God as working out salvation. Consequently, Irenaeus' conception of the Trinity was economic, for example, engulfing both the inner reality of God in Himself and His acts of salvation in human history. This view, due to its lack of philosophical speculation, was considered naive and was overcome by later theological reflection.

3. Origen (c. 185-c. 254)

At the zenith of the Alexandrian School, Origen's thought represented the first attempt to overcome heresies by way of a systematic approach to theology. Unfortunately Origen developed his approach to theology not on the basis of Scripture alone, as Irenaeus had endeavored, but rather on the basis of Neoplatonic philosophical ideas. These ideas, to a large extent, regulated Origen's conception of God's nature: God is the one, simple, timeless, spaceless, immutable, impassible, invisible, intellectual, personal reality (*On First Principles* 1. 1. 6; 1. 2. 4, 6; 1. 3. 4 [ANF 4:245, 247, 252, 253]).

Origen attempted to express the biblical revelation about the Trinitarian God within the same Neoplatonic philosophical categories. In so doing he moved from the economic-historical level in which Scripture reveals the Godhead to the immanent, timeless, spaceless level corresponding to the nature of God in Himself. Thus the Father alone is the simple and unoriginated cause of everything (*ibid.* 1. 3. 5 [ANF 4:253]). To explain the divine "multiplicity" of hypostases, Origen devised the idea of eternal generation, according to which the Son is timelessly generated by the Father (*ibid.* 1. 2. 4, 6 [ANF 4:247]). The Holy Spirit, though belonging to the unity of the Trinity, belongs to a lower ontological status than the Son. The Father, as source of everything, has the highest ontological rank, even above the Son (*ibid.* 1. 3. 4, 5 [ANF 4:252, 253]). A clear, twofold subordinationism is implicit in Origen's interpretation of the immanent Trinity. Origen conceives the Trinity as eternally active as Creator, benefactor, and provident (*ibid.* 1. 4. 3; Butterworth edition 1973). The Trinity's blessed and ruling power "exercises control of all things" (*ibid.*). God's power does not involve the everlasting existence of temporal creation. However, following basic dualistic Platonic ontology, Origen taught that all things "have always existed in wisdom, by a prefiguration and preformation" (*ibid.*1. 4. 3, 5). This constituted the basis for the doctrine of divine predestination. What has been made by God in Creation is what was already made, and therefore predestined, in God's eternal activity.

4. Trinitarian Heresies

From the second to the fourth centuries A.D. some unsuccessful conceptualizations of the biblical teaching regarding the Godhead were formulated. Dynamic Monarchianism, Modalistic Monarchianism, and Arianism were efforts at understanding the Trinity from the intellectual background provided by Neoplatonism in the tradition of Justin Martyr and Origen.

Dynamic Monarchianism was initiated by Theodotus (c. 190) and more technically developed by Paul of Samosata (second half of the third century). This position was built on Adoptionism, the christological heresy according to which Christ was a mere man upon whom the Spirit descended, anointing Him with divine powers at the time of His baptism, thus "adopting" Him as Son. Consequently, in the being of the eternal God there is no plurality of persons. The idea of an eternal, immanent Trinity is replaced by the idea of God's "dynamic" presence in Christ through the indwelling Spirit. Monarchianism holds that God is not a plurality of Persons but rather one sovereign, eternal being; "dynamic" means that the one God is connected with the man Jesus Christ through impersonal spiritual power.

Modalistic Monarchianism was initiated by the end of the second century by Noetus of Smyrna (c. 200). As with Dynamic Monarchianism, Modalistic Monarchianism also claimed that there is only one God, the Father. If Christ were God, as Christian faith maintained, then He must be identical with the Father. Father and Son are not two different divine persons but, rather, names that refer to the same God involved in different activities at different times. The Spirit plays no role except as another word to designate the Father. In Modalistic Monarchianism, "monarchy" affirms that God is one, namely the Father, while "modalism" states that God the Father is able to adopt a special mode of historical revelation in Jesus Christ the Son. Modalistic Monarchianism is a heresy to the Trinitarian position because it rejects the idea of Trinity, both in the immanent and economic levels.

Sabellian Modalism thought of God as a monad, which expressed itself in three successive historical operations, namely, the Father, the Son, and the Holy Spirit. By including the Holy Spirit and placing the Father at the same level with the other persons, Sabellianism improves Noetus' version of modalism. Yet the Trinity of persons is recognized only as modes of divine self-manifestations and not as belonging to the being of God Himself.

Arianism was originated by Arius (c. 250-336), who approached the understanding of the Immanent Trinity within a conception of God closer to Aristotelianism than Platonism and Neoplatonism. Even though Arianism shared Origen's conception of God as immutable, timeless, and simple, it rejected the idea of emanation implicit in his concept of eternal generation of the Son. Precisely because of God the Father's simplicity and immutability, Arius was convinced that His essence is not communicable through emanation or generation. On the other hand, God's timeless transcendence required a mediator who could execute God's purposes in space and time. Thus, Arius replaced Origen's idea of an eternal generation with the idea of creation out of nothing, a creation described as "before" and "outside" time, yet "there was a time when he [the Son] was not" (O'Carroll 26). The Son is, therefore, the most exalted creature, not to be compared with the rest of Creation, and Himself Creator of the world. The Holy Spirit is created by the Son and subordinate to him. Arianism, then, is the most severe distortion of the Trinitarian concept of God, bringing Monarchianism and Subordinationism to their extreme expression.

5. Council of Nicea (325)

The first ecumenical council met in Nicea to address the threat presented by Arianism, which it decisively condemned. The council affirmed the divinity of the Son, pronounced the doctrine of the eternal generation of the Son—the Son is "born of the Father, that is of the substance of the Father" and set forth the much-discussed consubstantiality (homoousios) of Father and Son. Finally, it affirmed the Holy Spirit as an afterthought by saying "And [we believe] in the Holy Spirit." In 381 the second Ecumenical Council met in Constantinople and proclaimed what is known as the Nicene-Constantinopolitan Creed, which enlarged Nicea's statement by explicitly affirming the divinity of the Holy Spirit.

6. Augustine (354-430)

In Augustine's works the patristic synthesis of Neoplatonism and Scripture reaches its most articulated and influential formulation. According to Augustine God is timeless, simple, immutable, self-sufficient, impassible, omniscient, and omnipotent (Confessions 7. 11; 12. 15; 11. 11; 11. 13; 13. 16 [NPNF-1 1:110, 167, 180, 196]; On the Holy Trinity 1. 1. 3; 5. 2. 3 [NPNF-1 3:18, 88]; The City of God 11. 10; 22. 1 [NPNF-1 2:210, 479]). On this basis, Augustine brought the doctrine of the Trinity to its classical theological expression in his book On the Holy Trinity. Unlike the Cappadocian Fathers, Augustine started with the conception of the oneness of God, and from there he moved to His threeness. The oneness of God was conceived by Augustine in relation to the consubstantiality (identity of substance) of the persons. God's simple, timeless essence is not only the ultimate ground for His ontological oneness, but it also replaces the Father as the fountainhead of the Trinity, thus becoming the source from which the persons and their unity are deduced.

Augustine is unhappy with the word "persons," probably because it suggests the idea of separate individuals. He believes that the term is used "not in order to give a complete explanation by means of it, but in order that we might not be obliged to remain silent" (*On the Holy Trinity* 5. 9 [NPNF-1 3:92]). Augustine's theory is that the persons are unchangeable, original, subsistent relations. He takes the ideas of eternal generation and procession and uses them to define the relations. Persons, thus, are reduced to the relations of begetting, being begotten, and proceeding. Within this framework and advocating the procession of the Holy Spirit from the Father and the Son (*Filioque*), Augustine advances his idea that the Holy Spirit, as subsistent person, is the mutual love of Father and Son, the consubstantial bond that unites them. There are reasons to wonder whether this view does justice to the biblical revelation about three different and independent subjects. The *Deo uno* seems to take over the *Deo trino*. Trinity is replaced by monarchy.

The timelessness of God's simple essence gives rise to the interpretation of God's foreknowledge-predestination-providence as the divine eternal sovereign causation of multiplicity, temporal creation, and history (see *The City of God* 22. 2 [NPNF-1 2:480]). The Platonic duplication of eternity in time is not produced by a Demiurge but rather by God who is conceived as creating both the world of ideas and their duplication in time *(ibid.)*.

7. The Athanasian Creed (c. 430-500)

The Athanasian Creed, also known as Quicunque, is considered to be the definitive expression of Catholic belief in the Trinity. Drawn up by an unknown author, this creed shows the influence of Augustine's theology of the Trinity. It explicitly expresses the simultaneous plurality and oneness of God: "The Father is God, the Son is God, (and) the Holy Spirit is God; and nevertheless there are not three gods, but there is one God" (Denzinger 15). It declares the divinity of persons not only by explicitly calling each one God and Lord but also by adjudicating to each one, respectively, the divine qualities of uncreatedness,

immensity, eternity, and omnipotence. It clearly distinguishes the three different persons, who are not to be confused (against Sabellianism). Unfortunately a subtle form of Monarchianism and ontological subordinationism is preserved when the differences of the persons are explained metaphysically by recourse to the ideas of generation and procession. Thus the Father is not begotten, while the Son is begotten from the Father, and the Holy Spirit proceeds from the Father and the Son (an expression of *Filioque*). The oneness of the Trinity is explained on the basis of its divine substance or nature: "The divine nature of the Father and of the Son and of the Holy Spirit is one" (Denzinger 39).

C. Medieval Period

Theological reflection during the Middle Ages articulated in a systematic way the logical consequences of the Augustinian synthesis. Unlike Augustine, however, Thomas Aquinas (1225-1274), the most prominent representative of scholastic theology, developed his theology on an Aristotelic philosophical foundation.

Thomas Aquinas did not formulate a new conception of God, but rather, building on Augustine, he brought the classical doctrine of God to a level of technical specificity and inner coherence not attained by former expositors. His system of thought built on his own Christian interpretation of Aristotle. Aquinas dealt first with the doctrine of God who is described as timeless, one, simple, immutable, perfect, and good (*Summa Theologica* 1a. 20. 4; 1a. 11. 3; 1a. 3. 6, 7; 1a. 9. 1; 1a. 4. 1; 1a. 6. 1). Once the doctrine of God is completed, the doctrine of the Trinity is brought in for lengthy discussion (*ibid.* 1a. 27-43). The one and simple essence or substance of God is understood in analogy to the workings and characteristics of the human intellect; more precisely, in the likeness of the Aristotelian interpretation of the intellect. Consequently, the persons in the Godhead refer not to independent centers of knowledge and activity as the biblical record declares. That would imply Tritheism. Persons are rather real distinctions within the simple absolute divine essence. The distinctions, which determine the persons as subsistent within the essence, are relations within the essence, and the relations are conceived as originating from the generation of the Son and procession of the Holy Spirit. Thomas integrates the classical teaching on the eternal generation and procession of the Spirit as necessary "results" of God's intellect (the Father) that, in expressing itself, produces in itself a Word (the Son). Moreover, God is not only knowing but also simultaneously loving. Love arises from the two divine persons, Father and Son, in an act that is described as unitive movement, a kind of return. That movement issuing from both the Father and the Son precipitates an eruption within themselves, namely the Holy Spirit, that becomes as real as they. The Holy Spirit is the act in which the love that issues from and unites the Father and the Son is consummated. Thus a threefold distinction of mutual opposition (paternity, filiation, spiration-procession) is established within the simple essence of God as identical with it. These subsistent relations, understood as opposition within the simple essence of God, are known as hypostases or persons. The relations, however, are identical with the simple essence. Thus, in the inner structure of the simple substance a certain relationality is revealed.

Thomas conceives foreknowledge, predestination, and providence as grounded in God's own timeless being (*ibid.,* 1a. 14. 13; 1a. 19. 3, 4; 1a. 22), thus continuing the Augustinian tradition. Aquinas' views on God are attractive and coherent within the philosophical system he chose to follow. However, since Aquinas' approach does not flow from Scripture, he is unable to present the inner coherence of the biblical view of God.

D. The Reformation

The theological concern of the Protestant Reformation centered on soteriological and ecclesiological issues. This emphasis may explain why the doctrine of God was not considered for revision. In general terms Protestantism reaffirmed the classical approach to God while at the same time intensifying or modifying some emphases. Additionally, the philosophical foundation for theology was not specifically addressed. Luther's and Calvin's theologies used biblical data and language extensively, thus giving the impression of being based only on Scripture. However, in their writings the Neoplatonic, Augustinian, and Ockamist influences are at work, in an implicit rather than explicit manner.

1. Martin Luther (1483-1546)

Luther's theology of God is based on God's revelation in Jesus Christ. From this basic starting point he draws a distinction between the revealed God and the hidden God. The revealed God is the revelation of God in Jesus Christ, in whom God reveals Himself as He really is, a God of love and justification. This is the work proper to God. Broadly speaking, the revealed God belongs to the historical level of immanence. The hidden God is the naked God beyond revelation (*Luther's Works* 5:44-46). According to Brunner, Luther in this level includes the wrath, mystery, and absolute power of God as well as our rational and legal knowledge of Him. Regarding the Trinity, Luther affirmed the traditional dogma. On the issue of God's actions, he intensified the Augustinian concepts of God's sovereignty, foreknowledge, and predestination, which would also be emphasized by Calvin. Luther's doctrine of God, however, falls short of faithfully including all biblical data on God.

2. John Calvin (1509-1564)

Calvin approached theology in a systematic way, following the tradition of Augustine. For him God is timeless, simple, impassible, immutable, and self-existent (*Institutes* 3. 21. 5; 1. 2. 2; 1. 13. 2; 1. 17. 13; 1. 18. 3; 3. 2. 6). Calvin reaffirmed the classical Augustinian position on the Trinity (*ibid.* 1. 13). Regarding the actions of God, Calvin even intensified the Augustinian view. On the basis of God's timelessness and immutability, foreknowledge and predestination were equated. Thus the sovereignty of God became the deployment of His eternal will for creation and humanity. Calvin's doctrine of God also falls short of faithfully including and integrating all biblical data on God.

3. Anabaptism

Also known as the Radical Reformation, Anabaptism developed in the sixteenth century as a pluralistic movement with a pietistic, practical, and biblical orientation. Because of the Anabaptist emphasis on practical Christian experience, theological issues were dealt with in relation to their practical application. With few exceptions, Anabaptists were orthodox in doctrine, accepting Nicene trinitarianism. They did not develop a speculative or biblical understanding of the Godhead but rather reaffirmed traditional teaching as the clarification of practical issues required. The trinitarian doctrine of God was important to them as a framework for ethical and communal life. Occasionally, however, their references to traditional doctrine may be read as a departure from it, as when Menno Simons refers to the Trinitarian persons not as modes or relations but rather as "three, true, divine beings" who "in deity, will, power, and works" are one *(Confession of the Triune God)*. Within this practical context, it is not surprising to find the Holy Spirit receiving a greater emphasis than in classical theology. Practical concerns tend to lean more on the work of the economic than on the nature of the immanent Trinity.

4. Jacobus Arminius (1560-1609)

Arminius formulated his approach to Protestant theology within an explicit philosophical framework. Following Aristotelic-Thomistic intellectualism, Arminius strongly agreed with the traditional view of God as timeless, simple, impassible, and immutable (Arminius 1:436-442; 2:34, 35). Arminius affirmed that God's foreknowledge of future free contingent human actions was caused by the future will and action

of human beings (3:66, 67; 3:482, 483). Specifically, a "middle or intermediate [kind of] knowledge ought to intervene in things that depend on the liberty of created *[arbitrii]* choice or pleasure" (2:39). Arminius felt uncomfortable with the idea of absolute predestination, according to which damnation and salvation are determined by God's immutable timeless decree "without any regard whatever to righteousness or sin, to obedience or disobedience" (1:212; cf. 1:211-247). Consequently, Arminius thought that salvation is the result of God's absolute decree, "in which he decreed to receive into favor *those who repent and believe"* (247). Arminius' theology moves within a philosophical rather than biblical matrix.

E. The Modern Period

The rise of the modern antimetaphysical trend developed since the Enlightenment has significantly influenced Christian theology. New philosophical trends became increasingly critical of the Platonic-Aristotelic tradition on the basis of which the classical understanding of God and theology had been cast. On the basis of Kantian, Hegelian, and Whiteheadian thought new theological interpretations were produced by liberal, avant garde theologians. In North America Whiteheadian Process Philosophy is becoming influential in the thinking of an increasing number of liberal as well as some conservative theologians. At the same time, the old classical understanding of God still continues.

1. Friedrich Schleiermacher (1768-1834)

Schleiermacher is considered the father of liberal theology because he devised a new ground on which Christian theology should build its doctrines. Theology, according to Schleiermacher, is not grounded in cognitive revelation, reason, or ethics, but in an inner religious experience identified as the feeling of absolute dependence on God. Since God is timeless, immutable, and simple (*Christian Faith* §52, §56), there is no place for distinctions within Him. Consequently, Schleiermacher dismissed the doctrine of the Trinity as second-order language that does not speak about the being of God in Himself. According to him the doctrine of the Trinity is inconceivable and contradicts divine simplicity; it is a theoretical construct produced by the speculative imagination of philosophy (§170-172).

2. Karl Barth (1886-1968)

According to Barth, God is one simple, timeless essence whose content is lordship or sovereignty. His personhood is one and identical with His essence. However, Barth also manages to believe in a Trinitarian God. Thus he reverses Schleiermacher's rejection of the classical doctrine of the Trinity, not only by adopting and developing it, but also by making it the structure of his entire *Dogmatics*. Barth follows Augustine's view that "persons" is a mere convention of speech that we are forced to use not to remain silent. The three persons are modes of existence of this one essence, required by the fact of revelation. In order to avoid tritheism, the modern idea of independent personality is not to be associated with them. In short, Barth's understanding of God and the Trinity is very close to that of Aquinas. The main differences between Barth and Aquinas are Barth's equation of God's simplicity with His sovereignty and the replacement of Aquinas' intellectualistic conception of the Trinity by analysis of the logic of revelation in Jesus Christ.

3. Alfred Whitehead (1861-1947)

Whitehead develops a metaphysical system whose capping piece is God. From a Platonic framework Whitehead builds his system under the influence of British Empiricism—John Locke (1632-1704) and David Hume (1711-1776). According to Whitehead, God is an entity that, like any other, must conform to the same metaphysical principles valid for the interpretation of the world. By applying the metaphysical principles of worldly entities to God, Whitehead arrives at the conclusion that God's

nature is dipolar. The primordial pole in God's nature is timeless, unlimited, conceptual, free, complete, potential, actually deficient, unconscious (Whitehead 521, 524). The consequent pole in God's nature is temporal, determined, incomplete, fully actual, and conscious (524). "The consequent nature of God is the fulfillment of his experience [knowledge] by his reception of the multiple freedom of actuality [the world process] into the harmony of his own actualization. It is God as really actual, completing the deficiency of his mere conceptual actuality [his primordial pole]" (530). This system allows God's timeless primordial pole to act only by means of "persuasion" or "lure" (522). God's temporal consequent nature knows and experiences the world, thereby completing himself and reaching full reality (actuality). According to Whitehead's system, God does not create the world; He saves it (526). God "saves the world as it passes into the immediacy of His own life." In this consists the "divine judgment" of the world (525).

"What is done in the world is transformed into a reality in heaven, and the reality in heaven passes back into the world. By reason of this reciprocal relation, the love in the world passes into the love in heaven, and floods back again into the world. In this sense, God is the great companion—the fellow-sufferer who understands" (532).

God and the world are, therefore, mutually interdependent. Even though Whitehead's criticism of classical thought is well taken, his dipolar view of God's nature has more in common with classical than with biblical thought.

4. Wolfhart Pannenberg (b. 1928)

Pannenberg is a leading neoclassical theologian writing at the end of the twentieth century. His God is infinite, timeless, omnipotent, and omnipresent (Pannenberg 1:397-422). The three divine persons are also described as three forms or modes of God's existence. Spirit, as essence of God, is to be understood not as intellect *(nous)* but rather as an impersonal force of life, further described in analogy to

Michael Faraday's idea of universal field. Knowledge about the three persons of the deity—their names and their distinctions—is derived from the biblical testimony that deals with the economic Trinity. The relationship between the immanent and economic Trinity is explained in connection with Pannenberg's understanding of God's action, which cannot involve the setting or the achievement of goals that would impinge on God's eternal self-sufficiency (384-396). God's action cannot be attributed to the immanent Trinity but rather to the immanent Trinity *ad extra,* that is, in relation to the world. God's activity *ad extra* is understood by Pannenberg as the self-actualization of the eternal God in time or, in other words, the temporal duplication of God's eternal life. Departing from Barth, however, Pannenberg does not apply the idea of eternal repetition to the duplication of persons in the immanent Trinity itself, but rather to the duplication of the eternal God the Father in space and time (the Son and the Spirit).

5. The "Open View" of God

The "open" designation seems to reflect the fact that this view calls for the openness of the eternal transcendent God of classical theology to the limitations and risks of the temporal world. The open view of God, also designated as "free-will theism," has developed as a direct result of Whitehead's influence on American Protestantism. This trend has gained acceptance not only among liberal Protestant theologians such as John B. Cobb, Jr. (b. 1925), but also among conservative evangelical theologians such as Clark Pinnock (b. 1937). The open view uses Whiteheadian understandings to replace the Platonic-Aristotelian framework of classical theology. Whitehead's views, consequently, are incorporated into theology only after suffering various degrees of reinterpretation and adaptation to Christian thinking. The more conservative proponents of the open view are forthright in their criticism of some aspects of Whitehead's system, such as the idea that God is not the absolute Creator and that God's way of acting in the world is limited to a persuasive mode, leaving no room for occasional coercive interventions (Hasker 139, 140). In spite of these criticisms, the open view of God implicitly assumes a modified version of God's dipolar nature. God is, at the same time, timeless and temporal. Unlike the timeless God of classical theism, the God of "free-will theism" is able to enter into direct relationships with His creatures within the past, present, and future sequence of time. However, by adopting the Whiteheadian, rather than biblical, view of divine knowledge, the open view limits God's knowledge to the past and present dimensions of time. In other words, the open view of God makes no room for divine foreknowledge of the free actions of human beings (Pinnock 124; Hasker 187). This conviction renders biblical prophecy uncertain. Moreover, divine providence cannot lead us to make the best long-term choice simply because God does not know the end from the beginning (Basinger 163).

F. Seventh-day Adventists

Seventh-day Adventists have limited themselves to dogmatic and theological statements, staying away from a systematic development of the Doctrine of God and the Trinity. Most theological statements have been produced within the context of studies about Christology, atonement, and redemption. In a very real sense, Adventist emphasis on Scriptures as the sole source of data for executing theology has given theological reflection on God a new and revolutionary start. Systematically distrustful and critical of traditional theological positions, Adventists were determined to build doctrines on the basis of Scripture alone. The difficulties implicit in this fresh approach may account for the scant number of Adventist statements on the doctrine of God. Among Adventists, developmental theological statements about the doctrine of the Trinity are mainly of three kinds: those that involved temporal subordinationism, those in which the classical interpretation of the doctrine on the Trinity is rejected, and those that affirm the Trinity as the biblical conception of the Christian God. Following a description of these, a brief reference to contemporary trends will be made.

1. Temporal Subordinationism

As early as 1854 J. M. Stephenson, writing on the atonement, clearly argued in favor of subordinationism, according to which Christ would have been temporally generated by the Father, that is, begotten by the Father (Stephenson 126). Being generated, Christ was divine, yet not eternal (*ibid.* 128); Stephenson accepted a semi-Arian Christology (cf. "Christology," *SDA Encyclopedia* 10:352-354). Other pioneers endorsing similar views were James White (1821-1881), Joseph Bates (1792-1872), Uriah Smith (1832-1903), J. H. Waggoner (1820-1889), E. J. Waggoner (1855-1916), and W. W. Prescott (1855-1944). Much should not be made of this erroneous teaching, however, since both E. J. Waggoner and Uriah Smith considered it compatible with, and not detracting from, the full divinity of Jesus as the "fulness of the Godhead bodily" (Col. 2:9, KJV; see also E. J. Waggoner 44; Smith 17).

2. Rejection of the Classical Doctrine

The rejection of the classical theological interpretation of the doctrine of the Trinity by some Seventh-day Adventist authors does not necessarily entail a rejection of the biblical revelation about the Trinity, because they reject the interpretation, not the facts themselves. The classical doctrine is frequently rejected on the basis of very weak arguments, such as that the word "Trinity" is not biblical or that the doctrine is against our God-given sense and reason. Sometimes the doctrine of the Trinity is rejected on the basis of wrong arguments, such as, for instance, that it teaches that the Holy Spirit is a person rather than an impersonal influence. However, more serious theological reasons have been submitted for rejecting the classical doctrine on the Trinity. Thus, some Adventist pioneers understood

that the classical interpretation of the immanent Trinity was incompatible with the economic Trinity as presented in Scriptures (Frisbie, in RH Mar. 12, 1857). Others clearly perceived that, should such an interpretation be accepted as correct, the biblical teachings about the historical actions of the Trinity would need to be radically reinterpreted, notably the teaching about the divine reality of Christ's atonement on the cross. James White found that the emphasis placed by the classical doctrine of the Trinity on the oneness of the immanent Trinity involved a lack of clarity regarding the distinctions among divine persons (*Day-Star,* Jan. 24, 1846) Loughborough went so far as to say that God is one person rather than three (RH Nov. 5, 1861), thus suggesting that the Father and the Son are the same person (Canright, in RH June 18, 1867; Bates 204, 205). Such a confusion of persons was correctly evaluated as involving the identification of Christ with the eternal God (J. White, in RH June 6, 1871), thus diminishing the divine status (J. White, in RH Nov. 29, 1877) of the historical Jesus Christ and His atonement (Stephenson 151; Hull, in RH Nov. 10 and Nov. 17, 1859; J. H. Waggoner 174). On the other hand, since early Adventists did not differentiate between biblical facts and their classical interpretation as conditioned by Greek, philosophical ideas, an antitrinitarian sentiment was pervasive during the first decades of Adventist history.

3. Affirmation of the Biblical Trinity

In spite of early temporal subordinationism, the tendency to think about the Holy Spirit in impersonal terms (Smith 10), and a strong critical stance against the classical doctrine of the Trinity, most Adventist thinkers have believed in the biblically revealed teaching that the Christian God is not circumscribed to the Person of the Father in heaven, but also includes the historical Jesus Christ and the Holy Spirit as divine Persons. The truth of the full divinity of Christ was specially emphasized by E. J. Waggoner in 1888. In 1892 the doctrine of the

Trinity was set forth explicitly when the Pacific Press reprinted Samuel T. Spear's article on the Trinity. Since Spear was not an Adventist, it is not surprising to find in his article a strong emphasis on the *Deo uno* of tradition and a remnant of ontological subordinationism regarding the person of the Son. With increasing levels of precision the Seventh-day Adventist Church affirmed the doctrine of the Trinity, first in the "unofficial" 1872 statement penned by Uriah Smith, and in the 1931 and 1980 official statements of belief. Ellen White's 1898 statement that "in Christ is life, original, unborrowed, underived" (DA 530) constituted the starting point both for the affirmation of the Trinity as an authentic, biblical teaching (Dederen 5, 12), and for a distinctive way of understanding it as a doctrine. Ellen White's statement dismissed not only the basic error included in both early Adventist Christology and doctrine of God, namely, the temporal subordinationism of the preexistent Christ, but it also signaled the necessary departure from the classical doctrine (Dederen 13), which involved the eternal, ontological subordination of the Son. In God's eternal being there is no eternal generation, and consequently, no eternal procession of the Spirit. The biblical concepts on the generation of the Son and the procession of the Holy Spirit must be understood as belonging to the historical personal acts of the Trinity in the work of Creation and redemption. In the being of God is an essential coprimordiality of three coequal, coeternal, nonoriginated persons. Moreover, Adventism conceives the idea of persons in its biblical sense, as referring to three individual centers of intelligence and action (Dederen 15). Finally, having departed from the philosophical conception of God as timeless and having embraced the historical conception of God as presented in the Bible, Adventists envisage the relation between the immanent and economic Trinity as one of identity rather than correspondence. The works of salvation are produced in time and history by the immanent Trinity (Guy 13) by way of its different Persons, conceived as centers of consciousness and action. Consequently, the indivisibility of God's works in history is not conceived by Adventists as being determined by the oneness of essence—as taught in the Augustinian classical tradition—but rather by the oneness of the historical task of redemption (Dederen 20). The danger of Tritheism involved in this position becomes real when the oneness of God is reduced to a mere unity conceived in analogy to a human society or a fellowship of action. Beyond such a unity of action, however, it is necessary to envision God as the one single reality which, in the very acts by which He reveals Himself directly in history, transcends the limits of our human reason (Prescott 17). In no way could human minds achieve what the classical doctrine about the Trinity claims to perceive, namely, the description of the inner structure of God's being. Together with the entire Creation, we must accept God's oneness by faith (James 2:19). Ellen White wrote: "The revelation of Himself that God has given in His word is for our study. This we may seek to understand. But beyond this we are not to penetrate. The highest intellect may tax itself until it is wearied out in conjectures regarding the nature of God, but the effort will be fruitless. This problem has not been given us to solve. No human mind can comprehend God. None are to indulge in speculation regarding His nature. Here silence is eloquence. The Omniscient One is above discussion" (MH 429).

4. Contemporary Trends

Generally speaking, contemporary Adventists have continued to center their theological interests in soteriological and eschatological matters. For this reason the technical discussion of the doctrine of God has not become an issue. However, while dealing with other related theological issues, such as atonement, justification, sanctification, and eschatology, a growing inclination to overemphasize the love, goodness, and mercy of God to the detriment of His justice and wrath be perceived in some authors (e.g., Provon-

sha 49). Some discussion has been initiated supporting the open view of God (Rice 11-58; see IX. E. 5).

X. Ellen G. White Comments

A. Speculative Study of God

"One of the greatest evils that attends the quest for knowledge, the investigations of science, is the disposition to exalt human reasoning above its true value and its proper sphere. Many attempt to judge the Creator and His works by their own imperfect knowledge of science. They endeavor to determine the nature and attributes and prerogatives of God, and indulge in speculative theories concerning the Infinite One. Those who engage in this line of study are treading upon forbidden ground. Their research will yield no valuable results and can be pursued only at the peril of the soul" (MH 427).

B. General Revelation

"The beauties of nature are an expression of the love of God for human intelligences, and in the Garden of Eden the existence of God was demonstrated in the objects of nature that surrounded our first parents. Every tree planted in the Garden spoke to them, saying that the invisible things of God were clearly seen, being understood by the things which were made, even His eternal power and Godhead" (UL 198).

"But while it is true that in the beginning God could be discerned in nature, it does not follow that after the Fall a perfect knowledge of God was revealed in the natural world to Adam and his posterity. Nature could convey her lessons to man in his innocence. But transgression brought a blight upon the earth and intervened between nature and nature's God. Had Adam and Eve never disobeyed their Creator, had they remained in the path of perfect rectitude, they would have continued to learn of God through His works.

But when they listened to the tempter and sinned against God, the light of the garments of heavenly innocence departed from them. Deprived of the heavenly light, they could no longer discern the character of God in the works of His hand" (8T 255, 256).

"The Gentiles are to be judged according to the light that is given them, according to the impressions they had received of their Creator in nature. They have reasoning powers, and can distinguish God in His created works. God speaks to all men through His providence in nature. He makes known to all that He is the living God. The Gentiles could reason that the things that are made could not have fallen into exact order, and worked out a designed purpose, without a God who has originated all. They could reason from cause to effect, that it must be that there was a first cause, an intelligent agent, that could be no other than the Eternal God. The light of God in nature is shining continually into the darkness of heathenism, but many who see this light do not glorify the Lord as God. They do not permit reason to lead them to acknowledge their Creator. They refuse the Lord, and set up senseless idols to adore. They make images which represent God and worship His created works as a partial acknowledgment of Him, but they dishonor Him in their hearts" (ST Aug. 12, 1889).

C. The Reality of God

1. God's Existence

"The existence and power of God, the truth of His Word, are facts that even Satan and his hosts cannot at heart deny" (FLB 90).

"Faith familiarizes the soul with the existence and presence of God, and, living with an eye single to the glory of God, more and more we discern the beauty of His character, the excellence of His grace" (1SM 335).

"Christ and the apostles taught clearly the truth of the existence of a personal God" (8T 266). "The existence of a personal God, the unity of Christ with His Father, lies at the foundation of all true science" (UL 316).

"It is faith that familiarizes the soul with the existence and presence of God; and when we live with an eye single to His glory, we discern more and more the beauty of His character" (RH Jan. 24, 1888).

2. God as Mystery

"Let human beings consider that by all their searching they can never interpret God. When the redeemed shall be pure and clean to come into His presence, they will understand that all that has reference to the eternal God, the unapproachable God, cannot be represented in figures. It is safe to contemplate God, the great and wonderful God, and Jesus Christ, the express image of God. God gave His only begotten Son to our world, that we might through His righteous character behold the character of God" (18MR 222).

"If it were possible for us to attain to a full understanding of God and His word, there would be for us no further discovery of truth, no greater knowledge, no further development. God would cease to be supreme, and man would cease to advance. Thank God, it is not so. Since God is infinite, and in Him are all the treasures of wisdom, we may to all eternity be ever searching, ever learning, yet never exhaust the riches of His wisdom, His goodness, or His power" (Ed 172).

"The great condescension on the part of God is a mystery that is beyond our fathoming. The greatness of the plan cannot be fully comprehended, nor could infinite Wisdom devise a plan that would surpass it" (RH Oct. 22, 1895).

"In speaking of His pre-existence, Christ carries the mind back through dateless ages. He assures us that there never was a time when He was not in close fellowship with the eternal God. He to whose voice the Jews were then listening had been with God as one brought up with Him" (ST Aug. 29, 1900).

D. Divine Attributes

1. God's Eternity

"In the word, God is spoken of as 'the everlasting God.' This name embraces past, present, and future. God is from everlasting to everlasting. He is the Eternal One" (8T 270; see below under predestination).

2. God's Immutability

"From beginning to end, God's requirements set forth His eternal truth. His law is the test of character. His covenant with man declares the immutability of His counsel. God is truth. He declares that He will not alter the thing that has gone out of His mouth" (19MR 182).

"'Till heaven and earth pass,' said Jesus, 'one jot or one tittle shall in nowise pass from the law, till all be fulfilled.' The sun shining in the heavens, the solid earth upon which you dwell, are God's witnesses that His law is changeless and eternal. Though they may pass away, the divine precepts shall endure. 'It is easier for heaven and earth to pass, than one tittle of the law to fail.' Luke 16:17. The system of types that pointed to Jesus as the Lamb of God was to be abolished at His death; but the precepts of the Decalogue are as immutable as the throne of God" (DA 308).

"There is no such thing as weakening or strengthening the law of Jehovah. As it has always been, so it is. It can not be repealed or changed in one principle. It is eternal, immutable as God Himself" (ST Mar. 20, 1901).

3. God's Love and Wrath

"In the councils of heaven the Lord planned to reshape the broken, perverted characters of man, and to restore to them the moral image of God. This work is termed the mystery of godliness. Christ, the only-begotten of the Father, assumed human nature, came in the likeness of sinful flesh to condemn sin in the flesh. He came to testify to the unchangeable character of the law of God that had been impeached by Satan. Not one jot or tittle of it could be changed to meet man in his fallen condition. Christ lived the law in humanity, in order that every mouth might be stopped, and that Satan might be proved an accuser and a liar. Christ revealed to the world the character of God as full of mercy, compassion, and inexpressible love" (*ibid.* July 2, 1896).

"Christ came to reveal God to the world in His true character, as a God of love, full of mercy, tenderness, and compassion. The thick darkness with which Satan had endeavored to surround the throne of Deity was swept away, and the Father was again manifested to men as the Light of Life" (SW Apr. 28, 1908).

"The law of God, from its very nature, is unchangeable. It is a revelation of the will and the character of its Author. God is love, and His law is love. Its two great principles are love to God and love to man" (GC 467).

"Then those who pierced Him will call on the rocks and mountains to fall on them and hide them from the face of Him that sitteth on the throne and from the wrath of the Lamb, for the great day of His wrath has come, and who shall be able to stand? 'The wrath of the Lamb'—One who ever showed Himself full of infinite tenderness, patience, and long-suffering, who having given Himself up as the sacrificial victim, was led as a Lamb to the slaughter to save sinners from the doom now falling upon them because they would not allow Him to take away their guilt" (21MR 350).

"That Lamb whose wrath will be so terrible to the scorners of His grace will be grace and righteousness and love and blessing to all who have received Him. The pillar of cloud that was dark with terror and avenging wrath to the Egyptians, was to the people of God a pillar of fire for brightness. So will it be to the Lord's people in these last days. The light and glory of God to His commandment-keeping people are darkness to the unbelieving. They see that it is a fearful thing to fall into the hands of the living God. The arm, long stretched, strong to save all who come unto Him, is strong to execute His judgment upon all who would not come unto Him that they might have life" (TMK 356).

"Riches, power, genius, eloquence, pride, perverted reason, and passion, are enlisted as Satan's agents in doing his work in making the broad road attractive, strewing it with tempting flowers. But every word they have spoken against the world's Redeemer will be reflected back upon them, and will one day burn into their guilty souls like molten lead. They will be overwhelmed with terror and shame as they behold the exalted one coming in the clouds of heaven with power and great glory. Then shall the bold defier, who lifted himself up against the Son of God, see himself in the true blackness of his character. The sight of the inexpressible glory of the Son of God will be intensely painful to those whose characters are stained with sin. The pure light and glory emanating from Christ will awaken remorse, shame, and terror. They will send forth wails of anguish to the rocks and mountains, 'Fall on us, and hide us from the face of him who sitteth on the throne, and from the wrath of the Lamb; for the great day of his wrath is come, and who shall be able to stand?'" (RH Apr. 1, 1875).

"God is slow to anger. He gave the wicked nations a time of probation that they might become acquainted with Him and His character. According to the light given was their condemnation for refusing to receive the light and choosing their own ways rather than God's ways. God gave the reason why He did not at once dispossess the Canaanites. The iniquity of the Amorites was not full. Through their iniquity they were gradually bringing themselves to the point where God's forbearance could no longer be exercised and they would be exterminated. Until the point was reached and their iniquity was full, the vengeance of God would be delayed. All nations had a period of probation. Those who made void God's law would advance from one degree of wickedness to another. Children would inherit the rebellious spirit of their parents and do worse than their fathers before them until God's wrath would fall upon them. The punishment was not less because deferred" (2BC 1005).

"The Sun of Righteousness shall arise upon those who have kept the commandments of God. Those who think that they can set their will against God's will are in the greatest danger. Those who wish to be covered in the day of God's anger must be true to God now" (ST June 2, 1890).

4. Transcendence

" 'Not that any man hath seen the Father, save he which is of God, he hath seen the Father. Verily, verily, I say unto you, He that believeth on me hath everlasting life.' This is the absolute Godhead. The mightiest created intellect cannot comprehend Him; words from the most eloquent tongue fail to describe Him. Silence is eloquence (7BC 914). 'The secret things belong unto the Lord our God: but those things which are revealed belong unto us and to our children forever' (Deut. 29:29). The revelation of Himself that God has given in His word is for our study. This we may seek to understand. But beyond this we are not to penetrate. The highest intellect may tax itself until it is wearied out in conjectures regarding the nature of God, but the effort will be fruitless. This problem has not been given us to solve. No human mind can comprehend God. None are to indulge in speculation regarding His nature. Here silence is eloquence. The Omniscient One is above discussion. Even the angels were not permitted to share the counsels between the Father and the Son when the plan of salvation was laid. And human beings are not to intrude into the secrets of the Most High. We are as ignorant of God as little children; but, as little children, we may love and obey Him" (MH 429).

E. Divine Activities

1. Predestination

"Wonderful possibilities are provided for every one who has faith in Christ. No walls are built to keep any living soul from salvation. The predestination, or election, of which God speaks includes all who will accept Christ as a personal Saviour, who will return to their loyalty, to perfect obedience to all God's commandments. This is the effectual salvation of a peculiar people, chosen by God from among men. All who are willing to be saved by Christ are the elect of God. It is the obedient who are predestinated from the foundation of the world. 'To as many as received him, to them he gave power to become the sons of God,' even to as many as believed on him" (GH June 11, 1902).

"But known unto God are all His works, and from eternal ages the covenant of grace (unmerited favor) existed in the mind of God. It is called the everlasting covenant; for the plan of salvation was not conceived after the fall of man, but it was that which was 'kept in silence through times eternal, but now is manifested, and by the Scriptures of the prophets, according to the commandment of the eternal God, is made known unto all the nations unto obedience of faith' (Rom. 16: 25, 26, ARV)" (ST Dec. 15, 1914).

2. Creation

"In the work of creation Christ was with God. He was one with God, equal with Him. . . . He alone, the Creator of man, could be his Saviour" (TMK 18).

"God designs that the Sabbath shall direct the minds of men to the contemplation of His created works. Nature speaks to their senses, declaring that there is a living God, the Creator, the Supreme Ruler of all" (PP 48).

"I was shown that the law of God would stand fast forever, and exist in the new earth to all eternity. At the creation, when the foundations of the earth were laid, the sons of God looked with admiration upon the work of the Creator, and all the heavenly host shouted for joy. It was then that the foundation of the Sabbath was laid. At the close of the six days of creation, God rested on the seventh day from all His work which He had made; and He blessed the seventh day and sanctified it, because that in it He had rested from all His work. The Sabbath was instituted in Eden before the fall, and was observed by Adam and Eve, and all the heavenly host. God rested on the seventh day, and blessed and hallowed it. I saw that the Sabbath never will be done away; but that the redeemed saints, and all the angelic host, will observe it in honor of the great Creator to all eternity" (EW 217).

3. Providence

"In the annals of human history the growth of nations, the rise and fall of empires, appear as dependent on the will and prowess of man. The shaping of events seems, to a great degree, to be determined by his power, ambition, or caprice. But in the word of God the curtain is drawn aside, and we behold, behind, above, and through all the play and counterplay of human interests and power and passions, the agencies of the all-merciful One, silently, patiently working out the counsels of his own will. The Bible reveals the true philosophy of history" (Ed 173).

"If you watch and wait and pray, Providence and revelation will guide you through all the perplexities that you will meet, so that you will not fail nor become discouraged. Time will outline the beauty and grandeur of Heaven's plan. It is difficult for human minds to comprehend that God in His providence is working for the world through a feeble instrument. To know God in the working out of His providence is true science. There is much knowledge among men, but to see the designs of heavenly wisdom in times of necessity, to see the simplicity of God's plan revealing His justice and goodness and love, and searching out the hearts of men—this many fail to do. His plan seems too wonderful for them to accept, and thus they fail to be benefited. But Providence is still in our world, working among those who are grasping for the truth. These will recognize the hand of God. But His Word will not be revered by those who trust in their own wisdom" (11MR 348).

F. The Trinity

"The Godhead was stirred with pity for the race, and the Father, the Son, and the Holy Spirit gave Themselves to the working out of the plan of redemption. In order fully to carry out this plan, it was decided that Christ, the only-begotten Son of God, should give Himself an offering for sin. What line can measure the depth of this love? God would make it impossible for man to say that He could have done more. With Christ He gave all the resources of heaven, that nothing might be wanting in the plan for man's uplifting" (CH 222).

"There are three living persons of the heavenly trio; in the name of these three great powers—the Father, the Son, and the Holy Spirit—those who receive Christ by living faith are baptized, and these powers will cooperate with the obedient subjects of heaven in their efforts to live the new life in Christ" (Ev 615).

"Before the disciples shall compass the threshold, there is to be the imprint of the sacred name, baptizing the believers in the name of the threefold powers in the heavenly world. The human mind is impressed in this ceremony, the beginning of the Christian life. It means very much. The work of salvation is not a small matter, but so vast that the highest authorities are taken hold of by the expressed faith of the human agent. The eternal Godhead—the Father, the Son, and the Holy Ghost—is involved in the action required to make assurance to the human agent, . . . confederating the heavenly powers with the human that men may become, through heavenly efficiency, partakers of the divine nature and workers together with Christ" (UL 148).

"Those who have by baptism given to God a pledge of their faith in Christ, and their death to the old life of sin, have entered into covenant relation with God. The three powers of the Godhead, the Father, Son, and Holy Spirit, are pledged to be their strength and their efficiency in their new life in Christ Jesus" (AUCR Oct. 7, 1907).

"The rite of baptism is administered in the

name of the Father, and of the Son, and of the Holy Ghost. These three great powers of heaven pledge themselves to be the efficiency of all who submit to this ordinance, and who faithfully keep the vow they then make" (6MR 27).

G. The Eternal Father

"All these spiritualistic representations are simply nothingness. They are imperfect, untrue. They weaken and diminish the Majesty which no earthly likeness can be compared to. God cannot be compared with the things His hands have made. These are mere earthly things, suffering under the curse of God because of the sins of man. The Father cannot be described by the things of earth. The Father is all the fullness of the Godhead bodily, and is invisible to mortal sight" (Ev 614).

H. The Eternal Son and His Work

"A complete offering has been made; for 'God so loved the world, that he gave his only-begotten Son'—not a son by creation, as were the angels, nor a son by adoption, as is the forgiven sinner, but a Son begotten in the express image of the Father's person, and in all the brightness of his majesty and glory, one equal with God in authority, dignity, and divine perfection. In him dwelt all the fullness of the Godhead bodily" (ST May 30, 1895).

"The Son is all the fullness of the Godhead manifested. The Word of God declares Him to be 'the express image of His person'" (BTS Mar. 1, 1906).

"In Christ is life, original, unborrowed, underived" (DA 530).

"The divine nature in the person of Christ was not transformed in human nature and the human nature of the Son of man was not changed into the divine nature, but they were mysteriously blended in the Saviour of men. He was not the Father, but in Him dwelt all the fullness of the Godhead bodily" (6MR 112, 113).

" 'In him dwelleth all the fullness of the Godhead bodily.' Men need to understand that Deity suffered and sank under the agonies of Calvary. Yet Jesus Christ whom God gave for the ransom of the world purchased the church with His own blood. The Majesty of heaven was made to suffer at the hands of religious zealots, who claimed to be the most enlightened people upon the face of the earth" (7BC 907).

"In Christ is gathered all the glory of the Father. In Him is all the fullness of the Godhead bodily. He is the brightness of the Father's glory, and the express image of His person. The glory of the attributes of God are expressed in His character. The gospel is glorious because it is made up of His righteousness" (ibid. 907).

"In Christ dwelt the fullness of the Godhead bodily. This is why, although He was tempted in all points like as we are, He stood before the world, from His first entrance into it, untainted by corruption, though surrounded by it. Are we not also to become partakers of that fullness, and is it not thus, and thus only, that we can overcome as He overcame?" (ibid.).

"But the Sun of Righteousness shines forth into the midnight darkness of superstition and error, and rolls back the cloud, and presents Himself as the one in whom dwelleth all the fullness of the Godhead bodily, as the exact representation of the Father. This is his message to the world: 'And this is life eternal, that they might know thee the only true God, and Jesus Christ, whom thou hast sent' " (ST June 27, 1892).

"Jesus Christ was the foundation of the whole Jewish economy. The world's Redeemer was symbolized in types and shadows through their religious services. The glory of God was revealed in Christ within the veil until Christ should appear in the world and display to the world all the fullness of the Godhead bodily. In Christ we behold the image of the invisible God; in his attributes we see the attributes of the character of the Infinite. Jesus said: 'I and my Father are one.' 'He that hath seen me hath seen the Father'" (ibid. Aug. 29, 1895).

I. The Eternal Holy Spirit and His Work

"The Comforter that Christ promised to send after He ascended to heaven is the Spirit in all the fullness of the Godhead, making manifest the power of divine grace to all who receive and believe in Christ as a personal Saviour" (HP 336).

"The Holy Spirit has a personality, else He could not bear witness to our spirits and with our spirits that we are the children of God. He must also be a divine person, else He could not search out the secrets which lie hidden in the mind of God" (Ev 617).

"We need to realize that the Holy Spirit, who is as much a person as God is a person, is walking through these grounds" (*ibid.* 616).

"The Holy Spirit is the Comforter, in Christ's name. He personifies Christ, yet is a distinct personality" (20MR 324).

"Before this the Spirit had been in the world; from the very beginning of the work of redemption He had been moving upon men's hearts. . . .

"The Holy Spirit is Christ's representative, but divested of the personality of humanity, and independent thereof. Cumbered with humanity, Christ could not be in every place personally. Therefore it was for their interest that He should go to the Father, and send the Spirit to be His successor on earth. No one could then have any advantage because of his location or his personal contact with Christ. By the Spirit the Saviour would be accessible to all. In this sense He would be nearer to them than if He had not ascended on high" (DA 669).

"The Spirit was to be given as a regenerating agent, and without this the sacrifice of Christ would have been of no avail. The power of evil had been strengthening for centuries, and the submission of men to this Satanic captivity was amazing. Sin could be resisted and overcome only through the mighty agency of the third person of the Godhead, who would come with no modified energy, but in the fullness of divine power. It is the Spirit that makes effectual what has been wrought out by the world's Redeemer. It is by the Spirit that the heart is made pure. Through the Spirit the believer becomes a partaker of the divine nature. Christ has given His Spirit as a divine power to overcome all hereditary and cultivated tendencies to evil, and to impress His own character upon His church" (*ibid.* 671).

"The Comforter that Christ promised to send after He ascended to heaven, is the Spirit in all the fullness of the Godhead, making manifest the power of divine grace to all who receive and believe in Christ as a personal Saviour" (Ev 615).

XI. Literature

Arminius, Jacobus. *Writings.* 3 vols. Grand Rapids: Baker, 1956.

Augustine. *The Trinity.* Washington, D.C.: Catholic University of America Press, 1963.

Barth, Karl. *Church Dogmatics.* 4 vols. Trans. G. T. Thompson. Edinburgh: T. & T. Clark, 1936-1962.

Basinger, David. "Practical Implications." In *The Openness of God: A Biblical Challenge to the Traditional Understanding of God.* Ed. Clark Pinnock. Downers Grove, Ill.: InterVarsity, 1994. Pp. 155-176.

Bates, Joseph. *The Autobiography of Elder Joseph Bates.* Battle Creek, Mich.: Steam Press of the Seventh-day Adventist Publishing Association, 1868.

Brunner, Emil. *The Christian Doctrine of God.* Trans. Olive Wyon. Philadelphia: Westminster, 1949.

Cullmann, Oscar. *The Christology of the New Testament.* Rev. ed., trans. Shirley C. Guthrie and Charles A. M. Hall. Philadelphia: Westminster, 1963.

Davidson, Richard M. *Typology in Scripture: A Study of Hermeneutical* tupos *Structures.* Berrien Springs, Mich.: Andrews University Press, 1981.

Dederen, Raoul. "Reflections on the Doctrine of the Trinity." *Andrews University Seminary Studies* 8 (1970): 1-22.

De Margerie, Bertrand. *The Christian Trinity in History.* Trans. Edmund J. Fortman. Still

River, Mass.: St. Bede's, 1982.

Denzinger, Henry. *The Sources of Catholic Dogma.* Trans. Roy J. Deferrari from Henry Denzinger's *Enchiridion Symbolorum.* St. Louis: Herder, 1957.

Erickson, Millard J. *Christian Theology.* 3 vols. Grand Rapids: Baker, 1990.

Feuerback, Ludwig. *The Essence of Christianity.* New York: Harper and Row, 1957.

Fortman, Edmund J. *The Triune God: A Historical Study of the Doctrine of the Trinity.* Philadelphia: Westminster, 1972.

Froom, LeRoy. *The Prophetic Faith of Our Fathers.* 4 vols. Washington, D.C.: Review and Herald.

Grenz, Stanley J., and Roger E. Olson. *Twentieth-Century Theology: God and the World in a Transitional Age.* Downers Grove, Ill.: InterVarsity, 1992.

Guy, Fritz. "What the Trinity Means to Me." *Adventist Review,* Sept. 11, 1986.

Harnack, Adolf. *History of Dogma.* 7 vols. Trans. Neil Buchanan. New York: Dover, 1961.

Hasel, Gerhard F. "The Meaning of 'Let Us' in Gn 1:26." *Andrews University Seminary Studies* 13 (1975): 58-66.

Hasker, William. *God, Time, and Knowledge.* Ithaca, N.Y.: Cornell University Press, 1989.

————. "A Philosophical Perspective." In *The Openness of God: A Biblical Challenge to the Traditional Understanding of God.* Ed. Clark Pinnock, Downers Grove, Ill.: InterVarsity, 1994. Pp. 126-154.

Heppenstall, Edward. *The Man Who Is God: A Study of the Person and Nature of Jesus, Son of God and Son of Man.* Washington, D.C.: Review and Herald, 1977.

Hill, J. William. *The Three-Personed God: The Trinity as a Mystery of Salvation.* Washington, D.C.: Catholic University of America Press, 1982.

Jewett, Paul K. *God, Creation, and Revelation: A Neo-Evangelical Theology.* Grand Rapids: Eerdmans, 1991.

Johnson, Aubrey R. *The One and the Many in the Israelite Conception of God.* Cardiff: University of Wales Press, 1961.

Kelly, J.N.D. *Early Christian Doctrines.* London: Adam & Charles Black, 1968.

Küng, Hans. *Does God Exist? An Answer for Today.* Trans. Edward Quinn. New York: Vintage, 1981.

Ladd, George Eldon. *A Theology of the New Testament.* Grand Rapids: Eerdmans, 1974.

Lewis, Gordon R., and Bruce A. Demarest. *Knowing Ultimate Reality: The Living God.* Grand Rapids: Zondervan, 1987.

Moltmann, Jürgen. *The Trinity and the Kingdom: The Doctrine of God.* Trans. Margaret Kohl. San Francisco: Harper, 1991.

O'Carroll, Michael. *Trinitas: A Theological Encyclopedia of the Holy Trinity.* Wilmington, Del.: Michael Glazier, 1987.

Pannenberg, Wolfhart. *Theology and the Philosophy of Science.* Trans. Francis McDonagh. Philadelphia: Westminster, 1976.

————. *Systematic Theology.* Vol. 1. Trans. Geoffrey W. Bromiley. Grand Rapids: Eerdmans, 1991.

Pelikan, Jaroslav. *The Christian Tradition: A History of the Development of Doctrine.* 5 Chicago: Chicago University Press, 1971-1989.

Pinnock, Clark, et al. "Systematic Theology." In *The Openness of God: A Biblical Challenge to the Traditional Understanding of God.* Ed. Clark Pinnock. Downers Grove, Ill.: InterVarsity, 1994. Pp. 101-125.

Prescott, W. W. *The Saviour of the World.* Takoma Park, Md.: Review and Herald, 1929.

Provonsha, Jack W. *You Can Go Home Again.* Washington, D.C.: Review and Herald, 1982.

Rahner, Karl. *The Trinity.* Trans. Joseph Donceel. New York: Herder and Herder, 1970.

Rice, Richard. "Biblical Support for a New Perspective." In *The Openness of God: A Biblical Challenge to the Traditional Understanding of God.* Ed. Clark Pinnock. Downers Grove, Ill.: InterVarsity, 1994. Pp. 11-58.

Sanders, John. "Historical Considerations." In *The Openness of God: A Biblical Challenge to the Traditional Understanding of God.* Ed. Clark Pinnock. Downers Grove, Ill.: InterVarsity, 1994. Pp. 59-100.

Seventh-day Adventists Answer Questions on Doctrine: An Explanation of Certain Major Aspects of Seventh-Day Adventist Belief. Washington, D.C.: Review and Herald, 1957.

Smith, Uriah. *Looking Unto Jesus.* Battle Creek, Mich.: Review and Herald, 1897.

Spear, Samuel T. "The Bible Doctrine of the Trinity." New York *Independent,* Nov. 14, 1889. Reprinted in M. L. Andreasen, *The Book of Hebrews.* Washington, D.C.: Review and Herald, 1948. Pp. 115-124.

Stephenson, J. M. *The Atonement.* Rochester, N.Y.: Advent Review office, 1854.

Veloso, Mario. *El compromisio cristiano: un estudio sobre la actualidad misionera en el evangelio de San Juan.* Buenos Aires: Zunino, 1975.

Waggoner, E. J. *Christ and His Righteousness.* Oakland: Pacific Press, 1890.

Waggoner, J. H. *The Atonement.* Oakland: Pacific Press, 1884.

Whitehead, Alfred North. *Process and Reality: An Essay in Cosmology.* New York: Macmillan, 1929.

Christ: His Person and Work

Raoul Dederen

Introduction

At the center of the Christian religion is Jesus Christ. Beyond the acceptance of a set of fundamental beliefs, in its inmost essence our religion is first and foremost a commitment to a Person: Jesus Christ. The same is true of the Christian message. The gospel is about an event at the center of which is Jesus Christ. Christianity does not go back merely to an early community of believers. It is rooted in Jesus of Nazareth. Christianity is Christ. But who is He?

The aim of this article is to make a reflective and systematic study of the person and mission or work of Jesus Christ, however brief and selective, based on the Scriptures, par-ticularly on the NT. The starting point in this study is that the Gospels are historically authentic and dependable materials describing what Jesus did and said. The remainder of the Scriptures, both OT and NT, are likewise recognized as trustworthy and reliable sources. After all, the person and work of our Lord, as well as their implications, are a matter of revelation more than of human thought.

This article will consider various aspects of the person and work of Jesus Christ, namely His person, death, resurrection, ascension, high priestly ministry, and second coming according to the following outline.

I. The Word Became Flesh

A. The Incarnation

In approaching an examination of the biblical teaching regarding Jesus Christ, it seems best, as the apostle John did in the prologue to his Gospel, first to draw attention to one of the most astounding assertions found in the Scriptures: that the Word, who "was with God" and "was God" (John 1:1), "became flesh" (verse 14). Not only did the Word become flesh, but He "dwelt among us" (verse 14). The term literally means "tabernacled among us" or "pitched his tent among us." This powerful expression of the incarnation of the Word is also a clear intimation of His preexistence.

1. Christ's Preexistence

Both explicitly and by implication, the NT tells us that Jesus, as the Word, existed before His birth in Bethlehem. His existence did not begin when He was born in Judea. Not only do we find on Jesus' lips a considerable number of references to the fact that He was "sent" by the Father (cf. Matt. 5:17; 15:24; Mark 1:38; 10:45; Luke 19:10; John 5:23), which may be regarded as mere allusions to His prophetic mission, but in explicit terms He stated His heavenly origin, that He "came" or "descended" from heaven to earth: "I came from the Father and have come into the world" (John 16:28; cf. Matt. 20:28; Luke 19:10). "He who comes from above is above all; he who is of the earth belongs to the earth, and of the earth he speaks; he who comes from heaven is above all. He bears witness to what he has seen and heard" (John 3:31, 32). And again, "No one has ascended into heaven but he who descended from heaven, the Son of man" (John 3:13), or "What if you were to see the Son of man ascending where he was before?" (John 3:62).

Not only did our Lord assert that He existed before coming into this world, in glory and in close communion with the Father (John 17:5), but He did not hesitate to affirm that "before Abraham was, I am" (John 8:58), a phrase reminiscent of the OT "I am who I am" (Ex. 3:14), the name by which God announced Himself to Moses in the wilderness as self-existent and eternal. This is no longer mere preexistence; it is eternal preexistence. "The saying is sure and worthy of full acceptance," insists Paul, "that Christ Jesus came into the world to save sinners" (1 Tim. 1:15; cf. 3:16). To the Colossians he writes, "In him all things were created, in heaven and on earth, . . . all things were created through him and for him. He is before all things, and in him all things hold together" (1 Tim. 1:16, 17; see Creation II. C). He existed before His birth in Bethlehem.

Nor is the OT silent on the subject. Micah sets forth the Messiah who was to come as one who would have existed prior to his birth in Bethlehem Ephrathah, "whose origin is from of old, from ancient days" (Micah 5:2) or "from everlasting" (KJV). Isaiah describes the same promised Messiah not only as "Wonderful Counselor," "Prince of Peace," but as "Mighty God" and "Everlasting Father" (Isaiah 9:6).

The teaching that the Son of God existed before He was born in Bethlehem and "descended" from heaven, where from all eternity He had shared the Father's glory, is a vital factor in our understanding of His person and work. It points out that His birth was not simply that of a great man, but rather the entering into the human condition of One who in the most intimate way was identified with God.

2. Christ's Incarnation

The concept of Christ's preexistence is further developed by the NT writers. Thus John, referring to the preincarnate Word, explains that the Word, who "was in the beginning with God," "became flesh and dwelt among us" (John 1:2, 14). John unequivocally writes "became flesh," not merely "showed Himself in" or "appeared as" flesh. At a definite time, as the aorist tense in the original underlines it, the Word became human. Jesus came from above and an incarnation, a term of Latin origin meaning "becoming in flesh," took place.

That our Lord Jesus Christ, the eternal Son of God, became human for our salvation is probably the one tenet of the Christian faith that is basic to all others. In a celebrated passage Paul speaks of Jesus as the one who "was in the form of God," but "emptied himself" ("made himself of no reputation," KJV), took "the form of a servant" and "became obedient unto death, even death on the cross," before His subsequent exaltation (Phil. 2:5-11). The word *morphē*, "form," denotes the essential characteristics and qualities in contrast with those that are merely incidental and changeable. The apostle is asserting here that the preexistent Word had the essential characteristics of God. He was God. Then Paul notes that, humbling Himself, the Word took the "form" of a servant, once again the essential characteristics and qualities that make a human being what it is. He became fully human. This was no metamorphosis, so frequent in Greek myths, but a genuine incarnation. Nor was it merely the appearance of humanity, but genuine humanity. Christ's humanity was real and complete. A preexistent divine Being humbled Himself and took human nature. A genuine incarnation occurred.

Numerous other allusions to the Incarnation are found throughout Paul's Epistles, some quite strong (2 Cor. 8:9; Col. 2:9; 1 Tim. 3:16; Heb. 2:14; 5:7). In Galatians 4:4, 5 we are told that "when the time had fully come, God sent forth His Son, born of woman, born under the law, to redeem those who were under the law, so that we might receive adoption as sons." Paul refers the whole transaction to the Father, who thus fulfills the plan of redemption. God's Son was born of a woman. The same purpose is underlined when, toward the end of his life, the apostle asserts that "the saying is sure and worthy of full acceptance, that Christ Jesus came into the world to save sinners" (1 Tim. 1:15). We may have felt the need of a teacher, an example, a revealer, an interpreter of God's will, a bulwark against evil. We may find all this in Him, and more, but at the core of them all He is God and Saviour.

3. The Virgin Birth

From the Scriptures we learn that our Lord became incarnate by being conceived through the power of the Holy Spirit in the womb of Mary, a virgin (Luke 1:26-35; Matt. 1:18-21). There is no evidence here of the kind of Greek myth common in the first century A.D., no reference to a marriage of deities, no mythological version of a birth account, but only a statement in sober and simple language concerning a sovereign act of the Holy Spirit.

Christ's incarnation and virgin birth imply both deity and humanity. John voices no mere truism when he insists that "Jesus Christ has come in the flesh," and makes this confession the crucial test of truth (1 John 4:2). He means rather that One who had His being eternally in the unity of the Godhead became human through an unrepeated act of God, without relinquishing His oneness with God. By the word "flesh" he does not mean a physical body only, but a complete human person. One should not miss the point.

To a modernized, secularized, positivistic mentality that has lost the capacity to wonder, Christ's preexistence, incarnation, and virgin birth seem all too often just myths that an educated mind can no longer hold. To the NT writers, however, it is only in an incarnation that God can be truly known (cf. John 1:18). Christ's preexistence, incarnation, and virgin birth are all one piece. They are not an isolated doctrine, a foreign piece improperly introduced into the Christian faith. They constitute a word about divine grace and human helplessness. They are part of the total drama of redemption, and to discard them is to create a hole in the fabric of the biblical understanding of Christ's person and mission.

B. Human and Divine

1. The Humanity of Christ

The assertion that Jesus was truly human is everywhere present in the NT. The One who came to be regarded in a variety of exalted ways through the titles that were given to Him was nevertheless a genuine human being. Everything that is said in the Epistles, the Gospels, and the book of Acts points to this fact. That He was a genuine human being is an all-pervasive assumption that probably accounts for the almost incidental way in which the NT writers present Jesus' humanity. Paul was merely summarizing what everybody recognized when he wrote that Christ was "born of woman, born under the law" (Gal. 4:4), of a certain family and descent (Rom. 1:3). He felt no need to elaborate on it.

a. The biblical evidence. A closer look at the Gospels underlines the same common assumption. He was born in the city of David (Matt. 2:1; Luke 2:4-11), lived in Palestine, and was put to death in Jerusalem under Pontius Pilate (Matt. 27:11-50; John 18:28–19:37). His mother's name was Mary (Mark 6:3), and though His sisters' names are not recorded, His brothers' names were James, Joseph, Simon, and Judas (Matt. 13:55, 56). In the picture drawn by the evangelists one may discern the features of real humanity. He ate (Mark 2:16), slept (Matt. 8:24), and grew tired (John 4:6) like other humans. He was obedient to His parents while growing up (Luke 2:51), increasing in wisdom and in stature (Luke 2:40, 52). Repeatedly He is depicted as seeking information through questions (Matt. 7:3, 4; 9:28; Mark 7:18, 19; Luke 7:24-28; John 11:34; 18:34). He knew sorrow and anxiety (Matt. 26:37; cf. John 11:35; 12:27), as well as temptation (Matt. 4:1). He was acquainted with hunger (Matt. 4:2) and thirst (John 19:28). He enjoyed the friendship of others (John 11:5) and was conscious of their hatred and jealousy (John 7:7; 15:18; Mark 15:10). He was a man of prayer (Matt. 14:23; Mark 1:35; Luke 11:1) who exercised faith (Matt. 4:4; John 11:41). We read also of His angry glance (Mark 3:5), of a loud cry which He uttered when alone on the cross (Matt. 27:46), as well as of the open jubilation of His joy (Luke 10:21). Nothing is lacking to convey the apostles' conviction that we have before us in Jesus a genuine human being who came "in the likeness of men" (Phil. 2:7), one thing alone excepted, He "knew no sin" (2 Cor. 5:21); He was the blameless "Lamb of God, who takes away the sin of the world" (John 1:29).

b. A human way of life shaped by scriptural principles. People certainly treated Jesus as one of them, laughing at Him when He refused to agree that Jairus' daughter was dead (Luke 8:53) or falsely criticizing Him as "a glutton and a drunkard" (Matt. 11:19). He was mocked and beaten by people who obviously saw no reason why they could not get away with their infamy (Luke 22:63). The object of their scorn and criticism was a real man. His whole way of life was human, down to His full trust in the OT Scriptures as God's revealed Word.

As a member of a community of faith nurtured by the OT Scriptures, He regarded the OT writings as inspired and authoritative. He consistently treated its historical narratives as straightforward and dependable records of facts. In the course of His teaching He made reference to Abel (Luke 11:51), Noah (Matt. 24:37-39), Abraham (John 8:56), Sodom and Gomorrah (Matt. 10:15; 11:23, 24), Isaac and Jacob (Luke 13:28), the wilderness serpent (John 3:14), Solomon (Luke 11:31; 12:27), Elijah (Luke 4:25, 26), Jonah (Matt. 12:39-41), and many other OT individuals and incidents. He made it plain that His own views and teachings were based on the principles and teachings of Scripture (Matt. 19:16-22; 26:24; Luke 4:1-13; 18:31-33). He could preface a quotation of Scripture by "Moses said" (Mark 7:10), "well did Isaiah prophesy" (verse 6), or "David himself, inspired by the Holy Spirit, declared" (Mark 12:36). But, as is clear from the context, these statements and injunctions derived their authority from the fact that they were commandments of God (cf. Matt. 19:4, 5; Gen. 2:24). He also set His stamp of approval on statements found in Genesis 1 and 2 (Matt. 19:4, 5; Mark 10:6-8). The narratives that seem least acceptable to the modern mind were more than once the very ones He felt no hesitation to choose for His illustrations.

It is of particular significance that after His resurrection, when He appeared to His disciples prior to His ascension, Christ busied Himself with the exposition of Scripture (Luke 24:25-27, 44, 45). It is safe to say that as a man His whole life was conditioned by His understanding of the OT Scriptures as the Word of God. In every crisis or any other important moment in His life, the OT emerges in a fashion that underlines that He lived by its light and heard the voice of God in its pages.

2. A Sinless Human Nature

In one's assessment of the human nature of Jesus, it is necessary to take account of another clear testimony of the NT concerning His sinless character, addressed clearly in a number of statements. The Epistle to the Hebrews affirms that Jesus "in every respect has been tempted as we are, yet without sin" (Heb. 4:15). Peter, who knew Him well, refers to Jesus as "the Holy One of God" (John 6:69), adding that He "committed no sin; no guile was found on his lips" (1 Peter 2:22). John affirms that "in him there is no sin" (1 John 3:5), while Paul's witness is that Christ "knew no sin" (2 Cor. 5:21). Equally important is Jesus' own testimony: "I have kept my Father's commandments" (John 15:10). "I always do what is pleasing to him" (John 8:29). In the same vein He asked His hearers, "Which of you convicts me of sin?" (verse 46).

Part of Christ's mission was to be truly human. He possessed the essential characteristics of human nature. He was "flesh and blood" (Heb. 2:14), and in all things like His fellow human beings (verse 17). His humanity did not correspond to Adam's humanity before the Fall, nor in every respect to Adam's humanity after the Fall, for the Scriptures portray Christ's humanity as sinless. Conceived by the Holy Spirit, His birth was supernatural (Matt. 1:20; Luke 1:35), so much so that the angel sent by the Father told Mary that "the child to be born will be called holy" (Luke 1:35).

He came "in the likeness of sinful flesh" (Rom. 8:3). He took human nature in its fallen condition with its infirmities and liabilities and bearing the consequences of sin; but not its sinfulness. He was truly human, one with the human race, except for sin. He could truthfully say "He [Satan] has no power over me" (John 14:30; *en emoi ouk echei ouden,* lit. "has nothing in me"). Jesus took human nature, weakened and deteriorated by four thousand years of sin, yet undefiled and spotless. "In him," writes John, "there is no sin" (1 John 3:5).

The uniform witness of Scripture to the sinlessness of Jesus does not mean that He could not have sinned. While it is true that Scripture tells us that God does no evil and cannot be tempted (James 1:13), it is fitting to point out that Jesus, as a human being, could have sinned, though He did not. He refused to break His intimate relationship with the Father. There were genuine struggles and temptations, some of enormous intensity, as His struggle in Gethsemane to do the Father's will shows (Luke 22:41-44).

"Thanks be to God for his inexpressible gift," writes Paul (2 Cor. 9:15). The mystery of Christ is beyond adequate expression. For indeed Christ's sinlessness is not merely a matter of moral perfection, but the foundation of His sacrificial death. His sinlessness is not simply a statement about Christ-in-Himself but also of Christ-for-us, of Christ as our Saviour. Because He is holy and sinless, He is fully qualified to be for sinners Lord, Redeemer, and High Priest. This holiness, this sinlessness of Jesus, is the moral presupposition of the atonement which will be considered later (see II. C-E).

3. The Deity of Christ

a. Christ's titles. Alongside these declarations on Christ's true and genuine humanity, something of the place assigned to Jesus in early Christian belief may be gained from a study of the names and titles which Jesus Himself used or others gave Him. Though the titles listed here do not amount to a systematic presentation of Jesus' person and mission, they undoubtedly make an important contribution toward it.

(1) Messiah/Christ. It seems logical to begin with "Messiah," since the Christian church owes its name to the Greek equivalent *Christos,* the "Anointed One." The Hebrew word relates to the deliverer figure whom the Jews awaited and who would be God's agent in the inauguration of a new age for God's people. Both the Hebrew and Greek terms are derived from roots meaning "to anoint." Evidently, by calling Him "Christ," the NT writers regarded Jesus as specially set aside for a particular task.

The title *Christos* occurs more than 500 times in the NT. Although there was more than one concept of Messiahship among Jesus' contemporaries, it is generally recognized that by the first century Jews had come to look on the Messiah as someone in a special relationship with God. He would usher in the end of the age, when the kingdom of God would be established. He was the one through whom God would break through into history for the deliverance of His people. Jesus accepted the title "Messiah," but did not encourage its use; for the term carried political overtones that made its use difficult. Though reluctant to avail Himself of it in public to describe His mission, Jesus rebuked neither Peter (Matt. 16:16, 17) nor the Samaritan woman (John 4: 25, 26) for using it. He knew Himself to be the Messiah, as seen in Mark's report of Jesus' words about giving one of His disciples a cup of water "because you bear the name of Christ" (Mark 9:41). Everything depended on the content put into it, as indicated in Jesus' reply to Peter at Caesarea Philippi. Shortly after the latter's confession that indeed Jesus was "the Christ, the Son of the living God" (Matt. 16:16), Jesus stressed the fact that "the Son of man must suffer many things" (Mark 8:31; cf. Matt. 16:21). Rejecting the idea of political Messiahship, He reinterpreted the Messianic office in a way radically different from current interpretations. If He considered Himself to be the Messiah, it was in the context of OT fulfillment, i.e., the consciousness that He was God's agent for the redemption of God's people, a redemption understood in a spiritual rather than a nationalistic sense.

Christ's resurrection clarified and certified His title as Messiah. Indeed, in the context of the Resurrection and of the outpouring of the Holy Spirit Peter at Pentecost declared that "God has made him both Lord and Christ, this Jesus whom you crucified" (Acts 2:36). From the first, the theme of Christian preaching and teaching is "Jesus as the Christ" (Acts 5:42). So deep was the conviction of the early church on this point that "Christ" soon became practically a proper name for Jesus. The gospel they proclaimed was "the gospel of Jesus Christ, the Son of God" (Mark 1:1). Among other things, the title Messiah or Christ had come to mean for the early disciples the anointed King of the promise.

(2) Christ as Lord. While Christ or Messiah was a title of particular significance to Jewish Christians, the title "Lord" (Gr. *kyrios*) had greater meaning for Gentiles. It was not adopted, however, from Gentile sources but taken from the OT, where in its Greek version it was used to render Yahweh (Gen. 2:4) and Adonai (Joshua 3:11; Ps. 8:1, 9). In secular Greek, "Lord" might be simply an indication of respect ("Sir," Matt. 13:27; John 4:19, or "master," Matt. 10:24; John 15:15). Throughout the Hellenistic world "lord" was also used to address the divinities of the mystery cults as well as the emperor. In more than one instance, to apply it to Jesus was in effect to equate Him with Deity, as may best be seen in Thomas' confession of faith, "My Lord and my God" (John 20:28).

By referring to Jesus as Lord, the early church intended to declare Him as standing above the human level, a proper object of worship (Acts 7:59, 60), worthy of prayer (verses 59, 60) and trust (Acts 16:31; Rom. 10:9), author of our salvation (Acts 15:11; 1 Thess. 5:9). "He is Lord of lords and King of kings" (Rev. 17:14; cf. 19:16), who shares with God in His nature, granting us grace as well as peace (Phil. 1:2; 2 Thess. 1:2), comforting our hearts and establishing us in all good works (2 Thess. 2:16,

17). In its Christian use the title implies the absolute sovereignty of Jesus over all aspects of life and faith, and it denotes deity. To Christians Christ is the "only Master and Lord" (Jude 4), whom every believer is called to "put on" (Rom. 13:14), for whose sake every disciple is ready to risk his or her life (Acts 15:26), even to die (Acts 21:13). He simply is the "Lord and Savior Jesus Christ" (2 Peter 1:11; 2:20). Here again, Christ's resurrection brought home to the early believers the true meaning of the lordship of Christ, for, as Peter told the crowds at Pentecost, it was by this event that God made Him both *Kyrios* and *Christos:* "Let all the house of Israel therefore know assuredly that God has made Him both Lord and Christ, this Jesus whom you crucified" (Acts 2:36).

(3) Son of God. "Messiah" and "Lord" are titles that could be understood in a functional sense, as intimating God's action and purpose in a particular man. "Son of God," another title ascribed to Jesus in the NT, points beyond His mere function. It points to the relation of that person with God in His being. Jesus Christ is more than God's man, the instrument of God's action. He is the Son of God. His relation to God goes beyond the functional. It is ontological. This is the radically new dimension that the NT brought to the understanding of the title "Son of God." Beyond the divine action in Him is divine being. The Son is "in the bosom of the Father" (John 1:18). Something of the Father's being is in the Son.

"Son of God" in the NT could mean much or little. Its meaning is based on the distinctive use of the term in the OT. It could be used of angels (Job 1:6; 38:7). The king is occasionally called God's son (2 Sam. 7:14; Ps. 2:7). Righteous people are called sons of God (Gen. 6:2); likewise Israel, considered collectively, is spoken of as God's son (Ex. 4:22; Hosea 11:1). But when the phrase is used of Jesus, the evidence shows that it is not to be understood in the same sense as in other cases. He is called "my beloved Son, with whom I am well pleased" (Matt. 3:17). Mark opens his Gospel with the phrase "Jesus Christ, the Son of God" (Mark 1:1). Matthew 2:15 applies "my son" of Hosea 11:1 unambiguously to Jesus. Peter's confession at Caesarea Philippi, "You are the Christ, the Son of the living God" (Matt. 16:16), is accepted without question by Jesus, who attributes it to divine revelation (verse 17). Those who accused Him of saying "I am the Son of God" (Matt. 27:43; cf. John 19:7) must have heard Him use the title. In the Synoptic Gospels it is clear that Jesus accepted the title and thought of Himself as God's Son (Matt. 11:27; Mark 13:34). The title comes into its fullest meaning in John's Gospel, where in many instances the expression "the Son" is used rather than "the Son of God," which is another way of bringing out Jesus' unique condition. God and His Son are uniquely bound to each other (John 3:35; 5:19, 20). Jesus Himself laid claim to this title (John 10:36), and the Jews understood the way in which He claimed God as Father to mean that He was making Himself "equal with God" (John 5:18).

Outside the Gospels, the NT writers define the Christian message as "the gospel concerning His [God's] Son" (Rom. 1:3). Already early in His ministry, Paul could summarize the Christian way as "faith in the Son of God" (Gal. 2:20). The Epistle to the Hebrews not only states but emphasizes the divine sonship of Jesus the Christ. Christ is superior to OT prophets (Heb. 1:1, 2), He is "Son" because "he reflects the glory of God and bears the very stamp of his nature" (verse 3). His position is that of Son, and on that basis He is superior to the angels (verses 4, 5) and greater than Moses himself (verses 5, 6).

In the most complete sense the Son partakes of the same nature as the Father. He possesses the same attributes (John 5:21; 8:58; 21:7), performs the same works (Matt. 9:2; John 5:24-29), and claims equal honor with the Father (John 5:23; 14:1). Just as the Resurrection heightens the meaning of the titles we considered earlier, it maximizes "Son" as well, for in Paul's words, Jesus was "designated Son of God in power . . . by his resurrection from the dead" (Rom. 1:4). If Christ's unique sonship might have been obscure before His death, it certainly was no longer so after His resurrection.

b. Jesus as God. In at least three instances, the biblical writers speak quite clearly of Jesus as God. In the first of these (Heb. 1:8, 9), Psalm 45:6, 7 is presented as what God says to the Son: "But of the Son he says, 'Thy throne, O God, is for ever and ever, the righteous scepter is the scepter of thy kingdom. Thou hast loved righteousness and hated lawlessness; therefore God, thy God, has anointed thee with the oil of gladness, beyond thy comrades.'" In this passage the Son, who is superior to angels (Heb. 1:4–2:9), Moses (Heb. 3:1-6), and the Levitical high priest (Heb. 4:14–5:10) is addressed as God. As does the Father, Jesus possesses the divine nature.

The second explicit statement is found in John 1:1: "In the beginning was the Word, and the Word was with God, and the Word was God." While it is true that there are exceptions to the rule, the anarthrous use (i.e., without an article) of "God" in 1:1c ("and the Word was God") distinguishes the predicate from the subject of the verb "to be," thus confirming the rendering "and the Word was God." In addition, the omission of the article emphasizes the quality and the character of the Word. Having distinguished the Word from God the Father (verse 1b), John affirms that He shares the same nature with the Father. In the first of the three crisp clauses of verse 1, John affirms the absolute, supratemporal existence of the Word. He existed in the beginning, before time and Creation. This eternal subsistence, however, was not in isolation, for John adds that "the Word was with God." He was distinguishable from God, yet in communion with Him, in a true sense identical with God. This indeed the apostle affirms by declaring unambiguously that "the Word was God." The predicate "God" in the third sentence of this outstanding declaration occupies a position of emphasis, probably to prevent inadequate inferences as to the nature of the Word. Eternally preexistent and in personal intercommunion with the Father, the Word, identified as Jesus of Nazareth in verse 14, is intrinsically divine.

Nowhere in the NT is Jesus more clearly identified as God than in the final passage, where in response to the invitation of Jesus to touch His wounds, Thomas, a skeptical disciple, utters the words "my Lord and my God" (John 20:28). The confession is the more significant in that it went unrebuked by Jesus (verse 29; cf. Rev. 19:10). Just as Israel had honored Yahweh as "My God and my Lord" (Ps. 99:8), so Christians could refer to Jesus as "my Lord and my God" and "honor the Son, even as they honor the Father" (John 5:23).

c. Jesus' divine consciousness. John's Gospel has preserved a considerable number of assertions made by Jesus Himself that bear witness to His divine self-consciousness. He repeatedly asserted that He was of higher-than-earthly origin and nature. He taught that He had "descended from heaven" (John 3:13). He affirmed, "You are from below, I am from above; you are of this world, I am not of this world" (John 8:23). He further declared, "I came from the Father and have come into the world" (John 16:28). These convey assertions of preexistence, made even more explicit in the question, "What if you were to see the Son of man ascending where he was before?" (John 6:62), or in His prayer, "Father, glorify thou me in thy own presence with the glory which I had with thee before the world was made" (John 17:5).

This awareness of being ontologically divine is further expressed in several remarkable "I am" sayings. "I am the bread of life" (John 6:35), "I am the light of the world" (John 8:12), "I am the door" (John 10:7), "I am the good shepherd" (verse 11), "I am the resurrection and the life" (verse 25), "I am the way, and the truth, and the life" (John 14:6), "I am the true vine" (John 15:1).

Jesus does not merely bring or give bread, life, light, or resurrection. He is each of them. To Jewish ears these "I am" affirmations must have aroused associations of the divine, for in the LXX, the Greek translation of the He-

brew OT, the same emphatic "I am" is frequently used by God Himself (cf. Deut. 32:39; Isa. 41:4; 43:10; etc.). The same inference is clearly underlined in other passages in which the Lord uses the "I am" formula, without adding a predicate modifier, for instance in John 8:24, 28 and 13:19. The most striking is found in John 8:58: "Truly, truly, I say to you, before Abraham was, I am." Outraged, His opponents "took up stones to throw at him" (verse 59), obviously regarding Jesus' statement as a blasphemous assertion of equality with God, of changelessness, a claim to deity.

4. One Person—Truly Divine, Truly Human

Having concluded that the NT teaches that Jesus of Nazareth was at the same time truly divine and truly human, one still faces one of the most difficult of all christological problems and an issue of the greatest importance: How can there be two natures and yet but one person? Although we may find it difficult to answer the question, the Scriptures encourage us to consider the mystery of God, even Christ (Col. 2:2, 3); and Jesus Himself tells us that a true knowledge of Him is possible through revelation (Matt. 11:25-27; 16:17).

First it must be established that the view according to which in Jesus two natures were united in one person is required by Scripture itself. We have noted that the Scriptures do indeed represent Christ as having a divine nature and a human nature. That these are united in one person is constantly assumed rather than formally expressed in the NT, which portrays Jesus as one person, one undivided personality in whom the two natures are inseparably united. Thus Paul speaks of Christ as a descendant of David according to His human nature (Rom. 1:3) and as "Son of God . . . according to the Spirit of holiness" (verse 4)—two natures in a single person. In the Epistle to the Hebrews one finds from the very start a systematic development of Christ's two natures in one person. The first chapter proclaims Christ's deity (verses 2, 3, 6, 8, 10-12), while the second chapter elaborates on His humanity (verses 9, 14, 16, 17). The same personal union is recounted in Paul's description of Christ as being in the very form (i.e., nature) of God, yet, regarding His humanity, making Himself nothing, taking the very nature ("form," again) of a servant, and being made in human likeness (Phil. 2:6-8). John, likewise, attests that the Word, who is God, became flesh, and that Christ, having a divine and a human nature, dwelled among humans (John 1:1-18).

This conviction was so strong among early believers that without the slightest hesitation, the apostles apply qualities of both humanity and deity to the same person. Thus the One who upholds all things by the word of His power grew and became strong in stature and in wisdom. He who was before Abraham was born in a manger. The One who dies is the One who fills all in all. In some instances the two natures are held in tension in a simple, compact phrase, such as they "crucified the Lord of glory" (1 Cor. 2:8). Statements like these are neither contradictions nor absurdities when perceived in the light of the human-divine personal union set forth in the Scriptures. They make sense only if one assumes that these two natures were united in a single person, the God-man.

II. His Ministry and Death

Early Christians were not averse to ascribing both humanity and deity to Jesus of Nazareth. Still, while concerned about who Jesus was (Matt. 16:13-17), they showed even greater interest in His mission and work. An increasingly clearer grasp of who He was helped them to understand better what His unique person enabled Him to do for them.

A. The Work He Came to Do

A careful reading of the NT shows that its writers were convinced that there was a purpose to Jesus' coming. He did not simply "appear," nor was He merely a gifted Galilean with special insights in the ways of God. He was "sent" by the Father, a statement that appears some 40 times in John's Gospel alone. The Lord Himself frequently indicated consciousness of being commissioned to His task by God. Two words are used to describe this sending: the general word *pempō* and the more specific *apostellō,* which shows an intimate connection between sender and sent. As God's anointed Servant, Jesus felt that there was a decree for Him to execute. Luke brings this out quite forcefully by using the Greek verbal form *dei* ("must" or "it is necessary") some 18 times (Luke 2:49; 4:43; 9:22; 24:44; etc.). Rather than considering Himself as merely one among many other divine messengers, Jesus knew Himself to be the Messenger-Son (Mark 12:6, 7). As the Father had set Him apart, sent Him into the world (John 10:36), and given Him authority (John 8:42; Matt. 9:6), it was not for Him to do His own will (John 4:34; 5:30; 6:38). Several purposes of His work and mission are more particularly underlined in the Scriptures.

1. To Confirm God's Promises

The Word became human to confirm the promises made by God to the fathers, beginning with the Protoevangelium in Genesis 3:15 and continuing throughout the OT (Isa. 7:14; 9:6; Micah 5:2). Two lines of predictions concerned the coming of the Son: He was to come as Saviour from sin as prefigured in the sacrifices of the OT (Gen. 4:3, 4; Lev. 1:3-9; 17:11) and announced by the prophets (Isa. 52:13, 14; 53:3-6; Dan. 9:26; Zech. 13:1, 7), and as King of His kingdom (Gen. 49:9, 10; Ps. 2; Jer. 23:5, 6).

2. To Establish the Kingdom of God

It was imperative for Jesus to ensure the recognition of the sovereignty of God and the establishment of His kingdom on earth (Matt.

4:17; Luke 19:11-27). In the Synoptic Gospels the central theme of Jesus' preaching, the kingdom of God, was announced as something that would appear in the future and yet was a reality already present, manifested in His own person and ministry (Matt. 12:28). The kingdom was where He was. The secret of being part of it, present or future, lay in belonging to Him (Matt. 7:23; 25:41).

3. To Impart the Knowledge of God

Inasmuch as knowledge of God is essential to eternal life, it was part of the mission of Christ to impart this knowledge (John 17:3). In the OT God was revealed as Creator and Ruler (for instance, Ps. 33:6; Isa. 40:12-17; 45:18; Jer. 10:12), though not infrequently as the Father of the chosen people (such as Deut. 32:6; Isa. 22:21; 63:16; Mal. 1:6). Jesus helped sinners think of God with trust and reverence, with love as well as with awe, as a Father who knows what things we need before we ask Him and who withholds no good things from His children. This revelation could be made only by the Son (Matt. 11:27; Luke 10:22), through His deeds even more than through His teaching, because it was enclosed in Him (John 14:7-10), an incarnate revelation that appeals to the love of the heart and calls for the surrender of the will.

4. To Be the Servant of God

The servant idea plays an important role in the NT understanding of the work and mission of Jesus. He Himself insisted that He had come "not to be served but to serve" (Matt. 20:28). The idea of the servant of God comes directly from four Isianic songs known as the servant songs (Isa. 42:1-4; 49:1-6; 50:4-9; 52:13–53:12). Though it has been debated whether the servant in these songs is an individual or refers to Israel collectively, the task of the servant in these passages is more intelligible if an individual is in mind. He is God's anointed (Isa. 42:1), called to establish justice on earth (verses 1, 3, 4), extend a ministry to Gentiles (verses 1, 4; Isa. 50:4) as well as to Israel (Isa. 49:5, 6a), be God's agent in worldwide salvation (verses 1-6), yet fulfill his task by voluntarily submitting himself to a substitutionary death (Isa. 53:4-6, 8, 10-12).

In a strongly worded fulfillment formula, Jesus directly quoted Isaiah 53:12, attesting His consciousness that the OT servant figure was being fulfilled in Him (Luke 22:37). Matthew, likewise, in the context of Jesus' healing ministry, cites Isaiah 53:4 as fulfilled in Jesus (Matt. 8:17). So does Luke when recording Philip's encounter with the Ethiopian eunuch, specifically apply to Jesus a direct quotation from Isaiah 53:7, 8 (Acts 8:32, 33). In Peter's first Epistle several direct allusions to the suffering Servant show that the apostle must have had the Isaiah passage in mind (1 Peter 2:22 = Isa. 53:9; 1 Peter 2:24a = Isa. 53:12; 1 Peter 2:24b = Isa. 53:5; 1 Peter 2:25 = Isa. 53:6).

As part of His mission, the Word who was in nature very God (Phil. 2:6) took the very nature of a servant (verse 7) in order that the divine life be manifested to humans in servant form (verses 5-7). He became obedient, even unto death, to reveal true humanity and present to the Father the perfect obedience due from humanity.

5. To Leave an Example

Jesus conceived of His mission as one of obedience to the Father's will. In picturesque language He claimed that His food was to do God's will (John 4:34) and clearly stated that He had not come down from heaven to do His own will "but the will of him who sent me" (John 6:39; cf. 5:30). Unlike the first Adam the Second Adam abode in His Father's love (John 15:10; cf. 14:31), was eager to please Him (John 8:29) and to accomplish the work of Him who sent Him (John 4:34). This involved a constant conflict with evil, for "he learned obedience through what he suffered," and was "made perfect" (Heb. 5:8, 9) through suffering (Heb. 2:10; cf. Matt. 26:39-45; Luke 22:42-46).

This truth is used to support an unrelenting appeal to the exemplary nature of Christ's life and ministry. Called to be "conformed to the image of his Son" (Rom. 8:29), Christians are exhorted to "put on the Lord Jesus Christ, and make no provision for the flesh, to gratify its desires" (Rom. 13:14; cf. Col. 3:10), to be imitators of Christ (1 Thess. 1:6), to abide in Christ and walk as He walked (1 John 2:6), to "walk in love," after the pattern Christ gave us (Eph. 5:2; cf. 1 Peter 3:8, 9). In a classic case in point, when addressing slaves and exhorting them to be submissive to their masters, even when suffering unjustly, Peter explains, "For to this you have been called, because Christ also suffered for you, leaving you an example, that you should follow in his steps" (1 Peter 2:21).

6. To Heal the Weak and Sick

Jesus came to heal. Far from manifesting contempt toward the weak and the sick, He showed that His mission and work were closely bound up with the frail and feeble of body and spirit. He healed many (Matt. 4:23). "Wherever he came, in villages, cities, and country, they laid the sick in the market places" (Mark 6:56; cf. Luke 4:40). "Great multitudes gathered to hear [Jesus] and to be healed of their infirmities" (Luke 5:15), "and the power of the Lord was with him to heal" (verse 17). This clearly was part of His mission. The twelve whom Jesus sent out were charged to proclaim the kingdom of heaven and to "heal, raise the dead, cleanse lepers, cast out demons" (Matt. 10:5-8; cf. Luke 10:8, 9).

Jesus viewed the presence of illness as a result of the Fall. Since His mission was to destroy the works of the devil, He made every effort to heal the sick and diseased. Yet His miracles of healing were more than spectacular wonders. Commenting on His healing activities in Capernaum, Matthew specifies that Jesus' healing ministry was the fulfillment of a prophecy made by Isaiah concerning the mission and work of the divinely appointed Servant: "He took our infirmities and bore our diseases" (Matt. 8:17; Isa. 53:4). Though Matthew makes no reference to an atoning element, he sees a clear connection between the Servant's work and human sickness in Jesus' healing ministry. His healing activities were part of the plan of God and of the work of Christ. They showed that the One who was to come in due time was now among them. They established the supernatural basis of the unique divine self-revelation that accompanied them.

7. To Make Sin Exceedingly Sinful

Included in Christ's gracious task was a revelation of the true moral condition of humanity. To produce in human beings a consciousness of guilt, repentance, faith, hope, and love was indispensable to His work. His conduct and His teaching made sin exceedingly sinful. His presence and ministry actually produced a sense of sin (Luke 5:8; 7:36-50). He was the very embodiment of the gospel. While it condemned sin, it invited the sinner to receive forgiveness and enter into union with the victorious One who from the first had overcome the world (Matt. 4:1-11; John 16:33). Corrupted sinners eventually rejected and killed Him, thereby further disclosing the depth of human guilt and need.

8. To Be a Faithful High Priest

Christ came to be qualified to act as a faithful high priest. He became flesh to enter into every human experience, apart from sin, that He might be fit as high priest (Heb. 2:17, 18). Christ's work reappropriated the threefold ministry of the high priest of OT times: to present annually the atoning sacrifice for the sanctuary and the whole congregation, to intercede for the faithful, and to bless the people (Lev. 4:16-21; 16:1-28).

9. To Save Sinners Through His Death

The mission of Christ involved His death. He came "to destroy the works of the devil" (1 John 3:8) and "to take away sins" (verse 5), thus delivering all those who were living as slaves of the devil (Heb. 2:14, 15). As Paul wrote to Timothy, "The saying is sure and worthy of full acceptance, that Christ Jesus came into the world to save sinners" (1 Tim. 1:15). This, however, could be accomplished only "through death," as the Hebrews statement stipulates (1 Tim. 2:14). He might have come to judge the world, but the joyful cry is that He came specifically to save sinners. The necessity of the Incarnation and the purpose of Christ's mission are God's response to sin. A self-giving death as a sacrifice for sin was a chief part of His work.

B. A Work Foretold in the OT

1. A Fact Present in Christ's Mind

Christ's death was not an afterthought or an accident, but the accomplishment of a definite purpose in connection with the Incarnation. The Gospels record sayings attesting that this fact was present in Christ's mind at an early stage of His ministry. The tragic note heard early in the Fourth Gospel (John 3:14, 15) finds corroboration in the Synoptic accounts (Matt. 9:15; Mark 2:19, 20; Luke 5:34, 35). As soon as He was recognized by His disciples as the Christ of prophecy (Mark 8:29), Jesus turned their attention to what He regarded as the true characteristic of His mission, namely that "the Son of man must suffer many things, and be rejected by the elders and the chief priests and the scribes, and be killed, and after three days rise again" (Mark 8:31; cf. Matt. 16:21).

The saving purpose of that death was clearly understood. Most pointed among His sayings is the statement that He came "not to be served but to serve, and to give his life as a ransom for many" (Matt. 20:28; Mark 10:45). While the first two Gospels are closely parallel in their accounts of the institution of the Last Supper (Matt. 26:26-29; Mark 14:22-25), to Mark's "This is my blood of the covenant, which is poured out for many" (Mark 14:24), Matthew adds the words "for the forgiveness of sins" (Matt. 26:28). In Matthew's addition Jesus is giving a theological interpretation of His coming death.

To Jesus, His death and its attendant

events were foretold by the OT prophets and part of a divine plan (Matt. 26:54, 56; Luke 22:37 = Isa. 53:12; Luke 24:44; John 17:12 = Ps. 41:9), which He anticipated and accepted. Of His own accord He was laying down His life; no one was taking it from Him. Until the end He had the power to lay it down and the power to take it back (John 10:17, 18; cf. Matt. 26:53).

2. A Conviction Shared by the NT Writers

In common with Jesus, the NT writers held that the OT foretold the gospel story, at least in types and symbols. In their eyes, Isaiah's picture of the Servant of the Lord was a prophecy of Christ (Matt. 18-21; Acts 8:32-35; 1 Peter 2:21-25). This view is particularly apparent regarding the passion of Christ. Peter insisted that "what God foretold by the mouth of all the prophets, that his Christ should suffer, he thus fulfilled" (Acts 3:18). Paul reminded the Corinthian believers that "Christ died for our sins in accordance with the scriptures" (1 Cor. 15:3), the necessity of which he found in the OT writings (Acts 17:2, 3). He also professed, this time before King Agrippa, that he had proclaimed nothing but what Moses and the prophets said would come to pass, "that the Christ must suffer" (Acts 26:22, 23). "He himself," writes Peter, "bore our sins in his body on the tree, that we might die to sin and live to righteousness. By his wounds you have been healed" (1 Peter 2:24). The latter words are a direct quotation from Isaiah's description of the substitutionary sufferings of the Servant to come (Isa. 53:5) and part of the broader Isaiah 52:13–53:12 passage mentioned above, in which the suffering Servant, having been vindicated, actually saves His persecutors and intercedes for the transgressors.

The apostles did not hesitate to point to specific prophecies, such as the prophecy of Christ's betrayal (Ps. 41:9-11; Acts 1:16), that of His crucifixion and the events surrounding it (Ps. 22:1, 7, 8, 18; Matt. 27:39-41; Mark 15:34; John 19:23, 24), as well as that of His resurrection (Ps. 16:8-10; Acts 2:22-28). Matthew reminded his readers that Zechariah had foretold the selling of Christ for thirty pieces of silver (Zech. 11:12, 13), a prophecy fulfilled in Judas' crime of betraying Jesus (Matt. 26:15). The same OT prophet predicted the smiting of the shepherd that the sheep may be scattered (Zech. 13:7; Matt. 26:31).

Their view is stated concisely in 1 Peter 1:10-12: "The prophets who prophesied of the grace that was to be yours searched and inquired about this salvation; they inquired what person or time was indicated by the Spirit of Christ within them when predicting the sufferings of Christ and the subsequent glory. It was revealed to them that they were serving not themselves but you, in the things which have now been announced to you by those who preached the good news to you through the Holy Spirit sent from heaven."

Years earlier, to those astonished at the healing of a man lame from birth, the same apostle explained that all the prophets, "from Samuel and those who came afterwards, also proclaimed these days" (Acts 3:24).

3. A Death of Utmost Importance

From what we saw regarding the mission and work of Christ, it should come as no surprise that, contrary to the facts in the case of ordinary human beings, the death of Christ, as well as His life, is of utmost importance. It is the high point of all four Gospels. John, for instance, devotes 12 of his chapters to Christ's public ministry, and nine to the events surrounding His passion—the sufferings of Christ between the night of the Last Supper and His death and resurrection. Matthew devotes one fourth of his Gospel to the last week of Christ's ministry, Mark about one third, Luke more than one fifth. The cross occupies a central place in the Gospels; it is the intended climax of their narratives.

A death by crucifixion was bloody and cruel, a terrifying horror, particularly for first-century Jews. It reminded them that one hanged on a tree was accursed by God (Deut. 21:22, 23). Yet that hateful cross is at the very center of Jesus' mission and God's plan. John sees it as an event of world salvation (cf. John 3:13, 14; 12:32). Because at the end of a life of commitment to the Father, He went to His death innocently, voluntarily, and in accordance with the will of His Father. Jesus' death has infinite atoning property.

C. The Atonement: Background Factors

At the very heart of the Christian religion is a cross, and on that cross the Son of God effected the sinner's salvation. The atonement means that in His death Jesus Christ dealt fully with the problem that sin had created. Whatever needed to be done, He did. Before reviewing the NT teaching on Christ's atoning life and death, let us define our terminology and briefly consider some key underlying factors brought out by the NT, which deserve particular attention.

1. The English Word "Atonement"

The English words "to atone" and "atonement" do not correspond etymologically with any Hebrew or Greek word that they translate. They are derived from the phrase "at one," and etymologically stand for harmony of relationship. To be "at one" with someone is to be in harmonious relationship with him or her. Likewise, "atonement" means "at one-ment," or "reconciliation." Progressively, however, in theological parlance, the terms have taken a more restricted meaning, no longer expressing their original intention but the process by which the obstacles to reconciliation are removed. Thus, "to atone for" a wrong is to take some action that cancels out the ill effects of alienation and brings harmonious relationships.

2. An Original Harmonious Relation

A key underlying foundation of the biblical doctrine of atonement is the assumption that God and humans are ideally one in life and interests. From Genesis to the Apocalypse it is everywhere assumed that God and humans should be in harmonious relation, at one.

Such is the picture of Adam and Eve in Eden (Gen. 1; 2; 3). In both OT and NT this assumption stands over against the fact that there is a radical breach in this unity (Gen. 3:22-24; Isa. 59:1, 2; Rom. 5:12; Eph. 2:1). Human life in its unregenerate state is estrangement from God. Human beings "sit in darkness" (Luke 1:79; cf. John 12:46), are "alienated from the life of God" (Eph. 4:18), "estranged and hostile in mind, doing evil deeds" (Col. 1:21), and "without God in the world" (Eph. 2:12). They are "hostile to God" (Rom. 8:7) and enemies of God (Rom. 5:10). Not only is this true of Gentiles (Rom. 1:23, 25, 26) but also of Jews, who pride themselves on their possession of the law (Rom. 3:9, 23). "There is no man who does not sin" echoes the OT (1 Kings 8:46); "there is none that does good, no, not one" (Ps. 14:3).

3. The Cause of the Estrangement

The cause of this estrangement from God is likewise plainly delineated. It is our sin, our persisting disobedience to the will of God. Underlying sin is the idea of law and a lawgiver, for "sin is lawlessness" (1 John 3:4). The lawgiver is God. The sinfulness of sin lies in the fact that while it is transgression of the law, sin is first and foremost rebellion against a person, against God, even when the wrong we do is to others or to ourselves (cf. Gen. 39:9; Ps. 51: 4). Far from being something impersonal and foreign to God, the law is a transcript of His character and will. Obeying or disobeying it is a serious matter, not because we are relating to an impersonal document, but because the law is understood as a way of relating to a personal God. Nor should one lose sight of the fact that violation of the law carries serious consequences: a liability to retribution, especially death, which is the sequel of sin. By His very nature, as the Scriptures assert, God is neither complacent nor indulgently indifferent to transgression. "God is not mocked," explains Paul, "for whatever a man sows, that he will also reap" (Gal. 6:7). The law of retribution for the unrepentant sinner finds expression in the solemn warning,

"the wages of sin is death" (Rom. 6:23). Indeed, explains the apostle, the sinner is already "dead through . . . trespasses and sins" (Eph. 2:1).

This does not mean that God holds aloof in cold contempt from sinners or turns from them with resentment. The same Scriptures that declare uncompromisingly God's unremitting antagonism to sin (Isa. 59:1, 2; Hab. 1:13; cf. John 1:29) and the harsh consequences that follow it portray a loving God, merciful and slow to anger (Ex. 34:6; Deut. 7:6-8; 1 John 4:8, 16). He draws near again and again, seeking to deliver sinners from the evil that is destroying them, and holding them apart from God (Gen. 3:9; Jer. 3:11-14; Hosea 6:1; Luke 13:34). In a final gesture of love and mercy He has come in His Son Jesus, who "came to seek and save the lost" (Luke 19:10) and died at the hands of sinful humans, for our sake, for those who were still sinners. "While we were yet sinners Christ died for us" (Rom. 5:8; see Law; Sin IV. A, B).

4. The Atonement and Christ's Death

The atoning work of Christ is closely associated with His death on the cross. Though not ignoring the importance of Christ's life, on this point the NT writers speak with one voice. "We were reconciled to God by the death of his son" (Rom. 5:10). "He himself bore our sins in his body on the tree" (1 Peter 2:24). "He is the expiation for our sins" (1 John 2:2). Sinners find themselves utterly unable to do anything to save themselves or to extricate themselves from their sinful condition. Their plight is serious indeed. They cannot cleanse themselves of sin (Prov. 20:9), and no deeds of law will ever enable them to stand before God justified (Rom. 3:20; Gal. 2:16). Hence the atonement, to accomplish for sinners what needed to be done, had to be made by someone else in their behalf. Christ is utter self-giving, even in death. He is the means of our return to God. Through Him we have access to the Father (Eph. 2:18), an access to be appropriated by faith (Eph. 3:12), faith in Him "whom God put forward as an expiation by his blood, to be received by faith" (Rom. 3:25).

There is no disputing that the NT proclaims the means of atonement as the gift of God to sinners, proceeding from the loving heart of God. In a most celebrated biblical statement we read that "God so loved the world, that he gave his only Son, that whoever believes in him should not perish but have eternal life" (John 3:16). This agrees with the words of Paul, for whom the cross is not only the measure of the love of Christ but of the love of God Himself: "In Christ God was reconciling the world to himself" (2 Cor. 5:19). "God shows his love for us in that while we were yet sinners Christ died for us" (Rom. 5:8). "He . . . did not spare his own Son, but gave him up for us all" (Rom. 8:32). For Paul, the final proof of God's love for sinners was the cross. The apostle does not, however, differentiate between the love of God and the love of Christ. Both are seen in the cross. "The life I now live in the flesh I live by faith in the Son of God, who loved me and gave himself for me," explains the apostle (Gal. 2:20). "For the love of Christ controls us, because we are convinced that one has died for all; therefore all have died" (2 Cor. 5:14).

5. A Divine Work

These statements make it evident that in the work of salvation the Father and the Son are completely at one. This is important in that it attests that our salvation comes to us with all the majesty of God the Father behind it. It is a divine work in its fullest sense. The idea that the cross expresses the love of Christ for us while He wrings atonement from a stern and unwilling Father, perfectly just but inflexible in insisting on punishment, is a caricature of NT thinking. To some extent, the need for reconciliation may be seen in the wrath of God against sin (Rom. 1:18; 2:5; cf. 1 Thess. 1:10), but the atonement takes place because God the Father loves us and in His Son makes provision for our salvation. Not alone did the Father conceive and initiate the plan of salvation; He was in Christ actually carrying it forward to completion.

D. Christ's Atoning Work: The NT Teaching

Besides these background factors, the NT uses several terms, metaphors, and symbols in its attempt to explain how Christ is able to cancel the effects of sin and reconcile the sinner to God. Throughout two thousand years of Christian history various theories have emerged, attempting to explain how this was done. None has succeeded in being universally accepted. Clearly, there is an essential mystery about the atonement: humans cannot fully comprehend how it works. But some points the Scriptures make clear, and any satisfactory understanding of the atonement must reckon with them.

1. A Sacrificial Death

Not surprisingly, the atoning death of Christ is expressed frequently in terms taken from the OT sacrificial system. In the OT atonement it is usually said to be obtained by sacrifices (Ex. 29:36; Lev. 4:20; Num. 15:25). Thus, the daily sacrifice or continual burnt offering seems most perfectly to have embodied the sacrificial idea through its vicarious character. This offering was not related to any particular transgression, but was maintained as the appropriate means for a sinful people to approach a holy God. The guilt, sin, and trespass offerings were necessary to atone for the sin that inherently was an offense against God's law, hence against God Himself (see Sanctuary I. C. 3). This offense had to be set right. Yet it is written of the atoning blood, "I have given it for you upon the altar to make atonement for your souls" (Lev. 17:11). The sacrifices were not the sinners' expedient remedy for their own redemption; they were designed by God and operated within the sphere of the covenant and covenantal grace. Nor did any value inherent in the sacrificial victim secure the atonement. Atonement was secure because the sacrifice was the divinely appointed way to obtain it. The victims were to be unblemished (Lev. 1:3; Deut. 15:21), denoting the necessity of perfection. Without attempting to confine the atonement to a single act, we cannot doubt that the death of the victim was the important thing (Lev. 1:5; 3:2; 4:4). This is again indicated in the general character of the sacrificial rite itself. The daily sacrifice was carried out in the OT context that recognizes that death is the penalty for sin (Gen. 2:16, 17; Eze. 18:4, 20), yet the God of the OT graciously told His penitent people that the death of a sacrificial victim would substitute for the death of the sinner. So clear is this connection that in the NT, the Epistle to the Hebrews can sum it up by declaring that "without the shedding of blood there is no forgiveness of sin" (Heb. 9:22).

At the same time, the NT asserts that the sacrifices of old were not, as such, the root of the remission of sins. In fact, Hebrews shows great concern to point out their inadequacy, except as types. They could not cleanse the conscience of the worshiper from guilt, but were mere ordinances set forth until a time of reformation (Heb. 9:6-10), a clear reference, in the context, to Christ's incarnation. The fact that mere animals were offered (Heb. 10:4) and that the offerings had to be repeated (verses 1, 2) shows clearly enough their inability to atone. The Epistle to the Hebrews finds in Jesus fulfillment and extension of the OT sacrificial system. Thus we read that the ritual services of the earthly sanctuary were "symbolic for the present age" (Heb. 9:9, *parabolē*), until Christ's coming (verse 10), "until faith should be revealed" (Gal. 3:23; cf. Heb. 13:11, 12).

The death of Christ, explain the NT writers, is a sacrifice for sin. John the Baptist, at the beginning of Jesus' ministry, saw Him in the role of a sacrifice: "Behold, the Lamb of God, who takes away the sin of the world" (John 1:29). More specifically, Paul viewed Christ's death as sacrificial: "Christ, our paschal lamb, has been sacrificed" (1 Cor. 5:7). He did not die because He was unable to resist enemies who conspired to destroy Him. He "was put to death for our trespasses" (Rom. 4:25); He came to die for our sins, "a fragrant offering

and sacrifice to God" (Eph. 5:2). His blood was "poured out for many for the forgiveness of sins" (Matt. 26:28). The book of Hebrews, again likening the work of Christ to the OT sanctuary services, depicts Him as the high priest who entered the heavenly tabernacle to offer a sacrifice, "not the blood of goats and calves, but his own blood, thus securing an eternal redemption" (Heb. 9:12).

The frequent references to Christ's blood are likewise suggestive of a sacrificial death. Paul, who speaks of the blood of Christ almost as often as he refers to His death, writes that "we are now justified by his blood" (Rom. 5:9); that there is "expiation by his blood" (Rom. 3:25); that "in him we have redemption through his blood" (Eph. 1:7); that we are brought near to God "in the blood of Christ" (Eph. 2:13); that Christ has reconciled all things to Himself "making peace by the blood of his cross" (Col. 1:20).

These statements, as well as Jesus' own references to His blood as the "blood of the covenant, which is poured out for many" (Mark 14:24), or Peter's to the "precious blood of Christ, like that of a lamb without blemish or spot" (1 Peter 1:19), remind us that blood means life violently taken away, in this case offered in sacrifice. Some have contested this view on the ground that in some OT passages (more particularly Gen. 9:4-6; Deut. 12:23) the shedding of blood is *only symbolic* of the life released by Jesus and does not imply that His life must be given as a sacrifice. The evidence, however, does not seem to support this interpretation. There is little doubt that these biblical statements establish that blood was identified with life. But what specific meaning does this have in connection with sacrifice? In Leviticus 17:11, the most often quoted statement, God states that "I have given it for you upon the altar to make atonement for your souls; for it is the blood that makes atonement, by reason of the life." For blood to be placed on the altar required death, understood as the giving up of life. Moreover, the Epistle to the Hebrews, in its comments on OT sacrificial rites, links "the blood of Christ" with the clause "a death has occurred which redeems" (Heb. 9:14, 15), thus underlining that blood in a sacrificial sense means more than life, although the latter is clearly included. The concept of blood strikes one as more meaningful than death. It draws attention to life as well as death.

2. A Vicarious Death

Jesus Christ "died for us" (1 Thess. 5:10). He did not die merely by the hands of His enemies or as the result of His own sin or guilt. He died specifically for us. "While we were yet sinners, Christ died for us" (Rom. 5:8). He gave Himself "for us" (Eph. 5:2) and became a curse "for us" (Gal. 3:13). Christ was our representative, as succinctly expressed by Paul in 2 Corinthians 5:14: "One has died for all; therefore all have died." The death of the representative counts as the death of those He represents. But "representative" is a term that may mean much or little. It needs to be made more precise. If indeed Christ, sinless as He was, came to share the awful weight and penalty of sin, it is difficult to avoid the conclusion that He died not only "for me" ("for my sake" or "in my behalf") but also "in my stead," especially since because of His life and death I need no longer die.

It is, of course, no secret that some reject out of hand the older language of substitution on the ground that it is too heavily laden with misleadings, even false connotations. Yet a variety of NT statements indicates that in His death Christ did indeed take our place. In two of the Synoptic Gospels one can find Jesus' well-known ransom saying, "the Son of man came not to be served but to serve, and to give his life as a ransom [lytron] for many [anti pollōn]" (Matt. 20:28; see also Mark 10:45). "Ransom" is what is paid to free from captivity, a sum given in exchange, usually for a person. The term clearly suggests substitution. So does anti (translated "for"), a preposition which essentially means "instead of," "in the place of." In His death Jesus took

our place, identifying Himself with sinners. From this identification, nevertheless, His soul shrank (Matt. 26:36-39, 42-44; Luke 22:41-44). This gives meaning to His cry of dereliction, "My God, my God, why hast thou forsaken me?" (Mark 15:34). Why should Jesus be in an agony as He contemplated death? Was it fear of the torture He was undergoing? Many lesser than He have faced death calmly. What He shrank away from was not death as such, but the death that was the death of sinners, that death in which He, the Sinless One, would experience the horror of being separated from the Father, forsaken by Him. To this Paul seems to have referred when he wrote that God, "for our sake [hyper], . . . made him to be sin who knew no sin, so that in him we might become the righteousness of God" (2 Cor. 5:21). Christ became something which He had not been. It must mean that in an unfathomable way He took the place of those who would themselves otherwise suffer death. The apostle did not want to say that Jesus was a sinner, but he went as near as possible, conveying the thought that God regarded Him in the same way as He regarded sinners.

"Ransom" (lytron) is part of a word group found in several NT passages, usually translated "to redeem" or "redemption," as in Romans 3:24; Ephesians 1:7; Titus 2:14; Hebrews 9:12, 15; 1 Peter 1:18, 19. "Ransoming," rather than "deliverance," is the essential meaning of these sayings. A "ransoming" and vicarious (substitutionary), death is one description chosen by the NT writers to explain to the early believers what happened at the cross. Paul addresses the same thought time and again, though in most instances he uses the preposition hyper rather than anti. Hyper is generally used in the representative sense of "for" or "on behalf of," though it sometimes borders on anti, "instead of," as, for instance, in 2 Corinthians 5:15 and 1 Timothy 2:6. So Christ died on our behalf and in our place. In fact, "ransom" has its true and proper sense in Paul when the apostle comments that Jesus "gave himself as a ransom [antilytron]

177

for all *[hyper]*" (1 Tim. 2:6), a statement reminiscent of the ransom passage in both Matthew and Mark. Here *anti* and *hyper* are used side by side. Noteworthy also is the fact that in this statement the word *lytron* is compounded with *anti*. The force of this combined word meaning "substitute-ransom" attests that the passage points to an interpretation of the death of Christ perceived as an act undertaken by Jesus in the place of others.

The substitutionary concept is also evident in 1 Peter 2:24: "He himself bore our sins in his body on the tree." Likewise in Hebrews 9:28, which speaks of Christ as "having been offered once to bear the sins of many." This is not to be understood to mean merely that Jesus put up with the frustrations and difficulties involved in living among sinful people. The meaning of "bearing sin" is made clear by several OT passages where the context shows that bearing sins means bearing their penalty. Thus God is recorded as saying, "The soul that sins shall die. The son shall not suffer for [Heb. "bear"] the iniquity of the father, nor the father suffer for [Heb. "bear"] the iniquity of the son; . . . the wickedness of the wicked shall be upon himself" (Eze. 18:20). Likewise in Numbers 14:34, Israel's 40 years of wandering in the wilderness is described as the bearing of the penalty of their sin of rebellion against God. Christ's bearing of our sins is a reference to His bearing our penalty.

In the face of this imposing body of evidence it seems difficult to deny that substitution is one approach adopted by the NT to explain the work, that is the life and death, of our Lord Jesus Christ.

3. The Expiation-Propitiation Dimension

The death of Christ has also an expiatory and, in the biblical sense, a propitiatory dimension. This aspect of Christ's death is expressed by the *hilaskomai* word group, which appears in one of the most crucial sections of Paul's letter to the Romans: "They are justified by his grace as a gift, through the redemption which is in Christ Jesus, whom God put forward as an expiation *[hilastērion]* by his blood, to be received by faith" (Rom. 3:24, 25). While derivatives of the *hilaskomai* word group have traditionally been translated "propitiation," "to propitiate," many modern theologians have rendered them "expiation" or "to expiate." To expiate means to put an end to, to cancel the guilt incurred, to pay the penalty for a crime. To propitiate, on the other hand, signifies to appease, to conciliate, to gain or regain someone's favor. It refers to the turning away of anger, usually by the offering of a gift. There is no doubt that this was the prevailing use in classical and Hellenistic Greek.

Modern scholarship has reacted against the traditional view that the death of Christ effected an appeasing of the wrath of God against sin, by virtue of which the sinner becomes the recipient of God's gracious gift of love. It has shown that, in most instances, when derivatives of the *hilaskomai* word group are used as religious terms in the LXX, which many regard as providing the background of Paul's thought, they are not to be understood as conveying the same meaning as found in secular sources. These words do not denote "propitiation," "appeasement," as in the pagan usage, but rather the removal of guilt or defilement. One ought not to think, therefore, of God as a capricious or vindictive deity whose wrath has been placated or appeased by the sacrifice of Christ, who thus changed God's mind toward sinners.

These are important conclusions, the results of valuable study. Still, one should be forgiven for asking whether the final word has been said. There is little doubt that the pagan views of wrath and propitiation are absent from the scriptural view of God. The God of the Bible is not a being who can be propitiated or placated after the fashion of ancient pagan deities. In the context of the *hilaskomai* word group, Christ's death is an expiation for our sins, a removing of guilt and the defilement of sin. Yet to say that all idea of wrath and propitiation is foreign to it seems to ignore the thought of various scriptural statements.

The celebrated Romans 3:21-26 passage, for instance, in which the apostle most compellingly sets forth the redemption which God has provided in Jesus Christ is, in truth, the culmination of a process of reasoning that began with the pronouncement of God's wrath against sin, "For the wrath of God is revealed from heaven against all ungodliness and wickedness of men" (Rom. 1:18) and which, in successive steps refers to God's wrath and judgment (Rom. 2:2, 4, 5, 8, 16; 3:4-6). The sinner's redemption, explains Paul, was obtained through the death of Christ, "whom God put forward as an expiation by his blood, to be received by faith" (verse 25). It seems difficult to deny that in the context of the first three chapters of the Epistle, Christ's expiation holds an element of propitiation. Wrath and judgment have occupied too important a place in this closely knit piece of reasoning not to lead the reader to look for some expression indicative of their cancellation in the process that brings salvation to the believer. Christ is that which expiates and propitiates, the means of which is indicated in the following phrase, "by his blood" (verse 25). Those who are of faith (verse 25a) have seen their guilt removed and God's wrath turned aside. Christ has voluntarily taken them upon Himself, God having "made him to be sin who knew no sin" (2 Cor. 5:21), and for our sake forsaken Him as He died on the cross. God so dealt with sin in Christ that sin is no longer a barrier between Him and humans.

A clue to the meaning of *hilastērion* in this passage is provided by Hebrews 9:5, the only other use of the term in the NT. Here it is translated "the mercy seat," the lid of the ark, in the Most Holy Place, where the atoning blood was sprinkled once a year (Lev. 16:11-14; see Sanctuary I. B. 1). Some have suggested that the same translation be retained in Romans 3:25; and much could be said for retaining it, as Luther did.

That some may have come to reject the whole idea of divine wrath and of propitiation as unworthy of the Christian view of God is understandable, for God is love, and nothing is more certain in the Scriptures. To explain wrath away as an impersonal expression, pointing merely to a process of cause and effect, however, is not to do full justice to Paul's thought. The term does not express anger in the sense in which it is so frequently ascribed to our own human experience, a wrath either capricious or uncontrollable, often an irrational outburst of passion, but rather the reverse side of God's relentless love, as well as His stern reaction to evil.

It is actually the combination of God's holiness, of His reaction against sin and His unshakable love for sinners, that sets forth the context in which the Scriptures refer to expiation-propitiation. God is holy. Christ suffered in our place, satisfying "the just requirement of the law" (Rom. 8:4), thus removing the obstacle to the pardon of the guilty. God's holiness made the penalty for sin inescapable. God took upon Himself His own decreed penalty. His love endured it in our stead, making the pardon possible and overcoming the divine-human alienation. What the holiness of God required, His love provided. On the cross the holiness of God's love is forevermore revealed and the love of the holy God fully manifested. Here justice and mercy kiss each other.

Some 40 years after Paul, the apostle John wrote, referring to Christ, "he is the expiation [propitiation] for our sins" (1 John 2:2), summing it all up in a most stirring fashion, "In this is love, not that we loved God but that He loved us and sent His Son to be the expiation [propitiation] for our sins" (1 John 4:10). We have here one of those resounding statements that mean so much for the understanding of the Christian view of the cross. John plainly affirms that God Himself, in His love, provided the costly Gift that cancels our guilt and turns God's wrath aside. In the apostle's words, God "loved us and sent his Son to be the expiation [propitiation] for our sins." Because of the cross we know with an unshakable conviction that God is love and eminently love. It shows us that love does not gloss over sin but effectively grapples with it. Christ's death, as an expiation-propitiation put forth by God Himself, is a demonstration, a proof of God's love and righteousness (Rom. 3:26). "Expiation" and "propitiation" may not be ideal words for our purpose, but for lack of more appropriate terms, we may have to use them with care. Moreover, our concern is with facts more than with words. They witness to two great realities, i.e., the reality of sin and of its seriousness on the one hand, and on the other the depth of God's love, which provides the gift which deflects the wrath from sinners and which is "to be received by faith" (verse 25). To eliminate either dimension from the love of God is to rob God's love of much of its apostolic meaning.

4. Justification

The concepts we have considered thus far—sacrifice, redemption, substitution, and expiation-propitiation—describe important aspects of Christ's life and death. Yet there are other metaphors of atonement. One of them, dominating Paul's letters to the Romans and the Galatians, is that of justification of sinners by the grace of God. (See Salvation III. A. 1.) This approach defines the saving significance of Christ's life and death by relating them to God's law (Rom. 3:24-26; 5:16-21). In substance, the apostle argues that God is just in condemning and punishing sin, merciful in pardoning and accepting sinners, and sovereign in exercising both attributes harmoniously together through Christ Jesus (Rom. 3:23-26). The biblical meaning of "justify" is to declare, accept, and treat as just. It is basically a legal term, a forensic term denoting a legal process culminating in a verdict of acquittal and excluding all possibilities of condemnation (cf. Prov. 17:15; Rom. 8:33, 34).

But then, since we are all sinners (Rom. 3: 9, 23), and all face judgment (2 Cor. 5:10; Rom. 14:10), deserving condemnation, how can Paul paradoxically affirm that God justifies the ungodly (Rom. 4:5)? His answer is that Christ has provided the way. Jesus Christ, acting on the sinners' behalf, has fulfilled "the just requirement of the law" (Rom. 8:4). By His blood, He has put away their sins (Rom. 3:25; 5:9). Through His obedience to God His people have been accepted as lawkeepers (Rom. 5:19), for through His life of righteousness and His dying the death of the unrighteous, He has redeemed them from the curse of the law, having Himself become a curse for them (Gal. 3:13). Just as one man's trespass led to condemnation, "one man's act of righteousness"—His sinless life and death—"leads to acquittal and life for all men" (Rom. 5:18). God made Him "our righteousness" (1 Cor. 1:30).

Not only does God save sinners, but He also saves them justly, in a way that accords with what is right. Far from compromising God's judicial righteousness, Christ's sacrificial life and death actually demonstrated it. God's law was not altered or suspended for our justification, but fulfilled by Christ, the Second Adam, acting in our name. In Paul's words, Christ's death proved that God "himself is righteous and that he justifies him who has faith in Jesus" (Rom. 3:26). By setting forth Christ, in whom sin was actually judged and treated as it rightly deserved, as an expiation for sin, God revealed the ground on which He is able to forgive and accept repentant sinners as His children, without compromising His own justice (verse 26). Provision has been made for all to be saved.

This, adds Paul, is "to be received by faith" (verse 25). Faith is not the ground of justification but the instrumental means by which Christ and His righteousness are appropriated, the outstretched empty hand that receives righteousness by receiving Christ. Justification is essentially a matter of relationship restored, which is what the word "atonement" stands for.

5. Reconciliation

Reconciliation is one more of the fundamental concepts derived from the early church's attempt to explain the nature and meaning of the cross. The work of Christ was perceived as having to do with reconciliation and the way it was effected. Although Paul alone in the NT uses the terminology, and does so in only four passages (Rom. 5:10, 11; 2 Cor. 5:18-20; Eph. 2:11-16; Col. 1:19-22), the concept of reconciliation is important in the apostle's understanding of the work of Christ. (See Salvation III. A. 2.)

Reconciliation has to do with the restoration of a broken relationship. It is a personal category. When there has been a state of enmity or hostility between people, and they have come to be of one mind again, one may speak of reconciliation. As noticed earlier, the whole thrust of the Bible is toward the fact that sin created a barrier between unregenerate humans and God, not to mention among humans themselves. Paul speaks of sinners as "estranged and hostile in mind" (Col. 1:21), or simply as "enemies" of God (Rom. 5:10), "by nature children of wrath" (Eph. 2:3). There is need of reconciliation. Since all four passages state that humans are to be reconciled to God, some have concluded that the state of enmity is on one side only, it has been argued that reconciliation merely requires a change in us, a return to God. There is truth in this, yet from the biblical perspective it is not the complete picture, which insists that here, too, God's holiness and the cross remain central.

In Romans 5:10, for instance, Paul writes that "while we were enemies we were reconciled to God by the death of his Son." There was enmity, but reconciliation occurred. As in human affairs, it occurred by taking out of the way the root cause of the quarrel, in this case it was sin. Humans are unable to remove it, so God put it out of the way. In the clearest possible terms, Paul tells us that whatever else the biblical doctrine of reconciliation involves, God initiated and accomplished reconciliation in Christ. Here again the place of the cross of Christ is critically important, for the apostle tells us in no uncertain terms that "we were reconciled to God by the death of his Son" (Rom. 5:10; cf. Col. 1:20).

Closely allied to this consideration is the observation that this took place because God loves us. Paul asserts that "God shows his love for us in that while we were yet sinners Christ died for us" (Rom. 5:8), "for the ungodly" (verse 6). For the NT, the love of God does not mean that sin can be passed over lightly or simply dismissed, but that sin is dealt with. This is no indulgent amnesty, but true forgiveness and reconciliation, thanks to the cross of Christ. The Father is the author of reconciliation. "All this is from God," argues Paul, "who through Christ reconciled us to himself and gave us the ministry of reconciliation; that is, God was in Christ reconciling the world to himself, not counting their trespasses against them, and entrusting to us the message of reconciliation. So we are ambassadors for Christ, God making his appeal through us. We beseech you on behalf of Christ, be reconciled to God" (2 Cor. 5:18-20).

Reconciliation is not something in which we have the decisive part. It is primarily an act of God, initiated by His love, by virtue of which God no longer counts our trespasses against us. It has to do not only with our attitude toward God, but also with God's attitude toward us, as a result of which He no longer looks upon us as enemies or holding a hostile status. Nor is it primarily a change in the sinner's attitude toward God, but an objective event accomplished by God for our salvation. The change of attitude on the sinner's part, involving a cessation of hostility toward God, occurs as a result of the reconciling work of Christ, not as its cause. It was "while we were enemies" that we were reconciled to God by the death of His Son (Rom. 5:10). No wonder Paul feels forced to add, "We . . . rejoice in God through our Lord Jesus Christ, through whom we have now received our reconciliation" (verse 11). Note that reconciliation is something to be "received," something that exists objectively before we experience it. What was effected was outside of and prior to our human response. It implies that God Himself became reconciled to man through the life and death of Christ. Here again, the death of Christ made it possible for a holy God to do for sinners what otherwise He could not have done.

Reconciliation with God brings inward peace of mind to the sinner (cf. verse 1). It also induces reconciliation of sinners with their neighbors. The classic biblical testimony is Paul's discussion in Ephesians 2 of one of the bitterest enmities in the ancient world, that between Jew and Gentile. Those who were at one time alienated, "strangers to the covenants of promise, having no hope and without God in the world," were "brought near in the blood of Christ. For he is our peace, who has made us both one, and has broken down the dividing wall of hostility, . . . that he might create in himself one new man in place of the two, so making peace, and might reconcile us both to God in one body through the cross, thereby bringing the hostility to an end" (Eph. 2:12-16). This is not an accidental by-product of the sinner's salvation. It is an integral part of it, part of living out the implications of our reconciliation with God. Once our reconciliation with God is effected, our reconciliation with each other should follow.

E. The Extent of the Atoning Deed

Bolstering their view of predestination by an appeal to the passages of Scripture that speak of Christ's giving His life for His sheep (John 10:1-15, 26, 27), for the church (Acts 20:28; Eph. 5:25), or for many (Mark 10:45), and to statements that seem to limit the object of Christ's intercession to the disciples and those whom they would win (John 17:9, 20, 24), some have insisted that Christ's atonement is limited in its design to those who are actually saved, to a select group chosen by God.

It appears, however, that the NT writers uphold an atoning deed perceived as universal in intent, available to all sinners, yet effective only when individually accepted. Thus, John describes the purpose of Christ's coming in universal terms (John 3:16, 17) and His death

as dealing with the sins "of the world" (John 1:29; 1 John 2:1, 2; cf. 4:14). Paul, likewise, speaks of Jesus as dying "for all" (2 Cor. 5:14, 15) or as giving Himself "as a ransom for all" (1 Tim. 2:6). Both 2 Peter, which asserts that God wills that "all should reach repentance" (1 Tim. 3:9), and the Epistle to the Hebrews, which bluntly declares that Christ tasted death "for every one" (1 Tim. 2:9), reemphasize the early church's understanding of God's offer of salvation as unrestricted.

To say that Christ died for all does not exclude the idea that He died for the elect and that His death is unquestionably efficacious for them. The larger circle includes the smaller one, as Paul tells us when he writes that God is "the Savior of all men, especially of those who believe" (1 Tim. 4:10). The atonement is intended for all, addressed to all, and sufficient for all, but it benefits only those who of their own will have responded to it in faith. (See Salvation I. D.)

The preceding survey of the purpose of Christ's mission has shown how vast and deep the atonement of Christ is. Guided by the Spirit, the NT writers strive with the inadequacy of human language as they seek to present us with what that divine event means. The various figures of speech with which Paul and the others explain it shed light on many dimensions of our sinful condition. We have referred to such aspects as sacrifice, redemption, substitution, expiation-propitiation, justification, and reconciliation. All these points are important, and none is to be neglected. Yet none is sufficient to cover all of the various aspects of the meaning of the cross. There is much more to it. The atonement stands for more than something negative, i.e., the putting away of sin and the removal of enmity. It opens the way to a new life in Christ. That new life of gratitude and growth in Christ, fruit of the atonement, is far from an insignificant facet of the Christian experience. The biblical doctrine of the atonement leads to that.

III. The Exalted Lord

A. The Risen Christ

However central the event, the NT message, even in the Gospels, does not conclude with the cross. The Gospel writers go right on to speak of the resurrection (Matt. 27:51-28:20; Mark 16; Luke 24; John 20; 21). The gospel that Paul received through revelation (Gal. 1:12) began by declaring "as of first importance" that "Christ died for our sins in accordance with the scriptures, that he was buried, that he was raised on the third day in accordance with the scriptures" (1 Cor. 15:3; cf. verse 1). Thus, the death and resurrection of Jesus Christ were proclaimed as belonging together to the very heart of the gospel. Paul's reluctance to refer to one without the other is reflected in Romans 8:34: "Christ Jesus, who died, yes, who was raised from the dead."

1. A Fundamental Event

Even so, as far as its place and its significance in the whole Christ-event are concerned, the Resurrection usually has been understood poorly. A large number of Christians have viewed Christ's resurrection mainly as the strongest possible evidence of their future resurrection to a life of eternal glory (cf. Phil. 3:20, 21; Rev. 21:1–22:5). By itself the Resurrection did not seem to have much importance in the work of redemption. We were redeemed by the cross, and by the cross only. The NT church, however, understood the resurrection of Jesus with its completion in the ascension, as central to, not simply confirmatory of, the Christian faith. For the early believers the Resurrection was the origin rather than the end of the story, in a sense the cornerstone of the Christian faith (1 Cor. 15:14, 17). It was seen not as a typical instance of resurrection in general but as a unique event. Nor was it a mere resuscitation, which brought Jesus back to this life to die again, as in the case of Lazarus or the son of the widow of Nain. His was the resurrection of the Messiah, the means chosen by God to designate Jesus as the Christ, the Son of God (Acts 2:36; Rom. 1:4).

The early disciples' faith built on the life and ministry of Christ was shattered to pieces at the cross. As the book of Acts tells us, the Resurrection viewed as a mighty declaratory act of God (Acts 2:24, 32; 1 Peter 1:21; cf. Eph. 1:19, 20) reinterpreted and reestablished the faith aroused by Jesus' life, and for the first time gave Him His true place as Lord and Christ (Acts 2:36; Rom. 1:4). Through the Resurrection Jesus was proclaimed not only Messiah and Lord, but "Author of life" (Acts 3:15), "Savior" (Acts 5:31), and "judge of the living and the dead" (Acts 10:42). Under the impact of the Resurrection the ambiguities that surrounded His life and death disappeared.

2. The Empty Tomb

Apart from the soldiers who guarded the tomb (Matt. 28:4), no one actually saw Jesus rising from the grave. But several found an empty tomb, and many more saw the risen Lord. Some of these appearances occurred in or near Jerusalem, others in Galilee. According to the biblical accounts, the Lord appeared to the women who went to the tomb prepared to anoint His body (verses 9, 10), Mary Magdalene (John 20:11-18), Simon Peter (Luke 24:34; 1 Cor. 15:5), two disciples on their way to Emmaus (Luke 24:13-31; Mark 16:12, 13), the 11 and other disciples gathered on the evening of the resurrection day (Luke 24:33, 34; John 20:19-23), Thomas a week later (verses 26-29), seven disciples by the sea of Galilee (John 21:1-19), the 11 gathered on a mountain in Galilee (Matt. 28:16, 17)—which appearance many regard as the same as that to the 500 brethren mentioned by Paul (1 Cor. 15:6), the disciples who saw Jesus ascend into heaven from the Mount of Olives (Luke 24:50, 51; Acts 1:6-9), James (1 Cor. 15:7), and Paul on the road to Damascus (Acts 9:1-19). Neither the Gospels nor Paul provide a chronological list of all the facts. Variations in detail, such as the sequence, number, and names of the women who visited the tomb, and the number of angels, are not hard to tabulate. These difficulties regarding details offer no insuperable objections when one remembers that each author selected the facts that he regarded most appropriate to his goal. Diverse interests seem to have determined the perspective from which the different aspects of the facts were underlined. But apart from details of description, the basic witness is remarkably unanimous. There is no evidence of a later fabrication or agreed-upon story.

3. A Physical Resurrection

Several common features characterize all of these appearances. They were granted to those who were already disciples of Christ. "God," as Peter declared to Cornelius, "made him manifest; not to all the people but to us who were chosen by God as witnesses" (Acts 10:40, 41). These manifestations were assurances given to those who had previously accepted Him. All scriptural records testify to a physical, bodily resurrection. The evangelists speak of touching Jesus (John 20:27), of eating (Luke 24:41-43) and conversing (John 21:9-22) with Him. This counteracts the Greek tendency to make of the resurrection an abstract, noncorporeal event. Indeed, it would have been inconceivable for first-century Jews to think of a resurrection except in bodily terms. A bodiless resurrection would have seemed an absurdity to them.

There is an underlying unity between the Jesus the disciples had known over the years and the risen Lord. He Himself emphatically declared, "A spirit has not flesh and bones as you see that I have" (Luke 24:40), adding "see, . . . it is I myself " (verse 39). Yet all depict the same phenomenon, that of a body identical yet changed, transcending the limitations of the human nature—barred doors did not exclude it (Luke 24:31; John 20:10, 26)—yet capable of manifesting itself within its parameters. In Pauline language it had "put on the imperishable" (1 Cor. 15:53). The disciples, at times at least, did not recognize Jesus initially as He stood before them (John 20:14; 21:4, 12). It seems significant that the two evangelists who insist most on the physical character of Christ's appearances (Luke 24:39-43; John 20:20, 27; 21:9-14) are those who mention that He had already, by the time of the appearances, "[entered] into his glory" (Luke 24:26) and been "glorified" (John 13:31; cf. 20:22 with 7:39). Mark states explicitly that Jesus "appeared in another form" (Mark 16:12).

By ruling out a priori the miraculous, the modern mind has tended to deny the resurrection of Christ as a historical fact of supernatural character. Some have suggested that the disciples merely stole the body and hid it away; some have insisted that Jesus was alive after the crucifixion and burial merely because He never really died, but merely fainted. Others have proposed that since there probably was a number of similar tombs in the burial area, the women, misled by the darkness, went to the wrong tomb, one that was indeed empty because it always had been. Still others have urged that the disciples did not actually see a risen Christ, but rather as a result of their faith in Him and their strong longing for Him, imagined that they saw Him and heard Him speak to them. In more recent years Christ's resurrection is no longer explained away, but demythologized and reinterpreted as a way of announcing that in Jesus of Nazareth God has, in a unique way, broken into human history and has come to stay. The *fact* of the resurrection, we are told, has no real relevance, since its crucial importance is as a factor in faith and not in history.

None of the theories that have been set forth to account for the empty tomb and Christ's appearances seems adequate, nor does any combination of them. Having seen Him, the disciples make no attempt to explain what took place. For them, Christ's resurrection was God's act (Acts 2:24, 32; Rom. 6:4; 1 Peter 1:21), the fulfillment of OT prophecies (Acts 2:25-36; 1 Cor. 15:4), a part of God's eternal purpose for the salvation of sinners. That the disciples, beaten and dispirited at the time of the Crucifixion, a few weeks later should have boldly confronted those who had condemned Jesus, and proclaimed His resurrection and lordship, is the real evidence for the resurrection as a historical fact (Acts 2:22-24; 3:14, 15; and especially 4:10). From the very beginning and with great power they testified to the Resurrection of their Lord (Acts 2:24; 4:33), leaving to God the things they could not understand.

4. The Significance of Christ's Resurrection

For the NT writers the resurrection of Jesus Christ is a new act of God, a historical event that occurred in the history of this world. Its theological importance cannot be overrated.

The christological significance of the Resurrection is considerable. For the apostles, its primary significance lay in the fact that it was the divine confirmation of Jesus' claims regarding His person and work. All that evil hands had done had been overturned by God's vindicating action: "This Jesus . . . you crucified and killed by the hands of lawless men. But God raised him up" (Acts 2:23, 24; 10:39, 40). Their constant emphasis was not only that Jesus was risen but that God had raised Him, or that He had been raised (Acts 2:32, 36; 3:15; 4:10; 5:30; Rom. 4:24, 25; 6:4; 8:11; 1 Cor. 15:4, 15; 2 Cor. 4:14; Gal. 1:1; Heb. 13:20; 1 Peter 1:21; etc.). By His resurrection Jesus was "designated Son of God in power" (Rom. 1:4; cf. Acts 13:33). It marked the beginning of His exaltation as Lord and Christ (Acts 2:29-36; Phil. 2:9-11), reflecting Jesus' own postresurrection statement that "all authority in heaven and on earth has been given to me" (Matt. 28:18). By raising Him from the dead, God "glorified his servant Jesus" (Acts 3:13) and appointed Him judge of the world (Acts 10:42; 17:31; cf. John 5:22, 27). As "the living one" He holds "the keys of Death and Hades" (Rev. 1:18).

Beyond these Christward dimensions, the Resurrection also has significance for sinners.

It is a saving event, for, in Paul's terms, Jesus "was put to death for our trespasses and raised for our justification" (Rom. 4:25). There is no salvation except for those who confess with their lips that "Jesus is Lord" and believe in their hearts "that God raised Him from the dead" (Rom. 10:9). Those who have been "baptized into his death," united with Him in a death like His, shall also be "united with him in a resurrection like his" (Rom. 6:3-5; Resurrection I. A. 2. a). Waiting for that day, and having been "crucified with Christ" (Gal. 2:20) unto sin, they have been buried with Him by baptism, "so that as Christ was raised from the dead by the glory of the Father, [they] . . . too might walk in newness of life" (Rom. 6:4; cf. 8:9-11; Eph. 2:4-7; Col. 2:12; 3:1-3) and "bear fruit for God" (Rom. 7:4; cf. 1 Peter 1:3). As Paul sees it, Christ's resurrection is of cardinal importance: "If Christ has not been raised," he writes, "then our preaching is in vain, and our faith is in vain. . . . If Christ has not been raised, your faith is futile and you are still in your sins" (1 Cor. 15:14-17). Our preaching, our faith, and our salvation do not take place apart from Christ's resurrection. In it we have the pledge of the consummation of God's redeeming purpose.

B. The Ascended Lord

According to the Scriptures, Christ not merely rose from the dead; He also ascended to heaven as the God-man and our Mediator. Christ's ascension is a major factor in the life of Christ as well as that of Christians. No complete view of Jesus Christ is possible unless the ascension and its consequences are included. Indeed, our Lord's heavenly ministry and Second Coming are inconceivable apart from it.

1. The Scriptural Evidence

The only detailed account of the ascension is given in Acts 1:2-11. The same event, reported much more briefly, is preserved in Luke 24:51 and in Mark 16:19. Several statements in the Gospels attest that it was anticipated by our Lord during His earthly ministry (Luke 9:31, 51; John 6:62; 7:33; 14:12, 28; 16:5, 10, 28). It is also mentioned or implied in several passages in Acts (2:33-35; 3:21; 7:55, 56; 22:6-8; 26:13-15). To those, additional references and allusions may be found, as in Philippians 2:9; 1 Timothy 3:16; Hebrews 1:3; 2:9; 12:2; 1 Peter 3:22; Revelations 1:13; 5:6. The event is more than adequately evidenced.

The record in the book of Acts is sometimes contested because of its picture of a body ascending, against the law of gravity or because it seems to suggest that heaven is located a short distance above the earth, an untenable picture in the eyes of modern science. The NT writers, for all that, see no greater difficulty in the ascension than in Christ's resurrection or His incarnation. To them it is part and parcel of God's plan of redemption and no more wonderful than the other two. Besides, there is no reason to assume that Luke, whose writing is that of a careful historian who verified his facts from original sources and eyewitnesses (Luke 1:1, 2; cf. Acts 1:1, 2), would not have verified the details of their experience in this particular instance also.

2. The Ascension's Relation to Christ

The ascension signaled the exaltation and glory of the risen Christ once His work on earth was accomplished (Phil. 2:9). It meant for Him the clear confirmation of His victory (Eph. 4:8) and the resumption of His face-to-face fellowship in glory with the Father (John 17:5). God had now "hyperexalted" *(hyperypsōsen)* Him (Phil. 2:9).

In their endeavor to describe our Lord's ascended life, the NT writers repeatedly use the statement of Psalm 110:1: "The Lord says to my lord: 'Sit at my right hand, till I make your enemies your footstool,' " which is quoted directly in Matthew 22:44; Mark 12:36; Acts 2:34, 35; 1 Corinthians 15:25; Hebrews 1:13; 10:12, 13, and indirectly in various passages which speak of Jesus being (Acts 2:33; Rom. 8:34), sitting (Eph. 1:20; Col. 3:1), or standing (Acts 7:55, 56) at God's right hand till all His enemies are subdued. A careful reading shows that many of these statements not only merely emphasize the historic fact of Christ's ascension on a certain day but denote His ascension as a continuous function. This point of view is seen also in Romans 8:34 and 1 Peter 3:22 where the two apostles declare that Jesus *"is* at the right hand of God." The symbolism does not imply that Christ is idle. On the contrary, its meaning is unmistakable. It expresses the exaltation and glory of the ascended God-man. The Resurrection has begun the great change; the Ascension conveys the distinct impression that Christ had gone to His Father and that all power has been put into His hands.

3. Its Relation to Believers

Christ's ascension is also of particular importance for Christian believers. For Christians, rather than denoting physical remoteness, it implies His spiritual nearness (Matt. 28:20). He is "alive for evermore" (Rev. 1:18). In God's own words, His "throne . . . is for ever and ever" (Heb. 1:8). In the NT, from the time of the ascension on, the constant assurance is that Christ is living and that in His life believers live. The ascension enabled Him to send forth the Holy Spirit (John 16:7; Acts 2:33) to convict the world of sin (John 16:8), indwell His disciples (John 14:17), edify and instruct them (John 14:25, 26; 16:14, 15), giving them power to witness (Acts 1:8; 4:8, 31), creating a new and radiating fellowship (Acts 2:41-47; 2 Cor. 13:14; Phil. 2:1, 2). Though ascended on high, He continues to instruct His own through the gift of the Spirit, who was to teach them all things (John 14:26) and guide them into all the truth, not speaking on His own authority, "for he will take what is mine and declare it to you" (John 16:14). This is illustrated by the outpouring of the gift of prophecy upon the church, "the testimony of Jesus is the spirit of prophecy" (Rev. 19:10; see God VII. C; Gifts X. D).

C. Christ's High Priestly Ministry

1. The Scriptural Evidence

He who has passed through the heavens" is now our great high priest (Heb. 4:14; cf. 6:20) in the heavenly sanctuary, the real tabernacle—as opposed to the shadowy, earthly one (Heb. 8:1, 2), maintaining a ministry of intercession on our behalf (Heb. 7:24, 25), ever interceding for us (Rom. 8:34). The high priesthood of Christ is one of the great themes of the Epistle to the Hebrews (2:17; 3:1–4:14, 15; 5:10; 6:20; etc.). He "has entered . . . into heaven itself, now to appear in the presence of God on our behalf" (Heb. 9:24). While His sacrifice for sin was made once for all on the cross (Heb. 7:27; 9:28; 10:11-14), the ascended Christ is making available to all the benefits of His atoning sacrifice. He is now both priest and priestly victim. As the Scriptures show, Christ's ministry in heaven is as essential to the salvation of sinners as His death on the cross.

2. Two Distinctive Ministries

The two distinctive ministries that the Levitical priests carried out in the earthly tabernacle were a pictorial representation of the plan of salvation. They typified, or illustrated, Christ's ministry in heaven. (See Sanctuary III. D.) This is the meaning of the references in Hebrews to the priests and high priests performing their ministries in the earthly sanctuary (Heb. 4:14, 15; 6:20; 7:27; 8:3; 9:7, 12, 24). The daily Levitical ministry in the holy place of the earthly sanctuary was essentially a ministry of intercession and reconciliation, symbolizing the truth that through Christ's ministry as intercessor the repentant sinner has constant and confident access to the Father (Heb. 4:14-16; 7:25; 10:19-22; see Sanctuary). Once a year, on the Day of Atonement, the Levitical high priest, and he alone, performed a ministry revolving around the cleansing of the sanctuary and of God's people, making atonement for both (Lev. 16:16-20, 30-32). On that day, said the Lord to Moses, "he [the high priest] shall make atonement for the sanctuary" and "for the priests and for all the people of the assembly" (Lev. 16:33). That day was intimately related to a work of judgment (Lev. 23:29; see Sanctuary I. C. 3. a, b) and in its typical functions foreshadowed the final judgment process that eradicates sin. The Scriptures indeed tell us that a judgment precedes Christ's second coming, for He returns in glory to give to all according to their works (Matt. 16:27; 25:31-46; cf. Rom. 2:6). The time when Christ was to begin this antitypical ministry of cleansing and judgment has been specified in Daniel 7-9, leading to A.D. 1844. (See Judgment III. B. 1.)

3. Ascended to Rule and to Fill All Things

The NT adds that Jesus also ascended to heaven that He might rule over and fill all things (Eph. 4:10; Rev. 1:5). He is seated far above all rule, authority, and power, both in this and in the coming age (Eph. 1:21). He was exalted, that in His name "every knee should bow" throughout the whole universe (Phil. 2:10). In Peter's words, He "has gone into heaven and is at the right hand of God, with angels, authorities, and powers subject to him" (1 Peter 3:22). All authority in heaven and on earth has been given to Him. He "is the head of the church" (Eph. 1:20-23; 5:23; Col. 1:18), the priest-king, and His kingship assures us that good will triumph over evil.

D. Christ's Second Coming

1. The Scriptural Evidence

Closely associated with Christ's ascension and high-priestly ministry is His coming again. For though He had come to this world to found the kingdom of God and fulfill the true spiritual meaning of the Messianic hope, He stated that the object of His mission would not be fully attained in that first coming. There was to be a break in His visible connection with earthly affairs (Matt. 16:21). He would depart for a time (John 14:19; 16:7), but He promised He would come again to carry on His work to complete fulfillment (John 14:1-3) and bring the kingdom of God to its supreme triumph and glory (Matt. 25:31-46; see Second Coming I. D. 4).

The biblical concept of our Lord's second coming is expressed by such terms as *parousia* ("presence," "arrival," or "coming"), often of a ruler or king (as in Matt. 24:27, 37, 39; 1 Cor. 15:23; 1 Thess. 2:19; 3:13; James 5:7, 8; 2 Peter 1:16; 3:4); *apokalypsis* ("disclosure," "revelation") in glory (Luke 17:30; 1 Cor. 1:7; 2 Thess. 1:7, 8; 1 Peter 1:13); *epiphaneia* ("manifestation" or "appearing"), a term used of Christ's incarnation (2 Tim. 1:10) and of the Second Coming (2 Thess. 2:8; 1 Tim. 6:14; 2 Tim. 4:1, 8; Titus 2:13). These terms stress the thought that the Christ, who has now withdrawn to the Father's presence and is pursuing His high-priestly ministry, will come again in visible glory, unveiling His true nature. The OT "day of the Lord," modified in reference to Christ as "a day" (Acts 17:31), "that day" (Matt. 7:22; 2 Thess. 1:10; 2 Tim. 1:18; 4:8), "the day of our Lord Jesus Christ" (1 Cor. 1:8), "the day when the Son of man is revealed" (Luke 17:30), "the day of Jesus Christ" (Phil. 1:6) or "of Christ" (verses 10; 2:16), or "the last day" (John 6:39, 40; 12:48), clearly emphasizes that Christ's return (Matt. 25:31; Mark 8:38; Acts 1:11; 1 Cor. 4:5) is part of God's expected schedule at the end of time. (See Second Coming I. B.)

2. The Manner of Christ's Return

Christ's second coming will be personal (Matt. 24:36; Acts 1:7), universally public and visible (Luke 17:23, 24; Rev. 1:7), audible (1 Thess. 4:16), and in power and glory (Matt. 24:30; 2 Thess. 1:7). He will return to gather the redeemed (Matt. 24:31; 25:32-34). The righteous dead will be raised (1 Cor. 15:23, 52, 53; 1 Thess. 4:16), and the righteous living at the time will be transformed, incorruptible, passing into the resurrection existence without dying (1 Cor. 15:52, 53; 1 Thess. 4:17; cf. Heb. 11:40; see Second Coming I. E). Though certain, the time of the Lord's return is unknown.

A considerable number of NT passages represent it as startling and unexpected. In spite of statements which represent the Second Coming as preceded by certain manifest signs, which give evidence of its nearness (Matt. 24:5, 7, 9, 29), its approach will be like that of a thief stealing into the house without warning (Luke 12:39, 40). The signal event is to come suddenly and unexpectedly, "at an hour you do not expect" (Matt. 24:44), yet it is near "at hand" (1 Peter 4:7; James 5:8, 9; 1 John 2:18). Since "that day and hour no one knows" (Matt. 24:36), Jesus and the NT writers urge believers to maintain an attitude of expectant preparedness, to look forward and be prepared at all times for the Lord's return (Matt. 24:44; 25:1-12; James 5:9) and to seek personal purity (2 Peter 3:11, 12; 1 John 3:2, 3).

3. The Triumph of the Kingdom

Barring the interlude of the millennium (see Millennium I. C) Christ's glorious return will signal the final triumph of His cause and the establishment and consummation of the kingdom of God, which is also the kingdom of Christ—in truth the kingdom of both (Matt. 13:41; 16:28; Luke 22:30; John 18:36; Col. 1:13; 2 Peter 1:11; Eph. 5:5). Paradoxically, Jesus announced that the kingdom, which will come in glory at the end of the age (Matt. 25:31-46), had, in fact, come into history and was already present in His person and mission: "The time is fulfilled, and the kingdom of God is at hand; repent, and believe in the gospel" (Mark 1:15; cf. Matt. 12:28).

Though Satan's destruction awaits the end of the millennium (Rev. 20:10), Jesus could say that the kingdom was present in the midst of them (Luke 17:21). The interval before the celebration of victory is both of uncertain duration and of relative unimportance. The decisive event was our Lord's death and resurrection. His second coming, though of utmost importance, is essentially its consummation. The work of Christ accomplished at His first coming inaugurated the eschatological epoch (Heb. 1:2; 1 John 2:18; 1 Peter 1:20). The

Christian believer now lives "between the times," between the "already" and the "not yet," awaiting Christ's "appearing and coming" (literally "the manifestation of his presence," 2 Thess. 2:8), experiencing now already the assurance of His presence, His high-priestly ministry, and His coming as "King of kings and Lord of lords" (Rev. 19:16).

By entering this evil age and invading the domain of Satan, Christ created a present spiritual realm in which the blessings of God's reign are already experienced (Col. 1:13), even eternal life (John 3:16). In His words, "He who believes in the Son has eternal life" (John 3:36; cf. 1 John 5:12). This eternal life we owe to Christ's life, death, and resurrection, which have introduced a new phase of the kingdom of God. It is something that may be enjoyed in the present, although its full implications await a consummation yet to come. In the meantime, Christ's followers are exhorted to love, wait for, and hasten the coming of their Lord (Luke 12:35-37; 1 Cor. 1:7, 8; 1 Thess. 1:9, 10; 2 Peter 3:11, 12). They are to look to the *parousia,* not with dread but with confidence and joyous expectancy as their "blessed hope" (Titus 2:13), because of what the returning Lord already has done for them at the cross and during His high-priestly ministry of intercession (Rom. 8:34; Heb. 4:15, 16).

E. Calling for a Response

The preceding survey has shown that the Christ of the Bible is the eternal Son of God, who became flesh, manifested Himself, and declared Himself, to be the unique Son of God. He showed Himself both sinless and sovereign over all Creation. The Christ of Scripture, freely and by design, gave Himself as a ransom for sinners and died on the cross so that those who believe in Him would be delivered from the guilt and the penalty of sin. The same Christ rose from the dead with flesh and bones, bearing the evidences of the Crucifixion. He ascended into heaven as our High Priest. The Christ of the Bible will come again soon in glory and power, to bring to an end the age in which we live.

All this has been God's doing. Throughout the whole of Scripture there is constant emphasis on God's initiative in our salvation. At the same time, there is an equally clear call to respond to God's grace. Sinners and saints alike are exhorted not to be content to gaze upon Him or to admire Him, but to walk in His steps, to become imitators of Him, until they are changed into the same image. God's call is not merely to salvation, but to a close walk with Him, to "abide in" Christ or simply to be in Jesus (John 15:4, 7). In the vine allegory Jesus expressed the idea of abiding in the double form of "abide in me, and I in you" (John 15:4; cf. verse 5). The branches, He insists, become useless except they abide in the vine—a most vivid way of expressing the centrality of Christ's life in the ongoing life of the believer. Equally important, the one who walks in Christ walks as Christ walked (1 John 2:6), keeps His commandments (1 John 3:24), shows love of the highest kind (1 John 4:12). The striking frequency with which John addresses the concept of "abiding" in his First Epistle (1 John 2:6, 24, 27, 28; 3:6, 24; 4:12, 13, 15, 16; cf. 2:10, 14; 3:9, 14, 17) points out John's eagerness to stress the source of power of the new life.

Paul likewise, with equal force and clarity, expounds the implications for each of us of God's plan of salvation in Jesus Christ. What happened to Christ affects every believer in Him, for whosoever is "in Christ . . . is a new creation" (2 Cor. 5:17). The new creation implies new principles of living, new interests, new moral values, new ways of thinking. An incorporation has occurred, for "all of us who have been baptized in Christ Jesus were baptized into his death" (Rom. 6:3). One's whole pattern of life is controlled by dwelling in Christ (cf. 1 Cor. 4:17).

So exhaustless and powerful is the scriptural idea of the believer's relationship with Christ that Paul adds to his "in Christ" concept that of a "Christ in us" notion. This was undeniably Paul's own experience: "It is no longer I who live, but Christ who lives in me" (Gal. 2:20). This experience was meant to be the norm, for the apostle prays that his Ephesian converts may experience the same blessing: "that Christ may dwell in your hearts through faith" (Eph. 3:17). This is made possible by means of the indwelling of the Holy Spirit. The concept is difficult to fathom—Paul himself refers to it as a mystery (Col. 1:27), but he is deeply convinced of its truth, wondering how much of it the Corinthian believers may have understood (2 Cor. 13:5).

A genuine proclamation of the gospel concerning the life and death of Jesus Christ will not only announce that Christ lived and was crucified for us. It will also proclaim that through conversion and baptism we were crucified with Him and now live the life of the resurrection. This is no mere statement of belief, but as set forth in the Scriptures, a daily experience until, in the fullness of time, Christ will have come again.

IV. Historical Overview

The purpose of this section is to survey some influential lines of thought that through 2,000 years of Christian history have been advanced concerning the person and work of Jesus Christ, with particular emphasis on the person of Jesus Christ. Limitations of space preclude a fuller assessment of theologians. I hope, however, to identify the main trends so that today's readers may be able to locate themselves more clearly in relation to the thinking of the Christian world around them.

A. The Ancient Church

As the Christian church extended its missionary outreach, the need to proclaim the gospel across cultural lines, on the one hand, and the rather naturally inquisitive impulse of the Hellenistic mind, on the other, tested the limits of Christian orthodoxy, in this case conformity to the Christological confession established by the NT writers. From the earliest stages of this development, the Word, or *Logos,* was set forth as holding a unique role in the salvation of sinners, for He was at one and the same time divine and human. The understanding of such a union is an issue of such unlimited significance that exaggerations were not long in appearing. Unfortunately, in most instances, the evidence regarding the various schools of thought later condemned as heretical is fragmentary, usually provided by their opponents, and hence not always reliable.

1. Denying the Reality of the Two Natures

The earliest Christian heresies denying the reality of the two natures in Christ came from opposite extremes. Docetism and Gnosticism, on the right, downplayed, if not denied, the humanity of Jesus for the sake of His divinity, while Ebionism, on the left, stressed Jesus' humanity at the expense of His divinity.

The *Ebionites* understood Jesus in the light of a strong monotheism, rooted in their Jewish background. They regarded Jesus as the natural son of Joseph and Mary, rather than the eternal Son of God, surpassing others in righteousness and endowed for the vocation of Messiah by the descent of the divine Spirit upon Him at His baptism.

Conversely, *Docetism*—from the Greek verb *dokein,* "to seem"—held that the divine Word did not actually become flesh but merely seemed to be human. As such, Docetism was part of a broad cultural trend that drew a sharp contrast between the spiritual or immaterial world and the world of matter. The latter was regarded as evil; the former alone was praiseworthy and sublime. It followed that the union of the divine and the human in Jesus was inconceivable, a mere appearance. Christian Docetists saw no difficulty in accepting the full deity of Jesus, but He had suffered and died only in appearance. It was a most dangerous heresy, which by the beginning of the third century, seems to have affected many intellectual Christian congregations.

2. Denying the Integrity of the Two Natures

Such early Christian authors as Justin Martyr (c. 100-165), Theophilus of Antioch (late second century), Melito of Sardis (d. c. 190), Irenaeus (c. 115-202), Tertullian (c. 160-c. 40), and Origen (c. 185-c. 254) attempted to meet these challenges by returning to a more biblical standpoint. Even so, their conception of Christ was often determined more by current philosophical trends than by the historic revelation found in the NT writings, leading some of them to Christological ambiguities.

Aiming at preserving the uniqueness of God the Father, Monarchians reacted vigorously against the Trinitarian views increasingly promoted among Christians. For them the Word was essentially less than God. This was the essence of the Arian heresy, which denied the integrity of the two natures in Christ. Arius (c. 250-c. 336) compelled the Christian church to settle the issue of the relation between the Father and the Son. Insisting on the absoluteness of God, he maintained that God is the one and only, utterly transcendent, who did not create by direct contact with the world but did so through the Son, whom He antedated as any human father does his son. Unlike the Father, the Son had a beginning. He was brought into existence out of nothing and before time by the Father Himself. Hence, though called God, He is not God the way the Father is. There was a time when He was not; His nature is not the same as the Father's.

3. The Nicene Response

Arius was condemned at the First Council of Nicaea in 325. In his struggle against Arius, Athanasius (c. 296-373) upheld the unity of the essence of the Father and the Son, no longer on the basis of a philosophical doctrine of the nature of the Word, but on the basis of the work of redemption accomplished by the Word incarnate. God alone, taking human flesh, could have accomplished it.

The Nicene creed reads in part, "We believe. . . . In one Lord Jesus Christ, the Son of God, begotten of the Father, only-begotten, that is, of the substance of the Father, God of God, Light of Light, true God of true God, begotten, not made, of one substance (*homoousios*) with the Father." There is a certain ambiguity in the term "substance." Christian tradition has understood it to be that which is common to all the individuals in a particular class, in this case the Godhead. Though specifically denounced, Arianism lived on in various forms for several centuries.

4. The Relationship Between the Two Natures

A crucial period in the Christian understanding of the person of Christ followed Nicaea. It extended from the middle of the fourth century to the middle of the fifth and was dominated by two opposing schools of thought: one in Alexandria, Egypt, the other in Antioch, Syria. Each attempted to address the issue as to how the eternal Son, truly God, could at the same time be truly man. The Alexandrians were concerned principally with preserving the divinity of Jesus. They focused on the unity of the humanity of Jesus with the divine Word. The Antiochenes were interested chiefly in Christ's humanity. They adopted a looser approach to the unity of the divine and human in Jesus. The former stressed that the *Word* took on flesh; the latter that the Word became a *human being*. Exaggerations soon followed.

a. Apollinaris. Disciple of Athanasius, Apollinaris (c. 310-390), took the Alexandrian view to an extreme. By teaching that in Jesus the divine Word took the place of the human mind *(nous)*, the seat of sin, he denied a full moral development and genuine humanity in Christ. His position was explicitly condemned at the Council of Constantinople in 381.

b. Nestorius. Conversely, in his effort to stress Christ's complete humanity, Nestorius (d. c. 451) tended to exaggerate the distinction between the two natures. His sustained objection to the use of the term *theotokos* ("bearer" of God) in reference to Mary gave his opponents grounds to assert that he was in fact denying Christ's divinity. He was perceived as thinking of the two natures, if not as two persons, at least as existing separately side by side, joined in a purely moral union.

c. Eutyches. In opposition to Nestorius, Eutyches (c. 378-454), one of Cyril of Alexandria's disciples, contended that in the incarnate Christ divinity and humanity coalesced in one, an outlook implying the denial of the two natures in Christ.

5. The Chalcedonian Definition

Eventually a council convened at Chalcedon (451) to bring the controversy to a conclusion. It condemned both Nestorius' and Eutyches' views, maintaining the unity of the person as well as the duality of natures. This council taught Christians to confess Christ as fully divine and fully human, to be acknowledged in two natures, "without confusion, without change, without division, without separation."

The Chalcedonian Definition can hardly be called a resolution of the Christological problem in answer to the question as to *how* the two natures are united in Christ Jesus. It has nothing to offer but four negative prepositions. It has been subjected to much criticism, especially in modern times. Nevertheless, if, to express the reality of God in Christ, the terms "person" and "nature" may no longer coincide in meaning with their modern English equivalents, they seem to have been adequate in their days. In their endeavor to express the inexpressible, the Council Fathers sought, by means of paradoxes, to bring human speech into the presence of the mystery of the Incarnation. Still, the formula satisfied neither side fully. The controversy continued in some areas with Monophysites, Monothelites, and Adoptionists exchanging charges and countercharges.

B. The Middle Ages

Medieval theologians added little of significance to the doctrine of the person of Christ. They accepted the authority of the Nicene and Chalcedonian statements while showing greater interest in heavily speculative, if not abstract, reflections regarding such items as Christ's consciousness, knowledge, freedom, virtues, capacity for suffering, and subjection to the Father. A few distinct points were stressed by Augustine (354-430) regarding Jesus, which Thomas Aquinas (1225-1274) further developed. The latter turned his attention more particularly to the mode of union in Christ, attempting to define and distinguish between the meanings of "nature" and "person."

1. Focusing on the Work of Christ

Medieval theologians, indeed, tended to focus on the work rather than on the person of Jesus Christ, more particularly His work of atonement. By the end of the eleventh century the long-prevalent view of Christ's death as a ransom paid to the devil began to fall into disrepute. It contended that through His death, Christ our representative paid a ransom to Satan who had acquired rights over humans by the fall of Adam and, fearing Christ's influence, was happy to accept the transaction. A victim of his own pride, and unaware of the efficacy of Christ's death, however, he deceived himself thinking he could overcome and hold Christ, who rose triumphant from the grave.

a. Anselm of Canterbury. In his book *Cur Deus Homo? (Why Did God Become Man?)*, Anselm of Canterbury (1033-1109) challenged the traditional view. The first theologian to frame a theory of the necessity of the Incarnation and the atonement in Christ, Anselm contended that sin robs God of the honor which He is due. He argued that in keeping with the demands of His own holy nature, God's honor needs vindication, either by punishment or by satisfaction. God's mercy prompted Him to seek it in the way of satisfaction. Sin, being an infinite offense against God, required a satisfaction equally infinite, one that God alone could provide. Yet the satisfaction had to be at once human and divine. This answered the question: Why did God become a human being? God Himself, Christ took the place of man and by His death made complete satisfaction to divine justice. His death was not a ransom paid to Satan, but a debt paid to God. In its essentials Anselm's formulation continues to find staunch protagonists wherever the Scriptures are accepted as God's Word.

b. Abelard. Some 40 years later Peter Abelard (1079-1142) rejected both the traditional view and Anselm's theory. In his *Epitome of Christian Theology* and his *Commentary on Romans,* he advocated a different view of sin. For him, the essence of sin was contempt for God's will. It resides more in peoples' evil intentions than in their actions, in agreeing to the evil inclinations of the mind. Since, from Abelard's perspective, there is no principle in God that requires satisfaction on the part of the sinner, Christ's life and death did not serve to satisfy divine justice but to arouse in sinners an answering repentance and love, which are their reconciliation and redemption. Christ's death is the supreme revelation of God's love. To many, however, the saving event appears to have been reduced to a tragic martyrdom, leaving little room for the inexorable necessity undergirding the cross. This view led to the exemplarist theory of the atonement and has come to be referred to as the moral influence theory.

C. The Reformation

The sixteenth century Reformers did not challenge the doctrine of Christ formulated by the Council of Chalcedon. They tended however to replace earlier emphases with a more existential stance, an approach that focused on one's encounter with the living Christ and on the "benefits of Christ," a theology of the cross rather than of glory.

1. The *Communicatio Idiomatum* Issue

A deep-seated disagreement set in among the Reformers in the context of their controversy about the Lord's Supper. Invoking the old doctrine of *communicatio idiomatum* (the "communication [interchange] of properties" between the divine and human natures of Jesus Christ), and on that basis insisting on the "real presence" of the body and blood of Christ in the bread and wine of the Communion service, Luther asserted that likewise there was a material interpenetration of qualities or attributes between the divine and human natures in Christ.

To Zwingli (1484-1531), his main opponent on the issue, Luther's view exhibited a dangerous Eutychian tendency, a fusion of natures which Chalcedon had rejected. Calvin (1509-1564), who also taught a communication of attributes, denied that the divine attributes could be imparted to the human nature of Christ. In his view the properties of both could be attributed to the same *person,* so that Christ could be said to be omniscient while at the same time having limited knowledge.

2. Of Christ's States and Offices

In two other areas the Reformers made their most original contribution to Christology, which was widely accepted and developed among Roman Catholics as well as Protestants. The Reformers introduced the doctrine of the two states of Christ, humiliation and exaltation. This distinction was not intended to supersede the doctrine of the two natures but to supplement it by giving fuller recognition to the dynamic aspect of Christ's life and ministry, presenting them in terms of a sequence of two states. They also fostered the doctrine of the three offices of Christ as prophet, priest, and king, first set forth by Calvin and subsequently taken up by Lutheran and Roman Catholic theologians.

D. Modern Times

The debate regarding the person and natures of Christ resumed in the eighteenth century under the impact of the Enlightenment, whose adherents distrusted all authority and tradition in their search for truth. Radically disrupting the medieval theological worldview, reason, rather than revelation, was set forth as the final arbiter of truth.

1. A Monumental Shift

The monumental shift in outlook that occurred during the Age of Reason led many intellectuals to restate historic Christian doctrines in terms inconsistent with biblical authority but more resonant with modern thought and its emphasis on literary criticism. Having already rejected the possibility of miraculous and otherwise supernatural elements, a roster of thinkers, starting with Hermann Reimarus (1694-1768) and continuing to the time of the World War I, endeavored to reconstruct the life of the "historical Jesus." Underlying the search was the assumption that the real Jesus, the "Jesus of history," would prove to be radically different from the "Christ of faith," the theological Jesus urged by theologians and church councils. Christologies "from above" set forth during the precritical era, when there was no question as to the historical reliability of the Bible and which started with the preexistent Word of God, who came down from heaven to save sinners, were progressively replaced by Christologies "from below." Indebted to the Enlightenment, Christologies "from below" produced a Jesus who, no longer divine, was essentially a religious moralist and reformer, the ideal man of modern liberalism, crucified because his views were ahead of his time. Although its author shared the basic historical method of the liberal searchers, Albert Schweitzer's book *The Quest of the Historical Jesus* (1906; trans. into English, 1910) spelled the end of the liberal quest for the Jesus of history.

2. Friedrich Schleiermacher

In this context Friedrich Schleiermacher

(1768-1834) reacted against both rationalism and formalist orthodoxy. In his attempt to win the educated classes back to religion, which he defined as built on a feeling of absolute dependence on God, he pictured a Christ whose uniqueness consisted in the fact that He possessed an unequaled "god-consciousness" of utter filial dependence upon the Father. Rejected as inadequate, the two-nature doctrine merely intended to express the truth that God was in Christ. Like us in nature, Jesus was yet distinguished from us by a God-consciousness so absolute and unbroken as to constitute "the veritable existence of God in Him." No one since the Reformation has exercised greater influence on present-day Christology than Schleiermacher.

3. Albecht Ritschl

Likewise reacting against the over-intellectualism of both orthodoxy and liberalism, Albrecht Ritschl (1822-1889) approached Christian doctrines in terms of value judgments and accordingly stressed what Christ did for us rather than what He is in Himself. Christ was a mere man, but in view of His teaching, His example, and the work He accomplished, He is worthy to be called God. Ritschl's influence has been second only to that of Schleiermacher.

4. Kenoticism

In contrast, Gottfried Thomasius (1802-1875) and other Kenoticists held that at the time of His incarnation the divine Logos laid aside His divine attributes of omnipotence, omniscience, and omnipresence. On the basis of Philippians 2:7, they sought to maintain the reality and integrity of Christ's dual nature and to underline the magnitude of His humiliation by becoming human.

E. Contemporary Approaches

The twentieth century has seen an astounding profusion of approaches to the Christological issues. An adequate survey is far beyond the scope of this article. Mention will be made of only a few of the more significant developments, more particularly those that suggest untried or unchartered approaches, though none seems entirely new.

1. Karl Barth's Trinitarian Christology

In a conscious reaction to what he regarded as the fundamentally erroneous outlook of liberal theology, with its confident attitude toward science and its stress on feeling, Karl Barth (1886-1968), with passionate fervor reaffirmed the classical orthodox statements of the first five centuries regarding the person of Christ. There were shifts in his thinking, and some of his views are not entirely free from the liberal presuppositions of the nineteenth century, but throughout his long and influential career Barth advocated a return to the Christ of Scriptures, of which he believed the Reformers to be the most authentic exponents. It was unquestionably a major shift. For Barth everything had to be seen in the light of Jesus Christ. The Jesus of history and the Christ of faith were one and the same. Without hesitation he proclaimed Jesus Christ as very God and very man, the virgin birth, substitutionary atoning death, resurrection, and other features of a Christology from above. Though it would be an overstatement to imply that in the recovery of these Christological emphases he returned in all essentials to the plain teachings of the Scriptures, Barth unquestionably raised the long-neglected biblical approach to Christology to a position of theological importance and study. Much of this came by way of reaction to R. Bultmann's drastic Christology.

2. Rudolf Bultmann's Demythologized Christ

Approaching the NT from a radical point of view, Rudolf Bultmann (1884-1976) argued that its writers did not describe factual history but added mythological elements to the original history of Jesus. They wrote in categories and terms of the ancient world picture, unacceptable to modern people. He invited his readers not to repeat the mistake of older liberals, who merely rejected a literal incarnation, literal miracles, a literal atonement, a literal resurrection, and a literal ascension. His method, as he saw it, was no longer rejection, but an anthropological reinterpretation. Our task today is to find out what religious truths and experiences the NT writers attempted to express by means of these myths, demythologize them and the person of Jesus, and "translate" them into current, relevant human existential categories. This approach amounted to a radical transformation of the biblical messages.

3. D. M. Baillie's Paradoxical Christology

In his excellent book *God Was in Christ* (1948) Donald M. Baillie intended to present the mystery of the Incarnation, not to solve the problem. He suggested a paradoxical Christology, i.e., that the most helpful approach to the mystery of the union of true God and true man is to accept it as a paradox, one of the constellation of paradoxes characteristic of the biblical revelation. To ignore or eliminate the element of paradox from it is to lose the Incarnation.

4. Oscar Cullmann

Where Bultmann placed little confidence in history, Oscar Cullmann (*Christ and Time*, 1951) insisted that Christ's incarnation and Calvary occurred in time. What the NT sets forth is not an existential mythologized interpretation of the Christ-event but a salvation-history interpretation. One discovers who Jesus is by finding out what He has actually done for us in human history; hence Cullmann's careful study of Christ's titles (*The Christology of the New Testament,* 1959).

5. Process Christology

In a revival of Irenaeus' endeavor to interpret the Incarnation as the crown and consummation of God's ongoing work in creation and so achieve a clear integration between creation and redemption, some twentieth-century theologians have seen in the philosophy of process a way of addressing the Christological problem in a fresh way. The new view was powerfully reinforced by the increasing acceptance of the theory of evolution. It was cogently articulated in Alfred N. Whitehead's (1861-1947) process philosophy. Whitehead's metaphysic has been gradually adopted and applied to theology, and by extension to Christology, by such advocates as Charles Hartshorne (b. 1897), Norman Pittenberg (b. 1905), John Cobb (b. 1934), and David Griffin (b. 1939). In process theology God is no longer static or immobile. He is always moving forward, cocreating history with humans. Always in a state of flux, through His intercourse with the changing world He is in process of becoming other than what He is now. While seeming to pay little, if any, attention to such issues as sin, Christ's preexistence and virgin birth, the Crucifixion and Resurrection, process Christologies show a strong and unquestioning commitment to the humanity of Jesus and to His place in history. At the same time, if God appeared in Jesus in an unsurpassed degree, it does not seem unthinkable, in principle at least, for this revelation to be surpassed in the future.

6. Wolfhart Pannenberg

In his *Jesus—God and Man* (1968), one of the major Christological treatises of the century, Wolfhart Pannenberg (b. 1928) argues that all history, being under the control of God, is a revelation of God. But this revelation needs to be deciphered. A theologian may decipher it in history by clues found in the OT eschatological and apocalyptic writings, a vision which becomes clear in the resurrected Christ. There is much to justify high appreciation of several aspects of Pannenberg's Christology, especially his stout defense of Christ's resurrection, which he perceives as an utterly historical event. One still experiences difficulty with his methodology which at times cites the biblical text, at other times Hegel, and at still other times argues from modern anthropological science.

7. Liberation Theologies

Liberation theology, together with its Christological corollary, is a critique of the traditional approach to theology, both Roman Catholic and Protestant, which are seen as too philosophically oriented, too cerebral, and too divorced from the sufferings of life. It arose in the late 1960s in Latin America as a reaction to widespread suffering and oppression decried as unjustifiable assaults on human dignity. Its principal exponents are, on the Roman Catholic side, Gustavo Gutiérrez of Peru (b. 1928), Jon Sobrino of El Salvador (b. 1938), Leonardo Boff of Brazil (b. 1938), and Juan Luis Segundo of Uruguay (b. 1925). On the Protestant side is Hugo Assmann of Brazil (b. 1933). For them, theology is critical reflection on praxis, beginning with a commitment to the oppressed. As a form of praxis, it must be directed toward changing the existing order.

Over against Chalcedonian Christology, whose Christ is perceived as supporting the current oppressive political and economic order, Christ is seen primarily as the liberator, a political rebel, concerned for the poor and social outcasts. It is essentially a Christology from below, starting from the man Jesus, then reflecting on His divinity. While its selective use of Scripture poses problems, liberation Christology has also offered an important corrective to overly spiritualized conceptions of the mission of the church.

Likewise, Black theology is unquestionably concerned with the issue of liberation. While liberation theology arose primarily within the Roman Catholic Church in South America, Black theology emerged in the 1960s and 1970s within Black Protestant communities in North America. The movement has many facets and nuances, characterized by various models, such as Martin Luther King, Jr. (1929-1968), Stokeley Carmichael (b. 1941), Malcolm X (1925-1965), James Cone (b. 1938), and J. Deotis Roberts (b. 1927). All emphasize the uniqueness of the Black experience and the need to develop a uniquely Black theology and Christology, since both reflect the Western or Greek methodological framework in which White theologians, assuming the superiority of Western culture did theology. This is another form of oppression.

Black Christology places strong emphasis on the historical Jesus, the oppressed One whose life and ministry were bound up with the oppressed. Even His declaration that the kingdom of God was at hand meant that slavery and oppression were about to end. At the same time, Black Christology propounds a basically biblical view of Christ's divinity, incarnation, and resurrection, while the salvation He brought in is usually expressed in terms of what He does or can do for the transformation of Black consciousness. Black theologians have rightly reminded us of the universality of Christ.

Feminist theology—and its understanding of Christ—is also regarded by many as a form of liberation theology, as the older term "women's liberation" suggests. Its efforts are directed toward achieving justice, freedom, and equality for women.

For virtually all feminist theologians the appropriate starting point for doing feminist theology is not the transcendent God and some communication of divine, but human, experience, regarded as the source and criterion of truth. Along with Latin American and Black liberation theologies, feminist theology is reflection upon fundamental issues in the light of experience, more specifically women's experience, concerns, and needs. Of late the movement, which began in the 1970s, has become increasingly heterogeneous. Thus, as far as Christology is concerned, some are ready to reject Jesus as a qualitatively unique incarnation of God, as in Mary Daly (b. 1928). Others, such as Carter Heyward (b. 1945) and Rita Brock (b. 1950), generalize the meaning of incarnation to include all persons; still others rather explore alternative interpretations of Jesus and select one that sees Him as a champion of the cause of women, as does Rosemary Radford Ruether (b. 1936).

Traditional Christology is rejected because of its predominantly male symbols for God and its male Saviour figure, which are seen as supporting patriarchialism with its belief in domination by males. The maleness of Jesus, it is argued, has been used to provide the norm of humanity, with the female being somewhat a second rate, or less than ideal, human being, with important implications for the issues of leadership in the church, for instance. It is also affirmed that the very claim that God was fully and uniquely present in a perfect *male* human, Jesus, and through Him brought salvation to all, does not justly represent the dynamic relation between God and *all* people. Because Christology has been, and continues to be, done predominantly by men in a particular culture, articulating men's questions and yearnings concerning the divine-human relationship, feminist theologians believe that women's experience has been omitted if not disregarded. Thus Christology needs to be dismantled and rearticulated in more egalitarian ways, in ways that contribute to the feminist quest for wholeness. Feminist theologians have, among other things, helped to clarify the doctrines of man and salvation. Since both male and female have been created in the image of God, men's inhumanity to women is an obvious manifestation of the sinful human condition. Still, the prompting that Christians give up such basic conceptions as the qualitatively unique divinity of Jesus Christ seems to be excessive.

8. *The Myth of God Incarnate*

More recently the publication of *The Myth of God Incarnate* (1977) by British theologians created quite a stir, probably because of its provocative title, for in actual fact it did not contain much that was new. Its authors are of the opinion that the doctrine of the Incarnation is no longer intelligible. Jesus is presented as a man appointed by God for a special role within the divine purpose. The concept of Jesus as God incarnate, living a human life, is regarded as a late conception, a mythological or poetical way of expressing His significance for humans. Since the contributors do not recognize the NT as authoritative and show a deep skepticism toward its reliability, the volume is almost entirely silent about the soteriological significance of Jesus, and His resurrection plays hardly any role at all. The book virtually revives the old liberal position of the nineteenth century and offers no real alternative to the historic doctrine of the Incarnation.

9. The Jesus Seminar

Since 1985, members of the Jesus Seminar have been advocating a "radical reformation" of Christianity, claiming that Jesus of Nazareth should be set free from the scriptural and creedal prison in which Christians have incarcerated Him. Applying both conventional critical methods of text analysis and other more disputed rules of evidence, the scholars of the controversial seminar have eventually concluded that no more than 20 percent of the sayings—and even fewer of the deeds—attributed to Jesus in the Gospels are authentic. Among the castoffs are the virgin birth, the Lord's Prayer, the sayings from the cross, most of His miracles, His bodily resurrection, and any claims of Jesus to divinity. The Jesus that remains is basically a social critic and secular sage akin to a Jewish Socrates.

10. Roman Catholic Christology

From the time of Aquinas to the middle of the twentieth century, Roman Catholic Christology focused principally on the ontological question: Who is Jesus in Himself? Only secondarily was the soteriological issue, Who is Christ for us? addressed.

The shift from an uncritical to a critical study of the NT, the move from a static to an evolutionary and existential understanding of human existence, as well as the development of historical and political consciousness as reflected in liberation theologies, contributed to the change from the medieval method to the twentieth-century approach. Here, as in Protestant Christology, two main methods are discernible: Christologies from above, represented in the works of Piet Schoonenberg (b. 1911), Hans Urs von Balthasar (1905-1988), and even Teilhard de Chardin (1881-1955), begin with the preexistent Word of God, who comes down from heaven to take human flesh. Christologies from below as advocated by Karl Rahner (1904-1984), Hans Küng (b. 1928), Walter Kasper (b. 1933), and Edward Schillebeeckx (b. 1914) begin with the Jesus of history. Moreover, Latin American theologians like Leonardo Boff (b. 1938) and Jon Sobrino (b. 1938), while stressing the historical Jesus over the Christ of faith, contend that orthodoxy is always to be linked with orthopraxy and God's concern for the poor and oppressed.

F. Current Crosswinds

At this time the Christological debate is fluid and its future course difficult to predict. The Chalcedonian Definition of "one person in two natures" has had lasting success, even in the twentieth century. There is fairly general agreement that in its attempt to remain faithful to the biblical testimony, the classical statement should be read as a beginning, not as an end. It was a creed born in crisis, which served its purpose long beyond its time. It may have lost some of its adequacy, not because the answer it has given is wrong, but because the questions asked presuppose a frame of reference that now has changed. The issues of Chalcedon are very much in the NT itself. They continue to need to be addressed.

G. Seventh-day Adventists

Seventh-day Adventists advocate a Christ-centered theological system. They view Christ as Creator, Redeemer, Lord of the Sabbath, High Priest, and soon-returning King.

They did not always accept the historic Christian doctrine of the Trinity, however. In the early decades they rejected it as unscriptural, Roman Catholic, contrary to reason, and demanding a two-nature Christology regarded as denying a divine atonement. Having formerly been members of the Christian Connection, James White (1821-1881) and Joseph Bates (1792-1872) among others, held to a form of Arianism regarding Christ's preincarnational origin. Some regarded Him as a created being; most, as an emanation from the Father. They did not deny His divinity or His right to be called God and to be worshiped as such; they mainly argued that, as begotten by the Father, Christ had a beginning and was made equal to the Father by the Father's pleasure. Their understanding of the Incarnation led to a one-nature Christology in which the preexistent divine Word, derived from the Father but not coeternal with Him, was transformed into human existence to die a divine and perfect atonement. Claiming that during His incarnation Christ was both human and divine was perceived as setting forth His death as a mere human sacrifice rather than a divine atonement.

A major shift occurred when, immediately after 1888, E. J. Waggoner (1855-1916) began to stress the Incarnation as a dwelling of the divine Word *in* sinful flesh, to live as divine Word a perfect human life. Here in a mysterious way the divine nature was united to fallen flesh with all its sinful tendencies, for the very purpose of triumphing over human sin and providing a similar power to human beings. Although his is still basically a one-nature Christology, the role played by the human flesh in Waggonner's understanding of Christ prepared the way for a two-nature Christology and a Trinitarian confession, as pointed out by Norman Young. At the same time, though starting in the 1870s, E. G. White played a considerable role in the gradual recognition of the Trinitarian viewpoint. From 1931 on, the Trinitarian understanding of God, along with Christ's full equality with the Father and a dual-nature Christology, has been an essential part of Adventist fundamental beliefs.

While all have upheld the sinlessness of the incarnate Christ, differences of opinion have persisted among Adventists regarding the nature of His humanity, whether or not He shared in the evil tendencies of the fallen human nature. Unlike the majority of early Adventists, in recent times many have adopted the view that while taking the fallen human nature, Christ did not partake of any of its sinful propensities or inclinations.

In a similar fashion, from an earlier position that viewed Christ's death at the cross as a supreme sacrifice but limited the word "atonement" to His heavenly ministry, SDAs gradually broadened their understanding of the atonement to include both the cross and Christ's heavenly ministry. In it the benefits of His atoning sacrifice on the cross are made available to believers. Each part is perceived as a finished work, yet both are required to make the atonement complete. Traditionally, Adventist authors have understood Christ's atoning death as a penal substitutionary sacrifice. In more recent times some have advocated a view reminiscent of Abelard's moral influence interpretation.

From the days of their earliest writers, Seventh-day Adventists, as their name emphasizes, have insisted that their High Priest will soon return to this earth to consummate the purpose for which He came the first time. They have been unanimous in emphasizing that this Second Coming is not a "spiritual" coming, or something that coincides with one's conversion or happens at death, but a visible, glorious event, with Christ descending from heaven as King of kings and Lord of lords.

V. Ellen G. White Comments

Ellen G. White has written much on the person and work of Jesus Christ. What follows is a representative sampling of her statements on the subject. Other articles dealing with specific dimensions of our topic, such as Christ as Creator, His deity, His priestly ministry, and His second coming, will provide the reader with additional reflections.

A. The Word Became Flesh

Regarding the knowledge of Christ, Ellen G. White writes:

"In Christ all fullness dwells. He [Paul] teaches us to count all things but loss for the excellency of the knowledge of Christ Jesus our Lord. This knowledge is the highest science that any man can reach. It is the sum of all true science. 'This is life eternal,' Christ declared, 'that they might know thee the only true God, and Jesus Christ, whom thou hast sent' " (MS 125, 1907; 7BC 905).

She explains that, as to the incarnation of the everlasting preexistent Word of God, "Christ was God essentially, and in the highest sense. He was with God from all eternity, God over all, blessed forevermore. The Lord Jesus Christ, the divine Son of God, existed from eternity, a distinct person, yet one with the Father" (1SM 247). "In Christ is life, original, unborrowed, underived" (DA 530). "The doctrine of the incarnation of Christ in human flesh is a mystery, 'even the mystery which hath been hid from ages and from generations' (Col. 1:26). It is the great and profound mystery of godliness. 'The Word was made flesh, and dwelt among us' (John 1:14). Christ took upon Himself human nature, a nature inferior to His heavenly nature. Nothing so shows the wonderful condescension of God as this" (1SM 246, 247). "Laying aside His royal robe and kingly crown, Christ clothed His divinity with humanity, that human beings might be raised from their degradation, and placed on vantage-ground. Christ could not have come to this earth with the glory that He had in the heavenly courts. Sinful human beings could not have borne the sight. He veiled His divinity with the garb of humanity, but He did not part with His divinity. A divine-human Saviour, He came to stand at the head of the fallen race, to share in their experience from childhood to manhood. That human beings might be partakers of the divine nature, He came to this earth, and lived a life of perfect obedience" (RH June 15, 1905).

"Christ, the Light of the World, veiled the dazzling splendor of His divinity and came to live as a man among men, that they might, without being consumed, become acquainted with their Creator" (MH 419). "Christ had not ceased to be God when He became man. Though He had humbled Himself to humanity, the Godhead was still His own" (DA 663, 664).

B. A Fallen Humanity

Not only is Jesus of Nazareth the incarnate Word, fully divine; He is also fully human. "That He might accomplish His purpose of love for the fallen race, He became bone of our bone and flesh of our flesh. . . . Divinity and humanity were mysteriously combined, and man and God became one" (FLB 48). "Christ, who knew not the least taint of sin or defilement, took our nature in its deteriorated condition" (1SM 253). "Jesus accepted humanity when the race had been weakened by four thousand years of sin" (DA 49). "He took upon His sinless nature our sinful nature" (MM 181).

At the same time, however, E. G. White explains that "He was to take His position at the head of humanity by taking the nature but not the sinfulness of man" (ST May 29, 1901).

Furthermore, "He was unsullied with corruption, a stranger to sin; yet He prayed, and that often with strong crying and tears. He prayed for His disciples and for Himself, thus identifying Himself with our needs, our weaknesses, and our failings, which are so common with humanity. He was a mighty petitioner, not possessing the passions of our human, fallen natures, but compassed with like infirmities, tempted in all points even as we are" (2T 508, 509).

Jesus "took upon Himself human nature, and was tempted in all points as human nature is tempted. He could have sinned; He could have fallen, but not for one moment was there in Him an evil propensity" (5BC 1128).

C. Two Natures in One Person

The Christian doctrine of two natures in the one person of Christ is clearly set forth. "Now, of the human: He 'was made in the likeness of men: and being found in fashion as a man, He humbled Himself, and became obedient unto death.' He voluntarily assumed human nature. It was His own act, and by His own consent. He clothed His divinity with humanity. He was all the while as God, but He did not appear as God. He veiled the demonstrations of Deity, which had commanded the homage, and called forth the admiration, of the universe of God. He was God while upon earth, but He divested Himself of the form of God, and in its stead took the form and fashion of a man. He walked the earth as a man. For our sakes He became poor, that we through His poverty might be made rich. He laid aside His glory and His majesty. He was God, but the glories of the form of God He for a while relinquished" (RH June 15, 1905; 5BC 1126).

"Was the human nature of the Son of Mary changed into the divine nature of the Son of God? No; the two natures were mysteriously blended in one person—the Man Christ Jesus" (21MR 418). "He exhibited a perfect humanity, combined with deity; . . . preserving each nature distinct" (GCB Oct. 1, 1899; 5BC 918).

D. Christ Our Example

Laying hold of His Father's power, Christ is our example. "The obedience of Christ to His Father was the same obedience that is required of man. Man cannot overcome Satan's temptations without divine power to combine with his instrumentality. So with Jesus Christ; He could lay hold of divine power. He came not to our world to give the obedience of a lesser God to a greater, but as a man to obey God's holy law, and in this way He is our example. The Lord Jesus came to our world, not to reveal what a God could do, but what a man could do, through faith in God's power to help

in every emergency. Man is, through faith, to be a partaker in the divine nature, and to overcome every temptation wherewith he is beset" (MS 1, 1892; 7BC 929). "Therefore Jesus was 'in all points tempted like as we are' (Heb. 4:15). He endured every trial to which we are subject. And He exercised in His own behalf no power that is not freely offered to us. As man, He met temptation, and overcame in the strength given Him from God" (DA 24).

E. A Sacrificial Death

Christ's death, as Ellen White saw, was a sacrificial death, foreshadowed in the OT sacrificial offerings. Describing the meaning and implications of the cross, she referred to categories such as substitution, ransom, expiation, propitiation, reconciliation, all reminiscent of the biblical vocabulary. "Upon Christ as our substitute and surety was laid the iniquity of us all. He was counted a transgressor, that He might redeem us from the condemnation of the law. The guilt of every descendant of Adam was pressing upon His heart. The wrath of God against sin, the terrible manifestation of His displeasure because of iniquity, filled the soul of His Son with consternation" (DA 753).

"And now the Lord of glory was dying, a ransom for the race" (*ibid.* 752). "Our ransom has been paid by our Saviour" (1SM 309). "[Christ] humbled Himself to man's nature. He did this that the Scripture might be fulfilled; and the plan was entered into by the Son of God, knowing all the steps in His humiliation, that He must descend to make an expiation for the sins of a condemned, groaning world" (RH June 15, 1905; 5BC 1127). "Christ became the propitiation for man's sin. He proffered His perfection of character in the place of man's sinfulness. He took upon Himself the curse of disobedience" (1SM 237). "Through Christ, Justice is enabled to forgive without sacrificing one jot of its exalted holiness. . . . Justice moved from its exalted throne, and with all the armies of heaven approached the cross. There it saw One equal with God bearing the penalty for all injustice and sin. With perfect satisfaction Justice bowed in reverence at the cross, saying, It is enough" (MS 94, 1899; 7BC 936).

F. A Demonstration of God's Love

"The death of God's beloved Son on the cross shows the immutability of the law of God. . . . [It] gives evidence to man of its changeless character" (2T 201). Yet in order to avoid any misunderstanding, Ellen White writes, "This great sacrifice was not made in order to create in the Father's heart a love for man, not to make Him willing to save. No, no! 'God so loved the world, that he gave his only-begotten Son' (John 3:16). The Father loves us, not because of the great propitiation, but He provided the propitiation because He loves us" (SC 13). "Christ's death proves God's great love for man" (AA 209). In addition, she contends, "Who can contemplate the unfathomable love that was manifested upon the cross of Calvary in the death of Christ, that we might not perish, but have everlasting life—who can behold this and have no words with which to extol the Saviour's glory?" (MB 43, 44).

G. Christ's Resurrection

Christ's resurrection signaled the end of Satan's kingdom and the assurance that for the believer death is just a sleep:

"When Jesus was laid in the grave, Satan triumphed. He dared to hope that the Saviour would not take up His life again. He claimed the Lord's body, and set his guard about the tomb, seeking to hold Christ a prisoner. He was bitterly angry when his angels fled at the approach of the heavenly messenger. When he saw Christ come forth in triumph, he knew that his kingdom would have an end, and that he must finally die" (DA 782).

"He arose from the tomb enshrouded with a cloud of angels in wondrous power and glory—the Deity and humanity combined. He took in His grasp the world over which Satan claimed to preside as his lawful territory, and by His wonderful work in giving His life, He restored the whole race of men to favor with God" (1SM 343).

"Christ became one with humanity, that humanity might become one in spirit and life with Him. By virtue of this union in obedience to the Word of God, His life becomes their life. He says to the penitent, 'I am the resurrection and the life' (John 11:25). Death is looked upon by Christ as sleep—silence, darkness, sleep. He speaks of it as if it were of little moment. 'Whosoever liveth and believeth in me,' He says, 'shall never die' (John 11:26). 'If a man keep my saying, he shall never taste of death' (John 8:52). 'He shall never see death' (John 8:51). And to the believing one, death is but a small matter. With him to die is but to sleep" (ibid. 302, 303).

H. Christ's Ascension

Commenting on Christ's last days with the disciples and on the significance of His ascension to heaven, Ellen G. White remarks: "The time had come for Christ to ascend to His Father's home. As a divine conqueror He was about to return with the trophies of victory to the heavenly courts. Before His death He had declared to His Father, 'I have finished the work which Thou gavest Me to do' (John 17:4). After His resurrection He tarried on earth for a season, that His disciples might become familiar with Him in His risen and glorified body. Now He was ready for the leave-taking. He had authenticated the fact that He was a living Saviour. His disciples need no longer associate Him with the tomb. They could think of Him as glorified before the heavenly universe" (DA 829).

"When Christ ascended to heaven, the sense of His presence was still with His followers. It was a personal presence, full of love and light. . . . [Jesus] had ascended to heaven in the form of humanity. They knew that He was before the throne of God, their Friend and Saviour still; that His sympathies were unchanged; that He was still identified with suffering humanity. He was presenting before God the merits of His own precious blood, showing His wounded hands and feet, in remembrance of the price He had paid for His redeemed. They knew that He had ascended to heaven to prepare places for them, and that He would come again and take them to Himself" (SC 73, 74).

I. Christ's High Priesthood

On Christ's priestly ministry and glorious return other articles in this volume may be consulted. However, the following quote deserves attention here. "The intercession of Christ in man's behalf in the sanctuary above is as essential to the plan of salvation as was His death upon the cross. By His death He began that work which after His resurrection He ascended to complete in heaven" (GC 489).

The person and work of Christ inspired in Ellen White a profound spirit of praise to God. She writes: "'Not unto us, O Lord, not unto us, but unto Thy name give glory, for Thy mercy, and for Thy truth's sake' (Ps. 115:1). Such was the spirit that pervaded Israel's song of deliverance, and it is the spirit that should dwell in the hearts of all who love and fear God. In freeing our souls from the bondage of sin, God had wrought for us a deliverance greater than that of the Hebrews at the Red Sea. Like the Hebrew host, we should praise the Lord with heart and soul and voice for His 'wonderful works to the children of men.' Those who dwell upon God's great mercies, and are not unmindful of His lesser gifts, will put on the girdle of gladness and make melody in their hearts to the Lord. The daily blessings that we receive from the hand of God, and above all else the death of Jesus to bring happiness and heaven within our reach, should be a theme for constant gratitude. What compassion, what matchless love, has God shown to us, lost sinners, in connecting us with Himself, to be to Him a peculiar treasure! What a sacrifice has been made by our Redeemer, that we may be called children of God! We should praise God for the blessed hope held out before us in the great plan of redemption, we should praise Him for the heavenly inheritance and for His rich promises; praise Him that Jesus lives to intercede for us" (PP 289).

VI. Literature

From the enormous amount of literature on the person and work of Jesus Christ, the following list selects publications that survey the field and have contributed to this article. The basic books remain the Gospels according to Matthew, Mark, Luke, and John, all too often neglected. Among the more important works in English—written from different standpoints—are:

Adams, Roy. *The Nature of Christ.* Hagerstown, Md.: Review and Herald, 1994.

Baillie, Donald M. *God Was in Christ: An Essay on Incarnation and Atonement.* New York: Charles Scribner's Sons, 1948.

Barth, Karl. *Church Dogmatics.* 4 vols. Edinburgh: Clark, 1956.

Berkouwer, G. C. *The Person of Christ.* Grand Rapids: Eerdmans, 1954.

Boff, Leonardo. *Jesus Christ Liberator.* Maryknoll, N.Y.: Orbis, 1978.

Brunner, Emil. *The Mediator.* Philadelphia: Westminster, 1947.

Cave, Sydney. *The Doctrine of the Person of Christ.* New York: Charles Scribner's Sons, 1925.

Cullmann, Oscar. *The Christology of the New Testament,* 2nd ed. Philadelphia: Westminster, 1964.

Erickson, Millard J. *Man's Need and God's Gift: Readings in Christian Theology.* Grand Rapids: Baker, 1976.

———. *The Word Became Flesh.* Grand Rapids: Baker, 1991.

Forsyth, P. T. *The Person and Place of Jesus Christ.* Boston: Pilgrim, 1909.

Grenz, Stanley J., and Roger E. Olson. *Twentieth Century Theology.* Downers Grove, Ill.: InterVarsity, 1992.

Guthrie, Donald. *New Testament Theology.* Downers Grove, Ill.: InterVarsity, 1981.

———. "Jesus Christ," *Zondervan Pictorial*

Encyclopedia of the Bible. Ed Merrill C. Tenney and Stevan Barabas. Grand Rapids: Zondervan, 1975. Vol. 3, pp. 497-583.

Harris, Murray J. *Jesus As God: The New Testament Use of "Theos" in Reference to Jesus.* Grand Rapids: Baker, 1992.

Hendry, George. "Christology," *A Dictionary of Christian Theology.* Ed. Allan Richardson. London: SCM, 1969. Pp. 51-60.

Heppenstall, Edward. *The Man Who Is God.* Washington, D.C.: Review and Herald, 1977.

Hick, John, ed. *The Myth of God Incarnate.* London: SCM, 1977.

Holbrook, Frank B. *The Atoning Priesthood of Jesus Christ.* Berrien Springs, Mich.: Adventist Theological Society, 1996.

Kelly, J.N.D. *Early Christian Creeds,* 3rd ed. London: Longman, 1972.

Ladd, George Eldon. *A Theology of the New Testament.* Grand Rapids: Eerdmans, 1974.

Larson, Ralph. *The Word Was Made Flesh: One Hundred Years of Seventh-day Adventist History, 1852-1952.* Cherry Valley, Calif.: Cherrytown Press, 1986.

Marshall, I. Howard. *I Believe in the Historical Jesus.* Grand Rapids: Eerdmans, 1977.

McGrath, Alester E. *The Making of Modern German Christology: From the Enlightenment to Pannenberg.* Oxford: Blackwell, 1986.

Meyendorff, John. *Christ in Eastern Christian Thought.* Washington, D.C.: Corpus, 1969.

Moltmann, Jürgen. *The Crucified God.* London: SCM, 1974.

Morris, Leon. *The Apostolic Preaching of the Cross.* Grand Rapids: Eerdmans, 1980.

———. "Atonement," *New Bible Dictionary,* 2nd ed. Ed. J. D. Douglas et al. Downers Grove: InterVarsity, 1982. Pp. 104-106.

———. *New Testament Theology.* Grand Rapids: Zondervan, 1986.

O'Collins, Gerald. *Christology: A Biblical, Historical, and Systematic Study of Jesus.* Oxford: Oxford University Press, 1995.

Oden, Thomas C. *The Word of Life.* San Francisco: Harper and Row, 1989.

Pannenberg, Wolfhart. *Jesus—God and Man,* 2nd ed. Philadelphia: Westminster, 1977.

Pelikan, Jaroslav. *Jesus Through the Centuries: His Place in the History of Cultures.* New Haven, Conn.: Yale University Press, 1985.

Ramm, Bernard. *An Evangelical Christology: Ecumenic and Historic.* Nashville: Thomas Nelson, 1985.

Rowden, Harold H. *Christ the Lord: Studies in Christology Presented to Donald Guthrie.* Downers Grove, Ill.: InterVarsity, 1982.

Runia, Klass. *The Present-day Christological Debate.* Downers Grove, Ill.: InterVarsity, 1984.

Schillebeeckx, Edward. *Jesus: An Experiment in Christology.* New York: Seabury, 1979.

Sobrino, Jon. *Christology at the Crossroads.* Maryknoll, N.Y.: Orbis, 1978.

Vick, Edward W. H. *Jesus: the Man.* Nashville: Southern Publishing, 1979.

Wallace, Ronald S. "Christology," *Baker's Dictionary of Theology.* Ed. Everett E. Harrison, et al. Grand Rapids: Baker, 1972. Pp. 117-123.

Wallenkampf, Arnold V., and W. Richard Lesher, eds. *The Sanctuary and the Atonement: Biblical, Historical, and Theological Studies.* Washington, D.C.: Biblical Research Institute, 1981.

Webster, Eric C. *Crosscurrents in Adventist Theology.* Berrien Springs, Mich.: Andrews University Press, 1992.

Whidden, Woodrow W. II. *Ellen White on the Humanity of Christ.* Hagerstown, Md.: Review and Herald, 1991.

Young, Norman H. "Christology and Atonement in Early Adventism." *Adventist Heritage* 9 (Fall 1984): 30-39.

The Doctrine of Man

Aecio E. Cairus

Introduction

Even though "theology" literally means "a discussion or study of God," man is one of its most important subjects. God revealed Himself as the Father of the human race (Matt. 6:9), through a Son who is not ashamed to claim human beings as His brothers and sisters (Heb. 2:11), and in the Spirit who takes humanity as His abode (1 Cor. 6:19).

While not feeling the perplexity and despair so often encountered among philosophers, biblical writers still pose the questions What is man? and Who am I? The Bible sets those questions in a context of reverence for God's works (Ps. 8:4) and His condescension toward humankind (Job 7:17), of thankfulness prompted by His grace (2 Sam. 7:18; Ps. 144:3), and humility facing the vastness of the task He has assigned (Ex. 3:11). We should do likewise.

"Theological anthropology" (the study of man from a biblical viewpoint) is usually discussed in connection with cosmology (which deals with the created universe), protology (the original state of affairs in the world), hamartiology (the vastly different state of affairs introduced by sin), and eschatology (the doctrine of the last things).

This is reasonable, for things acquire meaning in their natural context (hence the connection with cosmology). Though this relationship is now obscured by the consequences of sin, the origin of a being and its destiny disclose its nature. The nature of human beings is thus revealed in their creation (protology) and future state (eschatology).

In this essay "man" is used in a generic sense as found in Genesis 1:27, and refers to both men and women.

I. Man's Original State

A. Biblical Information

Although there is a great deal of information about man and his origin scattered throughout the Bible, the first two chapters of Genesis discuss the subject specifically and have been a cardinal source for theological reflection through the centuries.

Regrettably, in modern times the narratives contained in those chapters are often no longer seen as a single unit but as two diverging Creation narratives. Indeed, Genesis 2:4 begins a new narrative (the Paradise story), distinct from Genesis 1:1–2:3 (the Creation story), but is complementary to it. (See Creation I. B. 1-3.)

The Creation story offers an account of the origin of life and joy through God's creativity. The Paradise narrative explains the rise of death and affliction in the world through man's disobedience. Allusions to creative acts of God reappear, but with a different agenda. The variant order of their presentation answers to internal needs of the narrative, not to a different conception of the chronology of events. The Paradise story has continuity of thought with the Creation story, as well as affinity in language and structure. The meaning of different parts within the story may be completely missed unless this unity is recognized.

The matter of dietary regulations is but one example of this unity. In Genesis 1:29, 30 the first human pair is commanded to eat "every plant yielding seed" and every "tree with seed in its fruit"—grains and fruit. The animals, on the other hand, are to eat "green plants." Thus, the garden of fruit trees of Genesis 2:8,

9 was the logical place for Adam and Eve. In his first comment to the woman, the serpent showed he was clearly aware of the limitation of his own diet. His words could well be translated, "So what if ['ap ki] God said 'you must not eat from any tree in the garden!'" (see Gen. 3:1).

Some may argue that Genesis 1 and 2 were not intended to describe how everything was created, but only by whom and for what purpose. To the contrary, the "how" of Creation shows us the nature of the human creature. To portray this is the obvious intention of the biblical author.

B. God's Image in Man

The key text for basing the affirmation that human beings were created in the image of God is Genesis 1:26, 27: "Then God said, 'Let us make man in our image, after our likeness; and let them have dominion. . . .' So God created man in his own image, in the image of God he created him; male and female he created them."

1. Man's Place in Creation

To ascertain the place of the human pair in God's creation consideration must be given to the divine purpose for creating human beings, the meaning of "image of God," and biblical associations with that phrase.

a. God's purpose in creating man. The Bible differs from ancient thinkers (Plato, for instance) who affirmed that God had to create a world in order to express Himself. God was not constrained by His own nature to create anything, but freely decided to do so in such a way that His goodness, wisdom, and power—His "glory"—might be manifest, as intimated in Psalm 19:1-4.

It is true that mankind exists for God's glory, but not because He wants them as some kind of cosmic choir to sing His praise. Rather, they contribute to God's glory because they were designed in a most praiseworthy manner for a loving fellowship with Him (cf. Ps. 100:1-4).

b. God's self-portrait. According to the Creation story, God first delineated three pairs of environments: light was separated from darkness (day one, Gen. 1:3-5), water was separated from air (day two, verses 6-8), and dry land and its vegetation were separated from the sea (day three, verses 9-13). He then proceeded to fill those environments with inhabitants: light bodies appropriate to the luminous and dark firmaments (day four, verses 14-19), flying beings for the air and swimming beings for the waters (day five, verses 20-23), and land beings for the earth covered with vegetation (day six, verses 24, 25). (See Creation I. A. 1-10.)

Not until this task had been finished was everything ready for the appearance of man. "Then God said: 'Let us make man in our image, after our likeness. . . .' So God created man in his own image, in the image of God he created him; male and female he created them" (verses 26, 27).

This *creation in the image of God* should not be confused with *being* essentially the image of God. The sun projects an image of itself on the surface of a lake. A painter paints on canvas an image of the same heavenly body. The two are not sun images in the same sense. One is self-projected and shares in the nature of the sun itself, being a part of its radiance. The other is made by design in the image of the sun, but consists of pigments on canvas and has not emanated from the star itself.

Christ is, in virtue of His own nature, an eternal image of God. He "is the radiance of God's glory and the exact representation of his being" (Heb. 1:3, NIV). Indeed, "He is the image of the invisible God" (Col. 1:15). As such, He Himself is the Creator and Maker of man in the image of God (verse 16), though the whole Deity was no doubt involved in the expression "Let *us* make." Humans are an image of God, not as an extension of His being, but as a portrait achieved by His creative design.

c. Biblical associations of the image-of-God concept. Heathen thinkers conceived the world as an image of its Creator. In contrast, Scriptures reserve creation in the image of God for man alone (Gen. 1:26, 27; 1 Cor. 15:49). The context surrounding the expression in Genesis 1:26, 27 associates this image with a position at the summit of all material creation.

This may be shown in the progression found in the text through the successive days of Creation week, from mere energy (light) and inorganic matter in atmosphere, ocean, and land, to plant and animal life, culminating in humankind. There is also a change in the approval formula, from "it was good" before the creation of man (verses 4, 12, 18, 21, 25), to "it was *very* good" afterward (verse 31). Furthermore, the Deity deliberates only before the creation of man (verse 26).

The uppermost position of man is evident in the special attention he receives when God breathes life into him (Gen. 2:7). Furthermore, Adam cannot find adequate companionship among the animals (verse 20). The dignity associated with the position of man as God's image is underlined in Genesis 9:6, where the death penalty is demanded for those guilty of murder. Anything that threatens human life is to be considered an attack on the God it represents.

2. The Content of the Image

It is not immediately obvious in what precise sense we bear the image of God. If the accent is placed on resembling God, how can puny human beings resemble the Infinite? Everything in the human body answers to environmental needs. Our form, size, and configuration are linked to conditions on planet

Earth. Does God's environment resemble ours? Or should we limit resemblance to spiritual aspects? If so, are spiritual characteristics less unworthy of Deity than the physical? Thinkers of all ages have addressed these questions. A survey of their answers appears in the historical section (V). Here we concentrate on the biblical answers.

In order to specify the content of the image of God, we need to look at the divine intention as expressed in Genesis 1:26: "Let us make man in our image, after our likeness." This intention is important because it shows that the human being did not merely turn out in the image of God, but was carefully designed to be such. God's image is far more than the often-unconscious self-projection in any creative activity. This statement of intention also allows insight into God's larger purpose. (See Creation I. A. 12.)

The idea of the human creatures as an image of God primarily points toward their role as God's representative over the lower creation (verses 26, 27; Ps. 8:6-8). Man's function was to be analogous to God's in His sphere. This is indeed the import of the phrase "image of [a] god" applied to a human being in the ancient Near East; for example, Pharaoh was "the living image" of Amon or Ra. Bearing God's image, then, does not imply so much resembling God as representing Him. Man is God's collaborator (Gen. 2:4-6, 15) and lieutenant (Ps. 8:3-8; 115:16).

On the other hand, resemblance, though not the focal idea, cannot be excluded. The representational functions of human beings cannot subsist without communication with their Maker. Physical, intellectual, social, and spiritual endowments, as well as the ability to commune with God, are therefore integral to the concept of God's image. Since God's image in human beings is brought about in order to place them in dominion over lower nature, it must involve everything that enables humankind to rule in their sphere as God rules in His.

The NT emphasizes resemblance to God in the area of knowledge (Col. 3:10), righteousness and holiness (Eph. 4:24). This underlines the original goodness of humans, derived from a Creator preoccupied with making everything "very good." Self-portraits of a caring and loving God could not help being themselves grateful and loving. As such they would have found goodness and compliance with God's instructions totally natural. The image of God in man also includes the moral nature.

Far from leading to the abuse of nature, as sometimes charged by humanistic ecologists, dominion over nature makes human beings accountable before God for their actions in the natural world. Abuse is more apt to come from those who have access to, but not full ownership of, a heritage. The account of the full dominion given to humanity only emphasizes that nature conservation is in its own interest. God gave to human beings not merely an access to the natural resources of the earth, but the full stewardship thereof (Gen. 1:26). According to Scripture, nature is man's precious heritage. (See Stewardship I. B.)

3. The Original Righteousness

Physical, intellectual, social, and spiritual faculties are closely related to the dignity of a person, an essential aspect of being an image of God (1 Cor. 11:7). With all modesty and reverence we marvel at God's bounty to endow us with those faculties; we celebrate the accomplishments of mankind (Ps. 8). At the same time we may stumble upon the paradox of such an image of God behaving in a most ungodly way, as even highly civilized nations have shown in recent history. How can we still call this creature "an image of God"?

The paradox hinges on one of our dearest faculties: freedom. Our imagehood implies dependence on God, for something can be an image only in those respects in which it conforms to its model. Freedom, on the other hand, opens the way to autonomy and consequently to nonconformity. Still, autonomy leads to independence only when the free agent has his or her own agenda to follow. Differing agendas presuppose different principles and aims. We may willingly accept our condition as images of God and recognize our humble dependence, freely consenting to the principles of His kingdom, or we can reject it, turning freedom into rebellion.

"God made man upright" (Eccl. 7:29). He was certainly not perfect in the sense of having attained everything he was capable of attaining; for instance, he required instruction (Gen. 2:16, 17), particularly about the test of the tree of knowledge. Much was at stake in this test, intended to develop his moral maturity (James 1:2-4).

The moral condition in which our first parents were created is usually described as innocence, meaning that their virtue (freedom from moral wrong) was as yet untried. Virtue presupposes the ability to choose, or free will. Though the Bible says little about the human will, it does value human freedom highly. OT social legislation removed captives and slaves from the dismal status usual in antiquity and made it impossible to deal with a fellow Israelite as with mere chattel. The God of Israel assumes the role of Redeemer (Isa. 41:14; Jer. 50:34) or Liberator of His people (Isa. 61:1).

Jesus Christ understood His mission in the same light (Luke 4:16-21). This liberation, however, was not merely sociopolitical. The NT emphasizes man's bondage to sin (Rom. 3 and 7) as a consequence of his fallen nature. What a mere knowledge of God's will or law could not effect, Jesus obtained by remaining sinless (Rom. 8:3) and being obedient to the point of death on a cross (Phil. 2:6-8). In this way He became the Redeemer of those in bondage to sin (Heb. 2:15) and hence to death, "for the wages of sin is death, but the free gift of God is eternal life in Christ Jesus our Lord" (Rom. 6:23).

But such liberation is not universal or automatic. It comes only to those who willingly receive Christ (John 1:12) and results in freedom, not to revert to autonomous self-will, but to love God and neighbor under the "law of liberty" (James 2:12). "For you were called to freedom, brethren. Only do not use your freedom as an opportunity for the flesh, but through love be servants of one another" (Gal. 5:13).

Many biblical terms express the power of personal choice and decision including Hebrew *ḥāp̱ēṣ* and *rāṣôn;* Greek *thelēma.* More important, exhortation and moral instruction throughout the Scriptures cannot be explained without the assumption of human freedom and power to choose. God's will is free and unlimited; He has also given freedom of will to His created beings.

The will of God, the standard of goodness, is not abstruse or difficult to find. Even in the present state, a human being easily approves what is right, agreeing that the divine instructions are good (Rom. 7:15-18). But in the present sinful state the human will is captive to sin and requires divine grace to attain God's good purpose (verses 24, 25). In his original, upright state man was able to follow the divine instructions. God designed a universe free from death (Rom. 8:21), presupposing the ability to adhere strictly to His guidelines (Gen. 2:17). Alas, God's creatures could also (and did) choose death with equal freedom. (For other comment on "The image of God," see Sin I. A, C; Lifestyle I. A. 2.)

C. Sexuality in Its Original State

1. The Human Need of Companionship

While it is clear from Genesis 2 that man and woman were not created simultaneously, Genesis 1 disregards the time lapse. God created human beings as both male and female (verse 27). "Adam" is not truly a personal name in Hebrew, but a collective noun that may be translated "humankind" (NRSV) or "people" (cf. Gen. 5:2, KJV). The specific term for a male human, *'iš,* makes its debut in the Bible after the mention of the female, *'iššāh* (Gen. 2:23).

The Paradise story records a short time in

which only one human being was in existence, but for this there was no approval formula, only the reverse: "It is not good that the man should be alone" (verse 18). Following the pattern of relationships in the Godhead (John 17:24), meaningful existence for human beings needed to have a social dimension. The short lapse with only one 'ādām was intended to show him that he lacked a counterpart in the animal creation and thus stood in need of a "fit helper," or suitable companion. The ideal expressed in Creation was for man and woman to form a whole in which they were to be mutually complementary and interdependent. An isolated couple does not fulfill all the requirements for the social dimensions of man, but the creative procedure shows the importance of this dimension in God's plan.

The Bible thus places the function of sexuality in the context of fellowship, intimacy, and complementation on which genuine humanity is predicated. This conception is by far more advanced than the ideas of mere procreation, re-creation, or "release of tension" to which sexuality has often been reduced.

2. The Creation of Woman

Many interpreters have noted the significance of the way the woman was created (Gen. 2:21, 22). She was taken from the man's side—not his head or his feet—suggesting essential equality. The word ṣēlā', translated "rib" in this passage, is elsewhere rendered "side," as in the symmetrical counterpart to a leaf of a double door (1 Kings 6:34), the matching second wing of a building (Ex. 26:26, 27), the opposite slope of a mountain (2 Sam. 16:13). By preserving the sense "side" we may underline the equality and complementarity of man and woman. Together, man and woman formed humankind, created in the image of God, to help and support each other. To both together God gave dominion over the earth and its contents (Gen. 1:28).

According to Genesis 2:20, God created for Adam an 'ēzer, often translated "helper." However, the Hebrew word does not imply subser-

vience as the English term may; it can mean "support" or "benefactor" and is regularly used of God, who helps human beings (Ps. 33:20; cf. Ps. 54:4). Furthermore, the phrase kᵉnegdô, translated "fit for him," comes from a term meaning "in front of," suggesting that the companion God created for the man was to be his counterpart, his complement. (See Creation I. B. 7.)

Some authors have read into the account of Genesis 2 a divinely ordained hierarchy of the sexes. Woman, created for the sake of man (verses 18-20), had a derivative existence and was named by the man, who in this way indicated his authority over her (verse 23). In the biblical accounts of woman's creation, however, the story does not move from superior to inferior. In Genesis 1 the movement is the opposite, from lower creatures to higher ones; and in Genesis 2 it goes from incompleteness to wholeness. Physical derivation does not imply subordination: man is not subordinate to the ground. Matthew Henry argues that the woman was "dust double-refined, one removed further from the earth." In Genesis 2:23 Adam remarks on his wife's generic identification, "woman" or "wife," but does not give her a proper name until after the entrance of sin (Gen. 3:20).

The balance of biblical evidence is far from clearly supporting any superiority of the male. The submission of wives was a consequence of the disharmony in human relationships introduced in the world by sin (verse 16; II. B. 5). Paul enjoins submission of wives to their husbands who love them as Christ loved the church, as they love themselves (Eph. 5:21-33; see Marriage I. E. 1).

3. The Meaning of Marriage

Marriage institutions are part of human culture and vary widely over time and space. They did not originate in culture, however, but in God's design for the world. The establishment of the human couple is found among God's creative actions of the sixth day (compare Genesis 1:26-31 with 2:4-25). After God "built" the woman and brought her to him, "the man said: 'This at last is bone of my bones and flesh of my flesh; she shall be called Woman, because she was taken out of Man'" (Gen. 2:23). The specific terms for "man" and "woman" (Heb. '*iš* and '*iššāh*) when related to each other, connote "husband" and "wife," respectively. Here they have precisely those connotations, since the union of the first human pair is discussed.

In biblical times a male '*ādām* became a man/husband ('*iš*) when he took a woman/wife, just as she became a woman/wife ('*iššāh*) only at the time she was taken. This allusion points to the importance of sexuality for human identity.

Being married is not required to be fully man or woman; being a person is something much more basic than being a man or a woman. Yet human sexuality modifies and helps to define our personhood. Furthermore, sexual fulfillment is achieved only when a personal relationship based on total commitment, such as occurs in marriage, underpins and sustains the sexual relationship.

In marriage "a man leaves his father and his mother and cleaves to his wife, and they become one flesh" (verse 24). In many ages and places, customs have allowed a man and a woman who were almost total strangers to marry. In an uncanny way married life soon welded the couple into a union as close as blood ties ("flesh and bones" in the Hebrew idiom, compare Judges 9:2 and 2 Samuel 5:1). Intimacy causes the pair to stick together as counterparts cut from the same block of material. Over time spouses come to think, speak, and act alike; they "became one flesh."

That two should become one is "a profound" mystery (Eph. 5:32), foreshadowed in the way God instituted marriage. He literally made the first husband and wife from the same flesh and bones, as counterparts of the same body, and brought them together for a sturdy, lifelong union. This creative procedure should be viewed as illuminating the meaning of wedlock.

D. The Original Unity of Humankind

Contrary to the speculation that some races descend partially (by "amalgamation") from humanlike beings created apart from Adam, Acts 17:26 upholds the principle that the human race contains no other blood than that of Adam and Eve: "From one man he [God] made every nation of men, that they should inhabit the whole earth; and he determined the times set for them and the exact places where they should live" (NIV). This truth also links the solidarity of all people in the consequences of the fall of Adam (Rom. 5:12, 19) and, for all, in the possibility of salvation through Christ (1 Cor. 15:21, 22).

Animals were created "according to their kinds" (Gen. 1:21, 24, 25), which means "of various kinds" (cf. Gen. 6:20; 7:14; Lev. 11; Deut. 14; Eze. 47:10). This takes into account various species within each category, for instance, the diverse "beasts of the earth." Though humans appear in the Creation story as a category by themselves, nothing of the sort is said of them. They came originally in a single variety.

Science confirms this biblical information. The same biological variables, as well as the same psychological traits and cultural constants, are present in all human races. Differences among human races involve nothing but recombination, enhancement, or partial suppression of characteristics common to all of humankind.

To the best of scientific knowledge, races originated through inbreeding and genetic drift in times of population scarcity and dispersal. Philologists can now trace languages to a common stock; indeed the whole of linguistic and genetic evidence available to us points to a common origin for humankind.

Though not concerned with races as such, Genesis 11 stresses the original unity of humankind, even after the Flood. "The whole earth had one language" (verse 1) in the first generation after the catastrophe. That generation, just as Adam and Eve, were commanded to "fill the earth" (Gen. 9:1).

Under an autocratic leadership, however (Gen. 10:8, 9), they disobeyed the divine command (Gen. 11:4) and concentrated in Southern Mesopotamia (verse 2). For the good of this and all succeeding generations God disbanded them, enforcing cultural and linguistic diversity among different groups (verse 8; compare divisions among Semites, Japhetites, and Hamites in Genesis 10). This forced dispersal might well have provided the first opportunity for the genetic drift and inbreeding responsible for the racial diversity observable today among humans.

Biblical authors always emphasized the theological consequences of that original unity. Thus, Amos 9:7 explains that God sustains the same essential relationship with all ethnic groups of the earth, whether Semites (Israel), or Hamites (Philistines). The privileges of Israel depend on covenantal relationships, not on natural heredity.

E. Inner Life and Its Organic Support

1. The Wholeness of the Human Person

Human existence occurs on various levels: natural/supernatural, internal/external. As an image of God, a man or woman acts upon the natural world while keeping a unique relationship with God (supernatural level). On the natural level there is an inner life (thought, feelings, reason, memory, will, aesthetic appreciation, etc.) that far transcends that of the animals, while the outer organic life (nutrition, sleep, reproduction, etc.) is largely common to both.

Given the prominence of inner, relational life in humanity, it is no wonder that attempts have been made to conceive man as dual in nature. Inner and relational life takes place, according to the dualistic conception, within an entity, variously called "spirit" or "soul," immaterial in nature, which resides within our material organism, is able to function independently from it, and of which animals are deprived. Some divide human nature into three: body, soul, and spirit. For our purposes, both positions may be comprised under dualism, since in both, only one of the parts of human nature (spirit in one case, soul in the other) is really important, being separable and able to function independently. In these conceptions, the rest is secondary.

Dualism is generally associated with the idea that, separated from the organism in death, a soul or spirit goes on functioning forever ("immortal soul"). Nonetheless the same terms (soul or spirit) are often applied to expressions of the inner life itself rather than to an independant entity in which they supposedly live.

2. Biblical Monism

Opposed to dualism is biblical monism, the position according to which all expressions of the inner life depend on the whole of human nature, including the organic system. The components of a human being function as a unit. There is no separable soul or spirit capable of conscious existence apart from the body. Thus the words "soul" or "spirit" describe intellectual, affective, or volitive manifestations of the personality.

It is becoming increasingly clearer to theologians in various Christian denominations that the Bible views human beings as monistic. The *Interpreter's Dictionary of the Bible* affirms: "By Yahweh's communication of the vitalizing breath to the earthen man he had fashioned, we are not to conclude that man is compounded of two separate entities, body and soul—the view characteristic of Orphism and Platonism. To use the now classic phrase, the Hebrew conceived of man as an animated body, not as an incarnated soul."

All occurrences of the words "soul" and "spirit" in the Bible can be understood, in context, as referring to functions of the individual psyche or the activity of the whole person. This is true both in the OT of the terms *nepeš* or *rûaḥ,* and in the NT of the corresponding terms *psychē* and *pneuma,* which are translated "soul" or "spirit." In no single instance do we read of an immortal entity within man, a soul or human spirit that is able to function independently from the material body.

3. "Soul" and "Spirit" in the Bible

The account of man's creation in Genesis 2:7, has been sometimes interpreted as the infusion of a "soul" or immaterial substance into a material organism. But that inference is contrary to the record. It states that man was molded of the "dust from the ground," just as the animals of his environment were "brought forth" from the earth (Gen. 1:24; 2:19), only with more individualized attention and care. Then God "breathed into his nostrils the breath of life," which man shares with birds, reptiles, mammals, and other animals (Gen. 1:30; 7:22), and he "became a living being," a *nepeš ḥayyāh* like them (Gen. 1:20, 24).

The adjective *ḥayyāh* means "alive." Though *nepeš* is often translated "soul" in our versions, its usage for both man and beast (verses 20, 24, 30; 2:19; 7:21) shows that there is nothing immortal, or even pertaining to higher functions, about it. In its most basic sense the Hebrew word means "throat, gullet," from which the idea of "appetite" derives. "Appetite," in fact, is how the RSV translates it in Isaiah 5:14. The same translation could also be employed instead of "soul" in Genesis 34:3. In Isaiah 5:14 the term parallels "mouth" (cf. also Hab. 2:5) and could be advantageously so translated in Proverbs 25:25 (the thirsty "soul" enjoys cold water) and other places.

Related to the verbal root *npš,* "to breathe," *nepeš* figuratively means "life," as in Deuteronomy 24:6 and many other places. In Proverbs 8:35 it stands in contrast with "death" and parallels *ḥayyim,* another term for "life" (cf. *ḥayyāh* above). The meaning "life" can similarly be determined from the context of passages such as 1 Samuel 28:9; Psalms 30:3; 124:7; Proverbs 7:23; 19:18. The content of the term, however, is more active than merely sentient or vegetative life. In Genesis 2:7, then, the overall sense of the combination *nepeš ḥayyāh* is "an animated living being." Man *is* a soul rather than having one.

Thus neither the elements constituting man, nor the procedure applied at Creation, as depicted in Genesis 2:7, involve anything like a "soul" in the dualistic sense. Human beings are superior to animals, not because of the number of their basic components, but because they differ qualitatively from animals (Eccl. 3:19). This precludes the dualistic position.

Although death was not a part of the original world, biblical information about the process of dying likewise contradicts dualistic thought. In biblical terms death is described as a reversal process in which man, a ground creature, goes back to the ground (Gen. 3:19) and in expiring returns to God the breath (*rûaḥ,* lit. "wind," often translated "spirit"), which is symbolic of the life force leased to him, as well as to other living creatures (Gen. 6:17; 7:15, 22), in the beginning (Eccl. 12:7).

No personal or conscious entity survives the reversal process of death (Ps. 6:5; 30:9; 88:10; 115:17; 146:4; Eccl. 9:5, 6; Isa. 38:18, 19). The reversal can be turned around only at the resurrection. Thus all hope of a life beyond the grave centers on the resurrection (1 Cor. 15:16-23; cf. John 6:39, 40). Resurrection alone, not a disembodied state, can rescue the deceased from meaninglessness (Luke 20:37, 38). As William Tyndale, the English Bible translater and martyr, pointed out centuries ago, those who place disembodied souls in heaven, hell, or purgatory "destroy the arguments wherewith Christ and Paul prove the resurrection." (See Death I. A. 3, 4; Resurrection I. A.)

II. Man's Present State

A. Biblical Information

According to the first chapters of Genesis, the first humans were destined to a happy existence as God's helpers in Eden. In that "royal palace garden" (which is the literal meaning of "paradise") they would serve God (Gen. 2:15) and enjoy close communion with Him (cf. Gen. 3:8). The first pair could take advantage of a life-sustaining principle found in closeness to God by means of eating the fruit of the tree of life (Gen. 2:9; 3:22).

Such happiness did not obtain for long. The turning point came with sin, the betrayal of God's trust and explicit orders. These concerned another tree, linked to "the knowledge of good and evil," a Hebrew idiom implying self-dependent ability to judge and decide for oneself, usually associated with age (Deut. 1:39; 1 Kings 3:9; Isa. 7:15, 16).

Though the first humans were created as adults, they were still dependent on God for their moral decisions. As noted before, however, they chose autonomy, following the lead of the serpent: "So what if God said 'You must not eat from any tree in the garden'!" This betrayal made them unfit for intimacy with God and its attending benefits.

While the Genesis narrative is quite straightforward, chapter 3 needs revealed interpretation. The nature of the "serpent," a clever character (verse 1) touting "knowledge of good and evil" as a means to "become like God" (verse 5) and who seduced the human couple, promising that they would escape the death sentence determined for disobeying God (verse 4), is rather enigmatic in Genesis. According to the NT, behind the disguise stood the devil (Rev. 12:9), a spirit opposed to God (both "devil" and "Satan" mean "adversary"). He was one who once had been in the truth (John 8:44), and had already led astray many heavenly spirits in rebellion (Jude 6; Rev. 12:4, 8).

There are allusions to the fall of this being in the OT (Isa. 14:4-23; Eze. 28:1-10); mention of it is also made in intertestamental writings (Jubilees 10:8; 11:5; Damascus Document 3, 4; 2 Enoch 31:3). The NT confirms this description, denouncing him for inciting sin in humanity (Luke 22:3, 31; John 13:27; Acts 5:3; 1 Cor. 7:5) and for opposing the work of salvation (Mark 4:15; 1 Thess. 2:18). He also carries the ultimate responsibility for death (John 8:44; Heb. 2:14).

The idea of being "like God" in Genesis 3:4, 5, 22 applies, then, to the devilish attempt to establish a self-centered existence, ignoring God's law and denying one's creaturely dependence on Him (Isa. 14:13, 14; Eze. 28:2; cf. the Edenic setting in verses 13-15). Much more than an isolated act of disregard for divine authority, then, was at stake in the temptation of Adam and Eve. By their fall they joined in a cosmic rebellion against God.

However, God dealt mercifully with the sinners. They were not executed immediately but expelled from Paradise. No longer in the garden, Adam and Eve were surrounded by a hostile environment and, as God had announced in His judgment, they became prey to sorrow, pain, thankless toil, exploitative relationships, and ultimately death (Gen. 3:14-19). The Bible thus shows sin as the mainspring of evil in the human condition.

B. Sin the Pervasive Reality

The momentousness of Adam and Eve's rebellion and its pervasive consequences are addressed in Romans 5:12-20. They appear in order to clarify the cruciality of their antithesis: Christ's obedience at the cross as the opening of the door of salvation for the entire human race.

1. Romans 5:12

According to Romans 5, sin and death in humanity derive originally from Adam rather than from each individual person. Paul stresses repeatedly that a single action affects the whole of humanity. In verse 12, "sin came into the world *through one man*"; in verse 15, "many died *through one man's trespass.*" In Romans 5:18, 19 *"one man's"* trespass and disobedience led to condemnation, while *"one man's"* obedience and act of righteousness brought life.

In verses 12-14, Paul offers evidence of how far-reaching are the effects of the sin that started with a single person. First, everyone sins (cf. Rom. 3:9-20). If everyone started his or her own line of sins, independently from Adam, someone, at sometime, might be able not to sin. Since this does not happen, it follows that we do not start out independently. In the second place, there was death even when there was no special revelation of commandments as in Eden or at Sinai. At those times, even though sin did exist as a violation of conscience, it lacked the aggravating character of being the transgression of a written norm. If it were true that everyone receives only the consequences of his or her own sin, the people of those times, not being as guilty as Adam, should not have been punished by death as he was. The fact that they died shows that their death was a consequence of Adam's sin. (See Sin III. B; Death I. C. 1.)

2. A Misunderstood Passage

Romans 5:12 contains a bone of contention for translators and interpreters. The word "because" in the RSV stands for the Greek *eph' hō*, literally translated "on which." The Vulgate translated *in quo omnes peccaverunt*, "in whom all sinned." This translation gives basis to the concept of "original sin," by which every descendant of Adam, having sinned in Adam, is personally held accountable for the first sin.

However, "in whom" is not the idea expressed by the Greek *eph' hō*, but *en hō*, a common Pauline phrase (cf. Rom. 2:1; 7:6; 8:3, 15; 14:21, 22; 16:2). Furthermore, nothing in the context requires a theory of transmission of blame. The phrase *eph' hō,* means "on the basis of which" and may legitimately be translated as "because of which or whom." This would fit the context well: Sin and death entered the world through one man, because of whom all sinned (cf. Rom. 5:19). The RSV use of "because" is misleading: one expects "because" to be followed by the cause, whereas what follows *eph' hō* in Romans 5:12 is the effect. "Because all men sinned" should not, then, be understood as the reason that "death spread to all men." Such an interpretation does not fit the context. Rather, that all have sinned shows the validity of the rest of the verse: Sin and death spread throughout the world, beginning with Adam. The understanding of the verse is confirmed by its analogy to the next point in Paul's presentation. In verses 13 and 14, he argues that because people of all times have died, we must accept that death derives from Adam and not from personal sin.

This passage shows that if sin depended only on the individual exercise of free will, there would be no reason some saintly hero could not have avoided sin altogether. The lack of any such example in human history is proof of the fact that we cannot avoid sin. The pervasive power of sin that dwells within us (cf. Rom. 7:17) fatally translates itself into sinful thoughts, words, or actions at some point in the life of every human being. The pervasiveness of the power of sin is matched only by the saving power of the gospel.

Long before Paul wrote about the "sin which dwells within me" (verses 17, 20), God had pronounced the mind of man "evil from his youth" (Gen. 8:21); pointing to an innate ethical bias toward iniquity. The book of Job abundantly reflects on the somber condition of man who, starting from his lowly birth on this earth, is irremediably "unclean" in the eyes of God (Job 14:1-4). Describing the sinful human condition, Job exclaimed, "Who can bring a clean thing out of an unclean? There is not one" (verse 4); and God affirmed to Jeremiah, "the heart is deceitful above all things, and desperately corrupt" (Jer. 17:9).

3. Irresistible Tendencies

According to the NT the unregenerate person, faced with the revealed will of God, is unable to fulfill or even fully appreciate it (Eph. 4:18). The mind "is hostile to God; it does not submit to God's law, indeed it cannot; and those who are in the flesh cannot please God" (Rom. 8:7, 8).

A careful education, the exercise of will-power, or any other human device is ineffective against an evil nature with its self-centered propensities. Barring God's grace, the propensities of human nature inevitably lead to moral ruin. Hence the need for conversion before attempting to reform one's life. (See Salvation I. E.) Evil propensities remain even after conversion, but not in their former irresistible power. Through regeneration a new life is possible, as will be shown in the next section.

In any case, the menacing character of sin does not reside on the superficial level of its fruits so much as in its deep-seated roots in human nature. Sin is "systemic" in our life. The "sin which dwells within me" (Rom. 7:17, 20) is the reason that "the evil I do not want is what I do" (verse 19). Scripture here calls the indwelling cause of evil deeds "sin," which shows that the biblical concept of sin includes propensities, not merely evil deeds.

When speaking of the depraved human will a single exception must be made. Jesus Christ was sinless, though in every other way "like his brethren" (Heb. 2:17) in His human nature. In contrast with the rest of us, who are by nature "the children of wrath" (Eph. 2:3), He was from conception "the holy one" (Luke 1:35, NIV). He was never involved in sinful deeds (1 Peter 2:22) and the evil one had absolutely "no power" over Him (John 14:30; lit. "nothing in me"). A fuller discussion of this topic belongs to the biblical doctrine of Christ (see Christ I. B. 2), but an awareness of this exception to the doctrine of human depravity is important here.

4. Triumph Over Tendencies

Irresistible as it is for the unconverted person, any tendency or propensity can and should be fought and conquered with supernatural aid. The unavoidable defeat of our inborn resources can be turned around through the new birth from above (John 3:5-8). Christ Himself opened the way to victory. He was incarnated in the same sinful world that surrounds Christians. He "condemned sin in the flesh" (Rom. 8:3) by doing the will of God. As numerous NT passages show, all believers are expected to "follow" (Matt. 10:38) and "imitate" Him (Eph. 5:1, 2).

As pointed out by the apostle in Romans 7:22-25, attaining obedience is a miracle of the power of Christ's grace. While Paul's mind delighted in the law of God, "another law" was "at war with the law of" his mind. His only hope of deliverance was in Jesus Christ. The extent to which this deliverance may be realized in the present life of Christians deserves more detailed consideration and belongs to the doctrine of salvation. (See Salvation III.) For the description of the present state of the human race, it must suffice to remark that we are delivered from bondage to sin, not to negligent carelessness, but to fight a war against it, in a conflict that is strenuous even for the dedicated Christian.

Though help is available to overcome sin, the price of victory is continuous vigilance in spiritual warfare (Rom. 13:12; 2 Cor. 10:4; Eph. 6:10-13; 1 Peter 5:8, 9). This conflict is rooted in the dual nature of the converted, born from the flesh and from the Spirit (Gal. 5:17).

Christians are painfully aware of the reality that at times they do not behave in a fully Christian way. With Paul they can assert, "I of myself . . . serve the law of sin" (Rom. 7:25). Left to themselves, they easily fall into the trap of admiring God's will and self-confidently attempting to fulfill it without the requisite divine strength.

But even when winning battles, man's present condition, with its continuing need for struggle, is still precarious. Nor can we always count on coming out unscathed from warfare. Jesus instructed His disciples to pray daily for forgiveness (Matt. 6:12) and instituted the ordinance of foot washing to represent the continuing need for the Christian to be cleansed from the stain of sin (John 13:10, 12-17; see Ordinances II. A-D). The same epistle which proclaims that the power found in the new birth is able to overcome sin (1 John 5:4), also warns that whoever denies the presence of sin in his or her life practices self-deception (1 John 1:8) and blasphemously contradicts God (verse 10).

Because of an innate bent toward sin, complete deliverance will be celebrated only at the Second Coming. This bent can be resisted with the help of the indwelling Holy Spirit, but will not go away before that time. Not until then will every sinful tendency and every imperfection disappear; then and only then "we shall be like him" (1 John 3:2).

5. Human Depravity and Effects on Society

Inherent depravity is an expression of our solidarity, as human beings, with our first parents (Eph. 2:3). Sharing a common origin in Adam and Eve (Acts 17:26), we could not possibly inherit the originally unwarped will that they lost when they failed at the great trial (Gen. 3; 6:5). Conversely, if they had passed their trial successfully, we would have been as surely established in righteousness as we are now in sin.

In Eden God announced that sin would result in sorrow, pain, thankless toil, exploitative human relationships, and death (Gen. 3:14-19). This description perfectly fits the human experience.

We suffer because, estranged from God, we have lost the privileges found in closeness to Him. But we also inflict suffering on one another through fresh sins. Not only has our vertical relationship with God suffered, the horizontal relationship with other creatures has been damaged. Our interrelation with nature has been radically altered since Eden; it now

threatens to become an ecological nightmare, with famine and disease in its sequel. Marriage was perverted first into servitude and next into a dispensable travesty. Other instances of perverted horizontal relationships include class exploitation, slavery, economic inequities, national and ethnic wars, and other evils deeply ingrained in social structures. Indeed, many now conceive these structures as the root of all evils—a fragmentary diagnosis, dangerously reduced to some of the horizontal components of sinfulness. (See Sin V.)

C. Death, the Ultimate Enemy

1. Death as a Penalty for Sin

Because sin is not only a breach of commandments but primarily a rebellion against the Creator, a personal being, He must deal with it in a just manner. While it is true, to a certain extent, that sin itself includes punishment and has natural consequences (Prov. 5:22; Gal. 6:7), there are also penalties directly meted out by divine justice (Ex. 32:33; Matt. 25:41).

At times, especially when God is dealing with His people, divine punishment is corrective. The Bible compares it with the valuable discipline applied in the home for the education of a child (Ps. 94:12; Heb. 12:5-12). Some wish to accept as legitimate only this kind of punishment, intended to reform the evildoer. However, reform has its own agenda, which differs from the purposes of justice. Deserved punishments could be greater or lesser than those needed for behavior modification.

For strict justice to exist, retribution is irreplaceable. This should not be confused with rancor or vindictiveness. In the latter, a spirit of revenge controls the punishment, and justice again is forced to take a secondary place. Divine retribution, on the other hand, is guided by justice without revenge, administered in infinite love. (See Judgment II. E.)

God has determined to put out the cosmic rebellion by persuasion and love, not by brute force. For this reason alone the existence of sinners is tolerated for a time, while the mercy of God calls each one to repentance (2 Peter 3:9). But the sinfulness of creatures and the holiness of God cannot eternally coexist. Since the Lawgiver is also the Creator, the sinful rebellion of creatures fully deserves annihilation. This death penalty, about which our first parents were forewarned (Gen. 2:17), is therefore the just and fair wages of sin (Rom. 6:23).

Death as the penalty of sin is emphasized throughout the Scriptures. The unrepentant sinning "soul" (person) will die (Eze. 18:4), will be "cut off" (Ps. 37:9, 34) or destroyed (*kārat*, same Hebrew term as in Jeremiah 11:19), will perish (Ps. 68:2; cf. John 3:16) or "be no more" (Ps. 37:10; cf. verse 20). Such a person will be burned up as "stubble" (Isa. 40:24; Mal. 4:1; Matt. 13:30; 2 Peter 3:10; Rev. 20:15; 21:8) for "eternal destruction" (2 Thess. 1:9).

2. The Undoing of Death

According to the biblical data already reviewed, the original conditions of the human existence allowed both continual life in communion with God (the access to the tree of life; conditional immortality) and death (without the survival of personality in any form) through rebellion and disobedience. If the human race, as God intended, had become established in righteousness, their life truly would have become eternal.

Romans 5:12-14 has shown how Adam and Eve brought about depravity and death for themselves and all their descendants. We should also notice the symmetrical and opposite work of Christ, providing atonement for the whole race as a second Adam, in the following verses (15-19). According to 1 Corinthians 15:21, 22, "For as by a man came death, by a man has come also the resurrection of the dead. For as in Adam all die, so also in Christ shall all be made alive."

Thus the sentence of death unconditionally inherited by all from Adam is also unconditionally offset by a resurrection won by Christ for all. Because of the Resurrection, the end of present human life, a consequence of the sin of Adam and not of our own sins, cannot separate us from God eternally. This "first" death merely terminates the life of people of all times who, when resurrection cancels it out, will be able to receive God's promises together (Heb. 11:39, 40).

The resurrection of Christ inaugurated and guaranteed the same experience for all "who belong to Christ." This will happen "at his coming." After that Christ will destroy all His enemies (1 Cor. 15:23-25). "The last enemy to be destroyed is death" (verse 26).

Eternal life, then, is to be received as an actual gift only by those who belong to Christ at His second coming. However, Christians can claim it, even now, on the surety of the work of Christ. "God gave us eternal life, and this life is in his Son. He who has the Son has life; he who has not the Son of God has not life" (1 John 5:11, 12; cf. 1 John 1:2; 5:20).

At the close of the millennium those who opposed God, all of His enemies, will also be resurrected, but only to be judged and destroyed at the "resurrection of judgment" (John 5:28, 29). That destruction will be final. (See Millennium I. C. 3; Death I. F. 5; Judgment III. B. 3.) For this reason the "second death" is to be feared (Rev. 20:6): "Blessed and holy is he who shares in the first resurrection! Over such the second death has no power." This second death separates human beings from God eternally. It is not the consequence of Adam's sin but of each person's joining the rebellion against God and rejecting the provisions of His grace.

The enemies of God are finally to be utterly destroyed and all the effects of sin (Heb. 2:14; Rev. 20:14). Those who believe on Christ will be, from the time of His second coming on, eternally safe; there is no further possibility for sin or sinful natures to become a reality again. A single pulse of harmony will beat in the entire universe.

3. The Value of an Annihilating Retribution

In spite of the emphasis of Scripture on

definitive destruction as the retribution due to unrepentant sinners (e.g., 2 Thess. 1:9; Rev. 20:14; see II. C. 1), traditional Christendom follows a doctrine of eternal pain as the reward of the wicked. This doctrine results directly from a belief in a separable, immortal human "soul," already shown to be groundless (I. E. 1-3).

However, once the biblical concept of man is recovered, it is easy to see that an eternal, personal existence is impossible for the lost. God has made even a miserable existence, unavailable to man on an endless basis once the right relationship with Him was cut off (Gen. 3:22, 23). This is so because life is a gift of God for those who belong to Christ only (Rom. 6:23; John 3:16); indeed "he who has not the Son has not life" (1 John 5:12). Such a one "shall not see life" (John 3:36) and can exist for a limited time only, because there is no "eternal life abiding in him" (1 John 3:15).

At this point we need to consider the meaning of "eternal destruction" (2 Thess. 1:8). In view here is not an eternal destroying process, just as "eternal redemption" (Heb. 9:12) is not an eternal redeeming process. Clearly in both cases the meaning is a destruction or redemption that lasts for eternity, whose consequences are eternal.

In 2 Thessalonians 1:8, 9 the wicked "suffer the punishment of eternal destruction and exclusion from the presence of the Lord." The Greek verb *tinō,* translated "suffer the punishment," simply means to pay a penalty or be punished. In addition, the context shows that the punishment is "exclusion from the presence of the Lord," which presence is the reward of the righteous. This does not deny suffering as part of the punishment; pain will indeed result from the "flaming fire" of the day of "vengeance" (2 Thess. 1:7, 8), but this pain will not be "eternal punishment."

Similar considerations apply to Matthew 25:46, where the wicked "go away into eternal punishment, but the righteous into eternal life." The word *kolasis,* here used for "punishment," has a root meaning "to cut short," hence "to suffer loss." Here, as in 2 Thessalonians, the punishment is the loss of the reward of the righteous. This loss is as eternal as is life for the righteous. The rewards of both righteous and wicked are equally definitive.

The Bible does not speak of eternal torture or pain for the wicked, although the agents of destruction, such as fire and smoke, are called eternal (Matt. 25:41; Rev. 14:11). The wicked are thrown into a formidably unrelenting medium which guarantees that no residue will be left. Phrases such as "eternal fire" are applied in Scripture to the fate of cities such as Sodom (Jude 7) or the mystical Babylon (Rev. 19:3), of which no remains whatsoever survive, as Scripture clearly states (2 Peter 2:6; Rev. 18:8, 9; see Death I. F. 5; Millennium I. C. 3. e).

III. Man's Future State

While it is tempting to indulge in bold speculations about the future state of humanity, such a subject can be dealt with only cautiously, "for our knowledge is imperfect. . . . Now we see in a mirror dimly, but then face to face. Now I know in part; then I shall understand fully" (1 Cor. 13:9, 12). On the other hand, biblical revelation does allow us to state facts.

Dualistic thought has accustomed Christendom to think of the future state, or "heaven," in ethereal and immaterial terms. Among other factors, this is due to an overemphasis on the value of spirit and to ignoring the biblical fact that all the righteous will receive their rewards at the same time, at the Second Coming. Since the deceased righteous are imagined as disembodied, conscious entities, and represented as receiving their rewards as they die, they are placed in a "heaven" of this kind. The Bible, however, speaks of two real places where the saved will live: one temporary and another permanent.

A. Temporary Dwelling of the Saved

There is indeed a heaven where God and the angels dwell (1 Kings 8:30, 39; Ps. 11:4; 53:2; 80:14; 102:19; Matt. 5:16, 45, 48; 6:9), from which Christ came at His incarnation (John 3:13, 31; 6:38) and into which He ascended after His resurrection (Heb. 9:24). From here, too, He will descend at His second coming, when He will take the righteous to Himself (John 14:1-3; 1 Thess. 4:13-18; 1 Peter 1:4).

This heaven will be a temporary abode for the righteous. There they will share in the duties of judgment, a royal prerogative described in the Bible in kingly terms (Dan. 7:22, 26; 1 Cor. 6:2, 3; Rev. 3:21; 20:4) associated with heavenly glory. But these duties will cease after the final destruction of the wicked; then the righteous will inherit the new earth (Rev. 21:1-7; see Judgment III. B. 2; Millennium I. C. 2).

B. The Permanent Home of the Saved

The promise of a new earth occurs first in Isaiah (65:17, 21-23; 66:22, 23), in the context of the purification of the holy land from the pollution of idolatry. Though some aspects of those OT prophecies, conditioned by the obedience of Israel, are no longer in force, as a whole they are reaffirmed in the NT (Matt. 5:5; 2 Peter 3:11-13; Rev. 21:1; see Apocalyptic II. B. 1).

This confirms the symmetry between protology and eschatology. There will be a "regeneration" (KJV) or "renewal of all things" (Matt. 19:28, NIV), a "restitution" (KJV) or time "for God to restore everything" (Acts 3:21, NIV) according to His original plan, after which all things will remain forever in conformity with His will (Heb. 12:27).

God's plan includes an earthly home for human beings (Ps. 8:6-8). Man, created on the sixth day with the rest of land creatures (Gen. 1:24), was formed from the dust of the earth (2:7), and essentially linked with it (3:19; cf. Ps. 115:16). Land was always an important ingredient in covenantal promises (Gen. 12:7; 13:14, 15; 15:18; 17:8; 26:3, 4), not exhausted in Palestine but passed on to the whole world, the future inheritance of God's people (Rom. 4:13; Heb. 11:13).

These "new heavens and new earth" are not to be conceived as a different kind of cosmos. The terms employed in the promise of Isaiah 65:17 derive ultimately from Genesis 1, where they are carefully defined. "Heavens" is the name given by the Lord to the atmospheric expanse (verse 8) in which birds fly (verse 20); "Earth" is the land surface (verse 10). Accordingly, the new heavens and new earth will be, not some strange new interstellar space or a new planet, but the life-supporting environment of our own world—renewed, renovated, and cleansed by purifying fire (2 Peter 3:10-13; Ps. 102:26, 27; Heb. 12:27, 28). Few details of a material character are given in the Bible, undoubtedly because the relational plane of existence is much more important than the physical environment.

Relationships in the new earth will be characterized by righteousness (2 Peter 3:13). Just as rebellion against God at the time of the fall of Adam and Eve drove lesser living forms toward aggressive behaviors through the curse of sin (Gen. 3:14-19), so the universal pulse of harmony among God's creatures will drive them toward peace through God's blessing (Isa. 11:5-9; see II. C. 2).

Since sin is forever excluded from this home, the saved are securely established in righteousness and safe from all consequences of sin, such as death or pain, fulfilling God's original intent (Rev. 21:4). The whole history of human sin, suffering, and evil will appear then as a mere detour in the execution of the divine design. (See New Earth II.)

C. The Future Body

A description of biblical monism (or unitary conception of man, see I. E. 2 above) would be incomplete without dealing with the future body of the saved, however briefly. Biblical eschatology places the reward of the saved firmly on the new earth.

Already in the days of Paul some dualists had reduced Christian hopes for the final destiny of the saved to a purely incorporeal state (2 Tim. 2:18). Thanks to Paul's efforts to oppose this error and to the clear testimony of Scripture about the resurrection of Christ and the raising of the righteous in the last day (Rom. 8:11, 23; 1 Cor. 6:14-20; 15:20, 23, 53; Col. 1:18; Rev. 1:5), even traditional Christianity has retained the concept of a future body for eternity.

Later dualists, however, have taken refuge in the words of Paul in 1 Corinthians 15:44-49 to minimize the physicality of the body of the resurrected saints. Paul is here dealing with an argument, common among Sadducees and various heretics of his time, employed to deny resurrection on the basis of the understanding that our present body is incapable and/or unworthy of eternal preservation (verse 35). He counters that necessary change does not break continuity, just as there is continuity between a seed of corn and the emerging plant (verses 36-41). He then recognizes (taking distance from extreme Pharisaic postures holding an identical form after resurrection [2 Baruch 50:2]) that changes are to be made in the body of the saved (verses 42, 43): "So it is with the resurrection of the dead. What is sown is perishable, what is raised is imperishable. It is sown in dishonor, it is raised in glory. It is sown in weakness, it is raised in power."

Paul then continues, "It is sown a physical body, it is raised a spiritual body" (verse 44). The adjective given in the English translation by the RSV and other versions as "physical," is rendered as "natural" by the KJV and NIV. By opposing "spiritual" to "physical," Paul's statement has been perceived as suggesting an immaterial body, while by opposing "spiritual" to "natural," some have obtained an idea of a body in itself "supernatural," hence widely different from the one created in the beginning. The Greek original, however, conveys no such ideas. The contrasting pair of adjectives "physical/natural" and "spiritual" is in the original Greek *psychikos* and *pneumatikos*. As seen before, both *psychē* and *pneuma* are used for functions of inner life. Literally, it is sown a "psychic" body; it is raised "pneumatic." Therefore we have here no contrast or opposition between material and immaterial, or a natural and a "supernatural" body. Our present body is described in this verse in metaphysical terms such as those used for the resurrected body. Since the "psychic" condition of this present body does not preclude its physicality, why would the future "pneumatic" condition of our body preclude it?

The adjectives *psychikos* and *pneumatikos* designate characterizations and descriptions. They are not complete definitions. Ours is a "psychic" body, not because we are limited to a "psyche," but because we are endowed with it—and much more, including a physical system. We must then ask how a "psychic" body can be contrasted with a "spiritual" one. In the NT the *psychē* is a vital principle of the living being and often designates the whole person (for example, Matt. 2:20; John 10:11; Acts 2:41-43; Rom. 2:9; 16:4; 2 Cor. 12:5; Phil. 2:30). But several times it is contrasted with *pneuma*. In those passages, *psychē* is a purely natural principle present in the unconverted (hence the translation of *psychikos* as "natural" in 1 Corinthians 15:44, KJV and NIV). *Pneuma,* in contrast, is sometimes identified with the renewal of the inner man (1 Cor. 2:14, 15; Jude 19) brought about by God's Spirit, which will be completed in the glorification after the resurrection, in itself an event sometimes described as the work of the Holy Spirit (Rom. 1:4; 8:11).

For this reason, the present body may be described in 1 Corinthians 15 as "psychic," since it is endowed with *psychē,* but not "pneumatic" yet, since that must wait until the resurrection. The contrast between a "psychic" and "pneumatic" body, then, exactly parallels the contrast between "perishable" and "imperishable," "weak" and "powerful," or "dishonored" and "glorious" found in the preceding verses. It adds no new concepts about the constitution of such a body.

The concept might well be translated, "it is sown a body endowed with natural life, it is raised a body endowed with supernatural life/ spirit." A supernatural life for a natural body was available in Eden through the tree of life. The verse implies nothing against the materiality of the future body, nor against a return to the pristine conditions of our earth.

Indeed, since the resurrected body will be similar to Christ's (Rom. 8:23; 1 Cor. 15:23; Phil. 3:21; Col. 3:4), we must think of it as endowed with life and spirit, but also with flesh and bones, which He specifically declared He possessed in His resurrected state (Luke 24:39).

Our physical bodies may be considered among our humblest endowments. Even so, they still evidence that we are "fearfully and wonderfully made" (Ps. 139:14, KJV and NIV), and should not be excluded from the "restoration of all things," but, on the contrary, should serve to characterize that time as "the redemption of our bodies" (Rom. 8:23; see Resurrection II).

IV. Impact of the Biblical Doctrine of Man on the Christian's Life

God's creation of the first human pair by a sovereign act shows His power and wisdom. In this sense, we were created for His glory. Man was placed at the summit of Creation as an "image of God," representing the Godhead before the rest of the creatures of this world. Part of this responsibility is to represent God and, to a degree, resemble Him. The original state included dependence on God and conformity to His will. Because we have been made in God's image, "little less than God" (Ps. 8:5), we should be motivated to an optimistic search for progress, at the same time soberly acknowledging our responsibility to the Creator, other created beings, ourselves, and lesser forms of life.

The importance of human sexuality lies in the fact that we can enjoy companionship and intimacy with others. God made, not two persons of different gender, but rather a couple destined to have a harmonious and complementary relationship. Thus the Bible underlines the importance of the social dimension of humanity. Marriage, although not a requirement for a full human life, was designed from Creation to be a source of personal fulfillment.

Because God made male and female equally in His image, there is equality between sexes. However, after the Fall, Adam and Eve were told that one of the results of sin would be, for the good of the pair, the male's loving and caring rulership of the family. Throughout the Bible, women occupy places of dignity and responsibility. However, Christ went beyond the customs of His time and place to show deference toward women. This understanding of women should guide in a Christian man's treatment of women.

In God's sight all races are equally made in His image. While animal categories in the Creation story were multiform, human beings were of only one variety. Racial diversity concerns secondary aspects of human beings, originated in genetic variations as populations dispersed. An understanding of the essential unity of humankind is vital for comprehending the doctrine of salvation.

The biblical view of the human person is unitary, not dual. Inner life always depends on its external support, the biological organism. Soul and spirit are only intellectual, affective, or volitional expressions of the whole person. All human interactions and relationships must take into account the fact that a human being does not consist of separable parts. All of a person lives and all of a person dies. The biblical understanding of the nature of man helps us to integrate the physical as well as the spiritual aspects of our personality in order to achieve a healthier, more harmonious, more energetic approach to life.

That a dead person lies in the grave, unfeeling and unknowing, until the resurrection makes the time spent in the grave but a blinking of an eye. The hope of resurrection after the sleep of death is dear to the heart of Christians and lightens their grieving.

The evils of our existence are traceable to sin. Our first parents coveted a knowledge of good and evil or ethical autonomy, and by eating the forbidden fruit disabled themselves for communion with God. Once deprived of this relationship, people became subject to suffering, exploitative relationships, and finally death. Thus, evil is unmasked, not as a legal resident in the universe, but as an intruder to be fought, conquered, and destroyed.

Disguised as a serpent, Satan caused the fall of Adam and Eve. He still continues his attempts to deceive human beings. Once close to God, Satan now leads a cosmic rebellion against God, which Adam joined, causing sin to pervade humanity. Evil as only a social mishap is an illusion. We are in reality contending against "spiritual hosts of wickedness in the heavenly places" (Eph. 6:12). Sin comprises not only evil deeds but also their resident cause in the inner self. To achieve godlikeness requires constant vigilance; ultimately, the grace and strength of God will gain the victory.

Since sin is rebellion against God, it deserves retribution. Divine retribution means both correction and penalty. While the rebellion will ultimately be extinguished through persuasion and love, those who persevere in impenitence will "reap" for themselves total annihilation by means of the "second death." All human beings are subject to the first death, but its effect is merely to synchronize the rewards of those living in different ages; it will be unconditionally canceled by a resurrection. The second death is the penalty for personal sins, while the first is the effect of Adam's sin. Those who accept Christ's sacrifice and atonement can look forward in certainty to the reward of eternal life, sure that He has paid the penalty of the second death for them.

Although we know little about the future life, we can be sure of it. We can also know that the redeemed will live a physical existence. Heaven will be the temporary dwelling place of the saved while they participate in the judgment of those who have not been saved. The permanent home of the redeemed will be this earth, restored to its pristine condition. Eternal righteousness will be ensured. In their glorified, spiritual bodies, the redeemed will spend eternity with Christ in His eternal home.

The knowledge of the value God places on the human person should fill us with grateful joy. At the same time, we should feel a sense of responsibility, not only to care for our own selves, but to take to heart the welfare of our brothers and sisters who also have been created in the image of God.

V. Historical Overview

A. Monism and Dualism

Dualism entered Christianity via Greek thought. On this Enrique Dussel, a Roman Catholic theologian, writes: "The Christian understanding of man was formed within the horizon of Hebrew thought and developed homogeneously in primitive Christianity. However, Christendom (which is a culture not to be confused with Christianity) originated as a Hellenization of the primitive experience, substituting another language and other logical instruments of interpretation and expression instead, therefore falling into a mitigated dualism" (17).

Even before the classical Greek philosophical schools, there was in Greece a dualistic tradition (Orphism, Pythagoreanism) that stressed inner faculties of man as a divine element contrasting with the inferior (material) body. The intellect was to be strengthened by exercise, while the body was to be kept in subjection through asceticism.

Plato (fourth century B.C.) taught idealism: ultimate reality is purely spiritual, and the body nothing but a tomb for the soul (a Greek pun: *sōma, sēma*, "body, grave"; *Gorgias* 493). The soul antedated earthly existence, was uncreated and immortal, and migrated from one body to another after death (*Phaedo* 75, 76). Aristotle proposed an alternative view, according to which body and soul are two aspects of the same basic reality: matter and form of man. The platonic tradition, however, asserted itself in spite of Aristotle. Gnosticism and Neoplatonism stressed only the body-versus-soul opposition, denying the biblical doctrine of resurrection.

Primitive Christianity had to contend with a decadent Graeco-Roman society which had loose morals but great admiration for Platonism. Some early Christian writers denounced Gnosticism and its attending dualism as inimical to the biblical doctrine of the creation by God of the material world. Justin Martyr (c. 100-c. 165), converted when he was shown that the soul was not immortal but "ceases to exist," denounced as heretics those who expect, not a resurrection but "that their souls, when they die, are taken to heaven" (*Dialogue With Trypho* 5, 6, 80). While earlier extant Christian material is scant, it suffices to show that martyrs, when facing death, made their hope to hinge upon the resurrection, not upon any preceding meeting with God, at the same time expressing monistic convictions (Clement *1 Corinthians* 24-26; Polycarp *Martyrdom* 14).

Later, however, Neoplatonism made inroads into Christianity. Starting at Alexandria, a learning center for Greek philosophy and Christian theology, prejudice against the body as the seat of sexual and other passions developed among Church Fathers, and asceticism was adopted as a model of piety.

Church scholars still maintained the biblical doctrine of Creation and the resurrection of the flesh, but simultaneously gradually accepted the idea of a separable soul. They thought that after separation by death, the soul awaited, consciously or not, the resurrection. While this soul was no longer preexistent (as in Platonism or in the extreme views of Origen), but individually created, it was from that time on eternal.

In the Middle Ages the intermediate state between death and resurrection came to be a conscious state. The departed soul was summoned to a judgment, which anticipated the results of the final judgment after the resurrection, determining whether it would enjoy the presence of God. This enjoyment, however, might be deferred by a period of purification prior to entry into the presence of God. Such a delay might itself be avoided by the living of an ascetic life designed to achieve full forgiveness in this life. This doctrine of purgatory was further developed in the West, with indulgences as an alternative to physical mortification.

Toward the end of the Middle Ages, less dualistic Aristotelian ideas, long suppressed in Christendom but now reintroduced to Europe via the Spanish Judeo-Arabic culture, caught the attention of Scholastics, including Thomas Aquinas. He tried to assimilate the Aristotelian concept of soul as form and body as matter of man. The logic of such a position pointed in the direction of a soul inseparable from the body. But to conciliate his thought with church tradition, he posited a thoroughly immaterial *mens* (mind) and maintained that the soul "preternaturally" survived the decomposition of man at death. He thus fell short from the biblical view of man.

In 1513 the more extreme (Averroist) Aristotelian ideas were condemned by Pope Leo X. Only four years later, excesses in the preaching of indulgences sparked the Reformation. While the thrust of the message of Luther (1483-1546) was on righteousness by faith, in his response to the bull of Leo X, he also attacked the recently reaffirmed doctrine of the immortality of the soul as another of "these endless monstrous fictions in the Roman rubbish heap of decretals" (*Weimar Ausgabe* 7:131, 132). His solution at the time: souls sleep until the resurrection.

The issue was much debated among Protestants; Luther himself wavered. The Anglican Church never quite rejected purgatory;

the rest did. Soul sleep, defended by Tyndale, Milton, early Baptists, and many others, was rejected by the influential Calvin (1509-1564). Many scholars, pastors, and Christian groups, however, have always noticed and accepted biblical monism. In our century, noted theologians such as E. Brunner, R. Niebuhr, and O. Cullmann upheld it. Even more recently, disturbed by the traditional view of hell as endless agony and torment, such noted evangelicals as J. W. Wenham, J. R. Stott, and Clark H. Pinnock likewise have endorsed the scriptural doctrine of soul sleep. But it still needs to reach the general public: "Twenty years [after Oscar Cullmann's classic essay], . . . lay people still place their hope in the immortal soul, even while a growing chorus of biblical scholars and theologians are saying, mostly among themselves, that this is a pagan doctrine" (Myers 78).

B. Adventist Rejection of Inherent Immortality

Early Millerite Adventists gradually acquired this truth from Scripture. Since the issue was widely debated in the eighteenth and nineteenth centuries, individual members of the Advent movement no doubt held this truth privately. For instance, the Argentinian Francisco Ramos Mexia, a Sabbatarian and early "Adventist" of Scottish Presbyterian heritage, wrote around 1816 an acute comment on the words of Acts 2:34 in the margin of his personal copy of Manuel Lacunza's *Venida del Mesías en gloria y magestad,* III, 293, "For David did not ascend into the heavens." He inferred from this text that "Man, together with his soul or what you may call it, will dissolve: 'To dust thou shall return.' But he will later raise from it, Gentlemen!"

As a public tenet of faith, this truth was first championed among Millerite Adventists by George Storrs, a former Methodist minister. He became convinced of the mortality of the whole human being in 1841 by reading a tract published six years before by one Henry Grew. The following year he also accepted

Adventist teaching of Christ's return through the influence of Charles Fitch. Since *The Signs of the Times* chided in 1842 another Adventist minister for preaching this scriptural truth, Storrs defended it in *Six Sermons* and started the *Bible Examiner,* a periodical devoted to the issue.

Charles Fitch joined him in this endeavor in 1844 in spite of the opposition of William Miller and other leaders of the movement. Nor could the latter prevent this doctrine from quickly taking deep roots among Millerite Adventists, as shown already by the 10 fundamental beliefs of the Millerites adopted in 1845 by the Albany Conference. One of them declared that the inheritance of the saved is not received at death but at the Second Advent.

Though the Millerites split later into several bodies, all of them kept a belief in the mortality of the entire man. Among Seventh-day Adventists R. F. Cottrell and James White defended this concept in the pages of the *Review and Herald,* starting from 1853. The final annihilation of the wicked was included in the "Declaration of the Fundamental Principles of Seventh-day Adventists" published by *Signs of the Times* in 1874.

C. Universality of Sin

At times Christians have lost view of the biblical doctrine of the universality of human sin. Pelagius (fifth century), in a well-meaning but misguided endeavor to preach self-control, taught that the sin of Adam merely set a bad example, but did not affect our ability to choose. In the eyes of God newborn children are in the same state as Adam before his fall into sin. For this reason, in every age some people have been able to withstand temptation and not sin; the majority, of course, are in need of God's grace for salvation (see Augustine, *On the Proceedings of Pelagius* 23 [NPNF-1 5:193]).

Augustine (354-430), contemporary of Pelagius, easily showed the unscriptural character of Pelagianism. The nonexistence of sinless humans is one of the truths stressed by Scripture (1 Kings 8:46; Ps. 143:2; Prov. 20:9; Eccl. 7:20; Rom. 3:10-23; 1 John 1:8-10). Sin is a power to be conquered only by the born-again person sustained by the grace of God, and not by naked willpower. At the same time, however, Augustine taught that, far from being born as Adam before the Fall, we all are born with his guilt (original sin) and with such a corrupt or depraved will that we are not able even to choose the way of salvation without the aid of God's grace. From the utter depravity of man he further concluded that saving grace must be irresistible, and therefore some people (those who become lost) have not been elected by God to be saved. This doctrine is known as double predestination, since non-election to salvation is tantamount to reprobation.

The church of his times accepted his criticism of Pelagius, but rejected double predestination. A synod in Orange (A.D. 529) accepted original sin, the need for grace, and the operation of the Holy Spirit in us to choose faith and salvation. On the other hand it reminded Christians that grace is not irresistible: those who oppose the truth resist the Holy Spirit. According to this synod, then, nobody is predestined to be lost. Such was the consensus of the church for centuries.

When the Reformation came, a renewed emphasis on salvation by grace through faith and not through works (which are a product of the human will) made some of the rejected views of Augustine attractive again. Different theologians, however, had varying convictions on the matter. Luther (1483-1546) stressed the bankruptcy of the human will, while his friend Melanchthon (1497-1560) allowed an important place in salvation to free will in cooperation with grace. Calvin (1509-1564) embraced double predestination, even though in Calvinistic Holland Arminius (1560-1609) championed a single and universal call to salvation. This view implies that grace is not irresistible, since many will not be saved. Grace may be rejected, and even if accepted one may later fall from it.

Those who partially rejected the views of Augustine came to be known as semi-Pelagianism. Catholic semi-Pelagianism rejected double predestination. Protestant semi-Pelagianism abandoned as well the idea of original sin. What we inherit from Adam is not guilt, but depravity. We are born with evil propensities or tendencies, the roots of sin, which in the course of life fructify in sinful thoughts, words, or actions.

D. Adventist Thought

In the development of their beliefs Seventh-day Adventists have been more concerned with the practical teachings of Scripture than in developing a systematic theology. Some subjects have received more attention than others. Thus, historically, Seventh-day Adventists may be classified as largely Arminian in understanding (QOD 402-406), although, just as in Protestantism at large, there are varying emphases (Heppenstall 107-128; Gulley).

VI. Ellen G. White Comments

A. Man's Place in Creation

"He who set the starry worlds on high and tinted with delicate skill the flowers of the field, who filled the earth and the heavens with the wonders of His power, when He came to crown His glorious work, to place one in the midst to stand as ruler of the fair earth, did not fail to create a being worthy of the hand that gave him life. The genealogy of our race, as given by inspiration, traces back its origin, not to a line of developing germs, mollusks, and quadrupeds, but to the great Creator. Though formed from the dust, Adam was 'the son of God.'

"He was placed, as God's representative, over the lower orders of being. They cannot understand or acknowledge the sovereignty of God, yet they were made capable of loving and serving man" (PP 45).

"The Lord created man out of the dust of the earth. He made Adam a partaker of His life, His nature. There was breathed into him the breath of the Almighty, and he became a living soul. Adam was perfect in form—strong, comely, pure, bearing the image of his Maker. . . .

"Adam was crowned king in Eden. To him was given dominion over every living thing that God had created. The Lord blessed Adam and Eve with intelligence such as He had not given to any other creature. He made Adam the rightful sovereign over all the works of His hands. Man, made in the divine image, could contemplate and appreciate the glorious works of God in nature" (1BC 1082).

B. Creation in the Image of God

"When Adam came from the Creator's hand, he bore, in his physical, mental, and spiritual nature, a likeness to his Maker. 'God created man in his own image' (Gen. 1:27), and it was His purpose that the longer man lived the more fully he should reveal this image—the more fully reflect the glory of the Creator. All his faculties were capable of development; their capacity and vigor were continually to increase. Vast was the scope offered for their exercise, glorious the field opened to their research. The mysteries of the visible universe—the 'wondrous works of him which is perfect in knowledge' (Job 37:16)—invited man's study. Face-to-face, heart-to-heart communion with his Maker was his high privilege. Had he remained loyal to God, all this would have been his forever. Throughout eternal ages he would have continued to gain new treasures of knowledge, to discover fresh springs of happiness, and to obtain clearer and yet clearer conceptions of the wisdom, the power, and the love of God. More and more fully would he have fulfilled the object of his creation, more and more fully have reflected the Creator's glory" (Ed 15).

"Every human being, created in the image of God, is endowed with a power akin to that of the Creator—individuality, power to think and to do. The men in whom this power is developed are the men who bear responsibilities, who are leaders in enterprise, and who influence character. It is the work of true education to develop this power, to train the youth to be thinkers, and not mere reflectors of other men's thought. Instead of confining their study to that which men have said or written, let students be directed to the sources of truth, to the vast fields opened for research in nature and revelation. Let them contemplate the great facts of duty and destiny, and the mind will expand and strengthen. Instead of educated weaklings, institutions of learning may send forth men strong to think and to act, men who are masters and not slaves of circumstances, men who possess breadth of mind, clearness of thought, and the courage of their convictions" (ibid. 17, 18).

"Created to be 'the image and glory of God' (1 Cor. 11:7), Adam and Eve had received endowments not unworthy of their high destiny. Graceful and symmetrical in form, regular and beautiful in feature, their countenances glowing with the tint of health and the light of joy and hope, they bore in outward resemblance the likeness of their Maker. Nor was this likeness manifest in the physical nature only. Every faculty of mind and soul reflected the Creator's glory. Endowed with high mental and spiritual gifts, Adam and Eve were made but 'little lower than the angels' (Heb. 2:7), that they might not only discern the wonders of the visible universe, but comprehend moral responsibilities and obligations" (ibid. 20).

"Man was to bear God's image, both in outward resemblance and in character. Christ alone is 'the express image' (Heb. 1:3) of the Father; but man was formed in the likeness of God. His nature was in harmony with the will of God. His mind was capable of comprehending divine things. His affections were pure; his appetites and passions were under the control of reason. He was holy and happy in bearing the image of God and in perfect obedience to His will" (PP 45).

"In the creation of man was manifest the

227

agency of a personal God. When God had made man in His image, the human form was perfect in all its arrangements, but it was without life. Then a personal, self-existing God breathed into that form the breath of life, and man became a living, breathing, intelligent being. All parts of the human organism were put in action. The heart, the arteries, the veins, the tongue, the hands, the feet, the senses, the perceptions of the mind—all began their work, and all were placed under law. Man became a living soul. Through Jesus Christ a personal God created man and endowed him with intelligence and power" (8T 264).

C. Creation of the Woman

"God Himself gave Adam a companion. He provided 'an help meet for him'—a helper corresponding to him—one who was fitted to be his companion, and who could be one with him in love and sympathy. Eve was created from a rib taken from the side of Adam, signifying that she was not to control him as the head, nor to be trampled under his feet as an inferior, but to stand by his side as an equal, to be loved and protected by him. A part of man, bone of his bone, and flesh of his flesh, she was his second self, showing the close union and the affectionate attachment that should exist in this relation. 'For no man ever yet hated his own flesh; but nourisheth and cherisheth it.' . . . 'Therefore shall a man leave his father and his mother, and shall cleave unto his wife; and they shall be one' " (PP 46).

D. The Meaning of Marriage

"God celebrated the first marriage. Thus the institution has for its originator the Creator of the universe. 'Marriage is honorable' . . . ; it was one of the first gifts of God to man, and it is one of the two institutions that, after the Fall, Adam brought with him beyond the gates of Paradise. When the divine principles are recognized and obeyed in this relation, marriage is a blessing; it guards the purity and happiness of the race, it provides for man's social needs, it elevates the physical, the intellectual, and the moral nature" (*ibid.* 46).

E. Free Will

"God placed man under law, as an indispensable condition of his very existence. He was a subject of the divine government, and there can be no government without law. God might have created man without the power to transgress His law; He might have withheld the hand of Adam from touching the forbidden fruit; but in that case man would have been, not a free moral agent, but a mere automaton. Without freedom of choice, his obedience would not have been voluntary, but forced. There could have been no development of character. Such a course would have been contrary to God's plan in dealing with the inhabitants of other worlds. It would have been unworthy of man as an intelligent being, and would have sustained Satan's charge of God's arbitrary rule" (*ibid.* 49).

F. Original Righteousness

"Adam and Eve, at their creation, had a knowledge of the law of God. It was printed on their hearts, and they understood its claims upon them" (1BC 1104).

G. The Fall

"Eve really believed the words of Satan, but her belief did not save her from the penalty of sin. She disbelieved the words of God, and this was what led to her fall. In the judgment men will not be condemned because they conscientiously believed a lie, but because they did not believe the truth, because they neglected the opportunity of learning what is truth" (PP 55).

"There was nothing poisonous in the fruit itself, and the sin was not merely in yielding to appetite. It was distrust of God's goodness, disbelief of His word, and rejection of His authority, that made our first parents transgressors, and that brought into the world a knowledge of evil. It was this that opened the door to every species of falsehood and error" (Ed 25).

"Adam yielded to temptation and as we have the matter of sin and its consequence laid so distinctly before us, we can read from cause to effect and see the greatness of the act is not that which constitutes sin; but the disobedience of God's expressed will, which is a virtual denial of God, refusing the laws of His government. . . .

"The fall of our first parents broke the golden chain of implicit obedience of the human will to the divine. Obedience has no longer been deemed an absolute necessity. The human agents follow their own imaginations which the Lord said of the inhabitants of the old world was evil and that continually" (1BC 1083, 1084).

H. Conditional Immortality

"In order to possess an endless existence, man must continue to partake of the tree of life. Deprived of this, his vitality would gradually diminish until life should become extinct. . . . None of the family of Adam were permitted to pass that barrier [angel guard to Eden, Gen. 3:24] to partake of the life-giving fruit; hence there is not an immortal sinner" (PP 60).

"Upon the fundamental error of natural immortality rests the doctrine of consciousness in death—a doctrine, like eternal torment, opposed to the teachings of Scriptures, to the dictates of reason, and to our feelings of humanity" (GC 545).

I. Sinful Tendencies

"Man was originally endowed with noble powers and a well-balanced mind. He was perfect in his being, and in harmony with God. His thoughts were pure, his aims holy. But through disobedience, his powers were perverted, and selfishness took the place of love. His nature became so weakened through transgression that it was impossible for him, in his own strength, to resist the power of evil. He was made captive by Satan, and would have remained so forever had not God specially interposed. It was the tempter's purpose to thwart the divine plan in man's creation, and

fill the earth with woe and desolation. And he would point to all this evil as the result of God's work in creating man. . . .

"It is impossible for us, of ourselves, to escape from the pit of sin in which we are sunken. Our hearts are evil, and we cannot change them. 'Who can bring a clean thing out of an unclean? not one.' 'The carnal mind is enmity against God: for it is not subject to the law of God, neither indeed can be.' Education, culture, the exercise of the will, human effort, all have their proper sphere, but here they are powerless. They may produce an outward correctness of behavior, but they cannot change the heart; they cannot purify the springs of life. There must be a power working from within, a new life from above, before men can be changed from sin to holiness. That power is Christ. His grace alone can quicken the lifeless faculties of the soul, and attract it to God, to holiness" (SC 17, 18).

J. Life Only in Christ

"The Bible clearly teaches that the dead do not go immediately to heaven. They are represented as sleeping until the resurrection. . . . In the very day when the silver cord is loosed and the golden bowl broken . . . , man's thoughts perish. They that go down to the grave are in silence. They know no more of anything that is done under the sun. . . . Blessed rest for the weary righteous! Time, be it long or short, is but a moment to them. They sleep; they are awakened by the trump of God to a glorious immortality. 'For the trumpet shall sound, and the dead shall be raised incorruptible. . . . So when this corruptible shall have put on incorruption, and this mortal shall have put on immortality, then shall be brought to pass the saying that is written, Death is swallowed up in victory.' . . . As they are called forth from their deep slumber they begin to think just where they ceased. The last sensation was the pang of death; the last thought, that they were falling beneath the power of the grave. When they arise from the tomb, their first glad thought will be echoed in the triumphal shout: 'O death, where is thy sting? O grave, where is thy victory?' " (GC 550).

K. Resurrection

"Our personal identity is preserved in the resurrection, though not the same particles of matter or material substance as went into the grave. The wondrous works of God are a mystery to man. The spirit, the character of man, is returned to God, there to be preserved. In the resurrection every man will have his own character. God in His own time will call forth the dead, giving again the breath of life, and bidding the dry bones live. The same form will come forth, but it will be free from disease and every defect. It lives again bearing the same individuality of features, so that friend will recognize friend. There is no law of God in nature which shows that God gives back the same identical particles of matter which composed the body before death. God shall give the righteous dead a body that will please Him" (6BC 1093).

L. New Earth

"A fear of making the future inheritance seem too material has led many to spiritualize away the very truths which lead us to look upon it as our home. Christ assured His disciples that He went to prepare mansions for them in the Father's house. Those who accept the teachings of God's word will not be wholly ignorant concerning the heavenly abode. And yet, 'eye hath not seen, nor ear heard, neither have entered into the heart of man, the things which God hath prepared for them that love him.' . . . Human language is inadequate to describe the reward of the righteous. It will be known only to those who behold it. No finite mind can comprehend the glory of the Paradise of God.

"In the Bible the inheritance of the saved is called 'a country.' There the heavenly Shepherd leads His flock to fountains of living waters. The tree of life yields its fruit every month, and the leaves of the tree are for the service of the nations. There are everflowing streams, clear as crystal, and beside them waving trees cast their shadows upon the paths prepared for the ransomed of the Lord. There the wide-spreading plains swell into hills of beauty, and the mountains of God rear their lofty summits. On those peaceful plains, beside those living streams, God's people, so long pilgrims and wanderers, shall find a home" (GC 674, 675).

VII. Literature

Andreason, R. S. *On Being Human.* Grand Rapids: Eerdmans, 1982.

Barth, K. *Church Dogmatics.* 4 vols. Edinburgh: T. & T. Clark, 1936-1962.

Brunner, E. *The Divine Imperative.* Philadelphia: Westminster, 1957.

Cullmann, O. *Immortality of the Soul or Resurrection of the Dead?* New York: Macmillan, 1958.

Dussel, E. *El Dualismo en la Antropologia de la Cristianidad.* Buenos Aires: Guadalupe, 1974.

Flick, M. and Z. Alszeghy, *Antropologia Teologica.* Salamanca, N.Y.: Sigueme, 1985.

Froom, L. E. *The Conditionalist Faith of Our Fathers,* 2 vols. Washington, D.C.: Review and Herald, 1965-1966.

Gulley, N. "In Every Way but One." *Adventist Review,* Jan. 25, 1990.

Heppenstall, Edward. *The Man Who Is God.* Washington, D.C.: Review and Herald, 1977.

Johnsen, C. *Man, the Indivisible.* Oslo: Universitetsforlazet, 1971.

McDonald, H. D. *The Christian View of Man.* Westchester, Ill.: Crossway Books, 1981.

Myers, D. C. *The Human Puzzle.* San Francisco: Harper and Row, 1978.

Niebuhr, R. *The Nature and Destiny of Man.* New York: Charles Scribner's Sons, 1943.

Olsen, V. Norskov. *Man, the Image of God.* Hagerstown, Md.: Review and Herald, 1988.

Rice, R. *The Reign of God.* Berrien Springs, Mich.: Andrews University Press, 1985.

Seventh-day Adventists Answer Questions on Doctrine. Washington, D.C.: Review and Herald, 1957.

Shea, W. H. "The Unity of the Creation Account." *Origins* 5 (1978): 9-38.
———. "Literary Structural Parallels Between Genesis 1 and 2." *Origins* 16 (1989): 49-68.
Smedes, L. B. *Sex for Christians*. Grand Rapids: Eerdmans, 1975.

Vaucher, A. F. *L'histoire du salut*. Dammarie-les-Lys, France: Vie et Santé, 1951.
Wolff, H. W. *Anthropologie des alten Testaments*. Munich: Kaiser Verlag, 1973.
Zurcher, J. *The Nature and Destiny of Man*. New York: Philosophical Library, 1969.

Appendix A
Status of Women in the Bible

Where patriarchy held sway, as in the ancient Near East, women were relegated to a very unfavorable position. But even there, at least among the Hebrews, women and girls appeared publicly in everyday life and on sacred occasions (Gen. 24:13; Ex. 2:16; Deut. 12:12; Judges 21:21), could inherit in the absence of brothers (Num. 27:8), and were consulted before marriage (Gen. 24:39, 58). Proverbs 31:10-31 shows the wide variety of fields open to a woman. Positive examples such as Sarah, Rebekah, and Abigail, as well as Jezebel and Athaliah on the negative side, reveal the strength of women's influence, which in certain cases (Deborah, Judges 4; 5) was far-reaching and decisive for their nation.

Paul points out that the husband is head of the wife (1 Cor. 11:3) and that Adam was created before Eve (verses 7-9; 1 Tim. 2:13). Because of this situation, the apostle suggests that women use certain headdress styles (1 Cor. 11:5-7) and behave in certain ways in the congregation (1 Cor. 14:34-36; 1 Tim. 2:11, 12). On the other hand, the apostle offsets the derivation of the female from the male by affirming the interdependence of the two sexes (1 Cor. 11:11, 12). Paul also accepts the participation of properly attired women in public prayer and prophecy (verse 5). As seen elsewhere in the NT, women were highly influential in Christian congregations (Acts 9:36; 13:50; 17:4; Rom. 16:6, 12), served as instructors (Acts 18:26; Rom. 16:3), "deaconess" (Rom. 16:1), and coworkers in Paul's apostolic labors (Rom. 16:7; Phil. 4:3).

Christ Himself was more open than His peers in His dealings with women, struggling to win their souls (John 4:27), instructing them in spiritual matters (Luke 10:39), healing them on the Sabbath (Luke 13:10-13), boldly defending them (Mark 12:40; 14:6), ignoring their "uncleanness" (Luke 8:43-48), surrounding Himself with them (verse 2; Matt. 27:55, 56), and generally enhancing the potential and value of women, as His apostles did also (Gal. 3:28).

Appendix B
Husband/Wife Relationships

A related issue is hierarchy within marriage itself. After sin, God cursed the serpent (Gen. 3:14) and the ground (verse 17), foretelling the consequences upon the man and the woman (verses 16-19). She would suffer in childbirth; "in pain you shall bring forth children, yet your desire shall be for your husband, and he shall rule over you" (verse 16). Indeed, since the man would have to toil a hard and ungrateful soil, the brunt of rearing a family would be borne by the woman. In spite of these difficulties, which could easily discourage the woman from intimacy with her husband, she would experience a desire for him, which would thus help to sustain their union. In the changed relationships of the world affected by sin, she would lose part of her former autonomy and become subject to her husband. His rule, however, should not be tyrannical. The term for "rule," *māšal*, may imply a beneficent, compassionate government, like that of God (2 Sam. 23:3), and even connote protection and love, as in Isaiah 40:10, 11. These aspects of the husband's role are emphasized by Paul in

1 Corinthians 11:3 and Ephesians 5:23.

Paul also instructed wives to respect the authority of their husbands, particularly in the church setting (1 Cor. 11:2-16; 14:34-38; 1 Tim. 2:11-14). The precise scope of those instructions is difficult to assess, since we lack precise information on the situation that prompted them. Perhaps the wives of some catechumens had become stumblingblocks by assuming airs of spiritual superiority over their husbands. If so, Paul wanted the instruction of the new convert, the "new man in Christ," to follow the same pattern as the creation of the first man—the head of the family should be "formed" first (1 Tim. 2:12, 13). Some wives may have been interfering when the church assembly *(ekklēsia)* transacted its business. Paul would then stress the need to respect legitimate authorities.

In any case, within the context of a sinful world, the submission of wives is actually a blessing for the home, just as hard work and toil are a blessing in disguise for man. We should humbly accept God's judgments. Christians look forward to a time when the curses pronounced in Eden will disappear (Rev. 22:3). Paul's advice, "Wives, be subject to your husbands" (Eph. 5:22), should not, then, be absolutized any more than his injunction "Slaves, be obedient to those who are your earthly masters" (Eph. 6:5). Both admonitions have permanent value, but should be implemented in accordance with the institutions, conditions, and mores of the particular societies in which we live, unless these are condemned by Scripture.

Sin

John M. Fowler

Introduction

Nowhere in the annals of literature is the problem of sin so seriously dealt with as in the Bible. Its opening pages portray graphically the entrance of sin into human history, and its closing pages victoriously proclaim the eradication of sin from the universe. Between is depicted the continual human struggle with sin and God's promise and provision for redemption from sin. God's relationship with humanity, focused on the eradication of sin and the reconciliation of forgiven humanity with Himself, is one of the great themes of the Scriptures. Paul expresses this theme as well as any: "For our sake he [God] made him [Christ] to be sin who knew no sin, so that in him we might become the righteousness of God" (2 Cor. 5:21).

Contemporary culture dismisses sin as a preoccupation of the gullible few who take the Bible seriously. Sin may be seen as a behavioral problem with no relevance to either God or any divine norm for human life, or it may be acknowledged as moral imperfection but attributed to human developmental deficiency or a sudden outburst of emotional imbalance or biological drive. However, the Bible portrays sin for what it is: that which has come in between the Creator and the human and brought about a gulf between God and the human race. The gulf is so vast and unbridgeable by human means that God had to send His Son Jesus (John 3:16) "to be sin" for us so that "in Christ God was reconciling the world to himself, not counting their trespasses against them" (2 Cor. 5:21, 19).

How is sin defined? What makes it so serious in divine-human relations? What is its origin? Where lies its power? These and other related questions form the scope of this article, approaching the problem of sin from the perspective of the Bible and Christian history.

I. Humanity Before Sin
  A. The Image of God
  B. Divine Plan for Humanity
  C. Sin and the Image of God
II. Biblical Terminology
  A. In the OT
    1. *Haṭṭā'ṭ*
    2. *'Awôn*
    3. *Peša'*
    4. *Reša'*
    5. Summary
  B. In the NT
    1. *Hamartia*
    2. *Parakoē*
    3. *Parabasis*
    4. *Paraptōma*

    5. *Anomia*
    6. *Adikia*
    7. Summary
III. The Origin of Sin
  A. Prehuman and Angelic
  B. The Fall of Humanity
    1. A Historical Act
    2. A Responsible Act
    3. A Spiritual and Moral Act
    4. The Temptation and Fall
IV. The Nature and Essence of Sin
  A. Sin as Rebellion Against God
  B. Sin as Broken Relationship
  C. Sin as a State
  D. Sin as a Specific Kind of Evil
  E. Sin as Falling Short
  F. Sin as Transgression

I. Humanity Before Sin

The biblical account of humanity prior to sin presents man and woman in a state of goodness. Each day of Creation ended with the divine pronouncement that it was "good" (Gen. 1:4, 10, 12, 18, 25). But on the sixth day, having created Adam and Eve, God proclaimed that "it was very good" (verse 31). The reason for such a pronouncement is to be found not only in the fact that the creation of Adam and Eve climaxed the creative activity of God so far as to what would occupy this earth, but also in the fact that the creation of humanity involved elements of divine exclusiveness. A solemn divine council preceded human creation. The members of the Godhead united together and decided, "Let us make man in our image, after our likeness" (verse 26). A divine decree bestowed upon Adam and Eve "dominion" over the created order on the earth. With these twin blessings—the image of God and dominion—unavailable to other creatures on earth, God crowned Adam and Eve "with glory and honor" (Ps. 8:5-8).

Even as they exercised "dominion" over all that was on land, in air, and under the sea (verses 6-8), Adam and Eve were to live in moral and spiritual relationship with the Creator. God made them upright (Eccl. 7:29), with the highest possible potential in intellect, in moral and spiritual goodness, and in perfect and harmonious relationship with the Creator and within the race. They were created free moral agents with no bias or propensity toward evil. But they were not mere automatons. Their relationship and obedience to their Creator were to be the result of free choice, arising out of unconditional love and supreme regard for the Creator's will for them, revealed in moral principles and norms of conduct. The bestowal of free choice did not necessitate a yielding to sin, but rather made Adam and Eve creatures of responsibility and accountability.

A. The Image of God

The uniqueness of Adam and Eve above all other creatures is defined in the Creator's pronouncement "Let us make man in our image, after our likeness" (Gen. 1:26). Some theologians have made a distinction between "image" and "likeness": the former indicating natural graces with a rational mind and free will, retained after the Fall; the latter constituting original righteousness with life of the Spirit, lost after the Fall, but regained by grace.

However, the "image of God" motif, so central to the biblical account of Creation, is the most powerful expression of the dignity and the uniqueness of the human being. It endows the human person with unique dignity and worth. Humans are matter, yet above matter; they are creatures, yet above other creatures; they bear the image of God, yet they are not God.

What constitutes the image of God has been a subject of theological debate throughout history, and numerous identifications have been made: physical likeness, rationality, individuality, free will, understanding, freedom of choice, dominion, relationship of person to person, unity in diversity ("male and female" [verse 27]), etc.

In spite of varied positions, we are not left without clue as to what constitutes "the image of God." The NT presents the good news of salvation in Christ Jesus, by which forgiveness of sin and reconciliation of the sinner with God are made possible (2 Cor. 5:19). This process of salvation and reconciliation removes the "old self" and creates a "new self"—indeed a new creation, a theme prominent in the NT, particularly the writings of Paul. Paul speaks of this new person as one renewed in knowledge, holiness, and righteousness (Col. 3:10; Eph. 4:21-24). If these characteristics constitute the image of the redeemed, restored human being, by implication we may affirm that the original image of God must have constituted knowledge, holiness, and righteousness, which in their ultimate and purest sense in part define the nature of God.

Hence God's image is to be understood in those characteristics of being and relationships with which God chose to share part of Himself. To be holy, to be morally upright, to love righteousness, to live and relate on the basis of love, to be just and fair, to choose harmony with all that is good and beautiful, to be creative and obey the Creator's laws, to comprehend that which is divine and to shun that which is in disharmony with God's will, to be individually unique, yet collectively harmonious—these and other characteristics that come to mind when one thinks of God are included in the image of God.

Ultimately, the image of God is the opposite of the image of sin. Thus the triune God's declaration "Let us make . . . in our image" reveals that man as a sinner had no origin in the divine mind but is the result of human choice. The image of God defines the human being as God's child—a status of warmth, intimacy, and growth in Him that no other creature can have. Central to the concept of the image of God is a God-human relationship—loving, responsive, permanent, and fulfilling. This relationship makes sin's impact serious, for the entry of sin in Eden not only ruptured the God-human relationship but made the human a rebel by choice against the Creator. This rebellion led to a status of lostness. But the lostness need not be forever, for the God who created the human made provision even before the foundations of the earth were laid (Eph. 3:9-11) to redeem humanity from just such a contingency and restore fully His image through the death of His own Son. (See Creation I. A. 12; Man I. B.)

B. Divine Plan for Humanity

Being created in His image, God planned for Adam and Eve and their progeny a twofold destiny. Foremost, acknowledging God as sovereign of the universe, they would render to Him alone their total allegiance and worship. The eternal command of God has been always, "Fear God and give him glory, . . . and worship him who made heaven and earth" (Rev. 14:7). Exclusive worship of and total allegiance to God permeate the Bible, and these God zealously guards for Himself. Worship is simply giving God His worth: unreserved praise, unconditional obedience, and absolute gratitude. In this He admits no competition: "You shall have no other gods before me" (Ex. 20:3). The first commandment is not limited to gods external to human self, but includes self. To acknowledge God as the supreme sovereign and the only object of worship and service demands at once that self be stripped of pride, pretension, and deviation. A deliberate and radical rejection of self's desire to be its own god is the basis of the only proper and adequate relationship of humanity with God. It was Eden's model and Jesus' prescription of true worship: "You shall love the Lord your God with all your heart, and with all your soul, and with all your mind. This is the great and first commandment" (Matt. 22:37, 38). To place God first in all that we think and do, to see everything from His perspective and to do nothing without reference to Him, to absorb His priorities as our own and to devote all we are to fulfill those priorities, to put aside everything that comes between self and God and to choose His will and way at any cost is the great and first biblical commandment. Anything that deviates from that is contrary to God's design for humanity.

Second, the human family was to have dominion over the created order. In placing them on this earth as guardians, God created a stewardship of the highest order. Extending over the nonhuman order of Creation, this appointment marked a special relationship within the entire human family to descend from Adam and Eve. God's command "Be fruitful and multiply" (Gen. 1:28) was an invitation to humans to participate creatively in the establishment and the continuation of their race. Such an act recognizes a fellowship of responsibility among humans, fostering a human unity, bearing a certain similarity to divine unity among the three persons of the Godhead, in whose image humanity was formed.

Hence "the image of God" denotes not only a creative affinity with the Creator but also a responsibility for worship and fellowship that flow from such affinity. Further, it extends the fellowship to embrace all mankind.

C. Sin and the Image of God

But both history and experience testify that the ideal intended in the image of God lies shattered. While humans exercising part of the image of God (for example, reason and intellect) creatively soar to reach for the skies or probe deeply the mystery of life, they resist living under the provisions of the image of God with respect to the worship of the Creator and the demands of human fellowship, equality, and dignity. The human being who splits the atom to light an entire city also uses the same atom to destroy it. One spends a whole life extending the frontiers of knowledge or establishing a cure for an unknown killer, while another pauses not a moment to understand the seriousness of killing millions just to please some ignoble fantasy of building a lasting empire.

Whatever happened to the image of God? Surely humanity has not lost it completely. While we cannot deny that sin has caused enormous degeneracy in every area of human life, individually and collectively, we cannot conclude that sin has destroyed completely the image of God. Marred yes, but destroyed no. Further, if the image were totally destroyed, human reasoning and creativity would be difficult to fathom, and instances of love and sacrifice for the sake of the other so often witnessed in history would be enigmatic. Jesus' parable of the lost coin (Luke 15:8-10) provides a key relative to the status of the image of God after sin. Although the coin was lost and covered with dust, still it retained the inscription of the reigning power. Just as the coin bore that inscription even in its lost status, so with humanity. Human beings are lost because of sin; they lead a life of alienation from the Creator; they are marred and bruised by the power and influence of sin; but still the image of God in them is not totally destroyed. The image is latent in every human soul.

But latency of the image of God in no way minimizes the enormity of the legacy of sin both individually and collectively. Witness history and experience. A massive disorder, a persistent chaos, a continuing social disturbance, and a pathology of collective hatred seem to characterize human history. Within the soul, there rages war between the ideal and the real, and between competing drives, ambitions, and passions. Created a "little lower than the angels" (Ps. 8:5, KJV), the human often sinks to the level of a brute.

To what shall we attribute this universal plight? To heredity and environment, as naturalists would argue? To social and economic exploitation, as Marxists would suggest? To an inevitable process of determinism, as evolutionists would urge? Or shall we turn to the Word of God: "All have sinned and fall short of the glory of God" (Rom. 3:23)? The Bible looks at men and women in a realistic way and unhesitatingly diagnoses the human predicament as a condition of fallenness because of sin. Humanity was created to live on the high ground of fellowship with God and harmonious relationship with each other. But sin intruded, interrupted the human-divine fellowship, and poisoned the relationship between members of the human community.

The modern mind may find little or no meaning for the word "sin," but its presence is undeniable. The Bible interprets the human predicament from the perspective of God, and calls upon human beings to trace their individual and collective malady to sin: "Ah, sinful nation, a people laden with iniquity, offspring of evildoers, sons who deal corruptly! They have forsaken the Lord, they have despised the Holy One of Israel, they are utterly estranged" (Isa. 1:4).

II. Biblical Terminology

The Bible uses a rich range of terms to denote the concept of sin. While each word may convey a particular shade of meaning, a study of the most common words in both the OT and the NT underscores the theme that sin relates to a status of rebellion of humans against God, leading to their disobedience to God's will. A brief review of some of the key words used in the Bible to describe sin will assist in establishing a biblical definition.

A. In the OT

The OT uses a variety of words for "sin," but four stand out for their richness and frequency.

1. Ḥaṭṭā't

In noun form ḥaṭṭā't appears about 293 times in the OT. The basic meaning is "missing the mark," "missing a target," as in shooting an arrow (Judges 20:16; cf. Job 5:24). The theological use of the word underscores an act, a way, a lifestyle that deviates from what God has marked out. Hence sin is what misses God's standard (Lev. 5:5, 16; Ps. 51:4).

Thus ḥaṭṭā't denotes sin as an act or attitude that causes a person to miss the marks essential and expected to maintain the right relationship between the human being and God. Sin is a break in one's relationship with God.

2. 'Āwôn

'Āwôn is a deeply religious term. It occurs some 229 times, almost always rendered as "iniquity" before God, including the idea of punishment (Gen. 4:13; 15:16). The word carries the root idea of crookedness (Lam. 3:9). It also refers to falsehood, deception (Ps. 36:3), and vanity (Prov. 22:8, KJV; Isa. 41:29, KJV). Sin is that which twists away from God's straightforwardness and involves perverse behavior (Gen. 15:16; Isa. 43:24). Thus 'āwôn in its theological meaning goes further than ḥaṭṭā't in that it carries the additional notion of wrongful intention.

3. *Peša'*

Peša' occurs some 135 times in the OT. It signifies deliberate, premeditated, willful violation of a norm or standard. It also denotes a refusal to submit to rightful authority. It differs from *ḥaṭṭā't* in that the act is not inadvertent, but a deliberate revolt, rebellion, or transgression. The word is used to refer to a breach of contract, a willful break of an arrangement (1 Kings 12:19; 2 Kings 1:1; 8:20, 22). The element of "willfulness" and "revolt," carried into theological vocabulary, makes this word a much more serious form of sin than others (Isa. 1:2; Jer. 3:13; Hosea 7:13; 8:1), so serious that only unselfish and outgoing "love" can cover the rebellion that is *peša'*. Job 34:37 uses *ḥaṭṭā't* and *peša'* together: "For he adds rebellion *[peša']* to his sin *[ḥaṭṭā't]*."

4. *Reša'*

Reša' means "turbulence" and "restlessness" and appears 30 times in the OT. It is used to describe the status of the wicked who are "like the tossing sea; for it cannot rest" (Isa. 57:20). The term literally means "out of joint," "to be loose." Thus the term can refer to the unsteady status of the wicked who are tossed back and forth and live in confusion. In some references (Ex. 23:1 and Prov. 25:5), *reša'* is used to denote the sense of being wicked, and hence guilty of a crime. The term also refers to being guilty of hostility to God and His people (Ex. 9:27).

5. Summary

The OT vocabulary for sin is primarily theological in nature. Although these words vary in shades of meaning, there is a fundamental unity in their projection of sin: that sin is a failure, a deviation, a crookedness, a rebellion with respect to divinely prescribed norms and expectations. Sin is "missing the mark" and coming short of God's expectations. It is an act committed against the will of God, an iniquity against Him. It is a life of open, deliberate

rebellion against God's will and way. It involves a life out of joint, broken loose from its intended divine anchor, and as a result tossing up and down in a sea of wickedness. Further, sin is first and foremost a motivation, an action, a status of revolt against God. "Against thee, thee only, have I sinned, and done that which is evil in thy sight," writes David (Ps. 51:4), giving us a classic definition that sin is primarily an act of going against the will of God. Even though David's act was against Bathsheba and her husband, he, under the prompting of the Holy Spirit, confessed that what he did was not a behavioral shortcoming but a transgression of God's will and law. Sin is precisely that: a rejection of God, and from that flows an equally unacceptable relationship with fellow beings.

B. In the NT

The predominant theme of the NT is Jesus—His life and work as the redeemer from sin. As such the NT deals graphically with the seriousness of sin in terms of its ultimate cost—the life of the Son of God in the death of whom God's grace and forgiveness are made available to the human race. Whatever the NT says to underscore the deadliness of sin and its enormous cost to God, it is said in the light of the greatness and glory of the cross that once for all dealt the deathblow to the power of sin.

Of the many Greek words the NT uses to depict the enormity of sin, five are significant.

1. *Hamartia*

In the NT *hamartia* is the most frequently used word for sin, translated as such nearly 175 times. It literally means "missing a mark," such as in target practice. In classical Greek, the word is almost always used to indicate a negative failure rather than a positive transgression. In the NT, however, the word is used to describe something of a serious magnitude that places the sinner at a distance from, and in opposition, to God. *Hamartia* connotes an individual's deliberate failure to attain God's standard (Matt. 1:21; Rom. 5:12, 13; 1 John 1:9). Further, *hamartia* denotes human decision to be hostile to God (John 9:41; 19:11; 1 John 1:8). *Hamartia* is universal (Rom. 3:23), and its power has kept humanity under its grasp (verse 9). The power of sin is so heinous and its grasp so vicious that Paul almost personalizes *hamartia* and says that it rules (Rom. 5:21) and lords over us (Rom. 6:14), and that we have become its slaves (verses 6, 17, 20).

2. *Parakoē*

Parakoē literally means "a failure to hear," or an "unwillingness to hear." Often one hears only what one wants to hear, and in an ultimate sense sin means closing one's ears to God so as not to listen to Him but to oneself. The word appears three times and is generally translated in the NT as "disobedience" (Rom. 5:19; 2 Cor. 10:6; Heb. 2:2).

3. *Parabasis*

The NT uses *parabasis* seven times. In its verb form, the word means "to go across," "to pass beyond," and hence to go into a forbidden territory. The noun form describes a deliberate breach of the law, a violation of a commandment, a going into a forbidden zone. Hence it is translated "transgression" (Rom. 4:15; Gal. 3:19) or "violation" (Heb. 2:2, NIV).

4. *Paraptōma*

Paraptōma, used 23 times, indicates a "falling while one ought to be standing." It signifies a slip, a fault, and is commonly translated "trespass" (Matt. 6:14,15; Rom. 4:25; 5:15), and "transgression" (11:11, 12, NIV). Of all the words for sin, this one denotes the least deliberate act.

5. *Anomia*

Anomia appears 14 times in the NT. It suggests contempt or violation of *nomos,* the law. Most of the time the KJV translates it as "iniq-

uity" (Matt. 7:23; 13:41; 23:28; 24:12; Rom. 4:7; Heb. 1:9). The word describes the condition of a person who lives and acts contrary to the law. The well-known formula of 1 John 3:4 defines sin as "the transgression of the law" (KJV) and "lawlessness" (RSV).

6. *Adikia*

Adikia carries the ethical nuance of "unrighteousness" or the absence of righteousness, and is translated "wickedness" (Rom. 1:18, 19) and "wrongdoing" (2 Peter 2:15; 1 John 5:17). The NT also uses it in the sense of injustice or crime toward a fellow being. First John 3:4 and 5:17 equate *hamartia* with *adikia*.

7. Summary

While a review of the biblical terminology for sin is helpful in understanding the complexity of the concept of sin, these terms alone or collectively do not lead us to a precise scriptural definition of sin. The most fundamental feature of sin as portrayed in the scriptural theme of God dealing with the problem of sin is that it is a rebellion directed against the lordship and sovereignty of God and a refusal to accept His authority in one's life, conduct, and destiny. A denial of God is at the root of sin, and it may take different forms and activities involving ethical, moral, and spiritual relationships and dimensions.

Thus the biblical terminology shows that sin is not a calamity fallen upon the human unawares, but the result of an active attitude and choice on the part of the human. Further, sin is not the absence of good, but it is "falling short" of God's expectations. It is an evil course that the human has deliberately chosen. It is not a weakness for which humans cannot be held responsible, for the human in the attitude or act of sin deliberately chooses a way of rebellion against God, in transgression against His law, and fails to hear God's Word. Sin attempts to pass beyond the limitations God has set. In short, sin is rebellion against God.

III. The Origin of Sin

The origin of sin is an enigma that cannot be fully unraveled. However, one certainty remains beyond question. God is not the author of sin. Neither God's omnipotence nor His responsibility for creating the universe can be employed to justify the notion that God must somehow be responsible for sin. James cautions: "Let no one say when he is tempted, 'I am tempted by God'; for God cannot be tempted with evil and he himself tempts no one; but each person is tempted when he is lured and enticed by his own desire" (James 1:13, 14). The text is clear. On the one hand, the text sets forth in no uncertain terms that God "cannot be tempted" and that He "tempts no one." That is to say, no human being who knows the biblical portrayal of the character of God and the relationship He longs to maintain with humanity can ever say, "I am tempted by God, and therefore God is responsible for my sin." On the other hand, the text identifies the locus of where temptation and sin spring forth: "Each person is tempted when he is lured and enticed by his own desire." Therefore, the admonition "Let no one say . . ." is a warning against ever considering God as the source of sin. To think so is to ignore the biblical data. The Bible firmly insists that God is in no way responsible for sin. God is "holy, holy, holy" (Isa. 6:3). How can He who is so thoroughly holy be responsible for anything unholy? God is so distant from sin and His character so averse to iniquity that Habakkuk implores God's people not to look at Him as the source of evil, even though the presence of evil is so real and so cruel: "Art thou not from everlasting, O Lord my God, my Holy One? . . . Thou who art of purer eyes than to behold evil and canst not look on wrong" (Hab. 1:12, 13).

This message of God's absolute holiness, goodness, and truth permeates the Scriptures. He is "a God of faithfulness and without iniquity, just and right is he" (Deut. 32:4). He loves truth and He "is not a man, that he should lie, or a son of man, that he should repent" (Num. 23:19). He abhors evil (Ps. 5:6; Prov. 6:16), and is grieved that sin has separated humanity from Him (Isa. 59:2). There is an absoluteness about His character: He is "the Rock, his work is perfect; for all his ways are justice" (Deut. 32:4). How can such a God be the source of sin?

Further, the NT picturesquely describes the distance between God and sin: "God is light and in him is no darkness at all" (1 John 1:5). To bridge the gulf separating the human from God and to provide rescue from the realm of darkness, God made the utmost sacrifice of love in sending His "only Son" that we might not perish in sin (John 3:16). Stand at the cross and ask the question Can God be responsible for sin? What we see on the cross is God's eternal answer to the problem of sin. For sin at its core stands in opposition to God. God seeks and saves the lost; sin tempts and leads humans into destruction. God is love and hates sin; sin begets hatred, jealousy, and destruction. To ascribe the origin of sin to God is, therefore, not only unbiblical but, according to Scripture, blasphemous. Hence it is necessary to reject philosophic and deterministic notions that argue for the inevitability of sin, with God somehow being its author.

But the question remains: How did sin originate? Even though the Bible does not deal directly and exhaustively with the origin of sin in the universe, there is sufficient evidence to conclude that the origin of sin is prehuman and that sin entered into our world through the transgression of Adam and Eve.

A. Prehuman and Angelic

Even though the biblical data concerning the origin of evil in prehuman history is limited, sufficient is known to locate sin's origin in Satan. According to John, "the devil has sinned from the beginning" (1 John 3:8). The Bible teaches that long before the creation of the human race, God created a host of angels whose abode is the courts of heaven and whose duty is to do God's biddings. They worship God continually and act as His messengers by doing and revealing His will in both heaven and earth. In everything they do, they seek to praise and worship the Creator (Rev. 5:11, 12).

Angels, like human beings, were created good, but a fall occurred among them. The leader of these fallen angels was Satan, whom Jesus described as "a murderer from the beginning" and "the father of lies" (John 8:44). When Jesus accused the Pharisees of being "of your father the devil" (verse 44), He was tracing the ultimate source of sin to Satan. Jesus further said, "I saw Satan fall like lightning from heaven" (Luke 10:18), and the Apocalypse portrays a war in heaven in which Satan, "deceiver of the whole world," was cast out of heaven and fell to the earth (Rev. 12:7-9). The war between Christ and Satan, between good and evil, ending in the apocalyptic triumph of Christ over Satan, is a theme that runs throughout the Scriptures. As to when this war began and when Satan and his angels were cast out of heaven, the Bible is silent, but sufficient intimation is given that this occurred before the creation of Adam and Eve. (See Great Controversy I. B; II. A-C.)

No doctrine of sin can be complete without an understanding of this great controversy theme between Christ and Satan, between good and evil. The sovereignty and character of God are at its center. When Lucifer caused the revolt in heaven against God (verses 7-9), and when the revolt reached its climax, God had no alternative except to cast the fallen angelic host from heaven. What was the sin that caused the fall of angels? Paul's warning that no recent convert should be appointed a bishop lest he be "puffed up with conceit and fall into the condemnation of the devil" (1 Tim. 3:6) suggests that pride and self-conceit was the sin. Jude 6 suggests that the fallen angels "did not keep their own position but left their proper dwelling." From these two texts we infer that the sin of the fallen angels was dissatisfaction with their status and a desire to be like God. The angelic sin, therefore, is a desire to cross the boundaries of creaturehood and become like the Creator. By its very essence the Creator-creature relationship has an inbuilt demarcation. While the Creator extends life, love, and fellowship to the creature, the creature in turn is to respond in love, obedience, and praise to the One who made the creature's life possible. A crossing of this line, a rupture in this Creator-creature relationship, a desire to become like God, is the creature's rebellion against the Creator. Here lies the problem whereby the angels "did not keep their own position," and they were thrown out of their dwelling. If a desire to become gods had led the angels to fall, then it is not difficult to understand why the devil held out that possibility to Eve in tempting her to eat the forbidden fruit.

Defiance of God's prerogative to set limitations upon His creatures, combined with self-pride wanting to set itself as God (see Isa. 14:12-14), was the sin that caused war in heaven between Christ and Lucifer, foremost of the angels. In this war Satan was ready to take rebellion to its ultimate end, leading God to cast the rebels out of heaven.

B. The Fall of Humanity

With respect to the human race sin originated in the Garden of Eden with an act of rebellion on the part of Adam and Eve. Genesis 3 outlines the introduction of sin into this world. The first sin of our foreparents points to four significant factors that singly or in combination affect the course of sin in human life.

1. A Historical Act

Throughout history some theologians have defined the Fall narrative of Genesis 3 as allegory, dismissing it as myth without historical basis. Some refer to it as a suprahistorical event, incomprehensible for those of us who live in history. But for a correct understanding of the essence, nature, and destiny of sin, its historicity cannot be dismissed or undermined. Its beginning, its impact on the drama of human history, its defeat on the cross, and its final eradication at the final judgment are portrayed in Scriptures as historic mileposts, reaching from rebellion to restoration. To deny historicity to any of these events is to deny the authority and the authenticity of the Scriptures as the Word of the living God and to deny the sovereign Lord of history Himself.

The NT endorsement of Genesis 3 as a historical narrative means we cannot dismiss it as a myth or disregard it as irrelevant to our understanding of the nature of sin. The NT affirms the historic veracity of Adam in five passages (Rom. 5:14; 1 Cor. 15:22, 45; 1 Tim. 2:13, 14), and of the serpent twice (2 Cor. 11:3; Rev. 12:9). Paul wrote: "For as in Adam all die, so also in Christ shall all be made alive" (1 Cor. 15:22). This passage assures the believers that all who are committed to Christ shall experience resurrection from the dead at the time of His second coming. Paul's readers are to have no doubt regarding the resurrection. He argues that the resurrection is as real as Jesus Christ, who lived, died, and rose again—all historical events of a few years before the Epistle was written. Further, the apostle offers a twofold argument: Adam brought death, but Jesus brings life. In so arguing, Paul recognizes the historic reality of Adam, Jesus, the Second Coming, death, and the resurrection. To Paul and the NT church, the sin of Adam and Eve and resultant death were not allegories, but historical facts. Sin is real, not an illusion.

Again Paul argues for the historicity of the Genesis narrative in 2 Corinthians 11:3: "But I am afraid that as the serpent deceived Eve by his cunning, your thoughts will be led astray from a sincere and pure devotion to Christ." He does not see the serpent as a myth, but as a historic instrument through which Satan deceived Eve. Paul makes no historic difference among Christ, Eve, and the serpent. Likewise, in Romans 5:12-19, Paul contends that the entry of sin into this world is a historic act, introduced by the disobedience of real people; likewise, salvation from sin was accomplished in history by the person of Jesus.

To Paul, nothing in Genesis or in the NT is a myth—sin, serpent, righteousness, Adam, Eve, Christ, Satan, salvation, and resurrection are all real. Add to this the dramatic picture of the Apocalypse equating the serpent with the "Devil and Satan, the deceiver of the whole world" (Rev. 12:9). We have no basis to deny the historicity of the events that plunged the human race into sin. Nor can we categorize those events as myths or as of prehistorical irrelevance.

2. A Responsible Act

The eating of the forbidden fruit by Adam and Eve was an act indulged in by volition and responsibly executed. Adam and Eve had been told clearly that they were not to eat of the tree of the knowledge of good and evil, "for in the day you eat of it you shall die" (Gen. 2:17). The choice was unambiguously laid out: allegiance to their Creator or to someone else. Essentially, the test lay not in eating the particular fruit but in choosing to obey or disobey God. The trial of Adam and Eve was necessary to test their love and loyalty to God and to allow for growth and maturity of character. Had they successfully resisted the temptation, eternal life and happiness would have been the result. But when our first parents chose the fruit, they were clearly, responsibly, exercising their free choice, itself a gift from God. No one, not even Satan, coerced their choice. Of their own free will they chose to disobey God and ally themselves with Satan. As such their act was one for which they were responsible. God could not be held accountable for their act of disobedience and for their choice to reject Him. Theirs was an act of willful, deliberate rebellion. In that lay their sin.

3. A Spiritual and Moral Act

The eating of the fruit by our first parents was more than an innocent experiment in curiosity. It was a failure of a spiritual and moral test. God's creative purpose in bringing Adam and Eve into existence is that God's glory may be manifest (Isa. 43:7) and that a divine-human relationship could be a real possibility. This glory cannot be established and this relationship cannot exist and mature without a sound, tested moral and spiritual relationship. By "moral and spiritual" we mean two or more persons relating to each other on the highest possible level of fellowship in which all parties exercise unselfishness for the sake of the other. We may call this a covenant of fellowship. God has already shown how unselfish He is in creating Adam and Eve in His own image and entrusting them with dominion over the created order. Unfortunately, Adam and Eve failed the test: They chose not to live in the unselfish order of the divine requirement, and at the first opportunity translated their inner motive of rebellion into an outward act of disobedience by eating the forbidden fruit. They yielded to self's greatest temptation—to be like God, to be their own masters in moral and spiritual realms. Eve broke the relationship with God even before she touched the fruit. Her sin lay in the willful choice she made: placing her will and wish above and prior to the will and wish of her Maker. In her sin we see sin's essence: making one's will rather than God's will the ultimate law of life. Hence sin is not to be considered simply a moral shortcoming, a spiritual failure, a momentary betrayal, a privation, or an act of disobedience. Sin is all these, but at its core it directs human beings to choose as their god someone or something other than the Creator. Sin is a spiritual substitute.

4. The Temptation and Fall

The temptation of Adam and Eve had both an outer and an inner component. The external component was the tree of the knowledge of good and evil. Adam and Eve were forbidden to go near the tree and to partake of its fruit. There was nothing injurious or evil about the tree or its fruit. It would be a test of their love and loyalty to God. The inner component was much more complex. It tested the moral fiber and the spiritual choices of our first parents: They had to choose between the sov-

ereign Lord and the usurper; between self-abandonment and self-enthronement; and between a life of love, trust, and obedience to God and a life of selfishness and rebellion.

The sin of Adam and Eve is to be located not in their creatureliness but in their attempt to cross the boundaries of creatureliness and arrive at equality with the Creator, a suggestion placed before them by the serpent. While God did not create Adam and Eve with a propensity to sin, He did endow them with the freedom of choice. God created them "very good," and expected in them a response of willing, joyful, and loving obedience. That obedience must be not by coercion but by willing choice.

The temptation itself was not a surprise to Adam and Eve. God had told them of the forbidden tree, the forbidden fruit, and the consequences of disobedience. The atmosphere of open communion between God and Adam and Eve no doubt provided opportunity for extended and frequent conversation between God and our first parents on God's plan for them and this earth. Since the fall of Lucifer, the foremost of angels, had preceded the creation of Adam and Eve, it is unthinkable that God would not have warned them of the devious nature of the fallen angel and his possible attack on the newly created handiwork of God. Inasmuch as God does not allow His creatures to be tempted beyond their strength to withstand (1 Cor. 10:13), He did not permit Satan to approach Adam and Eve in all his dazzling splendor, and Satan chose the medium of a serpent.

Temptation in itself is no excuse for sin. God, who shared His image and likeness with human beings, has given sufficient strength and power to resist temptation and to flee from it (James 1:12-14). Human freedom is given by God not to choose that which will degrade or destroy that freedom but to choose the high and lofty way that will magnify that freedom for the glory of God and the growth of the human being. Hence the yielding to temptation and the responsibility for sin rest with

243

the individual (Prov. 4:23).

Satan tempts in many ways, but his objective remains always the same: defiance of God. To Eve, Satan came through the form of a beguiling serpent (see John 8:44; 1 John 3:8; Rev. 12:9) with a question: "Did God say, 'You shall not eat of any tree of the garden'?" (Gen. 3:1).

The question is an invitation to express doubt and sit in judgment on God's commandment. When that happens sin has already taken root, for sin, before it becomes an act, finds its expression in doubt and disbelief. An analysis of the conversation between Eve and the serpent and the resultant consequence of eating the fruit and sharing it with Adam reveals all the fundamental elements of sin—distrust in God's Word, disobedience, unbelief, disloyalty, rebellion, self-centeredness, placing human bonds over divine relationship, denial of moral responsibility for one's act, cover-up, shame, guilt, flight from consequences, and fear.

The Fall narrative underscores that distrust in God preceded the act of sin. To the serpent's query, Eve could have given a direct answer or completely ignored it, making allegiance to her Maker her first priority. Instead, her elaborate answer included even the possibility of death as punishment for eating the fruit or touching it. This gave the tempter the opportunity he was waiting for: to sow the seeds of doubt in God's Word, to suggest how arbitrary God is, to make her believe that there is no such thing as death, and to instill in her how selfish God is in placing such limitations upon her freedom. With the seed sown in a willing soil, the tempter was ready to reap the harvest. The conversation moved from the forbidden tree to the why of divine restriction, and at the suggestion of the serpent, the forbidden seemed "good," a "delight," and a thing "to be desired" (verse 6).

Eve and Adam ate. "Then the eyes of both were opened, and they knew that they were naked" (verse 7). Thus the Fall unveiled the paradox of sin. Their eyes were opened, but opened to see not their innocence but their nakedness. They learned the difference between good and evil but lost the power to abide by the good. They earned the eternal pursuit of becoming like gods, but they could not even live fully as human beings. They were afflicted with a profound sense of guilt (verse 7), alienation from God (verses 8-10), depravity and fallenness (verses 11-13), and death (verses 19-24). Painfully but surely, Adam and Eve learned that sin is a hard taskmaster, but a faithful paymaster. "For the wages of sin is death" (Rom. 6:23; see Great Controversy II. C. 5).

IV. The Nature and Essence of Sin

The predominant biblical view of the nature and essence of sin is that of personal estrangement from God. As such, it is relational at its core and rebellious in its expression. It is evil but a specific kind of evil. It is universal, but its locus is the human heart. It is an act as well as a state. It is selfishness, raising itself in pride against the Creator.

A. Sin as Rebellion Against God

An analysis of the origin of sin in heaven and in Eden clearly denotes that sin began as a rebellion against God and His will. Lucifer's claim "I will make myself like the Most High" (Isa. 14:14) and the tempter's offer to Eve that she in self-assertion "will be like God" (Gen. 3:5) are indicative that sin is a rebellion against God and His expressed will. The Genesis narrative provides penetrating evidence that sin is not so much an overt action as an inward, God-defying attitude that expressed itself in the external act of eating the forbidden fruit. The fact that Eve knew what God had said yet went against God's word makes her disobedience an act of intentional revolt. Later Isaiah expressed a similar thought: "Sons have I reared and brought up, but they have rebelled against me" (Isa. 1:2). In his magnificent prayer Daniel confessed Israel's sin as "we have sinned and done wrong and acted wickedly and rebelled, turning aside from thy commandments and ordinances" (Dan. 9:5). Thus the essence of sin is revolt against God, refusal to be subject to Him (Rom. 8:7), and enmity against God (Rom. 5:10; Col. 1:21).

This principle is demonstrated clearly in the Pentateuch in the incident of the golden calf. God did not view that act as one of error but as a rebellion, and charged Israel as such: "Remember and do not forget how you have provoked the Lord your God to wrath in the wilderness; . . . you have been rebellious against the Lord" (Deut. 9:7). Likewise, David's outcry, as noted already, shows that sin is an act against God: "Against thee, thee only, have I sinned, and done that which is evil in thy sight" (Ps. 51:4). In such a rebellion both *hamartia* (sin as failure) and *anomia* (sin as lawlessness) combine to produce a defiance and transgression of the will of God (1 John 3:4). Consequently, the transgressor wants to be his or her own God—rebellion comes full circle.

B. Sin as a Broken Relationship

The first scene in Genesis after the Fall is Adam and Eve hiding themselves from God (Gen. 3:8-10). Sin as a rebellion fractured the relationship that existed between God and Adam and Eve. Holiness and sin cannot face each other. "Your iniquities have made a separation between you and your God, and your sins have hid his face from you" (Isa. 59:2). The separation between God and human brings about a state of guilt (Isa. 53:6; Jer. 2:22; Eze. 22:4). Guilt in its emotive experience leads to loss of peace (Isa. 48:22), inner misery (Micah 7:1), and self-pity (Eze. 20:43). The basic symptom of this broken relationship with God is inward restlessness, as Isaiah says: "But the wicked [*rāšā'*] are like the tossing sea; for it cannot rest, and its waters toss up mire and dirt. There is no peace, says my God, for the wicked" (Isa. 57:20, 21).

Paul adds another dimension to this rela-tional aspect by stating that relationship with God calls for a life lived in faith. In Romans 14:13-23, the apostle sets forth two kinds of living: a life lived in the sphere of faith from which proceeds acts of faith, and a life lived apart from faith. Then Paul offers a definition of sin that is crucial to the relational dimension of sin: "For whatever does not proceed from faith is sin" (verse 23).

The rupture in relationship is not restricted to the vertical dimension alone, but extends to the horizontal. After the eviction of Adam and Eve from Eden, the horizonal rupture manifests itself when Cain murders his brother Abel and daringly refuses to own responsibility for his act (Gen. 4:8-10). The confrontation between God and Cain over the murder of Abel is twofold: On the one hand, it affirms a moral responsibility of one human being for the other; and on the other, it connects that responsibility with an accountability the human being should ever have toward God. Sin attempts to break this responsibility and escape from any accountability. Hence the vertical disorder inevitably leads to a horizontal disorder. However one may want to correct the latter and establish a harmony within the human community, any such attempt will eventually fail in the absence of the divine dimension, and thus human history becomes a story of sin and broken relationships.

Wherever fractured relationship reigns—be it between parent and child, husband and wife, pastor and parishioner, neighbor and neighbor—there lies sin with its flag of egocentrism hoisted high to capture power for oneself, to trample the right of the other, and to defy the righteous plans of God.

Further, sin's ruptured relationship impacts not only vertically and horizontally, but internally as well. The human heart is sick internally because of sin, and individuals cannot relate adequately to themselves or to their external environment because of sin.

Isaiah 53:6 confirms both sin's universality ("all we like sheep have gone astray") and individuality ("we have turned every one to his own way"). The prophet sees sin as both collective ("ah, sinful nation, a people laden with iniquity" [Isa. 1:4]) and as individual ("Woe is me! For I am lost" [Isa. 6:5]). Sin has had its devastating effect on the individual level so that the human being is described as "deceitful . . . and desperately corrupt" (Jer. 17:9), "rebellious . . . lying" (Isa. 30:9), and morally "unclean" (Isa. 64:6). Further, Paul argues that sin has darkened the intellect and has led the individual to unnatural acts that lower the human being from the status of being a human (Rom. 1:12-28).

The moral condition of the individual is filled with every kind of wickedness: "evil, covetousness, malice. Full of envy, murder, strife, deceit, malignity, . . . gossips, slanderers, haters of God, insolent, haughty, boastful, inventors of evil, disobedient to parents, foolish, faithless, heartless, ruthless" (verses 29-31).

To this devastating status of the individual sinner, Paul adds in Romans 7 the moral dilemma that each person faces: "I do not understand my own actions. For I do not do what I want, but I do the very thing I hate. . . . I can will what is right, but I cannot do it. For I do not do the good I want, but the evil I do not want is what I do" (verses 15-19).

Torn within oneself, the sinner finds a relational contradiction within. The power of sin is so overwhelming that the human being is powerless to break the intense pressure of the real over the ideal. So the person cries out: "Wretched man that I am! Who will deliver me from this body of death?" (verse 24). Such helpless wretchedness is the end result of the broken relationship.

C. Sin as a State

The biblical concept of sin further portrays its complexity by describing it as a state. Sin not only pervades the whole person but it takes abode in the human heart (Rom. 7:20). Like an enemy who invades a country and becomes its occupying power, sin has taken over the human mind and body to become the ruling power. The takeover is so complete, the depravity is so total, that "nothing good dwells" within a sinner (verse 18). Thus Paul shows that sin is not simply an act, a moral failure, or even an abnormal force. Sin is a demonic power that invades the human heart and reigns there. It becomes the controlling power of the thoughts, emotions, and actions of the individual. Paul uses expressions such as "flesh" (Rom. 8:6) and "the law of sin" (verse 2) to indicate that sin is a state with its seat in the human heart, and from there it controls the outward activities of the individual. The flesh is not simply the body; the law of sin is not simply a series of rules. The flesh is human nature apart from God; the law of sin is the status of rebellion against God. It is this nature and status, in perpetual rebellion against God and wanting to overthrow God from one's life, that constitutes sin as a state.

What results from an occupation so complete? The tragedy of a divided, confused personality: "The desires of the flesh are against the Spirit, and the desires of the Spirit are against the flesh; for these are opposed to each other, to prevent you from doing what you would" (Gal. 5:17).

Sin reduces the human person, the crown of God's creation, the bearer of God's image. Sin is no longer restricted to individual acts, but portrayed as a state of the being, controlling the very members of one's personhood (Rom. 7:20, 23). The remarkable gifts of the being—the power to think, to choose, to create, to persuade—have fallen prey to sin so that the "ought" and the "is," the "ideal" and the "real" stand in constant conflict in the human mind and action.

Paul is acutely sensitive to a war within him, a dichotomy of tragic proportions such that while he delights in the law of God in his inmost self, he finds himself captive to the law of sin (verses 22, 23). What he does not wish to do is what he does, and what he wishes to do, that he is unable to do. A corrupt and sinful nature yields sinful acts. As Jesus said, "For out of the heart come evil thoughts, murder, adultery, fornication, theft, false witness, slander" (Matt. 15:19).

D. Sin as a Specific Kind of Evil

Sin is not only evil, but a specific kind of evil. Not all evil is sin. Sickness and natural calamities such as earthquakes, tornadoes, and floods can be spoken of as evil in that they cause injury and affect the normalcy of life. Sin is not such an evil. It is a spiritual, moral, and ethical evil. Further, sin is not just an isolated act, but the outward expression of an inward revolt. Humans are not sinners because they commit sin, but they sin because they are sinners. Sin is an evil that affects the vertical relationship with God, the horizontal relationship with human beings, and the internal relationship with oneself. The biblical terminology examined above demonstrates the specificity of sin. Ḥaṭṭā'ṭ defines not simply evil, but an act of sin that misses God's standard (Lev. 5:5, 16; Ps. 51:4). 'Awôn carries the idea of "iniquity" before God (Gen. 4:13; 15:16) and indicates that sin is crookedness (Lam. 3:9), falsehood, deception (Ps. 36:3), and vanity (Prov. 22:8, KJV; Isa. 41:29, KJV). Likewise the NT words, such as hamartia, parabasis, anomia, adikia, and others define sin as a specific act perpetrated by human volition in violation against God's will and law.

Sin is not merely a passive disaster that has fallen upon humanity unawares. It is an active revolt against God on the part of Adam and Eve in the exercise of their free, but wrongful, choice. The specific nature of sin on the part of our first parents consisted in distrust of God's word, rejection of His authority, placing their will in opposition to God's will, and coveting a position that was not theirs. Self-centeredness, pride, revolt, a God-denying opposition, and covetousness all reveal how specific the sin of our forebears was. Add to this the moral and spiritual dimension involved in the rejection of God's authority and the deliberate choice of alternative authority in obeying the deceiver, and the specific nature of sin as rejection of God becomes amply clear and irrefutable.

The specific acts of sin manifest in different acts of commission and omission (for the latter, see J below). The list is as exhaustive as human experience and as pervasive and perverse as human behavior. As an example, Paul's list will suffice: "The works of the flesh are plain: fornication, impurity, licentiousness, idolatry, sorcery, enmity, strife, jealousy, anger, selfishness, dissension, party spirit, envy, drunkenness, carousing, and the like" (Gal. 5:19-21). For other lists of sin, see Matthew 15:19; Mark 7:21, 22; 1 Corinthians 5:9-11; 6:9, 10; Ephesians 4:25-31; 5:3-5; 1 Timothy 1:9, 10. Matthew 12:31, 32 speaks of one sin that is unpardonable: the sin against the Holy Spirit. (See God VII. C. 5.)

E. Sin as Falling Short

The primary words for sin in the OT (ḥaṭṭā'ṭ) and the NT (hamartia) mean to miss the mark or fall short of an expected standard. The moral dimension of the meaning of these words, when applied to sin, suggests that the individual has missed God's standard of behavior or lost God's way of living. This idea of falling short is not simply a violation of a specific law or set of laws but a mental attitude of alienation from God. Moreover, the NT idea of hamartia denotes sin not as the Greeks conceived of evil as an error committed by human deficiency and ignorance, but as a moral and spiritual shortcoming against a personal God before whom the sinner stands accountable. The biblical concept of sin thus makes it abundantly clear that sin is not a result of ignorance, human deficiency, rational inadequacy, or bodily finiteness, but an act of choice by which God's law for human existence is defied, disobeyed, and fallen short of. This emphasis cannot be missed when we take the Fall seriously; for in Eden we see not an imperfect couple, but a set of human beings, fresh from the hands of the Creator, endowed with all goodness, crowned with moral and spiritual fullness, without any bias or propensity toward evil. Adam and Eve were children of God (Isa. 1:2), but children who by their deliberate, rebellious choice fell short of God's expectations.

Paul writes, "Since all have sinned *[hamartanō],"* all "fall short of the glory of God" (Rom. 3:23). It is a falling short of the goal that God in love set for His creatures, and that goal was one of eternal communion and glory with God (1 Cor. 11:7). God did not set a goal that could not be achieved. His expectations were not unreasonable. But when we reject His goals and choose our own, when we set aside His will for us and choose our own wishes, we are setting up our own standards and rejecting God's. Any attempt to replace God's will and law with our own is falling short of His expectations, hence is sin.

F. Sin as Transgression

"Whosoever committeth sin transgresseth also the law: for sin is the transgression of the law" (1 John 3:4, KJV). John summarizes the biblical idea that sin *(hamartia)* is the "transgression of the law *[anomia],"* "lawlessness" (RSV). In linking *hamartia* and *anomia,* the apostle underlines the central role of law in defining sin. Sin is not simply an act of human failure; it is an act of rebellion against the law of God. The law of God is the transcript of God's character. It defines who God is and what He expects from His creatures. God's character of love, righteousness, and holiness, transcribed in the form of the Ten Commandments, specifically constitutes the norm by which human life is to be lived and judged. Living within the parameters of this law is living in perfect relationship with the Giver of the law. It is this principle that reveals the seriousness of God's requirement to Adam and Eve. Even though the law was not spelled out in the form of the Ten Commandments, the requirement placed upon Adam and Eve reflected God's norm for human life. The sin of our foreparents was one of rebellion against this law. It was lawlessness.

Paul also links sin to law, and argues that where there is no law there can be no sin (Rom. 5:13). Sin cannot be understood for what it is unless placed within the context of a moral universe, governed by the law of the Creator.

Hence the gravity and specificity of sin lie in one's choosing to go against the law of God, to indulge in "lawlessness," to assert that life can be lived independent of God. The enormity of sin as "lawlessness" is further noted in 2 Thessalonians 2:7, 8, where Paul personalizes it in describing the antichrist as "the lawless one." Thus, those who sin have no place in their lives for the One who gave the law. Sin, by virtue of being lawlessness, becomes godlessness.

The law is not an arbitrary obligation imposed upon humanity, but derives its role from the nature of God as He relates to humanity. When God charged Adam and Eve that the difference between life and death lay in their unconditional obedience to the law that He had spelled out for them, God was not being arbitrary. The command not to eat the forbidden fruit did not arise from a stern master, but from a loving, gracious Creator who wanted to establish a relationship with His creatures on the basis of a love that chose to respond in love.

The creature cannot ask, "Why any law at all?" A creature shall always be a creature, and the Creator shall always be the Creator. The difference between the two is God's sovereignty and a creature's finiteness. The law reflects that sovereignty and delineates that finiteness with limitations within which a creature shall exist and operate. Outside of that limit the relationship between the Creator and the creature is ruptured. The prescription of that limit does not mean arbitrariness, but the preservation of order and relationship.

The codifying of the law on Mount Sinai and the fact that God wrote the law with His fingers on tables of stone further affirm that the principles of the law are as enduring as God Himself. Jesus illuminated the law and summarized its eternal relevance in a relationship based upon love to God and to fellow human beings (Luke 10:27).

As a reflection of God's character, the law is "holy and just and good" (Rom. 7:12), and is given for the happiness of humans, even if they did not realize or understand it. Its moral and spiritual principles are not mere prohibitions, but comprehensive, universal guidelines that guarantee, when obeyed, joyful relationship with God and within the human community. But the transgression of that law puts human beings in a state of lawlessness, rebellion, and disobedience. Sin, therefore, is not merely breaking a code, but a refusal to live in a sound relationship with God.

G. Sin as Selfishness and Pride

An essential part of the nature of sin is self-centeredness and selfishness. After all, sin originated in self-seeking in the case of both Lucifer and our foreparents. If love to God is the essence of all virtue, if abandonment of self to choose God and abide in Him is the end objective of life, it follows that a love of self that displaces the primacy of God in life is sin.

The fall in heaven and in Eden illustrates how self-desire to go beyond its limitations to become like God ended in the tragedy of sin. Indeed, self-centeredness may be considered a root from which many other acts of evil spring. Greed, immorality, covetousness, arrogance, and envy, all are the result of an unwarranted love of self. Jesus consistently called for a denial of self and saw in self-centeredness an antithesis of what God expects human life to be (Luke 17:33). Likewise, Paul saw that "the mind that is set on the flesh is hostile to God; it does not submit to God's law, indeed it cannot" (Rom. 8:7).

Self-centeredness at its core is hostility to God and places self above all other relationships; therefore it cannot have any role in the Christian's moral and spiritual life. So Paul admonishes, "Do nothing from selfishness or conceit, but in humility count others better than yourselves" (Phil. 2:3). He further argues in Romans 7 that the desire to keep self enthroned is the main obstacle in the pursuit of good, and only Jesus can deliver from this obstacle. Indeed, selfishness was so crucial to Paul's concept of sin that he used the strongest possible theological language and called for the crucifixion of self to the point that the Christian can say, "It is no longer I who live, but Christ who lives in me" (Gal. 2:20). The force of the argument is inescapable: to be self-centered is the opposite of being Christ-centered. Salvation is thus seen as a radical shift from self to Christ. What is crucial in Christian discipleship is a daily experience of taking up the cross, crucifying self, and "being transformed by the renewal of your mind, that you may prove what is the will of God, what is good and acceptable and perfect" (Rom. 12:2; cf. Luke 9:23; Gal. 2:20).

Allied with self-centeredness is pride. In fact, the essence of pride is a distorted and disproportionate view of self that drives a person from a position of dependence to a disastrous attempt at independence. Was that not the reason for the fall of Lucifer (Isa. 14:12-15)? Satan, in turn, instilled in Adam and Eve this inordinate pride to be their own master, and ever since human nature has been infected with pride (Rom. 1:21-23). If pride was the undoing of Lucifer, it still remains the undoing of men and women who can easily "be puffed up with conceit and fall into the condemnation of the devil" (1 Tim. 3:6; cf. 2 Tim. 2:26).

Pride paves the way for destruction (Prov. 11:2; 16:18; 29:23). It is an attitude that God hates (Prov. 8:13), and is included in a list of vices that proceed from "within, and . . . defile a man" (Mark 7:23). To Paul pride and self-righteousness were at the root of unbelief. He insists that the gospel has no place for "boasting" (Rom. 3:27), that no one has any reason to glory in the achievement of salvation (1 Cor. 1:26-31; Eph. 2:9), and that true love is free from arrogance and self-conceit (1 Cor. 13:4). Indeed pride is so sinful that God scatters and resists the proud and exalts and favors the meek (see Prov. 3:34; Luke 1:51-55; James 4:6; 1 Peter 5:5).

This condemnation of pride as sin must not be taken to mean that adequate self-worth and self-image have no place in Christian teaching. On the contrary, Jesus' command "You shall love your neighbor as yourself" (Matt. 19:19) and Paul's perception "By the grace of God I am what I am" (1 Cor. 15:10) authenticate proper self-confidence and self-worth. Self must seek excellence, strive for fulfillment, and reach the highest possible goal. God does not wish mediocrity for His creatures. But when self asserts itself in such a way that it strives to be independent of God and tramples down fellow beings to achieve its goal, it has crossed its boundaries and plunged itself into sin. The difference between self-centeredness and self-abandonment is the difference between sinful pride and godly meekness.

H. Sin as an Enslaving Power

Sin is not only an act and a principle, but is also an enslaving power. It not only estranges but enslaves. Jesus said that "every one who commits sin is a slave to sin" (John 8:34). Just as the character of the fruit depends on the character of the tree, so are our actions determined by our hearts (Matt. 12:33-35). The acts of sin are merely outward and visible expressions of an inward disease that has gripped our emotions, thoughts, will, and the power to act. "The heart is deceitful above all things, and desperately corrupt; who can understand it?" (Jer. 17:9). It is this inner corruption, the inner propensity toward sin, that enslaves us.

Writing to the Romans, Paul portrays vividly the power and the grip of sin. He speaks of sin as reigning (Rom. 5:21). The word "reign" comes from the noun *basileus,* which means "king." Sin is a king, and humans are its woeful subjects. Paul also says that outside of Christ we are slaves to sin (Rom. 6:6, 7). As a master, sin exercises power and ownership, ruling over "your mortal bodies, to make you obey their passions" (verse 12). So deadly and powerful is the enslaving grip of sin and so faithful is sin in paying—its "wages . . . is death"—that Paul pleads that the sinner's only recourse is to accept "the free gift of God . . . eternal life in Christ Jesus our Lord" (verse 23).

Paul places utmost significance on the en-

slaving aspect of sin in human life. The imagery of a slave owner, common in Paul's time, comes to his help as he personifies the power of sin. As sinners we are under the bondage and power of sin. In Romans 6 Paul thinks of sin as a power, as a ruler. Sin is not a matter over which we have control so that at one moment we may sin and at another we may not. Rather, the apostle considers sin as the master, and we are the slaves. Sin is the power, we are the ruled, so that it is not we who rule over sin, but sin rules over us. How shall we be freed from this enslavement? Not by ourselves. Jesus is the answer: "even as the Son of man came not to be served but to serve, and to give his life as a ransom *[lytron]* for many" (Matt. 20:28; cf. Mark 10:45).

Lytron represents the purchase money for redeeming slaves. The root idea is clear: that the enslaving power of sin is so gripping over the human race that the "Son of man came . . . to give his life" as the ransom for many. To whom was the ransom paid is not under purview here, but Jesus shows the enormity of the enslaving power of sin and the cost of redemption. Paul carries the same thought in his exposition on redemption (Rom. 3:24-31; 1 Cor. 1:30; Eph. 1:7, 14; Col. 1:14). Paul's burden is to show that through the death of Christ, the redemptive price of sin has been paid, and a new kingdom of righteousness has displaced the old kingdom of sin. Those who have accepted the death of Jesus are "no longer . . . enslaved to sin" (Rom. 6:6). Through Christ the reign of sin is over (verse 12); sin's enslaving power is broken. Those who were once slaves to sin have now become God's "instruments of righteousness," and sin "will have no dominion" over them (verses 13, 14).

I. Sin as Guilt and Pollution

Insofar as sin is an individual act, a want of conformity to the law of God, it includes guilt, deserving punishment. But insofar as sin is a principle taking its abode in human nature, it includes pollution. The Bible speaks of individual acts of sin for which a person is found guilty and worthy of punishment (Matt. 6:12; Rom. 3:9; Eph. 2:3). It also speaks of a pollution that has corrupted human nature (Job 14:4; Ps. 51:2, 7; Isa. 1:5; Eph. 4:20-22). This pollution corrupts the heart and makes it "deceitful above all things" (Jer. 17:9), darkens the understanding (Eph. 4:18), makes the imagination evil and vain (Gen. 6:5; Rom. 1:21), gives birth to "evil talk" (Eph. 4:29), defiles the mind and the conscience (Titus 1:15), and makes the human being "dead through the trespasses and sins" (Eph. 2:1). Such is the picture of the natural human. But this does not mean that a person cannot have sound imagination, good affections, lofty speech, and intelligent understanding. What it does mean is that an unrenewed person has no capacity within to have a saving knowledge of God.

To the concept of sin as guilt and pollution, the Bible also adds uncleanness and impurity. The inhabitants of Jerusalem are offered deliverance from "sin and uncleanness" (Zech. 13:1). The entire sanctuary services of the OT were to deal with the individual and corporate iniquity, impurity, and uncleanness that resulted in Israel. In the NT Paul speaks of God giving up people "in the lusts of their hearts to impurity, to the dishonoring of their bodies among themselves" (Rom. 1:24). Again the apostle speaks of sexual sins as "impurity" and "greater and greater iniquity" and charges the newly baptized members to turn from this impurity and iniquity to "righteousness for sanctification" (Rom. 6:19). First Thessalonians 4:7, 8 charges that "God has not called us for uncleanness, but in holiness," and anyone who disregards this and indulges in acts of uncleanness does so not only against human beings but also against God and the Holy Spirit. The vocabulary of impurity, iniquity, and uncleanness used to denote the seriousness of sin in polluting both the individual and the collective community underscores that sin involves a serious cost not only in the separation that it causes between God and humans but also in the process of reconciliation and redemption: "The blood of Jesus his Son cleanses us from all sin" (1 John 1:7; see Sanctuary I. C. 2).

J. Sin as Neglect of Duty

The biblical portrayal of sin includes acts of both commission and omission. The first is seen in Genesis 3, where Adam and Eve deliberately disobeyed the expressed command of God and revolted against His will. Most sin is of that nature: transgression of God's law, an act of hostility against God or against a fellow human being, or a status of broken relationships. The second kind of sin—that of omission of duty—is illustrated in Genesis 4. This chapter does include a sin of commission— the murder of Abel; but also a sin of omission. Cain's denial that he was his brother's keeper (Gen. 4:9) shows up a sin of omission common in human history.

Humanity was created to be in fellowship with one another, and where that fellowship is broken by acts of omission or commission, to that extent sin reigns. Hence the divine demand: "He has showed you, O man, what is good; and what does the Lord require of you but to do justice, and to love kindness, and to walk humbly with your God?" (Micah 6:8). Jesus echoed similar concern in Matthew 25 for moral and spiritual duty to fellow human beings, and He warned that a failure to meet such duties can keep one out of the kingdom. "Whoever knows what is right to do," writes James, "and fails to do it, for him it is sin" (James 4:17).

K. Summary

From what the Bible reveals, sin must be defined and understood out of the relationship in which God placed the human being to Himself. From the Creation and Fall narrative to the simple definition that sin is "the transgression of the law" of God (1 John 3:4, KJV), the entire biblical data places sin as a particular state and act of the human against God. Out of this basic idea emerge several defining precisions.

1. Sin is a revolt against God. Although

God created humans free, they were not totally autonomous; nor were they intended to shape their destiny apart from God. Humans were created in a relationship of dependence on and fellowship with their Creator, subject to norms established by Him. When Adam and Eve revolted against this revealed will of God, sin entered this world. So sin is first and foremost placing one's will in opposition to God's will (Deut. 9:7; Isa. 1:2; Rom. 8:7).

2. Sin is a broken relationship. Both as a state and an act sin separates humans from God, and brings about a rupture in basic relationships that God wanted His creatures to enjoy. These relations include fellowship within the human community and right and joyful understanding of the role of self. Sin is a rupture in relationship in all its dimensions—vertical, horizontal, and internal (Gen. 4:8-10; Isa. 53:6; 59:2; Jer. 17:9; Rom. 7:5-10).

3. Sin is a state that pervades the whole human being. It has taken abode in the human heart, controls the cognitive, the emotional, the physical, and the spiritual dimensions of human existence. The remarkable gifts with which the Creator endowed the human being have come under the sway of sin, and that sin is the reigning monarch of the human heart. It is responsible for sinful actions (Matt. 15:19; Rom. 7:15-20; 8:2, 6).

4. Sin is a specific act of evil. It is an act that misses God's standard. It includes specific acts perpetrated by human volition in violation of God's will and law. These acts can be against God as a person and against fellow human beings, acts that have their origin and motivation in sin as the reigning monarch of the heart and are expressed outwardly (Lev. 5:5, 16; Ps. 51:4; Gal. 5:19-21).

5. Sin is falling short of God's expectations. Humanity was created to be children of God, and that status involves living within God's ideal. But by sin humanity has missed the moral, spiritual, and relational mark God had set (Isa. 1:2; Rom. 3:23; 1 Cor. 11:7).

6. Sin is lawlessness. It is the transgression of God's law, specified to Adam and Eve in no uncertain terms and to humanity as a whole in the form of the Ten Commandments which constitute the basic part of the moral law, the transcript of God's character (Luke 10:27; Rom. 5:13; 2 Thess. 2:7, 8; 1 John 3:4).

7. Sin is selfishness and pride. Sin originated in self-seeking to be God in the case of both Lucifer and our first parents. Any assertion of self to deny its creaturehood and dependence to seek place with God is sin. Self-centeredness is hostility to God, and it expresses itself in pride and self-conceit (Prov. 11:2; 16:18; Luke 17:33; Rom. 1:21-23; 3:27; 8:7; Gal. 2:20; Phil. 2:3; 1 Tim. 3:6; James 4:6).

8. Sin is an enslaving power. "Every one who commits sin is a slave to sin" (John 8:34). The bondage and power of sin make sinners so helpless and so distant from righteousness that they cannot free themselves from the rulership and ownership of sin, until they come to Christ, who has broken the enslaving power of sin and offers redemption to those who are under its power (Matt. 20:28; Mark 10:45; Rom. 3:24-31; 6:6,7; 1 Cor. 1:30; Eph. 1:7, 14).

9. Sin is guilt and pollution. As an individual act, sin brings guilt and punishment. But as a principle abiding in the heart, sin includes pollution. Sin, being unclean and impure, defiles the whole human personhood, and it is the blood of Jesus that cleanses us from all sin (Gen. 6:5; Ps. 51:2, 7; Isa. 1:5; Zech. 13:1; Matt. 6:12; Rom. 1:21, 24; 3:9; Eph. 2:3; 4:20-22; 1 John 1:7; see Man II. B. 3-5; Salvation I. E).

V. Consequences of Sin

The results of sin are numerous. While we cannot enumerate all of them here, we can look at them as they have affected human beings, God, and the environment.

A. Consequences for Human Beings

1. For Adam and Eve

From the Fall narrative we learn that the results of sin for Adam and Eve were immediate. They lost their innocence. A sense of fear, shame, and guilt took hold of them so that they could not enjoy the privilege they once had—that of face-to-face communion with God (Gen. 3:8-10). Adam and Eve discovered the enormous cost of sin: sin shut them out from God and they entered into a state of alienation and estrangement, passed on to their posterity. As a remission for sin, innocent blood was shed for the first time in history (verse 21), establishing the truth for themselves and their posterity that "without the shedding of blood there is no forgiveness of sins" (Heb. 9:22). The relationship between Adam and Eve, intended to be one of purity and harmony, suffered, and seeds of criticism and faultfinding germinated (Gen. 3:12). Work that was to be a joy became drudgery (verse 19). Having children and parenting, intended as joyful participation in the creative activity of God, became a source of pain in childbearing (verse 16) and sadness when brother rose against brother (Gen. 4:8-10). The two who were created to live in obedience forever had to die (Gen. 5:5), and death passed upon all humanity.

2. For the Human Race

Through the disobedience of Adam and Eve, sin entered the world, and through sin all its tragic consequences (Rom. 5:12-19). By the time of Noah, "the Lord saw that the wickedness of man was great in the earth, and that every imagination of the thoughts of his heart was only evil continually. And the Lord was sorry that he had made man on the earth" (Gen. 6:5, 6).

Sin has no excuse (Rom. 1:20), and its nature is so hostile to God that its effect on sinners is enormous. "They became futile in their thinking and their senseless minds were darkened" (verse 21). Their hearts became impure, and they dishonored their bodies among themselves and "exchanged the truth about God for a lie" (verses 24, 25). Both men and women fell prey to unnatural perversions, and "they were filled with all manner of wickedness, evil, covetousness, malice." They were "full of envy, murder, strife, deceit, malignity," and much more (verses 26-31).

Perhaps the most devastating consequence of sin for the human race is its power to alienate humanity from God (Isa. 59:1, 2; Micah 3:4) and make them subject to physical, moral, mental, and spiritual deficiency (Rom. 5:6, 10, 12-14, 18, 19; 6:20). Not only has sin disrupted God's relationship with human beings, but it has also poisoned the relationship among human beings. The issues that humanity struggles with today—the divisive elements of economic exploitation, racial prejudice, pride, greed, wealth and hypocrisy, hatred and discrimination based on gender, nationality, language, ethnicism, and all other alienating and violent factors within the human community—are a result of sin (Deut. 15:7, 8; 25:13-15; Isa. 32:6, 7; Micah 2:1, 2; James 5:1-6).

The ultimate consequence of sin for the human race is death: "It is appointed for men to die once" (Heb. 9:27). Death did not come as a surprise to Adam and Eve, for God had forewarned them of it (Gen. 2:17). Paul writes of its universality: "Sin came into the world through one man and death through sin, and so death spread to all men because all men sinned" (Rom. 5:12). While death is a natural consequence of sin, it is also the final penalty that comes to all unrepentant sinners in the form of the second death or final annihilation (Matt. 25:41; Rom. 6:23; Jude 12; Rev. 2:11; see Man II. C. 1; Death I. B. 3; F. 3-5).

3. For the Physical World

One specific way sin has had its impact on the world is the presence of evil. The Bible makes an objective difference between good and evil (Isa. 5:20; Amos 5:14, 15), and points out the reality of evil. But evil is not eternal; nor can it be traced to matter or to the body, as some have tried to do. Evil began with sin, and sin originated in revolt against God and in the misuse of the creaturely will (Rom. 5:12-18; 2 Cor. 11:3). Just as God is not responsible for the origin of sin, He is not responsible for the presence of evil in the physical and moral worlds. But the reality of evil cannot be denied; it is a real force, a horrible corruption of the good. The moment Adam and Eve sinned, evil resulted in both the physical and moral worlds.

Since that moment vast changes have taken place in the physical world. The thorn and the thistle (Gen. 3:17, 18), the aftermath of the Flood (Gen. 7:12), the desert and the wilderness, the groaning of the earth for deliverance (Rom. 8:19-22) are some of the word pictures the Bible uses to describe the effect of sin upon the world. The turbulent sea, the quaking earth, the flood, and the drought, the famine, and the pestilence were not in God's original plan for the earth.

Not all evil is necessarily sin, but all sin is evil. Natural catastrophes, such as floods, tornadoes, earthquakes, and war, are evil in that they bring about human suffering. God at times allows them as acts of judgment in history. Often when evil in history raises its head in either individual acts of suffering or communal genocide, we tend to ask, Why this evil? Where is God? While such questions may reflect human emotion at the point of exhaustion or human failure to understand the course of ups and downs of history, of one thing Christians are confident: God is not the author of evil. The sinful human heart lies at the source of all such evil, and will be so revealed at the end-time divine judgment. Even physical suffering on the part of the Christian need not be attributed to sin but rather understood in terms of spiritual blessing (James 1:2-4, 1 Peter 1:7); it is chastening, not penal, and should not separate us from the love of God (Rom. 8:38, 39).

Moral evil arises from human sinful inclinations (James 1:13-15). The propensity to sin and toward evil is in itself a consequence of Edenic sin, and the human heart is constantly prone to sin (Ps. 51:5; Rom. 7:23; James 1:15), awaiting opportunity to commit the act.

The results of sin will continue on earth until the formation of the new heaven and new earth in God's final act of judgment and purification of the earth and all that is in it (2 Peter 3:10-13; cf. Rev. 21:1-4).

B. Consequences for God

Although the Bible does not address directly the consequences of sin upon the Godhead, there are intimations of what sin has meant to God. The first is Adam's accusation that he sinned because of "the woman whom thou gavest to be with me," and then Eve's agreement with Adam that she sinned because "the serpent beguiled me" (Gen. 3:12, 13). One reason the biblical data argues that sin is hateful to God is precisely this: that sin has the audacity to accuse God of being the reason for it.

The serious nature of sin and the necessity that God deal with it once for all is revealed to the universe in the step He took to crush the author of sin by sending His Son (verse 15; John 3:16). God's love for the sinner cost Him the life of His Son. "For our sake he made him to be sin who knew no sin, so that in him we might become the righteousness of God" (2 Cor. 5:21).

God's relationship with Adam and Eve was open and free, face-to-face. Sin disrupted this relationship (Gen. 3:8-10; Isa. 59:1, 2), but God's love for humanity was so great that He kept open various channels of communication with His erring creatures: nature (Ps. 19:1), human relationships (Ps. 103:13; Isa. 54:5), Scripture (2 Tim. 3:16, 17), Jesus (John 1:1, 14, 18; Heb. 1:1-3), and the Holy Spirit (John 7:37-39; 16:8-14). Just as the Creator's original plan of eternal relationship with Adam and Eve was based upon love, trust, and obedience to Him, so was His design for Adam's progeny after the Fall. The design was the same: a relationship based on love, trust, and obedience. Subsequent to the Fall, God chose to express these principles as the moral law and codified them after their liberation from Egyptian bondage during the Exodus sojourn (Ex. 20:1-17).

Even as the redemption of the human race became a paramount priority with God after the Fall, so did judgment. The final consequence of sin for God is to meet the challenge of the usurper, the evil one. On that final day of judgment Satan and his followers, along with sinners who have rejected God's grace, will be destroyed forever, and a new earth and a new heaven shall come into being (Rev. 21:1-4). What was lost in Eden is restored.

VI. The Extent and Elimination of Sin

Both human experience and Scripture reveal the extent of sin. Sin plays no favorites. It has affected every race, nation, tongue, and people. Its effects can be seen in the moral and spiritual shortcomings of humans everywhere. The moral, social, sociological, and behavioral upheavals of the world need not be placed at the door of psychological maladjustment or economic deficiency, but at the door of sin. This extent of sin does not imply its permanence. God's plan of salvation includes the elimination of sin. We now turn to sin's extensiveness, transmission and penalty, the wrath and justice of God, and sin's eradication.

A. The Extensiveness of Sin

1. The Cosmic Effect of Sin

What was our solar system like before the Fall? What were the climatic conditions on earth? Such questions cross our minds when we realize the enormity of sin and its effect on the created order. The Bible remains largely silent on these matters.

However, Paul's argument that "we have become a spectacle to the world, to angels and to men" (1 Cor. 4:9) suggests that we are an exhibit before the universe, an exhibit in which is demonstrated the struggle between righteousness and sin, Christ and Satan. The battle for the lost human race is real. Both God and Satan have a stake in it. A biblical example of this is Job, in whom Satan took such an extraordinary interest as to challenge God to let him test Job's fidelity to God. Satan insisted that Job would fall if he was allowed to afflict him physically. With Adam and Eve, appetite was Satan's instrument. In the case of Job, affliction and persecution were Satan's choice. Satan touched Job at the very core of his heart—his children—and with them took his possessions and his health. "In all this Job did not sin" (Job 1:22; 2:10). The biblical portrayal of the character of Job as a spectacle before heaven indicates that all heaven is interested in what has been happening on earth since the Fall. Sin and its history are noted in heaven and its effect continually watched by the angelic world. This is obvious from the statement of Jesus that "there is joy before the angels of God over one sinner who repents" (Luke 15:10). This joy expresses itself in continuous praise and worship in heaven, with "the voice of many angels, numbering myriads of myriads and thousands of thousands, saying with a loud voice, 'Worthy is the Lamb who was slain'" (Rev. 5:11, 12).

Only God knows the total consequences of Adam's Fall. However, the Bible assures us that all that was lost through Adam is to be regained through Christ's sacrifice.

2. The Universality of Sin

The universal extent of sin is a fact of our everyday experience. The entire race lives in a threefold revolt of sin in relationships: revolt against God, revolt among fellow human beings, and revolt within oneself. The universality of that revolt shouts out the universality of sin.

Human longing to be free from guilt and to discover inner calm and peace is another indication of universal malice. Behavioral scientists may assign to this longing any name they

255

choose, but Christian anthropology must squarely face the universal reality of sin, called by its right name: a rebellion against, and an alienation from, God. The Gospels recognize the universal nature of this alienation and proclaim a cure equally universal (John 3:16).

The OT plainly teaches that "there is no man who does not sin" (1 Kings 8:46). During the time of Noah, sin became so universal and human imagination so corrupt that the Lord is presented as regretting His creation of humans (Gen. 6:6). While the Psalmist acknowledged he was conceived in sin and that as an individual he was guilty of sin (Ps. 51:4, 5), he was forced to lament that "no man living is righteous" (Ps. 143:2). And the wise man raises a historical challenge: "Who can say, 'I have made my heart clean; I am pure from my sin'?" (Prov. 20:9).

Who indeed can? "All we like sheep have gone astray; we have turned every one to his own way" (Isa. 53:6). The malignancy of sin has so polluted the human being that "from the sole of the foot even to the head, there is no soundness in it, but bruises and sores and bleeding wounds" (Isa. 1:6). The entire race stands helpless and hopeless before the tyrannical might of sin: "We have all become like one who is unclean, and all our righteous deeds are like a polluted garment. We all fade like a leaf, and our iniquities, like the wind, take us away" (Isa. 64:6).

The Epistle to the Romans is unique in its presentation of the power and universality of sin. Sin is so vile and universal that God has abandoned the human race to lustful hearts of "impurity," to "dishonorable passions," to "a base mind and to improper conduct" (Rom. 1:24, 26, 28). No one can escape this pollution and burden of sin, for "all men . . . are under the power of sin" (Rom. 3:9). "None is righteous, no, not one" and "no one does good, not even one" (verses 10, 12).

Sin's universality permeates Paul's agonizing cry: "All have sinned and fall short of the glory of God" (verse 23). If anyone should even dare to say that such is not the case, the Bible condemns such a person as a liar (1 John 1:8-10).

Recognizing the universality of sin, God has made provision for the salvation of the entire human race, Jew or Gentile, rich or poor, male or female. "For God so loved the world that he gave his only Son, that whoever believes in him should not perish but have eternal life" (John 3:16).

B. The Transmission of Sin

We have reviewed sin's origin and results. It appears both as an act and a state. We have examined its nature and essence, including its cosmic nature and universality. Each human being at one time or another comes to realize a moral shortfall, a spiritual deficiency that the Bible calls sin. But the question is How did this originate? Adam sinned. Am I a sinner because of his sin? Or am I a sinner because I have sinned?

A major passage addressing the question of linkage between Adam's sin and that of his posterity is found in Romans 5:12-19. Here the apostle locates the source of sin and subsequent death in Adam's fall. Paul's ultimate objective is to show that in spite of that heritage, the descendants of Adam have cause to "rejoice in God through our Lord Jesus Christ, through whom we have now received our reconciliation" (verse 11).

How can such reconciliation be possible? The act of Jesus Christ is an individual act. His death may be God's sacrifice for sin, but how can that individual act save others from sin? Lest his readers raise such a question, Paul immediately turns their attention to Adam and brings in a comparison with Christ. "As sin came into the world through one man and death through sin, and so death spread to all men because all men sinned" (verse 12), so "one man's act of righteousness leads to acquittal and life for all men" (verse 18). Paul does not pause to give a theological lesson on how sin was transmitted from Adam to the human race. He speaks only of the reality of the human situation, that Adam sinned and therefore the whole world lies in sin. "Death reigned through that one man" Adam, so shall those who receive grace and "the free gift of righteousness reign in life through the one man Jesus Christ" (verse 17). Similarly, "by one man's disobedience many were made sinners, so by one man's obedience many will be made righteous" (verse 19). Paul repeats that comparison in 1 Corinthians 15:21, 22: "For as by a man came death, by a man has come also the resurrection of the dead. For as in Adam all die, so also in Christ shall all be made alive."

If Romans 5:12-19 is read with the intention of finding out *how* the transmission of sin through Adam or of righteousness through Jesus takes place, we shall reach nowhere. That was not Paul's intention. But if the passage is read with the intention of showing that sin in human experience is real, and salvation through Jesus Christ is also real, then we come to the joyous discovery that sin is a defeated foe and through Jesus Christ we can overcome the problem of sin in human life.

All we can say from Romans 5:12-19 is that sin originated with Adam. Sin is universal in that all have sinned. Sin brings separation between God and humanity. Because of Adam's sin, we have inherited this separation from God and more—a propensity to sin, wrongful tendencies, perverted appetites, debased morals, as well as physical degeneracy. Tendency to sin or temptation to sin is not sin. Neither constitutes a revolt against God. Yielding to sin and committing the act of sin, thus transgressing the law of God, alienate us from God and make us guilty before Him. We are held responsible for our own sin, but thanks to God, we are offered forgiveness for that sin and acceptance before God because grace reigns "through righteousness to eternal life through Jesus Christ our Lord" (verse 21).

C. Death, the Penalty for Sin

Justice and reason demand that personal revolt against God and violation of His expressed will should be met with a penalty. Sin cannot be allowed to continue without just and necessary punishment. God had warned Adam and Eve that such a penalty was sure to follow transgression of His commandment (Gen. 2:16, 17). The object of the penalty is not simply reformation of the offender or a deterrent to further transgression, although these may be incidental in the life of a sinner. Penalty must be understood in terms of God's wrath and justice.

1. The Wrath of God

God's wrath arises from His holiness and righteousness, and is His response of revulsion toward sin. Since sin is universal, His wrath also is universal. In the biblical portrayal of God's wrath, it appears not so much an emotion or anger as the outcome of deep opposition of His holiness to evil. Divine wrath must not be understood in human terms such as jealousy, vengeance, or vindictiveness. God's wrath is the natural reaction of God's holy love against sin. It is God's moral outrage against human revolt. Without such outrage ultimately manifested in letting His Son die on the cross for the sins of the world, God could not remain God. The most poignant picture of God's wrath against sin is seen in the Lamb of God on the cross. It is God's love that drove Jesus to the cross, and it is His love that manifests itself in wrath against sin.

According to Paul, God's wrath has a present and future aspect. In the present, God hands over sinners to the consequences of their sin, and they find themselves under the power and grasp of sin and ultimately death (Rom. 1:18-22; 6:23). Against this background of total human helplessness, God reveals His grace and righteousness through Jesus Christ and "for our sake he [God] made him [Christ] to be sin who knew no sin, so that in him we might become the righteousness of God" (2 Cor. 5:21). Thus on the cross, "the wrath of God against sin, the terrible manifestation of His displeasure because of iniquity, filled the soul of His Son with consternation" (DA 753).

The future aspect of God's wrath is eschatological, manifest in final judgment to all things associated with sin (Rom. 2:6-8; Rev. 20:9).

2. The Justice of God

God's justice requires that He carry out the sentence of death predicated to disobedience (Gen. 2:17). Whatever meaning is given to death, it is the consequence of sin. Human beings are born in a state of separation from God, the source of life. Consequently, their bodies and minds do not have the optimum capacity that the Creator intended. There is the first death, a result of Adam's sin, common to all. Furthermore, there is the second death that terminates the career of sin. The Bible refers to this as the second death (Rev. 20:6), which is the "wages of sin" (Rom. 6:23). The second death is eternal death, which comes to all the impenitent when the wicked are eternally annihilated (Matt. 10:28; see Judgment III, IV; Man II. C. 3; Death I. G. 1).

This second death is by choice. Romans 6:23 clearly places two offers before all: the wages of sin to those who refuse to accept Jesus, and the gift of eternal life to those who accept Him.

D. The Eradication of Sin

The eradication of sin was made possible by the atoning death of Jesus, whom "the Father has sent . . . as the Savior of the world" (1 John 4:14). The central focus of the Bible rests on God's redemptive activity, culminating in Calvary, where "at the right time Christ died for the ungodly" (Rom. 5:6). The cross on which the ultimate sacrifice was offered (Heb. 9:26) was God's way of dealing with sin. There Jesus "was wounded for our transgressions, he was bruised for our iniquities; upon him was the chastisement that made us whole, and with his stripes we are healed" (Isa. 53:5).

The central thought of these and other passages dealing with God's redemptive activity focuses on Christ's substitutionary death for our sins. Paul says that "Christ died for our sins in accordance with the scriptures" (1 Cor. 15:3). John writes: "You know that he appeared to take away sins" (1 John 3:5). Peter adds: "He himself bore our sins in his body on the tree, that we might die to sin and live to righteousness" (1 Peter 2:24). The death of Jesus was the culmination of the entire sacrificial system of the OT, the ultimate offering for the sins of humanity (see John 1:29, 36; Heb. 9:28; 10:4). Paul adds, "For our sake he [God] made him [Jesus] to be sin who knew no sin, so that in him we might become the righteousness of God" (2 Cor. 5:21).

Thus the substitutionary death of Jesus on the cross—the sinless one dying for the sins of all—crushed the force of sin and the power of its originator and made possible the redemption of us all.

The final eradication of sin from the universe is reserved for the future, to take place following the millennium, the day of the Lord when "the heavens will pass away with a loud noise, and the elements will be dissolved with fire, and the earth and the works that are upon it will be burned up" (2 Peter 3:10). The final elimination of sin is an eschatological event, when God will pass His judgment upon Satan and all his followers, and "their lot shall be in the lake that burns with fire and sulphur, which is the second death" (Rev. 21:8; see Christ II. C-E; Millennium I. C. 3).

VII. Historical Overview

A. The Early Church

The postapostolic church did not immediately systematize a formal doctrine of sin. In almost all cases, doctrinal formulation developed as a reaction to what was perceived as ideas and positions contradictory to the simple statements of the Scripture. For example, only when the Gnostics represented sin as a necessary evil, having its source in a cause independent of God and beyond human control, did the church rise to correct the error by saying that sin was not a necessary evil, and that it entered the world by an act of free will by our first parents. The early church was content in saying that all humans are sinners; that sin came into the world by the disobedience of Adam; that it is universal in that all have sinned; and that redemption from sin has been made possible by Christ.

Irenaeus (c. 115-202) distinguished between the "image of God" and the "likeness of God." He defined the former as the endowments of a rational mind, a free will, which Adam retained after the Fall. The latter was the life of Spirit, which was lost after the Fall, but restored by grace manifest in the Incarnation. God came down to sinful human beings so that they could climb up to God. Origen (c. 185-254), following the Platonic theory of pre-existence, held that human souls sinned in a previous existence, and therefore all entered the world in a sinful condition. Imprisoned in human bodies, the souls begin a pilgrimage back to God when they accept the gospel—a process of salvation and restoration.

Eastern and Western churches dealt with the problem of sin differently in their polemic with Gnosticism. The East viewed humans more optimistically, holding that the Fall did not result in the loss of free will, nor did the Fall pass on guilt to succeeding generations. While conceding that sin was a deprivation with the resultant loss of purity, it did not hold that deprivation meant a bent toward evil. The Western church held a more pessimistic view of human nature: All sinned in Adam and inherited evil tendencies.

B. Pelagius and Augustine

When they first propounded their views on sin, Pelagius and Augustine represented two different understandings. Their impact on Christian thought has persisted through the ages.

1. Pelagius

Pelagius (c. 350-425), a British monk, taught in Rome during the latter part of his life. His theology proceeded from the assumption that if persons are truly human, they must possess the freedom to choose responsibly. Therefore, each human is born into the world in the same condition as that of Adam prior to the Fall, innocent and free from inherited or depraved tendencies. Thus human beings are perfectly able to obey God, just as Adam had been when he was created. But of course people do sin. Pelagius acknowledged this fact but explained it not on the basis of imputation or inheritance, but by the power of bad examples that persons tend to imitate. Individuals are accountable only for the sins they personally and consciously commit. Pelagius held that physical death was not a penalty for sin. Adam, whether he had sinned or not, would have eventually died. He was created corporeal, and, therefore, mortal—as are all his descendants. Thus, infants who died unbaptized are admitted to eternal life, with no need of cleansing from original sin.

The Synod of Carthage (418) condemned Pelagianism.

2. Augustine

Augustine (354-430), the bishop of Hippo, wrote extensively on sin. He refuted the Pelagian teaching that human beings had the duty of striving toward perfection. He argued that perfection could not be achieved by human effort because human beings were guilty and offensive to God, and had no power—not even desire—to change their moral nature.

Augustine taught that before the Fall, Adam possessed limited free will—the ability to choose freely between two predetermined alternatives, good and evil. When Adam chose to exercise the ability to sin, he lost the ability to refrain from sinning. He no longer had the freedom to choose; he could only decide to do evil. Whenever he did evil, he did so by the exercise of his will, which was now so completely corrupt that it longed for evil alone.

Augustine taught that "original sin" was the sin of the entire human race, not merely of Adam. This was so because all humans were "seminally present" in Adam. When Adam sinned, the entire human race sinned in and with him. All humans are conceived in sin (Ps. 51:5). The means of propagating the race is also the means of propagating original sin. The sexual desires experienced by fallen human beings are intrinsically evil and sinful.

The human will inevitably succumbs to lust because it is no longer free to choose moral purity or chastity. For this reason, human beings cannot be saved by their own effort or merit but only by the love and grace of God. The regeneration of an individual could be achieved only by the supernatural work of the Holy Spirit. A sinner is not capable even of cooperating with this work. Salvation is purely a gift of God, given in His sovereign mercy and foreknowledge.

C. Middle Ages

During the Middle Ages the nature of sin continued to be debated. Especially important was the emergence of a classification of sins as mortal and venial. The first was a deliberate turning away from God with a clear consent of the will; it caused a loss of sanctifying grace and must be confessed to a priest. The second did not wholly deprive the soul of sanctifying grace. Penance—fasting, flogging, pilgrimage, and other forms of asceticism—was considered a way to atone for one's wrongdoing and to control passions leading to sin. Because penance took so much time from the activities of daily life, "commutation"—often the payment of money—came to replace it, a forerunner of "indulgence" that in its crudest form allowed people to prepay the penalty of not yet committed sins.

1. Anselm

Anselm of Canterbury (1033-1109) defined original sin as the "absence of goodness,"

the goodness that every person ought to have. Thirteenth-century Scholastics followed his lead, and held further that in the Fall the human person had not suffered a total corruption of the spiritual nature, but lost only some gifts, such as holiness, immortality, wisdom, and dominion. Sin, they said, is an infinite offense against God and requires infinite satisfaction.

2. Thomas Aquinas

Thomas Aquinas (c. 1224-1274) made a distinction between "image" and likeness." He defined the image as consisting chiefly in the person's intellectual nature, inherent in which are the virtues of rationality, capacity for virtue, and an apitude for understanding and loving God. At the Fall, Adam did not lose this image. "Likeness" represents a "supernatural endowment of grace" that consists of love and obedience to God. This was forfeited at the Fall and restored at baptism.

According to Aquinas, sin is of two kinds: mortal and venial. When a human soul is so rebellious that it turns away from God, it has committed mortal sin. But when there is disorder in the soul, but not to the extent of turning away from God, there is venial sin. Aquinas distinguished between the two sins by suggesting that the aversion to God in mortal sin is like death, and the disorder in venial sin is like sickness. In mortal sin, the principle of life is lost; the sin itself is a willful transgression of a serious nature, such as apostasy, murder, adultery. These sins are forgiven only by the sacrament of penance, involving confession, absolution by a priest, and may even require payment of indulgences. In the case of venial sin, the damage is repairable by acts of prayer, fasting, and almsgiving.

D. Reformation

1. Martin Luther

Martin Luther (1483-1546) taught that before the Fall, Adam was inclined only toward good. After the Fall he and his descendants were subject to sin. The human race became a *massa perditionis* (lump of perdition). Human nature is sinful and full of concupiscence. All sins are mortal. With other Reformers, he denied the distinction between mortal and venial sins.

While sin includes outward acts and attitudes such as despising God, heart impurity, and disobedience, it is above all lack of faith. Unbelief, the turning away from God is the essence of human sin.

In his writings on original sin Luther opposes the Scholastics, who shared some of pelagius' views. he describes original sin as corruption of the whole person, including the lower nature (concupiscence) and the higher powers (understanding and will). Thus the natural person neither loves God nor longs after Him, but is content to find full satisfaction for mind and spirit in the created things. Just as the will is impotent to do good, so human beings are unable to prepare worthily to receive grace. hence, the human will is in bondage and it is free only to do evil. Without free will humans depend entirely on grace for conversion.

2. John Calvin

John Calvin (1509-1564) held that human nature changed substantially after the Fall so that humans are able to do civil good but not moral good. That is, people can do good as defined and prescribed by other human beings, but not as required by God. Fallen human beings cannot ruse above their fallen condition.

Sin is not merely the committing of sinful acts; it is also "hereditary depravity and corruption." Sin is the vitiated state in which humanity has existed since the Fall. It has brought about the miserable enslavement of the will. Thus, everything in human beings is corrupt, including intellect, heart, and will. Even the good works of Christians are imperfect, tainted by sin, for they are produced by intrinsically evil beings.

Since the human will is dead as far as any spiritual good is concerned, it takes an act of God to arouse spiritual willingness in human beings. Calvin's emphasis on the omnipotence of God eventually led him to formulate his doctrine of predestination, which affirms that even before the Fall or Creation, God in His eternal counsel and wisdom predestined some of His creatures to salvation and others to damnation.

3. Ulrich Zwingli

Zwingli (1484-1531) believed in the absolute authority of the Bible, and would not permit anything in religion or religious practice that could not be supported from the Scriptures. He considered original sin as a moral disease, but did not attribute to it guilt. He believed that faith was essential to salvation, and that the focus of this faith was the death of Christ. Although he considered sin as an act of individual rebellion against God, he accepted unconditional predestination to salvation, but taught that only those who heard and rejected the gospel were predestined to be damned.

4. Anabaptist Reformers

In addition to mainstream Reformers such as Luther, Calvin, and Zwingli, the Reformation movement gave rise to the Anabaptists, whose influence continues to the present time. They taught that sin is the transgression of God's law and is an individual revolt against God's will. Thus they insisted sin is an individual act and not a corporate act. Therefore, forgiveness of sin is based on individual repentance and confession of sin to God, having had faith in the atoning sacrifice of Jesus. Hence they opposed infant baptism on the ground that infants cannot understand either sin or the need for forgiveness.

E. Post-Reformation

1. Jacob Arminius

Jacob Arminius (1560-1609), a Dutch theologian, reacted to the entire soteriological system of Calvinism, in particular to its teachings on predestination. According to Arminius, Adam, in his original state, was fully capable of total and voluntary obedience to God. Because of sin, he became destitute of original righteousness and exposed to misery and death. This infirmity was passed on to his descendants. As a result, without God's help human beings are wholly unable to obey God or attain eternal life. The Fall resulted in total depravity. However, from the very first dawn of consciousness, God imparts to each individual "prevenient grace," a special influence of the Holy Spirit, which restores free choice and enables the hearer of the gospel to respond freely to the call of Christ.

The evil tendencies and the sinful state might be called sin, but they do not, in and of themselves, involve guilt or punishment. The inborn tendencies to evil are only imputed as sin when one consciously and voluntarily appropriates and ratifies them through personal, actual sin, in spite of God's grace and power to the contrary. The responsibility for sin and eternal loss rests entirely on the determinations of the human will.

2. The Council of Trent

The Council of Trent (1545-1563) held that as a result of sin, Adam lost the superadded gift of righteousness. The council also held that Adam's sin, by propagation, more than by example, injured the human race, with the exception of Mary. Although the council did not specifically state what was transmitted from Adam to the human race, it said that the human race received a nature devoid of righteousness, with an inclination to sin. The council held that in spiritual life, free will was weakened but not lost. The council also commanded that infants be baptized in order that they may be purified from the contamination inherited from their parents.

F. Seventeenth to Nineteenth Centuries

1. Federal Theology

Federal theology had its origin in Johannes Cocceius (1603-1669), a Dutch theologian, it maintains that Adam was not only the natural head of the human race but also its federal representative. Adam's sin was immediately imputed to all his descendants. The Westminster Confession (1647) affirmed this position.

Federal theology maintains that Adam was constituted, by God's sovereign appointment, the representative of the entire human race. God's covenant with Adam included all human beings. On condition of obedience, God agreed to bestow eternal life on Adam—and thus on all human beings. The penalty for disobedience was corruption and death for Adam and all his descendants. All are born corrupt because they were representatively incorporated in the sin and guilt of Adam. This representative incorporation is the root of each person's inherent disposition to sin, a federal relationship that all confirm by their own sinful acts.

2. Mediate Imputation

Mediate imputation is closely associated with Josua Placaeus of seventeenth-century France. Placaeus taught that we derive a corrupt nature from Adam, and that corrupt nature, not Adam's, is the basis of condemnation of the human race. The Synod of Charenton (1644) rejected that position. Placaeus responded that original sin was indeed more than hereditary corruption, but its imputation was mediate, following the actual sins committed by human beings born depraved both physically and morally. Thus he made a distinction between immediate and mediate imputation and denied that imputation was immediate.

3. John Wesley

John Wesley (1703-1791), the founder of Methodism, maintained that God provides human beings with prevenient grace, a spark of divinity that is God's antidote to original sin, which he defined as the corrupt nature of the soul before God. With this ability of self-determination, human beings are capable of choosing between good and evil. And so when the gospel is presented, human beings are in a position to respond positively to its saving news or reject it.

Wesley taught that both justification and sanctification are essential in dealing with sin. Justification is Christ's forensic declaration that we are righteous; sanctification is the restoration of the human will so that it might freely cooperate with God. After accepting the salvation offered in Christ, human beings could proceed to christian perfection, which, to Wesley, was the heart of the gospel. By perfection he meant a state in which the love for God and our neighbors rules our tempers, words, and actions. The innate and inevitable presence of bodily imperfections, which all humans inherit from fallen Adam, renders impossible the attainment of sinless perfection of the body until the final and complete transformation occurs at the resurrection.

Wesley distinguished between proper and improper sins. A proper sin is known and voluntary, whereas improper sins consist of errors, ignorance, and infirmities in speech or behavior.

4. New School Theology

New School Theology—so-called because it went against traditionally held Calvinistic teachings on sin and predestination—was formulated by Nathaniel Taylor, a New England theologian of the early nineteenth century. The school rejected federal theology and denied the imputation of Adam's sin. It claimed that unregenerate human beings can respond to the sacrifice of Christ without waiting for the Holy Spirit to take the first step. Revivalists such as Charles G. finney and Lyman Beecher popularized this position in the mid-nineteenth century.

5. Realistic School

This school of thought was seminally Augustinian. It flourished in the mid-nineteenth century. William G. T. Shedd, one of its chief proponents, maintained that God imputed to each of Adam's descendants guilt, depravity, and punishment of death, for the reason that the race was in Adam seminally, in undistributed form. Human nature is an unindividualized unity, and it existed in its entirety in Adam. When Adam sinned, not only did he sin, but also each person who comes into the world because of that unindividualized unity that Adam was. Because all persons are guilty coagents with Adam, our first parents were no more guilty of the first act than their descendants. Adam's sin is not ours because it was imputed to us; it was imputed to us because it is properly our own.

According to the realistic school, sin began with self-seeking, and pride was the mother of all sin. Corruption is inherited and synonymous with guilt. The results of sin are such evils as enmity, hatred, and obstinacy.

G. Twentieth Century

From the eighteenth century on, rationalism rose to question the traditional teaching about sin and punishment. Some such as Rousseau (1712-1778) held that people may be deceived but cannot be corrupted. Others, disavowing the literal interpretation of Genesis, saw sin as a resistance to the universal God-consciousness (Schleiermacher, 1768-1834), and as a product of selfishness and ignorance (Ritschl, 1882-1889). But the twentieth century saw the rise of neoorthodoxy, the social gospel, and liberation theology emphasizing varying views of sin.

1. Neoorthodoxy

Neoorthodoxy sought to uphold the gravity of human alienation from God while at the same time setting aside aspects of the Fall and sin that traditional theology has upheld. Karl Barth (1886-1968), proclaiming his dependence on the Reformation and the Bible, defined sin as "nothingness," "a contradiction of God's positive will and breach of the divine covenant." Each person reenacts the story of Eden, and finds perversion and depravity. No aspect of the human being is unaffected by sin:

there is nothing good that dwells in the human being. No capacity for God remains in human nature; therefore, the Spirit must create a point of contact before human beings can come to belief.

Emil Brunner (1889-1966) argued that the notion of original sin is completely alien to biblical thought. He held that each person sins individually, and within the individual there is a capability that enables them to apprehend the gospel and respond to it; else there would be no point in preaching.

Reinhold Niebuhr (1892-1971) held that humans stand in a paradoxical relation of freedom and finitude, of being free and bound. As such they experience anxiety—the internal precondition of sin. Niebuhr denied the Augustinian concept of original sin, but also disputed the liberal view that considered sin a weakness. To him, original sin is not inherited, but a fact of life. Niebuhr stressed that the root of sin lies in self attempting to assert its independence and be like God.

2. Social Gospel

In different ways, promoters of the social gospel have rejected the traditional view of sin. Ritschl viewed sin as individual deeds arising out of ignorance or a failure to realize ethical values, a seeking after that which is inferior. While justification is revealed by Christ, it is made effective only in reconciliation, which is human's work. Other social gospel advocates find the root of sin in economic exploitation and class oppression.

3. Liberation Theology

Liberation theology defines sin in terms of oppression, exploitation, and social injustice. The sin of pride dehumanizes people and causes them to be greedy. It is more societal than individual. Sin should not be understood primarily in religious terms, but rather in terms of social, political, and economic oppression of the poor. It is the exploitation of the rich over the poor, of the haves over the have-nots. It includes not only social injustice but also the rape of the environment. Thus sin is transmitted through the corrupt network of institutions, relationships, attitudes, and social selfishness, especially corporate selfishness.

H. Adventist Understanding

For 20 centuries after Jesus died on the cross for the sins of the human race, the history of the doctrine of sin has witnessed many contours—from total denial of its reality to indifference to its depravity and deadly grip. In between are a wide variety of teachings, from literal biblical views to a mixture of philosophic speculations and social preoccupations.

Against this background, we turn to Seventh-day Adventist teaching on the doctrine of sin. Even before their official organization in the 1860s, Seventh-day Adventists were seriously concerned with the problem of sin. Most of them were Millerites who expected that Jesus would return around 1844. In anticipation of that event, moral and spiritual readiness in terms of obedience to God's law was characteristic of the Adventists. When Jesus did not return in 1844, one group continued the study of God's Word, discovered the Sabbath and sanctuary truths, and later officially named themselves Seventh-day Adventists. The discovery of truths such as the Sabbath and a pre-Advent judgment that began in 1844, along with continued proclamation of the certainty and imminence of Christ's second coming, drove the early Seventh-day Adventists to be ready to meet history's final climax. While that spirit of readiness expressed itself in their practical concern with the problem of sin and living a life of obedience to the Decalogue, their Methodist roots kept their interest in perfection very much alive.

Adventist understanding of sin is rooted in the biblical concept of the great controversy, a cosmic conflict involving superhuman powers of good and evil. The conflict began in heaven with the rebellion of Lucifer, leading to his expulsion from heaven along with one third of the angels who joined him (Isa. 14:12-14; Rev. 12:3-9). The central issue of the conflict is the character of God: Is He a God of love or a tyrant forcing allegiance upon His creatures? With the expulsion of Satan, the controversy moved its venue from heaven to earth and has been a part of history ever since. Seventh-day Adventists believe that the cross of Jesus not only made salvation possible but has ensured the victory of God over Satan. Sin and Satan and their adherents will be finally eradicated from this universe when at the close of the millennium the great controversy will be ended. (See Great Controversy V. D. 1-3.)

The Adventist understanding of sin, its origin, and how God chose to deal with it, is best set forth in the writings of Ellen G. White. Her understanding is developed in the first few chapters of her book *Patriarchs and Prophets*. The entire section is an exposition of the biblical data on sin, and represents the Adventist understanding of the biblical concept of sin. The exposition can be outlined in nine major theses: 1. God is love, and He expects all His creatures to acknowledge Him and pay allegiance to Him out of love. 2. Lucifer, the chief of angels, sought to obtain homage due only to the Creator by acts of pride and deception. 3. As a result, the perfect harmony that characterized heaven was shattered, and Lucifer and his followers were expelled from heaven. Sin began with Lucifer. 4. At the end of the creation of the world, God placed Adam and Eve, made in His image, as stewards in charge of His creation, with the condition that their close relationship with God was dependent on their obedience to His revealed will. 5. Adam and Eve, at the behest of the temptation of Satan, rebelled against God and declared their independence. 6. Thus sin began, with all its consequences, including depravity and death. 7. God immediately announced the plan He had made long before the foundations of the earth were laid, that His Son would redeem the fallen race by offering Himself as a ransom for sin. 8. Those who accept the Son

will receive forgiveness and eternal life. 9. God will bring about the final elimination of sin at the eschatological judgment associated with the return of Jesus after the millennium and the establishment of the new heaven and the new earth.

These are the major teachings around which the Adventist understanding of sin is built. Adventists do not stress the idea of original sin in the sense that "personal, individual moral guilt adheres to Adam's descendants because of his [Adam's] sin. They stress, instead, that his sin resulted in the condition of estrangement from God in which every human being is born. This estrangement involves an inherent tendency to commit sin" (Neufeld 1351).

The year 1888 marks an important clarification in the Adventist understanding of sin and righteousness. Until then justification by faith was dealt with meagerly in Seventh-day Adventist books and periodicals. Emphasis was on obedience to the law, so much so that when E. J. Waggoner and A. T. Jones insisted on the doctrine of righteousness by faith alone at the world session of the church in Minneapolis in 1888, many, including the church leadership, did not initially accept it.

Among Adventists, the history of the doctrine revolved mostly around the issue of perfection. The fixation on perfection arose from early Adventist identification of themselves with the 144,000 of Revelation 14:1; 7:4, a special group who are said to be spotless and blameless. This, in combination with the NT eschatological goal that at the end of time God will have a church "without spot or wrinkle or any such thing" (Eph. 5:27), led some Adventists to argue for perfection here on earth. Others disagreed, and suggested that sinless perfection is possible only as a gift of God's grace bestowed at the time of the Second Coming upon those who have remained faithful to Him. This does not mean, however, that Adventists disclaim victory over sin in this present life. Far from it. Their position is the same as that of the apostle: "My little children, I am writing this to you so that you may not sin; but if any one does sin, we have an advocate with the Father, Jesus Christ the righteous; and he is the expiation for our sins, and not for ours only but also for the sins of the whole world" (1 John 2:1, 2).

The Adventist affirmation of the ultimate triumph of God in the eschatological eradication of sin is expressed in these forceful words:

"The great controversy is ended. Sin and sinners are no more. The entire universe is clean. One pulse of harmony and gladness beats through the vast creation. From Him who created all, flow life and light and gladness throughout the realms of illimitable space. From the minutest atom to the greatest world, all things, animate and inanimate, in their unshadowed beauty and perfect joy, declare that God is love" (GC 678).

VIII. Implications for Christian Life

The doctrine of sin is a significant teaching of the Bible. Without a proper understanding of its reality and an adequate appreciation of its seriousness, we cannot have a full and deep discernment of the nature of God or the nature of humanity and its destiny. Nor can we understand the complexity of life and its environment.

A. Nature of God

The doctrine of sin reveals to us the nature of God. It shows us that God is not a vengeful tyrant or arbitrary dictator of the universe, demanding from His creatures absolute obedience. If anything, the origin of sin teaches us that God chose to trust His creatures with the power of choice, and that He shared with humanity part of His creative power. Further, the doctrine of sin teaches us that God is love and just. Even though His justice demanded that Adam and Eve be immediately destroyed because of the pollution of sin they brought into the world, God's love stepped in and met the demands of His justice in the provision He made for the eventuality of sin. Sin reveals to us that "God so loved the world that he gave his only Son, that whoever believes in him should not perish but have eternal life" (John 3:16).

B. Nature and Dignity of Humans

The doctrine of sin shows us that the human person did not evolve from a lower stage to a higher stage, as evolution holds. Rather it teaches that we were created in the image of God, in His likeness, a little lower than angels. God has conferred upon us a unique dignity, and to us He gave the dominion of rulership over this earth. The concept of the image and the likeness affirms to us that God shared part of Himself with us and endowed us with imagination, intellect, and creativity.

C. Greatness of God's Love

The doctrine of sin has its implication for our understanding of the greatness and richness of the love of God. Not only has He loved us and made provision for our salvation, but He in turn has made it possible for us to be sharers of love with each other. Indeed the creation and operation of the ideal human family is one of God's magnificent gifts, to be understood only when we know and see the alternative available in the destructive nature of sin. Further, the operation of Christian fellowship without regard to alienating factors such as race, color, ethnicity, language is possible only because of the redemptive love of God. In the absence of that redemptive love, we see only the presence of chaotic sin.

D. Power Over Temptation

The doctrine of sin teaches us the reality and power of temptation. Not just in the Garden of Eden, but in human existence and struggle, we continue to encounter the tempter with his subtleties and dangerous cunningness. But the history of sin shows us that we need not become victims of temptation:

through the grace of a loving God we can become conquerors.

E. Moral Accountability

The doctrine of sin carries a strong implication that human life cannot be lived in gray areas of indifference. Sin must be called by its right name, and a moral line must be drawn between that which is wrong and right. Therefore, the external moral law and the internal law of conscience unite to remind us that we are not and cannot be like God. Nor are we brutes without accountability for our actions. As a community of human beings, we have a commitment to shared values, and values have meaning only within the context of the glory of God.

F. Meaning and Purpose of Life

The doctrine of sin also shows that history has meaning and life has purpose. An understanding of sin shows us that in history, "when the time had fully come" (Gal. 4:4), Jesus resolved the problem of sin, and again in the fullness of the end-time, Jesus will return to eradicate sin and establish God's kingdom of righteousness. Thus Christian eschatology assures us that sin will be finally eradicated.

Not the least, the study of sin reveals the loving and relational nature of God. This appears in the first act of God after Adam sinned, which was to search for him, establishing links of intimate communication.

IX. Ellen G. White Comments

A. Humanity Before Sin

"In what consisted the strength of the assault made upon Adam, which caused his fall? It was not indwelling sin; for God made Adam after His own character, pure and upright. There were no corrupt principles in the first Adam, no corrupt propensities or tendencies to evil. Adam was as faultless as the angels before God's throne" (1BC 1083).

"It certainly was not God's purpose that man should be sinful. He made Adam pure and noble, with no tendency to evil. He placed him in Eden, where he had every inducement to remain loyal and obedient. The law was placed around him as a safeguard" (*ibid*. 1084).

B. The Origin of Sin

"We need the authentic history of the origin of the earth, of the fall of Lucifer, and of the introduction of sin into the world. Without the Bible, we should be bewildered by false theories. The mind would be subjected to the tyranny of superstition and falsehood. But, having in our possession an authentic history of the beginning of the world, we need not hamper ourselves with human conjectures and unreliable theories" (2MCP 742).

"It is impossible to explain the origin of sin so as to give a reason for its existence. . . . Nothing is more plainly taught in Scripture than that God was in no wise responsible for the entrance of sin; that there was no arbitrary withdrawal of divine grace, no deficiency in the divine government, that gave occasion for the uprising of rebellion" (GC 492, 493).

"Adam yielded to temptation and as we have the matter of sin and its consequence laid so distinctly before us, we can read from cause to effect and see the greatness of the act is not that which constitutes sin; but the disobedience of God's expressed will, which is a virtual denial of God, refusing the laws of His government" (1BC 1083).

C. The Nature and Essence of Sin

"When man sinned, all heaven was filled with sorrow; for through yielding to temptation, man became the enemy of God, a partaker of the Satanic nature" (ST Feb. 13, 1893).

"It is not safe for us to enter into controversy with Satan, or to linger to contemplate the advantages to be reaped by yielding to his suggestions. Sin is blinding and deceiving in its nature. Disobedience to God's commandments is too terrible to be contemplated for a moment. Sin means dishonour and disaster to every soul that indulges in transgression of God's holy law, which is immutable" (RH Oct. 9, 1894).

"The aggravating character of sin against such a God cannot be estimated any more than the heavens can be measured with a span. God is a moral governor as well as a Father. He is the Lawgiver. He makes and executes His laws. Law that has no penalty is of no force" (LDE 241).

"All sin is selfishness. Satan's first sin was a manifestation of selfishness. He sought to grasp power, to exalt self. A species of insanity led him to seek to supersede God. And the temptation that led Adam to sin was Satan's declaration that it was possible for man to attain to something more than he already enjoyed—possible for him to be as God Himself. The sowing of seeds of selfishness in the human heart was the first result of the entrance of sin into the world" (7MR 232, 233).

"Man was originally endowed with noble powers and a well-balanced mind. He was perfect in his being, and in harmony with God. His thoughts were pure, his aims holy. But through disobedience, his powers were perverted, and selfishness took the place of love. His nature became so weakened through transgression that it was impossible for him, in his own strength, to resist the power of evil. He was made captive by Satan, and would have remained so forever had not God specially interposed" (SC 17).

D. Consequences of Sin

"Sin not only shuts away from God, but destroys in the human soul both the desire and the capacity for knowing Him. Through sin, the whole human organism is deranged, the mind is perverted, the imagination corrupted; the faculties of the soul degraded. There is an absence of pure religion, of heart holiness. The converting power of God has not wrought in transforming the character. The soul is weak, and for want of moral force to overcome is polluted and debased" (PK 233).

"Every act of transgression, every neglect or rejection of the grace of Christ, is reacting upon yourself; it is hardening the heart, depraving the will, benumbing the understanding, and not only making you less inclined to yield, but less capable of yielding, to the tender pleading of God's Holy Spirit" (SC 33).

"[Sin] defaces the divine image, frustrates God's purpose in man's existence, degrades his God-given powers, narrows his capacity, leads to unholy imaginations, and gives loose rein to unsanctified passions. Sin! how hateful in the sight of God! Holy angels look upon it with abhorrence" (RH June 3, 1880).

"Man through sin has been severed from the life of God. His soul is palsied through the machinations of Satan, the author of sin. Of himself he is incapable of sensing sin, incapable of appreciating and appropriating the divine nature. Were it brought within his reach there is nothing in it that his natural heart would desire it. The bewitching power of Satan is upon him. All the ingenious subterfuges the devil can suggest are presented to his mind to prevent every good impulse. Every faculty and power given him of God has been used as a weapon against the divine Benefactor. So, although He loves him, God cannot safely impart to him the gifts and blessings He desires to bestow" (6BC 1099).

"The sin of man has brought the sure result—decay, deformity, and death. Today the whole world is tainted, corrupted, stricken with mortal disease. The earth groaneth under the continual transgression of the inhabitants thereof" (1BC 1085).

"To the angels there seemed to be no way of escape for the transgressor. They ceased their songs of praise, and throughout the heavenly courts there was mourning for the ruin sin had wrought. Out of harmony with the nature of

God, unyielding to the claims of His law, naught but destruction was before the human race. Since the divine law is as changeless as the character of God, there could be no hope for man unless some way could be devised whereby his transgression might be pardoned, his nature renewed, and his spirit restored to reflect the image of God. Divine love had conceived such a plan" (ST Feb. 13, 1893).

E. The Extent and Elimination of Sin

"Justice demands that sin be not merely pardoned, but the death penalty must be executed. God, in the gift of His only-begotten Son, met both these requirements. By dying in man's stead, Christ exhausted the penalty and provided a pardon" (AG 139).

"The death of Christ upon the cross made sure the destruction of him who has the power of death, who was the originator of sin. When Satan is destroyed, there will be none to tempt to evil; the atonement will never need to be repeated; and there will be no danger of another rebellion in the universe of God. That which alone can effectually restrain from sin in this world of darkness will prevent sin in heaven. The significance of the death of Christ will be seen by saints and angels. Fallen men could not have a home in the paradise of God without the Lamb slain from the foundation of the world" (5BC 1132).

"Behold the cross of Calvary. There is Jesus, who gave His life, not that men might continue in sin, not that they may have license to break the law of God, but that through this infinite sacrifice they may be saved from all sin" (TM 161, 162).

"We must realize that through belief in Him it is our privilege to be partakers of the divine nature, and so escape the corruption that is in the world through lust. Then we are cleansed from all sin, all defects of character. We need not retain one sinful propensity. . . . As we partake of the divine nature, hereditary and cultivated tendencies to wrong are cut away from the character, and we are made a living power for good" (7BC 943).

F. Implications for Christian Life

"Notwithstanding our unworthiness, we are to remember that there is One who can take away sin, and who is willing and anxious to save the sinner. With His own blood He paid the penalty for all wrongdoers. Every sin acknowledged before God with a contrite heart, He will remove" (ibid. 970).

"Do you believe that Christ, as your substitute, pays the debt of your transgression? Not, however, that you may continue in sin, but that you may be saved from your sins; that you, through the merits of His righteousness, may be reinstated to the favor of God. Do you know that a holy and just God will accept your efforts to keep His law, through the merits of His own beloved Son who died for your rebellion and sin?" (RH July 24, 1888).

"To follow the word of the Lord, to embrace the truth, involves cross-bearing and self-denial; but it is not safe to do otherwise than to bear the cross. As you see the light, walk in the light. Let a solemn, unalterable purpose take possession of you, and resolve in the strength and grace of God, that henceforth you will live for Him, and that no earthly consideration shall persuade you to disown the divine law of ten commandments, and thus disown your Saviour and your God. Seek your counsel of God, and you will find that the path of obedience to His commandments is the path of the just, that 'shineth more and more unto the perfect day.'" (RH Oct. 9, 1894).

"The Christian life is a warfare. . . . In this conflict of righteousness against unrighteousness we can be successful only by divine aid. Our finite will must be brought into submission to the will of the Infinite; the human will must be blended with the divine. This will bring the Holy Spirit to our aid; and every conquest will tend to the recovery of God's purchased possession, to the restoration of His image in the soul" (MYP 55).

X. Literature

Berkhof, L. *Systematic Theology*. Grand Rapids: Eerdmans, 1941.

———. *The History of Christian Doctrines*. Grand Rapids: Eerdmans, 1975.

Berkouwer, G. C. *Sin*. Grand Rapids: Eerdmans, 1971.

Bromiley, Geoffrey W. and others, eds. *International Standard Bible Encyclopedia*. Grand Rapids: Eerdmans, 1979.

Brunner, Emil, *Man in Revolt: A Christian Anthropology*. Trans. Olive Wyon. Philadelphia: Westminster Press, 1947.

Evangelical Dictionary of Biblical Theology. Ed. Walter A. Elwell. Grand Rapids: Baker, 1990.

Guthrie, Donald. New *Testament Theology*. Downers Grove, Ill.: InterVarsity, 1981.

Kittel, G., and G. Friedrich, eds. *Theological Dictionary of the New Testament*. 9 vols. Grand Rapids: Eerdmans, 1964-1974.

Ladd, George E. *A Theology of the New Testament*. Grand Rapids: Eerdmans, 1974.

The New International Dictionary of the Bible. Ed. Merrill C. Tenney. Grand Rapids: Zondervan, 1963.

Neufeld, Don F., ed. *The Seventh-day Adventist Encyclopedia*. Washington, D.C.: Review and Herald, 1976.

Niebuhr, Reinhold. *The Nature and Destiny of Man*. 2 vols. New York: Charles Scribner & Sons, 1964.

Schaff, Phillip. *The Nicene and Post-Nicene Fathers,* First Series. 14 vols. Grand Rapids: Eerdmans, 1971.

"Sin." *Interpreter's Dictionary of the Bible*. Nashville: Abingdon Press, 1962.

Strong, Augustus H. *Systematic Theology*. 3 vols. Valley Forge, Pa.: Judson, 1961.

Whidden II, Woodrow W. *The Soteriology of Ellen G. White*. Ph.D. dissertation, Drew University, 1989.

Wilson, William. *New Wilson's Old Testament Word Studies*. Grand Rapids: Kregel Publications, 1987.

Zachrison, Edwin Harry. *Seventh-day Adventists and Original Sin: A Study of the Early Development of the Seventh-day Adventist Understanding of the Effect of Adam's Sin on His Posterity*. Ph.D. dissertation, Andrews University, 1984.

Salvation

Ivan T. Blazen

Introduction

Salvation is the universal theme of Scripture. All other major themes are subdivisions or explications of it. The form of salvation varies, but the underlying structure is the same: God visits His people and delivers them from those problems or powers that imperil their existence. From the beginning, when God clothed the guilty and shamed parents of the human race, to the day when God's people enter the New Jerusalem, God is viewed as dynamically involved with the deliverance of the human race. This is so much the case that the word "Saviour" is not only coordinated with the name "God," but becomes a definition of it, a name for God. As God is the "God of our salvation" (1 Chron.

16:35; Ps. 79:9; Hab. 3:18), so He is called and sometimes addressed as "Savior" (2 Sam. 22:3; Isa. 43:3; 45:15; Jer. 14:8; Luke 1:47; 1 Tim. 1:1; 2:3; Titus 1:3; 2:10; Jude 25). God may employ various human agents to effect His purposes, but it is He alone who saves (Isa. 43:11; 45:21). "Deliverance belongs to the Lord" (Ps. 3:8), who has, does, and will deliver people "out of all their troubles" (34:17). He wishes none to be lost (2 Peter 3:9), but all to be saved (1 Tim. 2:4), through Jesus' name (Matt. 1:21; Acts 4:12; 1 Thess. 5:9; Rom. 10:13). In sharing human suffering Jesus has become the pioneer and source of eternal salvation to all who follow Him (Heb. 2:10; 5:9).

I. Biblical Words and Foundational Concepts

A. *The Terminology of Salvation*

The vocabulary of Scripture is rich in words that correspond to the word "salvation." The Hebrew Bible contains a number of significant expressions, which, while having their own nuances, are often synonymous with each other.

The frequently occurring term *nāṣal,* which means to pull or draw out, signifies the rescue or deliverance of a person. God is a refuge and fortress because he delivers from deadly dangers (Ps. 91:3) and rescues his people for long life (verses 14-16). Two other terms for deliverance are *mālaṭ* and *pālaṭ.* They contain the ideas of escape and bringing to security or safety. The most notable occurrence of *mālaṭ* is in Joel 2:32, where it refers to eschatological salvation during the terrors of the day of the Lord. Further nuances to the concept of deliverance are found in *gā'al* and *pādāh,* which, when used with reference to salvation, carry the sense of God's putting forth special effort or paying a ransom (Ex. 6:6; 15:13; Ps. 77:14, 15; Isa. 43:3, 4; Jer. 50:34).

The word *ḥāyāh* adds to the dimension of God's grace and providence working in history to save or preserve life. This is illustrated by Lot, whose life was spared from the destruction upon Sodom by the mercy of God (Gen. 19:16, 19), and Joseph, through whom God, contrary to the evil intent of his brothers, overruled to save many lives (45:5, 7, 8; 50:20).

The most extensive and significant of the words for salvation in the Old Testament are *yāša'* and its cognates. The basic meaning is that of being brought from a narrow or oppressive environment into a spacious one, from bad into good circumstances where life flourishes and protection from enemies occurs (Ps. 18:18, 19). The salvation which the *yāša'* family of words contemplates is rooted in history and affects past, present, and future. In the past God's salvation is seen in His deliverance of the Hebrew slaves from Egypt. In the present it manifests itself in God's freeing His people from every kind of negative situation in which they are constrained or confined. With respect to the future, God will act again for His people, for His salvation never ends (Isa. 51:6). So effective will be God's salvation that the people will speak of salvation and praise rather than violence and destruction (60:18). Future salvation can be seen further in such texts as Isaiah 43:11-21; 51:1-6; 62:1-12; Jeremiah 46:27; Ezekiel 36:24-30, 33-38; Zechariah 8:7, 8, 13; 9:14-17; 10:6, 7.

In the LXX, the Greek version of the OT utilized by the earliest Christians, and in the NT, the Greek word that is the greatly favored translation of the Hebrew words for salvation is *sōzō* and its cognates. These words emphasize spiritual, moral, and eschatological deliverance. By God's action human beings are delivered from sin and Satan, suffering and death. In harmony with the OT, where salvation is past, present, and future, a person who experiences God's salvation was saved (Rom. 8:24; Eph. 2:5, 8), is being saved (1 Cor. 1:18; 15:2), and shall be saved (Matt. 24:13; Rom. 5:9, 10). Contrary to those who hold that the sum and substance of salvation is in the past ("realized eschatology") or in the present (existentialist viewpoints), future salvation must be underlined as well, for in the NT approximately one fifth of the occurrences of *sōzō* words refer to salvation in the end time.

In addition to the *sōzō* group the NT utilizes *lytroō* and its derivatives, *lytron, lytroomai, antilytron, lytrōsis, lytrōtēs,* and *apolytrosis* (a crucial term). This word family speaks of the freedom made possible through God's action in Jesus Christ. Sometimes, as in certain uses of *lytroō* in the LXX (Ps. 31:5 [30:6]; 103:4 [102:4]; Isa. 43:1), or in some NT passages, there may be no suggestion of payment or ransom (Luke 24:21; 21:28; Rom. 8:23; Eph. 4:30). In other cases the notion of price is clearly present (Rom. 3:24, 25; Eph. 1:7; 1 Peter 1:18, 19). Consequently, the full meaning of this word includes three ideas: bondage, freedom, and (often) price. Similar to the *lytroō* words is the word *rhyomai,* which means to deliver, rescue, save, or preserve.

B. The Historical Character of Salvation

The OT sees salvation as taking place in history, rather than in myth and ritual, as in the ancient Near Eastern religions. God's deliverance of Israel from Egypt is the supreme demonstration of His saving action and presages His salvation in the future. The contention of Isaiah 43:11 that there is one God and Saviour is applied to the Exodus in Hosea 13:4. God's concern for Israel manifested itself in His rescue from Egyptian bondage, deliverance at the Red Sea, care in the wilderness, and guidance into Canaan (Deut. 6:21-23; 11:3-5; 26:8, 9). The Exodus from Egypt by the power of God (7:19) was the focus of Israel's faith. This saving history was recited in confessional statements (6:20-24; 26:5-9; Joshua 24:2-13), rehearsed as the preamble to the Law (Ex. 20:2; Deut. 5:6), connected with the major festivals (Deut. 16:1-3, 9-12; Lev. 23:39-43), celebrated in psalms of praise (Ps. 66:1-7; 78:11-16; 105; 106; 135:8, 9; 136:10-16), and used as the interpretive key for understanding the meaning of special rituals in the life of Israel (Ex. 13:3-16, especially verses 8 and 14).

In saving His people out of Egypt, God slew Leviathan, a symbol for antidivine forces. Psalm 74:12-14 says that God crushed the heads of the dragon Leviathan. In 89:8-10 Leviathan reappears under the name of Rahab (cf. Isa. 51:9), and God's victory in the Exodus is again recounted, for God dries up the sea, crushes Rahab, and scatters the enemies of God. What God did at the Exodus gives promise of what He will do for Israel's redemption in the future. Isaiah 27:1 prophesies that God will slay Leviathan, the fleeing serpent or sea dragon. The story of future salvation, of which the Exodus is the prototype, is complete when the dragon, expelled from heaven (Rev. 12:7-9) and attempting to destroy the church (verses 13-17) as Pharaoh did Israel, is defeated along with the beast to whom the dragon had given its power (Rev. 13:1, 2; 19:20; 20:10).

The salvific power of God manifested in the Exodus was to be revealed again in the deliverance of God's people from their exile in Babylon and Persia (Isa. 49:8-26; 44:28-45:17). In a striking manner the language of the Exodus is utilized in depicting this return (Isa. 43:16, 17; 48:21; 52:12).

Moreover, in the NT, salvation in Jesus is patterned after the Exodus deliverance. Parallels include redemption by blood (Ex. 12:1-13; Rom. 3:24, 25; Eph. 1:7), coming out of Egypt (Hosea 11:1; Matt. 2:15), "This is my son" (Ex. 4:22; Matt. 3:17), the number 40 and the wilderness motif (Ex. 16:35; 34:28; Num. 14:33; Matt. 4:2; Luke 4:2). Further, the death of Jesus is described in terms of the Passover lamb (1 Cor. 5:7; 1 Peter 1:19), and baptism and the Lord's Supper are viewed as counterparts to Israel's experience with Moses in the sea and the reception of manna from heaven and water from a rock (1 Cor. 10).

Thus the Exodus, the greatest event of salvation prior to the coming of Christ, is woven into the fabric of the biblical portrayal of salvation history. It may be concluded that God's salvation in the Exodus explained Israel's past, gave meaning to its present, inspired hope for its future, illumined the story of Christ and the earliest Christians, and is the promise of final victory over evil for the church. In all of this God was, is, and will be the Saviour. The part of human beings, as at the Exodus, is to stand still and see the salvation of the Lord (Ex. 14:13, 14; cf. 2 Chron. 20:17). What the Exodus is to the OT, the life, death, and resurrection of Jesus are to the NT.

C. That From Which God Saves

In the biblical portrayal of salvation God saves from many negative realities. First, there is salvation from those who endanger people. These include the wicked (Ps. 37:40), violent (Ps. 140:1, 4, 5), bloodthirsty (Ps. 59:2), persecutors (Ps. 7:1; 142:6), deceivers (Ps. 43:1; 144:7, 8, 11), hateful (2 Sam. 22:18), enemies (Num. 10:9; 2 Sam. 22:4; Ps. 18:3; 31:15; Luke 1:69, 71), and nations bringing servitude or struggle (Judges 15:18; 2 Kings. 13:5; 2 Chron. 20:17; Micah 6:4).

Second, God saves from difficult or dangerous situations or problems. These include trouble in general (Ps. 34:6, 17; 54:7; 81:7), distress (1 Sam. 10:19; Ps. 107:13, 19), tribulation (1 Sam. 26:24), violence (2 Sam. 22:3; Ps. 22:20), illness (Matt. 9:21; Luke 8:36), fears (Ps. 34:4), (even the fear of death [Heb. 2:15], and death itself (Ps. 6:4, 5; 56:13; 68:19, 20; 116:8; Heb. 5:7).

Third, God delivers from mankind's sinful state and its consequences. Here Scripture speaks of lostness (Luke 19:10), iniquities or transgressions (Ps. 39:8; 51:1-9; 79:9; Matt. 1:21), bloodguiltiness (Ps. 51:14), corrupt society (Acts 2:40), the present evil age (Gal. 1:4), the dominion of darkness (Col. 1:13), subjection to the prince of the air, passions of the flesh (Eph. 2:1-5), and God's wrath (Rom. 5:9).

D. The Persons Whom God Saves

According to Scripture the recipients of God's salvation are those who, prompted by God's covenant love and grace, realize their need and show humble dependence upon God. They are responsive and receptive toward Him. In the NT they are spoken of as persons of faith. Contrary to charges that basing salvation upon faith cheapens the human response to mere intellectual belief or assent, biblical faith is a receptivity to all God gives and commitment to God of all a person is and has. Because of this the personal actualization of redemption requires repentance (Mark 1:14, 15; Luke 3:3; Acts 2:37, 38; 3:19; Rom. 2:4; 2 Cor. 7:10) and its fruits (Matt. 5:1-12; Luke 3:7-14). In harmony with this, the Hebrew Scriptures see God working savingly for those who fear (reverence) Him and hope in Him (Ps. 33:18-22), those who trust in Him (Ps. 22:4, 5; 86:2) and call upon Him (Ps. 55:16; 107:13), the humble and contrite (Ps. 34:18; Job 22:29), those who wait for God (Isa. 25:9) and take refuge in Him (Ps. 37:40), those who manifest covenant faithfulness or loyalty (Hab. 2:4), the upright in heart (Ps. 7:10), and those who seek God's precepts (Ps. 119:94). Thus, in the light of a wholistic biblical teaching, the faith that grasps salvation is the movement of the heart, mind, and life toward God. Faith and faithfulness are two sides of the same coin of relationship to God.

E. Humanity's Need for Divine Salvation

1. The Reality and Results of Sin

Sin is the ultimate human problem, for which divine salvation is the only solution. (For full treatment of sin, see Sin.) Beginning in pride and the desire to be like God (Gen. 3:4; Isa. 14:1-20; Eze. 28:1-19), sin is a universal actuality (1 Kings 8:46; 2 Chron. 6:36; Job 4:17; Ps. 14:1-3; Eccl. 7:20; Isa. 9:17; Dan. 9:11; Rom. 3:9-11, 23; 5:12, 19; 1 John 1:8, 10). It has resulted in universal condemnation and death (Rom. 5:14-18; 6:23; James 1:15).

2. The Nature of Sin

Since salvation is so directly connected with the reality of sin, the meaning of sin must be clarified so the nature of salvation may be more clearly apprehended.

a. Sin as deed. The first and most immediate way in which sin manifests itself is as a misdeed. The scriptural indictment of humanity's sinful actions is described in Romans 1:18–3:20. Even supposed righteous deeds are as unclean rags (Isa. 64:6).

b. Sin as depravity of the heart. However, sin is more than a misdeed. It may end in an action, but it begins in the inclination of the heart. Scripture testifies that sin is a perversion of a person's heart and will, moral nature, and innermost being. The depth of the heart's pollution is graphically described in Genesis 6:5; Isaiah 1:5, 6; 29:13; Jeremiah 11:8; 16:12; Matthew 7:18-23; and James 1:14, 15; 4:1, 2.

c. Sin as enslaving power. The Bible describes sinful actions as the product of living under the rule of an alien, evil, and enslaving power such as is described in Romans 5-8. Always occurring in the singular except in Romans 7:5, sin is pictured as a king or lord (Rom. 5:12-14, 21) to whom humans yield themselves in obedient service (Rom. 6:6, 12, 13). Like a harsh tyrant or wicked taskmaster, sin holds people in slavery (verses 6, 16-18, 20; 7:14) and pays them wages (Rom. 6:23). Like a demon it can dwell in a person (Rom. 7:17, 20), deceive that person (verse 11), as the serpent deceived Eve (Gen. 3:13), and even effect death in the person (Rom. 6:16, 23; 7:11, 14). Its suppression of mankind can be produced by the imposition of its own law (Rom. 7:23; 8:2) or, by subversively working its destructive purposes through God's law (Rom. 7:8, 11, 13; cf. 1 Cor. 15:56). It can lie dormant or suddenly spring to life, stirring the sinful passions to action (Rom. 7:5-9). Sin as a power stands opposed to God (Rom. 6:23) and, like a criminal, is condemned by God (Rom. 8:3). To speak of sin as a power expresses the paradox that sin is something we do, and yet which precedes and determines our doing. In sinning it is we who sin, yet not we ourselves (Rom. 7:17, 20). Thus, in what we do, we are really acting out the power of sin which controls us.

3. Salvific Needs Because of Sin

When sin is considered to be an act of wrongdoing, the sinner is called upon to repent, confess, be baptized, and receive forgiveness of sins and cleansing from guilt (Acts 2:38; 2 Peter 3:9; 1 John 1:9). This is the experience of justification.

When sin is regarded as the evil inclination of the heart or will, the sinner needs a new heart and right spirit (Ps. 51:10). God promises to supply these very gifts (Eze. 11:19; 36:26). This speaks to the issues of regeneration, conversion, and sanctification.

When sin is viewed as an enslaving, death-dealing power—a radicalizing of the concept of sin as an evil heart—what is necessary is more than repentance, forgiveness, or a change of heart. An exchange of lordships from that of sin and death to that of Christ and life is required (Rom. 6). Only under Christ's lordship is there true freedom.

In summary, the sinner's needs vis-à-vis the three aspects of sin are forgiveness, renewal, and freedom under a new Lord. These lie at the heart of the biblical message of salvation and will be spelled out in section III.

II. The Divine Plan of Salvation

A. *God's Decision in Eternity*

The salvation of humankind does not result from a divine afterthought or improvisation made necessary because of an unexpected turn of events after sin arose. Rather, it issues from a divine plan for man's redemption formulated before the founding of this world (1 Cor. 2:7; Eph. 1:3, 14; 2 Thess. 2:13, 14) and rooted in God's everlasting love for humanity (Jer. 31:3).

This plan encompasses eternity past, the historical present, and eternity future. It includes such realities and blessings as election and predestination to be God's holy people and bear likeness to Christ, redemption and forgiveness, the unity of all things in Christ, sealing with the Holy Spirit, reception

275

of the eternal inheritance, and glorification (Eph. 1:3-14). Central to the plan is the suffering and death of Jesus, which was not an accident of history nor the product of merely human decision, but was rooted in God's redemptive purpose (Acts 4:27, 28). Jesus was in truth "the Lamb slain from the foundation of the world" (Rev. 13:8, KJV).

Cohering with the reality of a plan are Jesus' statements as to why He came into the world. He came to fulfill the law (Matt. 5:17), to call sinners (Matt. 9:13), to be a friend of outcasts (Matt. 11:19), to seek and save the lost (Luke 19:10; cf. 1 Tim. 1:15), and to serve others and give His life as a ransom for them (Mark 10:45). All that He does is in His Father's name (John 5:43) and according to His will (verse 30). As the revealer of God (John 1:14, 18; 14:7-10), He brings people to God (verse 6) and to the eternal life or salvation that God grants to everyone who has faith in Him (John 3:15-17; see Great Controversy I. A).

B. God's Covenants in Time

1. The Essence and Unity of God's Covenants

The way by which God's eternal decision for human salvation is effected is through God's covenants in time. Although the Bible speaks of covenants in the plural (Rom. 9:4; Gal. 4:24; Eph. 2:12), there is only one basic covenant of salvation in Scripture. It is promissory in character—the blessings and salvation of God are given by God, not earned by human beings—but looks for humanity's response of faith and obedience. The heart of this covenant is God's steadfast love, spoken of throughout Scripture and at times equated with the covenant (Deut. 7:9; 1 Kings 8:23; Neh. 9:32; Dan. 9:4). The plural, covenants, means that God advances His saving purpose by restating His covenant in various ways to meet the needs of His people in different times and settings. Each form of the covenant plays its part in His unitary purpose of salvation.

2. The Adamic, Noachic, and Everlasting Covenants

The Adamic covenant refers to God's promise in Genesis 3:15, called the Protoevangelium (first announcement of the gospel), according to which, in its ultimate meaning, Christ the seed would conquer the evil one (Rom. 16:20). The Noachic covenant is a promise of grace and life. God vows to preserve creaturely life upon the earth (Gen. 6:18-20; 9:9-11). As a promise of mercy for all, this covenant is called an everlasting covenant (verse 16). The "everlasting" concept is also used for the Abrahamic covenant (Gen. 17:7, 13, 19; 1 Chron. 16:17; Ps. 105:10), the Sinai covenant with its Sabbath emphasis (Ex. 31:16), the Davidic covenant (2 Sam. 23:5; Isa. 55:3; Eze. 37:26, 27), the new covenant promise of the restoration of Israel (Jer. 32:40, restating 31:33; Eze. 16:60), and the sacrifice of Jesus (Heb. 13:20).

3. The Abrahamic, Sinaitic, and Davidic Covenants

The Abrahamic covenant of grace (Gen. 12:1-3; 15:1-5; 17:1-14) is fundamental to the entire course of salvation history (Gal. 3:6-9, 15-18). Through Abraham's seed, referring not only to his numberless descendants, but in particular to his one descendant, Christ (verse 16), God would bless the world. All who would be a part of Abraham's seed would find God to be their God, and they would be His people. Circumcision would be a sign (Gen. 17:11) of this already existing right relation to God constituted by faith (Gen. 15:6; Rom. 4:9-12).

The Sinaitic covenant, given in the context of redemption from bondage (Ex. 19:4; 20:2; Deut. 1-3) and containing God's sacrificial provisions for atonement and forgiveness of sin, was also a covenant of grace and a reiteration of major emphases in the Abrahamic covenant (special relation of God to His people: Genesis 17:7, 8 with Exodus 19:5, 6; a great nation: Genesis 12:2 with Exodus 19:6 and 32:10; and obedience: Genesis 17:9-14; 22:16-18 with Exodus 19:5 and throughout the Pentateuch). When the people broke the Sinai covenant, Moses prayed that God would remember His promises made in the Abrahamic covenant (Ex. 32:13). The special emphasis upon the law at Sinai indicated that the fulfillment of the Abrahamic covenant awaited a people for whom the reality of God's grace would be exhibited by obedience. Israel could not become a blessing for the world until it first lived as God's people and a "holy nation" (Ex. 19:6).

The Davidic covenant is interconnected with both the Abrahamic (Eze. 37:24-27) and the Mosaic (2 Sam. 7:22-24). In this covenant David would be a prince and king over Israel (verse 8; Jer. 30:9; Eze. 37:24, 25) and would build God's house or sanctuary (2 Sam. 7:7-13; Eze. 37:26-28). In this place God, who in the Abrahamic and Sinaitic covenants wanted to be their God and them to be His people, could dwell with them.

4. The New Covenant

The promise of a new covenant first occurs in Jeremiah 31:31-33. It is lodged in the context of Israel's return from exile and the blessings that God would grant. As the breaking of the covenant at Sinai (verse 32) brought Israel into exile, so the remaking of this covenant would preserve them and be their hope for the future. The content of this new covenant was the same as that of Sinai. There was the same God-people relationship and the same law (verse 33). The Sinaitic covenant was not outmoded or old, but broken. Reconstitution of this covenant would be premised upon forgiveness of the people's sins (verse 34) and the guarantee that God would place His covenant law (and reverence for Him, Jer. 32:40) within the hearts of His people (Jer. 31:33). This would bring about the intimate knowledge of God among all God's people (verse 34) and the full and lasting actualization of the covenant at Sinai. In Ezekiel 36:25-28, the internalization of God's law is because of God's renewing the heart

and putting His Spirit within it as the motive force of the new obedience.

In harmony with the emphasis on forgiveness (Jer. 31:34) and the Spirit (Eze. 36:37), the New Testament extends the concept of the new covenant to the blood of Christ, which brings forgiveness of sins (Matt. 26:28; Luke 22:20; 1 Cor. 11:25; Heb. 9:15; 12:24) and to the ministry of the Spirit, which brings life (2 Cor. 3:6).

5. The Old Covenant

The concept of an "old covenant" is explicitly referred to only in 2 Cor. 3:14, but is implied in Paul's use of "two covenants" in Galatians 4:24 and in the references in Hebrews to a "first covenant" (8:7, 13; 9:1, 15, 18), "second covenant" (9:7), and "better covenant" (7:22; 8:6).

Paul's statements on the covenants in 2 Corinthians and Galatians can be properly understood only in terms of his polemic against Judaizing opponents whom he saw as making the law, rather than Christ, central. Within this polemical context the old covenant in 2 Corinthians 3:14 stands for the Mosaic code of Sinai (verse 15) as read with a veil over one's eyes, that is, read non-Christologically as mere letter. As such it kills (verse 6). When the veil is removed in Christ (verses 15, 16), and one perceives the law's true content and meaning, what is seen is the life-changing glory of the Lord (verse 18) rather than the glory of the law. And to be related to the Spirit of the Lord, in contrast with the letter alone, brings freedom (verse 17) and life (verse 6; cf. Rom. 7:6).

In terms of Galatians it is clear that stress on obedience to law must never be separated from the primacy of a faith relationship with God. When that happens the law does not achieve its goal of leading to life (as originally intended, Deut. 6:24; Rom. 7:10), but leads rather to condemnation (Gal. 3:10, citing Deut. 27:26). Paul's equation of the Sinai covenant with bondage in Galatians 4:24, 25 should be explained from this perspective. The Sinai covenant, originally resting upon the reality of God's redemption of Israel from bondage, His promise to be their God and they His people, and containing a sacrificial system teaching atonement and forgiveness, was not a system of bondage. However, when law is separated from promise and faith from works, the covenant is perverted, and slavery rather than freedom results. The proper relationship between promise and law is found in Galatians 3:15–4:7. Here Paul argues that the only way to be justified is through the Abrahamic covenant of grace received through faith. The law of Sinai was not contrary to the promise to Abraham (Gal. 3:21), but fostered it by leading to Christ (verse 24) so that "what was promised to faith in Jesus Christ might be given to those who believe" (verse 22). The law's function as "custodian" ceases when a mature relationship with Christ is formed (verse 25; 4:1-5).

For Hebrews the reason for a second or better covenant is that God found the promises of the people at Sinai faulty, for they broke them (Heb. 8:8, 9). There was need for better promises (verse 6), and Hebrews explains these in terms of the new covenant promises of Jeremiah 31:33, where God reaffirms the covenant of Sinai and promises divine enablement to keep it. Further, there was need for a better sacrifice (Heb. 9:23) that could bring the reality of cleansing from sin (Heb. 10:2-4). The sacrificial laws of the Sinai covenant were indeed a shadow of the good things coming, but not the "true form of these realities" (verse 1). Thus, the first/second covenant motif of Hebrews is related to promise-fulfillment and type-antitype modes of thought.

III. Components of Salvation

As noted in I. E. 3, three aspects of the sin problem must be addressed. The solution of the problem lies in a new relationship with God, a new assurance before God, and a new life from God.

According to biblical teaching, especially as articulated by the apostle Paul, all the elements of salvation are found only "in Christ" (e.g., Eph. 1:1-14). This phrase, or its equivalent, which occurs in Paul's writings 164 times, refers to a personal relationship with Christ rather than to a merely legal status. An examination of its usages reveals that it is an experiential reality involving the most intimate union possible between the risen Christ and the believer. Because the believer is united with the risen Lord through the indwelling of His Spirit, he or she is made a part of the saving events of Christ's death and resurrection and included in the body of Christ, the church. As a result, the believer personally receives all the blessings of salvation which flow from Christ and exist in the fellowship of believers.

A. A New Relationship With God

The new relationship with God includes justification, reconciliation, and adoption.

1. Justification and Righteousness

a. Terminology. The verb "justify" is based upon the Hebrew *ṣadaq,* which means to be just or righteous and, in the causative *(hiphil)* form, to give a verdict in favor of, to treat or declare as righteous, to acquit, to vindicate, to restore to the right. The Hebrew nouns *ṣedeq* and *ṣᵉdāqāh* mean justice, rightness, or righteousness in terms of conformity to the relationship with God stipulated in His covenant law. The adjective *ṣaddîq* means just, lawful, or righteous. Corresponding to these Hebrew terms, and with essentially the same meanings, are the Greek verb *dikaioō,* the adjective *dikaiōs,* and the noun *dikaiosynē.* The nouns *dikaiōsis* and *dikaiōma* denote justification, though the latter term may also mean just requirement.

b. Forensic background of justification. The Hebrew and Greek verbs are forensic, meaning that they are to be understood in terms of the pronouncement that a judge renders in a legal case. If the judge finds for the accused, a verdict of acquittal or justification

278

is rendered; if he finds against the accused, the verdict is one of condemnation.

This forensic usage, with its covenantal context in the relationship between God and Israel, is the primary background for the NT teaching of justification by faith. However, this background, while vital to the biblical teaching, does not exhaust it. Court judgments and relationships are translated into the higher key of forgiving grace and a personal relationship between humans and God. The concept of God as judge is exceeded, though not superseded, by the concept of God as Father. The forensic language of justification flows into the theology of the inexhaustible and superabounding riches of God's gift of grace in Christ.

c. Antecedents. In Scripture, the apostle Paul most fully expounds the doctrine of justification. However, his exposition finds its preparation in the OT and particularly in the teaching of Jesus. The OT, with such emphases as the reckoning of righteousness or non-reckoning of sin (Gen. 15:6), the equation of righteousness with God's redemptive activities (Ps. 31:1; 143:11, 12), the forgiveness of the grossest sins and sinners (2 Chron. 33:1-13; Ps. 51), and the replacement of dirty apparel with clean or rich clothing (Zech. 3:1-5), supply foundational concepts for NT reflection on justification.

The image of clothing in Zechariah has affinity with Jesus' teaching on the wedding garment in Matthew 22:1-14. In order to be properly attired for the king's wedding banquet (an earthly illustration relating to entry into the kingdom of heaven), one needs a wedding robe. Without it one has no legitimate place at the wedding despite the gracious invitation received. The parable does not speak of what the robe signifies or how one gets it, but Scripture provides answers elsewhere. In Isaiah 61:10 exultant joy is heard because God "has clothed me with the garments of salvation, he has covered me with the robe of righteousness." The same note of joy is struck in the parable of the prodigal son when the father, representing God, joyously grants a robe

to his son (Luke 15:22). Galatians 3:26, 27, referring to those who have become God's justified children through faith and baptism into Christ, says that these are they who "have put on Christ." Thus, in the wider context of Scripture, the robe in the wedding parable may ultimately be seen as God's righteousness given in Christ.

In the story of the Pharisee and the publican (Luke 18:9-14) it is not pride in one's goodness or legal accomplishments that qualifies for God's verdict of justification but a repentant spirit and an earnest appeal for God's mercy. Even if every duty were to be performed, humans would still be unworthy servants (Luke 17:10). Thus, God's justifying grace is always needed.

Jesus' teaching on becoming right with God is seen in His deeds, for Jesus welcomed sinners and ate with them (Mark 2:15-17; Luke 15:2). This coheres with Jesus' parables of God's seeking, restoring grace, even for those who have moved far from Him (Luke 15:3-32). Jesus may not have used the phrase "righteousness by faith," as did Paul, but this teaching was a vital part of His mission and message.

d. The righteousness of God. The letter to the Romans, with important assists from Galatians and Philippians, is Scripture's most salient source for understanding justification by faith. Romans 1:16, 17 establishes the thesis of the entire letter. Verse 16 declares that the gospel, as the proclamation of God's Son as Christ and Lord (verses 3, 4), is the power that will most certainly lead everyone who has faith to salvation. Verse 17 explains that the gospel leads to salvation because in it the righteousness of God is being revealed. The connection of thoughts between verse 16 and verse 17, as well as the contrast with wrath in verse 18 (cf. Rom. 3:19, 20 with 21), shows that God's righteousness is a saving reality. The unrighteousness and wrath from which God's righteousness saves are described in Romans 1:18–3:20. Here the sordid reality of human sin is painted, and the wrath that rightly falls upon sinners is pictured as past (God handed them over [Rom. 1:24, 26, 28]), present (verse 18), and future (Rom. 2:2, 5, 8, 9). The conclusion of the matter is reached in the judgment scene of Romans 3:19, 20, where the whole world is guilty and no appeal to works is valid. Lost humanity awaits the sentence of death, the wage sin pays (Rom. 6:23). Over against this picture of sin and wrath, Romans 3:21 again takes up the theme of God's righteousness begun in Romans 1:16, 17. "But now" introduces the reversal of lostness under sin and wrath by the revelation of God's righteousness which creates a new beginning for those who receive it by faith (Rom. 3:22).

The view of God's righteousness as a saving activity comports with a significant class of usages found in the OT, particularly in Isaiah and the Psalms. In a number of texts God's righteousness is coordinated with, or synonymous to, His salvation or deliverance. Isaiah 46:13 states: "I bring near my deliverance [righteousness], it is not far off, and my salvation will not tarry; I will put salvation in Zion." Verses of the same import are Isaiah 51:5; 56:1; 59:16; 61:10. The synonymity is apparent, for God is one who announces "vindication [righteousness], mighty to save" (Isa. 63:1). Indeed, God is "a righteous God and a Savior" (Isa. 45:21; see also Ps. 24:5; 31:1; 40:10; 51:14; 71:15; 143:11). In certain texts God's righteousness is coordinated with His steadfast love or mercy (Ps. 36:5, 6, 10; 89:14).

This equation of righteousness with salvation or mercy in Isaiah and the Psalms gives a biblical precedent to what is already clear from the contextual connections of righteousness in Romans 1-3. We may deduce that the righteousness of God points not so much to an attribute of God but, in the dynamic mode of Hebrew thought, to a divine redemptive activity that puts people who are in the wrong into a right relationship with God. It is a covenantal concept.

e. Facets of justification

(1) Justification as a right relationship with God. In justification a person in a wrong (broken) relationship to God comes into a right relationship with Him. This would be better seen if the words "justify" and "justification" (based upon the Latin Vulgate, which assumes a "making just," *justum facere*) had been translated "rightify" and "rightification." All the terms begin with the stem *dik* in Greek and, therefore, are best begun with the stem *right* in English. In this way the interconnection between justification and righteousness is immediately evident. That the two are in fact synonymous (except where righteousness words are used in a strictly ethical sense, as in Romans 5:7; 6:13) is shown in two ways. First, while Paul announces his topic for Romans as the righteousness of God (1:17; 3:21), he goes on to speak mostly of justification. Second, justification and righteousness are equated in Romans 4:5.

(2) Justification as acquittal. A meaning of justification directly related to its forensic or juridical background is "acquittal," the opposite being "condemnation." This contrasting word pair is found in Deuteronomy 25:1; Proverbs 17:15; Matthew 12:37; Romans 5:16, 18; 8:33, 34; and 2 Corinthians 3:9. Thus, in justification, God saves sinners from condemnation for their sins (Rom. 8:1) by acquitting them of all charges.

(3) Justification as the reckoning of righteousness. The most important passage for understanding justification is Romans 4. Here Abraham, whom Jews considered a paragon of virtue, is brought forth to illustrate what the forefather of God's people found, and what his descendants may find as well (verses 1-5, 22-24). If the best need God's righteousness, so do all. That Abraham was justified by his good works is denied in verse 2 by Paul's declaration that Abraham could not boast before God. The implication is that if one cannot boast in the Creator's presence, justification cannot be by works. Thus, verse 2 shows us what Abraham did not find. Verse 3, quoting Genesis 15:6, describes what he did find, namely a divine reckoning of righteousness to him when he believed God. The line of argument

in verses 1-6 reveals three major stages: the divine promise of blessing, the human response of faith, and the divine pronouncement of righteousness. In other words, faith is declared to be a right response to God's grace and indicative of a right relationship with Him. Righteousness, or a right standing with God, does not result from the promise or faith by itself but from the cause-effect interaction between the two. The promise elicits faith, and faith receives the promise. The argument in Romans 4:3 is that if divine righteousness is reckoned, it can never be considered as man's achievement, but only as God's grace. Verse 4 indicates how things operate on the human level: people work and get pay for it, not grace. Verse 5, on the other hand, indicates how things operate on the divine level: by abandoning working for righteousness in favor of trusting (having faith in) the God who justifies the ungodly, this trust or faith is reckoned as righteousness.

To speak of the ungodly as being justified or reckoned as righteous was a revolutionary statement. To Paul's Jewish contemporaries it seemed supportive of ungodliness—hence the charges against Paul in 3:8 and 6:1, 15—and directly contrary to the Hebrew Scriptures, which say that God will not acquit the wicked (Ex. 23:7) and that those who do so are an abomination to God (Prov. 17:15). In this world of thought it is the just whom God pronounces just (cf. 1 Kings. 8:32). What answer can be given to the apparent ethical dilemma Paul's words pose? According to the Psalms, God himself is justified in His condemnation of evil (51:4). What warrants then, His justifying the ungodly rather than the godly? In Psalm 143:2 we read, "Enter not into judgment with thy servant; for no man living is righteous before thee." In this light, God's judgment upon the unrighteous could only be "Guilty!" However, Paul teaches that God does enter into judgment with His unrighteous people and, incredibly, the verdict is not "Guilty!" but "Righteous!" What supports this seeming contradiction? First, it must be remembered that Paul, in harmony with verse 2, taught that everyone was under the power of sin and short of God's glory (Rom. 3:9, 23). Thus, if anyone were to be justified, it would have to be from among the ungodly. Second, Paul did not teach merely that God justified the ungodly, but that He justified the ungodly who placed their faith and trust in Him. These are people who have repentantly responded "Yes!" to God's verdict upon sin and have cast themselves upon His mercy. This is already a new alignment with God, a saying "Amen!" to God. The Hebrew verb 'āman, from which the English "Amen" is derived, is the word in Genesis 15:6, quoted in Romans 4:3, for Abraham's believing God. To have faith is, indeed, the right response to God. Third, justifying faith is in the atoning sacrifice that God has provided (verse 25). This accords with the sacrificial system of Israel, whereby acceptance with God was achieved through sacrifice, and with those numerous OT passages where forgiveness is granted to the penitent (e.g., Ps. 51).

(4) Justification as divine forgiveness. In Romans 4:6-8 Paul comes to the heart of the matter. As he has discussed Abraham and a prominent text, Genesis 15:6, so now he discusses David and another prominent text, Psalm 32:1, 2. Since the OT stipulated that an important testimonial was to be established by at least two witnesses (Deut. 17:6), Paul presents Abraham and David as witnesses from the law and the prophets to righteousness by faith (Rom. 3:21). In fact, he uses the testimony of David to explain more fully the meaning of the reckoning of righteousness to Abraham. Here he seems to be applying Rabbi Hillel's second rule of biblical interpretation, *gezerah shawah,* "equivalency of expressions," (cf. Strack 93, 94). According to this principle, a word or phrase found in one text of Scripture could be explained by the meaning it bears in another text. Since the word "reckoned" appears not only in Genesis 15:6 but also in Psalm 32:1, 2, Paul uses the latter text from Psalms, with its threefold parallelism, to illumine the former text

from Genesis. Justification comes to mean forgiveness of sin, covering of sin, or not reckoning sin to the believer (Rom. 4:7, 8). Put otherwise, guilt is gone, sin no longer appears for judgment, and all charges are dropped. That God does not reckon sin finds a meaningful echo in 2 Corinthians 5:19: "God was in Christ [at the cross] reconciling the world to himself, not counting their trespasses against them." Thus, forgiveness lies at the heart of justification.

The concept of forgiveness is furthered by other significant terms and concepts that Scripture uses to define and explain it. As to terminology, the reality of forgiveness is represented in the Hebrew Bible by the pictorial language of covering (kāpar [Ex. 29:36; Lev. 8:15]; and kāsāh [Neh. 4:5; Ps. 32:1]); wiping away (māhāh [Ps. 51:1]); and lifting away or removing (Gen. 50:17). The concept of atonement is associated especially with kāpar, but also with nāśā'.

In the Greek NT forgiveness is portrayed as a sending away (the verb aphiēmi [Matt. 6:12, 14, 15; Rom. 4:7]; and the noun aphesis [Matt. 26:28; Acts 5:31; Col. 1:14]); being gracious to (charizomai [Luke 7:43; 2 Cor. 2:7; Col. 2:13]) or merciful to (hilaskomai [Luke 18:13 and hileōs, Heb. 8:12]); covering (kalyptō [James 5:20; 1 Peter 4:8], and epikalyptō [Rom. 4:7]); dismissing (apolyō [Luke 6:37]) or wiping away (exaleiphō [Col. 2:14, connected with forgiveness in verse 13]). The idea of atonement is found in the hilaskomai family of words.

Forgiveness of sins, as the removal of barriers to reconciliation and fellowship with God, is of fundamental importance for Hebrew-Christian faith. In biblical hope it was an outstanding blessing of the Messianic age (Isa. 43:25; Jer. 31:34; 33:8; 50:20; Micah 7:18, 19). Its significance should be viewed from both a manward and a Godward side. As to the former, humanity's state of separation from God and liability to God's wrath because of sin (Isa. 59:2; Rom. 1:18; 2:3, 5, 8, 9) can end only in eternal death (Rom. 6:23) without the forgiveness of God. If God's forgiveness is not received by the sinner, God's seeking love will remain unfulfilled and joy will be lost in heaven (an inference from Luke 15:6, 7, 9, 10, 23, 24). The great desire of God to forgive is implied in Jesus' last prayer, when on the cross, despite the heinousness of the crime against Him, He entreated: "Father forgive them, for they know not what they do" (Luke 23:34). The message of Scripture is that God, like the waiting father in the story of the prodigal son (Luke 15:11-24), longs to forgive the repentant sinner. When he acknowledges: "Father, I have sinned against heaven and before you" (verse 18), he will receive God's compassion and acceptance (verse 20), forgiveness and cleansing (Ps. 51:1, 2, 7, 9; 1 John 1:9).

As to the extent of forgiveness, Scripture represents God as saying that He has removed our sins from us as far as the east is from the west (Ps. 103:12); that He has cast them into the depths of the sea (Micah 7:19) or behind His back (Isa. 38:17); that He has blotted them out or swept them away (Ps. 51:1, 9; Isa. 43:25; 44:22) and will remember them no more (Jer. 31:34). When His work has been done, all of one's sins are forgiven (Luke 7:47; Col. 2:13). Indeed, it was for the sins of the whole world that Christ died as an atoning sacrifice, efficacious through faith (Rom. 3:25).

The prerequisites for, or concomitants of, the personal reception of forgiveness are repentance, confession, and baptism (Mark 1:4; Acts 2:38; 3:19; 1 John 1:9); faith (Acts 10:43; James 5:15); and union with Christ (Eph. 1:7; 4:32).

Although forgiveness is available to all, not all will be forgiven. There is no forgiveness for those who attribute to Satan the miraculous healing work of Jesus through the power of the Holy Spirit (Matt. 12:31, 32), the so-called unpardonable sin. When divine power is rejected, there is nothing more God can do to save (Heb. 6:4-6). We are called upon not to "reject him who warns from heaven" (Heb. 12:25) and outrage "the Spirit of grace" (Heb. 10:29).

Furthermore, if those who have been forgiven by God do not forgive others (Col. 3:13), they will not be forgiven in the final judgment (Matt. 6:12, 14, 15; Luke 6:37). The forgiveness called for is unlimited. Followers of Jesus are to practice, not a sevenfold but seventy-times-seven forgiveness (Matt. 18:21, 22), in contrast with the unrenewed person's desire for not merely a sevenfold vengeance but one that is "seventy-sevenfold" (Gen. 4:23, 24). That those who have obtained the incalculable forgiveness of God are to manifest forgiveness toward others is dramatically portrayed in the parable of the unmerciful servant (Matt. 18:23-35). Forgiving others from the heart (verse 35) is called a necessity (*dei*, "it is necessary" [verse 33]). This parable reinforces a centerpiece of Jesus' teaching: "Be merciful, even as your Father is merciful" (Luke 6:36).

(5) Justification as eschatological life and new creation. Justification also involves the gift of new life. Romans 5:18 teaches that Jesus' act of obedience at the cross leads to "justification of life" (literal translation of *dikaiōsis zōēs*). The words "of life" (genitive case in Greek) may be rendered "life-giving justification" or "justification which issues in life." In harmony with this, Romans 4:17 utilizes two great realities to explain the fullness of justification: Creation (God "calls into existence the things that do not exist") and Resurrection (God "gives life to the dead"). In other words, justification is a new creation in which God brings life to those who are spiritually dead (cf. Eph. 2:1-5). "If any one is in Christ, he is a new creation; the old has passed away, behold, the new has come" (2 Cor. 5:17). In Galatians, where justification is the main theme, Paul argues that what really counts with God is a new creation (Gal. 6:15). This coheres with Paul's rabbinic background according to which, when a Gentile was converted to Judaism, he was considered to be a new creature through the forgiveness of all his sins. Romans 6:4 speaks of one who has been united to Christ as having newness of life ("newness of Spirit" [Rom. 7:6]), meaning the eschatological life of the age to come. This new life, made available through the Spirit, is the foundation for ethical transformation, for the life brought by the Spirit is to be conducted under the guidance of the Spirit and bearing its fruit (Gal. 5:22-25).

(6) Justification as exchange of lordships. An element without which the full implications of justification will not be seen is found in Romans 6. The occasion for the chapter was the misunderstanding of Paul's teaching on justification by faith alone apart from the law (Rom. 3:21–4:25). His teaching had been misconceived to mean that believers could unconcernedly perform evil so that good might come (Rom. 3:8), or that they could continue in sin that grace might abound (Rom. 6:1). This was an erroneous deduction from Paul's teaching that when the law was revealed at Sinai, far from sin being abated—the Jewish position—trespasses abounded, only to be met by the superabounding of grace (Rom. 5:20). Paul's Jewish critics thought such a construction tantamount not only to justification of the ungodly but to the justification of ungodliness. Paul wrote Romans 6 to explain that justification did not mean this. His primary argument is that in the life of believers there has taken place a transfer or exchange of lordships. Sin used to be lord (verses 17, 20) but, as a result of baptism into Christ and His death (verses 3, 4), death to sin's lordship has occurred and the lordship of Christ has begun. In the forensic language of Romans 8:3, Christ judicially condemned sin in the flesh; thus, sin has lost its case in court. It is thereby deprived of authority over, or custody of, the life of one joined to Christ.

It is illuminating that the Greek word employed in Romans 6:7 to state that freedom from sin's reign has taken place is *dikaioō*, which is the word ordinarily meaning "to justify." This word, when used in the passive voice with the preposition "from" *(apo)*, means being freed from (cf. Acts 13:39, where forgiveness is coordinated with being freed from). This finds its parallel in the passive of *eleutheroō* (to free) in combination with "from" *(apo)* in Romans 6:18, 22. There can be no question that for Paul justification, in addition to forgiveness of sins, involves freedom from the old lordship of sin. When this freedom takes place, it is the root out of which the fruit of sanctification emerges. Justification is a far more powerful reality than a mere legal adjustment in the books of heaven. It is a dethroning of that illegitimate authority that prevents a sanctified life, and the establishment of that divine authority that enables it. Perhaps this is why Paul can twice move from justification to glorification without mentioning sanctification between (Rom. 5:2; 8:30). Justification, in the full Pauline sense, implies the concept of sanctification as moral growth predicated upon the believer's transfer to the lordship of Christ.

(7) Justification as community. Justification has a corporate as well as individual dimension. It creates the people of God. As persons are set right with God they are also brought into a right relationship with each other and become one body (Rom. 12:4;15:7; 1 Cor. 12:12, 13; Eph. 4:4, 5). Forged is a community in which status, ethnicity, race, and gender no longer operate as barriers to fellowship, since all are children of God through faith, one in Christ Jesus, and members of the household of God (Luke 15:1, 2; Gal. 2:12; 3:26, 28; Eph. 2:13-19).

(8) Justification as the reality of righteousness. It is common to say that in justification believers are treated as though they were righteous, or as if they had not sinned. This language is appropriate on two grounds. First, when righteousness is defined in a moral sense as perfect obedience to God's holy law (SC 62), justification must mean that sinners are treated as though they were righteous. And since, for Christ's sake, they are granted life instead of death, they are being treated as if they had not sinned. Second, the language of "as if we were righteous" is appropriate in a polemical situation with the Roman Catholic view that in justification we are not declared righteous, but are actually so by virtue of an infusion of grace and righteousness into the soul.

However, when righteousness or justification is looked upon in its primary relational sense of being set into a right relationship with God, with all its salvific benefits, there can be no "as if." When God says believers are right with Him, accepted by Him, forgiven by Him, reconciled to Him, adopted by Him, and granted life by Him as our Lord, they really are (cf. 1 John 3:2). Thus, in a relational sense, one can appropriately speak of "being made righteous," as in the RSV translation of Romans 5:9.

f. The ground of justification. "Since, therefore, we are now justified by his blood, much more shall we be saved by him from the wrath of God" (Rom. 5:9). That which both makes possible and expresses the justification of sinful man is the cross of Christ, considered as a vicarious, atoning sacrifice whereby humanity's sin is forgiven and God's wrath is averted.

The sacrificial character of Christ's death is seen in a number of passages. One of the most important is Romans 3:25, 26. Here, the way by which God justifies the sinner and the nature of the redemptive act which brings it about (verse 24) are described. According to this text, God set forth Christ as an atoning sacrifice. Its efficacy was to be received by faith and its purpose was to show God's righteousness vis-à-vis His forbearance in passing over former sins (verse 25). When this exhibition of divine righteousness took place, it would be seen that God was righteous and the one who puts in the right the person who has faith in Jesus (verse 26). To understand the thought of this passage it is necessary to go back to Romans 1:16, 17. Here it is stated that the proclamation of the gospel is the medium through which God leads people of faith to salvation because in the gospel God's righteousness is being revealed. The revelation of God's saving righteousness, stated in the present tense in verse 17, is picked up again in Romans 3:21, put into the past tense, disconnected from the law as its vehicle (for the law can work only wrath, Rom. 4:15), and connected with the cross (Rom. 3:25). It is at the cross that God's justifying grace, which liberates from sin (verse 24), is shown. In other words, the saving righteousness of God, which in the present is being actively revealed and appropriated through the gospel (Rom. 1:17), is the very righteousness that was first manifested in the historical event of Jesus' death (Rom. 3:25). When God put forward Jesus as a *hilastērion* (atoning sacrifice), the saving righteousness of God was fully exhibited. To use the word *hilastērion,* in terms of biblical and extrabiblical evidence, is to make a sacrificial reference. A proper interpretation of *hilastērion* must have regard for three main components of Paul's thought found in Romans 1:16–3:25. First, Paul emphasizes God not as the recipient of the *hilastērion* but as the provider of it (Rom. 3:25). In other words, the fact that God put forward Christ as a sacrifice shows that the cross, while an event in history, is not an event outside of God that moves Him to be gracious to us, but is an event inside of God by which He expresses His sacrificial love for us (cf. Rom. 5:8; Eph. 5:2; 1 John 4:10). God in self-sacrifice bears the pain and guilt of sin within Himself and gives us the pardon. Accordingly, God does not love us because of the atonement but, because He loves us, He provided the atonement. Second, Paul stresses two further components: the fact of sin and the reality of wrath. The translation and meaning of *hilastērion* must also deal with these issues that stand in a cause-effect relationship to each other. Because of sin, God necessarily manifests wrath.

Two major translations of *hilastērion* are propitiation and expiation, the former emphasizing the removal of wrath and the latter the cleansing or wiping away of sin. Each translation has merit, but expiation is better, for the deepest problem is not wrath, but sin which causes wrath. If sin can be expiated, wrath can be averted. An excellent and less abstract rendering, which avoids the controversy that has raged between proponents of propitiation or expiation and is most intimately expressive of the central element of the OT sanctuary services, is the visually powerful translation "sacrifice of atonement" (NIV, NRSV). Such a translation easily connects with all three necessary constituents of *hilastērion* in Romans 1:16–3:25 and the words "by his blood" in Romans 3:25. This phrase should be directly joined with *hilastērion* rather than "through faith." The NRSV well translates the first half of the verse: "Whom God put forward as a sacrifice of atonement by his blood, effective through faith." The appropriate contextual understanding of *hilastērion,* therefore, is a bloody sacrifice offered by (rather than to) God which atones for sin, and hence, turns away His just wrath from sinners who accept the sacrifice. (See Christ II. D. 3.)

According to the second half of Romans 3:25, the function of the cross is to exhibit God's saving righteousness by dealing with the problem of "former sins." These are the sins of the entire world before the cross and, by implication, throughout all time after the cross. The resolution of former sins comes through the saving righteousness of God according to which Christ, as the divine sin offering, bears God's full judgment against sin and offers God's full mercy to sinners.

The first half of Romans 3:26 stands in parallel with the latter half of verse 25—both speak of the exhibition of God's righteousness in His setting forth Christ as a *hilastērion.* The sacrificial gift of His Son—by which the unconditional love of God is demonstrated, the rebellious sin of mankind is expiated, and the wrath of God is obviated— shows that God is a righteous *(dikaiōs)* God who "rightifies" *(dikaiounta)* believers. The same Greek word, in different forms, is used in this verse to describe both the nature and work of God. The resultant meaning is that through the atoning sacrifice God is shown to be One who acts in consistency with His own righteous character, which takes sin seriously, as He deals graciously with sinners. His justice is not compromised in His bestowal of mercy.

The position that Christ's death was a vicarious sacrifice is substantiated by a number of passages. Romans 8:3 declares that Christ, who took on the likeness of our sinful flesh, came "for sin," meaning "as a sin offering." The phrase "for sin" *(peri hamartias)* is used in the Greek LXX for sin or guilt offerings, as in Leviticus 5:6, 7 and Isaiah 53:10. This thought most probably lies behind the statement God "made him to be sin" in 2 Corinthians 5:21. God made Christ a sin offering, and He did this for us. This means, as Galatians 3:13 says, that "Christ redeemed us from the curse of the law, having become a curse for us." This in turn accords with 1 Peter 2:24, "He himself bore our sins in his body on the tree."

Jesus, the fountainhead of the NT understanding of His sacrificial death, said that He had come "to give his life as a ransom for many" (Mark 10:45) and that the bread and wine of the Last Supper represented His broken body and the blood that would be "poured out for many for the forgiveness of sins" (Matt. 26:26-28). It is clear that Jesus accepted the OT proposition that "the life of the flesh is in the blood" and, therefore, "it is the blood that makes atonement, by reason of the life" (Lev. 17:11; cf. Heb. 9:22: "Without the shedding of blood there is no forgiveness of sins"). As John the Baptist calls Jesus the "Lamb of God, who takes away the sin of the world!" (John 1:29), and Paul says that "Christ, our paschal lamb, has been sacrificed" (1 Cor. 5:7), so Peter explains that we were ransomed "with the precious blood of Christ, like that of a lamb without blemish or spot" (1 Peter 1:18, 19). The concept of blood found here is obviously sacrificial, as also in Romans 5:9; Ephesians 1:7; 2:13; Colossians 1:20; Hebrews 9:12-14; 13:12; and Revelation 5:9. The blood motif is strong in Hebrews, where Jesus' death is called a sacrifice in the most explicit terms (9:26, 28; 10:11, 12, 14). In Ephesians also, Paul sees this death as a sacrifice and connects it with the love of Christ who gave Himself up for us (5:2).

In addition many texts affirm that Christ died for us for *(hyper)* our sins (Rom. 5:6, 8; 1 Cor. 15:3; 2 Cor. 5:14, 15, 21; Gal. 1:4; 2:20; Eph. 5:2; 1 Thess. 5:9, 10). On the other hand, Romans 4:25 uses the preposition *dia,* "because of," with the verb *paradidōmi,* "hand over." This construction parallels the LXX of Isaiah 53:12, where the Servant of the Lord is "handed over" for our sins. Likewise, Peter uses a number of phrases from Isaiah 53, applying them to the circumstances of Jesus' death (1 Peter 2:22 is from Isaiah 53:9; phrases in 1 Peter 2:24 come from Isaiah 53:4, 5, 12; and 1 Peter 2:25 reflects Isaiah 53:6). This use of Isaiah 53, where it is certain that the Servant dies a vicarious death for sinners, clarifies the nature of Christ's death.

This evidence makes clear that Jesus' death not only represents sinners (2 Cor. 5:14, 15) but substitutes for them, for by it Jesus bears the guilt and penalty, judgment and wrath, which, sinners personally would have borne. (See Christ II. D. 1, 2.)

g. The reception of justification. Scripture is unequivocal about the way one receives justification. It can be only by faith, since it comes from God through the sacrifice of Jesus. Being God's work, it cannot be man's, for then Christ would have died for no reason (Gal. 2:21). The NT does not teach the extremes of righteousness by works or righteousness by fate, but righteousness by faith.

Paul employs a variety of expressions to indicate that faith is the means of receiving a new standing before God and a new relationship with God. All these expressions are translated "by faith" and include *ek pisteōs* (Rom. 1:17; 3:30; 5:1; 9:30; 10:6; Gal. 2:16; 3:7, 8, 11, 12, 24; 5:5); *dia pisteōs* (Rom. 3:22, 30; Gal. 2:16, with both *ek* and *dia;* 3:14; Eph. 2:8); *epi pistei* (Phil. 3:9, containing *dia pisteōs* as well); and *pistei* (the simple dative case, Rom. 3:28). Romans 1:17 contains the pregnant expression *ek pisteōs eis pistin* (from faith to faith), meaning "by faith alone," "faith from beginning to end." What is *not* found is *dia pistin,* accusative case, and meaning "on account of faith." This could be misconstrued as making the human activity of faith the ground of justification rather than the means of appropriating a divine activity.

That justification is received through faith alone is supported in Galatians 2:15–3:18 by appeal to a number of witnesses. These include the experience of Peter and Paul (2:15-21), the Galatians (3:1-5), and Abraham (verses 6-9), as well as the witness of the law and the prophets (verses 10-12), the death of Christ (verses 13, 14), and the covenant made with Abraham 430 years prior to the giving of the law on Sinai (verses 15-18).

Summarizing the full and varied scriptural data on the nature of saving faith, it can be said that faith is surrender to the verdict, gift, and claim of God. Faith surrenders to God's verdict: "All have sinned and fall short of the glory of God" (Rom. 3:23). It surrenders to God's gift: "They are justified by his grace as a gift, through the redemption which is in Christ Jesus" (verse 24). And it surrenders to God's claim: "And he died for all, that those who live might live no longer for themselves but for him who for their sake died and was raised" (2 Cor. 5:15). Saving faith includes belief in the fundamentals of the gospel message (verses 3, 4; 1 Thess. 4:14), trust in God and His word (Rom. 4:19-21), and total commitment to God (Luke 13:25-33; Rom. 1:5: "The obedience of faith").

2. Reconciliation

a. Terminology and basic significance. The word "reconciliation" is basically a NT term and translates the verb *katallassō,* sometimes *apokatallassō,* and the noun *katallagē.* The main passages in which the term occurs are Romans 5:10; 2 Corinthians 5:17-21; Ephesians 2:11-19; and Colossians 1:19-22. The inner sense of the concept is most fully represented in the latter two passages. In Ephesians 2:11-19 the Gentiles are spoken of as "separated from Christ" and "alienated from . . . Israel." As a result of the blood of Christ, those who were once "far off have been brought near" (verse 13), and have received the message of peace (verses 14, 15, 17), the ending of hostility (verses 14, 16), and the reality of oneness with the covenant people of God (verse 14). In Colossians 1:19-22 Paul emphasizes the reconciliation of those who were "estranged and hostile in mind" (verse 21). Once again peace is made available through the blood of the cross (verse 20). These passages show that reconciliation is the process by which enmity is removed and fellowship restored. When two parties are reconciled, the war is over, and the alienation is gone. That is why a synonym for reconciliation is peace, which refers to the joining again of two who have been at war. This can be seen from Romans 5:1-11, which begins with peace and ends with reconciliation.

b. Relation to justification. Reconciliation is another way of talking about justification, as the parallelism between Romans 5:9 (justified by His blood) and 5:10 (reconciled by His death) shows. The essential synonymity of the two terms is seen in 2 Corinthians 5:18, 21. In verse 18 reconciliation is coordinated with God's not counting our trespasses, an expression found in Paul's discussion of justification in Romans 4:8. In 2 Corinthians 5:21 reconciliation, the subject of verses 18-20, alternates with the word "righteousness," a word intimately connected with justification. To say "so that we might become the righteousness of God in him" is, in this context, the same as saying "so that we might be reconciled to God through him."

c. Reconciliation as objective. While reconciliation involves the experience of restored relations with God, it is first an objective event before it is subjective. According to 2 Corinthians 5:18, 19, 21, reconciliation is achieved by the event of the cross. This objective event in the past history of salvation is the presupposition for the proclamation of reconciliation, whereby the possibility for humans to be reconciled with God on the existential level is made available through the apostolic appeal to "be reconciled to God" (verse 20). In the apostolic preaching the already-won reconciliation projects itself toward every person, and seeks lodgment in the experience of those who believe.

In Romans 5 Jesus dies for people while they are still sinful. The saving event is apart from them and before the emergence of faith. In fact, through the preaching of the gospel, Jesus' death is the originating cause of faith. It is likewise in the letter to the Ephesians. Through the death of Jesus, which in principle breaks down the wall of hostility between Jews and Gentiles, these diverse peoples are reconciled to God. What the gospel announces, therefore, is that people are to enter the new situation of reconciliation already existing "in Christ Jesus" (Eph. 2:13), who "is our peace" (verse 14).

d. **The objects of reconciliation.** The idea that God is won to reconciliation by an event outside Himself that influences or enables Him to once more hold fellowship with mankind is foreign to the NT. Investigation of the texts that speak specifically to the issue of who is reconciled leaves an unambiguous result. While the concept of God's wrath logically suggests that God is reconciled to man, as well as man to God, by the death of His Son, this is not the actual emphasis in the NT. Despite the fact that God's wrath is manifested against sinful humanity, it is He who, through the presentation of His Son as crucified, creates the conditions whereby reconciliation is possible. In fact He is present in that sacrifice, wooing erring mankind to Himself. The scriptural data are clear that God or Christ is the reconciler and we the reconciled (2 Cor. 5:19; Rom. 5:10; Eph. 2:16; Col. 1:21, 22).

As a result of God's reconciling activity not only does peace with God result (Eph. 2:17, 18; cf. Rom. 5:1), but peace with one another is made available in Christ (Eph. 2:14-16) and required by Christ (Matt. 5:23, 24).

3. Adoption

a. **Relation to justification and sanctifica-**tion. Adoption is a correlate of justification. A right relationship to God and being God's child go together. Like justification, adoption has a background in law and refers to the legal process of being "placed as a son" (the literal translation of the Greek *huiothesia*). There is also a relationship to the primal sense of sanctification, according to which people are set apart to belong to God as His people.

b. **Biblical usage.** In the OT, adoption is not a clearly identified or regularly practiced custom. This perhaps is because of the acceptance of polygamy in Israel's life, leaving little chance that one would be without an heir, and to Levirate marriage where, in the case of a husband's death, another family member would guarantee the family succession. In the OT one does not find adoption either as a technical term or as a part of the law. The closest to a formula appears in Psalm 2:7 where, with reference to the coronation of God's king on Zion (verse 6), God says: "You are my son, today I have begotten you." What was true of God's king, as he ascended the throne of Israel, was true of God's people as God delivered them from Egypt: "When Israel was a child, I loved him, and out of Egypt I called my son" (Hosea 11:1). It is undoubtedly to this event that Paul refers when he says that to Israel was granted, among other great privileges, "sonship" or "adoption" (Rom. 9:4).

Thus it was natural to think of the new Israel of God, the church (Gal. 6:16), as containing within itself the adopted members of God's household (Rom. 8:15; Gal. 4:5; Eph. 1:5). The reality of adoption is quite poignant when, in Ephesians 1:5, it is declared that the goal of God's predestination of us to adoption was "for himself" *(eis auton)*. Incredibly, God wanted us to belong to Himself as His children. Indeed, believers can exclaim: "See what love the Father has given us, that we should be called children of God; and so we are" (1 John 3:1). This can happen because, through reception of Jesus Christ and faith in His name, God has given believers the right to be called children of God, "who were born, not . . . of the will of man, but of God" (John 1:12, 13).

c. Roman adoption and its theological significance. While the theological origin of Paul's use of the concept of adoption lies in Israel's calling as God's son, it was undoubtedly the Roman custom of adoption that permitted certain conclusions to be drawn about the status of the Christian before and with God. In particular, through a complex symbolic sale, the adopting father bought his new son from the real father. Once the sale was finalized, the son came under the complete authority of his adopting father. This could be an austere reality depending upon the character and purpose of the adopting father. However, it carried with it certain important benefits. The son, completely severed from his old family relationships, gained all the rights of the new family. In a very realistic way the adopting father became his new father. The adoptee's debts were canceled and he became as full an inheritor of his new father's wealth as a blood son would be. It was a totally new life that awaited him and, if he had a family, his children also became part of the new family. In like manner, believers become real children of their heavenly Father, whence they or the Spirit of God cry "Abba! Father!" (Rom. 8:15; Gal. 4:6). Their debt of sin is canceled, and they become heirs of God and fellow heirs of Christ (Rom. 8:17; Gal. 4:7). They are not to be considered criminals in relation to a judge or slaves in relation to a master, but children in relation to a father who loves them. Furthermore, their present adoption (the "already") is a pledge of the eschatological fullness of adoption to come (the "not yet") when they will receive new bodies fit for God's new world to come (Rom. 8:23).

B. A New Assurance Before God

1. Present Assurance of Final Salvation

Though one may be hesitant to use the expression "I am saved" because of the mis-

conceptions concerning grace (the advocacy of "cheap grace") and discipleship ("Once saved, always saved, no matter what I do"; cf. 1SM 314, 315, 373; COL 155), which can arise from this basically correct statement, assurance of salvation and the conviction that "he who began a good work in you will bring it to completion at the day of Jesus Christ" (Phil. 1:6) may be joyfully affirmed. This theme is developed in Romans 5.

Drawing conclusions from the fact that believers have been justified, Paul argues that in the present they have peace with God, access to grace, joy, and hope for glorification in the future (Rom. 5:1-3). This hope will not fail, for it is based upon the already existent reality of God's love impressed upon the heart through the gift of the Spirit (verse 5). The context of this love is that, unlike human beings, who might be willing to give themselves for a good or righteous person (verse 7), Christ died for us while we were morally weak, ungodly, sinners, and enemies toward God (verses 6-8). The conclusion is that if God was willing to do the hardest thing—give His Son to die to justify or reconcile enemies, how much more will the risen Christ be willing to save His new friends from the ultimate wrath of God (verses 9, 10). Thus, believers can rejoice in their reconciliation (verse 11), for it promises glorification to come. As Romans 8 argues, absolutely nothing will be able to separate God's people from His love (verses 38, 39). The reality of justification, therefore, involves the reality of complete and lasting assurance.

2. Eternal Life Now Through God's Gift of His Son

Complementing Paul's language of justification by faith is John's vocabulary of eternal life by believing. The events of Jesus' life, which John calls signs, point to the identity of Jesus as the Messiah and Son of God and to the reality of eternal life through believing in Him (John 20:31). By believing in His name, by receiving Him, we gain the right to become children of God (John 1:12), with eternal life, the life of the Son (John 14:6), as a present reality (John 3:36; 4:14; 5:24; 6:40, 47-51, 57, 58; 10:27-30; 1 John 5:9-13). Three passages may be highlighted. According to John 5:24, the believer does not come into a judgment of condemnation, but has already passed from death to life. In John 10:27-30 the Father and the Son are united in protecting those who hear and follow the true shepherd. They hold the sheep so tightly that nothing can snatch them away and thus deprive them of the eternal life that the Shepherd gives His sheep. Furthermore, 1 John 5:9-13 was written precisely so that believers might "know" that they have eternal life, since the one who has the Son (is united to Him through faith) has life (verse 11). This sure knowing of the Christian, spoken of by John, finds a counterpart in Paul who, in speaking about the glorification that God decreed for believers before the ages (1 Cor. 2:7), declares that believers have been granted the Spirit of God so as to "understand" the gifts bestowed on them by God (verse 12).

3. Assurance Through Faith and Judgment According to Works

a. Judgment passages: Their purpose and significance. Scripture teaches that while justification is completely apart from works (Gal. 2:16; Rom. 3:20; Titus 3:5), there remains a judgment according to works for believers (see Matt. 7:21-23; 18:23-35; 25:31-46; Rom. 14:10, 12; 1 Cor. 3:13; 4:5; 6:9; 2 Cor. 5:10; Gal. 6:7, 8; Eph. 5:5, 6; 1 Thess. 4:6; Heb. 10:26-31). These texts contain warnings not only against following a course of life that would bring one into judgment, but against being deceived by the idea that there will be no judgment.

While those who maintain a faith relationship with Christ need have no fear of God's judgment or anxiety concerning salvation, three points are clear from the various judgment passages: (1) Christians, precisely those who are justified by faith, come into this judgment; (2) the judgment is according to one's works; and (3) two destinies are possible to those who have professed Christ: eternal life

or death. No one need be lost, however. The very reason for the judgment texts is to prevent this by awakening people to faithfulness to God, who has been faithful to them.

As the biblical texts on God's love and grace do not allow for the false view, "Never quite saved at all, no matter what Christ has done," so the judgment texts disallow the erroneous view, "Once saved, always saved, no matter what I do." Salvation is always a gift, but the gift does not remain when the Giver is rejected as the Lord of one's life.

b. The Christological premise of the judgment. The relationship between justification by faith and judgment according to works is best understood in the Christological setting of the relationship between Jesus as Saviour (stressing the gift of God), and Jesus as Lord (stressing the claim of God). To magnify His gift is to magnify His claim. The more radically one perceives and receives the love of God in the Saviour, the more a life of love, discipleship, and service for the Lord is created.

The self-giving love of Christ for others, revealed in His life and death, is the very essence of His reign and the basis of moral insight. What is to be done for Him is deducible from what He has done for us. We are called to love one another as Christ loved us (John 13:34; Eph. 5:25); to forgive as God has forgiven us (Matt. 18:32, 33; Eph. 4:32); and to live our new life in accordance with the Spirit who gave us life (Gal. 5:25). Thus, in Christ's act of self-giving, redemption was accomplished and the call to discipleship was disclosed.

To live in harmony with the Lord's claim is not an attempt to save oneself by one's own works. It is rather to have one's life shaped by the deliverance Christ brings. To be unwilling to live in accord with His claim is to reject Him as Messiah and the kingdom He brings. Christ cannot be king to those who are unwilling to be His subjects.

This means that the assurance of Christ's love and salvation plays a key role in living for Christ and modeling His love. Far from assurance leading to immorality (Rom. 3:8; 6:1, 15), it is the indispensable foundation for the new moral walk (verses 3, 4; 7:4; 8:2-4).

c. Resolving the tension. The tension between justification by faith and judgment according to works remains unresolved by any of several proposed conceptions. First, justification has been seen as all important and judgment according to works as a mere vestige of Jewish apocalyptic thought. This view disregards the frequency and stringency of the judgment texts in the NT and their application to believers. Second, the judgment texts, rather than being understood as a call to repentance and doing God's will have been reduced to merely exposing what humans could not do and the consequent need for divine forgiveness. This misses the biblical teaching that those who have been forgiven are to do God's will and that only the foolish, who are not grounded upon Jesus' words, do not (Matt. 7:21, 24-27; 18:32, 33; John 8:11). Third, some have distinguished between an initial justification by faith and a final justification by works of perfection. This view forgets that God's mercy will still be needed in the judgment (Matt. 5:7). Fourth, it has been urged that since God's verdict of justification is already present, the final judgment of believers cannot deal with salvation or lostness but only with ranks of blessedness in heaven. Such an understanding comports neither with the description of the lostness of certain professed believers (Matt. 7:21-23; 18:32-35; John 15:6; Rom. 8:13; 1 Cor. 3:17; 6:9; 10:6-12; Gal. 5:19-21; Eph. 5:5, 6; 1 Thess. 4:6; Rev. 21:8, 27; 22:15), nor with the silence of Scripture on any hierarchy in heaven.

A better view, which takes seriously all the scriptural data, might be termed the dynamic, salvation-historical view. It contains the two poles of the Bible's teaching of the "already" of salvation begun, and the "not yet" of salvation completed. Its essence is that there is only one justification, which is only by faith (Rom. 1:17) and which accompanies the believer from faith's inception to the final judg-

ment, where its reality is attested by its fruits. In the judgment God looks for justification with its fruit, not in the sense of "faith plus works saves," but of justification as the source of sanctified living. Failure to give due regard to judgment according to works discounts the "not yet" aspect of salvation history with its unfolding significance of the cross until every foe is put down and Christ is Lord of all (cf. 1 Cor. 15:24, 25). Judgment according to works teaches that the cross puts believers under the reign of Christ as Lord as well as Saviour. It tests whether we are indeed His workmanship, walking in the good works He planned for us (Eph. 2:10).

The secret of the final judgment in its relation to works is contained in Jesus' saying "Blessed are the merciful, for they shall obtain mercy" (Matt. 5:7) and illustrated by the parable of the unmerciful servant (Matt. 18:23-35). The paradoxical truth is that mercy is for the merciful. Unlike Jewish teaching that justice without mercy would be the operative principle of the final judgment (2 Esdras 7:33), Jesus taught that mercy would be shown to those who had been merciful to others. The merciful need mercy because, although the character of Christ can be imitated and approximated, it can never be equaled (2T 549, 628). Consequently, two realities are necessary in the judgment: (1) the fruits of justification must be present; and (2) justification must continue its function of pardon.

d. The result for assurance. The conclusion that may be drawn is that if justification grants assurance, judgment guards it from the dangerous illusion that assurance is possible without a committed relationship to, and following of, Christ. Good works do not impart assurance, but the One who motivates such works does. According to 1 Corinthians 10:1-12, all was well with Israel as long as they followed Christ the rock, but when they desired evil, destruction resulted. This judgment upon spiritually privileged Israel shows that those who think they stand assured of their salvation, while disregarding the lordship of

Christ, should take heed lest they fall (verses 11, 12). Amid their assurance, they must realize that they have the security of being God's children only as people who remain exposed to temptation. The biblical teaching of the judgment reminds believers of this and gives a proper foundation for true assurance, that is, living for Him who died and rose for them (2 Cor. 5:15; see Judgment II. D).

C. A New Life From God

There are a number of life-changing processes which Christ as Saviour, through the power of the Spirit, makes possible and Christ as Lord makes necessary.

1. Regeneration

a. The basic concept. Regeneration refers to that creative process of God whereby the natural person, unable to fathom or fulfill spiritual things (1 Cor. 2:14–3:3), becomes a spiritual person who can appreciate the Word of God and begin to practice its way of life. Thus, regeneration covers both awakening to spiritual life and its flowering. Sin has reduced human beings to slavery; only God's intervention can bring freedom. Accustomed to evil, humans are unable to do good (Jer. 13:23). They may wish to do so, but will not be successful, for evil always lies close at hand (Rom. 7:18, 21). In this situation (verses 5, 9, 11, 13; Eph. 2:1), a person can be made alive and empowered to good works only by the God of love who is rich in mercy (Eph. 2:4, 5, 10).

b. Biblical usage. The OT has no specific word for regeneration, but speaks of it in terms of circumcision of the heart: "And the Lord your God will circumcise your heart and the heart of your offspring, so that you will love the Lord your God with all your heart . . . that you may live" (Deut. 30:6; cf. 10:16; Jer. 4:4). Accordingly, Paul describes real circumcision as being "a matter of the heart, spiritual and not literal" (Rom. 2:29). Further, he says that believers have been circumcised "by putting off the body of flesh in the circumcision of Christ" (Col. 2:11), referring to the rending of Christ's body on the cross.

A variant of heart circumcision is the concept of God giving His people a new heart and a new spirit by which they will be able to walk in His way (Eze. 11:19, 20; 18:31; 36:26, 27). Thus, regeneration is an initial change of heart and a subsequent change of walk. This accords with the new covenant promise in Jeremiah 31:33: "I will put my law within them, and I will write it upon their hearts" (cf. Jer. 24:7; 32:39, 40). The Psalmist prays for this experience: "Create in me a new heart, O God, and put a new and right spirit within me" (Ps. 51:10).

In the NT, other ways are employed to express the reality of regeneration. John's Gospel announces that those who have gained the right to become children of God by believing (1:12) were born not by any human process or intention, but by the will of God (verse 13). Indeed, without being born from above, that is, by baptismal water and the Spirit, no one can enter the Kingdom of God (John 3:3, 5). Only by the Spirit can the change be made from flesh and the natural person to spirit and the spiritual person (verse 6). The work of the Spirit is like the wind that blows as it wills, which man cannot forecast. Thus, the regenerative process is God's doing, in the inscrutable wisdom of His power.

Titus 3:5, which contains emphases similar to those of John 3:5, speaks of "the washing of regeneration" (*palingenesia,* from *palin,* "again," and *genesia,* "birth" or "genesis") and renewal (*anakainōsis,* literally "to be new again") in the Holy Spirit. The connection between baptism and the Spirit is evidenced here. As with John 3:5 one cannot help recalling the baptism of Jesus, at which time He was empowered for His ministry by the Spirit. The concept of renewal in Titus 3:5 coheres with its usage in Colossians 3:9, 10, according to which believers "have put off the old nature with its practices and have put on the new nature, which is being renewed (*anakainoō*) in knowledge after the image of its creator." A similar concept is found in Ephesians 4:22-24.

Here believers are urged to put off the old man and put on the new, and a parallel is drawn between the old man being corrupted by deceitful lusts and the new man being renewed *(ananeoō)* in the mind. Furthermore, the new man is said to have been "created" *(ktizō)* in God's likeness. This recalls the creation of Adam at the beginning of time. A reference to God's creative power is also present in Ephesians 2:10, where believers are said to be God's workmanship, created for good works.

In 1 Peter the idea of a new birth occurs both in the compound verb *anagennaō* (1:3, 23), which in verse 3 is connected with Christ's resurrection, and in the adjectival phrase "newborn babes" in 2:2. Peter's point is that since Christians are newborn babies, they are meant to grow in salvation through spiritual nourishment. Consequently, regeneration refers both to God's power, which produces new birth and the subsequent growth.

Scripture teaches that regeneration is made possible by the will of God (John 1:13), the Spirit of God (John 3:5; Titus 3:5), and the word of God, identified with the preached word of the gospel (James 1:18, 21; 1 Peter 1:23, 25).

As believers are regenerated in the present, so at the end of time the world will be made new *(palingenesia,* Matt. 19:28) by the same power at work in spiritual renewal now (Rom. 8:21).

2. Repentance and Conversion

a. **Terms used for repentance.** "Repentance" is another word indicating a change. It is derived from a number of Hebrew and Greek terms. In Hebrew there are two basic terms. One is the verb *nāḥam,* which usually refers to God's change of attitude and action toward people (Gen. 6:6; Ex. 32:14). This is dependent first upon the people's willingness to repent (Jer. 18:8). If so, God's wrath is altered to graciousness (Joel 2:13). If not, God changes His mind about the good He intended to do for them (Jer. 18:10). *Nāḥam* further expresses sorrow or regret over creating people who have turned to evil (Gen. 6:6). (It can also express human sorrow over wrong, Judges 21:6, 15; Jer. 31:19). Another factor in God's change of mind is whether intercession has been made for His people, as when Moses pleaded that God would repent of punishing them (Ex. 32:12), and remember His covenant to multiply them and give them a land (verse 13). God responds by staying His wrath (verse 14).

The other Hebrew term is the verb *šûb* by which God asks His unfaithful people to turn away from sin (1 Kings 8:35; Neh. 9:35; Isa. 59:20; Eze. 3:19) and return to Him in covenant faithfulness (Deut. 4:30; Neh. 1:9; Jer. 3:14; 4:1). Sometimes *šûb* and *nāḥam* become synonymous (Ex. 32:12, with the translations "turn" and "repent").

In the Greek NT the main word for repentance is the verb *metanoeō* or noun *metanoia,* which indicates an afterthought that leads to a new evaluation and results in a "change of mind" (Matt. 3:8). The verb *metamelomai,* like the Hebrew *nāḥam,* expresses regret or sorrow for sin (Matt. 21:29, 32), but can also mean to change one's mind (2 Cor. 7:8). Greek words intimately related to the concept of repentance are the verb *epistrephō,* "to turn," "return" (Luke 1:16, 17; Acts 11:21), or "be converted" (Luke 22:32; Acts 3:19; James 5:20), and the noun *epistrophē,* "conversion" (Acts 15:3).

b. **Meaning and content of repentance.** The concept of repentance, so prominent with that of judgment in the prophets (Hosea 6:1; Joel 2:1-14), was the essence of John the Baptist's message (Matt. 3:2; Mark 1:4), a major part of the teaching of Jesus (Mark 1:14, 15), required by Peter (Acts 2:38; 3:19), utilized by Paul (Acts 26:20; Rom. 2:4), demanded by John the revelator (verses 5, 16, 21, 22; 3:3, 19) and at the heart of Judaism as well as monotheism. In Scripture this concept is fundamental to the theme of salvation. A number of important ingredients are found in it.

Two elements may be considered presuppositions of repentance. First is the acknowledgment that one is a sinner (Ps. 51:3, 4; Luke 15:18, 19) and second is the sorrow of a broken heart (Joel 2:12, 13), for "godly grief produces a repentance that leads to salvation" (2 Cor. 7:10).

Essential to repentance is a change of mind. The sinner discovers a new perspective on his or her status, relationships, motives, values, and sins. Of the prodigal Jesus said, "But when he came to himself" (Luke 15:17), indicating that he had not been himself or in his right mind. Sin involves irrationality and madness. To repent is to note how wrong one has been. What is needed, however, is more than a change of mind, typically a Greek way of looking at repentance. What is needed is the practical Hebrew concept of a change of direction, a turning around, and a returning to the source of life and moral understanding. Thus, after coming to himself the prodigal vowed to return to his father (verse 18). As in this experience, repentance involves both turning away from sin and returning to God (Acts 9:35; 11:21; 15:19; 26:20; 2 Cor. 3:16; 1 Thess. 1:9; 1 Peter 2:25) and the righteousness He both requires and supplies. Turning is the key idea. In a poignant appeal God says in Ezekiel: "I have no pleasure in the death of the wicked, but that the wicked turn from his way and live; turn back, turn back from your evil ways; for why will you die, O house of Israel?" (33:11; cf. 18:30-32). When people do return they will find that God is "gracious and merciful, . . . abounding in steadfast love" (Joel 2:12, 13).

The product of turning away from sin to God is what the Bible calls the "fruits that befit repentance" (Luke 3:8). These include compassion, generosity and sharing, honesty and integrity, and nonviolence or peaceableness (verses 10-14; cf. the list in Eze. 33:14, 15).

Thus repentance involves a complete and radical transformation of the life. It is not merely a presupposition of conversion, but is conversion at the deepest level. As such it leads to salvation (2 Cor. 7:10) and life (Acts 11:18).

c. Motivation for repentance. Two basic factors motivate repentance. The first is the reality and preaching of judgment. This is true throughout the writings of the prophets, and in the message of John the Baptist (Luke 3:7-9), Jesus (Luke 13:1-5), Paul (Rom. 2:3, 5), and John the revelator (Rev. 2:16, 22). The warnings of judgment are positive rather than negative, for their purpose is to keep people from judgment. God's warnings are meant to save life, not to destroy it.

The deepest motivating factor is the love and goodness of God. Paul declares: "Do you not know that God's kindness is meant to lead you to repentance?" (Rom. 2:4). Peter agrees that God is not willing "that any should perish, but that all should reach repentance" (2 Peter 3:9). When one reads in Scripture about God's earnest appeals for sinners to return to Him and receive life instead of death (Eze. 33:11; Joel 2:12), appeals explicitly connected with God's grace, mercy, and steadfast love (Joel 2:13), it is clear that God's love for sinners is the ultimate basis for repentance. When Scripture dramatically portrays the joy in heaven over a sinner who repents (Luke 15:6, 9, 23, 24, 32), this powerfully implies that God's love draws forth repentance. And when the prodigal realizes the good he left behind in his father's house, a good that now manifests itself in his father's eager compassion upon his return, it becomes obvious that God's love is cause and human repentance is response.

God's love is made effective upon the heart by His Spirit as He directs the sinner to the cross of Christ (Rom. 5:5-8). When Jesus was lifted up, He would draw all to Himself (John 12:32, 33). He was "the Lamb of God, who takes away the sin of the world" (John 1:29). It is only as this message is preached that the possibility of repentance is created. Repentance is a gift (Acts 5:31; 11:18) in that it is a divinely influenced reaction to the promise of salvation proffered by the God of love and grace.

3. Sanctification

Sanctification, or holiness, is one of the most frequent, important, and all-embracing concepts in Scripture. It has to do with God and man; with relationships, worship, and morals; with every period of life, whether past, present, or future; and with every element of the world, including times and places, objects and rituals. It is so significant that believers are admonished to strive "for the holiness without which no one will see the Lord" (Heb. 12:14).

In the Hebrew Scriptures the term is found as a verb, *qādaš,* to "set apart, sanctify," or "make holy" (approximately 170 times); a noun, *qōdeš,* "holiness" (about 470 times); and as an adjective, *qadôš,* "holy" (almost 120 times). In the Greek NT the concept appears in the form of the verb *hagiazō,* "to sanctify," "make holy," or "consecrate" (28 times); the nouns *hagiasmos,* "holiness" or "sanctification" (10 times); *hagiōsynē,* "holiness" (three times), and *hagiotēs,* "holiness" (one time); and the adjective *hagios,* meaning "holy" or, used as a noun, "saint" or "holy one" (233 times).

a. The meaning of sanctification

(1) Sanctification as a new relationship and status. Justification, reconciliation, and adoption are not the only relational concepts. Sanctification in its primal sense is also a relational word. The basic meaning is to be set apart or separated, as illustrated by the seventh day of creation, which God set apart or sanctified to be His special day (Gen. 2:3; Ex. 20:8-11). In this sense the word "sanctification" does not have a moral connotation, but by implication does have a moral goal. This can be seen in Leviticus 19:2, where God says to Israel: "You shall be holy; for I the Lord your God am holy." God is holy in that He is separate from all other so-called gods, from the created world of nature and creaturely life, and from all injustice or unrighteousness. He is different, unique, transcendent. While He is holy in and of Himself, so He can be called the "Holy One" (Isa. 10:17; Hosea 11:9; etc.) or "Holy One of Israel" (2 Kings 19:22; Ps. 71:22; Isa. 1:4; cf. 6:3), His people are holy only in a derivative sense by virtue of relation to Him. By His own action He has consecrated

them to Himself. This holiness, inherent in the new relationship God has established, is to be exhibited concretely and visibly by following God's will in every area of life (Lev. 19:3-37). By their actions His people affirm that He is the Lord their God (verses 4, 10, 12, 14, 16, 18, 25, 30-32, 34, 37). These frequent statements of God's lordship over His people are reminders of the new relationship which has been established and the new faithfulness that is, therefore, expected. Continuance as a kingdom of priests and holy nation is contingent upon obeying His voice and keeping His covenant (Ex. 19:5, 6).

Sanctification's relational root, out of which moral fruit grows, is found in 1 Corinthians 1:2. Notwithstanding the many serious ethical and theological problems the Corinthians had, Paul still addresses them as "those sanctified in Christ Jesus, called to be saints." The perfect tense in Greek, used in the word "sanctified," points to a completed action in the past which has continuing results in the present. As a result of God's call, the Corinthians already had been sanctified or set apart as His people. This is sanctification in the relational, rather than moral sense. While sanctification understood morally is the work of a lifetime (AA 560), sanctification in the relational sense, whereby we become God's property and people, is, like justification, the work of a moment. This is corroborated by 1 Corinthians 6:11, which places washing, sanctification, and justification alike in the past, as the product of the activity of Christ and the Spirit. The fact that sanctification can be coupled with justification as a past event and even listed before justification, shows that both sanctification, in the relational sense, as well as justification, are twin roots of moral growth. That sanctification, on one side of its meaning, is a definitive event in the past is also seen in the book of Hebrews where it refers to the purification of the believer through the sacrifice of Jesus (10:10, 29; cf. 13:12). Other texts pointing to a definitive sanctification in the past are Ephesians 5:25, 26, and Acts 20:32 and 26:18. Both these texts use the perfect tense of the participle and the second says that this past sanctification is by faith. In 2 Thessalonians 2:13 sanctification by the Spirit and belief (faith) in the truth are coordinated. Further support for accomplished sanctification is found in 1 Peter 1:2, which describes believers as "chosen and destined by God the Father, and sanctified by the Spirit for obedience to Jesus Christ." The fact that "chosen and destined," which come just before "sanctified," are in the past tense indicates that "sanctified" is also past. As such, sanctification is the precondition of future obedience to Jesus Christ.

In the sense discussed so far, sanctification refers to God's setting apart of a people to belong to Himself and His service. This idea is also found in 1 Corinthians 1:2, where the Corinthians have been sanctified and "called to be saints." The words "to be" are not in the Greek text and should not be understood as referring to a status that will take place in the indefinite future. By virtue of the fact that the Corinthians were already sanctified, they were already saints. The same Greek root is used for both sanctification and saint. In order to show the intimate connection of the words in English it would be better to translate "saintification," rather than "sanctification" (a word that derives from the Latin *sanctus,* "holy," and *facere,* "to make"). Because people belong to Jesus Christ they can be called saints (Rom. 1:6, 7). For this reason Paul addresses his letters to the saints. They have become such by God's action in sanctifying them or setting them apart. The word "saint," which almost always occurs in the plural, means "the people of God" or "God's own people."

(2) Sanctification as moral growth in goodness. According to 1 John 3:2 we, as believers, do not know what we shall be, but we know that when Christ appears we shall be like Him. Until that time we undergo a process of purification, with Christ as the norm of purity (verse 3). What takes place from the time of being set apart for Christ to the time when we shall be like Christ is sanctification as a progressive process of moral change by the power of the Holy Spirit in cooperation with the human will. Out of the root of sanctification as belonging emerges sanctification as becoming. The former, as the "already" of God's consecrating activity, leads to the "not yet" of God's conforming activity. In heaven itself there will be a ceaseless approaching unto God.

One of the most important passages of Scripture for sanctification as moral change is Romans 6. In this chapter Paul affirms that the Christian who has died to sin as the lord of his or her life no longer lives under its domination (verses 2, 14). With the crucifixion of the old self, sin's power over the body and the necessity to serve sin have been broken (verse 6). This definitive death has taken place through baptism, by which the Christian is not only united to Christ as new Lord but also united with the foundational events of salvation, Christ's death and resurrection (verses 3, 4). In verses 1-14 Paul sets death and life into juxtaposition eight times (2, 4, 5, 8, 9, 10, 11, 13), thereby showing their indissoluble connection, and indicating that death is not an end of itself, but the precondition for new life. Since Christ's death was a death to sin's power (not in His life, but as that which attacked His life), and His resurrection a living for God (verse 10), so one united to Christ is to consider himself dead to sin and alive to God (verse 11).

In this state of union with Christ, where sin has lost its authority and living for God is the new reality, three major consequences follow for the believer. The first is a walk in newness of life (verse 4). Newness of life is a reference to the eschatological life of the age to come. Christians have been grasped by this life, and their lifewalk in this world is transformed by it. What Paul says here finds an illuminating parallel in Galatians 5:25, where the gift of life from the Spirit sponsors walking in accord with the Spirit. This walk is characterized by the fruit of the Spirit described in verses 23, 24, 26, rather than the works of the flesh pictured in verses 19-21. In Colossians 3:1, 2 Paul adds that as a result of having been raised with Christ, the Christian is to seek the things that are above, where Christ is (Col. 3:12–4:6), instead of the sinful things of earth (Col. 3:5-9). Thus the believer's participation in the realities of the age to come is manifested and attested by the way that person conducts his or her moral life.

The concept of walking occurs 95 times in the NT. A number of these are found in Johannine passages that speak of believers walking in the light or in the darkness, walking as Christ walked, or in the truth (John 8:12; 11:9, 10; 12:35; 1 John 1:6, 7; 2:6, 11). However, it is the Pauline writings that place the greatest emphasis upon, and give the most varied descriptions of, the nature of the Christian's ethical walk. Dealing with things to be avoided, Paul refers to conduct that bears the stamp of the old eon. As long as Christians are in this world, they must necessarily walk "in the flesh," i.e., in the sphere of human existence (Gal. 2:20), but they must not walk "according to the flesh," meaning in accord with the world's rather than God's norms of behavior. For Paul, "according to the flesh" stands in contrast with "according to the Spirit" (Rom. 8:4, 5). In Galatians 5:16-25, walking in the Spirit is the only way to overcome walking in the flesh (cf. Rom. 8:13), for the flesh desires to prevent our doing the good we wish to do (Rom. 7:15, 17-20). Furthermore, Christians are not to walk as mere humans (1 Cor. 3:3), devoid of high spiritual principles, or according to the course of this world and the power at work in the children of disobedience (Eph. 2:2). This includes vanity of thought and a dissolute life (Eph. 4:17, 19). Christians will also refuse to practice (walk in) "underhanded" methods (2 Cor. 4:2) or to involve themselves in reveling and drunkenness, debauchery and licentiousness, quarreling and jealousy (Rom. 13:13).

Instead, they are to walk in Christ (Col. 2:6) in a manner appropriate to their gospel calling (Eph. 4:1), which includes love (Eph. 5:2) and faith (2 Cor. 5:7). With respect to non-Christians they should conduct themselves with wisdom (Col. 4:5) and earn their respect by being self-sustaining (1 Thess. 4:12), rather than living in idleness (2 Thess. 3:6, 11). They are to behave as children of light (Eph. 5:8) and as the wise who know how to redeem the time during evil days (verses 15, 16). In a word, believers are to walk in a way that pleases God (1 Thess. 4:1). What pleases God is sanctified living (verse 3), and this includes purity in sexual relations (verses 3-8), "for God has not called us for uncleanness but in holiness" (verse 7).

The second consequence of the union of believers with Christ is that they need not, and therefore should not, let sin reign in their mortal bodies, to obey their continuing desires (Rom. 6:12). Though the old self has been crucified and sin's sovereignty over the body has been broken, the body still belongs to the old eon—that is why it is called "a mortal body"—and therefore has continuing desires. These are the avenues through which sin seeks to regain control over its former subjects. Hence, while Christians are freed from the reign of sin, they are not freed from sin's influence this side of the resurrection. The only thing that can keep sin from reestablishing its rule is what ended it, the grace of God (verse 14). Christians remain temptable through the old bodily appetites, but the power of God's Spirit can prevent these from becoming deeds of the flesh (Gal. 5:16-25).

The third consequence of union with Christ is that believers are asked to yield their members to God as weapons of righteousness instead of to sin as weapons of wickedness. This is the Christian warfare, and its reality helps to define the implications of death to sin mentioned in Romans 6:2. Death to sin does not mean that sin has no further relation to the life of the believer. Rather, having been freed from sin as lord, believers are to fight sin as enemy. Released from sin's sovereignty, they are to battle its solicitation. They have peace with God, but are to be aggressively hostile to sin.

In this struggle believers are to be "strong in the Lord" and "put on his armor" so that they may withstand the fiery darts of the evil one (Eph. 6:10-17). However, they must take heed lest, by thinking they stand above the struggle with temptation, they fall (1 Cor. 10:12). But this need not happen, for God has made a way of escape (verse 13).

The sanctification of the Christian is a constant movement forward. The will of God cannot be reduced to any fixed level of attainment. (Phil. 1:27; cf. Eph. 4:1). The reason for this is that Christ is the norm of Christian existence (Phil. 1:21) and what believers have learned about Him is to determine their behavior (Eph. 4:20). He teaches the truth they are to follow, and as Lord, illustrates in His own existence the principles of love, humility, and service believers are to emulate (Phil. 2:1-8). The example of Christ in suffering also calls for imitation; believers are to "follow in his steps" (1 Peter 2:21-23).

To consider Christ in this way is to see that there is no end to the journey of sanctification. There is fulfillment, but not finality; further advances are always to be made. One may already be living to please God, exemplifying love itself, but is to do so more and more (1 Thess. 4:2, 9, 10, 12). In the language of 2 Peter 1:5-7, God's people are to supplement faith with virtue, virtue with knowledge, knowledge with self-control, self-control with steadfastness, steadfastness with godliness, godliness with brotherly affection, and affection with love. The fundamental reason for the "more" of these texts is the inexhaustible nature and challenge of Christ's love, not the power of sin to render believers impotent to truly effect the good.

Furthermore, Christian love is to abound with knowledge and discernment so that the excellent may be approved, purity achieved, and a filling with the fruits of righteousness realized (Phil. 1:9). Such discernment does not take place by worldly conformation but by the mind's transformation. This alone enables the believer to prove God's will as to the good, acceptable, and perfect (Rom. 12:2). Thus, the sanctified life involves a continual quest to learn what pleases God in all the circumstances of life (Eph. 5:8, 9; 1 Thess. 4:1). This is a dynamic standard that calls to ever-deepening moral insight and fulfillment.

b. Sanctification and perfection

(1) Terminology. In the OT, the concept of perfection is represented chiefly by the words *tāmîm* and *šālēm,* which mean complete, whole, and full. In the Greek NT, perfection is connected with the word *teleios,* which means complete or mature—that which has reached its goal (*telos* in Greek).

In the OT, imperfect humans can be called perfect; for example, Noah (Gen. 6:9); Abraham (17:1), and Job (Job 1:1). The qualifiers of the word "perfect" as applied to these individuals are such traits as walking with God (Gen. 6:9, 17:1), fearing God, and turning away from evil (Job 1:1). The perfect person, seen here in these and other texts (Deuteronomy 18:13; Psalm 101:2, 6, in which the word "faithful" alternates with perfect or blameless; and Proverbs 11:5), is one whose heart and way are turned toward God. There is wholeness of commitment to God and His will. The heart aspect of this is seen by the fact that *šālēm* is often used with the word "heart" to indicate undivided dedication to God and His law (1 Kings 8:61). In the NT being *teleios* (perfect) is predicated of God, who asks for the same in humans (Matt. 5:48). In Romans 12:2 God's will is said to be perfect, and humans are called to know it. However, in neither Testament is perfection or blamelessness equated with sinlessness. For example, in the OT, persons like Noah and Abraham, with their weaknesses, were called perfect. In the NT, though the children of the kingdom are summoned to be perfect (Matt. 5:48), they are also to pray for forgiveness of their trespasses (Matt. 6:12, 14, 15). Thus, perfection contains aspiration as well as attainment.

It is likewise in 1 John. John speaks of the perfecting of God's love in the believer (2:5; 4:12, 17, 18) and connects this with keeping God's commandments and walking as Christ walked (2:4, 6). Nevertheless, John declares that those who make a claim to sinlessness are liars in need of God's forgiveness (1:8-10). It is correct then to say that "the sanctified heart is in harmony with the precepts of God's law" (AA 563), but that "sanctified lips will never give utterance to such presumptuous words" as "'I am sinless; I am holy'" (*ibid.* 561, 562), for this would dishonor God (*ibid.* 561). Sanctification is always movement forward; perfection always lies ahead.

(2) Relation of perfection to sanctification. Perfection is the consummation of sanctification, and because it calls from the future, sanctification must continually deepen. If perfection as a state were ultimately realized, sanctification as growth would be ultimately stultified. However, the implications of Jesus' teaching suggest that perfection is, in a meaningful sense, realizable, as in the statement "Be perfect" (Matt. 5:48), and "If you would be perfect" (Matt. 19:21). A dialectic seems to be involved. For sanctification it can be said: "You are, and yet, you are not"; for perfection: "You are not, and yet you are." Paradoxically, perfection as present is sanctification; sanctification as future is perfection. This means that the two realities are part and parcel of the same reality—likeness to God.

Philippians 3:12-16 is the best expression of the paradox of perfection as present and future. Against his opponents who propounded a realized eschatology, according to which they were already living the perfection of the resurrected life (cf. 2 Tim. 2:17, 18), Paul asserted that he had not yet obtained this perfection (Phil. 3:12). By sharing Christ's sufferings, becoming like Him in His death, he hoped to attain the resurrection from the dead (verse 11) and the perfection it would bring. In consequence, he was moving on to the perfection of the future. This meant making Christ fully his own, because Christ had already made him His own (verse 12). The consciousness of totally belonging to Christ propelled Paul into the quest for future perfection (verse 13). In

the race of this life, Paul was pressing on for the day when Christ, as in the Olympic games, would call him up to receive his prize of perfection (verse 14). Surprisingly, he then exhorts: "Let those of us who are mature [Greek, "perfect"] be thus minded" (verse 15). What Paul had denied as present is here said to be present. In other words, those who are perfect now are those who realize that perfection is ahead! And yet, paradoxically, "Let us hold true to what we have attained" (verse 16). What is to come in its fullness is now here in part (Phil. 1:6).

(3) Love the key to perfection. In 1 Thessalonians 3:13 and 5:23, while the word *teleios* itself does not occur, the concept of perfection is expressed in terms of unblamableness and being sanctified wholly, in every aspect of one's being. Significantly the perfect sanctification of 3:13 is tied to love. It is as our love increases to one another now (verse 12) that our hearts are established unblamable in holiness at the coming of Christ. Future holiness is based on present love. Love is the center of perfection's meaning, for it is the greatest commandment (Mark 12:28-34) and the fulfillment of all the commandments (Rom. 13:8-10; Gal. 5:14). Love is the way by which faith works (verse 6), the test of the presence of eternal life (1 John 3:15-18; 4:20, 21), and the true knowledge of God (verses 7, 8). Indeed, God is love (verse 8). By love the world knows who Christ's disciples are (John 13:35). When Jesus taught that kingdom people were to be perfect as God is perfect, He meant that they were to love and care for all, as God does (Matt. 5:44-47). Luke correctly grasps the meaning when he says, "Be merciful, even as your Father is merciful" (Luke 6:36). This does not weaken the depths of the challenge, but puts it into the right key. The heart of perfection is compassionate love. This love is even greater than faith and hope (1 Cor. 13:13), for these are exercises of humans alone. Love is the prime characteristic humans share with God.

(4) Perfection's Parousia. First Corinthians 13 points out the imperfect character of many of the values Christians prize now (verses 8, 9) and announces a complete change: "But when the perfect comes." This gives a new perspective. Perfection is not so much something we reach, as something that reaches us; not so much that which we attain, as something which grasps our lives from beyond. The God of grace came to us the first time in His earthborn Son, who gave His life for our sins. He will come a second time "not to deal with sin but to save those who are eagerly waiting for him" (Heb. 9:28). The Parousia (coming) of Christ for His own will be the consummation of His setting them apart in sanctification at the beginning of their Christian lives. It will be also the intersection between present moral growth by the power of God and perfecting the redeemed eternally through His love and grace. Until that day of final perfection, "we all, . . . beholding the glory of the Lord, are being changed into his likeness from one degree of glory to another; for this comes from the Lord" (2 Cor. 3:18).

IV. Practical Implications of the Doctrine of Salvation

The biblical doctrine of salvation is of ultimate relevance for experience because it says that the deepest needs of human life are not left to mindless chance, luck, or fate. They are under the control of the Almighty, who has loved us with an everlasting love. His salvific interest in us extends from eternity past into the limitless future. Human life is set within the circumference of God's eternal plan for our good. Thus, our lives may be lived with faith, hope, and love rather than anxiety, fear, and egocentricity. In meeting the saving God we learn how we may add our interest and effort to the saving of others; in encountering the love of God, how we may love one another as He loves us. Thus, salvation changes our individual lives in the here and now and gives us impetus to challenge those societal structures that hold people in bondage. By experiencing the freedom that God provides, we are inspired to cooperate with Him in helping to improve the conditions of others so that we can live together as brothers and sisters, as children of a loving Father. To know we are God's elect (not in an exclusive but an inclusive sense) can help us to journey through this world and life although things on every side are falling apart. Further, since salvation is for all, every saved sinner is a brother or sister to every other. Thus, salvation forges community and brings us all together in love and respect, worship and service, until that day when a loud voice from God's throne will say: "Behold, the dwelling of God is with men. He will dwell with them, and they shall be his people, and God himself will be with them" (Rev. 21:3; see Sabbath III. C).

V. History of the Doctrine of Salvation

A. The Apostolic Fathers

According to the NT, grace is an eschatological event effected by God on humanity's behalf prior to human decision for God. God reconciles mankind to Himself through the once-for-all sacrifice of Jesus and, in an entirely free act, declares sinful humans who respond to the message of the cross to be free of condemnation and in a right relation to Himself. Grace therefore, is strictly a transcendent reality. It is not in any way inherent in man nor does it become a property of man. It remains always and entirely a gift.

This fundamental understanding becomes altered radically in the Apostolic Fathers, which includes the *Didache,* the *Letter of Barnabas, 1 and 2 Clement,* the *Shepherd of*

Hermas, and the *Letters of Ignatius.* Already by the second century, in these writings God's gift of grace becomes subsidiary to God's call to live a new life of obedience in response to the enlightenment Christ has brought. So, while Christ, now more a teacher of ethics than a saviour from sin, gives the knowledge of the truth, religion focuses primarily on humanity's acts before God, which bring justification, instead of God's acts for humanity, the definitive source of justification. God's grace falls from grace, and the gospel becomes a new law. Jesus the person is displaced by Jesus' precepts, and faith is replaced by following an example.

B. From the Apostolic Fathers to Augustine

1. Irenaeus

In the second century Irenaeus, in his *Against Heresies,* taught that salvation occurs not so much through the cross of Christ as through His entire incarnate life. By identifying fully with humankind in every stage of its existence and being obedient where Adam was disobedient, Jesus restores humanity to fellowship with God and makes possible the renewal of God's image and the creation of God's likeness. He becomes what we humanly are, so that we might become what He divinely is. In this theory of recapitulation, the idea being drawn from Ephsians 1:10, Christ sums up in Himself all that had been lost in Adam, reverses the death that Adam brought, and crushes the head of Satan (the *Christus Victor* motif).

2. Tertullian

Tertullian, theologian of the Western Church in the third century, paved the way for the development of a number of teachings relating to salvation. One of these was original sin. Tertullian held that in Adam the souls of all were potentially present, so that when Adam fell, all fell with him, a theory called Traducianism from the Latin word meaning "transmit." From Adam sin is transmitted to

all. Anticipating Anselm, Tertullian also taught the idea of satisfaction. Those who have been baptized must not only confess their sins, but make satisfaction for them. (For Anselm, Christ makes the satisfaction.) Satisfaction is rendered by repentance and through tears, fasting, prayers, and almsgiving. Without this satisfaction there is no forgiveness. Thus humanity's merit secures God's forgiveness, and temporal mortifications discharge eternal punishments. Good deeds also gain merit in the satisfaction view. Tertullian thus laid the basis for the merit system of Catholicism and for the conception and practice of penance. In his emphasis upon Christ's victory over all the evil forces, he added his support to the concept of *Christus Victor.*

3. Origen

Origen, an Alexandrian scholar of the first half of the third century, was not only the greatest expert in Scripture of any writer in the early church, but his theological system was the most important achievement of the pre-Nicene church. Two aspects of his teaching on salvation stand out. First, he very strongly stressed the *Christus Victor* motif. Christ had a lifelong struggle with the evil forces but, through His death and resurrection, defeated them. Two relevant texts were Colossians 2:15 in which Christ, by His death, despoils the powers of evil, and 1 Corinthians 15:24-28, which announces the triumph of the resurrected Christ over all His enemies, including death. Second, in a subordinate thought to that of the defeat of the evil powers, Origen emphasized that Christ's death was a ransom, as in Mark 10:45. The question was: To whom was the ransom paid? Origen answered that since it could not have been to God, it must have been to the devil, for it was he who held us captive until the soul of Jesus was paid to him. But the devil was deceived, for he did not realize that he could not bear the torment of holding Christ's soul (Origen *Commentary on Romans* 2.13). Here Origen struck two notes that were to be heard repeatedly until the time of Anselm in the eleventh century: the idea that the cross of Jesus was the bargain made with the devil to ransom sinful humans from his dominion, and that the devil was tricked by what Christ did. A very pictorial representation of the latter point is found in Augustine who suggested that the cross, the price of our salvation, was held out to the devil like a mousetrap, baited with Christ's own blood (Augustine *Sermon* 130. 2 [NPNF-1 6:499]).

4. Eastern Theologians and Athanasius

In the fourth century Athanasius was the most important voice among Eastern theologians who affirmed that salvation involved a form of human deification as a result of Christ's incarnation. By the divine Christ's becoming like us, He restored us to God's image, and we become like Him. Important texts used by proponents of this view were Psalm 82:6, which speaks of God's people being "gods"; 2 Peter 1:4, which sees believers becoming partakers of the divine nature; and 1 Corinthians 15:49, which tells of bearing the image of the heavenly man as we have that of the earthly man.

5. Augustine and the Pelagian Controversy

The issues involved between the opposite and competing theologies of Augustine and Pelagius have remained crucial to the present day. Pelagianism found significant support in the Eastern Church, but was eventually condemned in both East and West. However, it has lived on and resurfaced time and again in the life of the church.

Pelagius, a person of high repute and learning, was a monk of British origin who came to Rome about the year 380. A man of great moral fervor, he was appalled by the moral laxity of Roman Christians and sought to elevate their ethical standards. He could advocate a high morality because he was optimistic about human nature. Human beings were basically good and, notwithstanding the sin of Adam, were able to choose the good. The fact that God gave His law to humankind indicated that man was able to perform this law for, in the words of Pelagius, "He has not willed to command anything impossible, for he is righteous; and he will not condemn a man for what he could not help, for he is holy" (Pelagius *Epistle to Demetrius* 16). Pelagius did not believe that man was a slave to sin and thus rejected the concept of original sin. "Everything good and everything evil, in respect of which we are either worthy of praise or of blame, is *done by us,* not *born with us."* We are born without virtue or vice, and before the exercise of our will there is nothing in us but what God stored there (Pelagius *On Free Will,* in Augustine *On Original Sin* 2. 13 [NPNF-1 5:241]). Since, in accord with Eastern views of Creation, each person's soul came into being independently and directly at the time of conception or birth (thus rejecting Traducianism), there is no fundamental connection with Adam and nothing that could be passed on from him to others in the way of original sin. Thus, being without congenital spiritual defect, each individual does evil or good originally. God has given man the possibility to choose the right, and each person is responsible for the exercise of his freedom to choose. Cohering with the concepts of human freedom and responsibility was Pelagius' doctrine of grace. Grace has a twofold meaning. On the one hand, there is the natural grace of Creation, which has to do with God's gift of reason and will, by which man is able to avoid evil. On the other, there is the external grace of enlightenment by which God, through such instruction as the Ten Commandments and the Sermon on the Mount, shows us how to conduct our lives, and thus motivates us toward His will. In this view grace is not a supernatural power that changes man from sin to goodness. Because man has sinned, especially through environmental influences, God offers him pardon, which is operative in adult baptism (infants need no baptism, but are in Adam's pre-Fall condition). Once baptized, however, man has both the duty and the ability to live for God. If he wishes, he can keep God's commands without sinning. Whether he has done so will be seen in the final judgment, where his works will determine his destiny. God's predestation refers to His foreknowledge, not decision, of who will choose to live for Him (Kelly 360).

Augustine, who had worked out his views before the Pelagian controversy, was the complete opposite of Pelagius. Because of Adam's sin, he affirmed, humanity has lost its original possibility not to sin. Human beings in their fallen condition, inherited from Adam, cannot help sinning. The will of humanity has been corrupted and, without the prevenient grace of God that awakens the possibility to choose for God, humans will inevitably choose evil. With prevenient grace, however, humans receive new supernatural beginnings. This grace predisposes and prompts the will before a human being ever wills. Thus, salvation begins by God's direct initiative. Prevenient grace is followed by cooperating grace, whereby God assists the person's will once it has been prompted to follow. This is succeeded by sufficient grace, which enables one to persevere in the good. The climax of God's bestowal of grace is efficient grace, which is the power for actually effecting the good. In all this God's grace is irresistible (Augustine *On Rebuke and Grace* 34-38 [NPNF-1 5: 485-487]) and based upon God's predestination, by which He has determined who among the mass of sinful humans will receive His supernatural grace. Thus, salvation is from God alone and for those He wills alone.

A compromise position is that of the so-called semi-Pelagians, whose most able exponent was John Cassianus, a monk of Marseilles. The semi-Pelagians believed that as a result of the Fall humanity's body became mortal, and his moral nature became corrupt. However, while his ability to freely will was corrupted, it was not entirely lost (as in Augustinianism). Contra Pelagius, grace was needed, for sin has produced moral impotence. However, since man is a free agent, he can cooperate with God. In positions contrary to Augustine they affirmed that: (1) sometimes the initiative in salvation was by God's grace, sometimes by humanity's will; (2) grace was not irresistible; and (3) predestination of some rather than all was not true. God wished all to be saved, and thus, as in Pelagius, predestination is allied with foreknowledge rather than foreordination. Semi-Pelagianism, though debated for decades, did not receive conciliar approval, but has persisted in the church as containing viable alternatives to the extremes of Pelagianism and Augustinianism.

C. Medieval Scholasticism

1. Anselm

In medieval times two figures stand out as proponents of views on salvation which have significantly affected the course of Christian thought. The first was Anselm, archbishop of Canterbury in the eleventh century. Anselm became known not only for his ontological argument for God's existence but especially for his contribution to the theology of the atonement found in his *Cur Deus Homo*. Anselm rejected the ransom theory that had reigned supreme some nine hundred years from the time of Origen. In rather tightly knit logic Anselm contested the view that God, as Creator of the world, owed the devil any legal rights (Anselm *Why God Became a Man* 1. 7). In place of this, he proposed his own version of the idea of satisfaction. This new view made sense in the setting of feudalism in Anselm's day. In feudal society it was the duty of the serf to preserve the honor of his lord. If he did not do so, an appropriate punishment, which would render satisfaction to the honor of his lord, had to be made. Likewise in the spiritual realm. Sinful humans had brought dishonor upon God. This necessitated that a proper reparation be paid so that God's honor could be restored. However, God demanded a satisfaction that no sinful human could make and something extra that no future obedience, already due God, could satisfy. Further, because God was the Lord of the universe, the satisfaction given to Him had to be greater than all the universe, except for God. Consequently, since the price for sin was one which only God could pay but which humanity was under obligation to pay, it was necessary for the God-man to pay the satisfaction price for humankind (*ibid.* 2. 6). Christ, as both God and sinless human, could give what was not already owed to God, His life. Thus, His voluntary death constituted full satisfaction for the sins of humankind.

2. Abelard

Another answer of a totally different kind was given by Abelard, a French monk and one of the most acute thinkers of the first half of the twelfth century. Abelard rejected not only ransom and expiatory concepts but in particular the satisfaction theory of Anselm. He proposed instead what has been called the moral influence theory of the atonement. This view was a counterbalance to the very legal argument of Anselm, and is found in his Romans commentary and in *Epitome of Christian Theology*. In his expositions Abelard could utilize such traditional ideas as price, sacrifice, and merit, but the concept that captivated him and became central to his thought was that of divine love awakening the human response of love. Abelard raised the question as to how the death of God's innocent Son could so please the Father that through it God brings about reconciliation. The answer was that by Christ taking our nature and persevering even to death in instructing us by word and deed, He so closely attached Himself to us as to beget in us true love, which would be willing to endure anything for His sake. In harmony with Jesus' saying that there is no greater love than to lay down one's life for his friends, our redemption is that supreme love which is inspired in us by the passion of Christ, a love which both frees from slavery to sin and gives the freedom of being sons of God. As a result, fear is banished and we are filled with love for Christ. In a word, justification is the kindling of God's love in humanity's heart in view of the cross (Abelard *Commentary on Romans* 3. 26; 5. 5). Thus, love is the motive, method,

and result of God's redemption. Abelard offers no theory as to how the cross manifests God's love, but he is content to announce that the love shown in the cross is the central datum of faith. However, inasmuch as Abelard stresses Christ's identification with humanity, his understanding of how love is shown may well be caught by saying that Christ suffered with rather than for the sinner (Reid 11).

D. Reformation Thought and Catholic Reaction

1. Luther

Martin Luther's search for peace with God, which led him into the rigors of the monastic life which he greatly intensified in severity, found its resolution when he discovered the meaning of the revelation of the "righteousness of God" in Romans 1:17. He felt reborn with heaven's door opened when he found that this revelation was not of God's righteous wrath, by which He punishes the sinner, but of God's saving righteousness, by which the sinner may gain a right standing with God and freedom from condemnation. The sinner, as a passive receptacle, without any righteousness of his own, receives the alien righteousness of God by which he can stand in God's presence without fear. This righteousness or justification, which is a declaration of the change in the sinner's status rather than an infusion of goodness into his soul, as in Augustinianism, is grounded in the obedience of Christ in His life and atoning death on the cross.

This means, in accordance with Scripture, that salvation can be only by faith alone, by grace alone, and by Christ alone. For Luther, Christ is our righteousness, and this reality can be apprehended only by faith, for faith connects one with Christ. Since original sin cannot be eradicated in this life, and humanity's will is in bondage outside of Christ, faith must be God's gift that He works in humanity. This carries with it the idea of predestination, and Luther was strongly predestinarian. He can speak of justification as both a completed event—the sinner has been forgiven and is right with God—and as an event that initiates a process that will change the believer's interior life into likeness to Christ (McKim 91, 92). Since the latter will not be accomplished until the transformation of this body of death at the resurrection, the sinner remains *simul justus et peccator,* at the same time righteous (in his or her relation to God) and sinner (one who still has imperfections and sinful deeds). Though one remains a sinner, good works follow faith as its fruit and as the attestation of justification.

2. Calvin

John Calvin accepted the basic premises of the Lutheran Reformation on justification by faith, but brought a closer relationship between justification and sanctification by speaking of both of these realities as given to believers simultaneously by virtue of their incorporation into Christ (Calvin *Institutes* 3. 16. 1). The resultant union with Christ means that while justification and sanctification may be distinguished, they can never be separated. These two gifts are parts of one union with Christ. A troubling aspect of Calvin's teaching was his strong advocacy of double predestination as seen in the following statement in his *Institutes:* "By predestination we mean the eternal decree of God, by which he has decided in his own mind what he wishes to happen in the case of each individual. For all men are not created on an equal footing, but for some eternal life is preordained, for others eternal damnation" (3. 21. 5). One result of predestination to salvation was that it implied total assurance of final salvation. One predestined by God's sovereign decree could not be lost.

3. The Council of Trent

The Council of Trent met in 25 sessions from 1545 to 1563. While interested in reform in every area of the church's life, the bishops and theologians who made up the council believed that what they said on justification, in response to Luther, would be their most important theological work (Jedin 2:171). Their answer to the Reformation teaching of justification by faith alone through the imputation of Christ's alien righteousness is found in chapter 7 of the council's decrees. Here the council speaks of the prevenient grace of God that calls sinners, apart from any merits in themselves, and disposes them by God's quickening grace to effect their own justification by assenting to and cooperating with God's grace. While God's Spirit is active in this, humans are not passive (a direct counter to Reformation thought), for they have the ability to reject God's grace. But to be righteous they need God's grace. Following the preparation that prevenient grace makes possible comes justification, which is not merely forgiveness of sins but also the sanctification and renewal of the inner self. Here justification is said to be, in essence, sanctification, which was the position of Augustine. The formal cause of justification is the justice of God by which He makes us to be truly just within ourselves through the renewing of the spirit of our mind and the implantation in the heart not only of faith (as in the Reformers) but also of hope and love (Grensted 173-177; Toon 68, 69). Furthermore, the council anathematized anyone who taught that free will was wholly lost after Adam's fall, that a justified person must believe that he or she is assuredly a member of those predestined to salvation, and that that person cannot sin or lose grace.

We see here a number of important emphases: Justification as sanctification rather than leading to sanctification, as in Reformation thought; justification as intrinsic rather than extrinsic, infused rather than imputed, making righteous rather than pronouncing righteous; man as actor and cooperator rather than passive; atonement having to do not only with the Godward side but the humanward insofar as human beings are changed thereby; and a rejection of the view that a person once saved is always saved, no matter what sins are committed.

E. Arminianism and Methodism

1. Jacobus Arminius

A reaction to the predestinarian teachings of Calvinism found its strongest voice in Jacobus Arminius. The launching point for Arminius' position was a focus on the order of God's decrees. Did God first decree election and reprobation, and then permit the fall so as to make effective the decree (the supralapsarian position), or did He foresee and permit humanity's fall and then decree election so as to bring salvation (the infralapsarian position). Arminius, while called upon to defend supralapsarianism, decided against it and argued for freedom in humans, which was contrary to Calvinism. Arminius charged that predestination, as understood in Calvinism, made God the author of sin. Further, while he did not deny election, he based it not on an arbitrary divine decree but on God's foreknowledge of humanity's faith. Arminius' views were developed in his Five Articles, which contained the following elements (Bettenson 376, 377): (1) In eternity God determined to save those who would believe and persevere in faith and to condemn unbelievers; (2) Jesus died for all and has thus procured salvation for all, but this is effective only for believers; (3) humans, because of sin, have no ability in themselves or by the exercise of free will to do good; this is possible only by the renewing power of the Holy Spirit; (4) even the regenerate cannot do good or resist temptation without the grace of God; (5) believers can by the grace of God win the victory against Satan, sin, the world, and their own flesh, but whether they can lose their salvation must be studied further.

2. John Wesley

Wesley, who lived in the eighteenth century, was Arminian in his theological stance, as was the Anglican Church of which he was a part. The wellsprings for his concept of salvation lay in views on the atonement. Wesley, like evangelicalism today, taught that Christ's death was a penal and substitutionary sacrifice which propitiated God's just wrath, satisfied his justice, and thus enabled God to forgive sin in a way consistent with his holiness. Christ's atoning death made possible justification and sanctification. Justification included forgiveness of sins and acceptance of the sinner by God. The former covered the past, and the latter involved a new relationship with God in the present. He did not stress imputed righteousness because it might imply antinomianism. The new birth, a real change in us, which accompanied justification and yet was distinct from it, formed the transition from justification to sanctification. By sanctification one was saved from sin's power and root and restored to God's image. Sanctification had as its outcome, even in this life, the perfection of the believer, entire sanctification. In his book *A Plain Account of Christian Perfection*, Wesley tells what perfection is not (12. 2). It is not being perfect in knowledge, being free from mistakes, infirmities and temptations, or being without the need to continually grow. Thus, for Wesley, perfection was not a static, but a dynamic reality, not a "perfected perfection" but a "perfecting perfection" (Collins 118, 119). Wesley saw perfection as overcoming pride, self-will, evil tempers and thoughts, and restoring the mind of Christ (*A Plain Account of Christian Perfection* 12). For him, "entire sanctification" was "love excluding sin; love filling the heart, taking up the whole capacity of the soul" (Wesley *The Scripture Way of Salvation* 1. 9).

Wesley's perfection requires a distinction between two kinds of sin: "proper sin," which involves deliberate violations of God's law, and "improper sin," which comes from human ignorance and weakness. The first can be avoided, but not the second. Thus, perfection is relative. Where anyone is short of absolute perfection, Christ's atonement continues to avail (Ward 471, 472; Williams 179). Consequently, for Wesley no one becomes so perfect as to be without the need of forgiveness and dependence upon Christ (see Williams 177).

VI. Seventh-day Adventists

Seventh-day Adventists see themselves as heirs of and builders upon the Reformation insights into biblical teaching on justification by grace through faith alone, and restorers and exponents of the fullness, clarity, and balance of the apostolic gospel.

Adventist soteriology is connected with biblical eschatology and is set within the context of the overarching Adventist concept of the great controversy between Christ and Satan. posed to earth, has to do with the character of God, whether He is just and merciful, and with the law of God, whether it can be kept, and how its claims are to be satisfied once sin has entered.

In their explication of the solution to the great controversy, Adventists, through study, reflection, and divine guidance, have concluded that salvation contains no thread of human devising (1SM 396). It is the product of God's grace alone, which effects a new status and right relationship of sinners with God and, arising from that relationship, transforms them into the image of Christ. At the heart of Adventism is the Christological understanding that Christ is both Saviour and Lord. "If we accept Christ as a Redeemer, we must accept Him as a Ruler" (FW 16). As Saviour, Christ offers to mankind the gift of salvation and, as Lord, He calls for walking in newness of life (Rom. 6:4), manifesting the fruit of the Spirit (Gal. 5:22), and obedience to God's law (Rom. 8:4; Rev. 14:12) as the "service and allegiance of love," "the true sign of discipleship" (SC 60). Adventists have included both these elements under "righteousness by faith." "Our only ground of hope is in the righteousness of Christ imputed to us, and in that wrought by His Spirit working in and through us" (*ibid.* 63). To be righteous by faith means in the full sense that we have received from God both our title to heaven (justification) and our fitness for heaven (sanctification) (DA 300). Only by a faith union with Christ can these two great soteriological realities occur. Indeed, when justification has produced a new people in whose hearts Christ is present and His law is written, the great controversy will be over, and Christ will come again.

In Adventist thought the question of satisfying the claims of God's broken law is answered in the death of Christ and its result upon those who accept the efficacy of that death by faith. At the cross, in an act of divinely offered, voluntary, substitutionary, and representative sacrifice, by which the validity of God's law was forever upheld and the penalty of God's law was forever satisfied, Christ died for and in place of sinners. In this event, which both procured and expressed their forgiveness, self-giving rather than self-seeking love was seen to be the law of life for the universe (cf. DA 20, 21). It is this love and the law it represents that, in fulfillment of the new covenant promise (Jer. 31:33; Heb. 8:10), is written upon the hearts of believers. When this love, which is the character of Christ, is perfectly reproduced in God's people, that is, when it floods their souls, dominates their lives, and motivates their actions, Christ will come (COL 67-69). In Adventist thought God is waiting and working for the reproduction of Christ's character in His people. The loveliness and "matchless charms of the character of Christ" (4BC 1178), experienced and expressed in God's people, will answer all the charges of the evil one and bring closure to the great controversy.

Adventist thinking on the atonement sees it as containing two stages: Christ's sacrifice for sin on the cross and His priestly ministry in the heavenly sanctuary. There He applies for believers the salvific benefits of His death. This heavenly ministry of forgiveness and reconciliation is climaxed by the cleansing of the sanctuary, beginning in 1844 (Dan. 8:14; cf. Heb. 9:23). This event entails an "investigative" or "preadvent" judgment through which is revealed who the true people of God are, whose record of sins may be totally expunged. In contrast are those who are merely professed people of God for whom the ultimate efficacy of Christ's sacrifice cannot be applied since, in their lives, the reflected character of Christ, which the cross makes possible, has not been revealed. In consequence of this judgment, when Christ returns, His verdict and reward will be with Him and will be rendered when all meet before the throne of God (Rev. 20:11-15).

When the saving activity of God has run its full course and restored the image of God in humankind, then not only the inhabitants of this world but those of the universe, for whom the redemption of this world has been a lesson book (DA 19), will confess what Scripture has declared to be true: "God is love" (1 John 4:8; GC 678).

VII. Ellen G. White Comments

A. God's Purpose to Save

The plan of salvation is "an unfolding of the principles that from eternal ages have been the foundation of God's throne" (DA 22).

1. Everyone Can Find Deliverance

"Every man is free to choose what power he will have to rule over him" (*ibid.* 258).

2. How We Are Saved

"His love is drawing us to Himself. If we do not resist this drawing, we shall be led to the foot of the cross in repentance. . . . Then the Spirit of God through faith produces a new life in the soul. The thoughts and desires are brought into obedience to the will of Christ. . . . The law of God is written in the mind and heart" (*ibid.* 176).

3. God Spares Nothing for Our Salvation

"The gift of Christ reveals the Father's heart. . . . It declares that while God's hatred of sin is as strong as death, His love for the sinner is stronger than death. Having undertaken our redemption, He will spare nothing, however dear, which is necessary to the completion of His work. . . . The whole treasury of heaven is open to those He seeks to save" (*ibid.* 57).

4. Sinner's Inability to Resist Evil

"Through disobedience, his [humanity's] powers were perverted, and selfishness took the place of love. His nature became so weak-

ened through transgression that it was impossible for him, in his own strength, to resist the power of evil. He was made captive by Satan, and would have remained so forever had not God specially interposed" (SC 17).

5. Christ's Righteousness: Title and Fitness for Heaven

"The proud heart strives to earn salvation; but both our title to heaven and our fitness for it are found in the righteousness of Christ" (DA 300).

6. Sinners Accounted Righteous

"It was possible for Adam, before the fall, to form a righteous character by obedience to God's law. But he failed to do this, and because of his sin our natures are fallen, and we cannot . . . perfectly obey the holy law. . . . But Christ has made a way of escape for us. . . . If you give yourself to Him, and accept Him as your Saviour, then, sinful as your life may have been, for His sake you are accounted righteous. Christ's character stands in place of your character, and you are accepted before God just as if you had not sinned" (SC 62).

7. More Than Forgiveness

"Forgiveness has a broader meaning than many suppose. . . . God's forgiveness is not merely a judicial act by which He sets us free from condemnation. It is not only forgiveness *for* sin, but reclaiming *from* sin" (MB 114). "It means taking away our sins, and filling the vacuum with the graces of the Holy Spirit" (COL 420).

B. Christ's Atoning Death

"The sacrifice of Christ as an atonement for sin is the great truth around which all other truths cluster. . . . Every truth in the word of God, from Genesis to Revelation, must be studied in the light that streams from the cross of Calvary. I present before you the great, grand monument of mercy and regeneration, salvation and redemption—the Son of God uplifted on the cross" (GW 315). "Hanging upon the cross Christ was the gospel" (7-A BC 456).

Christ's suffering "did not begin or end with His manifestation in humanity. The cross is a revelation to our dull senses of the pain that, from its very inception, sin has brought to the heart of God" (Ed 263).

1. Atonement Not Cause of Divine Love

"The atonement of Christ was not made in order to induce God to love those whom He otherwise hated; and it was not made to produce a love that was not in existence; but it was made as a manifestation of the love that was already in God's heart" (ST May 30, 1895).

"The atonement of Christ was not the cause of God's love, but the result of that love. Jesus died because God loved the world" (RH Sept. 2, 1890).

"The Father loves us, not because of the great propitiation, but He provided the propitiation because He loves us. Christ was the medium through which He could pour out His infinite love upon a fallen world. 'God was in Christ, reconciling the world unto himself.' God suffered with His Son, in the agony of Gethsemane, the death of Calvary; the heart of Infinite Love paid the price of our redemption" (SC 13, 14).

2. Treated as We Deserve

"Christ was treated as we deserve, that we might be treated as He deserves. He was condemned for our sins, in which He had no share, that we might be justified by His righteous-

ness, in which we had no share. He suffered the death which was ours, that we might receive the life which was His. 'With His stripes we are healed'" (DA 25).

3. Necessity of Cross for Forgiveness

"There could have been no pardon for sin had this atonement not been made. Had God pardoned Adam's sin without an atonement, sin would have been immortalized, and would have been perpetuated with a boldness that would have been without restraint" (RH Apr. 23, 1901).

4. Unity Between Justice and Mercy

"His [Christ's] object was to reconcile the prerogatives of justice and mercy, and let each stand separate in its dignity, yet united. His mercy was not weakness, but a terrible power to punish sin because it is sin; yet a power to draw to it the love of humanity. Through Christ justice is enabled to forgive without sacrificing one jot of its exalted holiness" (GCB 1899, 102).

5. Sin Punished in Christ

"Our sins were laid on Christ, punished in Christ, put away by Christ, in order that His righteousness might be imputed to us, who walk not after the flesh, but after the Spirit" (ST May 30, 1895).

6. The Atmosphere of Grace

"In the matchless gift of His Son, God has encircled the whole world with an atmosphere of grace as real as the air which circulates around the globe. All who choose to breathe this life-giving atmosphere will live" (SC 68).

C. The Role of Faith

"Through faith we receive the grace of God; but faith is not our Saviour. It earns nothing. It is the hand by which we lay hold upon Christ, and appropriate His merits, the remedy for sin" (DA 175).

1. Faith Is . . .

"It [faith] is an assent of the understanding to God's words which binds the heart in willing consecration and service to God, who gave the understanding, who moved on the heart, who first drew the mind to view Christ on the cross of Calvary. Faith is rendering to God the intellectual powers, abandonment of the mind and will to God" (FW 25).

2. Christ Dishonored by Our Unbelief

"We look to self, as though we had power to save ourselves; but Jesus died for us because we are helpless to do this. . . . At this very time He is . . . inviting us to come to Him in our helplessness and be saved. We dishonor Him by our unbelief. It is astonishing how we treat our very best Friend, how little confidence we repose in Him who is able to save to the uttermost, and who has given us every evidence of His great love" (1SM 351).

3. Victory in Christ

"The omnipotent power of the Holy Spirit is the defense of every contrite soul. Not one that in penitence and faith has claimed His protection will Christ permit to pass under the enemy's power. The Saviour is by the side of His tempted and tried ones. With Him there can be no such thing as failure, loss, impossibility, or defeat; we can do all things through Him who strengthens us. When temptations and trials come, do not wait to adjust all the difficulties, but look to Jesus, your helper" (DA 490, 493).

4. Problems With Saying "I Am Saved"

"We are never to rest in a satisfied condition, and cease to make advancement, saying, 'I am saved.' When this idea is entertained, the motives for watchfulness, for prayer, for earnest endeavor to press onward to higher attainments, cease to exist. No sanctified tongue will be found uttering these words till Christ shall come" (1SM 314).

"Never can we safely put confidence in self or feel, this side of heaven, that we are secure against temptation. . . . Even when we give ourselves to Christ and know that He accepts us, we are not beyond the reach of temptation" (COL 155).

D. Hope for the Weakest

"The Saviour would have passed through the agony of Calvary that one might be saved in His kingdom. He will never abandon one for whom He has died. Unless His followers choose to leave Him, He will hold them fast" (DA 483).

1. Don't Be Discouraged by Shortcomings

"We shall often have to bow down and weep at the feet of Jesus because of our shortcomings and mistakes; but we are not to be discouraged. Even if we are overcome by the enemy, we are not cast off, not forsaken and rejected of God. No; Christ is at the right hand of God, who also maketh intercession for us" (SC 64).

2. Let the Mind Dwell on Christ, Not Self

"When the mind dwells upon self, it is turned away from Christ, the source of strength and life. Hence it is Satan's constant effort to keep the attention diverted from the Saviour. . . . The pleasures of the world, life's cares and perplexities and sorrows, the faults of others, or your own faults and imperfections—to any or all of these he will seek to divert the mind. Do not be misled by his devices. . . . We should not make self the center, and indulge anxiety and fear as to whether we shall be saved. All this turns the soul away from the Source of our strength. Commit the keeping of your soul to God, and trust in Him. . . . He is able to keep that which you have committed to Him" (*ibid.* 71, 72).

3. The Weakest Saint Stronger Than Satan

"Satan is constantly at work, but few have any idea of his activity and subtlety. The people of God must be prepared to withstand the wily foe. It is this resistance that Satan dreads. He knows better than we do the limit of his power and how easily he can be overcome if we resist and face him. Through divine strength the weakest saint is more than a match for him and all his angels, and if brought to the test he would be able to prove his superior power" (5T 293).

4. Holy Spirit and Regeneration

"The Holy Spirit was the highest of all gifts that He could solicit from His Father for the exaltation of His people. The Spirit was to be given as a regenerating agent, and without this the sacrifice of Christ would have been of no avail. The power of evil had been strengthening for centuries, and the submission of men to this satanic captivity was amazing. Sin could be resisted and overcome only through the mighty agency of the Third Person of the Godhead, who would come with no modified energy, but in the fullness of divine power. It is the Spirit that makes effectual what has been wrought out by the world's Redeemer. It is by the Spirit that the heart is made pure. Through the Spirit the believer becomes a partaker of the divine nature. Christ has given His Spirit as a divine power to overcome all hereditary and cultivated tendencies to evil, and to impress His own character upon His church" (DA 671).

5. Complete Recovery From Sin

"The plan of redemption contemplates our complete recovery from the power of Satan. Christ always separates the contrite soul from sin. He came to destroy the works of the devil, and He has made provision that the Holy Spirit shall be imparted to every repentant soul, to keep him from sinning. . . . A holy temper, a Christlike life, is accessible to every repenting, believing child of God" (*ibid.* 311).

6. A Great Change

"Our lives will reveal whether the grace of God is dwelling within us. A change will be seen in the character, the habits, the pursuits. The contrast will be clear and decided between what they have been and what they are" (SC 57).

7. The Test of Conversion

"Who has the heart? With whom are our thoughts? Of whom do we love to converse? . . . If we are Christ's, our thoughts are with Him, and our sweetest thoughts are of Him" (*ibid.* 58).

E. Sanctification: Work of a Lifetime

"Sanctification is not the work of a moment, an hour, a day, but of a lifetime. It is not gained by a happy flight of feeling, but is the result of constantly dying to sin, and constantly living for Christ. Wrongs cannot be righted nor reformations wrought in the character by feeble, intermittent efforts. It is only by long, persevering effort, sore discipline, and stern conflict, that we shall overcome. We know not one day how strong will be our conflict the next. So long as Satan reigns, we shall have self to subdue, besetting sins to overcome; so long as life shall last, there will be no stopping place, no point which we can reach and say, I have fully attained. Sanctification is the result of lifelong obedience" (AA 560, 561).

1. How to Surrender to God

"You cannot change your heart, you cannot of yourself give to God its affections; but you can *choose* to serve Him. You can give Him your will; He will then work in you to will and to do according to His good pleasure" (SC 47).

2. Obedience the Fruit of Faith

"While good works will not save even one soul, yet it is impossible for even one soul to be saved without good works" (1SM 377).

3. Obedience as Carrying Out Our Own Impulses

"If we consent, He will so identify Himself with our thoughts and aims, so blend our hearts and minds into conformity to His will, that when obeying Him we shall be but carrying out our own impulses. The will, refined and sanctified, will find its highest delight in doing His service. When we know God as it is our privilege to know Him, our life will be a life of continual obedience. Through an appreciation of the character of Christ, through communion with God, sin will become hateful to us" (DA 668).

4. Perfection of the Soul in Christ

"While we cannot claim perfection of the flesh, we may have Christian perfection of the soul. Through the sacrifice made in our behalf, sins may be perfectly forgiven" (2SM 32).

5. Holy in Our Sphere

"With our limited powers we are to be as holy in our sphere as God is holy in His sphere. To the extent of our ability, we are to make manifest the truth and love and excellence of the divine character" (1SM 337).

6. God's Ideal for His Children

"God's ideal for His children is higher than the highest human thought can reach. 'Be ye therefore perfect, even as your Father which is in heaven is perfect.' This command is a promise. The plan of redemption contemplates our complete recovery from the power of Satan. Christ always separates the contrite soul from sin. He came to destroy the works of the devil, and He has made provision that the Holy Spirit shall be imparted to every repentant soul, to keep him from sinning" (DA 311).

7. Perfection as Perfect Submission

"It may take time to attain perfect submission to God's will, but we can never stop short of it and be fitted for heaven. True religion will lead its possessor on to perfection" (3T 538).

8. Christ Gives Victory Over Inclinations and Lusts

"Christ came to this world and lived the law of God, that man might have perfect mastery over the natural inclinations which corrupt the soul. The Physician of soul and body, He gives victory over warring lusts. He has provided every facility, that man may possess completeness of character" (MH 130, 131).

9. Character Revealed by Habitual Words and Acts

"The character is revealed, not by occasional good deeds and occasional misdeeds, but by the tendency of the habitual words and acts" (SC 57, 58).

10. Christ's Perfection for Those Who Are Trying

"When it is in the heart to obey God, when efforts are put forth to this end, Jesus accepts this disposition and effort as man's best service, and He makes up for the deficiency with His own divine merit" (1SM 382).

11. Perfection Is Progressive

"The germination of the seed represents the beginning of spiritual life, and the development of the plant is a figure of the development of character. There can be no life without growth. The plant must either grow or die. As its growth is silent and imperceptible, but continuous, so is the growth of character. At every stage of development our life may be perfect; yet if God's purpose for us is fulfilled, there will be constant advancement" (Ed 105, 106).

"Day by day the believer is working out before men and angels a sublime experiment, showing what the gospel can do for fallen human beings" (AA 483).

12. The Perfect See Their Defects

"Those who are really seeking to perfect Christian character will never indulge the thought that they are sinless. Their lives may be irreproachable, they may be living representatives of the truth which they have accepted; but the more they discipline their minds to dwell upon the character of Christ, and the nearer they approach to His divine image, the more clearly will they discern its spotless perfection, and the more deeply will they feel their own defects" (SL 7).

VIII. Literature

Anselm. *St. Anselm: Basic Writings.* Trans. S. N. Deane. 2nd ed. La Salle, Ill.: Open Court, 1962.

Barclay, William. *The Mind of St. Paul.* New York: Harper, 1958.

Bettenson, Henry, ed. *Documents of the Christian Church.* New York: Oxford University Press, 1947.

Cave, Sydney. *The Doctrine of the Work of Christ.* London: London University Press, 1947.

Collins, Kenneth J. *Wesley on Salvation: A Study in the Standard Sermons.* Grand Rapids: Francis Asbury, 1989.

Green, E.M.B. *The Meaning of Salvation.* Philadelphia: Westminster, 1965.

Grensted, L. W. *A Short History of the Atonement.* Manchester: Manchester University Press, 1962.

Hengel, Martin. *The Atonement.* Trans. John Bowden. Philadelphia: Fortress, 1981.

Heppenstall, Edward. *Salvation Unlimited.* Washington, D.C.: Review and Herald, 1974.

Jedin, Hubert. *A History of the Council of Trent.* 2 vols. Edinburgh: Thomas Nelson and Sons, 1961.

Johnson, Alan F., and Robert E. Webber. *What Christians Believe: A Biblical and Historical Summary.* Grand Rapids: Zondervan, 1989.

Kelly, J.N.D. *Early Christian Doctrines.* 2nd ed. London: Adam & Charles Black, 1958.

Knight, George R. *The Pharisee's Guide to Perfect Holiness: A Study of Sin and Salvation.* Boise: Pacific Press, 1992.

LaRondelle, Hans K. *Christ Our Salvation.* Mountain View, Calif.: Pacific Press, 1980.

Landa, Paul J. "Medieval Perspectives on the Atonement." In *The Sanctuary and the Atonement: Biblical, Historical and Theological Studies.* Ed. Arnold V. Wallenkampf and W. Richard Lesher. Washington, D.C.: Biblical Research Institute, 1981.

McGrath, Alister. *Justification by Faith: What It Means to Us Today.* Grand Rapids: Academie, 1988.

McKim, Donald K. *Theological Turning Points: Major Issues in Christian Thought.* Atlanta: John Knox, 1988.

Mozley, J. K. *The Doctrine of Atonement.* New York: C. Scribner's Sons, 1916; London: Duckworth, 1915.

Reid, George. "Why Did Jesus Die?" *Adventist Review,* Nov. 5, 1992.

Righteousness by Faith Consultation. "The Dynamics of Salvation." *Adventist Review,* July 31, 1980.

Rodríguez, Angel Manuel. "Salvation by Sacrificial Substitution." *Journal of the Adventist Theological Society* 3, No. 2 (1992): 49-77.

Strack, Herman L. *Introduction to the Talmud and Midrash.* Philadelphia: Jewish Publication Society of America, 1931.

Taylor, Vincent. *Forgiveness and Reconciliation.* New York: St. Martin's Press, 1946.

Toon, Peter. *Justification and Sanctification.* Westchester: Good News, 1983.

Torrance, Thomas F. *The Doctrine of Grace in the Apostolic Fathers.* Grand Rapids: Eerdmans, 1960.

Ward, Cedric. "The Atonement in Wesley's Theology." In *The Sanctuary and the Atonement: Biblical, Historical and Theological Studies.* Ed. Arnold V. Wallenkampf and W. Richard Lesher, 464-477. Washington, D.C.: Biblical Research Institute, 1981.

Wesley, John. *A Plain Account of Christian Perfection.* London: Epworth, 1968.

Williams, Colin W. *John Wesley's Theology Today.* Nashville: Abingdon, 1960.

Death: Origin, Nature, and Final Eradication

Niels-Erik A. Andreasen

Introduction

Death is ever with us, regardless of age, position, or financial situation. Whatever attempts are made to dress it in acceptable garb, death remains our ultimate—and currently invincible—enemy. Despite flowers and speeches, death is an ugly specter lurking in everyone's experience. Furthermore, it is not only ubiquitous and repulsive but also incomprehensible.

In different times and places death and what ensues have been explained in diverse manners, yet there is no clear answer to the problem of death except in the Scriptures. Indeed, even those who take the Bible seriously often misunderstand its teaching on this topic.

This article considers the biblical teaching on death: what it means, where it came from, what happens to those who die, and finally, how death will be eradicated. Seen from this biblical perspective, death, loathsome as it may be, loses its stranglehold on human existence. Paul put it well: "Death is swallowed up in victory" (1 Cor. 15:54).

I. Biblical Exposition

A. Terminology and Definitions of Humans

The Bible's distinctive understanding of death comes to clear expression in its terminology. This will be clarified by an examination of the words and expressions for death, followed by a consideration of the biblical definition of life and death.

1. Words for Death in the OT

The root *mwt*, "died," as well as its nominal derivatives *(māwet, t^emûṯāh, māmôṯ)* occurs approximately 1,000 times. Although *mwt* is a common Semitic root, appearing prominently in Ugaritic literature and with an Egyptian equivalent, it has no plausible etymology. The basic verbal meaning is simply "to die," primarily with reference to people, occasionally to animals (Gen. 33:13), and only rarely to plant life (Job 14:8). Figurative usage, applying the word to the loss of property (Gen. 47:19) or of wisdom (Job 12:2), is rare indeed in the Bible, though common in our time (e.g., deadpan, dead bolt, deadweight). The unusual expression "his heart died within him" (1 Sam. 25:37) may indicate a loss of courage on the part of Nabal (he lost heart). However, it could also indicate a real, as opposed to a figurative, cessation of heart function, which in OT symbolism would indicate brain death. This is to say, Nabal suffered a stroke, or as the Bible puts it, "he became as a stone." This would also explain the following verse (38): "And about ten days later the Lord smote Nabal; and he died."

A related root *gw'*, "die," occurs in parallel to *mwt* (Job 3:11; 14:10), but may indicate death as the termination of life following some deprivation or misfortune (cf. Zech. 13:8; Ps. 88:15). In the *pilpel* and *hiphil* stems the verbal form of *mwt* is translated "kill," "put to

death." Here it joins several other related verbs such as *hārag*, "kill," "slay"; *rāṣaḥ*, "kill," "murder"; the rare *qāṭal*, "kill"; and *nākāh*, "strive," "smite."

The nominal form *māwet*, "death," simply characterizes death as the opposite of life and marks its end (Deut. 30:19; Prov. 18:21; Jer. 8:3). Finally, the OT speaks of death and dying by means of several unique expressions, for example, "breathed his last" (Gen. 25:8), "gathered to his people" (49:33), "slept with his fathers" (1 Kings 2:10).

Note should also be taken of the word *š^e'ôl*, "realm of death," which etymologically may be related to *šā'āh*, "lie waste," "be devalued," and which refers to the nether world (Isa. 14:9; Ps. 139:8), to the realm of death (Ps. 18:5; Hosea 13:14), to the insatiable grave (Prov. 27:20), and theologically speaking, to the absence of God, worship, and the normal life processes (Isa. 38:18; Ps. 6:5).

Throughout the OT the words for death point to a single understanding: the complete termination of life, its expressions, and functions.

2. Words for Death in the NT

The words *thanatos*, "death"; *thnētos*, "mortal"; *thanatoō*, "kill"; *thnēskō*, "die"; and derivatives are common Greek terms with an extensive usage in extrabiblical literature. They refer to death and the certain end of life, but according to classical Greek usage, not to the end of human existence. For in classical usage death was thought to affect only the body, not the soul, which was believed to be liberated at death and to live on afterward. However, the NT usage of these same words reveals a different meaning altogether. Here they refer "dying" or "being dead" to the end of life, that dreadful end and fearful lot of all people (1 Cor. 15:54, 55; Heb. 2:15; Rev. 6:8). Consequently, in contrast with classical usage, dying is never portrayed in heroic terms in the NT, not even the death of Christ (Matt. 26:36-46). Rather, death always represents the enemy of life and of people, indeed, the last enemy (1 Cor. 15:26). It is never a natural transition from one segment of human existence to another (TDNT 3:15).

Nekros, "dead" or "dead person or body," and *nekroō,* "put to death" or "kill," confirm this meaning of death. To be dead *(nekros)* means to be lifeless (Acts 28:6; Rom. 7:8), distinct from being alive (Mark 12:27), therefore in a figurative sense, separated from God, unfortunate, lost (Luke 15:24, 32; Heb. 6:1; 9:14; Rev. 3:1). The dead, rather than being "released" from life into a better existence, have in fact been conquered by a demonic power, the enemy of God (Rev. 20:11-15).

The NT special expressions for death include the irenic *koimaō,* "sleep" (John 11:11), but generally emphasize the negative view of death, for example, *apollymi,* "destroy," "bring to a bad end" (Matt. 21:41); *paradidōmi,* "deliver" (Rom. 4:25); *mellō teleutan,* "about to end" (Luke 7:2); *eschatos echō,* "having one's last" (Mark 5:23).

In NT terminology as well, death is characterized as the end of life, and as the enemy of God and humankind. Thus the entire biblical terminology for death and dying combines to portray a single understanding of death, namely, the termination of all existence for the whole human being. In this respect the biblical terminology corroborates the biblical descriptions of human nature in life and in death.

3. The Nature of Life and Death

In light of terminology and definitions, the biblical portrayal of human nature in life and in death takes on new and clear meaning. From a functional point of view, death is the opposite of the life God has created: whatever life is, death is not. This appears clearly expressed in the first biblical formula of human existence: "Then the Lord God formed man of dust from the ground, and breathed into his nostrils the breath of life; and man became a living being" (Gen. 2:7). Human life may be schematized as follows: dust of the ground (*'āpār min hā 'ªdāmāh*) + breath of life *(nišmat hayyîm)* = living being *(nepeš hayyāh).*

Each term deserves brief attention. Dust of the ground (*'ªdāmāh*) indicates that the material substance of humankind (*'ādām*) is "dust," or earth itself (*'ªdāmāh*). Hereby humankind is characterized as earthly and mortal, in the sense of possessing no inherent life. The body formed from the dust of the ground contained no divine material or life-giving elements enabling this form of dust to live independently. Next, God added His life-animating breath *(nešāmāh),* which is sometimes called spirit. It did not constitute a separate substance poured into the lifeless, empty form shaped of dust, but simply the divine life-giving power that transformed the dust into a living being. Hereby the Bible indicates that the life-breath does not represent a second entity, added, like an ingredient, to the body, capable of a separate existence, but an energizing power from God that transformed the earthen body into a living being *(nepeš hayyāh).* One of the root meanings of *nepeš* is "open throat," through which a person breathes, eats, and speaks. This leads to the derived meanings of "vibrant," "living," "energetic." The KJV translates *nepeš* as "soul," but the word refers to a whole, living being. In other examples, a "soul" *(nepeš)* can touch (Lev. 7:21), be bought as a slave (Lev. 22:11), eat (17:15), or crave certain foods (Deut. 12:20).

When this formula of human life is reversed, as in death, the life-breath is expired by the living being and returned to God, who gave it, leaving only the dust of the earth, so that the process of creation has been undone. This, in fact, represents the common biblical way of describing the moment of death: "Abraham breathed his last and died" (Gen. 25:8). "His illness was so severe that there was no breath left in him" (1 Kings 17:17). "If he should take back his spirit to himself, and gather to himself his breath, all flesh would perish together, and man would return to dust" (Job 34:14, 15). "When thou takest away their breath, they die and return to their dust" (Ps. 104:29). "And the dust returns to the earth as it was, and the spirit returns to God who gave it" (Eccl. 12:7). "All go to one place; all are from the dust, and all turn to the dust again" (3:20).

This biblical formula of life and death rejects all possibilities that anything except the survivors' memory of a person survives death. Ancestor worship, the belief that the spirits of ancestors live on after death and that the survivors must feed them, appease them, and follow their instruction, remains a delusion, no matter how real it appears to many traditional societies in the world. Not the spirit, but only the survivors' memory of the ancestor remains after death. That memory of a life well lived, the accomplishments realized, and the character traits of the deceased are kept also in the mind of God, and remain the finest legacy a person can leave behind after dying. Therefore, the Bible's rejection of soul immortality, ancestor worship, and the like does not leave us impoverished or deprived of the presence of our loved ones, but enriched with the memory of them, the things they did, the lessons they taught, and the character they developed. (See Creation I. B. 3.)

4. Wholism and Human Nature

The formula for human life, clearly expressed throughout the Bible, leads to a wholistic understanding of human nature. "The Hebrew conceived man as an animated body and not as an incarnate soul" (Robinson 70). Human nature, whether in illness or health, at birth or at death, does not constitute a composite of parts, each of which can be viewed or treated separately from any other part. The contemporary expressions "psychosomatic illness" and "whole-person care" represent recognition of this understanding of human nature, that a human being is a single whole and must be treated as such.

The biblical terminology for human nature corresponds consistently to this wholistic view. Thus the Hebrew word *bāśār,* "flesh" (Ps. 38:3), and the Greek words *sōma,* "body" (Rom. 7:24), and *sarx,* "flesh" (Gal. 4:13, KJV), do not portray a part of a person, namely, the body as opposed to the soul, but the whole person viewed from a certain perspective, namely that of human infirmity. Similarly, the Hebrew term *nepeš,* "soul" or "being" (Gen. 2:7), and the Greek *psychē,* "soul" or "life" (Rom. 16:4), refer to a person's existence, terminating at death, so that the soul has no existence without physical life. Other terms describing human nature—Heb. *rûaḥ,* "spirit" [Isa. 19:3]; Gr. *pneuma,* "spirit" [1 Cor. 7:34]; Heb. *lēb,* "heart," "mind" [Ps. 90:12] are used to represent human existence in its totality. (See Man I. E. 1-3.)

Since the Bible maintains a wholistic understanding of human nature, death does not divide body from soul so as to permit the soul to continue existing (soul immortality). Rather, death brings the whole life to a complete end. No function of human life survives death. This wholistic understanding of human nature holds great importance for health care, social services, education, and other services provided for those in need. It means that when attempting to cure or care for a particular problem, the entire person must be considered. Physical and psychological ailments are intertwined. Mind, heart, and body must be considered in true education. Spiritual and mental disorders must be addressed together. In short, the biblical understanding of human nature holds wide-reaching consequences for critical issues facing our society.

5. Death and the Memory of Life

Others' memory of the life of the deceased is the one aspect of human existence that survives death. All aspects of the present life reach their end at death, but the memory of a life well lived lingers on, not in material monuments for the dead, but in the living memory maintained for a time in the mind of the survivors, and preserved forever in the mind of God

(Isa. 49:15; Neh. 13:14, 22, 31). Therefore, the memory of the personality and character of the deceased who lived and died faithful to God is preserved in the hope that death, which struck them down, will itself be struck down at the last day by God, who then will return life to all those from whom it has been taken (1 Cor. 15:54-57). The character of the deceased, as remembered by the survivors and preserved in the mind of God, provides the connection between this life and the resurrected life.

6. Awaiting the Resurrection

No one, whether saint or sinner, receives the final reward, salvation or damnation, at death. That must await the resurrection. "For the hour is coming when all who are in the tombs will hear his voice and come forth, those who have done good, to the resurrection of life, and those who have done evil, to the resurrection of judgment" (John 5:28, 29; cf. Dan. 12:2). Death does indeed seal everyone's fate according to what was done in life, but the dead themselves are, as it were, naked and unclothed, meaning unconscious of any human activities, as in sleep, awaiting the resurrection, the judgment, and their respective rewards (2 Cor. 5:1-4, 10; Heb. 9:27). All matters associated with eternal life or death must therefore follow the resurrection, either the resurrection unto life, leading to an imperishable body, immortality (1 Cor. 15:52-54), and the eternal presence of God (1 Thess. 4:17) for God's saints, or the resurrection unto death, bringing destruction and eternal obliteration for those who have rejected the salvation of God (Matt. 25:31-46; Rev. 20).

Immortality belongs to God alone (1 Tim. 6:15, 16). No human being can possess this gift, except conditionally (Gen. 2:17) or ever lay claim to it as long as death reigns in the world (Rom. 5:12). By overcoming death, Christ Jesus our Saviour has brought life and immortality to light in the gospel (2 Tim. 1:10). By abolishing death at the end of this present world when Christ returns, God will bestow immortality upon His saints (1 Cor. 15:51-55; see Resurrection I-III).

B. Death: Its Origin, Agents, and Influence

Having considered the terminology for death, the definitions of life and death, and the transition from life to death, we turn next to the origin, agents, and influence of death. How does the Bible describe the cause of death, the agents responsible for it, and the presence of death in the world?

1. The Cause of Death

The Bible attributes the origin of death to sin. "Therefore as sin came into the world through one man and death through sin, and so death spread to all men because all men sinned" (Rom. 5:12). On a personal level, sin is offense against God (Ps. 51:4; Luke 15:21). It represents the opposite of God (Isa. 1:2-6) and a departure from His character, for "all have sinned and fall short of the glory of God" (Rom. 3:23). Thus the cause of death can be traced back to a personal confrontation between God and sinner. (See Man II. A, B; Sin III. A, B.)

According to the Bible, the first introduction of the concept of death was made by God Himself following the Creation: "You may freely eat of every tree of the garden; but of the tree of the knowledge of good and evil you shall not eat, for in the day that you eat of it you shall die" (Gen. 2:16, 17). The expression "shall die" (Heb. *môt tāmût*) is emphatic, meaning that death is inevitable, following upon the offense of disobedience.

This passage from Genesis 2 brings God, the sinner, and death into close proximity, though without implying any causal relationship between God and death. However, by reporting the possibility of death already in the story of Creation, the Bible reminds us that death is never far removed from life. Although the tempter's lie, "you will not die" (3:4), implies that life is invincible because it comes from God, the Bible teaches otherwise, noting that death has the potential of following close upon the heels of the very life God has created. Indeed, death may be considered the counterpart, or opposite, of life. Even the tempter (the serpent), who brought sin and death to humankind at first, originally was one of the living creatures made by God Himself (Gen. 3:1) but subsequently became an agent of death.

If we wish to inquire further into the origin of death, according to the Bible we must not seek it at the opposite end of the universe, far from where God resides, as proposed by certain ancient religions, but rather somewhere near God's throne. There an evil power set about to undo or reverse the life-giving activities of God. Nowhere does the Bible recognize the independent existence of a "god" of death, a counterpart of the God of life, reigning in the underworld at the opposite end of the universe, such as the gods Mot (Syria), Nergal (Mesopotamia), Osiris (Egypt), and Hades (Greece). Instead, behind Genesis 1-3 lie events that transpired in the very presence of God.

According to 1 John 3:4, 8, sinners are lawless persons, individuals who confront and oppose the principles and leadership of God by giving their allegiance to the devil, who has been sinning from "the beginning." That event occurred in heaven (Rev. 12:7-9) in a war pitting Michael, the archangel of God, and His supporters against the dark forces of the devil, also referred to as the dragon, the ancient serpent, and Satan, the deceiver. Although defeated (thrown down to earth, [verse 9]), the devil emerged with "the power of death" (Heb. 2:14), a power underwritten by sin and death.

Aspects of this composite picture tracing the beginning of lawlessness, sin, and death to the activities of the devil are further illuminated in the OT. Lucifer, one of God's creatures, the bright morning star (Isa. 14:12), is typified by the arrogant king of Babylon (verse 4), who is brought low into death at the very moment he exalts himself against God by attempting to usurp His heavenly throne (verses 13-15). Similarly, the prince of Tyre (Eze. 28:2), typifying one of God's perfect creatures, is sent down to the pit to die a death of disgrace (verses 8, 16-19) because he presumes to be divine in God's very presence (verses 6, 13, 14). Sin, and thus death, originated within one of God's own creatures in proximity to God through an act of lawlessness. It originated in creaturely pride and arrogance before the Creator. Thus God's creature, Lucifer, became the devil.

Following this fall from God's presence, the devil, functioning under titles such as serpent (Gen. 3:1) and Satan (Job 1:6), successfully deceived our first parents, through sin establishing claim upon this world. The devil claimed temporary authority over life and death, but as Job understood accurately, ultimately his life would rest in the hands of God (Job 1:21; 19:13-27).

By tracing the origin of death to a being near the throne of God Himself, Scripture does not imply that sin and death are somehow part of divine nature. Monotheism remains absolute in Scripture. No other gods, evil or good in nature, compete with the only God for rulership in the world. Neither does God Himself possess two conflicting natures, one good and the source of life, the other demonic and the source of death. Nor does Scripture suggest the concept of dualism, where two conflicting divine forces, one good and the other evil, struggle for power and leadership in the world. There is no place in worship services for practices designed to ward off sin and death by appeasing a threatening evil power.

Despite their origin in God's presence, sin and death are never traced to God Himself, to a divine being, but always to a created being, one of God's creatures gone astray. Thus none can rightly accuse God, the life-giver, of causing death. Neither does He disregard the sin introduced by one of His creatures. Rather, at great cost to Himself, He takes full personal responsibility for it.

Nowhere is the struggle between life and

death that rages across this world more intense than in God's very presence. Revelation 12:7-9 reports that actual war arose in heaven over this issue, leading to the defeat of the devil and a host of other evil beings, who were expelled from the presence of God and held imprisoned until judgment (2 Peter 2:4). Therefore, the fight to overcome sin and death, carried forward by God Himself, did not leave Him unscathed, but involved Him deeply and personally, ultimately leading to the death of His Son (Rom. 5:6-11).

As a result, the expulsion of the devil and his angels from the presence of God (Luke 10:18; 2 Peter 2:4; Jude 6; Rev. 12:9) becomes a promise of the final expulsion of sin and death from the whole creation of God (Rev. 12:7–20:15). In short, the origin of death near the throne of God does not imply that He *is* responsible for any of it, but that He *takes* responsibility for all of it. Beyond this, the Bible does not inform us further about the original "mystery of lawlessness" (2 Thess. 2:7) or the origin of death. (See Great Controversy I. B; II. A-E.)

2. The Agents of Death

In light of Bible teaching regarding its origin, death never can be seen as a natural, inevitable consequence of God's creation or as a normal segment of life. It is presented as an interruption of life, an unnatural intrusion, an enemy invading foreign territory. When through lawlessness sin claimed dominion over the world and the entire human family, death began to exercise its power over all living beings.

To explain more vividly how death exercises this power in the world, Scripture speaks in some detail about the agencies of death. Once sin and death were introduced among humans, the warfare between good and evil that began in heaven continued on earth. "For we are not contending against flesh and blood, but against the principalities, against the powers, against the world rulers of this present darkness, against the spiritual hosts of wickedness in the heavenly places" (Eph. 6:12). Demonic powers, foremost of which is the devil, exercise the power of death and hold all people hostage in the present world (Heb. 2:14, 15). Only the power of the Lord can defeat them (Eph. 6:10, 11), and only the armor of God can protect against the "flaming darts of the evil one" (verse 16).

Specific terms are used in Scripture to portray the agencies exercising the power of death on earth:

a. Satan. The most familiar biblical term for the agent of death is Satan (Job 1:6-12; 2:1-7; 1 Chron. 21:1; Zech. 3:1; Matt. 16:23; Mark 1:13; Acts 26:18; Rev. 20:2). When first describing this supernatural adversary, the OT uses the word *haśśāṭān,* "the satan," with an article, indicating that the word functions as a title meaning "accuser," "slanderer," "tempter." In 1 Chronicles 21:1 and the NT references it occurs as a proper noun, Satan, synonymous in meaning with the term *diabolos,* "devil" (Matt. 4:1; Mark 1:13); the old serpent *(ophis)* and the great dragon (Rev. 12:9); the deceiver of nations (20:2, 3). In the OT this agent of death had access to heavenly beings (Job 1:6; Zech. 3:1), whereas according to the NT, he had lost that privilege (Luke 10:18, 19; Rev. 12:9). Here Satan is the fallen enemy of God, committed to destroying the church (Rev. 12:9, 10, 13, 14), and awaiting his own destruction, as well (20:2; cf. verses 9, 10).

b. The devil (*diabolos*). This term, which occurs frequently in the NT, is a synonym for Satan. The devil tempts, misleads, murders, betrays, leads into sin, attacks, judges, and commands death (Matt. 4:1-11; 13:39; John 8:44; 13:2; Eph. 6:11; 1 Tim. 3:6; Heb. 2:14; 1 Peter 5:8; 1 John 3:8; Rev. 2:10; 12:9; 20:2, 10). He will suffer destruction at the end of the world (Rev. 12:9; 20:10). Beliar (or Belial), meaning "worthlessness" (2 Cor. 6:15), is an alternate name for the devil and is also applied to the antichrist.

c. The demons. Demons (Matt. 17:18; Luke 4:41), called unclean or evil spirits (Mark 1:23; 5:2) and evil angels (Rev. 12:7, 8), are all agents of destruction and death, often represented as secondary agents associated with and responsible to Satan. The Philistine deity Beelzebub and its altered form Beelzebul, literally "lord of flies"/"lord of filth," are variant names for the prince of demons and, indeed, the devil himself (Matt. 12:24; Mark 3:22; Luke 11:15).

d. The serpent. While claiming to enhance life, the serpent actually became an agent of death (Gen. 3:1; Rev. 20:2) and is called more "crafty" or "subtle" (Heb. *'ārûm*) than all God's other creatures. The serpent assumes this role so insidiously that a permanent association was created between Satan and serpent as the being who first introduced sin and death to the world (Rev. 12:9; Gen. 3:13, 14). Consequently, the serpent also received a punishment more severe than any other creature by being cursed to crawl on its belly and eat dust (Gen. 3:14), a symbol of defeat and humiliation.

e. Leviathan and Rahab. Considered malevolent gods by some ancient peoples, Leviathan and Rahab appear in the OT (Isa. 27:1; 51:9) as symbols of God's enemies, who obstruct His works and threaten His people. Both are identified symbolically with the sea (sea serpent, sea monster, or the like) to indicate that their activities are life threatening. The context of the references to these powers reveals that their defeat and destruction by God coincides with the redemption of His people in the final conflict between good and evil (27:1; 51:9-11).

f. Pestilence *(deber)* and plague *(rešep̱).* The latter appears as a malevolent deity in Ugaritic literature *(ršp),* but in the OT simply in lists of life-threatening disasters (Deut. 32:24; Ps. 78:48-50). The same is true of *deber,* which does not carry any sacred connotation but merely illustrates deadly aspects of divine punishment. Thus it appears in lists that include snares, traps, tempests, arrows, asp, cobra, snake, and serpent (Ps. 91:3-13). It is used with reference to the plagues in Egypt (Ex. 9:3; cf. 5:3). In Habakkuk 3:5 these two

agents accompany God's judgment upon His enemies.

The emerging picture presents an army of evil forces, physical and spiritual, confronting the world and its inhabitants with destruction and untimely death. The Bible does not present death as the natural end of life, but rather as a constant threat to life, unavoidable but never to be tolerated, accepted, or embraced. It represents the enemy of God and of life, of whom the Bible warns: "Be sober, be watchful. Your adversary the devil prowls around like a roaring lion, seeking some one to devour" (1 Peter 5:8).

3. The Universality of Death

Like sin, death originated near the very presence of God, entering this world through the experience of temptation, deception, and destruction. At once all life became infected by it. "Therefore as sin came into the world through one man and death through sin, and so death spread to all men because all men sinned" (Rom. 5:12). Thus each person born into the human family experiences the grip of sin upon life and the terrible power of death at work in the world.

The biblical account of the Fall (Gen. 3; 4; 6) vividly describes the process of the spread of sin and death in the world. It began with two individuals, a man and a woman. The first human experience of the Fall is expressed in God's question followed by His judgment. The question, "Where are you?" (3:9), is personal and concerns individuals who hid themselves from God. The judgment, "You shall die" (2:17), is equally personal—an individual death sentence, from which there is no escape, pronounced on one guilty person standing before God. But sin and death cannot be contained within the individual, for human nature itself is marred by sin, becoming "fallen," or flawed.

Genesis 4 describes everyday life in the first human family and shows how sin and death immediately spread horizontally as brother killed brother. Sin and death now reveal a social dimension, indicated by God's second question followed by His second judgment. The question, "Where is Abel your brother?" (verse 9), is social and concerns the immediate members of a small social group, the family. The judgment, "You shall be a fugitive and a wanderer on the earth" (verse 12), concerns society, which has been broken apart at the most fundamental level—the immediate family.

Genesis 4:23 records the arrogant song of Lamech before his wives, stating that a young man has been murdered as punishment for a slight offense. Life has become cheap and death prevalent. Sin and death have invaded the entire human race, indeed, the whole world (Gen. 6:1-8). Much later the prophet explained the pervasiveness of death as follows: "All flesh is grass, and all its beauty is like the flower of the field. The grass withers, the flower fades, when the breath of the Lord blows upon it; surely the people is grass" (Isa. 40:6, 7).

Not content to spread horizontally, the consequences of sin also extend vertically, in depth and height, and with them comes death. The individual's life from cradle to grave is infected with sin and subject to the curse of death (Ps. 51:3-5). Society as a whole suffers from sin and death in such an aggravated way (Isa. 1:6) that desolation and death threaten people, land, and institutions (verses 7-9; see Sin IV. A-K).

When we inquire about the cause of death, we are returned to that first creaturely rebellion against God, the original mystery of lawlessness (2 Thess. 2:7), before human experience with it. But our inquiry into the cause of sin also directs us to the first human experience of temptation and fall, as well as its impact on the human family and our world. The answer to the first of these questions is philosophical and historical. Death has a source that can be located in time, prior to Creation, and in space, near the presence of God (Isa. 14:12-14).

The answer to the second question reminds us that death has a source within human experience, as well, in the fall into sin, followed by our continued rebellion against God (1:2-6). Thus we lay the cause of death at the door of God's ancient adversary when he chose darkness instead of light, but we acknowledge that the human race has become God's adversary as well. The Bible describes this experience as a fall from grace and expulsion from God's life-giving presence, represented by the tree of life (Gen. 3:22-24).

Since the first human beings were created sinless, perfect, in the image of God and after His likeness (1:26, 27), it follows that the fall into sin did grave damage to that divine image. This broken image of God is shared by all human beings as a consequence of being born into this world, so that all have sinned and will partake of death (Rom. 5:12). Nevertheless, as a broken mirror still can reflect an image, imperfect but still recognizable, so fallen human beings still can reflect the image of God their Creator, imperfectly but still recognizably. Scripture affirms this difficult concept already in the account of the Fall (Gen. 3) by including within it the first assurance of redemption (verse 15)—the restoration of the image of God in His creation. Meanwhile the world has become the scene of spiritual warfare, a struggle between life and death for the continued existence of the human race (verses 14-19). Thus the fall from grace, marring the image of God, has alienated the entire human race from God, leading to condemnation and death for all (Eph. 4:18; Rom. 5:12). But thanks to the gift of God's grace, offered freely to everyone who believes in Jesus Christ, that broken image is restored, leading to eternal life (Rom. 5:15-21; see Salvation I-IV; Great Controversy II. E).

C. The State of the Dead

The spread of sin and death into the whole world has made death a present and common human experience. Like an unwelcome guest making frequent calls, death walks boldly into our families to claim our loved ones. This raises questions about the state of the dead and leaves those who remain with the sad task of mourning their loss and returning their deceased to the earth in a way that harmonizes with the biblical understanding of death.

1. Burial and the Grave

The Bible contains only sparse information about funerals and burial. Among the specific practices may be noted the common custom of closing the eyes of the dead (Gen. 46:4), perhaps to indicate the resemblance of death to sleep (I. C. 4). The family embraced the body (50:1) and prepared it for interment, probably without delay, since ordinarily no attempts were made to preserve the body.

The body was buried fully clothed or wrapped (Matt. 27:59; John 11:44); soldiers could be buried with their weapons (Eze. 32:27); and by NT times at least, spices were added to the burial clothes (John 19:39, 40). Embalming, mentioned in only two cases, involving Jacob and Joseph (Gen. 50:2, 26), appears to follow Egyptian customs (verse 3). The use of a coffin in the case of Joseph (verse 26) also seems to represent an Egyptian practice. Cremation, as in the case of King Saul and his sons (1 Sam. 31:12), does not appear to be a common custom (cf. 1 Chron. 10:12, which omits the reference to Saul's cremation, and Amos 2:1, which denounces the burning of the remains from the royal tombs).

Ordinarily the body would be interred, either in a subterranean pit or grave (Joshua 24:32), perhaps in a natural or cut cave in the rock (Gen. 23:8, 9; 50:5; Matt. 27:60), or in a human-made burial chamber of some kind (1 Kings 14:31). The common Hebrew word for grave (*qeber*) means simply a pit dug or cut in the earth, while the Greek word (*mnēmeion*) suggests the idea of a memorial, referring to a marker, inscription, or even a structure containing the chamber in which the dead were deposited. In later periods, and commonly by NT times, secondary burial of the bones in ossuaries (small receptacles of stone or clay) was practiced.

Poor people appear to have been buried in common graves (2 Kings 23:6; Jer. 26:23), whereas the rich could afford elaborate tombs (Isa. 22:16), perhaps with a memorial marker (2 Sam. 18:18). Some tombs belonged to the family, so that the dying could express their desire to be buried in the tomb of their fathers (Gen. 49:29-33; Judges 8:32; 2 Sam. 19:37). Consequently, large tombs might be vacated of old remains and subsequently reused.

Mourning for the dead accompanied burial activities and included tearing one's garments (Gen. 37:34), putting on sackcloth (2 Sam. 3:31), placing earth on the head (Joshua 7:6), and weeping aloud (Luke 8:52). At times a shorter or longer funeral lament might be composed to express pain, sorrow, and loss (2 Sam. 1:17-27; Jer. 22:18). The biblical understanding of death naturally contributes to a general lack of prescribed funeral rites and a marked economy in the ritual associated with burials (Gen. 23:2; 37:34; Deut. 34:8; 1 Sam. 25:1; Jer. 22:18; Matt. 9:23; Luke 23:55–24:1). Other rites associated with ancient funerals were prohibited in Scripture (Lev. 19:27, 28; Deut. 14:1). Touching a corpse would render a person unclean (Num. 5:2; 19:11-19); additional strictures applied to the priests (Lev. 21:1-4, 10-12).

Clearly, the Bible draws a sharp line between life and death, between the living and the dead. The two sides are separate, no contact exists between them, and no attempt must be made to cross that line. The funeral and burial remain orderly, respectful, and simple procedures for disposing of the corpse while remembering a life and mourning its loss.

2. The Region of Death

The Bible has little to say about the dead after their funeral, since the biblical concept of human nature holds that the dead have no existence apart from life in the body. Consequently, the Bible speaks of the buried only by means of verbal images expressing the total loss of life.

Thus it pictures the dead as the recent departed who have now joined, or rest with, their ancestors in the chambers of the tomb (Gen. 15:15; 1 Kings 14:31). Proverbs 2:18 and 5:5

depict the way there as a downward slope toward death, the path to *šeʾôl*. Elsewhere we observe the picture of a hall where death lurks (7:27; 9:18). Like a city it has gates through which the dead must pass (Job 38:17; Isa. 38:10). It is characterized by gloom, darkness, and shadows (Job 10:21, 22; Ps. 143:3), dust (Ps. 7:5; Gen. 3:19), and silence (Ps. 94:17; 115:17), with maggots present (Isa. 14:11).

Several technical terms describe the region of death. *Šeʾôl*, with the probable meaning of a waste, valueless place, conveys a symbolic representation of the grave (Gen. 37:35; 1 Kings 2:6; Prov. 1:12). By its gates (Isa. 38:10), or mouth (Ps. 141:7), live those who are near death, about to be swallowed up by its insatiable appetite (Isa. 5:14; Hab. 2:5), or to be caught in its snares (2 Sam. 22:6; Ps. 18:5). There can be no return without divine intervention. Parallel expressions to *šeʾôl* include *ʾereṣ taḥtît*, "underworld" (Eze. 31:14); *ʾabaddôn*, "place of destruction" (Job 26:6; Ps. 88:11; Prov. 15:11), and *šaḥat*, "pit" (Isa. 38:17; Ps. 16:10).

The NT term *hadēs*, translated "death" or the "realm of death" (Luke 10:15; Acts 2:27, 31; Rev. 1:18; 20:13, 14), corresponds closely to the OT term *šeʾôl*.

The popular belief that *hadēs* represents an intermediary place of punishment awaiting the unrighteous at death is familiar from the popular Jewish story found in the Palestinian Talmud, which may provide the background for Jesus' parable of the rich man and Lazarus (Luke 16:19-31; cf. Jeremias 183-187). The story tells of a rich tax collector who after a splendid funeral found himself in hades seeking water to quench his thirst while a poor scholar whose passing was hardly noticed reached Paradise. The focus of the story is upon hades, conceived as an intermediary place of purification. In adapting this story for His own purposes, however, Jesus overturned its conclusion about *hadēs* and transformed it into a parable about moral responsibility in the present life, before one's fate is sealed at death. By setting aside the popular beliefs

found in the original story about a second chance to make things right in *hadēs,* as in purgatory, Jesus restored the original biblical understanding of *hadēs* in the sense of *šeʾôl,* "grave." Jesus knew no doctrine of purgatory.

The emphasis upon death as punishment for unrighteousness is given additional vivid expression in the term Gehenna (Gr. *geenna,* Heb. *gêʾhinnom*). Designating the valley south of ancient Jerusalem used for refuse disposal as well as for Molech worship (2 Kings 23:10; Jer. 7:31, 32), it became associated with death and punishment and is generally translated "hell" in the NT (Matt. 5:22, 29, 30; 23:15; Mark 9:43-47; James 3:6). However, here it signifies a fate as much as a place, namely, death resulting from unrighteousness.

The region of death, then, is variously designated as the grave, *šeʾôl, hadēs, geenna,* and hell. Each of these terms refers simply to the grave, where the dead are interred. In terms of its character, the grave, the region of death, represents that which is diametrically opposed to the region of God (Ps. 139:8), and the place from which mortals cannot return (Job 17:11-16). A person enters the "region" of death alone and cannot return from it except in the resurrection.

3. The Condition of the Dead

In graphic poetic form the Bible describes the realm of death. When the dead king of Babylon arrives in the grave, *šeʾôl* figuratively "rouses the shades to greet you, all who were leaders of the earth" (Isa. 14:9). Such biblical descriptions of the state of the dead are symbolic, along with the speaking cypresses and cedars (verse 8), and beds of maggots and blankets of worms (verse 11). Such images of the condition in death underscore the conclusion that at death all ordinary life processes as we know them cease. In death work, and thus rewards, cease (Eccl. 9:5). Love, hate, and envy perish, along with participation in life's events (verse 6). Thought, knowledge, and wisdom no longer exist (verses 5, 10). The dead cannot lay plans (Ps. 146:4), and there is neither remembrance of the dead (Ps. 6:5; Eccl. 9:5) nor praise of God after death (Ps. 88:10, 11; 115:17; Isa. 38:18). The dead remain in the grave (Acts 2:29, 34).

4. Death as Sleep

In place of all the above-mentioned figurative descriptions of the state of the dead, the Bible favors the metaphor of sleep to describe the condition in death (Deut. 31:16; 1 Kings 2:10; Job 14:12; Dan. 12:2; Matt. 9:24; 27:51, 52; John 11:11; Acts 7:60; 1 Cor. 15:18, 51; 1 Thess. 4:13). This felicitous metaphor, commonly occurring throughout the Bible, receives special attention by Jesus in the report of Lazarus' resurrection. In conveying the most startling miracle Jesus ever performed, namely, the resurrection of someone whose body had begun to decay, this story is primarily instructive. Jesus is teacher first and miracle worker second. He instructs His distraught friends about God's life-giving power, His own death and resurrection, the nature of death, and the resurrection hope (John 11:1-44).

As the narrative unfolds, Jesus first informs His disciples that "Lazarus has fallen asleep," whereupon they cheerfully suggest that Lazarus surely will recover. When they discovered that Lazarus had actually died, Thomas responded passionately, "Let us also go, that we may die with him" (verse 16). Jesus apparently at first employed the gentle image of sleep in order to soften the blow Lazarus' death would bring to his close friends, while preparing them for the coming miracle of resurrection, to be understood as an awakening from sleep. The condition of sleep, with its apparent unconsciousness, well portrays the condition in death. Moreover, sleep normally is followed by an awakening, vividly symbolizing the resurrection from the dead (verse 23).

The resurrection of Lazarus is pivotal in John's Gospel, for it draws the battle lines between Christ and His opponents. He stated His case clearly (verses 40-42), while His opponents were determined to put Him to death (verse 53).

Death, a natural consequence of sin, remains the inevitable fate of human beings. The finality of death is underscored by the decomposing body on the fourth day. No life remains; existence has ended. But Lazarus is asleep, waiting to be awakened by God Himself. The metaphor of sleep used for death thus points at the same time to the finality of death and to the possibility of the resurrection. It is fundamental to the teaching of Christ.

Of all the biblical metaphors for the state of the dead, that of sleep is the most important, enabling us to speak gently and naturally about the dead in a way that does not frighten the survivors. It portrays the experience of dying as slipping into an unconscious state in which all normal mental functions such as thinking, planning, loving, hoping, and believing cease (cf. Eccl. 9:5, 6, 10; Ps. 88:3-7). The symbol of sleep illustrates well both the biblical understanding of death and its concept of resurrection, an event similar to an awakening (1 Thess. 4:15-18).

D. The Occult and Spiritualism

The belief in an after-death existence is clearly expressed in the classical Greek writings; it also enjoyed widespread popularity in the ancient Near East. The story of Saul and the witch of Endor (1 Sam. 28:3-19) and the many Israelite tombs containing pottery deposited for the use of the dead indicate that this belief was not entirely unknown among ancient Israelites. Nevertheless, the Bible roundly condemns this concept. Therefore, attempts to communicate with the dead through the occult, spiritualism, or the use of a medium also are condemned as a superstition to be vigorously combated (Ex. 22:18; Lev. 19:31; 20:6, 27; Deut. 18:9-13; Isa. 8:19, 20).

The unusual story about Saul and the woman at Endor tells of the king's desperate attempts to communicate with the dead prophet Samuel through a medium. The story makes clear that Saul by this time was suffering mental deterioration (1 Sam. 19:9-17; 28:3-10), that he attempted to consult God through the dead Samuel when dreams, Urim, and living prophets failed to answer him (1 Sam. 28:6). Evidently he talked only to the woman of Endor, the medium. It is possible to conclude on the basis of the context that only he, and not the woman of Endor, claimed to recognize Samuel in the apparition, while only the woman was able to see anything. Meanwhile, the "ghost" coming up from the earth, described by the woman as a god, and looking like an old man wrapped in a robe, was identified by Saul on the basis of her less-than-detailed description as the one he was seeking, namely, Samuel (verses 11-14). In short, the story bears no testimony to the actual presence of the dead prophet.

More important, Saul learned nothing from the experience except what he already knew from previous reports given by Samuel while the prophet was still alive (verse 17; cf. 1 Sam. 15:23, 27, 28). That message Saul feared and hoped to overturn. The satanic element in this story lies in the false idea that one can gain otherwise unavailable information from the dead through a spirit medium. The attempt at impersonation of a dead person is roundly condemned in the OT story as deceptive and useless, and the work of demonic agencies aided by a medium. No information can be gained from the dead, for in fact, they know nothing (Eccl. 9:5, 6).

Against this fundamental principle we can now place some unusual biblical descriptions of the state of the dead, recognizing that we deal with metaphoric language portraying the loss of human existence following death. For example, the Bible speaks of the dead as shades *(rᵉpā'îm)* characterized by their inability to live and communicate with God and humanity (Ps. 88:10; Prov. 2:18, 19; 21:16; Isa. 26:14). The term *rᵉpā'îm,* "shades," does not designate a quality of existence, such as soul *(nepeš)* or "spirit" *(rûaḥ)* would portray. In fact, the word nowhere describes a being who can be said to live in any manner associated with normal human existence. Indeed, death, the condition of the *rᵉpā'îm,* implies the ab-

sence of all consciousness. Rather than being ghosts enjoying some presumed minimum existence in death, the *rᵉpā'îm,* in fact, share all the known characteristics of the dead. They know nothing (Eccl. 9:5). They cannot talk or praise God (Ps. 6:5; 88:11; 115:17), their thinking and planning have ceased (146:4), they do not sense God's presence (Job 7:21), and they have no hope (Isa. 38:18).

E. Unusual NT Passages Dealing With Death

A few texts pose unusual questions in light of the general biblical understanding of life and death. However, a brief review of the weight of evidence indicates fundamental harmony with the biblical concept of the non-immortality of the soul. For an extensive examination of these passages the reader is referred to commentaries.

1. Luke 23:43

At first glance this short verse appears problematic. "Truly, I say to you, today you will be with me in Paradise." If read with a pause (or comma) after the words "Truly, I say to you," this verse states that Jesus invited the second thief on the cross to accompany him to Paradise that day, implying continued soul existence after death. The meaning becomes altered dramatically if the pause (or comma) follows the word "today." In this case Jesus would promise, "Truly, I say to you today," indicating a present promise of a future entrance into eternal life. Unfortunately, the oldest Greek manuscripts come without punctuation, so we must examine this verse in its context to determine its precise meaning. The intention of the verse is clear and simple: to offer the repentant thief on the cross salvation. The other thief also asked for rescue, but without repenting and acknowledging Christ (verse 39). For this he is corrected by the repentant thief (verse 41). Thus there is no discussion of eternal reward or punishment, about entrance to heaven or hell. Instead, the immediate context is the subject of salvation on a day of extreme trouble for three men. In His reply Jesus offered immediate assurance of salvation to the repentant thief.

It is worth noting that the thief asked modestly to be remembered by Christ when He would come into His kingdom, whereas Jesus offered him His company in Paradise (salvation). Once again the quality, not the timing, of the thief's request and Jesus' response remains primary. Evidently Jesus realized that He Himself would not enter His kingdom that day or even the next day (John 20:17), but He still wanted to give His newfound friend assurance of salvation "today." Thus Luke 23:43 teaches assurance of salvation, but not admission to the kingdom, on the day of death.

2. 2 Corinthians 5:1-10 and Philippians 1:19-26

These two Pauline passages appear problematic on the surface, for they seem to favor death over life on the grounds that death would bring the faithful into a special, immediate relationship with their Lord. But closer examination of these texts reveals a different perspective, harmonious with the rest of the Bible.

The apostle divides human existence into three phases. The first, consisting of the present life in the flesh, is illustrated by an earthly tent in which we live and labor or by which we are clothed (2 Cor. 5:1, 2; Phil. 1:22, 24). The second phase, representing death, is illustrated by nakedness, a state of being unclothed (2 Cor. 5:3, 4). The apostle desires to avoid this phase through the experience of translation (1 Cor. 15:51-57; 2 Cor. 5:4), for nakedness represents an awkward condition in which he cannot benefit the church with his ministry (Phil. 1:24). Elsewhere Paul refers repeatedly to death as a sleep, confirming that death represents an inactive period of waiting, an interlude during which the apostle is unable to benefit the church, while not yet enjoying the presence of his Lord (1 Cor. 15:6, 51; 1 Thess. 4:14). The third phase is represented by the life of resurrection and is illustrated by a building, a house not made with hands but made by God (2 Cor. 5:1). Clearly this phase represents the apostle's ultimate aspiration, for it will bring him near the Lord (verses 6, 8; Phil. 1:23).

Since this third phase is separated from the first earthly phase only by unconscious sleep with no sense of the passing of time for the deceased, it is natural for the text to juxtapose these two phases (Phil. 1:23). Only a resurrection from the dead or a translation from the living, not death itself, will bring the apostle to the last phase. For reasons already stated, he would rather not die (be unclothed) if he could choose translation, although he will of course accept either life or death from the hand of God in such a manner that whatever comes, his witness and ministry will be enhanced thereby (2 Cor. 5:9; Phil. 1:20-25). As for death, the state of nakedness, the apostle joins the biblical witness in decrying it and hoping for the day when "what is mortal may be swallowed up by life" (2 Cor. 5:4; see Resurrection I. A. 2. a).

3. 1 Thessalonians 4:14

The texts mentioned above help us to interpret others that appear to imply some existence after death but prior to the resurrection of God's saints. In 1 Thessalonians 4:14 we read that God brings with Christ those who have fallen asleep. The troubling question concerns those saints who have died and whom God will bring along with Christ. They will not accompany Christ from heaven to earth, but rather they will be raised from the grave to accompany Christ to heaven, as evidenced by the context (cf. 1 Cor. 6:14; 2 Cor. 4:14). The question in this passage concerns those who have died (or are fearful of dying) in the Advent hope. Will they be worse off than those who are alive and waiting for the return of their Lord? The apostle assures the living who fear death before the second coming of Christ that they will not be left behind (1 Thess. 4:15), but that those who have died in the Advent hope will rise to meet their Lord first, even before He turns His attention to those who are still alive (verses 16, 17). Hence, God's company with His saints at the end of time follows upon their resurrection from the dead and precedes the translation of the living. (See Revelation I. A. 2. a.)

4. Hebrews 12:23 and Revelation 6:9

Two texts speak of "spirits" and "souls" as though they were persons who had died. In the first is found the expression "spirits of just men made perfect" (Heb. 12:23), and the second refers to souls under the altar, "slain for the word of God and for the witness they had borne" (Rev. 6:9). Together they illustrate two different uses of symbolic language.

In the first case, the apostle draws a distinction between two groups: the original Hebrews who came to Mount Sinai (Heb. 12:18, 19), and the Christian Hebrews, to whom the Epistle is addressed and who have come to Mount Zion (verse 22). They are invited to approach the throne of God, where Christ serves as high priest (Heb. 4:16). Among those assembled at Mount Zion, symbolically representing the church of God or the heavenly Jerusalem, are innumerable angels, the firstborn enrolled in the kingdom, God our judge, and the just made perfect. As with that first assembly at Mount Sinai (Heb. 12:18-21), this second gathering at Mount Zion consists of God's saints, angels and humans, and Hebrew Christians, the firstborn of faith through the new covenant mediated by Jesus. They are not disembodied saints but real people, to whom the apostle appeals, "See that you do not refuse him who is speaking" (verse 25).

The second passage symbolically describes events under the fifth seal (Rev. 6:9-11). It reports on the fate of Christian martyrs not yet avenged by God for their innocently spilled blood. Like the blood of innocent Abel crying to heaven for help (Gen. 4:10), so the blood of these martyrs, symbolically speaking, calls for God to attend to their case. The imagery of speaking blood is familiar in the Bible (cf. Heb. 12:24). It refers to the voice of

the life represented by that blood, a life taken or given through the spilling of blood. It may speak of justice and revenge (in the case of Abel and the saints under the altar) and of grace and forgiveness (in the case of Christ). It is the blood, the innocent life wrongly taken from these martyrs, not disembodied souls, that calls out from under the altar for God to bring justice to the earth. The answer comes back with a twofold assurance. First, they are given a white robe indicating that God has not forgotten them, that the righteousness of Christ has enveloped them, and that they will not be left behind in the resurrection (cf. 1 Thess. 4:15). Second, they are told to wait (since two more seals remain to be opened) and to rest a little longer in their grave (Rev. 6:11). In this symbolic presentation of the resurrection hope held by those who died long ago, the dead play no active role but must patiently wait for the time established by God. This confirms the biblical understanding that the dead rest in the grave until called forth at the time of the resurrection.

F. The Resurrection and the Eradication of Death

We have noted that death is not merely a natural transition in human existence, but a power that reigns over life, brings it to an end, and destroys it. Death also brings punishment for sin, even at the hand of God. Still, it remains the enemy of life and of God. Therefore, the final eradication of death is preceded by the resurrection, through which the power of death is broken. This in turn brings the reign of death to its end, and finally death itself is eradicated. (See Second Coming I. G. 1-3; Resurrection I, II; New Earth.)

1. The Reign of Death

In describing the reign of death, the Bible personifies death as an existence, a dominion, a power to be reckoned with in this world. "Yet death reigned from Adam to Moses" (Rom. 5:14), and "because of one man's trespass, death reigned through that one man" (verse

17). This reign of death implies that death holds dominion over the present world and its inhabitants. Jeremiah speaks of death as an enemy with power to break into human life anywhere, at will, and without regard or consideration for victims. "For death has come up into our windows, it has entered our palaces, cutting off the children from the streets and the young men from the squares" (Jer. 9:21). Death exercises this power through sin (Rom. 5:17) and the devil (Heb. 2:14) and imposes it upon all people, for all have sinned (Rom. 5:12, 13). Conversely, "no man has . . . authority over the day of death" (Eccl. 8:8).

2. Death as the End of Life

While the reign of death all too often causes an unnatural interruption of life, as in the case of a mortal illness, fatal accident, or capital punishment, it also simply brings to an end a life that has run its course through the process of aging—itself a gentle form of death.

At 175 years of age "Abraham breathed his last and died in a good old age, an old man and full of years, and was gathered to his people" (Gen. 25:8). In advising Job on righteous living, Eliphaz promised, "You shall come to your grave in ripe old age, as a shock of grain comes up to the threshing floor in its season" (Job 5:26). Upon meeting his favorite son again, Jacob said to Joseph, "Now let me die, since I have seen your face and know that you are still alive" (Gen. 46:30). In recommitting himself to Christ, the apostle Paul exclaimed, "For to me to live is Christ, and to die is gain" (Phil. 1:21).

These passages and others suggest that the Bible acknowledges death as a release, a natural end to life, and in the case of a long and difficult life, even as a welcome release. Often the Bible reports the death of people in a disinterested way, simply as the end of their life. This corresponds to the present attitude of "coming to terms" with death, because it is unavoidable and one must therefore "get it over with" one way or another. Is the Bible inviting us to "come to terms with death"?

With the exception of the special case of Philippians 1:21, which expresses the apostle's total commitment to Christ in life and death, the examples cited of peaceful death actually focus upon the achievements in life rather than upon death and therefore should not be interpreted as an accepting attitude toward death.

A more precise understanding of the Bible's view of death in old age requires us to focus upon the ravages that aging brings upon life. Here it becomes clear immediately that waiting for death, even following a rewarding life, is neither desirable nor satisfactory. Thus, "the years of our life are threescore and ten, or even by reason of strength fourscore; yet their span is but toil and trouble; they are soon gone, and we fly away" (Ps. 90:10).

This text also warns of the often problematic nature of inactivity toward the end of life. Perhaps the most interesting passage is Ecclesiastes 12, the sad confession of an old man. "Remember also your Creator in the days of your youth, before the evil days come, and the years draw nigh, when you will say, 'I have no pleasure in them'" (verse 1). The next verses deplore the experience of old age, despite the wisdom and serenity it might be expected to bring. The sad fact remains that life comes to a swift and sad end and cannot be brought back. "Man goes to his eternal home, and the mourners go about the streets" (verse 5).

Perhaps a time may come in this gradual deterioration of life when death will seem a tolerable or even welcome escape, but according to the Bible the whole process is neither desirable nor tolerable. In fact, aging itself is an intrusive form of advancing death, which belongs to the curse of sin and is never desired (Eccl. 12:1-7). It represents a time when God's protection is especially needed (Ps. 71:18). The sad death scene of Jacob, surrounded by his sons and grandsons in Egypt, shows how old age prevents the patriarch from returning to the Promised Land. In reality it constitutes a sad and ultimately unacceptable conclusion to life—one that somehow must be overcome. "Then Israel said to Joseph, 'Behold, I am about to die, but God will be with you, and will bring you again to the land of your fathers'" (Gen. 48:21). Then he gave the following instruction: "I am to be gathered to my people; bury me with my fathers in the cave that is in the field of Ephron the Hittite" (49:29).

In Jacob's plea to his sons that he not be left behind, we see illustrated the Bible's opposition to death, considering it an unacceptable answer to life, even to a long and rich life, for it threatens the very promise of God. However, the patriarch's request also holds out hope for a future that even death cannot thwart—a hope anchored in the promise of God that Israel will inherit the Promised Land.

3. Death as Destruction

Death does not always arrive at the end of a long life; it may also walk boldly into the middle, striking fear and terror. The Bible presents that possibility as a frightening experience, indeed, some of the most courageous persons in the Bible—Moses, David, and the apostle Paul—were not always heroic in the face of death. During one of his confrontations with the unstable King Saul, David exclaimed to his friend Jonathan, "There is but a step between me and death" (1 Sam. 20:3). Much later, Christ Himself would not seek death except according to the will of His Father (Luke 22:42).

Such fear of death, especially of the untimely intrusion of death into life, characterizes the whole Bible and underscores a special biblical understanding of death: it does not represent the natural or unavoidable end to the present life followed by an ongoing existence on a different level, so that the heroic person may meet it courageously. Rather, death without the resurrection hope represents the end of all life, the absence of God, total darkness. Seen from the biblical perspective, the fear of death without the resurrection hope remains the most fundamental fear experienced by human beings. It is the fear of being left

alone, for to die means to be alone; it is the fear of facing God's judgment without atonement. By dying this way on behalf of sinners, Christ guaranteed that no human being ever needs to face death without hope.

It is not surprising then that the person facing death, timely or untimely, whether surrounded by family and friends or alone, whether believer or unbeliever, often spontaneously calls upon God. "The cords of Sheol entangled me, the snares of death confronted me. In my distress I called upon the Lord; to my God I cried for help" (Ps. 18:5, 6). Conversely, when God is near, the fear of death is overcome. "Even though I walk through the valley of the shadow of death, I fear no evil; for thou art with me; thy rod and thy staff, they comfort me" (23:4).

In the biblical setting, life-threatening experiences leading to the fear of death are similar to those we meet today. Illness, war, and natural calamities are the most common. Thus serious illness was associated with death and brought about fear. The poisonous food prepared by one of Elisha's servants from hastily gathered ingredients brought out the cry "O man of God, there is death in the pot!" (2 Kings 4:40), and all stopped eating. Hezekiah's dangerous illness threatened him with death, frightened him, and sent him to God in prayer. "Then Hezekiah turned his face to the wall, and prayed to the Lord. . . . And Hezekiah wept bitterly" (2 Kings 20:2, 3).

War brought untimely death to young men and untold suffering to surviving widows, orphans, and parents. Scripture is particularly aware that warfare hurts the soldiers on both sides of the battle lines in a senseless waste of life (2 Sam. 2:12-17). But the pain is equally deep in those to whom a report of death is brought from the battlefield. "O my son Absalom, my son, my son Absalom! Would I had died instead of you, O Absalom, my son, my son!" (18:33).

Natural catastrophes, as little understood in Bible times as today, were occasionally considered "acts of God" then as now. The sailors in the ship bound for Tarshish with Jonah on board were afraid of the storm (Jonah 1:5). In fact, the raging sea is often mentioned as a cause for fear of death (Ps. 107:23-32), as is the burning desert (Isa. 43:1, 2, 16-20).

These threats to life raised the specter of untimely death and led to fear of death, even among the greatest heroes in Scripture. For example, when faced with unimaginable catastrophes, Job did not "charge God with wrong" (Job 1:22), but neither did he accept death readily, though tempted to do so and encouraged by his friends to think that way (Job 15:1-6; 18). Instead, at the moment when his personal suffering weighed most heavily upon him (19:1-22), he affirmed God's gift of life above all the catastrophes disrupting his life. Job feared death greatly, but he trusted God more (verses 23-27).

4. Death as Punishment

The Bible frequently speaks of death as a punishment for sin, "for the wages of sin is death" (Rom. 6:23). This understanding of death recalls Genesis 2:17: "for in the day that you eat of it you shall die." Once more we meet this idea in the covenant laws advocating capital punishment, such as "whoever strikes a man so that he dies shall be put to death" (Ex. 21:12). The flood of water upon the earth and the destruction of Sodom, Gomorrah, and the other cities of the plain, represented divine punishment by death (Gen. 6:6, 7; 19:15-28; cf. 2 Peter 3:6, 7; Jude 6, 7).

In the history of Israel's wars of conquest we read of such capital punishment upon guilty people. "Now go and smite Amalek, and utterly destroy all that they have; do not spare them, but kill both man and woman, infant and suckling, ox and sheep, camel and ass" (1 Sam. 15:3). The prophets also pronounce similar punishment on individuals who had affronted God in a serious and unrepentant manner (Amos 7:16, 17). And the apostle Peter on God's command sent the scheming Ananias and Sapphira out to instant death (Acts 5:1-11).

It may seem strange that the Bible should pronounce such severe punishment upon sinners and use as an instrument of punishment that which is most antithetical to the character of God. Indeed, the Bible presents this divine activity as out of character: "For the Lord will rise up as on Mount Perazim, he will be wroth as in the valley of Gibeon; to do his deed—strange is his deed! and to work his work—alien is his work!" (Isa. 28:21). Death, that which God likes the least in His universe, thus becomes His instrument to protect what He likes the most, namely, life.

That perspective governs all the biblical references to death as a human punishment; it must never become a likable solution. At best it may be a necessary solution instituted for protecting life and guarding the security of society. Such a restriction to the death penalty does not come easily to human judges in the heat of the moment, as seen, for example, in the story of Saul's election. "Then the people said to Samuel, 'Who is it that said, "Shall Saul reign over us?" Bring the men, that we may put them to death.' But Saul said, 'Not a man shall be put to death this day, for today the Lord has wrought deliverance in Israel'" (1 Sam. 11:12, 13). Unhappily, King Saul did not remain so generous later in his reign, but attempted to use capital punishment to further his own cause (1 Sam. 14:36-46). Abuse of the death penalty can follow all too easily, such as using it for reasons other than the protection of life, perhaps to take revenge (2 Sam. 3:27) or for personal greed (1 Kings 21:8-14), or following on complete misapprehension of what is right and wrong, true and false (Acts 8:1).

All these experiences of death represent different aspects of the wages of sin, which through Adam fell upon the entire human race. This death comes to all, righteous and unrighteous alike, with the exception of those who experience translation, for example, Enoch, Elijah, and those among God's children who are alive at Christ's appearance (Gen. 5:24; 2 Kings 2:11; 1 Thess. 4:17). It proceeds from the dreadful separation between the human family and God and from the reign of terror by the devil in this world, all consequences of sin. Small wonder that, faced with so certain a prospect of death, some would attempt to come to terms with it, saying, "We have made a covenant with death, and with Sheol we have an agreement" (Isa. 28:15), but that treaty will be annulled (verse 18). In short, the power and reign of death are such that no human possibility exists for arranging a compromise with it or for coming to terms with it. Only God can break this reign of death and destroy its dominion over life by a new creative act, the resurrection.

5. The Second Death

The Bible refers to a second death (Rev. 20:14). Unlike the first death, which comes upon all humans because of sin, the second death is God's final punishment upon unrepentant sinners. (See Sin VI. C. 1, 2; Man II. C. 1-3.)

Divine judgment upon the impious in the last day appears repeatedly in biblical eschatology (Dan. 7:11; Joel 3:2, 3; Matt. 24:37-39; Luke 17:26-30; 2 Cor. 5:10; 2 Peter 3:5-7). This punishment must not be confused with the death common to all descendants of Adam, a fate from which the Second Adam, Jesus Christ, will bring an escape for the righteous (Rom. 5:18). The second death is God's direct punishment of sinners who have not repented and sought salvation in Jesus Christ. Facing this prospect so overwhelms the guilty with despair that they will actively seek death over life (Rev. 6:15-17).

A special case of God's judgment upon sinners is associated with the final eradication of death. The book of Revelation identifies that judgment as the second death, from whose punishment no appeal can be heard, no confession of sin made, or forgiveness offered (Rev. 20:6, 7). It follows a second "resurrection of condemnation" (NRSV) after the millennium (John 5:28, 29; Rev. 20:5; see Millennium

I. C. 3. e), leading to the ultimate death sentence. At this time sinners no longer can bear witness to God, express repentance, or find salvation. Only evil, war, hatred, deception, and the final judgment remain. This is followed by God's destruction of death and hades themselves (Rev. 20:14), leading to the creation of a new heaven and a new earth (Rev. 21, 22).

In His justice and fairness God does not limit resurrection to His saints, those "faithful unto death" (Rev. 2:10), but extends it to all, including those who never sought it but chose to live under the power of death (Rev. 20:11-13). For such people, together with Satan and his agents, there awaits the second death (verses 14, 15).

Following the second resurrection, death no longer is a power to be broken, but a presence to be eliminated. No longer does it hold sway over God's saints or reign on earth. It is but an ugly relic of the past with no opportunity ever to reassert its power. Hence its elimination is simple, swift, final, and undisputed (verse 14). The power of death has been overturned by the resurrection; now the presence of death is removed, making way for immortal life, illustrated here by God's constant presence with His saints and the permanent absence of death, the remembrance of death, or even sorrow for death (Isa. 25:8; Rev. 21:3, 4).

6. The Resurrection Hope

The hope of resurrection, a new creative act by God, appears already in the OT. Job 14:7-17 expresses the realization that without divine interference, death will be final (verses 7-12). Only when God, longing for His lost creatures, restores them to life, can the reign of death be broken (verses 14-17). This hope in the midst of suffering rises to a crescendo in the Redeemer passage of Job 19:23-27. It is also clearly expressed in the eschatological prophecies (Isa. 25:8, 9; Dan. 12:2). Hope for a resurrection of the dead received increasing prominence in the noncanonical writings between the Testaments and became a cardinal doctrine for the Pharisees in Christ's time.

By NT times the resurrection hope is firmly established in both the Gospels and the Epistles (Matt. 22:31, 32; Luke 20:27-38; John 11:24; 1 Cor. 15:51-53; 1 Thess. 4:13-18; Heb. 11:19). Jesus gave advanced assurance of this hope by raising the dead to life (Matt. 9:23-25; Luke 7:11-17; John 11:38-44), an assurance God affirmed by raising Christ from the dead, whereby all believers may enjoy eternal life (John 3:16; 5:25-29; 6:39, 40; 1 Cor. 15:20-23; 1 Peter 1:3). This new life, available through faith in Christ, will become immortal life, not at death, but following the resurrection at Christ's second coming, when those who are asleep will be called forth to new life (1 Cor. 15:51-53; 1 Thess. 4:13-18; see Resurrection I. A, B; Second Coming I. G. 2).

7. The Eradication of Death

Following the resurrection, God's gift of eternal life to all who believe in Christ will signify the end of the power of death and break its dominion over humankind (2 Tim. 1:8-10). Christ accomplished this through His own death and resurrection: "For we know that Christ being raised from the dead will never die again; death no longer has dominion over him" (Rom. 6:9; cf. Rev. 1:18). A resurrection, unlike a resuscitation, does not cheat death of its power in the last minute but effectively breaks the power of death. Hence "death no longer has dominion over him" (Rom. 6:9).

The key to death's demise is in Christ's resurrection, which unlocks the prison that holds all people captive, "for if we have been united with him in a death like his, we shall certainly be united with him in a resurrection like his" (verse 5). The resurrection removes the last vestiges of power from death. Thus "when the perishable puts on the imperishable, and the mortal puts on immortality, then shall come to pass the saying that is written: 'Death is swallowed up in victory.' 'O death, where is thy victory? O death, where is thy sting?'" (1 Cor. 15:54, 55).

G. Ultimate Destinies

The power of death was broken by Christ's death and resurrection. The reign of death in the world will end when He comes again to receive His saints. The presence of death will be forever eradicated in the lake of fire at the "second death." Two distinct destinies stand before all those who have suffered under the curse of sin and its wage of death. There is the sad destiny of faithless people, who will suffer God's last judgment and final eradication. Or there is the joyful destiny of all those who have accepted the assurance of eternal life.

1. Time, Duration, and Outcome of the Divine Judgment

Since the Bible clearly teaches that death is a sleeplike condition characterized by complete unconsciousness, it follows that execution of judgment upon the dead does not occur in an intermediate period between death and resurrection. According to the Bible, no hellfire is presently burning for the punishment of sinners who have died. Similarly, no disembodied souls of saints who died believing in Christ presently enjoy the blessings of the new earth. God's rewards and punishment await the resurrection.

This raises a question about the way we understand the Bible passages describing what appear to be long periods of terrible suffering for sinners, e.g., that the punishment of the faithless will include eternal punishment (Matt. 25:46), and the torment of the wicked will last "for ever and ever" (Rev. 14:11; 20:10). The expression "for ever and ever" (Gr. *eis tous aiōnas ton aiōnōn*) means literally "into ages of ages." Similar expressions serve elsewhere to indicate continuity, for example, "Thy throne, O God, is for ever and ever" (Gr. *eis ton aiōna tou aiōnos*). The parallel OT text in Psalm 45:6 (cited in Heb. 1:8, 9), "Your divine throne endures for ever and ever," employs a corresponding Hebrew expression: *'ôlām,* "age" (the same word is used in Exodus 21:6, where the liberated slave serves "for ever" [KJV], that is, for life). These terms do not by themselves denote the length of time during which they are active. Rather, they express unbroken duration of an action, the extent of which is determined by its subject.

If therefore we read these and related passages dealing with the destruction of sinners along with the figurative descriptions of this destruction, the Bible concept becomes clear. In every instance, the destructive agents (burning, worms, pestilence, rot, water, floods, wind, darkness, warfare, birds of prey, fire, and brimstone) will perform their destructive work completely, with no possibility of survival (cf. Isa. 66:24; Eze. 38; 39; Zech. 14:12; Mal. 4:1; Matt. 7:19, 26, 27; 8:12; Mark 9:43-48; Luke 17:26-30; Rev. 19:17-21). The emphasis throughout is upon complete and irrevocable destruction (cf. Jude 7). Consequently, punishment in the region of the dead, whether šᵉ'ôl or hadēs, cannot indicate unending periods of suffering (cf. Mark 9:43-47), but are simple references to complete destruction.

The references to the time frame of the final destruction or eternal existence ("for ever and ever") are determined by the object of destruction or preservation respectively. When we speak about the reign of Christ, the expression "for ever and ever" means "without ceasing," but when the subject turns to the destruction of sinners, the same expression simply means "until sin and sinners are completely eradicated from the earth." In the same vein, the saints who receive immortality at the final resurrection will exist forever, similar to God Himself, who is immortal. However, sinners do not receive immortality, and since they possess no inherent immortal soul, their punishment can last only as long as their destruction lasts. Then existence for them will end. (See Judgment III. B. 3; Great Controversy V. D. 3.)

2. Assurance of Eternal Life

The promise of eternal life in Christ to all who believe in Him, and the hope of immortality when Christ returns to defeat the power of death, give assurance to all believers. There is no need of vain speculation about natural inherent immortality, about reincarnation at death, or about a fleeting spiritlike existence of the soul following death. For Scripture teaches that the reward of the righteous, the assurance of every believer, is in a new creation, a resurrection of the body from the dead into newness of life.

How certain is that assurance? According to the apostle Paul, it is underwritten by the love of God: "For I am sure that neither death, nor life, nor angels, nor principalities, nor things present, nor things to come, nor powers, nor height, nor depth, nor anything else in all creation, will be able to separate us from the love of God in Christ Jesus our Lord" (Rom. 8:38, 39). With this assurance Christians can face even the terror of death with courage, for though they fear death greatly, they trust God more and have accepted His promise of eternal life.

Once this biblical understanding of death—its origin, nature, and final eradication—is firmly embedded in the mind of the believers, they have no real fear of death. Naturally, they remain apprehensive about dying, mourn the loss of loved ones, and long for the resurrection. But they will never again fear suffering in purgatory or eternal hellfires. Spirits or disembodied souls of loved ones do not frighten them, for they know these do not exist. Dreams of reincarnation of the soul or a reuniting of the human soul with the universe after death will be dismissed as false fancy. Instead, when facing death, either their own or that of a loved one, they comfort one another with these words: "And the dead in Christ will rise first; then we who are alive, who are left, shall be caught up together with them in the clouds to meet the Lord in the air; and so we shall always be with the Lord" (1 Thess. 4:16, 17). They will cherish the ultimate victory over death and its sting with the words of the apostle: "Thanks be to God, who gives us the victory through our Lord Jesus Christ" (1 Cor. 15:57).

II. Historical Overview

A. *At the Dawn of History*

Records from the ancient Near East speak of death as an inescapable fate. Only the gods, but not humankind, were endowed with immortality, according to the ancients. The story of Adapa (perhaps the Mesopotamian Adam) tells how the wisest of men forfeited the opportunity to enjoy eternal life: "Come now, Adapa! Why didst thou neither eat nor drink? Thou shalt not have (eternal) life!" (ANET 102). Similarly, the Gilgamesh epic's central theme is human mortality. Young King Gilgamesh, ignoring any thought of death, embarked upon a vigorous life filled with courageous, even dangerous, achievements. But when death claimed his friend, he set out to search for everlasting life, only to be told, "When the gods created mankind, death for mankind they set aside, life in their own hands retaining" (*ibid.* 90). But that did not deter the ancients' quest of eternal life.

In ancient Egypt magnificent monuments to the dead and expansive burial practices testify to a preoccupation with death and a belief in life after death. Death is the fate of all mankind—as certain as the setting sun. "What does it mean that I must go to the desert of the kingdom of the dead? It has no water, it has no air, it is so deep, so dark, so endless!" (Beyerlin 11). However, an ancient pyramid text (2500-2300 B.C.) expressed the hope that dead King Unis would still live: "O King Unis, thou hast not at all departed dead, thou hast departed living!" (ANET 32). Evidently Egyptians thought it possible to escape death by leading a pure life and appealing for mercy and justice before the gods of the nether world, as indicated in the book of the dead (*ibid.* 34-36).

The people of Israel arrived relatively late on the scene in the ancient world. Hence, the Bible writers cannot have been unfamiliar with the popular thinking about death in Mesopotamia and Egypt. Yet Scripture sets out a clear and unambiguous position on the matter. According to the OT, the people of Israel also recognized the inevitability of death. "You are dust, and to dust you shall return" (Gen. 3:19). But in distinction from their neighbors, the people of Israel did not attempt to circumvent the reality of death by various means but sought to understand its true meaning. "Lord, let me know my end, and what is the measure of my days; let me know how fleeting my life is!" (Ps. 39:4). The unique understanding of death in ancient Israel, distinctive from that of other peoples of the ancient Near East, encouraged them first to accept the inevitability of death, then to come to terms with its reality, not in defiance or vain hope of an afterlife, but in the presence of God.

Facing death, Job said, "The Lord gave, and the Lord has taken away; blessed be the name of the Lord" (Job 1:21). This does not suggest that ancient Israel considered death a friend or a tolerable conclusion to life. On the contrary, like its neighbors, Israel viewed death as a terrifying enemy, intruding upon life and disrupting it. "For death has come up into our windows, it has entered our palaces, cutting off the children from the streets and the young men from the squares" (Jer. 9:21; Eccl. 12:1-8). To make this reality of death understandable, the Hebrew Scriptures explained it as an unconscious, sleeplike state, without a surviving soul, and void of any normal human activities and experiences (Ps. 146:3, 4; Eccl. 9:10).

Like its neighbors, Israel was anxious for the defeat of death so that life could continue, but not through human effort, courage, or skill, by which death might be robbed of its prey. Rather, according to the people of Israel, death's life-threatening activities ultimately would be curtailed only by God Himself through three divine gifts. First, His gift of children to carry on with the purposes of life. "Then Israel said to Joseph, 'Behold, I am about to die, but God will be with you, and will bring you again to the land of your fathers'" (Gen. 48:21). Second, His (rare) gift of translation into a new life, without the experience of death, ascribed to Enoch (Gen. 5:24) and Elijah (2 Kings 2:11), and perhaps implied by the psalmist with the words "Thou dost guide me with thy counsel, and afterward thou wilt receive me to glory" (Ps. 73:24). Third, His great gift of resurrection from death. "And many of those who sleep in the dust of the earth shall awake, some to everlasting life, and some to shame and everlasting contempt" (Dan. 12:2).

This remarkable understanding of death, which challenged the views of the earliest civilizations and which seems so contemporary, even modern in our time, was not to last.

B. Greek, Roman, and Jewish Concepts

The biblical understanding of death, unique in the ancient world, provided only one contribution to the later Western and Christian thought about the matter. Greek philosophy provided a second. Prior to the emergence of the philosophers, in the time of Homer (ninth century B.C.), the Greeks believed that death brought an end to consciousness and thought, leaving only a bodiless, shadowy, unconscious "existence" (*Iliad* 23:69-107; *Odyssey* 11:204-223). The popular myth of Orpheus tells of the hero's near successful attempt to gain his wife's release from the underworld. However, with the arrival of the early Greek "scientific" philosophers in Asia Minor (seventh to fifth centuries B.C.), questions arose about the nature of life, reality, and, naturally, death. For example, Heraclitus (c. 544-484 B.C.) concluded that fire constitutes the ultimate essence in the world, and that the human soul is part of that fire (*On the Universe* 20, 67, 77). Hence the soul survives death, whereas the human body at death merely changes into a different form.

In the same vein, immortality through participation in something greater than individual life came to expression in the Greek city (*polis*). Pericles' funeral oration for those who died for their city (reported by Thucydides, *The Peloponnesian War* 2.35-46) speaks of those dying for the citizens and being remembered by and in the city for their deed. In these cases, immortality does not derive from an inherently immortal soul, but from belonging to an eternal reality, either physical (e.g., universal immortal fire) or social (e.g., the city).

However, by the time of Socrates (470-399 B.C.) and Plato (427-347 B.C.) soul immortality came to clear expression in public discourse, as illustrated, for example, in the *Phaedo,* which records the last hours of Socrates' life. Socrates expressed his belief that at death the soul is freed from the impure body to live on independently, released from the corporeal.

"Of course you know that when a person dies, . . . it is natural for the visible and physical part of him, which lies here in the visible world and which we call his corpse, to decay and fall to pieces and be dissipated. . . . But the soul, the invisible part, which goes away to a place that is, like itself, glorious, pure, and invisible . . . will it, if its very nature is such as I have described, be dispersed and destroyed at the moment of its release from the body, as is the popular view? Far from it. . . . The truth is much more like this. If at its release the soul is pure and carries with it no contamination of the body, because it has never willingly associated with it in life, but has shunned it, . . . then it departs to that place which is, like itself invisible, divine, immortal, and wise. . . . But, I suppose, if at the time of its release, the soul is tainted and impure, because it has always associated with the body and cared for it and loved it, . . . it will, I imagine, be permeated with the corporeal. . . . So the soul which is tainted by its presence is weighted down and dragged back into the visible world. . . . The shadowy apparitions which have actually been seen there [in graveyards] are the ghosts of those souls which have not got clear away, but still retain some portions of the visible, which is why they can be seen" (*Phaedo* 80c-81d).

This sharp etching of soul immortality did not immediately enjoy universal acceptance. Aristotle (384-322 B.C.) called into question Plato's emphasis on formal existence in distinction from individual existence, pointing instead to the fact that forms of concepts have existence only in the material world. Thus one can hardly speak of a noncorporeal existence of the soul, for only God is spirit without body. "But we must return from this digression, and repeat that the affections of soul are inseparable from the material substratum of animal life" (*On the Soul* 1. 403b. 17).

This skepticism was reiterated by some Latin writers, among them Lucretius (98-55 B.C.), who concluded, "Therefore, death is nothing to us, it matters not one jot, since the nature of the mind is understood to be mortal . . . so when we shall no longer be, when the parting shall have come about between body and spirit from which we are compacted into one whole, then sure enough nothing at all will be able to happen to us who then will no longer be" (*On the Nature of Things* 3. 830-842).

However, that did not prevent the speculation of Socrates and Plato, complete with its vivid illustrations of the soul's continuing existence, from entering popular beliefs that have persisted to our own time. It was thought comforting to those who mourned death and those who faced it, especially untimely death from persecution, war, or illness. Even the thinking of Jewish people, who had grown up with the scriptural heritage, felt its influence. For example, 2 Maccabees 6:30 reports the death of pious Eleazer with these words: "I am enduring terrible sufferings in my body under this beating, but in my soul I am glad to suffer these things because I fear him." And 2 Maccabees 12:43-45 describes a sin offering of 2,000 silver drachmas for the purpose of making atonement for the dead.

By the time of the early church two conflicting understandings of death had emerged, each responding to the problem of death in a different way: the Bible's understanding of death as the certain end of life, which can be restored only by a new re-creative act of God, and the Greek understanding of death as the beginning of new life, with its affirmation of the soul's continued existence after separation from the body at death. O. Cullmann explained this difference dramatically in his illustrative contrast between the ways Jesus and Socrates personally faced the experience of dying (Cullmann 19-27).

The Bible, as illustrated by the experience of Jesus, presents death as a foe, the enemy of God and the destroyer of life, from whose grip God will release His saints into a new life in the resurrection body. Greek thought, illustrated by the experience of Socrates, portrays death as a welcome friend, releasing souls long imprisoned in the body into a new life of the spirit. Jesus' realistic presentation of death carries the dying of all ages forward in the resurrection hope, whereas the fanciful portrayal of death by Socrates offers the dying nothing at all. These two pictures of death, sharply drawn already when the church began, invited Christians and the whole Western world to choose between them.

C. The Early and Medieval Church

The contrast between the classical (Greek) understanding and the biblical (Hebrew) concept of death is profound. But these apparently incompatible understandings became blended in Christian teaching, the result being the medieval understanding of life, death, the fate of the soul in purgatory, resurrection, and the final judgment. This teaching emerged slowly from a long, uneven development lasting nearly a thousand years.

In popular opinion the Platonic definition of death as the release of the soul from the body immediately upon death became generally accepted in the early church. That claim remains unsubstantiated. The biblical view of death as an unconscious state (sleep) awaiting the resurrection continued to be heard in the early centuries of the church. Ignatius of

Antioch (c. A.D. 107) wrote, "Labour together with one another; strive in company together, run together, suffer together, sleep together [in death], and awake together [in the resurrection], as stewards, and associates, and servants of God" (*To Polycarp*, 6. 9, 10 [ANF 1: 95). Irenaeus of Lyons (c. A.D. 180), using the principle of recapitulation, taught that as Jesus Christ after His death awaited the resurrection, so also the souls of His disciples at death would go to "the invisible place allotted to them by God, and there remain until the resurrection, awaiting that event; then receiving their bodies, and rising in their entirety, that is bodily, just as the Lord arose, they shall come thus into the presence of God" (*Against Heresies* 5. 31. 2 [ANF 1:560). Of course, Irenaeus speaks here of the soul in distinction from body and spirit, but hardly in a Platonic sense, for only the resurrection can restore life. Refusal to speculate about the soul also characterized the Cappadocian Gregory of Nyssa (c. A.D. 335-395), who held that the soul must always be with the body. "There is nothing, then, to hinder the soul's presence in the body's atoms, whether fused in union or decomposed in dissolution. . . . Therefore, the soul exists in the actual atoms which she has once animated, and there is no force to tear her away from her cohesion with them" (*On the Soul and Resurrection*).

On the other hand, Origen of Alexandria (c. A.D. 200) prepared the way for the bold intrusions of Platonic concepts regarding the soul into Christian theology (*On First Principles* 4. 1. 36 [ANF 4:381]) with the result that eventually death became reduced to a relatively minor step in an ongoing process of purification of the soul. That position received further development in the hands of the Latin Fathers beginning with Tertullian (A.D. 160-240). Now the soul was understood to be practically as corporeal as the body, its post-death existence described in considerable detail: "All souls, therefore, are shut up within Hades: . . . Why then, cannot you suppose that the soul undergoes punishment and consolation in Hades in

the interval, while it awaits its alternative of judgment, in a certain anticipation either of gloom or of glory? . . . No one will hesitate to believe that the soul undergoes in Hades some compensatory discipline, without prejudice to the full process of the resurrection, when the recompense will be administered through the flesh besides" (*Treatise on the Soul* 58 [ANF 3:234, 235]). Augustine of Hippo (A.D. 354-430) spoke of the time between death and resurrection when the soul is kept in "a hidden retreat, where it enjoys rest or suffers affliction just in proportion to the merits it has earned by the life which it led on earth" (*Enchiridion* 109).

Thus, in the fourth century A.D., the emerging medieval understanding of death was clearly outlined, with only details remaining to be filled in. To be sure, the biblical notion of a bodily resurrection remained prominent as the final step in the soul's journey to perfection. For Thomas Aquinas (A.D. 1225-1274), the resurrection of the body remained a necessity because the soul by its very nature needs a body, human happiness depends upon it, and final punishment for sin cannot be meted out to a bodiless soul. Nevertheless, the Platonic belief in ongoing existence after death became more firmly entrenched. The soul's existence after death was predicated upon the need for divine justice in human experience, and such justice consists of rewards or punishment—the inevitable lot of every incorporeal soul (*Summa Theologiae* 3, Suppl. 75. 1, 2).

The remaining component of the medieval picture of death which still needed further development concerned purification of the soul through penance. By this means the Roman Catholic Church imposed upon contrite sinners an obligation or a "satisfaction" to purify them in preparation for receiving God's ultimate reward at the resurrection. Unfinished works of satisfaction in this life would be completed after death as follows: "The punishment of purgatory is intended to supplement the satisfaction which was not fully completed in the body" (*ibid.* 71.6).

The ultimate expression of this view, illustrated by Dante, attributes to the incorporeal soul all the faculties of the body (so that it can take full advantage of the purification process after death), with its accompanying shift of attention away from the resurrection to the determinative period between death and resurrection. As a result, the resurrection was reduced in importance to merely confirming the outcome of the temporary purgation. This view of death prevailed during the High Middle Ages.

D. The Sixteenth-Century Reformation and Subsequent Developments

The Protestant Reformation introduced what would become a turning point in Christian teaching on death. Martin Luther (1483-1546) took issue with the system of penance and its corollary, purification of the soul in purgatory. They clashed with his understanding of salvation discovered during study and meditation upon Scripture. In His Word God offers to us two ways, he concluded: salvation through faith and damnation through unbelief. He makes no mention of purgatory, which, therefore, must not be admitted, "because it obscures the benefits and grace of Christ" (*Table Talk* 3695). This conclusion regarding an intermediate state following death would have a lasting impact upon later Protestant advocates of the soul's nonimmortality.

On the matter of soul immortality, however, Luther himself was not consistent. At times he affirmed the teaching of medieval theologians that the soul enjoys a separate existence from the body. But when describing the condition of the soul between death and resurrection, he occasionally accepted the NT picture of soul sleep, as follows: "For the human soul sleeps with all senses buried, and our bed is like a sepulcher. Yet in it there is nothing troublesome or burdensome. Thus, the place of the dead has no torments. . . . Our death and resurrection will also be like this. We depart, and we return on the Last Day, before we are aware of it" (*Lectures on Genesis,* Gen. 49:33). The Lutheran Church did not follow Luther's inconsistent lead on conditional immortality, essentially reverting to the medieval traditions (cf. Althaus 410-417).

John Calvin (1509-1564) also rejected speculation about the soul's intermediate state (in purgatory) as "neither lawful nor expedient" (*Institutes* 3. 25. 6), but he affirmed the immortality of the soul and refuted those who denied it, including Miguel Servetus (1511-1553), who with Calvin's consent suffered execution for this and other heresies. In fact, Calvin affirmed that the human soul is "something essential, separate from the body" (*ibid.* 1. 15. 2). Hence, the souls survive the body at death, "where in glad expectation they await the enjoyment of promised glory. . . . The lot of the reprobate is . . . to be held in chains until they are dragged to the punishment appointed for them" (*ibid.* 3. 25. 6).

Although the Reformers challenged and rejected the medieval teachings concerning the soul's purification in purgatory, the Platonic concept of the soul's immortality survived the Reformation and remained a permanent fixture in much of popular Christianity. On this point, at least, Platonic speculation appears to have overwhelmed biblical realism, although perhaps not completely.

In time, and from various quarters, the genuine biblical position reemerged, namely, that death ends all life, that no soul survives it, that it may be compared to sleep because it involves unconsciousness, and that life returns to the deceased only in the resurrection.

For example, John Milton (1608-1674) wrote, "The death of the body is the loss or extinction of life. The common definition, which supposes it to consist in the separation of soul and body, is inadmissable" (*Christian Doctrine* 1. 13).

The new philosophies of rationalism and empiricism lent their support to this view of death by rejecting Platonic speculation about a reality that could not be tested. John Locke (1632-1704), commenting upon Genesis 2:17, explained, "I must confess that by death here,

I can understand nothing but a ceasing to be (that is, the losing of all actions of life and sense)" (*The Reasonableness of Christianity* 1).

Among many church leaders who also defended the biblical position belongs Francis Blackburne (1704-1787). "Hence to suppose the souls of dead men to be alive, conscious and active, and capable of happiness and misery, from the death of the first man, to the resurrection of the very last, and to pretend to *demonstrate* this by reason and philosophy, is plainly to overturn the whole Christian system" (*A Short Historical View of the Controversy Concerning an Intermediate State,* 69, in CFOF 2:211, 212). Nevertheless, he observed, "it is remarkable that Protestants, who have on most occasions refused to be governed by *tradition,* seem to have submitted to it in this matter with the most implicit deference" (*ibid.* xiv, in CFOF 2:210).

In more recent years, reacting to the traditional understanding of death and more particularly to its corollary, the historic doctrine of hell, noted evangelical theologians such as J.R.W. Stott, Clark H. Pinnock, and J. W. Wenham, along with Oscar Cullmann, have argued convincingly in favor of conditional immortality. Far from dogmatizing about the position to which they have come, they are pleading for a frank dialogue among Christians on the basis of the Scriptures.

E. The Seventh-day Adventist Position

In the mid-nineteenth century this minority position, advanced by eighteenth-century clergymen and scholars on both sides of the Atlantic, was adopted by the young Seventh-day Adventist Church for the following reasons: (1) It represents the biblical view, free of philosophical speculation and ecclesiastical tradition, particularly the tradition of the soul's purification in purgatory already deplored by the Reformers; (2) it was held by the early church, reemerging during and after the Ref-

ormation; (3) it affirms the familiar biblical portrayal of death as a sleeplike unconsciousness, rejecting the view of the soul's continued existence after death; (4) it supports the biblical teaching that immortality is not inherent in the nature of the soul, or bestowed at death, but granted only at the resurrection from the dead; (5) it underscores the NT emphasis on Christ as the only way to eternal life without consideration of any merits accruing to the soul following death.

This is sometimes referred to as the "conditionalist position" because it attaches certain conditions to the gift of immortality, namely, acceptance of God's salvation by grace through faith in Jesus Christ by the condemned sinner. That gift alone, and no inherent natural quality of the human soul, is the condition for immortality.

The immediate impetus leading Seventh-day Adventists to adopt the conditionalist position was provided by a Methodist minister, George Storrs (1796-1867). His views, published as *An Enquiry: Are the Souls of the Wicked Immortal?* in 1842, attracted the attention of early Adventists James White (1821-1881), Joseph Bates (1792-1872), E. G. White (1827-1915), J. N. Andrews (1829-1883), D. M. Canright (1840-1919), and U. Smith (1832-1903). The conditionalist position became firmly and permanently anchored in Seventh-day Adventist teachings, recognized as a doctrinal "pillar" based squarely on the teachings of Scripture.

Ellen White gave this understanding of death and the nonimmortality of the soul careful and extended attention in several of her writings, confirming its place in Seventh-day Adventist theology. First, she regarded it as "present truth," meaning a central and pertinent biblical principle that corrects popular and widespread interest in spiritualism, which is viewed as a delusion first introduced into the world by the devil (Gen. 3:4) and subsequently promulgated by paganism and false Christendom. This delusion claims that sinners do not die, but live on as disembodied souls capable of communication with the living (EW 262; GC 531-562).

Second, White emphasized that as the consequence of sin, death is caused by human disregard of God's law, including nature's law and the laws of health. This insight, in turn combined with her wholistic understanding of human development, eventually brought about Seventh-day Adventist commitment to health care and education (CD 21, 40; PP 68).

Third, White underscored the biblical understanding of death as unconscious sleep, from which God alone can awaken the saints in the last resurrection at the second coming of Christ. The NT promise "For as in Adam all die, so also in Christ shall all be made alive" (1 Cor. 15:22) focuses attention upon the death and resurrection of Christ, especially its eschatological teachings about the Second Advent, when the power of death shall be broken and the eternal kingdom of God restored (DA 787; GC 545, 547, 549, 550, 645; PK 239).

The wholistic understanding of human nature, coupled with the teaching of conditional immortality, has been advocated consistently from the pulpit of the Seventh-day Adventist Church since its founding, at times in the face of opposition from other Christian and secular traditions (cf. Zurcher, Johnston). It has been an integral part of the church missionary work among non-Western cultures with strong beliefs in life after death, such as ancestor worship, spirit worship, or reincarnation. Although it was once a minority position, conditional immortality became widely accepted in the first half of the twentieth century by theologians and church leaders from many confessions (cf. CFOF 2:747-1034).

F. Current Crosswinds

A growing acceptance of conditional immortality continued into the second half of the twentieth century (cf. Anderson, Cullmann, Harris, Thielicke). During this period, however, several new conflicting developments entered the discussion. Increasingly, representatives from the social sciences, medicine, and ethics have joined theologians and philosophers in studying death. As a result, the earlier focus on theological questions dealing with the meaning of life and the destiny of persons has turned toward various anthropological, psychological, medical, and ethical questions. Special attention is given to the process of dying and the way in which both the dying person and family members and friends left behind cope with that process, as well as the role played by therapists, counselors, and clergy.

The medical profession has given attention to human experiences near the borders of life and the way they may be extended or crossed, due in part to the ability of medical science to "bring back to life" patients who for all practical purposes have momentarily ceased living. This ability to manipulate the life processes through medical technology, particularly at the border between life and death, has introduced new ethical concern about the quality of human life and the meaning of the human soul. Specific concerns have been raised that medical science applied to the human body may do injustice to the inner being of a person and the quality and dignity of human life. As medical costs escalate, renewed questioning is bound to arise, on the one hand, regarding heroic intervention designed to prolong a human life ebbing away toward death, and, on the other hand, regarding euthanasia or professional assistance with death for terminally ill persons whose life has become unbearable.

Given this context of new ideas, problems, and issues, Eastern and Western understandings of life and death have met to challenge the biblical understanding in new and, to traditional Christians, unfamiliar ways (cf. Hick). For example, the concept of reincarnation, or transmigration of the human soul from one body to another at death, has caught the attention of some in the West who simply cannot accept the idea that human life ends at death, given all the scientific ingenuity at our disposal. In its most crude form it holds that the soul of a person may return to life after death in the body of some other kind of being on its way toward perfection. More common in the West is the belief that a person's soul participates in some larger soul or life force, shared with other beings and retained after death. This participation, some believe, can be experienced already in the present life through experiences induced by ritual, meditation, or even drugs.

These new concepts of immortality challenge the biblical teachings of conditionalism as much as the older concepts of the soul's survival, purification in purgatory, and ascent to God. However, a large number of contemporary Jewish and Christian believers and theologians, among them Seventh-day Adventists, continue to affirm the concept of conditional immortality with its two corollaries, the wholistic approach to human beings and the resurrection hope in eternal life. The reasons are: (1) It helps explain and respond to the puzzling contemporary psychological and medical experiences with death, the so-called life-after-life experiences, for in the final analysis all these experiences have not reduced the number of funerals—death remains the final end of life; (2) it harmonizes with a wholistic view of human nature and the biblical understanding of human life as a miraculous gift of God; (3) it is realistic about the nature of death, with specific reference to the unity of the physical and spiritual aspects of life; (4) it correctly takes into account both the divinity of God and the humanity of humankind, thereby affirming the incarnation of God in Christ, the reality of salvation in Jesus Christ, and the resurrection hope, which brings comfort to those left behind.

III. Ellen G. White Comments

A. *Importance*

E. G. White early emphasized the importance of this doctrine (sometimes referred to as the "state of the dead"), regarding it as "present truth" about which the believers must have a "thorough understanding." The context of the following paragraph, first published in 1858, is satanic "delusions," "spiritualism," and the claim that the living can communicate with the dead.

"I saw that the saints must have a thorough understanding of present truth, which they will be obliged to maintain from the Scriptures. They must understand the state of the dead; for the spirits of devils will yet appear to them, professing to be beloved relatives or friends, who will declare to them unscriptural doctrines. They will do all in their power to excite sympathy and will work miracles before them to confirm what they declare. The people of God must be prepared to withstand these spirits with the Bible truth that the dead know not anything, and that they who thus appear are the spirits of devils" (EW 262).

Later, two whole chapters in her book *The Great Controversy* were devoted to this subject (GC 531-562). Here she affirms that the delusion first introduced by the serpent in Genesis 3:4 with the promise "you will not die" has spread throughout the whole world in the form of spiritualism (*ibid.* 561, 562). The biblical truth, on the other hand, remains as follows: "The Bible declares that the dead know not anything, that their thoughts have perished; they have no part in anything that is done under the sun; they know nothing of the joys or sorrows of those who were dearest to them on earth" (*ibid.* 556).

1. The Origin of Death

In developing this biblical teaching further, E. G. White observes the following points regarding the origin and nature of death:

Death is traced back to the power of Satan. "For his transgression, Moses came under the power of Satan—the dominion of death" (EW 164).

Sin is the source of this satanic power, which removes its victims from the sphere of

God. "He [Satan] determined to cause their fall, that, having separated them from God and brought them under his own power, he might gain possession of the earth and here establish his kingdom in opposition to the Most High" (GC 531).

2. The Causes of Death

While in a general sense death is presented as the wages of sin (EW 294), E. G. White writes extensively about these wages with specific illustrations of how they are paid. For example:

Poor health habits can bring premature death. "Premature decay and death are the result of walking away from God to follow the ways of the world. He who indulges self must bear the penalty. In the judgment we shall see how seriously God regards the violation of the laws of health" (CD 40).

General disobedience of God's law leads to death. "It was the first time he [Adam] had ever witnessed death, and he knew that had he been obedient to God, there would have been no death of man or beast" (PP 68).

Neglect of nature's law also threatens life. "And when premature death is the result of our violation of nature's law, we bring sorrow and suffering to others; we deprive our neighbors of the help we ought to render them in living; we rob our families of the comfort and help we might render them, and rob God of the service He claims of us to advance His glory. Then, are we not, in the worst sense, transgressors of God's law?" (CD 21).

In short, death has become the fate of the wicked. "While life is the inheritance of the righteous, death is the portion of the wicked" (GC 544).

3. The Nature of Death

However, death does not transport the righteous directly to heaven and the wicked straight to hell.

"Many are comforted with the assurance that their loved ones are enjoying the bliss of heaven, and without suspicion of danger, they give ear 'to seducing spirits, and doctrines of devils' " (GC 552). Further, "and how utterly revolting is the belief that as soon as the breath leaves the body the soul of the impenitent is consigned to the flames of hell!" (*ibid.* 545).

Rather, death is a sleeplike condition. "Christ represents death as a sleep to His believing children. Their life is hid with Christ in God, and until the last trump shall sound those who die will sleep in Him" (DA 527).

The sleep of death will last but a moment, as it were. "To the Christian, death is but a sleep, a moment of silence and darkness" (*ibid.* 787).

Thus during death there is no experience of consciousness, whether of knowledge, planning, or thought. "Many expected to hear from Lazarus a wonderful account of scenes witnessed after death. They were surprised that he told them nothing. He had nothing of this kind to tell. Inspiration declares, 'The dead know not anything. . . . Their love, and their hatred, and their envy, is now perished' (Eccl. 9:5, 6)" (*ibid.* 557, 558).

Only the resurrection will interrupt death. "They that go down to the grave are in silence. . . . They sleep; they are awakened by the trump of God to a glorious immortality" (GC 550).

Therefore, death is not a frightening experience to the righteous person. "To the believer, death is but a small matter. Christ speaks of it as if it were of little moment. 'If a man keep my saying, he shall never see death,' 'he shall never taste of death.' To the Christian, death is but a sleep, a moment of silence and darkness. The life is hid with Christ in God, and 'when Christ, who is our life, shall appear, then shall ye also appear with him in glory' (John 8:51, 52; Col. 3:4)" (DA 787).

B. On the Soul's Immortality

The doctrine of the soul's immortality receives considerable attention and is regarded as false and dangerously deceptive.

The doctrine is satanic in origin. "And this

is the evidence that the incestuous, drunken Amnon was at death immediately transported to the abodes of bliss, there to be purified and prepared for the companionship of sinless angels! A pleasing fable indeed, well suited to gratify the carnal heart! This is Satan's own doctrine, and it does his work effectually. Should we be surprised that, with such instruction, wickedness abounds?" (GC 539).

This doctrine is found nowhere in the Bible. "The doctrine of consciousness after death, of the spirits of the dead being in communion with the living, has no foundation in the Scriptures, and yet these theories are affirmed as truth" (Ev 603).

Nevertheless, the doctrine has entered the Christian church. "And the declaration of the serpent to Eve in Eden—'Ye shall not surely die'—was the first sermon ever preached upon the immortality of the soul. Yet this declaration, resting solely upon the authority of Satan, is echoed from the pulpits of Christendom and is received by the majority of mankind as readily as it was received by our first parents" (GC 533). "The theory of the immortality of the soul was one of those false doctrines that Rome, borrowing from paganism, incorporated into the religion of Christendom. Martin Luther classed it with the 'monstrous fables that form part of the Roman dunghill of decretals.' (E. Petavel, *The Problem of Immortality*, p. 255). Commenting on the words of Solomon in Ecclesiastes, that the dead know not anything, the Reformer says: 'Another place proving that the dead have no . . . feeling. There is, saith he, no duty, no science, no knowledge, no wisdom there. Solomon judgeth that the dead are asleep, and feel nothing at all. For the dead lie there, accounting neither days nor years, but when they are awaked, they shall seem to have slept scarce one minute.' (Martin Luther, *Exposition of Solomon's Booke Called Ecclesiastes*, p. 152)" (GC 549).

C. The Defeat of Death

The antidote to death is the resurrection and its power.

"So was the faith of this woman rewarded. Christ, the great Life-giver, restored her son to her. In like manner will His faithful ones be rewarded, when, at His coming, death loses its sting and the grave is robbed of the victory it has claimed" (PK 239).

The resurrection would be unnecessary if the righteous ascended to heaven immediately at death. "If for four thousand years the righteous had gone directly to heaven at death, how could Paul have said that if there is no resurrection, 'they also which are fallen asleep in Christ are perished'? No resurrection would be necessary" (GC 546, 547).

Thus only Christ holds the key to life and death. "He who Himself was soon to die upon the cross stood with the keys of death, a conqueror of the grave, and asserted His right and power to give eternal life" (DA 530).

Only those righteous people who live when Christ returns will experience translation and never face death. "Beside Him are two heavenly beings, in close converse with Him. They are Moses, who upon Sinai had talked with God; and Elijah, to whom the high privilege was given—granted to but one other of the sons of Adam—never to come under the power of death" (*ibid.* 421). "The living righteous are changed 'in a moment, in the twinkling of an eye.' At the voice of God they were glorified; now they are made immortal and with the risen saints are caught up to meet their Lord in the air" (GC 645).

Those who experience neither translation nor destruction face only death—the second death.

"In consequence of Adam's sin, death passed upon the whole human race. All alike go down into the grave. And through the provisions of the plan of salvation, all are to be brought forth from their graves. 'There shall be a resurrection of the dead, both of the just and unjust'; 'for as in Adam all die, even so in Christ shall all be made alive' (Acts 24:15; 1 Cor. 15:22). But a distinction is made between the two classes that are brought forth. 'All that are in the graves shall hear His voice, and shall come forth; they that have done good, unto the resurrection of life; and they that have done evil, unto the resurrection of damnation' (John 5:28, 29). They who have been 'accounted worthy' of the resurrection of life are 'blessed and holy.' 'On such the second death hath no power' (Rev. 20:6). But those who have not, through repentance and faith, secured pardon, must receive the penalty of transgression—'the wages of sin.' They suffer punishment varying in duration and intensity, 'according to their works,' but finally ending in the second death. Since it is impossible for God, consistently with His justice and mercy, to save the sinner in his sins, He deprives him of the existence which his transgressions have forfeited and of which he has proved himself unworthy. Says an inspired writer: 'Yet a little while, and the wicked shall not be: yea, thou shalt diligently consider his place, and it shall not be.' And another declares: 'They shall be as though they had not been' (Ps. 37:10; Obadiah 16). Covered with infamy, they sink into hopeless, eternal oblivion" (ibid. 544, 545).

But the righteous will overcome death with Christ in His resurrection.

"Nowhere in the Sacred Scriptures is found the statement that the righteous go to their reward or the wicked to their punishment at death. The patriarchs and prophets have left no such assurance. Christ and His apostles have given no hint of it. The Bible clearly teaches that the dead do not go immediately to heaven. They are represented as sleeping until the resurrection (1 Thess. 4:14; Job 14:10-12). In the very day when the silver cord is loosed and the golden bowl broken (Eccl. 12:6), man's thoughts perish. They that go down to the grave are in silence. They know no more of anything that is done under the sun (Job 14:21). Blessed rest for the weary righteous! Time, be it long or short, is but a moment to them. They sleep; they are awakened by the trump of God to a glorious immortality. 'For the trumpet shall sound, and the dead shall be raised incorruptible. . . . So when this corruptible shall have put on incorruption, and this mortal shall have put on immortality, then shall be brought to pass the saying that is written, Death is swallowed up in victory' (1 Cor. 15:52-54). As they are called forth from their deep slumber they begin to think just where they ceased. The last sensation was the pang of death; the last thought, that they were falling beneath the power of the grave. When they arise from the tomb, their first glad thought will be echoed in the triumphal shout: 'O death, where is thy sting? O grave, where is thy victory?' (verse 55)" (ibid. 549, 550).

IV. Literature

Althaus, P. *The Theology of Martin Luther.* Philadelphia: Fortress, 1966.

Anderson, R. S. *Theology, Death and Dying.* Oxford: Blackwell, 1986.

Bailey, L. R., Sr. *Biblical Perspectives on Death.* Philadelphia: Fortress, 1979.

Beyerlin, W., ed. *Near Eastern Religious Texts Relating to the Old Testament.* Philadelphia: Westminster, 1978.

Bultmann, R. "Thanatos." *Theological Dictionary of the New Testament.* Vol. 3, pp. 7-25.

Cullmann, O. *Immortality of the Soul or Resurrection of the Dead?* New York: Macmillan, 1958.

Eichrodt, W. *Theology of the Old Testament.* Philadelphia: Westminster, 1967. Vol. 2.

Froom, LeRoy. *The Conditionalist Faith of Our Fathers.* 2 vols. Washington, D.C.: Review and Herald, 1965, 1966.

Harris, M. J. *Raised Immortal: Resurrection and Immortality in the New Testament.* Grand Rapids: Eerdmans, 1983.

Hick, J. *Death and Eternal Life.* New York: Harper and Row, 1976.

Jeremias, J. *The Parables of Jesus.* Rev. ed. New York: Scribner's, 1963.

Johnston, R. M. "After Death: Resurrection or Immortality?" *Ministry,* Sept. 1983, pp. 7-10.

Jungel, E. *Death: The Riddle and the Mystery.* Philadelphia: Westminster, 1974.

Kaiser, O., and E. Lohse. *Death and Life.*

Translated by J. E. Steely. Nashville: Abingdon, 1981.

Küng, H. *Eternal Life: Life After Death as a Medical, Philosophical, and Theological Problem.* Garden City, N.Y.: Doubleday, 1984.

Mills, L. O., ed. *Perspectives on Death.* Nashville: Abingdon, 1969.

Nickelsburg, G.W.E. *Resurrection, Immortality, and Eternal Life in Intertestamental Judaism.* Cambridge, Mass.: Harvard University Press, 1972.

Pritchard, J. B., ed. *Ancient Near Eastern Texts.* Princeton, N.J.: Princeton University Press, 1955.

Provonsha, J. W. *Is Death for Real? An Examination of Reported Near-Death Experiences in the Light of the Resurrection.* Mountain View, Calif.: Pacific Press, 1981.

Rahner, K. *On the Theology of Death.* New York: Herder and Herder, 1972.

Robinson, H. W. *Inspiration and Revelation in the Old Testament.* Toronto: Oxford University Press, 1946.

Thielicke, H. *Living With Death.* Grand Rapids: Eerdmans, 1983.

Tromp, N. J. *Primitive Conceptions of Death and the Nether World in the Old Testament.* Rome: Pontifical Biblical Institute, 1969.

Wolff, H. W. *Anthropology of the Old Testament.* Philadelphia: Fortress, 1973.

Zurcher, Jean R. *The Nature and Destiny of Man.* New York: Philosophical Library, 1969.

Resurrection and Glorification

John C. Brunt

Introduction

Every Christian's hope for the future is based on the resurrection of Jesus Christ and the promise that His resurrection assures resurrection and eternal life for those who believe in Him (1 Cor. 15:20, 21; 2 Cor. 4:14).

Christ's return to life after His death on the cross assures Christians that His promises are reliable and that all those who commit their lives to Him in trust can look forward to eternal life that is not subject to death. This resurrection occurs at the return of Christ (1 Cor. 15:51, 52; 1 Thess. 4:16). For those who have died in Christ it will mean a return to life from the unconscious sleep of death. For believers in Christ who are alive when He returns it will mean transformation to an immortal existence in the new earth. For all who are in Christ it will include a new body, glorified and no longer subject to death (1 Cor. 15:42-44). In a separate resurrection the wicked rise to face the total destruction of the second death (Rev. 20:5-10).

This consistent biblical perspective of the resurrection of the dead is both different from and incompatible with the popular belief in the immortality of the soul.

The article begins by exploring the biblical material on the resurrection and glorification of believers, then reflects on the significance of the doctrine, and ends with a survey of various understandings of resurrection and life after death from a historical perspective.

I. The Biblical View of the Resurrection

Both testaments contribute to the biblical teaching on the resurrection. In the NT all theological thought about the resurrection of the believers is integrally related to the resurrection of Jesus Christ. (See Christ III. A. 1-4.) This explicit theological link is so strong in the NT and so permeates NT material that it demands treatment separate from the OT, where the specific picture of Jesus' resurrection was not yet known.

A. The New Testament

This section is divided into two parts. The first gives an overall summary of the NT teaching on the resurrection of the believers. This is the view of the "forest" to give a wholistic understanding of the New Testament material. From it a clear and consistent picture emerges.

It is also important to see what the individual trees contribute to the forest. Each NT writer adds a distinctive contribution to this consistent picture, its richness to be grasped only when we appreciate these distinctive contributions. Therefore, the second section will treat the individual NT writers to see how the unique perspective of each contributes to the consistent whole.

1. Summary

All NT thought about the resurrection of the believer grows out of the resurrection of Jesus Christ. Jesus declares Himself to be "the resurrection and the life" (John 11:25). But He goes far beyond declaration; He demonstrates His power over death when He raises Lazarus from the dead. Even this crowning miracle does not assure victory over death forever. Only His own resurrection from the tomb on the third day guarantees that death will be swallowed up in victory.

Christ's resurrection is the "first fruits" (1 Cor. 15:20, 23) that not only precedes the resurrection of the believer but assures it and provides the foundation for it. In this sense, Christ's resurrection is already the beginning of the final resurrection. It is an eschatological event—already the beginning of the end.

All Christian hope is founded on Christ's resurrection. Humans have no natural immortality. God alone has immortality (1 Tim. 6:15, 16). Death is an unconscious sleep (John 11:11; 1 Thess. 4:13) and, rather than being a transition to another kind of life, is simply the negation of life. Since God is the Lord of life, death

is an enemy (1 Cor. 15:26), against which humans have no power or hope in and of themselves. (See Death I. A. 6; F. 6.)

God promises, however, that just as Christ was raised, Christians also have the hope of resurrection (1 Thess. 4:14, 15; 1 Cor. 15:20-23). According to 1 Thessalonians 4:13-18 and 1 Corinthians 15:51-57, this resurrection coincides with the second coming of Jesus Christ, an event universally visible, and is accompanied by the call of the archangel and the sound of the last trumpet. At that point those who have died in Christ are resurrected and those believers who are alive are transformed, given immortality, and caught up with the resurrected ones to meet the Lord and be with Him forever.

In this new state of immortality and eternal fellowship with God believers do not shed their material bodies, but enjoy the kind of bodily existence God originally intended before the entrance of sin into the world. In 1 Corinthians 15:35-46 Paul affirms that this new glorified, or spiritual, body is not an immaterial body but a recognizable body with continuity and identity from earthly life. It is "spiritual," not in the sense that it is not physical, but that it is no longer subject to death. Both believers who have died and those alive at the return of Christ receive the same imperishable body. It differs from the present body only in that it is perfect, free of all the imperfections caused by sin in the world, and in that it is no longer subject to death.

This resurrection of the righteous at the second coming of Christ is not the only resurrection about which the NT speaks, however. It also speaks clearly of a resurrection of the unjust, or the wicked (Acts 24:15; John 5:28, 29). According to Revelation 20:5, 7-10, this second resurrection, or resurrection of the wicked, does not occur at the second coming of Christ, but 1,000 years later, after Satan has been bound for a millennium and the saints have reigned with Christ. At that point the wicked are resurrected and attempt to take the Holy City, which descended to the earth prior to their resurrection. This demonstrates their unchangeable unwillingness to accept Christ's rule despite all evidence. They are then destroyed with Satan, and the earth is remade into a new earth, where Christ will dwell with the saints forever. Revelation also speaks of a special resurrection in which those who crucified Christ will awake to witness His second coming (Rev. 1:7; see GC 637 in V. C).

We may therefore summarize the various resurrections found in the NT in the following way:

1. The resurrection of Jesus—the basis and foundation for the believer's resurrection, clearly stated in the Gospels (Matt. 28:6; Mark 16:6; Luke 24:5-7; John 21:14).

2. The resurrection of certain saints accompanying Jesus' resurrection (Matt. 27:52).

3. The special resurrection of those who crucified Christ to see Him come (Rev. 1:7).

4. The resurrection of the righteous when Jesus returns at the beginning of the millennium (e.g., 1 Cor. 15; 1 Thess. 4).

5. The resurrection of the wicked at the end of the millennium (Rev. 20).

Throughout the NT this good news about the resurrection is far more than interesting data about the future. It transforms life in the present by investing it with meaning and hope. Because of their confidence about their destiny, Christians already live a new kind of life. Those who live in the hope of sharing the glory of God are transformed into different people. They can even rejoice in suffering, because their lives are motivated by hope:

"Therefore, since we are justified by faith, we have peace with God through our Lord Jesus Christ. Through him we have obtained access to this grace in which we stand, and we rejoice in our hope of sharing the glory of God. More than that, we rejoice in our sufferings, knowing that suffering produces endurance, and endurance produces character, and character produces hope, and hope does not disappoint us, because God's love has been poured into our hearts through the Holy Spirit which has been given to us" (Rom. 5:1-5).

A more detailed treatment of the NT mate-rial will survey the individual writers to discover the contribution each makes to this NT teaching. We begin with Paul, because his letters were the first major portion of the NT to be written, and because he wrote in more detail on the theology of resurrection than did other writers in the NT.

2. Individual Writers

a. Paul. Although Paul spends little time on the events of Christ's life, His death and resurrection are constant themes in Paul's letters. When Paul speaks about what is of "first importance" for believers, it is that "Christ died for our sins in accordance with the scriptures, that he was buried, that he was raised on the third day in accordance with the scriptures, and that he appeared" (1 Cor. 15:3-5). Characteristically, Paul uses the passive voice for the resurrection—Christ *was raised* by God. The full discussion of 1 Corinthians 15 below will show how all hope for eternal life is based on Christ's resurrection.

Paul's first major discussion of the resurrection of the believers is found in the first of his extant letters, specifically 1 Thessalonians 4:13-18. Here he raises the issue because of an apparent misunderstanding among the Thessalonians, who are grieving about those who have died. They seem to be ignorant of the fate of these deceased loved ones. Paul responds by stressing that they should not grieve as those who have no hope, but should instead turn their attention to the hope of the second coming of Christ and the resurrection of the dead to occur at that time. He does not say the deceased loved ones are alive or conscious, but speaks of their current state as sleep and focuses attention on the time when Christ will return. Then the Lord will descend with a cry of command, the archangel's call, and the trumpet of God. Those who are alive will not have an advantage over those who have died. The latter will rise to new life; then those who are alive will be caught up with them to meet the Lord in the air and be with Him forever. Here Paul clearly builds a future hope for those who have died, as well as for the living when Christ returns.

The meaning of the phrase "God will bring with him those who have fallen asleep" (verse 14) has been disputed. Some have seen in it support for the immortality of the soul, assuming that God is bringing souls with Him from heaven to be reunited with bodies at the resurrection.

Several important considerations speak against this. First is context. There is no mention of souls. The entire passage focuses on the resurrection and the call to those who have "fallen asleep" to rise at the resurrection. There is no mention of reuniting body and soul.

Second is the parallelism in the passage itself. In quite literal translation the passage reads "For since we believe that Jesus died and rose again, in the same way, through Jesus, God will also bring with him those who have fallen asleep." It could be, however, that the phrase "through Jesus" should go with "those who have fallen asleep," as some suggest. But wherever one places this difficult phrase, the parallelism with the first part of the sentence suggests that "bringing with him" refers to bringing these deceased believers to life through the resurrection in the same way that Jesus Himself died but rose again. This is the plain sense of "in the same way," which links the two parts of the sentence. Thus both context and syntax support the idea that the phrase "God will bring with him" in verse 14 means that God will bring them to life with Jesus as He brought Jesus to life at the Resurrection.

A final consideration comes from a somewhat similar statement in 2 Corinthians 4:14: "knowing that he who raised the Lord Jesus will raise us also with Jesus." The preposition *syn* ("with") is used in both passages, which supports the argument from both context and syntax that bringing those who had fallen asleep *with* Jesus refers to bringing them to life with Jesus.

This passage, then, teaches that the Christian hope is based on the resurrection of Christ. As He rose again, so God will raise those who have died in Christ. This will occur at the Second Coming, at the same time as those living in Christ meet with them in the air to be with the Lord forever.

In 1 Corinthians 15 Paul responds not merely to a misunderstanding but to false teaching on the part of some who deny the resurrection. It is the fullest passage on the resurrection in the NT.

Again Paul bases the believers' hope firmly on the foundation of Jesus Christ's death and resurrection. The apostle begins by reaffirming that the death and resurrection of Christ is of first importance (verses 3, 4). Then he reminds the Corinthians of Christ's resurrection appearances to Cephas, the twelve, more than 500 brethren at one time, James, all the apostles, and finally to Paul himself, although the final appearance was out of schedule with the rest (verses 5-8). In other words, Paul affirms that in his experience on the Damascus road he actually met the risen Jesus Christ and became himself a witness of the Resurrection.

In verses 12-19 Paul gets to the point at issue. Some said there was no resurrection of the dead. It is impossible to say what motivated this thinking, but the presence of other elements in Corinth similar to the type of thinking found in later Gnostic heresies suggests the possibility that at least a group of Corinthians may have been influenced by an earlier version of this heresy. Paul's response is one of incredulity. If Christ is preached as raised, how can they say there is no resurrection? These verses make it clear that for Paul an integral package includes Christ's resurrection, the believer's resurrection, and meaningful Christian faith. If any part of the package is removed, all is lost. Without the Resurrection, preaching is vain, faith is futile, Paul is misrepresenting God, and believers are still in their sins and are of all people most to be pitied. These are strong words, but Paul is explicit about each item.

In verse 20 Paul leaves behind the ifs of the

previous paragraph and reaffirms that Christ has in fact been raised from the dead. He then emphasizes that this was not a solitary act, but is bound with the believers' hope for the resurrection. Christ is the "first fruits," an analogy drawn from the OT festivals. His resurrection is the assurance that more is to come. Paul turns to the analogy of Adam and Christ. Death came through Adam in a way that affected all humans. Now life comes through Christ. Christ's resurrection reveals His victory over every power and authority, even death. In a format typical of the NT the resurrection of Christ and the believer's resurrection are tied together theologically.

In verses 29-34 Paul again returns to the theme of verses 12-19, giving additional reasons that the Corinthians' denial of the resurrection makes no sense. Why are some people baptized for the dead if there is no resurrection? (Unfortunately these people and their practices are unknown.) And why would Paul face death every day if there were no resurrection?

Next, the apostle turns to a possible objection from his readers and takes up the question of how the dead are raised and what kind of body those resurrected will have. Since this section (verses 35-50) is covered below in the discussion of glorification, it suffices here to note that for Paul the resurrection is much more than the resuscitation of a corpse. It involves transformation into a new body no longer subject to death. Paul calls this a "spiritual" body.

Finally, Paul's focus turns to the second coming of Christ, designated as the "last trumpet" (verse 52). In almost poetic form he points his readers to the instantaneous transformation to occur when mortality gives way to immortality. At that time, when the dead are raised and they, along with the living, are transformed to immortality, death will be swallowed up in victory. According to Paul, understanding this will lead Christians to an enduring commitment to do the Lord's work, knowing that their labor is not in vain (verse 58).

In this passage Paul shows that belief in the resurrection, both Christ's and the believers', is an absolute part of Christian faith. Without this perspective Christian faith is futile. Theologically he also ties these two resurrections together, showing that God's demonstration of His power and purpose in the resurrection of Jesus gives hope to Christians. Finally he shows that the resurrection body will be a new, glorified body, no longer subject to death, and that this will occur at the second coming of Christ, when the living righteous also will be transformed to immortal life.

Closely related to the subject matter of 1 Corinthians 15 is 2 Corinthians 5:1-5; and although the word "resurrection" is not used, the enigmatic character of the passages requires its inclusion here. Paul contrasts the "earthly tent" of our present existence with a "building from God" not made with hands, which is our future hope.

Some have held that here Paul supports the idea of the immortality of the soul by referring to the body as an earthly tent, a temporary vessel filled by the eternal soul. But a closer examination of the passage shows this not to be the case. Nowhere does Paul speak of a soul or of any existence apart from the body. There is no hint of division of humans into two parts. Rather, Paul can speak of the earthly tent being "destroyed," not being separated from a soul. Paul uses the metaphor of being naked, or unclothed, for what would occur without the earthly tent. He does not desire this state. If for Paul an intermediate state were one of conscious existence of the soul with Christ, one would hardly expect him to reject it. Paul does not wish to be unclothed, however; he wishes to be *further* clothed, which he identifies as occurring when what is mortal is swallowed up by life. This is an obvious parallel to the hope he sets forth in the latter part of 1 Corinthians 15, where mortality will give way to immortality at the sound of the trumpet when Christ returns.

Thus it becomes evident that Paul is

speaking here of the resurrection, as specifically cited in verse 15, even though he does not use the term. The present mortal existence is like an earthly tent. It is not secure. The object of the metaphor is not a part of the person, but the person as a whole. Paul has no desire for death, which he compares to nakedness, or being unclothed. Rather, he wishes to be further clothed by being transformed to a new, immortal existence, which he compares to a building from God. This new state expresses God's will for His people, and He has given the Spirit as a guarantee, or down payment, that assures us that such hope is not vain. Thus we see significant continuity between the thought of this passage and 1 Corinthians 15. (See Death I. E. 2.)

To limit a study of Paul's perspective on resurrection to a few major passages that address the issue in detail would miss much of the richness of Paul's thought. References to Christ's death and resurrection permeate his letters. Several important theological themes emerge from these references.

One of the most important is participation with Christ in death and resurrection. For Paul, Christ's death and resurrection are much more than historical events with effects for the believer. To have faith in Christ is to identify with Him and His mission. In Philippians 3 Paul speaks of his willingness to count everything else loss for the sake of Christ: "That I may know him and the power of his resurrection, and may share his sufferings, becoming like him in his death, that if possible I may attain the resurrection from the dead" (verses 10, 11). He goes on to make it clear that he has not yet attained this, but he presses on toward the goal.

This theme is displayed vividly in Paul's discussion of the Christian life in Romans 6. Here Paul uses the illustration of baptism to speak to the question of whether Christians may go on sinning because they are saved by Christ's grace. For Paul the experience of identification with Christ in baptism precludes any attitude that takes sin lightly. Paul says: "For if we have been united with him in a death like his, we shall certainly be united with him in a resurrection like his. We know that our old self was crucified with him so that the sinful body might be destroyed, and we might no longer be enslaved to sin. . . . So you also must consider yourselves dead to sin and alive to God in Christ Jesus" (Rom. 6:5-11).

A second important theme is closely related to that of participation with Christ in His death and resurrection. Faith in Christ means sharing the newness of life demonstrated in the resurrection. Although Paul is clear that the actual resurrection of the body is *not yet* but occurs in the future at the Second Coming (see Phil. 3:12; 1 Cor. 15:52; 1 Thess. 4:16; and 2 Tim. 2:18), there is an *already* aspect to the resurrection. Already the believer shares in newness of life, as seen above in Romans 6:5, 6, 11. This theme recurs in Ephesians 2:3-7, where Paul speaks to Gentiles once in their sins but now "raised . . . up with him, and made [to] sit with him in the heavenly places," an amazing metaphor for the Christian's present experience with Christ. Yet even here Paul points beyond to what Christ will do in the coming ages (verse 7). He defines this new life further in 2 Corinthians 5:15 by showing that newness of life means a new focus of existence: "And he died for all, that those who live might live no longer for themselves but for him who for their sake died and was raised."

Identification and participation with Christ is a sharing in His death and resurrection. It involves a new life now, characterized by a new focus and purpose and a willingness to share in Christ's suffering. In this sense the Christian already shares in the power of Christ's resurrection. The Christian experience also involves a hope that can be realized only in the future when Christ returns, the dead are resurrected, and the living believers are transformed to immortal life.

b. The Synoptics and Acts. Because of the nature of the Gospels, their teaching concerning the resurrection of the believers is less explicit than in Paul's writings. In the Gospels the primary emphasis with regard to resurrection is the story of Jesus' resurrection. Although Luke-Acts is the only one of the Synoptics to include explicit instruction about the resurrection of believers, all the Gospel writers in some way tie Jesus' resurrection to His power to give life to the believer.

In Matthew the Resurrection not only is predicted beforehand (Matt. 16:21; 26:32) and announced after the fact to the women (Matt. 28:6), but the resurrected Jesus also appears to the disciples in Galilee and gives them the gospel commission (verses 16-20).

In one incident, recorded only by Matthew, the relationship of Jesus' resurrection to that of the believers is emphasized especially. Matthew tells us, "The tombs also were opened, and many bodies of the saints who had fallen asleep were raised, and coming out of the tombs after his resurrection they went into the holy city and appeared to many" (Matt. 27:52, 53). No mention is made of who these saints were, but they obviously became living exhibits that Jesus was the firstfruits of the resurrection and that His resurrection assures the believers that they can also be among "saints" who will come from the grave.

MSS differ with regard to the ending of the Gospel of Mark (Mark 16:9-20). Whatever conclusions one reaches with regard to this textual variant, the resurrection of Jesus is still evident. It is also clear that Christ's resurrection is integrally related to the life of the believer.

Mark emphasizes Jesus' role as the suffering-servant Messiah. He also points to the true nature of discipleship as following in the footsteps of Jesus by taking up the cross. The theological center of Mark is found in chapters 8-10, where Jesus three times predicts His own death and then calls His disciples to servanthood. Each of these predictions also includes an assertion that Jesus will rise in three days (Mark 8:31; 9:31; 10:34). This prediction of resurrection gives meaning to Jesus' subsequent call to discipleship and promise of life. In the words "For whoever would save his life will lose it; and whoever loses his life for my sake and the gospel's will save it" (Mark 8:35) we see the connection between Jesus' resurrection and the believer's hope for life.

The same connection is apparent when Jesus shows His power to raise the dead in Mark 5. When Jesus says that Jairus' daughter is not dead but only sleeping, the people laugh, for she obviously is dead. But Jesus is able to raise her to life. Thus a picture forms of Jesus not only as the one who rises from the dead but who also raises others from the dead. This picture is confirmed when the angel announces to the women who come to the tomb, "He has risen, he is not here" (Mark 16:6).

In his Gospel, Luke records the announcement of Jesus' resurrection by the angels at the tomb (Luke 24:4-7). He also notes the appearance of the resurrected Christ on the road to Emmaus (verses 13-32) and to the disciples in the upper room (verses 33-43). Furthermore, Luke deals with the believer's resurrection. Specific information on the resurrection appears also in Acts. Jesus is recorded as declaring that rewards for what is done in this life will be received at the resurrection. "But when you give a feast, invite the poor, the maimed, the lame, the blind, and you will be blessed, because they cannot repay you. You will be repaid at the resurrection of the just" (Luke 14:13, 14).

In Acts, Luke refers to one of Paul's speeches proclaiming that this resurrection also will include the unjust. Paul says, "I worship the God of our fathers, believing everything laid down by the law or written in the prophets, having a hope in God which these themselves accept, that there will be a resurrection of both the just and the unjust" (Acts 24:14, 15). Luke also pictures Paul tying the believers' resurrection to Christ's by emphasizing that Christ is the first to rise from the dead (Acts 26:23).

c. The Johannine writings. For John the central expression used in the Gospel to convey the Christian hope is "life" or "eternal life."

Following C. H. Dodd, many have stressed the theme of "realized eschatology" in John, which holds that the believer already experiences eternal life through Christ. There can be no doubt that this theme is present. For John there is a present reality, or an *already,* to eternal life. But this by no means negates the reality of a future hope defined in terms of resurrection.

One of the most instructive passages for seeing the juxtaposition of realized and future eschatology and its significance for an understanding of the believer's resurrection is John 5:19-29. In one sense at least three different resurrections are mentioned in this passage.

The first is the spiritual renewal of life that the believer currently possesses in Christ. This is clearly the focus of verses 24, 25: "Truly, truly, I say to you, he who hears my word and believes him who sent me, has eternal life; he does not come into judgment, but has passed from death to life. Truly, truly, I say to you, the hour is coming, and now is, when the dead will hear the voice of the Son of God, and those who hear will live."

Notice that the hour *now is* for this resurrection. Those who believe already have eternal life and have already passed from death to life. This emphasis uses different language from Paul, but the idea is similar. Paul spoke of walking "in newness of life" (Rom. 6:4), while John speaks of having eternal life. Both point to the significant reality of new life that the believer experiences in Christ, an experience so overwhelming that it can be defined only in eschatological terms.

John goes on to point to an hour that is coming and says, "Do not marvel at this; for the hour is coming when all who are in the tombs will hear his voice and come forth, those who have done good, to the resurrection of life, and those who have done evil, to the resurrection of judgment" (John 5:28, 29).

Here we see two additional resurrections, both clearly in the future. This is no longer reference to present spiritual experience. In the future those in the tombs will come forth. John does not identify the time of either of these resurrections; he only differentiates between the resurrections of the just and unjust.

The picture is the same in the next chapter, where John depicts Jesus as the bread of life. In John 6:54 Jesus says, "He who eats my flesh and drinks my blood has eternal life, and I will raise him up at the last day." Here again present reality and future hope are juxtaposed. The one who identifies with Christ has eternal life now. But in addition he or she will be raised at the last day. Again the future hope is presented in terms of the resurrection of the dead. Here, however, John goes one step further than in chapter 5, identifying the time of the resurrection of the just: it will occur at the last day. No mention is made here, however, of the resurrection of the unjust.

The resurrection is prominent in another of Jesus' discourses in John. In chapter 11 Jesus proclaims that He is the resurrection and the life. In characteristic Johannine style this word from Jesus is connected with a deed that serves as a sign and points to it: in this case, the resurrection of Lazarus. Jesus restores Lazarus to life after four days, demonstrating that He is the resurrection and the life.

Here John wishes to show his readers that the Christian hope in the resurrection is more than the then current general belief in the resurrection of the dead. Martha already believes in the resurrection of the dead. She expresses confidence that her brother, Lazarus, will rise again in the resurrection at the last day (verse 24). But Jesus has something more to reveal to her. What she does not yet know is that Jesus Himself is the basis of her hope in the resurrection, and He offers more than the hope of a future event.

Jesus offers her His own personal presence as the resurrection and the life. Resurrection is more than a future event. It is a living hope made real through the presence of Jesus. And what is true for Martha is true for all believers. That living hope renders the present death of no ultimate consequence. This is why Jesus can say that whoever lives and believes in Him shall never die (verse 26). And even if a person does die, there is the assurance of life again (verse 25). In fact, the present reality of hope has meaning only because of the future promise of the resurrection. The present reality of life in Christ liberates the believer from the fear of death, because it guarantees the future hope, as well.

Therefore, we see in John a combination of present and future reality. Christ Himself is the resurrection and the life. Those united with Him already experience a life so radically new that it can only be called eternal life. They also live in hope, knowing that even if they die, at the last day they will be resurrected to live with Christ forever.

John assumes, of course, that readers remember what he said in chapters 5, 6, and 11 by the time they come to the final section of the book that tells the story of the cross and Resurrection. The ultimate sign that Jesus is the resurrection and the life is His own resurrection. Yet for John the glorification and exaltation of Jesus is by no means limited to the Resurrection. The cross too lifts Jesus up as Saviour.

John makes this point by playing on a term with a double meaning. The phrase "lifted up" can be a technical reference to crucifixion. But it can also refer to figurative uplifting, or exaltation, as found in passages such as Luke 18:14. John purposely uses the term stressing the double meaning to show that Jesus is exalted in His crucifixion (John 12:31-33). For John, both Jesus' crucifixion and resurrection reveal His saving power.

As John presents Jesus' resurrection, he is especially interested in showing that those who were not present and did not physically see the risen Christ are at no disadvantage when it comes to believing on Jesus and accepting Him as the resurrection and the life. His is the only Gospel to recount the Resurrection appearance to Thomas. First, Jesus met the disciples without Thomas and breathed on them the Holy Spirit (John 20:19-24). Thomas would not believe the disciples' report of this incident until eight days later when Jesus again appeared, this time with Thomas present. After Thomas expressed his belief, Jesus responded, "Have you believed because you have seen me? Blessed are those who have not seen and yet believe" (verse 29).

Why can those who have not seen still believe? Because, according to John, believing comes not from mere seeing but from the work of the Holy Spirit after Jesus was resurrected and glorified. Several times (e.g., John 2:22; 12:16) the disciples fail to understand Jesus' actions. Only after the Resurrection do they "remember" and see the significance of what Jesus had done. This remembering is more than recalling. It brings a new understanding that makes Jesus' life real to the believer. This is the bringing to remembrance that the promised Spirit accomplishes (John 14:26). Through this action of the Spirit every believer has access to the meaning of Jesus' life and is at no disadvantage when compared with those who actually saw Jesus and were with Him.

Therefore, the account of the resurrection of Jesus shows how it is possible for John's readers to believe and experience eternal life. John makes it clear that this is the purpose of his book: "that you may believe that Jesus is the Christ, the Son of God, and that believing you may have life in his name" (John 20:31). As we have seen, this *life* includes the present experience of life with Christ and the future hope of the resurrection.

In the book of Revelation John brings to a climax the NT emphasis on the hope for resurrection and eternal life that every believer has in the light of Christ's resurrection. At the same time this book brings a new contribution. Revelation is the only book to be specific about the difference in time between the resurrection of the righteous and that of the wicked.

John immediately portrays Jesus as the resurrected one: "the faithful witness, the firstborn of the dead, and the ruler of kings on earth" (Rev. 1:5). No doubt this portrayal had special meaning to the first readers of the book. They were facing persecution from the emperor. At least one Christian, Antipas at Pergamum, had been martyred for his faith (Rev. 2:13). Now they hear that Jesus was not only the original "faithful witness," who now rules the earthly emperors, but also the "first-born" from the dead. In other words, He is not only living again after death, but He is the firstborn, the one who leads the way, ensuring the hope of the resurrection for His followers. In Revelation 1:18 John further emphasizes this point by declaring that Jesus, as the one who was dead and is now alive forever, has the keys of death and hades (the grave, or place of the dead). He not only has conquered death but offers His victory over death to others, as well. Therefore, they do not need to fear the earthly emperor, who cannot thwart Christ's victory.

This point is emphasized repeatedly in Revelation. For example, the church at Smyrna is told that it will suffer persecution and some will be thrown into prison, but it is also promised that those who are faithful unto death will receive Christ's crown, which is life itself (Rev. 2:10). For this reason John encourages the believers to consider it a victory, not a defeat, when one of them suffers martyrdom. The devil has used his fiercest weapon, death, to overcome faith, and has failed. Not even death has been able to dissuade the faithful, and since Christ has conquered death, they have been victors. Thus in Revelation 12:11 John can say of the faithful: "And they have conquered him [the devil and Satan (verse 9)] by the blood of the Lamb and by the word of their testimony, for they loved not their lives even unto death."

Christ's victory over death is finalized in chapters 20 and 21. In chapter 20 death and hades are thrown into the lake of fire and destroyed; death has no more power. In chapter 21 Christ and His people share a new heaven and a new earth, where "he will wipe away every tear from their eyes, and death shall be no more, neither shall there be mourning nor

crying nor pain any more, for the former things have passed away" (verse 4; see New Earth II. B. 3).

The time between the resurrections of the righteous and wicked is defined in Revelation 20 as a 1,000-year period during which Satan is bound. At the beginning of this period the righteous are resurrected (verse 4) and reign with Christ for 1,000 years. The first half of verse 5 is a parenthetical statement declaring that "the rest of the dead did not come to life until the thousand years were ended." The "rest of the dead" must be the wicked, since verse 4 has already spoken of the righteous. After the parenthetical statement in verse 5, John continues the line of thought of verse 4 and adds, "This is the first resurrection." That the reference to "first resurrection" points back to verse 4 and the resurrection of the righteous is obvious by what follows in verse 6, where John declares those who participate in it "blessed" and repeats that they reign with Christ 1,000 years. Thus John points to a "first" resurrection of the righteous at the beginning of the 1,000 years. Those who participate in it reign with Christ during the 1,000-year period. (See Millennium I. C. 1-3.)

The resurrection of the wicked occurs 1,000 years later, when the "rest of the dead" come to life. No detail about this resurrection is given, but it is assumed in verses 7-10, for the wicked are alive when Satan is freed from his prison for a little while and attempts to rally the wicked to surround the Holy City. This effort collapses in what John calls the "second death" (verse 14), when the devil, the wicked (those whose names were not found in the book of life, according to verse 15), and death itself are destroyed in the lake of fire.

d. Other New Testament writings. The book of Hebrews accepts the resurrection and emphasizes Christ's high-priestly ministry on behalf of believers and its significance for Christian life. The resurrection of the dead is included in the "elementary doctrine of Christ" (Heb. 6:1, 2), beyond which the readers of the book are now to move. This hardly means, however, that the resurrection is unimportant.

Its importance appears especially in chapter 11, which presents the great witnesses of faith. Here an important part of faith is trust in God's power to raise the dead. The author interprets Abraham's willingness to obey God and sacrifice Isaac as this kind of faith. He was willing to be faithful because "he considered that God was able to raise men even from the dead" (verse 19). Faith in the resurrection is bolstered by the fact that faithful women of old "received their dead by resurrection" (verse 35; probably a reference to the event recorded in 2 Kings 4:8-37). Thus for the author of Hebrews the "faith" that is so important includes trust in God's ability to raise the dead.

In 1 Peter, as in the book of Revelation, Christians who face at least some degree of persecution are addressed. Christians "may have to suffer various trials" (1 Peter 1:6) and find themselves "aliens and exiles" (1 Peter 2:11). The apostle encourages his readers and motivates them to faithfulness by showing that Christ's resurrection gives them both hope for the future and help for the present.

After his greeting and a brief blessing Peter begins by proclaiming that Christians have been "born anew to a living hope through the resurrection of Jesus Christ from the dead" (1 Peter 1:3). Again we see the close connection between the resurrection of Christ and the believer's hope. To live in hope is nothing less than a new birth to a new life. It is a life of confidence in God that transcends the present difficulties. Faith and hope can be placed in God, because God raised Christ and "gave him glory" (verse 21). So for Peter the assurance of hope for the future that the Resurrection brings also transforms the present existence into a new life of confidence. But this hope does more for the present. According to 1 Peter 3:21, the Resurrection also enables one to have a clear conscience. This occurs through baptism, but it is the Resurrection that gives baptism its power. Peter does not go on to explain this as Paul does in Romans 6, but presumably the fact that Christ has conquered death

and evil and that all authorities are now subject to Him frees the Christian from all sources of condemnation and makes Christ's forgiveness the last word.

The NT demonstrates a consistent picture of the importance of the Resurrection, the connection between Christ's resurrection and ours, and the firm reality of hope for future life, as well as the enrichment of our present existence that future hope brings.

B. The Old Testament

When we understand how inexorably the entire NT links Jesus Christ's resurrection with that of the believer, it should be neither surprising nor alarming that the OT is much less explicit about the resurrection. In the NT both the specific shape of the believer's resurrection and the theological significance of this resurrection grow out of God's revelation in Christ Jesus, especially as seen in His resurrection. What we find in the OT is much more implicit, with only a handful of explicit references to the resurrection.

1. General Perspectives on the Future Life

OT writers cannot point back to the resurrection of Christ as the foundation of hope for life in the future. In addition, the OT "thought world" was much more oriented to the community than is ours, and therefore often presented hope for the future in terms of the nation's or community's future. This aspect is often hard for individualistic modern readers to understand. In the OT world one's identity and destiny were bound up with one's participation in a community. For us the basic element of human life is the autonomous individual; for the OT person the basic element of life was the social unit, whether family, clan, or nation. (For a survey of God's promises with regard to Israel, see Remnant/Three Angels I. A, B; and 4BC 25-38.)

Nevertheless, several strong emphases in the OT point to a significant continuity with NT teaching at an implicit level. These include emphases on the body as good, on the wholeness of human beings, and on hope for life in God. In opposition to all forms of thought that depreciate the body or hope for escape from it, the doctrine of the resurrection offers a life-affirming and body-affirming perspective. The OT consistently shares this perspective. For example, in the Creation story God creates human beings, male and female, in His own image (Gen. 1:27) and affirms that what He has created is "very good" (verse 31). Never does the OT set forth bodiless existence as possible or desirable.

Closely related to this positive regard for the body is a strong emphasis on the wholeness of human beings. This wholistic perspective is also revealed in the Creation account. When God created human beings from the dust of the ground, He did not place a soul in them, but rather animated the physical body with the breath of life, and the human being became a living soul, or whole being (Gen. 2:7). Human beings are bodies enlivened by the breath of life. (See Man I. E. 1-3; Death I. A. 4.) The OT view of death grows out of this wholistic understanding of human beings. It describes death as sleeping with the fathers (Deut. 31:16), going down to the pit or cistern (Eze. 31:16; 32:24), lying down in the dust (Ps. 22:15), or, as is most often the case, going to the grave, or sheol.

A third important OT emphasis relating to the doctrine of the resurrection is hope for life in God. Throughout the OT Yahweh is the source of life and hope. Israel is to teach its children to set their hope in God (Ps. 78:7). Jeremiah can refer to Yahweh as the "hope of Israel, its savior in time of trouble" (Jer. 14:8). This conviction that God is the source of life, healing, and restoration includes the confidence that God can both end life and restore it, as Hannah shows when she prays, "The Lord kills and brings to life; he brings down to Sheol and raises up" (1 Sam. 2:6).

This ability to restore life is often applied to the nation as a whole in keeping with the strongly community-oriented worldview of the OT. This is true in Ezekiel 37, for instance,

where the prophet sees in vision a valley full of dry bones. He is asked whether they can live. At first he reflects the question back to God, but he is then commanded to prophesy to the bones. When he does, there is a great rattling, the bones come together, life is breathed into them, and they live again and stand on their feet (verses 1-10).

Almost all commentators recognize that this vision does not explicitly refer to the resurrection of individuals, for according to the interpretation of the vision as given in verse 11, the vision is about the "whole house of Israel." In the face of national disaster (the Babylonian captivity) the people have expressed their hopelessness by using an apparently popular expression that their bones are dried up (e.g., Prov. 17:22). Now God answers that hopelessness with a vision that vividly portrays and promises the restoration of the nation, the whole house of Israel.

Interpretation of the vision continues in Ezekiel 37:12-14, but the language changes. God opens graves and raises Israel up from their tombs. Although this interpretation is not without its difficulties, some see here a major transition in the text from the restoration of the nation as a whole to the resurrection of individuals in the nation who have died. This confidence in God's power to restore the nation, beautifully portrayed in Ezekiel 37, since it is based on the metaphor of individuals returning from the grave, shows that the idea of humans returning from death was not unfamiliar to Israel.

God's power over individual death is evidenced by at least three resuscitations in the OT. Although these are different from the final resurrection, in which the body is raised to immortality, they show clearly that the OT includes confidence in God to restore individual life from the dead. All three occur in relationship to Elijah or Elisha. In the first Elijah brings the son of the widow at Zarephath back to life (1 Kings 17:17-24). In the second Elisha does the same for the Shunammite woman's son (2 Kings 4:18-37;

see also 8:1-5). Finally a man accidentally buried in Elisha's grave returns to life when he comes in contact with the prophet's bones (2 Kings 13:21).

This brief review shows that the OT picture of hope should not be limited to a few explicit texts that specifically deal with resurrection. These explicit passages add to the picture, however.

2. Specific Passages Dealing With Resurrection

Three specific OT passages dealing with resurrection merit special attention. Admittedly, Job 19:25-27 presents difficulties; however, the conviction of life after death is clear. Other passages are Isaiah 26:19 and Daniel 12:2.

a. Job 19:25-27. Here Job's confidence that God will be his *gō'ēl,* or kinsman-redeemer, even beyond his death is clear. This expression of hope comes at the end of a long section in which Job poignantly laments his situation. Repeatedly he points to God as the one who has brought catastrophe upon him (see especially verses 8-13). Job can find no justice, and, to make matters worse, all of his friends and family have deserted him (verses 13-19). He wishes that his lament were written in a book or engraved in a rock with an iron pen so that it would never be forgotten (verses 23, 24). But in verse 25 the mood changes, and Job expresses confidence that his Redeemer will vindicate him and he will see God.

Typically in the OT this kinsman-redeemer is the one who buys back property that has been sold (Lev. 25:25-34), avenges murders (Num. 35:16-28), and provides heirs for one who died without them (Deut. 25:5-10; Ruth 4:1-6). Throughout the OT Yahweh presents Himself to Israel as a kinsman-redeemer (e.g., Ex. 6:6; Ps. 77:15; Isa. 44:24).

Although there are significant translation difficulties in the passage, and although it does not design to offer an explicit description of the biblical teaching about the resurrection, Job clearly expresses confidence that

God's redeeming and restoring power transcends both his present problems and death. "At last," after the destruction of his skin, Job will see his Redeemer with his own eyes (Job 19:25-27).

b. Isaiah 26:19. Isaiah 24-27 forms a section that seems to anticipate a more apocalyptic style than generally is found in the preexilic prophets. This section begins with the announcement that Yahweh will lay waste the earth and make it desolate because of the transgressions of the people and their violation of the covenant. Interspersed among the prophet's announcements of doom and responses of lament by the people, however, one finds expressions of trust and praise. In fact, the section ends with the promise that God will gather His scattered people back to the land of Israel, and the captives from Assyria and Egypt will return to worship Yahweh on the holy mountain at Jerusalem (Isa. 27:12, 13).

Among the expressions of hope in the section are Isaiah 25:8 and 26:19. The former announces that Yahweh will swallow up death forever and wipe the tears from all faces. Nothing is explicit about the means Yahweh will use to accomplish this victory, however. But the latter passage does refer to the resurrection of righteous who have died.

In Isaiah 26:13-15 the people acknowledge that they have served other gods, but these gods are now dead and will not live. They are shades who will not arise. The analogy of birth provides the occasion for further lament in verses 16-18. The people have been like a woman in labor, but the labor has produced nothing. In other words, the people have not been able to effect their own deliverance.

Then the mood changes with verse 19, which picks up on the language applied to the false lords in verse 14 and turns it around as an expression of hope for the people of Israel. "Thy dead shall live, their bodies shall rise. O dwellers in the dust, awake and sing for joy! For thy dew is a dew of light, and on the land of the shades thou wilt let it fall."

Several translation problems in this verse go beyond the scope of this article. For example, in the first line the Hebrew has "my body" in place of "their bodies." The shift in pronouns makes it difficult to determine who is speaking to whom in this verse. Is the speaker Yahweh, the prophet, or the people? Even though it is impossible to say with certainty, several things are clear. The "shades," who have gone to the grave, will live, and bodies will arise from death, causing singing and joy.

All of this makes it most natural to take this verse as an address to Yahweh. But it still leaves open two possibilities. Is Yahweh being addressed by an individual who expresses confidence in a personal resurrection? The contrast between "their bodies" and "my body" supports this. The former would refer to the righteous dead, and the latter to the individual speaker. Or is this the collective nation speaking, so that the message is similar to Ezekiel 37 and refers to the restoration of the fortunes of the nation? The final promise at the end of Isaiah 27 regarding the return of captives from Assyria and Egypt supports this. The weight of evidence tilts toward the former (Hasel 272-276). Although little detail is given about the resurrection in this passage, a resurrection of the body is clearly in view.

c. Daniel 12:2. Here we find a clear, definite reference to the resurrection of individuals in the OT. "And many of those who sleep in the dust of the earth shall awake, some to everlasting life, and some to shame and everlasting contempt." Here we see two resurrections, one for the righteous and one for the wicked.

The word "many" causes difficulty. Does Daniel foresee only a partial resurrection, or is "many" used in a colloquial way for "all," as was sometimes the case in Semitic thought? For some the use of the word "many" in OT passages such as Isaiah 53:12 and in NT passages such as Mark 14:24 and Romans 5:15 is sufficient to show that in Semitic thought the term is too broad to rule out the fact that Daniel is referring to all of the dead when he speaks of the resurrection. Others, such as Hasel (279-281), argue that Daniel is pointing to a special resurrection.

Ellen White (GC 637) quotes this passage when presenting the special resurrection of those who "died in the faith of the third angel's message" and come forth from the tomb to witness the Second Coming along with those who crucified Jesus (see I. A. 1 and EGW quotations at the end of this article). In any case, resurrection at the end of time is presented as a clear reality.

This survey of the OT reveals that the resurrection is less explicit than, yet theologically consistent with, what the NT teaches. Human hope is not in the immortality of an internal portion of a human being, but rather in God's wholistic restorative, re-creative power.

Clearly, resurrection was not new to the Jews of Jesus' day. Jesus was asked which one of seven brothers would be the husband of one widow "in the resurrection" (Matt. 22:23-29). Martha expressed confidence in the "resurrection at the last day" (John 11:24). While the idea does appear in intertestamental literature (see IV. B), it is evident that the OT provides ample basis for belief in resurrection.

II. Glorification of the Righteous

The word "glorification" refers to the postresurrection condition and experience of both Jesus and the believer. Because of the close connection between the resurrection of Jesus and that of the believer, it is important to begin with the postresurrection experience of the "first fruits" or "firstborn," whose resurrection serves as a model. As Paul says: "We await a Savior, the Lord Jesus Christ, who will change our lowly body to be like his glorious body" (Phil. 3:20, 21).

A. The Glorified State of Jesus

After the Resurrection Jesus did not simply return to live with the disciples in continuous fellowship as He had before. Rather, Jesus "appeared" to them at various times (see 1 Cor. 15:5-8). These appearances often began and ended abruptly. They were limited to a short period of time between the Resurrection and Ascension, specified as 40 days by Luke (Acts 1:3). Paul implicitly substantiates that the appearances occurred over a short time by making Christ's appearance to him on the Damascus road a chronological anomaly. He says Christ appeared to him as one "untimely born" (Gr. *ektrōma* [1 Cor. 15:8]). Yet even though the appearance to Paul was a *chronological* anomaly, Paul nevertheless considered it an appearance of the risen Christ, akin to the appearances to the other apostles.

All of this means that there was a certain discontinuity between the nature of Jesus before and after the Resurrection. This discontinuity is further seen in the fact that Jesus appears suddenly to the disciples when the door is shut (John 20:19) and vanishes suddenly out of sight (Luke 24:31). Obviously there is a mystery about Jesus in His glorified state.

Yet the emphasis of the Gospels is clearly on continuity rather than discontinuity. Luke and John especially wish to demonstrate that the Resurrection is real and the glorified body of Jesus is not a phantom or spirit but has continuity with earthly life as He had lived it as a human.

Jesus' encounter with Mary showed that He could be recognized by His voice (John 20:16). When the disciples on the road to Emmaus did not recognize Him, Luke makes it clear that it was because their eyes were kept from it (Luke 24:16). Mary could "hold" on to Jesus (John 20:17), and Thomas could see His scars (verse 20) and even be invited to put his finger in the scars (verse 27). Jesus even ate in their presence (Luke 24:43). But probably the strongest support for continuity comes in verses 36-39 where the idea that the risen Jesus is a "spirit" is explicitly rejected.

Here the continuity of the glorified Jesus with His preresurrection past is boldly stated. The glorified body is not a spirit. Jesus is recognized by the disciples. They can "handle" Him. He has "flesh and bones." Certainly Luke intends this picture of Jesus to serve as a model for the resurrection of the believer, as well. But Paul is most explicit of all about the postresurrection state of the believer.

B. The Glorified State of the Believer

For the believer too there is both continuity and discontinuity between the earthly body and the glorified, resurrection body. According to Paul, the discontinuity can be summed up in one basic fact: the earthly body is subject to the law of sin and death. It is mortal. It cannot overcome death, the enemy. Only Christ has power over death, and the resurrection body is a body that participates in Christ's victory and has received immortality. Paul's description of the resurrection body is found in 1 Corinthians 15:35-50, but before surveying Paul's thought in this passage it is necessary to note how Paul uses certain anthropological terms in general.

Four words are important here: "flesh," "body," "soul," and "spirit." In no case does Paul use any of these terms to refer to a part of a human being as distinguished from the rest. Rather, in each case Paul has various expressions of the whole person in view. These terms are used to point to different aspects of human existence. As J.A.T. Robinson showed in his study of the concept of body in Paul's thinking, both "flesh" and "body" can refer to the whole human person, but there is a difference in emphasis. "Flesh" (Gr. *sarx*) emphasizes humans in contrast with God—humans in mortality and in worldliness. It shows human solidarity with earthly existence. It can be neutral, showing that humans live in the world, or can denote sinfulness as humans living for the world (Robinson 19-25). Herold

Weiss (106) puts it well when he says that *"flesh* emphasizes the fact that men and women live in an ecological system in which sin and death are part of the life cycle."

According to Robinson, "body" (Gr. *sōma*) emphasizes the human that can be raised and is equivalent to our word "personality" (26-28). He contrasts the two terms by saying, "While *sarx* stands for man, in the solidarity of creation, in his distance from God, *sōma* stands for man, in the solidarity of creation, as made for God" (31).

"Soul" is most often used simply for the whole human being in the sense of "person" or "human life." Yet it too has a distinctive emphasis. H. Weiss (106, 107) sums this up by saying that "soul" "designates the kind of life peculiar to Adam and all his descendants. Basically, it is a life that is fragile, capable of being extinguished by a small accident." "Soul" emphasizes human fragility and vulnerability more than sinfulness, as "flesh" often does.

Finally, the word "spirit" has a distinctive meaning in Paul as well. It does not emphasize the immaterial, or nonphysical. Instead, it points to human life empowered by God. "Spirit" is unique to God and is made available to humans through Jesus Christ. In contrast with "flesh," it is life under the power of God rather than the power of sin and death. In contrast with "soul," it is life that participates in God's power rather than Adam's vulnerability. With these definitions in mind, we are ready to turn to Paul's presentation of the resurrection and glorification of believers.

Paul begins with an analogy that stresses both continuity and discontinuity. As a seed is buried in the ground, dies, and then sprouts forth to a new reality, so Christians die and, at the resurrection when Christ returns, come forth to a new existence. The Corinthians should not find this impossible to believe. There are different kinds of bodies for humans, animals, birds, and fish; the Christian will experience yet another kind of existence. But it is important to see where the discontinuity lies for Paul. What is new about this existence lies precisely at the point of human mortality and vulnerability.

Paul's contrasts in 1 Corinthians 15:42-49 make this clear:

Old	New
Sown perishable	Raised imperishable
Sown in dishonor	Raised in glory
Sown in weakness	Raised in power
Sown soullike	Raised spiritlike
Analogous to the man of dust	Analogous to the man of heaven

The RSV translation of the fourth contrast in this list is extremely misleading. It contrasts the "physical body" with the "spiritual body," and this could be taken to signify a material versus nonmaterial body, which is not part of Paul's thinking. Paul is contrasting the vulnerable body with the empowered body. For Paul the glorified resurrection body is the body freed from its vulnerability and its captivity to sin and death, freed to live as God originally intended.

Paul ends this passage with a statement that could be understood to contradict Luke 24:39. There Jesus demonstrated to the disciples that His postresurrection existence was one of "flesh and bones." In 1 Corinthians 15:50 Paul says, "I tell you this, brethren: flesh and blood cannot inherit the kingdom of God." There is no problem, however, when we remember Paul's distinctive use of the word "flesh." In Luke Jesus uses it to emphasize the physical reality of the postresurrection body. Paul assumes the physical reality and uses "flesh" to connote life oriented to a sinful world. Thus the two verses are not contradictory.

The glorified body will retain its identity with the preresurrection body and will be recognizable to other saints who have known the individual in this life. This is evident from 1 Thessalonians 4:13-18, where Paul comforts believers who have lost loved ones with the assurance that they will meet them again after the resurrection. (See Man III. C.)

362

III. The Significance of the Doctrine

A. *For Theological Understanding*

Any understanding of salvation would be incomplete without the doctrine of the resurrection of the believer. God's intent is the full restoration of the life that He originally intended, which will overcome the tragedy of sin and death. Atonement can be complete only when God's creatures are transformed to immortality and are freed of their mortality. This is why Paul's statements in 1 Corinthians 15 are so strong. Without the Resurrection, preaching and faith are vain (verse 14), faith is futile, and we are still in our sins (verse 17).

Although the full restoration of life and victory over sin and death have not yet become reality, already they are anticipated in the experience of hope made possible by the promised resurrection. The word "hope" is not used here in the popular sense of the word. In everyday speech hope often means nothing more than a wish with little or no basis. The NT concept of hope is nothing less than a new kind of existence characterized by assurance and confidence. To hope for the resurrection is not to wish for it, but to live in an atmosphere of assurance and confidence that already anticipates its reality.

This assurance is possible because the resurrection of the dead has already begun with Jesus. Jesus' resurrection not only assures the future resurrection of the believers but also begins it. This is what it means for Jesus to be the firstfruits of the resurrection. For this reason His resurrection can never be understood as merely the resuscitation of a corpse. It was rather an eschatological event in which Jesus took on a glorified body and thus both began and insured the resurrection of the righteous. He has done more than promise life to His disciples; He has effected it. Christians live in confidence, therefore, certain that they look forward to the real hope of life in the future. Jesus' resurrection is more than a life-enriching idea or a symbol of the meaning that life can have in the present, although it is that, as well. It is the assurance of resurrection and eternal life for the believer. Apart from this assurance, neither Christian soteriology nor eschatology can be understood.

The believer's new existence of confident assurance is characterized by fellowship with the risen Christ and participation in His body, the church. For the Christian the resurrection is not simply an event in the past or a hope for the future, but a present participation in fellowship with the risen Christ. We have already noted Paul's emphasis on this participation. For him, fellowship with the risen Christ meant sharing in both the death and resurrection of Christ.

This analogy was much stronger for Paul than it is for most modern readers. We are far more individualistic and can conceive of partnership with Christ only between us and Him. Paul could not. The locus of participation in Christ's resurrection and fellowship with Him was only in connection with the body of believers, in which the risen Christ makes Himself known and directs the body as its head. Christ is not simply identical with the body; He is its head. It is His body, and partnership with Him is fellowship in it.

This corporate nature of participation with Christ is much clearer when the NT concept of resurrection, as opposed to the notion of the immortality of the soul, is understood. It means that all receive the final reward together as community. As Hebrews 11:39, 40 proclaims, not even the great models of faith have yet received their final reward, for God had a better plan: "And all these, though well attested by their faith, did not receive what was promised, since God had foreseen something better for us, that apart from us they should not be made perfect." Sakae Kubo (136) is therefore right when he writes: "The resurrection of the dead is not an individual but a community affair. The righteous dead all rise up together, and those alive receive translation at the same time. We die individually, but we rise up together. All enjoy the blessings of eternity together."

This new existence of confident hope and participation with Christ is described in many terms and illuminated by many metaphors in the NT. But ultimately it is one's trusting participation in this experience (which Paul calls faith) that qualifies a person for the resurrection and ultimate salvation.

The doctrine of the resurrection can be fully appreciated only against the backdrop of a correct biblical understanding of death. Teachings such as the immortality of the soul or reincarnation, which deny either the wholistic reality or the finality of death from a human perspective, cannot give adequate emphasis to the glory of the resurrection, which overcomes death and mortality, the enemy of life, with a new God-given immortality. In the resurrection God does what human, finite, mortal power could never do. The resurrection is not merely the transition from one form of life to another; it is nothing less than the re-creation of that which had ceased to exist, and which now lives again through God's immortal power. (See Death I. F. 6, 7; G. 2.)

B. For Practical Experience

The biblical teaching about the resurrection has practical implications for everyday life. We will survey three areas where this is especially true.

First, it gives the believer a proper understanding of the body. God is both the Creator and Redeemer of the body, which shows that physical life is good. It is no accident that the Corinthians, at least some of whom had a problem with their understanding of the resurrection, also had problems with their attitude toward the body. Apparently some of them felt that it was perfectly acceptable to participate in sexual immorality with a prostitute (1 Cor. 6:16), while others thought that it was best for a man not to touch a woman, even in marriage (1 Cor. 7:1). Paul refuted both, and it

is no accident that he used the doctrine of the resurrection in his argument. He affirms that the body is good, and warns about sinning against it. The body is for the Lord, and the Lord is for the body (1 Cor. 6:13). It is a temple of the Holy Spirit (verse 19). The Christian should glorify God in his or her body (verse 20). All of this can be said because Paul knows that God will raise the body (verse 14).

If God values the body enough to restore it and raise it for eternity, Christians ought to value it as well. This has implications not only for sexuality but for health, as well. The very fact that a human being is a whole person, not a soul imprisoned within a body, looking for escape, as was taught by some Greek philosophers, implies a value for and a positive attitude toward the body. Christian hope is a life-affirming and body-affirming hope. (See Health.)

Second, the doctrine gives the Christian an appropriate, realistic attitude toward death. Naturally, if bodily life is valuable, Christians will promote life and fight death. Death will not be viewed as a friend, a natural part of life, or just another of life's passages, as it is considered in much of today's literature. The Christian will make no mistake about it: death is an enemy. But at the same time it is a defeated enemy. This means that we can fight it with confidence, knowing that its temporary victories will not prevail. We can be on the side of health, peace, and all else that promotes life without being discouraged and fearful that the enemy we fight will finally win.

This realistic view of death, which neither embraces it nor cowers before it, but recognizes it as a defeated enemy, also helps the Christian avoid other pitfalls, as well. The whole endeavor of channeling and attempting to communicate with the dead is ruled out, for if there is no immortal soul and the dead are in a state of unconscious sleep, then all such supposed communication is some kind of deception. The biblical picture helps us avoid such deceptions. (See Death I. D.)

Finally, the doctrine of the resurrection

gives the Christian a realistic attitude toward life and work in the present world. Some have argued that Christians, who look toward a future world, inevitably become apathetic about this one. This should be far from true. The life-affirming nature of their hope compels them to work for life here; the corporate nature of their hope compels them to work for the good of others. But they are also realistic. They know that their work is a participation in and anticipation of God's ultimate work. This keeps them from making an idol of their own efforts. Their trust in God to raise them at the last day enables them to put their lives on the line for the sake of the kingdom. In other words, they see their lives as valuable, but not ultimate. Life is a gift, to be embraced and valued, but not selfishly preserved at the cost of violat-

ing one's responsibility to God and others.

The vision of the coming reality of God's glory compels us to a specific posture in the present, that is, to work patiently and courageously in our world in a manner dictated by the way of Christ, the way from suffering to glory. Christians are free to give themselves in service with and for Christ, even if it means being "faithful unto death," in full confidence that there really is a crown, which is life.

To do anything less than this is to return to the old existence and death. But to give one's life in service in the hope of the resurrection is already to participate in life itself. John sums it up well: "We know that we have passed out of death into life, because we love the brethren. He who does not love abides in death" (1 John 3:14).

IV. Historical Overview

A. Ancient World

The ancient Near East knew no doctrine of life after death corresponding to the biblical teaching on the resurrection. However, in Mesopotamian literature the power to revive the dead was ascribed to Ishtar and Marduk (ANET 384, 437). The Greeks believed in the immortality of the soul and conscious life after death but knew nothing of a resurrection as taught in the Bible.

B. Judaism

During the intertestamental period the resurrection played a prominent role in Jewish thought, although ideas about it differed and not all accepted it. J. Charlesworth notes (68) that the belief in resurrection "was not the sole possession of the Pharisees. It is found in many types of literature, notably in 2 Maccabees, the Psalms of Solomon, and the common weekly prayer, the Eighteen Benedictions." However, George W. E. Nickelsburg concludes that "there was no single Jewish orthodoxy on the time, mode, and place of resurrection, immortality, and eternal life" (180).

Belief in the resurrection of the dead is

taught, for example, in 2 Maccabees 7:9: "The King of the universe will raise us from the dead and give us eternal life." Likewise, Psalms of Solomon 3:12 affirms that "those who fear the Lord shall rise up to eternal life." Other streams of Judaism emphasized views different from these. Josephus (c. A.D. 37-c. 100) confirms the testimony of the NT that the Sadducees did not believe in the resurrection (*Wars* 2. 165; *Antiquities* 18. 4. 16). The book of Jubilees (second century B.C.) seems to support a belief in the immortality of the soul: while the bones of the righteous rest in the earth, their spirits increase in joy (23:31).

Immortality of the soul was clearly taught by the diaspora philosopher Philo of Alexandria (c. 20 B.C.-c. A.D. 50). Abel's blood crying out from the ground shows the deserving dead live an incorporeal life (*Questions on Genesis* 1. 70); the translation of Enoch shows the same (1. 85). Philo, however, was not the only Jew to follow Greek philosophical ideas. The effect of this Hellenistic influence on views of the afterlife can be seen in archaeological remains of burial places. For example, first-century Jewish grave inscriptions at Beth She'arim, in Palestine, contain Greek ideas on the immortality of the soul, even when written in the Hebrew language.

Modern Judaism has tended to dissociate itself from the idea of a corporeal resurrection. The Reform movement went so far as to remove references to resurrection from the prayer book. Rather than being taken literally, resurrection is often understood as a symbol of the ultimate salvation of the whole person, body and soul.

C. Early Church

Heretical ideas concerning the resurrection seem to have appeared very early. In 1 Corinthians 15 Paul seems to refute either a negation of the resurrection or erroneous views regarding it. In 2 Timothy 2:17, 18 Paul names two teachers who falsely hold that the resurrection has already happened. Perhaps these were related to those mentioned in 2 Thessalonians 2:2, who affirmed that the day of the Lord had already come.

From the time of the earliest Fathers through Augustine, who set the course for the medieval period, the resurrection of the body was affirmed by the Fathers of the church against challenges from two directions. The first came from the non-Christian critics, who ridiculed the resurrection as an absurdity. The second came from the Gnostics, who held that all matter, including the body, was evil, and thus salvation in the body through a resurrection was unthinkable.

Yet as the Fathers defended the resurrection on these two fronts a significant development took place. The influence of the teaching of the immortality of the soul was combined with resurrection in ways that robbed the latter of its original power and meaning.

Already by the end of the first century Clement of Rome defends the doctrine of the resurrection against critics by using various illustrations, such as the cycles of day and night, sleeping and waking, the sowing of seed, and the legend of the phoenix, which rises from the ashes.

The first major discussion on the resurrection comes in the mid-second century in Justin's *Fragments on the Resurrection*. Here Justin attempts to make the Christian idea of resurrection understandable to the Greco-Roman mind. He argues that the resurrection is consistent with the thought of the Greek philosophers. He differentiates between body and soul but does not see the latter as immortal. The Christian's hope is in the resurrection of the body.

One tractate of the Gnostic Nag Hammadi Library is called *The Treatise on Resurrection*. In this work, probably dating from the second century, the Saviour, our Lord Christ, swallows up death by raising Himself and transforming Himself into an imperishable Aeon. This is a "spiritual" resurrection, not a resurrection of the body. At death believers leave the body behind. The resurrection is merely a disclosure of those who have risen; to one who believes, it is already a reality.

Irenaeus (c. 115-c. 202) combats this kind of position in *Against Heresies* (5. 3-7). The soul is mortal and is only a part of the person, not the whole. The whole person, including body and soul, will be saved. Christian hope is based on a bodily resurrection.

Athenagoras, also writing in the second century, takes a different position, one destined to grow in popularity. He too defends the resurrection against many of the same objections, but he sees persons made up of an immortal soul and a body. Death is a separation of soul and body. Resurrection is the reuniting of the two, because God willed that the proper nature of human beings was to live with a body (*Resurrection of the Dead* 1-25).

Tertullian (c. 160-c. 240) is even further from the NT *(Against Marcion* 9, 10; *On the Resurrection of the Flesh)*. The soul is not only immortal but corporeal, possessing a peculiar kind of solidarity that enables it to perceive and suffer. But since the soul cannot fully act without the body, body and soul must be reunited in a resurrection of the body before a person can face either eternal torment or eternal salvation.

Origen (c. 185-254) presents a similar view of death and of the reuniting of body and soul (*On First Principles* 3. 6), but he argues that since the immortal cannot cease to be and since God will restore all things, everyone will eventually be saved, even if for some this comes only after death. In his view, the resurrection occurs when all rational souls are restored and receive a spiritual body.

Gregory of Nyssa (c. 330-c. 395) carries even further the speculation about the nature of the soul in his *On the Soul and the Resurrection,* but the real climax of this trend to combine the resurrection of the dead with the immortality of the soul comes with Augustine (354-430). He discusses the subject in book 22 of *The City of God,* but a more succinct presentation can be found in *Faith, Hope and Charity,* chapters 23 and 29. Augustine defends the resurrection of the body against the Platonists, who deny that the body can inherit the kingdom. All will rise again in a re-creation that restores the body from the totality of the matter of which it originally consisted. But again, this is really a reuniting of the body with an immortal soul, which has continued to live after death. After death the separated soul stays in a place specially reserved for it. It receives either rest or tribulation depending on the course of its earthly life. After the resurrection the righteous will live in eternal happiness, but the wicked will experience the second death, which for Augustine is the eternal punishment in which the soul is not permitted to leave the body forever.

Although the resurrection of the dead is still affirmed at this point, its nature is very different from anything found in the Bible. Increasingly the immortality of the soul has been combined with resurrection in ways that change resurrection from the re-creation of the whole person to the reuniting of the body with a conscious soul that has already been experiencing either suffering or peace. This prepared the way for increasing speculations about purgatory throughout the medieval period.

D. Middle Ages

The most important theological figure during the medieval period is Thomas Aquinas (1225-1274). He includes a treatise on the resurrection in his *Summa Theologica.* He not only affirms a resurrection of the body (Supplement to Part 3, Question 75) and places it at the end of the world (Question 77), but even speculates on such questions as whether hair and fingernails will be resurrected (Question 80), whether one will be the same age as at death or young again, whether one will be the same height, and whether both sexes will be present (Question 81). It is clear, however, that for Aquinas, resurrection means the reuniting of body and soul.

E. From the Reformation to the Enlightenment

In spite of the fact that they continued to hold to a doctrine of natural immortality, the Reformers generally spoke out against purgatory, in Roman Catholic thinking an intermediate state in which the dead were purified through suffering. In addition, they all held to the reality and importance of Christ's resurrection, as well as the resurrection of believers, which that makes possible. Beyond these agreements there was much diversity. Reformers differed on how the resurrection related to the immortality of the soul and the intermediate state, and whether the resurrection body was the same as the earthly one.

Luther (1509-1564) reveals a good bit of ambiguity and diversity. On the one hand, when combating the doctrine of purgatory, he seems to suggest that Christians who have died are unconscious as they await the resurrection (*Commentary on Ecclesiastes* 9:6). Earlier in his same commentary on Ecclesiastes, however, he argues that it is not "certain that souls are immortal" (*ibid.* 3:20).

In his *Table Talk,* Luther seems to recognize this ambiguity and points to the incomprehensible nature of the mystery of the resurrection, as well as the intermediate state.

He says, "It's true that souls hear, feel, and see after death, but how this occurs we don't understand" (5534). In response to a further question about the meaning of the creed's proclamation about Christ descending into hell, Luther replies that it must be believed but cannot be understood *(ibid.)*.

Calvin argues for both resurrection and immortality. He explains that the Sadducees were wrong in holding that there was no resurrection and that the soul was mortal (*Institutes* 3. 25. 5). Further, he refutes two errors: that the soul sleeps or is nonexistent during death and that a different body is united with the soul at resurrection (3. 25. 6). Resurrection is the reuniting of body and soul, in which the new body is of the same substance as the former, but of a different quality (3. 25. 8).

Calvin carries both his argument and denunciation further in the *Psychopannychia,* where he argues against those who believe that the soul exists, but hold that it sleeps in a state of insensibility from death to the resurrection, and against those who deny the real existence of the soul. (See Death II. D.) Calvin maintains that the soul is a substance and truly lives with both sense and understanding after death until the resurrection (Calvin 419, 420).

Perhaps the Westminster Confession, written by an assembly of Presbyterians of England and Scotland in 1646, presents as well as any other document the essentials of the Protestant consensus, which is still the position of most conservative Protestants:

"At death the body returns to dust and the soul to God; the immortal soul either is received into heaven or cast into hell. At the last all the dead shall be raised up with the self-same bodies . . . which shall be united to their souls forever.

"The bodies of the unjust shall, by the power of Christ, be raised to dishonor; the bodies of the just, by his Spirit, unto honor, and be made conformable to his own glorious body" (Leith 228, 229).

It was inevitable that after the Reformation,

the Enlightenment—with its emphasis on universal reason, freedom from dogma, and skepticism toward miracle—would have difficulty with the doctrine of the resurrection. Although deists already had raised questions about the resurrection, the work of Reimarus (1694-1768) constituted a watershed. Reimarus, a professor at Hamburg, held that Jesus had been strictly a moral teacher who remained a Jew, never sought to overturn the ceremonial law, and did not intend to start a new religion (Reimarus 98-102). When Jesus died, He did not rise from the dead, as the many contradictions in the Gospel narratives show. Rather, the disciples, who did not wish to return to work, stole the body (153-164; 244, 245).

Although few followed the extreme position of Reimarus, questions about faith, reason, and history with regard to the resurrection continued to grow more and more crucial.

F. Modern Times

Three major streams of thought in modern Christianity diverge on the issue of the resurrection. The Roman Catholic tradition continues to see the resurrection as the reuniting of the body and soul and continues to emphasize the immortality of the soul. It still gives place to a doctrine of purgatory, though with less elaboration than was once the case.

The liberal Protestant tradition shows great diversity in its views of resurrection and afterlife. There has been a tendency, however, to see the concept of afterlife and of many other eschatological elements in Christianity as in some way symbolic of present experience and not actual events to take place in the future.

On the other hand, conservative or evangelical Protestants place strong emphasis on the literal return of Christ in the future, accompanied by the resurrection. Although there is much diversity over the specific scenario, most evangelicals hold to the immortality of the soul and see the resurrection as the reuniting of body and soul.

In the context of the neoorthodox debate Oscar Cullmann has raised questions about the immortality of the soul. He attempts to show that the NT doctrine of the resurrection of the dead is incompatible with belief in the immortality of the soul (Cullmann 15). In the interim between death and resurrection at the last day one is in a state of anticipation that shares the tension of the interim time (46-54).

In the evangelical tradition prominent thinkers such as John Stott and Clark Pinnock have more recently criticized the doctrine of the immortality of the soul as giving an incomplete hope for the future in contrast with the bodily resurrection of Christ, which points to a total salvation, not only of human spiritual life, but of all creation, including the physical (Stott 313-320; Pinnock 16, 17).

Rudolph Bultmann has claimed that the resurrection of Jesus must be demythologized to discover its true meaning, which was the rise of faith in the disciples (Bultmann 1951, 1:305). This rise of faith makes possible a new existence, which is the promised eschatological life. He rejects a literal Second Coming and resurrection of the dead by saying that the mythical eschatology of the NT is now "untenable for the simple reason that the parousia of Christ never took place as the New Testament expected. History did not come to an end, and, as every schoolboy knows, it will continue to run its course" (Bultmann 1957, 5).

Neoorthodox theologians such as Barth and Brunner disagree with aspects of Bultmann's approach, but also appropriate the resurrection existentially. Barth rejects Bultmann's interpretation of Easter as the rise of faith in the risen Lord, for faith in the risen Lord springs from its historical manifestation (*Dogmatics* 3. 2. 443). The resurrection of Jesus and His appearances must be accepted as genuine history (447). Yet this does not mean that the Resurrection is an ordinary historical event open to all observers. It is rather God's revelation in which the hidden being and work of Jesus Christ are exposed and exhibited. There is a "sacred incomprehensibility" about the Resurrection (4. 2. 146).

Brunner presents a similar view when he speaks of Easter as a "hole" through which something else becomes visible. The Resurrection "is a *Factum,* certainly, but not one which can be fitted into a series . . . of historical events. . . . In all this whatever becomes historically visible is only the echo of this happening. It is super-history, eschatological history, hence it is no longer historical at all" (Brunner 583). The resurrection of the body signifies the continuity of the individual personality after death.

A number of theologians in the Bultmannian tradition have broken at least partially with Bultmann in regard to the Resurrection. Wolfhart Pannenberg (128-133) affirms the historicity of the Resurrection but denies its corporeality. Jürgen Moltmann maintains that "Christianity stands or falls with the reality of the raising of Jesus from the dead by God" (165). This reality is more than the birth of faith as Bultmann held (173). To recognize the resurrection of Christ is to recognize in this event the future of God for the world (194). The Resurrection is a matter of promise and hope.

Although both Moltmann and Pannenberg corrected an important element in Bultmann, it would be a mistake to understand them as confirming a literal resurrection of the dead for the believer. In this regard J. Christiaan Beker (103) is correct when he observes that "in fact, whether intentionally or not, these theologians of hope construe the end-time more as an event in the realm of ideas than as an actual event. The kingdom of God constitutes for them the final goal and meaning of history."

Most conservative Christians have rejected the entire tradition characterized by Bultmann and have affirmed the historical literalness of both the resurrection of Jesus and the believers. Often, however, this insistence on the verity of the Resurrection has been combined with the concept of the immortality of the soul, so that the resurrection is seen as the reuniting of body and soul. The conservative emphasis often has included attempts to prove the Resurrection with various kinds of evidence from both the Bible and history, with little effort to speak to the problems of faith and history.

More recent evangelicals have addressed such issues, however. For example, G. Elton Ladd (263-284) affirms the historicity of the Resurrection and argues that those who cannot accept the nature of Christian faith as disclosed in the Bible bring with them presuppositions foreign to biblical faith (267-271). Against Bultmann, Ladd argues that an objective fact occurred in a garden outside Jerusalem. Yet Ladd also wants to show that the Resurrection is much more than history.

"The resurrection of Jesus is no less than the appearance upon the historical temporal scene of something which is eternal. . . . It is no 'disturbance' of the normal course of events; it is the manifestation of something utterly new. Eternal life has appeared in the midst of mortality" (273).

According to Ladd, this "supra-historical" event cannot be established and known by historical reconstruction and methodology, for historical proofs cannot compel faith, which comes by hearing (280). This does not divorce faith and reason, for they are in alliance, but not identical. The Resurrection can be accepted only by faith, but by a faith created by the Holy Spirit, who uses historical witnesses as instruments to elicit faith, but not proofs to compel it (281).

G. The Seventh-day Adventist Position

Since the entire biblical section is an explication of the Seventh-day Adventist understanding of the resurrection, this section will touch only briefly on the history of the doctrine in Adventist understanding.

The basic picture of the resurrection accompanying the Second Coming was already present in the preaching of William Miller. He taught that the resurrection of the righteous would occur before the millennium and that the resurrection of the wicked would take place at its end. (See Damsteegt 38-40 and Nichol 506, 507.)

The earliest articles on the resurrection to be published in the *Review and Herald* were reprinted from other sources. The first, on December 9, 1852, was taken from the *Midnight Cry* (1843). A well-developed discussion of the two resurrections, 1,000 years apart, appeared in the September 27, 1853, issue, but it had been published already in 1843. A third one, on April 18, 1854, came from a Baptist source.

In 1856 Loughborough wrote an original article for the *Review and Herald* entitled "Is the Soul Immortal?" (Dec. 11), in which he argued that the only hope of a future life was grounded in a literal resurrection. J. H. Waggoner analyzed the biblical evidence for the resurrection of the wicked in a *Review and Herald* article published February 5, 1857. (See Death II. E.)

Thus throughout its history the Seventh-day Adventist Church has consistently affirmed that Christians can look forward to the resurrection of the just at the second advent of Christ, and that those who die before Christ's return wait in unconscious sleep until the whole person is resurrected. Adventists have also held that the resurrection of the wicked will occur 1,000 years later at the end of the millennium.

The consistency of this position can be seen in the various statements of belief that the church has adopted. In one of its earliest published statements of belief in 1872, belief in the wholeness of human beings and the resurrection is included. This statement affirms that Christ was raised for our justification (No. 2) and that the dead will be brought out of the grave by a bodily resurrection: the righteous in the first resurrection at the second advent of Christ and the wicked at the second resurrection 1,000 years later (No. 21). At the last trump the living righteous are changed and become immortal (No. 22; Land 232-236).

A statement issued in 1931 proclaims that God only has immortality, that humans are inherently sinful and dying, and that immortality and eternal life come only from the gospel as a free gift of God (No. 9). Statements 10 and 11 reaffirm the unconscious state in death, as well as the two resurrections.

The most recent statement of belief, voted and published in 1980, reads as follows:

"The wages of sin is death. But God, who alone is immortal, will grant eternal life to His redeemed. Until that day death is an unconscious state for all people. When Christ, who is our life, appears, the resurrected righteous and the living righteous will be glorified and caught up to meet their Lord. The second resurrection, the resurrection of the unrighteous, will take place a thousand years later (Rom. 6:23; 1 Tim. 6:15, 16; Eccl. 9:5, 6; Ps. 146:3, 4; John 11:11-14; Col. 3:4; 1 Cor. 15:51-54; 1 Thess. 4:13-17; John 5:28, 29; Rev. 20:1-10)." (*SDA Yearbook* 1991, 8.)

V. Ellen G. White Comments

A. On the Resurrection of the Righteous

"The Pharisees believed in the resurrection of the dead. Christ declares that even now the power which gives life to the dead is among them, and they are to behold its manifestation. This same resurrection power is that which gives life to the soul 'dead in trespasses and sins' (Eph. 2:1). That spirit of life in Christ Jesus, 'the power of his resurrection,' sets men 'free from the law of sin and death' (Phil. 3:10; Rom. 8:2). The dominion of evil is broken, and through faith the soul is kept from sin. He who opens his heart to the Spirit of Christ becomes a partaker of that mighty power which shall bring forth his body from the grave" (DA 209, 210).

"Christ became one flesh with us, in order that we might become one spirit with Him. It is by virtue of this union that we are to come forth from the grave—not merely as a manifestation of the power of Christ, but because, through faith, His life has become ours. Those who see Christ in His true character, and receive Him into the heart, have everlasting life. It is through the Spirit that Christ dwells in us; and the Spirit of God, received into the heart by faith, is the beginning of the life eternal" (*ibid.* 388).

"To the believer, Christ is the resurrection and the life. In our Saviour the life that was lost through sin is restored; for He has life in Himself to quicken whom He will. He is invested with the right to give immortality. The life that He laid down in humanity, He takes up again, and gives to humanity" (*ibid.* 786, 787).

"The voice that cried from the cross, 'It is finished,' was heard among the dead. It pierced the walls of sepulchers, and summoned the sleepers to arise. Thus will it be when the voice of Christ shall be heard from heaven. That voice will penetrate the graves and unbar the tombs, and the dead in Christ shall arise. At the Saviour's resurrection a few graves were opened, but at His second coming all the precious dead shall hear His voice, and shall come forth to glorious, immortal life. The same power that raised Christ from the dead will raise His church, and glorify it with Him, above all principalities, above all powers, above every name that is named, not only in this world, but also in the world to come" (*ibid.* 787).

"The resurrection of Jesus was a type of the final resurrection of all who sleep in Him. The countenance of the risen Saviour, His manner, His speech, were all familiar to His disciples. As Jesus arose from the dead, so those who sleep in Him are to rise again. We shall know our friends, even as the disciples knew Jesus. They may have been deformed, diseased, or disfigured, in this mortal life, and they rise in perfect health and symmetry; yet in the glorified body their identity will be perfectly preserved. Then shall we know even as also we are known (1 Cor. 13:12). In the face radiant with the light shining from the face of Jesus, we shall recognize the lineaments of those we love" (*ibid.* 804).

371

"The Thessalonians had eagerly grasped the idea that Christ was coming to change the faithful who were alive, and to take them to Himself. They had carefully guarded the lives of their friends, lest they should die and lose the blessing which they looked forward to receiving at the coming of their Lord. But one after another their loved ones had been taken from them, and with anguish the Thessalonians had looked for the last time upon the faces of their dead, hardly daring to hope to meet them in a future life.

"As Paul's epistle was opened and read, great joy and consolation was brought to the church by the words revealing the true state of the dead. Paul showed that those living when Christ should come would not go to meet their Lord in advance of those who had fallen asleep in Jesus. The voice of the Archangel and the trump of God would reach the sleeping ones, and the dead in Christ should rise first, before the touch of immortality should be given to the living" (AA 258).

"All come forth from their graves the same in stature as when they entered the tomb. Adam, who stands among the risen throng, is of lofty height and majestic form, in stature but little below the Son of God. He presents a marked contrast to the people of later generations; in this one respect is shown the great degeneracy of the race. But all arise with the freshness and vigor of eternal youth. In the beginning, man was created in the likeness of God, not only in character, but in form and feature. Sin defaced and almost obliterated the divine image; but Christ came to restore that which had been lost. He will change our vile bodies and fashion them like unto His glorious body. The mortal, corruptible form, devoid of comeliness, once polluted with sin, becomes perfect, beautiful, and immortal. All blemishes and deformities are left in the grave. Restored to the tree of life in the long-lost Eden, the redeemed will 'grow up' (Mal. 4:2) to the full stature of the race in its primeval glory. The last lingering traces of the curse of sin will be removed, and Christ's faithful ones will appear in "the beauty of the Lord our God," in mind and soul and body reflecting the perfect image of their Lord. Oh, wonderful redemption! long talked of, long hoped for, contemplated with eager anticipation, but never fully understood.

"The living righteous are changed 'in a moment, in the twinkling of an eye.' At the voice of God they were glorified; now they are made immortal and with the risen saints are caught up to meet their Lord in the air. Angels 'gather together his elect from the four winds, from one end of heaven to the other.' Little children are borne by holy angels to their mothers' arms. Friends long separated by death are united, nevermore to part, and with songs of gladness ascend together to the City of God" (GC 644, 645).

"Christ was the first fruits of them that slept. It was to the glory of God that the Prince of life should be the first fruits, the antitype of the wave sheaf. 'For whom he did foreknow, he also did predestinate to be conformed to the image of his Son, that he might be the first-born among many brethren' (Rom. 8:29). This very scene, the resurrection of Christ from the dead, had been celebrated in type by the Jews. When the first heads of grain ripened in the field, they were carefully gathered; and when the people went up to Jerusalem, these were presented to the Lord as a thank offering. The people waved the ripened sheaf before God, acknowledging Him as the Lord of the harvest. After this ceremony the sickle could be put to the wheat, and the harvest gathered.

"So those who have been raised were to be presented to the universe as a pledge of the resurrection of all who believe in Christ as their personal Saviour. The same power that raised Christ from the dead will raise His church, and glorify it with Christ, as His bride, above all principalities, above all powers, above every name that is named, not only in this world, but also in the heavenly courts, the world above. The victory of the sleeping saints will be glorious on the morning of the resurrection. Satan's triumph will end, while Christ will triumph in glory and honor. The Life-giver will crown with immortality all who come forth from the grave" (1SM 305, 306).

"As the little infants come forth immortal from their dusty beds, they immediately wing their way to their mother's arms. They meet again nevermore to part. But many of the little ones have no mother there. We listen in vain for the rapturous song of triumph from the mother. The angels receive the motherless infants and conduct them to the tree of life" (2SM 260).

B. On the Resurrection of the Wicked

"A spirit of fanaticism has ruled a certain class of Sabbathkeepers there; they have sipped but lightly at the fountain of truth and are unacquainted with the spirit of the message of the third angel. Nothing can be done for this class until their fanatical views are corrected. Some who were in the 1854 movement have brought along with them erroneous views, such as the nonresurrection of the wicked, and the future age, and they are seeking to unite these views and their past experience with the message of the third angel. They cannot do this; there is no concord between Christ and Belial. The nonresurrection of the wicked and their peculiar views of the age to come are gross errors which Satan has worked in among the last-day heresies to serve his own purpose to ruin souls. These errors can have no harmony with the message of heavenly origin" (1T 411, 412).

"At the close of the thousand years, Christ again returns to the earth. He is accompanied by the host of the redeemed and attended by a retinue of angels. As He descends in terrific majesty He bids the wicked dead arise to receive their doom. They come forth, a mighty host, numberless as the sands of the sea. What a contrast to those who were raised at the first resurrection! The righteous were clothed with immortal youth and beauty. The wicked bear the traces of disease and death.

"Every eye in that vast multitude is turned to behold the glory of the Son of God. With one voice the wicked hosts exclaim: 'Blessed is he that cometh in the name of the Lord!' It is not love to Jesus that inspires this utterance. The force of truth urges the words from unwilling lips. As the wicked went into their graves, so they come forth with the same enmity to Christ and the same spirit of rebellion. They are to have no new probation in which to remedy the defects of their past lives. Nothing would be gained by this. A lifetime of transgression has not softened their hearts. A second probation, were it given them, would be occupied as was the first in evading the requirements of God and exciting rebellion against Him" (GC 662).

C. On the Special Resurrection

"Graves are opened, and 'many of them that sleep in the dust of the earth . . . awake, some to everlasting life, and some to shame and everlasting contempt' (Dan. 12:2). All who have died in the faith of the third angel's message come forth from the tomb glorified, to hear God's covenant of peace with those who have kept His law. 'They also which pierced him' (Rev. 1:7), those that mocked and derided Christ's dying agonies, and the most violent opposers of His truth and His people, are raised to behold Him in His glory and to see the honor placed upon the loyal and obedient" (ibid. 637).

VI. Literature

Barth, K. Church Dogmatics. Edinburgh: T. and T. Clark, 1936-1962.

Beker, J. C. Paul's Apocalyptic Gospel: The Coming Triumph of God. Philadelphia: Fortress, 1982.

Brunner, E. The Mediator. Trans. by Olive Wyon. Philadelphia: Westminster, 1947.

Bultmann, R. "New Testament and Mythology." In Kerygma and Myth: A Theological Debate, ed. Hans W. Bartsch, 1:1-44.

London: SPCK, 1957.

———. *Theology of the New Testament.* 2 vols. Trans. Kendrick Grobel. New York: Charles Scribner's Sons, 1951.

Calvin, J. *Tracts and Treatises in Defense of the Reformed Faith.* Vol. 3. Grand Rapids: Eerdmans, 1958.

Charlesworth, James H. *The Old Testament Pseudepigrapha and the New Testament.* Cambridge: Cambridge University Press, 1985.

Cullmann, O. *Immortality of the Soul or Resurrection of the Dead? The Witness of the New Testament.* New York: MacMillan, 1958.

Damsteegt, P. G. *Foundations of the Seventh-day Adventist Message and Mission.* Grand Rapids: Eerdmans, 1977.

Dodd, C. H. *The Interpretation of the Fourth Gospel.* Cambridge: University Press, 1953.

Hasel, G. F. "Resurrection in the Theology of Old Testament Apocalyptic." *Zeitschrift fuer die Alttestamentliche Wissenschaft* 92 (1980): 267-284.

Kubo, S. *God Meets Man: A Theology of the Sabbath and Second Advent.* Nashville: Southern Pub. Assn., 1978.

Ladd, G. E. "The Resurrection of Jesus." In *Christian Faith and Modern Theology.* Ed. Carl F. H. Henry. New York: Channel, 1964. Pp. 263-284

Land, G., ed. *Adventism in America.* Grand Rapids: Eerdmans, 1986.

Leith, J. H. *Creeds of the Churches.* Chicago: Aldine, 1963.

Moltmann, J. *Theology of Hope: On the Ground and the Implications of a Christian Eschatology.* New York: Harper and Row, 1967.

Nichol, F. D. *The Midnight Cry.* Takoma Park, Md.: Review and Herald, 1944.

Nickelsburg, G.W.E., Jr. *Resurrection, Immortality, and Eternal Life in Intertestamental Judaism.* Harvard Theological Studies, 26. Cambridge: Harvard University Press, 1972.

Pannenberg, W. "Did Jesus Really Rise From the Dead?" *Dialog* 4 (Spring 1965): 128-133.

Pinnock, C. "The Incredible Resurrection: A Mandate for Faith." *Christianity Today,* Apr. 6, 1979.

Pritchard, J. B., ed. *Ancient Near Eastern Texts.* Princeton, N.J.: Princeton University Press, 1955.

Reimarus, H. S. *Fragments.* Ed. Charles H. Talbert. Trans. Ralph S. Fraser. Philadelphia: Fortress, 1970.

Robinson, J.A.T. *The Body: A Study in Pauline Theology.* Studies in Biblical Theology. No. 5. London: SCM, 1952.

Schwarz, R. W. *Light Bearers to the Remnant.* Mountain View, Calif.: Pacific Press, 1979.

Stott, J.R.W., and D. L. Edwards. *Essentials: A Liberal/Evangelical Dialogue.* London: Hodder and Stoughton, 1988.

Weiss, H. *Paul of Tarsus: His Gospel and Life.* Berrien Springs, Mich.: Andrews University Press, 1986.

The Sanctuary

Angel Manuel Rodríguez

Introduction

Christ's death and resurrection from the grave lie at the very heart of the plan of salvation. Calvary was God's final answer to the human predicament. Christ's sacrifice is described as "once for all" (Heb. 10:10), valid "for all time," hence unrepeatable (verse 12). Nothing can be added to the cross in order to supplement its atoning and expiatory power. Jesus, who in His own life was victorious over the tempter (Matt. 4:1-11; Heb. 4:15), came to destroy the works of the devil (1 John 3:8). His victory over the forces of evil makes possible our own victory over sin (Rev. 12:11), as well as the final eradication of evil from our world (Rev. 20:9-15). The NT's emphasis on the finality of Christ's atoning death has led some to conclude that His work for our salvation came to an end at the cross. This calls for further clarification.

Having accomplished on earth the work for which He came (John 17:4, 5; 19:30), Christ was "taken up . . . into heaven" (Acts 1:11) "to save those who draw near to God through him, since he always lives to make intercession for them" (Heb. 7:25), till at His second coming He will appear "not to deal with sin but to save those who are eagerly waiting for him" (Heb. 9:28). Between these two poles, the cross and the Lord's glorious return, Christ functions as royal priest "in the sanctuary and the true tent which is set up not by man but by the Lord" (Heb. 8:2), the advocate (1 John 2:1) and intercessor for those who believe in Him (Rom. 8:34). As our high priest, Christ is ministering the benefits of His sacrifice to those who draw near to Him, a ministry as essential to our salvation as His atoning death.

The priestly ministry of our heavenly high priest was prefigured in the OT sacrificial system, especially as seen in the Hebrew sanctuary, made according to a "pattern" shown by God to Moses (Ex. 25:9) and pointing to the heavenly sanctuary. The sanctuary services were a lesson book in salvation. For this reason, the study of the sanctuary and its services not only clarifies the meaning of the rituals followed, but it also sheds light on the heavenly ministry of Christ.

I. OT Sacrificial System

In exploring the richness and depth of the biblical doctrine of the priesthood of Christ, we must consider the witness of both the OT and NT. For the Christian both Testaments form an indivisible unity of divine revelation. There is one Author of Scriptures who in the past revealed Himself through different instruments and who now has spoken to us through the Son (Heb. 1:1, 2). The unity of that revelation is suggested by its emphasis on one Saviour. Jesus Himself made clear that Scriptures "bear me witness" (John 5:36) and that Moses wrote about Him (verse 46). On the road to Emmaus Christ opened the Scriptures to two disciples, "and beginning with Moses and all the prophets, he interpreted to them in all the scriptures the things concerning himself" (Luke 24:27). Scriptures witness to only one eternal gospel of salvation (Rev. 14:6), proclaimed to Israel as well as to us (Heb. 4:2). In the OT God revealed the gospel to His people through Messianic prophecies, symbols, and types. (See Interpretation III. E. 3.) Therefore, in our effort to understand the work of our Lord, we will listen to both Testaments; they shed light on each other.

A. The Sacrificial System in Patriarchal Times

Sacrifice belongs to the very infrastructure of biblical theology and religion. Interestingly, the origin of sacrifice is not explicitly stated anywhere in the OT. The first time one is mentioned no particular reason is given for it and the issue of its origin is not addressed (Gen. 4:2-5). In subsequent records, the meaning of the sacrifice is implied but not openly discussed.

1. Origin of the Sacrificial System

The sacrificial system of the OT originated immediately after the Fall. In Eden God revealed Himself as the Redeemer of the human race. The penalty of eternal death was not applied to Adam and Eve at once because the Lord provided a means of redemption through which He would put an end to the serpent, the devil, and his works (Gen. 3:15; cf. Rom. 16:20; Heb. 2:14). God's gracious act in providing Adam and Eve with garments of skin was in fact a promise of redemption; when we place Genesis 3:21 in its theological context, the implicit death of the animal becomes a sacrificial act. Adam and Eve, after committing sin, were destined to experience ultimate death (Gen. 2:17). Surprisingly, their life was preserved. But precisely in that life-threatening context the death of an animal took place. The death penalty was not executed on them but on the animal. The death of the animal provided the means of restoring their relationship with the Lord.

Out of death came hope and restoration. That God made the garments and dressed the erring pair suggests that God did for them what they were unable to do for themselves. He graciously enabled them to approach Him, to live in His presence. Those same concepts belong to the theology of the sanctuary and its services later in the OT. What is embryonic or hinted at in Genesis 3 becomes a full-blown theological body of ideas in the Israelite sacrificial system. Adam and Eve were already benefitting from Christ's sacrifice.

2. General Characteristics of the System

Worship and sacrifice are inseparable in the patriarchal narratives. A place of worship was identified by its altar (Gen. 8:20; 12:7; 26:25). Several sacrifices and/or sacrificial acts are mentioned in Genesis, but the burnt offering appears to have been the most common (8:20; 22:3, 7). Reference is made, however, to a libation in 35:14. The term "priest" is used for the first time in 14:18 to designate Melchizedek, king of Salem who worshiped the "God Most High." Abraham acknowledged him as a rightful priest by giving him the tithe. As priest, Melchizedek received the tithe and blessed the patriarch (verses 18-20; see Stewardship I. C. 3).

3. Specific Sacrifices

a. Sacrifice of Cain and Abel. Most of the sacrifices mentioned in the patriarchal narratives were bloody. The significant exception is the one brought by Cain (Gen. 4:3). According to Hebrews 11:4 Abel offered his sacrifice by faith and God accepted it. Cain's offering was not an expression of faith but of his own convictions. Abel's faith in the atoning sacrifice of Christ revealed itself in unquestioning obedience. The sacrifice brought by Abel illuminates the meaning of sacrifice. Offering a sacrifice required the combination of proper inner attitude and obedience to external rituals. Whenever God accepted a sacrifice, He also accepted the offerer. Therefore, a sacrifice was instrumental in the preservation of

one's relationship with God (Gen. 4:7).

b. Sacrifice of Noah. The next mention of sacrifices is found in Genesis 8:20. After the Flood, Noah offered burnt offerings to the Lord. The context suggests that these sacrifices were an expression of gratitude for God's loving care for Noah and his family. The idea of expiation also seems to be present. The narrative states that God "smelled the pleasing odor"; He accepted the sacrifice and determined not to destroy again all living creatures (verse 21). By accepting the sacrifice God committed Himself to restore and preserve His relationship with humankind.

c. Sacrifice of Abraham (Gen. 22). God tested Abraham by asking him to present Isaac as a burnt offering (verses 1, 2). Thus Abraham was given the opportunity to reveal the true strength of his faith. God intervened and saved the life of Isaac, thus ending the test. But the narrative does not end there. The Lord provided a ram to be sacrificed in place of Isaac, indicating the importance of sacrificial substitution. The death of the sacrificial victim was required to preserve the life of Isaac and the relationship between God and Abraham. In Genesis 20 and 21 Abraham is described as one who did not always walk blamelessly before the Lord. He lied regarding Sarah his wife (Gen. 12:10-20; 20:1-18) and did not wait for the Lord to fulfill the promise of the son (Gen. 21:1-7). Yet the Lord asked him to pray for the king and gave him a son through Sarah. God seemed to have ignored Abraham's sin. The tension between a God who condemns sin and yet uses as His instrument a man who has violated the covenant is solved in Genesis 22. God was ready to withdraw the promise from the patriarch, leaving him without future and bringing the covenant to an end. But when Abraham showed, through his faith, his willingness to restore the covenant relationship with God, the Lord provided the sacrificial victim needed to expiate his sin and to restore his future (Gen. 22:15-19). On Mount Moriah, where the sacrifice was made, the temple was later built. The mount was symbolically called

"The Lord will provide" (verse 14) as a testimony to what God did for Abraham. The biblical writer adds, "It is said to this day, 'On the mount of the Lord it shall be provided' " (verse 14), indicating that the people had appropriated for themselves the experience of Abraham. Whenever they went to the mount of the Lord they too believed that He would provide a substitute for them. Salvation was understood to come from the Lord, bringing deliverance through substitutionary sacrifice (cf. Isa. 53).

B. The Israelite Sacrificial System

The book of Exodus introduces the Israelite sanctuary as a center of worship, mediation, and sacrifice. It describes the physical structure and the furniture of this unique place. The book also gives instructions concerning the consecration of the priests and provides some of the most important theological ideas associated with the sanctuary. The book of Leviticus details the sacrificial system, the sanctuary services, and the festivals.

1. The Israelite Sanctuary

The architectural concept of the structure was simple: the first apartment was the "holy place" (Ex. 28:29), and the second "the most holy" place (Ex. 26:33). The tabernacle courtyard, with its entrance eastward, was protected by a curtain. The entrance to the tabernacle was also protected by a curtain, suspended from five pillars of acacia wood overlaid with gold and resting in bronze sockets (verse 37). The two apartments inside the tabernacle were divided by a veil richly embroidered with figures of cherubim and hung from four wooden pillars overlaid with gold (verses 31-33). The structure of the tabernacle consisted of wooden frames overlaid with gold, resting on bases of silver (verses 15-30) and protected by four tent coverings (verses 1-14).

In the courtyard was an *altar of sacrifices* with a horn on each of its corners (Ex. 27:1-8). Throughout the OT the altar is associated with the presence of the Lord; through it the Isra-

elites had access to Him (Ps. 43:4). *A laver* between the altar and the entrance to the sanctuary (Ex. 30:17-21) was used by the priests to wash their hands and feet before officiating at the altar or before going into the tabernacle (verse 20). It was an appropriate symbol of spiritual cleansing from sin (cf. Acts 22:16; Eph. 5:26; 1 Cor. 6:11).

Inside the sanctuary, in the holy place, was a *table* (Ex. 25:23-30). On it were 12 loaves of bread, wine, and incense. These elements reminded Israel that God provided their daily bread and would ultimately provide the "bread of life" (John 6:48-51). Opposite the table on the south side was *the lampstand*, made of solid gold decorated with almond-shaped cups and flowers. Its shape—a central shaft with three branches on each side (Ex. 25:31-40)—and the use of floral terminology suggest a stylized tree of life. Zechariah associates the lampstand with God's omnipresence (Zech. 4:11) and with the power of the Spirit of the Lord (verse 6). In the NT Christ is the light of the world (John 8:12). *The altar of incense,* placed by the veil, had a horn on each corner (Ex. 30:1-10). It was used to burn incense twice a day before the Lord, thus representing prayers ascending to God (cf. Ps. 141:2). According to the NT Christ's merits are the fragrance that make our prayers acceptable before the Lord (Eph. 5:2; Rev. 5:8; 8:3, 4).

The ark of the covenant, located in the Most Holy Place, was a wooden box overlaid with gold inside and outside (Ex. 25:10-22). In it God commanded Moses to place the tables of the Ten Commandments (verse 16). A slab of pure gold, called a "mercy seat" (*kappōreṭ,* "that which expiates"), covered it; on this cover stood two cherubs facing each other. Between the cherubs the glory of God revealed itself, granting forgiveness to repentant sinners. The ark symbolized God's presence among His people. There He revealed His will to Israel (verse 22). There He showed His willingness to expiate the sins of His people. There was symbolized the presence of God as king and leader of

Israel, caring and providing for His people (1 Sam. 4:3; Ps. 80:1; 99:1).

2. Priesthood

Apparently God intended to have representatives from all the tribes of Israel minister at the sanctuary, but during the incident of the golden calf at Sinai the tribe of Levi alone remained loyal to the Lord. For this reason the Levites were chosen to serve in the sanctuary instead of the firstborn of Israel (Ex. 32:25-29; Num. 3:11-13; 8:16-18). The priesthood became hereditary, belonging exclusively to Aaron's family (18:6, 7), while the rest of the tribe served in related sanctuary tasks. The responsibilities of the priests were many and varied, but their main task was religious: to be mediators between God and His people.

a. God's representatives before the people. To the people, they taught the *tôrāh,* God's instructions to the nation (Deut. 33:10; Lev. 10:11). Closely related to this activity was the priestly duty of revealing God's will to those who sought divine guidance, particularly through the Urim and Thummim (Num. 27:21), two precious stones placed on the high priest's pectoral, through which God provided answers when consulted. The priests also functioned as judges in the sanctuary. In fact, the highest tribunal of the land operated at the central sanctuary (Deut. 21:5; 17:8-13). In addition the priests were responsible for blessing the people in God's name (Num. 6:22-27; Deut. 10:8).

b. The people's representatives before God. This was symbolically illustrated by the two precious stones placed on the shoulders of the high priest's ephod. On each of these were engraved the names of six of the tribes of Israel (Ex. 28:9-12). The 12 precious stones on the priestly breastpiece had the same function (verse 29). In the person of the priest the people had access to God's presence. But the mediatorial role of the priests reached its highest significance through the sacrificial system. During the daily services *(tāmîd)* the priests performed several important rites. They placed on the altar of burnt offering one sacrifice in the morning and another in the evening (Lev. 6:9, 12, 13; Num. 28:3-8). As part of the *tāmîd* the high priest went into the holy place to dress the lamps and to burn incense before the Lord (Ex. 30:7, 8). The priests presented the sacrifices brought by the Israelites to make atonement for them (Lev. 1:5-9; 4:25, 26). The high priest officiated when a sacrifice was offered on behalf of the community (verses 1-21). As the representative of the people before God, he was allowed to enter the Most Holy Place once a year. On the Day of Atonement he performed specific rituals to cleanse the sanctuary from the sins and impurities of the people of Israel, making the daily cleansing final (Lev. 16; 23:26-32). The duties of the priests and high priest pointed symbolically to Christ as our mediator before the Father.

The Levites assisted the priests (Num. 18:1, 5). They also guarded the sanctuary (Num. 1:53; 3:38). Their main task was to dismantle, transport, and reassemble the sanctuary (Num. 1:48-54). They did not, however, participate in priestly functions (Num. 18:3).

3. Sacrifices and Offerings

The spiritual needs of the Israelites were satisfied primarily through the sacrificial system, which allowed them to express their devotion and adoration, their deepest feelings and needs. Each sacrifice had its special significance.

The *burnt offering* (Heb. *'ōlāh,* "ascending offering") was totally burned on the altar. The person who brought it laid the hand on the head of the victim (Lev. 1:4) and prepared the animal for the priest to perform the blood ritual and place the sacrifice on the altar. This sacrifice could be a votive or freewill offering (Lev. 22:17-19). It was also an expiatory offering through which the person was accepted before the Lord; in 1 Samuel 13:12 the burnt offering was associated with the idea of "entreating the Lord," a phrase often used in the context of God's anger or displeasure (Ex. 32:11; 1 Kings 13:6). Thus, the burnt offering appears in the context of propitiation. It was an expression of worship, gratitude, thanksgiving, joy, and total dedication of the offerer to God. Since the individual was constantly in need of forgiveness, it was also a means of expiation.

The *peace offering* (*š^elāmîm*, "peace/well-being offering") was a voluntary sacrifice brought as a thanksgiving or votive or free-will offering (Lev. 7:11-18). The sacrifice was a joyful occasion (see 1 Sam. 11:14, 15; 1 Kings 8:63) and served to strengthen the covenant relation through communion with God and other Israelites (Deut. 27:7). Most of the meat was given to the offerer who ate it before the Lord with family and friends (Lev. 7:15). Part of the flesh went to the priest (verses 32-34). The laying on of hands and the blood ritual indicate that this sacrifice also had an expiatory function (Eze. 45:15, 17).

The *sin offering* was a sacrifice for the removal of sin. One type was offered when a priest or the community sinned unintentionally (Lev. 4:1-21) and the other when a layperson sinned unintentionally (verses 27-31). The procedure for each was slightly different. When a priest brought the sacrifice, the blood was sprinkled inside the tabernacle and some of it was put on the horns of the altar of incense. The rest of the blood was poured out at the base of the altar of sacrifices and the flesh of the animal was burned outside the sanctuary. In the case of a layperson, some of the blood was applied to the horns of the altar of burnt offering and the rest was poured out at the base of the altar. Some of the flesh was eaten by the priest. This sacrifice expiated any unintentional violation of the covenant law.

According to Leviticus 5:1-6 this sacrifice also expiated the intentional violation of God's will, for the sins listed are intentional. (The phrase "it is hidden from him" could be translated "it is hidden by him" [verses 2, 4].) Intentional sin was not outside the expiatory function of the sacrificial system. Only high-handed sins were not forgiven because the

individual broke completely from the Lord (Num. 15:30). In summary, the sin offering expiated unintentional sins that contaminated the person morally, ethically, or ritually. It also addressed intentional sin expressed through the individual's willingness to reveal a wrong action, a sin, or a state of uncleanness. This sacrifice dealt with the problem of moral and cultic impurity.

The *guilt offering* freed the individual from a state of guilt incurred before the Lord through the unintentional misappropriation of the holy and for cases of suspected sin (Lev. 5:15, 17; Num. 6:12). The Lord allowed the sinner to bring a guilt offering in order to restore peace of mind. A guilt offering was also required for the expiation of the intentional sin of misappropriating someone's property and denying it (Num. 5:5-8) and for sexual intercourse with a betrothed slave girl (Lev. 19:20-22). Whenever possible, restitution and compensation were required in addition to the sacrifice. The procedure for this sacrifice was the same as for the sin offering (Lev. 7:7). The only difference was that its blood was "thrown on the altar round about" (verse 2) and was not placed on its horns. Through the sacrifice, atonement was made for the repentant sinner (Lev. 5:18).

The *meal offering* was a nonbloody offering. The term *minḥāh*, translated "meal offering," means "gift, tribute." This offering accompanied all burnt offerings and peace offerings and consisted of wheat grain or flour, oil, and incense (Num. 15:3-11). The drink offering made from grapes was probably poured out at the base of the altar of burnt offerings. As an offering from the fruits of the land, the *minḥāh* was a recognition of God's gracious provisions. It also may have been an expression of the person's willingness to preserve the covenant relationship with the Lord (Lev. 2:13).

The various sacrifices indicate that the sacrificial system addressed all the spiritual needs of Israel. Some were primarily expiatory, like the sin and guilt offerings. Others did not emphasize expiation although they did atone for the individual (e.g., various kinds of peace offerings). Adoration, consecration, thanksgiving, joy, devotion, communion, fellowship, covenant loyalty, atonement, and much more were expressed through the sacrificial system. That each sacrifice included an element of atonement suggests that without it none of the gifts brought by the people were acceptable to the Lord. The theological richness of the Israelite sacrificial system pointed symbolically to the infinite value and efficacy of the sacrificial death of Christ.

C. Functions of the OT Sanctuary System

To better understand the typological significance of the sanctuary and its contribution to the understanding of Christ's high priestly ministry, the different functions of the sanctuary should be studied in detail.

1. Theological Aspects of the Israelite Sanctuary

God's request for a tabernacle among the Israelites came after they left Egypt and made a covenant with God (Ex. 25:8). This suggests that redemption precedes access to the sanctuary because only those who have been redeemed and have entered into a covenant relationship with God can enjoy full communion with Him. The sanctuary is, in a sense, an attempt to restore to the Edenic state of close fellowship with God.

a. Meeting place. The sanctuary is a meeting place for God and humans. Its name, "Tent of Meeting," shows this function: to provide a space where God and His people can meet (Ex. 40:32). The idea of encountering God is important in the book of Exodus. Through Moses, God made an appointment with the Israelites at Sinai (Ex. 3:12). They traveled to that mountain, prepared for the meeting (Ex. 19:10, 11), and on the third day met the Lord (verse 18). Sinai became the first Israelite sanctuary (verse 12; 24:2-5, 12). The Hebrew sanctuary perpetuated the Sinai experience, a place where God met with His people (Ex. 29:43; Ps. 68:17).

b. Center of divine revelation. God's glory was revealed at Sinai (Ex. 24:16, 17); it dwelt later in the sanctuary (Ex. 40:34, 35). This glory was not merely the brightness of His presence (Ex. 24:17), but especially the mystery of His person. The impenetrable light of His glory testified to His immanence and His transcendence (Ex. 33:18-23). From the sanctuary God continued to reveal His will to His people. The Ten Commandments, proclaimed by God from Sinai (Ex. 20:1-17), were now proclaimed from the sanctuary (Ex. 25:22). Also from the sanctuary God revealed His power as king and judge; this power reached beyond the borders of Israel to the whole world (Ex. 15:17, 18; 23:23; Amos 2:5). His localized presence in the sanctuary did not limit Him in any way.

c. Center of worship. For the Israelites, meeting with God at the sanctuary was an act of worship (cf. Ps. 95:6). This was particularly true during the festivals when they came joyfully to praise the Lord (Ps. 68:24-26; 132:7). The people of Israel also went to the sanctuary with their concerns and needs, hoping to find refuge and comfort in God (Ps. 43:2, 4, 5). At times they came to confess their sin, seeking forgiveness from the Lord in order to be counted among the righteous (Ps. 32:1, 2, 5, 11). There they received blessing and righteousness from the Lord (Ps. 24:3-5).

d. Place of access to the heavenly sanctuary. According to Exodus 25:9 the tabernacle was to be built following the "pattern" (*tabnît*) that the Lord showed Moses on Mount Sinai (cf. verse 40). This concept needs study because it sheds light on the true nature of the Israelite sanctuary. The noun *tabnît* is derived from the verb *bānāh,* "to build." In the OT *tabnît* refers to a structure (Ps. 144:12), a pattern or model for a building (2 Kings 16:10; 1 Chron. 28:11-19), an image or figure of something (Deut. 4:16, 18; Ps. 106:20; Isa. 44:13; Eze. 8:10; 10:8), or a replica (Joshua 22:28). It usually describes a three-dimensional object and in most cases presupposes the existence of an original.

The question is whether *tabnît* in Exodus 25:9 is a model pointing to the heavenly sanctuary as the original. If it can be shown that there was in the Israelite faith an awareness of the existence of a heavenly sanctuary, the use of *tabnît* in Exodus would point to that original. The OT testifies that behind the earthly sanctuary lay a more sublime structure, a dwelling of God in heaven. This heavenly abode was shown to Moses and served as a model for the sanctuary he was to build. References to the heavenly sanctuary are found in the Psalms and the prophetic books. The psalmist affirms that the throne of God is in His heavenly sanctuary (Ps. 11:4) and that from His heavenly dwelling the Lord observes what takes place on earth (Ps. 33:13, 14; 102:19; 113:5, 6). Different terminology is used to refer to God's heavenly abode: "holy temple" (Micah 1:2; Hab. 2:20); "temple" (2 Sam. 22:7; Ps. 18:6); "sanctuary" (Ps. 60:6; 150:1); "dwelling" or "place" (Isa. 18:4; Micah 1:3); and possibly "house" (Ps. 36:8). Since God's dwelling is in heaven it is not strange to find "heavens" *(šāmayim)* used as a designation for His heavenly "sanctuary" (Ps. 20:6; 102:19), as well as "dwelling place" (1 Kings 8:39, 43, 49). Even God's throne is used as a metonym for His heavenly sanctuary (Ps. 11:4; 93:2; Dan. 7:9).

These two sanctuaries, the heavenly and the earthly, were closely related. The earthly provided a point of access to the heavenly (Isa. 6:1-7). The efficacy of the Israelite sanctuary was determined by its relationship with God's celestial temple. Solomon was fully aware of the connection between the two. He prayed that whenever a person made an oath in the Temple in Jerusalem, God would hear from heaven and act (1 Kings 8:31, 32); that whenever the people asked for forgiveness, He would hear from heaven and forgive their sins (verse 34; cf. verses 36, 39, 43). The efficacy of the rituals performed in the earthly sanctuary depended on what took place in the heavenly one.

To that heavenly reality the term *tabnît* points in Exodus 25:9, 40. Since the earthly was modeled after the heavenly, we can point to certain correspondences between the two. First a functional correspondence is suggested. The heavenly sanctuary is the place in the universe where the transcendental God meets with His heavenly creatures. Solomon asked, "Will God indeed dwell on the earth?" His surprising answer was, "Behold, heaven and the highest heaven cannot contain thee; how much less this house which I have built!" (1 Kings 8:27). God cannot be circumscribed by space, yet He condescends to dwell among His creatures, to enter their sphere of action, to dwell on earth and in heaven in order to make Himself accessible to them (cf. verses 29, 30).

This heavenly temple, a meeting place for God and His creatures, is also a center of worship. There God's angels, His heavenly hosts, and "all his works, in all places of his dominion" praise Him as Lord enthroned in the heavens (Ps. 103:19-22). There also He reveals His will to them and they listen and obey (verses 20, 21). The heavenly council praises Him because He is incomparable (Ps. 89:5-7). From the heavenly sanctuary God interacts with His people on earth, not just by listening to their prayers but also by coming down and rescuing them from their distress and the oppression of their enemies (18:6, 14-19; 20:2, 6). More important, from His dwelling in heaven God grants forgiveness to His people (1 Kings 8:30, 34, 49, 50) and teaches them the right way (verse 36).

If the heavenly served somehow as a model for the earthly there must be some type of structural relationship between the two of them. This correspondence should not be defined in terms of the size or the materials used in the construction of the earthly sanctuary, but rather in the architectural concept of the structure. The architectural concept can take different shapes and sizes, and different materials can be used in building the structure, but the underlying concept remains unchanged. The two-apartment structure of the earthly sanctuary points not only to a two-apartment heavenly sanctuary, but also to the two-phased ministry of Christ in that place. Of course, the heavenly sanctuary is infinitely superior to the earthly. This would be expected of a place in the universe that unites the finite with the infinite, the Creator with His creatures, the transcendental One with His creation.

2. Sanctuary, Covenant, and the Nature of Sin/Impurity

a. Covenant and holiness. God's nature is uncompromisingly holy (Lev. 19:2). His holiness defines Him as singular and separated from the world of sin and death that humans experience. To enter into a covenant relationship with God means to be allowed to participate in His holiness (Ex. 19:6). When the covenant was instituted, the law was read to the people and the blood of the sacrificial victims was sprinkled on the altar, representing the presence of God and the people (Ex. 24:5-8). The people were called to imitate God's holiness through obedience to the covenant law (Lev. 19:2; 20:7, 8). Only through sin and impurity could this covenant relationship be threatened or disrupted.

b. Sin and covenant. The vocabulary for sin in the OT is rich (see Sin II. A). Within the context of the sanctuary services three views of sin are particularly important. The first understands sin (*ḥēṭ'*, "sin, fault, missing of the mark") as a failure to perform a particular duty, i.e., to obey the covenant law (Lev. 4:2; Isa. 42:24). The second designates sin (*'āwôn*, "iniquity, perversion") as an activity that is crooked or wrong, a perversion of what is right (e.g., Job 33:27). Third, the true nature of sin is expressed with the word *pešaʿ* (crime, rebellion). The term was used to refer to the breaking of a covenant between two nations (2 Kings 1:1; 8:20, 22). In a theological context *pešaʿ* defines sin as an act of rebellion against the covenant and the Lord of the covenant (Isa. 1:2; Jer. 3:13; Amos 2:4, 6-8). *Pešaʿ* describes humans as possessing a naturally an-

tagonistic spirit toward God. Because they rebelled against Him (Gen. 3), sin is now mysteriously interwoven in human nature (Ps. 51:5; 143:2). The problem is located in the human heart and from there sin springs to life (Jer. 11:8; 17:9; 18:12). This claim of independence from God brings the covenant relation to an end.

c. Impurity and covenant. The main thrust of the cultic regulations revolved around the opposite poles of holiness and uncleanness. Holiness is foreign to humans and to creation in general; it is the exclusive possession of God. He sanctifies objects, places, time, and in a very particular way He sanctifies His people (Lev. 22:9, 16). An improper contact between the holy and the common results in profanation; a contact between the holy/clean and the unclean results in contamination. Impurity and uncleanness threaten practically everything; even the clean can come under their power (Lev. 11:39).

Theologically speaking, "impurity" was a metaphor expressing alienation from God and fellow humans. The unclean person was not to come into contact with other people and was excluded from the sanctuary. Such a person had no meaningful relationships and was, therefore, dead to society. Thus, in Leviticus impurity is fundamentally associated with the sphere of death and disease (Num. 6:6, 7, 11; Lev. 13; 14).

The impure person entered into the sphere of death. Deprived of social interaction with the covenant community and of access to the covenant Lord in the sanctuary, the person became an outcast to the covenant relationship. This understanding of uncleanness suggests that sin and impurity are in essence synonymous. Both terminate the covenant relation through involuntary or voluntary violations of covenant law.

d. God's reaction to sin/impurity. God is not indifferent to the covenant violations of His people. His concern for their loyalty is based on the fact that outside the covenant relationship death reigns. To step outside the covenant is to enter the realm of death, impurity, and alienation from God. The person who breaks away from the Lord incurs guilt and bears his or her own iniquity (Lev. 4:3; 5:2-4). The phrase "to bear one's iniquity or sin" is used in the OT in the sense of being "responsible for one's own iniquity" (Lev. 5:1, 17; 17:16; 19:17; 20:17, 20), and therefore, is liable to punishment (Lev. 7:20, 21; 19:8). God's anger is provoked by the violation of the covenant law (Lev. 26:28). This anger can take the form of redemptive punishment or discipline (verses 14-26). It can also lead to the dissolution of the covenant relationship (verses 27-33), and ultimately to death (cf. Lev. 15:31; 18:24-28).

3. Resolution of the Sin Problem

The resolution of the sin problem among the Israelites was not essentially different from what it had been in the patriarchal religious system. God desired to forgive the sin of His people and showed it through the sacrificial system. The forgiveness (Lev. 4:20) and cleansing (Lev. 12:8) needed by repentant sinners was provided at the sanctuary. To be forgiven, those who were bearing their sin brought a sacrificial victim to the Lord (Lev. 5:5, 6). The sacrificial system functioned within a redemptive and legal frame of reference which took seriously any covenant violation. Within that context, forgiveness was a divine gift, a glorious manifestation of God's love. In essence the Israelite sacrificial system was God's gift of love to the covenant people. To the Israelites God gave the sacrificial blood to use as a means of atonement (Lev. 17:11). Out of His grace He gave the priesthood to Aaron and his sons (Num. 18:7). The Levites, chosen to assist Aaron, were God's gift to the priests (verses 8, 9).

The sanctuary services illustrated the way the Lord dealt with the sin problem. Its services consisted of two ministrations: the daily rituals and the annual service on the Day of Atonement. An exploration of these should provide a better understanding of God's plan for the final resolution of the sin problem through Christ.

a. Daily services. Each day the priests ministered in the court and the holy place of the tabernacle on behalf of God's people. Twice every day a public sacrifice was offered for all (Ex. 29:38-42). In addition, repentant sinners came to the sanctuary bringing their sacrifices, seeking atonement through the mediation of the priest. Different aspects of these sacrifices deserve attention.

(1) Laying on of hands. Hands were laid on every sacrificial animal, but only in Leviticus 16:21, where sin and impurity are transferred to the goat for Azazel, is the ritual explicitly connected with the transference of sin. Laying on of hands was also practiced on noncultic occasions to express the idea of transfer and, in some cases, substitution (Lev. 24:14; Num. 8:10; 27:18-23). In the daily sacrifices the repentant sinner transferred to the victim his or her sin/impurity. This ritual seems to have been accompanied, at least in some cases, by a confession of sin on the part of the penitent (Lev. 5:5, 6; 16:21).

(2) Slaughtering the animal. The sacrificial victim was usually killed by the offerer, although sometimes the priest slaughtered it (Lev. 1:14, 15; 5:8). Sin and penalty cannot be separated from each other. Sin was transferred to the sacrifice as was its penalty.

(3) Ritual of the eating of flesh. According to the Levitical legislation, a portion of the flesh of the sin offering belonged to the priests and was to be eaten in a holy place (Lev. 6:17, 18, 25, 26; 7:6, 7). By eating the flesh of the sacrificial victim the priest bore the sins of the people and thus made atonement (Lev. 10:17). This vicarious act did not affect his holiness. The sinner came to the sanctuary bearing sin and transferred it to the sacrificial victim. Finally the priest carried the sin and brought it before the Lord, thus making atonement for the sinner (Ex. 28:38). Whenever a priest brought a sacrifice for his own sin, he was not allowed to eat the flesh of the sacrifice. He could not bear his own sin with-

out dying (Lev. 22:9).

(4) Blood ritual. The blood of some sacrificial victims was taken into the holy place by the priest and sprinkled seven times in front of the veil (Lev. 4:6). Sprinkling could mean consecration (Ex. 29:21; Lev. 8:11) or cleansing (Lev. 14:7, 51; 16:19; Num. 8:7). Whenever the flesh was not eaten the blood was taken to the holy place, making these two rituals interchangeable. Their meaning was the same: sin was brought before the Lord, transferred to the sanctuary.

Leviticus 17:11 reads, "For the life *[nepeš]* of the flesh is in the blood; and I have given it for you upon the altar to make atonement for your souls *[nepeš]; for it is the blood that makes atonement, by reason of the life [nepheš]."* God assigned to the blood of the sacrificial animal an expiatory function on behalf of the people, accepting it in exchange for the life of the person. This interpretation of the blood ritual holds for all sacrificial blood (verse 8).The expiatory function of blood as life is limited in verse 11 to its use on the altar. Blood belongs exclusively to God and by returning the blood of the sacrifice to Him on the altar, sinners were allowed to transfer their sin by means of a mediating priest to the sanctuary. That is, for the time being, the sanctuary assumed their sin and guilt. God accepted the sacrifice as a substitute for the sinner. In anticipation of the ultimate offering for sin, the mediated blood atoned and expiated the sin of the offerer.

(5) Expiatory value of all sacrifices. All sacrifices had an expiatory function, but the expiatory force of the sacrifice was determined by the blood ritual and by what happened to the flesh of the victim. The blood ritual of the sin offering was complex because its primary function was to make atonement for the sinner. The blood of the guilt offering was tossed or scattered on the sides of the altar of burnt offering and the priest ate the flesh. Restitution and compensation were also required in the blood ritual. The blood of the burnt offering—a multi-purpose sacrifice—was tossed on the sides of the altar, and the whole sacrificial victim was burnt on the altar. The main function of the peace offering was not expiatorial, but the laying on of hands and the tossing of the blood on the sides of the altar suggested an expiatorial aspect.

Since all sacrifices established or strengthened good relations between God and the individual, every sacrifice had, to some extent, an expiatory function. More than any other book of the OT, Leviticus indicates that humans are essentially impure, never free to approach God by themselves. Every bloody sacrifice dealt with this existential problem, even when the primary function of the sacrifice may not have been expiatory.

(6) The daily burnt offerings. There was always a burnt offering on the altar on behalf of the people of Israel (Ex. 29:38-42; Num. 28:3-8), suggesting that the daily acceptance of the nation by God was made possible through the sacrificial lamb on the altar. As a nation Israel depended on the constant expiatory power of this sacrifice.

(7) Transfer and contamination. There is a sense in which the transference of sin, in connection with the daily sacrifices, did not contaminate the victim, the priest, or the sanctuary. The illegal violation of the sanctity of the sanctuary was a contamination, but in that case the sinner was to die (e.g., Lev. 15:31; 20:2, 3; Num. 19:13). Sin was transferred to the sacrifice, to the priest, and to the sanctuary; but they all remained holy. Here we confront a paradox. The person who took the flesh of the sin offering outside the camp to burn it was to wash his clothes and bathe his body before returning to the camp (Lev. 16:27, 28). Yet, the flesh of the animal, described as "most holy" (Lev. 6:24), was a source of contamination. The ashes of the red heifer (Num. 19:1-10) were mixed with water and sprinkled for cleansing on a person who touched a dead body (verses 11-13). Yet, the person who did the sprinkling was contaminated (verse 21). Cleanness and uncleanness were together in this rite. Some-

thing similar happened with the blood: in some respects it was a source of impurity (Lev. 12:7), in others it was a means of purification.

In the context of atonement, holiness and sin, life and death, purity and impurity, are brought together in an unfathomable, paradoxical relation. The Lord brings them together, and out of this encounter atonement and forgiveness emerge victorious. The holy instrument came into contact with the unclean and yet remained holy, providing a remarkable prefiguration of the mystery of Christ's sacrifice (2 Cor. 5:21).

The daily services contributed to the resolution of the sin problem by providing for the individual and the nation a daily means of atonement. Through sacrifice and priestly mediation, the sin of the penitent was transferred to the sacrificial victim. God allowed the Israelites to return blood to Him on the altar, through the ministry of the priest, as a substitute for the life of the sinner. God assumed responsibility for sin in the sense that He was willing to bear the iniquity ('āwôn), the transgression (pešaʻ), and the sin (ḥēṭ') of His people through forgiveness (Ex. 34:7).

b. Annual service: Day of Atonement. Once a year the high priest had access to the Most Holy Place (Lev. 16). On this day the Israelite sanctuary service reached its climax and ultimate goal. The purpose of the Day of Atonement included several closely related elements.

(1) Final cleansing of the people. The sanctuary was to be cleansed "because of the uncleannesses of the people of Israel, and because of their transgressions, all their sins" (verse 16; cf. verses 21, 30, 34). The accumulation of these terms for sin designates all kinds of sin, meaning that the sins expiated on the Day of Atonement were not limited to any one category of wrong. The rituals of the Day of Atonement purified the sanctuary and the altars (Lev. 16:16, 18; Ex. 30:10), yet, those rituals benefited the people because their cleansing was final. This is suggested in Leviticus 16:33: "He shall make atonement for the sanc-

tuary, and he shall make atonement for the tent of meeting and for the altar, and he shall make atonement for the priests and for all the people of the assembly." The space "contaminated" was the sanctuary, and atonement was made to cleanse it. But since through the daily services the sin and impurity of the Israelites were transferred to the sanctuary, its removal on the Day of Atonement made their cleansing final.

(2) God judges Israel. In the sanctuary God functioned as the judge of His people. In the Psalms, which were used in the temple services, God is often praised as judge of His people and of the world (Ps. 9:19). He is the one who judges Israel, and the psalmist is not afraid to be judged by Him (Ps. 7:7, 8). As judge God searches the minds and hearts of the righteous (verse 9; 139:1, 23). It is God who vindicates the righteous in the judgment (Ps. 17:2; 26:1, 2; 35:24; 43:1).

The Day of Atonement was a holy convocation, a day when the people were to afflict or humble themselves (Lev. 23:27). The same verb (humble) appears with fasting in Isaiah 58:3, 5, but humbling oneself probably included more than fasting (cf. Ps. 35:13). Fasting expressed the individual's dependence on and need of God. On the Day of Atonement the Israelites felt and expressed their dependence on God and their desire to preserve the covenant relationship with the Lord, because only He could make their cleansing final.

This day was also a day of rest, a ceremonial sabbath during which no work was to be done (Lev. 16:31). All Israelites were to humble themselves before the Lord, totally dependent on God and abstaining from all secular activity. The resting of the people contrasts with the activity of the high priest in the sanctuary. While they rested, he was active on their behalf before the Lord. The final cleansing they could not accomplish through their actions, the priest would accomplish for them.

On the same day, the Lord judged the Israelites. He evaluated whether or not they had humbled themselves, whether or not they were really depending on His cleansing power and forgiving grace (Lev. 23:29). He also evaluated whether or not they were resting in Him (verse 30). Those who did not afflict themselves and did not rest in the Lord were found guilty and could no longer be part of God's people (verse 30). The individual who, through pride and self-reliance, rejected God's atoning grace made useless the benefit of the daily services.

(3) Vindication of God and His sanctuary. Through the daily sacrifices, the confessed sins of repentant sinners were transferred to God's sanctuary. Sin and impurity were only allowed to come into the very presence of God to make atonement for them. But not even atoned-for sins could stay in God's holy dwelling indefinitely. As long as those sins remained, the resolution of the sin problem was not yet final. The Day of Atonement proclaimed that holiness and sin, purity and impurity, had nothing in common. Sin and impurity were foreign elements permitted by God to remain temporarily in His presence in order to preserve those whom He loved. But at an appropriate moment God would remove from His presence those elements and those who chose to identify themselves with sin/impurity.

On the Day of Atonement God returned sin/impurity to its true source and originator. The second goat from the people was for Azazel; that is, it represented Azazel (Lev. 16:8). While the meaning of this name is not clear, the parallelism between "for the Lord" and "for Azazel" indicates that Azazel was a personal being, probably a demonic figure. Azazel comes into the picture after Aaron finishes the cleansing of the sanctuary. This goat is not involved in the expiatory rituals of the Day of Atonement. This goat bore all the iniquities of the people of Israel (verse 22; *nāśā' 'āwôn*). Here the phrase does not mean to bear the sin of someone vicariously, for only here is the phrase "to bear all their iniquities" followed by a destination: a solitary land. The expression means "to carry iniquity away" to the wilderness and has no expiatory overtones. The rite of the scapegoat was a rite of elimination of sin/impurity, not a sacrificial act.

The placing of sin/impurity on the goat representing Azazel indicated the demonic origin of sin/impurity and returned it to its place of origin. This demonic power, far from being a threat to the Lord, is controlled by Him. While Israel rests, the Lord reveals His power over evil and all demonic forces. The Day of Atonement is, therefore, a proclamation of God's sovereignty and of the supremacy of holiness over sin/impurity. This undoubtedly points to the consummation of God's redemptive plan for the human race through Christ.

The daily and annual services in the Israelite sanctuary were intertwined in the resolution of the sin problem in the OT. Instead of removing the sinner from His presence, the Lord cleansed the sinner in order to preserve the covenant relationship. In the daily services the sin/impurity of the penitent was transferred, through a sacrificial substitute, to the sanctuary, and the person was left at peace with God. Once a year the daily atonement met its consummation in the removal of that sin/impurity from the presence of God, making the daily cleansing final. On the Day of Atonement God examined the quality of the faith commitment of His people. Those who kept their daily faith relationship with the Lord were preserved; those who violated and rejected it were separated permanently from the covenant community. God showed Himself to be a loving and powerful God, able to save and to overcome the forces of sin. Thus the OT sacrificial system outlined in shadows and types the plan of redemption centered in the coming Messianic Redeemer.

II. Christ's Priesthood in the NT

A. *Limitations of the Typical System*

This examination of the typological fulfillment of the sacrificial system in Christ concentrates on Hebrews and Revelation. But since the sacrificial interpretation of the death of Christ is found throughout the NT, other texts also will be examined. The typical system had serious limitations, the recognition of which is not merely a NT phenomenon. The psalmist knew that it was impossible for humans to redeem themselves, to pay a price for their own lives (Ps. 49:7). Only God could pay the ransom (verse 15). Sacrifice was only the expression of a contrite heart seeking forgiveness from God (Ps. 51:16-19). The OT pointed to a time when those limitations would be removed through the perfect sacrifice of the Servant of the Lord (Isa. 52:3–53:12), described as the perfect Lamb who died a vicarious sacrificial death (verse 11).

The NT identifies the limitations of the old system in order to magnify the greatness of the new. Thus the covenant with Israel is seen in Hebrews as having a limited temporal function (8:7-13). The Israelite sanctuary was only a shadow, a type, a copy, of the original sanctuary in heaven, not the true one (verses 2, 5). The Levitical priesthood was inadequate because it could not attain perfection (Heb. 7:11), that is, it could not take away the sin problem. To illustrate: The typical Levitical priesthood could only role-play the genuine priestly ministry of Christ, who through His sacrifice and mediation could indeed "put away sin" (Heb. 9:26; 10:4).

B. *Superiority of the New Order*

The pastoral concern of the Epistle to the Hebrews is expressed in expositions and exhortations. The faith of the believers to whom the letter was addressed seems to have deteriorated so that they were attracted once more to Jewish faith and practices. The author of Hebrews exhorts them to remain faithful to the faith they once accepted (3:13, 14; 4:1; 12:12, 13). Throughout the letter the writer argues for the superiority of the work of Christ over the ritual, sacrificial system, emphasizing its ineffectiveness to purge sin and the repetitious nature of its services over against the once-and-for-all sacrifice of Christ "to put away sin" (9:26). Hebrews contrasts the old and new in order to demonstrate that through Christ a new and superior exodus has taken place. The achievements of the new exodus are far better than those of the old, and the redemption it has initiated is eternal, that is to say, unrepeatable, because its benefits are permanent.

1. Better Covenant

The new system established through Christ brought into existence the new covenant announced by Jeremiah (Jer. 31:31-34; Heb. 8:8-12). The new covenant is superior to the old because its mediator is the Son of God (Heb. 8:6; 9:15). He who is human (Heb. 2:5-18) and divine (Heb. 1:1-4) is able to bring God and humans into a covenant relationship. He is also the sacrificial victim through whose blood the covenant was ratified (Heb. 12:24; 9:15-18). Christ is called the "surety of a better covenant" (Heb. 7:22) because He guarantees the permanency of the new covenant. The contrast between the two covenants leads the apostle into a discussion of the sanctuaries under each of the covenants (Heb. 8; 9).

2. Better Sanctuary

a. Heavenly sanctuary in Hebrews. The author of Hebrews follows the Exodus pattern: redemption, covenant, and sanctuary. The sanctuary of the new covenant is superior because it is heavenly (Heb. 8:1, 2; 9:24). Here Hebrews relies on Exodus 25:9, 40, finding there a reference to God's true heavenly sanctuary, which antedates the earthly. The heavenly sanctuary served as a model for the earthly, which could be called the antitype (Heb. 9:24, Gr. *antitypos*). Inasmuch as the tabernacle is a copy of the original, it is inferior, described as a "shadow" of the heavenly. As a copy and shadow, the earthly sanctuary pointed to the heavenly one and so testified to its own transitoriness (verse 11).

In Hebrews the heavenly sanctuary is real; Christ entered there after His ascension (4:14-16; 6:19, 20; 9:24; 10:12) and is performing a priestly work there (7:27). For the apostle, Christ is a divine person who took on humanity and became one of us (2:14), suffered under the pressure of temptations (5:7, 8), died on the cross (12:2), ascended to heaven (4:14), and entered into the heavenly sanctuary (9:24). For the author of Hebrews the reality of all these experiences is unquestionable.

Hebrews, following the teachings of the OT, argues for a real sanctuary in heaven. Passages that seem to suggest a metaphorical interpretation of the heavenly sanctuary, under closer scrutiny support a literal interpretation. The noun *ta hagia* (the sanctuary) in Hebrews designates the sanctuary as a whole and not one of its two apartments. This is suggested particularly by the fact that *ta hagia* is used in parallelism with "tent" (*skēnē;* 8:2), which in the OT designates the tabernacle. Moreover, when the author of Hebrews refers to the holy place, *hagia* is used without the article; and when the reference is to the Most Holy Place, *hagia hagiōn* is employed. This emphasis on the earthly sanctuary as a copy of the heavenly, coupled with a discussion of the two apartments of the earthly (9:1-7), suggests that the author of Hebrews understood that the heavenly sanctuary was a bipartite structure. However, the idea is not developed, since the apostle's main interest is to make clear that the heavenly sanctuary, where Christ ministers, is superior to the earthly. (See Appendix A.)

b. Heavenly sanctuary in Revelation. The heavenly sanctuary is mentioned a number of times in Revelation. In 14:17 the *naos* (temple) is "in heaven"; in 11:19 the language is even more precise: "God's temple in heaven." "Temple" and "tabernacle" *(skēnē)* are used as synonyms in 15:5 and are also described as being "in heaven." This two-apartment structure contains a holy place with lamps (4:5) and an altar of incense (8:3, 4); it also has a Most Holy Place with the ark of the covenant (11:19). God's throne is in the sanctuary (4:2-8; 7:15). Salvation (7:10) and intercession (8:2-4) are accomplished there; because of that, the temple is the object of attack of the evil forces (13:6). While the heavenly sanctuary is described in the colorful language and imagery of the earthly types, Revelation 4 and 5 make clear that the earthly sanctuary was but a pale copy of the vastly superior and glorious heavenly one. At the end of the book we are informed that in the New Jerusalem there is no temple (21:22); the whole city serves as God's tabernacle, the place where He dwells with His people (verse 3; cf. 7:15).

3. Better Priesthood

The heart of the message of Hebrews is that "we have such a high priest, one who is seated at the right hand of the throne of the Majesty in heaven" (8:1). From the beginning of the Epistle Christ's priestly work is announced (1:3); reference is made to it in each succeeding chapter until its full development in 7:1-28.

a. Christ's priesthood and the Aaronic priesthood. Hebrews shows that Jesus met the basic qualifications for the Levitical priesthood far better than did the Aaronic priests. The typological significance of their priesthood found antitypical fulfillment in Him.

High Priestly Requirements

Aaronic Priesthood
1. Must be human (Heb. 5:1)
2. Must be appointed by God (verse 4)
3. Must sympathize with sinners through self-control (verse 2; *metriopatheō,* "moderate one's passions")

4. Must have something to offer: blood of animals (verses 1, 2)

5. Must officiate in a sanctuary: an earthly one (Heb. 9:1-7)

Christ's Priesthood

1. Christ was human (Heb. 2:14) as well as divine (1:1-3)

2. Christ was appointed by His Father (5:5, 6)

3. Christ sympathizes (*sympatheō,* "be compassionate") with sinners (4:15)

4. Christ offered Himself as a sacrifice (7:27)

5. Christ officiates in the heavenly sanctuary (8:2)

b. Christ's priesthood and Melchizedek. While the Aaronic priesthood prefigured Christ's priestly activity, the NT leaves no doubt that the new priesthood would do away with the old. The old covenant would be replaced by the new, the typical sacrifices would be concluded by the true, and the Levitical priesthood would give place to the order of Melchizedek (Heb. 7:11, 12, 18, 19; 8:13; 10:3-10). Thus, the priesthood of Christ was not only the antitype of the Aaronic priesthood, but also the fulfillment of the Messianic prophecy found in Psalm 110:4, in the light of which Hebrews examines Genesis 14:17-20. In the discussion of the priesthood of Melchizedek, the superiority of Christ's priesthood is demonstrated (Heb. 7:1-28).

The incident narrated in Genesis 14 provides information to show that the priesthood of Melchizedek is superior to that of Aaron. This is demonstrated first, by noting that Abraham gave his tithe to Melchizedek (Heb. 7:2, 4-6). Second, by blessing Abraham, Melchizedek showed himself superior to Abraham (verses 6, 7). Third, the priesthood of Melchizedek remains forever (verse 3). In Hebrews Melchizedek foreshadows the priesthood of Christ (verse 3).

The prediction of Jesus' priesthood according to the order of Melchizedek indicated that the Aaronic priesthood was transitory (verses 11-14), and perfection—that is, salvation from sin—was not possible through the Aaronic priesthood. This meant that God intended to change the priestly law, making it possible for one who was not a descendant of Aaron to become high priest. Once the new High Priest after the order of Melchizedek arrived, the typical priesthood would end (verses 15-19). Christ became priest, not on the basis of genealogical ties, but by a divine declaration. His priesthood is permanent because His life is indestructible.

In reality Jesus Christ is the only true priestly mediator between God and the human race. The priesthoods of Aaron and Melchizedek serve only as role models of Christ's effective ministry. "For there is one God, and there is one mediator between God and men, the man Christ Jesus, who gave himself as a ransom for all, the testimony to which was borne at the proper time" (1 Tim. 2:5, 6).

The superiority of Christ's priesthood is based on its establishment by a divine oath. It is also superior because "he holds his priesthood permanently, . . . for ever" (Heb. 7:24). His priesthood is, therefore, unchangeable. Finally, Christ is a superior priest because He is sinless and does not have to offer sacrifices to expiate His own sins (verses 26, 27). His ministry is totally on behalf of others (verse 25).

4. Better Blood/Sacrifice

The limitations of the Israelite economy became most evident in the area of the effectiveness of the sacrificial system. None of the daily sacrifices had the power to take away sin and impurity; neither did the Day of Atonement sacrifices (Heb. 10:4). Christ's blood is superior because it deals with human uncleanness (sin) and alienation from God by cleansing the conscience (Heb. 9:14) and perfecting the worshiper (Heb. 10:14). This perfection is to be understood as the removal of all obstacles that hinder a person's access to God. The blood of Jesus cleanses from sin (1 John 1:7; Rev. 1:5; 7:14), in a once-and-for-all sacrifice (Heb. 7:27; 10:12).

III. Christ's Ministry in the Heavenly Sanctuary

A. Inauguration of the Heavenly Sanctuary

The ministration of the Aaronic priesthood in the holy place of the sanctuary every day and in the Most Holy Place once a year typified the work of Christ in the heavenly sanctuary, depicting two aspects of Christ's mediation within salvation history. References to the moment when Christ began His priestly work in the heavenly sanctuary are found in Daniel, Hebrews, and Revelation.

1. Daniel and the Inauguration of the Heavenly Sanctuary

The Messianic prophecy recorded in Daniel 9:24-27 was given as an answer to Daniel's prayer on behalf of his people and the city of Jerusalem. The prophet was informed that 70 weeks of grace were to be granted to Israel. This period, divided into seven weeks, 62 weeks, and one week, respectively, is prophetic and represents, following the year-day principle of prophetic interpretation, 490 years. (See Apocalyptic II. D; Judgment III. B. 1. a.) The most important aspect of this prophecy is the coming of the Messiah, who is anointed after 69 weeks and dies in the middle of the seventieth week. Through His death transgression comes to an end by the righteousness He provides. When the prophecy is fulfilled ("sealed"), sin is brought to an end because divine forgiveness is now available. Iniquity has been atoned for and a Most Holy Place is anointed (verse 24).

The phrase "most holy" is never applied to a person in the OT. When it refers to the Most Holy Place it takes the article, which does not appear here. In the absence of the article "most holy" refers to the sanctuary and/or to things connected with it. The idea of anointing a "most holy place" corresponds to the anointing of the earthly sanctuary (e.g., Ex. 30:26-29; 40:9-11). Daniel refers to the anointing or dedication of the heavenly sanctuary when Christ would begin His priestly work.

This unparalleled Messianic prophecy predicts the dedication of the heavenly sanctuary using terminology employed in the dedication of the earthly sanctuary. In addition, the chronology of the prophecy itself points to that event. It begins with the anointing of the Messiah. His death, which brings in forgiveness, puts an end to the sacrificial system (Dan. 9:27). Finally, the heavenly sanctuary where the Messiah would carry out His priestly work would be anointed. According to this prophecy, all this would take place near the end of the 70 prophetic weeks.

2. Hebrews and the Inauguration of the Heavenly Sanctuary

Hebrews contrasts the old Exodus with the new and shows special interest in the initiation of the religious institutions. The making of the old covenant (9:18-20) and of its earthly sanctuary (verses 1-10, 21) are particularly mentioned. The author is also interested in the initiation of Christ's priestly work in the heavenly sanctuary that inaugurated a way of access to God (10:20). The verb *enkainízō* means "to dedicate, to inaugurate, to renew," and is used in verse 18 to refer to the inauguration of the first covenant. Another reference to the inauguration of Christ's ministry in the heavenly sanctuary occurs in verses 11, 12, where the verb "to inaugurate" is not used, but we find concepts associated with it. *Ta hagia* (sanctuary) refers here to the entire sanctuary and not just to the Most Holy Place (see Appendix A).

Christ is described as arriving, for the first time after His ascension, at the heavenly sanctuary and entering it after obtaining eternal redemption. The Greek construction of verse 12 suggests that Christ first secured redemption and then entered into the sanctuary. On the cross Christ obtained redemption; in the heavenly sanctuary He is applying the benefits of His redemptive work to those who repent of their sins and believe. As in times of old, access to the sanctuary was preceded by a sacrificial act of redemption. The blood of Christ is contrasted in verse 12 with the blood of "goats and calves," used in the inauguration of the earthly sanctuary. Christ's blood makes possible the initiation of His high priestly ministry.

Since the heavenly sanctuary preexisted the earthly one, the inauguration was not so much of the sanctuary as of Christ's ministry. God had heretofore forgiven human beings on the basis of Christ's coming death and priesthood (Rom. 3:25; Heb. 9:15). After His ascension, forgiveness was based on a completed sacrifice. This inauguration marked the beginning of Christ's application of the merits of His already-past life and atoning death.

3. Revelation and the Inauguration of the Heavenly Sanctuary

The scene described in Revelation 4 and 5 is a heavenly one (4:1); the place is the heavenly sanctuary. God's throne is there (4:2); seven lamps are located there (4:5); bowls full of incense are mentioned (5:8); and a Lamb is present (5:6). One of the purposes of this vision is to throw light on the enthronement of Christ as king and high priest in the heavenly sanctuary. In the first vision of the exalted Lord (Rev. 1:12-16), Christ is described as a high priest (verse 13; cf. Ex. 28:4) walking among seven lampstands. He is also described as a king sitting with His Father on the throne (3:21).

In Revelation 5 the Lord is sitting on His throne with a scroll in His right hand that no one can open (verses 1-4). God's throne is surrounded by His heavenly council and the angelic hosts. Then the "Lion of the tribe of Judah, the Root of David," appears (verse 5; cf. Isa. 11:1). He is described as a slain lamb because even though He is the exalted Lord his sacrifice retains its efficacy (verse 6). He is worthy to receive the scroll and open it (verses 9, 10), and to rule over the nations and their destiny (verse 13). He is worthy to take His position as king and priest in the heav-

enly sanctuary because He died to pay the ransom for the world (verses 9, 12). Surrounded by the praises of heavenly beings, the Son is enthroned as king and high priest. From this point on in Revelation, the Lamb is associated with God on His throne (see 22:3).

B. Christ's Mediatorial Work: Daily Services

1. Mediation and the Daily Services

In Hebrews Christ's sitting at the right hand of God (10:12, 13) and His intercessory work are described in the context of the daily services of the earthly sanctuary (7:27; 10:11). He entered the heavenly sanctuary to minister on behalf of His people (6:20; 9:24). At His ascension He began to fulfill the typical function of the daily services in the earthly sanctuary. Paul understood this priestly work of Christ as mediatorial (Rom. 8:34; 1 Tim. 2:5). Daniel saw the Messiah, the Prince of the Host (cf. Joshua 5:13-15), performing the daily services (the *tāmîd*) in the heavenly sanctuary (Dan. 8:11, 12).

In Revelation every one of the visionary cycles of the book is introduced by a sanctuary scene. Three of these deserve special mention here. The first introduces the messages to the seven churches (1:10-20). The exalted Christ appears to John as a high priest walking among seven lampstands representing the seven churches. Through His ministry on behalf of the churches He comforted and encouraged believers. The mention of lamps suggests ministry in the holy place. The second sanctuary scene, already discussed, introduces the cycle of the seven seals (4; 5) and depicts Christ's enthronement as king and high priest. The third scene serves as an introduction to the seven trumpets (8:2-5). Here John sees another angel ministering before the altar of incense in the holy place of the heavenly sanctuary (verse 3). This angel is probably Christ because, according to Exodus 30:7, 8, the responsibility of burning incense on the altar rested primarily on the high priest. Before the altar of incense, the angel mediates the prayers of the saints by mingling them with incense burning on the live coals on the altar (Rev. 8:3). This is a description of Christ's ongoing ministry in the heavenly sanctuary, presenting on behalf of repentant sinners His sinless life and atoning death, symbolized as sweet-smelling incense.

2. Specific Aspects of Christ's Mediation

Christ's work encompasses more than His ministry on behalf of humanity. Through His death He reconciled to God "all things, whether on earth or in heaven" (Col. 1:20). This cosmic reconciliation will reach its consummation at the end of the great controversy, before the destruction of the evil powers, when every creature in heaven and on earth will "confess that Jesus Christ is Lord, to the glory of God the Father" (Phil. 2:10, 11). Meanwhile, through Christ God preserves the universe and keeps it together (Col. 1:17; Heb. 1:3).

God revealed Himself in a unique way in Christ (John 1:14). Through the Son God speaks (Heb. 1:2) and reveals His will to the Christian community (Heb. 12:25). His speaking also takes the form of a blessing. Through Christ God has blessed believers "with every spiritual blessing in the heavenly places" (Eph. 1:3; cf. Gal. 3:14).

Through Christ's sacrificial death human beings are brought to God and continue to have access to Him (Eph. 2:18; 1 Peter 3:18). Christ appeared before God in the heavenly sanctuary as our forerunner; thus we are free to approach God in full confidence through Him (Eph. 3:12; Heb. 10:20).

Forgiveness is mediated from God to humanity through Christ (Eph. 4:32). Through Christ repentance reaches the human heart (Acts 5:31). Even after conversion, sin besets Christians, making it possible for them to fall. In such cases there is an Advocate who can represent the sinner before God and through whom one can be forgiven (1 John 2:1, 2).

Uncleanness is the natural condition of the human heart. In order to restore unity between God and humanity, cleansing is necessary. This cleansing, necessary whenever believers sin (Heb. 9:14), is available through Christ (1 John 1:9). Believers were once sanctified through the blood of Christ (Heb. 10:29), but Christ continues to establish their hearts in holiness (1 Thess. 3:13). They are called, like ancient Israel, to be holy because God is holy (1 Peter 1:15, 16). But that holiness reaches Christians through the work of Christ in the heavenly sanctuary.

Christians are in constant need of mercy and grace (Heb. 4:16). Because of Christ's priestly work believers can "draw near to the throne of grace" to receive these benefits. The priests drew near to God when performing their services. Christians now have the same privilege through Christ who mediates God's love through these benefits.

Through Christ God cleansed those who believed, that they might serve Him (Heb. 9:14). Christ, as high priest, is always willing to provide the assistance needed by those who are tempted (Heb. 2:18). The power to overcome reaches them through Christ, who equips them with whatever they may need in order to do God's will, working in them that which pleases God (Eph. 2:10; Heb. 13:20, 21). Through the blood of the Lamb they can overcome evil (Rev. 12:11). Through Christ, His followers receive the Spirit who enables them to be victorious over the sinful nature and to obey God's law (Rom. 8:2-4, 9, 14).

The book of Revelation describes Christ as a mediator presenting the prayers of the saints before God (8:2-4). Jesus told the disciples to present their prayers to God in His name and assured them that God would listen and answer (John 16:23, 24). The exalted Lord is the only channel of communication between God and the believer. Every aspect of the Christian experience is mediated by Christ, who lives to intercede on behalf of those who approach God through Him. This aspect of the ministry of Christ will continue until He leaves the heavenly sanctuary at the Second Coming.

C. Christ's Work of Judgment:
The Day of Atonement

1. The Day of Atonement in Hebrews

There are in Hebrews some clear references to the Israelite Day of Atonement. In Hebrews 9:25, 26 and 10:1-10 the sacrifice of Christ and those offered on that day are contrasted. Christ's sacrifice is described as unrepeatable and His blood as superior to the sacrifice offered by the high priest in the earthly sanctuary on the Day of Atonement. Christ does not need to offer Himself again and again (9:25), since He did it "once for all" (10:10, 11). The comparison is not between the ministry of the high priest in the Most Holy Place and Christ's work in the heavenly sanctuary, but between the effectiveness of Christ's blood and the limited function of animal blood in the old system. The purpose of the references to the Day of Atonement in Hebrews is to show the superiority of the sacrifice of our Lord.

Hebrews 9:23 is significant in the discussion of the typological meaning of the Day of Atonement. Scholars have been surprised by the statement that heavenly things need to be purified. However, it is not difficult to interpret this passage once it is recognized as a reference to the Day of Atonement. Here is a clear indication that Christ performs in the heavenly sanctuary a work of cleansing that is the typological equivalent of the work of the high priest in the earthly sanctuary on the Day of Atonement. The passage does not state that this cleansing takes place immediately after Christ's ascension, but that the heavenly sanctuary is also in need of cleansing. This typology is not developed, neither is the time element discussed. Nevertheless, the typological connection is significant because it recognizes that Christ's mediatorial work encompasses the theological content of the annual services of the Israelite sanctuary. In addition, the context suggests that the cleansing of the heavenly sanctuary is connected with Christ's death on the cross as sin bearer (verses 26, 28) and with His work before the Father on behalf of His people (verse 25).

2. The Day of Atonement in Daniel

With its emphasis on cleansing, judgment, and vindication, the apocalyptic visions of Daniel project the imagery of the Day of Atonement to the very end of earth's history. The cleansing is connected directly to the heavenly sanctuary and to the work of the Messiah as king and priest. The visions introduce the time element, making it possible for the reader to identify a specific moment within salvation history when the Messiah would begin His work of final cleansing, judgment, and vindication in the heavenly dwelling of God.

a. Daniel 8:13, 14: Day of Atonement. In Daniel 8:13, 14—a part of the vision beginning with 8:1—the prophet uses Israelite sanctuary language to describe the work of the little horn and the work of the Prince of hosts, Christ, in the heavenly sanctuary. Thus a linguistic and theological relationship is established between this passage and the book of Leviticus. The symbols used to represent political powers are a ram and a he-goat (verses 20, 21), both clean animals used as sacrificial victims. The word "horn" has cultic overtones (cf. Lev. 4:7), as do "truth" (Dan. 8:12; cf. Mal. 2:6), and "transgression" (Dan. 8:12; Lev. 16:16). Several terms for "sanctuary" are used: *mākôn* (place, Dan. 8:11: designates God's earthly [Isa. 4:5] and heavenly sanctuaries [1 Kings 8:39]); *miqdāš* and *qōdeš* (sanctuary, Dan. 8:11, 13). In the tabernacle context the word "hosts" refers to the Levitical guard (Num. 4:3, 23). The verb "taken away" (Dan. 8:11) is also used in Leviticus to designate the removing of the parts of the sacrifices that belonged to God (e.g., Lev. 4:10). The heavenly beings in Daniel 8:13 are "holy ones," establishing another connection with sanctuary terminology. The *tāmîd*, "the continual," designates the daily work of the priest in the holy place. Since the "Prince of hosts" is a heavenly being (cf. Joshua 5:14) the sanctuary in Daniel 8:9-14 must be the heavenly one.

The main concern of this vision is the attitude of the little horn toward the sanctuary and the priestly work of the Prince (verses 11, 12). It attacks the host of heaven, defeats them (verse 10), and goes after the Prince and the sanctuary. This spiritual attack is described in military terms. The *tāmîd* is taken away from the Prince, and the foundation/place of the sanctuary is cast down and rejected. Then, in a spirit of rebellion/transgression (verse 12), the little horn sets up its own force to control the *tāmîd*. The "truth" associated with the sanctuary is obscured by this anti-God power (cf. Dan. 7:25). The cultic language used by Daniel makes it clear that the little horn does not contaminate the sanctuary; the attack on the sanctuary profanes it (cf. Dan. 11:31), but does not contaminate it. The sanctuary is treated by the horn-power as a common place. The little horn somehow affects the Prince's *tāmîd*, or continual mediation in the holy place. The question of the horn's interference with the mediatorial work of the Prince in the Most Holy Place is addressed in Daniel 8:13, 14. Here two difficulties surface: the debated meaning of *niṣdaq* and the length of the 2300 days.

(1) The meaning of niṣdaq *in Daniel 8:14.* The verb *niṣdaq* has been translated in different ways: The sanctuary will be "cleansed," "restored," "reconsecrated," "restored to its rightful state," or "will emerge victorious." Two considerations make it difficult to decide how to translate this verb: (a) The verbal form employed by Daniel is not used anywhere else in the OT; (b) only here does this verb relate to a physical structure. However, these problems are not insurmountable. The primary use of the root *ṣādaq* is legal, designating the restoration of the legal rights of a person falsely accused of a crime (Ps. 7:8; 9:4; Isa. 50:8, 9). The righteous are declared innocent and the accusers condemned (2 Chron. 6:23; Deut. 25:1). This legal use includes the idea of salvation. God's righteousness is His saving action on behalf of His people (see Ps. 98:2-9; Isa. 1:27, 28). Righteousness as salvation implies the destruction of the oppressor, resulting in the restoration of harmony and order (see Ps. 71:2-4; 143:11, 12).

The root *ṣādaq* is closely associated with the sanctuary services. In Leviticus "purity," obtained through atonement, was required for access to the sanctuary. In the book of Psalms "righteousness" *(ṣᵉdāqāh),* granted as a gift from the sanctuary (24:3-5), was required. The righteous were not only those who remained loyal to the Lord (Ps. 15:2-4), but also those whose sins had been forgiven (32:1, 2, 11). The word "righteousness" describes the gates of the temple (118:19), the priestly dress (132:9), and the sacrifices offered to the Lord (4:5; 51:19). The root *ṣādaq* is also used as a synonym for purity (Job 4:17; 17:9; Ps. 18:20). Isaiah 53:11 illustrates this meaning: "By his knowledge shall the righteous one, my servant [the Messiah], make many to be accounted righteous [*ṣādaq,* declared righteous]; and he shall bear their iniquities." The many were declared righteous not because they were righteous or clean, but because the Servant removed their sin, their uncleanness, by bearing it Himself. Thus, to be declared righteous by God is also to be purified, cleansed from sin.

According to Daniel 8:14 the little horn's interference with the daily priestly ministration of Christ in the heavenly sanctuary will end with the cleansing/vindication of that sanctuary. The *niṣdaq* of the sanctuary would impact on the sanctuary and God and His people, who would then be vindicated. Only such a rich root as *ṣādaq* could express both cleansing and vindication, combining legal and redemptive concerns in a sanctuary setting, bringing the resolution of the sin problem to its consummation.

According to Daniel, at some point during the eschatological day of atonement the desecration of the priestly work of the Messiah perpetrated by the little horn will be redressed by its destruction. In the OT the desecration of the sanctuary was redressed through the extermination of the sinner and not through sacrificial expiation (Jer. 51:11; Eze. 7:22; 25:3).

The death penalty was pronounced against any Israelite who profaned the sanctuary (Eze. 23:39, 46-49) or sacrificial offerings (Lev. 19:8). Resolution came, so to speak, through the death of the culprit. Daniel applies this same legal principle to the desecrating power of the little horn. The result of its evil actions will be rectified through a powerful manifestation of the holiness and righteousness of God at the close of the eschatological day of atonement. This results in the extermination of the horn. But this eschatological day of atonement includes more than the destruction of this evil power.

(2) The 2300 evenings-mornings: The time frame for the vindication is given by the phrase "until 2300 evenings-mornings." The phrase "evenings-mornings" is used in Genesis 1 to designate each day of Creation week. In the sanctuary services certain activities were referred to as taking place evening and morning, that is, every day (Ex. 27:20, 21; Lev. 24:2, 3). The 2300 evenings-mornings are a period of 2300 prophetic days, which, according to the year-day principle, represent 2300 years. (See Judgment III. B. 1. a; Remnant/Three Angels V. B.)

The beginning of this prophetic period is suggested in Daniel 8:13, which may be translated as follows: "Until when [will] the vision, the daily/continual, and the transgression causing horror, make both the sanctuary and the host a trampling?" This literal translation separates the noun "vision" from "daily." Most versions translate "the vision of the daily," limiting the question to the period during which the little horn was active. But the Hebrew does not allow for this. The first noun is in the absolute state (it has an article and long vowels), which suggests that a comma should be placed after it. The term *ḥāzôn* is used in verses 1 and 2 to refer to the vision of the different animals. The question in verse 13 is about the time for the completion of the vision of verses 1-12: the emphasis is on the termination of the vision and what is to follow.

Because the 2300 days/years begin during the activity of the ram, that is, from the time of the Medo-Persian empire (verse 20), the vision would run from then until the beginning of the cleansing of the heavenly sanctuary. A more specific date for the beginning of the 2300 years is provided by the connection between Daniel 8 and 9. There are clear terminological connections between the two. In 9:23 Gabriel tells the prophet, "Understand the vision." The term for "vision" *(mar'eh)* is the same one used in 8:26, 27 to refer to "the vision of the evenings and the mornings," the part of the *ḥāzôn* (vision) of chapter 8 that had to do with the time period. Gabriel interpreted to Daniel the vision but did not explain the part concerning the 2300 years. At the end of chapter 8 Daniel stated that he did not understand the *mar'eh.* In chapter 9 Gabriel came to assist Daniel in understanding the *mar'eh,* the "vision" of the time period. In both chapters the verb "understand" is used (Dan. 8:23-27; 9:22, 23) and both concern the sanctuary. In 9:24 the sanctuary is dedicated and its services begin, while in 8:14 the same sanctuary is cleansed. These relations connect the time prophecy of the 70 weeks to the 2300 years. The verb "decreed" in 9:24 also means "to cut off," as is seen in Mishnaic Hebrew and in texts found in the city of Ugarit (1300 B.C.). The implication is that the 490 years were "cut off" from the 2300 years. The 490 years began with the decree to rebuild Jerusalem made by Artaxerxes in 457 B.C.; that decree is also the starting point for the 2300 years. The end point of that period would fall in A.D. 1844. Then the sanctuary would be cleansed/vindicated. At this particular time within salvation history Christ would begin the second aspect of His mediatorial work in the heavenly sanctuary, as described in Hebrews 9:23.

b. Daniel 7: the judgment. Daniel 7 contains an important judgment scene that is parallel to the sanctuary section in 8:13, 14. In this scene are given a description of the initiation of the judgment (verses 9, 10), its conclusion (verses 13, 14), and a short interpretation (verses 26, 27; see Judgment III. B. 1. a).

A correct understanding of the function and purpose of this judgment requires the clear establishment of its place within the sequence of events in the vision. Daniel saw four beasts: one like a lion (verse 4); one like a bear (verse 5); another like a leopard (verse 6); and the fourth, undescribable, with ten horns (verse 7). Daniel saw another horn coming out and uprooting three of the ten. This little horn spoke against God, persecuted the saints for three and a half times (360 x 3 + 180 = 1260 days/years), and changed or attempted to change the law and the times (verse 25). The judgment scene is introduced as the little horn speaks great words against God (verses 11, 25); its persecution of the saints had already gone on for three and a half times. As a result of the judgment, the little horn loses its dominion and is destroyed. After this the Son of man and the saints receive God's eternal kingdom (verse 27). The judgment described in Daniel 7 takes place shortly after the three and a half times, yet before the little horn is destroyed and the kingdom of God is established forever.

The judgment scene is clearly heavenly. God is there with His council. In addition, thousands of His messengers are present to serve Him and to witness the judgment. The cosmic nature of this judgment is thus emphasized.

Several elements in the vision indicate that this judgment is investigative, not executive. The reference to books (verse 10) is a strong indication of its investigative nature. The "books" contain the records of the lives of those who are judged, who are not there in person but whose life records are available for scrutiny. The OT contains several references to celestial books, all of them associated with God's people (see Ps. 69:28; Dan. 12:1). The books in the judgment scene of Daniel (see Judgment III. B. I. c.) contain the records of the lives of God's servants. The court judges them and decides in their favor (Dan. 7:22). They are vindicated before the universe and can now possess the kingdom. This interpretation is confirmed by comparing this judgment scene with Daniel 12:1, 2, where Michael receives the kingdom after the defeat and destruction of the enemy from the north (Dan. 11:45). Then the saints are delivered and a resurrection takes place. Those resurrected to eternal life have their names written in *the* book (Dan. 12:1), suggesting that the investigative judgment examines also the records of those who died trusting in the Lord. Their names were investigated and retained in the books because their sins were blotted out from the records.

The judgment of Daniel 7 is also vindicative; it declares the righteous ones worthy of inheriting the kingdom of God. Observed by God's intelligent creatures, this judgment vindicates God's government, the way He has dealt with sin and salvation, and His actions before His vast universe. The little horn is not judged favorably as are the saints; it is condemned. In the biblical understanding of legal proceedings, innocent persons falsely accused of crime went to the temple court asking the Lord to judge them to vindicate them (Ps. 7:8, 9; 26:1, 2). The vindication of the righteous ones confirmed the evilness of the wicked accuser (Ps. 35:1; Zech. 3:1-4); in order to restore them, the one causing the disruption was neutralized, condemned, and deprived of power. The situation of the little horn in Daniel 7 parallels this type of judicial process.

c. Meaning of the cleansing/vindication of the sanctuary in Daniel. There is a clear connection between the judgment scene in Daniel 7 and the section concerning the heavenly sanctuary in Daniel 8:13, 14. The two describe in parallel form the history of the world from the prophet's time to the time of the end. Each chapter adds new elements, throwing light on the nature of the great controversy and on specific events within salvation history. The investigative judgment and the cleansing of the sanctuary complement each other, enriching our understanding of Christ's mediatorial work in the heavenly sanctuary shortly before the Second Coming. The book of Daniel looks forward to the time when the salvation of God's people will be final. They are already the saints of the Most High, having received the cleansing benefits of the sacrificial death of the Messiah (9:24, 27), who can, therefore, represent them in the heavenly court (7:13, 14, 18). The vindication/purification of the sanctuary (8:14) makes the vindication/purification of God's people final before the universe. Their sins are blotted out from God's dwelling and they inherit the eternal kingdom of God.

On the Day of Atonement God judged His people. The vindication/purification of the sanctuary in Daniel also includes judgment. The verb used by Daniel to refer to the cleansing of the sanctuary is primarily a legal term, yet in it legal and cultic aspects are brought together, making possible interpretation of the priestly work of the Prince in juridical-redemptive terms. This judgment seeks primarily to vindicate God's people, as is seen in Daniel 7, where the saints are judged and acquitted. God's people remain in an attitude of complete dependence on God under the most distressing circumstances. The records of their lives are examined and their sins are blotted out; at the same time the names of false believers are removed from the books (cf. Ex. 34:33; Lev. 23:29, 39). Those whose names are preserved in the books, including the dead saints, inherit the kingdom (Dan. 7:22; 12:1, 2). Thus the sanctuary is cleansed.

The priestly ministry of the Prince (Dan. 8:11) is performed on behalf of God's people. The purification of the sanctuary (verse 14) shows that the involvement of the sanctuary is an effective way of disposing of the sin problem and that the transfer of sin to the sanctuary in no way affects God's character. The cosmic judgment in Daniel 7 points precisely to this dimension of God's concern for His own reputation and for the holiness of His dwelling place. The final resolution of the sin problem takes place before God's creatures who are allowed to open the books and examine them. As a result of this process the instrument of salvation, the Son of man, is recognized as universal king (verse 14). God's contact with sin then comes to an end; the sanctuary is cleansed/vindicated.

3. The Day of Atonement in Revelation

The book of Revelation shows progression in Christ's work in the heavenly sanctuary. In the first part of the book Jesus is ministering in the holy place (8:3-5). But in Revelation 11:19 John is taken into the Most Holy Place of the heavenly sanctuary, where he sees the ark of the covenant. This points to the beginning of the second aspect of Christ's mediatorial work, that of judgment. In Revelation 15:8 we are informed that this work of judgment has come to an end: The temple is "filled with smoke from the glory of God and from his power, and no one could enter" (cf. Lam. 3:44). The visibility of the ark not only indicates movement from one area to another, it also reminds the reader of the law of God deposited inside the ark. This law is the standard by which God judges (cf. James 2:8-13). The antitypical day of atonement is here introduced.

a. Investigative judgment. According to Revelation Christ is involved in an investigative judgment. He "searches mind and heart" and gives to all according to their works (Rev. 2:23). It is, therefore, important for believers to hold fast what they have until He comes (2:25; 3:11). If they are conquerors their names will not be blotted out from the book of life and Christ will represent them before the Father and the angels (3:5). This suggests that some names will be blotted out from the book of life and that commitment to and reliance on Christ's power determines what happens to an individual's name.

Revelation pays particular attention to events on earth while the cleansing/vindication of the heavenly sanctuary is taking place. While God in heaven is determining whose names will remain in the books, on earth the Lord is gathering His remnant through the message of the three angels (Rev. 14:6-11; see Three Angels V. B-D). Revelation 14 begins with a description of the remnant (144,000) standing before God, victorious over the evil powers that threatened their lives (verses 1-5). The second part of the chapter (verses 6-11) introduces the means employed by God to gather a remnant from every nation, tribe, tongue, and people (verse 6). God's messengers proclaim once more His eternal gospel, calling humans to fear and worship the Creator because "the hour of his judgment has come" (verse 7). The urgency of this message is based on the fact that God is now making judicial decisions in the heavenly sanctuary. He is separating true from false worshipers. The last part of Revelation 14 describes the second coming of Christ under the symbol of a harvest (verses 14-20), indicating that the investigative judgment ends shortly before the Advent.

The same ideas are discussed in Revelation 7. Here the remnant (144,000) who are sealed before the wrath of God is poured out are presented as able to stand before the Lord at His coming. The sealing is a judicial process by which the members of the true remnant are identified, evaluated, and preserved. This imagery is also found in Ezekiel 9:1-4. In contrast with the idolaters, who must be destroyed, the faithful remnant are identified and marked to separate them from the impenitent covenant violators. Revelation 7:9-12 describes the remnant gathered before the throne of God.

Prior to the above victory scene the judgment in the heavenly sanctuary is proclaimed by the remnant who are described as those who keep the commandments of God, who have remained loyal to God's covenant (Rev. 12:17; 14:12). They call the rest of God's people to come out of Babylon before Christ's mediatorial work ends (Rev. 18:1-4).

b. Beginning of the judgment. The investigative judgment, according to Revelation, begins after the prophetic periods of Daniel and Revelation have been fulfilled. In Revelation 10:6 John hears a mighty angel saying that "there should be time no longer" (KJV). The RSV, as well as other versions, incorrectly translates *chronos* (time) as "delay." Revelation 10 refers back to Daniel 12, where several prophetic time periods appear. Time periods are very important in Daniel (7:25; 8:14; 9:24; 12:11, 13) and Revelation (9:15; 11:3; 12:6). The 2300 days/years of Daniel 8:14, ending in 1844, are the longest of these periods. The angel of Revelation 10:6 states that all these prophetic periods have been fulfilled. Only the consummation of salvation is still future (verse 7). In this context John, representing God's remnant, is told, "You must again prophesy about many peoples and nations and tongues and kings" (verse 11). This is the same task as that of the three angels in Revelation 14:6-11.

The proclamation of the three angels' messages is a work of rebuilding and restoration, as indicated in Revelation 11:1, where John is told to "measure the temple of God and the altar and those who worship there." The symbolism points to the Day of Atonement since only on that day did the temple, the altar, and the people go through a cleansing experience (Lev. 16). But here they are measured rather than cleansed. The verb "to measure" suggests a process of evaluation (cf. Matt. 7:2) and may express the idea of judgment. Thus Revelation 11:1 refers to what is taking place in heaven. Measuring can also express the ideas of preservation (2 Sam. 8:2) and restoration or rebuilding (Eze. 41:13, 15; Zech. 2:2-8). This second possibility would suggest that the sanctuary which is being measured or evaluated in heaven is at the same time being restored on earth, establishing thus a connection between what goes on in heaven and its impact on earth. This work of restoration is suggested by the command to "again prophesy" (Rev. 10:11). The restoration on earth of the truth about the sanctuary and Christ's ministry there is necessary because "the beast" has attacked the tabernacle of God for 1260 days/years (Rev. 13:5, 6; cf. Dan. 7:25; 8:12). In addition the whole earth is about to be deceived by the dragon who presents himself as the rightful object of worship over against the Creator.

c. Results of the investigative judgment.
The investigative judgment, which is taking place in heaven and is being proclaimed in the setting of the gospel, has several purposes, all of them related to the day of atonement. This judgment vindicates God's people and reveals beyond a shadow of doubt that they have been washed in the blood of the Lamb (Rev. 7:14). They have preserved their covenant relationship with the Saviour. Consequently, they will enter God's temple in heaven to serve Him (verse 15). At the same time, the vindication of God's people results in the condemnation of God's enemies. Revelation 18:20 states, "God has given judgment for you against her [Babylon]!" In vindicating His people God in fact condemns the evil powers; at this time He judges and avenges the blood of the martyrs (Rev. 6:10).

Above all, the investigative judgment serves to vindicate God Himself. The full impact of the cross is analyzed and God is found to be merciful, righteous, and holy. All His judicial actions are revealed as righteous (Rev. 15:4) and the redeemed shout, "Just and true are thy ways" (verse 3). The dwellers of heaven praise the Lord saying, "Hallelujah! Salvation and glory and power belong to our God, for his judgments are true and just!" (Rev. 19:1, 2; see 11:16-18).

Finally, the investigative judgment leads to the cleansing of the universe. At the Second Coming, God's people are removed from earth and taken into the presence of God in heaven (Rev. 7:9; 14:1), while their enemies are destroyed (Rev. 19:19-21). Only the dragon is left alive to wander on this desolate planet for a thousand years (Rev. 20:1-3; see Millennium I. C). The true Azazel is finally unveiled in all his evil; the true originator of sin is unmasked before the universe and made responsible for the sin problem. The typical goat Azazel finds its antitype in the dragon left alone in the wilderness of a desolate planet.

After the millennium comes the executive phase of the judgment. Satan and the wicked ones, who come to life at the end of the millennium, meet before God to listen to their sentence (verses 11, 12). The books are opened once more and the records of their lives are analyzed. Then, sin and sinners, together with originator and instigator of sin, are eradicated from the universe. The cleansing that began in God's sanctuary reaches cosmic proportions. (See Judgment III. B. 3.)

D. Summary

Christ's mediatorial work in the heavenly sanctuary is a well-documented biblical teaching. At His ascension He inaugurated His priestly work of applying to believers the benefits of His expiatory/propitiatory death on the cross. Christ's work has two aspects: The first was prefigured through the daily services in the earthly sanctuary and began at the ascension. In it Christ mediates God's loving grace to His people and represents them before God. The second aspect of Christ's priesthood was typified by the work of the high priest in the Most Holy Place on the Day of Atonement. Hebrews refers to this dimension of Christ's ministry; Revelation shows Jesus performing His work in the two apartments; and Daniel places the initiation of the antitypical day of atonement at a specific moment within salvation history, at the end of the 2300 days/years, in 1844. This aspect of Christ's work is a development of His mediatorial service and does not put an end to His daily work of intercession and mediation. In this second phase, a juridical-redemptive-eschatological aspect is initiated and added to His priesthood.

The second phase of Christ's ministry is the consummation of His work of vindication, judgment, a cleansing of the universe from sin, sinners, and Satan. God in Christ assumes responsibility for the sins of His people. Every confessed sin found in the heavenly records is credited to God's Son. But that process must come to an end or the sin problem will never be completely solved. At some point the records must be closed. This involves a work of investigation and judgment, which results in the vindication of God's people. The names of false believers are removed from the book of life. The justification of true believers is reaffirmed, their names are preserved in the heavenly book of life, and their sins are blotted out from the records. God is vindicated by showing to the universe that His judicial deci-

sions are just, that sin and holiness have nothing in common, and that God is a merciful, loving, and righteous Lord. This revelation of God's holiness, power, and grace is possible only through the Lamb, who completes the defeat of the dragon to its consummation by blotting him out of God's universe.

IV. Implications of Christ's Sacrifice and Priesthood for Christian Experience

It was through the study of the earthly sanctuary services and their symbolic meaning, together with Daniel 8:14 as a point of departure, that Adventism came into existence as a historical movement, developed its doctrinal identity, and identified its mission. We are confronted here with a foundational and vital aspect in Adventist thought. This type of development was possible because Daniel 8 included a time prophecy that identified 1844 as a significant date in God's calendar and also because chapters 8 and 9:23-27 pointed to Christ's work of redemption. This salvific task is connected in those passages not only with the cross but also with Christ's ongoing mediatorial work in the heavenly sanctuary. The exploration of the sanctuary services and its symbolic meaning resulted in the Adventist doctrine of the sanctuary and provided a theological perspective that unlocked a biblical system of beliefs of great relevance for God's people. Among those relevant elements are the following:

1. The OT teaching on the sanctuary provides a unique perspective from which to study the plan of redemption. It illuminates the development of that plan within history, identifying its key components and, in conjunction with the prophecies of Daniel, even showing the precise time of their fulfillment. This typical system centers on the work of Christ and provides an integrated view of His ministry. The progression in Christ's work in the sanctuary is clearly seen: He is Sacrificial Victim, High Priest, Mediator, Judge, Advocate, and King.

2. The end of the 2300 years in 1844 reminds us that salvation history is still in progress and did not come to an end with Jesus' death on the cross. God is developing His plan as He intended and anticipated. God is still active within world history, leading it to His own goal, the establishment of His kingdom on earth. The prophetic periods serve as landmarks within history, heralding the completion of God's plan of redemption.

3. Daniel 8:14 and the sanctuary inform us that Christ is now performing the last aspect of His high priestly work in the heavenly sanctuary. The antitypical day of atonement is in progress and God is judging His people. We are approaching the very end of God's mercy. Soon we will face the final confrontation between the forces of God and Satan. Certainly this eschatological orientation of Christ's priestly ministry in the Most Holy Place of the heavenly sanctuary is rooted in the cross. While the end of sin was clearly seen at the cross, the final eradication of sin is now, through Christ's mediation, approaching its consummation.

4. Christ's work of mediation and judgment calls us not only to actively proclaim God's eternal gospel in the setting of the three angels' messages, but also challenges us to evaluate our relationship with Christ. Our religious experience should be marked by a humble dependence on the Saviour. While the sanctuary is being cleansed, our spiritual life also should be cleansed from sin. This personal cleansing takes place by means of

repentance and forgiveness through Christ.

5. The investigative judgment occurring in heaven now is a testimony to the way God and the universe take every human being seriously. Through Christ's ministry in the sanctuary, God deals with human beings on an individual basis, reaffirming their dignity and value in Christ who represents them as their Advocate. The redeemed will join the heavenly family, not as strangers but as well-known family members who sympathize with and respect the rest of God's family.

6. The investigative judgment signifies that human decisions and actions have a cosmic impact. What we are, think, and do is preserved indelibly in the heavenly records. Far from being cause for stress and fear, this reality should be a source of joy. What we do, what we are, is not lost in the vastness of time and space but preserved within God's sanctuary. Every prayer, good deed, encouraging word, or expression of love is preserved as a witness to the manifold wisdom of God, who is able to transform sinful human beings into new and holy creatures. While sin—human weakness, rebellion, error, and failure—is also recorded there, forgiveness is constantly available to those who approach God through Christ, the believers' Advocate. In the investigative judgment, sins committed by those who remain in a covenant relationship with Christ are not counted against them because they were counted against Christ at the cross. Those sins are blotted out, to be remembered no more. The Christlike character of the believer is fixed for eternity.

7. The cleansing of the heavenly sanctuary points in a special way to the moral nature of God, the moral arbiter of the universe, which is accountable to Him. The believer should find comfort in knowing that an all-powerful and all-loving personal God is in charge of the universe. To restore the universe and preserve its order, judgment and accountability are indispensable. Since judgment is based on God's law, His people are characterized as those who keep the divine commandments in loving response to His justifying grace.

8. The cleansing of the sanctuary testifies to the fact that evil is not eternal. It will come to an end, as with shouts of joy and praise God's loyal creatures recognize that sin and evil are extinguished through divine justice and love. The cross demonstrates that the Son agreed with the Father in His judgment on sin and took it upon Himself. In the divine plan Christ has become for repentant sinners both substitute and surety. The OT sanctuary shows that sin cannot simply be forgiven by passing over it lightly. The sin problem can be fully resolved only when evil is removed from God's presence and its true source identified and exterminated. At the end of His ministry in the heavenly sanctuary Christ will come to deliver His people from the power of their enemies, especially from death. Satan or Azazel is recognized throughout the universe as the source and originator of sin, and his extinction is decreed. To deal improperly with sin would mean to perpetuate it; therefore it must be totally and forever eradicated. Then the victory of God and the Lamb over the powers of disruption will be final. Holiness and impurity will be separated forever and the harmony of God's love will rule over a healed universe.

9. The salvific significance of the cross is enriched through the study of Christ's priesthood. While the cross was the greatest revelation of God to the universe, indispensable to the resolution of the sin problem, that revelation is not fully understood. Its yet-to-be-understood dimensions will occupy the thoughts of the redeemed throughout eternity. Christ's indispensable priestly ministry in the heavenly sanctuary constantly uncovers the richness of the cross, making its merits available to whoever comes to the Father through Him.

V. The Priesthood of Christ in History

A. Early Church

The Church Fathers did not explore in detail the priestly work of Christ in heaven. Their main emphasis was on Christ's priestly work on the cross where He offered Himself as a sacrifice (Origen *Commentary on John* 1:40 [ANF 9: 318, 319). Athanasius recognized the continuity between the sacrifice of Christ on the cross and His priestly ministry in heaven where Christ was performing a work of propitiation, redemption, sanctification, and judgment (*Discourse Against the Arians* 1. 11. 41; 2. 14. 7 [NPNF-2 4:330, 351]), as did Augustine (c. 354-430; *Sermon* 8. 1; 87. 1; *Tractates on the Gospel of John* 22. 5 [NPNF-1 6: 284; 7:146]). However, the church introduced additional mediators through whom forgiveness of sin was granted to believers. Among the most important were the priests (Origen *Homily on Leviticus* 2.4; *Homily on 1 Corinthians* 24). To that was added the mediation of the saints and apostles in heaven (Origen *Exhortation to Martyrdom* 30; *On Prayer* 11. 2; *Homily on Numbers* 10. 2).

The reality of the existence of a heavenly sanctuary was practically overlooked in the patristic literature. It would appear that Greek dualism made it difficult for the Church Fathers to accept the reality of a heavenly sanctuary. The tendency was to speculate on the meaning of the Israelite sanctuary, using a mystical or allegorical approach. Even those who wrote on Hebrews spiritualized the heavenly things (Chrysostom *Homily on Hebrews* 14. 3 [NPNF-1 14:433]). Irenaeus identified God's temple with the believer (*Against Heresies* 5. 6. 2 [ANF 1:532]) while others, more often, identified it with the church (Augustine *Enchiridion* 56; Methodius [d. 311] *The Banquet of the Ten Virgins* 5. 7 [ANF 6:328]).

B. Middle Ages and Reformation

The Church Fathers laid a foundation for the interpretation of the Israelite sanctuary and Christ's priestly work during the Middle Ages. The sacrificial death of Christ was always recognized, but His mediatorial work as high priest continued to be supplemented by the work of many saints. During this period the idea of the mediatorial work of virgin Mary, the mediatrix, was popularized in the church. The interpretation of the heavenly sanctuary as the Christian church became the prevailing theological opinion. The Venerable Bede (c. 673-735), at the beginning of the Middle Ages, wrote an influential volume on the Israelite tabernacle. It was an allegorical exposition of Exodus 24:12–30:21 in which he argued, following patristic writers, that the tabernacle was a symbol of the church. He suggested, in a more precise way, that the tabernacle represented the present church, and the temple of Solomon, the future one. For centuries the ecclesiological interpretation of the sanctuary was the predominant view.

The nature of the atonement became an important subject of discussion during the Middle Ages. The most influential work produced on this subject was *Cur deus homo? (Why Did God Become Man?),* written by Anselm (c. 1033-1109). It was a most powerful exposition of the sacrificial death of Christ as our substitute, through whom God's justice was fully satisfied. Other expositions on the doctrine of atonement were developed as a reaction to Anselm, among them the moral influence theory of atonement of Peter Abelard (c. 1079-1142).

The Reformers, in their sincere concern for the church, called Christians back to the Bible as the only source of faith and practice. Consequently, Martin Luther stressed the all-sufficiency of Christ as our atoning sacrifice and only mediator before the Father. Luther said He was "at the right hand of God, not in order to be idle and while away His time there, but to save us all from sin, death, and the power of the devil" (*Sermon* 37 on John 3:23). Luther reaffirmed the biblical description of Christ as priest and concluded that we can "be sure, yes, completely sure, that Christ appears and is a Priest before God" on our behalf (*Lecture on Hebrews* 9:24). John Calvin developed the concept of the three offices of Christ—prophet, king, and priest—which have become a traditional feature in Protestant theology. Christ's priestly work has two parts: (1) His work at the cross, and (2) His intercession in the heavenly sanctuary before the Father. Calvin defined that work of intercession as Christ's "continual application of His death for our salvation. That God does not then impute to us our sins, this comes to us; because He has regard to Christ as the intercessor" (*Commentary on John* 2. 1). Calvin used the language of Hebrews to refer to the heavenly sanctuary, but Luther seemed to understand the holy place of Israelite sanctuary as symbolizing the militant church and the Most Holy Place representing the triumphant church (*Lectures on Hebrews* 9. 2).

English Puritan theologians demonstrated great interest in the high priestly ministry of Christ in the heavenly sanctuary. In his *Expositions on Hebrews* (1668-1880) Puritan theologian John Owen underscored the importance of Christ's ministry in the heavenly sanctuary: "The actual intercession of Christ in heaven . . . is a fundamental article of our faith, and a principal foundation of the consolation of the church" (on Heb. 7:23-25). He specifically noted that "the actual application of grace and mercy unto us depends on his appearance before God, and the intercession wherewith it is accompanied" (on Heb. 9:24).

Puritan writers based their understanding of Christ's priesthood on the book of Hebrews and the typological nature of the Israelite sanctuary services. The very "existence of a heavenly sanctuary was standard theology among Puritans divines" (Ball 109). This heavenly sanctuary was the model shown to Moses. Owen noted that the Israelite sacrificial system and the priesthood delineated and pointed to the totality of Christ's work of salvation (*Expositions on Hebrews* 8. 5).

The priestly work of Christ provided for the believer, among many other things, forgiveness of sin, access to God, assurance of salvation, spiritual power, and a glorious hope. His all-sufficient ministry made unnecessary the intervention of any other mediator between God and the believer; one who attempted to obtain help elsewhere, according to David Dickson, denied Christ (Ball 117). The study of the activities of the Day of Atonement led some to observe that the ritual took place after the daily services; that is to say, the setting for the ritual was one of salvation. Likewise Christ began His priestly work after He offered Himself as a salvific sacrifice. Puritan authors believed that the Day of Atonement had legal and judicial significance. On that day the people were not only blessed but also judged. Puritan thinkers made no chronological distinction between the typological fulfillment of the daily and annual service of the Day of Atonement (Ball 115).

C. Modern Period

Modern scholarship rejects the historicist approach to the interpretation of the prophecies of Daniel and Revelation. The atoning significance of the death of Christ is recognized by conservative Christians, but His high priestly mediation continues to be a neglected area. The reality of the heavenly sanctuary in Hebrews is taken by some scholars as an image used to designate the presence of God rather than a locality (Guthrie 196). Others take it simply as figurative, poetic language (Hagner 117), or as language to designate the individual believer whom Christ indwells (Stedman 996-998).

D. Adventist Understanding

During the nineteenth century there was in North America a great interest in the second coming of Christ. One of the most influential leaders of this revival was William Miller (1782-1849). His studies of the prophecies of Daniel led him to conclude that the "purification of the sanctuary" of Daniel 8:14 referred to the return of the Lord (the cleansing of the earth from sin), and that the 2300 years would end in 1843/1844. He and his followers finally established that Jesus would come back on October 22, 1844. The failure of the prediction resulted in the Great Disappointment.

Some Millerites searched for an explanation of the disappointment. They carefully examined the chronology of the 2300 days and concluded that it was correct, and that the mistake was in the event. Hiram Edson suggested that at the end of the 2300 years Christ entered the Most Holy Place to perform a special work before returning to earth. Owen R. L. Crosier developed that idea through a study of the Israelite sanctuary services in conjunction with the book of Hebrews. He concluded that there were two sanctuaries: one earthly and the other heavenly. Daniel 8:14, he argued, was a reference to the heavenly sanctuary and Christ's work in it. Attempting to define Christ's priestly work in a more precise way, he indicated that it had two phases: one began at the Ascension, corresponding to the work in the holy place; and the other, beginning in 1844, corresponding to the work in the Most Holy Place. This was a typological fulfillment of the work of the high priest in the Israelite sanctuary. The antitypical day of atonement was the time from 1844 to the end of the millennium, the consummation of salvation history. Sacrifice for sin was made on the cross; the priestly mediation of Christ, through the merits of His blood, made atonement for the sins of repentant sinners. The Israelite sanctuary was defiled by open rebellion and through the confession of sin. Defilement through confession took place when sin was transferred to the sacrifice and, through its blood, to the sanctuary. It was concluded that the heavenly sanctuary was defiled by the confessed sins of God's servants.

The study of the Most Holy Place in the earthly sanctuary led the Adventist believers to study the ark of the covenant in which the Ten Commandments were placed. Under the influence of Hiram Edson, E. G. White, and O.R.L. Crosier, a connection was established between the sanctuary ritual system, the Ten Commandments, and the Sabbath. As a result, a Sabbatarian Adventist group of believers came into existence. The study of the sanctuary also resulted in a better understanding of the final judgment. Joseph Bates suggested that the judgment scene in Daniel 7 and the hour of God's judgment in Revelation 14:6 were references to the work of Christ after 1844. This idea was developed by others, particularly by James White. It was concluded that the cleansing of the heavenly sanctuary included the investigative judgment of God's people, followed by the judgment of the wicked and the final disposition of Satan, represented by the figure of Azazel in Leviticus 16 (Damsteegt 85-92; Maxwell 119-157). The connection between Daniel 7 and 8 and Revelation 14:6-12 provided for the early Adventists a sense of mission to the world, a mission prophetically represented in the messages of the three angels. But the doctrine of Christ's priesthood also had an experiential dimension. While Christ was performing the cleansing of the sanctuary in heaven God's people on earth were to cleanse their lives from sin through the work of the Spirit.

The study of the biblical evidence led Adventists to conclude that a theological definition of the atonement should include the cross as the place of the atoning death of Christ, as well as His priestly ministry in the heavenly sanctuary. Refinement in the understanding of the investigative judgment, also called the pre-Advent judgment, concluded that it does not inform God but reveals His justice. In fact, "God condescends to show them His justice and His righteousness in His dealing with sinners," while at the same time the "investigative judgment is a revelation of love and loyalty to God at its best" (Heppenstall 209, 216).

The Adventist understanding of Christ's priestly ministry in the heavenly sanctuary is significantly different from that of other Christians. There have also been dissenters on the topic within the church: Albion Fox

405

Ballenger (1861-1921), W. W. Fletcher (1879-1947), Louis Richard Conradi (1856-1939), E. B. Jones (fl. 1919-1949), and during the 1980s Desmond Ford. At approximately the same time the General Conference was inaugurating a Daniel and Revelation Committee, assigned to reexamine the teachings of these books and the Adventist understanding of them. Although the committee's work was broad in scope, it included questions raised by Ford. They continue to be of interest for church members as evidenced by the publication and sales of popular books on the subject. Some of the writers put great emphasis on the symbolism of almost every detail of the ritual, while others concentrate on the typological significance of its services.

The doctrine of Christ's priesthood, together with the prophetic interpretation of Daniel 8:14, provides the Seventh-day Adventist Church with a historical identity. Adventists see their movement, not as a historical accident, but as the result of God's special intervention in human affairs. The fulfillment of Daniel 8:14 in 1844 validates the presence of Seventh-day Adventists in the world, and particularly in the Christian community. As the initiation of Christ's heavenly ministry coincided with the outpouring of the Spirit on the fledgling church (Acts 2:33), so the beginning of the antitypical day of atonement coincided with the birth of the Seventh-day Adventist Church.

VI. Ellen G. White Comments

A. The Israelite Sanctuary Services

"The system of Jewish economy was the gospel in figure, a presentation of Christianity which was to be developed as fast as the minds of the people could comprehend spiritual light" (FE 238).

"The gospel of Christ reflects glory upon the Jewish age. It sheds light upon the whole Jewish economy, and gives significance to the ceremonial law. The tabernacle, or temple, of God on earth was a pattern of the original in heaven. All the ceremonies of the Jewish law were prophetic, typical of mysteries in the plan of redemption" (ST July 29, 1886).

"A lesson was embodied in every sacrifice, impressed in every ceremony, solemnly preached by the priest in his holy office, and inculcated by God Himself—that through the blood of Christ alone is there forgiveness of sins. How little we as a people feel the force of this great truth! How seldom, by living, acting faith, do we bring into our lives this great truth, that there is forgiveness for the least sin, forgiveness for the greatest sin" (RH Sept. 21, 1886)!

"Thus in the ministration of the tabernacle, and of the temple that afterward took its place,

the people were taught each day the great truths relative to Christ's death and ministration, and once each year their minds were carried forward to the closing events of the great controversy between Christ and Satan, the final purification of the universe from sin and sinners" (PP 358).

"The incense, ascending with the prayers of Israel, represents the merits and intercession of Christ, His perfect righteousness, which through faith is imputed to His people, and which can alone make the worship of sinful beings acceptable to God. Before the veil of the most holy place, was an altar of perpetual intercession, before the holy, an altar of continual atonement. By blood and by incense, God was to be approached—symbols pointing to the great Mediator, through whom sinners may approach Jehovah, and through whom alone mercy and salvation can be granted to the repentant, believing soul" (FLB 197).

"The law of God, enshrined within the ark, was the great rule of righteousness and judgment. That law pronounced death upon the transgressor; but above the law was the mercy seat, upon which the presence of God was revealed, and from which, by virtue of the atonement, pardon was granted to the repentant sinner. Thus in the work of Christ for our redemption, symbolized by the sanctuary service, 'mercy and truth are met together; righteousness and peace have kissed each other' (Ps. 85:10)" (PP 349).

"The daily service consisted of the morning and evening burnt offering, the offering of sweet incense on the golden altar, and the special offerings for individual sins. And there were also offerings for sabbaths, new moons, and special feasts.

"Every morning and evening a lamb of a year old was burned upon the altar, with its appropriate meat offering, thus symbolizing the daily consecration of the nation to Jehovah, and their constant dependence upon the atoning blood of Christ" (*ibid.* 352).

B. The Sacrifice of Christ

"As the sin bearer, and priest and representative of man before God, He entered into the life of humanity, bearing our flesh and blood. The life is in the living, vital current of blood, which blood was given for the life of the world. Christ made a full atonement, giving His life as a ransom for us. He was born without a taint of sin, but came into the world in like manner as the human family. He did not have a mere semblance of a body, but He took human nature, participating in the life of humanity" (7BC 925).

"The reconciliation of man to God could be accomplished only through a mediator who was equal with God, possessed of attributes that would dignify, and declare Him worthy to treat with the Infinite God in man's behalf, and also represent God to a fallen world. Man's substitute and surety must have man's nature, a connection with the human family whom he was to represent, and, as God's ambassador, he must partake of the divine nature, have a connection with the Infinite, in order to manifest God to the world, and be a mediator between God and man" (RH Dec. 22, 1891).

"Christ, in counsel with His Father, instituted the system of sacrificial offerings: that death, instead of being immediately visited upon the transgressor, should be transferred to a victim which should prefigure the great and perfect offering of the Son of God.

"The sins of the people were transferred in figure to the officiating priest, who was mediator for the people. The priest could not himself become an offering for sin, and make an atonement with his life, for he was also a sinner. Therefore, instead of suffering death himself, he killed a lamb without blemish; the penalty of sin was transferred to the innocent beast, which thus became his immediate substitute, and typified the perfect offering of Jesus Christ. Through the blood of this victim, man looked forward by faith to the blood of Christ which would atone for the sins of the world" (ST Mar. 14, 1878).

"The rivers of blood that flowed at the harvest thanksgiving, when the sacrifices were offered in such large numbers, were meant to teach a great truth. For even the productions of the earth, the bounties provided for man's sustenance, we are indebted to the offering of Christ upon the cross of Calvary. God teaches us that all we receive from Him is the gift of redeeming love" (RH Nov. 10, 1896).

C. The Heavenly Sanctuary

"The question, What is the sanctuary? is clearly answered in the Scriptures. The term 'sanctuary,' as used in the Bible, refers, first, to the tabernacle built by Moses, as a pattern of heavenly things; and, secondly, to the 'true tabernacle' in heaven, to which the earthly sanctuary pointed. At the death of Christ the typical service ended. The 'true tabernacle' in heaven is the sanctuary of the new covenant. And as the prophecy of Daniel 8:14 is fulfilled in this dispensation, the sanctuary to which it refers must be the sanctuary of the new covenant" (GC 417).

"The heavenly temple, the abiding place of the King of kings, where 'thousand thousands ministered unto Him, and ten thousand times ten thousand stood before Him' (Dan. 7:10), that temple filled with the glory of the eternal throne, where seraphim, its shining guardians, veil their faces in adoration—no earthly structure could represent its vastness and its glory. Yet important truths concerning the heavenly sanctuary and the great work there carried forward for man's redemption were to be taught by the earthly sanctuary and its services" (PP 357).

"The matchless splendor of the earthly tabernacle reflected to human vision the glories of that heavenly temple where Christ our forerunner ministers for us before the throne of God. The abiding place of the King of kings, where thousand thousands minister unto Him, and ten thousand times ten thousand stand before Him (Dan. 7:10); that temple, filled with the glory of the eternal throne, where seraphim, its shining guardians, veil their faces in adoration, could find, in the most magnificent structure ever reared by human hands, but a faint reflection of its vastness and glory. Yet important truths concerning the heavenly sanctuary and the great work there carried forward for man's redemption were taught by the earthly sanctuary and its services.

"The holy places of the sanctuary in heaven are represented by the two apartments in the sanctuary on earth" (GC 414).

D. Christ's High Priestly Work

"The ministration of the earthly sanctuary consisted of two divisions; the priests ministered daily in the holy place, while once a year the high priest performed a special work of atonement in the most holy, for the cleansing of the sanctuary. Day by day the repentant sinner brought his offering to the door of the tabernacle and, placing his hand upon the victim's head, confessed his sins, thus in figure transferring them from himself to the innocent sacrifice. The animal was then slain. 'Without shedding of blood,' says the apostle, there is no remission of sin. 'The life of the flesh is in the blood' (Lev. 17:11). The broken law of God demanded the life of the transgressor. The blood, representing the forfeited life of the sinner, whose guilt the victim bore, was carried by the priest into the holy place and sprinkled before the veil, behind which was the ark containing the law that the sinner had transgressed. By this ceremony the sin was, through the blood, transferred in figure to the sanctuary. In some cases the blood was not taken into the holy place; but the flesh was then to be eaten by the priest, as Moses directed the sons of Aaron, saying: 'God hath given it you to bear the iniquity of the congregation' (Lev. 10:17). Both ceremonies alike symbolized the transfer of the sin from the penitent to the sanctuary" (ibid. 418).

"As Christ's ministration was to consist of two great divisions, each occupying a period of time and having a distinctive place in the heavenly sanctuary, so the typical ministration consisted of two divisions, the daily and the yearly service, and to each a department of the tabernacle was devoted" (PP 357).

"Jesus stands in the holy of holies, now to appear in the presence of God for us. There He ceases not to present His people moment by moment, complete in Himself. But because we are thus represented before the Father, we are not to imagine that we are to presume upon His mercy, and become careless, indifferent, and self-indulgent. Christ is not the minister of sin. We are complete in Him, accepted in the Beloved, only as we abide in Him by faith" (ST July 4, 1892).

"Our great High Priest completed the sacrificial offering of Himself when He suffered without the gate. Then a perfect atonement was made for the sins of the people. Jesus is our Advocate, our High Priest, our Intercessor. Our present position therefore is like that of the Israelites, standing in the outer court, waiting and looking for that blessed hope, the glorious appearing of our Lord and Saviour Jesus Christ. . . . Type met antitype in the death of Christ, the Lamb slain for the sins of the world. The great High Priest has made the only sacrifice that will be of any value. . . .

"In His intercession as our Advocate Christ needs no man's virtue, no man's intercession. Christ is the only sin bearer, the only sin-offering. Prayer and confession are to be offered only to Him who has entered once for all into the holy place. Christ has declared, 'If any man sin, we have an advocate with the Father, Jesus Christ the righteous.' He will save to the uttermost all who come to Him in faith. He ever liveth to make intercession for us. This makes of no avail the offering of mass, one of the falsehoods of Romanism" (7BC 913).

"The Son of God . . . has fulfilled His pledge, and has passed into the heavens, to take upon Himself the government of the heavenly host. He fulfilled one phase of His priesthood by dying on the cross for the fallen race. He is now fulfilling another phase by pleading before the Father the case of the repenting, believing sinner, presenting to God the offerings of His people. Having taken human nature and in this nature having overcome the temptations of the enemy, and having divine perfection, to Him has been committed the judgment of the world. The case of each one will be brought in review before Him. He will pronounce judgment, rendering to every man according to his works" (*ibid.* 929).

"What is Christ doing in heaven? He is interceding for us. By His work the threshold of heaven is flushed with the glory of God which will shine upon every soul who will open the windows of the soul heavenward. As the prayers of the sincere and contrite ones ascend to heaven Christ says to the Father, 'I will take their sins. Let them stand before you innocent.' As He takes their sins from them, He fills their hearts with the glorious light of truth and love" (*ibid.* 930).

"The intercession of Christ in man's behalf in the sanctuary above is as essential to the plan of salvation as was His death upon the cross. By His death He began that work which after His resurrection He ascended to complete in heaven. We must by faith enter within the veil, 'whither the forerunner is for us entered' (Heb. 6:20). There the light from the cross of Calvary is reflected. There we may gain a clearer insight into the mysteries of redemption. The salvation of man is accomplished at an infinite expense to heaven; the sacrifice made is equal to the broadest demands of the broken law of God. Jesus has opened the way to the Father's throne, and through His mediation the sincere desire of all who come to Him in faith may be presented before God" (GC 489).

"By His spotless life, His obedience, His death on the cross of Calvary, Christ interceded for the lost race. And now, not as a mere petitioner does the Captain of our salvation intercede for us, but as a conqueror claiming His victory. His offering is complete, and as our intercessor He executes His self-appointed work, holding before God the censer containing His own spotless merits and the prayers, confessions, and thanksgiving of His people. Perfumed with the fragrance of His righteousness, these ascend to God as a sweet savor. The offering is wholly acceptable, and pardon covers all transgression. To the true believer Christ is indeed the minister of the sanctuary, officiating for him in the sanctuary, and speaking through God's appointed agencies" (ST Feb. 14, 1900).

"Christ, our Mediator, and the Holy Spirit are constantly interceding in man's behalf, but the Spirit pleads not for us as does Christ, who presents His blood, shed from the foundation of the world; the Spirit works upon our hearts, drawing out prayers and penitence, praise and thanksgiving. The gratitude which flows from our lips is the result of the Spirit's striking the cords of the soul in holy memories, awakening the music of the heart.

"The religious services, the prayers, the praise, the penitent confession of sin ascend from true believers as incense to the heavenly sanctuary, but passing through the corrupt channels of humanity, they are so defiled that unless purified by blood, they can never be of value with God. They ascend not in spotless purity, and unless the Intercessor, who is at God's right hand, presents and purifies all by His righteousness, it is not acceptable to God. All incense from earthly tabernacles must be moist with the cleansing drops of the blood of

Christ. He holds before the Father the censer of His own merits, in which there is no taint of earthly corruption. He gathers into this censer the prayers, the praise, and the confessions of His people, and with these He puts His own spotless righteousness. Then, perfumed with the merits of Christ's propitiation, the incense comes up before God wholly and entirely acceptable. Then gracious answers are returned" (1SM 344).

"Our crucified Lord is pleading for us in the presence of the Father at the throne of grace. His atoning sacrifice we may plead for our pardon, our justification, and our sanctification. The Lamb slain is our only hope. Our faith looks up to Him, grasps Him as the One who can save to the uttermost, and the fragrance of the all-sufficient offering is accepted of the Father. Unto Christ is committed all power in heaven and in earth, and all things are possible to him that believeth. Christ's glory is concerned in our success. He has a common interest in all humanity. He is our sympathizing Saviour" (7BC 948).

"Attended by heavenly angels, our great High Priest enters the holy of holies and there appears in the presence of God to engage in the last acts of His ministration in behalf of man—to perform the work of investigative judgment and to make an atonement for all who are shown to be entitled to its benefits" (GC 480).

"In the typical system, which was a shadow of the sacrifice and priesthood of Christ, the cleansing of the sanctuary was the last service performed by the high priest in the yearly round of ministration. It was the closing work of the atonement—a removal or putting away of sin from Israel. It prefigured the closing work in the ministration of our High Priest in heaven, in the removal or blotting out of the sins of His people, which are registered in the heavenly records. This service involves a work of investigation, a work of judgment; and it immediately precedes the coming of Christ in the clouds of heaven with power and great glory" (ibid. 352).

"The blood of Christ, while it was to release the repentant sinner from the condemnation of the law, was not to cancel the sin; it would stand on record in the sanctuary until the final atonement; so in the type the blood of the sin offering removed the sin from the penitent, but it rested in the sanctuary until the Day of Atonement.

"In the great day of final award, the dead are to be 'judged out of those things which were written in the books, according to their works' (Rev. 20:12). Then by virtue of the atoning blood of Christ, the sins of all the truly penitent will be blotted from the books of heaven. Thus the sanctuary will be freed, or cleansed, from the record of sin. In the type, this great work of atonement, or blotting out of sins, was represented by the services of the Day of Atonement—the cleansing of the earthly sanctuary, which was accomplished by the removal, by virtue of the blood of the sin offering, of the sins by which it had been polluted.

"As in the final atonement the sins of the truly penitent are to be blotted from the records of heaven, no more to be remembered or come into mind, so in the type they were borne away into the wilderness, forever separated from the congregation" (PP 357, 358).

"It was seen, also, that while the sin offering pointed to Christ as a sacrifice, and the high priest represented Christ as a mediator, the scapegoat typified Satan, the author of sin, upon whom the sins of the truly penitent will finally be placed. When the high priest, by virtue of the blood of the sin offering, removed the sins from the sanctuary, he placed them upon the scapegoat. When Christ, by virtue of His own blood, removes the sins of His people from the heavenly sanctuary at the close of His ministration, He will place them upon Satan, who, in the execution of the judgment, must bear the final penalty. The scapegoat was sent away into a land not inhabited, never to come again into the congregation of Israel. So will Satan be forever banished from the presence of God and His people, and he will be blotted from existence in the final destruction of sin and sinners" (GC 422).

"This is the great day of atonement, and our Advocate is standing before the Father, pleading as our intercessor. In place of wrapping about us the garments of self-righteousness, we should be found daily humbling ourselves before God, confessing our own individual sins, seeking the pardon of our transgressions, and cooperating with Christ in the work of preparing our souls to reflect the divine image" (7BC 933).

VII. Literature

Ball, Bryan W. *The English Connection: The Puritan Roots of Seventh-day Adventist Belief.* Cambridge, Eng.: James Clarke, 1981.

Bede: On the Tabernacle. Tr. Arthur G. Holder. Liverpool: University Press, 1994.

Damsteegt, P. Gerard. "Historical Background (Early Nineteenth Century)," "Among Sabbatarian Adventists (1845-1850)," and "Continued Clarification (1850-1863)." In *Doctrine of the Sanctuary: A Historical Survey.* Ed. Frank B. Holbrook. Silver Spring, Md.: Biblical Research Institute, 1989. Pp. 1-118.

Ellingworth, Paul. *The Epistle to the Hebrews: A Commentary on the Greek Text.* Grand Rapids: Eerdmans, 1993.

Feldeman, Emanuel. *Biblical and Post-Biblical Defilement and Meaning.* New York: KTAV, 1977.

Guthrie, Donald. *The Letter to the Hebrews.* Grand Rapids: Eerdmans, 1983.

Hagner, Donald A. *Hebrews. New International Biblical Commentary.* Peabody, Mass.: Hendrickson, 1990.

Hasel, Gerhard F. "Studies in Biblical Atonement I: Continual Sacrifice, Defilement/ Cleansing and Sanctuary." In *The Sanctuary and the Atonement.* Ed. Arnold V. Wallenkampf, W. Richard Lesher. Washington, D.C.: General Conference of Seventh-day Adventists, 1981. Pp. 87-114.

Heppenstall, Edward. *Our High Priest.* Washington, D.C.: Review and Herald, 1972.

Holbrook, Frank B., ed. *Symposium on Daniel: Introductory and Exegetical Studies.* Washington, D.C.: Biblical Research Institute, 1986.

————. *The Seventy Weeks, Leviticus, and the Nature of Prophecy.* Washington, D.C.: Biblical Research Institute, 1986.

————. *Issues in the Book of Hebrews.* Silver Spring, Md.: Biblical Research Institute, 1989.

————. *The Atoning Priesthood of Jesus Christ.* Berrien Springs, Mich.: Adventist Theological Society Publications, 1996.

Johnsson, William G. *In Absolute Confidence.* Nashville: Southern Pub. Assn., 1979.

————. "The Significance of the Day of Atonement Allusions in the Epistle to the Hebrews." In *The Sanctuary and the Atonement.* Ed. Arnold V. Wallenkampf, W. Richard Lesher. Washington, D.C.: General Conference of Seventh-day Adventists, 1981. Pp. 380-393.

Lane, William L. *Hebrews 9-13.* Dallas: Word, 1991.

Levine, Baruch A. *In the Presence of the Lord.* Leiden: E. J. Brill, 1974.

Maxwell, C. Mervyn. "The Investigative Judgment: Its Early Development." In *Doctrine of the Sanctuary: A Historical Survey.* Ed. Frank B. Holbrook. Silver Spring, Md.: Biblical Research Institute, 1989. Pp. 119-157.

Milgrom, Jacob. *Leviticus 1-16.* New York: Doubleday, 1991.

Olsen, V. Norskov. "The Atonement in Protestant Reformation Thought." In *The Sanctuary and the Atonement.* Ed. Arnold V. Wallenkampf, W. Richard Lesher. Washington, D.C.: General Conference of Seventh-day Adventists, 1981. Pp. 452-463.

Owen, John. *An Exposition of Hebrews.* 4 vols. Evansville, Ill.: Soverign Grace Publishers, 1960.

Rodríguez, Angel Manuel. "El santuario y sus servicios en la literatura patrística." *Theologika* 7 (1992): 22-79.

Seventh-day Adventists Answer Questions on Doctrine. Washington, D.C.: Review and Herald, 1957.

Shea, William H. *Selected Studies on Prophetic Interpretation.* Silver Spring, Md.: Biblical Research Institute, 1992, rev. ed.

Stedman, Ray C. *Hebrews*. Downers Grove, Ill.: InterVarsity, 1992.

Wallenkampf, Arnold V., and W. Richard Lesher, eds. *The Sanctuary and the Atonement*. Washington, D.C.: General Conference of Seventh-day Adventists, 1981.

Appendix A
Ta Hagia in Hebrews

A. Hebrews 8:1, 2

In Hebrews 8:2 we find the first use of the noun *ta hagia* to designate the heavenly sanctuary. *Ta hagia* is a plural adjective with an article, meaning "holy things," or, collectively, "the holy." It is used in the Greek version of the OT (LXX) to refer to the Israelite sanctuary. In Hebrews Christ is a minister in *ta hagia,* further defined as "the true tent which is set up not by man but by the Lord." The term "tent," *skēnē,* without modifiers, is normally used in the LXX to designate the Israelite tabernacle as a whole. In Hebrews 8:2, both nouns refer to the heavenly sanctuary; between the two is the conjunction "and" *(kai),* which here functions as an epexegetical or explicative *kai,* bringing in a second noun to define the first in a more precise way. Thus, Christ is ministering in the sanctuary *(ta hagia),* the true, heavenly tabernacle *(skēnē).* Here *ta hagia* refers to the heavenly sanctuary in its entirety.

B. Hebrews 9:1-10

In Hebrews 9:1 the earthly sanctuary is called *to hagion kosmikon,* "the earthly holy place." A singular noun with a definite article is used *(to hagion)* to designate the sanctuary of the first *(prōtē)* covenant. This sanctuary had two apartments, here called "tents" *(skēnē).* The first is called *hagia,* literally, "holies," without a definite article, for with the article *ta hagia* designates the sanctuary as a whole and not merely one of the compartments (cf. 8:2). The second tent is called the *hagia hagiōn,* literally, "holy of holies." In verse 6 the priests enter continually into the first tent to perform their daily responsibilities. In verse 7, on the annual Day of Atonement, only the high priest enters the second tent. A contrast is implicit between the daily access of the priests to the holy place every day and the yearly access of the high priest once a year to the Most Holy Place.

The heavenly sanctuary appears in verse 8, which seems to introduce an evaluation of the earthly sanctuary. The Holy Spirit has revealed to the believer that "the way into the sanctuary *[ta hagia]* is not yet opened as long as the first tent is still standing" (RSV and NASB translate "outer tent," whereas the Greek clearly states "first tent." In verses 2-6 the "first tent" is the holy place of the earthly sanctuary. If that were still so in verse 8, the text would be saying that as long as the daily services in the holy place were being performed, there was no access to the Most Holy Place *(ta hagia)* of the earthly sanctuary. Such an obvious conclusion would not require the intervention of the Holy Spirit. Here, however, *ta hagia* refers to the heavenly sanctuary. This would mean that as long as the holy place *(prōtē skēnē)* of the earthly sanctuary was functioning, access to the heavenly sanctuary was not available. Verse 8 would then suggest that access to the heavenly sanctuary was possible only through the second tent (the Most Holy Place) of the earthly sanctuary. But that, we would argue, is not the way Hebrews interprets the Israelite tabernacle.

The second solution to this exegetical problem is to take *prōtē skēnē* as a designation for the Israelite sanctuary as a whole. The contrast then stands between the first sanctuary, *prōtē skēnē,* and the heavenly *ta hagia,* "sanctuary." This is supported by the following considerations.

1. In Hebrews 8 and 9 two covenants and their respective sanctuaries are in view. The old covenant is called the first, and the new covenant, the second (8:7). The old covenant had an earthly sanctuary consisting of two

compartments (9:1); likewise, also the second covenant (verse 8). These two sanctuaries are contrasted in verse 8.

2. According to Hebrews neither the holy place nor the Most Holy Place of the earthly sanctuary provided free and permanent access to God. Limited access was available to the high priest once a year but not to the people. The whole sanctuary was needed to provide complete, unhindered access to God. Thus *prōtē skēnē* in verse 8 should not be limited to the holy place.

3. Beginning with 9:8 there is a shift from spatial considerations to temporal ones, as indicated by the temporal particle *eti,* "while, as long as." The contrast is between the sanctuaries of two different ages: "The way into the sanctuary is not yet opened *as long as* the first tent is still standing." The *prōtē skēnē* is placed now in the context of temporal discussions and taken to refer, not to the space in front of the Most Holy Place, but to the tabernacle of the first covenant. The term *skēnē* would thus designate the sanctuary as a whole (cf. 8:2).

A shift to a temporal discussion is also indicated by verses 9, 10. According to verse 9 the problem with the ministry in the *prōtē skēnē* was that the gifts and sacrifices offered there could not perfect the conscience. This limitation applied not only to the daily services but also to the annual services. This suggests the use of the phrase "first tent" to designate the sanctuary as a whole. In verse 10 the time element is expressed clearly: The services in the earthly sanctuary were to last "until *[mechri]* the time *[kairos]* of reformation," that is, until the coming of Christ (verse 10). The shift from spatial to temporal considerations is even more clear if the phrase, "which is symbolic *[parabolē,* "illustration"]* for the present age [*kairos,* "time"]," in verse 9, is taken to designate the age when the *prōtē skēnē,* the earthly sanctuary, was functioning. The meaning would then be that the earthly sanctuary itself was an illustration of the fact that free and final access to God was

not yet a reality and verse 10 would introduce the new time when the deficiency was to be eliminated. We would then have two sanctuaries in two different periods.

4. When the author of Hebrews establishes a contrast between the earthly and heavenly sanctuaries, he normally takes the earthly sanctuary as a whole. For instance, the sanctuary "made with hands" is the earthly sanctuary in its entirety, which is then contrasted with the heavenly one (9:24). In 8:2 the sanctuary which was "set up by man" is the earthly, with its holy and Most Holy places, and is contrasted with the heavenly sanctuary *(ta hagia).* Thus a contrast between the earthly holy place and the heavenly sanctuary is unlikely in 9:8. The contrasts between the two sanctuaries suggest that the heavenly one is also a bipartite structure.

In conclusion, verse 8 contrasts the earthly sanctuary, called "first tabernacle," with the heavenly *ta hagia.* Both sanctuaries are visualized in their entirety. *Ta hagia* is the heavenly sanctuary and not a part or section of it. The apostle has concluded, through the illumination of the Spirit, that as long as the earthly sanctuary was functioning, the way to the heavenly sanctuary was not yet open; the very existence of the earthly sanctuary illustrated that fact. The coming of Christ's death, resurrection, and ascension opened a way to the heavenly sanctuary (cf. 10:19, 20).

C. Hebrews 9:11, 12

The Greek of this long sentence is syntactically difficult; however, certain aspects of its meaning are clear.

1. The main clause can be identified: "He entered once for all into the sanctuary *[ta hagia]."* Here the new priestly work of Christ in the heavenly sanctuary is introduced in contrast with the old system; "but" is adversative. Nothing indicates that in the main clause *ta hagia* designates the Most Holy Place in the heavenly sanctuary; it means here the same as in 8:2 and 9:8, the whole sanctuary.

2. In verse 11 the phrase "the greater and

more perfect tabernacle (not made with hands, that is, not of this creation)" refers to the heavenly sanctuary. Already "tabernacle" *(skēnē)* was used in 8:2 to designate the heavenly sanctuary. The implicit contrast here is between the heavenly "tent" and the "tent" made by Moses (8:5). Hence, the heavenly tent and *ta hagia* in verse 12 refer to the same entity, the heavenly sanctuary.

While the previous aspects of the verse are clear, the relationship of the four subordinate clauses to the main one is complex:

"Through [*dia*, "by means of, through"] the greater and more perfect tent"
"Not made with hands, that is, not of this creation"
"Not [*oude*, "neither"] by [*dia*] the blood of goats and calves"
"But by [*dia*] his own blood"

The four clauses are closely related. The second modifies the first, clarifying by antithetical parallelism the nature of the "greater and more perfect tabernacle." The two must stay together in any interpretation of the sentence. The third is introduced by the negative "neither" *(oude),* which is rather unusual or even unexpected. In Greek *oude* joins negative sentences of the same type. While the previous clause is negative, it is not of the same type. This suggests a stylistic change, making the presence of "neither" *(oude)* tolerable. The use of the preposition "by" *(dia)* suggests that a new element or idea is being introduced. The last clause is obviously related and directly connected to number three. This is suggested by the presence of the adversative particle *de,* "but," and another use of *dia.* The parallelism is antithetic.

These clauses, which are connected one to the other in pointing back to the first clause, are theologically important to what the author is trying to say. On the basis of theological content, the four can be grouped into two. The first two state the superiority of the sanctuary of the new covenant by implicitly contrasting it with the earthly sanctuary made by humans and belonging to this creation. The last two state the uniqueness of the new sacrificial blood by contrasting it, again implicitly, with the blood of animals used in the old covenant. The contrasts are expressed in an elegant way by combining positive and negative clauses.

A *Positive*
  "through the greater and more perfect tent"
B *Negative*
  "not made with hands, that is, not of this creation"
B *Negative*
  "not by the blood of goats and calves"
A *Positive*
  "but by his own blood"

By way of these subordinate clauses the theological content of the main clause is greatly enriched. To the fact of Christ's entrance into the heavenly sanctuary is added the information that the sanctuary in which Christ functions as priest is immensely superior to the earthly one and that the priestly blood is likewise superior.

The passage does not state that Christ entered the heavenly sanctuary by means of (or through, *dia*) the greater and more perfect tent. While *dia* in the first clause remains difficult, the interpretational problem becomes more acute if the clause is tied to the main verb ("he entered"). In the first subordinate clause *dia* should be related to the first part of the main clause, "but Christ arrived as high priest." The preposition *dia,* "through," could refer to the means or agency He uses in performing His priestly work: "Christ arrived as high priest by using the greater and more perfect tent." The same notion applies to the use of the preposition *dia,* which introduces the subject of blood in the third clause. The idea of this long sentence is that after He arrived as high priest, Christ used in His priestly work a superior sanctuary and His own blood. Then He entered into that sanctuary after securing eternal redemption. This is in perfect agreement with what is said elsewhere in Hebrews. The NEB has captured in its translation the real intent of the author of Hebrews: "But now Christ has come, high priest of good things already in being. The tent of his priesthood is a greater and more perfect one, not made by men's hands, that is, not belonging to this created world; the blood of his sacrifice is his own blood, not the blood of goats and calves; and thus he has entered the sanctuary once and for all."

D. Hebrews 9:24, 25

This passage, in particular verse 24, has been interpreted to mean that the heavenly sanctuary is heaven itself. The thought expressed is the same found in 9:11, 12: Christ entered the heavenly sanctuary, which served as a model for the earthly. As the original, the heavenly is superior. The first part of verse 24 expressed a negative statement: Christ did not enter into a sanctuary made with hands. The noun "sanctuary" is *hagia* without the definite article. The article is not necessary because the modifiers make the noun definite. *Hagia* refers to the sanctuary as a whole without reference to any section of it. The sanctuary made with hands is again contrasted with the "true one" stressing the reality of the heavenly sanctuary (cf. 8:2).

According to Hebrews, Christ did not enter into an inferior sanctuary, but "into heaven itself." Here the sanctuary and heaven are not equated. In the first part of verse 24 *hagia* refers to both sanctuaries—to the one that is "a copy" and the other that is "the true one." The author seems to have used "heaven" by itself for stylistic reasons. To avoid using *hagia* again and in an effort to be brief and move on to the second point in the argument, the word "sanctuary" is intentionally omitted. The context helps identify what was omitted. Christ entered "into [the sanctuary which is in] heaven." In the OT "heaven" is used as a designation for God's heavenly dwelling;

therefore, since God's sanctuary is in heaven, "heaven" can be used to refer to it without making heaven itself God's sanctuary. This is not a peculiar interpretation of the passage but what the author has stated previously. It also agrees with the understanding in Hebrews of the heavenly sanctuary as the "real one." In verse 25 *ta hagia* designates the earthly sanctuary. The text deals with the Day of Atonement and one could argue that the noun refers to the Most Holy Place; however, on that day the high priest officiated in the whole sanctuary and not only in one of its apartments. In this verse also *ta hagia* should be understood as designating the earthly sanctuary in its entirety. Had the author of Hebrews wanted to refer to the "Most Holy Place," the phrase used in 9:3 could have been chosen.

E. Hebrews 10:19, 20

In verse 19 the believer has confidence and freedom to enter the heavenly sanctuary by virtue of Christ's blood. *Ta hagia* does not point to any particular section of the heavenly sanctuary but to the sanctuary itself. Christ entered there and by virtue of His death we have access to it.

In verse 20 the veil of the temple seems to be equated with the flesh of Christ: "By the new and living way which he opened for us through the curtain, that is *[tout' estin]*, through his flesh." "That is" *(tout' estin)* is used often in Hebrews to explain the immediately preceding noun (see Heb. 2:14; 7:5; 9:11). If so used here, *tout' estin* makes the veil equivalent to the flesh of Christ. Such an interpretation creates problems, which make it untenable. For one, it implies that in order to enter the sanctuary, Jesus went through His own flesh (the veil). This could not be applied to His experience on the cross because going through the veil is something that takes place in the heavenly realm. In addition, the term "veil" is used in a very concrete and local way in the rest of the Epistle (6:19, 20; 9:3). There is no evidence in 10:20

that "veil" is being used in a metaphorical or symbolic way.

The phrase *tout' estin* is also used in Hebrews to refer back to a noun other than the immediately preceding one (see 13:15). This ambiguity allows *tout' estin* to refer back to "the way," the other noun in the verse. In that case the way of access to God, through the veil, is the flesh of Christ, i.e., His incarnation, death, and resurrection. The genitive phrase "of his flesh" would, then, be a genitive of dependence connected to "way": "the way . . . , that is, [the way] of his flesh." This interpretation is grammatically and contextually valid, and agrees with the understanding of the heavenly sanctuary in concrete and local terms as presented in the rest of Hebrews.

Appendix B
Hebrews 6:19, 20

These verses belong to a chapter that contains an exhortation to Christian hope. The problem phrase involves "the inner shrine behind the curtain," where Christ has entered. In Greek it reads, *eis to esōteron tou katapetasmatos,* "into the interior of the veil." This phrase is similar to the LXX of Leviticus 16:2: *eis to hagion esōteron tou katapetasmatos,* "into the sanctuary within/behind the veil."

There are obvious similarities; but at the same time there are differences. The rather general nature of the statement and the immediate context in Hebrews indicate that the apostle was not even suggesting that Christ entered into the Most Holy Place immediately after His ascension to fulfill the typological meaning of the Day of Atonement. Items vital to this interpretation are the following:

1. The term *katapetasma* is ambiguous. It is employed in the LXX to refer to the veil at the entrance to the courtyard of the sanctuary (Num. 3:26), to the first veil at the entrance to the holy place (Ex. 26:37), and to the veil in front of the Most Holy Place (verses 31, 33). By itself the term cannot be used to determine which of the veils is intended. In Hebrews 9:3 the term is specific; "the second veil." The lack of specificity in 6:19 indicates that the reference is not to the second veil, and that the author does not define the specific area of the sanctuary into which Christ entered.

2. In Hebrews 6:19 the preposition "behind/within" *(esōteron)* is used in a different way than in Leviticus 16:2, where it specifies a place within the sanctuary as indicated by the noun "sanctuary" *(to hagion)* preceding it. In other words, in Leviticus 16:2, "within the veil" designates a specific area inside the "sanctuary." On the other hand, in Hebrews 6:19 *esōteron* is used, not as a preposition but as a noun. It is preceded by a definite article: *"eis to,* "into *the* interior of the veil," rather than "within the veil." There is no mention of the sanctuary in Hebrews 6:19; instead the prepositional phrase *(eis to esōteron katapesmatos)* suggests the sanctuary as a whole and does not point to any particular section within the heavenly sanctuary. "Veil" could well refer to the veil at the entrance of the sanctuary which provided access to the sanctuary itself.

3. That the phrase "into the interior of the veil" does not refer to the Most Holy Place is also suggested by comparing 6:19 with 7:19. Here the old priestly law, with its restrictions, is eliminated by the introduction of a "better hope, . . . through which we draw near to God." The concept of "hope" is followed here, as in 6:19, by a cultic concept.

6:19	7:19
"A hope"	"A better hope"
"that enters into the interior of the veil"	"through which we draw near to God"

Hebrews 7:19 elucidates the meaning of 6:19. Entrance into the interior of the veil is understood to mean "to come near to God," a phrase used in the OT to describe the service of the priests in the sanctuary (Lev. 21:21, 23),

but never to refer to the high priest's ministry in the Most Holy Place. The phrase is also applied to the individual who approaches God in worship and prayer (Isa. 29:13). According to Hebrews, hope in Christ provides access to the heavenly sanctuary. The text does not discuss the specific place within the heavenly sanctuary where Christ entered after His ascension. That Christ entered the sanctuary means that He has full access to God.

4. Contextual considerations rule out the discussion of the antitypical day of atonement in Hebrews 6:19, while the Day of Atonement is clearly in view in Leviticus 16:2 . In Hebrews 6:13-20 the discussion concerns the certainty of God's promises to Abraham. Because God fulfilled those promises to the patriarch, Christians are encouraged to hold fast to their hope knowing that God's promises are reliable. That hope brings certainty be-

cause it is anchored in God's very presence, the heavenly sanctuary, where Christ entered as our forerunner.

Finally, the parallelism between 6:19 and 10:19-22 suggests that in 6:19 the author may have had in mind Christ's entrance into the heavenly sanctuary at the initiation of His high priestly work.

6:19, 20	10:19-22
Christ entered	Christ inaugurated
the veil	the veil
high priest	high priest
the interior of the veil	draw near

Moreover, the aorist tense in 6:20—"Christ entered" (eisēlthen)—points to a particular moment in time when He entered for the first time into the heavenly sanctuary, i.e., after His ascension.

Creation

William H. Shea

Introduction

Creation is the basic event with which the history of the world and humanity begins. It is also basic to the history of the salvation of the human race since it was shortly after Creation that human beings fell into sin. The account of the Fall is given in Genesis 3. The basic account of the Creation precedes that narrative in Genesis 1 and 2. Quite naturally, therefore, the Bible begins with the account of Creation. In other passages of the OT, however, there are other major statements about Creation. In any study of this doctrine those texts need to be taken into account.

In addition to the OT, the NT likewise teaches the doctrine of Creation. Several points are emphasized here. The first is that Jesus Christ was active in Creation. The second is that He is Lord over His creation. Finally, there is the matter of the new creation. In NT statements on the subject, such as in Revelation, the new creation is related to the old. It is like it, but differs from it in certain respects. It will be more advanced and refined than the original creation. From this general perspective the texts themselves may now be considered.

I. Creation in the Old Testament

A. Genesis 1

The primary statement on the creation of the world is found in Genesis 1. Here is described the way God set up the world for its inhabitants, both animal and human. Since no human being was present at the time God did this, we are dependent upon revelation for a view of the world as it came to be fitted up during Creation week. God did this by a series of separate and discrete acts. The record indicates that these acts spanned a period of seven days. Each of those days consisted of one light and one dark period, as have all days since that time. Thus at Creation the Creator set up a framework and then revealed to us just what that framework was. Not only was the Sabbath set aside for special uses at that time, but it marked the end of God's special creation. This was the original model for the unit of time known as the seven-day week.

1. In the Beginning

Genesis 1:1 begins with a dependent prepositional phrase, "in the beginning." Genesis 1:1 is part of the context of Genesis 1:2 and the rest of the chapter. The point of the phrase was simply to give a brief description of the world as it was when God began to work His special works upon it. Some have translated this opening dependent phrase as "when God began to create." While that language may be more free than the original Hebrew, it does convey the idea that the concern here is with the creation that follows rather than the pre-existing state. The text acknowledges the fact that the inert earth was in a watery state before the events of Creation week, but it is not especially concerned with identifying how long it may have been in that state.

The verb used in this opening sentence is *bārā'*, properly translated "created." This verb is used in the Bible only to designate an activity of God. Human beings and God may make things *('āśāh)*. God may make, using the same verb, but only God can create in the way that is indicated by *bārā'*. Thus, only God can create the matter that was later shaped in Creation, but both God and human beings can reshape that matter in various ways.

The subject of the verb *bārā'* is God, here called by the general word for God in Hebrew, *'elōhim*. He is the subject of all of the verbs for creating, making, and shaping in Genesis 1. The one true God is introduced in the first sentence of the Creation account; He is the One who acts all the way through this account. No other God disputes with Him about what He creates, as in extrabiblical polytheistic creation stories. He is sovereign over Creation, and it obeys His will as it rises to its newly organized state. The biblical Creation account is emphatic: This one sovereign God is the only true Creator.

2. The Heavens and the Earth

The first objects of this creative activity identified in the text are the heavens and the earth. Some have taken the "heavens" as a reference to the universe. The way to evaluate this interpretation is to see how the phrase "heavens and the earth" is used in the rest of this narrative. An examination of those occurrences shows that the word "heavens" does not focus upon the universe, but rather upon the atmospheric heavens that surround this earth. Those were the "heavens" that God addressed when He divided the firmament on the second day of Creation week. Those were the heavens in which the birds flew after their creation on the fifth day (Gen. 1:20). Thus the focus of the use of the phrase "heavens and the earth" in Genesis 1 is upon this earth, not the universe or the starry heavens. This shows the geocentric emphasis of this Creation account.

Oriented to the scientific method, modern thought comes to this account thinking of an observer of the earth standing outside of it or looking down upon it. That is not the point of view from which this narrative was written. The Creation acts were revealed and recorded as if they had passed before an observer positioned upon the earth, not outside of its systems. That point of view makes some elements in the narrative more understandable.

3. The Creation of Light on Day One

Genesis 1:3 says that on the first day of the Creation week God spoke light into existence, to penetrate the watery darkness of this earth. A question has arisen here in relation to the fourth day of Creation. On that day God said, "Let there be lights in the firmament of the heavens." The text identifies those lights as the greater light (the sun), the lesser light (the moon), and the stars (Gen. 1:14-16). Since today we know of light only from these natural sources and from human-made sources, it is difficult to conceive how God made light on day one without the assistance of these astronomical bodies.

Two different answers have been given to this question. The first is that the astronomical bodies were actually there all the time, giving off their light, but from the earth those bodies were hidden from view by a dense cloud cover surrounding it, the watery firmament above. On the fourth day this cloud cover or watery envelope was reorganized to make more visible the astronomical bodies involved. This theory remains possible, but at present there is no direct evidence to support it.

The other way this feature has been explained is that the light present upon the first three days of Creation week came directly from God Himself. He subsequently delegated that task to the astronomical bodies identified on the fourth day. There is a biblical parallel to such an occurrence in Revelation 21:23. There the New Jerusalem will not need light from the sun or the moon because God Himself will provide light. That could also have been the case during the first three days of Creation week.

Human beings later came to worship the astronomical bodies that provided them with light. God may have wished to avoid that possibility by creating light apart from the sun and moon, which later became the objects of worship. Our worship is due the One who created nature; it is not due to nature itself.

4. The Time Element for the Days of Creation

The account of each of the first six days of Creation week ends with a dateline. That dateline has a standard formula. It reads, "There was evening and there was morning, day one [or second, third, etc.]." It has been suggested that these were not literal 24-hour days, but long ages through which the earth and the elements in it evolved to their later state.

The language of the date formula excludes this possibility. Each statement contains four elements. First is the verb "to be," which is actually written out twice. Then come the portions of the day as related to darkness and light, evening and morning. Third, the day is given a number. Finally, there is the word for "day" itself. In this complex date formula it is stated that the time elements occurred, that they made up the day, and that the whole day was numbered. When other evidence in the OT is compared with this type of date formula (see Gen. 33:13; Ex. 12:18; Neh. 5:18), there can be no doubt that the writer was speaking of the 24-hour period of light and dark which made up one whole day. Adding the other elements of this formula to the word "day" gives a specificity that requires the limited and local application of this phrase in time.

5. The Division of the Firmament on Day Two

The watery firmament, or envelope, around the earth already existed before the second day of Creation. On this day God divided, or separated, it into two main portions, the water above and the water below. The emphasis is upon the waters above, here referring to the atmospheric heavens. The Hebrew word (verse 8) might be translated as "sky" (NIV). It is that portion of the space above the earth in which water collects in the clouds.

6. The Division of Dry Land and the Seas on Day Three

The primordial state of the earth was described in Genesis 1:1 as covered with water. The first two days of Creation did not change that situation. The earth is heir to that situation, since about 70 percent of its surface is still covered with water—the seas.

Those seas made way for dry land on the third day. Just how God accomplished this is not known. Whether He created great ocean basins or heaped up the mountains, we do not know. We know only that land did appear at this time and that as a consequence the earth

became usable and occupiable by plants, animals, and human beings. The plants that came forth were divided into three main categories: "vegetation, plants yielding seed, and fruit trees bearing fruit in which is their seed" (verse 11). The emphasis is upon their perpetuation, for the seed mentioned was to propagate them, "according to their own kinds."

The phrase "according to its kind" (verse 11) deserves attention because it gave rise to a special understanding of nature in the nineteenth century known as the fixity of species. According to this interpretation the species existent upon earth were fixed and limited to the original species that God had created during Creation week. All of the known species were thought to be the direct descendants of those original species. The same was thought to be true of the species of the animals that were taken into the ark by Noah.

This theory was based upon a false linguistic premise. It derived from a particular translation of *lᵉmînēhû*, which was interpreted as applying to what are known as species today. Since the progress in genetics over the last century has indicated that there is descent with modification, this older interpretation is certainly wrong on a biological basis.

Closer examination of this word in the biblical text also reveals that this theory is wrong on a biblical basis. In Genesis 1 this word is used for plants (verse 12), birds and fish (verse 21), and land animals according to their three categories (verses 24, 25). Thus this word is used for major classifications or divisions in the plant and animal kingdoms. In Leviticus 11, however, the same word is used for much smaller divisions of the animal world. It is used four times in the section on birds (verses 14-19), three times in the section on insects (verse 22), and once in the section on those animals that crawl on the earth (verse 29). In each of these cases this word is used for individual animals that a modern zoologist would probably identify as a species. The same distinctions are found in the parallel passage of Deuteronomy 14.

Thus the word translated "according to its kind" is used in Genesis 1 for large divisions of the plant and animal world and then in Leviticus 11 and Deuteronomy 14 for small divisions. It cannot refer to species in both cases. A dissection of the word *le mînēhû* itself helps to clarify the idea. The *le* prefix is a preposition, meaning "to," "for," "by," or "according to." The middle part is a noun, *mîn,* meaning "kind," "class," or "species." The suffix is a possessive pronoun, showing to whom something belongs. The translation "according to its kind" is legitimate and best understood as an idiomatic expression referring to "the different kinds of" plants or animals. Another interpretation is that the middle part of the word is the preposition *min,* "from"; in this case the phrase would mean "according to that from which it comes." In either case, the phrase may be used at any level and referring to any class of plants or animals, regardless of how narrowly or broadly defined that group is. Whereas the idea of plants bearing seeds "each according to its kind" (Gen. 1:12) seems to refer to genetic links, *le mînēhû* simply points to "different kinds," a variety. Thus the nineteenth-century concept of the fixity of species has no biblical, linguistic, or biological basis.

7. The Appearance of the Astronomical Bodies on Day Four

In the narration of the fourth day, the sun and moon are called the greater light and the lesser light. The reason for not using the actual names for these heavenly bodies could well be that by the time this record was written by Moses, the sun and moon (and the stars) were deified and worshiped. To avoid any concession to that view, their names were not even mentioned in Genesis 1:16-18. They were simply astronomical bodies at the beck and call of the Creator. They held no independent existence apart from Him. He made them and they served His purposes, especially with regard to marking time and seasons for human beings.

8. Literary and Historical Relations Between Days One to Three and Four to Six

There is a thematic relationship between the first three days of Creation week and the following three days. The subject of the first day, light, appears again on the fourth day. The subject of the second day, the division of the firmament, reappears on the fifth day. Birds and fish fill the two divisions of the firmament. The subject of the third day, the dry land and its plants, is related to Creation on the sixth day: The animals and human beings were to fill up the space on that dry land and consume its plants as food. Thus day one is related most directly to day four, day two is related most directly to day five, and day three is related most directly to day six.

These relations are literary in nature, but they also represent accurately the creative activity of God. He made His creation in this order and way. Given His omnipotence, He could have done all of this creating in one day or even one second, but He did not. He chose rather to pace His creative acts, revealing them one by one. We have come to know these events through the biblical revelation. Other beings were involved. The angels undoubtedly looked on as these events took place, and Job 38:7 suggests other worlds may have viewed this new creation.

Thus the orderly march of creative activities on these days of Creation demonstrated the love, care, and organization of the God we serve. He set up the world in an orderly fashion and then filled it. At the end of the first three days of Creation the world was beautiful but empty of fish, fowl, or land animals. At the end of the next three days it was beautiful and full of living creatures. It was all the more beautiful for being filled in that way. Space had found its occupants; promise had met its fulfillment.

9. The Creation of Birds and Fish on Day Five

The occupants of the upper space of the

firmament, the sky, were the birds. They are, of course, marvelously adapted to their environment. The creation of all of the marine organisms documented here includes even the great *tannînim,* presumably whales. These great creatures were the product of the Creator's virtually instantaneous creation. According to evolutionary theory, an animal this large would have required long ages to evolve.

10. The Creation of Land Animals and Human Beings on Day Six

The first third of this portion of the narrative tells of the creation of land animals (Gen. 1:24, 25). Then comes the account of the creation of human beings, both male and female, more detailed than the account of any other element in Creation week. Finally, Genesis 1:29, 30 tells of the assignment of the diet of both the land animals and human beings.

In verse 24 the word for "kinds" (here *l^emînāh*) is used in a general sense: all the kinds of land animals. In verse 25 it is applied to three individual groups: the beasts of the earth, the cattle, and the creeping animals. The story points to a large variety of animals.

11. Poetry in Genesis 1

The stately cadences of Genesis 1 have raised the question of whether there is poetry in this account. One reason these verses sometimes look like poetry is the parallelism of thought, which is characteristic of Hebrew poetry. But Genesis 1 lacks poetic meter and could be more accurately described as poetic prose. One exception is found in verse 27. The parallelism, and even meter, can be seen both in Hebrew and English:

"So God created man in his own image,
in the image of God he created him;
male and female he created them."

The same verb "to create" appears in all three lines. The name for God appears twice and is understood in the last line. The word for image is used twice and is understood in the last line. In the Hebrew text these lines are very even, with a similar number of words and syllables in each line. Thus this little unit of the Creation story qualifies as fully poetic. It is expanded in the complementary account of Creation in Genesis 2.

The verb at the beginning of Gen. 1:26, where the creation of human beings is first contemplated, is in the first person plural, "Let *us* make man in *our* image." This occurs in the prose part of the account, not in the poetic section. One cannot, therefore, explain away this plurality in the account as a mere literary feature. It is of grammatical significance and, therefore, of theological and historical import. Both male and female forms of the human race manifested the image of God in Creation. As originally created, both bore the express image of their Creator. There was an equality here that was damaged and distorted by the Fall. (See Man I. C.)

12. The Image of God

The phrase "image of God" has elicited major comments from theologians through the Christian Era (see Man I. B; Sin I). The emphasis in these writings has been upon the rational powers and freedom of choice granted to human beings at Creation. In scholastic theology this was taken to include the state of moral righteousness before the Fall. Since the Reformation, Protestant theologians have tended to place their emphasis upon the latter quality. Another portion of this discussion has questioned to what extent the Fall and sin have obliterated or disfigured this original state. A distinction has also been made between that original state that was enjoyed by Adam and Eve and that state to which regenerated Christians are elevated in their spiritual experience with God. In general, the latter has been seen as quite different from the original state enjoyed at the time of Creation.

The word used in Genesis 1:27 for "image" is *ṣelem,* well known in Hebrew and its ancient cognate languages. It was used primarily for images of the gods that were placed in temples. These were thought to represent the appearance and functions of the gods. The Bible is unique in its use of this word: in the ancient world the gods were made in the images of human beings, whereas in the Bible humans were made in the image of God.

Moderns have shied away from the physical aspect of this phraseology. Ancient Hebrews did not. Their conceptions of the world and what was good about it were much more tangible than ours. This is shown in the Creation story, where, after each day's creation, the products of those creative acts were pronounced "good," and after it was all done it was all pronounced "very good." This view of the material world and its inhabitants was characteristically Hebrew.

That the image of God, in which man and woman were created, includes a physical likeness is part of the conception conveyed by the original word used here. This likeness also suggested rational powers with which to think God's thoughts after Him. In their unfallen state Adam and Eve were pure and sinless. To that extent they were like God morally, even though they soon lost this state through their transgression. The likeness to God also extends into the realm of emotions. God is an emotional being. We have abundant evidence for this in the Bible. He loves His creatures. He is not the cold, dispassionate, and removed god of the deists; He is the present and active God who is in touch with His creatures. The story of the Bible after the Fall is the story of God in search of His fallen creatures. He expresses, in both the OT and the NT, His love for those creatures. It is natural, therefore, that creatures made in His likeness and image should also reflect those aspects in their creaturehood.

Philosophers who have placed emphasis upon the rational aspects of the image of God in human beings have stressed a correct point. One can also agree that this involves the freedom of choice with which Adam and Eve were endowed in the Garden of Eden. To these powers, however, should also be added the physical aspects of that image. While we may not presently understand just how that aspect of the image was worked out, it still should have been present in some features. Given the wholistic view of human beings in the OT, the emotional life that goes with the physical being should also be stressed. Thus to be created in the image of God ultimately means that human beings bear a likeness to Him in terms of their rational powers, their freedom of choice, their original moral purity (now damaged by the Fall), their physical appearance, and their emotional life. To be created in the image of God means to have received a comprehensive likeness of the Creator.

13. The Diet of Humans and Animals

At this point a relationship between the third and sixth days of Creation surfaces. On the third day God created the vegetation, plants, and trees. These already existed when Adam and Eve and the land animals were created on the sixth day. One of the first things that all these creatures needed was food to sustain them. This their Creator already had provided even before they were created.

The original diet assigned to Adam and Eve during Creation week included "every plant yielding seed which is upon the face of all the earth, and every tree with seed in its fruit" (Gen. 1:29). To the animals was given "every green plant" (verse 30). Not only were Adam and Eve vegetarians in their original created state, but so were the animals. This left no room for animal predation before the Fall.

The wisdom of this original diet has been demonstrated in modern times. Scientific studies upon a comprehensive group of subjects have demonstrated that, on the average, vegetarian Seventh-day Adventists in the United States live seven years longer than do their nonvegetarian counterparts in the general population. As these studies have continued, that average figure has risen. Thus the wisdom of the Creator in His assignment of the original diet has been amply demonstrated by modern science. Certainly God knows what is the best food for His creatures.

14. The Creation of the Sabbath on Day Seven

The division between Genesis 1:31 and 2:1-4, as all other chapter divisions in the Bible, was made centuries after the first writing of the book. The record of the seventh day belongs with that of the other six. This is evident from the designation of this day as "seventh day" three times in this passage. The name "Sabbath" is not used here, but the verb *šābat* appears with its original root meaning, "to cease." Thus God "ceased" His work on this day. One can see, therefore, how this day received its name. Sabbath was first of all the days God ceased His work and then, in reflection upon that fact, the day that human beings ceased from their work. On this day God rested; He ceased from all of His creative activity. He did not physically need this rest, for He is omnipotent, but His divine rest serves as an example for us. It is the divine rest given to human beings.

The second divine activity in Genesis 2:1-4 is that of blessing this particular day. God had already blessed the birds and fish that He created on the fifth day, as well as Adam and Eve on the sixth day (Gen. 1:28). Thus the divine blessing had been given to objects created, but not to a day. In this case the divine blessing was pronounced on a unit of time, not on objects created within that unit of time.

God's blessing was placed upon the seventh day for a special purpose. The blessings on animals and human beings had to do especially with biological productivity. The blessing on the Sabbath, on the other hand, was intended to make it spiritually fruitful. The animals could not understand the blessing bestowed on this day, but Adam and Eve could. From the Creator Himself, the first pair learned of the special blessing that God had pronounced on the seventh day.

Another blessing given to Adam and Eve in Genesis 1:28 was dominion over the animal world. The Sabbath expresses a dominion, too, but not the dominion of Adam and Eve over the creation. Rather, it expresses the dominion of God over Adam and Eve and over all that He had created. Thus the Sabbath not only memorializes Creation; it is also the day that recognizes God's dominion over His creation. This responsibility was spelled out in more detail later in the fourth commandment; there, even the animals within the gates of Sabbathkeepers were to rest on that day (Ex. 20:10). They could not recognize and observe the Sabbath in a spiritual sense, as did human beings, but they still could benefit from the physical rest of that day.

God rested, or "ceased," on the seventh day; He then blessed the day. Finally, He sanctified it, or set it apart for a holy use. The verb *qādaš,* "to be holy," is here used in a causative form, meaning that God declared, or made, the Sabbath holy. In a similar way, God made holy the tabernacle constructed by the Israelites (Lev. 21:23); hence it came to be known as the "holy place" (*qōdeš* or *miqdāš* from the same root). In Exodus 40:9 the tabernacle is consecrated and becomes holy; both "consecrated" and "holy" come from the root *qādaš,* "to make holy," "to set apart." As the sanctuary was sanctified or holy space, so the Sabbath was sanctified or holy time, set apart for the use of God and His human creatures.

The sanctification of the Sabbath at Creation is important to the issue of whether the Sabbath is solely Jewish or belongs to the entire human race. Since all of this activity took place at the end of the Creation week when the first members of the human race were placed upon the earth, it is evident that the Sabbath was given to them. It was set apart and consecrated for them as representatives of all humanity. (See Sabbath I-IV.)

B. Genesis 2

A second Creation story begins in Genesis 2:5. Critical scholars commonly set this chapter off as coming from another literary source.

This position misunderstands the nature of the relationship between these two chapters, which are related to each other on the principle of repetitive parallelism. Throughout the OT, and especially in poetry, parallelism is a basic literary device. The ultimate example of this kind of repetition is found in the book of Job, in which the arguments are presented in poetry. Job's friends go through three major cycles of arguments divided into nine subsections. God answers all of this in His final three discourses. To the ancient reader the repetitive parallelism heightened the interest in the story as it came to its climax. In Genesis 2, therefore, one would expect to find parallel statements on Creation, given the importance of the topic.

1. Similarity of Subject

One evidence that Genesis 2 is a parallel statement to Genesis 1 is the similarity of the subjects treated. Both stories begin with reference to the creation of heaven and earth (Gen. 1:1; 2:4). The division of the seas on the second day is paralleled by the division of the rivers in 2:10. The creation of the animals on day 6 is reflected in the reference to the creation of the animals in 2:19. The provision of food for man and animals on the third and sixth days of Creation in Genesis 1 is developed in Genesis 2:16 to include the food for Adam and Eve. The dominion over animals given to man in 1:28 is now spelled out in the naming process mentioned in 2:19. Finally, the creation of human beings, male and female, is described in much more detail.

Repetitive parallelism, however, does not slavishly repeat what has been given before. Rather, it states the subject matter in a new and complementary way that elaborates upon what has gone before. That is what Genesis 2 does with Genesis 1. In 1:27 the creation of human beings is referred to in a brief poetic statement, which is then developed in the prose of Genesis 2. Genesis 2 expands upon what has gone before; it does not negate or contradict it.

2. The Use of Divine Names

The divine name Elohim is used exclusively in Genesis 1. The divine name used in Genesis 2:4-25 is Yahweh. This difference has led critical scholars to posit different sources for the two chapters. This position entails some difficulties. First, there is no contrast between the use of Elohim in chapter 1 and Yahweh in chapter 2. In Genesis 2:4-25 God is called Yahweh Elohim, not dropping the name used in Genesis 1 but adding another divine name. Thus Elohim is now specified in more detail as Yahweh Elohim.

The difference between these two names is the difference between the generic and the personal. Elohim, or its more common Near Eastern form El, was used in all Semitic language societies of the Fertile Crescent. Thus the name Elohim would have been understood in all those societies. On the other hand, each of these societies had its own personal and individual gods: Marduk in Babylon, Ashur in Assyria, Milcom among the Ammonites, Chemosh in Moab, and Qaus in Edom. Yahweh was the specific and personal name used for the true God of the Israelites; no other god in the ancient world used that name.

Genesis 1 would, therefore, have been understood by other inhabitants of the ancient world as a general statement on Creation using the general name for God that they all knew. Genesis 2, on the other hand, is a specific statement about the creation of man and woman, connected only with Yahweh, the true God of Israel. The general God who set up the cosmos in Genesis 1 is, in actuality, the personal God that is specified by this complementary use in chapter 2.

The writer moves from the general to the specific identification of God because of the objects described as created in the second account: man and woman, Adam and Eve. They were personal human beings and responded to their Creator God in a way that no other part of His creation could, directly to the personal God who created them. It was altogether fitting and appropriate, therefore, to identify that God in a personal and intimate way because of the personal nature of His creation. While the use of different divine names in Genesis 1 and 2 is theologically important, it does not mean that the stories come from different sources.

3. Literary Structure

Genesis 1 was organized and written in a parallel type of literary statement. The first three days' activities were directly paralleled by those creative activities that took place on the next three days.

Genesis 1 was the macroscopic view of Creation, how the world was set up for its inhabitants. In Genesis 2 we move to the microscopic parallel. In essence, the microscope focuses on the second half of the sixth day of Creation week. As the telescope was used for the creation of Genesis 1, the microscope comes into play in Genesis 2. The text narrows to focus on the creation of man and woman.

Genesis 2 is not organized in a directly parallel fashion. The creation of man is presented first, and the creation of woman is presented last. These two creative acts occupy parallel positions at the beginning and the end of the narrative. Between these two are other paired elements. Those paired elements involve statements about the garden and the rivers. Both statements on the creation of man and woman in this chapter contain a preliminary assertion on conditions that preceded that creation. In the case of the creation of man, that preliminary statement focuses upon the plant world and the fields. In the case of woman, that preliminary statement focuses upon the animal world (verses 18-20).

The Special Creation of Genesis 2 is described in a unique way. In Genesis 1 God spoke the various objects into existence. He said, "Let there be . . . ," and the object mentioned appeared. In Genesis 2 a different approach is used. The verb employed for this divine activity is *yāṣar*, "to form, shape." God takes something that already exists—the dust

of the earth—and forms it. He shapes it into a man. But still it is not animate; it needs something more. God breathes into this form the breath of life, and it becomes a living "being" *(nepeš)*. This word is sometimes translated "soul," but the content of this passage clearly indicates that the whole being of Adam is taken into account here. Thus two elements made up Adam: the dust of the earth and the breath of life. Chemical analysis has shown that the human body is indeed made up of the same chemical elements that are found in the earth. The breath of life can simply be defined as the energy of God for life. When death occurs, as it later did to Adam and Eve, these two main elements break apart. The dust of the earth returns to the earth, and the breath of life returns to God, who gave that energy in the first place (Eccl. 12:7; see Man I. E; Death I. A. 3, 4).

The verb *yāṣar* is used for the work of a potter and the potter himself (Jer. 18:1-4). Thus the picture, in contrast with Genesis 1, is that of God working with His hands to make man, just as the potter molds and fashions the pot. But the divine Potter can do more than the human; He can make His product come alive. When God kneels down and breathes into the man's mouth, he does come alive. This is anthropomorphic, or "humanlike," terminology used for divine activities. We do not know exactly how God did this act of creation. But these verbs of activity express the loving concern and intimate contact of the Creator with His creatures as He created them.

4. The Garden Planted

In Genesis 2:8 God plants a garden, especially prepared for Adam and Eve. More than other locations, this special place was prepared by God Himself for the human pair. It had three kinds of trees. First, probably in abundance, were the fruit trees—good to eat, good to the taste, good to see, and good for nutrition. Two other trees were planted there: the tree of life and the tree of the knowledge of good and evil. They come into play later in the account.

5. The Four Rivers

Genesis 2:10 says that one river flowed out of Eden, and there it divided into four rivers. The names of the four rivers are given, but these names need not necessarily be identified with the postdiluvian rivers that carried those names, such as the Tigris and the Euphrates. Antediluvian names may well have been given to postdiluvian features of the surface of the earth. Something similar has happened with many place names from England taken to other parts of the British Empire. They were not the same places, but the names were brought over and reused. Thus the names give no clue regarding the location of the garden.

6. The Second Description of Eden

The first account of Eden (Gen. 2:8, 9) tells how God planted the garden and placed man there. The second Eden account indicates what man was to do there: to "keep it" (Gen. 2:15-17). Adam was placed in Eden as the gardener responsible for the garden. God also indicated to him from which of the trees he could eat and the one tree from which he could not eat: the tree of the knowledge of good and evil.

7. The Creation of Woman

Genesis 2:18-24 contains four main elements; the introduction, the action, the celebration of the action, and the resultant state. The introduction involves the story of Adam's naming the animals, which brings up a direct correlation with Genesis 1. There God named those objects which were made on the first three days: night and day, the sky, the seas, the earth. Adam named those objects that were created on the fifth and sixth days: the animals. What God named on the first three days Adam did not rename; what God left unnamed from the last three days was the province of Adam's naming activity. Thus this naming activity is complementary, part belonging to God and part belonging to Adam. The complementary nature of this activity strongly sug-

gests that these two narratives were the work of one and the same author, that they were not written by different authors or scribal schools separated by centuries.

This naming process sets the stage for the creation of woman by pointing out to Adam how alone he really was. Each of the animals that Adam named had a mate, but Adam was alone. God could have created Adam's mate at the same time that He created Adam, but He did not. In this way Adam gained a greater appreciation for his mate and insight into the loving care of the God who made provision for his need.

Since Eve was created from a rib taken from the side of Adam, and Adam was created from materials taken from the dust of the ground, Eve was made out of the same elements as was Adam. However, this was done in a more personal way than by simply shaping a mound of dust into the form of another being. Adam was put to sleep by God and one of his ribs was removed and made into the woman, Eve. The use of the rib expresses equality, in contrast with taking a bone from the foot to express inferiority or a portion of the skull to express superiority.

The immediate response of Adam when Eve was brought to him was to break into song because of his joy. The only truly poetic unit in the Creation account of Genesis 1 was 1:27, where God's intent to create human beings was expressed in a tricolon, a poetic unit consisting of three lines. That we may call the Song of the Creation of Man. In Genesis 2:23 we have the Song of the Creation of Woman. In this case the song was sung, the poetry pronounced, by Adam. There is a similarity and a dissimilarity between these two poetic units. The number of words used and the number of syllables pronounced are very close to equal. In 1:27, however, there is only one poetic unit, whereas in 2:23 there are two units of two lines each.

Not only does this poetic account of 2:23 express Adam's joy at meeting his helpmeet, it also says something about authorship. The rest of Genesis 2 was written in prose, just as the rest of Genesis 1 outside of verse 27 was written in prose. Thus these two parallel Creation narratives follow the same outline, and their poetic units are written in a very similar style. The same author followed the same outline in these parallel and complementary narratives. Taken together with the parallels already noted, this similarity gives strong evidence that these two narratives were written by one author, in complementary parallelism, so common in both Hebrew prose and poetry.

The last element in the story of the creation of woman has to do with the unified couple created thereby, and the consequences for future generations of the human race. Adam and Eve, the first couple, were to be an example of the close bond between husband and wife. No other human relations were to interfere with that bond (Gen. 2:24). Their lack of clothing at the time of their creation expresses the purity and perfection with which they came forth from their Creator's hand (verse 25; see Marriage I. A. 1-3).

C. Wisdom Literature: Job

Job 38-41 contains a magnificent statement regarding the creatorship of God, but these chapters can only be understood by reviewing the book of Job up to that point. God evaluated Job as upright and righteous, serving Him with his whole heart. Satan disputed this, saying that Job served God only for his own benefit. So God agreed to a test for Job. Satan was permitted to take almost everything away from Job, including his wealth and his family, but excluding his wife. Satan was even permitted to harm Job's body, but not to kill him.

Job's friends came to him to talk to him about his problems. They insisted that Job must have been suffering for his sins. Job protested that he did not know what sins he was suffering for. The argument went round and round. Job's friends were not convinced of his innocence, yet they could not point out any sins of Job. Job's fourth friend, Elihu, only added to this same argument.

Finally, God stepped in to reveal Himself. He did not tell Job what was happening, that he was enduring a test of his faith and righteousness, not being punished for his sins. Only later could readers see behind the scenes like this.

God answered Job by asking him rhetorical questions about his understanding of nature. As he realized how little he knew, Job was forced to acknowledge the wisdom of God in nature. Given the wisdom of God demonstrated in Creation, Job should be able to trust His Creator, even though he might not understand everything about his life.

Thus the wisdom of God demonstrated in His creation is at the heart of the book of Job. The final four chapters of Job provide a powerful statement that the God of the book of Job is the Creator and that His wisdom is demonstrated in Creation. It may have been marred by sin, but the basic demonstration of God's wisdom is still evident.

The order in Job follows the order of the Creation week in a general way. God's questions begin with queries about inanimate nature: "Where were you when I laid the foundation of the earth?" (Job 38:4). Of course, Job was not there; the question was rhetorical. The order of the questions in chapter 38 goes from the foundation of the earth, to the division of the seas and dry land (verses 8-11), to the division of time between light and dark (verses 12-15), and then back to the seas (verses 16-18). Then it returns to the subject of light and dark (verses 19-21).

The next section takes up the atmospheric elements (verses 22-30): snow, hail, wind, rain, thunder, ice, and frost. All of these God controls and has set in order and motion. Job cannot do this, neither can he explain how God does it.

Then come the stars in their constellations. Where was Job when they were set in order? Can he lead them forth or deflect their paths? Can he rearrange their governance of the seasons on earth (verses 31-33)? Impossible. This is the work and wisdom of God the Creator, with which Job has nothing to do.

Beginning with Job 38:39, God turns to animals and birds. The series begins with the lions and continues mostly with land animals; occasionally birds are interspersed. The series climaxes with two monstrous beasts, behemoth at the end of chapter 40, probably a hippopotamus, and leviathan in chapter 41, possibly a crocodile. Job had no part in the creation of any of this. It was all God's work, showing His wisdom in Creation.

Before this display of God's wisdom in return, Job was humbled and repented in dust and ashes, awed by the greatness of the Creator: "I know that thou canst do all things" (Job 42:2). Job learned that even in suffering he could trust the Creator, whose wisdom was demonstrated in His creation. From this insight came the final restoration of all things to Job (42:12, 13).

D. Psalms

1. Psalm 104

The outline of Psalm 104 follows the outline of the days of Creation in Genesis 1. It does not identify the days of Creation specifically, but follows the order of events of those days. It utilizes an anticipation of what would come about from those days; it looks forward to their potential, their function, and their benefit. The poetic language used here offers enormous possibilities for praising the God who created all.

The element created on the first day was the light that covered the earth, but in Psalm 104:2 it is God who is covered with light. From His radiant glory the light of Creation issues. Psalm 104 provides an answer to the long-standing question about the source of the light on the first day of Creation: The light that surrounded the person of God provided light for the earth (see I. A. 3). On the second day of Creation in Genesis 1 the firmament was divided. Psalm 104:3, 4 talks about the same element. God "stretched out the [atmospheric] heavens like a tent." The "tent" encompasses all of God's creatures on earth. The Lord not only made the atmosphere in which we live but also set it in motion.

The appearance of dry land on the third day of Creation week is told in a rather matter-of-fact way in Genesis 1. There God simply spoke and it was so. In Psalm 104 God "rebuked" the seas that stood over the land. Verse 6 begins with the earth covered with water before God brought forth the dry land. This section ends in verse 9 with the promise that He will not cover the earth with waters as before: neither the Noachic nor the primeval flood will recur. The center of this section describes the rising up of mountains and the sinking down of the valleys. Thus God shaped the earth.

While God does not allow the seas to cover the earth again, as they did before He brought forth the dry land, He still waters the earth. The watering necessary for the plants and animals and the earth itself is described in verses 10-13. A crescendo takes the waters of God higher and higher. The springs in the valley give drink to the animals of the field. Higher up come the birds in the trees. Finally, even the tops of the lofty mountains are watered by the cycle of nature that God has set up and energized.

Starting with Psalm 104:14, the creation of plants and their use for food are described, following the same pattern as the waters, in an ever-mounting crescendo. The food provided starts on the plain, where the cattle feed and humans labor to raise crops. From that region come the grapes and grain and olives, each with a place in the life of men and women. Above this come the majestic trees, even the great trees in the high mountains, the cedars of Lebanon (verse 16). These serve a purpose too, for the birds build their nests in them. There is even life above the timberline, for there the mountain goats scamper on the cliffs of the highest mountains. All of this comes forth from the dry land that was created on the third day.

Psalm 104 deals next with the heavenly

luminaries, but the order is different from that found in Genesis 1:14-19. Genesis 1 begins with the largest orb, decreases to the smaller light, and then goes to the smallest lights. Psalm 104:19 begins with the moon as evening comes on and the sun sets. Then it tells of the activities of the animals at night. After the hunt of the night the animals crawl back into their dens to rest and a new occupant of the land comes forth: humans rise and go forth in the sunshine to work in the fields. So the order of the elements of time is evening and morning, moon and sun, lions who work at night, and humans who work in the daylight—all as established by the time frame of Genesis 1, "there was evening and there was morning."

On the fifth day the firmament that had been divided on the second day was populated with birds above and fish below. In the psalm the sea teems with life (verse 25), even the great Leviathan, also mentioned in Genesis. The birds are not mentioned here, for they already have appeared in relation to the trees created on day three. Just as life was placed in the seas on day five, a new form of life appears on those seas. It is not a new kind of fish, but human beings, who travel over the seas in boats.

According to Genesis 1, first the animals and then humans were created on the sixth day. Humans are considered the crowning achievement of Creation. Strange to say, they are not even mentioned directly in the account of the sixth day in the psalm, which deals mainly with what has been provided for the sustenance of life on the earth. God is pictured as feeding His creatures from His hand as a gentle shepherd or zookeeper would: "When thou openest thy hand, they are filled with good things" (verse 28).

God completed the creation of man by breathing into him the breath of life. That final act is taken up in the psalm, but in another order (verses 28-30). Here we discover what happens when the breath is taken away: "When thou hidest thy face, they are dismayed; when thou takest away their breath

they die and return to their dust" (verse 29). Only then does the psalm tell about the giving of that creative spirit for life (verse 30). Breathing out the breath of life is not the end of the race nor the end of the species. God breathes His breath of life anew, and life arises in the next generation. The curse of sin and death has come, but the blessing and promise of God go on nonetheless; His people will overcome the enemy.

In Genesis the account of Creation week goes on to describe the seventh day. The psalm has something similar. On the Sabbath we recognize that God is our Creator; we honor Him in the commemoration of Creation. That is the first thing mentioned in Psalm 104:31. When God finished His creation, He said that it was "very good." In Psalm 104 He rejoices in His works (verse 31). But something more happens: He "looks on the earth and it trembles," He "touches the mountains and they smoke" (verse 32). This is the picture of a theophany, the manifestation of God's personal presence. This is what happens on the Sabbath when the Lord draws near to His people and makes Himself known. Struck with reverential awe, they render Him worship.

That worship is described in the next two verses. Human beings bring worship and honor and glory and praise to God (verse 33). This is not a onetime occurrence: The psalmist promises to carry on this activity as long as life lasts. The praises of the Lord are on the lips of the psalmist continually. Silence is another part of worship. In verse 34 the psalmist asks that silent meditation upon the Lord may be pleasing to God. Finally, this reflection upon worship ends with rejoicing (verse 35).

2. Psalm 19

The first half of Psalm 19 and the fourth day of Creation show considerable similarity. Both accounts involve the sun as a principal actor. In Psalm 19 the sun is given a functional assignment: to warm the earth each day. This half of the psalm has sometimes been seen as an ancient Canaanite hymn to the sun. That interpretation confuses poetic personification with theological deification; here we have the first, not the second.

The first four verses of this psalm tell who is praised by God's handwork in the heavens. Not the sun or the stars, but God their Creator is lauded (verse 1). This evident praise of God goes on day and night because God's handiwork is ever manifest in the sky. Special emphasis is given to the night sky. The stars are completely silent, but still they utter a speech of their own, not audible but visible. They show how powerful and magnificent God the Creator is.

The order in Psalm 19 is from the lesser bodies, the stars in verses 1-4, to the greater body, the sun described in verses 4-6. The sun speaks of the Creator also, but in a way different from the stars. The sun is more visible; its effects can be seen and felt more directly. The sun sheds its heat upon all; nothing is hidden from it (verse 6). All of this is ultimately the work of God, who has set in the sky the tent for the sun. The sun is not a strong man or a strong god; it is rather "like" a strong man. The personification leans upon a comparison to draw out the function of the sun. The stars with their speechless speech and the sun with its radiant heat are provisions of the true God and reveal His wisdom as well.

The second half of this psalm, verses 7-14, deals with what appears to be an entirely different subject, the law or Torah of God. That teaching of Yahweh is praised for its aid and comfort for the believer. Some commentators have seen this half of the psalm as so different that they have considered it an independent psalm in praise of the law, like Psalm 119, but that is not the case. There is an evident development between the two halves. The first half describes what may be called general revelation, the revelation of God in nature. The second half of the psalm describes what may be called special revelation, the revelation of God through His spoken and written word.

The use of the names for God is different in the two halves of this psalm. In the first half, the divine name used is Elohim, just as in Genesis 1. The divine name used in the second half of the psalm is Yahweh, just as in Genesis 2. Thus, to move from general revelation in nature in the first half of the psalm to special revelation in the second half of the psalm is also to move from a general revelation about God to a special revelation about the one true, personal God, Yahweh.

3. Psalm 8

The special emphasis of this psalm is on the creation of human beings. This psalm begins with the divine name Yahweh and His title, "our lord" (*ᵃdōnênû*), known throughout "all the earth" for what He has done, especially in Creation.

In Psalm 19 the stars uttered speechless speech. Here speech is spoken and heard, because it is uttered by created beings on earth. That speech, however, does not come from the wisest and most intelligent of humans; it comes from the mouths of babes (verse 2). Even the little ones can see the wisdom and greatness of God in His creation. Seeing God's wisdom and glory revealed in the heavens leads to reflection on the relative importance, or lack of importance, of human beings (verses 3, 4).

As the psalmist's view takes in the night sky, he can only reflect upon the puny insignificance of man in comparison with the starry splendor. The answer to the psalmist's rhetorical question is a surprise. Instead of confirming that humans are insignificant in comparison with all he sees, the psalmist affirms humanity's important place because of being created by God: "Yet thou hast made him little less than God" (verse 5; "angels" in Heb. 2:7).

Verses 6-8 refer to all the elements over which humans were to have dominion: birds, animals, and fish. A summary statement on this dominion is given first (verse 6): "Thou hast given him dominion over the works of thy hands; thou hast put all things under his feet." The next two verses enumerate the animate inhabitants of the earth under humanity's dominion. Psalm 8:5-8 is a restatement or amplification of the creation of human beings in Genesis 1:26, 27. Human beings still possess dominion over the animal world; unfortunately, they do not always exercise it wisely.

E. The Prophets

1. Amos

The three well-known Creator hymns of Amos are found in 4:13; 5:8, 9; and 9:5, 6. In these Amos adds that the Creator God is using the elements of nature to work out His judgments upon wicked and rebellious humankind and Israel.

The beginning of the first Creator hymn (Amos 4:13) describes the forming of the mountains. The picture is compatible with God's activities on the third day of Creation week. God, who formed the human mind, also knows humans' thoughts. This knowing becomes an important element in the prophet's messages, for the judgment of God is predicated upon His knowledge of the motives of the human heart and mind. Turning the morning to darkness not only refers to the succession of day and night, but also to the day of the Lord. The Israelites thought that the day of the Lord would be a day of light for them and of darkness for their enemies. Amos pronounced the reverse (Amos 5:18-20). Thus God controlled not only the physical motions of the sun and moon, which brought the light and dark parts of the day, He also controlled the ultimate destiny of human beings and nations.

The reference to treading upon the heights of the earth is common OT language for a theophany. Here the Creator-God comes in judgment, even though the details are not spelled out in this hymn.

In the second Creator hymn (Amos 5:8, 9) the stars are described as the creation of God. The doubled and inverted order "turns deep darkness into the morning, and darkens the day into night," indicates the progression of day and night, but also carries with it the notion of judgment and the day of the Lord.

The reference to the waters of the sea recalls the events of the second and third days of Creation week. In this case, however, God uses those waters differently. They still are under His control, but now they are used for destruction. They are floodwaters, not Noah's flood, but a locally destructive flood of judgment. Yahweh is the sovereign over nature and controls its forces. They served His purpose at Creation and continue to serve His purpose, even for judgment and destruction.

The language of theophany appears in the third Creator hymn (Amos 9:5, 6) in an even more forceful way. The aspect of judgment is clear: This approach of God acts upon the forces of nature and affects people, who mourn because of judgment.

This passage does not picture God's control over the Nile floods or any other river. Rather, it is a picture of what happens to the land when God passes over it with His theophanic appearance. While the first hymn simply referred to God's treading upon the mountains, in this third hymn He touches the earth, and it melts. Once it has melted, it behaves like the waves of a river.

2. Isaiah

a. Isaiah 40:26-28. The primary statement on Creation in the book of Isaiah, this prophetic narrative draws a number of contrasts between the true God and the false gods. In Isaiah 40:18-20 the idols are ridiculed as mere work of human hands. Yahweh's creatorship is introduced by a rhetorical question: "To whom then will you compare me, that I should be like him?" (verse 25). The answer is that no god can be compared with Yahweh. One line of evidence for this is that He created the host of heaven, the stars (verse 26). Such knowledge and action surpass by far the natural powers of man and the other gods. God not only knows their number but also the name of each. He not only created the starry host, He also superintends them and supports them.

Two dimensions of God's creatorship surface here. The existence of the everlasting God goes backward in time to eternity past. His creatorship also extends to the ends of the earth. There is nothing, even at the ultimate limits of the earth, that He has not created.

The note upon which Isaiah 40:26-28 ends becomes the key that Isaiah later uses to introduce other activities of the Creator God. These introductory statements, showing God as Creator, are found in Isaiah 42:5; 44:24; 45:12, 18; and 48:12, 13. Each of these Creation statements introduces a different prophecy. A theological relationship can be seen between the introduction and the prophecy that follows. Creation occurred in the past and manifested the might, power, and wisdom of God. Prophecy extends into the future, and the power and wisdom of the Creator God will yet be manifested in the future, when the events prophesied take place.

The major Creator statement in Isaiah 40:26-28 precedes all of the later formulas. In other words, all of the introductory statements point back to, and are derived from, that major statement. The God who gives prophecies is the same God who made the world. Two major differences set apart the true God from all of the false gods of the ancient world: God made the world and knows what will come to pass in the world that He made.

b. Isaiah 65 and 66: re-creation. With Isaiah 65:17 and 66:22 a new aspect of God's creative power is introduced. Here the inspired prophet looks ahead to a time when the earth will be restored: "For behold, I create new heavens and a new earth." This prophecy originally focused on the old Jerusalem (Isa. 65:18, 19). These were the conditions that God promised could have developed. But the prophecy was not met with a corresponding response of faith. Therefore, this original promise has been transferred to a renewed earth and a New Jerusalem, as is clear from the prophecies of Revelation 21, 22.

This idea is repeated and extended in Isaiah 66:22, 23, providing a parallel to the original Creation story. Isaiah 65:17 refers to the new heavens and the new earth, just as Genesis 1:1 referred to the creation of the old heavens and old earth. Isaiah 66:22 repeats the idea of new heavens and new earth, already found in Isaiah 65:17. Isaiah 66:23, however, adds a new idea to that repetition: people, along with their activities. One type of activity is singled out for mention—worship. That worship is connected with time, just as the appearance of human beings before their Creator was also connected with time in the Garden of Eden. Adam and Eve were created on the sixth day, or Friday, and their first full day on earth was the seventh-day Sabbath. The same type of activity is envisaged for the new earth. There are two parallel statements about creation in Genesis 1 and 2; there are two parallel statements, as well, about re-creation in Isaiah 65 and 66.

3. Jeremiah

a. Jeremiah 10:11-13: the true God and the false gods. Jeremiah continues Isaiah's rejection of false gods who cannot create. Jeremiah likewise extends the work of the Creator into the present.

In this passage Jeremiah identifies the false gods as nonfunctional; they did not make the heavens and the earth. Further, they shall cease to exist; they will perish from the earth and the heavens. Verse 12 identifies the true God in terms of His work in Creation: He made the earth, established the world by His wisdom, and stretched out the heavens.

Verse 13 makes an interesting addition to OT Creator language: "When he utters his voice there is a tumult of waters in the heavens, and he makes the mist rise from the ends of the earth. He makes lightnings for the rain, and he brings forth the wind from his storehouses." This language does not concern the past historical event of Creation, but the present experience and activities of God, the world, and God's people. Rain, wind, dew, and lightning are part of a present experience. The God who created those elements in the original Creation still controls them and uses them for His purposes.

b. Jeremiah 27:5: the Creator-God and the rise of Babylon. The setting of Jeremiah 27 is a conference in Jerusalem. Various kings of the west, including Zedekiah, king of Judah, have gathered in Jerusalem to plot against their overlord, Nebuchadnezzar of Babylon. Jeremiah is given a message for them, conveyed in the language of Creation: "It is I who by my great power and my outstretched arm have made the earth, with the men and animals that are on the earth, and I give it to whomever it seems right to me" (verse 5). Just as God had originally given the earth into the care of Adam and Eve, so now He had given the Near Eastern portion of it to Nebuchadnezzar. It was God's prerogative as Creator to do so, and men such as these western kings should not rebel against that decree or against Nebuchadnezzar, who was carrying it out.

c. Jeremiah 51:15, 16. The preceding statement about God's ownership and assignment of the earth raises a question: Did this mean that Nebuchadnezzar and Babylon would rule forever? The last major prophecy of the book of Jeremiah makes clear that this would not happen. Once again Creator language is used: "It is he who made the earth by his power, who established the world by his wisdom, and by his understanding stretched out the heavens" (Jer. 51:15). This verse is virtually the equivalent of Jeremiah 10:12. It tells again of God's threefold creation of the earth, the world, and the heavens. Jeremiah 51:15 is nearly a repetition of 27:5. Thus Jeremiah 27 and Jeremiah 51 are reciprocals. Jeremiah 27 is about the rise of Babylon, and chapter 51 is about its downfall. Each of these prophecies is preceded by an introductory Creator statement.

d. Jeremiah 32:17. In Jeremiah 32:17 we find a Creator statement of quite a different nature. Chapter 32 speaks of the city of Jerusalem being given into the hands of the Chaldeans, or Babylonians (verses 24-29). The city already was under siege when Jeremiah prophesied that it would fall.

As a prologue or introduction to that statement, Jeremiah gave a lengthy recital of the mighty works of God in history (verses 16-23). Creation is listed as the first of those: "Ah Lord God! It is thou who hast made the heavens and the earth by thy great power and by thy outstretched arm! Nothing is too hard for thee" (verse 17).

F. Other OT Creation Statements

Five main examples of Creation statements in the OT have been examined: Genesis, Job, Psalms, Isaiah, and Jeremiah. This does not exhaust the Creation materials in the OT; however, other statements can only be mentioned briefly. The Psalms contain more references to Creation than the other three mentioned above (8; 19; 104). Psalm 24:1 gives a basic statement of God's ownership. Psalm 33:6-9 gives an expanded view of Creation, concluding with the summary "For he spoke, and it came to be; he commanded, and it stood forth." Psalm 102:25-27 contrasts the eternal nature of God with the transient nature of His creation. Psalm 124:8 makes only a brief mention of the fact that the Lord made the heaven and the earth. Psalm 146:6 does something similar. Psalm 148 is a psalm of praise to God as Creator; inanimate nature personified praises Him, for He has made it all.

Other elements in wisdom literature deal with the Creation theme. Proverbs 8 presents a major statement on Creation. Here wisdom is personified and characterized as being present with God in the beginning, at Creation. A briefer expression appears in Proverbs 3:19, 20. Another statement on Creation is found in Zechariah 12:1 as an introductory statement to a prophecy of what the Lord will do in the future. Nehemiah 9:6 reveals that the idea of Yahweh as Creator continued to the end of the OT.

G. The Date of Creation

The OT does not give a precise date for the events of the Creation week of Genesis 1. It does, however, give some data that can be used to develop a general and approximate date for those events. As in much historical work, biblical chronology must work backward from the known to the unknown. The dates that are well known in the OT are those of the kings. Working backward, we get a date of approximately 970 B.C. for the beginning of the reign of Solomon.

Adding the 480 years of 1 Kings 6:1 to 970 B.C. gives an approximate date for the Exodus: c. 1450 B.C. Until this point the chronological picture is fairly clear; from the Exodus backward the evidence is less precise. Depending on which chronological scheme is used, the birth of Abraham can be figured as late as 1950 B.C. (using the 400 years of Gen. 15:13; cf. Gal. 3:17) or as early as 2170 B.C. (figuring 430 years of Egyptian sojourn [Ex. 12:40] + Jacob's being 130 years old when he went to Egypt [Gen. 47:9] + 60 years to the birth of Isaac [Gen. 25:26] +100 years to the birth of Abraham [Gen. 21:5]).

In addition to these discrepancies, from Abraham backward the only chronological information available is contained in the genealogies of Genesis 5 and 11. Following these lists, assuming that no generations are missing, one should be able to arrive at approximate dates for the Flood and for Creation. However, the Hebrew text differs significantly from the Septuagint in both genealogies. Following the Hebrew, Noah's flood would have occurred between 2300 and 2500 B.C., some 1650 years after Creation. Following the LXX, the Flood would have happened c. 3400 and Creation c. 5600 B.C.

Given the difficulties of using genealogies to compute chronology, the problems of interpretation of the texts, and the differences between the Greek and Hebrew recensions, one can only affirm that Creation took place much more recently than the evolutionary theory proposes. This earth's history probably began in the fifth millennium B.C.

II. Creation in the NT

The NT repeats some of the ideas about Creation found in the OT. It also adds some information not elaborated in the OT. Jesus Christ appears in Creation as the agent through whom the Godhead worked. Various passages in the NT state this, but Jesus Himself also demonstrated it in His work on earth. As the Re-creator and Healer He demonstrated that He also was the original Creator, who could now rectify creation damaged by sin. As part of that claim Jesus also held that He was Lord of the Sabbath (Matt. 12:8), the memorial of that original Creation.

The NT confirms the OT Creation account. It is evident that the Creation account of Genesis 1 was well known to the NT writers and was accepted as the standard account of beginnings. This is shown especially in the way the Creation account was used verbatim in the NT. Three of the seven days of Creation are cited directly in the NT.

In 2 Corinthians 4:6 we read, "For it is the God who said, 'Let light shine out of darkness,' who has shone in our hearts to give the light of the knowledge of the glory of God in the face of Christ." Just as God physically commanded light to shine upon the earth on the first day of Creation week, spiritual light shines in the human heart from God and Christ. The physical light of the first day of Creation week is accepted as the basis for this spiritual application.

In dealing with the question of divorce, Jesus referred to and quoted from both Genesis 1 and 2. To show what the original and divinely intended state of marriage was, Jesus said, "Have you not read that he who made them from the beginning made them male and female, and said, 'For this reason a man shall leave his father and mother and be joined to his wife, and the two shall become one flesh'?" (Matt. 19:4, 5). The reference to making male and female comes from Genesis 1:27, and the reference to the union of husband and wife comes from Genesis 2:24. Jesus knew this account from the scroll of Genesis and referred to the fact that His hearers could find it there. In this manner the account of the sixth day of Creation is confirmed by NT testimony.

The author of Hebrews draws out the lesson that Joshua did not give his people complete rest. That complete rest can only be found by believing in Jesus and accepting His salvation. The Sabbath is the memorial of this re-creation, just as it was the memorial of the completed creation in Genesis 2:1-4. Hebrews 4:4 refers to this fact: "For he has somewhere spoken of the seventh day in this way, 'And God rested on the seventh day from all his works.'" The source of this statement is Genesis 2:2, which the writer accepts as an original, physical, and historical event.

A. Creation Week as a Finite Transition Point in Time

Ten texts in the NT use "foundation of the world" terminology to identify the starting point for this world's history. Six of these refer to events that have taken place "since" or "from" the foundation of the world (Matt. 13:35; 25:34; Luke 11:50; Heb. 4:3; 9:26; Rev. 17:8). Four refer to events that took place "before" the foundation of the world (John 17:24; Eph. 1:4; 1 Peter 1:20; Rev. 13:8). Thus the NT writers knew Creation week as a finite point in time that divided the time and events before it from those that took place after it. As Bible writers referred to Creation, it was not vague or nebulous, but historically specific.

As already has been noted in Isaiah and Jeremiah, statements about the Creator God introduce various prophecies. Something similar appears in several NT passages, especially in Acts. In Acts 4:24 the believers addressed God as the Creator: "Sovereign Lord, who didst make the heaven and the earth and the sea and everything in them." This is virtually identical with Exodus 20:11, which has the same elements in the same order.

Paul used essentially the same formula while preaching to the Gentiles at Lystra: "Turn from these vain things to a living God who made the heaven and the earth and the sea and all that is in them" (Acts 14:15).

Paul took the same approach on Mars Hill. He began his speech there with Creation and a reference to the Creator God. After referring to the unknown god, he turned his hearers' attention to the "God who made the world and everything in it, being Lord of heaven and earth" (Acts 17:24).

Thus in Acts three times references to the Creator God introduce what follows. On a smaller scale this also appears in Ephesians 3:9, where Paul describes the mystery hidden for ages in God, "who created all things."

A more remarkable use of this formula is made by the angel of Revelation 10, who comes down to the earth in great glory, lifts his right arm to heaven, and swears an oath. The oath is taken in the name and title of the Creator-God, "by him who lives for ever and ever, who created heaven and what is in it, the earth and what is in it, and the sea and what is in it" (verse 6). The oath the angel swore has to do with prophetic time to the end of time; the reference of Creation in the oath assures that the prophetic time in question will come to an end.

B. Revelation and Faith in Creation

Nature's revelation of the true God appears in both Testaments. In the NT it is found in Romans 1:20, which shows that there was a general revelation in nature from which the Gentiles stubbornly refused to learn. They turned away into the darkness of their own immoral ways. But had they listened to the voice of God in nature, this need not have been so.

There was something missing when the Gentiles looked at the revelation of God in nature and yet did not learn about Him. Hebrews 11:3 tells us what that missing element was: "By faith we understand that the world was created by the word of God, so that what is seen was made out of things which do not appear." The reference to the "word" by which God created harks back to Genesis 1, where each event of the Creation week was brought about by God's speaking into existence objects and creatures.

C. Christ as Creator

The major new element introduced into Creation thought in the NT is Christ as Creator. What was hidden or only implied in the OT has now become clear in the NT. John 1:1-3 affirms Christ as Creator: "All things were made through him, and without him was not anything made that was made."

Colossians 1:16-19 makes a similar statement, with some of the same elements. Christ as Creator is emphatically present; verse 16 states, each time with a different preposition:

> "In him all things were created . . .
> all things were created through him
> ["all things were created," under-
> stood] and for him."

The use of these different prepositions emphasizes, as do all other features of this verse, the creatorship of Christ. Nothing lay outside His creative acts. But His creatorship did not stop there. The statement continues: "In him all things hold together." He is not only Creator, He is Sustainer. His work with Creation is an ongoing process.

The creatorship of Christ is also stated in Hebrews 1:2, but not as extensively as in John or Colossians. The same three-step succession is observed. Christ was first of all the Creator, for it was the Son "through whom also he created the world." This same Son is "upholding the universe by his word of power" (verse 3). This series goes on to say that "when he had made purification for sins, he sat down at the right hand of the Majesty on high" (verse 3). Thus, in the introduction to Hebrews also, Christ is Creator, Sustainer, and Purifier.

Just as the Sabbath and the original Creation were linked in the OT, so also these two elements are connected in the NT. The lead text is found in Mark 2:27: "And he said to them, 'The sabbath was made for man, not man for the sabbath; so the Son of Man is lord even of the sabbath.' " The first of these statements is positive, while the second is negative. The first tells what the Sabbath is, while the second tells what the Sabbath is not. Human beings were made on the sixth day, the Sabbath on the seventh. Humans were already in existence when the Sabbath was made; therefore, the day evidently was made for their use and benefit. Surprisingly, however, Adam was not made lord of the Sabbath. The "Son of man," Jesus Christ, holds that title.

A link between Creation, re-creation, and the Sabbath also appears in the Gospel of John. Two Sabbath miracles are recorded, in John 5 and John 9, with a number of similarities between the two. Jesus seems to have selected particular individuals for healing on the Sabbath day so that they might serve as special examples of something He wanted to teach about Himself and His relationship to the Sabbath.

These two miracles were performed in different ways; the first, merely by the spoken word. That was also the way the Creation was carried out, as described in Genesis 1. The next healing took place by the touch of the Master and His use of clay. That was the way man was created, according to Genesis 2. The body of Adam was formed from the dust of the earth and God breathed into it the breath of life. In John 9 the body was already operating, except for one portion, the eyes. To remedy that defect, Jesus put clay on the one part that had gone wrong.

The clear lesson is that Jesus was and is the Creator. He was the Creator in Genesis 1 and 2; He was the Re-creator in John 5 and 9. The function was essentially the same, for He created the whole as well as parts of the human body. Thus Jesus clearly taught that He was the original Creator and the use and application of the powers were ongoing.

D. Creation in the End-time Message

The book of Revelation contains more eschatology than any other NT book. As such, it points forward from the time when John received the vision to the end of time and beyond. The subject of Creation plays a part in the message and has some special links to the end-time.

The first reference to Creation in Revelation comes, indirectly, in Revelation 1:10. That passage gives us the time frame in which John received this vision, the Lord's day. We should, therefore, look for a particular statement connecting a day with the Lord. The only day of the week mentioned in that way in the Bible is the Sabbath. This is true both of the OT (Isa. 58:13) and the NT (Mark 2:28). Thus the day upon which John received this vision can be identified as a Sabbath. That day, in turn, was a memorial of Creation. (See Sabbath II. B. 3.)

The first major reference to Creation as such comes in Revelation 4. There John was shown the great heavenly throne scene, with God the Father seated upon the throne. Around the throne sat the 24 elders; the four living creatures were also positioned there. A considerable portion of the theology of this narrative can be seen in the words of the praise songs, particularly appropriate for the Sabbath.

The first song was sung by the four living creatures who praised God for His holiness, utilizing the *trisagion* adapted from the form in which the seraphim sang it in Isaiah 6:3 (Rev. 4:8). Then the 24 elders joined in the song, but now the content of the song was new, a song in praise of God as Creator (verse 11).

In Revelation 10 one finds a more eschatologically oriented Creation statement. As a mighty angel comes down to earth, he raises his right hand and swears a solemn oath as to the truthfulness of the message that he brings. He swears to God, "who lives for ever and ever, who created heaven and what is in it, the earth and what is in it, and the sea and what is in it" (verse 6). Accompanying the proclamation of this prophetic message is a renewed emphasis on God, who was and is Creator.

The same point is brought out by the first angel's message of Revelation 14, the first of three end-time messages that lead up to the Second Coming and produce the final harvest (14:6-14). Three main elements are identified in that message to be given to all parts and peoples of the earth: (1) a call to preach "the eternal gospel," (2) a call to announce that the pre-Advent judgment in heaven has begun (in A.D. 1844), and (3) a call to worship God as Creator in the end-time. (See Judgment III. B. 1.)

Revelation 14:7 not only calls attention to God as Creator; it affirms that we should worship Him as Creator. The most appropriate way to worship God as Creator is to worship Him on the day that He has set aside as the memorial to Creation, the Sabbath. In the end-time, therefore, we should look for a special message, a special preaching, a special call to worship God as the Creator by the use of His own designated memorial of Creation, the Sabbath. (See Remnant/Three Angels V. A, B; Sabbath III. E.)

E. The Ultimate Re-creation: The New Earth

Revelation 21 and 22 describe the grand culmination of the preaching of the gospel: The saints possess the ultimate physical kingdom of God. This description of the New Earth is only a faint reflection of what reality will be. One aspect of this renewal will be the fulfillment of various OT prophecies and promises that were not fulfilled to ancient Israel because of the failure of faith on the part of the people. Revelation 21 shows the connection in rather specific terms. According to verse 1, John saw "a new heaven and a

439

new earth; for the first heaven and the first earth had passed away, and the sea was no more." This harks back to the creation of heaven, earth, and sea as described in Genesis 1. Interestingly, in the new earth there are no more seas such as exist in this world. More specifically, this verse is modeled after Isaiah 66:22, which first gave the promise of the new heavens and the new earth. Here those promises come to full fruition in a way that was not envisaged by the OT prophets.

The first of the two visions at the end of Revelation focuses on the people who dwell in the new earth and the New Jerusalem. The second emphasizes the place where they dwell, with a detailed view of the New Jerusalem. This is just the reverse of the Creation narratives in Genesis 1 and 2. In Genesis 1 the world was created as the dwelling place of human beings. Then, in Genesis 2, the people, Adam and Eve, were put in that world. Now, in Revelation 21, the text talks about those who dwell there, and Revelation 22 refers to the place where they dwell.

The Bible begins and ends on the same note: Creation. Genesis 1 and 2 tell the story of the original Creation. Revelation 21 and 22 tell the story of the new re-creation. Both are accomplished by the Creator God; both are His works, not the construction of man. All that is enclosed between Genesis 1-2 and Revelation 21-22 is the history of the plan of salvation. (See God IV. C; New Earth III. A-C.)

III. Theology and Personal Experience

From the survey of the biblical texts which bear upon the doctrine of Creation various lessons may be drawn. Some of these may be more abstract or philosophical, but others come down to the level of personal experience and practice.

A. We Are His Creatures

The place to start deriving biblical lessons about Creation is our creaturehood. We are created beings. The biological processes that were set in motion at the time of Creation week are still in progress and have resulted in our existence today. Like God Himself did at the conclusion of that Creation week, we can stand back and say, "It is very good." This applies to our own personal existence; it applies to the wonders and marvels of the physical system with which our bodies function; and it applies to the world outside of ourselves as we survey all of nature, animate and inanimate, around us.

Since we are His creatures and He has made us, we should ultimately attribute all our accomplishments to Him. Our talents, our abilities, are ultimately the product of His design at Creation. Musical talents, business achievements, the getting of wealth, academic attainments, physical prowess, agricultural and industrial products, architectural design and construction, and the many other accomplishments of human beings are not to be denigrated, but rather appreciated as the product of beings created in the image of God. This reality demands utter humility before Him.

B. Worship of Our Creator

Not only does our understanding of our creaturehood place us in a logical and sensible relationship with our Creator, our fellow creatures, and the world about us, it should also lead us to a sense of reverential awe for the greatness of the God who created all things. We can express that sense of worship in corporate or individual ways.

Time and again in the account of Genesis 1 God is recorded as saying, "it is good," with the final benediction being "It was very good." This gives us pause to reflect upon the nature of the physical world. There is a view according to which matter is bad, but things in the realm of the spirit and philosophical thought are good. However, this is a false polarization; the two are not mutually exclusive. Hebrew thought, as expressed in the Bible, leads to a strong appreciation of the beauty and utility of the physical.

The Genesis account indicates that human beings were given prime responsibility for the care of the earth and all that it contains. They were given dominion over the birds, fish, and land animals that inhabit the earth. This does not mean that human beings are to dominate them to their detriment, but that they are to appreciate animals in their appropriate ecological niche.

The Bible is emphatic, especially in the OT, that God should be thought of as distinct and separate from His creation. This was not the view of the pagan world around ancient Israel, where the forces of nature were deified. Pagan polytheism depended upon approaching the gods with offerings to placate them and keep them favorably inclined toward the inhabitants of the land. In the Bible all of the forces of nature are impersonal; they are not deified and are ultimately under the control of one sovereign Creator.

C. Stewardship

Stewardship is another avenue of service to God the Creator (see III. A, B). As one cares for the land, the animals, and the wealth that one possesses, one should not only think of these as gifts from God but also as objects which should be given back to Him by sharing them with the less fortunate. (See Stewardship I. B; E. 2-4.)

D. The Historical Act of Creation

The Bible considers the creative acts of God as historical. They were so well known and recognized that the idea of God as Creator was reduced to a formula used to introduce prayers, prophecies, promises, and historical recitals of God's mighty acts. The creative acts of God in Genesis 1 were considered to be only the beginning of these mighty acts.

E. Worship of the Sustainer

The biblical texts surveyed make it amply clear that the ancients did not conceive of the Creator's activities as stopping at the end of Creation week. Rather, those activities still continue through biblical times until today. Both in the OT and the NT there are statements about God's creative work followed by references to His continued upholding of His creation. That includes each human being alive today. Were it not for God's sustaining power, none of our lives could continue.

F. The Revelation of God in Nature

The OT creation texts, especially those in Psalms, testify to the fact that we can see God's handiwork in nature. Nature speaks to us of nature's God. We cannot learn everything about God from nature, since the witness of nature to God has been damaged by sin; nevertheless, the natural world still testifies to the power and greatness of God. We do well to heed this witness.

G. Evolution Rejected

Evolutionary theory, which posits progress from lower to higher forms of life over extremely long periods of time, is not compatible with the biblical text either on a theistic or a nontheistic basis. OT and NT creation statements confirm the same point of view about God's creative work at the foundation of the world. There was a Special Creation at the time of the original Creation week. Modern science may dispute this, but it cannot do so on the basis of sound exegesis of the biblical text; it must do so only on the basis of extrabiblical factors.

H. Mission and Message

As has been pointed out in section II. D., on Creation in the book of Revelation, there is a last-day message to be given to the world. That message includes specific statements about the God of heaven as the Creator-God. That message of the Creator-God is to be given at a certain point in the scheme of salvation history, during a time known in the book of Daniel as the "time of the end." Attention is to be called to the Creator-God during that time when the Creator-God has been especially obscured in the thought of human beings. To remedy this situation, God as Creator needs to be recognized and preached. This is emphasized for the last time by the appearance of the mighty angel of Revelation 10 and the first angel of Revelation 14.

Through the ages the saints have looked forward to the coming kingdom of God. The OT outlines of that long-hoped-for kingdom are not entirely clear, but they have been refined by the eschatological promises of the NT. When God finally sets up His eternal kingdom, it will be quite different from the world as it is presently known. That re-

creation will necessitate a new and fresh exercise of His creative power. For that reason the Bible refers to this kingdom as "a new heaven and a new earth." The New Jerusalem will be even more glorious and wonderful than anything humans have known. The Lord God will sit on the throne at the center of the New Jerusalem in the earth made new. Those who place their trust in the Creator and Redeemer God will have the privilege of receiving the final fulfillment of their long-awaited hopes. Then the righteous will long enjoy the works of their hands, just as God will long enjoy the works of His creative hands.

IV. Historical Overview

A. The Ancient Near East

The hallmark of Creation stories from the ancient world is their polytheism. In these stories the creation of the world arose out of episodes of conflict and differences of opinion among the gods. In this tension the will of one god or one group of gods won out over the desires of another god or group of gods. In contrast, the Bible views Creation as the work of one sovereign God, who rules over all of nature and employs its forces and elements for His purposes.

1. The Assyrian View: Enuma Elish

In the Enuma Elish story two groups of gods were set against each other. One was led by the goddess Tiamat, who represented the waters, and her consort, Kingu. The other group was in disarray, and its members were looking for a leader. In the Babylonian version, Marduk was the god chosen to lead the opposing party, while in the Assyrian version, Ashur was chosen. In the stories, Marduk or Ashur defeated Tiamat and Kingu, and the goddess's body was sliced in half lengthwise to make the division between the waters above and the waters below. There is a faint resemblance here to the events of the second day

of the Creation account in Genesis 1. Possibly the name Tiamat may be related linguistically to the Hebrew word $t^e h \hat{o} m$, which is translated "depths" or "deep" in Genesis 1. Kingu was slaughtered also, and his blood was mixed with clay to make humankind. Some have seen here a faint resemblance to the sixth day of Creation in the biblical account.

2. The Old Babylonian Version: Atrahasis

The oldest copy of the Atrahasis Epic comes from the seventeenth century B.C. The original story undoubtedly goes back well before that time. The story begins with the lesser gods having to do most of the work for the greater gods. Eventually they became disgusted and decided to strike. Finally, a compromise was worked out in which human beings were to be created to carry the burden of the work.

After the decision to create mankind was made, the birth goddess became involved. She purified the clay necessary for the project, and a god named We-ila was slaughtered so that his blood could be mixed with the clay. When this specially prepared clay was ready, the birth goddess nipped off 14 pieces of it and incubated them. When the time came for the seven men and seven women to be born, some assistant birth goddesses came to help with the delivery, and so humankind was born. The similarity to the biblical account is that mankind was made out of the dust of the earth, or clay, but in the biblical account God did that on one particular day.

3. The Sumerian Genesis

The Eridu text is known from copies of tablets that date to about 1600 B.C. It probably had a much older oral and written history. The story tells of Creation, antediluvian life, and the Flood.

Unfortunately, the first 36 lines have been broken away from the beginning of the text. In these lines must have been the fuller recitation of Creation. We do have, however, a summary statement: "When An, Enlil, Enki and Ninhursaga [the birth goddess] fashioned the blackheaded people [the Sumerians] they had made the small animals of the earth to come up from the earth in abundance."

There are several similarities between this summary and the statements on these subjects in the biblical account. Humanity and land animals were created at the same time, and the animals were created in a similar way, from the earth. Their abundance is mirrored in the biblical account, according to which the earth, air, and waters swarmed with living creatures. The story focuses, however, on the Sumerians as the center of human creation, whereas the Bible makes Adam and Eve the ancestors of the entire human race. Polytheism shows in the cooperation of the main gods in this act of creation, and in the particular activity of the birth goddess in the process.

4. Ancient Egyptian Creation Myths

The fluidity of ideas about Creation is evident in a series of myths. At different times different gods were involved in the action of creation. Probably the most important creation text from Egypt is the one known as the Memphite Theology (ANET 4-6). In it the creator-god Ptah created by his spoken word with a modest resemblance to Genesis 1.

At different times different gods were presented as more prominent in the work of creation. Thus Amun, Aten, Atum, Ptah, and Khnum were all seen as the chief creator god at one time or another. The idea of conflict being involved in the process of creation is present in another myth known as "The Repulsing of the Dragon and the Creation" (*ibid.* 6, 7). Taking a parochial view, one text saw Thebes in Upper Egypt as the center of Creation (*ibid.* 8).

5. Greek Creation Theology

The date of Hesiod has been difficult to determine, although his writings were well known by the fifth century B.C. It is currently estimated that they came from around 800 B.C. He has given us his observations on creation in two different works. The description of the creation of the cosmos is told in his *Theogony,* and the story of the creation of the human race is told in his tale of Pandora and the Five Ages, recorded in *Works and Days.*

The story of the creation of the world is essentially sexual in Hesiod's *Theogony.* Into a framework of genealogies, stories about the gods have been inserted. Part of the purpose of this poem was to exalt Zeus, just as the Enuma Elish was written in support of the greatness of Marduk. The text goes through three main generations of the gods. The first (lines 116-210) includes the generations of Chaos, Eros, and some of the other gods and their children. The stories of the second generation of the gods tell of the origin of the children of the Titans, the children of Chronos, and other gods (lines 211-735). This section also tells of the creation of woman, but not man. It concludes with a story of war among the gods in heaven. The third-generation section of the work emphasizes the kingship and marriages of Zeus, along with stories of other gods (lines 736-880).

The story of Pandora, on the other hand, distinguishes between the good of maleness and the not-so-good of femaleness. Some have seen an echo of the biblical story of the fall of

443

Eve perpetuated here. From a biblical point of view it could be said that these stories deal more with the fall and the descent into evil than with the original creation. This descent was from a glorified golden age; this is a story of the devolution of the human race from that original state more than of its evolution upward on a ladder of progress.

B. Intertestamental Jewish Literature

We take 1 Enoch and Jubilees, both from the second-century B.C. pseudepigrapha, as examples of intertestamental literature. As would be expected on account of their derivation from the Hebrew Scriptures, they follow the outline of the Genesis creation. They diverge from the Genesis account to add details not found in the Bible and expansions going in different directions. The more expansionist of the two is 1 Enoch.

The Book of Jubilees deals with Creation much as does the Bible. In Jubilees 2 and 3 the language is similar to that of Genesis. Creation takes place in six days, in the same order as in Genesis, but with more details for each day. A prolonged section describes the seventh day, the first Sabbath. The purpose of this narration is to give a fixed point from which to begin the first cycle of sabbatical and jubilee years.

An important theme in 1 Enoch is the orderly cycle of nature, in which the stars, sun, and moon move in their orbits, and the winds, seas, and seasons observe their regular cycles. These cycles set the stage for the astronomical speculations in the latter part of the book. Of these regular cycles, the writer says, "All of them belong to him who lives forever. His work proceeds and progresses from year to year. And all his work prospers and obeys him, and it does not change; but everything functions in the way which God has ordered it" (1 Enoch 5:1-3). This idea certainly agrees with the OT vision of God's creating and sustaining activity.

According to 1 Enoch 10:17-22, there will be a new earth. It will be tilled in righteousness and planted with trees of blessing. Plants, trees, and vines will produce abundantly, and all pollution and iniquity will be eradicated.

C. First-Century Jewish Sources

It is quite natural that a historical work such as Josephus' (c. 37-c. 100) *Antiquities of the Jews* begins, after a discussion of its sources, with the story of Creation as told in Genesis. This section of Josephus' work covers book 1, chapters 27-42. The account follows the order of the biblical text. The expansion found here is modest.

When Josephus comes to Genesis 2, he goes directly to the creation of man without commenting on the state of the fields and garden. He describes the rivers of Genesis 2 by name and location. Regarding the Fall of Genesis 3, Josephus holds that the first pair briefly felt "happier" after they had eaten of the fruit of the tree of the knowledge of good and evil. Thus in summary, Josephus follows the canonical account of Creation rather closely and uses it for historical purposes, as an introduction to his history of Israel.

Philo of Alexandria, who lived and worked in the first half of the first century A.D., injects a new element into the story of Creation. The influence of Greek philosophy on Philo's thinking and writing is readily apparent in his interpretation of the biblical Creation account. While he stoutly maintained a central core of biblical religion back of the Creation account, he also interpreted the details of that account as figurative and symbolic *(On the Creation)*.

Philo's view of Creation shows how the account of Scripture has been reread and interpreted according to the principles of Greek philosophy. The dichotomy between the real and the ideal is perpetuated and makes the Creation into something that it was not when it came forth from the hand of God. In the Hebrew view this material creation was very good, but in the Greek and Philonic view, the spiritual or ideal was far superior to the material.

D. The Early Church: Origen and Augustine

Coming from Alexandria as he did, Origen (c. 185-c. 254)—not surprisingly—followed the Alexandrian method of exegesis, as previously represented in Philo. In Genesis 1 as in other scriptural passages Origen recognized a triple scene—literal, moral, and allegorical—of which he clearly preferred the last.

Augustine (354-430) took a very different view of the nature of the Creation record than did Origen. He noted that hours, days, months, and years are marked off by the movement of heavenly bodies which God set in motion (*City of God* 12. 15). While he was uncertain about the nature of the first three days of Creation week (*ibid.* 11. 6), he was clear on the nature of the creative acts themselves. These were not figurative or symbolic. Augustine also underlined that the harmony and unity in nature give evident praise to the wisdom of the Creator (*Confessions* 7. 13). Much of his emphasis was on the praise due the Creator, even from inanimate creation which Augustine personifies (*City of God* 11. 4). The seventh day of Creation week he took literally, but God's resting was spiritual (*ibid.* 11. 8).

Augustine gave much attention to the years in the genealogy of the antediluvians (Genesis 5). He compared the Hebrew and Greek manuscripts to attempt a definitive computation for their ages. He held that, on the basis of the calendar for the Flood, their years were like our years. From his discussion it is evident that he considered the antediluvians, including Adam and Eve, to be literal individuals, with literal birth and death ages (*ibid.* 15. 10-15). From his study he eventually concluded, on the basis of the day-age theory, that the world was not yet 6,000 years old (*ibid.* 20. 7).

E. The Medieval Period: Aquinas as an Example

The greatest work of Thomas Aquinas (c. 1225-1274) was his *Summa Theologiae*, the highest achievement of medieval theological systematization. Divided into three main sections, the first deals with God, His nature, and how all things have proceeded from Him. If in various areas reason is paramount for Aquinas, many of the fundamental Christian teachings, including the creation of the world, reach us through divine revelation. At the same time, such truths as the existence of God and Creation must not be considered as contrary to reason.

Most of his arguments for the existence of God derive from nature or Creation. The prime mover set Creation in motion; therefore, we know of him from that movement. As the first cause He caused this Creation to come into being and led its subsequent chain of causes. The damage that sin has caused to that perfect creation must, of course, be allowed for. Aquinas' argument for rational design in nature has been a favorite of modern scientists and philosophers. A kind of "secular theism" has grown up among moderns who can see the readily apparent design in nature and are led back to the Designer, even though they may not worship Him in a formal setting.

F. The Reformation: Martin Luther as an Example

Luther received his doctor's degree on October 18, 1512. A week later he began to lecture on Genesis. Unfortunately, these early lectures have been lost. We do have, however, his second set of *Lectures on Genesis,* which began on June 1, 1535. His lectures on the first five chapters give us a good idea about what the mature Luther thought about Creation (*Luther's Works,* vol. 1).

Luther believed in creatio ex nihilo, for he stated at the outset of that work that "we know from Moses that the world was not in existence before 6,000 years ago" (*ibid.* 1. 3). That the physical creation is treated quite literally in this work is evident in many passages. He wrote: "What Moses calls heaven and earth are not the kind they are now, but the crude and formless masses which they were up to that time. The water was dark; because it is lighter by nature, it surrounded the still formless earth itself, like an ooze or a dense fog. The primary matter, so to speak, for His later work God, according to the plain words of the Decalog (Exod. 20:11), did not create outside the six days but at the beginning of the first day" (*ibid.* 6).

The description of this state as "without form and void" Luther took as empty, unformed, and without anything animate present (*ibid.* 7).

Luther rejected the speculation of the philosophers here, too. He mentioned the Prime Mover of Aristotle (and Aquinas) but did not bother with this idea. Instead, he affirmed, "follow Moses and declare that all of these phenomena occur and are governed simply by the Word of God" (*ibid.* 30). Some aspects of the Creation account that he did not understand, Luther left with God to be believed by faith. About the dividing of the waters, he affirmed, "But He Himself wants to remain the only master of His order and the referee of His world. And so we should not be very inquisitive here" (*ibid.* 33).

It is of interest to see how little impact Creation had upon the creedal and catechetical statements that originated with the Reformation. In a survey of nine of these documents, only Luther's *Small Catechism* of 1529 included a statement on Creation, and then it was only a general assertion about God as the Creator of all. The reason for this evident lack is that the reformers were agreed on this subject, which was not a major point at issue between them and the Roman Church. This was perhaps the last time at which there was a reasonable degree of unity on this subject, for with the coming of the Age of Rationalism in the next two centuries, this consensus broke apart into very disparate views.

G. The Age of Rationalism

With the rise of scientific inquiry in the seventeenth and eighteenth centuries, new thoughts and ideas about the world and the universe came into the philosophical realm. The discoveries of Galileo, Kepler, Newton, Harvey, and others led to a new and mechanistic view of the operation of the universe. What started as a study of the laws that God had created in nature ended by isolating those laws from the God with whom they were at first associated. This was especially true in the case of Sir Isaac Newton (1642-1727). A devout Christian himself, he discovered in the world of physical laws things that led others to develop views that isolated those laws from God. The universe was on its own, and although it operated by law, those laws came to be seen as inherent in it.

As the universe came to be seen as independent of God, a divine Creator receded from the thought of the thinkers of the time. This led to the Deist view of the universe, the watchmaker's model. Like a great watchmaker, God had made the world; but then He had left it to run on its own, according to the laws that had been created with it. The watch was wound up, and it could now run on its own without God's assistance. This brought with it the corollary that God did not break into the natural operation of this world. Hence miracles were now ruled out, as was any direct revelation to prophets. There may have been an original Creator, but after creating the world He took little interest in it.

Only one step beyond that view was the idea that the human race did not need the watchmaker God either. Not only was the universe on its own, but it arose on its own, spontaneously, without the assistance of the watchmaker. These philosophical developments impacted the biblical account of Creation in two different but parallel ways. The first was through literary criticism of the biblical account, and the second was through the affirmation that science has demonstrated the inaccuracy of the biblical account of Creation. These two methods of evaluation of the biblical record continue to this day; the development of both is examined here, together with some of the challenges they have posed to the biblical account.

1. Literary Criticism of Genesis and the Creation Account

One of the earliest critics of the Creation story was Benedict Spinoza, a Jewish philosopher who lived in Holland (1632-1677). His comments were, however, merely a prologue to what was to come. The landmark study, with which the modern era of literary criticism of Genesis and the Creation story began, is the work of Jean Astruc, a French physician (1684-1766) who published his theory of the composition of Genesis in 1753. Astruc held to the Mosaic authorship of Genesis but proposed that Moses used sources and arranged these in four columns. Later scribes then rearranged these columns, thus providing for the present arrangement of the book. He explained the different use of the divine names in Genesis 1 and 2 as coming from different sources.

It did not take long to extend the idea of Astruc and separate these sources from Moses. This was done by Johann Eichhorn (1752-1827), who proposed that these sources originated from different times and scribes long after Moses. Other scholars of the nineteenth century added to this theory until the documentary hypothesis came together in its greatest synthesis, that of Julius Wellhausen (1844-1918) in his work *Die Komposition des Hexateuchs und der historischen Bücher des Alten Testaments* (3rd ed., 1899). This theory has continued to undergo modification. At present it is said that the four main sources of the Pentateuch—*J, E, D,* and *P*—are distributed over a period of about 500 years, from the days of David to postexilic times.

The two chapters at the beginning of Genesis are assigned to the *E* source and the *J* source, respectively. This is done on the basis of the presence of different divine names and different literary styles. Thus neither of these Creation accounts was written by Moses, but by later scribes. Since these accounts were written late in biblical history and

by different groups of scribes working at different times, they cannot be considered reliable history.

Conservative writers, both Jewish and Christian, have made extensive critiques of the documentary hypothesis. Notable among these are works by U. Cassuto (*The Documentary Hypothesis,* Eng. trans., 1961), M. H. Segal (*The Pentateuch,* 1967), and O. T. Allis (*The Five Books of Moses,* 1943). Section I. B. of this article has responded to those who follow the documentary hypothesis by pointing out features that link the two chapters with the same author. The precise match in word, syllable, and stress-accent counts between the two narratives clearly speaks against the production of Genesis 1 and 2 by different scribal schools, separated by four or more centuries. Furthermore, the use of two divine names has been shown to have theological meaning related to the function of God in the two chapters.

The documentary hypothesis fails to recognize the parallel, repetitious nature of Hebrew literature, both poetry and prose. The account in Genesis 2 is a parallel repetition of a few select elements found in Genesis 1, as is common in Hebrew parallel writing. Given that the Creation record is a major statement of the Hebrew Bible, its parallel repetition is to be expected.

In general, scholars tend to come in two different varieties: those who lump Israel together with the rest of the countries and cultures of the ancient Near East, and those who tend to separate Israel as distinct and unique. Literary critics have looked for those elements that separate the two Creation narratives of Genesis while overlooking those elements that bind the two narratives together. Above all, they have overlooked the main literary mechanism that ties them together, repetitive parallelism of thought.

Other techniques of analyzing the biblical text have followed the documentary hypothesis. One of these is form criticism, developed first by H. Gunkel (*The Legends of Genesis,*

1901). This school of thought emphasizes the "setting in life" that gave rise to the story and examines the units in which the narration has been transmitted. Gunkel attempted to connect the biblical Creation story with the Chaos creation myth of Mesopotamia (see IV. A. 1). Since the chaos theme has not survived to any significant extent in Genesis 1, Gunkel has affirmed that "we can *conjecture* a form of the account in which more personages appear and in which the world is created after a conflict of God with Chaos" (Gunkel, 74; italics supplied). The key operative word here is "conjecture." In other words, since Chaos is not present in the Bible text we have today, the account must be reconstructed in such a way as to make it tell the story of the battle with Chaos. Thus the Babylonian myth becomes the standard by which the biblical Creation account is reconstructed, even though the two narratives have very little in common.

2. Scientific Criticism of Genesis and the Creation Account

The first avenue through which the scientific sector has criticized the Creation account, and the Flood account along with it, has been the findings and theories of geology. While others preceded him, the foundation of modern evolutionary geology may be said to have been laid by James Hutton (1726-1797). As he examined the rock formations of his native Scotland and in England, he came to place great emphasis upon the slow action of erosion of moving water in wearing down the land and forming new rocks by deposition. This laid the theoretical foundation for uniformitarianism, which maintains that what is today has always been. If one assumes that the present is the all-encompassing key to the past, the uniformitarian assumptions become the measure of time in the past, which stretches out to an almost endless procession of cycles of erosion and deposition. With this basic proposal, geological time was extended far beyond anything that a recent biblical Creation could encompass. Georges Cuvier of

France (1769-1832) soon added his studies of the fossils to the strata that were deposited in this way.

a. Nineteenth century. An obscure English land surveyor named William "Strata" Smith added to this system by organizing the different rock systems he found in his work of surveying. Smith worked out the idea of "index fossils" for the strata of rock with which he was familiar and made a geological map of central England on this basis. The reception of this map was sufficient to encourage him to extend the geological mapping project to all parts of England. He was a contemporary of Cuvier but, because of his limited education, probably never became familiar with Cuvier's work of a similar nature.

While the work of Hutton, Cuvier, and Smith supported and extended the idea that vast periods of time were involved in depositing the geological strata and the fossils they contained, the mechanism for this progression was published in 1844. The author of the book, *Vestiges of the Natural History of Creation,* was not known at the time of its publication; only after his death was Robert Chambers, well-known publisher of the *Cyclopaedia of English Literature,* recognized as its author. This work held that the progression from invertebrates to fish, from reptiles to mammals and man, as found in the fossils, was one of succession or *evolution.* While the mechanism of evolution had not yet been proposed, the idea that these were successive life forms extending over long ages was in circulation well before Charles Darwin's time.

In the meantime, the principles of uniformitarian evolutionary geology had been crystallized by Charles Lyell (1797-1875). This approach to geology was presented in his book *The Principles of Geology;* the first of three volumes was published in 1830. Surprisingly, Lyell resisted the evolutionary implications of his work for a long time. He rejected Chambers' book *Vestiges* and resisted Darwin's theory when it was published. He finally capitulated and accepted it in his later years.

Lyell's *Principles of Geology* was well known and had a tremendous influence in bringing about a reorientation from the short biblical chronology for Creation to the extremely long timescale of uniformitarian geology. Darwin took Lyell's book along on his voyage on the *Beagle;* thus it served as a geological primer for the biological theory that he eventually worked out. His own theory of evolution depended upon selection and survival of the fittest to develop the succeeding species. This was published in his book *Origin of Species* in 1859.

A number of creationists opposed these ideas in the nineteenth century, but theirs was a somewhat different orientation from that of creationists of the twentieth century. One of the prominent earlier creationists was Louis Agassiz (1807-1873), who was especially well known for his work with fossil fish and for observation and theories about the development of glaciers.

b. Twentieth century. Many developments have taken place in the fields of geology, biology, and genetics that affect the view of these matters taken by scientists today. In the field of geology there has been a drift away from uniformitarianism. Geologists today, evolutionists or not, are more agreeable to admitting abundant evidence for catastrophes in the geological column. The difference between this view and that of creationists is that evolutionary geologists now see multiple catastrophes in the geological column, while creationists prefer to put most of these into one great catastrophe, the biblical flood. Whatever one does with evidence for the Flood also affects how one sees Creation before it.

Another field that has impacted the Christian's view of the world is radiometric dating as developed by physicists. Radiometric dating, which dates elements in the nonfossil-bearing (nonsedimentary) rocks, would put those elements and their volcanic deposition millions of years in the past. This could still be compatible with the Christian view of the creation in Genesis 1 if one allowed that the primordial planet existed in an inert state before Creation week and the advent of life on the earth. Radiocarbon dating is used to date dead organisms, organic material, but the method becomes more and more inaccurate farther back in history.

In the field of biology, genetics has had the most profound impact upon the theory of evolution. Darwin had only a rudimentary knowledge of genetics. He held that inherited characteristics were transmitted by spherules in the blood. At the same time that Darwin was working, the monk Gregor Mendel worked out the laws of heredity governed by genetics. Unfortunately, his work was lost and had to be rediscovered. It is now understood that changes in characteristics occur through mutations in the genes. This poses a problem for evolution, because more often than not mutations are harmful rather than helpful. An attempt was made to overcome the problem through the study of population genetics. If one takes a whole population of a species one may statistically overwhelm harmful mutations and select the helpful ones.

A major revolution has taken place in biology with the discovery of the dual heliacal form of the DNA molecule by Watson and Crick in 1953. What is now known to happen in reproduction is that the base pairs which bind the backbone of DNA together unzip, and the halves of the parental pairs join to make a new member of the species. This makes the evolution of species all the more difficult to hypothesize because of the immensity and complexity of the problem. A major research effort is now under way to determine all of the base pairs in the DNA of human genes and chromosomes. Since there are more than 3 billion base pairs which make up the human genome, the possibility that a being so precise and complex could have come about through evolution becomes infinitesimally small. The testimony of the marvelous wonders of genetics is the same as the testimony of the biblical writer who said that we are "fearfully and wonderfully made" (Ps. 139:14).

H. Seventh-day Adventist Contributions

Seventh-day Adventists have made major contributions to creationism in the twentieth century. The initial leader in this effort was George McCready Price (1870-1963). Self-taught in geology, he was critical of professional publications by geologists. He denied that there was order to the distribution of fossils through the geological strata and held that the geological strata were out of order in many places. Geologists do admit that in some places the strata are inverted, but they refer to these as deceptive conformities, which, they hold, have developed when the lower strata were thrust over the later strata. Price held that these inverted strata were deposited in the correct order and thus the theory of geologists was wrong on that point. He argued these criticisms in a series of books: *The New Geology* (1923), *The Predicament of Evolution* (1925), *Genesis Vindicated* (1941), and *Common-Sense Geology* (1946). Price could well be called the father of the twentieth-century creationist movement.

Price was not unchallenged, even within his church. A professor of biology at Pacific Union College, Harold W. Clark, took a different view of the geological strata and the fossils that they contained. Clark did more field work than Price had done and came to the conclusion that the strata and their fossils were found in the order in which evolutionary geologists said they were. That conclusion required the development of an alternate theory for their deposition, one that was compatible with the superposition of the fossils. Clark came up with the idea of "ecological zonation," that the fossils were buried in the order in which they occupied their ecological niches in nature. Thus the bottom dwellers were buried first, the fish were buried next. As swamp dwellers, the amphibians were buried above the fish, and finally the mammals, occupants of higher land, were buried last. Although this model does not answer all questions about the deposition of the fossils, it is accepted by many creationists as the best explanation currently available. (See Clark 1946, 1977.)

V. The Seventh-day Adventist View of Creation

Seventh-day Adventists hold that the record of Creation in Genesis 1 and 2 is literal and historical, just as was largely held until the eighteenth century. In Genesis we have a record of the mighty acts of God in Creation; but that record is only the beginning of His work on behalf of the inhabitants of this planet, for that record continues throughout the Bible. Thus the Creation account at the beginning of the Bible is but an introduction to the history of the plan of salvation.

For Seventh-day Adventists, the elements contained in the Genesis Creation story are not symbolic or spiritual. God saw that the matter that He created and used during Creation week was good, even very good. The biblical view is that the good of the spiritual is contained within matter, which is also good, not isolated or separate from it. This stands in contrast with the view of Greek philosophy, which has seen matter as bad and the spiritual, or ideal, as good.

Among the features of this account, which are held to be literal, are the references to time. Given the formula about the time elements, it is evident and clear that the writer of the text was referring to literal 24-hour days, each with its day and night. This gives a full basis and foundation for the seventh day as the conclusion to Creation week. That day was a day for the rest of God, in which He took into full account all of the good things that He had created, even the human beings with which His creative event culminated. For good reason God set that day apart, and blessed and sanctified it for the use of human beings.

Nature still reveals its grandeur and beauty even though it has been damaged by the effects of sin. Some of the later texts in the OT praise God for His wonderful creation, and the praise for God as the Creator continues all the way to the NT book of Revelation.

The date for this Creation week was only a few thousand years ago, in recent time, not millions of years ago. An inert planet may have been here before, but life was not created upon it until the recent Creation week that is described in Genesis 1. Nature provides a general revelation about God. This is acknowledged in various OT and NT texts. God's wisdom and power are demonstrated by the macrocosm and the microcosm of the physical world.

God still retains power over what He created. According to the OT, He could use His power to bring about judgments upon the nations around Israel and also on the people of Israel themselves when they turned away from Him and His covenant and acted wickedly. In these last days God will yet utilize those powers again in the same way. In the seven last plagues (Rev. 16) God will again demonstrate that He is Creator and Judge.

Before that time a special message needs to be given. It is a message about God as Creator. At a time when, as never before, humans refuse to recognize Him as Creator, a message is to be given which calls their attention to the Creator once more. This message is contained especially in the first angel's tidings of Revelation 14:6, 7, a special message which the Seventh-day Adventist Church feels called to proclaim. In calling the attention of the world to the Creator, we also call their attention to worship, which is best carried out on the day that the Creator set aside to commemorate His creation, the Sabbath.

Finally, the power of God will be exercised again, when He makes His new Creation, the new heavens and the new earth. Once again the earth will come forth from the hand of its Creator purified of sin. Restored to its Edenic beauty, the earth will become the home of the saved and will demonstrate to the universe that God is love, and that through His love He has restored everything to His people. Thus the creative and redeeming power of God will be fully demonstrated at the end of the great controversy.

In view of the biblical data available on the subject of Creation, the Seventh-day Adventist Church has drawn up and voted the following official statement on its view of Creation:

"God is Creator of all things, and has revealed in Scripture the authentic account of His creative activity. In six days the Lord made 'the heaven and the earth' and all living things upon the earth, and rested on the seventh day of that first week. Thus He established the Sabbath as a perpetual memorial of His completed creative work. The first man and woman were made in the image of God as the crowning work of Creation, given dominion over the world, and charged with responsibility to care for it. When the world was finished it was 'very good,' declaring the glory of God. (Gen. 1; 2; Ex. 20:8-11; Ps. 19:1-6; 33:6, 9; 104; Heb. 11:3.)" (*SDA Yearbook* 1981, 5).

VI. Ellen G. White Comments

A. Nature and Nature's God

"Nature is a power, but the God of nature is unlimited in power. His works interpret His character. Those who judge Him from His handiworks, and not from the suppositions of great men, will see His presence in everything. They behold His smile in the glad sunshine, and His love and care for man in the rich fields of autumn. Even the adornments of the earth, as seen in the grass of living green, the lovely flowers of every hue, and the lofty and varied trees of the forest, testify to the tender, fatherly care of our God, and to His desire to make His children happy.

"The power of the great God will be exerted in behalf of those that fear Him. Listen to the words of the prophet: 'Hast thou not known?

Hast thou not heard, that the everlasting God, the Lord, the Creator of the ends of the earth, fainteth not, neither is weary? There is no searching of his understanding. He giveth power to the faint; and to them that have no might he increaseth strength. Even the youths shall faint and be weary, and the young men shall utterly fall. But they that wait upon the Lord shall renew their strength; they shall mount up with wings as eagles; they shall run, and not be weary; and they shall walk, and not faint'" (ST Mar. 13, 1884).

"God is the foundation of everything. All true science is in harmony with His works; all true education leads to obedience to His government. Science opens new wonders to our view; she soars high and explores new depths; but she brings nothing from her research that conflicts with divine revelation. Ignorance may seek to support false views of God by appeals to science; but the book of nature and the written word do not disagree; each sheds light on the other. Rightly understood, they make us acquainted with God and His character by teaching us something of the wise and beneficent laws through which He works. We are thus led to adore His holy name, and to have an intelligent trust in His word" (*ibid.* Mar. 20, 1884).

B. Science and the Bible

"Rightly understood, both the revelations of science and the experiences of life are in harmony with the testimony of Scripture to the constant working of God in nature.

"In the hymn recorded by Nehemiah, the Levites sang, 'Thou, even Thou, art Lord alone; Thou hast made heaven, the heaven of heavens, with all their host, the earth, and all things that are therein, the seas, and all that is therein, and Thou preservest them all' (Neh. 9:6).

"As regards this earth, Scripture declares the work of creation to have been completed. 'The works were finished from the foundation of the world' (Heb. 4:3). But the power of God is still exercised in upholding the objects of His creation. It is not because the mechanism once set in motion continues to act by its own inherent energy that the pulse beats, and breath follows breath. Every breath, every pulsation of the heart, is an evidence of the care of Him in whom we live and move and have our being. From the smallest insect to man, every living creature is daily dependent upon His providence. . . .

"He who studies most deeply into the mysteries of nature will realize most fully his own ignorance and weakness. He will realize that there are depths and heights which he cannot reach, secrets which he cannot penetrate, vast fields of truth lying before him unentered. He will be ready to say, with Newton, 'I seem to myself to have been like a child on the seashore finding pebbles and shells, while the great ocean of truth lay undiscovered before me.'

"The deepest students of science are constrained to recognize in nature the working of infinite power. But to man's unaided reason, nature's teaching cannot but be contradictory and disappointing. Only in the light of revelation can it be read aright. 'Through faith we understand' (Heb. 11:3)" (Ed 130-134).

C. Authentic History of the Beginning of Our World

"The Bible is the most instructive and comprehensive history that has ever been given to the world. Its sacred pages contain the only authentic account of the Creation. Here we behold the power that 'stretched forth the heavens, and laid the foundations of the earth.' Here we have a truthful history of the human race, one that is unmarred by human prejudice or human pride. . . .

"There is harmony between nature and Christianity; for both have the same Author. The book of nature and the book of revelation indicate the working of the same divine mind. There are lessons to be learned in nature; and there are lessons, deep, earnest, and all-important lessons, to be learned from the book of God" (RH Aug. 19, 1884).

"The history of the world from the beginning is contained in Genesis. There it is revealed that all nations who forget God and discard His way and His sign of obedience, which distinguishes between the just and the unjust, the righteous and the wicked, the saved and the unsaved, will be destroyed. . . .

"The Lord calls upon all to study the divine philosophy of sacred history, written by Moses under the inspiration of the Holy Spirit. The first family placed upon the earth is a sample of all families which will exist till the close of time. There is much to study in this history in order that we may understand the divine plan for the human race. This plan is plainly defined, and the prayerful, consecrated soul will become a learner of the thought and purpose of God from the beginning till the close of this earth's history. He will realize that Jesus Christ, one with the Father, was the great mover in all progress, the One who is the source of all the purification and elevation of the human race" (3MR 184).

"We are dependent on the Bible for a knowledge of the early history of our world, of the creation of man, and of his fall. Remove the word of God, and what can we expect than to be left to fables and conjectures, and to that enfeebling of the intellect which is the sure result of entertaining error. We need the authentic history of the origin of the earth, of the fall of the covering cherub, and of the introduction of sin into our world. Without the Bible, we should be bewildered by false theories. The mind would be subjected to the tyranny of superstition and falsehood. But having in our possession an authentic history of the beginning of our world, we need not hamper ourselves with human conjectures and unreliable theories" (MM 89).

"The divine Mind and Hand has preserved through the ages the record of creation in its purity. It is the Word of God alone that gives to us an authentic account of the creation of our world" (RH Nov. 11, 1909).

D. God Not Indebted to Preexisting Matter

"In the formation of our world, God was not beholden to preexistent substance or matter. 'For the things that are seen were not made of the things which do appear.' On the contrary, all things, material or spiritual, stood up before the Lord Jehovah at His voice, and were created for His own purpose. The heavens and all the host of them, the earth and all things that are therein, are not only the work of His hand, they came into existence by the breath of His mouth.

"The Lord had given evidence that by His power He could in one short hour dissolve the whole frame of nature. He can turn things upside down, and destroy the things that man has built up in his most firm and substantial manner. 'He removeth the mountains; he overturneth them in his anger, he sweepeth the earth out of its place, and the billows thereof tremble and are astonished at his reproof; the mountains quake at him, and the hills melt, and the earth is burned in his presence' " (3MR 208).

"God has permitted a flood of light to be poured upon the world in the discoveries of science and art; but when professedly scientific men reason upon these subjects from a merely human point of view, they are sure to err. The greatest minds, if not guided by the Word of God, become bewildered in their attempts to investigate the relations of science and revelation. The Creator and His works are beyond their comprehension; and because these cannot be explained by natural laws, Bible history is pronounced unreliable.

"Those who question the reliability of the Scripture records have let go their anchor and are left to beat about upon the rocks of infidelity. When they find themselves incapable of measuring the Creator and His works by their own imperfect knowledge of science, they question the existence of God and attribute infinite power to nature.

"In true science there can be nothing contrary to the teaching of the Word of God, for both have the same Author. A correct understanding of both will always prove them to be in harmony. Truth, whether in nature or in revelation, is harmonious with itself in all its manifestations. But the mind not enlightened by God's Spirit will ever be in darkness in regard to His power. This is why human ideas in regard to science so often contradict the teaching of God's Word" (8T 257, 258).

"The theory that God did not create matter when He brought the world into existence is without foundation. In the formation of our world, God was not indebted to preexisting matter. On the contrary, all things, material or spiritual, stood up before the Lord Jehovah at His voice and were created for His own purpose" (*ibid.* 258, 259).

"God's government included not only the inhabitants of heaven, but of all the worlds that He had created; and Lucifer had concluded that if he could carry the angels of heaven with him in rebellion, he could carry also all the worlds" (PP 41; see GC 497).

E. The Sabbath as Old as the Earth Itself

"God has given us His commandments, not only to be believed in, but to be obeyed. The great Jehovah, when He had laid the foundations of the earth, had dressed the whole world in the garb of beauty, and had filled it with things useful to man—when He had created all the wonders of the land and the sea—instituted the Sabbath day and made it holy" (4T 247).

"When the foundations of the earth were laid, then was laid the foundation of the Sabbath, and the morning stars sang together, and all the sons of God shouted for joy. . . . God gave His law, and in the fourth precept of the Decalogue is His Sabbath, the very day on which we have turned aside from worldly business in order to observe it as a memorial of the creation of the heaven and the earth" (RH July 15, 1890).

"If man had always obeyed the fourth com-

mandment there never would have been an infidel in the world, because it testified that the Lord made the heaven and the earth, the sea and all that in them is; wherefore the Lord blessed the Sabbath day, and hallowed it" (1SAT 233).

"The Sabbath was made for all mankind, and was instituted in Eden before the fall of man. The Creator called it 'my holy day.' Christ announced Himself as 'the Lord of the Sabbath.' Beginning with creation, it is as old as the human race, and having been made for man it will exist as long as man shall exist" (ST Nov. 12, 1894).

F. Science, True and False, and Revelation

"To many, scientific research has become a curse; their finite minds are so weak that they lose their balance. They cannot harmonize their views of science with Scripture statements, and they think that the Bible is to be tested by their standard of 'science falsely so called.' Thus they err from the faith, and are seduced by the devil. Men have endeavored to be wiser than their Creator; human philosophy has attempted to search out and explain mysteries which will never be revealed, through eternal ages. If men would but search and understand what God has made known of Himself and His purposes, they would obtain such a view of the glory, majesty, and power of Jehovah, that they would realize their own littleness, and would be content with that which has been revealed for themselves and their children" (4SP 345).

"He who created the world and made the lofty mountains, who opened the fountains of the great deep, who formed the mighty rocks and the lofty trees, has given man power to appreciate these wonders of earth and heaven, power to understand the lessons drawn from them by Christ. But human intelligence could never have originated these lessons, and neither can man understand them only as God by His Holy Spirit sanctifies the observation. . . .

"Little confidence can be placed in human

reasoning. Were Christ in the world today, the veriest stripling in the schools would prate to him of so-called science. But Christ would answer: 'No man can serve two masters' " (RH July 3, 1900).

G. 1890 Statements Concerning the Flood

"The entire surface of the earth was changed at the Flood. A third dreadful curse rested upon it in consequence of sin. As the water began to subside, the hills and mountains were surrounded by a vast, turbid sea. Everywhere were strewn the dead bodies of men and beasts. The Lord would not permit these to remain to decompose and pollute the air, therefore He made of the earth a vast burial ground. A violent wind which was caused to blow for the purpose of drying up the waters, moved them with great force, in some instances even carrying away the tops of the mountains and heaping up trees, rocks, and earth above the bodies of the dead. By the same means the silver and gold, the choice wood and precious stones, which had enriched and adorned the world before the Flood, and which the inhabitants had idolized, were concealed from the sight and search of men, the violent action of the waters piling earth and rocks upon these treasures, and in some cases even forming mountains above them" (PP 107, 108).

H. Evidence of Changes Made by the Flood

"The rocks are among the precious things of earth, containing treasures of wisdom and knowledge. In the rocks and mountains are registered the fact that God did destroy the wicked from off the earth by a flood, and the broken surface of the earth reveals, in the gi-gantic rocks and towering mountains, that the Lord's power has done this because of the wickedness of man in the transgression of His law. The ever-varying scenery that meets the eye is the work of the God of wisdom, that in His stupendous works men may discern that there is a living God whose power is unlimited. The marvelous works of majesty are to refine the soul and to soften the roughness of man's nature, to help him in character building" (3MR 217).

I. On Mountains and Mountain Building

"I was so very weary I lay down on the seat and slept for two hours, and in doing this lost some interesting part of the scenery, but we made as much as possible of the rest of the journey.

"It was grand and magnificent. There were lakes and gorges and canyons and towering rocks, some of remarkable appearance. The mountain peaks, rising above mountain peaks. Some adorned with trees, some cultivated to the very top. The trail to them went zigzag, and how they could build their houses, and make their gardens and live up so high was a mystery to us. Chapels were built on the mountain heights, and villages were nestled in the mountain gorges. . . .

"We are filled with awe. We love to gaze upon the grandeur of God's works, and are never weary. Here is a range of mountains extending the whole length of a continent piled up one above another like a massive irregular wall reaching even above the clouds. That God who keeps the mountain in position has given us promises that are more immutable than these grand old mountains. God's Word will stand forever from generation to generation" (*ibid.* 214).

VII. Literature

Brueggemann, Walter. *Genesis*. Interpretation, vol. 1. Atlanta: John Knox, 1982.

Cassuto, Umberto. *A Commentary on the Book of Genesis.* Part 1, *From Adam to Noah.* Jerusalem: Magnes, 1989.

Clark, Harold W. *The New Diluvialism.* Angwin, Calif.: Science Publications, 1946.

———. *The Battle Over Genesis.* Washington, D.C.: Review and Herald, 1977.

Coffin, Harold G. *Origin by Design.* Washington, D.C.: Review and Herald, 1983.

"Evidences of a Worldwide Flood." In *The Seventh-day Adventist Bible Commentary.* Washington, D.C.: Review and Herald, 1953. Vol. 1, pp. 64-98.

Finegan, Jack. *Handbook of Biblical Chronology.* Princeton: Princeton University Press, 1964.

Gunkel, Herman. *The Legends of Genesis.* New York: Schocken, 1964.

Hasel, Gerhard F. "The Significance of the Cosmology in Genesis 1 in Relation to Ancient Near Eastern Parallels." *Andrews University Seminary Studies* 10 (1972): 1-20.

———. "The Meaning of 'Let Us' in Gn 1:26." *Andrews University Seminary Studies* 13 (1975): 58-66.

———. "The Sabbath in the Pentateuch." In *The Sabbath in Scripture and History.* Ed. K. A. Strand. Washington, D.C.: Review and Herald, 1982. Pp. 21-43.

———. "The 'Days' of Creation in Genesis 1: Literal 'Days' or Figurative 'Periods/Epochs' of Time?" *Origins* 21 (1994): 5-38.

Jacobsen, Thorkild. "The Eridu Genesis." *Journal of Biblical Literature* 100 (1981): 513-529.

Johnson, Phillip E. *Darwin on Trial.* 2nd ed. Downers Grove, Ill.: InterVarsity, 1993.

Lavallee, Louis. "Augustine on the Creation Days." *Journal of the Evangelical Theological Society* 32 (1989): 457-464.

Lewis, Jack P. "The Days of Creation: An Historical Survey of Interpretation." *Journal of the Evangelical Theological Society* 32 (1989): 433-455.

Maxwell, C. Mervyn. *God Cares.* Vol. 2, *Revelation.* Boise, Idaho: Pacific Press, 1985.

"Science and a Literal Creation." In *The Seventh-day Adventist Bible Commentary.* Washington, D.C.: Review and Herald, 1953. Vol. 1, 1976, pp. 46-63.

Shea, William H. "Literary Structural Parallels Between Genesis 1 and 2." *Origins* 16 (1989): 49-68.

———. "A Comparison of Narrative Elements in Ancient Mesopotamian Creation-Flood Stories With Genesis 1-9." *Origins* 11 (1984): 9-29.

———. "The Unity of the Creation Account." *Origins* 5 (1978): 9-38.

Speiser, E. A. *Genesis.* 3rd ed. Anchor Bible. Vol. 1. Garden City, N.Y.: Doubleday, 1981.

Webster, Clyde L., Jr. *The Earth: Origins and Early History.* Office of Education, North American Division of the General Conference of Seventh-day Adventists: Silver Spring, Md., 1989.

Wenham, Gordon J. *Genesis 1-15.* Word Bible Commentary. Vol. 1. Waco, Tex.: Word, 1987.

Westermann, Claus. *Genesis 1-11.* Minneapolis: Augsburg, 1984.

The Law of God

Mario Veloso

Introduction

In all societies, law as the basis of right conduct is vital to the well-being of people. From a theological point of view, law becomes even more important because it includes the law of God, in which divine requirements are made of human beings.

From a biblical standpoint, law often points to the Torah or Book of the Law, the Pentateuch, which is traditionally considered to contain 613 commandments. Yet the books of Moses have no monopoly on the topic. From Genesis through Revelation, the law is integral to the history of Israel, to the teaching of Jesus, and to the Epistles of Paul.

While different kinds of law are evident throughout the Bible—ceremonial laws, civil laws, health laws, community laws—the law of God is at the heart of the concept. The Decalogue, the moral law, is spiritual and shows the character of God. It transcends time and place, sharing the permanence of its Author.

God's law must be studied in relation to other topics. The Decalogue is part of God's covenant with His people. For Paul, law is closely related to grace. Ultimately law must be viewed in the light of the cross, for Christians the central event of history.

This article on the law explores the meaning, purpose, uniqueness, and permanence of the law of God. It also considers the application of the doctrine in everyday Christian life and in the life of the Seventh-day Adventist Church.

I. God's Law in the Scriptures

A. Definitions

Before analyzing the meaning of God's "law" as contained in Scripture, it is necessary to consider the words used for this concept and the kinds of divine law.

1. Words for Law

The most common word for law in the OT is *tôrāh*, meaning "direction," "instruction," or "law." While *tôrāh* carries this precise meaning, often it refers to the totality of divine instruction God gave His people (Gen. 26:5; Ex. 16:4; Isa. 1:10 and 8:20, where the RSV translates "teaching"). Psalm 119 uses several words to describe God's law ("testimonies" [verse 2]; "precepts" [verse 4]; "statutes" [verse 5]; "commandments" [verse 6]), all these terms are subsumed under one concept: *tôrāh*, the totality of the revealed will of God. In the word *tôrāh* were included the moral, ceremonial, and civil laws of Israel. Because God's "law" was the entire plan of salvation, Isaiah could affirm that the "coastlands wait for his law" (Isa. 42:4). The Pentateuch, the main source of this instruction, was called Torah or Law of God (Neh. 8:18; 9:3).

The NT uses the Greek *nomos* to represent *tôrāh*. The shades of meaning of *nomos* are varied, reflecting the rich meaning of its Hebrew original. Thus it may point to Scripture as the revelation of God's will (John 15:25), the Pentateuch in general (Matt. 7:12), or at times the Decalogue (James 2:10-12) or the ceremonial law (Acts 15:1).

2. Kinds of Law

The abundant legal material of the Bible embraces all aspects of life—health, diet, sexuality, work, community, cult, government, and even the relationship with the environment. Some of these laws are of universal application, while others were applicable only in certain times and places. However, all of them are *tôrāh*: divine instruction for God's people.

a. Nonuniversal laws. The nonuniversal laws were given to the nation of Israel, to be kept by its citizens and the strangers who sojourned with them. These ceremonial and civil laws were not intended to be observed by those who did not form part of God's people.

The *ceremonial laws* were regulations that God used to teach the plan of salvation through symbols and cultic practices. The OT makes it clear that these laws were already in practice soon after the Fall, as is shown by the story of Cain and Abel (Gen. 4:3-7). After the Exodus, the cultic regulations were expanded and recorded in Leviticus, describing the entire ritual system of Israel's sanctuary and, later, of the Jewish temple.

The ceremonial system was established to typify Christ's perfect offering on the cross. Christ was its foundation, its message, its expectation; it was also an expression of faith in Christ. But the system was not perfect because it was only a shadow or symbol of the real sacrifice for sin. It could not cleanse sinners from sin. It was only a promise that salvation would come by the offering and sacrifice of the Lamb of God and an expression of faith in that promise (Heb. 10:1-10).

The *civil laws* were given by God through Moses to the nation of Israel to regulate the life of the community. These laws were mostly an application of universal principles con-

458

tained in the second table of the Ten Commandments, which deal with relationships between human beings. The basic principle of the civil laws was justice in the public service of rulers and judges, and righteousness in all actions of the covenant people (Ex. 23:1-9; Deut. 16:18-20; Lev. 19:9-18).

b. Universal laws. God's interest in humans is manifested in laws given for and applicable for all persons, valid for all times and in all situations. Examples of these universal laws are natural laws, health and dietary laws, sexual laws, and the moral law of the Ten Commandments. All of these are important in the legal material of the Bible, but in the Ten Commandments we encounter a unique law governing the moral life of all human beings in all times and places.

B. The Nature of the Moral Law

The *tôrāh* was at the core of Hebrew thinking and practice. Israelites could not understand life or themselves without the law. For them history reached its climax in God's act of giving the law. Nothing was greater than the law because nothing else brought God so close to them as His magnificent presence at Sinai. Furthermore, this law shaped Israel's history afterward. Two things worked together to make Israel the people of God: One was the unmerited election of Israel by God (Deut. 4:37; 7:7; 10:15); the other, His unprecedented self-revelation to the entire nation (Ex. 20). The content of this revelation was the law. Therefore the law was at the same time a divine gift of grace and the expression of God's will, showing how His people should live.

The law showed that God gave Himself to Israel to be their God and elected them to be His possession (Ex. 19:4-6). It was a moral, ethical, social, and cultic monument. But the law was not a monument to be stationed in some prominent place; rather, it was a living monument. Although written in stone, God wanted to locate it in the hearts of His people (Ps. 37:30, 31; Jer. 31:33) so it could rule the entire life of every individual, of the whole nation, and even of all humanity.

The law was not only the revelation of God's will and grace but the revelation of His holiness. He could call His people to a holy life because He Himself was holy (Lev. 19:2). The law represented the character of God, His righteousness and perfection, His goodness and truth (Ps. 19:7, 8; 119:142, 172). Paul called it "spiritual" (Rom. 7:14) and affirmed, "So the law is holy, and the commandment is holy and just and good" (verse 12). Any violation of the law was a separation from God (Isa. 59:2), from Israel (Ex. 12:15, 19; Lev. 7:20, 21, 25, 27), and from life itself (Ex. 28:43; Deut. 18:20). It meant rebellion, apostasy, and death.

The way of life pointed out by God to His sons and daughters, both in times of old and now, is the same: a true moral life. Reading the whole content of God's revelation—OT and NT alike—gives a clear picture of the way God intends a "holy nation" and the Christian church to live: a life defined by words such as righteousness, justice, sanctification, obedience, holiness, and faith, a life that follows God's principles that are spelled out in the moral law. His people are to live a life with a moral character similar to God's.

1. The Decalogue

The Ten Commandments were given in negative terms for clarity and exactness. Such precision was needed then, as always, because of the human tendency to avoid responsibility and commitment through misinterpretation. There should be no misunderstanding about the will of God over moral matters for He is the sole determiner.

God provided two fundamental motivations when giving the Ten Commandments to Israel: (1) "I am the Lord your God"; and (2) I brought you out of bondage (Ex. 20:2; Deut. 5:6). Then He proclaimed the law as recorded in Ex. 20:2-17.

The Decalogue (Ex. 20:1-17; Deut. 5:6-21) has two main divisions and covers five areas. The two main divisions affect all relationships: those with God (first four commandments) and those with fellow human beings (last six commandments). The five areas are concerned with God, holiness, family, humanity, and one's neighbor.

The first, commandments one and two (Ex. 20:3-6), affirms that there is only one God. Relationship with Him must be exclusive and direct. He does not tolerate the infidelity of devotion to other nonexistent gods, nor does He allow any kind of intermediary symbol in worship, not even a humanly created image of God Himself.

The second area, the third and fourth commandments (verses 7-11), asserts that God's name and Sabbath are holy. The name of God must be revered and worshiped. It cannot be taken in vain because His name stands for God Himself, the only one who deserves worship. The holiness of the Sabbath is respected by observing that day which is holiness in time, a recurrent holiness uniting the Creator of the universe with the stewards of creation in an act of acceptance and integration. The observance of the Sabbath includes resting from common everyday activities, worshiping the true Creator-God, respecting the inviolability of the world of creation, restoring the integrity of the environment, and protecting the rights of those who work under our responsibility.

The third area, commandments five and seven (verses 12, 14), avers that family is sacred. Father and mother are to be honored. God also forbids infidelity to one's own marriage and the violation of anyone else's matrimony.

In the fourth area, the sixth and eighth commandments (verses 13, 15), humanity is inviolable. No one can take the life or the property of anyone else. This includes falsely testifying in court against the life of someone and defrauding or delaying the payment of wages (see Lev. 19:13).

In the fifth area, individuals and society must be protected, for evil words and sinful desires could destroy them. God prohibits bearing false witness (Ex. 20:16): perjury, speaking evil, suppressing the truth, or even being silent when somebody gives an unfair report about a person. God forbids the coveting of one's neighbor's house, spouse, servants, animals, or any possession that belongs to another (verses 16, 17).

In a moral law of only ten commandments, God covers all the desires and activities of the human family. Reflecting on God's law, David said: "Thy commandment is exceedingly broad" (Ps. 119:96). It is like God's "word," which is "firmly fixed." God's ordinances, laws, precepts, and testimonies are forever. In them the psalmist has delighted and through them God has given him life (verses 89-96).

2. The Law an Expression of God's Character

The law of God, and specifically the Ten Commandments, reflects God's character. The Decalogue has existed and will exist as long as His character remains unchanged. As God is ever the same (Ps. 102:25-27), so Christ is likewise "the same yesterday and today and for ever" (Heb. 13:8). The biblical writers see God's attributes in His law. Like God, "the law of the Lord is perfect" and "the commandment of the Lord is pure" (Ps. 19:7, 8). "The law," explains Paul, "is holy, and the commandment is holy and just and good" (Rom. 7:12). "All thy commandments are right" exalts the psalmist (119:172). John summarizes: "God is love" (1 John 4:8).

The context of John's definition is an explanation of the opposing spiritual activities of the antichrist (verses 1-3). Those who "are of God" will distinguish between what is "truth" and what is "error" (verse 6). The error of the antichrist is to deny the mission of Christ (verse 3). He "denies" Jesus (1 John 2:22), and in this he also disavows the Father because the Son and the Father are one (1 John 1:2, 3). This is a denial of fellowship and knowledge including the knowledge of God and fellowship of the Son. While the spirit of error represents satanic powers at work, the spirit of truth (1 John 4:6) is the work of the Holy

Spirit to establish a close fellowship with the Son by faith and to give the true knowledge of God by revelation (verse 13). Those who love God do His will (1 John 2:17) and "keep his commandments" (verses 3-6).

Knowledge of God as love is neither theoretical nor speculative. It is not an ontological knowledge of God—a knowledge of His being, rather a relational knowledge—a knowledge of His character. This powerful knowledge determines the way of life and the moral conduct of the person who loves God—he "ought to walk in the same way in which he walked" (verse 6). It produces a life in harmony with God's commandments, the same old ones that become new because they are grounded in love as a reality (verses 7, 8).

When the commandment is thus grounded in God's love it produces no fear of any kind, not even of the judgment, but "boldness," or "confidence" *(parrēsia)*. This confidence in the "day of judgment" (1 John 4:17) includes peace in the everyday judgment of our own conscience (1 John 3:21) and assurance in the final judgment at Christ's coming (1 John 2:28). The moral law defines the way a true Christian should live because it is the expression of God's character of love and "because as he is so are we in this world" (1 John 4:17).

When there was no sin the principle of love ruled the universe. Every created being loved God as Creator and others as itself. For this reason, when the lawyer asked Jesus, "Which is the great commandment in the law?" the Lord replied: "You shall love the Lord your God with all your heart, and with all your soul, and with all your mind. This is the great and first commandment. And a second is like it, You shall love your neighbor as yourself." Jesus finished by saying: "On these two commandments depend all the law" (Matt. 22:37-40).

3. The Law as a Foundational Principle

Love is the foundational principle of the moral law. This is revealed clearly in the OT as well as the NT. Quotations from Jesus and Paul may suffice to show this.

Following Jesus' answers to vital questions about the relationship of Israel with the Roman Empire and the truth of the Scriptures and the power of God to resurrect the dead, one of the scribes, recognizing that Christ had responded well, asked about the foundational principle of the law. He queried: "Which commandment is the first of all?" (Mark 12:28).

For the foundational principle of the law, Jesus referred to Deuteronomy 6:4, the passage that had constituted Israel's watchword through its entire history. He underlined the distinctive oneness of the true God as opposed to the multiplicity of gods in other nations. The first commandment of the one God was the commandment of love. "And you shall love the Lord your God with all your heart, and with all your soul, and with all your mind, and with all your strength" (Mark 12:30). The second commandment, quoted from Leviticus 19:18, He declared to be in the category of the first: "You shall love your neighbor as yourself." The foundational principle of the law is not self; it lies outside self. It is in the oneness of the loving God who requires the same kind of love from all His creatures. It is true love which loves God above all things and one's neighbor as oneself. Love permeates both the first and second commandments of the law, the foundational principle of both tables of the Ten Commandments.

The reaction of the scribe was both emotional and rational. "You are right, Teacher," he answered enthusiastically. Then rationally he gave his evaluation of Jesus' teaching: "You have truly said" (verse 32). When human emotions and reasoning agree with God's moral principle, the result is wisdom and a spiritual experience in tune with the kingdom of God. Ending the incident, Mark writes: "When Jesus saw that he answered wisely, he said to him, 'You are not far from the kingdom of God' " (verse 34).

With a clear understanding of the moral law as the commandments of love we now come to the way the law is fulfilled: "Owe no one anything, except to love one another; for he who loves his neighbor has fulfilled the law" (Rom. 13:8). To love one's neighbor means a permanent state of indebtedness, a continuous moral obligation. This is true of all God's commands as they "are summed up in this sentence, 'You shall love your neighbor as yourself' " (verse 9).

The concept that the Christian who loves fulfills the law—"love is the fulfilling of the law" (verse 10)—eliminates none of the Ten Commandments. On the contrary it provides an all-inclusive concept. God's intent and purpose for every one of the commandments is love. The entire law is incompatible with selfishness, hence it cannot be perfectly obeyed by mere outward conformity. True obedience must come from the heart and the spirit through love.

C. The Spiritual Nature of the Moral Law

The need for a spiritual obedience to the law comes from the very nature of God's law, which "is spiritual" (Rom. 7:14). Those who disobey the law are "carnal," and "sold under sin" (verse 14). Such persons have only "the form of religion," the outward look of piety (2 Tim. 3:5). Their obedience is not heartfelt; it is done merely to satisfy requirements and constitutes legalism, which is distinct from spiritual obedience to a spiritual law. While trying to fulfill the law of God, enemies of God are in constant conflict with God's law, because "the law is holy, and the commandment is holy and just and good" (Rom. 7:12).

The moral law, being good by God's design, never leads to anything bad, wrong, or destructive. What brings death is sin within us (verses 13, 21). Evil has enslaved human beings under the "law of sin" to the point of restraining the will that wishes to do good, forcing it to depart from the spiritual law of a spiritual God (verses 23, 21) to become a "wretched" person, carrying a "body of death" (verse 24).

The only solution to the enslaving force of sin is Christ: His person, His life, His substitutionary sacrifice (Rom. 8:1-4), His fulfillment of the law (Matt. 5:17, 18), and His teachings about the Ten Commandments (verses 1-48). His person and life convict us of sinfulness; His sacrifice sets us free from the law of sin; His fulfillment of the law confirms its moral value; and His teachings underline the spiritual dimension of the law.

Christ's fulfillment of the law shows clearly that He came to destroy sin, not to destroy or abolish the law of God. "Think not that I have come to destroy the law and the prophets; I have come not to abolish them but to fulfil them" (verse 17). While "law" here refers to the Pentateuch, in verse 19 and the rest of Matthew 5 Jesus clearly has in mind the spiritual dimensions of the Decalogue.

For Jesus the spiritual nature of the law is clear in the Sermon on the Mount. The prohibition of the sixth commandment, "You shall not kill," includes the anger that turns brother against brother (verses 22, 23) and the antagonistic attitudes that create adversaries (verse 25). The seventh commandment prohibits the lust of the heart as well as adultery (verse 28). The command to love our neighbor also demands love for our enemies, blessing those who curse us, doing good to those who hate us, and praying for those who persecute us (verses 43, 44). This spiritual expansion of the moral law is not intended to eliminate the law. Rather than teaching Christians "to break" the commandments, Jesus wanted them "to teach" and "to do" them (verse 19). This intention continues throughout Christian history. The book of Revelation, referring to the time of the end and the remnant of the Christian church, notes the continuing body of commandments and foresees faithful Christians keeping them (Rev. 12:17; 14:12).

D. The Purpose of the Moral Law

The moral law's purpose is not to solve the problem of sin. That comes only by the atoning sacrifice of Christ, which each Christian must accept by faith. God gave His law to provide definitions—to show how things really are—concerning life, God, and sin. Fulfilling another purpose, the law provides direction in the Christian's life, showing the way God would have His people live in gratitude, faith, and obedience.

1. To Provide Definitions

In the OT the law defined the state of well-being for each individual and for the entire nation. The Ten Commandments, as a summary of the Torah, defined the quality of a sanctified life before God. The Sabbath commandment, in turn, is the sign of a proper awareness of sanctification. God the holy one sanctifies a person; the works of the law cannot do it. "You shall keep my sabbaths, for this is a sign between me and you throughout your generations, that you may know that I, the Lord, sanctify you" (Ex. 31:13; cf. Eze. 20:12).

The same principle is carried into the NT. As a divine self-revelation the moral law defines God's character. The cross of Christ is at the center of this revelation. The will of God is supreme. He is the unchangeable sovereign of the whole universe. His law cannot be changed, because His will is perfect. But at the same time it is a good and acceptable will (Rom. 12:2) and He is a loving God. He loved us so much that He gave His beloved Son (John 3:16), gave life to our mortal bodies (Rom. 8:11), and gave us the Holy Spirit so that we, who could not be subject to the law of God, by the power of the Spirit could fulfill its requirements (verses 4-8).

A superficial way to eliminate sin would have been to invalidate the moral law. In this case Christ's sacrifice on the cross would not have been needed. But the reality of the Crucifixion proves that God did not abolish the moral law. It continues defining sin: Is the law sin? "By no means! Yet, if it had not been for the law, I should not have known sin" (Rom. 7:7). The law defines sin as disobedience to God, marks sin as offensive, and defines the state of human beings as deliberate rebellion against God.

There was sin in the world before God gave the moral law to Israel in written form. Adam and Eve had disobeyed a God-given commandment (Rom. 5:13, 14). Already sin was defined because they knew the law. Sin is disobedience to God, for the knowledge of sin is "through the law" (Rom. 3:20).

The law made sin more sinful—"law came in, to increase the trespass" (Rom. 5:20). Sin became a conscious act of disobedience to specific commandments, and the intentions of the flesh became fully visible (Gal. 5:17-19). Even the amount of sin increased. The coming of the commandment challenged sin, which responded by becoming more active (Rom. 7:9), producing more evil desires (verse 8), and causing well-intended persons to lose their way by deception (verse 11). As he did with Eve, Satan uses the commandment as a provocation to sin, in temptation, and as an instrument of condemnation (Gen. 3:3).

The law is "the power of sin" (1 Cor. 15:56). It makes sin an act of willful rebellion against God. Since the law provides information about sin, any sin becomes a clear act of the sinful will against God, an act of rebellion. Sin is a formal rebellion—"lawlessness" or lack of conformity with the law (1 John 3:4) and a spiritual rebellion—an act of unfaithfulness against God and a denial of Him (Rom. 14:23; Titus 1:15, 16).

Because of its capacity to define sin, the law can also convict of sin. Although the law provides no justification (Rom. 3:20), only wrath (Rom. 4:15) and condemnation, because of its role as a "custodian" (or "tutor," ASV) it brings us to Christ (Gal. 3:22-24). The goal/end of the law is Jesus Christ, "that every one who has faith may be justified" (Rom. 10:4).

The major function of the law is to affirm that God, the absolute sovereign over humanity, has claim over everyone and possesses the authority to demand obedience—not merely accidental obedience, but one that leads to a righteous and holy life. It is true that because of sin humanity no longer can live this type of life. But God is also powerful to provide the spiritual power needed for justification and sanctification. The moral law provides standards of behavior required for the believer to live in harmony with God and fellow human beings.

2. To Provide Direction

God's law provides direction for the life of His children. The way of living that God pictures for human beings is based on His intentions and principles. A person's desires or ideas, or a set of customs and practices established by a particular society, cannot be the basis on which humans should build their life. God spelled out His principles and absolutes for life and wrote them with unmistakable words in the Ten Commandments. These commandments are intended by God to bring life (Rom. 7:10) that is "holy and just and good" (verse 12).

Holy. Because it is an expression of God's will, His law can be only true, righteous, and holy. In Romans 7:7-13, Paul deals with the whole law and specifically with the tenth commandment: "You shall not covet" (Ex. 20:17). In this citation Paul affirms that the principles and absolutes of the law rule the entire life of a person, including actions and desires.

Just. As the expression of God's righteousness, the law is the standard of a righteous life. The life of Christ in obedience to the law shows that there can be no other righteous way than obedience to God's law. By obeying the law Jesus demonstrated that the law is just and can be kept.

Good. There is only one kind of moral good, the one that comes from God. He alone can distinguish what is good from what is not, distinguishing between good and evil. And He does so through the Ten Commandments. Obedience to the law leads to blessing and happiness. "The law of the Lord is perfect, reviving the soul; the testimony of the Lord is sure, making wise the simple; the precepts of the Lord are right, rejoicing the heart; the commandment of the Lord is pure, enlightening the eyes; the fear of the Lord is clean, enduring for ever; the ordinances of the Lord are true, and righteous altogether. More to be desired are they than gold, even much fine gold; sweeter also than honey and drippings of the honeycomb. Moreover by them is thy servant warned; in keeping them there is great reward" (Ps. 19:7-11).

E. The Moral Law and the Final Judgment

The Scriptures teach the reality of a final judgment to come (Matt. 12:36, 37; Rom. 14:10-12; 2 Cor. 5:10). While salvation is by faith in Christ's death on the cross, judgment is based on law: "So speak and so act as those who are to be judged under the law of liberty" (James 2:12). (See Judgment.)

The law judges in two stages. At present it convicts evildoers of transgression (v. 9): in the future, it will condemn them as sinners (verses 11, 12). The judgment day will be the time of "punishment" (2 Peter 2:9) and "destruction" for the ungodly (2 Peter 3:7). On the other hand, this will be the moment of deliverance and vindication to those who abide in God (1 John 4:17).

A person may lose freedom by breaking the law or by considering the works of the law as righteousness, thus failing to be justified (Gal. 2:16). However, bondage does not come from the law; slavery is the consequence of submitting to sin (Rom. 6:16-19). James presents the Decalogue as a "royal law," a "law of liberty," the norm of God's final judgment (James 2:8-12). Vindication in judgment comes not through good deeds, but through mercy, because "mercy triumphs over judgment" (verse 13). Apart from the loving mercy of Christ, accepted in faith and gratitude, no one can be saved.

II. The Perpetuity of God's Moral Law

As an extension of God's character, the law partakes of His perpetuity. Hence its authority among humans stands above time and place. From Genesis to Revelation, the law of God is presented as eternal.

A. *God's Law Before Sinai*

The Ten Commandments stem from the universal principle of love ruling in the universe before sin. All ten, including the fourth, may be identified in the patriarchal period between Adam and Moses.

1. The Ten Commandments in Genesis

The existence of law is implied as a prerequisite to the appearance of sin. While the Ten Commandments as found in Exodus are not specifically spelled out in Genesis, such principles underlie human responsibility.

The first table of the law, governing the relationship between humans and God, appears in several accounts. Jacob's instructions to his household in preparation for their worship of God at Bethel, provide an understanding of the first and second commandments. Jacob urged: "Put away the foreign gods that are among you, and purify yourselves, and change your garments; then let us arise and go up to Bethel, that I may make there an altar to . . . God" (Gen. 35:2, 3).

The third commandment, which forbids taking God's name in vain, is implied in Abraham's making his servant "swear by the Lord, the God of heaven and of the earth" that he would not take a Canaanite wife for Isaac (Gen. 24:3). Eliezer's commitment not to take the Lord's name in vain was evidence Abraham could trust him totally.

The fourth commandment, requiring observance of the seventh day Sabbath, clearly echoes what happened at the close of Creation week. "And on the seventh day God finished his work which he had done, and he rested on the seventh day from all his work which he had done. So God blessed the seventh day and hallowed it, because on it God rested from all his work which he had done in creation" (Gen. 2:2, 3).

The commandments of the second table of the law—governing human relationships—appear also in the background of the incidents recorded in Genesis. The fifth commandment, that children honor father and mother, is alluded to in the conversation of the Lord with Abraham about the destruction of Sodom and Gomorrah. There Abraham's way was to "charge his children and his household after him to keep the way of the Lord by doing righteousness and justice"; meant the Lord would "bring to Abraham what he has promised him" (Gen. 18:19).

The allusion to the sixth commandment, "You shall not kill," cannot be overlooked in the Genesis account of Cain's killing Abel (Gen. 4:8-11). The seventh, "You shall not commit adultery," is recognizable in Joseph's refusal of seduction by Potiphar's wife. "How then can I do this great wickedness, and sin against God?" (Gen. 39:9). The breaking of this commandment is also clearly repudiated in the story of immoral behavior by the people of Sodom (Gen. 19:1-10).

The eighth commandment, "You shall not steal," was well known among Joseph's brothers when, on their second journey to Egypt, the silver cup and the wheat money were found in Benjamin's sack. Joseph's brothers said: "Behold, the money which we found in the mouth of our sacks, we brought back to you from the land of Canaan; how then should we steal silver or gold from your lord's house?" (Gen. 44:8). The ninth commandment, condemning false witness and falsehood, appears in the story of Jacob's taking Esau's blessing with lies and deception. Jacob recognized this when he said to his mother: "Perhaps my father will feel me, and I shall seem to be mocking him, and bring a curse upon myself and not a blessing" (Gen. 27:12). The tenth commandment, forbidding coveting the neighbor's wife or property, is implied in the story of Abraham and Pharaoh (Gen. 12:13-20) and Abimelech and Pharaoh (Gen. 20:1-10). The king intended to take Abraham's wife and God prevented him from doing so because she was a married woman. The evil of coveting is also seen in Jacob's scheming to take his brother's birthright and blessing (Gen. 27).

We see that the law was well known in the beginning of human history. While no written book of law appears in Genesis, many incidents bear witness to the applied Ten Commandments so that the case for its existence and universal application must be accepted. There is also a clear statement from God to Abraham: "I will multiply your descendants as the stars of heaven, and will give to your descendants all these lands; and by your descendants all the nations of the earth shall bless themselves: because Abraham obeyed my voice and kept my charge, my commandments, my statutes, and my laws" (Gen. 26:4, 5).

2. Sin Before Sinai

Clearly, sin existed prior to the giving of the law at Sinai. The apostle Paul argues for the existence and operation of God's law at that time: "Sin indeed was in the world before the law was given, but sin is not counted where there is no law" (Rom. 5:13). In this way he indicates that the law existed before God wrote the Ten Commandments on tables of stone and gave them to Moses at Sinai. In all probability, the law existed in oral form.

Paul presents another strong argument for the existence of law before Sinai: the existence of death, which exists only as a consequence of sin. Paul points out that "death reigned from Adam to Moses" (verse 14). Death resulted from a "judgment" which brought the "condemnation" of sin (verse 16). There could be no sin or judgment if law does not exist. On this basis the existence of the law from Eden to Sinai is indisputable.

3. The Fourth Commandment Before Sinai

Exodus 16 provides a clear reference to Sabbath rest before Sinai, connected with the manna miracle. God announced: "Behold, I will rain bread from heaven for you; and the people shall go out and gather a day's portion every day, that I may prove them, whether they will walk in my law or not" (verse 4). On the sixth day the Israelites were to gather manna for two days, because on the Sabbath day they would find none in the field (verse 25). When some insisted on gathering manna on the Sabbath, God said to them: "How long do you refuse to keep my commandments and my laws?" The closing statement of the narration is simple: "So the people rested on the seventh day" (Ex. 16:27-30). (See Sabbath.)

B. The Ten Commandments at Sinai

If the Ten Commandments existed prior to Sinai, why was it assigned explicitly to the Israelite nation? The Ten Commandments were a God-given universal law. They expressed values God expected from every person of the world. However, in selecting Israel as His special people, and entering in a covenant relationship with them, He reiterated the ten-commandment law as a guide for their lives, now in written form.

He gave Israel other laws, civil and religious; however, the Ten Commandments were to provide the basis of Israel's moral life. They were and are the expression of God's character and the foundation of His universal government.

1. Uniqueness of the Ten Commandments

The uniqueness of the Ten Commandments, the moral law at Sinai, does not reside exclusively in its content, but also in the fact that God Himself wrote the Decalogue or "Ten Words" (the name given the Decalogue in Hebrew [Ex. 34:28]) on tables of stone and gave them to Moses.

Because of their unique circumstances of

origin, the Ten Commandments occupied a position in the Torah above any other Israelite law. They were given by God in the most spectacular divine self-revelation ever in national history. In the Ten Commandments God proclaimed the basis for His covenant with Israel. The Ten Commandments were the only part of the Torah proclaimed with thunder and lightning from a mountain top (Ex. 20:18-20) later to be written by God's own finger on two stone tablets (Ex. 31:18; 34:28; Deut. 4:13; 10:4).

The Ten imperative Words of God were to be honored under all circumstances by every Israelite. At Sinai, the moral law of the universe became the particular law of Israel without changing its general nature. Its universality was unaffected. For Israel it became foundation of all other national laws, some of which were limited to certain specific circumstances and for a given time. For example, certain sacrificial laws required designated sacrifice only in conjunction with specific sin, in effect only until the coming of the Messiah, to whom the sacrifices pointed.

The Ten Commandments were unique. They were located in a prominent place in the Pentateuch. They were spoken by God to the people. They were engraved on stone tablets by God Himself. They formed the foundation of other law codes. They had a specific name. And they were placed inside the Ark of the Covenant (Ex. 40:20; Deut. 10:2-5).

2. Importance of the Ten Commandments

The essence of the Ten Commandments is not their form, but the divine authority in their origin: God's transcendence, sovereignty, and will. At the heart of the law was its collective application to all Israel, His people, and to every individual member, His son and daughter. This special relationship gave the law a unique task— to safeguard and to maintain such a relation.

The importance of the proclamation of the law at Sinai lies not in the enumeration of legal norms, but in the majesty of God's presence and action (Ex. 19:16-25), the nearness of the Creator, and the proximity of the neighbor.

The Commandments represented love to God and love to one's neighbor (Deut. 6:5; 30:15, 16), love to one's neighbor. It was not merely external love, nor inward love alone. It was real, living affinity, a love that involved the entire personality and the total experience of life.

The law calls for personal commitment, not to a legal institution, but to God Himself. This is the most comprehensive relationship that human beings can ever live. It touches the mercies of the Lord and produces life, joy, delight, justice, righteousness, and salvation for the human being (Ps. 119:142, 156, 162, 174; Isa. 51:4-8).

Remembering the experience at Sinai, Moses reminded Israel that God had made a covenant with them at Horeb (Deut. 5:1-5). This covenant had a law (Deut. 4:44), the Ten Commandments. The law in Deuteronomy 5:6-21 is the same law as in Exodus 20. The small differences in detail found in the fourth commandment—liberation rather than Creation as the rationale for keeping the seventh day— were not intended as contradictions but as complements.

The Ten Commandments were the heart of the Torah. They were given for all humanity, and specifically for Israel within the particular framework of the covenant, apart from which they would never be understood. If treated as an isolated unit, their importance and significance, as well as God's purpose for them, would be missed.

The covenant required mutual obligation. The people committed themselves to obey the voice of the Lord, to keep the covenant, to obey God's commandments. At the same time, the Lord agreed to treat the people as His special possession among all the nations of the world. This particular treatment would make them: (1) a kingdom of priests, prepared to fulfill God's service or mission in the midst of humanity and to benefit all mankind; and (2) a holy nation, sanctified by a relationship with God and fully committed to Him through obedience (Ex. 19:5, 6).

In committing themselves to be God's people under His all-powerful action, God gave them the moral principles on which the covenant would be established. They are expressed in the precepts recorded in Deuteronomy 5:22-33. The Decalogue defined the relationship of the chosen people to God and to one another, both as members of the people of God and as members of the human family.

In addition to the Ten Commandments, designed for all humanity, God gave Israel other laws, intended to govern their special relationship with God. These included civil laws and health laws. But above all, the ceremonial law or sacrificial system was uniquely for Israel's spiritual benefit.

3. The Ceremonial Law

The sacrificial system began immediately after Adam and Eve fell into sin (Gen. 3:21) and continued through the patriarchal age, when Melchizedek appears as "priest of God Most High" (14:18). Its purpose was to point every believer to the coming Messiah and Saviour, the true sacrifice for their sin. We know of no recorded laws about sacrifices prior to Moses. At Sinai the sacrificial practice was enlarged, elaborated, and codified.

The ceremonial law, given because of the transgression of the moral law, consisted of sacrifices and offerings—symbols or types—pointing to future redemption. Its purpose was to teach sinners how to discern and accept beforehand the future offering for sin at the cross. It was an experiential aid to the understanding and acceptance of Christ's salvation, in symbols and types, before the sacrifice for that salvation became a reality.

At times the ceremonial system has been presented as in opposition to Christ. On the contrary, it was established to typify His perfect offering on the cross (Heb. 10:1). Its foundation was Christ. Its message was Christ. Its expectation was Christ. And its expression of faith was in Christ. The ceremonial system, however, was imperfect. It was only a type, a symbol, a shadow of a future reality. It could

not cleanse sinners from sin (verses 1-4). It could only promise that salvation would come by the offering and sacrifice of the Lamb of God.

The law of sacrifices and ceremonies defined a divinely ordained system of worship. It was a cultic application of the universal principles contained in the first table of the moral law. Its purpose was to express obedience to God and acceptance of His provision for sin through ceremonies until the reality symbolized by the ceremonies and sacrifices would come. While parts of ceremonial law are found in Exodus, Leviticus, and Deuteronomy, the major body of ceremonial laws is located in Leviticus, especially chapters 1-9. (See Sanctuary.)

Three principal features distinguished the ceremonial law: (1) its didactic nature, (2) its demand for obedience, and (3) its temporal nature. God intended it to teach the plan of salvation through Jesus Christ and to give an opportunity for believers to express their faith in Him and His future sacrifice by fulfilling the requirements of the ceremonial law. This law's validity would last only until the true sacrifice was made on Calvary's cross (Heb. 9:10).

C. The Ten Commandments in Jesus' Teachings

Jesus made no secret about His attitude toward traditional Jewish law and the Ten Commandments. While questioning or even disapproving the traditions of the elders (Mark 7:1-13), Jesus exalted the Ten Commandments, clearly affirming the perpetuity of the Decalogue.

1. Equality of the Ten Commandments

In addressing the equality of the Ten Commandments (Matt. 22:35-40), a lawyer posed Jesus a testing question: "Teacher, which is the great commandment in the law?" (verse 36). The lawyer subscribed to a hierarchy of importance. Rabbinical tradition held that wherever two commandments conflicted, obedience to the greater would release the person from obeying the lesser. For Pharisees, the first table of the law surpassed the second, so serving human beings could be more easily dispensed with.

Jesus' answer is based on two grounds: the content of Scripture and a denial of hierarchies. From the Scriptures He referred to two portions of the Pentateuch: (1) Deuteronomy 6:5, which commands loving the Lord; (2) Leviticus 19:18, which mandates loving one's neighbor. Regarding the implied hierarchy of the commandments, Jesus accepted the existence of two commandments. While the first was "great" (Matt. 22:38), the second one was no lesser. It was "like" it (verse 39), "equal" *(homoios)* in importance and validity. The order was not intended to permit any exception; both commandments were to be kept equally.

The controlling principle behind the moral law—a first table of four commandments related to God, and the second table with six about one's neighbor—is love. This love requires from us heart, spirit, mind: all of ourselves. From God's love springs the moral law, and the reflection of His love in human life provides the objective of the whole law.

2. Permanence of the Ten Commandments

The most direct teaching of Christ about God's law is located in the Sermon on the Mount: "Think not that I have come to abolish the law and the prophets; I have come not to abolish them but to fulfill them. For truly, I say to you, till heaven and earth pass away, not an iota, not a dot, will pass from the law until all is accomplished" (Matt. 5:17, 18).

Jesus was not planning to destroy or abolish the law. While the phrase "the law and the prophets" refers to the full revelation of God as in the OT, the "law" refers to the Torah or Pentateuch, at the heart of which lies the ten-commandment law.

In Matthew 5 Christ repeatedly referred to the moral law. Jesus spoke about "commandments" (verse 19), about "righteousness" (verse 20), and about the spiritual meaning of commandments such as "You shall not kill" (verses 21-26) and "You shall not commit adultery" (verses 27-30). These are clear references to the Decalogue. Jesus did nothing to destroy it; He fulfilled it. Christ also urged His listeners to teach and keep it (verse 19). The real destroyers of the law were the scribes in their traditional interpretations. In Matthew 15:1-6, Jesus illustrated this in relation to the fifth commandment of the Decalogue.

Jesus also clearly recognized the perpetuity of the Ten Commandments. "Till heaven and earth pass away, not an iota, not a dot" would "pass from the law" (Matt. 5:18). Then He stated what He required from His followers: obedience to the law. In view of this ("then" [verse 19]), one who "relaxes [undoes or breaks] one of the least of these commandments and teaches men so, shall be called least in the kingdom of heaven; but he who does them and teaches them shall be called great in the kingdom of heaven" (verse 19).

Jesus then proceeded to explain the meaning of the law forbidding murder and adultery. Respect for the letter of the law would fall short of fulfilling God's expectations. The law deals with external behavior as well as with internal motivation. Here Jesus was clearly saying that its moral definition would not end with His teachings but continue in His new kingdom of eternal life.

A similar point appears in Jesus' conversation with the rich young ruler (Matt. 19:16-26). The young man asked what he should do to have eternal life. Jesus answered, "Keep the commandments"; then He specified which ones: "You shall not kill"; "You shall not commit adultery"; "You shall not steal"; "You shall not bear false witness"—that is, the Decalogue. Here the word "commandments" *(entolē)* is used, whereas in Matthew 5:18, 19 both "commandments" *(entolē)* and "law" *(nomos)* are used. Both refer to the same thing: the Ten Commandments.

The specific law intended was clearly identified in the conversation. The rich young ruler had kept the Ten Commandments, but in a legalistic way—as an independent, moral, legal code. He lacked the most important part of the law: the Lawgiver. "Follow me," Jesus said (Mark 10:21). But the rich young ruler did not follow Jesus; he stayed with the law, and in so doing he was left with the same isolation and uncertainty. Salvation does not come from the code; it comes from the Lawgiver, the Saviour. Israel had known this from ancient times, but they had forgotten it. Because they lost the true meaning of the Ten Commandments, they had forgotten that these commandments were a revelation of God's will, calling for a close relationship with Him.

Under God's authority Jesus taught that obedience and following Him are compatible. In reality the two are so united that one without the other becomes only a pretense of Christian life. Legalistic obedience separates a person from Christ; true spiritual obedience to the law is nothing but the true way of life for the Christian who truly follows Jesus.

Jesus required wholehearted obedience to the law. When the Pharisees brought to Jesus the woman caught in adultery, He did not condemn her, but bade her: "Go, and do not sin again" (John 8:11). The incident had to do with obedience to the law. The scribes and Pharisees tried to put Moses and Christ in opposition (verse 5). They reminded Jesus that according to Moses the woman should die. Jesus, writing their sins on the ground, said to them: "Let him who is without sin among you be the first to throw a stone at her" (verse 7). If Jesus had in mind the abolition of the Ten Commandments, this would have been a perfect occasion to declare it. Instead, while forgiving her, He ratified the authority of the law. He said, "Do not sin again" (verse 11). This was His message whenever He forgave a sinner. The Ten Commandments of God's moral law had the same authority that God bestowed upon them at the beginning and obedience to all of them was still necessary.

3. The Sabbath Commandment

Jesus did not abolish the Sabbath. His controversies with the leaders of Israel about the Sabbath show that He carried on a work of reformation, rejecting Jewish traditions about the manner of Sabbath observance, but never abolishing it. This appears in the controversies over Sabbath labor (Matt. 12:1-8; Mark 2:23-28; Luke 6:1-5), healing (Matt. 12:9-13; Luke 13:10-17; John 5:2-18; 9:1-34), and casting out demons (Mark 1:21-27; Luke 4:31-37). In this reforming Jesus showed that He, not the Pharisees, was Lord of the Sabbath (Matt.12:8). He held that the seventh-day Sabbath was a blessing for the human family (Mark 2:27), as had been intended from the beginning (Gen. 2:1-3). He respected and observed the Sabbath by attending religious meetings and by teaching there (Luke 4:16). His closest followers continued respect for the Sabbath after His death. They "prepared spices and ointments"; then "on the Sabbath they rested according to the commandment" (Luke 23:56). (See Sabbath.)

D. The Law in Paul

Paul's view of the law appears in both his practice of the law, particularly his observance of the Sabbath, and his teachings. His personal obedience of the law appears in the book of Acts. His teaching on the law appears in his letters to the young churches he had founded. Some of his texts on the law have been misunderstood; therefore, they deserve special attention.

1. Paul's Observance of the Sabbath

The book of Acts covers the period from the resurrection of Christ to the imprisonment of Paul, some 30 years. In spite of what some have said regarding the annulment of the law at the cross, Paul observes the Ten Commandments. Luke notes several occasions on which Paul worshiped on the Sabbath day.

In Antioch of Pisidia, on his first missionary journey, the apostle "on the sabbath day . . . went into the synagogue and sat down" (Acts 13:14). He came not as a preacher but as a worshiper, which for an early Christian was the proper thing to do. Paul was invited to speak and his message was so compelling that "the next Sabbath almost the whole city gathered together to hear the word of God" (verse 44).

In Philippi, on his second missionary journey, Paul went on Sabbath to a "place of prayer" outside the city, by the riverside (Acts 16:13). Again, even in the absence of a synagogue Paul came to worship, not merely to reach a Jewish audience. He was a Sabbath observer. Luke notes that in Thessalonica he attended the synagogue for three successive Sabbaths (Acts 17:1, 2).

2. Paul's Teaching About the Law

Paul uses the word "law" in different ways. It may refer to the Mosaic Law (Gal. 4:21); to the whole OT (1 Cor. 14:21); to the Ten Commandments (Rom. 2:17-23; 7:7; 13:8-10); or to a specific law, such as the one that binds husband and wife (Rom. 7:2). He also uses the word "law" *(nomos)* in a figurative sense, such as when referring to the "law of evil" (verse 21) or "law of sin" (verse 25; see also Rom. 8:2; Gal. 6:2). While Paul does not give a precise definition each time he employs the term, usually its meaning is evident from the context.

Paul never refers to the "law" in the plural; the law is always one, the revealed will of the one God. The law, and more specifically the Decalogue, represents the divine mandate. It is the living will of God. This characteristic of the law leads Paul to a clear conclusion: the law cannot be abolished. "Do we then overthrow the law by this faith? By no means! On the contrary, we uphold the law" (Rom. 3:31). By the "principle of faith" (literally, *law* of faith) the believer obeys the law (verse 27).

While the law is upheld as good and just (Rom. 7:12), it does not provide justification or salvation. If justification is by faith, it cannot be by law. Justification—the restoration of the sinner's broken relationship with God—brings the person from independent, rebellious, and sinful separation to peaceful intimacy with God. It is achieved only through Jesus Christ, the only means of justification.

Receiving Him comes by faith, and by faith alone (Rom. 5:1-10).

Anyone who attempts to become justified by works is living "under law," not "under grace" (Rom. 6:14). To be just one must be in perfect obedience of the law. But the sinner is imperfect before the law and cannot attain justification by works. To escape such a conundrum, the sinner must accept Jesus Christ by faith. Paul's rejection of the law as the means of justification does not lead him to reject obedience to the law by the justified sinner who lives now in peace with God and walks according to the Spirit. For it is through Jesus Christ that "the just requirement of the law" can "be fulfilled in us, who walk not according to the flesh but according to the Spirit" (Rom. 8:4). This type of obedience is only possible for the sinner who is in Christ and lives with Him through the Spirit by faith.

a. **The purpose of the law.** In Romans 7:5-12 Paul discusses the purpose of the law. The law does not make anyone a sinner; sin does that. The law brings knowledge of sin and causes the sinner to know that he or she is living in sin. The law *(nomos)* "aroused" "our sinful passions" (verse 5). Contrary to the sinner's constant minimizing of the importance and effects of sin, the law makes a sinner see its real magnitude. Paul here specifies which law he is talking about: the one that says: "You shall not covet" (verse 7). The Ten Commandments are not sinful. Writing three decades after the cross, Paul finds nothing wrong with them. Through them Paul learned about sin. He came to have an intimate acquaintance with sin and the sinful experience. The problem of sin is not with the law, but with the individual. If there were no law, sin would still exist, but the individual would have no sense of guilt. The law brought guilt; wrong lies not in the law, but in the sinner. The feeling of guilt is created by sin; the law makes it known to the sinner's mind. "So the law is holy, and the commandment is holy and just and good" (verse 12).

Obviously here Paul speaks of the law of the Ten Commandments. The sinner is not holy, just, or good, and the law shows that. The law condemns sin, but Jesus delivers the sinner "from the law" by His death; so the sinner can "serve" God, obeying His law "in the new life of the Spirit" (verse 6).

In Galatians 3:19-29 Paul deals again with the purpose of the law. From Abraham onward, the history of Israel centered in the covenant, in God's promise. The core of Abraham's response was faith. Later God gave to Israel a law, a comprehensive system of life that helped them to understand the nature, experience, and scope of faith (verses 15-18). The law, this system of life, was not intended to take the place of the promise or to destroy it. Its object was not to produce righteousness or life. Life would come only through the promise, by faith in Christ.

In purpose the Jewish system was to be a "custodian," "tutor," or pedagogue (*paidagōgos* [verse 24]). The *paidagōgos* was not the teacher *(didaskalos)* but the slave who went with the boy to school to provide protection, to help carry school utensils, and to teach him good manners. The law—the total Jewish system of life—was not against the promise nor did it ever supersede the promise (verse 21). How ironic it would be for the pedagogue, a slave of the promise, to become the master of the child.

When Christ came, the promised life became no longer a promise but a full reality (verses 27, 29). Therefore the Jewish system of life was no longer needed (verse 25). There would no longer be a Jewish or Gentile way of life. There would be only sons and daughters, "offspring" and "heirs," of Abraham, through faith. There would be only one way of life, no longer centered in the "law" but in the "promise," the Christian way of life, totally centered in Christ.

The "law" given 430 years after the promise to Abraham, a tutor for the Jews but no longer so for Christians, was not the moral law in particular, but the total Jewish system of life. A Christianity without law would be amoral or immoral, which it is not. Christianity is a virtuous way of life, a life "clothed" with Christ. The verb *enduō* (to put on or clothe) means to take on the characteristics, virtues, and/or intentions of another and to become like the person one puts on. Becoming like Christ could never produce a way of life in opposition to a ten-commandment law, which Christ uniformly obeyed.

b. Law and freedom in Galatians. The commanding theme of Galatians is freedom in Christ. Christ gave Himself on the cross to grant us freedom (1:4). Hence the basis for Christian ethics and behavior is liberty (5:1), and the Christian invitation to Jews and Gentiles is to liberty (5:13). Since liberty is not an exhaustive definition of Christianity, however, some kind of explanation is required.

Liberty as the Christian way of life stands in contrast with the traditional Jewish way of life—bondage under the law (Gal. 3:13; 4:3, 5, 9), the pagan way of life and slavery to human passions (Gal. 1:4; 5:13, 24). In Galatians Paul uses four Greek words to picture liberty from different perspectives. Each adds to the understanding of liberty and law.

(1) Exaireō. From the perspective of the will of God (1:3-5), liberty means *deliverance,* rescue from the evil power that dominates "the present age." This salvation calls for the united work of God the Father and our Lord Jesus Christ, "who gave himself for our sins" (verse 4; cf. Gal. 2:20; Eph. 5:2, 25; 1 Tim. 2:6; Titus 2:14), and who also was given by God to save us (Rom. 4:25; 8:32; cf. John 3:16). Jesus Christ said that this rescue was the very purpose of His mission: He came "to give his life as a ransom for many" (Mark 10:45; cf. Isa. 53:5, 6, 12).

Liberty as salvation for humanity, together with the work of Christ to accomplish it, was "according to the will of our God" (Gal. 1:4). This agrees with the OT teaching that both salvation—also defined by Psalm 119 as liberty—and law (Torah) came from the will of God.

In Jesus' time, however, obedience to the Torah no longer meant submission to the will of God, for Torah was reworked by the Jewish leaders into a burdensome cultic and moral code, now the controlling principle for the nation and for every individual. As such it did not work for salvation but for bondage. The Jews needed deliverance from this concept. Such deliverance could not come from the law, which they had transformed into an enslaving force, but from Christ, through faith, the linking principle of relationship with the Saviour (Gal. 2:16-21).

(2) Eleutheria. From the perspective of obedience to the truth, liberty means *freedom* (verse 4; Gal. 5:1-13; cf. Rom. 8:21; 1 Cor. 10:29; 2 Cor. 3:17). Paul's concept begins with the biographical section of Galatians. He reports that false brethren spied on him to see if he obeyed the law in the matter of circumcision. Since he already had freedom in Christ he refused to return to "bondage." His "submission" was not to the law but to "the truth of the gospel" (Gal. 2:3-5, 14; cf. 2 Cor. 11:10; Col. 1:5).

In the Antioch confrontation, Paul rebuked Peter for not being "straightforward about the truth of the gospel" (Gal. 2:14). The Greek text says that Peter and his associates did not "walk straight" in the truth of the gospel. Their conduct was not steadfast, sincere; they were hypocrites pretending one thing and doing another. Besides accepting and knowing the truth, a proper conduct relates to the truth of the gospel. In 2 Corinthians 11:10 Paul speaks of "the truth of Christ." In Colossians 1:5, 6 he uses an equivalent expression: the "word of the truth, the gospel." The truth of the gospel is Christ, His will, His word: a will that brings freedom, a word that produces "fruit." Fruit, in this context, refers to Christian conduct and mission. The gospel requires submission to Christ. It makes Christ the deciding power in the life of a Christian. For Jews, this power lay with the law; for Gentiles it was their passions; for Christians it was Jesus Christ Himself. Laws and passions produce bondage; Christ gives freedom.

Christian liberty is not libertine. To the contrary, it is most stable, a committed and most righteous way of life. The reason is that the Christian does not make moral decisions as a slave of passions or rules, but as a free person in Christ. Because the will of the Christian is united with the will of Christ (Gal. 2:20) and empowered by the Holy Spirit, the Christian can decide and act in harmony with the fruit of the Spirit (Gal. 5:22, 23). All outward actions of the Christian are the result of a new relationship with Christ in liberty.

For this reason liberty is extremely important and the Christian must "stand fast" in it (verse 1). This concept reappears in the ethical section of the Epistle, where Paul refers to liberty in the context of obedience to the truth (verses 1-15). He explains that anyone who returns to bondage—Jews under the Torah, Gentiles under passions—has become "severed from Christ" (verse 4). For in Christ the only thing that counts is "faith working through love" (verse 6), which is equivalent to "obeying the truth" (verse 7). Through faith the Christian is free to love.

One danger, however, threatens this freedom: the flesh (verse 13). When God gave the law to Israel He wanted them to be united with Him under His will. But there was in the law the danger of legalism, which made the law, not God, the deciding moral power in life. When Christ came to set all human beings free, the danger reappeared on the side of libertinism, using liberty as an opportunity for the flesh (verse 13). This danger occurs because evil always tries to use every possible means to bring humanity under its power. Fortunately evil is limited; it cannot use God the Father, the Son, or the Holy Spirit to place humanity in bondage to the evil powers. For this reason, while eliminating the Torah and passions as ruling powers in the life of Christians, Paul could not and would not eliminate the power of Christ. There exists a moral Christian life, a life ruled by love in liberty through faith. This is the love of God who calls to liberty (verse 13), the love of Christ who provides liberty (verse 1), and the love of the Holy Spirit who produces the fruit (verses 22, 23) of obedience to the truth. The Christian obeys the truth (verse 7), walks in the Spirit (verse 25), and fulfills the law of Christ (verse 14).

(3) Exagorazō. In Galatians 3:13 and 4:5 this word presents liberty from the perspective of the work of Christ and points to *redemption.* With this word liberty is defined in more precise terms to include both the situation from which the Christian is liberated, the curse of the law, and the new situation attained by such freedom, that is, adoption into God's family.

To be free from the law means to be redeemed from its "curse" (Gal. 3:13). Paul says that those who belong to the works of the law are "under a curse" (verse 10). Only here does Paul use this expression; by it he means that redemption is freedom from being "enslaved" by the "elements of the world" (Gal. 4:1-9, 21-25; 5:1; cf. 2:4, 5). The Jews, on the other hand, were under the "curse" of the law. This curse could not be the law or disobedience to it, because Christ Himself became "a curse for us" (Gal. 3:13); that is, He took upon Himself the divine judgment for sin, so the believer could receive the blessing of Abraham and the promise of the Spirit (verse 14).

Paul quotes four OT passages to show what the curse of the law is (Deut. 27:26; Hab. 2:4; Lev. 18:5; Deut. 21:23). He does not speak of a radical separation between faith and law but of a radical separation between curse and justification. Curse is the consequence that comes to one who "does not confirm the words of this law by doing them" (Deut. 27:26). For a criminal the curse was death by being hanged on a tree (Deut. 21:22, 23). The curse was not the law, nor disobedience itself, but the consequence of disobedience. It was death. The law was intended to protect life; the one who observed it would live (Lev.18:1-5). But humanity disobeyed the law, and disobedience brought death. Under such conditions there was only one way to attain life: faith (Hab. 2:4). Humanity, however, could not live a life of faith, because it was under the curse of the

law. It must be liberated first by Christ's becoming a curse for us. Christ was not a criminal, but He was treated as one so that we criminals could be treated as though we were not criminals. Christ did not remove the law or obedience to the law by His death; He removed the curse. Christ liberated those who were under the curse by taking upon Himself the curse of the law. He died in place of the accursed ones.

A person who has been liberated from the curse of the law is no longer a slave but a son of God. The new adoption relationship resulting from freedom is with God Himself; in it the child of the Lawgiver delights to obey the divine will as expressed in the Ten Commandments. This brings to the believers everything that belongs to God; they become God's "heirs" (Gal. 4:5-7), not slaves "under the law," but masters *(kyrios)* "of all" (verse 1) and sons and daughters under the Spirit (verse 6). With immense gratitude they rejoice in their new state and by the indwelling Christ observe God's commandments.

(4) Stauroō. Liberty is defined by the word "crucify" in Galatians 5:24 and 6:14. Here we find the meaning of liberty and law in the context of the Christian way of life—the life of a new creature. The person who belongs to Christ has "crucified" the flesh (Gal. 5:24) and the world has been "crucified" to him (Gal. 6:14). The term *crucifixion* stands for an ethic of freedom that preserves the will. A voluntary death to the flesh, including passions and desires, is a commitment of the will. This text is closely connected to Galatians 2:19, 20, where personal spiritual crucifixion is an experience of togetherness with Christ. In this unity death is not a destruction of the will but the beginning of a new life. It is a way of life determined by the Son of God and lived willingly by faith. Law is defined in this context as living and walking in the Spirit (Gal. 5:25). Quoting the OT, Paul defines law as love (verse 14). Then he explains its meaning: walking in the Spirit (verse 16). And walking in the Spirit means freedom from the law (verse 18) and

freedom from passions (verse 24). This is a rejection of both Jewish and Gentile ethical systems. Legalism and libertinism are opposed to God because they take His place as the deciding power of the will. God gave the law not as a set of rules to keep, but as a revelation of His will. God gave freedom not for libertinism, but to provide for the operation of a free human will. Paul does not eliminate God's will or the exercise of the human will. He clarifies that the only way for these two wills to be in harmony is by living in the Spirit. Such a life requires keeping in step with the Spirit, being drawn into line by the Spirit (*stoicheō* [Gal. 5:25]). The emphasis is on the Spirit. He leads the will. For this reason Paul affirms that being crucified to the world and having the world crucified to us, or walking in the Spirit, is the "rule" of Christianity (Gal. 6:16). The standard of the new creation (verse 15)—the law of love (Gal. 5:14), the law of Christ (Gal. 6:2), the truth (Gal. 5:7)—has a clear ethical mandate.

The OT law and the law of Christ are linked by the word "fulfilled." The Ten Commandments are to be fulfilled under the moral intent of love (verse 14; 6:2). The text used to define the law as love is Leviticus 19:18, which speaks about love to one's neighbor. Therefore this law can point only to the Ten Commandments. And more than that, Paul speaks of fulfilling the whole of it, not a part (Gal. 5:14).

The reference to law in Galatians 5:3 differs from that of 5:14. The focus is different: the first focuses on the cultic laws; the second on the moral law. In both texts there is a reference to all the law, but with different words. The "whole law" in verse 3 *(holon ton nomon)* refers to the total of Torah regulations, even to the most insignificant one. Paul says that those who validated circumcision also needed to observe the whole Torah, including the cultic laws. In verse 14 the Greek says *pas nomos,* which suggests totality in terms of quality rather than quantity, drawing attention to the real quality of moral principles.

Another striking difference between these two references to the law is related to what has to be done with the law. The term used in relation to the cultic law is "to do" *(poieō),* which focuses on man's own work. The term used in relation to the moral law and the "law of Christ" (Gal. 6:2) is "to fulfill" *(plēroō),* which focuses on the work of the Holy Spirit. The context bears witness to Paul's distinction. Doing the law is the effort of human initiative and action; fulfilling the law is the initiative and work of the Spirit. Paul is really saying that the fulfillment of the Ten Commandments can be complete only through the work of the Holy Spirit. Obedience is the fruit of the Spirit.

In Galatians Paul brings us back to the beginning, before the proclamation of the Torah. He points out that what is important in the Christian moral life is the knowledge and fulfillment of God's will through the Spirit. This is the truth in moral terms. Here is the law of Christ. The only difference between the moral law of the Torah and the law of Christ lies in the way the Jews kept it, or "did" it—legalistically—and the way Christians were taught to fulfill it—with no legalism, only by faith through the work of the Holy Spirit, as a grateful submission to the will of God Himself.

c. Problem passages. While Paul's support of the law, specifically of the Ten Commandments, is clear, some of his statements appear to support the notion that the law lost its validity after the Crucifixion. Three such passages deserve careful study.

(1) Romans 10:4. Here Paul states: "For Christ is the end of the law, that every one who has faith may be justified." The phrase "end of the law" could be understood as "termination of the law," suggesting that the law would no longer be in force. However, two matters must be considered: the context of the phrase and the Greek word for "end."

In this passage Paul is describing his fellow Jews who, to a great extent, have failed to reach salvation. They pursued the law of Moses, but not in faith, and failed to attain righteousness. In fact, they stumbled over the "Stumbling Stone." While attempting to become righteous through the law, they failed to see Christ as the one to whom the law of Moses, with its ceremonies and sacrifices, pointed (Rom. 9:30–10:4).

The word *telos* has a rich gamut of meanings: from termination to fulfillment to obligation to aim or goal. In the NT the basic meaning is tied to "fulfillment"; however, *telos* can also be translated as aim or goal, issue or result, end or conclusion. One should remember that purpose and result, aim and goal, are but two sides of the same coin. In 1 Timothy 1:5, *telos* is used in the phrase "the *aim* of our charge is love." That is, love is the intended result of our preaching. Thus, "end" *(telos)* in Romans 10:4 can be seen to refer to Christ as the objective toward which the whole Jewish ritual or law pointed. Christ was the fulfillment of the OT figures and symbols, the culmination of the Torah, not the One who would abolish the law and end the validity of God's requirements for human beings.

(2) Ephesians 2:14, 15. In a passionate description of the way Christ has broken down the barriers that kept Gentiles from being God's people, Paul affirms that Christ "has broken down the dividing wall of hostility, by abolishing in his flesh the law of commandments and ordinances, that he might create in himself one new man in place of the two, so making peace." No longer must the Gentiles remain "alienated" and without promises or hope (verse 12). By His death Christ made Jews and Gentiles into one Christian church. To do this He abolished "the law of commandments and ordinances" (Gr., "the law of commandments consisting of decrees" [verse 15]).

In Acts we read of the difficulties for Gentiles and Jews in becoming one people. Only under mandate of a vision from God was Peter willing to take the gospel to the Gentile Cornelius (Acts 10:9-20). At the Jerusalem Council the main issue was whether Gentiles should become Jews before being accepted into Christian fellowship (Acts 15:1-29). Some believers went so far as to say: "It is necessary to circumcise them, and to charge them

to keep the law of Moses" (verse 5). After much discussion, the leaders of the church and the Holy Spirit agreed that circumcision was not necessary; Gentile Christians should abstain from food sacrificed to idols, from blood, and unchastity (verse 29). By not requiring Gentiles to follow Jewish ceremonies, the leaders were indeed opening the door to the Gentiles. They could not have extended their fellowship to those who did not practice the cultic ritual had not Christ made a new and better way possible, doing away with the need for rituals and ceremonies such as circumcision, ritual baths, and sacrifices.

(3) Colossians 2:13, 14. In Colossians 2 Paul describes the wonder of the salvation that Christ has made possible for them. Buried in baptism with Him, they were also circumcised in Christ (verses 11, 12). They had been "dead in trespasses" and "uncircumcision," but God had made them alive, He had forgiven their sins, and had "canceled the bond which stood against us with its legal demands." He had done this figuratively by "nailing it to the cross" (verses 13, 14). Because of Christ's triumphs over the evil powers, the Colossians were now free to enjoy the blessings of salvation (verse 15).

The key word in this passage is the "bond" or "certificate of debt" (NASB), translated from the Greek *cheirographon,* which appears only here in the NT. From nonbiblical literature we know that the *cheirographon* was a document written in one's own hand as a proof of obligation, hence, a note of indebtedness or a promissory note. Thus, what Jesus figuratively nailed to the cross was the condemnation that human beings incurred through sin.

This debt or condemnation is further identified as having legal demands against us. Not only was it hostile to us or against us; this note of indebtedness consisted of "decrees against us" (NASB). Interestingly this phrase that describes the promissory note includes one of only two Pauline occurrences of the same Greek word *dogma,* "opinion" or "decree"; the other appears in Ephesians 2:15. In both texts a system of regulations is evidently in view. In Ephesians the regulations have to do with ritual that separated Jews from Gentiles, especially circumcision. The context of Colossians 2:14 indicates regulations having to do with ceremonial celebrations and food (v. 16; see Sabbath). In both cases *dogma* has to do with Jewish ceremonial law. With the death of Christ the ceremonial system that pointed forward to Christ as the culmination of the entire legal system came to an end. No longer was it needed. Not so the moral law, including the Ten Commandments, which are a representation of the eternal character of God. It can be safely concluded that in these texts nothing is said or even intimated about the demise of the moral law.

E. The Law in the Writings of John

John, who was the last surviving apostle of Jesus Christ, was the last NT writer. He probably wrote his Gospel, Epistles, and Revelation in the last decade of the first century. Thus his writing took place some 30 years later than that of the Synoptic Gospels. Yet John's Gospel shows no real difference from the other Gospels in the way he presents Jesus' teachings on the law.

1. The Law in the Gospel of John

Reference was already made to John's Gospel in the section about Christ's teachings on the law (II. C). In this section our aim is to consider rather John's own understanding of the law. The way John conveys Jesus' life and teachings might shed light on his perception of the Ten Commandments. It could also point to changes in the Christian knowledge of and attitude toward the law.

John uses the word "law" more than Matthew does. It appears 14 times in John and eight in Matthew, but even so the question of the law is less central in John than in Matthew. John uses the word "law" (*nomos*) to refer to the Pentateuch (John 1:45), the whole

of the Old Testament (10:34), the law of Moses (7:23), a legal ordinance (18:31), and the Ten Commandments (1:17; 7:19). On the other hand, between chapters 10 and 15 John uses the word *entolē*, "command," 10 times. Among these are the "new commandment" of John 13:34 and two references to keeping Christ's plural commandments (John 14:15; 15:10). This section of the Gospel parallels to some extent the usage of *entolē* in the Epistles of John.

John's writings show no such contention in the Christian community over the law as that which appears in Pauline writings. The validity of the law is not contested. Against this background John's references to the law could be expected to be noncontroversial and not so direct as Matthew's recorded sayings, such as the one in the Sermon on the Mount about the perpetuity of the law (Matt. 5:18). John does not need to tell the Christian community that its numbers are under the obligation to fulfill the law, for that is a given.

John records two major incidents in his Gospel in which the Jewish leaders accused Jesus of breaking the Sabbath. The first was the healing of the paralytic at Bethesda (John 5:1-16); the second, the healing of the blind man at the Pool of Siloam (John 9:1-41).

In the first incident, John has Jesus giving a formal response to the accusations: "Jesus answered (*apekrinato*) them, 'My Father is working still, and I am working'" (John 5:17). The verb form suggests a public or formal defense. Jesus defended Himself, denying the accusation that He had transgressed the fourth commandment. He was simply doing the "work" of the Father on that Sabbath day, the work of creation and salvation. The verb John used to express the working of Father and Son is *ergazomai,* which John uses to refer to the saving work of Christ (verse 17; 6:32, 35; 9:4), and elsewhere applies to human beings in speaking of deeds "wrought in God" (John 3:21; cf. 6:28) or of laboring for the food that produces eternal life (6:27). The work of God was not that of a breadwinner, but that of mission. The Father and the Son "work" that nothing should be lost (verses 38, 39); they also work for the salvation of the world (John 4:34; 9:4; 12:49, 50). Since missionary deeds were not forbidden on Sabbath, Jesus was in full harmony with the fourth commandment of the moral law.

In John 9 Jesus is condemned for healing a blind man at the Pool of Siloam on a sabbath day. His enemies said, "This man is not from God, for he does not keep the sabbath" (verse 16). They also affirmed: "This man is a sinner" (verse 24). To show that they had the power to pass judgment on Jesus, they excommunicated the healed man (verse 34). But Jesus could not accept that the power of judgment lay with His enemies. He announced: "For judgment I came into this world, that those who do not see may see, and that those who see may become blind" (verse 39). Jesus was the only judge because, living in obedience to the law, He was not a sinner and the Father had committed all judgment to Him (John 5:22, 30). The condemnation of the judgment will come "on the last day" to those who do not believe or receive Christ's word, which is God's commandment (John 12:48).

In both cases, Jesus did not accept the accusation of breaking the Sabbath law. His healing of both the paralytic and the blind man were merely part of His divine activity. He had the right to save and judge human beings.

2. The Law in the Epistles of John

In the Epistles of John, the singular word *nomos,* "law," so frequently used in the rest of the NT, is never employed. In its stead, John uses the word *entolē,* "command" or "commandment." Of the 18 times the word *entolē* is used, 10 are in the singular and eight in the plural. The commandment of God is closely related to believing in Christ, in His mission, His love, and His power to give eternal life: "This is his commandment, that we should believe in the name of his Son Jesus Christ and love one another, just as he has commanded us" (1 John 3:23).

Harking back to the "new commandment" of John 13:34, the aged apostle presents the content of this special commandment: love (1 John 2:7, 8). The new commandment, which was new only in the sense of renovation and the reality of its fulfillment, enjoins Christians to love one another and God (1 John 4:21; 2 John 5). Even the reference to love in the new commandment is not new, as it was included in the instructions given by God through Moses (Lev. 19:18). Thus John can say that this is "no new commandment, but an old commandment which you had from the beginning." Yet this commandment is new in the sense that it is now working to transform the believers into the likeness of Christ (1 John 2:7, 8).

While God's commandment is one, it is also plural, the Ten Commandments of His moral law. John's emphasis is on *keeping* them. The word used five times by John is *tēreō,* to observe, to practice, to keep strictly. It expresses the idea of conforming the inner purpose of human desires and acts to the will of God as it is given in the commandments. For this reason John also describes God's commandments as a way of life, Jesus' way of life. John urges the "elect lady" to walk according to God's laws, just as Jesus instructed (2 John 6). Furthermore, keeping the commandments is seen as evidence that Christians know God (1 John 2:3, 4) and love Him (John 14:15).

The commandment of love does not refer to some kind of comfortable feeling only; it requires the actual practice of the Ten Commandments with their demand of love to God and to fellow human beings. The reference to the absolutes of God's commandments, with their ethical propositions that define a particular way of life, includes also the "doctrine of Christ" (2 John 9), which is not the doctrine about Christ but the doctrine *given by* Christ. John concludes: "Any one who goes ahead and does not abide in the doctrine of Christ does not have God; he who abides in the doctrine has both the Father and the Son" (2 John 9).

478

3. The Law in the Book of Revelation

John carries into the book of Revelation the same use of *entolē* as noted in John 10-15 and in his Epistles. In addition he stresses the same intimate relationship between law and faith—the commandments are always together with Jesus Christ—and the imperative of keeping the commandments.

The book of Revelation not only witnesses to the Christian's acceptance of God's commandments at the end of the first century; it points out their validity for the Christian church to the end of time. Thus the Ten Commandments are validated for the entire history of the Christian church until the second coming of Christ.

When John describes the remnant, the faithful Christians of the end time, he points specifically to their keeping of the commandments of God, in plural. "Then the dragon was angry with the woman, and went off to make war on the rest of her offspring, on those who keep the commandments of God and bear testimony to Jesus" (Rev. 12:17). The dragon is Satan (verse 9) and the woman stands for the people of God (cf. Isa. 54:5, 6; Jer. 6:2).

Satan has been at war against the church from the beginning; he will continue to fight it until the end. But the remnant will not yield to Satan's temptations. Faithful Christians will keep God's commandments until the very end of time; they will achieve this by faith in Jesus.

John describes the remnant as "those who keep the commandments of God and the faith of Jesus" (Rev. 14:12). The context makes reference to worshiping "him who made heaven and earth, the sea and the fountains of water" (verse 7). This may refer to the fourth commandment since this is the only place in the law where worship of the Creator is demanded. (See Sanctuary; Remnant/Three Angels.)

The perpetuity of the Ten Commandments is clear in the Bible. God's law is the whole scope of history: from Adam and Eve to the restoration of the planet. Only those who overcome with Christ will enter the new earth where there will be no place for transgressors. "He who conquers shall have this heritage, and I will be his God and he shall be my son. But as for the cowardly, the faithless, the polluted, as for murderers, fornicators, sorcerers, idolaters, and all liars, their lot shall be in the lake that burns with fire and brimstone, which is the second death" (Rev. 21:7, 8).

The law has always been an important element in God's government of the universe. Its validity is clearly attested and its authority will never be questioned by those who follow God. God's enemies have opposed His law in the past; they will continue to do so until the coming of the Lord. Then they will be destroyed and the conflict between good and evil will end, but God will forever continue using His law to define His absolutes for a moral life.

III. Law and Salvation

God's law is related to salvation in many ways. One of the most important of these interrelationships is that of the law with the covenant. Further, law and grace are often placed in opposition to each other; however, both are essential to salvation. Finally, at the heart of salvation is the cross, from which law cannot be divorced.

A. Law and Covenant

The first biblical reference to *tôrāh* comes in a revelation of God's will to Isaac in Gerar

(Gen. 26:5), when God told the patriarch to stay in the land the Lord had offered Abraham as a gift for himself and his descendants (Gen. 12:1-3). This gift included the possession of the land, the multiplication of his descendants, and the blessing for him and for all the nations of the earth (Gen. 26:1-4). These promises had been included in the covenant that God made with Abraham and all the generations of his descendants (Gen. 15:18; 17:7). For his part, Abraham obeyed God—kept His charge, His commandments, His statutes, and His laws.

The keeping of the law, in this context, means to adhere to Yahweh, His person, His instructions, and His will. For Abraham God's covenant and law were one and in harmony with the covenant (Gen. 12:1-3). Abraham did not keep God's revelations and instructions in an accidental or sporadic manner, but did so willingly and consistently. The promise of God sworn from Isaac "he confirmed a statute to Jacob, as an everlasting covenant to Israel" (1 Chron. 16:17; cf. 14-18). And when the promised Messiah came, the covenant and the law were bound together in Christ for eternity (Gal. 3:17).

The importance of the law, as well as its validity, lay in the will of God. The covenant demanded obedience to God, for God's law was the expression of His will and the basis of the covenant. Thus, when the people forgot the one God who expressed His will in the law, and obeyed the law as a set of formal principles of conduct or as cultic ordinances, God sent His prophet to say: "They have broken my covenant, and transgressed my law" (Hosea 8:1). Obedience without respect for God was rebellion. The only possible solution for such a condition was to draw up a new covenant. God said: "I will make a new covenant with the house of Israel and the house of Judah" (Jer. 31:31). Once more the will of God was clearly expressed in the covenant and the law: "I will put my law within them, and I will write it upon their hearts" (verse 33).

The law and the covenant revealed the will of God to the covenant people—His people. It revealed a spiritual unity that far surpassed the formalities of the cult or the correctness of behavior. It revealed the only way He could be their God, and they could be His people (verse 33).

To understand the relationship between Israel's system of law and the covenant one must realize that the word "covenant" is used in the Bible to describe a particular saving relationship between God and Israel. The covenant was initiated by God, freely accepted by Israel, and ratified by a sacrifice. The covenant relationship included God's promises and Israel's obligations, which were defined by the moral law that determined a particular way of life within the covenant. The civil laws established the identity of the nation; the ceremonial law helped the nation to fulfill the moral law and to understand the plan of salvation; and the health laws made possible a healthy long life within the covenant community.

The Bible mentions two covenants—the old and the new. While both express God's loving will, certain differences are evident. Both relate to God's law.

1. The Old Covenant

The old covenant is first referred to in Exodus 19, where God speaks to Moses about what He has already accomplished for Israel. He has liberated them from Egypt and has made them His people (verse 4). In consequence of His powerful acts in favor of Israel, God expected the people (1) to obey His commandments, and (2) to keep His covenant (verse 5). If Israel did so, God would accomplish His part: "Now therefore, if you will obey my voice and keep my covenant, you shall be my own possession among all peoples; for all the earth is mine, and you shall be to me a kingdom of priests and a holy nation" (verses 5, 6). All the people accepted the terms of the covenant, "All that the Lord has spoken we will do" (verse 8). A covenant was then drawn up and God gave them the Ten Commandments (Ex. 20) to show exactly how a covenant people should live.

Salvation/liberation and the covenant way of life were tied together as one expression of the will of God for His people. He made this clear by His mighty historical acts of liberating Israel from Egypt and giving them the Ten Commandments at Sinai. In the preamble of the Decalogue He said: "I am the Lord your God, who brought you out of the land of Egypt, out of the house of bondage" (verse 2).

Salvation and law have a proper relation, in

which there is no trace of legalism. Living the covenant way of life or obeying God's commandments is a consequence of His free and unconditional salvation. Israel was not to live as did the Egyptians or the Canaanites. They were to live as God instructed and for His glory: "You shall not do as they do in the land of Egypt, where you dwelt, and you shall not do as they do in the land of Canaan, to which I am bringing you. You shall not walk in their statutes. You shall do my ordinances and keep my statutes and walk in them. I am the Lord your God" (Lev. 18:3, 4).

According to the Epistle to the Hebrews, the old covenant was faulty (Heb. 8:7) and "ready to vanish away" (verse 13). But that covenant was not faulty in itself, nor was God's part in it at fault. It was made at God's initiative, based on what God had already done for Israel. The people had accepted the terms of the covenant and its way of life, and the ratification sacrifice had been properly carried out (Ex. 24:1-8). The fault of the old covenant was in Israel's attitude toward it, the way they attempted to keep it—in a spirit of legalism. Paul explains: "What shall we say, then? That Gentiles who did not pursue righteousness have attained it, that is, righteousness through faith; but that Israel who pursued the righteousness which is based on law did not succeed in fulfilling that law. Why? Because they did not pursue it through faith, but as if it were based on works" (Rom. 9:30-32). Righteousness by faith is the basis of Moses' teachings about the law and the foundation of the entire OT (see Deut. 30:11-14), as much as it is the basis of Paul's teachings in the NT. Explaining righteousness by faith in Romans 9 and 10, Paul quotes what Moses wrote in Deuteronomy 30:11-14. Both Paul and Moses speak about the same truth: righteousness, salvation, life, and even obedience are possible only by faith.

Israel, however, did not obey the law within the covenant relationship with God. The nation forgot God while still keeping its ties to the law. Keeping the law for the sake of doing the works of the law is pure legalism. This was not God's intention for Israel when He made a covenant with that people and gave them His Ten Commandments at Sinai.

The law and the covenant were only one piece of God's will. God was the center of both the covenant and the law. For this reason Moses told Israel, God "declared to you his covenant, which he commanded you to perform, that is, the ten commandments; and he wrote them upon two tables of stone" (Deut. 4:13). But Israel broke the old covenant.

2. The New Covenant

The invalidation of the old covenant prompted the need for a new covenant. "In speaking of a new covenant he treats the first as obsolete" (Heb. 8:13); but God did not change. The difference between the two covenants must be found in the attitude of God's people. In making the covenant God came close to the people to make them one with Himself: "You shall be to me . . . a holy nation" (Ex. 19:6). God spoke the covenant and the people replied: "All that the Lord has spoken we will do" (verse 8). Sadly enough many Israelites turned a covenant of grace into a system of salvation by works. "Ignorant of the righteousness that comes from God, and seeking to establish their own, they did not submit to God's righteousness." They "pursued the righteousness which is based on law," "they did not pursue it through faith, but as if it were based on works" (Rom. 9:30–10:3), thus perverting it.

The purpose of the new covenant was to produce the salvation relationship of the covenant without which obedience of faith to the law is impossible. Obedience of faith is God's will working through the Spirit with the free human will to fulfill the law within a relationship of faith. As part of the new covenant God promised: "I will put my law within them, and I will write it upon their hearts; and I will be their God, and they shall be my people" (Jer. 31:33). Through the prophet Ezekiel God promised: "A new heart I will give you, and a new spirit I will put within you; and I will take out of your flesh the heart of stone and give you a heart of flesh. And I will put my spirit within you, and cause you to walk in my statutes and be careful to observe my ordinances" (Eze. 36:26, 27). As a result, the way of the new covenant is joyful. So David understood it: "I delight to do thy will, O my God; thy law is within my heart" (Ps. 40:8). So, too, the Christian understands the way of the new covenant (Heb. 8:7-13; 9:15).

Two elements determine the nature of the covenant: the time of its ratifying sacrifice and the presence of the Spirit. The ratifying sacrifice of the old covenant was made first at Sinai. The ratifying sacrifice of the new covenant took place at Calvary. The old covenant was made at Sinai and immediately ratified with the blood of sacrificial animals (Ex. 24:5-8; Heb. 9:18-20). The new covenant was first made with Adam and Eve after they had sinned (Gen. 3:15), repeated to Abraham, and ratified by the sacrifice of Christ at the cross (Heb. 9:15).

The new covenant, according to Paul, is the covenant of "the Spirit," not merely in a written code as the old one (2 Cor. 3:6). The old covenant was written on tables of stone, while the new was to be engraved by the Spirit on the heart; their content did not change. The first one was outside the person; the second, within. Indeed, the law brings condemnation, unless the Spirit internalizes it and gives life. The covenant becomes obsolete the moment it is put outside of the person (Heb. 8:6). It becomes a new covenant when the converted person serves "not under the old written code but in the new life of the Spirit" (Rom. 7:6). There was only one law for both covenants: the Ten Commandments; the difference was in the kind of obedience. One was legalistic; the other, through the Spirit by faith.

The purpose of the two covenants was the salvation of humanity. Under the old covenant Israel tried to save itself by its own obedience to the law. Under the new covenant God promised to create spiritual unity between Himself and each human being. This He would do through the Holy Spirit in order to produce true obedience to the law by faith. Abraham responded to God by believing, and the Lord "reckoned it to him as righteousness" (Gen. 15:6). In the same way, Paul said that all Christians should "serve the living God" (Heb. 9:14).

3. Law and New Covenant

Obedience to the moral law is the result of the new covenant, established on better promises than those of the old (Heb. 8:6). The promise does not abrogate the law so Christians become free from obeying it. On the contrary, instead of being written on tables of stone, the law is engraved on the minds and hearts of God's people. Its continuity is thus forever established and the possibility of true obedience to the moral law realized. Obedience becomes a full reality in heart, mind, and deed.

Because under the new covenant the law is written by God in hearts and minds, obedience is spiritual and an action of the free will. Both the moral character of the law and the morality of Christian behavior are thus secured without falling into legalism.

B. Moral Law and Grace

As shown in the case of Abraham (Gen. 15:6; Rom. 4:1-5, 22; Gal. 3:6), the relationship between law and grace is the same in both Testaments; faith is always involved. All of Scripture indicates that because human beings have sinned, according to the law they must die. However, God's grace opens the possibility of salvation by faith in the sacrifice of Jesus Christ.

Grace cannot by itself solve the problem of sin. The cross, as the very center of God's grace operation, is an affirmation of the law through death and obedience. Christ did not eliminate the law; He suffered its sentence and obeyed its orders. Christ died the death that the law demanded of sinners. For sinners to have the possibility of salvation Christ became the "curse of the law"; He was hung on "a tree" (Deut. 21:22, 23). He was "made sin" for our sake (2 Cor. 5:21) and died on the cross, accursed by the law "for us" in order "that we might receive the promise" (Gal. 3:13,14). At the cross Christ fulfilled the sentence of the law and God demonstrated "his love for us" (Rom. 5:8).

What the grace of God and Christ eliminated at the cross was not the law but condemnation. "Law came in, to increase the trespass; but where sin increased, grace abounded all the more, so that, as sin reigned in death, grace also might reign through righteousness to eternal life through Jesus Christ our Lord" (Rom. 5:20, 21).

When Christians, through faith in Christ, accept God's grace they obey with love and gratitude. They also walk "in newness of life" (Rom. 6:4), experiencing by faith God's gracious forgiveness.

1. Improper Function of the Law: Legalism

If the moral law was not abrogated at the cross, it must be obeyed. But it is not obeyed to obtain justification or sanctification. Legalism is pretending to be accepted by God or to be able to remain in Him simply because of obedience. It is the foolish sin of self-righteousness and the gross mistake of missing the righteousness freely given by God's grace in Christ.

Paul affirms that the self-dependence of the legalism of his opponents led them to boasting, trusting in the flesh, seeking legal blamelessness, and attempting their own righteousness through the works of the law (Phil. 3:1-11). Those who embraced legalism and thus became "enemies of the cross of Christ" would not attain salvation but "destruction" (verses 18, 19).

Legalism leads people to think they can be saved by obeying the law. In so doing it turns away from grace, does away with faith, and perverts the gospel (Gal. 1:6, 7). A perversion of the gospel is no gospel at all. The Greek word for "perverting" means to turn things upside down. A political term, *metastrephō*

suggested revolutionary activities, indicating that Paul saw legalism as a rebellion against the grace of God and God Himself. Legalism misrepresents salvation and leads people away from salvation.

2. The Witness of True Obedience

In the Scriptures there is no opposition between law and grace, as if in OT times people were saved by obedience to the law (righteousness from the law), and in NT times, by grace (righteousness in Christ). The shift is rather from promise to fulfillment (Gal. 3; 4).

According to Romans 9:30–10:13, Israel obeyed the law as an instrument of self-righteousness but did not attain justification. This, however, was not always the case. At least two individuals are recorded as having been justified by faith: Abraham and David. Paul, quoting the OT, says that "Abraham believed God, and it was reckoned to him as righteousness" (Rom. 4:3). In an autobiographical psalm David said: "Blessed is he whose transgression is forgiven, whose sin is covered" (Ps. 32:1). Paul explains this as righteousness imputed "apart from works" (Rom. 4:6-8).

Obedience is not a means of obtaining salvation. On the contrary, it is the evidence of God's grace operating by faith in a person's life, the outworking of gratitude for salvation already received. Obedience is the only way to show that the power of God is at work in an individual. Witnessing in favor of oneself does not count; the true witness comes from the Holy Spirit. Obedience can happen only when the Holy Spirit is at work producing acts of obedience to the moral law. These acts a Christian performs by faith, only because the Spirit works through a converted life full of grace.

According to Ephesians 2:4-10, salvation, as a gift from God, is wholly "by grace . . . through faith." Good works, the works of obedience to the law, do not activate God's grace for justification or for sanctification. Salvation, including justification and sanctification, is a gift of the grace of God. Good works are an outgrowth of the new birth. "For we are his workmanship, created in Christ Jesus for good works, which God prepared beforehand, that we should walk in them" (verse 10). Therefore, obedience, being by grace, is the visible evidence that grace is working by faith in the life of a Christian person. (See Salvation.)

C. The Law and the Cross

At Calvary two important events related to the law took place. The first was the termination of the ritual system; the second was the reaffirmation of the moral law.

1. Termination of the Ritual System

The ritual system with all its ceremonial laws had one main objective: to announce the sacrifice of Christ and teach its meaning. When Jesus died on the cross, symbols gave way to reality; therefore, they were no longer needed. The Synoptic Gospels all note that after Christ died, "the curtain of the temple," which separated the holy from the Most Holy, "was torn in two, from top to bottom" (Matt. 27:51; Mark 15:38; Luke 23:45). Christ died at the time of the evening sacrifice, when the priest, after sacrificing the lamb, presented its blood before the veil. He was not allowed to go into the Most Holy Place, for only the high priest could enter the Holy of Holies, only once a year on the Day of Atonement. The tearing of the veil, allowing the priest to see inside the Holy of Holies, showed that the whole ritual system had come to an end.

Daniel had already prophesied that at His death the Messiah "shall confirm the covenant" and "put an end to sacrifice and offering" (Dan. 9:26, KJV; verse 27, NIV). The same concept is repeated in the NT. As the ritual system was only "a shadow of the good things to come" (Heb. 10:1), it was in force only "until the time of reformation" (Heb. 9:10), or "till the offspring should come" (Gal. 3:19).

When Christ died, the ritual system with its complex sacrifices and ceremonies ceased. The real sacrifice for sin had been made. With forgiveness offered freely, the cross "canceled the bond which stood against us with its legal demands; this he set aside, nailing it to the cross" (Col. 2:14). Christians should no longer be concerned with ceremonial food or drink, or the ceremonies of festivals, new moons, or annual sabbaths, because the whole ritual system was only a "shadow" of "things to come." The reality of this shadow, "the substance," was Christ's sacrifice (verses 16, 17). This was the only sacrifice that could purge the conscience and take away sin (Heb. 9:12-14; 10:4).

Just as Christ abolished the ritual system at the cross, He broke down "the middle wall of division" between Jews and Gentiles. The Jewish ceremonial system, given by God as a schoolmaster to bring everyone to the cross of Christ, had been made "enmity" and put the Gentiles "far off," alienating them from the commonwealth of Israel. By His sacrifice, Jesus brought about the reconciliation of Jews and Gentiles to God, and made them into one body (Eph. 2:11-18).

2. The Cross: Reaffirmation of the Moral Law

The cross is the greatest proof that the Ten Commandments could not be abolished or invalidated. If God had intended to abrogate the moral law, He could have easily done so before the cross. To say that it was necessary to fulfill the law before actually abolishing it would mean that God took the pain of sending His Son to the cross only to justify sinners *in* their sinfulness. Salvation would have come only by a legal formality, a deliverance from judgment, not from sin.

Abolishing the law instead of solving the sin problem would have perpetuated the existence of sin as a reality accepted by God Himself. At the cross Christ paid the demands of the law, in reality the demand of God, the Lawgiver. Christ died to destroy sin, not to abolish the moral law. The death of Christ did not free human beings from the authority of the law; on the contrary, it showed that the law is as ceaseless as God's justice. For this reason Jesus Christ said that He did not come to destroy the law but to fulfill it (Matt. 5:17).

The fulfillment of the law at the cross is its total affirmation: the affirmation of its verdict, the sentence of condemnation on sin executed (Rom. 5:6-21); the affirmation of its justice, the wages of sin paid in full (Rom. 6:23); the affirmation of its purpose, the full achievement of obedience to God performed (Phil. 2:5-16), with the perfect love of God being fully applied to humanity (Rom. 8:31-39); and the affirmation of its command, the requirements of the law established through faith in the cross (Rom. 3:19-31).

The cross affirms the moral law. "Do we then overthrow the law by this faith? By no means! On the contrary, we uphold the law" (verse 31).

IV. Practical Implications for Christian Living

Being moral, spiritual, and comprehensive, the ten-commandment law is a transcript of God's character. It conveys God's pattern of conduct for all human beings, worldwide and for all times. It is the only part of divine revelation chiseled by the very finger of God on tables of stone, thus underlying their lasting value and perpetuity.

Its twofold division derives from the two fundamental principles of love on which the kingdom of God operates: "You shall love the Lord your God with all your heart, and with all your soul, and with all your strength, and with all your mind; and your neighbor as yourself" (Luke 10:27; cf. Deut. 6:4, 5; Lev. 19:18).

This law is one of the instruments in the hands of the Spirit by which He convicts us of sin. Its purpose is to define sin and to convince us all of our sinfulness. The Spirit gathers us sinners at the foot of the mount of the law to hear the divine standard of righteousness and to place us under the conviction of sin and the condemnation of eternal death. In this hopeless condition He then leads us to the mount of Calvary and reveals to us the way of escape. Under deep conviction of sin we are ready to hear the good news of salvation through faith in the atoning life and death of Jesus Christ.

For this reason the law and the gospel work hand in hand in the redemption of sinful human beings. They cannot be enemies. The law cannot take away sin nor did Jesus come to take away the law, but rather the condemnation of the law. We cannot earn salvation by our good works or by a strict obedience to the ten-commandment law. Obedience is the fruitage of our salvation in Christ. It is the outward expression of deep gratitude in response to God's unfathomable love. Believers who come to understand how much Christ our Lord valued the law and magnified it in His life will be eager to follow in His steps.

In truth, it is to Christ's obedience that we owe everything. As the Scriptures tell us, just "as by one man's disobedience many were made sinners, so by one man's obedience many will be made righteous" (Rom. 5:19). The whole redemption of Christ consists in restoring obedience to its place. He brings us back to a life of obedience, of grateful obedience, of love obedience. Or have we forgotten, as Paul so fittingly asks, that we are servants "either of sin, which leads to death, or of obedience, which leads to righteousness" (Rom. 6:16)? Made righteous by the obedience of Christ, we are like Him and in Him servants of obedience unto righteousness. It is in the love obedience of One that the love obedience of many has its roots and its life.

Let this be the Christ we receive and love, and seek to be like. Let us prove the sincerity and strength of our faith in Him and the Spirit's supernatural power by accepting Christ the obedient One as the Christ who dwells in us.

V. Historical Overview

This brief history of how God's law has been viewed traces the main trends during Christian times.

A. Apostolic Fathers and Apologists

The writings of the apostolic fathers and the apologists, the earliest Christian writers following the New Testament Era, consist mainly of letters, sermons, treatises, and similar works. They do not present a systematic theological treatment of the Ten Commandments, nor do we find in them an exposition of this doctrine in theological terms. This is not to say that these early Christian writers had no theological concerns or rejected the doctrines to which they gave minimal attention. Their interest was mainly in exposition of their understanding of the Scriptures on specific issues, often matters debated in the churches.

Some of these demands arose from heretical movements developing among the churches. An example was Ebionism, so-called because of its teachings with respect to the law. Our understanding of this early group is limited by the fact that their own writings have not survived, and most of our information about them is derived from their enemies' reports.

The Ebionites mistakenly believed that the mission of Christ was not so much to save humanity as to call humans to obedience of the law. Although the law was at the core of their spirituality, they considered that the OT laws of sacrifices were an external addition to the law given by God, hence they rejected certain parts of the Pentateuch, but their understanding of Jesus' fulfillment of the law was in harmony with NT teaching. Christ's assertion that He came to fulfill the law, they said, did not mean He fulfilled it by terminating its binding nature, but in setting up an example that all should follow.

Irenaeus (c. 130-200) became one of the most important defenders of Christian faith, including in his work a discussion of law. In his *Against Heresies* he explained that Christ's teachings about the law in Matthew 5 were not meant to oppose the law, but to fulfill it in the sense of extending its meaning and expanding its scope. The law was given to instruct humans that they might learn to serve God, abstain from evil deeds, and resist the tendency toward performing them.

Clement of Alexandria (c. 160-215) championed the defense of Greek philosophy as God-given preparatory instruction by which the human mind is trained to receive the full truth as Jesus taught it. Clement's work, *Stromata,* maintains that the law was given by the Good Shepherd, whose law is the precept of knowledge. Those who obey that law cannot disbelieve or be ignorant of the truth. The law trains us to piety, prescribes what is to be done, and restrains from sin. Observance of the commandments attains a secure life for the entire human race because the law of God is the fountain of all ethics and the source from which the Greeks had drawn their laws.

Origen (c. 185-254), also of the Alexandrian theological school, produced several theological works, including *On First Principles.* There he explained his allegorizing spiritual interpretation of the Bible. For him the true sense of the Bible often is not apparent in what the text says, which he designates as literal or physical, but rather in what the spirit and soul can draw from the text, namely the moral and psychical sense, which discovers the hidden intellectual or spiritual sense of the Scriptures. Following this unusual hermeneutic, the OT and NT events are not to be seen as pure history, "nor even do the law and the commandments wholly convey what is agreeable to reason" (4. 1. 16). For Origen the law reported in Deuteronomy as a "second law" takes the form of an allegory relating to the first and second comings of Christ. Such an allegorical understanding of the law eliminates its importance for Christian living and behavior and introduces into Christian theology a way of thinking that is foreign to biblical teaching.

Augustine (354-430) is seen as the last of the Early Fathers and forerunner of medieval theology. When confronted with the ideas of Pelagius, a British monk, Augustine summarized the Pelagian teachings, one of which dealt with the law. Augustine reports that Pelagius taught that, along with the gospel, the law contributed to the kingdom. Freedom to obey or disobey the law has been given each human by the grace of God. Moreover, the law itself is a means of grace. In another anti-Pelagian treatise, *Against Two Letters of the Pelagians,* Augustine criticized the Pelagians for holding that grace has appeared to mankind in three stages, originally by natural creation, then by the law, and finally in Christ. Augustine denied that the law conveyed grace, arguing that grace was given to make human beings doers of the law, but salvation comes only by the blood of Christ.

B. Medieval Trends

Augustinian theology dominated the church in the Medieval period, however toward the close of the High Middle Ages the writings of Thomas Aquinas (1224-1274) moved Christian theology in new directions. His *Treatise on the Law* developed the idea that eternal law lies at the core of every law, including the natural law from which springs a universal morality. Yet natural law is incomplete, therefore must be perfected by divine law, specifically the Ten Commandments. In them God gave an explicit, detailed way of life. According to Thomas the gospel law is the high point of the divine law, for God's commandments are loving and include broader "counsels of perfection." These counsels do not share the level of obligation characterizing the Ten Commandments, but their purpose is to render easier the gaining of eternal happiness for those seeking greater perfection.

C. The Reformation

The Reformers introduced a new examination of the gospel from the Scriptures; however, treatment of the law retained much of the clear anthropological approach characteristic of the Middle Ages. While accepting the law as the expression of God's will, Martin Luther (1483-1546) held that much of God's will is perceived through the natural law that comes to our understanding through civil institutions such as the family and state. Following this comes the theological function of the law. For Luther the function of the law is, on the human side, a condemnation of humanity, and on God's side, the awakening of His wrath.

Luther saw a compelling contrast between the law and the gospel. The contrast lies beyond one's simple understanding that the law is God's "No" to sinful humans while the gospel is His "Yes" to repentant sinners. But from this dialectic relationship between law and gospel Luther developed his entire theology of justification, predestination, and ethics. This is not to say that he rejected the law, for in his eyes the law keeps the justified sinner, still as sinner, and leads him to acknowledge his desperate plight. Grace provides the answer.

In his *Commentary on Galatians* Luther affirmed that the whole law, ceremonial and moral, is "utterly abrogate" for the Christian, who is dead to the law. However, from another perspective the law remains, and the flesh must be subject to the law. A major theme of Luther's was Christian freedom. Christians are free from the law in the conscience but not so in the flesh, where it should be truly empowered.

The law, as Luther taught it, has a purpose for the unrighteous, as well as for Christians. It places sinners under restraints, limiting their evil actions. And Christians profit from this as well since no person is pious by nature. Furthermore, the law teaches how to recognize sin and how to resist evil, both of which are crucial to Christian life.

Other streams of thought were prominent

in the Reformation. Ulrich Zwingli (1484-1531) is remembered for his somewhat social views, and John Calvin (1509-1564) as the outstanding pioneer in today's evangelical movement.

Zwingli saw the law as "nothing but a manifestation of the will of God, and like God's will, eternal." God's law made all humanity guilty of death, but those who trust in Christ "cannot be damned by the law." Therefore the believer, dead to the law and living in Christ, no longer needs a law, for "whatever pleases God pleases him also." At the same time Christians are free from laws governing forms of worship. Because Jesus has fulfilled it, the law "can no longer condemn anyone." At conversion the believer was "set free and made a child of God," all fear of the law and of death being abolished.

Calvin addressed the law from two directions: a natural law written in the human conscience and the written law. The written law gives instruction regarding perfect justice and the perfect life. It is a mirror in which we see our sins, for it reveals God's will and shows that we do not fulfill His ideals. Salvation does not come by the fulfillment of the law because there is no justice in our own work. It comes through remission of sins. At the same time the law has several functions: it accuses sinners, admonishes believers, discloses human sinfulness, leads to grace, leads to Christ, protects the community from unjust individuals, shows God's righteousness, teaches that God is the Father of all humans, and urges believers to well-doing. Therefore the law is important in that it (1) points to God's justice, convincing all of injustice and sin, (2) destroys human arrogance so persons will accept God's mercy and have confidence only in His grace, (3) declares God's punishment for sin, which is death. Overall, the law is profitable for Christians, for it reminds them of those things that are acceptable to God and how to be righteous before the Lord.

Any review of the Reformation must note a movement called the Radical Reformation, its leaders called the Radical Reformers. They rep-resented a wing of the Reformation rejected by the major Reformers, but whose influence eventually became widespread. One of the leaders in this movement was Konrad Grebel, a Swiss Reformer critical of what he felt was an inadequate Lutheran reform. For him, emphasis should rest on the importance of the law engraven not on stone tablets, but on the tables of the heart. Balthasar Hubmaier, perhaps the most able of the Radical Reformers, cited what he called "distinguishable purposes" of the law, a threat of doom to the flesh, an aid and testimony against sin, and teacher of the path of piety.

D. The Modern Period

All doctrines, including the doctrine of the law, developed from the eighteenth to twentieth centuries under a tension between tradition and doubt, dogma and relativism. Religion retained the forms developed by tradition, but with a sense of restless dissatisfaction, particularly among the heirs of the Reformation. The result presents a picture of widespread disunity. John Bunyan (1628-1688), Puritan heir to the Radical Reformers and Calvinists, argued for an integration of law and grace. Later the Wesleyans advocated the closest connection between them in practical Christian life.

Orthodox Lutherans continued to teach sharp disjunction between law and grace. From this perspective they accused the Pietist wing of their church of confusing gospel with law. In response, Pietists insisted that within the doctrine of grace stands an imperative that we live in harmony with the law of God. Therefore there should be no setting one against the other as paradox.

In the nineteenth century the formation of the Seventh-day Adventist Church introduced into Christian discussion a fresh look at the law in the full Bible, OT and NT. Early Adventists gave little attention to integrating law and gospel, or to the question of obedience counted as good works. For them salvation was a gift from God through the sacrifice of Christ, by faith alone.

Although defending the Reformation principle of *sola scriptura,* their vigorous insistence on obedience to the law of God, specifically the Ten Commandments with its Sabbath mandate, provoked widespread response from their critics over the role of law. Many argued the law reached its conclusion in the ministry and sacrifice of Christ, thereby rendering the Sabbath no longer a part of Christian theology. Adventists developed powerful responses to such antinomianism, and their numbers grew rapidly, a key feature of their teaching being the perpetuity of the law of God.

Under influence of the social gospel late in the nineteenth century, with its politicized theology, discussion of the law of God lost specific purpose, sin becoming identified with selfishness. From this perspective humans sin against their higher self, against good persons, or the universal good, but not directly against God in the classic sense. With such developing secular mentality and decline of traditional Protestantism in the late-twentieth century, sin has often come to be redefined as a state of social injustice, a generalized social malaise, in brief a redefinition in political, economic, cultural, and psychological terms. Such developments have led to diminished interest, beyond limited circles, in the role of the law of God.

VI. Ellen G. White Comments

Ellen G. White's teachings about the law and the doctrine of the law in the Seventh-day Adventist Church are identical. Therefore in a study such as this they must be together. However, for the sake of identifying the relationship of Ellen G. White with the Adventist faith and to see their relationship better, this section is divided into two parts: the law in Ellen G. White's writings and the law in the doctrine of the Seventh-day Adventist Church.

A. The Law in Ellen G. White's Writings

Ellen G. White (1827-1915), a cofounder of the Seventh-day Adventist Church, is recognized by Adventists as an authoritative exponent of its doctrines and beliefs. Her writings about the law are abundant and consistent within themselves and with the Scriptures.

In 1846, under the influence of other Adventists such as Joseph Bates, she began to understand the necessary connection between the gospel and the law of God. The conviction came even more strongly after receiving a vision about the sanctuary in heaven, which also called attention to the fourth commandment. In relation to that vision she wrote, "Attention must be called to the breach of the law, by precept and example." She added, "I was shown that the third angel proclaiming the commandments of God and the faith of Jesus, represents the people who receive this message, and raise the voice of warning to the world to keep the commandments of God and His law as the apple of the eye; and that in response to this warning, many would embrace the Sabbath of the Lord" (LS 96).

In her first published pamphlet, in 1851, she notes that already in 1849 she had come to understand that God's commandments and the faith of Jesus—the law and the gospel—could not be separated. Therefore she presented the law of God, the sanctuary doctrine, and the faith of Jesus as the "principal subjects" of the "present truth" (EW 63).

Her concept of "present truth" expresses an overview of the doctrinal body that must be considered indispensable for all Christians in the time of the end, that is from 1844 until Christ's second coming. Because from her first writings she put the law in this category of doctrine, we can expect that she would not change her view on the law.

Prior to the General Conference session of 1888, where the doctrine of justification by faith was emphasized, Ellen G. White presented the law in clear language. In 1875 she wrote that the law of God was sacred, important, and its character was more exalted for those who accepted Christ as their Redeemer than for its original recipients (RH Apr. 29, 1875).

In 1884 she explained that the law is a complete rule of life given by God to humanity. If obeyed, through the merits of Christ, the obedient Christian shall live. If disobeyed, the transgressor will be condemned by its power (ST Sept. 4, 1884).

Two years later she stated that the holy, just, and good law brought from God the knowledge that is "to govern all human intelligences" (ibid. Apr. 8, 1886). Later in the same year she wrote that "there is no saving quality in law. The law condemns, but it cannot pardon the transgressor. The sinner must depend on the merits of the blood of Christ." Therefore "faith in Christ is necessary" (ibid. Aug. 5, 1886).

In 1887 her writings focused on the power of the judgment in the law. As a mirror it helps us "to discern the defects in our character," but it does not turn our good deeds into salvation, rather it leads us to repent and exercise faith in Jesus Christ (ibid. May 5, 1887).

At the General Conference session of 1888, held in Minneapolis, major confrontation arose between two groups of leaders, one group emphasizing the law, the other focusing on justification by faith. Ellen White favored the advocates of the gospel. At the same time she held to the same views on the law. In a sermon she delivered there on November 1, 1888, which followed J. H. Waggoner's presentation of the law as the instrument to demonstrate human sin, with Christ as the solution for sin, Ellen White said, "I know it would be dangerous to denounce Dr. Waggoner's position as wholly erroneous. This would please the enemy. I see the beauty of truth in the presentation of the righteousness of Christ in relation to the law as the doctor has placed it before us" (1888 Materials 164). Later in the same message she affirmed that "truth must be presented as it is in Jesus" and "Jesus will reveal to us precious old truths in new light," implying that the emphasis on Jesus Christ was new

light for that presentation of the precious old truth of the law (ibid. 165, 167).

Several brief quotations drawn from a single article published in 1890 may illustrate Mrs. White's presentation about the law following 1888. "The law spoken from Sinai is a transcript of God's character. . . . Our righteousness is found in obedience to God's law through the merits of Jesus Christ. . . . An infinite sacrifice has been made that the moral image of God may be restored to man, through willing obedience to all the commandments of God. . . . Man cannot possibly meet the demands of the law of God in human strength alone. His offerings, his works, will all be tainted with sin. A remedy has been provided in the Saviour, who can give to man the virtue of His merit, and make him colaborer in the great work of salvation. Christ is righteousness, sanctification, and redemption to those who believe in Him, and who follow in His steps. . . . We should dwell on the law and the gospel, showing the relation of Christ to the great standard of righteousness" (RH Feb. 4, 1890).

In the same year she wrote, "We want the sanctification that God Himself gives, and that sanctification comes through doing His law. . . . The only remedy that could be found for fallen man was the death of Christ upon the cross. Thus the penalty of transgression could be paid" (ibid. July 15, 1890).

In writing about the Pharisees' accusation against Jesus for breaking the law, Mrs. White wrote, "They whispered to one another that He was making light of the law. He read their thoughts, and answered them, saying—

" 'Think not that I am come to destroy the law, or the prophets: I am not come to destroy, but to fulfill.' Here Jesus refutes the charge of the Pharisees. His mission to the world is to vindicate the sacred claims of that law which they charge Him with breaking. If the law of God could have been changed or abrogated, then Christ need not have suffered the consequences of our transgression. He came to explain the relation of the law to man, and to illustrate its precepts by His own life of obedience. . . .

"The law is an expression of the thought of God; when received in Christ, it becomes our thought. It lifts us above the power of natural desires and tendencies, above temptations that lead to sin. God desires us to be happy, and He gave us the precepts of the law that in obeying them we might have joy" (DA 307, 308).

B. The Law in the Doctrine of the Seventh-day Adventist Church

The Seventh-day Adventist understanding of the law has been consistent through the years. From the original formulation of principal doctrines in the "1848 Bible Conferences" to the present time the law has been strongly endorsed.

Adventist doctrine makes a clear distinction between the moral law, or Ten Commandments, given by God for all human beings, and the ceremonial law of the ritual system with its regulations governing Jewish religious practice. This distinction requires a basis on which such distinctions can be supported. As with Christian theologians in general, numerous Adventist theologians have addressed the question, among the better known being M. L. Andreasen and Edward Heppenstall. In brief, the conclusion is that while Paul makes clear the cessation of Jewish ceremonial law, in no sense does the apostle suggest abrogation of moral law

as found in the Ten Commandments (Rom. 3:31; 7:7; Gal. 3:21).

At the General Conference session held in Dallas, Texas, in 1980 the delegates reformulated, essentially by extension, the basic Adventist statement of beliefs. Among the 27 statements the eighteenth addresses the law of God, reading: "The great principles of God's law are embodied in the Ten Commandments and exemplified in the life of Christ. They express God's love, will, and purposes concerning human conduct and relationships and are binding upon all people in every age. These precepts are the basis of God's covenant with His people and the standard in God's judgment. Through the agency of the Holy Spirit they point out sin and awaken a sense of need for a Saviour. Salvation is all of grace and not of works, but its fruitage is obedience to the Commandments. This obedience develops Christian character and results in a sense of well-being. It is an evidence of our love for the Lord and our concern for our fellow men. The obedience of faith demonstrates the power of Christ to transform lives, and therefore strengthens Christian witness. (Ex. 20:1-17; Ps. 40:7, 8; Matt. 22:36-40; Deut. 28:1-14; Matt. 5:17-20; Heb. 8:8-10; John 15:7-10; Eph. 2:8-10; 1 John 5:3; Rom. 8:3, 4; Ps. 19:7-14.)"

The teaching of Ellen White and the Adventist Church regarding the law are one and the same. Both are based on and shaped by biblical revelation.

VII. Literature

Andreasen, M. L. *The Faith of Jesus and the Commandments of God.* Washington, D.C.: Review and Herald, 1939.

Bible Readings for the Home Circle. Washington, D.C.: Review and Herald, 1914.

Bunch, Taylor. *The Ten Commandments.* Washington, D.C.: Review and Herald, 1944.

Facts for the Times. 4th ed. Battle Creek, Mich.: Review and Herald, 1893.

Hastings, H. L. *Will the Old Book Stand?* Washington, D.C.: Review and Herald, 1923.

Heppenstall, Edward. "The Covenants and the Law." In *Our Firm Foundation.* Washington, D.C.: Review and Herald, 1953.

Moore, Marvin. *The Gospel vs. Legalism.* Hagerstown, Md.: Review and Herald, 1994.

Nichol, Francis D. *Answers to Objections.* Washington, D.C.: Review and Herald, 1932.

Pelikan, Jaroslav. *The Christian Tradition.* 5 vols. Chicago: University of Chicago Press, 1971-1989.

Pierson, Robert H. *The Secret of Happiness.* Nashville: Southern Pub. Assn., 1958.

Richards, H.M.S. *What Jesus Said.* Nashville:

Southern Pub. Assn., 1957.

Schaff, Philip. *The Creeds of Christendom.* 4th ed. New York: Harper, 1919.

Seventh-day Adventist Bible Students' Source Book. Ed. Don F. Neufeld and Julia Neuffer. Washington, D.C.: Review and Herald, 1962. S.v. "Law."

Seventh-day Adventists Believe . . . A Biblical Exposition of 27 Fundamental Doctrines. Washington, D.C.: Ministerial Association, General Conference of Seventh-day Adventists, 1988.

Source Book for Bible Students. Washington, D.C.: Review and Herald, 1922.

Van Wyk, William. *My Sermon Notes on the Ten Commandments.* Grand Rapids: Baker, 1948.

Vaucher, Alfred F. *L'histoire du salut.* Dammarie-les-Lys, France: Signes des Temps, 1951.

Wilcox, Milton C. *Questions and Answers.* 2 vols. Mountain View, Calif.: Pacific Press, 1919.

The Sabbath

Kenneth A. Strand

Introduction

In both the OT and NT the weekly day for rest and special worship services was the seventh day of the week (Saturday), called the "Sabbath." This word was also applied to certain annual holy or festal days, though its main use was for the seventh day of the week.

In post-NT Christian history the word "sabbath" eventually came to be applied in certain traditions to Sunday, the first day of the week, and is still used by various Sundaykeeping Christians to designate Sunday. In this article, when the word "Sabbath" is spelled with an initial capital letter, it refers to the seventh day of the week.

The Hebrew root from which "sabbath" is derived is *šbt*, whose primary meaning is "to cease" or "desist" from previous activity. The noun form is *šabbāt*, and the verb is *šābat*. Modern English versions usually render the noun as "sabbath" and the verb as "to rest" (or sometimes as "to keep sabbath"). Although these renditions are correct and appropriate, the underlying concept of "cessation" suggests a relation to that which has preceded, rather than simply a recourse for weariness.

A further noun referring to the Sabbath in Exodus and Leviticus is *šabbātôn*, also derived from *šbt*, and often translated "solemn rest." Six of eleven times it appears in the phrase *šabbat šabbātôn* (Ex. 31:15; 35:2; Lev. 16:31; 23:3, 32; 25:4). The occurrence of *šabbāt* and *šabbātôn* together indicates intensification.

In the NT the word for "sabbath" is the Greek *sabbatōn,* or its apparent plural, *sabbata.* However, the latter may be simply a transliteration of the Aramaic *šabbetā,* which is the emphatic state of the singular noun. Thus when the term *sabbata* occurs in the NT, the context must guide as to whether the meaning is singular or plural.

Sometimes *sabbaton* in the NT refers to the entire week. For instance, in Luke 18:12 the Pharisee boasts that he fasts twice *tou sabbatou* (in the week). Also in a number of references the first day of the week is indicated by the numeral "one" with *sabbaton* or *sabbata* (Matt. 28:1; Mark 16:2, 9; Luke 24:1; John 20:1, 19; Acts 20:7; 1 Cor. 16:2), the noun "day" being clearly implied by the use of the feminine form of the numeral.

In Hebrews 4:9, the term *sabbatismos* is correctly translated as "sabbath rest." In this general section of Hebrews (3:7–4:13), which employs the Sabbath as a metaphor for spiritual rest, the noun *katapausis* (rest) also occurs eight times, and the verb *katapauō* three times.

I. The Sabbath in the OT

A. Pentateuch

1. General Overview

For the most part, *šabbāṯ, šāḇaṯ,* and *šabbāṯôn* are used in reference to the seventh day of the week, but various passages in the Pentateuch also utilize this kind of sabbath terminology for certain annual festivals and for the seventh ("sabbatical") year. In some instances it is used in a metaphorical sense as "rest" for the land.

Three passages in the Pentateuch specifi-cally link the seventh-day Sabbath with Creation: Genesis 2:1-3; Exodus 20:11; 31:13-17. A number of other passages refer to rest on the seventh day of the week. In the following discussion the Sabbath texts are analyzed in the order in which they occur in the Pentateuch. (See Creation I. A. 14.)

2. Sabbath References in the Pentateuch

a. Genesis 2:1-3. After a description of God's day-by-day activities during the first six days of Creation week, Genesis 2:1 gives a summary statement that Creation had been completed. Genesis 2:2, 3 states, "And on the seventh day God finished his work which he had done, and he rested on the seventh day from all his work which he had done. So God blessed the seventh day and hallowed it, because on it God rested from all his work which he had done in creation."

Several items in this passage deserve special notice: 1. Although the Hebrew noun *šabbāt* does not occur, the verb *šābat* appears in both instances that refer to God's resting from His work of Creation. 2. The seventh day of the week is prominent, with five references to it, three using the specific expression "seventh day" and two using the pronoun "it." 3. The statement takes the form of a chiasm or inverted parallel statement:

A. God finished his work (verse 2)
  B. And he rested on the seventh day from all his work which he had done (verse 2)
    C. So God blessed the seventh day and hallowed it (verse 3)
  B'. Because on it God rested from all his work which he had done (verse 3)
A'. In creation (verse 3, cont.)

This chiasm's two introductory statements (A and B) call attention to God's creative work and to His resting on the seventh day. The same two thoughts are presented at the conclusion of the chiasm, in reverse order (B' and A'). This leaves at the center of the chiasm (C) the reference to God's blessing and hallowing the seventh day. In a chiasm that takes this A-B-C-B'-A' form, the central item normally represents the text's major focus. Thus in Genesis 2:2, 3 the major focus is the statement that "God blessed the seventh day and hallowed it."

The Hebrew verb used for God's blessing of the seventh day is *bārak*, also used for God's blessing on animals and on humankind (Gen. 1:22, 28). This divine blessing is not static, but continues to have special meaning onward from the time when it is first given. The basic meaning of the Hebrew term translated "hallowed" or "sanctified" (from *qādaš*, "to be holy") is a "separating" or "setting apart" of something in fulfillment of a divine purpose and/or command. Thus the statement that God "hallowed" the seventh day not only distinguishes this day from the other six, but also reinforces the idea of a continuing special meaningfulness of this day for the human beings whom God had created. Something "set apart" has to be more than simply a memory relic of the past; it must have an ongoing significance. This hallowedness of the Sabbath is reiterated in various later Pentateuchal references (e.g., Ex. 16:23; cf. 31:14-16; 35:2) and the basic language of the entire statement in Genesis 2:2, 3 reappears in the Sabbath commandment of Ex. 20:8-11.

b. Exodus 5:5. Exodus 5:5 contains sabbath terminology in the statement "And Pharaoh said, 'Behold, the people of the land are now many and you make them rest *(šābat)* from their burdens!'" While the seventh day of the week is not specifically mentioned, the immediate context implies that this rest had religious significance.

c. Exodus 16. Exodus 16 contains the OT's first use of the Hebrew noun *šabbāt* (verse 23). In fact, in this passage the noun is used four times (verses 23, 25, 26, 29). The setting is the giving of manna to the children of Israel in the Wilderness of Sin two weeks before their arrival at Mount Sinai. According to Exodus 16:5, on the sixth day the Israelites were to gather and bring in "twice as much as they gather daily." Later in the chapter they are informed that on the seventh day no manna would appear (verses 25, 26) and that although the manna gathered on each of the other days would spoil overnight, that which was gathered on the sixth day would keep (verses 19-24). On the seventh day some people went out into the field to look for manna but found none (verse 27). God's response was, "How long do you refuse to keep my commandments and my laws? See! The Lord has given you the sabbath, therefore on the sixth day he gives you bread for two days; remain every man of you in his place, let no man go out of his place on the seventh day" (verses 28, 29). This wording gives the distinct impression that the Sabbath was already known to the Israelites.

d. Exodus 20:8-11. Exodus 20 sets forth the Ten Commandments given by God to Moses at Sinai. In this law the fourth commandment specifies that work should be done six days and that the seventh day is to be observed as a day of rest. The basis for this injunction is that "in six days the Lord made heaven and earth, the sea, and all that is in them, and rested the seventh day; therefore the Lord blessed the sabbath day and hallowed it" (verse 11).

The language used here summarizes the content of Genesis 2:2, 3, leaving no doubt that Exodus 20:11 points to the Creation Sabbath. Also significant is that the Sabbath commandment appears within the ten-commandment law, which in turn was the center of God's covenant. That this ten-commandment law was distinctive, with the other Pentateuchal laws as additions or commentary, is clear from the statement in Deuteronomy 5:22 that to these Ten Commandments God had "added no more"—i.e., the Decalogue was a complete entity in and of itself.

Furthermore, the covenant basis that is set forth in Exodus 20 for keeping the Ten Commandments, including the Sabbath commandment, is redemptive history, or more properly, divine redemption itself. The children of Israel had come into covenant relationship with Yahweh (see Ex. 19). Then in the preamble and historical prologue to the Decalogue, God states the prime element in the redemption which the Israelites had experienced: "I [Yahweh] am the Lord your God, who brought you out of the land of Egypt, out of the house of bondage" (Ex. 20:2). The Israelites had been redeemed from slavery, and this prior goodness of Yahweh provided the foundation for the covenant relationship in which the Israelites were, in turn, to be obedient to God's commandments.

At times the Sabbath and the concept of God's covenant became virtually synonymous (cf. Ex. 31:16). More than any of the other nine precepts of the Decalogue, the Sabbath provided a visible distinctive that set God's people apart from any and all who did not serve Yahweh. Thus in a very real way it embodied the true meaning of covenant relationship with God, for it identified Israel as a people in fellowship with their Creator and Redeemer.

Moreover, the Sabbath commandment is the only one in the Decalogue that has the three distinguishing marks of a seal impression: the *name,* the *office,* and the *domain* of the individual or entity whose authority the seal represents. Thus the Sabbath commandment may be considered the *seal* of the Decalogue. (See also the discussion of the Sabbath as "sign" in connection with Exodus 31:13-17 and Ezekiel 20:12, 20.) The Sabbath commandment is distinctive not only by containing the three essentials of a seal, but also by utilizing a unique introduction, the word "remember." This word may carry several concepts: to remember the Sabbath as an institution that is already time-honored; to remember, because there may be a danger of forgetting; and to remember with a forward look, because the Sabbath is so central to the ongoing covenant experience. Whatever nuance or nuances the term may have had in the context of its original statement at Sinai, one thing is certain: The word "remember" is emphatic as an introduction here, and serves to call special attention to the Sabbath commandment.

e. Exodus 23:12. After a reference to the "sabbatical year" in Exodus 23:10, 11, the following instruction is given concerning the seventh day of the week: "Six days you shall do your work, but on the seventh day you shall rest; that your ox and your ass may have rest, and the son of your bondmaid, and the alien, may be refreshed" (verse 12). For the "rest" commanded to the Israelites in covenant relationship with God, the verb is *šābaṭ,* whereas for the beasts of burden, the type of rest is simply *nûaḥ.* And for the "son of your bondmaid" and for the "alien," the niphal imperfect of *nāpaš*, "to refresh," is used. This Hebrew word does not necessarily imply recovery from weariness, though that element may be included; rather it suggests an enhancement in quality of life or the pleasure of rest from work that has been accomplished well. Thus the Sabbath should be a meaningful spiritual experience for both the Israelite servants and the aliens sojourning among the Israelites.

f. Exodus 31:13-17. In Exodus 31:13-17 we find a statement very similar to those in Genesis 2:2-3 and Exodus 20:11, but with several added features. 1. The keeping of God's Sabbath is a sign, not only of Creation (verse 17), but also of His sanctifying His people (verse 13). 2. The covenant relationship, earlier set forth in the context of the Decalogue (chaps. 19 and 20), is now explicitly applied to the Sabbath and termed "a perpetual covenant" (verse 16). 3. The penalty of death is decreed for profanation of the Sabbath (verses 14, 15). 4. The emphatic terminology *šabbaṯ šabbāṯôn*, "sabbath of solemn rest," is used for the first time (verse 15). 5. In reference to the Creation Sabbath, the statement speaks not only of God's resting, as in Genesis 2:2, 3 and Exodus 20:8-11, but also adds that God "was refreshed" (verse 17), obviously not in the sense of recovery from weariness, but rather as a pleasant relaxation subsequent to, and because of, God's completion of His work in producing a perfect Creation.

The use of the word "sign" in verse 13 is noteworthy. A sign is something that points beyond itself to reveal a more profound reality. With respect to the Sabbath, that reality is twofold: The Sabbath provides an ever-present assurance of God's sanctifying of His people (verse 13), and it serves as a constant reminder of God's Creatorship (verse 17). In both aspects, the *keeping* of the Sabbath is what gives it effectiveness as a sign (verses 13, 16).

g. Exodus 34:21. Exodus 34:21 reads, "Six days you shall work, but on the seventh day

you shall rest; in plowing time and in harvest you shall rest." Here the noun "Sabbath" does not occur, but "the seventh day" is explicitly indicated and the verb for both occurrences of "rest" is *šābaṯ*. That in an agricultural economy the Sabbath was to be kept faithfully during the two most crucial seasons for labor, "plowing time" and "harvest," emphasizes the great sanctity with which God had invested the day.

h. Exodus 35:2, 3. In Exodus 35:2, 3 the term *šabbaṯ šabbāṯôn* is used in a command to observe the seventh day as a "holy sabbath of solemn rest to the Lord." The death sentence for violation is once again decreed, with the added remark that "you shall kindle no fire in all your habitations on the sabbath day." Reference here is obviously to an unnecessary Sabbath task for the Israelites.

i. The book of Leviticus. Although the book of Leviticus has more occurrences of the terms *šabbāṯ* and *šabbāṯôn* than the other books of the Pentateuch combined, comparatively few of these refer specifically to the weekly Sabbath. References that do so are 19:3, 30; 23:3, 38; 24:8; and 26:2.

In 19:3, 30 and 26:2 the simple command is given, "You shall keep my sabbaths." In the first instance it occurs after a reference to the honoring of parents, and in the last two instances it precedes the expression "and reverence my sanctuary: I am the Lord." Leviticus 23:3 states briefly, "Six days shall work be done; but on the seventh day is a sabbath of solemn rest [*šabbaṯ šabbāṯôn*], a holy convocation; you shall do no work; it is a sabbath [*šabbāṯ*] to the Lord in all your dwellings." This text gives evidence that the Sabbath was not only to be a "solemn rest" but also a "holy convocation." The remainder of Leviticus 23 is devoted primarily to annual feasts, which are declared to be "besides the sabbaths of the Lord" (verse 38). Leviticus 24:5-8 specifies that each week on the Sabbath Aaron should replace the showbread in the sanctuary.

In Leviticus 16:31 the annual Day of Atonement is referred to as *šabbaṭ šabbāṭôn*. Also, in chapter 23 this day and various other annual days are set forth as "sabbaths" or "days of solemn rest." For four of these the sabbath terminology used is *šabbāṭôn* or *šabbaṭ šabbāṭôn:* the first day of the seventh month (the blowing of trumpets), the tenth day of the seventh month (Day of Atonement), and the first and eighth days of the feast of booths (23:24, 25, 27-32, 34, 36). The first and seventh days of the Feast of Unleavened Bread and the day of Pentecost may also have been considered as sabbaths, though the Essene and Boethusian traditions in later Judaism interpreted the references to "sabbath" in verses 11, 15, and 16 to be weekly seventh-day Sabbaths. On all of the annual holy days, except for the Day of Atonement, no "laborious work" was to be done, but a stronger prohibition applied to that day: "No work" should be done (verse 28).

In Leviticus 25:2-6 sabbath language is again used, but the references are to the "sabbatical year." In Leviticus 26 several references to "sabbaths" (verses 34 [twice], 35, 43) are metaphorical, designating the future time when the covenant people of Israel, if disobedient, would be taken captive, so that the land could enjoy "sabbaths." In addition to the plural noun, the verb *šābaṭ* is also used, indicating that the land would have "rest" (verses 34, 35).

j. The book of Numbers. The book of Numbers refers to the weekly Sabbath in two contexts. In 15:32-36 an account is given of a man gathering sticks on the Sabbath and consequently suffering the death penalty for what was obviously a flagrant violation of Sabbath regulations. In 28:9, 10 there is a stipulation that on the Sabbath two one-year-old male lambs were to be sacrificed as a burnt offering in addition to the regular daily burnt offering.

k. Deuteronomy 5:12-15. The final Pentateuchal reference to the Sabbath occurs in Deuteronomy 5:12-15. Here Moses reiterates the Sabbath command in wording quite similar to that in Exodus 20:8-11, except for one main feature: Instead of a reference to the Creation Sabbath, the rationale for observing the Sabbath is God's rescue of the Israelites from slavery in Egypt. "You shall remember that you were a servant in the land of Egypt, and the Lord your God brought you out thence with a mighty hand and an outstretched arm; therefore the Lord your God commanded you to keep the sabbath day" (verse 15).

Some commentators take this statement to be evidence that the Sabbath was a relatively new institution, adopted by Israel on the basis of the Exodus, and not connected with a Creation Sabbath at all. Such a conclusion is unwarranted for several reasons: 1. The language used in verse 15 indicates that this verse represents Moses' own elaboration of the Decalogue. 2. The book of Deuteronomy itself is a recital of Israel's wilderness experience, and this context makes a reference to the deliverance from Egyptian slavery particularly appropriate. 3. The mention of Israel's rescue from Egyptian bondage in no way negates the fact that Israel was well aware of the Sabbath as a Creation institution, a fact evidenced in Exodus 20:11 and 31:17. 4. The deliverance-from-Egypt motif in connection with the Decalogue is not new in Deuteronomy 5, for it had already occurred in conjunction with the giving of the Decalogue in Exodus 20 (see I. A. 2. d).

Yahweh's deliverance of Israel from Egyptian bondage was the redemptive act that gave evidence of His prior goodness and provided the basis for the covenant relationship between Him and His people. The preamble and historical prologue set forth in Exodus 20:1, 2 are repeated in Deuteronomy 5:6: "I am the Lord your God, who brought you out of the land of Egypt, out of the house of bondage." In extant ancient political covenants which have this same type of form, the suzerain's prior relationship to the vassal ruler (and/or forebears), including raising the vassal to kingship, was foundational for the vassal's commitments to the suzerain. Similarly Yahweh's prior goodness to the Israelites was foundational for their commitments to Him as stipulated in the Ten Commandments. It should not come as a surprise, therefore, that Moses should set forth as a basis for keeping the Sabbath commandment the fact that Yahweh had brought the Israelites out of Egypt "with a mighty hand and an outstretched arm" (Deut. 5:15). The specific mention of this comes, moreover, in the normal flow of Moses' thought, for after his reiteration of the part of the Sabbath commandment requiring that strangers and servants be allowed to rest (verse 14), he immediately gives the counsel, "You shall remember that you were a servant in the land of Egypt" (verse 15).

In this reiteration of the Decalogue Moses declares the definitive nature of the Decalogue as a discrete and complete entity. In Deuteronomy 5:22 Moses states that when God had spoken the Ten Commandments, He "added no more." Furthermore, the standing of the Decalogue as the one and only body of apodictic law (broad statements of principles, universal in character) in the Pentateuch also sets it apart as unique, particularly so when it is compared with the Pentateuch's multitude of "case-law" instructions. God chose to make the Sabbath an integral part of the "moral law," thus emphasizing and enshrining its moral nature. For any human being to separate it from the other nine commandments of the Decalogue or to declare it to be "ceremonial" flies in the face of what God Himself has proclaimed.

B. Historical Books, Psalms, and Prophets

In Israel's OT history subsequent to that covered in the Pentateuch, references to the Sabbath are comparatively fewer than in the books of Moses. However, the evidence for Israel's continuing observance of the seventh day of the week as the Sabbath is clear and has not been seriously disputed by modern OT scholarship. In the following synopsis, we follow a basically chronological presentation of the biblical data.

1. Eleventh- and Tenth-Century References

The earliest post-Pentateuchal references to Sabbath observance are found in 1 and 2 Chronicles. Samuel the prophet and David established various persons "in their office of trust" (1 Chron. 9:22). Among these were certain Kohathites who "had charge of the showbread, to prepare it every Sabbath" (verse 32). Again, when David "was old and full of days," he "assembled all the leaders of Israel and the priests and the Levites" (23:1, 2), arranging various temple duties (23:1–28:21). In this context, there is reference to burnt offerings to the Lord "on sabbaths, new moons, and feast days" (23:31). The same days are mentioned in Solomon's communication with Hiram of Tyre for help in building the Temple (2 Chron. 2:4). After the Temple was built and dedicated, Solomon offered the required offerings on those same days (8:13). Thus there is evidence of liturgical continuity with the Pentateuchal prescriptions that distinguished the three categories of "holy convocations" from the ordinary days.

2. Ninth-Century References

Two ninth-century Sabbath references appear in 2 Kings. The first of these (2 Kings 4:18-37) reports that when the son of a Shunammite couple died suddenly, the mother requested that her husband provide a donkey and a servant so that she could travel to visit the prophet Elisha. Not knowing that their son was dead, the father queried, "Why will you go to him [Elisha] today? It is neither new moon nor sabbath" (verse 23). This oblique reference to the Sabbath thus provides evidence for the religious nature of that day. It was obviously a day considered especially appropriate for visits to God's prophets.

The second reference, 2 Kings 11:4-20 (cf. 2 Chron. 23:1-11), reports the coup d'état organized by Jehoiada, the high priest, in which he overthrew Athaliah and placed 7-year-old Joash on the throne. The day was the Sabbath, at the time of the changing of the temple guard. This was a propitious time from the standpoint of having a double contingent of guards present for the coup. Moreover, the coup itself had spiritual dimensions in its ejection of Baal-promoting Athaliah, daughter of Ahab and Jezebel, and in its religious consecration of the new king as he stood by one of the two pillars at the temple entrance (verse 14).

3. Eighth-Century References

a. Historical literature. The earliest eighth-century reference to the Sabbath in the OT historical literature is a notation in 2 Kings 16:18 of King Ahaz' removal of the "covered way for the sabbath which had been built inside the palace." This, along with acts of desecration in the Temple itself (cf. verse 17), was "because of the king of Assyria" (verse 18) and thus a part of the apostasy of Ahaz under Assyrian influence. In 2 Chronicles 31:3, in connection with the great reform accomplished by Hezekiah, the king provided the "burnt offerings for the sabbaths, the new moons, and the appointed feasts."

b. Rebukes by the prophets Amos, Hosea, and Isaiah. Three of the earliest writing prophets—Amos, Hosea, and Isaiah—make pertinent references to the Sabbath. Amos, in his rebuke to the evildoers in the Northern Kingdom, quotes them as asking when the Sabbath would be over, "that we may offer wheat for sale, that we may make the ephah small and the shekel great, and deal deceitfully with false balances" (Amos 8:5). Hosea, too, brings an indictment against Israel, quoting the Lord as saying, "I will put an end to all her mirth, her feasts, her new moons, her sabbaths, and all her appointed feasts" (Hosea 2:11). Isaiah, in a sweeping complaint to Judah for mere formalistic religion, declares in a similar vein, "Bring no more vain offerings; incense is an abomination to me. New moon and sabbath and the calling of assemblies—I cannot endure iniquity and solemn assembly" (Isa. 1:13).

Amos, Hosea, and Isaiah thus provide evidence that Sabbath observance was considered normative for God's people in both Israel and Judah. The people in both kingdoms were, however, performing a heartless type of religious practice that included mere formalistic Sabbath observance.

c. Positive references in Isaiah. Isaiah furnishes some beautiful discussions of genuine Sabbathkeeping. The first of these, in Isaiah 56:2-8, takes the form of an extended beatitude. It pronounces a blessing upon the person "who keeps the sabbath, not profaning it, and keeps his hand from doing any evil" (verse 2). Then it reaches out to encompass foreigners and eunuchs (verses 3-7). The eunuchs who keep God's Sabbaths and hold fast to His covenant will receive "a monument and a name better than sons and daughters" (verse 5), and the foreigners "who join themselves to the Lord" and keep the Sabbath will be made joyful in God's house of prayer (verses 6, 7).

In Isaiah 58:13, 14, the Sabbath is mentioned within the context of a passage that expresses what a true fast involves. The specific Sabbath statement reads as follows:

"If you turn back your foot from the sabbath, from doing your pleasure on my holy day, and call the sabbath a delight and the holy day of the Lord honorable; if you honor it, not going your own ways, or seeking your own pleasure, or talking idly; then you shall take delight in the Lord, and I will make you ride upon the heights of the earth; I will feed you with the heritage of Jacob your father, for the mouth of the Lord has spoken."

Here the Sabbath is set forth as a day that God's people are to honor. They are to refrain from doing their own pleasure on that day. And God promises that He will, in turn, provide them with rich spiritual and temporal blessings. The expressions "my holy day" and "the holy day of the Lord" have a parallel in the term "my sabbaths" in Isaiah 56:4.

Isaiah's final reference to the Sabbath appears in 66:22, 23. Here an assurance is given concerning the future: "For as the new heaven and the new earth which I will make shall remain before me, says the Lord; so shall your descendants and your name remain. From new moon to new moon, and from sabbath to sabbath, all flesh shall come to worship before me, says the Lord."

4. Late-Seventh- and Sixth-Century References

a. Jeremiah. The prophet Jeremiah, whose prophetic ministry spanned some four decades from c. 626 to 586 B.C., reminded Judah's royalty and people that on the Sabbath they should refrain from carrying burdens into Jerusalem, from bearing burdens out of their dwellings, and from doing any work, as God had commanded their forebears (17:21, 22). He promised glory and longevity for Jerusalem for obedience, and threatened a devouring, unquenchable fire to the city's palaces for disobedience (verses 24-27).

Destruction did come to Jerusalem. In three campaigns Nebuchadnezzar subdued Judah, deported its inhabitants, and destroyed the temple. In this setting we find Jeremiah's one further clear reference to the Sabbath: The "Lord has brought to an end in Zion appointed feast and sabbath, and in his fierce indignation has spurned king and priest" (Lam. 2:6).

b. Ezekiel. Ezekiel, exiled to Babylon, refers repeatedly to Sabbathbreaking in contexts that also mention other aspects of apostasy. In Ezekiel 20:12-24 the prophet brings out forcefully the intent and effect of true Sabbathkeeping: "Moreover I gave them my sabbaths, as a sign between me and them, that they might know that I the Lord sanctify them" (verse 12); and "hallow my sabbaths that they may be a sign between me and you, that you may know that I the Lord am your God" (verse 20). These statements are in a context that reiterates Israel's wilderness experience at the time of the Exodus; thus they provide an obvious linkage to Exodus 31:13-17, where the Sabbath is referred to as a "sign" of God's sanctification of His people and of His Creatorship. They also reiterate the basic Pentateuchal emphasis on the Sab-

bath as a holy day (Ex. 20:8-11; Lev. 23:3) and on Israel as a holy nation or holy people (Ex. 19:6; Lev. 19:2).

In addition to reaffirming the meaning of the Sabbath as a "sign" (Ex. 31:13-17; see I. A. 2. f), Ezekiel has added an item: *knowledge* that the Lord sanctifies His people (20:12) and that Yahweh is their God (verse 20). This knowledge surely includes an intellectual awareness, but a far richer meaning also resides within the term: It includes and evidences the concept of a close *personal relationship.* For the ancient Hebrew, the matter of "knowing" involved first and foremost a relationship. And thus Ezekiel 20:12, 20 sets forth—indeed, instructs and commands—a deep, genuine, and continuing spiritual encounter between God and His people that bonds them to Him in the closest possible personal relationship.

Several further references to the Sabbath occur in Ezekiel's "ideal-temple" section in chapters 40-48. Here, "the Levitical priests, the sons of Zadok" (44:15), "shall keep my [God's] sabbaths holy" (verse 24). The prince was to furnish "the burnt offerings, cereal offerings, and drink offerings, at the feasts, the new moons, and the sabbaths" (45:17). Finally, on Sabbaths and at the time of new moons, the "gate of the inner court that faces east"—a gate "shut on the six working days"—was to be opened for worship and for the appropriate liturgical activities (46:1-3).

5. Fifth-Century References: Nehemiah

Nehemiah, the Jewish leader after the return from Babylon, makes three references to the Sabbath. The first is in a penitential prayer affirming that God had given to Israel "right ordinances and true laws, good statutes and commandments," and had made known to them the "holy sabbath," as well as "statutes and a law by Moses" (9:13, 14). This statement shows recognition, as late as the fifth century, of a distinction between the commandments that God gave directly, including the Sabbath, and the ordinances that God gave through Moses. This distinction was blurred in later Judaism.

The other two references are in connection with a Sabbath reform. The people promised to desist from engaging in commerce with the "peoples of the land" on the Sabbath and other holy days. They likewise promised to maintain the service of God's house, including the offerings for "the sabbaths, the new moons, the appointed feasts" (10:31-33). Later, when Nehemiah saw agricultural products prepared and traded on the Sabbath (13:15, 16), he ordered the city gates of Jerusalem closed "when it began to be dark . . . before the sabbath," and not opened "until after the sabbath" (verse 19).

II. The Sabbath in the NT

A. Gospels

The NT presents important information about Sabbath theology and Sabbathkeeping. In particular, the teachings and practice of Jesus reveal the fundamentals that should guide His followers in regard to the Sabbath. In this section we review the main instances wherein Jesus taught by example, by word, and through miracles of healing the essence of true Sabbath observance. In evaluating Jesus' Sabbath conflicts with the Jews, in which He even faced the charge of Sabbath-breaking, we must be aware of what was at stake: the question of the validity of the "oral law." The Sabbath disputes arose, not over matters prohibited in the OT, but in connection with the traditions that had developed during intertestamental times (see V. A. 2).

A basic principle enunciated by Jesus was that He came not to destroy the law and the prophets but to fulfill them (Matt. 5:17, 18). This principle was exemplified in His treatment of the Sabbath and other stipulations of the Decalogue, such as honoring one's parents and refraining from murder (verses 21, 22; 15:3-6). His whole attitude was one of exalting the divine law; but this caused Him to come into conflict with Jewish additions to, and interpretations of, that law. His Sabbath activities and teaching, as portrayed in the four Gospels, reveal a recapturing of the original intent of the Sabbath by returning to its full, inward, spiritual meaning.

Some of the references to the Sabbath in the four Gospels involve no controversy of Christ with the scribes and Pharisees, whereas others reveal some sort of polemical setting and/or aftermath.

1. The Sabbath in Noncontroversial Settings

a. Jesus' synagogue attendance. Jesus attended the synagogue on the Sabbath (Mark 1:21; 6:2; Luke 4:16, 31; 13:10). According to Luke 4:16, His "custom" was to go to the synagogue on the Sabbath. By synagogue attendance, Jesus manifested His positive attitude toward the Sabbath as a time for "holy convocation" (Lev. 23:3).

b. Sabbath counsel in Matthew 24:20. A statement in Jesus' eschatological discourse recorded in Matthew 24 indicates the same sort of positive Sabbath emphasis. In predicting the time when Roman armies would take Jerusalem, Jesus urged His disciples, "Pray that your flight may not be in winter or on a sabbath" (verse 20). The hardship of winter is readily understandable, but why would the Sabbath be mentioned? It is sometimes suggested that flight on the Sabbath would be difficult because of Jewish interference; however, if the Jews were occupied in warfare the Sabbath would be a propitious time to leave the city. Nor is there cogency to the concept that the "Sabbath-day's journey" would be a hindrance, for the type of Sabbathkeeping set forth in the Gospels implies Christian rejection of this extrabiblical device (moreover, even Rabbinic tradition allowed flight for the purpose of saving life). The implication of the text is that the disciples should pray that their flight not be on the Sabbath to avoid an experience that would diminish their ability to engage in normal Sabbathkeeping and thus lessen their sense of Sabbath sacredness.

c. Sabbathkeeping when Jesus was in the tomb. Luke 23:54-56 provides an example of Sabbathkeeping on the day that Jesus was in the tomb. The women noted where His body was laid, then "prepared spices and ointments," and on the Sabbath "rested according to the commandment." They waited until early on "the first day of the week" to return to the tomb to anoint the body, but found it empty (Luke 24:1-3). The "commandment" that they had observed was obviously the Sabbath commandment of the Decalogue. Their continued Sabbath observance at the time of Jesus' death indicates that they followed His own example of Sabbathkeeping. It also undercuts the theory that Jesus had a negative attitude to the Sabbath that supposedly provided a basis for later rejection of the Sabbath.

d. Earliest recorded healings. The earliest recorded examples of healings by Jesus on the Sabbath appear not to have raised any controversy. Both Mark and Luke describe the healing of a demoniac who interrupted the synagogue service in Capernaum on a Sabbath (Mark 1:21-28; Luke 4:31-37). Later, evidently on the same Sabbath, Jesus also healed Peter's mother-in-law of a high fever (Matt. 8:14, 15; Mark 1:29-31; Luke 4:38, 39). More healings followed after sundown (Matt. 8:16; Mark 1:32-34; Luke 4:40).

2. Sabbath Incidents Involving Controversy

a. Plucking grain on the Sabbath. The first Sabbath conflict recorded in the three Synoptic Gospels relates to whether it was lawful for Jesus' disciples to pluck wheat heads on the Sabbath (Matt. 12:1-8; Mark 2:23-28; Luke 6:1-5). The disciples picked heads of wheat and ate them after "rubbing them in their hands" (Luke 6:1). While the OT allowed persons going through a grainfield to so engage themselves to satisfy their hunger, the Pharisees challenged Jesus.

According to the oral law (later codified in the Mishnah and Talmuds), Jesus' disciples were guilty regarding two main categories of work prohibited on the Sabbath: reaping and threshing (see V. A. 2). Jesus defended the disciples, calling attention to David's eating showbread when he was hungry, and He referred also to the fact that the priests in the Temple did extra work on the Sabbath and were guiltless (Matt. 12:3-5). Likewise, His disciples now were guiltless. Jesus further stated, "I tell you, something greater than the temple is here" (verse 6), and also indicated that the Sabbath was made for man, not vice versa (Mark 2:27). All three Synoptics conclude with the forceful statement of Jesus that "the Son of man is lord of the sabbath" (Matt. 12:8; Mark 2:28; Luke 6:5; see Creation II. C).

b. Sabbath healings in the Synoptics. In Matthew 12:9-13, Mark 3:1-5, and Luke 6:6-10, there is record of the healing of an individual whose right hand was withered. The regulations as later codified in the Mishnah allowed that a sick or injured person could be treated on the Sabbath, but only if the situation was life-threatening. This case was chronic, and obviously not covered by this provision. Hence the scribes and Pharisees asked Jesus, " 'Is it lawful to heal on the sabbath?' so that they might accuse him" (Matt. 12:10; Luke 6:7). Jesus responded by asking, "What man of you, if he has one sheep and it falls into a pit on the sabbath, will not lay hold of it and lift it out?" (Matt. 12:11). Since rabbinical regulations allowed this, the basic question put to the Pharisees was whether less should be done for a human being (verse 12). Jesus confronted the Pharisees with an even stronger query: "Is it lawful on the sabbath to do good or to do harm, to save life or to kill?" (Mark 3:4). For them to omit doing good was considered doing evil. So the failure to heal the man with a withered hand would be contrary to their own basic principles. Jesus "looked around at them with anger, grieved at their hardness of heart" and healed the withered hand (verse 5).

Two further healings that raised questions are recorded by Luke: the "woman who had

had a spirit of infirmity for eighteen years" and the man with dropsy (13:10-17 and 14:1-6). In connection with these healings, Jesus again referred to the more humane treatment of animals on the Sabbath than what the scribes and Pharisees were willing to allow for human beings.

c. Sabbath healings in John. Two of Jesus' Sabbath healings are recorded only in the Gospel of John: in 5:2-9 that of a lame man at the Pool of Bethzatha (Bethesda), and in chapter 9 that of a man born blind. In the first case, Jesus healed the man and commanded him, "Rise, take up your pallet, and walk" (5:8). The man arose and did exactly as he was told (verse 9), thus demonstrating that his healing was real and complete. This activity led to controversy with the Jews (verses 10-16), inasmuch as the healed man had broken the law pertaining to bearing a burden on the Sabbath, one of the 39 main classes of work later codified in the Mishnah. Jesus put this healing action within the context of "My Father is working still, and I am working" (verse 17). God was constantly active in sustaining the universe and also in the work of redemption of human beings. Jesus claimed simply, but forcefully, that He was participating in this ongoing divine redemptive activity, an activity fully compatible with the intent of the Sabbath. (See Creation II. C.)

That more than physical healing was involved is evident by the words of Jesus when He later found the man in the Temple, "Sin no more, that nothing worse befall you" (verse 14). The wellness of the man involved a spiritual dimension along with the physical. The same dynamic is revealed by Jesus' healing of the paralytic in Capernaum (Matt. 9:1-7; Mark 2:1-12; Luke 5:17-25), whose sins Jesus forgave, giving evidence "that the Son of man has authority on earth to forgive sins" (Matt. 9:6). The message is precisely the same as the one proclaimed in the healing of the lame man at the Pool of Bethzatha. These miracles were thus a proclamation of Jesus' divinity and Messiahship.

In the case of the healing of the man born blind, the Pharisees accused Jesus of not keeping the Sabbath (John 9:16). But again, what Jesus had failed to observe was the Pharisaical rules of Sabbathkeeping, not Scriptural injunctions. Indeed, Jesus called this miracle a work of God (verse 3). Just before performing this healing, Jesus spoke words very similar in meaning to those He had pronounced in connection with the healing at Bethzatha. Now He said, "We must work the works of him [the Father] who sent me, while it is day" (verse 4). This miracle revealed again Christ's participation in the work of God the Father, and thus Jesus here too called attention to Himself as the Messiah, through whom divine grace and blessing are bestowed.

3. Significance of Jesus' Sabbath Healings

a. Reasons for the Sabbath healings. Jesus could have restricted His healing miracles to days other than the Sabbath, but He did not. In fact, the Gospels appear to place a special emphasis on the Sabbath healings, which engendered controversy with the Jews. Through them Jesus taught lessons about true Sabbathkeeping. More fundamentally, by these miracles He called attention to His divinity, to His oneness with the Father, and to His work of salvation. The controversy over Sabbath healings gave a heightened opportunity for Jesus to teach the vital truths pertaining to His salvific work. Moreover, that the two Sabbath healings mentioned by John took place in Jerusalem at the time of annual feasts enhanced Jesus' opportunity to proclaim truths vital for the salvation of human beings.

b. Healings as a proclamation of Jesus' mission. The two Sabbath healings recorded by John are noteworthy because of the discussion that followed and because they were links in a progression of events affirming Jesus' mission. When Jesus healed the lame man at the pool of Bethzatha and proclaimed that both He and His Father were working, the Jews understood this as a claim to equality with God and "sought all the more to kill him"

(John 5:18). Jesus put forth a number of significant points: (1) The Son does the same things that the Father does (verse 19); (2) "the Father loves the Son, and shows him all that he himself is doing; and greater works than these will he show him" (verse 20); (3) "as the Father raises the dead and gives them life, so also the Son gives life to whom he will" (verse 21); (4) the Father, who has life in Himself "has granted the Son also to have life in himself" (verse 26); (5) the Father "has given all judgment to the Son" (verse 22); (6) the person "who does not honor the Son does not honor the Father who sent him" (verse 23); and (7) those who hear Christ's word and come to Him have "eternal life" (verse 24; cf. verses 39, 40).

Jesus' teaching here, as in the following chapters, is that real life, "eternal life," is available to human beings and that they can receive it only through Him. This is, in fact, the basic message introduced by John at the outset of his Gospel: "In him was life, and the life was the light of men" (John 1:4).

"Eternal life," which has Christ as its one and only Source, is what Jesus' Sabbath healings are really about. In Jesus' discourse at the Pool of Bethzatha the term itself occurs twice (John 5:24, 39) and recurs in later chapters (John 6:27, 40, 47, 54, 68; 10:28; 17:2, 3). Jesus made clear that this abundant life (John 10:10)—a life of fullness, wholeness, richness— begins *now* qualitatively for those who accept Him and His salvation (see John 5:24). Christ also gives assurance that this life will be extended into eternity when He raises the dead "at the last day" (John 6:40; also cf. 5:28, 29; 6:39, 40, 54; 1 Cor. 15:51-54; 1 Thess. 4:16, 17).

B. Acts, Epistles, and Revelation

1. Acts

The evidence of the book of Acts indicates that after Jesus' resurrection the apostles continued to observe the Sabbath. In Antioch in Pisidia (in Asia Minor), Paul and Barnabas attended and participated in synagogue worship services two weeks in succession (Acts 13:14, 42-44). Some years later, during Paul's second missionary journey, Paul and Silas met on the Sabbath with a group of women gathered by the riverside in Philippi (16:12, 13).

When Paul reached Thessalonica, he went into the synagogue "as was his custom" (17:2; an expression similar to the one about Jesus in Luke 4:16). On the three Sabbaths that he was in Thessalonica he expounded "from the scriptures, explaining and proving that it was necessary for the Christ to suffer and to rise from the dead" (17:2, 3; RSV translates *sabbata* in verse 2 as "weeks" instead of "sabbaths," but since the account refers to Paul's activity in the synagogue, the translation "sabbaths" or "sabbath days" is undoubtedly correct).

Later Paul worked in Corinth for a year and a half (18:1-18). During the week he engaged in his occupation as a tentmaker (verse 3), but "in the synagogue every sabbath" he argued and "persuaded Jews and Greeks" (verse 4). However, during part of his stay in Corinth he taught "the word of God" (verse 11) in the house of Titius Justus because of the Jewish opposition he encountered in the synagogue (verses 6, 7).

The book of Acts thus records a number of instances of Sabbath observance by Paul and his companions. On the other hand, there is no account of these apostles having ever observed the first day of the week for worship services. Two references that have been suggested as evidence for regular Sunday worship services—Acts 20:7 and 1 Corinthians 16:2—are really nothing of the kind. The first actually refers to a night meeting for a special occasion (according to biblical reckoning, Saturday night); and the second suggests that money be laid aside *at home* (not in the church or synagogue) for a collection to be gathered later.

2. Epistles

Only two references in the NT Epistles use the word "Sabbath" (though with different Greek words, as we will note below):

Colossians 2:16 and Hebrews 4:9.

a. Colossians 2:14-17. Modern scholars recognize that Colossians 2:2-23 is polemic against heretical teachings, possibly gnostic in nature (see especially verses 8-11, 18-23). In this context we find a reference to God "having canceled the bond which stood against us" (verse 14) and the injunction therefore to "let no one pass judgment on you in questions of food and drink or with regard to a festival or a new moon or a sabbath," which "are only a shadow of what is to come," with "the substance" belonging to Christ (verses 16, 17).

Some versions translate the sabbath reference as "sabbath days." Whether the Greek used here, *sabbatōn,* is plural or singular is not clear. Many commentators have suggested that the text refers to the "sabbaths" or holy days of the Mosaic "ceremonial law," not to the weekly Sabbath.

Such commentators and interpreters, however, generally have not grappled with the fact that the reference in Colossians 2:16 seems comparable to the repeated OT references to a trilogy in the pattern of annual-monthly-weekly observances (in that order or in the reverse). It is not absolutely certain, of course, that the heresy at Colossae involved this threefold group of celebration days, therefore the terminology here might not be comparable to that of the OT. It is also possible that Paul was using the common literary device of inverted parallelism, thus moving from annual to monthly and then back again to annual festivals.

In any case, what must not be overlooked is the fact that the very context in which the trilogy of terms is mentioned in Colossians deals, not with days per se, but with *ceremonies.* The text refers to temporal celebrations in which "food and drink" were present. In short, Colossians is here dealing with a ceremonialism that had lost sight of Christ, who is the very substance to which the OT ceremonies pointed.

It is striking too that in the OT references to the trilogy of celebrations invariably deal, not with the observance of the days, but with the way in which those holy days were related to specifications of the "ceremonial law" (1 Chron. 23:31; 2 Chron. 2:4; 8:13; 31:3; Isa. 1:11-14; Eze. 45:17). A misguided emphasis on ceremony and a self-satisfaction with formalism could lead to a meaningless religious exercise, whether in OT or NT times. Colossians 2:16, 17 gives precisely the same kind of message as Isaiah 1:11-14; in neither case is the sanctity of God's appointed weekly day of worship in question. What is under attack in both instances is only a heartless "ceremonialism," with Colossians going on to countermand the judgmentalism of some advocates of now-obsolete ceremonial observances.

Thus the *sabbatōn* reference in Colossians 2:16 neither suggests nor implies that the seventh-day Sabbath itself was abolished. Moreover, the well-attested Sabbath practice of the apostles flies in the face of any and all attempts to use Colossians 2:16 as an evidence that the seventh-day Sabbath had been abrogated.

b. Hebrews 3:7–4:13. In the section of the book of Hebrews 3:7 through 4:13 the term *katapausis* occurs eight times (3:11, 18; 4:1, 3 [twice], 5, 10, 11), and the verb *katapauō* occurs three times (4:4, 8, 10). All are usually rendered "rest." The word *sabbatismos* occurs once (4:9), rendered "sabbath rest." Thus the idea of "rest," including "sabbath rest," is obviously a key concept here. This passage in Hebrews constitutes a hortatory/homiletical exposition of Psalm 95:7-11, which refers to the failure of the Israelites in their wilderness wanderings. Their failure led, in turn, to God's oath that they would not enter His rest.

This particular line of thought in the psalm is introduced by the appeal, "O that today you would hearken to his voice! Harden not your hearts, as at Meribah" (verses 7, 8). This statement is foundational to the entire passage in Hebrews (see 3:8, 13, 15; 4:7), with the word "rest" being used metaphorically to represent the salvation experience in Christ (cf. Matt. 11:28-30). This "rest" may also include a further, eschatological fulfillment. The book of Hebrews, in common with other NT literature, places stress both on the present faith experience and on the time of ultimate rewards (see Heb. 10:25 and Heb. 11).

In Hebrews 4:4, allusion is made to God's resting from His work at the time of Creation; the reference to the Sabbath (4:9, 10) draws upon this: "So then, there remains a sabbath rest for the people of God; for whoever enters God's rest also ceases from his labors as God did from his." Various interpretations have been given as to what is meant here by "sabbath rest." Because of the strong emphasis on patterning after God's example, some have claimed that it refers to Sabbathkeeping. On the other hand, it has been unwisely used to bolster weekly Sunday observance, in spite of the fact that Sunday is nowhere mentioned in the passage. The "another day" of verse 8 is not Sunday, but clearly refers to a *time* that is future to that of Joshua and the Conquest of Canaan.

In view of the "rest" concept within the entire pericope, those who interpret the statement about "sabbath rest" in a metaphorical sense appear to be doing the best justice to what is intended. Unfortunately and incorrectly, some exegetes have argued that because the Sabbath rest is here used metaphorically to typify an experience in Christ, this must be evidence that the weekly Sabbath had been abrogated. More cogent, however, is the opposite view, for unless the weekly Sabbath was indeed being observed by the addressees of the book of Hebrews, the force of the homiletical/theological argument would be lost. Thus although Hebrews 4:9, 10 does not deal primarily with Sabbath observance, it does provide indirect corroboration of apostolic observance of the seventh day of the week.

3. Revelation

Revelation 1:10 uses the expression "Lord's day" to designate the day when John received his vision on the Isle of Patmos. This term obviously stands in contrast with the Roman emperor's days: It exalts the Lord Jesus Christ over Domitian, who had banished John to Patmos and who enjoyed having himself referred to as "Lord and God."

Many interpreters have concluded that this was the first day of the week, or Sunday. However, not until about a century later do we find the earliest example of "Lord's day" used in a patristic source to signify the weekly Christian Sunday (see V. B. 2. b). Methodologically, it is not sound to read this usage back into the NT, where there is no prior or contemporary evidence for it. The Gospel of John, dating to perhaps a few years from the writing of Revelation and which should therefore be a particularly helpful source, consistently uses the designation "first day of the week" for Sunday. Not once does it use "Lord's day," a strange phenomenon if "Lord's day" were already the Christian designation for Sunday.

A minority of interpreters claim that John was carried in vision to the end-time, and that this is the meaning of his use of "Lord's day." There is no linguistic basis for such usage (the expression differs from "day of the Lord" and "day of Christ"). Moreover, since the first vision and several of the others have at least their initial sections pertaining to John's own day, it is untenable to invest the term "Lord's day" in Revelation 1:10 with future eschatological implications.

Several lines of evidence indicate, instead, that the seventh-day Sabbath was the "Lord's day" of Revelation 1:10: 1. This day had consistently been honored by Christ and His apostles through attendance at worship services; additionally, it was the day of which Christ expressly called Himself Lord (Matt. 12:8; Mark 2:28; Luke 6:5). 2. The book of Revelation is immersed in OT language and imagery, and therefore there may be special relevance for Revelation 1:10 in the fact that the OT refers to the Sabbath as

God's holy day (Isa. 56:4; 58:13; Eze. 20:12, 13, 16, 20, 21, 24; 22:8, 26; 23:38). Revelation shows a particular closeness to basic concepts and imagery in Ezekiel, and it is significant that Ezekiel is the OT prophet who most repetitively used the phrase "my [God's] sabbaths." 3. The message of the first angel of Revelation 14:6, 7 emphasizes Creation language that is similar to that in the Sabbath commandment of the Decalogue; this message is also linked with the psalm of praise ordered by King David at the time when the ark containing the Ten Commandments was brought to Jerusalem (see 1 Chron. 16:7-36). 4. The emphasis of the book of Revelation on the commandments of God (cf. Rev. 12:17; 14:12) suggests the totality of God's requirements, including Sabbath observance.

C. Summary of the NT Evidence

The NT evidence reveals that Christ and His apostles regularly honored the seventh-day Sabbath by attending "holy convocations" (usually in synagogues). Moreover, nowhere in the NT is there evidence of any other day being honored as a day of worship. Furthermore, there is no evidence of Sabbath-Sunday controversy in the NT. Whenever a major change in religious practice occurs, controversy inevitably ensues, as in the case of circumcision in the NT. But nowhere in the NT is there any polemic whatever regarding worship on the seventh day of the week. This fact becomes an added strong evidence for the continuance of Sabbath observance. In the NT period, the seventh day of the week was the one and only *Christian Sabbath*.

III. A Biblical Theology of the Sabbath

The axiom that religious practices are no better than the theology that informs and undergirds them applies to Sabbathkeeping and Sabbath theology as well as to all other facets of religious observance. This fact highlights the importance of having an intelligent Scripture-based understanding of genuine Sabbathkeeping. But there is also a further consideration: The Sabbath is not an end in itself, but a manifestation of an inward experience. For Christians, the center of religious experience is a personal relationship with Jesus Christ and through Him also with God the Father (John 14:9, 21, 23; 17:21-23, 26). This relationship is the heart of the experience reflected in the Sabbath. Every aspect of Sabbath theology, as well as the Sabbath practice that it informs, is an outworking of, and reflects a vital relationship with, the Godhead.

For a Sabbath theology to be valid, it must be Bible based, thoroughly rooted in the OT and NT. In this respect a theology of the seventh-day Sabbath is completely different from any so-called theology of the "Sunday sabbath," which has no divine word pertaining to it, for nowhere in the Bible is there any men-

tion of special sanctity for Sunday. On the other hand, Scripture contains numerous references that describe the nature of the seventh day of the week and declare that it is the day that God set apart for worship and rest.

In examining the theology of the Sabbath, we relate it to other biblical doctrines. The final picture should present an intertwined whole.

A. The Sabbath and the Doctrine of God

The basic question that we must ask is, "What does the Sabbath teach us about God?" The following list, though by no means exhaustive, draws attention to some of the main features of the nature, character, and activity of God that are illuminated by the Sabbath as set forth in Scripture.

1. God as Creator

God is the omnipotent Creator, whom human beings need to recognize and revere, and with whom they need fellowship in order to have fullness of life. This message comes through clearly in Genesis 1 and 2, as well as in the Sabbath commandment of the Decalogue and in various other Sabbath passages. The Creator provided the Sabbath as a blessing to human beings, who need the special fellowship with their Creator that the Sabbath memorializes and fosters.

We must remember that Christ, the divine Son of God, as well as God the Father, participated in Creation and in the establishment of the Sabbath. Without Christ "was not anything made that was made" (John 1:1-3); "in him all things were created, in heaven and on earth, visible and invisible" (Col. 1:16).

2. God as Redeemer

God is the all-sufficient Redeemer and Saviour, whose redemptive action precedes a covenant relationship with His redeemed people. Among the Scriptures we earlier noted, Exodus 31:17 and Ezekiel 20:12, 20 refer to the Sabbath as a sign of the lordship of Yahweh and to Him as the Sanctifier. Also, in direct connection with the Sabbath commandment in Exodus 20 and Deuteronomy 5, the Decalogue's historical prologue refers specifically to Yahweh's mighty redeeming act in saving His people from Egyptian bondage (Ex. 20:2; Deut. 5:6). Furthermore, Moses' reiteration of the Sabbath commandment contains a reference to God's saving activity (Deut. 5:15).

The Sabbath as a sign of redemption actually has precedence over the Sabbath as a memorial of Creation. Only those who are redeemed by Christ can truly recognize and understand what Creation means. Indeed, the example of God's redemption of the Israelites from Egyptian bondage leads our minds to the redemption made available through the life, death, and resurrection of Jesus Christ. That redemption is, in fact, what makes all lesser redemptions, including the Exodus from Egypt and Israel's deliverance from Babylon, efficacious and meaningful.

3. God as Covenant Maker

God loves fellowship with His created beings. This was demonstrated at Creation by His setting apart the Sabbath as a special day of fellowship with the human beings He had created. Christ's ministry on earth bears out this same lesson. He fellowshipped with His people on the Sabbath and daily manifested a close relationship with them. Just as the Sabbath was intended in biblical times to be a day for God's children to have special fellowship with Him and with their fellow worshipers, so its purpose is still the same today.

The sin problem and God's deliverance of human beings from it have brought an added dimension to God's fellowshipping with humankind. Those who accept the divine saving grace are distinguished from the rest of humanity by being placed in a covenant relationship with God. In the covenant that God made with Israel at Sinai, His prior goodness in delivering the Israelites from Egyptian bondage formed the basis for the relationship. And among that covenant's stipulations—the Ten Commandments—the Sabbath was so integral that it was itself referred to as "a perpetual covenant" (Ex. 31:16).

Covenants have mutual obligations. At Sinai, the great Sovereign Suzerain of the universe stooped down to enter a formal covenant with the people He had delivered from cruel bondage. That covenant guaranteed His continuing care and protection for them, but required in turn their obedience in manifestation of their loyalty to Him. The covenant relationship that was thus developed made Israel a "kingdom of priests and a holy nation" (Ex. 19:6). This description is echoed in the NT regarding the Christian church (1 Peter 2:9; Rev. 1:6). The NT new covenant, which is grounded directly in the salvation brought about at infinite cost to the Godhead, guarantees God's continuing care. But it also requires obedience to God's commandments in gratitude and loyalty to Him (Heb. 8:10; 10:16; cf. Jer. 31:31-33).

4. God as Giver of Good Gifts and Sustainer of His Creation

The Sabbath, in calling attention to God's

creative and re-creative activity, shows His generosity. In Eden He bestowed everything needed by His created human beings. This included life itself, human and divine fellowship, complete health and happiness, a perfect environment, and all the talents and mental and physical capabilities necessary for humanity to function well. Through the redemption and salvation made possible by Christ's sacrifice, all the blessings of a renewed fellowship with God are restored. Through Christ, human beings can receive forgiveness of sin, spiritual revitalization, and the joy and internal peace that only His salvation can bring. Beyond this, God provides physical blessings even to those who do not recognize Him. In the words of Christ, the Father in heaven "makes his sun rise on the evil and on the good, and sends rain on the just and on the unjust" (Matt. 5:45).

This statement by Jesus is a declaration that God is the Sustainer of all, who constantly watches over His created human beings and meets their needs. This aspect of the Father's and Christ's character and activity is also set forth in the pronouncement that Christ made after one of His Sabbath miracles of healing: "My Father is working still, and I am working" (John 5:17). Indeed, Christ's Sabbath healings are themselves a powerful witness to the fact that God is the great Sustainer as well as the Saviour and the Giver of all good gifts (James 1:17)

5. God as the Ultimate in Fairness

Yahweh is the ultimate in fairness. He "shows no partiality" (Acts 10:34). The seventh-day Sabbath is a very special token and demonstration of God's complete and unswerving fairness. It is a gift to mankind that is equally applicable and accessible to everyone. It comes everywhere with the same regularity and in the same amount. Furthermore, in connection with Sabbathkeeping among the ancient Israelites, God specified that all—the servant and the alien as well as the landowner (Ex. 23:12)—should have this one day every week free from their common labors, thus showing total impartiality.

6. God as Perfection

God is perfect. The basic witnesses to this are the facts of Creation and redemption, which the Sabbath serves to memorialize. In the beginning God's works were perfect, and they remained so until sin brought a blight upon His creation. The salvation that Christ offers is perfect. Jesus Christ is both the "pioneer and perfecter of our faith" (Heb. 12:2). Moreover, Christ's Sabbath miracles and His discourses in connection with them reveal the perfection of the Godhead in the work of salvation. Finally, we must note that the "new heaven and the new earth" which God will create will also be perfect (Isa. 66:22; Rev. 21:1-4).

7. Christ's Divinity

Christ is God. The Sabbath testifies to the divinity of Christ by means of His declaration that He is Lord of the Sabbath (Matt. 12:8) and through His Sabbath healing miracles. He is the Lord of the Sabbath because He made it. His healings involved not only supernatural physical cures, but also the forgiveness of sin and the granting of spiritual wholeness, giving indisputable witness to His divine nature and underscoring the truth of His claim to be one with His heavenly Father (John 5:17, 19, 20; 9:3-5; 10:30). Thus the Sabbath helps us to recognize the divinity of Christ. (For other aspects of the doctrine of God, see God I-VIII.)

B. The Sabbath and the Doctrine of Humanity

1. The Sabbath and Human "Createdness"

The inverse side to the question of what the Sabbath teaches us about God is "What does the Sabbath tell us about ourselves as human beings?" By calling our attention to Creation week, the Sabbath reminds us that we are created beings. As such, God has given us a variety of capabilities and talents, commensurate with the activities in which human beings can engage. Our first parents were created in the image of God, and that image has in certain ways lingered on, in spite of the distortions brought to it by sin. Among the capacities that God has given to the human family are those of fellowship, love, compassion, and the variety of emotions that we experience. Though some of these have been severely constricted or even obliterated by sin, God's redemption in Christ can and does restore them to those who accept Christ's saving grace.

The fact of our being created individuals carries with it a variety of aspects of "createdness" and "creatureliness." In our createdness, we are mortal. When God created human beings, He did not bestow upon them immortality, thus all human beings have been subject to death. God alone has immortality (1 Tim. 6:16). Only He can bestow immortality, and this He will do for His faithful followers when Christ returns (1 Cor. 15:51-54; 1 Thess. 4:15-17).

As the Sabbath leads us to consider our human "createdness" and "creatureliness," it reminds us that we are neither omnipotent nor omniscient, but that we live and perform solely within the limited sphere of life and capability that our Creator has bestowed upon us. This should foster in us a spirit of true humility, for the fact that all human beings owe their existence and talents to the same sovereign God leaves no room for any to boast. Indeed, the realization of our own human createdness should give us an attitude of respect and care for all other human beings. In addition, it should make us sensitive to our environment as we realize that God has made us caretakers of it.

2. The Sabbath as a "Leveler"

The Sabbath, by calling our attention to Creation and to our own createdness, has a "leveling" effect. As noted previously (III. A. 5), the Sabbath is equally accessible to all human beings with the same regularity and in the same quantity. In addition, God indicated the applicability of its rest to *all* persons, servants and aliens as well as property owners. The universality of the Sabbath is set forth also by Isaiah in his reference to its observance by "foreigners who join themselves to the Lord" (Isa. 56:6, 7). As a portion of time, the universality of the Sabbath places it within reach of all human beings, impartially and cost-free.

3. The Sabbath and Our Value to God

The Sabbath also teaches that we are of value to God and that He has given us remarkable potential. One of the expressions of His love for us is the very fact that He gave the Sabbath to the human beings whom He created, so that they could have special fellowship with Him. But all the other blessings—life itself, human fellowship, a beautiful environment, and intellectual and physical strength—have also come from Him. Thus human beings are capable of undertaking worthwhile and challenging enterprises that can result in valuable contributions to God and to society. God has given us a sequence of six days in which to do meaningful work. Just as He saw that what He had created in six days was "very good" (Gen. 1:31), we at the end of our six days of work can turn in gratitude to Him for what He has made possible for us to accomplish.

4. The Sabbath and Fellowship, Love, and Compassion

The Sabbath reminds us that God has bestowed on human beings the need for fellowship and the capacity to love, care, and be compassionate. The Sabbath was to be a day for holy convocation (Lev. 23:3). It was also a reminder to the ancient Israelites that because God had been very kind in delivering them from Egyptian bondage they should act compassionately, treating their fellow human beings with love and kindness.

C. The Sabbath and the Doctrine of Salvation

Sin disrupted God's original plan for the human beings He created, but through Christ that plan has been reinstated and is functional for all who accept His saving grace. The Sabbath has a role in dealing with the sin situation, for it is a sign of the sanctifying power and lordship of Christ. It helps us to realize our need of redemption, of salvation, of restoration. It turns our minds to Him who alone holds the remedy that overcomes the sin disease and its enslavement. The Sabbath, by pointing to Christ as the Redeemer, helps us to recognize our need for salvation and the infinite expense to God the Father and to Jesus in providing it.

The biblical basis for the soteriological significance of the Sabbath emerges from several considerations: 1. The obligation for keeping the Sabbath, along with the other nine commandments of the Decalogue, was set forth at Sinai in the framework of God's redeeming love and saving activity. 2. The Sabbath was declared to be a sign that Yahweh is the God of His people and that He sanctifies them. 3. Rightly observed, the Sabbath results in delighting oneself in God as set forth in Isaiah 58:13, 14. 4. Christ's Sabbath healings forcefully illustrate His power to heal spiritually as well as physically. Indeed, Christ is the only Saviour. It was He who redeemed Israel from Egyptian bondage (see 1 Cor. 10:1-4), and it is He who forgives sins and gives to sin-shackled human beings both freedom and wholeness.

As a concluding remark about the Sabbath in relationship to salvation, we repeat that for human beings in a world of sin the Sabbath as a sign of redemption has precedence over it as the sign or memorial of Creation. The work of "re-creation" must come to us first if Creation and our Creator are to have real meaning to us. This does not demean or lessen the importance of the Sabbath as a memorial of Creation, but simply calls attention to the vital fact that for human beings under the bondage of sin, a release from that bondage precedes and is basic to all knowledge of, and relationship to, God. Meaningful Sabbathkeeping occurs only within a personal fellowship with Christ.

D. The Sabbath and the Doctrine of the Church

As we have seen, the Sabbath is a "leveler" both by its very nature and by its keeping us aware of our createdness. But the Sabbath is also a "leveler" in its soteriological dimension, not only because of the need for salvation that is shared by *all* human beings, but because those who accept it in their lives are brought into a fellowship in which there "is neither Jew nor Greek, there is neither slave nor free, there is neither male nor female," but all are "one in Christ Jesus" (Gal. 3:28). This fellowship is Christ's *ekklēsia,* the Christian church.

The Sabbath as a sign of Christ's redeeming power gives it a role in creating loving respect throughout the entire Christian fellowship. It reminds us that we all share a common salvation and that the One who is our Lord and Saviour is also the Lord and Saviour of our Christian brothers and sisters. As we worship together from Sabbath to Sabbath, we grow in mutual love and respect. The bond among genuine followers of Christ becomes so close, in fact, that they are imbued with the spirit of Christ's saying, "Greater love has no man than this, that a man lay down his life for his friends" (John 15:13). When Jesus spoke these words, He undoubtedly thought of His own impending death, but His statement also had a predictive and promissory significance for all Christians. The statement carries the implication for the corporate life of the church that each individual member so loves his or her brothers and sisters in Christ as to be willing, ready, and happy to take death in their place. And indeed, early-church history testifies repeatedly that true Christians, when persecuted, fulfilled Jesus' words.

The ecclesiological aspect of the Sabbath has another important facet, one that relates to the work of the Holy Spirit for the upbuilding of the congregation and for its outreach to the world at large. This is God's giving of special gifts to the Christian community through the Holy Spirit, endowments that are appropriately called spiritual gifts (Rom. 12:4-8; 1 Cor. 12:4-11; Eph. 4:11-14). On the Sabbath various of these gifts are manifested publicly. Moreover, the fact that the Sabbath is a sign of redemption should make us grateful, not only for the gifts which the Holy Spirit has bestowed upon us, but for the gifts He has bestowed upon others. And as church members work together, they should seek to affirm the spiritual gifts of one another. (See Spiritual Gifts II.)

E. The Sabbath and the Doctrine of Last Things

Ancient Judaism had a saying that the Sabbath was a foretaste of eternity in this world (Mishnah *Tamid* 7. 4). It would not be surprising if NT Christians held a similar concept, but concerning this there is no entirely clear Scripture evidence. While the "rest" in Hebrews 3:7–4:13 may possibly be taken as referring to the new earth, the main emphasis is on the spiritual experience in Christ that begins in the present age. This experience is, of course, the beginning of eternal life and will continue in heaven and the new earth.

Despite the nearly universal disregard of the Sabbath among contemporary Christians, the Scriptures continue their call for its observance in honor of Christ as Creator and Redeemer. Such a condition inevitably involves the Sabbath in controversy.

The Sabbath will have a special place, as well, in the final crisis of this earth's history. Near the end of this age there will be an upsurge of demonic power. The wrath of Satan, the dragon of Revelation 12, is directed toward the remnant of the woman's (the church's) offspring (Rev. 12:17), and the nature and intensity of this wrath are subsequently elaborated in 13:11-17. This last-day remnant is described as keeping God's commandments and having the testimony of Jesus Christ (12:17). A false mark, the mark of the beast, is forced, with severe sanctions, upon the world (13:16, 17). This mark stands in contrast with God's sign, which is set forth in Scripture as the seventh-day Sabbath. Just as the Sabbath was a sign for the ancient Israelites that Yahweh was their God, in the end-time crisis it will be a sign of loyalty to God by those who keep *all* of His commandments. It will display the full trust of Christ's people in His saving power and will signify their rejection of the beast entity and the latter's mark. (See Remnant/Three Angels V; Great Controversy V. A-D.)

IV. The Importance of the Sabbath for Christians

Believers who observe the Sabbath according to the biblical instructions do so with joy, not by constraint. In the Sabbath they see evidences of God's love; they also understand that by observing the Sabbath they reciprocate His love. True Sabbathkeeping Christians think far less of Sabbath restrictions than of Sabbath privileges.

The Sabbath is the high day of the week. When God in His omniscience and goodness saw fit to create this world and do it in six days of creative work, He also saw fit to add one more day—a day of "cessation" or "rest"—to complete the seven-day week. That day is made even more special because Yahweh blessed it and hallowed it (Gen. 2:3). The Sabbath remains for humanity a particularly significant parcel of time, whose meaning and whose physical and spiritual blessings are today as rich as ever. Therefore, for us who live in this generation, the Sabbath's divine enrichments still apply and can be experienced fully. When through Christ's grace we accept and live in the joy of the Sabbath, it becomes truly *our* crowning day of the week.

The mature Christian experiences the Sabbath as a vital part of abundant life, the "eternal life" in Christ, which begins qualitatively now and is extended quantitatively to all eternity at the Second Advent. The growing Christian finds that the Sabbath provides closer fellowship with Christ, while at the same time that very fellowship with Christ—along with the spiritual rest, joy, and assurance that it gives—leads to a better understanding of the Sabbath and into enhancement in the experience of Sabbathkeeping. From both perspectives, the Sabbath is not a burden, but rather a pleasant release from the humdrum that so frequently fills the other six days of the week. It encapsulates, as it were, the "rest" in Christ, of which He spoke: "Come to me, all who labor and are heavy laden, and I will give you rest. Take my yoke upon you, and learn from me. . . . For my yoke is easy, and my burden is light" (Matt. 11:28-30).

The basis for both our Sabbath theology and our Sabbathkeeping is a close personal relationship with Christ, our Saviour. He is the Center from which all of our religious beliefs and activities radiate. Without Him they are null and void, for He is the perfect one, in and through whom alone we can grow up in valid and meaningful Christian experience.

Genuine Sabbathkeeping presupposes a "holiness" of life that is found only in Christ. In the OT, God emphasized repeatedly to Israel their need to be holy because He is holy (e.g., Lev. 11:44; 19:2; 20:26). This is a theme reiterated for Christians in the NT (1 Peter 1:15, 16). Ellen White has pointed out that "the Sabbath is a sign of Christ's power to make us holy" (DA 288) and that "in order to keep the Sabbath holy, men must themselves be holy" (*ibid.* 283). Another writer has aptly stated, "The Sabbath has no meaning at all unless creative power accomplishes its result in the life of the one who observes the day. Holiness *of* time must match holiness *in* time" (Kubo 49).

V. The Sabbath in History

A. Intertestamental Period and Early Judaism

1. Intertestamental Period

The intertestamental period (late fifth century B.C. through early first century A.D.) has many lacunae with regard to the precise development of Judaism and its practices. Nonetheless, some documentation exists.

a. The Elephantine Jews. Documentary evidence from Elephantine, an island in the Nile River in Upper Egypt, near modern Aswan, indicates that a colony of Jews existed there as early as the fifth century B.C. In the 1940s specialists studied a group of inscribed potsherds from this Elephantine Jewish colony. Two of these mention the Sabbath only obliquely, but nonetheless thereby give an awareness of the Sabbath. Two others, however, are more specific. In one case, a woman named Yislah is ordered to "arrange" ("bind" [?]) an ox on (or before[?]) the Sabbath, lest it become lost. In the other case, a certain task, possibly the receiving of a shipment of fish, was to be done prior to the Sabbath. Whatever religious syncretism may have existed in the practices of the Elephantine Jews, they displayed some concern for proper Sabbath observance.

b. Maccabean defensive war. By the outbreak of the Maccabean revolt (166-142 B.C.) against the Seleucid ruler Antiochus IV Epiphanes, the Jews had an established tradition of total noncombatancy on the Sabbath. Early in the Maccabean struggle, however, when the enemy troops routed and killed some thousand Jews (1 Macc. 2:31-38), the Maccabean leader Mattathias and his companions determined that *defensive* warfare was proper for the Sabbath (verses 39-41).

In 63 B.C. Pompey the Great, a Roman general, used the Sabbath days for military preparations such as raising earthworks against the walls of Jerusalem; finally, after a three-month siege, he entered the city on a Sabbath. Again in 37 B.C. it was on a Sabbath that the Romans captured Jerusalem.

c. The books of Judith and Jubilees. Two OT pseudepigraphical works provide information regarding the Sabbath. Judith and Jubilees both date to the mid-to-late second century B.C. The concept of nonfasting on the Sabbath occurs in both works. Concerning Judith (supposedly a heroine of the Exile period, but most likely a fictional character), it is reported that after her husband died of sunstroke during the barley harvest, "she fasted all the days of her widowhood, except the day before the sabbath and the sabbath itself" (Judith 8:2-6). The book of Jubilees prescribes the death penalty for Sabbath fasting (50:12, 13). The death penalty is also indicated for traveling, kindling a fire, slaughtering, trapping, and fishing, and making war on the Sabbath.

Among other activities prohibited on the Sabbath, on pain of death, are spousal cohabitation; discussion of business matters, including travel plans; drawing up water; and picking up anything to carry out of one's dwelling (50:8). The only types of permissible Sabbath activity relate to (1) eating, drinking, resting, and blessing God; and (2) burning frankincense and bringing gifts and sacrifices before the Lord (50:9-11). God and the angels are portrayed as having kept the Sabbath in heaven before it was made known to any human being on earth (2:30).

2. Rabbinic Tradition

The first comprehensive written codification of the oral law was the Mishnah, produced early in the third century A.D. This document furnishes a good picture of the type of legal tradition operative among the Jews in NT times. Although the Sabbath is mentioned in a number of the Mishnah's 63 tractates (or "books"), two of them are devoted specifically to the Sabbath and the "Sabbath-day's journey"—*Shabbath* and *'Erubin,* respectively.

The tractate *Shabbath* sets forth 39 main classes of work that must be avoided, and indicates numerous activities that fall under each of them. The main classes are the following: "sowing, ploughing, reaping, binding sheaves, threshing, winnowing, cleansing crops, grinding, sifting, kneading, baking, shearing wool, washing or beating or dyeing it, spinning, weaving, making two loops, weaving two threads, separating two threads, tying [a knot], loosening [a knot], sewing two stitches, tearing in order to sew two stitches, hunting a gazelle, slaughtering or flaying or salting it or curing its skin, scraping it or cutting it up, writing two letters, erasing in order to write two letters, building, pulling down, putting out a fire, lighting fire, striking with a hammer and taking out aught from one domain into another" (*Shabbath* 7. 2).

These 39 main classes have numerous subsections. For instance, quantity limitations were specified for products or objects that could be carried on the Sabbath: "straw equal to a cow's mouthful," "milk enough for a gulp," "rope enough to make a handle for a basket," and many others (*Shabbath* 7. 2–8. 7). Among further illustrations from the tractate *Shabbath* are the following: "Greek hyssop may not be eaten on the Sabbath since it is not the food of them that are in health" (14. 3). A person whose teeth are paining "may not suck vinegar through them but he may take vinegar after his usual fashion, and if he is healed he is healed" (14. 4). Various knots are listed that may not be tied or untied on the Sabbath, but one rabbi declared that nobody "is accounted culpable because of any knot which can be untied with one hand" (15. 1). If water was drawn from a well or cistern, a gourd weighted with a stone could be used; but if the stone should fall out, the person would be culpable (17. 6), presumably because the stone was not part of the vessel for drawing water but had been instead a burden within that vessel.

Work, as understood by the rabbis, meant *purposeful* activity, done in the *normal manner.* Thus, writing with one's foot or mouth or elbow, not being the ordinary way to write, was exempt from culpability. Further complicating the situation was the lack of agreement of the authorities on exactly what actions made a person culpable (*Shabbath* 12. 3-12. 5).

The tractate *'Erubin* relates to distances people could travel or move on the Sabbath, such as the 2,000-cubit "Sabbath-day's journey." This distance could be extended, however. If before sunset at the beginning of the Sabbath, an individual would go 2,000 cubits from the city where he lived and place there the amount of food for two meals and declare in the proper way that this was his *'erub,* that location would technically become his dwelling for the Sabbath. Then on the Sabbath itself he would be able to go to that place plus another 2,000 cubits beyond it, and thus a total of 4,000 cubits.

The *'erub* was also used in connection with the moving of objects from one dwelling to another. This overcame the four-cubit limitation on movement that pertained to individual residences. If food were placed jointly by occupants of neighboring dwellings in the common courtyard before the beginning of the Sabbath and the *'erub* declared, the various dwellings (and the common courtyard) could be considered as one larger dwelling. Thus, on that Sabbath, foodstuffs or other objects could be carried into the courtyard and back and forth among the participating dwellings. But there were restrictions: For instance, two outer courtyards making *'erub* with a courtyard between them would be allowed access to it, but the two outer courtyards were not allowed access to each other (*'Erubin* 4. 6). The various activities and circumstances involving the use of the *'erub* are multitudinous.

The foregoing examples from the Mishnah show how Rabbinic tradition both "fenced in" the law and liberalized Sabbath restrictions. For instance, the rigorous rules about moving objects on the Sabbath, based on the elaboration of the restrictions in Jeremiah 17:22, were mollified. A further illustration of the liberalizing attitude is that in order for there to be culpability for Sabbathbreaking, one's *complete*

act of work must be done in error. If persons "began the act in error and ended it wittingly, or if they began it wittingly and ended it in error, they are not liable: . . . unless both the beginning and the end of their act were done in error" (*Shabbath* 11. 6). If a person threw something on the Sabbath and then remembered it was the Sabbath, but the object was intercepted by another human being or a dog, or burned up, the individual would not be culpable. If an object were thrown to wound either a man or an animal, but before the wound was actually inflicted, the individual who threw the object remembered that it was the Sabbath, he would not be culpable for Sabbathbreaking.

The casuistry of the scribes in developing the oral law provided such a multitude of human restrictions and accommodations that only the teachers of the law were able to grasp and cope with the various nuances. The common people, by and large, were greatly bewildered, and thus gained a reputation for ignorance regarding the law.

In spite of such a cumbersome load of restrictions and modifications, ancient Judaism considered the Sabbath a day of special privilege and delight. On Friday evening the Sabbath was welcomed with special joy. The Sabbath noonday meal was to be particularly good, and by no means should it be missed. Sabbath rules were relaxed for certain occasions, such as religious festivals, and in cases of extreme emergency.

3. Essenes and Boethusians

Josephus refers to the Essenes as the strictest sect of the Jews. They were a minor, but nonetheless significant, party during the NT epoch. An Essene work composed probably not more than a century later than the book of Jubilees, and referred to as the Zadokite Document or the Damascus Document, gives numerous specifications concerning the Sabbath (10. 14–11. 18). Its general thrust parallels to a great degree that of the material in the book of Jubilees. However, the death sentence is not mentioned for Sabbathbreaking (possibly because by this time the "power of life and limb" was in Roman hands). Moreover, the Sabbathday's journey was not to be more than 1,000 cubits (half of that allowed by the Pharisees), although in going after an animal on the Sabbath to pasture it, a person could go 2,000 cubits. The Damascus Document also stipulates that infants should not be carried around on the Sabbath, that animals were not to be assisted in giving birth to their young on the Sabbath, and that if a newborn animal would fall into a cistern or a pit it should not be lifted out on the Sabbath. Josephus notes that the Essenes would not even allow defecation on the Sabbath (*Wars* 2. 8. 9)!

Although the Sadducees, the priestly aristocracy of the NT, were Hellenizers, they followed the norms of the Pharisaic party in basic Jewish religious observances. A Sadducean subgroup known as Boethusians appears to have approached the Essene rigors. In common with the Essenes Boethusians followed a solar calendar that eliminated the possibility of having the annual festivals ever fall on a weekly Sabbath. In their view this provided a safeguard for the Sabbath.

4. Philo and Josephus

At the time of transition to the NT epoch in the first half of the first century A.D. Philo of Alexandria provides insights into Sabbath theology and activities. These were given in an apologetic context and reflect the situation in Alexandria rather than Palestine. Philo speculates on the meaning of the number seven, refers to the Sabbath as the birthday of the world, and treats the philosophical meaning of rest, including the aspects of equality and freedom inherent in the Sabbath commandment (*Special Laws* 2. 15; and *Decalogue* 20).

As for practice, Philo refers to attendance at the synagogue on Sabbaths for the purpose of studying "philosophy"—i.e., the OT. Undoubtedly he used the term because of the philosophical orientation at Alexandria and his own philosophical bent. He states further that the Sabbath should be devoted solely to philosophy aimed at improvement of character and submission to conscience (*On Creation* 43). Jewish synagogues were "schools of good sense," where temperance, courage, justice, and other virtues were fostered (*Special Laws* 2.15). Utilizing leisure time in such places for the pursuit of wisdom was far superior, he felt, to the debilitating effect of spending time in sports and entertainment (*Moses* 2. 39).

Josephus, also, in the latter half of the first century A.D., speaks of the Jews setting the seventh day apart from labor and dedicating it to the learning of Jewish customs and laws (*Antiquities* 16. 2. 3). Moreover, he describes the practice of a priest in Jerusalem standing near the tower at the southwest corner of the Temple and blowing a trumpet to signal the approach of the Sabbath on Friday afternoon and also at the Sabbath's close on Saturday evening (*Wars* 4. 9. 12). He gives, as well, evidence of the normative Jewish tradition of nonfasting on the Sabbath, mentioning the requirement of eating the noon meal on the Sabbath (*Life* 279).

B. Sabbath and Sunday in the Early Church

1. The Origin of Sunday Observance

The precise sequence of events that led to the rise of a weekly Sunday is somewhat obscure. It is clear that Sunday observance did not originate as a substitute for the Sabbath. Not until the fourth century did Sunday begin to replace the Sabbath as a rest day; until then the weekly Christian Sunday had been a workday, with time set aside for special worship services.

An *annual* Sunday resurrection celebration may have been antecedent to the weekly Sunday observance that eventually came to be recognized as a resurrection festival. In the NT, the Jewish Passover was considered as typifying the real Paschal Lamb; likewise, the Jewish firstfruits celebration was considered as typifying Christ's resurrection (1 Cor. 5:7; 15:20).

According to Leviticus 23:11, the wave sheaf was to be offered on the "morrow after the sabbath." The Pharisees interpreted that day as the day after the Passover Sabbath. They killed the Passover lamb on Nisan 14, celebrated the Passover Sabbath on Nisan 15, and offered the firstfruits wave sheaf on Nisan 16, regardless of the day of the week on which those dates might fall. In contrast, the Essenes and the Sadducean Boethusians interpreted the "morrow after the sabbath" as the day after a weekly Sabbath, and thus *always* a Sunday.

Christians celebrated their Resurrection "firstfruits" festival *annually,* not weekly, and most likely kept it in harmony with their previous custom in the Jewish celebration of the firstfruits. Thus early Christians adopted both types of Jewish reckoning—the Pharisaic and the Essene-Boethusian—as is evidenced by the "Easter Controversy" of the late second century.

Eventually this *annual* celebration may have spread into a *weekly* one because of a variety of factors, such as anti-Jewish sentiment (especially prominent in Rome and Alexandria) and the downgrading of the Sabbath through the Sabbath fast. Furthermore, there is evidence to suggest that the seven weeks between Easter and Pentecost had special significance for certain segments of the ancient church, and a practice of honoring the Sundays during this season eventually may have spread throughout the year.

2. Sabbath and Sunday in the Second and Third Centuries

a. Earliest information. Three second-century references to a day of rest should be mentioned, because they have been argued as attesting either Sunday or Sabbath observance, though none specifically mentions either day. These are Ignatius of Antioch; Pliny, a Roman governor of Bithynia; and the *Didache*.

Around A.D. 115 Ignatius of Antioch wrote an epistle to the Magnesians in Asia Minor, in which he warned these Christians against an extreme variety of Judaistic practice. In *Magnesians* 9. 1, he speaks of "no longer sabbatizing but living according to the Lord's, in which also our hope has risen in him." This has often been interpreted as "no longer keeping the Sabbath, but living according to the Lord's day [Sunday]." The word "day" is not in the Greek, but has been supplied. In place of adding the word "day," one could supply the word "life," which would give the translation "living according to the Lord's life." Either meaning is possible by the Greek construction used, but "Lord's life" seems especially fitting in view of the fact that in it (or, by it) "our hope has risen in him [Christ]."

The expression "sabbatizing" reflects a general lifestyle rather than observance of a day. A fourth-century interpolator of Ignatius did not equate "sabbatizing" with Sabbath-keeping, but encouraged observance of both Sabbath and Sunday. His only objection was to the Jewish *type* of Sabbathkeeping (see V. B. 3. a). The context of Ignatius' statement—an appeal to the example of the OT prophets (8. 2–9. 1)—suggests that he was dealing with a *manner of life* rather than with days of worship. Those OT prophets, who no longer were sabbatizing and were living according to the "Lord's," did not keep the first day of the week, but kept the seventh-day Sabbath.

A letter of Roman governor Pliny to the Roman emperor Trajan in A.D. 112 speaks of practices of Christians in Bithynia. Some of these Christians had apostatized; and when interrogated by Pliny about their earlier beliefs and practices, they indicated that the extent of their wrongdoing had been that before sunrise on a "stated day" (or "fixed day") they had met and sung hymns to Christ as to a God (*Letters* 10. 96). This practice looks more like an annual resurrection-day sunrise celebration than it does the observance of either a weekly Sabbath or a weekly Sunday.

An instructional manual entitled *Didache,*

perhaps dating to the early second century, urges in its chapter 14 that "according to [or "on"] the Lord's of the Lord" there be assemblage, the breaking of bread, and the holding of Eucharist. This text has been interpreted as referring to a weekly Sunday celebration, to an annual Easter, or to the seventh-day Sabbath. The context and nature of the statement, however, makes a totally different suggestion seem more viable: that *instruction* (or "command" or "doctrine") is the noun to be supplied. This would give the reading, "according to the Lord's instruction."

b. Second-century Church Fathers. The earliest reference that reveals honor to Sunday as a day for weekly Christian worship comes from the *Epistle of Barnabas of Alexandria* (c. 130). In a thoroughly allegorical discourse, Barnabas refers to the Sabbath as a sign of the millennium and to the "eighth day" (Sunday) as a symbol of the new earth; he also seems to suggest that the "eighth day" is either the day being kept by Christians or the day that should be so kept (*Epistle* 15).

If Barnabas is somewhat ambiguous, Justin Martyr in Rome (c. 150) provides unequivocal evidence. In his *Apology* to the Roman emperor and senate, he describes the Sunday-morning worship service with which he was familiar (*1 Apology* 67). The service apparently took place in the very early morning. Recent scholarly examination, however, raises question whether section 67 may be a later interpolation. Justin's *Dialogue With Trypho the Jew* sets forth Justin's view of the superiority of Christianity over Judaism. In his polemic in this work Justin denigrates the Sabbath, as the following statement shows: "Do you [Trypho] see that the elements are not idle, and keep no Sabbaths? Remain as you were born" (23).

Toward the end of the second century Clement of Alexandria berated the Sabbath and favored the first day of the week. In a variety of speculative ways, Clement gave priority to the first day of the week. He is also the earliest Church Father to refer to the weekly Sunday

as "Lord's day," doing so in a curious and highly allegorical reference to the Greek philosopher Plato (428-348 B.C.): The "Lord's day Plato prophetically speaks of in the tenth book of the *Republic,* in these words: 'And when seven days have passed to each of them in the meadow, on the eighth they are to set out and arrive in four days' " (*Miscellanies* 5. 14).

Irenaeus of Gaul (fl. c. 175-200), applied "Lord's day" to Easter Sunday in his treatise *On Easter* (no longer extant). An unknown later writer indicated that for Irenaeus "Pentecost" was "of equal significance with the Lord's day." Thus Irenaeus' "Lord's day" was the annual Easter, for the comparison is obviously between two *annual* festivals (*Fragments From the Lost Writings of Irenaeus* 7).

c. Second-century apocryphal sources. Two apocryphal sources refer to "Lord's day," perhaps two or three decades earlier than Clement of Alexandria (though the dating is uncertain): The Gospel of Peter speaks of Christ's resurrection as occurring on the "Lord's day" but does not mention the keeping of either an annual or a weekly celebration of that day. The Acts of John relates that the apostle John broke his fast "on the seventh day, it being the Lord's day." In the latter source we find John traveling as a prisoner, and possibly the seventh day of the journey is intended. However, inasmuch as the church in the East did not fast on the Sabbath (see V. B. 3. b), John would be breaking his fast on that day. Neither of these two apocryphal sources deserves great credence. But the fact that the Acts of John and the book of Revelation both come from the Roman province of Asia suggests a common usage and meaning of the term "Lord's day" for the seventh-day Sabbath in these Acts and Revelation 1:10.

d. Third-century Church Fathers. During the third century A.D. Christian observance of Sunday on a weekly basis became rather widespread. However, there was as yet no basic controversy over the Sabbath, except in a few places, such as Rome, Alexandria, and the area around Carthage, which was influenced by Rome. Just as in NT times, such silence as to controversy would be an indication that generally throughout Christendom the status quo was being maintained.

In Rome and North Africa there were differences of view. In contrast to the earlier polemic of Justin Martyr, Hippolytus of Rome in the early third century strongly objected to fasting on both Sabbath and Sunday. In Rome the practice of fasting every Sabbath had arisen, making the Sabbath a day of gloom rather than of joy. Never was there a fast on Sunday, however, and Hippolytus argued for a similar honor for the Sabbath.

In North Africa, Tertullian, a contemporary of Hippolytus, at first seemed negative toward Sabbathkeepers, since he felt that their practice of not kneeling on the Sabbath was causing dissension (*On Prayer* 23). (In the Roman West, kneeling was considered a negative mode, not proper for a day of joy, and therefore Christian worshipers did not kneel on Sunday.) Later, however, he defended the Sabbath, vigorously opposing the Sabbath fast (*Against Marcion* 4. 12, 30, and *On Fasting* 14). We may conclude that in Rome and North Africa, the Sabbath had not entirely disappeared. Throughout the rest of Christendom the lack of polemic indicates that whatever Sunday observance did exist was not considered as interfering with the Sabbath.

3. Sabbath and Sunday in the Fourth Through Sixth Centuries

a. **Fourth century.** In the early fourth century Constantine's famous Sunday edict of March 7, 321, had a most striking bearing on both Sabbath and Sunday. It reads as follows: "On the venerable Day of the Sun let the magistrates and people residing in cities rest, and let all workshops be closed. In the country, however, persons engaged in agriculture may freely and lawfully continue their pursuits; because it often happens that another day is not so suitable for grain-sowing or for vine-planting; lest by neglecting the proper moment for such operations the bounty of heaven should be lost" (9BC 999).

This edict obviously lacked in Christian orientation, for it refers to Sunday as "the venerable Day of the Sun." Moreover, Constantine's regulations were not patterned after the OT Sabbath, for he exempted agricultural work, a type of work specifically prohibited in the Pentateuch. A further edict dated July 3 of the same year provided military regulations regarding Sunday.

Some sixty-five years later, in A.D. 386, the emperors Theodosius I and Gratian Valentinian forbade litigation and the payment of public or private debt on Sunday. Subsequent rulers extended restrictions even more, so as increasingly to "sabbatize" the Christian Sunday.

The earliest known ecclesiastical enactment rejecting Sabbath observance and replacing it with weekly Sunday observance comes from a regional council in Laodicea thought to have taken place about A.D. 364. In its Canon 29 this council stipulated, "Christians shall not Judaize and be idle on Saturday, but shall work on that day; but the Lord's day [Sunday] they shall especially honour, and, as being Christians, shall, if possible, do no work on that day. If, however, they are found Judaizing, they shall be shut out from Christ" (Hefele 2:316).

Loyalty to the seventh-day Sabbath did not succumb without a struggle. In fact, in the fourth century we find considerable polemic regarding Sabbath and Sunday. In contrast with the enactment of the Council of Laodicea, a fourth-century compilation known as the *Apostolic Constitutions* states, "Let the slaves work five days; but on the Sabbath-day [Saturday] and the Lord's day [Sunday] let them have leisure to go to church for instruction in piety" (8. 33) and, "But keep the Sabbath [Saturday], and the Lord's day festival [Sunday]; because the former is the memorial of the creation, and the latter of the resurrection" (7. 23). The same source contains several other similar statements (2. 36; 2. 47; 7. 36). At about the same time, the interpolator of Ignatius advised: "Let every one of you keep the Sabbath after a spiritual manner, rejoicing in meditation on the law. . . . And after the observance of the Sabbath, let every friend of Christ keep the Lord's Day as a festival, the resurrection day, the queen and chief of all the days" (*Magnesians* 9).

b. Fifth century. In the fifth century John Cassian (360-435) made reference to church attendance on both Saturday and Sunday, stating that he had even seen a monk who sometimes fasted five days a week but went to church on Saturday or on Sunday and brought home guests for a meal on those two days (*Institutes* 5. 26). Other statements of Cassian also refer to church services on both Sabbath and Sunday (*Institutes* 3. 2; *Conferences* 3. 1). Another Church Father who made favorable mention of both days is Asterius of Amasea. About the year 400 he declared that it was beautiful for Christians that the "team of these two days comes together"—"the Sabbath and the Lord's Day"—each week assembling the people with priests as their instructors (*Homily* 5, on Matt. 19:3).

Augustine (354-430), bishop of Hippo in North Africa, dealt in several of his letters with the controversy over Sabbath fasting (*Epistles* 36 [to Casulanus], 54 [to Januarius], and 82 [to Jerome]). In the letters to Casulanus and Januarius, he noted that the large Christian church in Milan did not observe the Sabbath fast (36. 32 and 54. 3, respectively).

Augustine made clear, as well, that Sabbath fasting was limited to Rome and some other places in the West (36. 27); churches in the East and "by far the greater part of Christendom" did not observe the Sabbath fast (82. 14). Cassian's testimony is similar, for he states that "some people in some countries of the West, and especially in the city [Rome]" were fasting on the Sabbath (*Institutes* 3. 10).

Especially interesting are the records of two church historians of the fifth century. Socrates Scholasticus (fl. c. 440) wrote, "Although almost all churches throughout the world celebrate the sacred mysteries [the Lord's Supper] on the sabbath [Saturday] of every week, yet the Christians of Alexandria and at Rome, on account of some ancient tradition, have ceased to do this" (*Ecclesiastical History* 5. 22). Sozomen, a contemporary of Socrates, wrote, "The people of Constantinople, and almost everywhere, assemble together on the Sabbath, as well as on the first day of the week, which custom is never observed at Rome or at Alexandria" (*Ecclesiastical History* 7. 19). It is pertinent to recall here that Rome and Alexandria were the only two cities displaying a negative attitude toward the Sabbath as early as the second century (see V. B. 2. b).

c. Sixth century. During the sixth century major steps were taken toward bringing about the demise of the Sabbath and promotion of Sunday observance. Certain theological rationales downplayed the importance of the Sabbath, but much more significant were the decrees of church synods and the ordinances of rulers. In A.D. 538, the Third Synod of Orleans forbade "field labours" so that "people may be able to come to church and worship" on Sunday (Hefele 4:209). Whereas Constantine's Sunday law had exempted agricultural labor from Sunday observance, now "field labours" were specifically included. This was a giant step toward applying the Pentateuch's Sabbath specifications to Sunday. The Second Synod of Macon in 585 and Council of Narbonne in 589 decreed further stipulations for very strict Sunday observance (*ibid.* 407, 422). Moreover, the ordinances of Macon "were published by King Guntram in a decree of November 10, 585, in which he enforced careful observance of Sunday" (*ibid.* 409). Thus a civil authority rendered support to the church, a phenomenon that grew in magnitude and scope during the next several centuries. By the end of the sixth century Sunday had supplanted the Sabbath well-nigh universally in Europe. It now served as the Christian weekly day of rest as well as of worship.

d. Sabbath and Sunday in Ethiopia. At least in some parts of the country or among certain groups of people in Ethiopia there developed a somewhat different relationship between Sabbath and Sunday. In the so-called *Egyptian Church Order,* apparently based on Hippolytus' *Apostolic Tradition* of the early third century, there is in the Ethiopic version a prescription stipulating that on both the Sabbath and first day of the week "the bishop, if it be possible, shall with his own hand deliver to all the people, while the deacons break bread." The same document indicates that both of these days were considered different from the "other days," and there is, in fact, even a reference to these two days as "sabbaths" (*Statutes of the Apostles* 66).

C. The Sabbath in the Middle Ages and Reformation Era

From the sixth century onward rigid Sunday observance developed in Europe. During the early Middle Ages the first day of the week increasingly came to be looked upon as having the characteristics of the Sabbath commandment of the Decalogue. There is no evidence in this period, however, of any widespread use of the word "sabbath" as a designation for Sunday. In Europe the expression "Lord's day" was the common one used for the first day of the week. But in Ethiopia, the tradition of considering both Saturday and Sunday as "sabbaths" continued on into modern times.

1. The Middle Ages

During the Middle Ages a Catholic theology developed concerning Sunday as fulfilling the Sabbath commandment. The concept was that the stipulations of the commandment remained intact, but the specific day had been changed from Saturday to Sunday by the Catholic Church. The specifications were considered to be moral and continuously binding, whereas the choice of the day itself was looked upon as ceremonial and therefore temporary, transitory, and subject to change by the church.

Several ninth-century sources reveal clear evidence of an awareness of Sunday's being a replacement for the Sabbath, such as Canon 50 of the Synod of Paris of A.D. 829. But the classical theological formulation came with Thomas Aquinas (d. 1274), who nevertheless did not think that the Sunday sabbath needed to be as strictly observed as the OT Sabbath. He stated that in its literal sense the "commandment to keep the Sabbath [in the Decalogue] is partly moral, and partly ceremonial"—moral in that human beings should set aside some time for concentrating on the things of God, and ceremonial as to the particular time set apart (*Summa Theologica* 2a2ae. 122. 4).

During most of the medieval period there is evidence of strong efforts by both ecclesiastical authorities and secular rulers to enforce Sunday observance. Nevertheless, some Christians in Europe refused to discard the Saturday Sabbath. Glimpses of such Sabbathkeepers come from the late Middle Ages: a case of Sabbathkeeping in England in 1402; a group of some 16 to 18 persons arrested in Douai, France, in 1420 because of their theological views and practices that included Sabbathkeeping; and Sabbathkeepers in Norway in 1435 and 1436. The information in each of these instances comes from the opponents of the Sabbathkeepers. However, in the early sixteenth-century documentary evidence from Norway cites ecclesiastical prohibition of Saturday Sabbathkeeping on the one hand, and of some small degree of clerical encouragement for such Sabbathkeeping on the other.

2. The Reformation Era

a. Major Reformers. Because Martin Luther (1483-1546), the pioneer Protestant Reformer, emphasized Christian freedom and opposed the numerous ceremonies and "ceremonial strictness" of the Roman Catholic Church, he felt that neither Sabbath nor Sunday was a divine requirement and that the Catholic sabbatizing of Sunday was invalid. Since, however, it was important to have one day each week for worship services, Luther selected Sunday, for this was the traditional weekly worship day on which people were accustomed to gather for church.

John Calvin (1509-1564) held a view similar to Luther's regarding the observance of Sunday as a convenience rather than a necessary requirement in fulfilling a divine prescription for weekly worship. Calvin differed from Luther, however, in rejecting the Catholic distinction between moral and ceremonial aspects of the Sabbath commandment, a distinction which Luther retained. Calvin believed that the Sabbath had been abrogated, with Sunday being substituted for it by the early Christian church. He also elucidated more clearly than Luther a theology of the Sabbath by pointing out three main functions: (1) the Sabbath is important for spiritual growth; (2) it is the anchor for public worship; and (3) it has social and humanitarian benefits in its practical concern for giving rest to servants. These elements were enunciated as early as his 1536 edition of the *Institutes of the Christian Religion.*

Martin Bucer (1491-1551), the prominent Reformer in Strassburg, was renowned for his spirit of openness and toleration, but rather strangely he heralded a strict Sunday observance. On Sundays no one was to perform "unnecessary corporal works," even useful ones, and "no works of the flesh" (remunerative labor, repayment of debts, sports, etc.) should be engaged in, nor should there be absenteeism from religious gatherings (*De Regno Christi* 2. 10). In 1532 Bucer and his colleagues went so far as to ask the Strassburg civil authorities to put an interdiction on all Sunday work except activities necessary to satisfy bodily needs. By 1534 the city passed an ordinance to this effect, with heavy financial penalties for noncompliance.

Close associates of Luther in Wittenberg, such as Philip Melanchthon (d. 1560), adhered basically to Luther's position. In Zurich, Ulrich Zwingli (d. 1531) and his followers treated their Sunday observance in much the same way. A notable exception was a former friend and colleague of Luther's, Andreas Bodenstein von Carlstadt (d. 1541), who, to the dismay of Luther, in 1524 published a treatise in which he set forth rather strict Sabbath observance. In it Carlstadt also indicated that Sunday was a day "which men have established" and referred to the Saturday Sabbath as a disputed matter.

Certain early-sixteenth-century English Reformers, such as William Tyndale (d. 1536), went further than Luther and Calvin in playing down the need for any specific day of the week as the day for congregational worship. In fact, Tyndale suggested that the main day for worship could be every tenth day, if this would be helpful toward counteracting superstition. In practice, however, he followed the usual custom, which dictated that the weekly gathering in England, as elsewhere, be on the first day of the week.

b. Sixteenth-century Sabbathkeepers. In Europe during the Reformation Era, Sunday was by far the predominant day for Christian worship services, but some groups made Saturday their main worship day. In a relatively few instances they observed both Saturday and Sunday.

The most striking example of seventh-day-Sabbath observance in Europe during the sixteenth century is that of a few Anabaptist groups. The detailed evidence concerning their beliefs comes by way of their detractors. In an effort to discredit these Anabaptists, their opponents detailed what the specific Anabaptist arguments were. This is true, specifically with regard to no-longer-extant writings about the Sabbath by the Anabaptists Oswald Glait and Andreas Fischer, who had accepted Saturday as the Sabbath c. 1527 and 1528. Their biblical arguments, from both the OT and NT, are very similar to those still set forth by those who observe the seventh-day Sabbath. They also referred to the first Sunday enactment as being issued by Emperor Constantine the Great.

In Spain, a reform movement led by Constantino Ponce de la Fuente (d. 1560) included observance of the seventh-day Sabbath.

Another such movement was inaugurated in Transylvania by Andreas Eössi toward the end of the sixteenth century, and flourished in the second decade of the following century. However, Simon Pechi, Eössi's successor in the leadership of these Transylvanian Sabbathkeepers, made the movement more Jewish than Christian. In the Nordic lands, a decree against Sabbathkeepers was issued in Norway in 1544, and a decade later a decree against Sabbathkeeping in Finland was issued by King Gustavus I Vasa, who ruled both Sweden and Finland. By the end of the sixteenth century there is evidence of Sabbathkeepers in Sweden. And from the Netherlands, France, Russia, and elsewhere in Europe, there are reports concerning Saturday Sabbathkeepers, but in some cases the Sabbathkeepers may have been Jews rather than Christians.

D. The Sabbath Among Puritans and Baptists

1. Puritan Sunday Sabbatarianism

The Protestant emphasis on Sunday as the "Christian sabbath" emerged in the late sixteenth century among the Puritans of England. For the Puritans, the day was honored not only with worship services, but with very strict prohibitions. This restrictiveness was not compatible, however, with the general attitude in England, especially among the Anglicans, who constituted the "Established Church." In the religious settlement made by Queen Elizabeth I there had been allowance for considerable latitude in religious belief and practice, a factor that made the Puritan stringency even more distasteful. In 1585, for example, the Queen opposed an attempt of Parliament to pass a law for stricter sabbath (Sunday) observance.

The Sunday sabbath became a strong bone of contention between the Puritans and the Anglican party. Nicholas Bownd's *Doctrine of the Sabbath* of 1595 was a Puritan clarion cry concerning the validity of the "biblical sabbath" (Sunday sabbath) for England as a "Holy Commonwealth." Bownd utilized a "transfer theory" for making Sunday the sabbath, claiming that the apostles themselves had changed the day from Saturday to Sunday.

Puritan Sunday observance called forth a response by King James I in 1618, in his *Book of Sports,* which set forth and supported the Anglican position. Serious debate followed, and later King Charles I reissued the *Book of Sports.* Anglicans held their main weekly worship services on Sunday, but after church attendance the people were free to engage in business pursuits, sports, or other entertainments. The practice of the Puritans was in stark contrast with this, as they seriously endeavored to make their Sunday sabbath conform to the OT Sabbath regulations. Puritanism, as it came to America in the 1620s and 1630s, carried with it this same attitude of very strict Sunday observance.

2. The Saturday Sabbath in England

Within the ranks of English Puritanism several groups emerged, including those who believed in adult baptism. These Baptists were, for the most part, also staunch Sundaykeepers. However, among them there arose certain prominent advocates of Saturday as the Sabbath. In studying the rationale for making Sunday a sabbath, they took the next logical step: they adopted *the very day* set forth in Scripture as the Sabbath.

John Traske (d. c. 1636) and Theophilus Brabourne (d. c. 1661) were among the early powerful exponents of Saturday as the true Sabbath. Nowhere in Scripture could they find a "transfer theory." What they did find was that the day of worship for Christ and His apostles had been Saturday. Beginning with a publication in 1628, Brabourne produced no fewer than four major works on the Sabbath over some three decades. Although it appears that under ecclesiastical pressure Brabourne finally returned to the Anglican position, in his publications he firmly advocated to the very end the observance of the seventh day of the week.

3. The Saturday Sabbath in the New World

In the New World (Western Hemisphere), Jewish immigrants were the first keepers of the Saturday Sabbath. The earliest Jewish settlers emigrated to Brazil from Portugal in 1502. Another group reached Mexico by 1521. Toward the end of the sixteenth century Jews settled in Argentina as well; and by the mid-seventeenth century, Jewish congregations were established in the Netherlands Antilles. The founders of the first Jewish congregation in what was later to become the United States were immigrants from Brazil who in 1654 established *Sherith Israel* in New Amsterdam (now New York).

Seventh Day Baptists were the first Christian Sabbathkeepers in the New World, the earliest documented observance of the Saturday Sabbath being that of Stephen Mumford, who in 1664 emigrated from England to Newport, Rhode Island. There he joined the Baptist congregation, influencing some of its members to adopt the biblical Sabbath and thereby arousing serious controversy. Eventually he drew the condemnation of that congregation upon himself and his converts. In December of 1671, together with some six or seven others, he withdrew from the Newport Baptist Church and founded the first Seventh Day Baptist community on American soil. These Sabbathkeepers elected William Hiscox, one of Mumford's converts, as their first pastor. Soon Seventh Day Baptists spread into other parts of New England and even farther to the west.

Seventh Day Baptists were ardent advocates of the Saturday Sabbath, publishing and disseminating literature on the subject. With growth in its membership and in the number of congregations in America, this group of Sabbathkeepers eventually organized into a fellowship of communions during the first years of the nineteenth century. In 1818 they officially adopted the name "Seventh Day Baptist." Their *Missionary Magazine* and *Protestant Sentinel* were launched in 1821 and

1830, respectively, and were replaced in 1844 by *The Sabbath Recorder.* One of the main objectives of these journals was promulgation of material regarding the seventh-day Sabbath. A tract society was established in 1835 (since 1844 bearing the name American Sabbath Tract Society), and by 1850 a series of 17 tracts and six books about the Sabbath had been published, including a reprint of George Carlow's *Truth Defended* of 1724.

In the early nineteenth century Argentine patriot Ramos Mexía (1773-1825) studied the Bible and became convinced of the validity of the seventh-day Sabbath. On his farm south of Buenos Aires, all work ceased every week on Sabbath.

E. Jews and the Sabbath in Modern Times

In spite of restrictions codified in the Mishnah and the Talmud, Jews throughout the Common Era have been joyous and ardent Sabbathkeepers. Pious Jews welcome and cherish the Sabbath hours as if they brought the visit of a queen or bride, two of the metaphors used to describe the Sabbath. In present-day Judaism, however, strictness about traditional Sabbath observance varies among the several major groups into which Judaism has become subdivided.

Certain Jewish writers of the nineteenth and twentieth centuries have made a considerable impact in developing theological thought about the Sabbath. Prominent among these are Samson Hirsch, Hermann Cohen, Leo Baeck, Martin Buber, and Franz Rosenzweig, who have set forth the Sabbath's relationship to God's sovereignty, human ethics, and general morality. Cohen sees, for example, the Sabbath as the initial step toward abolishing slavery, a concept paralleling Hirsch's reference to the Sabbath's placement of master and servant on equal footing as free persons.

Perhaps no other Jewish publication in recent times has had a greater impact on Sabbath theology, however, than Joshua Abraham Heschel's *The Sabbath: Its Meaning for*

Modern Man in 1951. Much of the same ethical concern of the previously mentioned Jewish writers, including the concept of the Sabbath as a "leveler," is evident in Heschel. One of his major themes is the universality of time. Among his beautiful descriptions of the Sabbath is "a palace in time," the title of his first chapter. He points out, as well, that whereas human beings compete for space, time is always available to everyone. However, the Sabbath is a special segment of time that stands apart from time in general. Indeed, the Sabbath is "the armistice in man's cruel struggle for existence" (29). But it is also more than this, for it is "a profound conscious harmony of man and the world, a sympathy for all things and a participation in the spirit that unites what is below and what is above" (31, 32).

F. The Sabbath in Seventh-day Adventist History and Practice

1. The Beginnings of Adventist Sabbathkeeping

The seventh-day Sabbath began to be kept by certain Adventists shortly after the Disappointment in 1844. Rachel Oakes, T. M. Preble, and Joseph Bates were the earliest Sabbath advocates. Ellen and James White soon accepted the teaching, which they presented in the "Bible Conferences" in 1848.

a. Rachel Oakes and T. M. Preble. Knowledge of the seventh-day Sabbath came to those who had been within the Millerite movement through two main avenues. One was Rachel Oakes (later married to Nathan Preston), a Seventh Day Baptist, who in early 1844 distributed Seventh Day Baptist publications among members of the Christian Brethren Church in Washington, New Hampshire. Through the influence of Oakes, Frederick Wheeler, a Methodist minister who had adopted the Adventist stance and who had this Washington church in his preaching circuit, began to observe the Sabbath about March of that year. Soon several members of the Farnsworth family and a few others also accepted the Sabbath. These formed the nucleus for the first group of Sabbathkeeping Adventists. By 1850 they joined with other Sabbathkeepers to become the nucleus of the SDA Church, which was officially organized in 1863.

The second avenue through which knowledge of the seventh-day Sabbath came to Adventist believers was an article by T. M. Preble, a prominent Millerite minister who frequently wrote for Adventist papers. He lived near Washington, New Hampshire, and may have learned of the Sabbath from someone in the Washington Christian Brethren Church. In August 1844 he began to keep the Sabbath. Moreover, he also prepared an article on the subject, published in the *Hope of Israel* of February 28, 1845. This article was later reprinted as a tract and in that form reached many Adventists, among whom was Joseph Bates.

b. Joseph Bates. Preble's article came to Joseph Bates's attention by March of 1845, and Bates took an immediate and strong interest in the material it presented. Bates himself soon began to write on the topic of the Sabbath, by May 1846, expressing his new convictions in a short section toward the end of a 39-page pamphlet entitled *The Opening Heavens*. This pamphlet had been inspired by his reading of O.R.L. Crosier's discussion of the heavenly sanctuary of Daniel 8:14. Strangely, in his *Opening Heavens* Bates did not connect the Sabbath with the ark of the testament in heaven mentioned in Revelation 11:19, but only with the ark in the ancient Israelite sanctuary.

Bates's first publication specifically on the Sabbath was his *Seventh Day Sabbath, a Perpetual Sign*, a 48-page tract that appeared in August 1846. Preble had referred to Daniel 7:25 as being fulfilled by the activity of the "little horn" in endeavoring to change "times and laws," and Bates followed Preble's reasoning in *Tract Showing That the Seventh Day Should Be Observed as the Sabbath* that "all who keep the first day of the week for '*the Sabbath*' are the *Pope's Sunday Keepers!!* and

God's Sabbath Breakers!!!" (10).

In his publication, however, Bates now began to move beyond the traditional Seventh Day Baptist expositions by suggesting a link between the Sabbath and the "Third Angel's Message" of Revelation 14:9-11. In his second edition (January 1847), in his *Vindication of the Seventh-day Sabbath* (January 1848), and in *A Seal of the Living God* (January 1849), he moved progressively to an understanding of the Sabbath as linked to the ark in heaven and also as representing the "seal of the living God" mentioned in Revelation 7.

c. James and Ellen White. Ellen Harmon apparently had her first contact with the Sabbath question in 1846, when with her sister and James White she visited Joseph Bates in New Bedford, Massachusetts. At that time she did not accept Bates's Sabbath views. On August 30, 1846, James White and Ellen Harmon were married, the same month in which the first edition of Bates's Sabbath tract appeared. The evidence in this tract led James and Ellen to begin to observe the Bible Sabbath and to teach and defend it during that very autumn (1T 75). The next April, Ellen had her first vision concerning the Sabbath (EW 32-35), a vision corroborating what had already been ascertained by careful study of the Bible and by much prayer.

d. The "Sabbath Conferences." During the earliest stage of their development, Sabbathkeeping Adventists had no formal organization; but in 1848 a number of them attended seven small local meetings. These later came to be called "Sabbath Conferences" because they were meetings of "friends of the Sabbath" interested in the "third angel's message" (Rev. 14:9-11). These conferences had a select agenda, including the Sabbath, and helped to bring a sense of unity to the rather widely scattered groups of Adventist Sabbathkeepers.

e. Time for beginning the Sabbath. Not until the 1850s did the time of day for commencing and closing the Sabbath become fully clarified for the growing number of Sabbath-

keeping Adventists. Although Seventh Day Baptists had observed a sunset-to-sunset Sabbath on the basis of scriptural evidence (e.g., Mark 1:32), Joseph Bates was of the opinion that the Sabbath should begin at 6:00 p.m. on Friday and end at 6:00 p.m. on Saturday (RH Apr. 21, 1851). Bates's view did not, however, find universal favor among the Sabbathkeeping Adventists. James White wrote in 1855, "We have never been fully satisfied with the testimony presented in favor of 6:00 o'clock" (*ibid.* Dec. 4, 1855). At that time, in addition to those who adhered to Bates's practice, some observed a midnight-to-midnight time frame, others used the sunset-to-sunset guideline, and still others thought that the Sabbath should begin on Saturday morning.

In view of these differing viewpoints, J. N. Andrews was assigned the task of making a thorough investigation of the subject. In his written report, which was published in the same issue of the *Review and Herald* as James White's comment, he demonstrated from the OT and NT that the biblical word "even" (or "evening") means sunset. Prior to this he had also presented his finding orally to an assembly of Sabbathkeeping Adventists, nearly all of whom had accepted his solution to the question. Among the dissenters were Joseph Bates and Ellen White, who still held to the 6:00 position. At the close of the assembly, however, Ellen White received a vision in which she was shown that the Sabbath should be observed from sunset to sunset. Some 12 years later James White could write that this vision "settled the matter with Brother Bates and others, and general harmony has since prevailed among us upon this point" (*ibid.* Feb. 25, 1868).

f. The Sabbath and prophecy/eschatology. At the outset Adventist Sabbathkeepers adopted, for the most part, the same rationale, arguments, and understanding that the Seventh Day Baptists had set forth regarding the Sabbath. The Seventh Day Baptists had strong scriptural arguments, from both the OT and the NT, but they failed to relate the Sabbath with other major theological concerns, including various aspects of prophetic fulfillment and the eschatological focus of certain passages of Scripture. The one notable exception was their attention to the prophecy of Daniel 7:25 and the related passage in Revelation 13:5, 6.

As Bates and others continued their study of the Sabbath, however, they soon came upon a connection with the three angels' messages of Revelation 14 (especially the third one). Further prophetic links emerged, such as the Sabbath as God's seal of Revelation 7, and the trade embargo and death decree depicted in Revelation 13:16, 17 as inclusions in expected forthcoming Sunday legislation. Bates himself, in his continuing publications, set forth these new insights, as well as making an integral connection between the Sabbath and the heavenly sanctuary. The Sabbath's connection with the sanctuary, accompanied by a call for revival as set forth in Revelation 14, became a major emphasis in the Sabbath theology of Bates and other of the Adventist "pioneers" who were forerunners (and for the most part founders) of the SDA Church.

g. Early publications on the Sabbath. The Sabbath took considerable space in some of the earliest SDA periodicals—for instance, in the *Present Truth,* which was inaugurated in 1849, and in its successor, *The Advent Review and Sabbath Herald,* from 1850 onward.

In 1861 J. N. Andrews published a 340-page book entitled *History of the Sabbath and First Day of the Week.* This rather comprehensive work was enlarged and revised for later editions. Andrews for the most part adhered to Seventh Day Baptist concepts and historical treatment, but he also did extensive reexamination of the basic historical sources. In addition, he cited many Sunday-keeping authors. L. R. Conradi took an interest in Andrews' work, and in 1891 translated his *History* into German. In 1912 he issued in English, as coauthor, an enlarged and substantially revised edition, indicated as being the "fourth edition."

2. Adventist Sabbath Practice

The SDA Church considers the Scriptures of the OT and the NT as the normative guide for its theology and practice. For this reason SDAs celebrate the seventh day of the week as the Sabbath. On it they endeavor to follow pertinent OT regulations, but especially the example of Christ in the NT, as to how the day should be treated. Based on the scriptural evidence, SDAs have adopted the practice of keeping Sabbath from sundown Friday night to sundown Saturday night. All of these hours are considered sacred to God. They are a time when personal pursuits and interests are set aside for spiritual refreshment. SDAs believe, moreover, that proper preparation for genuine Sabbath observance must be a *daily* practice of making Christ the Lord of the Christian's life, and therefore daily devotions and self-surrender to Christ are not to be neglected at any time.

On Saturday mornings (or in exceptional cases, on Saturday afternoons) SDAs have regular worship services. These normally consist of (1) Sabbath School, with a Scripture lesson study as the primary focus (usually in small groups or "classes," and with special sections devoted to youth and to children); (2) a short "missionary period" for setting forth plans for local missionary activity and Christian "help work"; and (3) the preaching service, in which the Scripture reading and sermon have the primary emphasis. On a quarterly basis the Sabbath morning preaching service includes celebration of the ordinances of footwashing and the Lord's Supper, patterned after Christ's example and instruction set forth in John 13:1-17; Matthew 26:26-30; 1 Corinthians 11:23-29.

In many SDA churches there are also sundown meetings on Friday and Saturday evenings. Where such services do not exist, or when attendance is not possible, personal or family devotions mark the beginning and the ending of the Sabbath. Business affairs and personal secular pleasures and entertainment (such as sports) are avoided by SDAs during the Sabbath hours. Frequently nature hikes (especially for children and youth), participation in local missionary-type outreach, and general spiritual fellowship with other SDAs or with non-SDAs are engaged in, as being in harmony with divine instruction for Sabbath observance. Although SDA physicians normally do not keep office hours on Sabbath, they do stay "on call" for aid to the sick, including persons who may be hospitalized. All essential personnel in SDA medical institutions must rotate Sabbath service time so that patients are always cared for, even though general routines are normally reduced during Sabbath hours.

The SDA position regarding the use of the Sabbath hours has aptly been set forth by Ellen White, whose writings are respected in the SDA Church: "The Sabbath is not intended to be a period of useless inactivity. The law forbids secular labor on the rest day of the Lord; the toil that gains a livelihood must cease; no labor for worldly pleasure or profit is lawful upon that day; but as God ceased His labor of creating, and rested upon the Sabbath and blessed it, so man is to leave the occupations of his daily life, and devote those sacred hours to healthful rest, to worship, and to holy deeds" (DA 207).

In keeping with the importance of Sabbath observance, a major volume entitled *The Sabbath in Scripture and History* was published in 1982. This work represents the combined effort and work of some 19 specialists and treats in detail the Sabbath throughout the OT and NT, as well as in Christian history. It also includes three chapters on Sabbath theology.

VI. Ellen G. White Comments

Ellen G. White has written so widely about the seventh-day Sabbath that only a sampling of her insights and counsels regarding it can be given here. Much of what she has written is occasional in nature, speaking to various specific situations requiring the same or similar counsels, a fact that accounts for a fair amount of repetitiveness in her treatment of the Sabbath. This survey presents typical or representative statements on major aspects of the Sabbath and Sabbathkeeping.

A. The Origin and Significance of the Sabbath

"In Eden, God set up the memorial of His work of creation, in placing His blessing upon the seventh day. The Sabbath was committed to Adam, the father and representative of the whole human family. Its observance was to be an act of grateful acknowledgment, on the part of all who should dwell upon the earth, that God was their Creator and their rightful Sovereign; that they were the work of His hands and the subjects of His authority" (PP 48).

"The Sabbath is not introduced as a new institution but as having been founded at creation. It is to be remembered and observed as the memorial of the Creator's work. Pointing to God as the Maker of the heavens and the earth, it distinguishes the true God from all false gods. All who keep the seventh day signify by this act that they are worshipers of Jehovah. Thus the Sabbath is the sign of man's allegiance to God as long as there are any upon the earth to serve Him" (*ibid.* 307).

"The Sabbath institution, which originated in Eden, is as old as the world itself. It was observed by all the patriarchs, from creation down. During the bondage in Egypt, the Israelites were forced by their taskmasters to violate the Sabbath, and to a great extent they lost the knowledge of its sacredness. When the law was proclaimed at Sinai the very first words of the fourth commandment were, 'Remember the Sabbath day, to keep it holy'— showing that the Sabbath was not then instituted; we are pointed back for its origin to creation" (*ibid.* 336).

"The fourth commandment is the only one

of all the ten in which are found both the name and the title of the Lawgiver. It is the only one that shows by whose authority the law is given. Thus it contains the seal of God, affixed to His law as evidence of its authenticity and binding force" (*ibid.* 307).

B. Human Need for the Sabbath

"God saw that a Sabbath was essential for man, even in Paradise. He needed to lay aside his own interests and pursuits for one day of the seven, that he might more fully contemplate the works of God and meditate upon His power and goodness. He needed a Sabbath to remind him more vividly of God and to awaken gratitude because all that he enjoyed and possessed came from the beneficent hand of the Creator" (*ibid.* 48).

"The Sabbath, as a memorial of God's creative power, points to Him as the maker of the heavens and the earth. Hence it is a constant witness to His existence and a reminder of His greatness, His wisdom, and His love. Had the Sabbath always been sacredly observed, there could never have been an atheist or an idolater" (*ibid.* 336).

C. Christ the Maker of the Sabbath

Ellen White repeatedly notes that Christ was with God the Father at Creation, active in the work of Creation, as the NT makes clear (John 1:1-3).

"Since He [Christ] made all things, He made the Sabbath. By Him it was set apart as a memorial of the work of creation. It points to Him as both the Creator and the Sanctifier" (DA 288).

"He [Christ] who made the Sabbath did not abolish it, nailing it to His cross" (*ibid.* 630).

"All things were created by the Son of God. . . . And since the Sabbath is a memorial of the work of creation, it is a token of the love and power of Christ" (*ibid.* 281).

"Christ, during His earthly ministry, emphasized the binding claims of the Sabbath; in all His teaching He showed reverence for the institution He Himself had given" (PK 183).

D. Christ's Sabbath-Observance Principles

In connection with conflict between Jesus and the Jewish leaders, Christ enunciated true biblical principles of Sabbath observance in contrast with the human-made restrictions:

"As the Jews departed from God, and failed to make the righteousness of Christ their own by faith, the Sabbath lost its significance to them. . . . In the days of Christ the Sabbath had become so perverted that its observance reflected the character of selfish and arbitrary men rather than the character of the loving heavenly Father. The rabbis virtually represented God as giving laws which it was impossible for men to obey. They led the people to look upon God as a tyrant, and to think that the observance of the Sabbath, as He required it, made men hard-hearted and cruel. It was the work of Christ to clear away these misconceptions. Although the rabbis followed Him with merciless hostility, He did not even appear to conform to their requirements, but went straight forward, keeping the Sabbath according to the law of God" (DA 283, 284).

"He [Jesus] had come to free the Sabbath from those burdensome requirements that had made it a curse instead of a blessing.

"For this reason He had chosen the Sabbath upon which to perform the act of healing at Bethesda. He could have healed the sick man as well on any other day of the week; or He might simply have cured him, without bidding him bear away his bed. But this would not have given Him the opportunity He desired. A wise purpose underlay every act of Christ's life on earth. Everything He did was important in itself and in its teaching. Among the afflicted ones at the pool He selected the worst case upon whom to exercise His healing power, and bade the man carry his bed through the city in order to publish the great work that had been wrought upon him. This would raise the question of what it was lawful to do on the Sabbath, and would open the way for Him to denounce the restrictions of the Jews in regard to the Lord's day, and to declare their traditions void.

"Jesus stated to them that the work of relieving the afflicted was in harmony with the Sabbath law. It was in harmony with the work of God's angels, who are ever descending and ascending between heaven and earth to minister to suffering humanity. Jesus declared, 'My Father worketh hitherto, and I work'" (*ibid.* 206).

"Christ would teach His disciples and His enemies that the service of God is first of all. The object of God's work in this world is the redemption of man; therefore that which is necessary to be done on the Sabbath in the accomplishment of this work is in accord with the Sabbath law. Jesus then crowned His argument by declaring Himself the 'Lord of the Sabbath'—One above all question and above all law. This infinite Judge acquits the disciples of blame, appealing to the very statutes they are accused of violating" (*ibid.* 285).

E. Sabbathkeeping and Holiness

Ellen White has repeatedly emphasized that mere formalistic Sabbathkeeping is meaningless or worse. True observance of God's Sabbath involves the sanctification of life which Christ gives.

"It [the Sabbath] declares that He who created all things in heaven and in earth, and by whom all things hold together, is the head of the church, and that by His power we are reconciled to God. . . . Then the Sabbath is a sign of Christ's power to make us holy. And it is given to all whom Christ makes holy. As a sign of His sanctifying power, the Sabbath is given to all who through Christ become a part of the Israel of God" (*ibid.* 288).

"The Sabbath was not for Israel merely, but for the world. It had been made known to man in Eden, and, like the other precepts of the Decalogue, it is of imperishable obligation. . . .

"No other institution which was committed to the Jews tended so fully to distinguish them from surrounding nations as did the Sabbath. God designed that its observance should designate them as His worshipers. It was to be a token of their separation from idolatry, and their connection with the true God. But in order to keep the Sabbath holy, men must themselves be holy. Through faith they must become partakers of the righteousness of Christ" (*ibid.* 283).

F. The Sabbath Through the Ages

"In the first centuries the true Sabbath had been kept by all Christians. They were jealous for the honor of God, and, believing that His law is immutable, they zealously guarded the sacredness of its precepts. But with great subtlety Satan worked through his agents to bring about his object. That the attention of the people might be called to the Sunday, it was made a festival in honor of the resurrection of Christ. Religious services were held upon it; yet it was regarded as a day of recreation, the Sabbath being still sacredly observed" (GC 52).

"From that day [the time when the law was given at Sinai] to the present the knowledge of God's law has been preserved in the earth, and the Sabbath of the fourth commandment has been kept. Though the 'man of sin' succeeded in trampling underfoot God's holy day, yet even in the period of his supremacy there were, hidden in secret places, faithful souls who paid it honor. Since the Reformation, there have been some in every generation to maintain its observance. Though often in the midst of reproach and persecution, a constant testimony has been borne to the perpetuity of the law of God and the sacred obligation of the creation Sabbath" (*ibid.* 453).

Ellen White also notes that among the Waldenses were some who "were observers of the Sabbath," and that in Ethiopia, too, Christians observed the Sabbath, even though they also abstained from labor on Sunday (*ibid.* 577, 578).

G. The Sabbath in the Final Crisis of Earth's History

"The Sabbath will be the great test of loyalty,

for it is the point of truth especially controverted. When the final test shall be brought to bear upon men, then the line of distinction will be drawn between those who serve God and those who serve Him not. While the observance of the false sabbath in compliance with the law of the state, contrary to the fourth commandment, will be an avowal of allegiance to a power that is in opposition to God, the keeping of the true Sabbath, in obedience to God's law, is an evidence of loyalty to the Creator. While one class, by accepting the sign of submission to earthly powers, receive the mark of the beast, the other choosing the token of allegiance to divine authority, receive the seal of God" (*ibid.* 605).

"But not one is made to suffer the wrath of God until the truth has been brought home to his mind and conscience, and has been rejected. There are many who have never had an opportunity to hear the special truths for this time. The obligation of the fourth commandment has never been set before them in its true light. He who reads every heart and tries every motive will leave none who desire a knowledge of the truth, to be deceived as to the issues of the controversy. The decree is not to be urged upon the people blindly. Everyone is to have sufficient light to make his decision intelligently" *(ibid.).*

"The Sabbath question is to be the issue in the great final conflict in which all the world will act a part. Men have honored Satan's principles above the principles that rule in the heavens. They have accepted the spurious sabbath, which Satan has exalted as the sign of his authority. But God has set His seal upon His royal requirement. Each Sabbath institution bears the name of its author, an ineffaceable mark that shows the authority of each. It is our work to lead the people to understand this. We are to show them that it is of vital consequence whether they bear the mark of God's kingdom or the mark of the kingdom of rebellion, for they acknowledge themselves subjects of the kingdom whose mark they bear" (6T 352).

"God has called us to uplift the standard of His downtrodden Sabbath. How important, then, that our example in Sabbathkeeping should be right" (*ibid.* 352, 353).

H. Preparation for the Sabbath

Preparation for the Sabbath should occupy the whole week, and in all preparation the spiritual dimension is paramount.

"We are not merely to observe the Sabbath as a legal matter. We are to understand its spiritual bearing upon all the transactions of life. All who regard the Sabbath as a sign between them and God, showing that He is the God who sanctifies them, will represent the principles of His government. They will bring into daily practice the laws of His kingdom. Daily it will be their prayer that the sanctification of the Sabbath may rest upon them. Every day they will have the companionship of Christ and will exemplify the perfection of His character. Every day their light will shine forth to others in good works" (*ibid.* 353, 354).

"When the Sabbath is thus remembered, the temporal will not be allowed to encroach upon the spiritual. No duty pertaining to the six working days will be left for the Sabbath. During the week our energies will not be so exhausted in temporal labor that on the day when the Lord rested and was refreshed we shall be too weary to engage in His service" (*ibid.* 354).

But while "preparation for the Sabbath is to be made all through the week, Friday is to be the special preparation day" *(ibid.):*

"See that all the clothing is in readiness, and that all the cooking is done. Let the boots be blacked and the baths be taken. It is possible to do this. If you make it a rule you can do it. The Sabbath is not to be given to the repairing of garments, to the cooking of food, to pleasure seeking, or to any other worldly employment. Before the setting of the sun let all secular work be laid aside and all secular papers be put out of sight. Parents, explain your work and its purpose to your children, and let them share in your preparation to keep the Sabbath according to the commandment" (*ibid.* 355, 356).

"On this day all differences between brethren, whether in the family or in the church, should be put away. Let all bitterness and wrath and malice be expelled from the soul. In a humble spirit, 'confess your faults one to another, and pray one for another, that ye may be healed' (James 5:16)" (*ibid.* 356).

I. The Sabbath in the Home

In her discussion of the Sabbath in the home, Ellen White's first instruction is that before "the setting of the sun [on Friday evening] let the members of the family assemble to read God's word, to sing and pray" (*ibid.*). Then regarding the Sabbath day itself, she declares:

"Let not the precious hours of the Sabbath be wasted in bed. On Sabbath morning the family should be astir early. If they rise late, there is confusion and bustle in preparing for breakfast and Sabbath school. There is hurrying, jostling, and impatience. Thus unholy feelings come into the home. The Sabbath, thus desecrated, becomes a weariness, and its coming is dreaded rather than loved.

"We should not provide for the Sabbath a more liberal supply or a greater variety of food than for other days. Instead of this the food should be more simple, and less should be eaten, in order that the mind may be clear and vigorous to comprehend spiritual things. . . .

"While cooking upon the Sabbath should be avoided, it is not necessary to eat cold food. In cold weather let the food prepared the day before be heated. And let the meals, though simple, be palatable and attractive. Provide something that will be regarded as a treat, something the family do not have every day" (*ibid.* 357).

"In pleasant weather let parents walk with their children in the fields and groves. Amid the beautiful things of nature tell them the reason for the institution of the Sabbath. Describe to them God's great work of creation. Tell them that when the earth came from His hand, it

was holy and beautiful. Every flower, every shrub, every tree, answered the purpose of its Creator. Everything upon which the eye rested was lovely and filled the mind with thoughts of the love of God. Every sound was music in harmony with the voice of God. Show that it was sin which marred God's perfect work; that thorns and thistles, sorrow and pain and death, are all the result of disobedience to God. Bid them see how the earth, though marred with the curse of sin, still reveals God's goodness" (*ibid.* 358).

"As the sun goes down, let the voice of prayer and the hymn of praise mark the close of the sacred hours and invite God's presence through the cares of the week of labor" (*ibid.* 359).

J. Travel on the Sabbath

Ellen White points out that travel on the Sabbath should be avoided as much as possible. But in "order to reach the churches that need our help, and to give them the message that God desires them to hear, it may be necessary for us to travel on the Sabbath." In such cases, "so far as possible we should secure our tickets and make all necessary arrangements on some other day" (*ibid.* 360). In addition, when "starting on a journey we should make every possible effort to plan so as to avoid reaching our destination on the Sabbath." And when "compelled to travel on the Sabbath we should try to avoid the company of those who would draw our attention to worldly things." Nevertheless, whenever "there is opportunity we should speak to others in regard to the truth. We should always be ready to relieve suffering and to help those in need." We should not, however, "talk about matters of business or engage in any common, worldly conversation" (*ibid.*).

K. Sabbath Meetings

"Wherever there are as many as two or three believers, let them meet together on the Sabbath to claim the Lord's promise.

"The little companies assembled to worship

God on His holy day have a right to claim the rich blessing of Jehovah. They should believe that the Lord Jesus is an honored guest in their assemblies. Every true worshiper who keeps holy the Sabbath should claim the promise: 'That ye may know that I am the Lord that doth sanctify you' (Ex. 31:13)" (*ibid.* 360, 361).

"The preaching at our Sabbath meetings should generally be short. Opportunity should be given for those who love God to express their gratitude and adoration" (*ibid.* 361). "Let none come to the place of worship to take a nap. There should be no sleeping in the house of God" (*ibid.*).

All should feel that they have "a part to act in making the Sabbath meetings interesting":

"You are not to come together simply as a matter of form, but for the interchange of thought, for the relation of your daily experiences, for the expression of thanksgiving, for the utterance of your sincere desire for divine enlightenment, that you may know God, and Jesus Christ, whom He has sent" (*ibid.* 362).

L. Further Concerns

With specific regard to the Sabbathkeeping practice of workers in SDA medical institutions, Ellen White pointed to the example of Christ, to the need for rest, and to the importance of the Sabbath as a sign between God and His people.

"Often physicians and nurses are called upon during the Sabbath to minister to the sick, and sometimes it is impossible for them to take time for rest and for attending devotional services. The needs of suffering humanity are never to be neglected. The Saviour, by His example, has shown us that it is right to relieve suffering on the Sabbath. But unnecessary work, such as ordinary treatments and operations that can be postponed, should be deferred. Let the patients understand that physicians and helpers should have one day for rest. Let them understand that the workers fear God and desire to keep holy the day that He has set apart for His followers to observe as a sign between Him and them" (7T 106).

"All our medical institutions are established as Seventh-day Adventist institutions, to represent the various features of gospel medical missionary work, and thus to prepare the way for the coming of the Lord" (*ibid.* 107).

Concerning the operation of public health-food restaurants, the following counsel is given:

"The question has been asked, 'Should our restaurants be opened on the Sabbath?' My answer is: No, no! The observance of the Sabbath is our witness to God, the mark, or sign, between Him and us that we are His people. Never is this mark to be obliterated" (*ibid.* 121).

A restaurant could, however, provide food packages on Friday for those who wish to take health foods home for use on the Sabbath (*ibid.* 121, 122).

Instruction has also been given regarding business plans and partnerships with those who do not respect the Sabbath:

"There is need of a Sabbath reform among us, who profess to observe God's holy rest day. Some discuss their business matters and lay plans on the Sabbath, and God looks upon this in the same light as though they engaged in the actual transaction of business.

"Others who are well acquainted with the Bible evidences that the seventh day is the Sabbath, enter into partnership with men who have no respect for God's holy day. A Sabbathkeeper cannot allow men in his employ, paid by his money, to work on the Sabbath. If, for the sake of gain, he allows the business in which he has an interest to be carried on on the Sabbath by his unbelieving partner, he is equally guilty with the unbeliever; and it is his duty to dissolve the relation, however much he may lose by so doing. Men may think they cannot afford to obey God, but they cannot afford to disobey Him. Those who are careless in their observance of the Sabbath will suffer great loss" (Ev 245).

The high standard which Ellen G. White sets forth as an absolute necessity in true Sabbathkeeping is well summed up in a statement quoted earlier: "In order to keep the Sabbath holy, men must themselves be holy. Through faith they must become partakers of the righteousness of Christ" (DA 283).

VII. Literature

Introductory Note: The literature regarding Sabbath and/or Sunday is massive. This listing is a select bibliography. Of the limited number of titles given, a few are not compatible with the views expressed in this chapter (especially so in the case of the books by Carson and Rordorf; these are listed simply because of the wide public attention they have received). In general, however, the selections will be supportive.

Andreasen, Niels-Erik. *The Old Testament Sabbath: A Tradition-historical Investigation.* Missoula, Mont.: University of Montana, 1972.

———. *Rest and Redemption: A Study of the Biblical Sabbath.* Berrien Springs, Mich.: Andrews University Press, 1978.

Andrews, J. N., and L. R. Conradi. *History of the Sabbath and First Day of the Week.* 4th ed., revised and enlarged. Washington, D.C.: Review and Herald, 1912.

Bacchiocchi, Samuele. *Divine Rest for Human Restlessness: A Study of the Good News of the Sabbath for Today.* Rome: Pontifical Gregorian University Press, 1980.

———. *From Sabbath to Sunday: A Historical Investigation of the Rise of Sunday Observance in Early Christianity.* Rome: Pontifical Gregorian University Press, 1977.

———. *Rest for Modern Man: The Sabbath for Today.* Nashville: Southern Pub. Assn., 1976.

Brunt, John. *A Day for Healing: The Meaning of Jesus' Sabbath Miracles.* Washington, D.C.: Review and Herald, 1981.

Carson, D. A., ed. *From Sabbath to Lord's Day: A Biblical, Historical, and Theological Investigation.* Grand Rapids, Mich.: Zondervan, 1982.

Dugmore, C. W. "Lord's Day and Easter." *Neotestamentica et Patristica* (Sup. NT, vol. 6). Leiden: Brill, 1962.

Hasel, Gerhard F. "Sabbatarian Anabaptists of the Sixteenth Century," Part I, *AUSS* 5 (1967):101-121; Part II, *AUSS* 6 (1968):19-28.

———. "Sabbath." *The Anchor Bible Dictionary.* Vol. 5, pp. 849-856.

Hefele, Karl Joseph von. *A History of the Councils of the Church.* 5 vols. Edinburgh: T. & T. Clark, 1883-1896.

Heschel, Abraham Joshua. *The Sabbath: Its Meaning for Modern Man.* New York: Farrar, Straus, and Young, 1951.

Horner, George, ed. and trans. *The Statutes of the Apostles or Canones Ecclesiastici.* Oxford, Eng.: Williams and Norgate, 1904.

Kubo, Sakae. *God Meets Man: A Theology of the Sabbath and the Second Advent.* Nashville: Southern Pub. Assn., 1978.

Lewis, A. H. *A Critical History of the Sabbath and the Sunday in the Christian Church.* Alfred Centre, N.Y.: American Sabbath Tract Society, 1886.

Liechty, Daniel. *Andreas Fischer and the Sabbatarian Anabaptists: An Early Reformation Episode in East Central Europe.* Studies in Anabaptist and Mennonite History, No. 29. Scottdale, Pa.: Herald Press, 1988.

———. *Sabbatarianism in the Sixteenth Century: A Page in the History of the Radical Reformation.* Berrien Springs, Mich.: Andrews University Press, 1993.

Odom, Robert L. *Sabbath and Sunday in Early Christianity.* Washington, D.C.: Review and Herald, 1977.

Rordorf, Willy. *Sunday: The History of the Day of Rest and Worship in the Earliest Centuries of the Christian Church.* Trans. A.A.K. Graham. Philadelphia: Westminster, 1968. (Originally in German: *Der Sonntag. Geschichte der Ruhe- und Gottesdiensttages im ältesten Christentum.* Zurich: Zwingli Verlag, 1962.)

Saunders, Herbert E. *The Sabbath: Symbol of Creation and Re-Creation.* Plainfield, N.J.: American Sabbath Tract Society, 1970.

Shea, William H. "The Sabbath in Extra-biblical Sources." *Adventist Perspectives* 3, No. 2 (1989): 17-25.

Strand, Kenneth A. "Another Look at 'Lord's Day' in the Early Church and in Revelation 1:10." *New Testament Studies* 13 (1967): 174-180.

———. *The Early Christian Sabbath: Selected Essays and a Source Collection.* Worthington, Ohio: Ann Arbor Publishers, 1979.

Strand, Kenneth A., ed. *The Sabbath in Scripture and History.* Washington, D.C.: Review and Herald, 1982.

Appendix
The Seven-Day Week and the Julian-Gregorian Calendar

Two items of technical nature deserve brief attention: the rise of the "Planetary Week," and the "Julian-Gregorian Calendar."

A. The "Planetary Week"

There is no evidence in the ancient world of any seven-day week aside from that of the Hebrews until the rise of the "Planetary Week" in *post*-OT times.

Quite early in their history both the Babylonians and the Greeks took an interest in astronomy. Since the planetary week has its days named after the sun, moon, and five planets of the solar system, it is obvious that astronomy or astrology lies in its background. Through a rather lengthy process of study of the heavens by Babylonians and Greeks, eventually there emerged, somewhere between 300 and 150 B.C., a sequence of the "seven planets": the sun and moon and the five planets known to the ancients. This sequence, was Saturn-Jupiter-Mars-Sun-Venus-Mercury-Moon. It was based on the "spatial" distance of each of the heavenly bodies from the earth as determined through astronomical calculations.

The astrology of Hipparchus (190-126 B.C.) in western Asia Minor influenced astronomical/astrological research in Alexandria, Egypt. In addition, the Egyptian priests about this time developed a day with 24 sixty-minute hours. In Alexandria, all the necessary ingredients for the creation of a planetary seven-day week were brought together about 150 B.C. These were the concept of planetary gods, originally developed by Babylonian priests; the mathematical and astronomical data produced by the Greeks; the system of 24 hours, an Egyptian innovation; and knowledge of the Hebrew weekly cycle.

The most complete information concerning the process involved in this astrological or planetary week comes from the Roman historian Cassius Dio, who wrote in the early third century A.D., at a time when this planetary week had gained universal acceptance in the Roman world. According to Dio (*Roman History* 37. 18, 19), the 24 hours of each day were believed to be ruled in sequence by the "seven planets" (including Sun and Moon). The planet ruling the first hour of a day gave that day its name. Since Saturn began the seven-planet sequence, Saturn would rule the first day. The first hour of the second day would be the "Sun's day," so that Sunday followed Saturday. In a similar manner all seven of the heavenly bodies were given authority over the first hour of a day, and gave their names to their days.

As the planetary week developed, Sunday, not Saturday, was given the priority as the first day of the week. This was because the Sun was by far the brightest celestial body. In the biblical pattern for the week, which had been spread widely throughout the then-known world by Jews of the Diaspora, the seventh day would be equivalent to the one called "Saturn's day" in the planetary week. This was actually attested by later Roman writers, who stated that as early as 63 B.C. the day on which the Jews held their Sabbath was "Saturn's day" (*ibid.* 37. 16. 2-4).

B. The Julian-Gregorian Calendar

In recent discussions it has sometimes been contended that the weekly cycle has been altered since ancient times, thus changing the sequence of the days. The main calendar that is used throughout the world today, called the "Gregorian Calendar," effected no weekly change from that of its predecessor, the "Julian Calendar" (instituted in 45 B.C. by Julius Caesar). Therefore, it is certain that the days of the week in NT times are still the same days of the week at present.

In the 12-month year of the Julian Calendar, the addition of a leap year every four years finally threw the calendar off by about 11 minutes and 14 seconds annually. Cumulatively, this amounted to approximately three days in every four centuries. In 1582 the vernal equinox occurred on March 11 instead of on March 21, the day when it had occurred at the time of the Council of Nicaea in A.D. 325. To remedy the discrepancy, Pope Gregory XIII decreed in 1582 that 10 days be dropped out of the reckoning, with the result that Thursday, October 4, was followed by Friday, October 15 (not by October 5). No adjustment or change was made in the weekly cycle.

In order to bring the calendar into better balance with the actual solar year, Gregory stipulated that the only century years that would have a leap day would be those divisible by 400, thus eliminating three of the Julian "leap days" every 400 years. The first such "century-leap-year" was 1600. In 1700 the "leap day" was omitted.

The Church

Raoul Dederen

Introduction

For a considerable time in the history of Christian thought interest in the doctrine of the church has been slight. It did not receive the careful attention that Christology and the doctrine of the Trinity received in the fourth and fifth centuries, the atoning death of Christ in the Middle Ages, or the issue of salvation in the sixteenth century. But among other factors, the ecumenical movement of the twentieth century, with its vision of *one* church of Christ, has contributed to making this doctrine a center of theological discussion.

The aim of this article is to deal, however briefly and selectively, with the references to the church in the Scriptures, more particularly in the NT. It intends to point out what the early church professed on the subject. We shall first consider Christ's relation to the church. Then we shall look at the nature and scope of the church, followed by an examination of its mission and government. Finally, we will give attention to the ordinances and marks of the church, followed by a survey of the historical development of this particular doctrine.

I. The Church in God's Plan

From beginning to end the Bible is concerned with God's purpose of creating a people for Himself, a people who would respond to Him in faith and obedience and who would be a source of blessings for all people(s). The call of Abraham, Isaac, and Jacob was intended to fashion such a people (Gen. 17:1-8; cf. 12:1-3; 15:1-6). So was the calling of Israel. When national Israel proved to be recalcitrant, seeking like Adam to be self-sufficient, God turned to the creation of a remnant (Isa. 37:31; Micah 2:12; 5:7, 8; Zeph. 3:13), through whom in His purpose redemption would be fulfilled. The divine intent to create out of Israel God's people is a continued study in the NT, where it finds its fulfillment in the Christian church.

The early Christian community known as the "church" is usually thought of as coming into existence at Pentecost, after Christ's death and resurrection. Its growth and organization were a gradual process. How far can its foundation and characteristics be traced back to the teaching and ministry of Christ Himself? Is the church a society founded by the Lord as an integral part of His work for humanity or a mere human institution that came into existence after the Resurrection as the community of those professing belief in Christ? Did the idea of the Christian church originate with Jesus, or was it a later development? This will be our first concern.

A. Christ's Intent

A cursory survey of the Gospels might lead one to conclude that Jesus was not interested in the church. Only twice is the term *ekklēsia* found on His lips, both of them in one Gospel (Matt. 16:18, 19; 18:17). Some even regard these sayings as a later retrojection in the ministry of the Lord by the early church. The virtual absence of the word "church" from the Gospels is a problem that demands attention, but only a flagrant neglect of basic evidence can obscure the fact that Jesus intended to create a visible community. The more the Synoptic evidence is studied, the more clearly the fact emerges that what Jesus established was something more than merely another theological school. He came to give birth to a fellowship of men and women under the kingship of God, a religious community of which He was the leader.

1. Gathering and Training Disciples

From the first Christ began to gather to Himself a number of disciples. At times there were large numbers of them (cf. Luke 6:17, 19; John 6:60), yet they were more than an unorganized mass of followers. From among them, explains Luke, Jesus chose 12 "whom he named apostles" (Luke 6:12, 13), and whom He set aside "to be with him, and to be sent out to preach" (Mark 3:14). Subsequent events show that the twelve were part of the system of training to which Christ devoted more and more of His time.

As the destined Messiah Jesus gathered a remnant community to Himself. Though reluctant to acknowledge Himself publicly as Messiah because of His rejection of a political and nationalistic messiahship, to some Jesus did not hesitate to affirm that the title was His (Matt. 16:16, 17; Mark 14:61, 62; 15:2; John 4:25, 26). A Messiah without a community was unthinkable to the Jewish mind. The concepts of disciples, a remnant, and messiahship were constitutive of a new community, a people of God, which is the Messiah's essential possession.

Christ also gave His followers memorable teachings about the manner of life they were meant to live, illustrated, for instance, in the Sermon on the Mount (Matt. 5-7), whose ethical demands presuppose a community. Those who attached themselves to Him were to be prepared to make the same sacrifices as their Master, to be cross-bearers (Matt. 16:24) and develop entirely new values in which world-gaining became of no importance compared with losing life for the sake of Jesus (Mark 8:34-36).

The Gospels show us also that those whom Jesus called were sent out on a mission. Theirs was a community with a mission. That the 12 (Mark 3:13-15), and later on the 70 (Luke 10:1, 7-20), were sent out on a mission did not happen by chance; it was part of a deliberate purpose of our Lord Himself. They had been called with this in view (Mark 6:7-13; Luke 10:1, 17-20). They, in turn, with the same end in view, were to pray "the Lord of the harvest to send out laborers into his harvest" (Luke 10:2). Christ's ministry aimed at the formation of a particular community.

2. The Shepherd and His Flock

The absence of the word "church" from the Gospels, except in Matthew 16:18 and 18:17, is explained to some extent by the occurrence of several other terms intended to describe the new people of God. This intent is reflected in Jesus' teaching on His "flock" and the "true vine." The "shepherd-and-flock" picture is prominent in both OT and NT (Ps. 23; 80:1; Luke 12:32; John 10; 21:15; cf. Matt. 26:31). It is true that "flock" and "church" are quite distinct in biblical history and usage, but they describe the same people of God. When He called all who would receive life from Him to follow Him (cf. Matt. 4:19; 8:22; Mark 2:14; 8:34; Luke 5:27; 18:22; John 1:43; 21:22), He called them, not only to Himself, but into a relationship closer than that of a natural family. That new family was not determined by flesh, but by those doing the will of God (Mark 3:33-35).

During the course of His ministry Jesus gathered a community around Himself. The supporting evidence for the community idea provides no reason to doubt that Jesus could have spoken about the church, as we find it in Matthew 16 and 18. The authenticity of the utterances, especially the first one, "I will build my church," has been called into question, but on grounds of minimal textual support. It is made up of rather arbitrary presumptions regarding the composition of this particular Gospel. There are no conclusive reasons for denying that Jesus' statements about the church are authentic, though they may refer to a looser concept than the organization and structure that later developed in early Christianity.

B. "Upon This Rock"

To Peter, on the ground of the apostle's believing confession that Jesus was "the Christ, the Son of the living God" (Matt. 16:16), Jesus stated, "You are Peter, and on this rock I will build my church, and the powers of death [Gr. "the gates of Hadēs"] shall not prevail against it" (verse 18). The personal phrase is prominent in the original text, "on this rock I will build *my* church." It indicates that Jesus deliberately intended to create a continuing community against which the "powers of death" would not prevail. This assurance was most important in the light of the imminence of

Jesus' own death. It is as if He had said, "I am soon to die (cf. verse 21), but I shall rise and be at work to build My church, with which I shall be till My return."

The meaning of the "rock" to which Jesus referred when He said, "You are Peter, and on this rock I will build my church" (verse 18), is also vital for a correct understanding of the church. Some have argued, on the strength of the wordplay in Aramaic, that "Peter" and "rock" are one and the same, that Peter is the rock on which the church is built, adding that the role that the Lord gave to the apostle was permanent and meant to be transmitted to his successors. There is no suggestion of this kind in the passage. As their later behavior toward Peter indicated, none of the disciples who heard Jesus make that statement understood it that way. For them Christ was the foundation of the household of God (1 Cor. 3:11) and its cornerstone (Eph. 2:20-22; 1 Peter 2:4-8). It is definitely more in harmony with the teaching of Scripture to understand Christ's statement to mean that Jesus as the Christ, the Son of God, or the confession thereof, is the foundation upon which the church is built.

In summary, there is no solid ground for maintaining that Jesus did not expect that a community of His disciples would come into existence after His departure. He directed His sayings and teachings to the formation of a visible society.

II. The Nature and Scope of the Church

We need next to inquire regarding the basic meaning of the word "church" in the NT, not to mention the nature and the scope of the society that the word describes. Since certain images used by the NT writers—especially by Paul—so effectively suggest the qualitative constituents of the church idea, we shall devote some space to them also.

A. The Biblical Terminology

The English word "church" and cognate terms in other languages (cf. Scottish *kirk,* Dutch *kerk,* German *Kirche*) are derived from

the Greek word *kuriakos,* "that which belongs to the Lord." It generally renders the NT *ekklēsia,* from *ek* (out, or from) and *klēsis* (to call), a term used among the Greeks of a body of citizens gathered to discuss the affairs of state.

Though it acquired a distinct Christian meaning, it has its own pre-Christian history. The term is in itself strong evidence of the connection existing between the OT and the NT. The LXX uses *ekklēsia* almost 100 times as a translation of *qāhāl,* "a meeting," "a gathering," "an assembly," "those called out," "gathered." It can refer to a gathering of men called up for military duty (Num. 22:4; Eze. 16:40) or to those who gather to do evil (Ps. 26:5). It is used readily of those who worship God (2 Chron. 30:13) as well as to describe the assembling of Israel before God at Horeb (Deut. 9:10; 10:4; 18:16). In Deuteronomy 31:30 "the congregation" (KJV) of Israel is gathered before the Lord for religious purposes. The term was applicable to meetings of all sorts; it is the people and the purpose that give significance to the *qāhāl.* The Hebrew *'edāh,* also a general term for "meeting," "assembly," "congregation," is usually translated into Greek as *synagōgē.* As mentioned earlier, the Greek *ekklēsia* was originally used to denote an assembly of free citizens called together by a public crier for the purpose of hearing an oration, usually in connection with public affairs. This meaning is still found in Acts 19:32, 39, 41.

The word thus came into Christian history with associations alike for the Greek and for the Jew. In Christian parlance *ekklēsia* denoted the "congregation" or community of those called by God, out of the world, to be His people. Theirs was the society of those who were free but always conscious that their freedom sprang from obedience to their Lord. This accent is made explicit in many cases, as for instance *"ekklēsia* of God" (1 Cor. 1:2; 10:32; Gal. 1:13; 1 Thess. 2:14; 1 Tim. 3:5).

On occasion the church is qualified as the church or churches "of Christ" (Rom. 16:16; Gal. 1:22) or "of the Lord" (Acts 20:28). Often this qualification is implicit, but even where the prepositional phrase is lacking, the context is clear: God in Christ is the authority that has constituted the *ekklēsia.* It belongs to God because He has called it into being, dwells within it, and rules over it.

B. The Church, Local and Universal

The NT writings refer to the church in two main ways. In most references it is a community of believers in a specific locality. Thus

Paul's letters are addressed "to the church of God which is at Corinth" (1 Cor. 1:2) or "to the church of the Thessalonians" (1 Thess. 1:1). The term is used in the same way in reference to Jerusalem (Acts 8:1; 11:22) or Cenchreae (Rom. 16:1). A small company of Christians meeting in a house for worship is also identified as a church (verse 5; 1 Cor. 16:19; Col. 4:15).

In a broader sense the term is used to refer to wider geographic areas or to denote the universal church, that is, the totality of the church. Thus we hear about "the churches of Galatia" (Gal. 1:2), "the churches of Christ in Judea" (verse 22; cf. 1 Thess. 2:14), Macedonia (2 Cor. 8:1), or Asia (1 Cor. 16:19), and find the word "church" used in a universal sense, as for instance in Ephesians 1:22; 3:10; Colossians 1:18. It is indeed in the same way that the Lord Himself had declared that He would build His church (Matt. 16:18).

For any adequate understanding of the NT view of the nature and scope of the church, both local and universal dimensions must be given full weight. The local congregation is the church, as for instance "at Corinth" (1 Cor. 1:2). Still, the local congregation is not regarded as merely a part or component of the whole church, but as the church in its local expression. The whole is in the part. The local visible *ekklēsia* is the whole church expressed locally in a particular time and space.

C. The Church and the Kingdom of God

If the church is the fellowship of those who have answered God's call and have come together in the name of Jesus Christ, one may consider the church as synonymous with the kingdom of God. Indeed there is a close connection between the two, yet they should not be confused.

1. The Kingdom as the Rule of God

According to the Synoptics the kingdom of God, or the kingdom of heaven, was the central theme of Jesus' preaching. In the NT the kingdom of God means primarily the rule of God, His authority as king, and secondarily the realm over which that reign is exercised. God's kingdom is synonymous with His rule. The kingdom of God, which is also the kingdom of Christ (cf. Matt. 13:41; Luke 22:30; Col. 1:13; 2 Tim. 4:1), is the redemptive rule of God in Christ. Its object is the redemption of sinners and their deliverance from the powers of evil (1 Cor. 15:23-28). Standing over against it is the kingdom of Satan (Matt. 12:26; Luke 11:18) and the "kingdom of the world" (Rev. 11:15), which oppose the working of God's kingdom and must be conquered (cf. Rev. 11:15.)

God's kingdom, which will come in glory at the end of the age (Matt. 25:31-46; cf. 13:36-43) and which will bring the rebirth of the material order (Matt. 19:28), has come into history in the person and mission of Christ (Luke 17:21). His whole ministry and preaching are marked by this dominant reality. In Christ the kingdom of heaven breaks into the domain of the evil one. The power of Satan is broken. All this is founded on the fact that Jesus is the Christ, the Son of God. The kingdom has come in Him and with Him. The kingdom has come, the kingdom will come, but it comes by the way of the cross. This good news, i.e., "the gospel of the kingdom" which Jesus Himself preached and taught (Matt. 4:23; 9:35), is to be "preached throughout the whole world as a testimony to all nations" before the end comes (Matt. 24:14), inviting people to repent and to accept God's rule in their lives. (See Second Coming I. D.)

2. The Role of the Church

Although there is an inseparable relationship between the two, the church is not the kingdom. The two are not equivalent, even in the present age. As noted, the kingdom is the rule of God. The church, in contrast, is the human community that lives under God's rule. Created in answer to the call of the gospel of the kingdom, the church witnesses to the kingdom. The kingdom is God's redeeming activity in Christ in the world; the church is the assembly of those called out of the world, who are redeemed and belong to Christ. The church is the manifestation of the kingdom or reign of God. As the organ or instrument of this kingdom, the church is called to confess Jesus as the Christ and to proclaim the gospel of the kingdom to the ends of the world.

D. A Faithful Israel

There is no question that from the NT evidence the church is vitally related to God's plan of salvation. The question is: How does the church relate to Israel? The matter has been and still is vitally debated.

1. Two Major Approaches

Some, seeing the differences between the two, insist that Israel and the church are two entirely separate peoples that cannot be mingled and must not be confused. God has two different programs that He is carrying out in history: one with Israel, the other through the Christian church. They maintain the distinction that recognizes Israel's calling as a nation among nations to the end of time (cf. Num. 23:9; Deut. 7:6-8). This interpretation allows for the literal understanding of OT prophecies portraying a most prosperous future for Israel as a nation.

Another position, emphasizing the similarities between Israel and the church, views the two essentially as one people of God, in continuity. Here, in NT times the term "Israel" represents no longer a national entity but the spiritual people of God, the new Israel. Because national Israel rejected its Messiah, God pursued His work of salvation by giving the kingdom "to a nation producing the fruits of it" (Matt. 21:43). This "chosen race," this "royal priesthood," this "holy nation," "God's own people," is the church (1 Peter 2:9).

2. A Covenant Relationship

What does appear in the Scriptures is that all of God's dealings with the Israelites in OT times were based on the covenant that originally had been ratified between Yahweh and

Abraham (Gen. 15:18; 17:2-7). God had chosen him with a clear purpose in mind, the ultimate salvation of all nations (Gen. 12:3). Mindful of His covenant with Abraham (Ex. 2:24), God renewed it with Israel at Mount Sinai, so that His universal purpose might be fulfilled. Israel was to be his "own possession among all peoples" (Ex. 19:5, 6), a "kingdom of priests" (verse 6), set apart to represent God to the world and the needs of the world to God. The election of Israel, like that of Abraham, however, did not involve the rejection of any other nation. Israel had been chosen for the sake of the world's salvation, for, said God, "all the earth is mine" (verse 5). He had elected both Abraham and Israel not to privilege but to service, to further His purpose for the nations.

The people of Israel pledged themselves to obey God (verses 1-8; Ex. 24:3-8). On His part, God promised, as a result of their obedience, to give them the land He swore to their fathers (Deut. 1:7, 8; cf. Gen. 15:18) and to endow them with unique physical, intellectual, and material blessings (Deut. 7:12-16; 28:1-6, 10, 13; 30:9, 10), setting them "high above all the nations of the earth" (Deut. 28:1). All these covenant blessings were predicated on Israel's whole-hearted cooperation with God's will (Deut. 4:5-8; 7:12-16). Impressed by Israel's witness and living examples, one by one the nations would unite with Israel in the worship and service of the true God (Deut. 28:1-14; Isa. 2:1-3; 19:18-22; 56:6, 7; 60:1-16; Zech. 8:20-23). It is important to note that this was a conditional covenant, as the introductory clause of the Exodus 19 passage sets forth: "If you will obey my voice and keep my covenant" (verse 5). Tragically, Israel became disobedient and an unworthy representative. Its defection led to the Babylonian captivity and the forfeiture of Canaan. After the Captivity, God renewed His covenant with Israel and restored the exiles to the land of the covenant as He had promised through His servants the prophets, who reminded Israel that the covenant promises would yet be fulfilled if they would be loyal to God (Isa. 14:1, 2; 27:12, 13; Jer. 16:14-16; 29:10-14; Eze. 34:11-16; Micah 2:12, 13).

3. The Church as Spiritual Israel

When the Messiah sent from God came, His own people "received him not" (John 1:11). Israel, as God's covenant people, was rejected. This time no assurance of reinstatement came from God, but Christ gave a verdict on the Jewish nation: "The kingdom of God will be taken away from you, and given to a nation producing the fruits of it" (Matt. 21:43). The privileges, promises, and blessing of the covenant relationship were transferred to the Christian church as spiritual Israel and as God's chosen instrument on earth.

Some of the OT prophecies made to national Israel would never be fulfilled, since they were made to a nation situated in the land of Canaan and were strictly conditional upon Israel retaining its status as the covenant people. Other promises that the OT directed to literal Israel are "spiritually" applied by the NT writers to the church. Thus after foretelling the rejection of Israel because of its sin, Hosea foresees its restoration (1:6, 9). God will make a new covenant with Israel (Hosea 2:18) and betroth His people to Himself forever (verses 19, 23). Rejected Israel would be restored. The NT applies the prophecy to spiritual Israel, the church. Referring to this new people that consists not of Jews only but also of Gentiles, Paul writes, "As indeed he says in Hosea, 'Those who were not my people I will call "my people," and her who was not beloved I will call "my beloved"'" (Rom. 9:25). Again, referring to Hosea 1:9, the apostle adds, "And in the very place where it was said to them, 'You are not my people,' they will be called 'sons of the living God'" (verse 26).

Joel, like Hosea, foresaw the restoration of Israel: "You shall know that I am in the midst of Israel, and that I, the Lord, am your God and there is none else. And my people shall never again be put to shame" (Joel 2:27). This promise is followed by the astounding prophecy of the outpouring of the Holy Spirit upon all flesh (verses 28, 29). This is clearly a promise to literal Israel, for the prophecy continues, "For behold, in those days and at that time, when I restore the fortunes of Judea and Jerusalem" (Joel 3:1). Nevertheless, on the day of Pentecost, when the Holy Spirit was given to the church, Peter, guided by the Spirit, declared, "This is what was spoken by the prophet Joel" (Acts 2:16). It can be concluded that both Paul and Peter meant that promises made to literal Israel were fulfilled to spiritual Israel, the church. Individual Jews would still be able to find salvation, but they would do so as believers in Christ (Rom. 9:6; 11:1, 2).

In many respects the church has taken the place of Israel, even to the point that not all who are descended from Abraham physically are his spiritual descendants. Paul stresses this point, for example in his Epistle to the Romans: "For he is not a real Jew who is one outwardly, nor is true circumcision something external and physical. He is a Jew who is one inwardly, and real circumcision is a matter of the heart, spiritual and not literal" (2:28, 29; cf. 4:16; 9:7, 8; Gal. 3:29). Abraham has been made "the father of all who believe without being circumcised" (Rom. 4:11). It is difficult for language to state more clearly that Abraham's spiritual seed, his true spiritual children, are men and women of faith, whatever their ethnic background. The church has become "the Israel of God" (Gal. 6:16; see Remnant/Three Angels I, II).

E. The Church, Visible or Invisible?

Close to the center of any view of the church lies the issue of the visible and invisible church. Some deny the existence of any church but the visible church, a visible institution, discernable by marks visible to all. To them the concept of the invisible church is a heretical doctrine. Others hold as emphatically that the church is invisible, embracing all who as true children of God are indwelled by His Spirit and known only to God. The distinction is not new. It should be noted that the disparity we are addressing here is not the same as the differentiation between the local and the universal church. What we are dealing with is the question of the extent to which the church is to be identified with its present institutional extension.

1. Two Extremes

Advocates of the first group regard specific organizational structures as part of the true church, especially if they can be traced back to Christ's day. Groups of persons may gather, organize themselves, study the Scriptures, sing hymns, worship God, and call themselves a church, but if they cannot trace themselves back historically to the apostles, preferably by means of an uninterrupted line of successors to the apostles, they are not a church.

No less earnest in their conviction are those who stress the priority of one's direct relationship to God through Jesus Christ. That is what makes one a Christian. It is the sum total of such born-again believers that constitutes a church. Whether assembled or not in a visible group, they make up the church. The visible organization is relatively unimportant, especially since membership in one of them is no guarantee of salvation. In some cases there is an unmistakable aversion to anything resembling a formal structure. The emphasis here is upon the quality of individual Christian living.

Perhaps, as is sometimes the case, the biblical solution to the problem lies between these two extremes. It is important to note that the Scriptures refer to both the visible and the invisible church, or more exactly to the visible and the invisible dimensions of the church.

2. The Priority of Faith and Repentance

When questioned about salvation Jesus assigned priority to an individual's faith and spiritual condition. To the disciples He said: "Truly, I say to you, unless you turn and become like children, you will never enter the kingdom of heaven" (Matt. 18:3). To the multitude He stressed that "whoever does not bear his own cross and come after me, cannot be my disciple" (Luke 14:27). To Nicodemus He stated that "unless one is born anew, he cannot see the kingdom of God" (John 3:3; cf. verse 5). Skeptical Jews were appalled by Jesus' statement that "he who believes [in Me] has eternal life" (John 6:47). Facing the same issue, the apostles likewise insisted on repentance, conversion, and faith in Christ. When Peter and others were asked, "Brethren what shall we do?" the reply was, "Repent, and be baptized every one of you in the name of Jesus Christ for the forgiveness of your sins" (Acts 2:37, 38). Peter's answer was the same in Acts 3:12-26 and 4:7-12. In reply to the Philippian jailor's question "What must I do to be saved?" (Acts 16:30), Paul plainly stated: "Believe in the Lord Jesus, and you will be saved" (verse 31). In none of these instances is there any suggestion that salvation depends on one's relation to a visible institution or group of believers.

3. A Bodily, Visible Church

Having recognized the priority of faith and repentance, it is difficult to minimize the equal importance given by the Scriptures to the visible dimension of the church. In response to the preaching of Peter and the other apostles, some 3,000 souls "received his word," were baptized, and were "added that day" to the 120 who had assembled in the upper room (Acts 2:14-41). On subsequent days others were added, so that this basic group which Luke calls "the whole church" (Acts 5:11), grew to some 5,000 (Acts 4:4). It is evident that these first Christian believers acted as a corporate and visible community. They "devoted themselves to the apostles' teaching" (Acts 2:42), had fellowship with one another (verse 42), observed the ordinance of baptism (verses 38, 41) and apparently the Lord's Supper (verse 42), met for prayer (verse 42), worshiped together (verse 46), and contributed to the support of the needy (verses 44, 45). These are undoubtedly characteristics of a visible and, however loosely, organized local church.

This first community of believers was a present, visible and palpable group, which caused a visible public uproar (Acts 17:6). The current tendency of playing off the church as an invisible entity against the visible and concrete form of the church seems to display ignorance of the biblical teaching that time and again attributes the existence of concrete and visible local churches to God or to Christ (cf. 1 Cor. 11:16; Gal. 1:22; 1 Thess. 2:14; 2 Thess. 1:4). The church, according to the NT, is not an invisible entity, nor a mental image. Indeed, an invisible church would be as unthinkable to biblical thought as a Messiah without a community. The church is bodily, visible, tangible. It has a definite structure with differentiated parts or "members." It is actual, both local and universal.

At the same time the church can be described as having an invisible dimension, which is not measurable by sinners, even when redeemed. They cannot adequately see the line that divides true and false believers, or identify who authentically belongs to the church and who does not. Not all who are nominally members of the church are in true and living communion with God. The believers within the visible church constitute the true church. From the teaching of the Lord Himself it appears that the visible community of God's people is likely to be mixed and not entirely uncorrupted in its membership. No mere acknowledgment of Him or even participation in His ministry is a guarantee of genuineness and acceptance by God (Matt. 7:21-23; Luke 13:22-27). Tares and wheat will grow together until harvest time (Matt. 13:24-30, 36-43).

It is possible on the one hand that there are persons within the visible church who are not true believers, therefore not actually part of the body of Christ. Conversely it is possible for some to be savingly related to Christ without belonging to the visible church. These are the focus of the gospel invitation to come out of Babylon and join God's visible church (Rev. 18:1-4; cf. John 10:16).

III. Biblical Images of the Church

NT writers used the term *ekklēsia* to refer to the body of believers. They also resorted to various cognate ways to further express their concept of the church. Among them, images and metaphors hold a prominent place. Because they so effectively suggest the characteristic and qualitative components of the church idea, these biblical images of the church deserve some attention. Of these we shall retain four: body, bride, temple, and people of God.

A. The Church as a Body

A major Pauline analogy for the church—and probably his most distinctive—is the body of Christ. The church is not a body per se; it is never described as a or the "body of Christians," but always as the body *in* Christ (Rom. 12:5) or the body *of* Christ (1 Cor. 12:27). Paul seems to use the metaphor of the body to express the oneness of the church with its Lord. His primary emphasis is on the unity of believers with Christ. He may well have gained this understanding of the solidarity of Christians with Christ from his Damascus road experience. There he was made to see that in persecuting Christians he was indeed persecuting Christ Himself. Christ's probing question was, "Saul, Saul, why do you persecute me?" (Acts 9:4; cf. 22:7; 26:14). Paul later impressed the same truth on his Corinthian converts, explaining that to divide the church was like dividing Christ (1 Cor. 1:13) and that in sinning against their brethren they were sinning against Christ (1 Cor. 8:12). This image stresses the unity of the church, whether local or universal, an organic unity within a body that stands in vital relationship to Jesus Christ.

This same concept of the oneness of the church—whether local or universal—is introduced by Paul when he deals with the problem of Christians' relations to one another. There is one body, with members having different functions, yet all equally honorable and necessary to the efficient working of the body as a whole. Believers are no longer their own, but baptized "into" him (1 Cor. 12:13); they are "in" Him and He is "in" them (Gal. 2:20). In that body they are all members one of another. This requires the recognition of mutual dependence (1 Cor. 12:12-26), in a communion *(koinōnia)* of righteousness and life in which each, however spectacular his or her role, must know the humility of receiving this function and gift from Christ for the sake of the whole body (Rom. 12:3-8; Eph. 4:11-16).

Emphasizing further the complete dependence of the church upon Christ, Paul introduces a new idea in his Prison Epistles, namely Christ as the head of the church (Eph. 1:22, 23; 4:15; Col. 1:18). Far from supporting the view that the church is an extension of Christ, he maintains a clear distinction between the head and the body. The head is exalted and occupies a unique position. As the head Christ is the source and the locus of authority that the whole body is to obey (Col. 2:10). Believers united with Him are nourished through Him (verse 19).

B. The Church as a Bride

The image of the church as the bride of Christ likewise argues for unity among believers and with Christ, particularly in the context of the biblical ideal of monogamous marriage (Gen. 2:24). Jesus Himself used the wedding imagery, though without explicitly identifying the bride (Matt. 25:1-13; cf. 22:1-14). At the same time the Lord, in sayings and in parables, represented His return as the coming of the Bridegroom (Matt. 25:6) and symbolized as a marriage feast (Matt. 22:1-14). Paul, reflecting on the image, specifically applied it to the church (cf. Eph. 5:25). Here, as elsewhere in the Epistle, the metaphor is applied to the universal church (cf. Eph. 1:22; 3:10, 21; 5:23, 27, 29, 32).

The metaphor involves the affirmation of the closest possible unity between Christ the head and the church as His bride, in view of the biblical doctrine that man and wife become "one flesh" (Gen. 2:24). There is no support, however, for the view that the apostle regarded the church as a literal incarnation or extension of Christ. As His bride, the church must remain pure and faithful to her one husband, Jesus Christ, surrendered without absorption and servant without compulsion.

C. The Church as a Temple

Early Christians who liked to think of their community as the New Jerusalem, the Holy City (Heb. 12:22), also thought of it as the Temple of God. It was indeed the presence of the Temple that made Jerusalem the Holy City. But rather than thinking in terms of the visible structure on Mount Zion (cf. Acts 17:24), they held that God had erected His people as a sanctuary by choosing to dwell among them (2 Cor. 6:16). The whole church was a "holy temple in the Lord" (Eph. 2:21); so were the congregations (1 Cor. 3:16, 17) and each individual believer (1 Cor. 6:19).

As a figure of the church this temple, though a single structure, is seen as *growing* into "a dwelling place of God in the Spirit" (Eph. 2:21, 22), "built upon the foundation of the apostles and prophets, Christ Jesus himself being the Chief cornerstone" (verse 20; cf. Mark 12:10). The church is "a spiritual house," explains Peter, in which individual believers are being built like living stones (1 Peter 2:5), hewed and shaped by the Lord for proper fitting. They are also priests (verse 9), whose duty, as it was in OT times, is a ministry of intercession and the offering of spiritual sacrifices (verse 5).

D. The Church as the People of God

To the images of body, bride, and temple, the NT adds the metaphor of the people of God. The idea of the people of God is frequently applied in the OT to the nation of Israel, chosen and protected by God (cf. Ex. 15:13, 16; Deut. 14:2; 32:9, 10; Hosea 2:23). In the NT likewise, the church is perceived as the continuation and consummation of God's covenant community. To his fellow believers Peter writes, "You are a chosen race, . . . God's own

people" (1 Peter 2:9), a statement clearly reminiscent of the Sinai covenant (Ex. 19:5, 6).

While in the NT "people of God" and related terms are used to describe OT Israel (Heb. 11:25; cf. Luke 1:68; Rom. 11:1, 2), they are also employed to designate the mixed Christian community of Jews and Gentiles (2 Cor. 6:14-16; 1 Peter 2:9, 10; cf. Rom. 9:25, 26). In a typical pattern of OT fulfillment, the NT sees the church as the true Israel (Rom. 9:6; Gal. 6:16) and the true seed of Abraham (Gal. 3:29; cf. Rom. 4:16; 9:7, 8). Far from using the term "people" as denoting a mere mass or mixture of individuals, ill-defined and lacking identity, the NT shares the OT conception of God's people. It sees the new people of God as a well-defined community, with an unambiguous sense of identity and mission. Here the definite article "the" should be preserved, "*the* people of God."

The concept emphasizes God's initiative: He chose. The church belongs to Him and He belongs to the church. Of God's decision Paul writes: "God said, 'I will live in them and move among them, and I will be their God, and they shall be my people' " (2 Cor. 6:16). As OT Israel was His because He redeemed and purchased it (Ex. 15:13, 16), so does the church belong to Christ because He redeemed it and "obtained [it] with his own blood" (Acts 20:28). God expects His church to be His with undivided loyalty, for Christ is eager to present it to Himself "without spot or wrinkle or any such thing, that she might be holy and without blemish" (Eph. 5:27).

E. A Few Pointers

This selection of images of the church is by no means exhaustive. An adequate review would require consideration of many more, such as the pictures of the church as a fortress, a vineyard, an army, a commonwealth, and a pillar of truth, to mention just a few. None of the separate figures can comprehend the total range of NT thought about the church. Yet all point to the church's dependence on the triune God and the interdependence of all members within the community.

In almost all of these expressions, whether local or in its totality, the church is seen as a profoundly theocratic reality whose origin and destiny are rooted in God. It is a Christocentric community, for it exists thanks to Christ's person and work. The church is also a charismatic reality, for the Holy Spirit weaves together its life. It is a new creation, an expression on earth of the kingdom of God. As God's chosen instrument of action in the world, it is entrusted with the task of sharing the good news worldwide, and taking part in the warfare between God and Satan. Oneness and wholeness are of the essence of its life, a oneness enriched by the gathering of men and women from all nations, tribes, tongues, and peoples.

The common existence of believers in Christ as His body, bride, temple, and people gives a sharper and richer picture of the nature and scope of the church than can be drawn on the basis of the term *ekklēsia* alone. They contain a wealth of viewpoints and possibilities of expression for elucidating more fully than *ekklēsia* can the place and significance of the church in the NT. There is also as part of the same symbols a functional dimension, a perception of the role and function of the church in relation to God's purpose for the world, which is our next task.

IV. The Mission of the Church

While the church may not be primarily defined in terms of its functions, these are nevertheless most important. The church is the body of Christ. Yet it has not been called to exist as an end in itself, but to fulfill God's purpose, i.e., to carry on the Lord's ministry in the world, to do what He would do if He were still on earth. This explains why, from that perspective, the church does not merely have a mission, the church is mission.

Throughout the Bible God is a God of sending, of mission. His characteristic approach to humans is by sending someone to speak to them for Him. "From the day that your fathers came out of the land of Egypt to this day, I have persistently sent all my servants the prophets to them, day after day," He said to the people of Judah (Jer. 7:25; cf. 26:5; 29:19; 35:15; 44:4). In the fullness of time He "sent forth his Son" (Gal. 4:4), again with a clear purpose. The Son, in turn, "sent out" the twelve, and later the seventy with a message regarding the kingdom of God (Luke 9:1, 2; 10:1, 9). To this mandate Christ added the post-resurrection commission recorded in Matthew 28:19, 20; Luke 24:46-48.

A. "Make Disciples of All Nations"

The final instruction Jesus gave to His disciples was to "go . . . and make disciples of all nations" (Matt. 28:19; cf. Acts 1:8). As Christ was sent into the world by the Father, so He sent His disciples (John 20:21). Their primary task, as well as that of the church, has always been the sharing of the gospel of Jesus Christ to the ends of the world. The members of the church have been called out of the world to be sent back into the world with a mission and a message. The call to evangelism springs from an unequivocal command of the Lord of the church.

B. Instruct the Believers

The edification of believers is another mission or function of the church. God, explains Paul, gave to the church apostles, prophets, evangelists and pastors (Eph. 4:11) "for the equipment of the saints, for the work of ministry, for building up the body of Christ, until we all attain to the unity of faith and of the knowledge of the Son of God, to mature manhood, to the measure of the stature of the fullness of Christ" (verses 12, 13).

Those brought to Christ were "to grow up in every way into Him who is the head, into Christ" (verse 15). In the early church the task of teaching (*disdaskō*) required that the truth and the duties of the gospel be more deliberately unfolded and applied. Teaching took place publicly in the Temple and in homes, among Jews and in the assembly of believers (Acts 4:2, 18; 5:21, 25, 28, 42; 18:11; 20:20). Its intent was to apply Christ's will to the daily life of the community as a word of instruction, of encouragement, and of consolation, to "live in Him" (Col. 2:6; 3:16; 1 Tim. 6:2; cf. 1 Cor. 14:3, 26) on the basis of "the word of God" (Acts 18:11), "the . . . counsel of God" (Acts 20:26, 27), or "the word of Christ" (Col. 3:16).

Edification may take different forms as it occurs on various levels. It could mean indoctrination of the members of the church in order to expound "the way of God more accurately" (Acts 18:26), teach believers the apostles' "ways in Christ" (1 Cor. 4:16, 17), or help them stand against heresies (Eph. 4:14, 15). The content of the preaching and of the more elaborate instruction was necessarily often the same (Acts 5:42; 15:35; Col. 1:28) and at times the preacher was also a teacher, especially in the case of the apostles (1 Tim. 2:7; 2 Tim. 1:11).

C. Care for the Needy and Suffering

While the early church gathered for instruction and fellowship, it also understood the responsibility of caring for the needy and suffering. Jesus was known for His ministry of healing, even raising the dead on occasion. He expected His disciples to follow in His steps (Matt. 10:5-8; Luke 10:1-12, 17) and clearly stated that acts of love done in His name would on the last day distinguish true believers from those who made empty professions of faith (Matt. 25:31-46). Time and again the apostles, likewise, underlined the importance of practical Christianity (cf. James 1:27; 2:1-7; 1 John 3:15-17).

Whereas believers should separate from worldly alliances (2 Cor. 6:14-18), they are "the salt of the earth" and "the light of the world" (Matt. 5:13-16). By their influence and testimony they are called to support those causes that promote the social, economic, and educational welfare of the human family. The primary mission of the church is unquestionably related to evangelism and the implementation of God's plan of salvation. Yet its members are invited to learn from the Lord, who though He subordinated physical and other material help to spiritual needs, showed concern and took action on behalf of the needy and suffering.

D. Glorify God

One more dimension of the mission of the church should be mentioned: the ascription of glory to the One who has created it through redemption in Jesus Christ. The words of the apostle Paul, that God has chosen sons and daughters unto Himself through Christ "to the praise of his glorious grace" (Eph. 1:6), suggest that the ultimate purpose of the church is the worship of God. So amazing is the display of God's purpose in creating the church and bestowing on it all blessings in Christ that the apostle exalts in an outburst of praise: "To him be glory in the church and in Christ Jesus to all generations, for ever and ever. Amen" (Eph. 3:21). Glorifying God is no mere duplication of teaching or edification. Whereas the edification focuses on the believers and benefits them, glorifying God focuses on praising and exalting the Lord. Though it is also intended to benefit the worshipers (Heb. 10:25), it centers its attention on who and what God is. Glorification of God finds its most intense expression in the book of Revelation, where the vision of God calls a chorus of praise addressed to the thrice-holy God with whom the Redeemer-Lamb is associated (Rev. 4:8-11; 7:11, 12; cf. 5:9-14).

Glory is brought to God in the church through a thankful response to His grace: "He who brings thanksgiving as his sacrifice honors [or 'glorifies'] me" (Ps. 50:23). Peter perceived the church as "a holy priesthood, to offer spiritual sacrifices acceptable to God through Jesus Christ" (1 Peter 2:5). This worship involves declaring "the wonderful deeds of him who called you out of darkness into his marvelous light" (verse 9). God is further glorified with the lives of believers "filled with the fruits of righteousness which come through Jesus Christ, to the glory of praise of God" (Phil. 1:10, 11).

E. At the Heart of the Mission: The Word

Let us finally consider the element that lies at the heart of all the functions of the church and gives shape to everything it does: its message, the content of what the church proclaims.

The essential nature of the apostolic preaching is clearly expressed in two main words used throughout the NT: *kērussein,* "to proclaim as a herald," and *euangelizein* "to tell good tidings." *Euangelizein* frequently characterizes the content of the good tidings, specifically as "the gospel" (*to euangelion,* 1 Cor. 15:1; 2 Cor. 11:7; Gal. 1:11), or more variously as "Jesus as the Christ" (Acts 5:42), "peace" (Eph. 2:17), or "the word" (Acts 15:35). Such expressions make plain that preaching and evangelizing in the early church were fundamentally the proclamation of good tidings from God, the heralding of Jesus Christ as Saviour.

Paul makes the most frequent use of the term "gospel." Although he often refers to it without qualifiers to define its meaning (cf. Rom. 1:16; 1 Cor. 4:15; Gal. 2:5, 14; Phil. 1:5; etc.), he has in view a specific body of facts. These are plainly set forth in such passages as Romans 1:3, 4; 1 Corinthians 15:1-11; and 2 Timothy 2:8, in which Christ's divine Sonship, His genuine humanity, redemptive death, burial, resurrection, and second coming are indicative of what the gospel includes. The speeches and events recorded in the book of Acts prior to Paul's ministry make it apparent that there was general agreement among early believers as to the content of the gospel (2 Tim. 2:23, 24, 32, 36; 3:15; 4:1, 2, 10-12; 7:56; 10:36, 39-43; etc.).

It was by no means a human gospel (Gal. 1:11) but "the word of truth" (Eph. 1:13; cf. Col. 1:5), built on revelation (Gal. 1:12), a word that cuts across all racial and social barriers (Rom. 1:16; Gal. 3:28) and is never obsolete (Jude 3). The gospel lay at the heart of the mission of the church, bringing forth evangelism, edification, worship, and social concerns.

F. The Ministry of the Spirit

1. "Filled With the Spirit"

In worshiping God and battling against a hostile world, the church is not left unassisted. As the Holy Spirit was upon Jesus throughout His ministry (cf. Matt. 3:13-17; Luke 4:1, 14, 18-21; Acts 10:38), so the Spirit would be with the apostles forever (John 14:16, 17). Pentecost saw the fulfillment of the Lord's promise, the Spirit "filled" them (Acts 2:4; cf. 4:8, 31; etc.), transforming individual believers. NT passages speak of the Holy Spirit as "coming" on the disciples (Acts 1:8; 19:6), being "given" by God (Acts 8:18; 15:8), or falling on them (Acts 10:44; 11:15). Whatever the terms, there is a firm consciousness that God in Christ has given the Holy Spirit to those who put their trust in Him, and that this gift is the necessary equipment for Christian service. So rich is the testimony of the NT in this respect that one is compelled to be selective.

As a person rather than a force or an influence, the Spirit bore witness with their spirit (Rom. 8:16), interceded for them (verses 26, 27), and sanctified them (Rom. 15:16; 2 Thess. 2:13). He taught them (1 Cor. 2:13), lived in them (2 Tim. 1:14), and empowered them (2 Cor. 3:6). Signal success in their witness (Acts 2:37-47) showed that the promise of the Father had been fulfilled (Acts 1:4, 5). Equally awesome and amazing was the Spirit's activity within the community of believers. He strengthened the church for its daily witness (verse 31), preserved its unity (Eph. 4:3, 4; Phil. 2:1, 2), helped the church in resolving controversies (Acts 15:8, 28, 29) and in selecting leaders (Acts 20:28). The Spirit's work in launching the Gentile mission comes out clearly in Acts 13:1-4, as well as His continued guidance as the mission expanded, opening and closing doors (Acts 16:6-10; 19:21; 20:22, 23). So widely did the Spirit's activities permeate the life of the NT church that there was hardly any aspect of life—individual or common—outside the sphere of His influence. (See God VII. C.)

2. The Gifts of the Spirit

To the empowerment of the Christian community, the Spirit added special gifts to individual believers (Rom. 12:6-8; 1 Cor. 12:4-11, 27-31; Eph. 4:11). These *charismata,* or gifts of grace, are not to be confused with the Christian virtues described as the fruit of the Spirit (Gal. 5:22, 23). They are apportioned by the Spirit to whom and as He wills (1 Cor. 12:11). Some of these gifts refer to the exercise of practical ministries, such as healing, the working of miracles, or administra-tion. Others concern the ministry of the Word of God, such as apostles, prophets, evange-lists. All are bestowed on the church "for the common good" (verse 7) and for the building up of the church (1 Cor. 14:12). They are intended to strengthen the believers in their faith and to enable them to perform their ministry in the church or among unbeliev-ers. The giving of the Spirit—and of His gifts—is represented by the apostles as the gift of the exalted Lord by which He carries on His work on earth (Acts 2:33; cf. John 7:39; see Gifts II).

V. The Government of the Church

The charismatic gifts of the Spirit do not exhaust the NT understanding of ministry, however, nor are they seen as dispensing with the need for a regular ministry. Thus, in his writings, more than once Paul refers to elders and bishops (cf. Phil. 1:1; 1 Tim. 3:1; 5:17, 19; etc.) as do Peter and James (1 Peter 5:1; James 5:14). The apostle must have had in mind a ministry of some sort when he beseeched the Thessalonian believers to "respect those who labor among you and are over you in the Lord" (1 Thess. 5:12). It is difficult to lead any group for any length of time without office-bearers of some kind, and there is evidence that the NT church did not try.

A. The Apostles' Ministry

As to organization in the early church, the NT writings are not as detailed as we might wish, yet they provide us with solid and im-portant data on the subject.

It seems evident from the Gospels that whereas Jesus intended to create a visible com-munity, He gave His disciples few formal pre-scriptions for its organization. Soon after His ascension there appears a well defined body of disciples led by the apostles (Acts 1:13-15; 2:14), with a clear sense of mission (Acts 2:37-41), showing strong signs of expansion (verse 41; 4:4; 6:7). The apostles emerge as the lead-ers and teachers of the community (Acts 37, 42; 3:1; 5:1-3).

In the course of time the increase in the num-ber of disciples and the same intense sense of mission (Acts 6:1-3) led the apostles to del-egate some of their functions to seven believ-ers who would help them in ministry (verses 4-6). The "word of God increased" (verse 7) and persecution caused an extension of the church to other parts of Palestine and beyond (verses 8-11). In "Phoenicia and Cyprus and Antioch" "a great number that believed turned to the Lord" (Acts 11:19-21), bringing up churches such as the one in Antioch (verse 26). Launched by the Holy Spirit and the Antiochian church, the mission of Paul and Barnabas led to the foundation of a large num-ber of other local churches, each of which was provided with elders appointed by Paul and Barnabas, but probably chosen by the local believers as in the case of the seven referred to in Acts (14:23; 6:3). Such elders were al-ready functioning in Jerusalem as recorded in Acts 11:30.

The recognition of the apostles' leadership is unmistakable. In the narrowest sense of that flexible word, the apostles were the 12 appointed by Jesus Himself (Matt. 10:1-4), Matthias replacing Judas, and Paul, though in a broader sense the term also applies to Barnabas (Acts 14:4, 14), James (Gal. 2:9), and Andronicus and Junias (Rom. 16:7). In the de-veloping structure of the church the 12 and Paul, having personally encountered the risen Lord and being individually commissioned by Him, occupy a unique position of authority. With the prophets, they are the foundation on which the church is built, Jesus being the cornerstone (Eph. 2:20). As foundation of the church they have no successors. They were the natural leaders and teachers of the Christian community.

B. Local Ministries

While the apostles exercised what may be broadly described as a general and global ministry, deacons and elders seem to have carried out theirs at the local level. Elders or presbyters, otherwise known as bishops or overseers—the terms are interchangeable in the NT (Acts 20:17, 28; Titus 1:5, 7; cf. 1 Peter 5:2)—performed duties that were chiefly spiritual and supervisory (Acts 20:17-28; 1 Peter 5:1-3; James 5:14). They labored among fellow believers and had charge "over [them] in the Lord" (1 Thess. 5:12), clearly in positions of leadership. Their permanent role is evidenced by the list of qualifications necessary for such leaders as found in 1 Timothy 3:1-7 and Titus 1:7-9. The same is true of deacons, whose work appears to have been spiritual as well as the care of the temporal business of the church (Acts 6:1-6, 8-14; 8:4-13, 26-40; 1 Tim. 3:8-13).

In other words, leadership functions in the earliest phases of the history of the church were predominantly in the hands of the apostles. As the church grew in size, the necessity of government, of instruction and discipline, caused some of the functions of the apostles' ministry to be implemented by local church members exercising their God-given gifts. A reasonably structured organization was developing. Much of the government of local churches rested in the hands of local congregations, whereas difficult questions which arose out of the great extension of the church were addressed in broader assemblies (cf. Acts 15:1-6).

C. Church Governance and the NT

Basically church government is a set of rules and regulations designed to facilitate the task of the church and the work of those involved in it. Some have seen in church government, or church order, a contradiction in terms, arguing that in the church the Spirit blows wherever He wills, that His work cannot be directed by human beings. From what we have seen thus far, it appears, however, that in the Scriptures the Spirit is not so "spiritual" that He can have nothing to do with order. The question remains as to which form is prescribed in the Scriptures. The NT, recording the life of the church from its inception, presents surprisingly little detailed information about the organization of the church, except in the book of Acts and in Paul's Pastoral Epistles.

1. Theories

Over the centuries three main theories of church government have emerged, each claiming some scriptural basis. The Episcopalian system is the government of the church by bishops (episkopoi). Though forms of the episcopal governance vary, the most widespread expressions of the system hold that Christ has entrusted authority and the government of the church directly and exclusively to bishops as successors of the apostles. The most highly developed form of episcopal government has vested authority especially in the bishop of Rome, regarded as the supreme bishop.

Congregationalism, the system of church government that stresses the role of the individual Christian and makes the local congregation the seat of the authority, also claims scriptural precedent. Here emphasis is put on the autonomy and independence of the local church. Christ alone is the head of the church. The governing power rests exclusively with the members of the congregation. Cooperative associations may exist when beneficial, but their role is strictly advisory.

The Presbyterial form of church government consists in the rulership by elders (presbyteroi) as representatives of the church. Authority is exercised by this office and more particularly by a series of representative bodies. Christ's authority is seen as bestowed on individual believers who delegate it to elders who represent them and exercise authority on their behalf, both locally and in a series of governing assemblies that include clergy and laity.

2. Basic Principles

Each of the current systems of church government may be able to point to some NT elements that justify its organization. There are, however, a few facts and principles set forth by the NT writers that should not be ignored.

To begin with, Christ is the head of the church and the source of authority in all things. His will, as revealed in the written word, is the ultimate standard by which the church is to determine its actions. While it might be said that He exercises His authority in the church through its leaders—as in the case of the apostles—this is not to be understood to mean that Christ has transferred His authority to His servants. Theirs is only a delegated, derived authority. These leaders, called by God and chosen by the congregation, are set aside to lead the church in the various aspects of its worldwide mission.

This is the form of church government toward which the church was moving in the days of the apostles. The Scriptures do not warrant the existence of an episcopal system, structuring the church along monarchial, if not imperial, lines. Nor do they call for a pattern in which each church or congregation is the complete church, independent of every other, rejecting any authoritative organizational structure over the local congregation. It appears rather that the biblical data set forth a basic representative form of church government in which much is made of the priesthood of all believers and of the gifts of grace bestowed by the Spirit,

while recognizing the authority of representative bodies. (See VII.)

3. Charismata and Institution

There has been debate not only over the precise nature of the charismatic gifts, but also over their place in the government of the church. Several functions of leadership in the church are described as "gifts" in Ephesians 4:11: apostles, prophets, evangelists, pastors, and teachers. They carried with them a degree of authoritative leadership. Moreover, as noticed earlier, that the churches referred to by Paul had a formal leadership is clear also from his appeal to the Thessalonians to respect those who "are over you (*proïstamenoi*) in the Lord and admonish you" (1 Thess. 5:12). The same participle is used later on of bishops (1 Tim. 3:4), deacons (verse 12) and elders (1 Tim. 5:17), which leads one to conclude that *proïstamenoi* designates the office/function of elders/bishops and deacons.

Addressing the issue as to how the institutional and the charismatic related to each other, some hold that the church needed no organization, since each believer was born of the Spirit and the recipient of at least one gift (1 Cor. 12:7; 1 Peter 4:10). In this view the need for institutional offices arose only when the charismatic ministry disappeared from the church, now unfaithful to its vocation. Others, pointing to the fact that several Pauline Epistles as well as the book of Acts attest to the importance of organization, maintain that the former theory simply glosses over the biblical data. It appears more tenable to assume that the *charismata* and the institutional ministries, such as elders, bishops, and deacons, existed side by side and that the mission of the church depended on both.

VI. The Ordinances of the Church

For the new "way" His incarnation, life and death would inaugurate, our Lord had appointed beforehand certain definite rites that all born-anew disciples would be called to observe, i.e., baptism and the Lord's Supper. Some

refer to them as ordinances, others as sacraments. Stemming from the Latin *ordo,* meaning "an order, a row," an ordinance refers to a practice ordained by the Lord. Sacrament, deriving from the Latin *sacramentum*—which was applied to things sacred or mysterious—may be defined as a rite in which spiritual realities are set forth by visible signs, suggesting for some the thought of something beyond the rite itself, seen as a visible sign participating in that reality. Both terms are foreign to the NT, yet both rites are at the heart of the expression of the church's faith.

A. Baptism

1. Antecedents and Origins

The ordinance of baptism may have derived its outward form from either Jewish proselyte baptism or from the rite administered by John the Baptist. Common to both was the presupposition of a break with the old life through the acceptance of the new. John's baptism, however, was addressed to Jews and was a call to "repentance for the forgiveness of sins" (Mark 1:4). In the case of the Lord's own baptism, the main emphasis was on commitment to a unique task, and consecration to His messianic ministry (cf. Matt. 3:15). Christian baptism expresses a radically new significance. Christ's incarnation, life, and death fulfilled God's salvation, and baptism in the name of Jesus indicates participation in this salvation through faith in Christ.

2. A Command

The command to baptize was part of Christ's Great Commission to the church to make disciples of all nations and to baptize them (Matt. 28:19). The command of our Lord was faithfully carried out by the disciples. Actual baptisms are recorded in Acts 2:38, 41; 8:12, 13, 16, 36-38; 9:18; 10:47; 16:15. The proclamation of the gospel called for a decision that ended in baptism. There is no trace in the NT of unbaptized Christians.

3. The Meaning of Baptism

In essence baptism is a simple rite that reflects the meaning of the gospel and of the plan of salvation it sets forth. The term itself comes from *baptizō* an intensive form of *baptō*,

to dip in or under. When referring to water baptism (Matt. 3:6; Mark 1:9; Acts 2:41), it carries the idea of immersing, of dipping a person under water. At the same time, since *baptizō* is used in various ways in the NT, including washing (Mark 7:4; Luke 11:38) and Christ's suffering and death (Mark 10:38, 39; Luke 12:50), it may be unsafe to make its original meaning the final argument for the mode of baptism. One should not ignore, however, the additional significance of the fact that several incidences of water baptism recorded in the NT involved immersion (cf. Matt. 3:6; Mark 1:5, 9, 10; John 3:23), a conclusion further sanctioned by the theological meaning given to the rite by the NT writers.

For Paul the meaning of baptism is first and foremost bound up with the saving events of Jesus' life, death, and resurrection, intrinsically contained in the conception of dying and rising with Christ. "Do you not know," asks the apostle, "that all of us who have been baptized into Christ Jesus were baptized into his death? We were buried therefore with him by baptism into death, so that as Christ was raised from the dead by the glory of the Father, we too might walk in newness of life" (Rom. 6:3, 4; cf. Col. 2:12). Paul's interpretation finds its full significance in baptism by immersion alone.

What Christ did for all sinners at Calvary is appropriated by each individual Christian in his or her baptism. In baptism Christians die with Christ, are crucified with Him (Rom. 6:6, 8; cf. Col. 3:3). His death frees them from sin (Rom. 6:7, 18). Risen with Christ, they begin a new life (verses 11-13; 7:4-6; Col. 3:1). The immersion into water is the outward form of one's immersion into Christ. The rising out of the water is the outward expression of the new life in Christ, of having "put on" Christ (Rom. 13:14; Gal. 3:27).

Immersion into water is also the outward form of a vital inner commitment to Christ. This is vividly described in Romans 6, for instance, by several words compounded with the preposition *syn*, meaning "with." We are buried together *(synetaphēmen)*, we have become a single plant with Him *(symphytoi);* the old nature is crucified together with Christ *(synestaurōthē).* If we died with Christ *(syn Christō)* we shall also live together with Him *(syzēsomen;* Rom. 6:4-6, 8). These various themes find a common focus in the fundamental thought of baptism as a drowning of the old life and an emergence into new life, a death and a resurrection.

4. Baptized Into One Body

Still, Christians are seen not only as baptized "into Christ" (Gal. 3:27) but also "baptized into one body," the church, the body of Christ (1 Cor. 12:13). If baptism is identification with Jesus Christ, it is at the same time identification with His body, the church. In Paul's words, "By one Spirit we were all baptized into one body" *(ibid.).* Christian baptism is baptism "in the name of Jesus Christ" (Acts 2:38; 10:48) or "in the name of the Lord Jesus" (Acts 8:16; 19:5), which, rather than referring to differing baptismal formulas, seems to refer to the theological import of baptism. It implies more particularly that those baptized belong to Christ, involving once again the notion of incorporation.

5. Believers' Baptism

It should be obvious at this point that this baptism is *believers'* baptism. If indeed it symbolizes the sinner's death to sin followed by a new life—the death, burial, and resurrection of Christ—baptism is an act of faith and a public testimony that one has been united with Him in His death and resurrection, a testimony to one's commitment to Christ. This explains why so often in the book of Acts proclamation, faith, repentance, and baptism are linked together. On the day of Pentecost, responding to the question "Brethren, what shall we do?" Peter replied, "Repent, and be baptized every one of you in the name of Jesus Christ for the forgiveness of your sins; and you shall receive the gift of the Holy Spirit" (Acts 2:37, 38). It is "when they believed Philip as he preached good news about . . . the name of Jesus" that inhabitants of a city in Samaria "were baptized" (Acts 8:12). In answer to the Philippian jailer's question "What must I do to be saved?" Paul answered simply, "Believe in the Lord Jesus, and you will be saved, you and your household" (Acts 16:30, 31). Soon afterward they were baptized (verse 33).

In each instance baptism was an expression of repentance and conversion, which implies that the household and families that at times are mentioned (cf. Acts 11:14; 16:15, 31-34; 18:8) met the conditions of baptism: they responded to the preaching of the word, confessing repentance and faith. There is no indication in the NT that infants were ever baptized. The general drift of the narratives is in a totally different direction. Immersion of believers was the practice in apostolic times. The introduction of any other form is unwarranted and bound to lead to misconceptions.

6. Baptism and the Holy Spirit

In various NT passages the gift of the Spirit is explicitly connected with water baptism, as in Acts 2:38; 8:14-17; 9:17, 18; 10:44-48; 19:1-7, and in the Gospels, as in Matthew 3:11; Mark 1:8; Luke 3:16; John 1:33; 3:5. In some instances the granting of the Spirit precedes baptism (Acts 10:44, 47); in others it follows it (Acts 2:37, 38; Mark 1:8). On two occasions the biblical narrative associates the laying on of hands with the imparting of the Spirit (Acts 8:12-17; 19:1-6). Yet one finds no NT teaching to the effect that the laying on of hands is the necessary condition or the moment when the Holy Spirit is imparted. In the case of Cornelius, the Spirit was given before baptism and without any outward sign such as the laying on of Peter's hands (Acts 10:44-48). Yet the apostle did not judge that after such an obvious mark of God's favor it was unnecessary for Cornelius and his household to be baptized in water. The two go together.

In the NT the baptismal ceremony is a whole, a unit not to be analyzed in its component parts. It is in the whole action that the Spirit is bestowed. There is no biblical baptism without the Spirit. Baptism is always baptism in water and in the Holy Spirit. (See Ordinances I.)

B. The Lord's Supper

The other biblically ordained rite for the life of the church is the Lord's Supper. Instituted by Christ Himself on the night in which He was betrayed (Matt. 26:20-30; Mark 14:17-25; Luke 22:14-23), the ordinance is referred to in the Scriptures as the "Lord's Supper" (1 Cor. 11:20), the "participation [or "communion"] in the body of Christ" (1 Cor. 10:16) and the "table of the Lord" (verse 21). Some speak of the "breaking of bread" (Acts 2:42; cf. verse 46), while others prefer the designation "eucharist," derived from the Greek *eucharisteō*, the term used for the giving of thanks before partaking of the elements (Matt. 26:27; 1 Cor. 11:24). It seems to have been part of a common meal, at least in Corinth, eaten in connection with the bread and the cup after the pattern of the Last Supper as described in the Synoptic Gospels.

The combined witness of the Synoptics leaves no doubt that the ordinance was instituted by Christ Himself. While there remain difficulties regarding the nature of the Last Supper and its relationship to the Jewish Passover, the Lord's Supper has all the marks of the paschal meal, whether described by the Synoptists or by Paul (1 Cor. 10:14-22; 11:23-34), who writes that "Christ, our paschal lamb, has been sacrificed" (1 Cor. 5:7). What began as a Passover ritual commemorating the exodus from Egypt and the establishment of the covenant at Sinai (Ex. 24) became the celebration of a new exodus, this time from sin, and the establishment of a new covenant to be sealed with Jesus' own blood.

1. The Meaning of the Lord's Supper

a. A look backward. Christ's command "Do this in remembrance of me" (1 Cor. 11:24) sums up the primary meaning of the Lord's Supper. It is first and foremost a memorial rite, not of all that Christ said and did, but more specifically of His redemptive death. As the Jewish Passover was a look backward, a reminder of God's mighty act in which He delivered Israel from the Egyptian bondage (Ex. 12:14; 13:3, 8, 9; Deut. 16:3), so the Lord's Supper, in which Christians partake of the bread and the wine, commemorates the decisive event that Christ effected at Calvary, the new "exodus" (cf. Luke 9:31), and His triumph over sin and death. The breaking of bread and the pouring of wine is the church's continual recollection of the fact and meaning of Christ's sacrificial death in which it originated (Acts 20:28), and which is the basis of our salvation.

b. A present reminder. The Lord's Supper also sets forth a present truth. Those who gather at "the table of the Lord" (1 Cor. 10:21) to eat the "Lord's supper" (1 Cor. 11:20) express visibly their present union with one another because of their union with the head of the church, Christ Himself. "Because there is one loaf," those who are many are one body, for they "all partake of the same loaf" (1 Cor. 10:16, 17). It is clear that for Paul the Lord's Supper provides a basis for unity. At the foundation of this ongoing relationship between God and His people is a covenant, a new covenant stressed in each of the accounts of the ordinance (Matt. 26:28; Mark 14:24; 1 Cor. 11:25).

c. A forward look. As a memorial of the past and reminder of the present, as instituted by Christ the Lord's Supper is also a forward look, a look to the Lord's second coming. Paul writes, "For as often as you eat this bread and drink the cup, you proclaim the Lord's death until he comes" (1 Cor. 11:26). The same eschatological motif was expressed by Jesus when He said, "I tell you I shall not drink again of this fruit of the vine until that day when I drink it new with you in my Father's kingdom" (Matt. 26:29; cf. Mark 14:25; Luke 22:16, 18). As the Jews in celebrating the Passover not only looked back to their deliverance from bondage but to a new deliverance by the Messiah they longed for, so the Christian fellowship at the Lord's table is a proclamation that the One who did come and is present among us has promised to come again.

d. Symbolic elements. In the Lord's Supper there is a real communion with Christ, though not with the idea that Christ's body and blood are present in the elements. Christ's body and blood are no more present today in the elements of bread and wine than they were when the Lord instituted the ordinance, took bread and gave it to the disciples, saying, "Take, eat; this is my body," then likewise took a cup and gave it to them, explaining, "Drink of it, . . . for this is my blood of the covenant, which is poured out for many for the forgiveness of sins" (Matt. 26:26-28). His instruction was clear: "Do this is remembrance of me" (1 Cor. 11:24, 25). The unleavened bread and unfermented fruit of the vine—which alone can appropriately symbolize the sinless perfection of the person of Christ—are shared "in remembrance of me"; they speak of sacrificial death and salvation and proclaim them until He comes.

Aside from Paul's discourse in 1 Corinthians 10 and 11, little is said in the Scriptures regarding the prerequisites for partaking of the Lord's Supper. Yet if by its very nature the ordinance denotes a spiritual relationship between the individual and the Lord, the Lord's table is set only for those who have a share in Him and in His salvation. A prerequisite may be inferred from Paul's urgent request that the church censure from the body those known to be living in open sin (1 Cor. 5:1-5). Still, Christ's attitude toward the disciple who betrayed Him should warn Christians against undue exclusiveness. (See Ordinances III.)

2. The Ordinance of Foot Washing

From the biblical perspective the Communion service is incomplete without its foot-washing rite. Just as He gave a more profound meaning to the Jewish Passover service, Christ invested foot washing, the OT hospitality rite, with deeper significance and made it an integral part of the Lord's Supper (John 13:1-5). Not only did His example impress on the minds of those present His life of meekness and service, but the Lord also used the event to prepare the self-centered and proud disciples (cf. Luke 22:24) to take part in the Lord's Supper.

The foot washing was to do more than clean their feet, soiled by the dusty and muddy roads, since after washing them, and referring to Judas, Jesus could say that they were clean, but not all of them (John 13:10, 11). A higher cleansing, a cleansing of the heart was part of Christ's intention when He instituted this ordinance. Its institutional, or lasting character, is clearly stated in Christ's instruction: "I have given you also an example, that you also should do as I have done to you," further emphasized by His remark "if you know these things, blessed are you if you do them" (verses 15, 17).

Does this ordinance have relevance to the present age beyond the clear lesson that the mark of Christian greatness is service? Christ's explanation to Peter that "he who has bathed *[louō]* does not need to wash *[niptō]*, except but his feet, for he is clean all over" (verse 10) seems to address our question. Like the disciples whose sandaled feet became dusty and needed washing again, so Christians baptized in Christ and cleansed by His blood as they walk the Christian life stumble and need Christ's cleansing grace to wash away the defilement. They need not be rebaptized: "He who has bathed does not need to wash, except for his feet." The ordinance of foot washing is a much needed confession of our self-centeredness and our need of Christ's grace as well as a renewal of our baptismal vows. The instruction to observe it, "I have given you an example, that you also should do as I have done to you" (verse 15; cf. verse 17), is as clear as the command regarding the Lord's Supper itself, "Do this in remembrance of me" (1 Cor. 11:24). The same verb *poieō* (to do) is used in both instances. There is no scriptural reason to understand either command in a merely symbolic sense. Jesus gave only two ordinances to the church, baptism and the Lord's Supper, which includes foot washing. None has lost its relevance. Both have been given for the edification of the church and the equipment of the saints for ministry. (See Ordinances II.)

VII. Church Authority

If the primary duty of the church is to worship and glorify God (cf. Eph. 1:3, 5, 11-14), the first task it was given by the risen Christ is that of evangelism (Mark 16:15; Luke 24:45-47; Acts 1:8). The church is not merely a gathering of people who come together to celebrate Jesus Christ and His teachings, but a people called together by God to witness, to bear Christ's name and to proclaim it (cf. 1 Peter 2:9). In the implementation of this commission the church is constantly confronted by the issue of authority. To what degree is it fulfilling Christ's intention? How, for instance, will the church make sure that in its teaching and proclamation it has not yielded to the cultural and philosophical assumptions of the various contexts in which it fulfills its mandate? Where shall it find the unfailing authority to resolve such issues?

A. The Ultimate Authority

As Creator, Redeemer and Sustainer, Lord and King of all creation (see Creation III), God alone is the source and ground of authority for the church. Yet our knowledge *of* God must be a knowledge *from* God, for only as He reveals Himself can He be known to His people. In revelation God discloses Himself to human beings and shares His will with them. This divine speaking reached a remarkable expression in the prophets who shared God's mind with His people (Heb. 1:1; see Revelation/Inspiration IV. D). Even so, the supreme expression of God's self-revelation is Jesus Christ, the incarnate Word of God (John 1:1-3, 14; 1 Tim. 3:16), at once the locus and the content of divine revelation (John 1:18; 3:31). In Him, as Saviour and Lord, divine revelation and authority find focus and finality.

In brief, the Word of God who holds authority over Christians and the church is known first and foremost as a person, Jesus Christ, who came to reveal the Father and proclaim the gospel of salvation. He also chose a handful of apostles so that His word and testimony might be faithfully proclaimed and interpreted after His death (Mark 3:13, 14). They were not merely witnesses to the crucified and risen Christ, but also commissioned and empowered by Him (Matt. 28:18-20; Acts 2:1-4; Rom. 1:1; Acts 13:2-4; 22:21) to preach the gospel (Acts 14:7, 21; 16:10; 1 Peter 1:12) and to share Christ with Jews and Gentiles (Acts 17:3; Rom. 10:17; 16:25; 1 Cor. 1:23; 2:2; 2 Cor. 1:19; etc.). They were the strongest authoritative human voices among the churches.

B. Apostolic Authority

Their authority, however, was not their own, for the gospel, Paul insists, enjoyed antecedent authority. Any apostle tampering with it was none of Christ's apostles (Gal. 1:8, 9). Whether "by word of mouth or by letter" (2 Thess. 2:15), in obedience to Christ the apostles announced the "word of God" (1 Thess. 2:13), which they expected believers to accept as a command of the Lord (1 Cor. 14:37). Speaking with the authority which "the Lord gave" them (2 Cor. 10:8) they occupied a crucial and unique position in the transmission of the word of God and the edification of the church (Eph. 2:20).

C. The Authority of Scripture

When their message found embodiment in the Scriptures, the Word that held authority over the Christian community and was known primarily as a Person came to be known secondarily in the form of the spoken and now written language of the NT. The latter found its place and function next to the OT writings, which from the very start had been the Bible of Christ and of the NT church. God was still the source and ground of authority, for the Scriptures, both OT and NT, are not merely a testimony to revelation but revelation itself. They are not an intrusion upon God's revelation in Christ but very much part of it, for Christ is their supreme content. Therein lies the authority of the Scriptures, since the only authoritative Christ Christians know is the Christ of the Bible.

D. Authority in the Local Church

At the level of the local congregation, the elders/bishops seem to have consistently enjoyed the greatest authority (see V. B). One of their main functions was general pastoral care and oversight (Acts 20:17-28; 1 Peter 5:1-3), with special tasks such as giving instruction in sound doctrine and refuting those who contradicted it (1 Tim. 3:1, 2; Titus 1:5, 9). Those who "[ruled] well" were to be "considered worthy of double honor," more particularly so if they labored in "preaching and teaching" (1 Tim. 5:17).

While the elders and deacons helped the apostles in the exercise of their ministry, much of government of the local churches rested in the hands of the churches themselves. It is evident that local congregations exercised authority with respect to the selection of local leaders (Acts 6:1-6; cf. 14:23). They appointed messengers to be sent to other churches (Acts 11:22) or to accompany apostles (2 Cor. 8:19), sometimes accrediting them by letter (1 Cor. 16:3). The local congregations also bore responsibility for purity in doctrine and practice. They were to "test the spirits to see whether they are of God" (1 John 4:1) or, in Paul's terms, to "test everything" and "hold fast what is good" (1 Thess. 5:21).

The same is true regarding the exercise of church discipline (Matt. 18:15-17). The Lord Himself noted that "whatever you bind on earth shall be bound in heaven; and whatever you loose on earth shall be loosed in heaven" (verse 18). The terminology was all too familiar to the disciples who heard Christ on that occasion. In synagogal and rabbinic usage it meant primarily the authority to prohibit and to allow something, to impose penalties on someone, or to acquit someone. The exercise of disci-

pline ranged all the way from private and caring admonition (cf. Matt. 18:16; Gal. 6:1) to disfellowshipping (Matt. 18:18; 1 Cor. 5:11, 13). Evidently the local congregation is to settle the conditions of membership and the rules of the house.

E. Authority of the Universal Church

Yet, according to the same Scriptures, it is evident that in the exercise of authority the local congregation does not live in isolation or independence from other local churches. Any theory of church authority, and therefore of church government, that fails to recognize the reality and unity of the universal church falls short of the biblical testimony. The relevance of the oneness of the church does not proceed, however, from its practical desirability or the need for amicable cooperation. Its basis lies in the very nature of the local church, which is not merely a section of the universal church but the church itself fully present in that particular locality, the church in local expression. Nor is the church universal the sum total of all local congregations. The church is one and indivisible, a unity expressed in a visible manner. This is clearly reflected in the way the word *ekklēsia* is often used in the NT (see II. A, B). The NT "body" metaphor reaffirms it. Christ does not have several bodies, but one, and that one body manifests itself in the unity and closeness of the whole church. This is of vital significance for the concept of church authority and its exercise.

If indeed Jesus intended His church to proclaim and share the gospel, one can hardly deny it the right to exercise a measure of administrative authority. In the realm of determining truths of revelation the role of the universal church is more particularly difficult and important. As "the pillar and bulwark of the truth" (1 Tim. 3:15) the church is called not only to teach the truth of the gospel but also to preserve and defend it. While "the faith . . . once for all delivered to the saints" (Jude 3) has been fixed by the last apostolic witness, it needs interpretation and application to new circumstances and emergencies.

The means by which this is done, in dependence on the Lord's promised guidance (John 14:15-17; 16:12, 13), is strikingly illustrated in Acts 15. This chapter tells of the gathering in Jerusalem of a large assembly of representatives from various churches (verses 2, 3) and the local apostles and elders (verse 4) to consider a divisive issue, the role of circumcision in salvation. After "much debate" (verse 7) Peter's reference to the Spirit's activity (verse 8) and James' final appeal to the Scriptures (verses 13-18), a decision was reached and sent forth to the believers elsewhere. The letter-decree sent out in the name of the apostles and elders (verse 23) was no mere recommendation, since soon afterward, on his second missionary journey, Paul and Silas, passing through various cities on their way to the region of Phrygia and Galacia (Acts 16:6) "deliv-ered to them for observance the decisions [Gr. *dogma*] which had been reached by the apostles and elders who were at Jerusalem" (verse 4). "Delivered to them for observance." The voice of the Spirit (Acts 15:28) speaking in the Scriptures and in the work of the gospel among Gentiles was distinctly heard by those assembled "to consider this matter" (verse 6). They were assured that their decision, reached after considerable difference of opinion and by means open to the church in all ages, was in harmony with Christ's will. They were confident that Christ's presence had been "in the midst of them" when thus "gathered in [His] name" (Matt. 18:20). Major assemblies that address matters pertaining to the church in general and that concern the preservation of unity, therefore exercising authority on a broader and more extended scale than a local congregation, are unquestionably warranted by Scripture.

VIII. The Characteristics of the Church

As soon as heresies arose it became necessary to point to certain marks by which God's church could be identified. The consciousness of this need was already present in the early church. Although the NT suggests a longer list than appears here, certain characteristics of the early Christian society seem more pronounced than others.

A. Faith

The fundamental characteristic is a living faith. According to the NT, the church is a society not of thinkers or workers, but of believers. "Believers," or "those who believed," is constantly used as a synonym for the members of the church (cf. Acts 4:4, 32; 5:14; 15:5; 18:27; 1 Thess. 1:7; 1 Tim. 4:12). Baptism, which from the start was the entrance rite into the church and a sign of belonging to the body of Christ, was essentially a rite of faith and of confession (Acts 2:44; 8:12; 16:31-33; 18:8). This church-building faith was no mere act of intellectual assent, but the symbol of an intimate union between the believer and Christ, which resulted in a new creation (2 Cor. 5:17).

B. Fellowship

From the very nature of faith follows the next mark, fellowship. This fellowship is primarily fellowship with Christ, who, though ascended to heaven (Acts 3:21), is yet sensibly present to His disciples (Gal. 2:20; cf. Matt. 18:20; 28:20). This fellowship with Christ *(koinōnia)* to which each Christian is called (1 Cor. 1:9) is also a "participation [or fellowship-*koinōnia*] in the Spirit" (Phil. 2:1), as well as a "fellowship [or communion-*koinōnia*] of the Holy Spirit" (2 Cor. 13:14) who mediates between Christ and the believer.

Equally important, this fellowship is also actively exercised toward the members of the Christian community. It was one of the chief characteristics of the primitive church (Acts 2:42). Since they were vitally joined to Christ, all believers were exhorted to stand in living relation to one another. The reality of their fellowship explains the frequent occurrence of the term "brethren" commonly applied to those who belonged to the fellowship: some 40 times in the book of Acts alone and more than 90 times in Paul's Epistles. It appears from the writings to the Corinthians that the Lord's Supper provides an unusual opportunity for the fellowship of Christians to express itself—a communion-fellowship in Christ's death and resurrection that entails a communion of heart and spirit among the participants themselves.

At the same time, though it is not the kingdom of God, the church has been "called out" of this world to express the kingdom's leavening presence within this world. All of the paradoxical ways in which God's reign brings a reversal of conventional human values are bound up in this modeling process (cf. Luke 22:24-30). The church is summoned to live out in this world the kingdom's openness toward all people, whether aligned with God or not (Matt. 5:43-48), while at the same time setting forces in motion that will break down oppressive barriers between Jew and Gentile, slave and master, man and woman (Gal. 3:28). Thus the prayer "thy kingdom come" expresses more than a pious wish. The kingdom advances in this world as the church models obedience to God's will on earth (Matt. 6:10; see Sabbath III. D).

C. Oneness

Oneness is another main characteristic of the church as depicted in the NT. Although there are many congregations, the church of Christ is but one church, one body of which Christ is the head. As Paul writes (Eph. 4:4-6), this body has "one Lord, one faith, one baptism, one God and Father of us all." This unity is perceived as a visible unity, as evidenced by Jesus' prayer urging that His disciples be one so that the *world* might know and believe (John 17:23, 21). Such a unity toward which Paul strove transcends the divisive elements of race, class, and gender (Gal. 3:28). It is not the result of a voluntary act of uniting on the part of the members of Christ's body, but a unity enabled by the Spirit, for the church has found oneness in Christ (Eph. 5:2-15).

Living in a variety of cultures, times, and places, the church may appear as disparate. The book of Revelation itself celebrates the Lamb who through the cross "didst ransom men for God from every tribe and tongue and people and nation" (Rev. 5:9). All, however, belong to one body, whose inner unity seeks and acquires outward expression in the profession of the same faith (Eph. 4:5, 13, 14) and Christian conduct in a visible church.

According to the Scriptures, this bond of unity is not found in the ecclesiastical organization of the church but in the preaching of the word of God. The word is what the apostles preached (Acts 4:31; 13:5; 15:35; 16:32; etc.), what the Gentiles gathered to hear and glorified (Acts 11:1; 13:44, 48), and what grew and multiplied (Acts 12:24; cf. 6:7; 13:49; 19:20). Divisions and a factious party spirit were strongly denounced (cf. 1 Cor. 11:18, 19; Gal. 5:20), along with false brethren (Gal. 2:4), false apostles (2 Cor. 11:13), and erroneous teaching departing from the apostolic doctrine (1 Tim. 6:3; 2 Peter 2:1). As Paul saw it, God "desires all men . . . to come to the knowledge of the truth" (1 Tim. 2:4). Thus there is indeed such a thing as "the truth" (2 Thess. 2:12, 13), "the word of truth" (Eph. 1:13; 2 Tim. 2:15), which must be preserved (Gal. 2:5), but which some, "puffed up with conceit" (1 Tim. 6:4), oppose, threatening the oneness of the church.

D. Holiness

Holiness is another leading characteristic of the church. Along with "believers," "saints" is one of the most frequently recurring designations for the members of Christ's body, especially in Paul's writings. In the NT the person, thing, or place, that is holy (Gr. *hagios*) belongs to God, hence is "separate" from sin and consecrated to God. This claim is underlined in such statements as "you are not your own; you were bought with a price" (1 Cor. 6:19, 20; cf. 1 Peter 1:18, 19).

The holiness or sainthood of the Christian community resides in its separation from the world in answer to God's call (2 Tim. 1:9), just as Israel of old was called to be a "holy" nation (Ex. 19:6; 1 Peter 2:9; cf. Lev. 20:26). The church is holy, set apart from the world, to refract the holiness of God and bring forth the fruits of the Spirit in a fallen world. Jesus called His disciples "out of the world" (John 17:6), though He regarded them as still "in the world" (verse 11) but "not of the world" (verse 14). The NT notion of holiness includes both implications: being set apart from the world and reaching out to a world in rebellion. The church cannot be holy while forsaking its mission and task of saving sinners.

Yet, side by side with the sense of outward holiness, the words "holy" and "saint" carry with them the meaning of ethical holiness. Christian holiness consists not merely in a status determined by one's relation to Christ, but also in a consecration to God that finds expression in character and conduct. At the same time the members of the church are called saints even when the evidences of holiness are sadly lacking. Thus Paul addresses by the title "saints" the members of the church at Corinth in which he found so much to reprove (2 Cor. 1:1). While holiness or sainthood is a Christian's outward calling and status as believer, the work of sanctification is going on and must continue to go on. As paradoxical as it may appear, the Corinthian believers are depicted at one and the same time as "sanctified in Christ" and "called to be saints" (1 Cor. 1:2). Those who are in Christ have consecrated themselves to Christ (2 Cor. 6:14-18), making "holiness perfect in the fear of God" (2 Cor. 7:1). Holiness is a growing and continuous experience in Christ, who "loved the church and gave himself up for her, . . . that the church might be presented before him in splendor, without spot or wrinkle or any such thing" (Eph. 5:25, 26; cf. Titus 2:14). The holiness of the church is intertwined in continuing human imperfection. The church is holy yet subject to infirmities.

E. Universality

With equal clarity, the NT insists on the universality or catholicity of the church. Too often misunderstood because of its partisan air, the word "catholic" refers not to a particular hierachical organization but to the fact that the Christian message is intended for all people, everywhere. The church is meant to embrace all nations (Matt. 28:19; cf. Rev. 14:6). It is not bound to a particular time or place, but encompasses believers of all generations, nations, and cultures.

Still the catholicity of the church does not lie in its worldwide outreach alone, but in the influence it exercises on all aspects of human life as well as in the church's possession of universal truth. Because Christ's love is addressed to all, the church offers the whole counsel of God to the whole world. It reaches out to the whole world with the whole truth as revealed by God (cf. Acts 20:27). The church teaches universally and from first to last all the teachings Christ has commanded (Matt. 28:20). Here again is a reliable test: The universal nature of the church has clear missionary implications.

F. Apostolicity

As the household of God, writes Paul, the church is "built upon the foundation of the apostles and prophets, Christ Jesus himself being the chief cornerstone" (Eph. 2:20). On that account, although the term itself is foreign to the NT, various Christians speak of the apostolicity of the church, some insisting even on a literal, linear, and uninterrupted apostolic succession by the laying on of hands as evidence of such apostolicity. What authenticates the church, it is claimed, is a visible and unbroken connection, which can be traced historically, between a present-day Christian community and the church of the apostles.

This view, however, seems to ignore the fact that in the NT the line of succession between the apostles and today's apostolic witness is conceived as a continuous line of faithfulness to the testimony of the apostles, sustained by the Holy Spirit. From the earliest days onward the disciples "devoted themselves to the apostles' teaching and fellowship" (Acts 2:42). The intimation is that the continuing church accepts and teaches the truths preached by the apostles, and lives the kind of life that they enjoined (2 Tim. 1:13, 14). Thus, Paul admonished Timothy, "And what you have heard from me before many witnesses entrust to faithful men who will be able to teach others also" (2 Tim. 2:2), adding that an elder/bishop must be "an apt teacher," able to "care for God's church," to "hold firm to the sure word as taught," and "to confute those who contradict" the apostolic doctrine (1 Tim. 3:2-7; Titus 1:5-9).

If the church, as apostolic, is grounded in the message of the apostles, it is apostolic also because it is sent into the world as Christ was sent (from *apostellō*, lit. to send forth, to send out on service, or with a commission). As Christ was sent (Matt. 10:40; 15:24; Mark 9:37; Luke 4:43; John 7:29) and the disciples were sent (Matt. 10:16; John 17:18), so the continuing apostolate is still being sent (John 20:21). Mission characterizes all that the church does. Apostolicity is a distinct mark of the true church. But any notion of apostolicity that fails to engage in faithfulness to the gospel and to mission is a misconceived view of apostolicity.

G. A Faithful Remnant

Tragically, persecution, apostasy, and corruption were to strike the church. Jesus Himself warned the disciples that "false prophets" would arise to lead them astray (Matt. 24:4, 24), that a period of "great tribulation" would come upon them (verses 21, 22). Paul likewise forewarned his fellow believers that after his departure "fierce wolves" would arise from among them, not sparing the flock, "men speaking perverse things, to draw away the disciples after them" (Acts 20:29, 30).

In spite of the apostasy, relentless persecution and tribulation, which, according to the book of Revelation, would last 1260 years (Rev. 12:6; cf. 12:4; 13:5; see Remnant/Three Angels III. A), at the end of a long and worthy line of

heroes of the faith, and with the arrival of "the time of the end," God would call a remnant (Rev. 12:17, KJV). "Remnant" in this passage, from which the "remnant church" is derived, is reminiscent of the OT usage of the term in which it described a minority remaining loyal to God (2 Chron. 30:6; Ezra 9:14; Isa. 10:20; Eze. 6:8, 9) and going forth to witness for Him (Isa. 37:31, 32; 66:19). God would raise up another chosen instrument to proclaim the apostolic message to earth's inhabitants.

The end-time remnant shows clear characteristics. John describes it as made up of those who "keep the commandments of God and bear testimony to [lit. "have the testimony of"] Jesus" (Rev. 12:17). Following in the steps of Christ, who kept His Father's commandments (John 15:10), and holding fast to "the faith which was once for all delivered to the saints" (Jude 3), the remnant is described here as being a commandment-keeping church, observing all of God's commandments. The remnant also has "the testimony of Jesus," which John later defines as "the spirit of prophecy" (Rev. 19:10; see Remnant/Three Angels IV. A; Gifts X. D).

In the context of end-time circumstances, the message and mission of the church are further outlined in Revelation 14:6-12. Three messages—coupled with that of Revelation 18:1-4—constitute God's last appeal to sinners to accept His gracious gift of salvation, as shown in the verses immediately following (14:13-16; see Remnant/Three Angels V. B-E; Judgment III. B. 1. a. [1]). From the proclamation of this last message there is gathered a people that John depicts (as in Rev. 12:17) as keeping the commandments of God (14:12), but adding "and the faith of Jesus." They are characterized by a faith similar to that of Jesus, reflecting His unshakable confidence in God and embracing all the truths of the Scriptures. The cross and the law are again brought together. God has loyal disciples in other communities, but He has called the remnant church once more to preach "the everlasting gospel" to the ends of the world (verse 6, KJV), to bear witness to Christ and prepare sinners for the Lord's second coming.

From beginning to end, these marks belong to the essential nature of the church: faith, fellowship, unity, holiness, universality, and faithfulness to the apostolic message. They are also intrinsically intertwined, and in their unity point to the authentic church of God.

IX. A Sober Look Into the Future

A. Living in a Pluralistic World

Our inquiry, however brief, into the nature, scope, mission, and marks of the church enables us to point out a few things regarding the church of the future. No one can predict what the coming decades will bring. Yet biblical prophecy and current trends suggest a likely scenario.

Committed to the scientific and technological worldview of human betterment through the seemingly relentless expansion that science and technology have made possible, Christians, worldwide and in increasing numbers, have become alarmed that the great forces our modern technology now wields might indeed lead humanity into a most dangerous world. At the same time the past two centuries have brought such overwhelming changes in the intellectual and social realms of our lives that on most questions the traditional answers offered by Christianity seem no longer relevant. With few notable exceptions, all over the Western world, traditionally a stronghold of Christianity, men and women are abandoning the church and its message. The trend is toward minority status for Christians.

The church finds itself today in a world radically different from what it has known for centuries. The "Constantinian era"—when church and society shared similar ideals—has come to an end. As a result Christians find themselves part of a community of believers who, by virtue of a personal, free, and explicit decision of faith, dissociate themselves from the current views of their social environment. The church of the future will have the characteristic of a "little flock," a true remnant, living in a pluralistic world in which God and the Scriptures will at best be merely one alternative among many others, if indeed the rest of society is tolerantly pluralistic, which, prophecy tells us, is far from assured.

This means that, in several ways, true Christians will be close to the early believers in the circumstances of their existence: diaspora in a neopagan world, a family of scattered congregations united in faith and fellowship around the teachings of the apostles, basic communities of belief that one enters only through total commitment. Dispersed and on the move, the church will be engaged in mission. Because of the sharp contrast with a secularized and un-Christian milieu, the remnant church—how befitting the description!—will have to find out why it should present a specific statement about God and salvation in the last days. The church will have to remain solidly founded on the Scriptures, close to the teachings of the prophets and the apostles, relying on the Holy Spirit. It will grow as a worldwide church where major local churches, regions such as Africa, Europe, or Asia, will have their own special character while maintaining the unity of faith and order so characteristic of the early church.

B. The Church, Militant and Triumphant

While in this world the church is a militant church, daily engaged in the battles of its Lord, and in warfare against satanic agencies. Its members are in constant conflict with the world, the flesh, and the powers of evil (Rom. 7:15-23; Gal. 5:17; 1 Peter 5:8, 9; 1 John 5:4; cf. 1 John 4:4).

If this side of the Lord's return the church is the militant church, the church of the New Jerusalem is the triumphant church. It is made up of faithful disciples and conquerors in this worldly battle. They have exchanged the sword for a palm of victory (Rev. 7:9) and the cross for a crown (2 Tim. 4:8; 1 Peter 5:4). The battle is over, the mission accomplished (Matt. 25:21, 23) and the redeemed, invited to the wedding feast of the Lamb (Rev. 19:9), eat and drink at Christ's table in His kingdom (Luke 22:28-30) and reign with Him for ever and ever (Rev. 22:5).

X. Historical Overview

A. The Ancient Church

1. Early Patristic Writings

The doctrine of the church was not a major issue in the early church. The early Church Fathers showed no particular awareness of the potential importance of the doctrine. In their writings, the church is generally represented as the *communio sanctorum,* the congregation of the saints, the chosen people of God. It is essentially a spiritual society, made up of Christians who, in spite of their different origins and backgrounds, are one in Christ, faithful to the teachings of the apostles, and growing in faith and holiness. When describing the church, the patristic writings often refer to it as the body of Christ (Ignatius, c. 105), the new Israel (Clement of Rome, c. 95; Justin Martyr, c. 150) or the temple of the Holy Spirit (Irenaeus, c. 180), among others, reminding one of the themes used by the NT authors. Few probed much further.

2. Toward an Episcopal Church

Shortly, however, a perceptible change came about. Already in the second century, persecution on the one hand and the rise of heresies on the other made it necessary to designate certain external characteristics by which the true catholic church (i.e., "universal" church) could be identified. The church began to be conceived in terms of an external institution, ruled by bishops as direct successors of the apostles and in possession of the true Christian tradition. While there is no convincing evidence that episcopacy, with its threefold ministry of bishop, priest (or presbyter), and deacon, is discernible as the primitive form of church government in the NT, it certainly made its appearance by the second century and in time became practically universal. The tranquillity with which this system was accepted in the various parts of the Roman Empire seems to show the extent to which the rise of the episcopate to a position of leadership met a felt need.

The general view was that the bishops stood in the place of the apostles, whose teaching office they continued. A particular *charisma* was attached to their office. As priests *(sacerdotes),* they stood as mediators between God and the people. In that capacity they offered sacrifices to God and introduced a new understanding of the Christian ministry as well as a new perception of the nature and characteristics of the church, with a highly sharpened distinction between clergy and laity.

3. The Cyprianic Doctrine of the Church

Cyprian, bishop of Carthage from 248 to 258, was to draw the lines together and develop for the first time an explicit doctrine of the episcopal church. His ecclesiology shows all the marks of a man trained in Roman law, legalistic, logical, and practical. Once more in the face of persecution and heresy, his two points of contention were the unity of the church and the authority of the bishop. On the basis of Matthew 16:18 Cyprian maintained that the church was founded on the bishops, the successors of the apostles. They were the lords of the church. They were the church, and whoever refused to submit to the rightful bishop was not in the church.

Together the bishops constituted a college, the episcopate. As such they represented the church. The unity of the church was found in the unity of bishops. Outside of the church there was no possibility to be saved. Heretics were challenged to produce the origin of their churches, to demonstrate the authority of their bishops through a direct line of ordination from bishop to bishop in such a way that the first bishop had as his teacher and predecessor one of the apostles.

Cyprian was the first to set forth distinctly and cogently the idea of a catholic church comprehending all true branches of the church of Christ and bound together by a visible and external unity. The desire to stem the rise of heresy had resulted in a concept of the church and of unity that would progressively deface the scriptural teaching on the nature and identity of the church.

Another tendency, however, manifested itself during those early centuries. While the major trend in the development of the church was toward an external centralization and control of the church, opposition movements, at times powerful, fiercely defied it. Characterized as heretics, these advocates regarded the true church as a fellowship of saints. They made the holiness of church members the real mark of the church. Thus Montanism in the middle of the second, Novatianism in the middle of the third, and Donatism in the beginning of the fourth century were born of a reaction against the gradual secularization and the increasing laxity and worldliness of the church. In various ways they strove for the purity of the church and insisted on rigorous life style and ecclesiastical discipline. (See Gifts XIII. A.)

4. Augustine and the Donatist Controversy

The Donatist controversy forced an accelerated pace of theological reflection on the nature and identity of the church. The Donatists were a group of Christians in Roman North Africa who argued that the church was a community of saints, within which sin had no place. The issue became particularly significant during the fierce persecution undertaken in 303 by the emperor Diocletian, who ordered that Christian books and churches be burned. Under pressure a number of Christians surrendered their copies of Scripture to their Roman persecutors to burn. When the persecution receded and many of these *traditores* "traitors" (lit., "those who handed over [the Scriptures]") returned to the church, the Donatists argued that those who lapsed under persecution needed to be rebaptized, and the bishops reordained.

The movement itself originated in the rejection of Caecilian as bishop of Carthage on the grounds that one such *traditor* had been involved in his consecration. By the time Augustine (354-430) returned to Africa some 75 years later and became bishop of Hippo, the breakaway faction, strongly sustained by North African nationalism, had established itself as the leading Christian body in the region.

The theological issues raised concerned the identity and the unity of the church on the one hand and the validity of sacraments celebrated even by unworthy ministers on the other. Augustine addressed them in the context of Cyprian's legacy and was able to resolve the tensions in a way that influenced all subsequent western theology. The church is holy not because of the moral character of its members, but on the basis of the endowments it has received from Christ. These include the faith of believers, Christ's teachings, episcopal succession, and the sacraments. The church must expect to remain to the very end a "mixed body" of saints and sinners, refusing to weed out those who have lapsed under persecution or for other reasons.

Similarly, explained Augustine, the sacraments of the church do not derive their validity from the worthiness of the minister (priest or bishop) who administers them. Their true minister is Christ. No minister, however holy, grants the grace of the sacraments he administers. The personal unworthiness of a minister does not compromise the validity of the sacrament or the efficacy of the grace it imparts. God alone is the Giver.

Augustine insisted that the Donatists could claim neither the unity nor the catholicity of the church. As an inevitable aspect of the life of the church, sin should never be the occasion or justification for schism. Besides, confined to North Africa, Donatists were only a small part of catholicity understood in its geographical sense. Local churches are true churches only insofar as they are part of the universal church.

Cyprian championed the concept of a universal church, with centralized authority and control. Augustine developed this theory into a system that laid the foundations for papal supremacy in western Christendom.

5. Prominence of the Roman See

As the episcopal system of church government expanded, five centers were held in particular esteem, i.e., Alexandria, Antioch, Constantinople, Jerusalem, and Rome. Rivalry developed between the leaders of these churches, especially those of Rome and Constantinople. By the end of the fifth century the bishop of Rome was clearly acquiring a position and role of special prominence. He intervened in the life of distant churches, took sides in theological controversies, was consulted by other bishops on doctrinal and moral questions, and sent delegates to distant councils. In view of the Matthew 16:18, 19 statement, claimed to have granted Peter primacy over the other apostles, as successors of Peter, the Roman bishops maintained that this priority rested upon a solid theological foundation. The eastern churches, which developed in the eastern Roman or Byzantine Empire, rejected the allegation, while consenting to a primacy of honor and recognizing the bishop of Rome as "first among equals" in the episcopal college.

B. In the Middle Ages

1. In the West: A Monarchical Episcopacy

The theologians of the Middle Ages, an era generally taken to date from about A.D. 500 to about 1500, contributed but a few elements to the development of the doctrine of the church. As elaborated by Cyprian and Augustine it appeared clearly stated and complete.

In the area of church organization, however, major changes occurred. The church itself developed into a close-knit, compactly organized, and increasingly absolute monarchy. After the break between the Christian East and West, traditionally dated 1054, and under the influence of such Roman Pontiffs as Gregory VII (1073-1085) and Innocent III (1198-1216), the claims of a primacy of honor ripened into a dogmatic insistence on the supremacy and monarchical status of the bishop of Rome, in accordance with contemporary models of government. Western Christendom became Roman Catholic, a church in which the relation of the faithful to the see of Rome was so predominant that it swallowed up the relations to the local bishop. Not only was the concept of the church as the *communio sanctorum,* the assembly of the saints, disregarded, but even the vision of the church as a communion of local churches was absorbed in the vision of a universal church under a universal primate. No longer the Vicar of Peter, the more traditional title of the Roman pontiff since the end of the fourth century, but the Vicar of Christ, originally an episcopal title, came to be exclusively identified with the bishop of Rome.

2. Protesting Voices

There was no lack of protesting voices. In the East, Orthodox churches pointed to the absence of specific declarations by any ecumenical council. In the West, Bede (d. 735), Paul the Deacon (d. c. 800), Hincmar, archbishop of Rheims (d. 882), Rabanus Maurus (d. 856), Gerbert of Aurillac, who later became Pope Sylvester II (d. 1003), among others, acknowledged the primacy of honor of the Roman see but contested the claims of popes to override the authority of metropolitan bishops. Pierre d'Ailly (d. 1420), Jean de Gerson (d. 1429), and other "Conciliarists" argued that such authority resided in the whole body of the faithful exercised through general councils.

Overt opposition to the Roman view grew steadily. Particularly outspoken in their protest were the twelfth-century Waldenses. Other opponents were clerics such as Robert Grosseteste, bishop of Lincoln (d. 1253); John of Paris (d. 1306); a German friar, Meister Eckhart (d. 1327); William of Ockham (d. 1349), an English Franciscan; John Wycliffe (d. 1384), English priest and theologian; and John Huss (d. 1415). The winds of dissension were stirring. The schism that Cyprian and Augustine denounced so vehemently eventually came in the sixteenth century. Before turning to these developments and their influence on the Christian doctrine of the church, we shall briefly consider the turn taken by the same doctrine in the eastern part of Christendom.

3. In the East: A Collegial Episcopacy

The development of the Christian church with its priesthood and episcopate was common to both eastern and western Christianity. The East, however, laid less stress on a solidification of the church into a thoroughly organized and monarchical hierarchy. The priestly and episcopal system never reached an established external authority for the whole church. In Eastern Orthodoxy, churches dwelled more on the local church as a eucharistic community in communion with the incarnate Christ and on the representation of His work of redemption in the rich mysteries of the liturgy.

In spite of burgeoning differences in language and culture, and a growing diversity in ecclesiastical customs, many expressions of unity and goodwill existed between the two "sister churches," western Catholicism and Eastern Orthodoxy. A slow process of estrangement led to a first mid-ninth-century separation and in 1054 to a final break between the Latin and Greek churches, a break that has persisted to our time.

Eastern Orthodoxy had little desire to challenge the primacy of honor allowed by various councils to the Roman see but firmly resisted western attempts to translate primacy into a supremacy over the universal church. No ecclesiastical see was entitled to claim supremacy over all the others. Autocephalous churches, involving the culture of local communities, are entitled as national churches to elect their own metropolitan bishop or patriarch and thus govern themselves, closely allied with the secular state. Some sees, those of Rome, Constantinople, Alexandria, Antioch, and Jerusalem, did, as the canons of early ecumenical councils had expressed it, possess a certain authority over sees within the same region, but this was perceived as a matter of ecclesiastical organization, not of divine right. None had an inherent juridical right over others. Together the bishops formed a collegial body, enjoyed an essential equality, and, in a General Council in search of the common mind of the church, exercised the totality of their episcopal authority.

C. The Reformation

Various social, political, intellectual, and religious factors contributed to the rise of the sixteenth-century Reformation.

1. Luther and the Church

As an Augustinian priest and professor of Scripture, Martin Luther (1483-1546) was convinced that the church of his day had lost sight of the Christian doctrine of grace. Central to his concern was the scriptural teaching that justification was by grace through faith alone, which came to deny the necessity for the mediatorial function of the church and of the priesthood.

In Luther's view, the church was essentially the spiritual communion of those redeemed by justifying grace, the ancient communion of saints. An episcopally ordained ministry was therefore not necessary to safeguard the existence of the church, but the faithful preaching of the Word of God was essential to its identity. Where the pure gospel was preached and the sacraments rightly administered there was the church. It was more important to preach the same gospel as the apostles than to be a member of an institution claiming to be historically derived from them.

From then on Luther's ecclesiology diverged increasingly from traditional Roman Catholic beliefs. His distinction between two aspects of the church, the one visible and the other invisible, allowed him to deny that the church is essentially an external society with a visible head. It also offered him opportunity to affirm that the essence of the church was to be found in the sphere of the invisible, i.e., in faith and communion with Christ. The most important thing for Christians was that they belonged to the spiritual or invisible church. This implied membership in the visible church, one, holy, catholic, and apostolic. It also explained the need for an outward ecclesiastical society understood as a number of baptized believers guided by a priest or a bishop under the gospel. At the same time Luther expected the Christian princes to grant protection to the church and, for the sake of Christian unity, to exercise considerable authority within the church in matters both social and ecclesiastical. As a result much of the authority of the pope and bishops passed to the Christian princes. Luther's views on the church were incorporated into his two *Catechisms,* the *Augsburg Confession* (1530), the *Articles of Schmalkalden* (1537), and the *Formula of Concord* (1537), all combined in the *Book of Concord* (1580). They became the chief standards of most Lutheran churches.

2. Calvin and the Church

During the 1520s Luther, Melanchthon, and other Reformers shared the belief that reunion with a reformed Catholic Church was mainly a matter of time. In the 1540s and 1550s, when all hopes of reaching a compromise collapsed, a second generation of "Protestant" theologians further pursued their distinctive understanding of the nature and identity of the church. John Calvin (1509-1564) stood out as one of the most prominent.

While his concept of the church fundamentally corresponds to Luther's, Calvin's realization that separation from the main body of the Roman Catholic Church might continue indefinitely led him to develop a more coherent and systematic ecclesiology. Some aspects are directly related to the purpose of this essay.

While recognizing that some traces of the true church could still be found in the Roman Catholic Church, Calvin regarded it as necessary, on scriptural grounds, to break with it. The Word of God "purely preached and heard" and the sacraments "administered according to Christ's institution" were the distinguishing marks of the church. This minimalist definition of the church, however, took on a new significance. Calvin included in it a specific form of church structure and administration, developing a detailed theory of church government based upon his study of the NT and generally referred to as "Reformed" or "Presbyterian." This form of church government recognizes that the authority of the church is vested in its members. Leadership derives its authority and responsibilities from the constituency, while executive responsibilities are delegated to representative bodies and officers.

Endowed by Christ with the necessary power and gifts, the church exercises authority in matters spiritual, such as the preservation of the Word, the framing of confessions of faith, and the exercise of discipline. The spiritual power of the church is to be distinguished from the temporal power. In the latter, Christian magistrates, exercising their Christian vocation, have as their appointed end to defend sound doctrine and the doctrinal position of the church, to promote general peace, and to prevent all public offenses against religion from arising and spreading among the people. Only when commanding anything against God are rulers to be disobeyed. Calvin insisted on a close union between church and state, reminiscent to some extent of the Roman Catholic teaching. Contrary to Luther, however, he advocated a more theocratic policy that subjected the state to the church. His views on the church have found their most systematic development in his *Institutes of the Christian Religion* (4. 1-20), and their strictest expression in the *Second Helvetic Confession* of 1566. They have been upheld for the most part by the Reformed churches.

3. The Radical Restoration

Almost from the start, and much to the consternation of the magisterial Protestant Reformers who persecuted them, "radical" or "separatist" groups of devoted Christians demanded absolute separation from secular society and the state churches. Here the church was a church of believers only, marked by spirituality and holiness. As a Spirit-guided company, it was to press further the revival begun by the magisterial Reformers, who were suspected of retaining too many tenets of the Roman Catholic faith. There was a need for a truly *restored* church rather than a mere *reformation*. This implied a "true church," gathered and disciplined on the apostolic model, without compromise.

Thus the real problem between Luther on the one hand and the Anabaptists (a name applied to them by their opponents) was not so much the issue of baptism as the mutually exclusive concepts of the church. Separatist ecclesiology called for separating from the unbelieving world and from the state, a view quite different from that of the magisterial Reformers, who saw the church and the state as practically coextensive and held that all citizens of a territory were to be members of the established church. For the radical Reformers, churches were local companies, gathered on the principle of a free, responsible faith and a regenerate life, with no rule, discipline, or hierarchy external to the local group, responsible to Christ for their government. Such separatist groups were many and varied. They included the Hutterites of Moravia, the Mennonites of Holland, and many smaller groups. The comprehensive designation of Anabaptists was often attached to the whole movement, though all did not adopt the policy of rebaptizing converts.

4. Anglicanism and the Church

In contrast with the other sixteenth-century Reformation movements, the Reformation in England started not with a dominant ecclesiastical leader but with Henry VIII's (1491-1547) political defiance of the pope. It continued as a religious system of doctrines and practices maintained by Christians in communion with the see of Canterbury, whether in England or abroad. From the start Anglicanism has insisted that its doctrine is both Catholic and Reformed. Along with the Reformers, it holds to the concept of the essentiality of the invisible church against the Roman Catholic claim of a visible hierarchical church centered upon the pope. The emphasis, however, remains on the visible church and the threefold ministry of bishop, priest, and deacon in continuity with the medieval church.

Within Anglicanism, the "Puritans," dissatisfied with halfhearted attempts at reform, sought a further "purification" of the Anglican Church along the lines of Calvin's teachings. Some among them came to advocate Congregationalism and complete separation of church and state. They demanded a regenerate membership and self-sufficient assemblies of believers independent of all external compulsion.

D. The Eighteenth and Nineteenth Centuries

1. The Age of Reason and the Church

With its distrust of all authority and tradition, and its belief that truth could be attained only through reason and experiment, the "Enlightenment" significantly affected the Christian doctrine of the church. The rationalists of this period—the seventeenth and eighteenth centuries—were mainly Deists. Arguing against revelation and the supernatural they held that the responsibility of human beings was to discern and live by the laws that God had laid down in Creation. While no outstanding treatise on the church was published during that time and the ecclesiologies set forth during the Reformation remained normative for Catholics, Lutherans, Reformed, Anglicans, and Congregationalists, some new ideas suggested by the spirit of the time proved quite influential.

To John Locke (1632-1704), who did believe that God revealed Himself in the Scriptures, the church was primarily an ethical society, an institution established for the improvement of moral standards. He also pleaded for mutual toleration of private religious convictions and fostered the idea that the separated Christian bodies were all more or less natural categories of Christianity. A spirit of toleration was gaining ground and the traditional concern for the unity of the one body of Christ dropped into the background.

As the intellect was in the ascendence in the second half of the seventeenth century, Lutherans, Reformed, and Roman Catholic theologians wrote vast and intricate dogmatic treatises intended to fortify their positions. Reacting against formalism and sterile scholastic theology, the most significant religious movements of the period laid stress on the importance of an individual conversion, a warm devotional life, and a puritanical discipline. Most influential among them were Pietism, which flourished in Germany, Methodism, pioneered in England by John and Charles Wesley, and Jansenism within Roman Catholicism. Eventually each movement led to the creation of a new church. At the end of the eighteenth century and the beginning of the nineteenth, Romanticism, a movement in literature and art, reassured feeling, a sense of wonder and of emotion, which encouraged a religious attitude in reaction to the rationalism of the day.

2. Friedrich Schleiermacher

In the aftermath of the Romantic Movement, contending that religion was based on intuition and feeling, Friedrich Schleiermacher (1768-1834), often described as the father of modern Protestantism, attempted to win the educated classes back to the Christian religion. He defined the latter as a sense and taste of the infinite, a feeling of total dependence upon God, independent of all dogmas. Although in the context of such strong individualism a doctrine of the church would seem to have little room, in his major works, *On Religion: Speeches to Its Cultural Despisers* (1799) and *The Christian Faith* (1821-1822), Schleiermacher paid much attention to the church.

His treatment of the nature and identity of the church was derived not so much from biblical or dogmatic sources as from ethics, philosophy of religion, and apologetics. The church, he maintained, is an association of those who share the same kind of religious feeling. It includes all religious communions whose religious consciousness senses the need of redemption. That redemption is made available by Jesus Christ, who constrains His disciples to a new corporate life. Within that one fellowship of believers, the church, a distinction must be made between a visible and an invisible church, although Schleiermacher prefers to use the antithesis of an outer and inner fellowship. Each is part of the church but in a different sense. Those who live in a state of sanctification belong to the inner fellowship. To the outer one pertain those on whom preparatory grace to recognize Christ is at work. This view of the origin and nature of the church is closely related to the doctrine of election and the conviction that there is no living fellowship with Christ apart from the indwelling work of the Spirit. Every nation will sooner or later come to Christ, a view that Scleiermacher regards as essential to the Christian faith.

3. Albrecht Ritschl

Equally influential, Albrecht Ritschl (1822-1889) reacted to the subjectivism of Schleiermacher and the philosophical idealism of Hegel. He found the foundation of Christian theology in God's revelation in Jesus Christ. Starting with the *facts* of Christ's life, Ritschlian theology is practical rather than speculative, concerned with the human will rather than with feelings. Hence its strong ethical emphasis with both personal and social implications.

The necessity of the church and of membership in it are repeatedly underlined by Ritschl. The church is the locus where men and women get to know and appropriate the redemption offered in Jesus Christ. The essential distinctive of this community is its acceptance of the moral teachings of Christ. The church is the fellowship of believers. Its unity is bound up with the pure preaching of the gospel and the pure administration of the sacraments. Organized for the conduct of worship, the Christian community is the church; engaged in common action inspired by love, it is the kingdom of God. Although related, the two are clearly distinct. Very much in accord with the predominant optimism of the day, this concept of the kingdom of God as the gradual ethical development of humankind bore little resemblance to the kingdom of God set forth in the NT.

4. Roman Catholic Ecclesiology

Roman Catholic ecclesiology was not unaffected by the intellectual challenges of the Enlightenment. The abiding inclination of official theologians and canonists to assert papal prerogatives was induced by the rise of nationalism within the church (Gallicanism, Josephinism, Febronianism) and the new theological liberalism of the nineteenth century. The First Vatican Council (1869-1870) marked the culmination of this development. It defined the pope's power as full and supreme over the whole Roman Catholic Church in matters of faith and morals as well as in those pertaining to the discipline and government of the church.

E. The Twentieth Century

Twentieth-century viewpoints on the nature and identity of the church present a pattern even more diversified than that of the Reformation. Representative figures or movements have been selected to give a general picture of the contemporary outlook.

1. Protestant Liberalism

Ritschl's theology and its ethical emphasis proved to be particularly influential in the last quarter of the nineteenth and the first part of the twentieth century, both in Europe and in the United States, and particularly on Protes-

tant liberals. Rooted in historical criticism of the Scriptures, indebted to Scleiermacher's understanding of religion as a feeling of total dependence upon God and to Rithschl's ethical approach, the emphasis of Protestant liberal theologians on the social gospel had a profound influence on their concept of the church. At best, churches were merely human organizations of people gathered together on the basis of their common religious and ethical concerns and for the task of spreading the "social gospel," which would pave the way for the coming kingdom. Credos and ecclesiastical dogmas were a matter of private opinion and often an obstacle to the radical transformation of society.

Dissatisfied with the condition of the liberal churches and provoked by the ecumenical impetus toward unity between the two world wars, a new generation of liberal theologians, often labeled "neoliberals," started making room for the church, insisting on a distinction between the spiritual church and the organized church. A church existed over and beyond the split denominations. Not just another social fraternity but a divine institution founded by God, it was the spiritual fellowship of all Christians committed to the reign of God. It might even require some inevitable structural organization.

2. The Ecclesiology of Karl Barth

In Karl Barth's theology, with its rejection of all natural theology and all religion grounded in experience and its effort to return to the basic principles of the Reformation, the doctrine of the church is more central than in that of many of his contemporaries. His language may not always be as clear as one may wish and his doctrine of the church may have evolved. Still, Barth has persistently articulated his views on the nature and identity of the church. In the fourth volume of his *Church Dogmatics* one finds Barth's fullest treatment of the issues involved.

The church is not a human institution, but an act of God, an event, a new and continuous creative work of God. Nor is it invisible, for to apply the idea of invisibility to the church would be to devalue it. The church is one, and on their way to the one church, divided churches should abandon their claim to be identical with the one church. Though constantly failing and falling in error, the church is holy, but only as the body of Christ. It is also catholic, to the extent that in each age it is faithful to its essence and seeks continual reformation. This also explains the church's apostolicity, that is, the fact that it remains under the normative authority and instruction of the apostles, in agreement with them and with their message. This distinguishes it from the false church.

The church, which exists for God, is also for the world. This twofold ministry calls for the proclamation of the gospel, and for its explanation as well as application to the situation in time and place of those who are addressed. The forms of this twofold ministry are multiple, but each form is laid upon the whole Christian community. All distinctions between clergy and laity, office-bearers and others, are rejected. No one has an office, but no one is ever "off-duty."

3. The Ecclesiology of Hans Küng

In two of his major works, *Structures of the Church* (1963) and *The Church* (1967), Hans Küng (1928-), the best known and most controversial Roman Catholic ecclesiologist of the twentieth century, constructs an ecclesiology primarily on the basis of the biblical data and the use of church history. When dealing with the origin of the church, ordination, apostolic succession, the local and the universal church, and the papal office, Küng uses church history and NT evidence, not so much to support current official teaching but to suggest alternative possibilities. The dividing line between Roman Catholic and Protestants strikes him as less sharp than traditionally thought. His most significant contribution to the discussion of issues regarding the nature and identity of the church may well lie in the insightful questions he raised before his difficulties with the Vatican

in 1979 involving the withdrawal of his license to teach Roman Catholic theology.

F. Current Crosswinds

1. The Ecumenical Movement

More recently the doctrine of the church has been thrown into the forefront by the rise and development of modern ecumenism. Since the primary concern of the ecumenical movement is the relationship of churches to each other, the issues related to the nature and identity of the church cannot be ignored.

Founded in 1948 as an outgrowth of the 1910 World Missionary Conference at Edinburgh, the World Council of Churches (WCC) has sought to bring about a visible communion of all Christians. This communion is perceived as having its basis in one baptism, the confession of the apostolic faith, and the common celebration of the Lord's Supper in a mutually recognized ministry. All are issues related to the Christian doctrine of the church. While itself devoid of any definite ecclesiology, the WCC has fostered a sense of communion among many churches that, while still far from complete, is regarded by many as the outstanding factor of twentieth-century church history. This convergence has found expression in the voted 1982 Faith and Order document *Baptism, Eucharist and Ministry*.

Some churches, often in light of their concern for scriptural truth, have not hesitated to voice their concerns and reservations regarding several ecumenical issues, particularly church government, the form and function of ministry, the specter of a superchurch, and the failure of the ecumenical movement in the area of world mission.

2. Roman Catholic Ecumenism

While opposed at first to the goals expressed by the WCC, the Roman Catholic Church opted for extensive cooperation with it. The Second Vatican Council (1962-1965), which, as far as church governance is concerned, viewed the Papacy in increasingly communal and collegial terms and explicitly articulated its longing for a reunion of all Christian churches, also recognized the existence of "sister churches" in Eastern Orthodoxy and the presence of "ecclesial dimensions" in others. Since then it has engaged in bilateral conversations with other churches, at the same time fostering its relationship with the WCC. Even so, John Paul II's encyclical *"Ut unum sint"* (That They May All Be One [1995]) and its renewed call to Christian unity has done little to break the stalemate and uncertainty regarding the future of the ecumenical movement.

3. The Postmodern Orientation

More recently postmodernism has left thinkers of all theological orientations in what seems a crisis of identity. With its questioning of the central assumptions of the Enlightenment epistemology, the postmodern mind no longer is confident that humanity is able through the objective use of reason to demonstrate the essential correctness of philosophic, scientific, and religious doctrines. It refuses to limit truth to its rational dimensions, thus dethroning the human intellect as the arbiter of truth. Not only are there other valid paths to knowledge and truth, but being far from universal and timeless, truth is essentially relative to the community in which people participate.

This major transition in thinking has enormous significance for one's understanding of the church, especially its nature and identity. It also poses a grave challenge to the church in its mission. It will be the task of emerging generation to think through the implications of this phenomenal change for the presentation of the Christian faith among conflicting interpretations of reality and for the scriptural doctrine of the church.

G. Seventh-day Adventists

From the very first, immediately after the Disappointment of 1844 (see Adventists I. D), Seventh-day Adventists (the name was not adopted until later years) have held that the three angels' messages of Revelation 14:6-12, coupled with the proclamation of Revelation 18:1-4, constitute God's last message of grace before Christ's return in power and glory. They believed their movement to be the only one to meet the conditions specified in these verses and in Revelation 12:17. At the same time they emphatically repudiated the thought that they alone belonged to the children of God. All who worship God in terms of His will as they understand it were seen as belonging to Him and potential members of the final remnant. Still, to them had been entrusted the task of summoning men and women everywhere to worship the Creator in view of the nearness of the judgment hour and to warn against succumbing to the great end-time apostasy foretold in Revelation 13 (see Remnant/Three Angels). Adventists still hold these views.

While united by several doctrines, the "little flock," a remnant indeed of former Millerites (see Adventists I. D), remained suspicious toward any doctrine of the church. Any ecclesiology would have represented a return to their former Babylonian condition. In the 1850s, however, the number of Advent believers started multiplying and growing increasingly widespread. In spite of determined opposition on the part of some, James White's calls to shun confusion, seek unity in faith and action, and to build the Advent movement on the principles of church order found in the NT, all for the sake of a more efficient outreach, proved successful. A doctrine of the church was slowly emerging.

With the organization of seven statewide conferences of churches in 1861 and 1862, and the creation of a General Conference in 1863, some 20 years after the Disappointment the foundations of a doctrine of the church had been laid and a pattern of ecclesiastical organization devised. The unique sense of mission conveyed by the urgency of the "three angels' messages" had greatly contributed to the founding of the Seventh-day Adventist Church, a name adopted in 1860.

From then on the church has been understood in its local and universal dimensions. To the traditional characteristics of one, holy, catholic (universal), and apostolic, Adventists have added keeping all of God's commandments and being endowed with the gift of prophecy. Organized for mission service, a group of local churches forms a conference, or otherwise named unit; and a group of these units forms a union conference. The unions, worldwide grouped under divisions, form the General Conference organization. The pattern is similar to the Presbyterian or representative form of church government; this time, however, on a worldwide scale. Recently a congregationalist form of church governance has been advocated in a few places.

Like the Anabaptists, Seventh-day Adventists have stood traditionally equidistant from magisterial Protestantism (Lutheran, Reformed, Anglican) and Roman Catholicism. They have promoted the authority of Scripture, believer's baptism, separation of church and state, religious liberty, a deep concern for the Great Commission, and the conviction that the church, built as closely as possible to the pattern of the NT, transcends national boundaries and local cultures. For them the church, whatever else it might be, is a community of baptized believers, rooted in the Scriptures and unrestricted in their missionary concern by territorial limitations.

XI. Ellen G. White Comments

From the very beginning Ellen White was deeply involved with the doctrinal and organizational developments of the Advent movement. As an inspired counselor she played a key role in the growing Adventist understanding of the doctrine of the church. She was always clear that the Seventh-day Adventist Church was God's church in the end-time and showed a far-reaching concern for its development, organization, and unity. Given the limitations of space, the following pages deal essentially with these particular aspects of Adventist ecclesiology.

There is no doubt in Ellen White's mind as to the existence and reality of God's church. "The Lord," she writes, "has a people, a chosen people, His church, to be His own, His own fortress, which He holds in a sin-stricken, revolted world" (TM 16). She further noted that He "has a distinct people, a church on earth, second to none, but superior to all in their facilities to teach the truth, to vindicate the law of God. God has divinely appointed agencies—men whom He is leading, who have borne the heat and burden of the day, who are cooperating with heavenly instrumentalities to advance the kingdom of Christ in our world" (*ibid.* 58). The church is "a channel of light, and through it He communicates His purposes and His will" (AA 163). "Nothing in this world is so dear to God as His church" (2SM 397), which "after Christ's departure was to be His representative on earth" (DA 291).

A. The Church: On Earth and in Heaven

"From the beginning, faithful souls have constituted the church on earth. In every age the Lord has had His watchmen, who have borne a faithful testimony to the generation in which they lived. . . . God brought these witnesses into covenant relation with Himself, uniting the church on earth with the church in heaven. He has sent forth His angels to minister to His church, and the gates of hell have not been able to prevail against His people" (AA 11).

"The church of God below is one with the church of God above. Believers on the earth and the beings in heaven who have never fallen constitute one church" (6T 366).

B. Christ and the Church: A Close Relationship

God's church is built on a rock. "That Rock is [Christ] Himself—His own body, for us broken and bruised. Against the church built upon this foundation, the gates of hell shall not prevail" (DA 413). "He the head, and the church the body" (Ed 268). As "head of the church and the Saviour of the mystical body" (AH 215; letter 18b, 1891), Christ "superintends His work through the instrumentality of men ordained by God to act as His representatives" (AA 360).

"Very close and sacred is the relation between Christ and His church—He the bridegroom, and the church the bride" (Ed 268). "In the Bible the sacred and enduring character of the relation that exists between Christ and His church is represented by the union of marriage" (GC 381).

C. There Are Tares Among the Wheat

Although it is the body of Christ, "the church is composed of imperfect, erring men and women, who call for the continual exercise of charity and forbearance" (5T 104). "[God] has a church, but it is the church militant, not the church triumphant. We are sorry that there are defective members, that there are tares amid the wheat" (TM 45).

"Some people seem to think that upon entering the church they will have their expectations fulfilled, and meet only with those who are pure and perfect. They are zealous in their faith, and when they see faults in church members, they say, 'We left the world in order to have no association with evil characters, but the evil is here also;' and they ask, as did the servants in the parable, 'From whence then hath it tares?' But we need not be thus disappointed, for the Lord has not warranted us in coming to the conclusion that the church is perfect; and all our zeal will not be successful in making the church militant as pure as the church triumphant" (TM 47).

And yet, "enfeebled and defective as it may appear, the church is the one object upon which God bestows in a special sense His supreme regard. It is the theater of His grace, in which He delights to reveal His power to transform hearts" (AA 12).

D. God's Appointed Agency for the Salvation of Sinners

As "the repository of the riches of the grace of Christ" (AA 9), the church is "God's appointed agency for the salvation of men. Its mission is to carry the gospel to the world. And the obligation rests upon all Christians. Everyone, to the extent of his talent and opportunity, is to fulfill the Saviour's commission. The love of Christ, revealed to us, makes us debtors to all who know Him not. God has given us light, not for ourselves alone, but to shed upon them" (SC 81).

God, indeed, has chosen to depend on the church to forward His work of salvation. Hence He baptized it with the Spirit's power and endowed it with every gift of grace needed to triumph over every obstacle (cf. 6T 432). To enable it to accomplish this task "the Holy Spirit was to descend on those who love Christ. By this they would be qualified, in and through the glorification of their Head, to receive every endowment necessary for the fulfilling of their mission" (ML 47). In apostolic times, "the church revealed the spirit of Christ and appeared beautiful in its simplicity. Its adorning was the holy principles and exemplary lives of its members. Multitudes were won to Christ, not by display or learning, but by the power of God which attended the plain preaching of His word" (5T 166).

In a description of rare beauty and power, prompted by one of Ezekiel's revelations, Ellen White describes God's intention for the church: "Wonderful is the work which the Lord designs to accomplish through His church, that His name may be glorified. A picture of this work is given in Ezekiel's vision of the river of healing: 'These waters issue out toward the east country, and go down into the desert, and go into the sea: which being brought forth into the sea, the waters shall be healed. And it shall come to pass, that everything that liveth, which moveth, whithersoever the rivers shall come, shall live: . . . and by the river upon the bank thereof, on this side and on that side, shall grow all trees for meat, whose leaf shall not fade, neither shall the fruit thereof be consumed: it shall bring forth new fruit according to his months, because their waters they issued out of the sanctuary: and the fruit thereof shall be for meat, and the leaf thereof for medicine' (Eze. 47:8-12)" (AA 13).

E. Gospel Order in the Early Church

Under the leadership of the apostles the work committed to the church developed rapidly. It became necessary to further distribute the responsibilities that thus far had been borne by the apostles. Seven men chosen by the Jerusalem church were set apart by the apostles, "an important step in the perfecting of gospel order in the church," explains Ellen White (*ibid.* 88, 89). Soon afterward, "as an important factor in the spiritual growth of the new converts, the apostles were careful to surround them with the safeguards of gospel order. Churches were duly organized in all places in Lycaonia and Pisidia where there were believers. Officers were appointed in each church, and proper order and system were established for the conduct of all the affairs pertaining to the spiritual welfare of the believers. This was in harmony with the gospel plan of uniting in one body all believers in Christ, and this plan Paul was careful to follow throughout his ministry" (*ibid.* 185).

Thus "the organization of the church was further perfected," explains our author, "so that order and harmonious action might be maintained" (*ibid.* 91, 92). "And now," she writes, "in these last days, while God is bringing His children into the unity of the faith, there is more real need of order than ever before; for, as God unites His children, Satan and his evil angels are very busy to prevent this unity and to destroy it" (EW 97).

F. Some Form of Organization Deemed Indispensable

In an extended chapter written after some 40 years of organizational development (TM 24-32), Ellen White reflected on various experiences that she regarded as intimately related to the growth of the Advent cause. Difficulties had to be met and evils corrected: "Our numbers were few. . . . The sheep were scattered in

the highways and byways, in cities, in towns, in forests" (*ibid.* 24). A handful of keen and dedicated faithful spent hours searching the Scriptures for truth and praying "that we might be one in faith and doctrine; for we knew that Christ is not divided" (*ibid.*). As their numbers increased "it was evident that without some form of organization there would be great confusion, and the work would not be carried forward successfully. To provide for the support of the ministry, for carrying the work in new fields, for protecting both the churches and the ministry from unworthy members, for holding church property, for the publication of the truth through the press, and for many other objects, organization was indispensable" (*ibid.* 26).

Though opposition was strong and had to be met again and again, the conviction prevailed that "organization was essential" (*ibid.*), "and marked prosperity attended this advance movement" (*ibid.* 27). "God has blessed our united efforts" and "the mustard seed has grown to a great tree," she concludes (*ibid.*).

There was an urge to avoid confusion and to see "the work . . . carried forward successfully." In other words an undergirding theological concern, i.e., the need to proclaim the gospel of Christ to the ends of the world before the soon return of the Lord demanded that consideration be given to some form of church government.

Any church organization should be in harmony with the testimony of Scripture. Recalling the experience of the early Christian believers, Ellen White remarked:

"The organization of the church at Jerusalem was to serve as a model for the organization of churches in every other place where messengers of truth should win converts to the gospel. Those to whom was given the responsibility of the general oversight of the church were not to lord it over God's heritage, but, as wise shepherds, were to 'feed the flock of God, . . . being ensamples to the flock' (1 Peter 5:2, 3); and the deacons were to be 'men of honest report, full of the Holy Ghost and wisdom.' These men were to take their position unitedly on the side of right and to maintain it with firmness and decision. Thus they would have a uniting influence upon the entire flock" (AA 91).

G. The Need for United Action

Some underlined the dangers involved in these efforts to "establish order," and insisted on choosing their own independent course. They had come to "believe that order and discipline are enemies to spirituality," that "all the efforts made to establish order are . . . a restriction of rightful liberty," to be "feared as popery" (1T 650).

To those Ellen White answered that "God has made His church on the earth a channel of light, and through it He communicates His purposes and His will. He does not give to one of His servants an experience independent of and contrary to the experience of the church itself. Neither does He give one man a knowledge of His will for the entire church, while the church—Christ's body—is left in darkness" (GW 443).

This, she holds, is true of every believer, and applies even to apostles and prophets as evidenced in the case of Paul. Though Christ had chosen to fit the apostle for a most important task and, on the Damascus road, had brought him into His very presence, He did not Himself teach Paul the lessons of truth. "Christ reveals Himself to him," she writes, "and then places him in communication with His church, who are the light of the world. They are to instruct this educated, popular orator, in the Christian religion" (3T 433). By directing Saul of Tarsus to the church, Christ acknowledged "the power that He has invested in it as a channel of light to the world" (ibid.).

H. Lesson From the Jerusalem Council

Years later, as the Judaizing believers introduced the issue of circumcision to the church at Antioch, "Paul knew the mind of the Spirit of God concerning such teaching" (AA 200). "He had been taught by God regarding the binding of unnecessary burdens upon the Gentile Christians" (ibid.). To find out about God's will, did he need to attend a gathering which at Jerusalem would address the issue? "Notwithstanding the fact that Paul was personally taught by God, he had no strained ideas of individual responsibility. While looking to God for direct guidance, he was ever ready to recognize the authority vested in the body of believers united in church fellowship" (ibid.). Here is a most interesting insight into the apostle's—and the early church's—understanding of the importance of united action in the service of God.

Equally significant is Ellen White's remark that the conclusion reached on that occasion by the Jerusalem council was sent out "to put an end to all controversy; for it was the voice of the highest authority upon the earth" (AA 196). Likewise, she was "shown that no man's judgment should be surrendered to the judgment of any one man. But when the judgment of the General Conference [in session], which is the highest authority that God has upon the earth, is exercised, private independence and private judgment must not be maintained, but be surrendered" (3T 492).

I. Beware of the Spirit of Domination

While urging that the church "move discreetly, sensibly, in harmony with the judgment of God-fearing counselors" (9T 257), Ellen White deemed that "the high-handed power that has been developed" by some, "as though position has made men gods," ought to cause fear among God's people (TM 361). She held that if a leader has fallen prey to "the spirit of domination," "feeling that he is invested with authority to make his will the ruling power, the best and only safe course is to remove him, lest great harm be done" (ibid. 362). "Those in authority," she explains, "should manifest the spirit of Christ. . . . They should go weighted with the Holy Spirit. A man's position does not make him one jot or tittle greater in the sight of God; it is character alone that God values" (ibid.). "The Lord," she is sure, "will raise up laborers who realize their own nothingness without special help from God" (ibid. 361).

J. God's End-time Church

In a chapter defining the difference between the remnant church and Babylon, our author writes: "God has a church on earth who are lifting up the downtrodden law, and presenting to the world the Lamb of God that taketh away the sins of the world" (ibid. 50). While describing that church as "standing in the breach, and making up the hedge, building up the old waste places" (ibid.), she reminds her readers that "God has called His church in this day, as He called ancient Israel, to stand as a light in the earth. By the mighty cleaver of truth, the messages of the first, second, and third angels [of Revelation 14], He has separated them from the churches and from the world to bring them into a sacred nearness to Himself. He has made them the depositories of His law, and has committed to them the great truths of prophecy for this time. Like the holy oracles committed to ancient Israel, these are a sacred trust to be communicated to the world. . . .

Nothing is to be permitted to hinder this work. It is the all-important work for time; it is to be far-reaching as eternity" (5T 455, 456).

In her second message to the General Conference session in 1913, Ellen White told her fellow Seventh-day Adventists that "the work that lies before us . . . will put to the stretch every power of the human being. It will call for the exercise of strong faith and constant vigilance. . . . The very greatness of the task will appall us. And yet, with God's help, his servants will finally triumph" (GCB May 27, 1913, 165).

K. The Church Triumphant

As to that triumph, our author makes clear that "the same power that raised Christ from the dead will raise His church, and glorify it with Christ, as His bride, above all principalities, above all powers, above every name that is named, not only in this world, but also in the heavenly courts, the world above. The victory of the sleeping saints will be glorious on the morning of the resurrection. Satan's triumph will end, while Christ will triumph in glory and honor. The Life-giver will crown with immortality all who come forth from the grave" (1SM 305, 306).

XII. Literature

Systematic theologies as well as relevant articles in Bible dictionaries, encyclopedias, and theological journals address this subject. The following list selects volumes that, along with this format, survey the field and have contributed to this article. Among the more important works in English—written from different perspectives—are:

Bannerman, D. Douglas. The Scripture Doctrine of the Church. Grand Rapids: Baker, 1976.

Barth, Karl. Church Dogmatics. Edinburgh: T. and T. Clark, 1936.

Beasley-Murray, George R. Baptism in the New Testament. London: Macmillan, 1962.

Berkouwer, Gerrit C. The Church. Grand Rapids: Eerdmans, 1976.

Bromiley, Geoffrey W. The Unity and Disunity of the Church. Grand Rapids: Eerdmans, 1958.

Calvin, John. Institutes of the Christian Religion. Book 4. Philadelphia: Westminster, 1960.

Cleveland, Earl E. The Church—Servant to the World. Grantham, England: Stanborough Press, 1983.

Damsteegt, P. Gerard. Foundations of the Seventh-day Adventist Message and Mission. Grand Rapids: Eerdmans, 1977.

Dana, H. E. A Manual of Ecclesiology. Kansas City: Central Seminar, 1944.

Dulles, Avery R. Models of the Church. Garden

City, N.Y.: Image Books, 1978.

Eastwood, Cyril. *The Priesthood of All Believers*. Minneapolis: Augsburg, 1962.

Ferguson, Everett. *The Church of Christ*. Grand Rapids: Eerdmans, 1996.

Flew, R. N. *Jesus and His Church*. London: Epworth, 1956.

Florovsky, Georges. *Bible, Church, Tradition: An Eastern Orthodox View*. Belmont, Mass.: Nordland, 1972.

Gilkey, Langdon. *How the Church Can Minister to the World Without Losing Itself*. New York: Harper and Row, 1964.

Goodall, Norman. *The Ecumenical Movement: What It Is and What It Does*. New York: Oxford University Press, 1964.

Hiscox, Edward T. *The New Directory for Baptist Churches*. Philadelphia: Judson, 1894.

Jay, Eric George. *The Church: Its Changing Image Through Twenty Centuries*. Atlanta: John Knox, 1980.

Kelley, Dean M. *Why Evangelical Churches Are Growing*. New York: Harper and Row, 1977.

Küng, Hans. *The Church*. New York: Sheed and Ward, 1968.

Ladd, George E. *Jesus and the Kingdom*. New York: Harper and Row, 1964.

Manson, Thomas W. *The Church's Ministry*. Philadelphia: Westminster, 1948.

McKenzie, John L. *Authority in the Church*. New York: Sheed and Ward, 1966.

Minear, Paul S. *Images of the Church in the New Testament*. Philadelphia: Westminster, 1960.

Newbegin, Lesslie. *The Household of God*. New York: Friendship Press, 1954.

Radmacher, Earl D. *What the Church Is All About*. Chicago: Moody, 1978.

Saucy, Robert L. *The Church in God's Program*. Chicago: Moody, 1972.

Schwarz, Richard W. *Light Bearers to the Remnant*. Mountain View, Calif.: Pacific Press, 1979.

Schweizer, Eduard. *Church Order in the New Testament*. London: SCM, 1961.

Watson, David. *I Believe in the Church*. Grand Rapids: Eerdmans, 1979.

White, Ellen G. *The Remnant Church*. Mountain View, Calif.: Pacific Press, 1950.

The Ordinances: Baptism, Foot Washing, and Lord's Supper

Herbert Kiesler

Introduction

Although performed in different ways, baptism, foot washing, and the Lord's Supper are three of the most ancient and important Christian ordinances, totally grounded in New Testament practice and teaching. Baptism is the door to the church, a symbol of renunciation of the old life and the adoption of a new life in Christ (Rom. 6:4). Foot washing points to humility and cleansing (John 13:10-16). Participation in the bread and wine of the Lord's Supper remembers Christ's broken body and spilt blood while looking forward to the Second Coming (Matt. 26:28; 1 Cor. 11:23-26).

I. Baptism

Of key importance to the topic of baptism is the biblical teaching on which it is based. The practical dimensions of the rite must also be considered, as well as the history of baptism through the centuries.

A. The Biblical Teaching on Baptism

The ordinance of baptism is rooted in the teachings of the NT with references found in several passages. This study notes the NT terminology for baptism and analyzes its major witnesses: John the Baptist, Jesus, and Paul. Additional attention is paid to baptism in Acts.

1. Terminology

The words "baptize" and "baptism" come from the Greek root *baptizō,* "to immerse." A related root is *baptō,* "to dip in or under," which occurs in several passages (Luke 16:24; John 13:26; Rev. 19:13), but never appears in reference to baptism. The root *baptizō* is used more than 60 times to denote the baptism by immersion of persons unto repentance, as in John's baptism, or following the resurrection, into Christ. The same root, found in Mark 7:4; Luke 11:38; and Hebrews 9:10, all applied to Jewish ceremonial washing. Five times the word points to the baptism of the Holy Spirit (Matt. 3:11; Mark 1:8; Luke 3:16; John 1:33; Acts 11:16), where no physical immersion is meant. In Mark 10:38 and 39 the term is used in a figurative way: to undergo, to suffer.

Not only does the word used support the idea of baptism by immersion, the details of baptismal stories in the NT clearly indicate immersion. For example, Matthew points out that "when Jesus was baptized, he went up immediately from the water" (Matt. 3:16), and John baptized at Aenon near Salim, "because there was much water there" (John 3:23). In Acts 8:38, 39, both Philip and the eunuch went down into the water and came up from it.

2. Baptism of John

The first NT references to baptism involve John the Baptist (see Mark 1:4, 5; Luke 3:3). According to Matthew 3:1-6, John the Baptist proclaimed a message of repentance in view of the approaching kingdom. As a result of his preaching, people from Jerusalem, Judea, and the Jordan region went to him and were baptized, confessing their sins.

John's baptism inaugurated the new life of the converted person, assuring the one baptized of forgiveness and cleansing from sin. In other words, John's baptism was characterized by a forward look to the coming judgment and redemption by the Messiah, who was to baptize with the Holy Spirit and with fire (Matt. 3:11).

Some scholars have pointed out similarities between the covenanters of Qumran and John the Baptist. For both, the end was near. Therefore, a drastic change was needed, a moral preparation through repentance and baptism. The community at Qumran never acknowledged the Messiah when He appeared, while John was His herald.

3. Baptism of Jesus

All four Gospels provide an account of the baptism of Jesus by John (Matt. 3:13-17; Mark 1:9-11; Luke 3:21, 22; John 1:31-34). Matthew points out that John was reluctant to baptize Jesus: "I need to be baptized by you, and do you come to me?" (Matt. 3:14). Jesus answered John, "Let it be so now; for thus it is fitting for us to fulfil all righteousness" (verse 15). Jesus did not receive baptism as a confession of guilt, but He identified Himself with the penitents of Israel who were responsive to the preaching of John (DA 111). Thus He took the steps that we are to take, doing the work that we must do. The baptism of Jesus was important because of His role in carrying out the plan of God in both judgment and redemption. It underscores baptism's deep significance for His followers.

Matthew, Mark, and Luke mention three things that took place after the baptism of Jesus: the heavens were opened, Jesus saw the Spirit of God descending like a dove, and a voice from heaven spoke, "This is my beloved Son, with whom I am well pleased" (Matt. 3:16, 17; cf. Mark 1:11; Luke 3:22). All three accounts point out that after the voice from heaven acknowledged Jesus as God's Son, the Spirit drove Him into the wilderness, where He was tempted by Satan (Matt. 4:1; Mark 1:12; Luke 4:1).

During His passion week the chief priests, scribes, and elders asked Jesus by what authority He worked (Matt. 21:23-27; Mark 11:27-33; Luke 20:1-8). He replied with a counter question: Was John's baptism of divine or human origin? Because they would not answer, Jesus refused to respond to their initial question. But Jesus fully endorsed the mission and baptism of John the Baptist (Matt. 11:11; 17:12, 13; Luke 7:24-28).

No NT writer brings the baptism of Jesus into relationship with Christian baptism. The reason for this seems simple: Although He was baptized with others, Jesus' baptism was unique, for He was baptized as the Messiah. However, though Jesus' baptism was singular, it still is related to our baptism, because the Messiah is the representative of God and man. According to Mark 1:11, a voice from heaven acknowledged Him as God's beloved Son. According to Galatians 3:26 all believers are sons and daughters of God through faith in Christ Jesus.

4. The Missionary Commission

All the Synoptic Gospels affirm that after the Resurrection Jesus gave His disciples a worldwide commission to preach and teach. Matthew's record of Christ's commission to His followers contains a threefold order: (1) Go and make disciples of all nations; (2) baptize them in the name of the Father, Son, and Holy Spirit; and (3) teach them to observe all that I have commanded you (Matt. 28:18-20). Here

Christ is portrayed as the exalted Lord, the universal sovereign and Messiah to whom is given all authority. Thus, Matthew concludes his Gospel by emphasizing the kingship of Jesus. It is this King who commands His disciples to go and "make disciples of all nations." In verse 20 Jesus specifies that disciples are made by instructing believers in regard to His teachings and commands; those who have become disciples are to be baptized. Baptism, then, is the public evidence of discipleship.

The gospel commission is the great charter of the church. Every believer is charged with the responsibility of teaching others the message of the kingdom of God. Believers are to share their faith and in this way to make disciples of all nations. Christians are to transcend national, ethnic, and other boundaries to reach people and win them for Christ and His kingdom.

Acceptance of Christ involves an intelligent act of the will. Instruction in the vital truths of the gospel before making that choice is important. Baptism is an evidence of belief (Mark 16:16), and follows instruction.

After His resurrection the Lord gave His disciples the commission to preach the gospel worldwide (Mark 16:15). In Luke 24:47 the emphasis is on repentance and the forgiveness of sins to be preached to all nations. These two key concepts, repentance and forgiveness of sins, are reminiscent of the message of John the Baptist.

5. Baptism in Acts

From the very first, Christian baptism was associated with repentance. Baptism in the name of the Lord Jesus not only symbolized cleansing from sin, it was also a sign that one no longer had a part in the rejection of the Messiah. It showed that one had become a disciple of Jesus and a member of His people.

In Acts 1:5 reference is made to both water baptism and baptism by the Holy Spirit. The latter became a reality on the day of Pentecost (Acts 2:1-4), and its purpose was to empower the disciples to become active participants in the global mission of the church. But baptism by the Holy Spirit did not abrogate the need for water baptism, for when the people had listened to Peter's sermon they asked how they should respond. Peter answered, "Repent, and be baptized every one of you in the name of Jesus Christ for the forgiveness of your sins; and you shall receive the gift of the Holy Spirit" (Acts 2:38).

During his mission to Samaria Philip preached the good news about the kingdom of God. As a result many were baptized, "both men and women" (8:12). It is noteworthy that "when the apostles at Jerusalem heard that Samaria had received the word of God, they sent to them Peter and John, who came down and prayed for them that they might receive the Holy Spirit; for it had not yet fallen on any of them, but they had only been baptized in the name of the Lord Jesus" (verses 14-16). The apostles did not confer the Holy Spirit upon the newly baptized believers, they simply asked the Lord to bestow the Spirit upon them as evidence of their acceptance by God.

As an effect of his vision encounter with the Lord on the Damascus road Paul was blinded. His sight was subsequently restored by Ananias through the laying on of hands. He was then filled with the Holy Spirit and later baptized (Acts 9:3, 4, 8, 17, 18). Ananias' instruction to Paul on this occasion was given with the words "Rise and be baptized, and wash away your sins, calling on his name" (22:16).

The baptisms of Cornelius and the Philippian jailer are of special interest because they were accompanied by divine intervention. Cornelius was the first Gentile to be baptized. In a vision Peter had been shown not to discriminate against the Gentiles. He was told, "What God has cleansed, you must not call common" (10:15). While Peter was preaching to Cornelius, the Holy Spirit fell on his Gentile listeners. In the light of this divine manifestation Peter did not hesitate to proceed with the baptism of Cornelius, along with some of his

relatives and friends (verses 44-48).

While Paul and Silas were praising the Lord during their imprisonment in Philippi a great earthquake occurred. The potential loss of prisoners so endangered the jailer that he was about to kill himself (16:25-34). Paul stopped him from doing this. In answer to the jailer's question "What must I do to be saved?" Paul and Silas told him that if he believed on the Lord Jesus he and his household would be saved (verse 31). The apostles then preached the word of the Lord to him and all who were in his house. As a result they were baptized (verse 33). Earlier in the same chapter the baptism of Lydia is also recorded (verses 14, 15).

These incidents of baptism referred to in Acts clearly present baptism as evidence that the believer accepts salvation through the redemptive act of Jesus. Baptism was also a public act during which the name of Jesus was confessed (8:12; 10:48; 16:30-33; 22:16), being preceded by preaching or study of the Word (8:12, 35; 16:32).

6. Baptism in the Pauline Writings

Paul's most extensive exposition of baptism is found in Romans 6:1-11, which must be seen in its broader context. In chapter 5 the apostle has shown that Jesus is the only solution to the sin problem—for "where sin increased, grace abounded all the more" (verse 20). In chapter 6 he points out that his readers have died to sin. He continues, "Do you not know that all of us who have been baptized into Christ Jesus were baptized into his death? We were buried therefore with him by baptism into death, so that as Christ was raised from the dead by the glory of the Father, we too might walk in newness of life" (verses 3, 4).

In verse 3 the apostle makes the point that the believer's relationship with Christ through baptism includes a relationship to His death. In verse 2 Paul indicates that a person who has accepted Jesus as his Lord and Saviour has died to sin. From this we can infer that the Christian, united with Christ in baptism, has finished with sin and lives now in the newness of life dedicated to God (verse 4).

Jesus made it plain that anyone who wishes to enter the kingdom of God needs spiritual regeneration, the result of the renewing of the heart by the Spirit of God and water baptism (John 3:5). In the same way Paul affirms that a candidate for the kingdom of glory must become a new creation (2 Cor. 5:17). As the result of a transformation of the entire being, this process involves death and burial of the carnal nature and resurrection to a new life in Christ in baptism (Col. 2:11, 12).

We hardly do justice to Paul's meaning in Romans 6:1-4, or to the chapter as a whole, unless we recognize the different senses in which Christians die to sin and are raised to new life. Since Christ died for all on the cross, Christians are buried with Him by baptism, giving up their wills and dying, as it were, with Him on that day, to allow Him to live His life through them, as the same apostle declares in Galatians 2:20 and 6:14. Christians die to sin and are raised up in their baptism; in this way they demonstrate their acceptance of God's offer of forgiveness through Jesus Christ. Through Him, Christians receive the ability to die daily to sin and to rise to newness of life through obedience to God. Finally, they die to sin when they die physically; they will be raised in the resurrection of life at their Lord's return.

Some have taken the punctiliar aorist verb "we died" in Romans 6:2 to mean that Christians are seen as having died with Christ in His death. However, Paul's intended meaning is best expressed as a reference to what happened to the Roman Christians—as indeed to all believers—at their baptism: death to sin.

According to Paul, by being baptized "into Christ Jesus" Christian believers are baptized into His death and raised to share in His risen life, to "walk in newness of life" (6:3, 4). By baptism they "put on the Lord Jesus Christ" (13:14; cf. Gal. 3:27). Christians may thus experience fullness of life (Col. 2:9, 10).

Paul understands baptism as an initiation into life in Christ, but also as an initiation into the corporate body of Christ, the church (cf. 1 Cor. 6:11; 12:13). Baptism does not stand for its own sake; it is always the door to the church. To belong to the church—the body of Christ—means that by their baptism Christians take on the responsibilities of the body. Membership in that body involves "forbearing one another in love," being "eager to maintain the unity of the Spirit in the bond of peace" (Eph. 4:2, 3), and doing away with barriers among fellow church members (Gal. 3:27-29). It also means employing the spiritual gifts conferred by the Spirit to build up the body so that it may reach "the measure of the stature of the fulness of Christ" (Eph. 4:11-13). Finally, becoming a member of the body commits Christians to the missionary task of the church (Matt. 28:18-20; see Church VI. A).

B. Practical Dimensions of Baptism

Several practical dimensions of baptism deserve consideration. Baptism opens the door to church membership. Further, the mode in which baptism is conducted and the age at which it is administered need consideration. Finally, the matter of rebaptism must be taken into account.

1. Entrance Into the Church by Baptism

By baptism Christians join the "one body" and become members of the community of faith (Acts 2:41, 42, 47; 1 Cor. 12:13). This is not membership in a club, which can be dropped at one's convenience, but membership in the body of Christ. Baptism thus involves repentance, faith, and surrender to the Lordship of Christ.

2. Mode of Baptism

The Bible teaches baptism by immersion. As noted before, the word "baptism" itself indicates immersion. New Testament examples, likewise, show baptism to be by immersion. Finally, Paul's reference to burial and resurrection in Romans 6:3-5 would be pointless unless total immersion was intended. Baptism by sprinkling or pouring does not conform to the biblical pattern or meaning of baptism by immersion.

When administering baptism, Christians commonly use the formula found in Matthew 28:19: "in the name of the Father and of the Son and of the Holy Spirit." To baptize in the name may mean into the family of, or upon the basis of authority delegated by, the triune God. In apostolic times the formula "in the name of Jesus Christ" or "in the name of the Lord Jesus" was used (Acts 2:38; 8:16; 10:48). Baptism in the name of Jesus only, rather than according to the formula of Matthew 28:19, may reflect Peter's exhortation to accept Jesus Christ as the Christ-Messiah, to confess Him publicly, and join His church.

3. Age of Baptism

Those who defend the practice of infant baptism appeal to the so-called *oikos* or "household formula." In their opinion this supports the view that children and/or infants were baptized in NT times. The following texts that speak of the conversion and baptism of a household are usually cited: (1) "I did baptize also the household of Stephanas" (1 Cor. 1:16); (2) Lydia "was baptized, with her household" (Acts 16:15); (3) the keeper of the prison at Philippi "was baptized . . . with all his family" (verse 33); (4) "Crispus, the ruler of the synagogue, believed in the Lord, together with all his household" (Acts 18:8); (5) "You will be saved, you and all your household" (11:14).

Some scholars maintain that Paul and Luke would not have mentioned the baptism of "households" if children had been excluded. However, on closer examination the arguments in favor of infant baptism grounded on these texts are based on silence. Such households would more likely have been their servants and possibly older children. A biblical basis for the practice of infant baptism is lacking. Of course, children of all ages were present in the early church. The church took a special interest in them because Jesus had considered them to be especially precious in God's sight (Matt. 18:3; 19:14). But no baptism of children is ever mentioned in the NT. Infant baptism, however, began only in postapostolic times, and no concrete evidence for this practice appears before the end of the second century.

In the light of Acts the preaching or the study of the Word and the candidate's confession and affirmation of faith in the Lord Jesus Christ preceded baptism (Acts 8:12, 13, 35-38; 16:30-33). All of this confirms the point that the baptismal candidate could not have been an infant. New Testament references to initiation assume that the recipients of baptism were adults, and that the dispositions required of them were conscious and deliberate renunciation of sin and idols, personal faith in Christ and allegiance to Him.

4. Rebaptism

As noted earlier, baptism brings a person into membership in the Christian church, to share the common privileges and responsibilities of the community. Whether baptism, which is the entrance ceremony to church fellowship, may or should be repeated is a often-asked question.

The only Bible passage dealing with rebaptism is Acts 19:1-7, where about 12 Ephesian disciples are rebaptized. The text itself poses no difficulty. The situation described is that of people who had once been baptized. In response to Paul's question "Into what then were you baptized?" they answered, "Into John's baptism" (verse 3). According to verse 5, the 12 were then baptized again. Apparently Paul did not consider their former baptism as valid or adequate.

The Ephesians are introduced as "disciples" who had not been baptized in the name of Jesus and were not aware of the Holy Spirit. John's baptism was based on an appeal for repentance and forgiveness (Mark 1:4; Luke 3:3). Christ's was different. The reason for their rebaptism, therefore, seems evident. They had received only John's "baptism of repentance."

Apparently Apollos had known only the baptism of John (Acts 18:25), but there is no mention of his rebaptism. Some of the apostles also must have received John's baptism (John 1:35-40), but there is nothing to indicate they were ever rebaptized. Thus one may conclude that some of the disciples and Apollos, although baptized with the baptism of John, were in possession of two important elements: their belief in Jesus and the presence of the Holy Spirit in their lives. Because these two elements were lacking in the baptism of the Ephesians, Paul considered their baptism invalid and rebaptized them. Evidently Paul held that rebaptism was in order because subsequent to their baptism they had received vital new truths. The reception of additional, basic truths warrants rebaptism.

Another reason for rebaptism may be apostasy. One who has openly violated God's laws and been disfellowshipped from the church must enter the body anew. On accepting Christ again that person will wish to signify renewed fellowship with Christ and the church by rebaptism. "When one has been baptized into Christ, rebaptism is called for only if there has been a definite apostasy from the beliefs and standards that fellowship with Christ requires" (6BC 373). On the other hand, rebaptism may be abused, as in the case of one who repeatedly apostatizes and requests rebaptism. On the topic of rebaptism for apostasy, the Scriptures are silent; therefore, caution must be exercised.

5. The Impact of Baptism on Christian Experience

A theoretical discussion of baptism is of little significance without consideration of its impact upon one's life. Baptism in itself does not guarantee newness of life. There is no sacramental power in the water as such. Baptism is, however, symbolic of cleansing from sin and moral defilement.

Once enlightened by the Holy Spirit, a person realizes his or her lost condition. Through repentance and confession one can be freed from the burden of sin and guilt and find full acceptance with God and freedom to live a new life in the Spirit. This new life is the result of a rebirth or regeneration. The apostle Paul likens the experience of rebirth or regeneration to the death and burial of the old life and resurrection to a new life. This is symbolized by baptism.

C. Conclusion

Key passages relating to baptism in the NT reveal that the concepts of confession, repentance, cleansing, death to sin, and rising to newness of life are closely associated with baptism. The rite also involves belief in Jesus, as well as the cleansing of the conscience. The idea of cleansing is dominant. Thus baptism essentially symbolizes cleansing from sin.

The believer is baptized into Christ and into the fellowship of the church. From the NT perspective the body of Christ is made up of individuals who have been baptized into Christ. They are in intimate union with Christ (Gal. 3:27), and at the same time they now enjoy fellowship with other members of the church.

D. Historical Overview

1. Antecedents to Baptism

A historical sketch of baptism should take into consideration antecedents to the Christian rite. For example, in Leviticus 15, ten verses prescribe washing and bathing to purify from uncleanness of different types (5, 6, 7, 8, 9, 11, 13, 21, 22, 27). Jewish purification baths, as evidenced in archaeological discoveries from the time of Herod's Temple, were common. In the Qumran community, these ablutions seem to have become extremely important, the hallmark of godliness. In mainline Judaism, the baptism of proselytes was part of their admission into the community of faith. None of these washings or baptisms, not even the baptism of John in the Jordan, had the significance of uniting the one baptized with divinity, as does baptism into Christ.

2. Postapostolic Period

During this period several changes occurred in the way baptism was administered and understood.

The *Didache,* a document (late first or early second century) that permitted pouring water three times on the candidate's head, in the name of the Trinity, when there was a shortage of water (*Didache* 7). Cyprian (c. 200-258) held that sprinkling and pouring were equally efficacious and that baptism did not consist in the submersion of the body but rather the application of "saving water" to the head (*Epistle* 75. 12). Those who could not be baptized by immersion for health reasons were sprinkled.

Infant baptism appears explicitly for the first time in Tertullian (c. 200) in a passage that opposes what appears to be a relatively new practice (*On Baptism* 18). A few years later Origen (c. 185-c. 251) claims that infant baptism was a tradition handed down from the apostles (*Commentary on Romans* 5. 9).

During the early centuries the baptismal rite was enlarged to include elaborate ceremonies. Baptismal services were deferred to certain holy days, especially Easter. This was an obvious departure from the NT practice in which baptism followed conversion. In the ceremonies of the third century, triple immersion was coupled with confession, anointing, and the laying on of hands. A baptismal eucharist followed. The triune formula (Matt. 28:19) was commonly used in baptism.

Influenced by Mithraic and Eleusinian mystery rites, Christians began to adopt the position that baptism imparted bliss to the initiate. For Tertullian (c. 200), water baptism brought forgiveness of sin, deliverance from death, regeneration, and the bestowal of the Holy Spirit (*Against Marcion* 1. 28).

3. Post-Nicene Church

From about the fourth century onward both infant and adult baptisms were practiced. By the fifth century infant baptism had become the common practice. In spite of the increasing popularity of infant baptism, certain prominent Christian leaders were baptized as adults. Ambrose of Milan (d. 397) was first baptized at the age of 34, even though his parents were Christians. Both Chrysostom (d. 407) and Jerome (d. 420) were in their twenties when they were baptized.

However, infant baptism gradually became the norm. When Gregory of Nazianzus (d. 390) was asked, "Shall we baptize infants?" he made the following compromising statement: "Certainly if danger presses. For it is better to be unconsciously sanctified than that they should depart from this life unsealed and uninitiated" (*Oratio* 40. 28).

Augustine (d. 430) was the first theologian to formulate a dogmatic theory of baptism, which stemmed from his controversy with the Donatists. He distinguished sharply between *sacramentum* and *res sacramenti,* the sacrament and the grace of which the sacrament is a sign. He held that it was possible to obtain the *sacramentum* (rite) without the *res* (grace). Augustine held baptism to be indispensable for salvation because people could be saved only within the church, to which baptism was the sole means of entrance. A layperson, even a heretic, might administer valid baptism. He undergirded the mystical efficacy of infant baptism with the docrine of original sin. In fact, he made infant baptism serve to cancel the guilt of original sin. Augustine realized that children themselves had no faith, hence they could receive forgiveness only through the mediation of the church. Conversion of the heart through faith would follow, depending upon the child's physical growth and maturity. At the Council of Carthage in A.D. 418 the church endorsed the rite of infant baptism: "If any man says that new-born children need not be baptized . . . let him be anathema."

4. Middle Ages

The scholastics systematized and elaborated the teachings of Augustine. They clearly distinguished between matter and form. The matter of baptism was water, while its form consisted of the words. Since both form and matter were instituted by God, the church had no right to alter the sacrament. In baptism all sins were forgiven. Children could experience forgiveness from original sin and adults from sins committed.

Thomas Aquinas (1225-1274), the foremost Catholic theologian, asserted that "baptism may be given not only by immersion, but also by affusion of water, or sprinkling with it." But he held that it would be safer to baptize by immersion, "because that is the most common custom" (*Summa Theologiae* 3a. 66. 7).

Aquinas believed that baptism brings everyone into actual contact with the flow of grace emanating from Christ. It confers the "character" of belonging to Christ, to His "body," the church. This character obtained in baptism enables the believer to receive the other sacraments.

5. Reformation

Luther was not entirely successful in correcting the predominant Roman Catholic view of his day on the inseparable connection between the outward means of grace, in this instance baptism, and the inward grace communicated by it. Over against the Anabaptists, he insisted that the effectiveness of the sacrament of baptism depended on its divine institution rather than on the faith of the recipients. Through the divine efficacy of the Word—apart from which the sacrament has no significance—the baptismal rite effected regeneration in children, although for adults this effect depended on the faith of the recipient.

Zwingli differed from Luther in his theological understanding of the sacrament as a sign, a ceremony, or a pledge that did not actually convey something. As a pledge of faith, baptism expressed the covenant relationship between God and His people, in a way similar to circumcision in the OT. Zwingli underlined the corporate significance of baptism by em-phasizing it as an act of reception into the church.

Calvin, on the other hand, denied that baptism, of itself, confers grace. As with the other means of grace, God appointed baptism as a means through which He works His grace in the hearts of sinners. He saw baptism as the initiatory sign by which the believer is admitted to the fellowship of Christ. The Lord appointed it as a sign and evidence of our purification from all sin. Calvin was quick to point out, however, that the only purification baptism provides is by means of "the sprinkling of the blood of Christ" (*Institutes* 4. 15. 2). The mode of baptism, whether performed by immersion or by sprinkling, was inconsequential (*ibid.* 19). Like Augustine, Calvin had a strong interest in predestination, especially in connection with the baptism of children. With Luther, he believed that the elect were sealed by grace through baptism. To both, baptism signified the beginning of a "new life" in the church. When a child numbered among the elect died without baptism, it suffered no harm in God's sight. Calvin was opposed to private baptism and he held that baptism was to be performed by the clergy.

The name "Anabaptists" (meaning "Rebaptizers") was given to a group of Protestants in the sixteenth century who concerned themselves with the restoration of the apostolic understanding of baptism. They insisted on the biblical teaching of repentance and discipleship as a basis for adult baptism. Thus they opposed the practice of infant baptism, for which they could find no NT justification.

6. Modern Era

During the age of pietism and rationalism there was no significant theological interest in baptism. Schleiermacher considered it the solemn act of reception into the "community of believers." In his opinion the baptism of children was meaningless unless followed by proper education. Baptism, he maintained, was incomplete unless it led to confirmation.

The question of infant baptism is alive in the contemporary Christian church. In 1943 Karl Barth delivered a serious challenge to infant baptism, calling it a "half-baptism" and pointing out its lack of scriptural basis (Barth 34-54). Erich Dinkler indicated that "there is no scriptural support in the New Testament for infant baptism" and that this question "must be 'concluded' theologically" (Dinkler 636). On the other hand, Oscar Cullman confidently affirmed that infant baptism was practiced in the early church as an admission rite, in place of Jewish circumcision (Cullmann 70). Likewise, Joachim Jeremias, while admitting that there is no clear example of infant baptism in the NT, still insists that the small children of believers were baptized (Jeremias 55).

At present there is a lack of unity on the form of baptism among the Christian communities. In its document entitled *Baptism, Eucharist and Ministry,* the Committee on Faith and Order of the World Council of Churches recommends the following parts in a baptismal service: (1) preaching on baptism; (2) invocation of the Holy Spirit; (3) renunciation of evil; (4) profession of faith in Christ and the Holy Trinity; (5) use of water; (6) recognition of the newly baptized members as sons and daughters of God called to be witnesses of the gospel. At the same time the baptism of infants is allowed (*Baptism, Eucharist and Ministry* 2-7).

7. Adventist Position

In 1861 B. F. Snook defended the practice of adult baptism by immersion against the prevailing practice of infant baptism, based on linguistic and biblical grounds. He maintained that both the classical and the sacred use of the Greek word *baptizō* could not possibly refer to pouring or sprinkling; it could only mean immersion. From a biblical perspective, Snook demonstrated that baptism is a memorial of the burial and resurrection of Christ (Col. 2:12). It is related to salvation and is to be administered for the remission of sins (Acts 2:38). It is also an initiation rite into the church to be preceded by repentance (Rom. 6:3; Gal. 3:26, 27; Snook).

E. J. Waggoner viewed baptism as a sign of the death and resurrection of Christ. He emphasized the fact that baptism is not a mere form but represents a burial with Jesus into His death, thus signifying putting off the old life, crucifying the old man, and taking on Christ's life in whom we rise to walk in newness of life (Waggoner 1891).

Adventists accept baptism as the biblical rite of admission to the church. This baptism, as both the evidence in the Scriptures and the practice of the early church testify, must be by immersion ("On Baptism" 6). This rite is administered to those who consciously and freely accept Christ as their Saviour and Lord, repent of their sins, and are thoroughly instructed in the beliefs of the church (*SDA Church Manual* 1990, 41-43). Thus, infants are excluded. Furthermore, Adventists have always rejected any view of baptism as an act which, in and of itself, imparts grace and effects salvation.

While rebaptism is relatively uncommon in the churches it is felt to be appropriate under two circumstances. When one who joins the church has previously been baptized by immersion, rebaptism is still encouraged because it is considered that the person has accepted new biblical truths since that previous baptism. At the person's request, the church may accept him or her by "profession of faith" without rebaptism, thus recognizing the validity of the baptism by immersion of other churches. When church "members have fallen away in apostasy and have lived in such a manner that the faith and principles of the church have been publicly violated, they should, in case of reconversion and application for church membership, enter the church as in the beginning, by baptism" (*SDA Church Manual* 1990, 51). This happens when one who "is truly reconverted" renews his or her "covenant with God" (Ev 375).

II. The Ordinance of Foot Washing

The practice of foot washing has never gained prominence in Christianity. The majority of contemporary Christians simply bypass this rite. When rightly understood, however, the ordinance of foot washing is an ideal preparation for the celebration of the Lord's Supper, as it was in the upper room.

A. New Testament Basis

Foot washing appears repeatedly in the Bible as a hospitable act on the part of a host who thus shows honor to his guests. Of the eight OT references to foot washing, six refer to this customary act (Gen. 18:4; 19:2; 24:32; 43:24; Judges 19:21; 1 Sam. 25:41); one refers to humiliation (Ps. 58:10), and one seems to be simply a matter of cleanliness (Cant. 5:3). In the NT, foot washing as a mark of gracious hospitality appears in Luke 7:44 and 1 Timothy 5:10.

The only biblical reference to foot washing as an ordinance is found in John 13:1-20. In this passage Jesus set an example of humility and true servanthood by washing the feet of His disciples. The disciples took this action very seriously and Peter even objected to Christ's washing his feet. In verse 14 Jesus invited His disciples to follow His example and to continue this practice, saying, "If I then, your Lord and Teacher, have washed your feet, you also ought to wash one another's feet."

John 13:1-20 not only narrates the first foot washing, it also deals with the meaning of this rite for the church at large. The key that unlocks the meaning of the rite of foot washing lies in the conversation between Jesus and Peter. The first of the symbolic overtones appears in verse 7, where Jesus speaks of the disciples' later understanding of the ordinance of foot washing. Without this cleansing a disciple loses his heritage with Jesus (verse 8): "If I do not wash you, you have no part in me."

Because of its structure, this passage is parallel to the "new commandment" of love in 13:34. Jesus' love for the disciples in life and even more in death here becomes the norm to follow (see 15:12; 1 John 2:6; 3:3, 7; 4:17).

These words transcend the literal meaning of removing the dust from someone's feet. While Peter and his brethren had been washed from sin and uncleanness in the "fountain opened for the house of David . . . to cleanse them from sin and uncleanness" (Zech. 13:1), they were still subject to temptation and evil. Thus they needed a higher cleansing that would wash away "the alienation, jealousy, and pride from their hearts" (DA 646).

"To have part with someone" (see John 13:8) means to have a share or a place with that person. In Matthew 24:51 the unfaithful servant is condemned to having a "part" with the hypocrites. In 2 Corinthians 6:15 a Christian has no "part" with unbelieving heathen. The meaning of this phrase can be understood better in the light of Jesus' promise to His disciples. If faithful, they would share in the life He was to gain (John 14:19). They would also be where He was (John 12:26; 14:3; 17:24) and would therefore share in His glory (see John 17:22, 24). The full love of Jesus and the Father would be revealed to them (John 14:21, 23). In John 13:14 Jesus gave an example, whose meaning transcends the narrow circle of the twelve. "If I then, your Lord and Teacher, have washed your feet, you [plural] also ought [opheilete] to wash one another's feet."

The verb opheilō has both a literal and a figurative meaning: in the first it means "to owe," as in having a debt; in the second it means to have an obligation, with the idea of "ought" or "must," and is followed by a second verb that shows what one is obligated to do (cf. Luke 17:10 where the servant's duty to his master is in view). Here the obligation is to wash each other's feet. The word expresses a moral obligation, something that needs to be done. The verbal tense indicates continued or repeated action rather than a one-time duty. Jesus clearly intended that the disciples should continue to discharge this obligation, following the example He had given them: "For I have given you an example, that you also should do as I have done to you" (John 13:15).

Finally, in John 13:17 Jesus calls for action on the part of the Christian community. "If you know these things, blessed are you if you do them." Jesus blends action together with coming to a knowledge of the truth (cf. John 3:21; 7:17; 8:31).

The rites of the Lord's Supper and foot washing were introduced to the small circle of the twelve apostles. After the resurrection of Jesus, however, Christian congregations celebrated the Lord's Supper (cf. Acts 2:42; 1 Cor. 11). The Lord's Supper became a significant part of corporate worship. Although the biblical record gives no additional account of the practice of foot washing, in the light of John 13 there is reason to believe that the ordinance was observed.

B. Significance of Foot Washing

Frequently foot washing is dismissed as an ancient Near Eastern custom without meaning in today's society. It is not seen as a valid mandate of Christ for His followers. However, by ignoring foot washing, modern Christians miss its deep theological meaning.

Foot washing, according to Jesus' words in John 13:10, does not replace baptism. "He who has bathed [Gr. *louō,* to take a bath] does not need to wash [Gr. *niptō,* wash something or a part of the body], except for his feet." Once a person has been baptized (bathed), there is no need for undergoing baptism anew each time a sin is committed or a desire for spiritual cleansing is awakened. Unless a believer lapses into open apostasy, no need exists for a complete bath (baptism), only for the washing of feet in representation of the removal of sin, following sincere repentance and confession.

The understanding of foot washing as representing forgiveness of postbaptismal sin is partly due to the occurrence of the word *katharos* in this verse. A cognate of this term

also appears in 1 John 1:7, 9 with explicit reference to forgiveness of sin through the blood of Jesus. Even though sin is not explicitly mentioned in verse 10 its presence is implied. The idea of the forgiveness of postbaptismal sin fits well with Jesus' emphatic language in verse 8, where Peter is told that he would have no part with Jesus because of postbaptismal sin that had not been removed by cleansing.

Also represented in the washing of feet is Jesus' giving of Himself, in life and death, to save human beings. The ordinance of foot washing memorializes Christ's humiliation in His incarnation (DA 650).

C. The Impact of Foot Washing on Christian Experience

In preparation for the Lord's Supper, the practice of foot washing leads the believer to a deeper appreciation of Christ's love, humility, and the meaning of genuine discipleship in terms of servanthood. The purpose of this ordinance is not merely the removal of dust from one's feet. This rite is a type of a higher cleansing of the heart, which is the source of alienation, jealousy, and pride. As believers stoop to wash each other's feet all thoughts of self-aggrandizement, pride, and selfishness are to give way to the spirit of love, humility, and fellowship. In this spirit one experiences union with God and with one another and is thus prepared to meet with the Lord in the celebration of His Supper.

The believer's desire to participate actively in the life and ordinances of the church is related to spiritual maturity. Lack of regular participation in the ordinances for a time should not be interpreted as a breach of covenant with the Lord. On the other hand, willful and lasting resistance to the ordinance of foot washing may be symptomatic of spiritual problems in a believer's life.

D. Conclusion

In the light of John 13:10 it is clear that the rite of foot washing is not to replace baptism, which is washing of the entire person from sin and defilement. The purpose of the ordinance of foot washing is to wash away postbaptismal sins. It is symbolic of a higher cleansing that washes away all feelings of pride, selfishness, and self-aggrandizement. Thus it is an ideal preparation for the celebration of the Lord's Supper.

From John 13:14 it is clear also that Christ has imposed a moral obligation upon His disciples, both of His immediate apostles and the wider circle of the church, to wash each other's feet. The symbolic act of foot washing should be an expression of a believer's sacrificial love toward fellow members. Persistent, willful nonparticipation may be interpreted as a voluntary severance from Christ (13:8).

E. Historical Overview

1. Until the Reformation

Mention of foot washing is absent from the *Didache* (late first or early second centuries), which gives instruction on several matters of church procedure, including the celebration of the Lord's Supper. However, prohibitions of foot washing enacted by later councils—probably due to excesses practiced in connection with the ceremony—indicate that the rite was known and practiced. Bishops washed the feet of priests in connection with certain special meals; the feet of the newly baptized were washed as part of the baptismal ceremony. Ambrose of Milan (fourth century) wrote that foot washing was "a help towards humility" (*Of the Holy Spirit* 1. Prologue). For Augustine (A.D. 354-430) foot washing was to be practiced for mutual confession and forgiveness (*On the Gospel of John* 58).

To a great extent, Christ's injunction to wash each other's feet was taken figuratively, as urging humility among Christians. Origen (c. 185-254), commenting on John's narration, called foot washing a symbol of humility. The *Apostolic Constitutions,* a late fourth-century collection of admonitions for Christians, refers to John's account of Jesus' washing of the disciples' feet, but only to remind the deacons

of their Lord's example of humility.

In Augustine's time it was customary for foot washing to be celebrated during Holy Week (*Letter to Januarius* 18). Bernard of Clairvaux, however, recommended foot washing as a "daily sacrament for the forgiveness of sins" (*De coena Domini* sermon).

In the Roman Catholic Church, laypersons did not participate in this service for centuries. Other Christians, however, practiced foot washing. The Celtic church, for example, kept the practice alive until it disappeared in the eleventh century. Albigenses and Waldenses had foot-washing ceremonies, but mainly limited the practice to the washing of visiting ministers' feet. In the Eastern Church the rite of foot washing was considered a "mystery" and practiced in monasteries and by the Czar himself once a year.

2. From the Reformation Onward

In his 1544 Maundy Thursday sermon on foot washing in the *Hauspostille,* Luther decried the hypocrisy of the ceremony as carried out by church leaders of his day and pleaded rather for true humility in personal relations. The practice of foot washing fell into disuse among Lutherans, who considered it "an abominable corruption." Foot washing was revived by the Moravians, who did not confine it strictly to Maundy Thursday, but the practice was later abolished by the Synod of 1818 (*New Schaff-Herzog* 4:339-340).

Anabaptists decided in favor of foot washing in the seventeenth century, accepting as still valid Christ's mandate in John 13:14 and Paul's injunction in 1 Timothy 5:10. They believed that through the sacrament of foot washing the sinner experienced cleansing through the blood of Christ and expressed deep humility. Their spiritual descendants, the Mennonites and Brethren, as well as some Baptist and Holiness groups, still practice foot washing.

3. In the Adventist Church

The Seventh-day Adventist Church is the

largest denomination that regularly observes the ordinance of foot washing in connection with the Lord's Supper. The first recorded instance of foot washing among Adventists took place after the Lord's Supper at the close of a meeting at Grafton, Vermont, in July 1844. Miller himself deemed foot washing a "promiscuous act" (Ferris 11, 12).

In 1845 the *Day-Star* published a running debate on foot washing as an ordinance. Its promoters stressed the importance of keeping all the commands of Jesus and showing love to the brethren. Its detractors linked the rite with fanaticism.

In 1849 James White published a collection entitled *Hymns for God's Peculiar People*. It included one titled "Washing Feet." The *Advent Review and Sabbath Herald* published on August 5, 1851, a report of a foot-washing service held a month earlier at Wheeling, New York. The separation of men and women at the service helped to secure general acceptance of the rite.

On January 1, 1859, before the organization of the Seventh-day Adventist Church,

Ellen White described a day of meetings in her diary: "In the eve the church followed the example of their Lord": they washed one another's feet and then partook of the Lord's Supper. Elsewhere she referred to the ordinance as follows:

"Duties are laid down in God's Word, the performance of which will keep the people of God humble and separate from the world, and from backsliding, like the nominal churches. The washing of feet and partaking of the Lord's supper should be more frequently practiced. Jesus set us the example, and told us to do as He had done" (EW 116).

In early Adventism the understanding of foot washing developed along different lines. Ellen White emphasized the Christocentric aspect of this important rite, while others placed greater emphasis upon the symbolic understanding (Oestreich 191-199). The continuation of the practice was confirmed when number 15 of the fundamental beliefs was voted by the church at the General Conference session held in Dallas in 1980. (See Church VI. B. 2.)

III. The Lord's Supper

Although it may be understood and practiced in different ways by diverse Christians, the Lord's Supper is of central importance to all believers. The rite instituted at Christ's Last Supper is called by different and usually interchangeable names: Eucharist, a giving of thanks for God's good gifts; Communion, emphasizing the fellowship with Christ; and the Lord's Supper, denoting the origin of the service. Several aspects of the topic deserve consideration. The most important in this article are its New Testament origin, its meaning for modern Christians, and practical aspects of its celebration.

A. The Lord's Supper in the New Testament

On the eve of His crucifixion Jesus celebrated the Last Supper with His disciples, as recorded by all three Synoptic Gospels (Matt.

26:26-29; Mark 14:22-25; Luke 22:14-20). Paul rehearses the story in 1 Corinthians 11:23-25. These four passages agree on the essentials of the narrative; in their differences they complement one another. Together they form the basis of Christian teaching on the Lord's Supper.

Interestingly, John's Gospel tells of the foot washing but not of the Last Supper. However, John 6:53 speaks of eating Christ's flesh and drinking His blood, suggesting the Lord's Supper.

1. The Last Supper in the Synoptics

In the Synoptics, Christ's Last Supper is closely connected with the celebration of the Passover. In spite of this relation, however, the Lord's Supper is new—a transformation of the Jewish ceremony, full of fresh and deep meaning. While the Passover had pointed forward to the death of Christ, the Lord's Supper would point back to the same event and remind Christ's followers of their Lord's sacrifice until His return.

a. The form: bread and cup. According to Matthew, Mark, and Luke, Christ instituted the Lord's Supper at the end of the Passover meal readied by the disciples in the upper room. Two elements, common in Jewish homes, made up this special meal.

Jesus took bread—undoubtedly the flat, round, unleavened bread of the Passover—and blessed it (Matt. 26:26; Mark 14:22), or gave thanks for it (Luke 22:19), and offered it to the disciples. The normal blessing pronounced over bread by the head of the household was, "Praised be Yahweh, our God, the king of the world, who makes the bread to come forth from the earth"; both blessing and gratitude were expressed in these words.

Likewise, Jesus took the cup, gave thanks, and invited the disciples to drink from it (Matt. 26:27; Mark 14:23; Luke 22:20). Perhaps the thankfulness would have been pronounced in the traditional blessing: "Praised be Yahweh, our God, the king of the world, who creates the fruit of the vine." The content of the cup is clarified later as the "fruit of the vine" (Matt. 26:29; Mark 14:25; Luke 22:18).

In Luke's Gospel the cup is shared before the bread, and a second cup closes the meal (verses 17, 20). It is possible that the first cup was part of the Paschal meal; thus it would not be part of the Lord's Supper. The narrations in Matthew and Mark, as well as in 1 Corinthians, note the sharing of bread first, followed by the one cup.

b. The meaning: communion and prophecy. Jesus clearly explained the significance of both bread and cup. The bread, He said, was His body; the cup, His blood (Matt. 26:26, 27; Mark 14:22, 23; Luke 22:20). By taking the bread and fruit of the vine, the disciples were entering into intimate communion with Him.

The blood was that of the covenant, "poured out for many" (Matt. 26:28; Mark 14:24), or more intimately, "for you" (Luke 22:20). By this pouring out, forgiveness of sins would be obtained (Matt. 26:28).

With His promise not to drink of the "fruit of the vine" again until He would drink it with His disciples in the kingdom, Jesus gave the assurance that He would be reunited with His friends (verse 29; Mark 14:25). Thus Jesus promised to participate with His disciples in the Messianic banquet (Isa. 25:6-8) in the kingdom of God (Matt. 22:1-10; Luke 14:15-24) in the day of the final consummation (Rev. 21:3-5). In spite of the imminent separation, there was a bright eschatological future. The celebration of the Last Supper was not only a backward look or a reflection on the redemptive action of God through Jesus Christ; it was also a forward look into the future, to the moment of His glorious return as prophesied in John 14:1-3.

Luke adds the phrase: "Do this in remembrance of me" (Luke 22:19). Jesus wished to be remembered in the celebration of the Lord's Supper until He returned. An OT parallel of this "remembrance" appears in the exhortation to remember the Passover (Ex. 12:14) as a symbol of God's benefits.

2. The Last Supper in 1 Corinthians

Paul refers to the Lord's Supper only in 1 Corinthians, in relation to problems regarding worship. In 10:16-21 he points out that partaking of the Lord's Supper makes the Corinthians participants in the body of Christ; likewise participating in pagan sacrifices implies fellowship with demons. In 11:17-34 Paul deals with irregularities in the Corinthian church's celebration of this special rite.

By means of rhetorical questions, Paul affirms that the "cup of blessing" is "participation in the blood of Christ" and the "bread we break" is participation in the "body of Christ" (1 Cor. 10:16). Like the Gospel writers, he uses the expression "cup" to represent its content. However, his main emphasis is not on form but on meaning: drinking the cup and eating the bread created fellowship with Christ and one with another. Christians who were part of the body of Christ could no longer have fellowship with demons or demon worshipers through ceremonial meals (verses 14-21).

The brief narration of the institution of the Last Supper in 1 Corinthians 11:23-25 may be the earliest written account of it, since the letter to the Corinthians was probably written in the midfifties, earlier than the Gospels. The words are most similar to those found in Luke. Paul may have heard the story from the apostles, though he informs the Corinthians that his teaching on the Lord's Supper came from the Lord Himself.

Paul stressed the "remembrance" aspect of the Lord's Supper by mentioning the phrase in relation to both bread and cup. But he emphasized even more clearly the prophetic element of the Communion: participation in it is a proclamation of faith in the Second Coming (verse 26). The apostle pointed out to the Corinthians that their celebration was not a true remembrance of Jesus, because they had forgotten the meaning of His life and death. They were busy with their individual pursuits of pleasure and social positioning. Paul countered this selfish behavior by urging them to remember the past and the future in order to live as Christians in the present.

Finally, Paul dealt with abuses in the community's celebration of the Lord's Supper. Some were participating in "an unworthy manner," which made them guilty of profaning the body and blood of the Lord (verse 27). His recommendation was that each should partake of the Lord's Supper after self-examination and fully discerning the meaning of the symbols (verses 28, 29). Failure to do this had already brought ill effects on the Corinthian Christians and would certainly bring further judgment upon them (verses 29, 30). In giving final instructions to the congregation on the correct way to celebrate the Lord's Supper, Paul also alluded to their transforming this special service into an occasion for gluttony and display (verses 33, 34).

B. The Theological Meaning of the Lord's Supper

Jesus Himself explained the basic meaning of the supper He instituted shortly before His crucifixion. What He said must form the basis of any theological reflection on the topic. Because Christians rightly consider themselves disciples of Jesus, the basic meaning of the Lord's Supper is the same today as it was for the twelve in the upper room.

When Jesus gave the bread and the cup to His disciples, He said, "This is my body" and "this is my blood"; these the disciples were invited to eat. A similar concept is found in John 6:51-58, where Christ clearly told His hearers that He Himself was the "living bread which came down from heaven," and that to have life they must eat His flesh and drink His blood. One who ate His flesh and drank His blood would "abide" in Him. In John 15 Christ uses a figure from agriculture to portray this same "abiding": the branch must remain attached to the vine. Obviously, it was impossible for those who listened to Christ literally to "eat" Him; it was also absurd to expect that His disciples would literally attach themselves to His person. Thus, the abiding, the eating, and the drinking must be figurative. Seen in this light, the cup and bread of the Lord's Supper are symbols of a greater reality. While not the substance of Jesus' body and blood, the cup and bread represent His broken body and spilt blood, His death on the cross and the saving gift issuing from it.

By eating and drinking, human beings take nourishment into their bodies. By food and drink they are physically strengthened as what they take becomes part of their very cells. By drinking the cup and eating the bread, Christ's disciples become partakers of Christ's life. Not only do they eat *with* Him in fellowship, they appropriate His qualities into their lives.

The cup represented the "new covenant," said Jesus (Luke 22:20). The covenant idea was clear in Jewish thinking. Yahweh had first covenanted of His own free will to bless Israel; the people had then agreed to love and obey Him. The breach in this covenant had resulted in the Babylonian deportation in 586 B.C. God had always wanted His law to be in the hearts of His people (Deut. 6:6; Ps. 37:31; Isa. 51:7), but they had failed Him. Jeremiah had already expressed the certainty of a new covenant—one not written on tables of stone but on the hearts of God's people (Jer. 31:33, 34). This new covenant was not new in that it meant a change in God's law or intention but in the means by which it was ratified. Jesus' own blood would confirm God's promises of salvation. In the Last Supper this new covenant became a reality. As the disciples partook of the cup, they participated in the provisions and power of that new covenant, made possible by Christ's death. Christ's blood was the symbol and the means of His voluntary and substitutionary atonement; it was the guarantee of the establishment of the new covenant.

In Bible times a covenant was often consummated with a meal. By eating together, the parties committed themselves to fulfill their pledges. By sharing the cup and bread with His disciples Jesus made a covenant with them. He would shed His blood for them, making possible their salvation; He also agreed to prepare for them a place in God's kingdom, to which He eventually would take them. Until then He would not drink again from the fruit of the vine (Luke 22:18).

Christ's disciples—both then and now—are waiting for the Father's kingdom. In pledge of His part of the covenant, Jesus offered His blood and His flesh. As their part of the agreement, Christians partake of the emblems of His sacrifice as evidence of their compliance with the terms of the covenant. Each time believers celebrate the Lord's Supper they look back to the cross and wonder at divine love. At the same time they look forward to the day when they will sit around God's table in the kingdom.

The blood of the new covenant is poured out in forgiveness (Matt. 26:28). Through the death of Jesus the sins of the human race are blotted out. The tender heart of Jeremiah's new covenant is coupled with divine forgiveness (Jer. 31:31-34). Drinking of the cup symbolizes the human acceptance of this gift of forgiveness.

Furthermore, since the whole community participates in the one cup and bread, the Lord's Supper becomes a unifying factor. By eating together, Christians draw closer one to another, as well as to their Lord.

Because of the benefits the Christian would derive from the Lord's Supper, Jesus admonished His disciples to celebrate it. The Greek verb tense suggests repeated action—not once but again and again. The celebration was to be "in remembrance" of the liberation from sin made possible by Christ's death, just as the Passover was observed in remembrance of Israel's liberation from Egypt. On the other hand, just as the Passover anticipated the sacrifice of Christ as Passover lamb, the Lord's Supper anticipated the victory of the Lamb in the kingdom.

In the celebration of the Lord's Supper, celebrants should not only reflect upon the fact and manner of Jesus' death but also—and most especially—on its present meaning and effect for the entire congregation of God's people. Attention should focus more upon the joy of victory of the Resurrection than upon the sadness of Christ's suffering and death. Celebration of the Lord's Supper is never complete, however, without reflection upon the seriousness of Christ's passion and death for us on the cross.

That the Communion service soon became known as the Eucharist or "giving of thanks" is not hard to understand. In it a person may indeed give thanks to God for the infinite gift of Jesus' life and death. This ceremony is a celebration of the Christian's fellowship with Jesus and His followers, forgiveness from sin, and expectant hope of the future kingdom.

As Paul pointed out to the Corinthians, the celebration of the Lord's Supper proclaims the Lord's death until He comes again (1 Cor.

11:26). Participation in the emblems of Christ's suffering is an act of proclamation of the certainty of the Second Coming. As a symbolic meal, the Communion service joins the believers' daily life and the promise of Christ's coming, and empowers the believer to give a witness to the Christian's glorious hope. (See Church VI. B. 1.)

C. The Practice of the Lord's Supper

The NT is virtually silent regarding the details of the celebration of the Lord's Supper. Little is said about the frequency, who may or may not participate, or even the exact nature of the bread and cup to be used. These practical aspects have been developed on the basis of scriptural principles.

1. Frequency of Celebration

The phrase "as often as you drink it" (see 1 Cor. 11:26) gives no indication of how often Communion is to be celebrated. No other instructions appear in the NT regarding the frequency of the Lord's Supper. Thus, different churches have developed their own patterns of celebration. Some Christians take Communion weekly or even daily.

2. Who May Participate

Paul warns the Corinthians not to participate in the Lord's Supper "in an unworthy manner," but rather to do so after appropriate self-examination (1 Cor. 11:27, 28). To grasp the meaning of the phrase "in an unworthy manner," one needs to consider also Paul's instructions to the believers regarding the "worthy life" and the context of his admonition. Christians are to "lead a life worthy of God" (1 Thess. 2:12), of their calling (Eph. 4:1), and "of the gospel of Christ" (Phil. 1:27). According to Colossians 1:9, 10, Paul prays that Christians may increasingly live a life worthy of the Lord, one pleasing to Him, doing good works in service to Christ.

According to 1 Corinthians 11:20, 22, certain individuals in the Corinthian church displayed an attitude contrary to Paul's definition of "worthiness." The greedy and selfish wealthy ones displayed a lack of concern for their poorer brethren. By their conduct they hurt the less fortunate members of the community and dishonored their Lord. They apparently failed to distinguish between a common meal at which, for example, a family would eat together, and the sacred Supper, when all social differences should have been put aside (see 6BC 765). Proper examination of their motives and attitudes would have shown them the correct way to act.

Those who have been baptized into Christ can come in confidence of God's grace, and participate in the Communion. Those who are not baptized believers would not have a true reason to participate. In the context of a believer's baptism, unbaptized children should be invited to observe as others take part. After proper instruction and baptism, they may join their fellow believers in the celebration of their Lord's death, resurrection, and soon return.

3. Unleavened Bread and Unfermented Wine

In view of the Jewish custom of removing all leaven from the home on the eve of Passover (Ex. 12:15, 19; 13:7), it can be safely assumed that the bread used at the Last Supper was unleavened. Furthermore, Paul equates leaven with sin (1 Cor. 5:7, 8), of which there was none in Christ. Thus, unleavened bread—normally made of whole-wheat flour mixed with oil, water, and salt—is used in the Communion service to represent the Lord's body sacrificed for all who believe in Him, regardless of time and place.

The descriptions of the Lord's Supper in both the Synoptics and Paul use the expressions "cup" and the "fruit of the vine" for the drink representing Christ's blood. The word "wine" is not used. Alcohol is a product of decay and death, unfit to symbolize the redeeming blood of Jesus. Thus, the use of fermented juice or alcoholic wine in the Communion service is not appropriate. The pressed juice of the grape correctly represents the blood of Christ, poured out for the forgiveness of many.

In her description of the Last Supper, Ellen White writes: "Christ is still at the table on which the paschal supper has been spread. The unleavened cakes used at the Passover season are before Him. The Passover wine, untouched by fermentation, is on the table. These emblems Christ employs to represent His own unblemished sacrifice. Nothing corrupted by fermentation, the symbol of sin and death, could represent the 'Lamb without blemish and without spot' " (DA 653).

D. Conclusion

In the Communion service the Lord offers us His great gifts of salvation: His body and blood, aptly symbolized by the unleavened bread and the pure juice of the grape. The bread represents Jesus as a person; the grape juice is a perfect symbol of His atoning blood. In the celebration of the Lord's Supper, Christians are not only conscious of Jesus' great sacrifice for their sins but also able to rejoice in the new covenant that guarantees present fellowship with Christ and future glory in His kingdom. Therefore, the Lord's Supper is an occasion for rejoicing, not mourning, although we will always be mindful of the high cost of our ransom, the precious blood of Christ, the Lamb without blemish or spot (1 Peter 1:16).

Baptism binds us to Christ in His death (Rom. 6:3, 4), a death He suffered in our stead and for our salvation. The Lord's Supper, likewise, is the proclamation of our Lord's death and resurrection, till He come (1 Cor. 11:26), but among Christians it points to the death that He Himself explained as the basis of the new covenant (Mark 14:24). Just as baptism celebrates one's fellowship with Christ and one's desire to be part of Christ's body, the Lord's Supper is a celebration by baptized believers of the redeeming event that brought them together.

While baptism expresses a convert's decision to belong to Christ, the Lord's Supper shows the church's desire to proclaim Christ's death as God's final act of salvation. The Lord's Supper is the means whereby those who have sealed their covenant with Christ join with Him in that sacrificial self-offering to the Father's will.

E. Historical Overview

1. Early Centuries

In the early church the Lord's Supper appears to have been celebrated in conjunction with a "love feast" *(agapē),* especially designed to benefit the poor. From Corinth (1 Cor. 11:17-22) onward, abuses marred the celebration, so that the Communion service was eventually separated from the fraternal meal (midthird century), as fasting became mandatory before taking Communion.

Several early-church writers mention the Lord's Supper. The *Didache* (late first or early second century) gives specific instructions on its celebration: the prayers are specified, with the cup being served before the bread; only baptized members could participate in this service intended to bring unity to the participants (9, 10). Ignatius (early second century) specified that only a bishop could lead out in the Communion (*Smyrnaeans* 8 [ANF 1:90]); he also affirmed that this rite was "medicine for immortality" (*Ephesians* 20 [ANF 1:57]). Justin Martyr (midsecond century) describes the weekly celebration of the Lord's Supper. He notes the use of wine mixed with water and the bread, which are "the flesh and blood of Jesus" through "the prayer of the Word" (*Apology* 1. 65-67 [ANF 1:185]).

Early in the church's history the bread and wine were considered as symbols. As time went on, these elements came to be considered as the very flesh and blood of Christ. For Irenaeus (c. 130-c. 200), the bread produced by the earth, "when it receives the invocation of God, is no longer common bread, but the Eucharist, consisting of two realities, earthly and heavenly" (*Against Heresies* 4. 18. 5 [ANF 1:486]). Hippolytus (c. 170-c. 236) gave strict orders that no crumb of the Lord's Supper should fall, "for it is the Body of Christ to be eaten by them that believe and not to be thought lightly of" (*Apostolic Tradition* 32. 2. 3). Cyril of Jerusalem (c. A.D. 347) urged catechumens to accept the transformation of the bread and wine, by the power of the Holy Spirit, into the body and blood of Christ (*Mystagogical Catecheses* 4. 9; 5. 7 [NPNF-2 7:152, 154]); this they were to do in unfaltering faith (*ibid*. 5. 20). Ambrose (339-397) wrote that the bread and wine "by the mysterious efficacy of holy prayer are transformed into the flesh and the blood" (*On the Christian Faith* 4. 10 [NPNF-2 10:278]).

As the priesthood developed a mediatorial role, the celebration of the Eucharist became the sacrifice of the Mass. Already Tertullian uses the term "sacrifice" for the bread and wine (Morgan 140-144). In 253 Cyprian wrote a letter in which he repeatedly affirmed that as the priest offered the wine, he was repeating Christ's saving sacrifice (*Epistle* 62 [ANF 5: 362, 363]). John Chrysostom (c. 347-407) called the Eucharist "the dread sacrifice, the unutterable mysteries" (*Homilies on Acts* 21 [NPNF-1 11:141]). Theodore of Mopsuestia (c. 350-428) pointed out that when the priest presented the bread and wine, Christ was being laid on the table to be sacrificed (*Catechetical Homilies* 15, 16).

2. Middle Ages

After the fifth century East and West came to hold different positions on the presence of Christ in the Lord's Supper. In the West Augustine (354-430) said that the sacrament was visible evidence of something invisible (see *First Catechetical Instruction* 26. 50). Furthermore, he pointed out the need for it to be taken spiritually, in faith, to be effective: "it is not that which is seen that feeds, but that which is believed" (*Sermon* 112. 5; cf. *Treatise on the Gospel of John* 25. 12; 26. 18). In the East the general belief was that once the elements were consecrated, they became identical with the body and blood of Jesus Christ. Thus,

John of Damascus (c. 675-c. 749) could argue that "the bread and wine are not merely figures of the body and the blood of Christ (God forbid!) but the deified body of the Lord itself" (*Orthodox Faith* 4. 13).

This controversy over the bodily presence of Christ in the bread and the wine continued for centuries. In 1050 Berengar of Tours taught that the elements were not actually changed, but represented the body and blood of Christ; they fed the soul in a spiritual way because they were received in faith. For this teaching he was accused of heresy and forced to accept a statement by Pope Nicholas II to the effect that after consecration the bread and wine became the true body and blood of Jesus. When he later resumed his original stance, he was again condemned and required to agree that the elements "underwent a *substantial* change into 'the real flesh of Christ' " (Barclay 70, 71).

In the early twelfth century, the much-debated word "transubstantiation" made its appearance. According to this concept, the substance of the elements was miraculously transformed into another. The bread and the wine actually became the body and blood of Christ, regardless of their outward appearance. The Fourth Lateran Council in 1215 ruled: "His body and blood are really contained in the Sacrament of the altar under the species of bread and wine, the bread being transubstantiated into the Body, and the wine into the Blood, by the power of God" (decree 1; Leith 58). Thomas Aquinas (1225-1274) affirmed that after the consecration, no more bread and wine remained: the body of Christ, not there before consecration, took its place. By God's power the whole substance of the bread is converted into the whole substance of the body of Jesus, a conversion "properly called transubstantiation" (*Summa Theologiae* 3a. 75. 2, 4).

Transubstantiation was thus the orthodox Roman Catholic position. It was officially set forth by the Council of Trent: "This holy Synod declares anew, that through consecration of the bread and wine there comes about a conversion of the whole substance of the bread into the substance of the body of Christ our Lord, and of the whole substance of the wine into the substance of his blood. And this conversion is by the Holy Catholic Church conveniently and properly called transubstantiation" (thirteenth session, chap. 4).

3. Reformation

The views of the Reformers concerning the Lord's Supper developed gradually and were never uniform. They agreed that the sacraments result in blessings when they are received by a person who enjoys a personal faith relationship with God. They held that the sacraments are effective only if they are partaken of in the sovereignty and freedom of the Holy Spirit. On the other hand, they denied that the Mass was a sacrifice offered to God and rejected the doctrine of transubstantiation.

Martin Luther (1483-1546) emphasized the Lord's Supper as "pure gospel," a gift from God, and a joyful communion with Christ within the fellowship of the church. He stressed the scriptural basis for the sacrament. Theologically, Luther followed Augustine, bringing out the need for faith, yet insisting that the words of Jesus, "This is my body," be taken literally. He also denounced the withholding of the cup from the common people and condemned the use of the expression "propitiatory sacrifice" for the Mass.

Luther opposed the teaching of transubstantiation, favoring instead the idea of "consubstantiation." Thus he indicated the presence of two substances, a combination of the body and blood of Christ with the bread and wine of the Communion.

In the Augsburg Confession of 1530, Philip Melanchthon affirmed "that the true body and blood of Christ are really present in the Supper of our Lord under the form of bread and wine" (article 10; Leith 71). Article 24 states that "the holy sacrament was not instituted to make provision for a sacrifice for sin—for the

sacrifice has already taken place—but to awaken faith and comfort our consciences" (*ibid.* 85).

Ulrich Zwingli (1484-1531), on the other hand, insisted on interpreting the words "this is my body" by the phrase "this signifies my body." It is difficult to determine exactly what he did believe in this matter. Though his writings contain statements that regard the Lord's Supper as a seal or pledge of what God is doing for the believer, Zwingli insisted on identifying the eating of the bread and drinking of the wine with faith in Christ and trustful reliance on His death. The elements were signs or symbols, figuratively representing spiritual truths or blessings.

John Calvin (1509-1564), the third of the great Reformation figures, refuted the idea that bread *became* the body of Christ. Neither could he fully accept Luther's idea that the body of Christ was present in the Eucharist, nor was he satisfied with Zwingli's view that the bread and wine were no more than signs. In a chapter of his *Institutes of the Christian Religion* where he argued against those who disagreed with him (4. 17), Calvin stressed the dynamic, joyful aspect of the Lord's Supper: it gave a foretaste of eternal life and was a pledge of the resurrection of the body. The bread and wine also stood for union with Christ through the work of the Spirit. Christ was in heaven and did not come down to the faithful; but by partaking of the emblems, believers were lifted to Him. All of this, Calvin admitted, was a mystery.

During the Reformation the form of the elements—wafers and white wine—was still used, as was the word "consecrate." As customs and attitudes were resistant to change, the former eucharistic practice was in many respects adapted to the new understanding of the sacrament.

The official position of the Church of England is expressed in the Thirty-nine Articles (revised 1571). Transubstantiation is "repugnant to the plain words of Scripture; the Body of Christ is given, taken, and eaten, in the

Supper, only after an heavenly and spiritual manner," by faith (Leith 276). The sacrament is not to be worshipped; it is a "Sacrament of our Redemption by Christ's death" *(ibid.).*

The Westminster Confession adopted in 1647 by the Church of Scotland postulates that the Lord's Supper is not a sacrifice, "but only a commemoration of that one offering up of himself, by himself, upon the cross, once for all, and a spiritual oblation of all possible praise to God for the same." Although "sometimes called by the names of the things they represent, to wit the body and blood of Christ; albeit, in substance and nature, they still remain truly and only bread and wine, as they were before" (Leith 225, 226).

4. Modern Era

In current discussions on the Lord's Supper, little attention is paid to historical developments of the doctrine and practice from the eighteenth century to the present. It would appear that modifications of the positions coming out of the Reformation and the Counter-Reformation have been minimal.

Regarding the Communion service, contemporary scholarship seems to be more committed to history than to theology. One of the main points at issue is the question concerning the identity of the Last Supper. Was it a Passover meal or does it conform to some other Jewish meal celebration? Also important is the dating of the Passover meal, which in the Gospel of John appears to differ from the day reported in the Synoptic Gospels. Issues of this kind have been addressed by Lietzmann, Bultmann, Jeremias, Marxsen, Patsch, and Schuermann, among others.

In 1982 the Faith and Order Commission of the World Council of Churches published a document to be submitted to the churches as a basis for further discussion of the ordinances. According to *Baptism, Eucharist and Ministry,* the Lord's Supper is a "gift which God makes to us through the power of the Holy Spirit." It is a thanksgiving to the Father and a memorial of Christ's sacrifice. It also anticipates the Parousia. Strong undertones of sacramental theology come through in the document which holds, for instance, that "the church confesses Christ's real, living and active presence in the eucharist" which is discerned by faith. Furthermore, "the sharing in one bread and the common cup . . . demonstrates and effects the oneness of the sharers with Christ and with their fellow sharers." This challenges "all kinds of injustice, racism, separation, and lack of freedom" (10-17).

5. Adventist Position

The Lord's Supper has been an essential part of SDA worship from the beginning of the movement. This may be attributed largely to the fact that the early members of the church had come out of Baptist, Congregationalist, Methodist, Presbyterian, and other churches that practiced the Lord's Supper.

One of the early records of an Adventist celebration of the Lord's Supper, dated August 18, 1848, relates that the attendees of the Sabbath conference held in Volney, New York, celebrated the Lord's Supper. Among early Adventists some favored the celebration of the Communion service once a year, because they considered it as a continuation of the Passover. As the organization developed, the Lord's Supper was celebrated once each quarter and became known as the "quarterly meeting."

The Seventh-day Adventist Church normally celebrates the Lord's Supper once each quarter, either in the Sabbath worship service or in a special service (see *SDA Church Manual* 1990, 78). The quarterly plan seems to come from the American Methodist tradition, but has been found satisfactory to most church members. Adventists feel that more frequent observance of the ordinances could possibly lead to a loss of the sacred spiritual significance of these sacred rites, reducing them to a mere formality.

Seventh-day Adventists practice open Communion, allowing all believing Christians to participate, although this has not always been so. Thus, George I. Butler, president of the General Conference from 1871 to 1874 and from 1880 to 1888, expressed opposition to open Communion (*Review and Herald,* May 27, 1873). In the 1890s Adventists changed their position regarding the closed Communion service, largely under the influence of publications by Ellen G. White.

According to the *SDA Church Manual,* "all who have committed their lives to the Saviour may participate" (1990, 80) in the Lord's Supper. This "open Communion" permits Christians from other churches to take part in an Adventist Communion service. On the topic Ellen White wrote: "Christ's example forbids exclusiveness at the Lord's Supper. It is true that open sin excludes the guilty. This the Holy Spirit plainly teaches. . . . But beyond this none are to pass judgment. God has not left it with men to say who shall present themselves on these occasions. . . .

"There may come into the company persons who are not in heart servants of truth and holiness, but who may wish to take part in the service. They should not be forbidden" (DA 656).

On the other hand, participants should examine their lives and make spiritual prepara-tion to come to the Lord's table. For this reason the *Church Manual* urges that the service be announced beforehand to allow members to "prepare their hearts and to make sure that matters are right with one another" (1990, 79). Likewise, children of church members should "learn the significance of the service by observing others participate. After receiving formal instruction in baptismal classes and making their commitment to Jesus in baptism, they are thereby prepared to partake in the service themselves" (*ibid.* 80, 81).

The *SDA Encyclopedia* points out that "throughout SDA history there has been little change in the understanding of the meaning of the Lord's Supper." The unleavened bread and unfermented grape juice always used (see *SDA Church Manual* 1990, 82) have normally been seen as symbols of the body and blood of Christ, and as reminders of Christ's passion and death. However, the Lord's Supper is more than a mere memorial meal, for Christ is present by His Holy Spirit. Participation in the Communion service by members of the body contributes to Christian growth and fellowship. The Communion service commemorates deliverance from sin, signifies corporate communion with Christ, and anticipates the Second Advent (*Seventh-day Adventists Believe* 199-203).

IV. Ellen G. White Comments

In our discussion of the ordinances we have focused our attention upon Scripture. In this section of the article we have included a number of key statements by Ellen G. White, for further study of this topic.

A. Baptism

1. Meaning of the Ordinances

"The ordinances of baptism and the Lord's supper are two monumental pillars, one within and one without the church. Upon these ordinances Christ has inscribed the name of the true God" (Ev 273).

"Baptism is a most sacred and important ordinance, and there should be a thorough understanding as to its meaning. It means repentance for sin, and the entrance upon a new life in Christ Jesus. There should be no undue haste to receive the ordinance. Let both parents and children count the cost. In consenting to the baptism of their children, parents sacredly pledge themselves to be faithful stewards over these children, to guide them in their character building. They pledge themselves to guard with special interest these lambs of the flock, that they may not dishonor the faith they profess" (6T 93).

2. The Necessity

"Christ made baptism the entrance to His spiritual kingdom. He made this a positive condition with which all must comply who wish to be acknowledged as under the authority of the Father, the Son, and the Holy Ghost. Those who receive the ordinance of baptism thereby make a public declaration that they have renounced the world, and have become members of the royal family, children of the heavenly King" (AG 143).

3. Step in Conversion

"The steps in conversion, plainly marked out, are repentance, faith in Christ as the world's Redeemer, faith in His death, burial, and resurrection, shown by baptism, and His ascension on high to plead in the sinner's behalf" (YI Feb. 1, 1874).

4. Repentance Required

Addressing the youth, Ellen White stated, "Repent ye and be converted, that your sins may be blotted out. There is no time for you to waste. Heaven and immortal life are valuable treasures that cannot be obtained without any effort on your part. No matter how faultless may have been your lives, as sinners you have steps to take. You are required to repent, believe, and be baptized. Christ was wholly righteous; yet He, the Saviour of the world, gave man an example by Himself taking the steps which He requires the sinner to take to become a child of God, and heir of heaven" (4T 40).

"John the Baptist came preaching truth, and by his preaching sinners were convicted and converted. These would go into the kingdom of heaven before the ones who in self-righteousness resisted the solemn warning. The publicans and harlots were ignorant, but these learned men knew the way of truth. Yet they refused to walk in the path which leads to the Paradise of God. The truth that should have been to them a savor of life unto life became a savor of death unto death. Open sinners who loathed themselves had received baptism at the hands of John; but these teachers were hypocrites" (COL 277).

5. Christ Is Example

"In the submission of Christ to the ordinance of baptism, He shows the sinner one of the important steps in true conversion. Christ had no sins to wash away, but in consenting to become a substitute for man, the sins of guilty man were imputed to Him. 'For he hath made him to be sin for us, who knew no sin; that we might be made the righteousness of God in him.' While God accepts Christ as the sinner's substitute, He gives the sinner a chance, with Christ's divine power to help him, to stand the test which Adam failed to endure" (YI February 1874).

6. A Pledge

"All who profess to be followers of Jesus Christ, in taking this step [in baptism] pledge themselves to walk even as He walked. Yet the course many pursue who make high profession shows that their lives are far from being in conformity to that of the great Pattern. They shape their course to meet their own imperfect standard. They do not imitate the self-denial of Christ, or His life of sacrifice for the good of others" (RH Aug. 16, 1881).

"Provision has been made that when man repents and takes the steps requisite in conversion, he shall be forgiven. When he is baptized in the name of the Father, the Son, and the Holy Ghost, these three great powers are pledged to work in his behalf. And man on his part, as he goes down into the water, to be buried in the likeness of Christ's death and raised in the likeness of His resurrection, pledges himself to worship the true and living God, to come out of the world and be separate, to keep the law of Jehovah" (1SAT 321).

7. Preparation of Candidates

"Before baptism there should be a thorough inquiry as to the experience of the candidates. Let this inquiry be made, not in a cold and distant way, but kindly, tenderly, pointing the new converts to the Lamb of God that taketh away the sin of the world. Bring the requirements of the gospel to bear upon the candidates for baptism" (6T 95, 96).

"The preparation for baptism is a matter that needs to be carefully considered. The new converts to the truth should be faithfully instructed in the plain 'Thus saith the Lord.' The Word of the Lord is to be read and explained to them point by point" (Ev 308).

8. Parental Responsibility

"After faithful labor, if you are satisfied that your children understand the meaning of conversion and baptism, and are truly converted, let them be baptized. But, I repeat, first of all prepare yourselves to act as faithful shepherds in guiding their inexperienced feet in the narrow way of obedience. God must work in the parents that they may give to their children a right example, in love, courtesy, and Christian humility, and in an entire giving up of self to Christ. If you consent to the baptism of your children and then leave them to do as they choose, feeling no special duty to keep their feet in the straight path, you yourselves are responsible if they lose faith and courage and interest in the truth" (6T 94, 95).

B. Lord's Supper and Ordinance of Foot Washing

1. Thankful Observance

"The ceremony of foot washing and the Lord's Supper, in its simplicity and spirituality, is to be observed with true solemnity, and with hearts full of thankfulness. Its participants are not to exhaust their powers of thought or their physical powers on outward forms and ceremonies. All the vigor of mind and the healthfulness of body are to be fresh to engage in the work of the gospel, to lead souls from sin into the upward path of holiness. In this ordinance is presented the necessity of economizing all the thoughts, all the energies, all the affections and faculties, to wear Christ's yoke, to come into partnership with Him in seeking to save the souls

that are perishing without God and without hope in the world" (RH June 21, 1898).

2. The Passover

"The Passover pointed backward to the deliverance of the children of Israel, and was also typical, pointing forward to Christ, the Lamb of God, slain for the redemption of fallen man. The blood sprinkled upon the doorposts prefigured the atoning blood of Christ, and also the continual dependence of sinful man upon the merits of that blood for safety from the power of Satan, and for final redemption. Christ ate the Passover Supper with His disciples just before His crucifixion, and the same night, instituted the ordinance of the Lord's Supper, to be observed in commemoration of His death. The Passover had been observed to commemorate the deliverance of the children of Israel from Egypt. It had been both commemorative and typical. The type had reached the antitype when Christ, the lamb of God without blemish, died upon the cross. He left an ordinance to commemorate the events of His crucifixion" (1SP 201).

3. Transition

"On the fourteenth day of the month, at even, the Passover was celebrated, its solemn, impressive ceremonies commemorating the deliverance from bondage in Egypt, and pointing forward to the sacrifice that should deliver from the bondage of sin. When the Saviour yielded up His life on Calvary, the significance of the Passover ceased, and the ordinance of the Lord's Supper was instituted as a memorial of the same event of which the Passover had been a type" (PP 539).

4. Meaning and Purpose

"Here our Saviour instituted the Lord's Supper, to be often celebrated, to keep fresh in the memory of His followers the solemn scenes of His betrayal and crucifixion for the sins of the world. He would have His followers realize their continual dependence upon His blood for salvation" (ST Mar. 25, 1880).

5. Administration of the Ordinances

"Every ordinance of the church should be so conducted as to be uplifting in its influence. Nothing is to be made common or cheap, or placed on a level with common things. Our churches need to be educated to greater respect and reverence for the sacred service of God. As ministers conduct the services connected with God's worship, so they are educating and training the people. Little acts that educate and train and discipline the soul for eternity are of vast consequence in the uplifting and sanctifying of the church" (6T 97).

6. The Elements

"The broken bread and pure juice of the grape are to represent the broken body and spilled blood of the Son of God. Bread that is leavened must not come on the Communion table; unleavened bread is the only correct representation of the Lord's Supper. Nothing fermented is to be used. Only the pure fruit of the vine and the unleavened bread are to be used" (RH June 7, 1898).

"The broken bread was a symbol of Christ's broken body, given for the salvation of the world. The wine was a symbol of His blood, shed for the cleansing of the sins of all those who should come unto Him for pardon, and receive Him as their Saviour" (ST Mar. 25, 1880).

7. Exclusiveness Forbidden

"Christ's example forbids exclusiveness at the Lord's supper. It is true that open sin excludes the guilty. This the Holy Spirit plainly teaches. But beyond this none are to pass judgment. God has not left it with men to say who shall present themselves on these occasions. For who can read the heart? Who can distinguish the tares from the wheat?" (Ev 277).

8. Perversion of the Ordinances

"The Corinthians were departing widely from the simplicity of the faith and the harmony of the church. They continued to assemble for worship, but with hearts that were estranged from one another. They had perverted the true meaning of the Lord's Supper, patterning [it] in a great degree after idolatrous feasts. They came together to celebrate the sufferings and death of Christ, but turned the occasion into a period of feasting and selfish enjoyment" (SLP 170).

9. The Ordinance of Foot Washing—Its Purpose

"The object of this service is to call to mind the humility of our Lord, and the lessons He has given in washing the feet of His disciples. There is in man a disposition to esteem himself more highly than his brother, to work for himself, to serve himself, to seek the highest place; and often evil surmisings and bitterness of spirit spring up over mere trifles. This ordinance preceding the Lord's Supper is to clear away these misunderstandings, to bring man out of this selfishness, down from his stilts of self-exaltation, to the humility of spirit that will lead him to wash his brother's feet. It is not in God's plan that this should be deferred because some are considered unworthy to engage in it. The Lord washed the feet of Judas. He did not refuse him a place at the table, although He knew that he would leave that table to act his part in the betrayal of his Lord. It is not possible for human beings to tell who is worthy, and who is not. They cannot read the secrets of the soul. It is not for them to say, I will not attend the ordinance if such a one is present to act a part. Nor has God left it to man to say who shall present themselves on these occasions" (RH May 31, 1898).

"Christ gave His disciples to understand that the washing of their feet did not cleanse away their sin, but that the cleansing of their heart was tested in this humble service. If the heart was cleansed, this act was all that was essential to reveal the fact. He had washed the feet of Judas; but He said, 'Ye are not all clean.' Judas brought a traitor's heart to this scene, and Christ revealed to all that He knew him to be the betrayer of his Lord, and that the washing of his feet was not an ordinance to cleanse the soul from its moral defilement" (*ibid.*, June 14, 1898).

"'If I then, your Lord and Master, have washed your feet; ye also ought to wash one another's feet. For I have given you an example, that ye should do as I have done to you.' Here is the object lesson: 'Ye also ought to wash one another's feet.' 'Verily, verily, I say unto you, The servant is not greater than his lord; neither he that is sent greater than he that sent him. If ye know these things, happy are ye if ye do them.' This ordinance is not to be treated in a mechanical way as a form. Its real object is to teach humility" (*ibid.*).

10. Foot Washing—Not to Be Deferred

"The ordinance of foot washing is not to be deferred because there are some professed believers who are not cleansed from their sins. Christ knew the heart of Judas, yet He washed his feet" (*ibid.*).

V. Literature

Bacchiocchi, Samuele. *Wine in the Bible: A Biblical Study on the Use of Alcoholic Beverages.* Berrien Springs, Mich.: Biblical Perspectives, 1989.

Baptism, Eucharist and Ministry. Faith and Order Paper No. 111. Geneva: World Council of Churches, 1982.

Barclay, W. *The Lord's Supper.* Philadelphia: Westminster Press, 1967.

Barth, Karl. *The Teaching of the Church Regarding Baptism.* London: SCM, 1948.

Biblisches Forschungskomitee der Euro-Afrika-Division. *Abendmahl und Fusswaschung.* Hamburg: Saatkorn Verlag, 1991.

Brown, Henry. F. *Baptism Through the Centuries.* Mountain View, Calif.: Pacific Press, 1965.

Cullmann, Oscar. *Baptism in the New Testament.* Chicago: Henry Regnery, 1950.

Dinkler, Erich. "Taufe im Urchristentum." In *Die Religion in Geschichte und Gegenwart,* 3rd ed. Tübingen: J.C.B. Mohr (Paul Siebeck), 1957-1965. Vol. 6, pp. 627-637.

Farag, Wadie. "Religious Foot Washing in Doctrine and Practice With Special Reference to Christianity." Ph.D. dissertation, Dropsie University, 1970.

Ferris, Roger. "The Ordinances of Foot Washing and the Lord's Supper in the Seventh-day Adventist Denomination." Seventh-day Adventist Theological Seminary, Washington, D.C., 1957.

Graybill, Ron. "Foot Washing in Early Adventism." *Review and Herald,* May 22, 1975.

————. "Foot Washing Becomes an Established Practice." *Review and Herald,* May 29, 1975.

Hastings, James, ed. "Feet-washing." *Encyclopaedia of Religion and Ethics.* 13 vols. Edinburgh: T. and T. Clark, 1908-1926.

Higgins, A.J.B. *The Lord's Supper in the New Testament.* London: SCM Press, 1952.

International Standard Bible Encyclopedia. 4 vols. Rev. ed. Grand Rapids: Eerdmans, 1979-1988.

Jeremias, Joachim. *Infant Baptism in the First Four Centuries.* Trans. David Cairns. Philadelphia: Westminster Press, 1960.

————. *The Eucharistic Words of Jesus.* Trans. Norman Perrin. 3rd German ed. by Norman Perrin. New York: Charles Scribner and Sons, 1966.

Johnsson, W. G. *Clean! The Meaning of Christian Baptism.* Nashville: Southern Pub. Assn., 1980.

Kodell, Jerome. *The Eucharist in the New Testament.* Wilmington, Del.: Michael Glazier, 1988.

Leith, John H. *Creeds of the Churches.* Atlanta: John Knox Press, 1973.

Lehmann, Helmut T., ed. *Meaning and Practice of the Lord's Supper.* Philadelphia: Mühlenberg Press, 1961.

Lynch, W. E. "The Eucharist a Covenant Meal" in *Contemporary New Testament Studies.* Ed. M. Rosalie Ryan. Collegeville, Minn.: Liturgical Press, 1965.

Morgan, James. *The Importance of Tertullian.* London: Kegan Paul, Trench, Trubner, 1928.

Morris, Colin. "An Examination of the Ordinances of Feet Washing Noting Groups That Have Practiced It Since the Reformation." Berrien Springs, Mich.: Andrews University Press, 1972.

New Schaff-Herzog Encyclopedia of Religious Knowledge. 13 vols. New York: Funk and Wagnalls, 1909.

Oestreich, Bernhard. "Die theologische Deutung der Fusswaschung in der Gemeinschaft der Siebenten-Tags-Adventisten." In *Abendmahl und Fusswaschung,* Biblisches Forschungskomitee der Euro-Afrika-Division. Hamburg: Saatkorn Verlag, 1991. Pp. 173-210.

Olsen, V. Norskov. "How the Doctrine of Baptism Changed." *Ministry,* July 1978.

———. "The Recovery of Adult Baptism." *Ministry,* September 1978.

"On Baptism." *Review and Herald,* Apr. 2, 1908.

Reumann, John. *The Supper of the Lord.* Philadelphia: Fortress, 1984.

Seventh-day Adventists Believe . . . A Biblical Exposition of 27 Fundamental Doctrines. Washington, D.C.: Ministerial Association, General Conference of Seventh-day Adventists, 1988.

Seventh-day Adventist Church Manual. Rev. ed. General Conference of Seventh-day Adventists, 1990.

Snook, B. F. *Christian Baptism.* Battle Creek, Mich.: Steam Press of the Review and Herald Office, 1861.

Thomas, John Christopher. *Footwashing in John 13 and the Johannine Community.* Sheffield, Eng.: JSOT Press, 1991.

Waggoner, E. J. *Thoughts on Baptism.* Battle Creek, Mich.: Seventh-day Adventist Pub. Assn., 1891.

Spiritual Gifts

George E. Rice

Introduction

Spiritual gifts figure prominently in the writings of the apostle Paul. He not only lists some of them, but also clearly delineates their function: to build up the church. The gifts were not for personal enjoyment or aggrandizement, but for the good of the body. Since these gifts existed in the early church, one could say that the Christian community was *charismatic,* though not in the sense usually given to the word today.

Paul taught that the gifts—including prophecy, teaching, apostleship, evangelism, speaking in tongues, and working of miracles—were to be exercised by Christians from all walks of life. From his letter to the Corinthians it is evident that some misused them, especially that of speaking in tongues.

While in some quarters great significance is attached to speaking in tongues, the NT makes it clear that other gifts are more important to the well-being of the church. Paul recommends the gift of prophecy as the most desirable. Therefore, a major portion of this article is given to a discussion of this gift.

A prophet is first of all one who speaks God's message. A secondary aspect of the prophetic task is to predict the future. The work of writing prophets may be included in the biblical canon. The work of oral prophets is no less prophetic, even if it is not written. In any case, the messages spoken or written by a prophet must harmonize with all of Scripture and serve to warn the world and edify believers.

From OT times there have been promises of special manifestations of the prophetic gift in the "last days." In this light, a study of Ellen G. White's exercise of the prophetic gift is undertaken.

I. OT Examples of Spiritual Gifts
   A. Prophecy
      1. Oral Prophecy
      2. Written Prophecy
   B. Miracles and Healings
   C. Wisdom and Knowledge
II. NT Doctrine of Spiritual Gifts
   A. Definition of Terms
   B. God-given Gifts
   C. Gifts Identified and Ranked
      1. Gifts Identified
      2. Gifts Ranked
      3. Nature of Each Gift
      4. Nature of Tongues
   D. Permanence of the Gifts
   E. Purpose of the Gifts
   F. Conditions for the Gifts
III. Counterfeit Gifts
   A. Prophecy
   B. Miracles
   C. Tongues
IV. The Prophetic Gift
   A. Definition of Terms
   B. The Prophetic Call
   C. Receiving and Communicating the Messages
      1. Visions
      2. Dreams
      3. The Word of the Lord
      4. Research Model
      5. Communicating the Message
      6. Illumination
V. Prophecy and the Canon
   A. Oral Prophecy
      1. Confirmatory Messages
      2. Sanctuary Singers
      3. Sons of the Prophets
   B. Written Prophecy

I. OT Examples of Spiritual Gifts

A thoughtful reading of the OT will show that the *charismata* (spiritual gifts) listed in the NT were also given to God's people before Pentecost. The only exceptions were the gifts of tongues and the interpretation of tongues.

A. Prophecy

Prophecy is the most prominent spiritual gift in the OT. God had told the people of Israel, "Hear my words: If there is a prophet among you, I the Lord make myself known to him in a vision, I speak with him in a dream" (Num. 12:6). The OT record abounds with the words and deeds of men and women who were given the prophetic gift. Although two broad categories of prophecy can be identified, some prophetic activity cannot readily be placed into one or two convenient categories. The following categorization—oral and written— is suggested as one approach to understanding the prophetic gift in the OT.

1. Oral Prophecy

Chronologically, oral prophecy predates the first written books of the OT canon. Before the Flood, God communicated with the descendants of Adam through prophets such as Enoch and Noah. Following the Flood, He chose prophets such as Elijah and Elisha.

611

Down through OT history God continued to communicate with His people through oral prophecy (see V. A).

2. Written Prophecy

The most ancient written prophecy we know is that of Moses. Human instruments were chosen by God and inspired by the Holy Spirit to communicate the counsel and purposes of God through written messages to His people. The prophets who fit into this category can be subdivided into two groups: (1) canonical and (2) noncanonical.

Canonical prophets are those whose writings are preserved in the Scriptures. Most of these are known by name; some are not. From Moses to Malachi, the works of the canonical prophets span the pages of the OT. Within these pages we become aware of the work of a second group of writing prophets—noncanonical prophets. Although their writings are not preserved in the Scriptures, their messages bore the authority of God. More will be said later about these two categories of written prophecy (see V. B).

B. Miracles and Healings

The OT abounds with accounts of God's breaking into human history and performing the miraculous. Throughout the years of desert wandering, Israel continually witnessed miracles. In the majority of instances, however, Moses functioned as the herald of the coming display of divine power, admonishing the people to behold the marvelous workings of God. Only on the few occasions when God used Moses as His instrument, as when fresh water was brought out of the rock, do we see the gift of miracles in his ministry.

Elijah was the herald of the three and one-half years of drought. God obviously informed Elijah of what He was about to do, and Elijah then informed Ahab (1 Kings 17:1-7). Again, at the word of the Lord, Elijah informed Ahab that rain was about to come; he prayed and the rain came (1 Kings 18:41-46). James, however, presents the whole experience as though

Elijah possessed the gift of miracles: "Elijah was a man of like nature with ourselves and he prayed fervently that it might not rain, and for three years and six months it did not rain on the earth. Then he prayed again and the heaven gave rain, and the earth brought forth its fruit" (James 5:17, 18).

However, the experiences of Elijah during the drought seem more like the gift of miracles. As the widow of Zarephath followed the instruction of Elijah, she had enough meal and oil to feed the prophet, herself, and her son throughout the drought (1 Kings 17:8-16). When the widow's son died, Elijah raised him to life (verses 17-24). At the word of Elijah 102 soldiers from Ahaziah were consumed by fire (2 Kings 1:9-14).

Upon receiving a double portion of Elijah's Spirit, Elisha not only possessed the prophetic gift, he also was given the gifts of miracles and healing. He turned bad water into wholesome water with the use of a little salt (2 Kings 2:19-22); multiplied oil for a grieving widow so she could pay her debts (2 Kings 4:1-7); raised the dead (verses 32-37); purged a pot of pottage from the poison of wild gourds by the use of meal (verses 38-41); multiplied 20 loaves of barley to feed 100 men (verses 42-44); cured Naaman of leprosy (2 Kings 5:8-14); and caused an axhead to float upon water (2 Kings 6:1-7).

C. Wisdom and Knowledge

The spiritual gift of knowledge exhibited in skillful craftsmanship was given to Bezalel of the tribe of Judah, Oholiab of the tribe of Dan, and others who worked under their direction in the construction of the tent tabernacle. God said to Moses, "See, I have called by name Bezalel . . . of the tribe of Judah: and I have filled him with the Spirit of God, with ability and intelligence, with knowledge and all craftsmanship. . . . And behold, I have appointed with him Oholiab . . . of the tribe of Dan; and I have given to all able men ability, that they may make all that I have commanded you" (Ex. 31:1-6).

The OT contains other outstanding examples of the gifts of wisdom and knowledge. Pharaoh recognized these gifts in Joseph when he said, " 'Can we find such a man as this, in whom is the Spirit of God?' So Pharaoh said to Joseph, 'Since God has shown you all this, there is none so discreet and wise as you are' " (Gen. 41:38, 39). The Scripture says of Daniel and his three friends, "As for these four youths, God gave them learning and skill in all letters and wisdom; and Daniel had understanding in all visions and dreams" (Dan. 1:17).

The gift of wisdom was also given for leadership. Joshua was "full of the spirit of wisdom, for Moses had laid his hands upon him;

so the people of Israel obeyed him" (Deut. 34:9). Wisdom for leadership was also given to the judges (Judges 2:16, 18; 11:29) and David (1 Sam. 16:13).

Illustrations of other *charismata* can be found throughout the OT. Solomon, for example, asked for the gift of discernment that he might judge the people wisely, "Give thy servant therefore an understanding mind to govern thy people, that I may discern between good and evil" (1 Kings 3:9). God granted his wish (verses 11, 12). The gifts of mercy and hospitality were given to the widow in Zarephath (1 Kings 17:8-16) and to the woman in Shunem (2 Kings 4:8-10, 21, 32).

II. NT Doctrine of Spiritual Gifts

The NT introduces and develops spiritual gifts as an endowment from Christ and imparted by the Holy Spirit. From what is presented there, we are able to identify the working of the Holy Spirit and the presence of His gifts in the OT. To begin a study of these gifts in the NT, it is necessary to define three terms used by NT writers.

A. Definition of Terms

Three words are used in the NT for the presence/gift of the Holy Spirit and the subsequent gifts that He dispenses to Christians. *Charis* (grace, favor) is the root of the word that Paul prefers for spiritual gifts: *charismata.* At its simplest level, it means "grace-gift." Except for its appearance in 1 Peter 4:10, it is used only by Paul (16 times), but not exclusively for spiritual gifts (e.g., Rom. 5:15, 16; 6:23; 11:29; 2 Cor. 1:11).

Pneumatikos (an adjective, "spiritual"), like *charismata,* is used almost exclusively by Paul (23 times), the exception being 1 Peter 2:5 where it appears twice. In 1 Corinthians 12:1 and 14:1 this adjective appears in the neuter gender and is used as a noun ("spiritual things" or "spiritual gifts"). Paul launches into his discussion of spiritual gifts by using *pneumatikos,* "Now concerning spiritual gifts, brethren, I do not want you to

be uninformed" (1 Cor. 12:1).

It is thought that *pneumatikos* was possibly the term used by the Corinthians to describe their experience in the Spirit *(pneuma)* in a letter addressed to Paul seeking counsel on spiritual gifts. Schatzmann (101) suggests that the term was chosen by the Corinthians because it expressed a certain spiritual superiority, and that Paul, having used it in verse 1, immediately shifts to *charismata* to underline their error.

The third term, *dōrea* (gift, used 11 times), is not used for spiritual gifts; however, its use by Luke (four times in Acts) is of interest. In each instance, *dōrea* is used for the reception of the Holy Spirit as a gift. Evidently when the Spirit is present in the life, *charismata* follow, according to 1 Corinthians 12.

Luke uses *dōrea* first in Acts 2:38, where the Holy Spirit is promised as a gift to those who repent and are baptized in the name of Jesus. In Acts 8:17-20 new believers at Samaria received the Holy Spirit when Peter and John laid their hands upon them. Seeing this, Simon wanted to buy the power by which he could endue whomsoever he wished with the Holy Spirit by the laying on of his hands. Peter replied, "Your silver perish with you, because you thought you could obtain the gift *[dōrea]* of God with money!" Third, in Acts 10:44-46, when Cornelius and his family believed the gospel, they received the gift *(dōrea)* of the Holy Spirit, which enabled them to speak in another language(s). Finally, in Acts 11:15-17, when reporting the conversion of Cornelius and his family to church leaders, Peter said that God had given to the Gentiles the same gift *(dōrea)* that had been given to the Jewish believers at the beginning.

B. God-given Gifts

Paul is unequivocal that spiritual gifts originate with the Father and the Son (Eph. 4:8, 11) and are apportioned to each individual as the Holy Spirit chooses (1 Cor. 12:11). In addition to this, the Spirit of God who understands the thoughts of God is given to Christians that they may understand and appreciate the gifts that are bestowed by Him (1 Cor. 2:10-13). Also, the Spirit is given by the Father to those who ask Him (Luke 11:13).

The experience of the Corinthian believers indicates that God intends all the gifts to be present and operative among His people. Paul points out that the "testimony of Christ" (the spirit of prophecy, Rev. 19:10) had been confirmed among them, thus there was no lack in spiritual gifts (1 Cor. 1:6, 7, see X. C for further discussion of this passage). Later (1 Cor. 14:1) Paul encouraged them to earnestly desire spiritual gifts *(pneumatikos),* especially prophecy. Twice Paul admonished Timothy not to neglect the gift that, through the laying on of hands, had been given him by God (1 Tim. 4:14; 2 Tim. 1:6).

According to the record in the Synoptic Gospels, the apostles possessed certain spiritual gifts long before Pentecost, thus giving evidence that they had been consecrated by the Holy Spirit and inaugurated into their public work. Luke 9:1 states that Jesus "gave them power and authority over all demons and to cure diseases" as He prepared them for their first field experience. In Matthew 10:8 He charged them to "heal the sick, raise the dead, cleanse lepers, cast out demons."

Having already been inaugurated by the Holy Spirit for public ministry (Luke 9:1) and empowered to heal the sick, raise the dead, cleanse lepers, and cast out demons (Matt. 10:8), the apostles received a deeper draft of the Spirit again when Jesus, during a post-resurrection appearance, breathed on them and said, "Receive the Holy Spirit" (John 20:22). The full power for world mission came later, at Pentecost (Acts 2:1-4). It was renewed again when the building in which the apostles were praying was shaken and they were all filled once more with the Holy Spirit and spoke "the word of God with boldness" (Acts 4:31). Thus the experience of the apostles provides a precedent for multiple "baptisms" of the Spirit.

The special attention given by Luke to the manifestations of the Holy Spirit at Pentecost (Acts 2:1-4), Samaria (Acts 8:14-24), Cornelius' home (Acts 10:44-48), and Ephesus (Acts 19:1-7) emphasizes two important facts. First, Jesus' commission to preach the gospel in Jerusalem, Judea, Samaria, and all the world (Acts 1:8) was realized. Second, the gift *(dōrea)* of the Spirit and the gifts *(charismata)* that He allocates are universal—being received by Jews, Samaritans, Romans, and Ephesians. Thus Luke establishes Peter's Pentecost statement as fulfilled, "For the promise [of the Spirit] is to you and to your children and to all that are far off, every one whom the Lord our God calls to him" (Acts 2:39).

C. Gifts Identified and Ranked

The apostle Paul identifies the various gifts that are given by the Holy Spirit. Two of the four passages below list individuals to whom gifts have been given for purposes of spiritual ministry.

1. Gifts Identified

1 Corinthians 12:8-10
"To one is given through the Spirit . . ."

1. Utterance of wisdom
2. Utterance of knowledge
3. Faith
4. Gifts of healing
5. Working of miracles
6. Prophecy
7. Ability to distinguish spirits
8. Various kinds of tongues

9. Interpretation of tongues

Romans 12:6-8

"Having gifts that differ according to the grace given to us . . ."

1. Prophecy
2. Service
3. Teaching
4. Exhorting
5. Contributing
6. Giving aid
7. Acts of mercy

1 Corinthians 12:28-30

"And God has appointed in the church . . ."

1. Apostles
2. Prophets
3. Teachers
4. Workers of miracles
5. Healers
6. Helpers
7. Administrators
8. Speakers in tongues
9. Interpretation of tongues

Ephesians 4:11

"And his gifts were that some should be . . ."

1. Apostles
2. Prophets
3. Evangelists
4. Pastors
5. Teachers

In 1 Corinthians 12:8-10 and Romans 12:6-8 Paul identifies spiritual gifts, while in 1 Corinthians 12:28 and Ephesians 4:11 he identifies spiritual ministries given to the church as a gift. Although the gifts listed in 1 Corinthians 12:8-10 and Romans 12:6-8 are operative within the spiritual ministries, they are not limited to these ministries, for spiritual gifts are given to all who accept Christ by the Spirit according to His will.

2. Gifts Ranked

Apostles are first in both lists of spiritual ministries, with prophets or prophecy second. Not only is the apostle first in the list, but in 1 Corinthians 12:28 Paul uses the adverb "first," which can mean first in time or first in place. If one restricts the meaning of this flexible word to those who encountered the Lord and were commissioned by Him, this gift might be considered to have ended. However, if the basic meaning of the word—one who is sent on a mission—is retained, "apostle" is equivalent to "missionary," with the first word derived from the Greek and the second from the Latin. Certainly mission—taking the good news to the world—was commanded by the Lord until the end of time (Matt. 28:18-20).

Apparently Paul did not attempt to rank the gifts by importance. In 1 Corinthians 12:8-10 he listed prophecy sixth, while in Romans 12:6-8 he placed it first. Tongues is next to last in 1 Corinthians 12 and does not appear at all in Romans 12.

There is the distinct possibility that the gifts in 1 Corinthians 12:8-10 are divided into three subgroups identified as wisdom, faith, and tongues. The gifts that belong to each group are connected by the Greek word *allos* ("another" of the same kind) while the next subgroup is identified by the word *heteros* ("another" of a different kind). Thus the utterance of wisdom and the utterance of knowledge are joined by *allos* and belong together as a subgroup. Faith begins a new subgroup, being separated from the wisdom group by the use of *heteros*. Healing, working miracles, prophecy, and distinguishing between spirits are all attached to faith by the use of the word *allos*. The gift of tongues, on the other hand, begins the third group, being separated from the faith subgroup by the use of the word *heteros,* while the interpretation of tongues is joined to tongues by *allos*.

3. Nature of Each Gift

The nature of the gift of tongues will be dealt with in some detail below and the gift of prophecy will occupy the remainder of this article, therefore the other gifts are considered briefly here.

a. Utterance of wisdom (1 Cor. 12:8). It is possible that "utterance of wisdom" is two gifts combined into one. The first is the gift of perception and understanding, with the ability to process what is perceived; the second is the gift of sharing the results in practical counsel that does not disrupt, but brings harmony and growth to those who hear.

b. Utterance of knowledge (verse 8). This gift also may consist of two parts. The first is the gift of study that penetrates the meaning of God's Word so that it becomes understandable; the second is the gift of communicating its meaning so that others may understand and be blessed.

c. Faith (verse 9). This gift claims God's

promises when the present and future hold no hope of fulfillment, and then presses ahead trusting God to work out His will.

d. Healing (verse 9). This gift brings relief from both physical and emotional suffering. God has prescribed prayer and anointing with oil as the usual method by which healing is to be sought (James 5:14, 15), but healing often is granted through prayer alone.

e. Working miracles (1 Cor. 12:10). Although generally thought of in conjunction with healing, this gift includes the ability to do anything that may be thought undoable through natural means.

f. Ability to distinguish between spirits (verse 10). This gift also is referred to as discernment. It is the gift of identifying the issues and motives that create conflicts. It also enables one to distinguish between truth and error, between true and false teachers or prophets.

g. Service (Rom. 12:7). This is the gift of performing tasks which may be unpleasant at times, to help others with a ready and cheerful spirit.

h. Teaching (verse 7). The gift of teaching and the utterance of knowledge are similar in some ways. The gift of teaching provides spiritual instruction in such a way that God's Word and will are understandable, and listeners are able to incorporate them in their lives.

i. Exhorting (verse 8). This gift comforts and encourages. It may also include the ability to focus otherwise random and vague ideas into understandable goals.

j. Contributing (verse 8). The gift of generosity includes giving systematically and cheerfully of one's means.

k. Giving aid (verse 8). This gift may refer to the giving of one's time and energy to meet human needs no matter how these present themselves.

l. Acts of mercy (verse 8). The gift to be compassionate to the needs and feelings of others, and to extend appropriate temporal and spiritual help.

4. Nature of Tongues

Of the gifts listed by Paul, tongues and prophecy engender the most discussion. Prophecy is dealt with in detail later (see IV), therefore it would be appropriate to give some attention to tongues at this point.

Many see the Delphic oracle as evidence that the tongues experience presented in 1 Corinthians 14 has its roots in Hellenistic religion. However, G. F. Hasel (47-49, 130-133) has shown that this popular comparison is under serious question as a result of recent research. It has been demonstrated that the Pythian priestess did not engage in *glossolalia* (ecstatic utterance of unintelligible speechlike sounds) when delivering her oracles.

Hasel (41-55) demonstrates further that the phrase "to speak in tongues" (*glōssa lalein*) "is never used outside the NT for what is today designated as glossolalia" or unintelligible speech. Such research makes it more and more difficult to understand "speaking in tongues" in the NT as an ecstatic, unintelligible speech.

There is no doubt that the gift of tongues in Acts 2 was *xenoglossia* (speaking in an unlearned human language). Twice Luke tells us the people heard the apostles' witness to the wonderful works of God in their own languages (verses 8, 11). In Acts 10:41-46 the Jews accompanying Peter understood Cornelius and the members of his household as they extolled God through the gift of tongues.

The apostles' gift of languages was permanent. Not only did they speak accurately the language(s) given to them, but the gift enabled them to speak their own language with a precision they did not have prior to Pentecost (AA 40).

When Paul laid his hands upon the 12 newly baptized "disciples" at Ephesus, the Holy Spirit granted them two gifts: "they spoke with tongues and prophesied" (Acts 19:6). The text does not indicate whether the experience of tongues was *xenoglossia* or *glossolalia,* but since the experience on the day of Pentecost is the criterion for identifying subsequent tongues experiences (Acts 10:44-46; 11:15-17), we may safely assume that previously unlearned human languages were spoken.

D. A. Carson (83) states that as far as Paul was concerned the gift of tongues is *xenoglossia:* "On balance, then, the evidence favors the view that Paul thought the gift of tongues was a gift of real languages, that is, languages that were cognitive, whether of men or of angels." Hasel maintains that the gift of tongues is the ability to speak in a real language, but denies that this speaking includes the language of angels. He further notes that this gift could not refer to "unintelligible speech of nonsense syllables" spoken so as to be understood only by God. Speaking in tongues is speaking in a "human language by which God's revealed 'mysteries' are made known to humankind" (Hasel 123, 126).

In both Romans 12 and 1 Corinthians 12 Paul uses the human body as a model of how the various gifts interrelate. Each gift has its place in God's plan; thus none is dispensable. If those that are thought to be least are absent, the whole body suffers (1 Cor. 12:14-26). Schatzmann (102) says, "None of the gifts of grace is worthless; and none is worth less than any other."

D. Permanence of the Gifts

Charismata are to be found in the church until Jesus comes. This is evident from three statements by Paul. First, in the introduction (1 Cor. 1:6, 7), he says that with the reception of the testimony of Christ the church was lacking none of the gifts as they waited for the "revealing of our Lord Jesus Christ" (see X. C for a study of this passage). Paul's point is clear: *charismata* will be operative among those anticipating the Second Advent, and as long as the Advent is delayed *charismata* will be present.

Second, in his great chapter on love, Paul says that our knowledge and prophecy are imperfect, but when the perfect comes the imperfect will pass away (1 Cor. 13:9, 10). That

which is perfect will be introduced at Jesus' return. Until then charismata will play their proper role in the ministry of the church.

Third, the spiritual ministries within which *charismata* function have been given to the church until all "attain to the unity of the faith and of the knowledge of the Son of God, to mature manhood, to the measure of the stature of the fullness of Christ" (Eph. 4:13). This will be realized only when Jesus appears the second time to change this "perishable nature" to "imperishable" and this "mortal nature" to "immortality" (1 Cor. 15:53).

E. Purpose of the Gifts

The NT makes it clear that *charismata* are given for the completion of the mission entrusted to the church. That mission includes introducing the gospel into new fields (Acts 1:8), proclaiming Christ with boldness (Acts 4:31), working signs and wonders to the glory of God (Acts 2:43; 5:12-16), strengthening fellowship and the spirit of community (Acts 2:44-47; 4:32-37), combating error with truth (Acts 6:10), and imparting the benefits of the various gifts for the nurturing of the saints (Rom. 1:11; 12:6-8; 1 Peter 4:10, 11).

In Ephesians 4:11-14, Paul emphasizes the gifts of spiritual ministries that God has given to the church, i.e., apostles, prophets, evangelists, pastors, and teachers. These ministries are to work together to nurture and upbuild the flock, as well as to proclaim the gospel to those outside the fold. Both clergy and laity are to participate in these ministries. As the various spiritual gifts and ministries distributed by the Spirit are employed for the salvation of souls, the church today can witness and have experiences similar to those of the early church following Pentecost. Each individual Christian is privileged to receive the Spirit's gifts in order to witness properly for Jesus; each member has the opportunity of using his or her gifts in the various ministries to upbuild the church.

Because *charismata* are given to enable the church to fulfill its mission to the world, the church of Christ is a charismatic church. Although today the word "charismatic" has become associated with ecstatic or emotional experiences during corporate and individual worship, in the NT charismatic denotes empowered for service—either individually or corporately.

F. Conditions for the Gifts

The idea of meeting certain conditions before receiving the Spirit and the gifts He dispenses causes uneasiness in some circles. But conditions are fundamental to NT teaching about spiritual gifts. For example, Peter informed his hearers that certain conditions must be met before the reception of the Holy Spirit—repentance and baptism in the name of Jesus for the remission of sin (Acts 2:38). Before the Sanhedrin he summarized the necessary conditions: the Holy Spirit is given to those who obey God (Acts 5:32).

Paul informed the Corinthians that an unspiritual person who is unable to understand and appreciate spiritual things does not receive the gifts of the Spirit (1 Cor. 2:13, 14). The jealousy and strife in the congregation at Corinth gave evidence that some among them were still of the flesh and not spiritual, thus not qualified to receive spiritual gifts.

Before Paul lists seven of the gifts (Rom. 12:6-8), he admonishes the Romans to present their bodies as living sacrifices to God, holy and acceptable, and not to be conformed to the world (verses 1, 2). Following the list of spiritual ministries, he appeals to the Ephesians to put off their old lifestyle, not to live as the Gentiles, and to be renewed and "created after the likeness of God in true righteousness and holiness" (Eph. 4:17-24). Paul admonishes Timothy to rekindle the gift that had been given to him, and reminds him that God has given to Christians the spirit of self-control (2 Tim. 1:7).

The matter of obedience raises profound questions. For example, is it possible for a Christian to live in violation of God's law and the teaching of Jesus while claiming the presence of the Holy Spirit and experiencing *charismata* (spiritual gifts)? The NT teaches that this is an impossibility (1 Cor. 2:14, 15). Therefore, when God's law is consciously disavowed and Jesus' teachings are persistently violated while spiritual gifts are claimed, the *charismata* are counterfeit gifts.

III. Counterfeit Gifts

At times people speak of the "perversion" of *charismata*. This may be misleading. Paul assures us that the Holy Spirit chooses the individual to whom a particular gift is given. "All these [gifts] are inspired by one and the same Spirit, who apportions to each one individually as he wills" (1 Cor. 12:11). It is not likely that the Spirit will dispense any gift to a person who will abuse or pervert the gift, for Paul says, "The unspiritual man does not receive the gifts of the Spirit of God, for they are folly to him, and he is not able to understand them because they are spiritually discerned" (1 Cor. 2:14). *Charismata* are given for service, not for self-gratification.

If the genuine gifts could be perverted, no doubt the perversion would be for selfish reasons. For example, selfishness motivated Simon Magus' desire to buy from Peter the power to give the Holy Spirit to whomsoever he wished (Acts 8:19). The greed for gain motivated the prophet Balaam to hire himself out to Balak, king of Moab, for the purpose of cursing Israel (Num. 22-24).

What appears at first as a perversion of *charismata* is in actuality a counterfeit of the gifts. This becomes clear if the nature of the great controversy is kept in mind. *Charismata* are given for mission and service—for the building and strengthening of the kingdom of God and for the penetration and destruction of the kingdom of Satan. It is a well-devised move on the part of the enemy to counterfeit the gifts that God has supplied to build and strengthen His church and to decimate Satan's kingdom, then use a counterfeit for his own purposes in the great controversy. Those involved with the counterfeit gifts think they have been baptized in the Holy Spirit, when it is not the Spirit of God that is operating in them. (See Great Controversy I-VI.)

A. Prophecy

As OT history reveals, there is little new in Satan's counterfeit of *charismata* in the end-time. The false prophets presented there do not pervert the genuine gift of prophecy, they are counterfeits—the devil's ploy to mislead and confuse if possible.

Israel was introduced early to the counterfeit. Balaam had been a true prophet of God, but by the time he appears in Israel's history he had lost the true gift because of the sin of greed. Continuing the pretense of being a prophet of God, he became a false prophet, a counterfeit (PP 439).

Israel was also warned, "When a prophet speaks in the name of the Lord, if the word does not come to pass or come true, that is a word which the Lord has not spoken; the prophet has spoken it presumptuously, you need not be afraid of him" (Deut. 18:22).

Many centuries later the test of a true prophet set forth in Deuteronomy became the issue in the confrontation between Jeremiah and Hananiah. Jeremiah prophesied that the Jews taken into Babylonian captivity would return to Palestine after 70 years (Jer. 25:11, 12; 29:10). Hananiah prophesied in the name of the Lord that they would return within two years (Jer. 28:3). Jeremiah told the people that if the word of the prophet who prophesied peace came to pass, they would know that God had spoken through him. Jeremiah then made a second prediction: Hananiah would die that very year (Jer. 28:9, 16). Both of Jeremiah's predictions came true: Hananiah died in the seventh month (verse 17), and the captives returned after 70 years.

But if the word of a genuine prophet does not come to pass, does that mean that he has become a false prophet, i.e., a counterfeit? Not necessarily, for God has laid out the principle of conditional prophecy (see VII).

B. Miracles

Jesus not only warned against counterfeit prophets at the end of time (Matt. 7:15-20; 24:24), but also against counterfeit miracle workers: "On that day many will say to me, 'Lord, Lord, did we not prophesy in your name, and cast out demons in your name, and do many mighty works in your name?' And then will I declare to them, 'I never knew you; depart from me, you evildoers' " (Matt. 7:22, 23).

"On that day" many who claim to have worked miracles in His name will seek entrance into the kingdom, only to be denied. These miracle workers, whom Jesus identifies as evildoers, will not have perverted the genuine gift of miracles, for as evildoers they could not possess that gift. Rather, they have played into the hands of the great deceiver; theirs are counterfeit miracles.

Paul predicted as much when he wrote to the Thessalonians, "The coming of the lawless one by the activity of Satan will be with all power and with pretended signs and wonders, and with all wicked deception for those who are to perish, because they refused to love the truth and so be saved" (2 Thess. 2:9, 10).

John points out that the preparations for Armageddon are rooted in deception. Three demonic spirits, working through their agents, counterfeit the gift of miracles, and the world leaders are deceived into an active role in the final battle between good and evil (Rev. 16:13, 14).

C. Tongues

The gift of tongues, as prophecy and miracles, has a counterfeit. The original gift on the day of Pentecost consisted of perfectly spoken human languages. Uttering sounds that cannot be identified with any human language is not a perversion of but a counterfeit of the genuine.

The emphasis placed upon tongues in the modern Pentecostal movement may be viewed as a perversion of their proper place in God's overall plan. For example, Pentecostals say that because the first manifestation of the Holy Spirit's "power was supernatural utterance in other languages," tongues must be viewed as the "normative evidence of the Pentecostal power in the lives of Christians" (Ervin 40).

But Paul asks, "Do all speak with tongues?" (1 Cor. 12:30). The use of the adverbial negative *mē* in the Greek construction of Paul's question is evidence that he knew the answer would be "no." The same apostle also says, "All these [gifts] are inspired by one and the same Spirit, who apportions to each one individually as he wills" (verse 11). To insist that all must speak in tongues before claiming baptism in the Holy Spirit is a perversion of Paul's teaching in 1 Corinthians 12 and 14, while speaking with utterances that do not compose a human language is a counterfeit.

It would also be a perversion of Paul's teaching on *charismata* to link the possession of a gift(s) with authority. The Corinthian enthusiasts may have misused the gift of tongues by setting themselves up as superior to the rest. As a result, spiritual authority, expressed in *glossolalia,* became anarchy and threatened the self-understanding of the community. Schatzmann notes, "It is safe to say that the charismatic authority of the individual believer receives (and maintains) its significance only in submission to the charismatic authority of the entire community" (99).

IV. The Prophetic Gift

The value of the prophetic gift can be appreciated only in light of its most treasured product. L. E. Froom (PFOF 4:966) explains, "The realization that the Bible, the express product of the gift of prophecy, is, next to Christ Himself and the Holy Spirit, God's best gift to man, lifts the gift of prophecy out of the realm of some strange vagary onto the highest plane in the operation of the marvelous plan of redemption."

Because a gift must have a recipient, it is necessary to ask two questions: (1) Who receives the gift of prophecy? and (2) What is the role of such persons in Christ's church?

A. Definition of Terms

Several words are translated "prophet" in the Bible. It would be helpful to identify the meaning these words convey. In the OT three words are translated "prophet." *Ḥōzeh* and *rō'eh* mean "seer" and stress the manner in which God communicates with the prophet, i.e., through visual representation. *Nābî'* is used most frequently and seems to have its roots in the idea "to announce." Thus a prophet is "an announcer" or "one who proclaims a message." An example of this function of *nābî'* appears in the case of Aaron who served as Moses' spokesperson in the court of Pharaoh (Ex. 7:1).

By combining the concepts contained in the three Hebrew words, we can say that prophecy in the OT is (1) a communication from God, which may or may not be predictive; (2) received by one who has been given the prophetic gift; and (3) to be proclaimed to a specific audience.

When the writers of the NT spoke about the messages of the prophets, usually they referred to the writers of the OT. Within the world of the NT, the Greek word *prophētēs* (prophet) not only bore the connotation of one who spoke on behalf of a god, but could refer also to a philosopher, teacher, historian, or a specialist in the sciences. Within the Christian community there were prophets also: men and women speaking on behalf of God.

B. The Prophetic Call

There is some debate whether the prophetic call and the bestowal of the prophetic gift constitutes a "prophetic office" or whether the gift is strictly functional. In any case, the Bible records various dramatic experiences connected with the call and the bestowal of the gift. For example, God spoke to Moses at the burning bush (Ex. 3; 4), Elijah placed his mantle over the shoulders of Elisha (1 Kings 19:19-21), Isaiah stood in God's presence and the burning coal from off the altar was placed upon his lips (Isa. 6), Jeremiah was informed that God had chosen him to be a prophet before he was born and had God touch his mouth (Jer. 1), Amos was recruited from among the shepherds of Tekoa (Amos 1), and Paul fell to the ground when overcome by the glory of the resurrected Christ (Acts 9:1-9).

Others are identified as prophets without any report of a spectacular, dramatic call. They appear in history, do their assigned task, and disappear. The silence does not negate the possibility of a dramatic experience when they were given the call, nor does it mean that they did not have the prophetic gift.

All true prophets, however, have one thing in common. Even though some are reluctant to assume the responsibility that God wishes to lay upon them, they bow in humble obedience before the One who calls. This attitude of submission comes from a heart that has been changed by the power of the Holy Spirit, and is reflected in the words of prophets such as Samuel, "Speak, for thy servant hears" (1 Sam. 3:10), and Isaiah, "Here I am! Send me" (Isa. 6:8).

The purpose of the prophetic gift is to provide a means of communication between God and humanity. Because God's acts in history have a significant effect on His people, God intends to keep them informed. Amos gives this assurance: "Surely the Lord God does nothing, without revealing his secret to his servants the prophets" (3:7).

The various prophetic communications recorded in the Scriptures show the functions of the gift, for example, to guide, counsel, exhort, instruct, comfort, unveil the future, reprove, warn of coming judgment, and call to revival, to mention a few. In summary, prophecy reveals the creative and redemptive acts of God as they center in Jesus. It provides a guidebook to be studied and obeyed by those who have fastened their faith upon the eternal hope.

C. Receiving and Communicating the Messages

True prophecy consists of a revelation from God and the proclamation of what has been revealed. Counterfeit prophecy always will include proclamation, but there will be no revelation that has its origin with God. Moses says, "If a prophet arises among you, or a dreamer of dreams, and gives you a sign or a wonder, and the sign or wonder which he tells you comes to pass, and if he says, 'Let us go after other gods,' . . . you shall not listen to the word of that prophet or to that dreamer of dreams" (Deut. 13:1-3). The dream, in this context, comes from a source other than God.

God affirmed to Aaron and Miriam that true prophets receive revelations from Him, saying, "Hear my words: If there is a prophet among you, I the Lord make myself known to him in a vision, I speak with him in a dream" (Num. 12:6). This statement sets forth the two most frequent means by which God communicates with a person who has been chosen to receive the prophetic gift. (See Revelation/Inspiration III, IV.)

1. Visions

The prophet in vision may see symbolic representations of events that will take place in the future, or see actual events as they happened in the past or are about to happen. A prophet can converse with God and angels; is informed about the affairs of nations, kings, and common people; and may be taken beyond time as we know it, beyond the close of the great controversy, to behold events that will take place in eternity.

The Scriptures describe physical phenomena during a vision that may be considered by some as part of an "ecstatic" experience. For example, Balaam describes being prostrated at the vision of the Almighty and hearing His words while his eyes remained open (Num. 24:3, 4, 15, 16). Daniel was left without physical strength, fell upon his face, and was in what seemed a deep sleep. He felt a hand touch him and set him upon his hands and knees. When he was commanded to stand upright, he was given strength and stood trembling, but apparently was not breathing (Dan. 10:8-11, 17). Paul was stricken by the light that flashed around him and left temporarily blind at the time of his first vision (Acts 9:3-8). John fell to the ground as though dead (Rev. 1:17).

Ellen White's physical condition while in vision was similar to that described above. These conditions have been reported in detail by numerous eyewitnesses. They include the loss of physical strength followed by supernatural strength, absence of breath, open eyes appearing to watch something in the distance, unconsciousness of surroundings, and for a time following the vision, all seeming dark. Although these physical phenomena capture the interest of people, the content of the message received from God is the real object of attention.

2. Dreams

God also informed Aaron and Miriam that He would communicate with a prophet through prophetic dreams. Messages received in dreams are not inferior to those given in visions; the difference is that they come when the prophet is asleep.

God also communicates through dreams with people who are not prophets. For example, through the symbol of an image King Nebuchadnezzar was shown in a dream the future course of human history. Daniel, a prophet of God, was given the interpretation of what Nebuchadnezzar saw in a "night vision" or dream (Dan. 2).

When asked how she knew whether God was communicating with her through a dream or if she was merely dreaming as all humans do, Ellen White said that the same angel who attended her in the dream of the night attended her during a vision of the day (A. White 1969, 7).

3. The Word of the Lord

Not all revelation comes through dreams and visions. In many places in the writings of the prophets the inspired writers refer to God's method of communication as "the word of the Lord came to me" aside from any reference to dreams or visions (cf. Jer. 1:4; Eze. 6:1; Hosea 1:1). This seems to have been primarily a revelatory audition from the Lord to the prophet.

4. Research Model

Luke outlines still another expression of true prophecy, referring to research. In the introduction of his Gospel, he claims eyewitnesses to the life and ministry of Jesus, along with ministers of the word, as his sources. There is no reference here to dreams and visions, though they are not necessarily excluded, but a clear mention of interviews, referring specifically to the fact that the things that were accomplished by Jesus "were delivered [paredosan] to us," i.e., transmitted to him (Luke 1:2).

Ellen White substantiates the dimension of research in the prophet's ministry: "God has been pleased to communicate His truth to the world by human agencies, and He Himself, by His Holy Spirit, qualified men and enabled them to do this work. He guided the mind in the selection of what to speak and what to write" (GC vi). To understand that divine inspiration includes not only dreams and visions given by the Holy Spirit, but also guidance by the Spirit in collecting information through research, should help readers accept the fact that in some instances both canonical and noncanonical inspired writers used sources in their literary productions.

5. Communicating the Message

Prophetic messages were communicated in various ways. Many were delivered orally to individuals or groups of people (2 Sam. 12:7-12; Acts 21:10-12). Some were sent by letter (Jer. 29; Rev. 2; 3; the NT Epistles are letters sent to churches or individuals by inspired writers). Through pantomime Ezekiel presented many of his messages to the captives in Babylon (Eze. 4; 5; 12, etc.).

Certain inspired writers used literary assistants in writing out the messages received from God. For example, Baruch assisted Jeremiah in recording all the instruction that the Lord had given him (Jer. 36:1-4). When the original source was destroyed by King Jehoiakim, Jeremiah dictated the messages over again to Baruch, with additions (Jer. 36:32).

Paul, too, seems to have had assistants who helped him prepare his Epistles. Tertius was the scribe for the book of Romans (Rom. 16:22). Some Epistles close with a greeting in Paul's hand, thus implying that someone assisted with the body of the letter, for example, 1 Corinthians, Colossians, 2 Thessalonians, and possibly Galatians. This may well have been the case for other Epistles also.

6. Illumination

The gift of prophecy is given for the edification of the church (1 Cor. 14:4). As the Spirit reveals messages, the prophet communicates these to the people so they will know the will of God. Recorded prophetic messages provide opportunity for numerous persons to be instructed in the will of God as it was revealed to the prophet.

Teachers and preachers who edify God's people by expounding His Word have the gift of exhortation (Rom. 12:8) or the gift of teaching (1 Cor. 12:28). As the teacher and preacher of the Word prepare their messages, the Holy Spirit enlightens their understanding. This experience is illumination, not the gift of prophecy. As the messages are delivered, the authority of each message rests in the inspired biblical passage from which it is drawn, not in anything possessed inherently by the teacher or preacher, nor in their experience of illumination. (See Interpretation II. D.)

V. Prophecy and the Canon

Because the OT and NT present such a diverse range of activities under the title of prophecy, it is difficult to assign to precise categories every instance of the prophetic activity of the Spirit reported in the Scriptures. The suggestion that prophecy may be divided into oral and written categories is only an attempt to provide two flexible categories into which the Spirit's prophetic activities may be placed. Also, embedded within the discussion of prophecy as a spiritual gift lies the question of authority and a prophet's relationship to earlier writings already accepted as canon. For the purposes of this study, it may be asked, What is the role of the prophetic gift after the canon has been closed?

A. Oral Prophecy

Oral prophecy predated the writings in the canon, existed simultaneously with the activities of the writing prophets, and is to be present among God's people until the end of time (Joel 2:28, 29). In this category are such OT prophets as Enoch and Noah before the Flood, and Elijah and Elisha after the Flood. Oral prophecy also existed during NT times as will be seen later (see VI). Lesser-known examples of oral prophecy are presented under the following broad categories.

1. Confirmatory Messages

In some instances men and women, moved by the Holy Spirit, spoke words intended to confirm faith, to comfort and bless God's people by manifesting His presence among them.

A few examples are cited here from both Testaments. The OT records the experience of the 70 elders who were chosen to assist Moses in judging the children of Israel. Following the instruction of the Lord, Moses gathered the 70 before the tent tabernacle, and "then the Lord came down in the cloud and spoke to him [Moses], and took some of the spirit that was upon him and put it upon the seventy elders; and when the spirit rested upon them, they prophesied. But they did so no more" (Num. 11:25). Two of the elders did not meet with the group, but the Spirit fell upon them and they prophesied as well (verses 26-30).

Although the Bible does not reveal what these elders said, and although they did not prophesy again, it is safe to assume that the gift of wisdom and discernment was given to them by the Spirit as they shared with Moses the responsibility of judging Israel. By permitting the 70 elders to prophesy under the power of the Spirit, God confirmed before Israel that these men had been chosen for a special work.

Israel's first king had a similar experience. He first prophesied as a sign that he had indeed been chosen by God to lead Israel (1 Sam. 10:1-13). The second time the Spirit moved upon Saul to prophesy He prevented him from taking David's life. At this time the men sent by Saul to kill David also prophesied (1 Sam. 19:18-24). Although neither Saul nor his armed men were prophets, their experiences convinced others that God was with David.

Following the death of King Saul, a group of men from Benjamin and Judah sought out David with the intent of joining him. David was willing to accept them if they had come as friends, but was not sure of their intent. "Then the Spirit came upon Amasai, chief of the thirty, and he said, 'We are yours, O David; and with you, O son of Jesse! Peace, peace to you, and peace to your helpers! For your God helps you.'" Recognizing that Amasai had been moved by the Spirit to speak these words, David accepted the men into his ranks, "and made them officers of his troops" (1 Chron. 12:18). There is no record that Amasai prophesied again; he was not a prophet.

The NT records the experiences of Elizabeth and Zechariah. Luke says that both were filled with the Holy Spirit; Elizabeth proclaimed a message from God with a loud voice and Zechariah prophesied (Luke 1:41, 67). Mary, the mother of Jesus, responded to Elizabeth's inspired statement with her beautiful hymn, "My soul magnifies the Lord" (Luke 1:46-55). There can be no doubt that Mary also spoke under inspiration. By introducing his Gospel with this trilogy of inspired statements, Luke indicates that prophecy had been restored to Israel and suggests the dawning of the Messianic age.

The OT prophet Joel foresaw the day when the prophetic gift would be given in abundance. As the Spirit of the Lord is poured out upon His people, "your sons and your daughters shall prophesy, your old men shall dream dreams, and your young men shall see visions" (Joel 2:28). Peter's application of this passage to the events of Pentecost is in harmony with the context of Joel's statement about the giving of the early rain (verse 23; see VI). The second part of Joel's statement relating to the latter rain promises to God's people a future experience similar to Pentecost.

2. Sanctuary Singers

A second category of oral prophecy may be illustrated by the sanctuary singers. Under David's direction three groups of singers were appointed to prophesy with lyres, harps, and cymbals during the sanctuary services. The sons of Asaph, who wrote many of the psalms preserved in the canonical book of Psalms, prophesied. The sons of Jeduthun prophesied under the direction of their father "with the lyre in thanksgiving and praise to the Lord." The sons of Heman, David's seer, also prophesied under the direction of their father "in the music in the house of the Lord with cymbals, harps, and lyres for the service of the house of God" (1 Chron. 25:1-8).

These singing groups were not made up of prophets, although Heman was a seer and Asaph wrote for the canonical book of Psalms. How could these singers prophesy on cue from their directors? No doubt they sang what had been written previously by those who were considered inspired. They were not prophets, but sang the inspired prophetic word to the glory of God, and thus, in that sense, they prophesied.

3. Sons of the Prophets

A third category of prophetic activity took place in the schools of the prophets founded and run by the prophet Samuel. The young men enrolled in these schools were called the sons of the prophets. Their studies centered on the law of God, instruction given by Moses, sacred history, sacred music, and poetry. In Samuel's day two such schools existed at Ramah and Kirjath-jearim (PP 593).

These schools and the sons of the prophets were in existence during the ministry of Elijah and Elisha, with schools at Bethel and Jericho (2 Kings 2:1-18; 4:1-7). A young man from among them was sent to Ahab with an oral message from God (1 Kings 20:35-43). Twice in the narrative he is referred to as a prophet (verses 38, 41). The 100 prophets that Obadiah hid in a cave from the anger of Jezebel and sustained with bread and water also may have come from among the sons of the prophets (1 Kings 18:3, 4). Although the Scriptures tell us little about these men, they were recognized as prophets and used by God to carry out His purposes.

B. Written Prophecy

Written prophecy is a message bearing the authority of God and communicated by the Holy Spirit through a chosen messenger in written form to the intended recipient(s). It can be divided into two categories: canonical and noncanonical.

1. Canonical

The canonical books of the Old and New Testaments are the authoritative voice of God speaking through His chosen instruments, the Bible writers. They present the truths that lead to eternal life, and all religious teaching must be tested by them.

2. Noncanonical

The canonical books introduce prophets whose writings were not intended for the canon. Among these in the OT are Nathan and Gad (1 Chron. 29:29) and Ahijah and Iddo (2 Chron. 9:29). Even though these prophets wrote nothing for the canon, they are identified as prophets. As such they were God's representatives and their messages bore His authority. As we will see later, Ellen White fits into this category as an end-time, writing, noncanonical prophet (see XI).

VI. Prophecy in the NT

With the opening chapter of Luke, the prophetic gift is seen in the hymns of Elizabeth, Mary, and Zechariah. All four Gospels record the prophetic ministry of John the Baptist. The prophetic gift remains operative throughout the experience of the apostolic church and manifests itself in the work of John the revelator at the close of the first century.

Twice Paul informs his readers that God has appointed prophets within the church (1 Cor. 12:28; Eph. 4:11). He goes a step further and says that the NT church was built upon the foundation of the apostles and prophets (Eph. 2:20). These prophets are NT prophets, for Paul says in Ephesians 3:4, 5 that the Spirit had revealed the mystery of

Christ to these apostles and prophets, which had not been made known to previous generations.

The Greek sentence structure of Ephesians 2:20 *(tōn apostolōn kai prophētōn)* and 3:5 *(tois hagiois apostolois autou kai prophētais)* suggests that both apostles and prophets fit into one category or are one and the same, i.e., the apostles are also prophets. However, as has been noted, there are prophets in the NT who were not apostles, for example, Agabus, Judas, Silas, and the four daughters of Philip.

Paul urges the Corinthians to seek spiritual gifts, especially that they might prophesy, because prophecy builds up the congregation by edification, encouragement, and consolation (1 Cor. 14:1-3). Only if tongues are interpreted for the benefit of the congregation is the gift of tongues equal to the gift of prophecy. So Paul says, "I want you all to speak in tongues, but even more to prophesy" (verse 5).

At this point Paul's rhetorical questions must be remembered, "Are all prophets? . . . Do all speak with tongues?" (1 Cor. 12:29, 30). Again, with the Greek adverbial negative (me) present in the question, the obvious answer is no. Therefore, although Paul wished all were

prophets and could prophesy, he knew that not all would receive the gift of prophecy.

On the basis of this understanding, the prophets of 1 Corinthians 14:29-33 fit into the category of oral prophets. They are not church members who, stirred by a sermon or hymn, wished to share a thought or two that happened to be impressed upon them. The words spoken by these prophets were to be weighed and evaluated by other prophets (hoi alloi); if accepted they would then be shared so that the message from God might be properly understood and appreciated by all.

VII. Conditional and Unconditional Prophecy

The idea that every prophecy uttered by a true prophet will come to pass, and that unfulfilled prophecy shows a prophet is false, will not stand in the presence of Scripture. The very fact that predictions made by prophets who have been proved to be true have not come to pass forces the consideration of at least two categories of prophecy: conditional and unconditional. (See Apocalyptic II. B.)

A. Unconditional Prophecy

Some prophecies in the Scriptures, by the very nature of their content, will be fulfilled regardless of the response of human beings. These include the great Messianic prophecies, the predictions of the end of human history as we know it and of the experience of sin, and predictions of the earth made new.

B. Conditional Prophecy

Prophecies that are not fulfilled may be labeled false. After all one must take into account statements such as, "When a prophet speaks in the name of the Lord, if the word does not come to pass or come true, that is a word which the Lord has not spoken; the prophet has spoken it presumptuously, you need not be afraid of him" (Deut. 18:22). Jeremiah also wrote, "As for the prophet who prophesies peace, when the word of that

prophet comes to pass, then it will be known that the Lord has truly sent the prophet" (Jer. 28:9).

On the other hand, there is in the OT canon an entire book devoted to a prophecy that was not fulfilled, but was still a genuine prophecy. Jonah came to Nineveh and cried, "Yet forty days, and Nineveh shall be overthrown" (Jonah 3:4). Based on the criteria set forth in Deuteronomy 18:22, Jonah would be considered a false prophet, for Nineveh was not destroyed within 40 days. However, Jonah was a true prophet who delivered the exact message that God intended should be given. Jonah's true prediction was not fulfilled because the people to whom it was addressed responded by repentance, proclaiming a fast and putting on sackcloth (Jonah 3:5).

The experience of Nineveh illustrates the basic principle of conditional prophecy as stated by Jeremiah: "If at any time I declare concerning a nation or a kingdom, that I will pluck up and break down and destroy it, and if that nation, concerning which I have spoken, turns from its evil, I will repent of the evil that I intended to do to it. And if at any time I declare concerning a nation or a kingdom that I will build and plant it, and if it does evil in my sight, not listening to my voice, then I will repent of the good which I had intended to do to it" (Jer. 18:7-10).

VIII. The Prophetic Gift and a Closed Canon

A genuine fear exists that if the prophetic gift extends beyond the end of the first century A.D., the authority of God's Word as it exists in the OT and NT canons will be compromised. Because of this fear many who believe the prophetic gift continues until Jesus comes see this gift as playing a minor role in the church. Some understand 1 Corinthians 14 to say that a message from a "Christian prophet" (1) is to be evaluated by the church; (2) does not bear the authority of God, i.e., it is not the Lord's command; and (3) can be either accepted or rejected. They further urge that Christian prophecy does not carry as much authority in the church as the gift of teaching, for teaching illuminates the Word of God while Christian prophecy lacks the authority of the canon.

We must be constantly on guard lest Scripture be challenged by placing other documents alongside it. In no way should there be a deemphasis of the Bible or teaching of doctrines contrary to Scripture. A careful study of the prophetic gift after the close of the canon should help Christians avoid these pitfalls.

A. Written Noncanonical Prophecy and a Closed Canon

Without question, the experience of the apostles is unique in two ways. First, they were eyewitnesses of the incarnate God. John marvels at the privilege that was given to him and his fellow apostles: "That which was from the beginning, which we have heard, which we have seen with our eyes, which we have looked upon and touched with our hands, concerning the word of life—the life was made manifest, and we saw it" (1 John 1:1, 2).

Second, the apostles were given the privilege of recording their experience under the divine inspiration of the Holy Spirit. "We . . . testify to it, and proclaim to you the eternal life which was with the Father and was made manifest to us—that which we have seen and heard we proclaim also to you. . . . And we are writing this that our joy may be complete" (verses 2-4).

The apostles' experience is not repeatable, but it is recorded for our benefit. What they heard and saw was the ultimate revelation of God (Heb. 1:1, 2), and through their record the readers of the NT canon can share in some degree their experience. The writings of the apostles, concluding with the book of Revelation, are a closed canon.

While the warning contained in Revelation 22:18, 19 prohibits adding to or deleting from the words of the prophecies found in Revelation, an important principle is established by this closing passage in the NT canon. By implication, no alteration of any canonical book is permitted. However, one should not dismiss lightly the possibility of further divine revelation.

When it is understood that written prophecy exists in two forms, canonical and noncanonical, it is possible to see that God may speak with authority to His people through the prophetic gift after the close of the canon and not compromise its position and authority. Ellen G. White, who among Seventh-day Adventists is recognized as chosen by God to receive the gift of prophecy, emphasized this when she pointed out that the Scriptures identify a number of persons who were given the prophetic gift but who had nothing to do with the writing of the Bible: "In like manner, after the close of the canon of Scripture, the Holy Spirit was still to continue its work, to enlighten, warn, and comfort the children of God" (GC viii).

B. Function of the Postcanonical Prophetic Gift

In recognition that God still speaks with authority to His people although the biblical canon is closed, it is necessary to determine the relationship between literary canonical prophecy and literary noncanonical prophecy and the function of the latter in the experience

627

of the church. Perhaps the most forceful way to present this relationship and function is to examine the attitude toward the Bible on the part of a literary noncanonical prophet and what Ellen White saw as her role in the church.

1. Exalt Scripture

Ellen White relates to the Scriptures in an entirely different manner from Joseph Smith or Mary Baker Eddy. While they hold their writings to be superior to the Bible, Ellen White gives supreme authority to God's Word. The following summarizes her position on the Bible: "In His word, God has committed to men the knowledge necessary for salvation. The Holy Scriptures are to be accepted as an authoritative, infallible revelation of His will. They are the standard of character, the revealer of doctrine, and the test of experience" (GC vii).

The Bible is identified as a chart and guidebook to heaven (1SM 15). Repeatedly in sermons and on the printed page, Ellen White held up the Word before the people with the assurance that it was the only rule of faith and practice. Emphasizing that God's Word was to be cherished and obeyed, she totally rejected the idea that the light given her through the prophetic gift was to take the place of the Bible (3SM 29).

2. Illuminate and Clarify Scripture

Although Ellen White claims inspiration of the Holy Spirit equal to that experienced by the Bible writers—"The Holy Ghost is the author of the Scriptures and of the Spirit of Prophecy" (3SM 30)—she recognizes her position as a literary noncanonical prophet. What she was inspired to write carries the authority of God, but it is (1) to take its place subservient to Scripture: "The Spirit was not given—nor can it ever be bestowed—to supersede the Bible; for the Scriptures explicitly state that the Word of God is the standard by which all teaching and experience must be tested" (GC vii); and (2) to illuminate and clarify Scripture: "Little heed is given to the Bible, and the Lord has given a lesser light to lead men and women to the greater light" (3SM 30).

Jesus told His disciples that when the Holy Spirit should come, He would lead them into a fuller understanding of all truth (John 16:13). Ellen White observes, "Yet the fact that God has revealed His will to men through His word, has not rendered needless the continued presence and guiding of the Holy Spirit. On the contrary, the Spirit was promised by our Saviour, to open the word to His servants, to illuminate and apply its teachings. And since it was the Spirit of God that inspired the Bible, it is impossible that the teaching of the Spirit should ever be contrary to that of the word" (GC vii).

3. Apply Scripture

Ellen White points out that the Scriptures abound with principles for proper Christian living, and that her testimonies, both general and personal, written under the inspiration of the Holy Spirit, are designed to call attention to these biblical principles. Her testimonies are not new revelations, but set out the plain lessons for life as presented in Scripture, that (1) errors may be corrected, (2) the right way may be seen more clearly, and (3) every person may be without excuse (3SM 31).

4. Reprove and Warn the Church

Ellen White pointed out that God regarded reproofs and warnings as an important phase of her prophetic work. She (1) continually reproved the church as well as individuals; (2) warned of errors into which they had strayed, both in belief and lifestyle; and (3) called all back to a closer relationship with God and a deeper study of His Word (1SM 46-48).

5. Protect From Doctrinal Error

Inspired by the same Spirit that inspired the Bible writers, and emphasizing the fact that Spirit-inspired writings would not contradict one another but be in perfect harmony, Ellen White further states, "The Bible must be your counselor. Study it and the testimonies God has given; for they never contradict His Word" (3SM 32). If the *"Testimonies* speak not according to this word of God, reject them. Christ and Belial cannot be united" (*ibid.* 32, 33).

Because of this agreement with the Bible, the messages of Ellen White have protected the Seventh-day Adventist Church from accepting doctrinal error and have helped to ground its members in biblical truth.

IX. Testing the Prophetic Gift

The human family has been swept into a great cosmic struggle between two spiritual powers (see III). Within this great controversy the forces of evil employ every means at their disposal to deceive people and misrepresent God, even using false prophets to achieve their goal. Jesus has warned, "false Christs and false prophets will arise and show great signs and wonders, so as to lead astray, if possible, even the elect" (Matt. 24:24). For this reason John tells the church that claims to the prophetic gift must be tested: "Beloved, do not believe every spirit, but test the spirits to see whether they are of God; for many false prophets have gone out into the world" (1 John 4:1).

Four primary tests may be applied to anyone who claims the gift of prophecy. All four must be met before the prophetic gift can be accepted as genuine.

A. "To the Law and the Testimony"

The first test compares the teaching of one who claims the spirit of prophecy with the teaching of the sacred canon. This principle was laid down by Moses as he spoke to Israel: "If a prophet arises among you, . . . and if he says, 'Let us go after other gods,' . . . you shall not listen to the voice of that prophet or to that dreamer of dreams. . . . But that prophet or that dreamer of dreams shall be put to death, because he has taught rebellion against the Lord your God" (Deut. 13:1-5). Isaiah emphasized the same principle many centuries later as he admonished Israel not to consult mediums or wizards; instead the people should go "to the teaching [*tôrāh* or law] and to the testimony!" He insisted that a source of information that did not speak

according to these had "no dawn," no light, in it (Isa. 8:20).

Because the Bible is the source of truth, the authoritative, infallible revelation of God's will, the revealer of doctrines, the standard of character, and the test of experience, what is set forth under the claim of the prophetic gift must agree with the Word. As Ellen White (GC vii) wrote, "Since it was the Spirit of God that inspired the Bible, it is impossible that the teaching of the Spirit should ever be contrary to that of the word."

Any doctrine, counsel, or prophecy that is at variance with what is presented in the Bible is to be rejected, for it does not come from the Spirit of God.

B. Prophets Known by Their Fruits

Jesus introduces the second test, "Beware of false prophets, who come to you in sheep's clothing but inwardly are ravenous wolves. . . . Thus you will know them by their fruits" (Matt. 7:15-20). The content of a prophet's message, as well as the effect of his own personal life, will testify to its origin. The lifestyle of one who has the genuine prophetic gift will be in harmony with the teachings of the Bible.

In addition, all must consider the kind of fruit produced in the lives of people who follow the teaching of a person who claims the prophetic gift. If the life of the one claiming to be a prophet and the effect of that person's teaching are in agreement with the Bible, the second test is passed.

C. Fulfilled Predictions

Although predicting the future is not the major work of a true prophet, attention must be given to predictions made. As already noted, prophecy may be either conditional or unconditional (see VII). God told Israel that when a prophet makes a prediction in the name of the Lord and the prediction does not come to pass, that prophet has spoken presumptuously (Deut. 18:21, 22). Likewise Jeremiah told King Zedekiah that when a prophet makes a prediction and it comes to pass, that prophet is a true prophet (Jer. 28:9). However, God has made provision for conditional prophecy (18:7-10).

In many prophecies conditions for fulfillment are plainly stated, but in others no conditions exist. On the basis of Jeremiah 18:7-10, it is clear that God's promises of blessings or threatenings of punishment rest upon conditions, whether stated or implied. The fulfillment of the prophecy depends upon the response to the prophetic message.

Therefore, predictions must be examined carefully, taking into account the principle of conditionality. In addition, the three other tests must be met by anyone who claims the prophetic gift.

D. Prophet Confesses Christ

As John admonishes Christians to test the spirits that lead people to speak and warns them against false prophets, he adds, "By this you know the Spirit of God: every spirit which confesses that Jesus Christ has come in the flesh is of God, and every spirit which does not confess Jesus is not of God" (1 John 4:2, 3).

This test is much broader than just claiming to believe that Jesus once lived on earth. In its fullest sense, this test encompasses everything that the Bible teaches about Jesus: that He is truly God and truly man, that He has existed from eternity, and that He is the word of God made audible. Jesus is Creator and Sustainer of heaven and earth, Source of life, and Light of all mankind. He was sinless and born of a virgin. He died an atoning death for sinners, was resurrected bodily, ascended to the right hand of the Father, ministers as High Priest in the heavenly sanctuary, and is soon

to return to earth to destroy sin forever and take His faithful people to heaven. This test is closely related to the first test. A true prophet will speak in agreement with the law and the testimony.

E. Additional Evidence of Prophetic Gift

In addition to the four major tests given above, several additional features help discriminate between the true and the false.

1. Physical Manifestations

Scripture notes at times physical phenomena in connection with revelations given by the Holy Spirit. The phenomena recorded at the time of Daniel's (Dan. 10) and Balaam's (Num. 24) experiences show certain similarities. John mentions some of these in connection with the revelations he received on the Isle of Patmos (Rev. 1; see IV. C. 1).

2. Timeliness of the Prophetic Message

Although the Bible sets forth sweeping predictions that span long periods of time, the majority of messages given to God's people in the Bible relate to their immediate situation and arrive precisely when needed for their guidance. The same is true in the post-canonical function of the gift of prophecy.

3. Certainty and Fearlessness of the Messenger

The confidence with which the true prophet speaks in the name of God helps to establish assurance among the people that God has indeed spoken. In delivering messages of rebuke, the prophet cannot be intimidated by the displeasure of the people. As God called Jeremiah to his prophetic ministry, He said, "Gird up your loins; arise, and say to them everything that I command you. Do not be dismayed by them, lest I dismay you before them. And I, behold, I make you this day a fortified city, an iron pillar, and bronze walls, against the whole land, against kings of Judah, its princes, its priests, and the people of the land. They will fight against you; but they shall not prevail against you, for I am with you, says the Lord, to deliver you" (Jer. 1:17-19).

4. Elevated Spiritual Nature of the Messages

While the messages of a true prophet may deal with the common issues of life, they will always be of a high, dignified nature and never reflect that which is cheap and vulgar, either in content or in language. Even in messages of rebuke, the prophets will draw the minds of the people to lofty spiritual principles that will build and strengthen their relationship with God.

5. Practical Nature of the Messages

In his Second Letter to Timothy, Paul stresses the practical nature of the messages sent by God and recorded in the Scriptures as "profitable for teaching, for reproof, for correction, and for training in righteousness, that the man of God may be complete, equipped for every good work" (2 Tim. 3:16, 17). Likewise, any true prophetic message will not present wild speculations, strange fantasies, or meaningless rambling.

X. End-time Manifestations of the Prophetic Gift

It is clear from the Scriptures that the prophetic gift is to be present among God's people until the end of time.

A. Evidence From Joel

Joel speaks of an abundant outpouring of God's Spirit upon His people, of young men seeing visions, old men dreaming dreams, and sons and daughters prophesying (Joel 2:28, 29). He even sets the time frame for this experience. There will be cosmic phenomena with the sun being darkened and the moon turned into blood. Disasters on earth are described cryptically as "blood and fire and columns of smoke." All of this is to precede immediately "the great and terrible day of the Lord" (verses 30, 31).

Along with other Early Christian believers, Peter viewed Christ's first coming as the last days (Heb. 1:2; 9:26; 1 Cor. 10:11; 1 Peter 1:20) and applied Joel's prophecy to the Pentecost experience (Acts 2:16-21), linking the gift of prophecy to the gift of tongues.

Joel's prophecy of the coming prophetic gift is set in the context of the early and latter rains (Joel 2:23-32). The refreshing, life-giving fall rains, which enabled the seed to sprout and take root, are called the early rain. The spring rain, which brought the grain to maturity and readiness for harvest, is called the latter rain. This phenomenon in the Palestinian agricultural cycle is a symbol of the spiritual refreshing that God gives to His people through His Spirit (Hosea 6:3). Peter, fully believing he was living in the last days, experienced the early rain. The latter rain is yet to come upon God's people at the end of time. (See Remnant/Three Angels V. E.)

B. Evidence From Jesus

Jesus said false prophets would appear, prophesy in His name, and then request admission into His kingdom; on that day He would say, "I never knew you; depart from me, you evildoers" (Matt. 7:15-23). These false prophets would be active at the end of time, showing signs and wonders and attempting to deceive the very elect (Matt. 24:24). The fact that these end-time prophets are labeled "false" suggests that the true would also be present.

C. Evidence From Paul

Paul begins 1 Corinthians with the assurance that spiritual gifts will be with the followers of Christ until the day He returns. Among these gifts is the "testimony of Christ" (to martyrion tou Christou [1 Cor. 1:6-8]). Since Paul is speaking of spiritual gifts, given by the Spirit, the "testimony" spoken of here must also be seen as a gift. Paul says that with the "testimony of Christ" the

Corinthians now lack none of the spiritual gifts.

The expression "testimony of Christ" may be understood in two ways. First, witness "to" Christ had been given among the Corinthians through the preaching of the apostle Paul. On the other hand, Christ was the source "of" the witness they had received. *Tou Christou* may be understood either as an objective genitive ("to Christ" or "about Christ" [RSV]), or as a subjective genitive ("of" or "from Christ" [KJV]). If a subjective genitive, it would parallel what John presents in Revelation. Having the gift of the "testimony of Jesus," the Corinthian Christians lacked none of the spiritual gifts.

Paul emphasizes what he says to the Corinthians by his instruction to the Ephesian church (Eph. 4:11-13). God has given to His church the gift of spiritual ministries that include apostles, prophets, evangelists, pastors, and teachers. These gifts are given to equip Christ's followers for the work of the ministry that has been given to them. This equipping continues until all have come into (1) the unity of the faith, (2) the knowledge of the Son of God, (3) full maturity, and (4) the measure of the stature of the fullness of Christ. Obviously Paul has his sights set on the day when Jesus returns, when His desire for the church will be finally realized.

D. Evidence From John

In Revelation, John confirms the biblical teaching that the prophetic gift will not only extend beyond his day, but will be manifested in the church at the end of time. Presenting a prophetic picture of the spiritual battle that already has been identified as the great controversy (see III), John links God's people with the prophetic symbol of a comely woman (Rev. 12:1, 2). The forces of evil, represented by a great red dragon, poise themselves to destroy her Child at birth, but He is caught up to the throne of God (verses 3-5).

Failing to destroy the Child, the dragon turns on the woman, attempting to destroy her throughout the centuries following the ascension of Jesus. Finally he attempts to destroy the remnant of her seed at the end of time (verses 13-17). The remnant of this woman has the testimony of Jesus (verse 17). Here, as in 1 Corinthians 1:6, the genitive is subjective, i.e., the testimony originates with Jesus. This is exactly the way "the testimony of Jesus Christ" (in referring to the Book of Revelation itself) and "testimony of Jesus" (in referring to OT Scriptures) are understood in Revelation 1:2, 9.

In Revelation 19:10 the meaning of *tēn martyrian Iēsou* is made clear. The angel says, "I am a fellow servant with you and your brethren who hold the testimony of Jesus [*tēn martyrian Iēsou*]. Worship God." And John interprets, "For the testimony of Jesus [*tēn martyrian Iēsou*] is the spirit of prophecy." John's attending angel identifies himself as a "fellow servant" with him and others "who hold the testimony of Jesus," which is "the spirit of prophecy." The fact that the terms "testimony of Jesus" and "spirit of prophecy" are synonymous with "prophet" is seen in Revelation 22:9, where the attending angel repeats his earlier statement but substitutes "prophet" for "testimony of Jesus": "I am a fellow servant with you and your brethren the prophets."

John makes it clear that the remnant that has the testimony of Jesus also has the prophetic gift.

XI. Role and Function of Ellen G. White in the Seventh-day Adventist Church

From its beginning the Seventh-day Adventist Church has accepted the biblical teaching of spiritual gifts (see XIII. E). Miracles of physical healing through prayer and the anointing of oil have been present from the very beginning of the church's existence. The gifts of teaching and administration have been apparent not only in the work of Ellen White, but in the ministries of her husband, James, and other prominent figures throughout the church's history. All of the other gifts have had an impact on the growth and development of the church in one way or another.

Emphasis here is on the prophetic gift as seen in the experience of Ellen G. White, and on the fruits of this gift as they are seen in her life and ministry, because this gift surpasses all other experiences of spiritual gifts in the church.

A. Ellen G. White

Ellen and her twin sister, Elizabeth, were born on November 26, 1827. Two of eight children, they lived on a small farm with their parents, Robert and Eunice Harmon, in Gorham, Maine. Shortly after the birth of the twins, the Harmon family moved about 12 miles east to Portland. At the age of 9 Ellen suffered a severe injury to the face by a stone thrown by a classmate. Unconscious for three weeks and not expected to live, Ellen made a slow and painful recovery. Her formal education came to an end.

In 1840, at the age of 12, Ellen gave her heart to God during a Methodist camp meeting. Two years later she was baptized by immersion in Casco Bay, Portland, Maine. In 1840 and 1842 the Harmon family attended Adventist meetings and accepted William Miller's teaching on the imminent return of Jesus. When Jesus did not return on October 22, 1844, Ellen and other Advent believers studied the Bible and prayed for light and guidance to take them through the difficult days ahead.

On one of these occasions, in December 1844, 17-year-old Ellen joined four other women for study and prayer. The Spirit of God rested upon her and she was given the first of approximately 2,000 visions that she was to receive during the next 70 years. In response to a vision shortly afterward, she began to travel from place to place with friends and relatives to share with fellow believers what had been revealed to her in the first and succeeding revelations.

In August 1846 Ellen married James White, a young Adventist preacher. A few weeks after their marriage the Whites began studying a 48-page pamphlet prepared by Joseph Bates in which the Bible teaching on the seventh-day Sabbath was set forth. Convinced by the biblical evidence, they accepted the Sabbath of the Scriptures. Six months later, on April 3, 1847, Ellen was shown in vision the law of God in the heavenly sanctuary with light around the fourth commandment.

Of the four sons born to the Whites—Henry, Edson, William, and John—only Edson and William lived to adulthood.

Through the study of the Scriptures and with guidance given through the prophetic gift, a growing, thriving body of Advent believers began to emerge out of the disappointment of October 1844. This little band of former Millerites adopted the name Seventh-day Adventist at a general meeting in 1860. On August 6, 1881, James White died in Battle Creek, Michigan. Ellen carried on her work in the United States, Europe, and Australia for 34 more years. She died at her home, Elmshaven, in St. Helena, California, on July 16, 1915, at the age of 87.

B. Ellen White's Self-understanding

As Ellen White looked back over her work, she felt that the word "prophet" did not adequately define her ministry. She preferred to be thought of as God's "messenger" for His people in the last days. Although others often referred to her as a prophet, she realized that her work embraced more than what was generally understood by that term; yet she did not seek personal honor and rewards. In addition to this, she was sensitive to the reproach brought upon the cause of Christ in her day by others who had boldly claimed the title of prophet (3SM 74).

Having been given the prophetic gift, Ellen White recognized the authority invested in her ministry as a literary, noncanonical prophet. On countless occasions, through voice and pen, she addressed leaders and laity alike with the realization that her words bore an authority from God. She was constantly aware that this authority did not rest within herself, but in the messages that God had given her to deliver. With this recognition came a sense of awe and unworthiness. (Regarding the relationship between Ellen White's writings and the sacred canon, see VIII. B.)

She saw her role as a spokesperson for God, a guide for the developing work of a church that would soon encircle the globe, and as a counselor to God's people preparing for the return of Jesus. Although she had no formal training in theology, her writings contain penetrating theological insights that unfold the meaning of Scripture passages that could otherwise be missed. This is especially true of the five books that make up the Conflict of the Ages series, which deal with the biblical record from Creation to the final destruction of sin: *Patriarchs and Prophets, Prophets and Kings, The Desire of Ages, The Acts of the Apostles,* and *The Great Controversy.*

In her role as God's messenger and through the guidance of the Holy Spirit, she saw her responsibility to take the lead in establishing: (1) church organization; (2) a global view of the total mission of the Seventh-day Adventist Church; (3) a foreign mission thrust that would carry the gospel to all the world; (4) hospitals, clinics, and medical schools; (5) health and temperance programs for both the church and the community; (6) an educational system that goes from the earliest training through graduate studies; and (7) publishing and printing establishments to put Christian literature into the hands of people.

C. The Seventh-day Adventist Church and the Role of Ellen White

One of the earliest statements in print that reflects growing recognition and support for the prophetic role given to Ellen White comes from the pen of Joseph Bates (1792-1872), one of the founders and early leaders of the Seventh-day Adventist Church. Bates had several opportunities to hear Ellen White relate the content of various visions she had received. Although he could find nothing in what he heard that was contrary to the Scriptures, he was alarmed by her claim of having received revelations from God. For some time he was unwilling to accept what he saw and heard as more than the result of her injury in childhood.

In 1847, after talking with other people who had seen Ellen White in vision and who had listened to her reports of what she saw, after witnessing for himself several occasions when she was in vision, and after conversing with Ellen herself, Bates concluded that he had seen and heard enough evidence for a decision. "I can now confidently speak for myself. I believe the work is of God, and is given to comfort and strengthen His 'scattered,' 'torn,' and 'pealed [sic] people,' since the closing up of our work for the world in October 1844" (21). Since Bates's early statement, administrators, ministers, and teachers have repeatedly expressed his thought in print.

The first published statement to come out of a general meeting of the church body appeared in the church paper, the *Review and Herald,* December 4, 1855. Joseph Bates, J. H. Waggoner, and M. E. Cornell were appointed during a business session to prepare a statement to be addressed to "the dear saints" on behalf of the conference regarding the "gifts" that had been given to the church. In a signed article, "Address of the Conference Assembled at Battle Creek, Mich., Nov. 16, 1855," Bates, Waggoner, and Cornell confessed on behalf of the whole body that the church had not fully appreciated or supported the spiritual gifts that God had given to the Sabbathkeeping Adventists. Special reference was made to "the visions." All the "saints" were called upon to render thanks to God for the spiritual gifts He had placed in the church, but especially for the gift of prophecy. In addition, all were admonished to read what had been printed from "the visions" and to be willing to submit their lives to the counsel given by God.

From 1867 on, reaffirmation of belief in spiritual gifts, and especially the gift of prophecy, has been a regular action of the world church in business session. The 1867 resolution reads as follows:

"*Resolved,* That we express our continued faith in the perpetuity of Spiritual Gifts during the gospel dispensation, and our gratitude to God that He has intimately connected the spirit of prophecy with the proclamation of the third angel's message" (RH May 28, 1867).

The fifty-fifth General Conference session, held in Indianapolis, Indiana, in July 1990, was no exception. On July 13 a resolution on the Spirit of Prophecy was introduced to the delegates and accepted by vote. It reads, in part:

"We are grateful to God not only for giving us the Holy Scriptures but also for giving us the last-day manifestation of the gift of prophecy in the life and work of Ellen G. White. Her inspired writings have been invaluable to the church throughout the world in countless ways" (AR July 26-Aug. 2, 1990).

A standing affirmation is found in the 27 fundamental beliefs of the Seventh-day Adventist Church. Belief No. 16 is a statement on spiritual gifts and ministries while No. 17 addresses "The Gift of Prophecy," and reads as follows:

"One of the gifts of the Holy Spirit is prophecy. This gift is an identifying mark of the remnant church and was manifested in the ministry of Ellen G. White. As the Lord's messenger, her writings are a continuing and authoritative source of truth which provide for the church comfort, guidance, instruction, and correction. They also make clear that the Bible is the standard by which all teaching and experience must be tested (Joel 2:28, 29; Acts 2:14-21; Heb. 1:1-3; Rev. 12:17; 19:10)" (*SDA Yearbook* 1981, 7).

D. Sources and Literary Helpers

During the 1980s attention was focused on Ellen White's use of sources, and widespread discussion followed. The fact that Ellen White quoted and paraphrased other authors in no way lessens her inspiration, nor has the Ellen G. White Estate attempted to cover up Mrs. White's practice. Indeed, in 1933 W. C. White (Ellen White's son) and D. E. Robinson (one of Ellen White's secretaries) prepared a 27-page pamphlet titled *Brief Statements Regarding the Writings of Ellen G. White,* which dealt openly with the issue of sources and literary helpers.

1. Sources

The authors noted that in the early years Ellen White was distressed over her difficulty in expressing in human language the content of the visions she received. However, she was given assurance by God that He would bestow grace upon her and give her the guidance that she needed to fulfill the responsibilities placed upon her.

"She was told that in the reading of religious books and journals, she would find precious gems of truth expressed in acceptable language, and that she would be given help from heaven to recognize these and to separate them from the rubbish of error with which she would sometimes find them associated" (White and Robinson; reprinted as a supplement to AR June 4, 1981).

In the introduction to the 1888 edition of *The Great Controversy,* Ellen White herself addressed the issue of sources: "In some cases where a historian has so grouped together events as to afford, in brief, a comprehensive view of the subject, or has summarized details in a convenient manner, his words have been quoted; but except in a few instances no specific credit has been given, since they are not quoted for the purpose of citing that writer as authority, but because his statement affords a ready and forcible presentation of the subject."

This statement has been reproduced in the introduction to the 1911 edition (xii) with two minor adjustments in wording.

It has long been known that canonical writers used both inspired and uninspired sources in their writings. As was noted earlier, Luke informs his readers about his sources of information on the life and ministry of Jesus. He clearly states that they came not from dreams and visions but from interviews with eyewitnesses and ministers of the word (Luke 1:1-4; see IV. C. 4).

The extent to which Ellen White's voluminous reading was reflected in her writings has come to be understood only in recent years. Although some have questioned her prophetic gift as a result of this knowledge, her use of sources does not present a problem to those who are aware of and understand the research model of inspiration (see IV. C. 4). In fact, the discussion over Ellen White's use of sources has enriched and broadened our understanding of inspiration. A recent study to isolate the literary sources behind *The Desire of Ages* is worthy of the attention of anyone wishing to examine this topic further. (See Veltman.)

2. Literary Helpers

Like Jeremiah and Paul (see IV. C. 5), Ellen White used literary assistants. In the early years her husband, James White, assisted her in getting letters ready to send and preparing manuscripts for publication. After James's death in 1881, W. C. White assumed this role. During those years when her literary production was the highest, her staff included several assistants. Their responsibilities ranged from typing manuscripts and letters to helping with grammar and spelling corrections. After typing Ellen White's handwritten material and making corrections in grammar and spelling, assistants would return it to Ellen White for careful reading. At this point she might add or subtract, and the material would be retyped. Only after another reading would it be ready for the press or the mail. None of the assistants was permitted to interject his or her own thoughts or concepts, as indicated in the following paragraph.

Ellen White's most trusted assistant, Marian Davis, was given responsibility for helping in book preparation. In comparing the work of her regular assistants and that of Marian Davis, Ellen White (MR 926) wrote: "My copyists you have seen. They do not change my language. It stands as I write it. Marian's work is of a different order altogether. She is my book-maker. . . . She does her work in this way. She takes my articles which are published in the papers, and pastes them in blank books. She also has a copy of all the letters I write. In preparing a chapter for a book, Marian remembers that I have written something on that special point, which may make the matter more forcible. She begins to search for this, and if when she finds it, she sees that it will make the chapter more clear, she adds it."

E. Fruit of a Life's Work

At her death in 1915 Ellen White had written more than 100,000 pages of material that appeared in the following forms: 24 books in circulation, two book manuscripts ready for publication, periodical articles exceeding 5,000, and approximately 200 tracts and pamphlets. In addition there were 6,000 typewritten letters and general manuscripts totaling approximately 35,000 pages and 2,000 handwritten letters, documents, diaries, journals, etc., which, when typed, comprise an additional 15,000 pages.

Since her death Ellen White's major books have been translated into more than 100 languages and dialects—*Steps to Christ* alone into approximately 150 languages. Additional translations of various books are constantly in preparation.

However impressive the volume of the literary production, of greater significance is the spiritual impact her writings have upon people's lives. The content of these writings—God's love expressed in the gift of His precious Son, the great controversy, the call to prepare for Jesus' return, the power of God's grace that enables victorious living, and other biblical themes exalted before the reader—has had an impact fully measured only when Jesus returns.

F. Custody of Ellen White's Writings

In 1912, at 85 years of age, Ellen White drew up a will that made provision for the care of her writings. Five men were named to act as trustees: W. C. White, her son; Clarence C. Crisler, one of her secretaries; Charles H. Jones, manager of the Pacific Press Publishing Association; Arthur G. Daniells, General Conference president; and F. M. Wilcox, editor of the church paper, the *Review and Herald.*

The will placed in their trust all copyrights, book plates in all languages, the general manuscript file, and all indexes relating to the file. She charged the trustees with the responsibility of (1) caring for all her published works and unpublished manuscripts, (2) improving the books and manuscripts, (3) securing and printing new translations, and (4) printing compilations from the letters, documents, articles, and manuscripts in the files.

The will also stipulated that the board of trustees would be both independent and self-perpetuating. Later the board was expanded to 15: seven members who serve for life and eight who hold five-year terms.

Serving under the direction of the board of trustees is a staff who carry on the daily work at the White Estate office at General Conference headquarters. These individuals research Mrs. White's writings on issues of current interest to the church and publish the results in articles for church journals, books, and documents filed at the White Estate office for the benefit of church leaders, laity, and other researchers. Staff personnel travel throughout the world field holding seminars on spiritual gifts, the Spirit of Prophecy as revealed in the life and work of Ellen White, and on topics of current interest that she addressed. Research centers are located at several sites around the world.

Utilizing modern technology, the White Estate has made available all of Ellen White's published, unpublished, and manuscript materials on CD-ROM disk.

XII. Impact of Spiritual Gifts

Spiritual gifts are the provision Jesus made for the advancement of the work that He commissioned His disciples to do after His ascension. The Holy Spirit, the Comforter, would come in Jesus' name to teach His followers by guiding them into further truth, to bring to remembrance the instruction given by Jesus, to empower them for their task, and to bestow gifts according to His will.

The followers of Jesus today are to seek these gifts just as earnestly as the Corinthians sought for them at Paul's urging (1 Cor. 14:1). These gifts, under the ministry of the Holy Spirit, will (1) equip church members for the work of ministry including winning people to Jesus, (2) build up the body of Christ, (3) lead into the unity of faith and knowledge of the Son of God, (4) develop spiritual maturity in Jesus, and (5) sustain spiritual growth toward the stature of the fullness of Christ (Eph. 4:11-13).

The end product of true spiritual gifts is a healthy and energetic church. Christians among whom these gifts function properly will "no longer be children, tossed to and fro and carried about with every wind of doctrine, by the cunning of men, by their craftiness in deceitful wiles" (Eph. 4:14).

XIII. Historical Overview

At its very inception the Christian church was a charismatic community. Having called the 12 apostles to be the nucleus of the new church, Jesus "gave them power and authority over all demons and to cure diseases" (Luke 9:1). As He sent them out two by two for their field experience, He said, "Heal the sick, raise the dead, cleanse lepers, cast out demons" (Matt. 10:8). Fortified by the Spirit's power (John 20:22; Acts 2:1-4; 4:31), the apostolic church was a dynamic, Spirit-filled community in which *charismata* (spiritual gifts) enabled the early Christians to carry out the commission of their Lord (Matt. 28:19, 20). In this sense the early church was a charismatic community.

The attitude of the Christian church toward spiritual gifts has varied over the centuries, however, as has the attitude of various groups within Christianity. The first part of this historical overview looks at an early attempt to regain the gifts that were once operative in the apostolic church. In the second part, the current attitude toward spiritual gifts among several Christian bodies is examined.

A. Montanism

During the last half of the second century A.D. a small group of Christians in the Roman province of Phrygia in Asia Minor focused their attention on reclaiming the gifts of the Spirit. In 172 Montanus, a recent convert from paganism, claimed the gift of prophecy. Within a short time he was joined by two women, Priscilla and Maximilla, who also claimed the gift. They identified their movement as "the New Prophecy," but their opponents referred to it as "the Phrygian heresy." By the fourth century the movement was known as "Montanism," after its founder. This was the church's first neo-Pentecostal movement.

1. View on Spiritual Gifts

Montanists believed that spiritual gifts were not restricted to the Apostolic Era, but were intended for all who believe. Evidence for this was found in the promise that in the last days God would pour out His Spirit, and "your sons and your daughters shall prophesy, your old men shall dream dreams, and your young men shall see visions" (Joel 2:28; Acts 2:17). The prophetic gift, of course, received the greatest emphasis because of the experiences of Montanus, Priscilla, and Maximilla.

Montanism grew out of a burning desire for spiritual renewal. The goal of its early adherents was to restore the church to its primitive simplicity, to experience again the *charismata* (spiritual gifts), and to have the assurance of the presence and guidance of the Paraclete or Holy Spirit. Montanism has been identified as a reactionary movement against the corruption then creeping into the church. It also reacted against the prevailing influence of Gnosticism and paganism, laxity of discipline, a developing hierarchy, and a growing disbelief in the validity of spiritual gifts in the experience of the church.

2. History's Assessment of the New Prophecy

When a group departs from the norm in religious practices, strange stories may spring up about those who are involved, and often these stories become accepted as fact. Montanists were no exception. Stories circulated early about apparitions of Christ and the Paraclete at Montanist meetings. Trances and convulsions with mass hysteria also were reported.

A. H. Newman (1:204) suggests that this early fanaticism was natural to the soil out of which Montanism grew. Phrygians were known for their excesses in the worship of the pagan goddess Cybele. In addition to gross immorality, they were suspected of ecstatic visions, wild frenzy, and self-mutilation.

Although there were calls from within the established church to recognize the presence of the prophetic gift and to come to an understanding with the Montanists, the ecclesiastical authorities rejected such a venture and turned on the followers of Montanus as heretics.

More recently scholars have been kinder, saying the Montanists should not be viewed as intellectual heretics because they differed from their fellow Christians only in the acceptance of "new prophecy." The roots of Montanism lay not in heresy or militant apocalypticism, but in a belief that the Spirit could speak to individuals in order to bring about proper Christian discipline (Fox 409).

N. Bonwetsch (486) points out that the "New Prophecy" made no claims to reveal further truth. Its utterances supported the church's tradition, defended the resurrection of the dead, and developed a rich eschatology. The aim of the movement was preparation for the soon return of Jesus—a preparation that should govern the entire life of the Christian.

D. Wright (23, 28, 29) concludes that: (1) the condemnation of Montanism was "a frantic resourcefulness" on the part of "Catholic critics" to find fault with a movement that was irregular rather than unorthodox; (2) the reasons for the widespread condemnation and excommunication of the "New Prophecy" are nowhere precisely specified; (3) "the rejection of the movement reveals as much about developing catholicism as it does about Montanism itself"; and (4) "Montanism was at worst fanatical rather than heretical."

3. Tertullian's Defense of Spiritual Gifts

Montanism won a staunch defender when the Latin Church Father Tertullian of Carthage (c. A.D. 160-230) accepted its teaching on spiritual gifts. According to R. Baus (203), Tertullian separated Montanism from the three original prophets and its Phrygian context. He saw the mission of Montanism as "bringing Christianity and mankind in general to adult maturity through the working of the Paraclete."

Those who view Montanism as a heresy claim that abnormal ecstasy accompanied the "New Prophecy" to the point that the person possessed by the Spirit became frenzied and began to babble and utter strange sounds. Wright (21-23), however, points out that there is no evidence of glossolalia, and that Tertullian, as he discussed the experience of ecstasy, "included scarcely any suggestion of glossolalia and little that was in a popular sense ecstatic." Ecstasy, as described by

Tertullian, was produced in a normal manner during sleep when human reason entered into direct relation with God; dreams and visions resulted.

For Tertullian, the presence of *charismata* was evidence of the presence and activity of the Holy Spirit. For the ecclesiastical authorities who were busy building a hierarchy, the presence of *charismata* made it clear that Montanism's "genuinely Christian aims were distorted by an immoderate exaggeration of their real significance, and that they represented a falsification of Christian tradition" (Baus 204). Thus Montanism has come to bear the label of heresy.

4. John Wesley and Montanism

Fifteen centuries later, however, John Wesley assessed the activities of the ecclesiastical authorities who condemned Montanus as those of "rich and honourable Christians," who always have numbers and power on their side ridiculing the real faith of "one of the holiest men of the second century." Wesley viewed Montanus as stressing obedience to divine law and love for God and humankind, but placing a stronger emphasis than others on manifestations of the power that flows from being filled with the Spirit (Smith 25).

B. General Christian View

The resistance manifested by early ecclesiastical authorities to *charismata* became the position of the church during the succeeding centuries. Physical healing, however, was exempt from denunciation.

1. Roman Catholicism

In the Roman Catholic Church, miraculous healings have been reported and accepted for centuries. Worldwide, thousands have claimed healings at various shrines dedicated to the virgin Mary or one of the saints. Relics reportedly passed down from Jesus and the apostles are claimed to have strengthened the faith of people who desired healing. Although most of the reported healings take place as a result of praying to Mary or one of the saints, healings by very devout individuals have been reported. Catholics have long looked upon miracles as authenticating their teachings.

2. Protestantism

Early Protestant reformers were taunted because they could not produce miracles as evidence for the truthfulness of the reformed teachings. This, perhaps, was a major factor contributing to the idea that developed within Protestantism that *charismata* had been withdrawn at the end of the Apostolic Age.

The work of the Holy Spirit, however, was not rejected by Protestantism. Instead of being revealed through spiritual gifts, the Spirit was transforming lives. His power was seen in overcoming sinful human nature and in a demonstration of the Christian attributes of righteousness, peace, and joy. The Holy Spirit in the life of the believer resulted in moral power. As T. Smith (25) points out, Luther and Calvin (sixteenth century) were wary "of those who seem to substitute mere human emotion for the Holy Spirit's work in transforming the moral natures of men and women." The Swiss and Dutch Anabaptists, on the other hand, wanted more emphasis on outward obedience, while the Mennonites emphasized the suffering brought about by obeying Jesus. All of these early reform movements minimized *charismata*.

Following Aldersgate, John Wesley (1703-1791) was more open to the concept of supernatural expressions of the Holy Spirit. In fact, he accepted the emotionalism exhibited by many of his followers, acknowledging "that trances, healings, miracles, and other extraordinary events might occur in the lives of believers" (Smith 25). George Whitefield, Wesley's fellow evangelist, became increasingly nervous over Wesley's openness to emotional expression, feeling that these demonstrations were not the primary focus of the Spirit's work.

But John Wesley was no charismatic. He and the Puritans of his day felt that the Quakers were far too emotional and did not rely sufficiently on the Scriptures to restrain demonstrations of what they called the Holy Spirit's power. In the nineteenth century many evangelists and churches agreed with Wesley. These included Charles G. Finney, R. A. Torrey, and other "higher life" evangelists. The holiness movement flourished among American Methodists and some Friends, Congregationalists, Baptists, and German-speaking members of the Evangelical and United Brethren churches. For them, obedience and love, not emotional ecstasy, were the real evidence of the Holy Spirit's presence.

With the rise of the charismatic movement in the late twentieth century, Protestantism again has become divided over the work of the Holy Spirit. The charismatic camp focuses on spiritual gifts, the extraordinary, and the emotional, while the fundamentalist camp stresses power for holy living.

C. Holiness Movements

John Wesley fully believed Paul's teaching that while we were sinners and enemies of God Jesus died for us (Rom. 5:8-10), and thus by His grace He made provision for our forgiveness and justification by faith in Him. He also emphasized Christian perfection as a second, instantaneous work of grace, preceded and followed by gradual growth in holiness. The concept that a sinner can reach perfection is the foundation upon which the various holiness churches are built. Among those bodies that do not identify themselves as Pentecostal, the work of the Holy Spirit is seen as relating to sanctification and holy living rather than *charismata*.

1. The Methodist Episcopal Church

During the late nineteenth century in the United States, the Methodist Episcopal Church spawned several smaller holiness denominations. The origin of these separatist churches is similar: (1) a strong leader within the Methodist Episcopal Church was forced out for various reasons; (2) he formed an independent holiness group; and (3) mergers with smaller holiness groups would then produce a new organized holiness denomination.

Two of the largest holiness churches to emerge from this process were the Church of the Nazarene and the Pilgrim Holiness Church. The eastern branch of the Church of the Nazarene was called the Pentecostal Church of the Nazarene, but later dropped the word Pentecostal so it would not be confused with the tongues movement that developed in the emerging Pentecostal churches in the early twentieth century. However, the founder of the Pilgrim Holiness Church, Martin Wells Knapp, stressed the spiritual gift of divine healing.

2. Pentecostalism

The Pentecostal churches within the holiness movement give special emphasis to spiritual gifts. The Wesleyan concept that conversion must be followed by the second blessing (sanctification) was expanded by Charles Fox Parham (1873-1929) to include baptism in the Holy Spirit verified by speaking in tongues. Some historians point to Topeka, Kansas (1901), as the birthplace of the Pentecostal movement. Parham was holding revival meetings there when "Agnes Ozman became the first person in modern times to seek and receive the experience of speaking in tongues as a sign of being 'baptized with the Holy Spirit' " (Melton 43). However, the revival on Azusa Street in Los Angeles (1906) under the preaching of William J. Seymour, who had studied under Parham in Houston, Texas, is more popularly known as the birth of modern Pentecostalism.

Based upon the message of John the Baptist, "I baptize you with water for repentance, but he who is coming after me is mightier than I, . . . he will baptize you with the Holy Spirit and with fire" (Matt. 3:11), Pentecostals view their water baptism as the Spirit baptizing them into Christ, while their second baptism is Christ baptizing them into the Spirit. After baptism in the Holy Spirit, it is believed, the individual will manifest at least one of the nine gifts enumerated by Paul in 1 Corinthians 12. The spiritual gifts most frequently emphasized, however, are tongues and healing.

The gift of tongues manifests itself in two ways: *glossolalia* and *xenoglossia*. Because only a few vowels and consonants are used, *glossolalia* cannot be classified as speaking in any language; it is rather a "verbalized religious experience" (Melton 41). *Xenoglossia*, on the other hand, is speaking a genuine foreign language by one who does not know that language.

G. Wacker (933, 934) also divides this gift into two categories. The "gift of tongues" is not shared by all Christians. It edifies the church when an interpreter is present. It also expresses the longings of the heart in private prayer. The second category, the "sign of tongues," is shared by all Christians. It is a supernatural sign that the speaker has been baptized by the Holy Spirit. Traditional Pentecostals believe that all of the recorded instances of Spirit baptism in Acts were accompanied by the "sign of tongues."

The gift of healing, as carried on in public meetings by Pentecostal healers, has raised objections in the minds of many Christians—not so much in regard to the reality of the healing as concerning the form and display accompanying the healing. Many are offended by the seeming overfamiliarity with God during prayer and the loud, demanding style of the "healer." Objections are also voiced over the psychology that is used to manipulate the audience.

The Pentecostal view of church history is portrayed in the following scenario: The Christian church began its existence as a charismatic church—a church empowered for mission by the Spirit through the presence of spiritual gifts. With the development of a hierarchy and clerical corruption, the gifts faded away and the church entered into the Dark Ages. The work of Protestant reformers began the process of restoration, but their work was not complete. A complete restoration of the charismatic church, empowered for mission by the Holy Spirit, is now found in the Pentecostal movement. The "early rain" fell on the apostolic church at Pentecost; the "latter rain" is now falling in the Pentecostal experience.

D. Modern Charismatic Movement

While mainline churches after World War II remained resistant to the Pentecostal experience and the presence of spiritual gifts in the modern age, R. Quebedeaux (967) points to three factors that contributed to the beginning of charismatic renewal among them in the 1950s: (1) Pentecostal phenomena among clergy and laity, (2) activities of the Full Gospel Businessmen's Fellowship International (FGBMFI), and (3) the ecumenical ministry of David du Plessis.

1. Full Gospel Businessmen's Fellowship International

The FGBMFI was founded by a group of businessmen and professionals (1951) from the Assemblies of God Church who had become disenchanted with growing clerical domination. Through their publication, *Voice,* reports of Pentecostal experiences began circulating. As ministers and laypeople from mainline churches heard of the reports, they joined FGBMFI and shared in these experiences. "Thus FGBMFI became the chief cornerstone in the foundation for charismatic renewal" (Quebedeaux 967).

2. David du Plessis

An Assemblies of God minister, David du Plessis, was the Pentecostal observer at various ecumenical meetings. His presence as a Pentecostal spokesman in ecumenical circles contributed much to bringing respectability to the Pentecostal experience and message among non-Pentecostal clergy and laity. By the mid-1950s Pentecostalism was accepted as a third force in world Christianity.

3. Mainline Churches

The rise of the charismatic movement in Protestant mainline churches began in 1960. In that year Dennis Bennett, rector of St. Mark's Episcopal Church in Van Nuys, California, reported to his parish his charismatic experience of speaking in tongues during a private prayer meeting. When the congregation split over the issue, Bennett was moved to a dying inner city church in Seattle, Washington. There he promoted *charismata,* and the church experienced phenomenal growth. This caught the attention of the mass media, and his experience was written up in both *Time* and *Newsweek.* Bennett received public support from hundreds of mainline ministers and priests. The charismatic movement had come to the attention of mainline Protestant churches, and many were ready to respond.

The movement first penetrated Catholicism in 1967 at Duquesne University (Pittsburgh, Pennsylvania) where two professors of theology led 20 students and faculty members into a neo-Pentecostal experience. From Duquesne the movement spread to the campus of Notre Dame University (South Bend, Indiana), then to the University of Michigan.

As the movement entered mainline, middle-class churches, the typical Pentecostal style of worship became more subdued, and formal liturgy was hardly affected. The practice of glossolalia, healing, and prophecy became the central feature of the midweek meetings.

Theologically, charismatic renewal emphasizes the authority of the Bible, personal commitment to Christ, and evangelism, as neo-evangelicalism does. But while neoevangelicals insist on doctrinal agreement for Christian unity, charismatics see Spirit baptism as the unifying force. In its endeavor to regain *charismata,* the charismatic movement has recaptured the experiential within Christianity.

E. Seventh-day Adventist Church

From its beginning, the Seventh-day

Adventist Church has firmly believed in and accepted the presence of *charismata*. Among the followers of William Miller, where the roots of the Seventh-day Adventist Church are to be found, the prophetic gift was given to William Ellis Foy and Hazen Foss. Foy was given visions relating to the Millerite movement in 1842 and 1844. Foss received a vision in late September or early October 1844, in which he witnessed the journey of the Adventist people to the city of God.

The little company of Millerites who were to form the Seventh-day Adventist Church knew of the experiences of Foy and Foss. Foy related what he had seen, but Foss refused to share the vision that he had received, even though he was instructed to do so in a second vision. Following continued refusal, he heard a voice speak to him, "You have grieved away the Spirit of the Lord." Horrified at this message, he called a meeting and attempted to communicate the vision, but was unable to recall it. "It is gone from me," he cried out; "I can say nothing, the Spirit of the Lord has left me" (*SDA Encyclopedia* 10:563).

Shortly after hope that Christ would return on October 22, 1844, was shattered, the prophetic gift was given again, this time to a young woman who was part of the little company of Millerites that later grew into the Seventh-day Adventist Church. Sometime during December 1844, Ellen G. Harmon (later White) received in Portland, Maine, the first of approximately 2,000 visions. Both Foy and Foss, who heard Ellen White relate the content of her first vision, confirmed that what she had seen had been shown to them earlier.

While Seventh-day Adventists believe that all of the spiritual gifts will exist in the endtime church for the completion of the gospel commission, the gift given to Ellen White has received the greatest attention. Believing that history is soon to close and that Jesus is about to return, Seventh-day Adventists look upon themselves as the remnant people of God identified in Revelation 12:17. This remnant keeps the commandments of God and has the testimony of Jesus, which John identified as the spirit of prophecy (Rev. 19:10; see X. D for further discussion).

Through the guidance of the prophetic gift bestowed on Ellen White, Seventh-day Adventists have avoided extremes experienced by other churches in connection with the interpretation of spiritual gifts. Three examples are: (1) extreme emotionalism in worship, (2) counterfeit speaking in tongues, and (3) counterfeit miracles.

1. Emotionalism

Millerites in the Methodist Church shared Wesley's acceptance of emotional experiences during worship. During a prayer meeting in 1843 the Spirit of God rested so powerfully upon young Ellen Harmon that she lost consciousness and was unable to return home that night. The Spirit rested on another person also, who was prostrated as though dead. He regained consciousness, but he too was unable to return home.

Early Adventist meetings carried over the enthusiasm of Methodism and were characterized by a chorus of hearty amens and loud voices praising God. On Christmas Eve 1850 Ellen White was given a vision of the perfect order of heaven and the glory of God filling the heavenly temple. On the basis of this vision and the accompanying instruction, she began (1) to call for church organization and (2) to move the church away from unhealthy and unnecessary excitement in worship. Speaking of the "exercises" (ecstatic experiences), she said, "I saw that there was great danger of leaving the Word of God and resting down and trusting in exercises. . . . I saw danger ahead" (5MR 227).

As the great controversy theme unfolded before her, Ellen White understood that Satan would try to counterfeit the work of the Holy Spirit by introducing emotionally charged experiences and spiritual highs during worship. This effort would increase during the closing moments of earth's history as the great deceiver would counterfeit the latter rain experience. From 1850 on, words of caution multiplied.

2. Tongues

In the early history of the Seventh-day Adventist Church, four documented experiences of speaking in tongues took place: (1) 1847, to guide a young man into the ministry; (2) 1848, in a meeting to decide when to begin the Sabbath; (3) 1849, guidance to missionary endeavor; and (4) 1851, a report of the presence and power of God.

On the second occasion a number of believers had gathered to study and pray about the correct time to begin the Sabbath, for there was a division of opinion on the subject. A Brother Chamberlain was "filled" with the Holy Spirit as the group prayed, and cried out in an unknown tongue. The interpretation was that he wanted a piece of chalk. With chalk in hand, he drew the face of a clock upon the floor, and indicated, under the "power," that the Sabbath was to begin at 6:00 p.m. Through further Bible study, however, Chamberlain's message was rejected, and sundown was finally established as the proper time, according to God's Word, to begin the Sabbath.

Ellen White was a witness to three of the four tongues-speaking episodes. However, she gave no support or endorsement to these experiences. Later she referred to unknown tongues as an unmeaning gibberish "which is unknown not only by man but by the Lord and all heaven. Such gifts are manufactured by men and women, aided by the great deceiver" (1T 412).

3. Miracles

Miracles of healing as a result of earnest prayer and the anointing of oil have been experienced among Seventh-day Adventists even to the present. Ellen White reported numerous occasions when physical healing took place as she joined others to anoint and pray for the suffering. But again she sounded a caution, because "Satan will exercise his power by working miracles. God's servants today could not work by means of miracles, because spurious works of healing, claiming to be divine, will be wrought" (2SM 54).

While Seventh-day Adventists recognize the presence of spiritual gifts in the church as dispensed by the Holy Spirit for the advancement of the gospel throughout the world, guidance through the prophetic gift given to Ellen White has led them to be cautious about accepting a gift as "genuine." They understand that Satan has the power to produce and work through counterfeit gifts. Therefore the position of the church is to examine closely each claim to a gift, testing it by God's Word to determine whether the gift is from the Holy Spirit and whether it produces the fruit of the Spirit.

XIV. Ellen G. White Comments

A. *Spiritual Gifts*

"The Holy Spirit was to descend on those in this world who loved Christ. By this they would be qualified, in and through the glorification of their Head, to receive every endowment necessary for the fulfilling of their mission. . . . All power in heaven and earth was given to Him, and having taken His place in the heavenly courts, He could dispense these blessings to all who receive Him.

"Christ has said to His disciples, 'It is expedient for you that I go away: for if I go not away, the Comforter will not come unto you; but if I depart, I will send him unto you' (John 16:7). This was the gift of gifts. The Holy Spirit was sent as the most priceless treasure man could receive. The church was baptized with the Spirit's power. The disciples were fitted to go forth and proclaim Christ" (TDG 341).

"The talents that Christ entrusts to His church represent especially the gifts and blessings imparted by the Holy Spirit. [1 Cor. 12:8-11 quoted.] All men do not receive the same gifts, but to every servant of the Master some gift of the Spirit is promised" (COL 327).

"The special gifts of the Spirit are not the only talents represented in the parable [Matt. 25:13-30]. It includes all gifts and endowments, whether original or acquired, natural or spiritual. All are to be employed in Christ's service" (*ibid.* 328).

"Here is a course by which we may be assured that we shall never fall. Those who are thus working upon the plan of addition in obtaining the Christian graces, have the assurance that God will work upon the plan of multiplication in granting them the gifts of His Spirit" (MYP 116).

"When the Saviour said, 'Go, . . . teach all nations,' He said also, 'These signs shall follow them that believe; In my name shall they cast out devils; they shall speak with new tongues; they shall take up serpents; and if they drink any deadly thing, it shall not hurt them; they shall lay hands on the sick, and they shall recover.' The promise is as far-reaching as the commission. Not that all the gifts are imparted to each believer. The Spirit divides 'to every man severally as He will' (1 Cor. 12:11). But the gifts of the Spirit are promised to every believer according to his need for the Lord's work. The promise is just as strong and trustworthy now as in the days of the apostles. 'These signs shall follow them that believe.' This is the privilege of God's children, and faith should lay hold on all that it is possible to have as an endorsement of faith" (DA 823).

"The promise of the Spirit is not appreciated as it should be. Its fulfillment is not realized as it might be. It is the absence of the Spirit that makes the gospel ministry so powerless. Learning, talents, eloquence, every natural or acquired endowment, may be possessed; but without the presence of the Spirit of God, no heart will be touched, no sinner be won to Christ. On the other hand, if they are connected with Christ, if the gifts of the Spirit are theirs, the poorest and most ignorant of His disciples will have a power that will tell upon hearts. God makes them the channel for the outworking of the highest influence in the universe" (COL 328).

"God has in store love, joy, peace, and glorious triumph for all who serve Him in spirit and in truth. His commandment-keeping people are to stand constantly in readiness for service. They are to receive increased grace and power, and increased knowledge of the Holy Spirit's working. But many are not ready to receive the precious gifts of the Spirit which God is waiting to bestow on them. They are not reaching higher and still higher for power from above, that, through the gifts bestowed, they may be recognized as God's peculiar people, zealous of good works" (8T 247, 248).

"Acknowledge the gift that has been placed in the church for the guidance of God's people in the closing days of earth's history. From the beginning the church of God has had the gift of prophecy in her midst as a living voice to counsel, admonish, and instruct.

"We have now come to the last days of the work of the third angel's message, when Satan will work with increasing power because he knows that his time is short. At the same time there will come to us through the gifts of the Holy Spirit, diversities of operations in the outpouring of the Spirit. This is the time of the latter rain" (3SM 83).

"Physical, mental, and spiritual gifts have been placed in our possession. In the Bible, God's will is plainly made known. God expects every man to use his gifts in a way that will give him an increased knowledge of the things of God, and will enable him to make improvement, to become more and more refined, ennobled, and purified" (TDG 137).

"Study this scripture carefully [1 Cor. 12:4-12]. God has not given to every one the same line of work. It is His plan that there shall be unity in diversity. When His plan is studied and followed, there will be far less friction in the working of the cause. . . .

"The Lord desires His church to respect every gift that He has bestowed on the different members. Let us beware of allowing our minds to become fixed on ourselves, thinking that no one can be serving the Lord unless he is working on the same lines as those on which we are working. . . .

"The work is hurt unless there are brought into it all the gifts that God has bestowed. Many times the progress of the work has been hindered because the laborers thought their gifts all that were necessary for its advancement" (PUR Dec. 29,1904).

B. Seek Daily Baptism of the Spirit

"I beseech the member of every church to seek now for the greatest blessing Heaven can bestow—the Holy Spirit. If in faith you seek for a greater measure of God's Spirit, you will be constantly taking it in and breathing it out. Daily you will receive a fresh supply" (UL 143).

"For the daily baptism of the Spirit every worker should offer his petition to God" (AA 50).

"Teach your children that it is their privilege to receive every day the baptism of the Holy Spirit" (CG 69, 70).

C. Ellen White's View of Scripture

"God committed the preparation of His divinely inspired Word to finite man. This Word, arranged into books, the Old and New Testaments, is the guidebook to the inhabitants of a fallen world, bequeathed to them that, by studying and obeying the directions, not one soul would lose its way to heaven.

"Those who think to make the supposed difficulties of Scripture plain, in measuring by their finite rule that which is inspired and that which is not inspired, had better cover their faces . . . for they are in the presence of God and holy angels. . . .

"And He [God] has not, while presenting the perils clustering about the last days, qualified any finite man to unravel hidden mysteries or inspired one man or any class of men to pronounce judgment as to that which is inspired or is not. When men, in their finite judgment, find it necessary to go into an examination of scriptures to define that which is inspired and that which is not, they have

stepped before Jesus to show Him a better way than He has led us.

"I take the Bible just as it is, as the inspired Word. . . .

"Brethren, let not a mind or hand be engaged in criticizing the Bible. It is a work that Satan delights to have any of you do, but it is not a work the Lord has pointed out for you to do" (1SM 16, 17).

"The Bible is written by inspired men, but it is not God's mode of thought and expression. It is that of humanity. God, as a writer, is not represented. Men will often say such an expression is not like God. But God has not put Himself in words, in logic, in rhetoric, on trial in the Bible. The writers of the Bible were God's penmen, not His pen. Look at the different writers.

"It is not the words of the Bible that are inspired, but the men that were inspired. Inspiration acts not on the man's words or his expressions but on the man himself, who, under the influence of the Holy Ghost, is imbued with thoughts. But the words receive the impress of the individual mind. The divine mind is diffused. The divine mind and will is combined with the human mind and will; thus the utterances of the man are the word of God" (*ibid.* 21).

D. Ellen White's View of Her Work

"These words were spoken to me: 'Your work is appointed you of God. Many will not hear you, for they refused to hear the Great Teacher; many will not be corrected, for their ways are right in their own eyes. Yet bear to them the reproofs and warnings I shall give you, whether they will hear or forbear' " (5T 74).

"In these letters which I write, in the testimonies I bear, I am presenting to you that which the Lord has presented to me. I do not write one article in the paper expressing merely my own ideas. They are what God has opened before me in vision—the precious rays of light shining from the throne" (*ibid.* 67).

"During the discourse, I said that I did not

claim to be a prophetess. Some were surprised at this statement, and as much is being said in regard to it, I will make an explanation. Others have called me a prophetess, but I have never assumed that title. I have not felt that it was my duty thus to designate myself. Those who boldly assume that they are prophets in this our day are often a reproach to the cause of Christ.

"My work includes much more than this name signifies. I regard myself as a messenger, entrusted by the Lord with messages for His people" (1SM 35, 36).

"In regard to infallibility, I never claimed it; God alone is infallible. His word is true, and in Him is no variableness, or shadow of turning" (*ibid.* 37).

E. Ellen White and the Prophetic Gift

"There are some occupying positions of responsibility who have had little experience in the working of the Holy Spirit. They do not appreciate the light in warnings, reproofs, and encouragement given to the church in these last days, because their hearts and minds have not been receiving the Spirit of divine grace. These persons are disposed to conceal the fact that in connection with the work of the third angel's message the Lord through the Spirit of prophecy has been communicating to His people a knowledge of His will. They think that the truth will be received more readily if this fact is not made prominent. But this is mere human reasoning. The very fact that this light coming to the people is not presented as having originated with human minds will make an impression upon a large class who believe that the gifts of the Spirit are to be manifested in the church in the last days. The attention of many will thus be arrested, and they will be convicted and converted. Many will thus be impressed who would not otherwise be reached" (1888 Materials 808, 809).

"As inquiries are frequently made as to my state in vision, and after I come out, I would say that when the Lord sees fit to give a vision, I am taken into the presence of Jesus and angels, and am entirely lost to earthly things. I can see no farther than the angel directs me. My attention is often directed to scenes transpiring upon earth.

"At times I am carried far ahead into the future and shown what is to take place. Then again I am shown things as they have occurred in the past. After I come out of vision I do not at once remember all that I have seen, and the matter is not so clear before me until I write, then the scene rises before me as was presented in vision, and I can write with freedom. Sometimes the things which I have seen are hid from me after I come out of vision, and I cannot call them to mind until I am brought before a company where that vision applies, then the things which I have seen come to my mind with force. I am just as dependent upon the Spirit of the Lord in relating or writing a vision, as in having the vision. It is impossible for me to call up things which have been shown me unless the Lord brings them before me at the time that He is pleased to have me relate or write them" (1SM 36, 37).

"Although I am as dependent upon the Spirit of the Lord in writing my views as I am in receiving them, yet the words I employ in describing what I have seen are my own, unless they be those spoken to me by an angel, which I always enclose in marks of quotation" (*ibid.* 37).

"The question is asked, How does Sister White know in regard to the matters of which she speaks so decidedly, as if she had authority to say these things? I speak thus because they flash upon my mind when in perplexity like lightning out of a dark cloud in the fury of a storm. Some scenes presented before me years ago have not been retained in my memory, but when the instruction then given is needed, sometimes even when I am standing before the people, the remembrance comes sharp and clear, like a flash of lightning, bringing to mind distinctly that particular instruction. At such times I cannot refrain from saying the things that flash into my mind, not because I have had a new vision, but because that which was presented to me perhaps years in the past has been recalled to my mind forcibly" (*ibid.* 36, 37).

F. Gift of Tongues

"The Holy Spirit, assuming the form of tongues of fire, rested upon those assembled. This was an emblem of the gift then bestowed on the disciples, which enabled them to speak with fluency languages with which they had heretofore been unacquainted. The appearance of fire signified the fervent zeal with which the apostles would labor and the power that would attend their work.

"'There were dwelling at Jerusalem Jews, devout men, out of every nation under heaven.' During the dispersion the Jews had been scattered to almost every part of the inhabited world, and in their exile they had learned to speak various languages. Many of these Jews were on this occasion in Jerusalem, attending the religious festivals then in progress. Every known tongue was represented by those assembled. This diversity of languages would have been a great hindrance to the proclamation of the gospel; God therefore in a miraculous manner supplied the deficiency of the apostles. The Holy Spirit did for them that which they could not have accomplished for themselves in a lifetime. They could now proclaim the truths of the gospel abroad, speaking with accuracy the languages of those for whom they were laboring. This miraculous gift was a strong evidence to the world that their commission bore the signet of Heaven. From this time forth the language of the disciples was pure, simple, and accurate, whether they spoke in their native tongue or in a foreign language" (AA 39, 40).

"The priests and rulers were greatly enraged at this wonderful manifestation, which was reported throughout all Jerusalem and the vicinity; but they dared not give way to their malice, for fear of exposing themselves to the hatred of the people. They had put the Master to death, but here were His servants, un-learned men of Galilee, tracing out the wonderful fulfillment of prophecy, and teaching the doctrine of Jesus in all the languages then spoken" (3SP 267, 268).

"There is a great work to be done in our world. Men and women are to be converted, not by the gift of tongues nor by the working of miracles, but by the preaching of Christ crucified" (ML 219).

G. Counterfeit Gifts

"Some of these persons have exercises which they call gifts and say that the Lord has placed them in the church. They have an unmeaning gibberish which they call the unknown tongue, which is unknown not only by man but by the Lord and all heaven. Such gifts are manufactured by men and women, aided by the great deceiver. Fanaticism, false excitement, false talking in tongues, and noisy exercises have been considered gifts which God has placed in the church. Some have been deceived here" (1T 412).

"There are wandering stars professing to be ministers sent of God, who are preaching the Sabbath from place to place, and have truth mixed up with erroneous sentiments, and throw out a strange jumble of views to the people. Satan has pushed them in to disgust intelligent and sensible unbelievers. Some of these have much to say upon the gifts, and are often especially exercised. They give themselves up to wild, excitable feelings, and make unintelligible sounds which they call the gift of tongues. A certain class seem to receive it, and are charmed with the strange manifestations which they witness. A strange spirit rules with this class, which would bear down and run over any one who would reprove them. God's Spirit is not in the work" (4SG-b 154, 155).

"The man who makes the working of miracles the test of his faith will find that Satan can, through a species of deceptions, perform wonders that will appear to be genuine miracles" (Mar. 156).

"The way in which Christ worked was to

preach the Word, and to relieve suffering by miraculous works of healing. But I am instructed that we cannot now work in this way, for Satan will exercise his power by working miracles. God's servants today could not work by means of miracles, because spurious works of healing, claiming to be divine, will be wrought" (2SM 54).

"Those who look for miracles as a sign of divine guidance are in grave danger of deception. It is stated in the Word that the enemy will work through his agents who have departed from the faith, and they will seemingly work miracles, even to the bringing down of fire out of heaven in the sight of men. By means of 'lying wonders' Satan would deceive, if possible, the very elect" (3SM 408, 409).

"The enemy of souls desires to hinder this work; and before the time for such a movement shall come, he will endeavor to prevent it by introducing a counterfeit. In those churches which he can bring under his deceptive power he will make it appear that God's special blessing is poured out; there will be manifest what is thought to be great religious interest. Multitudes will exult that God is working marvelously for them, when the work is that of another spirit" (GC 464).

XV. Literature

Aune, David E. *Prophecy in Early Christianity and the Ancient Mediterranean World.* Grand Rapids: Eerdmans, 1983.

Bates, Joseph. "Remarks." In *A Word to the "Little Flock,"* n.p., 1847. P. 21. Facsimile reproduction. Washington, D.C.: Review and Herald, 1944.

Baus, Karl. *From the Apostolic Community to Constantine.* Vol. 1 of *History of the Church,* ed. Hubert Jedin and John Dolan. New York: Crossroad, 1980.

Bonwetsch, N. "Montanus, Montanism." *The New Schaff-Herzog Encyclopedia of Religious Knowledge.* Ed. Samuel Macauley Jackson. New York: Funk and Wagnalls, 1910. Vol. 7, pp. 485-487.

Carson, D. A. *Showing the Spirit: A Theological Exposition of 1 Corinthians 12-14.* Grand Rapids: Baker, 1987.

Dunn, James D. G. *Baptism in the Holy Spirit.* Philadelphia: Westminster, 1977.

Ervin, Howard M. *Spirit Baptism: A Biblical Investigation.* Peabody, Mass.: Hendrickson, 1987.

Fox, Robin. *Pagans and Christians.* New York: Knopf, 1987.

Froom, Le Roy. *The Prophetic Faith of Our Fathers.* 4 vols. Washington, D.C.: Review and Herald, 1950-1954.

Grudem, Wayne. *The Gift of Prophecy in the New Testament and Today.* Westchester, Ill.: Crossway, 1988.

Hasel, Gerhard. *Speaking in Tongues: Biblical Speaking in Tongues and Contemporary Glossolalia.* Berrien Springs, Mich.: Adventist Theological Society, 1991.

Houston, Graham. *Prophecy: A Gift for Today?* Downers Grove, Ill.: InterVarsity, 1989.

Jemison, T. Housel. *A Prophet Among You.* Mountain View, Calif.: Pacific Press, 1955.

Melton, J. Gordon. *The Encyclopedia of American Religions.* 3rd ed. Detroit: Gale Research, 1989.

Newman, Albert Henry. *A Manual of Church History.* 2 vols. Philadelphia: American Baptist, 1904.

Paulsen, Jan. *When the Spirit Descends.* Washington, D.C.: Review and Herald, 1977.

Payne, J. Barton. *Encyclopedia of Biblical Prophecy.* New York: Harper and Row, 1973.

Quebedeaux, Richard. "Conservative and Charismatic Developments of the Later Twentieth Century." *Encyclopedia of the American Religious Experience: Studies of Traditions and Movements.* 3 vols. Ed. Charles H. Lippy and Peter W. Williams. New York: Charles Scribner's Sons, 1988. Vol. 2, pp. 963-976.

Schatzmann, Siegfried S. *A Pauline Theology of Charismata.* Peabody, Mass.: Hendrickson, 1987.

Smith, Timothy. "The Spirit's Gifts: Then and Now." *Christianity Today,* Mar. 19, 1990, pp. 25, 26.

Veltman, Fred. *Full Report of the Life of Christ Research Project.* Washington, D.C.: General Conference of Seventh-day Adventists, 1988.

Wacker, Grant. "Pentecostalism." *Encyclopedia of the American Religious Experience: Studies of Traditions and Movements.* 3 vols. Ed. Charles H. Lippy and Peter W. Williams. New York: Charles Scribner's Sons, 1988. Vol. 2, pp. 933-945.

White, Arthur L. *Ellen G. White.* 6 vols. Washington, D.C.: Review and Herald, 1981-1986.

————. *Ellen G. White: Messenger to the Remnant.* Washington, D.C.: Review and Herald, 1969.

Wright, David. "Montanism: A Movement of Spiritual Renewal?" *Theological Renewal* 22 (1982): 19-29.

Stewardship

Charles E. Bradford

Introduction

The biblical idea of stewardship is more than a narrow creedal statement. It is a dynamic principle under which the kingdom of God operates. Humans stand under the judgment of God, and Christian stewardship presses the question, Who is responsible for the care of God's creation and the gifts that He has shared with the human creature? These gifts are physical, spiritual, and intellectual. They come from the hand of the Creator: life, health, possessions, and even the planet itself. "Every good endowment and every perfect gift is from above, coming down from the Father of lights with whom there is no variation or shadow due to change" (James 1:17).

Stewardship is an essential element of faith. Time, talent, treasure, and temple (the body) are given to human beings to test their loyalty to the Creator. The whole concept is heightened by the eschatological pronouncement of Revelation 14:7: "Fear God and give him glory, for the hour of his judgment has come; and worship him who made heaven and earth, the sea and the fountains of water." This gives impetus, urgency, and timeliness to the doctrine.

The biblical concept of stewardship transcends and informs the whole of Christian teaching and doctrine. It embraces and connects many of the great doctrines of the church and becomes an organizing principle for understanding Scripture. The doctrine of Creation; the doctrine of humanity, redemption, and restoration; the doctrine of the Sabbath; and the doctrine of the church are inextricably bound up with the idea of stewardship. Stewardship also becomes the root of mission, the basis of sharing the gospel with the world.

A steward is a manager, and stewardship is management—the management of goods and gifts on behalf of another. Stewardship is trusteeship, and a trustee is one who holds property in trust. A trustee agrees to administer or exercise power for the benefit of another. A trustee holds legal title to property for the benefit of another person and carries out specific duties with regard to the property. A steward or trustee has a specific duty to the owner or beneficiary.

In the biblical sense stewardship means the grateful and responsible use of all God's gifts. Christian stewards are empowered by the Holy Spirit and commit themselves to conscious, purposeful decisions in the use of these gifts. For the committed Christian the stewardship principle becomes more than intellectual assent to doctrinal formulation; it becomes something to be lived out, shared, experienced. The stewardship principle is wrapped around all of life, and all of life becomes an outworking of this great principle that has been engraved upon the "tablets of human hearts" (2 Cor. 3:3).

I. Biblical View of Stewardship

There is no single OT or NT word that carries with it all that is associated with the word "stewardships." The doctrine does not rest on the exegesis of one word or even one passage. The doctrine, as understood and taught by Christians today, is broadly based and firmly rooted in the whole of Scripture. It draws upon the text of both testaments. The idea grows and becomes clearer under the ongoing illumination of a dynamic biblical witness (see Prov. 4:18).

A. Concepts and Words

1. "The One Over the House"

Expressed in the simplest terms, a steward is a person who is employed to manage and be responsible for the property or business affairs of another. The term may be simple, but the concept is broad. Clearly, a steward is a servant, but a servant with authority. This finds illustration in the almost-universal custom of appointing someone to care for "the house," a *majordomo*. Abraham's servant was "the oldest of his house, who had charge of all that he had"; that is, he administered all that Abraham had (Gen. 24:2).

Pharaoh said to Joseph, "You shall be over my house, and all my people shall order themselves as you command; only as regards to the throne will I be greater than you" (Gen. 41:40). "House" here stands for estate, domain, or realm. It can mean the domicile, those who live in the building, the affairs of the family, or the interests of an entire kingdom. Potiphar saw in Joseph someone who could be entrusted with the responsibility of managing his household: "So Joseph found favor in his sight and attended him, and he made him overseer of his house and put him in charge of all that he had" (Gen. 39:4).

Before becoming Pharaoh's administrator, Joseph had been put in charge: "And the keeper of the prison committed to Joseph's care all the prisoners who were in the prison; and whatever was done there, he was the doer of it" (verse 22). After becoming the one in charge of Pharaoh's house, Joseph employed his own steward to care for his house. When his brothers visited Egypt, Joseph "commanded the steward of his house" to return "each man's money in the mouth of his sack" (Gen. 43:19; 44:1). It is evident from the steward's reply to the brothers that Joseph has made him his confidant with reference to his family (Gen. 43:23).

At times "the house" comes to mean responsibilities expanded to include a city, province, or kingdom. "And the men of Judah came, and there they anointed David king over the house of Judah" (2 Sam. 2:4). In 2 Kings 10:5, the "palace administrator" was in charge of the royal "house." (The designation is also used in 2 Kings 15:5; Esther 8:2; Isaiah 22:15; 36:3.) In the Daniel narrative the prince of eunuchs is placed in charge of the four Hebrew worthies (Dan. 1:10). The word used for prince (*śar*) may also be rendered "steward," and refers to a captain, chief, general, governor, keeper, lord, master, ruler, or steward. As the concept develops it becomes clear that the steward cannot carry out his function without some measure of authority.

2. *Oikonomos* and *Oikonomia*

The NT takes OT ideas and joins them with first-century ideas, concepts, and words, thus enriching and enlarging the biblical teaching on stewardship. The most common Greek words used in relationship with stewardship are derived from *oikos* and *oikia*, "house." The *oikonomos* is one who keeps the house: the steward or manager. *Oikonomia* is the abstract noun, "management of the house," the meaning of which is often much broader.

The dishonest steward of Jesus' parable (Luke 16:2-4) is called an *oikonomos*, and his duties and responsibilities are called *oikonomia*, "stewardship." In 1 Corinthians 9:17 Paul speaks of *oikonomia* as the trust committed to him. Ephesians 1:10 uses the word *oikonomia* to refer to God's plan "to unite all things" in Christ. In Ephesians 3:2 the apostle speaks about the "stewardship of God's grace."

In Colossians 1:25 *oikonomia* is a God-given commission to "make the word of God fully known." In Titus 1:7 the bishop is called

a steward *(oikonomos)*, signifying that he has a stewardship obligation to discharge.

Oikonomos appears in Romans 16:23 in reference to the treasurer of the city. In 1 Corinthians 4:1, 2, Paul wants the church to think of him and his fellow workers as "servants of Christ and stewards of the mysteries of God." Further, he notes, "it is required of stewards that they be found trustworthy." Every Christian is an *oikonomos:* "As each has received a gift, employ it for one another, as good stewards of God's varied grace" (1 Peter 4:10).

B. Creation as the Basis for Stewardship

1. God's Gracious Act

The doctrine of stewardship has its origin in Creation. Any attempt to fully grasp the essence of stewardship must begin here. Indeed, one's understanding of the first three chapters of Genesis determines one's concept of God—the kind of person He is—His nature and character.

Whether implicit or explicit, the thought that God is the "landlord of ultimate concern" is embedded in Scripture. From the first words of Genesis Yahweh is seen as the Creator God. The biblical writers take this for granted. There is no attempt to prove what is patently clear. (See Creation III. A-C.)

2. God's Ownership

In Creation, God reveals Himself as the gracious God of steadfast love. His work in Creation gives insight into His character. He fashions the new world with care and skill. The world of the Master craftsman is infinitely beautiful. The psalmist encourages the people to "thank the Lord for his steadfast love, for his wonderful works to the sons of men" (Ps. 107:31; 111:4).

There is a bond between Creation and salvation throughout Scripture. The living God is both Creator and Redeemer. Before creating the world, He provided for a plan of salvation to meet the contingency of sin (1 Peter 1:18-20). Thus, in the person of Jesus, Creation, redemption, and grace were to come together. With man's fall, the truth about Creation linked with divine grace, which provides for a full re-creation of penitent sinners and the earth from the effects of human transgression. (See Salvation III. C.)

Creation was a gracious act of a loving God. His purpose in Creation was to populate the planet with intelligent beings who would be the object of His love. "For thus says the Lord, who created the heavens (he is God!), who formed the earth and made it (he established it; he did not create it a chaos, he formed it to be inhabited!): 'I am the Lord, and there is no other'" (Isa. 45:18).

3. Adam and Eve, God's Deputies

This gracious God made the human beings whom He had created in His image to be His representatives to care for the earth. "Let them have dominion over the fish of the sea, and over the birds of the air, and over the cattle, and over all the earth, and over every creeping thing that creeps upon the earth" (Gen. 1:26). The same command is repeated in verse 28.

In the account of Creation man and woman are summoned to be like the Creator, in whose image they were made. The human role is different from that of all other creatures. The moral imperative is applied only to them. Human creatures are given a special place in God's creation. God intimates special intentions and purposes in the creation of humanity; He speaks directly only to these human creatures (verses 26-30). Ellen White points out that "God created man a superior being; he alone is formed in the image of God, and is capable of partaking of the divine nature, of cooperating with his Creator and executing his plans" (SD 7).

God created the human pair in His image that they might fulfill His commission to have dominion. God created Adam and Eve with a specific task—to be stewards over creation.

So that they might carry out their task, He richly blessed them. Man's stewardship responsibility is a part of the image of God.

Adam was therefore specially designed to be God's representative. Only Adam and Eve, of all created beings, could be stewards under God, because only they were moral beings. "The first man Adam" (1 Cor. 15:45) was the head of the human race. As he came from the hand of the Creator he represented all that God intended humanity to be.

The narrative is carefully worded so as to make clear for all time (1) the sovereignty of God, His ownership and prior claim; (2) our assignment, "to dress and keep" the earth; (3) our responsibility and accountability, as moral beings, created in the image of God.

The deputy status of Adam and Eve continues even after the Fall, as the psalmist indicates: "Thou hast given him dominion over the works of thy hands; thou hast put all things under his feet" (Ps. 8:6; see Man I. B. 1, 2).

C. Reminders of God's Ownership

As Creator, God is also owner and sustainer of His creation. "The earth is the Lord's and the fulness thereof, the world and those who dwell therein" (Ps. 24:1). "For every beast of the forest is mine, the cattle on a thousand hills.... If I were hungry, I would not tell you; for the world and all that is in it is mine" (Ps. 50:10-12). By His might "he covers the heavens with clouds, he prepares rain for the earth, he makes grass grow upon the hills" (Ps. 147:8).

1. Tree of Knowledge of Good and Evil

In the Garden of Eden the tree of knowledge of good and evil served as a reminder that God has not relinquished title to His property. Stewardship has its limits. The steward has no right to use the owner's goods without reference to the owner's will. The tree of knowledge of good and evil was off-limits; it was a reminder and a warning that breach of the stewardship covenant carries its penalty. "And the Lord God commanded the man, saying, 'You may freely eat of every tree of the garden; but of the tree of the knowledge of good and evil you shall not eat, for in the day that you eat of it you shall die' " (Gen. 2:16, 17).

God will not allow humans to assume the position of proprietors. They will always be stewards, deputies. Should human beings be permitted to act as owners, they would soon arrogate to themselves the very prerogatives of deity. (See Sin III. B. 1-3.)

2. Sabbath

The first full day that Adam and Eve experienced was the Sabbath day, God's special day of rest (Gen. 1:31–2:3).

When examined in the light of the stewardship concept, the fourth commandment becomes a divine statement about human relationships. First comes the relationship with God. This day is the "sabbath to the Lord your God" (Ex. 20:10). In the Sabbath commandment the creatures are reminded of their finitude, their creatureliness. The Creator reminds the created that He retains title to His world. His earthborn children are vicegerents and stewards.

In the Sabbath commandment reference is made also to the relationship to fellow humans "In it you shall not do any work, you, or your son, or your daughter, or your manservant, or your maidservant, or your cattle, or the sojourner who is within your gates" (verse 10). The steward, as God's representative, is to make the Sabbath rest available to all God's creatures.

Into the succession of ordinary days God has placed a gift to those created in His image. We may even say that the Sabbath is a portion of eternity set in the midst of time.

The Sabbath also establishes relationships between Yahweh and human beings, who are always creatures, and between humans and the animals, and even between human beings and the earth. A relationship of dependence on God and worship of the Creator is clearly enjoined. In specifying that one must not keep the Sabbath alone, but in the company of others, God delineated proper relations among human beings. Finally, by exempting animals from work, the Creator showed how human beings could care for the dominion that had been placed under their feet (Birch 80).

Since the Sabbath has to do with time, human beings are made conscious of time's value. The statement "The sabbath was made for man" is followed by another: "The Son of man is Lord even of the sabbath" (Mark 2:27, 28). As a universal time gift, the Sabbath invests all other time with greater meaning. The deeper meaning of Sabbath is that Jesus is Lord of all—time, talent, treasure, and body temple. (See Creation I. A. 1-4; II. C; Sabbath I. A; II. A.)

3. Tithes and Offerings

In addition to the Sabbath, tithes and offerings remind us that only God is proprietor in the absolute sense. Of this the first pair were reminded by the tree whose fruit they were not to eat (Gen. 2:17). After sin and expulsion from the garden, this ownership truth was reinforced in the tithing principle.

In Genesis tithepaying appears as an already-known practice. Abraham paid tithe to Melchizedek, king of Salem and a priest of God Most High (Gen. 14:18-20). The same is recorded of Jacob, who promised Yahweh, "Of all that thou givest me I will give the tenth to thee" (Gen. 28:22).

The tithe was to be regarded as God's tenth. "All the tithe of the land, whether of the seed of the land, or of the fruit of the trees, is the Lord's: it is holy unto the Lord" (Lev. 27:30). The sacred tenth was an acknowledgment of Yahweh's ownership. "The earth is the Lord's, and the fulness thereof, the world and those who dwell therein" (Ps. 24:1; cf. 50:10-12; Haggai 2:8).

The Israelites were commanded to tithe all the yield of their seed, "which comes forth from the field year by year" (Deut. 14:22). In this way the covenant people showed love and respect for their God. In all things He was to be first. "Honor the Lord with your substance and with the first fruits of all your produce" (Prov. 3:9).

The record indicates that the practice of tithing continued after the exile. "Then all Judah brought the tithe of the grain, wine, and oil into the storehouses" (Neh. 13:12). Clearly the tithe was for religious purposes, including the support of priests and Levites: "To the Levites I have given every tithe in Israel for an inheritance, in return for their service which they serve, their service in the tent of meeting" (Num. 18:21). In postexilic times, "men were appointed over the chambers for the stores, the contributions, the first fruits, and the tithes, to gather into them the portions required by the law for the priests and for the Levites according to the fields of the towns; for Judah rejoiced over the priests and the Levites who ministered" (Neh. 12:44). This was to be done with joy and gratitude to the Provider who had given them "power to get wealth" (Deut. 8:18).

The tithe is tangible, reminding us that the physical creation has been pronounced good. Therefore, the command is to "honor the Lord with your substance and with the first fruits of all your produce" (Prov. 3:9). The returning of the tithe saves us from a false dichotomy between the spiritual and the material. Israel's God is the Giver of every good gift. He makes no radical differentiation between the so-called spiritual and the so-called natural. "He has made everything beautiful in its time" (Eccl. 3:11). Later Jesus would acknowledge tithing as something that "you ought to have done, without neglecting the others" (Matt. 23:23).

The returning of the tithe makes the worshiper a partner with God in concrete ways. There is an identification with the caregiving God, whose spirit of sacrificial love is taken on. God's interests and concerns become the believer's interests and concern. The covenant relationship is deepened.

The experience of the Jewish people under Nehemiah gives a remarkable insight into the tithing system. An entire people heartily entered into covenant with their God.

When all Judah brought the tithe of the grain, wine, and oil into the storehouses, Nehemiah appointed treasurers who were "counted faithful; and their duty was to distribute to their brethren" (Neh. 13:13).

At the end of the OT the prophet Malachi repeats Yahweh's requirement, together with a promise of rich blessings:

"Will man rob God? Yet you are robbing me. But you say, 'How are we robbing thee?' In your tithes and offerings. You are cursed with a curse, for you are robbing me; the whole nation of you. Bring the full tithes into the storehouse, that there may be food in my house; and thereby put me to the test, says the Lord of hosts, if I will not open the windows of heaven for you and pour down for you an overflowing blessing. I will rebuke the devourer for you, so that it will not destroy the fruits of your soil; and your vine in the field shall not fail to bear, says the Lord of hosts. Then all nations will call you blessed, for you will be a land of delight, says the Lord of hosts" (Mal. 3:8-12).

Failure to return the tithe is viewed as a breach of the covenant.

D. Examples of Stewardship

In addition to the tithe the Lord requested offerings. Yahweh complained that Israel was robbing Him in "tithes and offerings" (Mal. 3:8). When the Israelites made pilgrimage to Jerusalem they were expected to bring an offering or gift, a *mattānāh,* from the verb *nātan,* to "give" (Deut. 16:17). The same word is used to designate a gift given by a father to his child (Gen. 25:5) and God's gift of the priesthood to Aaron (Num. 18:7). The word suggests a gift prompted by a good and loving disposition of one person toward another (cf. Esther 9:22).

As a people in covenant relationship with God, Israel had received His richest gift, His grace. God had been merciful, gracious, and good to the nation. The Torah itself was a gift of God's grace. The appropriate response to this manifestation of plenteous grace is suggested in Psalm 96:8: "Ascribe to the Lord the glory due his name; bring an offering, and come into his courts! Worship the Lord in holy array." David exclaimed in awe: "But who am I, and what is my people, that we should be able thus to offer willingly? For all things come from thee, and of thy own have we given thee" (1 Chron. 29:14).

For a model of giving, Christians look to God, "who gives to all men generously and without reproaching" (James 1:5). Sons and daughters of the Father imitate the one who "makes his sun rise on the evil and on the good, and sends rain on the just and on the unjust" (Matt. 5:45). Believers are moved by God's unparalleled example, in that He "did not spare his own Son but gave him up for us all" (Rom. 8:32).

1. The OT

God has always ministered His grace to the world through individuals and His people Israel. They reveal His grace to the world and in a sense become channels of blessing. Certain individuals in the biblical record epitomize the principles of true stewardship.

a. Abraham. God's covenant promise was "I will make of you a great nation, and I will bless you, and make your name great, so that you will be a blessing" (Gen. 12:2). Abraham, the father of the faithful, stands out as an example of total commitment to Yahweh in covenant relationship. Of him God could say, "I have chosen him [Heb. "I have known him"], that he may charge his children and his household after him to keep the way of the Lord by doing righteousness and justice" (Gen. 18:19). Stewardship presupposes a trust relationship. Fidelity to God, commitment to His will, and obedience to His commands are the hallmark of the true steward. In His appearances to Abraham Yahweh made it clear that He wanted to make him trustee of the knowledge of God.

b. Joseph. One of Jacob's sons became the ideal steward of the OT. His story dominates the last part of the book of Genesis. Sold into cruel slavery, he rose to positions of prominence in Potiphar's house (Gen. 39:4, 5) and in the Pharaoh's kingdom (Gen. 41:39-41). Joseph understood his mission. He realized that "God meant . . . for good," the harsh treatment he had suffered, in order "that many people should be kept alive" (Gen. 50:20). In considering Joseph's life, the psalmist noted that God "had sent a man ahead of them" (Ps. 105:17). As God's steward, Joseph brought great blessings to Egypt. "The king . . . made him lord of his house, and ruler of all his possessions, to instruct his princes at his pleasure, and to teach his elders wisdom" (verses 20-22). "To the ancient Egyptian nation God made Joseph a fountain of life. Through the integrity of Joseph the life of that whole people was preserved" (AA 13).

c. Israel. God wished to make Israel a channel of His truth, grace, and blessing to neighboring nations. His people were to be His stewards. These were the terms of His covenant with them: "Now therefore, if you will obey my voice and keep my covenant, you shall be my own possession among all peoples; for all the earth is mine, and you shall be to me a kingdom of priests and a holy nation" (Ex. 19:5, 6). They would be richly blessed; they would lend to other nations but never need to borrow (Deut. 28:12).

God's material blessing on Israel would attract the attention of the world. It was God's intention that the nations should inquire as to the reason for Israel's unusual prosperity. This would open the way for Israel to give effective witness to the Source of blessings and to point out the necessity of obeying the God of heaven (Isa. 44:8; 49:6; Mal. 3:12). God made every provision for His chosen people to be stewards of His saving grace: "I am the Lord, I have called you in righteousness, I have taken you by the hand and kept you; I have given you as a covenant to the people, a light to the nations, to open the eyes that are blind, to bring out the prisoners from the dungeon, from the prison those who sit in darkness" (Isa. 42:6, 7).

2. The NT

a. Jesus as God's perfect steward. Jesus came into the world as God's chief steward, sent by the Father (John 5:36). Restoration, recovery, and redemption of a lost planet were the terms of reference and the parameters of His stewardship (Luke 19:10; Eph. 1:10). It was as if the lost section of the cosmos had been placed in His hands, for Him to rescue the people from sin's slavery (Matt. 1:21). He came to bring life (John 10:10). The Father gave Him authority for mission and judgment (Matt. 28:19, 20; John 5:22-27; 8:29).

Jesus is the administrator of the plan of salvation, as Paul points out in Ephesians 1:9-23. The plan hinges on Christ and His saving activities. He takes charge and superintends the project, while still in subjection to His Father, still in human flesh. God commends Jesus for being "faithful to him who appointed him" (Heb. 3:2). For this reason Jesus is worthy of "more glory than Moses as the builder of a house has more honor than the house" (verse 3). As a faithful son over God's house, He is Himself the medium of salvation. "Consequently he is able for all time to save those who draw near to God through him, since he always lives to make intercession for them" (Heb. 7:25).

b. Stewardship in Christ's parables. The idea of stewardship finds amplification in certain of the parables of Jesus. In Luke 12, for instance, faithful and unfaithful stewards are contrasted. The servants are warned to maintain a state of readiness—loins girded, lights burning—waiting their master's return. At the sound of the first knock they are to answer the door quickly. The exact hour of his coming is not known; it may be the second or third watch of the night. For doing his master's bidding, "the faithful and wise steward" will then be "set over all his possessions" (verses 42-44). But there is another kind of steward—the unfaithful one, who is not prepared for the master's coming. "The master of that servant will come on a day when he does not expect him and at an hour he does not know, and will punish him, and put him with the unfaithful" (verse 46).

The point of the story was accountability for the knowledge and gifts of God. "And that servant who knew his master's will, but did not make ready or act according to his will, shall receive a severe beating" (verse 47). Jesus made it clear that this parable was for the disciples. On them the manifold grace of Christ had been freely bestowed. As stewards of their master's gifts, they were to share with others. At the end of the age full account of their stewardship would be required (cf. Matt. 24:45-51; 25:14-30).

Stewardship is the main motif of the parable of the pounds (Luke 19) and of the parable of the talents (Matthew 25). The nobleman, or landowner, travels to a far country. He calls his servants together to give them instructions and tasks to perform while he is away. In each instance he expects that they will make a profit by the wise use of their capital. Luke 19:13 indicates that they are to do business with them while he was away. In Matthew he "entrusted to them his property" (Matt. 25:14). The servants understood their responsibility. The five-talent servant "went at once and traded with them." The one who received two did likewise (verses 16, 17). In both parables the servants who carried out their stewardship responsibilities in the absence of the landowner/nobleman were commended and rewarded. The wise steward identifies with the master and his interests. There will, however, be a time of review and evaluation at some future date. Judgment begins "with the household of God" (1 Peter 4:17).

In Matthew 25:31-46 stewards are judged on the basis of their treatment of the unfortunate—the prisoners, the sick, the destitute, and the homeless. Those who shared unselfishly are surprised that the King declares these deeds to have been done to Him. They are invited to "inherit the kingdom" (verse 34). Those who fail the evaluation are consigned to "eternal punishment" (verse 46).

As can be seen in these parables, steward-ship has its rewards and punishments. In every case the master of the house is uncompromis-ing—those who have received his capital are required to improve it. The standard of judg-ment is clear: "Every one to whom much is given, of him will much be required; and of him to whom men commit much they will de-mand the more" (Luke 12:48).

c. Stewardship in the apostolic church. The church in the apostles' day presented a dynamic demonstration of Christian steward-ship. The members of the community un-derstood what it meant to be stewards, individually and as a corporate body. They modeled well the principles of Christian stew-ardship by their attitude and practice. Each member stood ready to perform good works, show generosity, and share their means. Acts 2:44, 45 describes Christian stewardship in action: "And all who believed were together and had all things in common; and they sold their possessions and goods and distributed them to all, as any had need."

The early Christians felt responsible for each other, whether Jew or Gentile, through-out the empire. This ecumenical awareness de-veloped early. When the Jerusalem church suffered during the famine that was predicted by the prophet Agabus, the believers in the Gentile world gave liberally toward the relief effort. Paul saw this crisis as an opportunity to demonstrate genuine *agapē* love. The worldwide fellowship was strengthened and united in the task. "And the disciples deter-mined, every one according to his ability, to send relief to the brethren who lived in Judea; and they did so, sending it to the elders by the hand of Barnabas and Saul" (Acts 11:29, 30).

In 2 Corinthians 9:6, 7 Paul develops a the-ology of giving: "The point is this: he who sows sparingly will also reap sparingly, and he who sows bountifully will also reap bounti-fully. Each one must do as he has made up his mind, not reluctantly or under compulsion, for God loves a cheerful giver."

The unselfish giving of early Christians had its reflex action. "You will be enriched in every way for great generosity, which through us will produce thanksgiving to God; for the rendering of this service not only supplies the wants of the saints but also overflows in many thanksgivings to God. Under the test of this service, you will glorify God by your obedi-ence in acknowledging the gospel of Christ, and by the generosity of your contribution for them and for all others" (verses 11-13).

While caring for members of the household of faith and for all who were in need in the communities where they lived, church mem-bers were not to neglect their own families. Stewardship responsibility begins with caring for the needs of blood relations. Paul states this very emphatically: "If any one does not provide for his relatives, and especially for his own family, he has disowned the faith and is worse than an unbeliever" (1 Tim. 5:8).

The apostles also urged upon the church the duty of providing financial support for the gospel ministry. In verse 18 Paul appealed to the words of Jesus, "the laborer deserves his wages" (Luke 10:7; Matt. 10:10). In encourag-ing Timothy to honor the elders (verses 17, 18), he cites an OT dictum: "You shall not muzzle an ox when it is treading out the grain." (See Deut. 25:4; cf. Num. 18:21; Neh. 12:44, 45.)

Although Paul did not always accept the gifts of the churches for the support of his ministry, he insisted on his right to such sup-port. The requirement is still valid.

"If we have sown spiritual good among you, is it too much if we reap your material benefits? . . . Do you not know that those who are employed in the temple service get their food from the temple, and those who serve at the altar share in the sacrificial offerings? In the same way, the Lord commanded that those who proclaim the gospel should get their liv-ing by the gospel" (1 Cor. 9:11-14).

The early church was infused with the spirit of liberality. They took the words of the apostle Paul very seriously: "Each one must do as he has made up his mind, not reluctantly or under compulsion, for God loves a cheerful giver" (2 Cor. 9:7). The church of the apostles is a stewardship model for all time.

The church in the apostles' time set the pattern, provided the benchmark. As Joseph was in Egypt and Israel among the nations, so those who take on Christ's name are both responsible and accountable. The blessings God has given to them they, in turn, are to pass on to the whole world. Stewardship is sharing the incomparable riches of Christ with fellow human beings. "This is how one should regard us, as servants of Christ and stewards of the mysteries of God. Moreover it is required of stewards that they be found trustworthy" (1 Cor. 4:1, 2).

The faith community does not exist for itself. It exists for the distribution, the sharing, of God's manifold grace with a needy world. This grace is more than sentiment; it addresses concrete situations and real needs. Those needs may sometimes be spiritual or they may be material. The steward has no option but to meet these needs wherever found and on whatever level.

E. Biblical Stewardship: Applications

As God's deputies on earth, the first couple and their descendants have been entrusted the stewardship of God-given resources. These include divine grace, life, time, talents, wealth, and the earth itself. (See Lifestyle II. C. 5.)

1. Stewardship of Divine Grace

The greatest gift that human beings have received from God is eternal life (John 3:16), not only in the hereafter but also now (John 5:24; 10:10). This is the "good news" Jesus came to spread. Before His ascension He entrusted the unfinished task to His disciples: "Go therefore and make disciples of all nations, baptizing them in the name of the Father and of the Son and of the Holy Spirit, teaching them to observe all that I have com-

manded you" (Matt. 28:19, 20).

Paul recognized his obligation to share the gospel of grace: "For necessity is laid upon me. Woe to me if I do not preach the gospel!" (1 Cor. 9:16). But he did not limit the responsibility to himself or even to his fellow apostles. To the Corinthians he wrote that "God . . . through Christ reconciled us to himself and gave us the ministry of reconciliation" (2 Cor. 5:18). He commended the Thessalonians because the "word of the Lord sounded forth from . . . [them] in Macedonia and Achaia"; their faith in God had "gone forth everywhere" (1 Thess. 1:8). He also prayed that Philemon's sharing of his faith might "promote the knowledge of all the good that is ours in Christ" (Philemon 6).

Peter likewise spoke of the Christians' duty to preach the good news: "But you are a chosen race, a royal priesthood, a holy nation, God's own people, that you may declare the wonderful deeds of him who called you out of darkness into his marvelous light" (1 Peter 2:9). The Gentiles were to observe the life of the Christians and "glorify God" because of it (verse 12). The apostle also urged that believers "always be prepared to make a defense" of the hope in them (1 Peter 3:15).

Revelation 14:6-12 contains good news, "an eternal gospel" (verse 6) to proclaim to all the world. The focus is on the God whose promise and Word transcend the present gloomy situation and point to the glorious outcome described in the final chapters of Revelation. The good news is that God does love this planet and is determined to rescue and renew it so that His original purpose in Creation may be fulfilled. Sharing this vital message in its fullness is part and parcel of Christian stewardship.

The church, as a corporate body, is under constraint to model consistently an authentic stewardship community in an increasingly secular society. In order to do so it must rein in its tastes, resist conspicuous consumption, and imitate as closely as possible the way of living of the lowly Nazarene. This will help give credibility to the church's witness.

The individual Christian must not, however, look to the organization to assume his or her personal responsibility. If the stewardship motif says anything, it is that we are held accountable as individuals for doing the best we can with what we have, to the glory of God and to the service of fellow humans and all of creation.

In the end-time, the people of God are to join in the proclamation of the three angels' messages of Revelation 14. Because they have been the recipients of God's free salvation, they are under obligation to share the message of hope and life.

2. Stewardship of Life

Life is a gift of God and belongs to God, its source. But God has graciously entrusted life to the human race. Of it He requires wise administration.

God is the abundant Lifegiver, who delights in sharing life with His creatures. The biblical account throbs with the language of dynamic, irrepressible life. For example:

"And God said, 'Let the waters bring forth swarms of living creatures, and let birds fly above the earth across the firmament of the heavens.' So God created the great sea monsters and every living creature that moves, with which the waters swarm, according to their kinds, and every winged bird according to its kind. And God saw that it was good. And God blessed them, saying, 'Be fruitful and multiply and fill the waters in the seas, and let birds multiply on the earth' " (Gen. 1:20-22).

Adam became a living being after God "breathed into his nostrils the breath of life." He and Eve were instructed to "be fruitful and multiply, and fill the earth" (verse 28). Adam's stewardship responsibility was to join his Creator in engendering life and preserving the precious breath of life in all humans. Cain evidently recognized this responsibility, as is suggested by the way he responded to God. Because of his failure to preserve his brother's life, Cain was cursed by God, for the voice of Abel's blood cried forth from the ground (Gen. 4:10-12). God called Cain to account for denying his stewardship of his brother's life. He likewise holds us responsible for the life and welfare of our fellow human beings.

After the Flood Noah's sons were instructed as to how they, too, as responsible stewards, must treasure God's gift of life. "For your lifeblood I will surely require a reckoning. . . . Whoever sheds the blood of man, by man shall his blood be shed; for God made man in his own image" (Gen. 9:5, 6). By the solemn proclamation of the sanctity of life God made the life of human beings secure. "This warning is directed against homicide and suicide" (see 1BC 264).

The sacrificial system, instituted at the gates of Eden, in which the death that human beings deserved because of their sins was averted only by the death of a substitute, was an indication of the high premium God placed on human life. This redemption, or atonement, has always been precious and costly (Lev. 1:1-5; 1 Peter 1:18, 19). The cross of Calvary is the ultimate statement regarding the value of human life.

Human stewardship of life is enjoined in the Decalogue. The sixth commandment reads, "You shall not kill" (Ex. 20:13). In Leviticus 17:14 God's regard for life is shown in rules concerning blood: "For the life of every creature is the blood of it; therefore I have said to the people of Israel, You shall not eat the blood of any creature, for the life of every creature is its blood; whoever eats it shall be cut off."

Another evidence of God's high valuation of human life is seen in the divine instructions regarding the cities of refuge. Those guilty of manslaughter could flee there and be saved (Num. 35:11-15; Deut. 19:4-7). At the same time, the Israelites were commanded not to hate their neighbors or to bear grudges; rather they were to love their neighbors as themselves (Lev. 19:17, 18). This was part of their stewardship responsibility.

3. Stewardship of the Earth

As noted (I. C), "the earth is the Lord's and the fulness thereof, the world and those who dwell therein" (Ps. 24:1). At Creation everything was "very good" (Gen. 1:31). Millennia later Paul wrote, "The whole creation has been groaning in travail" (Rom. 8:22). Today, the earth reels under the weight of pollution and misuse.

The Israelites were taught that the earth must be given opportunity to renew itself. Every seventh year the land must also have its Sabbath (Lev. 25:2-7). During the sabbatical year the land was to lie fallow. No planting or pruning was to take place. If Israel gave the land its due rest, the Lord would see that no one lacked food. Another way in which God showed His concern for Israel's proper stewardship of the land appears in the command to allow new trees to grow up before their fruit was harvested. "But in the fifth year you may eat of their fruit, that they may yield more richly for you" (Lev. 19:23-25). Every Israelite was responsible for helping to maintain the vitality of the soil. By following God's rules for the land, the Israelites showed their allegiance to God, the owner and Creator of all the earth.

The stewardship of the earth, which God entrusted to Adam and Eve, still belongs to their descendants. We who inhabit the planet are responsible for its care. In the final judgment, the "destroyers of the earth" are destroyed (Rev. 11:18).

4. Stewardship of Talents and Abilities

Stewardship includes the judicious use of God-given abilities and talents. For the construction of the desert tabernacle, God gave "ability and intelligence, with knowledge and all craftsmanship" to those who were to do the work (Ex. 31:2-6). Centuries later Paul described the spiritual gifts bestowed on believers for the benefit of the church body (Rom. 12:4-8; 1 Cor. 12; Eph. 4:7-14; 1 Peter 4:10, 11). These gifts are skills and abilities, given by God and placed at the believers' disposal, to be used as the Spirit directs; they serve to enrich and upbuild the fellowship of believers. The church is a community of gifted people who serve the world. Proper stewardship of these gifts entails ministry and mission, reaching out to meet human need in Christ's name. (See Spiritual Gifts I, II.)

Christians must make the best possible use of their communication skills. Paul encouraged believers to let their "speech always be gracious, seasoned with salt" (Col. 4:6), to set "an example in speech" (1 Tim. 4:12), and to be characterized by "sound speech that cannot be censured" (Titus 2:8). As all other gifts, speech should be used to the glory of God and the blessing of others. Above all, the talent of speech should be cultivated and used to share the good news of Jesus with all who come into the believer's sphere of influence.

In His parables of the pounds and the talents, Jesus pointed out the importance of using what the master had entrusted to his servants (Luke 19:12-27; Matt. 25:14-30). The correct use of the master's means—that is, their multiplication—produced approval and reward. The talent that did not grow was taken away from the servant, who was condemned to outer darkness for failing to use his talent. While the story speaks of money, "talents" or "pounds" can be taken to refer to God-given abilities and talents for one's own self-development and the benefit of others.

II. Historical Overview

A. *Judaism*

Jews followed OT practices in tithes and offerings during the intertestamental period. For example, Tobit (second century B.C.) relates his fictional trips to Jerusalem for the yearly feasts, on which he took with him the first fruits and the tithes of his produce. He specifies, "Of all my produce I would give a tenth to the sons of Levi who ministered at

Jerusalem; a second tenth I would sell, and I would go and spend the proceeds each year at Jerusalem; the third tenth I would give to those to whom it was my duty" (Tobit 1:7, 8). Rabbinic sources tell us that the first tithe was collected yearly; the second was due in years 1, 2, 4, and 5 of the sabbatical cycle; the third tithe was given in the third and sixth years. Thus, every year except the seventh, a person paid two tithes.

The Mishnah contains tractates on tithes and offerings. *Terumoth* specifies the gifts that should be presented to the priest, the average amount of which should be one fiftieth of the produce. *Ma'aseroth,* the tractate on tithes, gives detailed instruction on which vegetables and fruits should be tithed. A third tractate explains the payment of second tithe.

At the same time, the biblical philosophy of returning tithes and offerings out of gratitude seems to have been eroding; giving became a way of getting something in return. The Wisdom of Sirach maintains that "almsgiving atones for sin" (3:30). Tobit affirms that "charity delivers from death and keeps you from entering the darkness" (4:10; cf. 12:8-10).

After the destruction of the Temple a great deal of importance was attached to the correct payment of tithes. The concept of a person's being "trustworthy in tithes" came into vogue, and those who did not pay tithe were considered to be second-class Jews. While tithe paying was not obligatory except in the land of Israel, there is evidence that Jews in the Diaspora also set aside their tithe.

B. Early Church

The church of the apostles understood itself to be a new community whose life was derived from the risen Christ. "To live is Christ" (Phil. 1:21). The Pauline expression "in Christ" signifies that the members of this body have a radical new orientation: "Therefore, if any one is in Christ, he is a new creation" (2 Cor. 5:17). Their stewardship practices were the outworking of the principles that Jesus taught and the apostles passed on to them: "For you know

the grace of our Lord Jesus Christ, that though he was rich, yet for your sakes he became poor, so that by his poverty you might become rich" (2 Cor. 8:9; cf. Phil. 2:5-8). However, after the apostles' demise the spirit of liberality and the grace dynamic waned. Gradually, good works, gifts to the poor, and support of the gospel ministry were no longer viewed as the outworking of the "grace of our Lord Jesus Christ" but as a means to secure salvation. Following this line of thought, Clement, bishop of Rome in the last decade of the first century, stated, "Good, then, are alms as repentance from sin; better is fasting than prayer, and alms than both." Furthermore, "alms lighten the burden of sin" (*To the Corinthians* 2. 16). In the *Shepherd of Hermas* (early second century), fasting was commanded as a sacrifice "noble, and sacred, and acceptable to the Lord" (*Simile* 5. 3).

The early church had no tithing system such as that known among Jews. According to Irenaeus (c. 130-c. 200), "those who have received liberty" no longer paid tithes as did the Jews, but "set aside all their possessions for the Lord's purposes, bestowing joyfully and freely not the less valuable portions of their property" (*Against Heresies* 4. 18. 2).

Tertullian (c. A.D. 200) describes the giving of Christians in Carthage. They were not to be compulsory, but voluntary: "as it were, piety's deposit fund." These gifts were to be used "to support and bury poor people, to supply the wants of boys and girls destitute of means and parents, and of old persons confined now to the house," and to care for those in prison for their faith (*Apology* 39).

Epiphanius, writing in the fourth century, pointed out that tithing was no more binding than circumcision or Sabbath observance. It had been given, he said, "to keep us from overlooking the 'iota,' the initial letter of the name of Jesus" (*Against Heresies* 1. 1. 8).

In the late fourth and early fifth centuries, voices began to be heard demanding that Christians pay tithe. Ambrose of Milan (340-397) affirmed that God had reserved one tenth of the grain, wine, fruit, cattle, garden, business, and even hunting; it was "not lawful for a man to retain what God had reserved for Himself." A good Christian should not taste his fruits before offering something of them to God (*Sermons* 33, 34). Augustine (354-430) maintained that Christians must pay tithes in order for their righteousness to exceed that of the scribes and Pharisees (Matt. 5:20; *Exposition on Psalm* 146. 7). In 576 the provincial Council of Tours directed Christians to pay their tithes. In 585 the Second Council of Macon prescribed excommunication for those who refused to pay tithe. However, tithe was not necessarily one tenth of one's income, but a stipulated donation.

C. The Middle Ages

The medieval understanding of salvation by merit greatly affected the idea of stewardship. The primary motive for giving was to save one's soul. Fees for different services were instituted: for marrying, for burying, for confessing, for saying a mass for the salvation of a dead person's soul. In order to raise money a religious body might pledge itself to far more masses than the priests could possibly say. The fees for saying masses, along with the sale of indulgences, were chief among the complaints that led to the Protestant Reformation.

From Constantine (d. 337) onward, the Christian church was a state church. As centuries passed, the distinction between ecclesiastical and state tithes and taxes became virtually impossible to distinguish. For example, Charlemagne (742-814) regulated the division of tithe into three parts: for the clergy, for the poor, and for church support. Penalties were enforced on those who failed to pay. In England a civil law enjoining the payment of tithe was passed in 787. A 1295 law ordained that tithes were to be paid on the gross value of all crops; it further dictated how the tithe was to be paid on milk, animals, wool, pastures, and even bees. Personal tithes were also required: tithe of the profits of business and trades. Again the word "tithe" did not necessarily connote one tenth.

In the medieval system of giving, voluntary giving as a stewardship of God's means was to a great extent lost. Giving was demanded by the church and the state. The spirit of stewardship that had characterized the first-century church was no longer recognizable.

D. Reformation

The Reformation was in many respects a reaction to the abuse of clerical power and the establishment of a merit system of salvation. It did not succeed, however, in destroying the symbiotic relation between church and state. Tithing was imposed, not so much by the church, as by the state. In Germany, from 1555 on, when Lutheranism was legalized and placed under the protection of the Lutheran princes, the right of ecclesiastical oversight—and with it the right to tithe—came into the hands of the territorial secular authority. Tithes gathered were for the support of the ministry, the maintenance of schools, and the care of the poor.

Even though most Protestants felt comfortable with secular enforcement of church legislation, some dissented. Ulrich Zwingli (1484-1531) strongly disagreed with the ecclesiastical system of tithing, holding that giving should be voluntary rather than mandatory. Other groups, such as the Anabaptists, the Quakers, and the English Separatists, were equally against ecclesiastical tithing. However, such dissenters were in the minority. It was generally understood and accepted that the state should care for its obligations by sharing its largess and using its power to enforce the church's financial levies upon its members.

On the Catholic side, the Council of Trent (1545-1563) declared that the payment of tithes was due God and that all who refused to pay them were to be excommunicated. However, this regulation was not enforced. The French Revolution brought tithing in the Roman Catholic Church to an end.

E. The North American Experiment

Even in colonial America it was difficult to draw effective lines of demarcation between church and state. The pattern of centuries with the state financing the church was too strongly ingrained and took many years to shake off. The American Revolution helped reverse the trends and practices of many centuries. But the great "American experiment" proved traumatic to the churches, which could no longer look to the state to finance their activities. Thrown on their own resources, the churches were forced to reexamine the apostolic model. The new situation was a blessing in disguise. Voluntary gifts actuated by the spirit of Christ were obviously the path to take, but church leaders had no history, no tradition, no past experience, to draw on.

Innovative church leaders devised various methods. Unfortunately, some were unworthy of the name Christian. Pew rentals, bazaars, suppers, games of chance, and lotteries were tried. Some clergy decried these "new" methods, pointing out that they were no better than the "old" methods of pre-Reformation days.

The American church can be credited with the revival of interest in Christian stewardship, although the emphasis was almost exclusively on the financial aspect. Church historians usually give the late 1800s as the beginning of the stewardship movement in America. From the outset the movement was fueled by the great interest in foreign missions. Later came the attempt to construct the theological base and the effort to bring practice and theory together in the local church. Many training programs and strategies were put in place, with varying degrees of success. In the year 1920 twenty-nine denominations from the United States and Canada came together at the call of a group of stewardship leaders in New York City to form the United Stewardship Council.

III. The Seventh-day Adventist Stewardship Experience

Most Christians would agree with the Seventh-day Adventist Statement of Fundamental Beliefs, which states:

"We are God's stewards, entrusted by Him with time and opportunities, abilities and possessions, and the blessings of the earth and its resources. We are responsible to Him for their proper use. We acknowledge God's ownership by faithful service to Him and our fellow men, and by returning tithes and giving offerings for the proclamation of His gospel and the support and growth of His church. Stewardship is a privilege given to us by God for nurture in love and the victory over selfishness and covetousness. The steward rejoices in the blessings that come to others as a result of his faithfulness" (*SDA Yearbook* 1999, 7).

Seventh-day Adventist history runs parallel to the development of the American religious scene. Born in the religious fervor of the missionary movement and forged specifically by the intense apocalypticism of the times (the great Second Advent movement) the Seventh-day Adventist Church developed a strong stewardship consciousness.

A. Finances

An entire chapter of the *Seventh-day Adventist Church Manual* is dedicated to gospel finance. There the Adventist concept of stewardship is set forth. The paragraph over "Stewardship" reads:

"Christians are God's stewards, entrusted with His goods, and the divine counsel is that 'it is required in stewards, that a man be found faithful' (1 Cor. 4:2). The question of stewardship in its fullest form covers many aspects of Christian life and experience, such as our time, our influence, and our service, but there is no doubt that the stewardship of our means is a vitally important phase of this question. It is one which concerns every member of the church. It involves our recognition of the sovereignty of God, of His ownership of all things, and of the bestowal of His grace upon our hearts. As we grow in the understanding of these principles we shall be led into a fuller appreciation of the way God's love operates in our lives" (*SDA Church Manual* 1995, 135, 136).

1. Tithes

In 1859 Adventists adopted a plan called Systematic Benevolence that encouraged regular giving, proportional in some way to one's income or property. Early in 1863 the *Review and Herald* suggested one tenth of one's income as a minimum contribution. "The children of Israel were required to give a tithe, or tenth, of all their increase. . . . And it cannot be supposed that the Lord requires less of His people when time is emphatically short, and a great work is to be accomplished in the use of their means in giving the last merciful message to the world" (RH Jan. 6, 1863). In 1876 the General Conference unanimously adopted a resolution stating: "We believe it to be the duty of all our brethren and sisters, whether connected with churches or living alone, under ordinary circumstances, to devote one tenth of all their income from whatever source, to the cause of God" (*ibid.* Apr. 6, 1876).

Adventist pioneers saw tithing as rooted in Scripture. Ellen White wrote many articles and devoted entire chapters in her books to the subject of gospel finance. The rendering of tithe and offerings was a requirement of gospel order. The motivation was evangelical: support of the gospel ministry and the spread of the message of salvation. By the year 1878 the tithing plan was well established in denominational policy and practice.

Around the world, church members and their children compute the tithe as one tenth of their income. Those who conduct their own businesses are encouraged to return the tithe on their earnings.

Tithe is used for the support of the gospel ministry, for the prosecution of the church's mission to the world. This is done on the basis of the OT use of tithe for the support of the Levites (Num. 18:21). The General Conference *Working Policy* states:

"The tithe is to be held sacred for the work of the ministry and Bible teaching, including conference administration in the care of churches and field outreach operations. The tithe is not to be expended upon other lines of work such as church or institutional debt paying or building operations" (V 05 05).

Local churches remit 100 percent of the tithe contributed by the members to the conference or mission. These associations of churches forward one tenth of the tithe received to the unions, which are groupings of conferences. Next, the unions send one tenth of the tithe they receive to the division, one of the 12 sections of the world church. Finally, the divisions send on one tenth of their income to the General Conference. Thus, church members, without reference to where they live, have a part in the mission of the church through the tithe, which they return to the local congregation.

The church sees in its financial plan "a larger purpose than appears in its financial and statistical reports. The arrangement is more than a means of gathering and distributing funds. It is, under God, one of the great unifying factors of the Advent movement" (*SDA Church Manual* 1995, 137).

2. Offerings

Recognizing that the Israelites were called upon to give at least a second tithe (Deut. 12:17, 18; 14:22-27) and possibly also a third one (Deut. 14:28, 29), early Adventist leaders encouraged believers to contribute freewill offerings for other church projects, above and beyond the 10 percent tithe. For example, in 1876 an additional "one third" offering (of the Systematic Benevolence quota) was suggested for the Tract and Missionary Society.

Later came other offerings, notable among them the weekly Sabbath School offerings. In 1878 penny boxes were placed near the door to receive funds for local Sabbath School expenses. Sabbath schools started collecting offerings for missions in 1885, providing members the opportunity of supporting a worldwide church. Part of the special offering taken on the last Sabbath of the quarter is designated for a special project which is highlighted throughout the quarter.

A variety of offerings is collected in local churches, either regularly or occasionally. Their use is carefully controlled by appropriate entities at the local church, the conference, the union, and the General Conference.

Serious, committed Christians, make certain that the funds entrusted to them by the Creator are used in His service. Through estate planning, church members may place their estate in the hands of trustees so that treasure which they handled wisely in life may continue to bring glory to God and serve human need even after their demise. This is good stewardship that brings satisfaction and fulfillment to the follower of Christ.

3. Department of Stewardship and Development

In 1966 the General Conference of Seventh-day Adventists organized what became known the next year as the Department of Stewardship and Development to assist conferences and world divisions in promoting stewardship awareness. This department was asked to prepare literature, training programs, and seminars for pastors and churches. In addition to practical, hands-on teaching, the department was to keep on the cutting edge of theological issues pertaining to stewardship. Walter M. Starks was chosen as the first director of the new department.

Further developments have ensued. In 1971 provision was made for stewardship secretaries in the local churches to promote stewardship of temple, treasure, talents, and time among members. In 1980 stewardship was connected with the Ministerial Association. At the creation of the Church Ministries Department in 1985, the official fostering of stewardship, through published materials and various

workshops and seminars, became a part of that new entity. In 1995, when some of these functions were divided, Stewardship became a separate department.

Although returning tithes and giving offerings is essential to the Seventh-day Adventist theology of stewardship, stewardship includes much more. Stewardship touches the whole of life, and its concepts inform the pressing questions posed today. These questions bring up the issues with which church members must grapple—environmental and social concerns, public and personal health concerns, the pressing issue of poverty, and all the perplexing questions that surround the beginning and end of human life and, of course, the use of earth's finite resources. The list is not exhaustive. But the biblical teaching about stewardship enables Christians to balance these apparently conflicting concerns in a manner that is pleasing to Jesus Christ who is Lord. The ongoing task for Christians is how to apply these great principles in today's complex world.

B. Earth

Human beings are at the mercy of nature, but at present the planet itself groans under the human attacks and is indeed threatened with distinction at the hand of humankind. By greed and wastefulness, often under the guise of advancing technology, humans have wounded Planet Earth unto death. The earth is filled with life-threatening toxic wastes. Natural resources have been dangerously squandered. In some cases the land has been robbed by overuse of its ability to produce. Even the seas have been plundered of their once-rich resources.

In such a world as this, Seventh-day Adventist Christians are called to live a simple life, without greed or waste. Recognizing that the resources of the earth are finite, they are to protect and conserve the environment. The church promotes vegetarianism as a healthful way to increase the availability of food. Schools and churches carry out varied and often creative ecological programs.

The observance of the seventh-day Sabbath, in loving response to the commandment (Ex. 20:8-11), provides an opportunity for Adventists to celebrate Creation along with the Creator. Individuals, families, and church groups frequently spend Sabbath afternoons in nature activities. These promote an understanding of the marvels of the natural world as well as the need for protecting God's creation.

In 1992 the Annual Council voted a document, "Caring for God's Creation," which presents the Seventh-day Adventist position on stewardship of the earth. We quote in part:

"The world in which we live is a gift of love from the Creator God, from 'him who made the heavens, the earth, the sea and the springs of water' (Rev. 14:7, NIV; cf. Rev. 11:17, 18). Within this creation He placed humans, set intentionally in relationship with Himself, other persons, and the surrounding world. Therefore, as Seventh-day Adventists, we hold its preservation and nurture to be intimately related to our service to Him. . . .

"Because we recognize humans as part of God's creation, our concern for the environment extends to personal health and lifestyle. We advocate a wholesome manner of living and reject the use of substances such as tobacco, alcohol, and other drugs that harm the body and consume earth's resources; and we promote a simple vegetarian diet. . . .

"We accept the challenge to work toward restoring God's overall design. Moved by faith in God, we commit ourselves to promote the healing that rises at both personal and environmental levels from integrated lives dedicated to serve God and humanity.

"In this commitment we confirm our stewardship of God's creation and believe that total restoration will be complete only when God makes all things new" (RH Dec. 31, 1992).

These statements signal a growing awareness on the part of Seventh-day Adventists of the impact of Christian stewardship on their interaction with God's world. The world and material substance are not bad in and of themselves; in fact, "all things bright and beautiful, all creatures great and small" are made by the Creator to be enjoyed by human beings (cf. Gen. 1:31). Christians are to treasure "the beauty of the earth." They should have respect for the earth, but they must not worship it. Throughout Scriptures God is always above and apart from Creation.

C. God's Grace

Revelation 14:6-12 contains good news, "an eternal gospel" (verse 6) to proclaim to all the world. The focus is on the God whose promise and Word transcend the present gloomy situation and point to the glorious outcome described in the final chapters of Revelation. The good news is that God does love this planet and is determined to rescue and renew it so that His original purpose in Creation will be fulfilled. Sharing this vital message in its fullness is part and parcel of Christian stewardship to which Adventists are committed.

Because of this aspect of stewardship, Adventists are dedicated to the ministry of bringing the gospel to everyone. Because they are stewards of God's grace, Adventists operate medical and educational institutions and relief organizations. They preach and teach, and they support those who carry out ministry. (See Lifestyle II. A.)

D. Life and Health

Contrary to Greek dualism, which perceived a human being as body and soul, the latter imprisoned in the first and eager to be set free from it, the Scriptures admit no such dichotomy. They speak of wholeness. Far from being despicable because it is earthly, the body is of major importance. Thus, in order to keep the mind and spirit in optimal condition, a person must care for the body, which is "a temple of the Holy Spirit" (1 Cor. 6:19). For this reason, "health reform and the teaching of health and temperance are inseparable parts of the Advent message" (SDA Church Manual 1995, 148).

In keeping with the biblical injunction, the Seventh-day Adventist Church has fostered healthful living among its members as well as others whom it may reach. Around the globe a well-developed system of medical institutions seeks to alleviate suffering and promote wellness. The *Church Manual* states, "We belong to God, body, soul, and spirit. It is therefore our religious duty to observe the laws of health, both for our own well-being and happiness, and for more efficient service to God and our fellow men" (*ibid.* 1995, 148; see Health; Lifestyle II. B).

In today's technological society, stewardship of the body includes life-and-death decisions, especially those relating to the termination of life through abortion or euthanasia. In harmony with the biblical teaching, Adventists are committed to the value and sanctity of human life. Two General Conference documents of 1992 deal with the issues.

The "Guidelines on Abortion" are based on "broad biblical principles" that life is a valuable gift from God and at the same time our response to God's will; yet it is our right and responsibility to make decisions regarding life. "Prenatal human life is a magnificent gift of God. . . . Thus prenatal life must not be thoughtlessly destroyed. Abortion should be performed only for the most serious reasons." Further, "the church does not serve as conscience for individuals; however, it should provide moral guidance." Decisions on abortion should be made by the individuals involved, aided by "accurate information, biblical principles, and the guidance of the Holy Spirit. Moreover, these decisions are best made within the context of healthy family relationships." Finally, "church members should be encouraged to participate in the ongoing consideration of their moral responsibilities with regard to abortion in the light of the teaching of Scripture" (RH Dec. 31, 1992; see Marriage II. F. 1).

Based on the same biblical principles, the document "Care for the Dying" appeals to practical and responsible Christian love.

"After seeking divine guidance and considering the interests of those affected by the decision (Rom. 14.7), as well as medical advice, a person who is capable of deciding should determine whether to accept or reject life-extending medical interventions." When the person is not capable of making such a decision, those closest to the individual should responsibly face the decision. Compassionate love should permeate the environment surrounding the dying. (See Marriage II. F. 2.)

"While Christian love may lead to the withholding or withdrawing of medical interventions that only increase suffering or prolong dying, Seventh-day Adventists do not practice 'mercy killing' or assist in suicide (Gen. 9:5, 6; Ex. 20:13; 23:7). They are opposed to active euthanasia, the intentional taking of the life of a suffering or dying person" (RH Dec. 31, 1992).

E. Time

Time is a precious gift of God. It is the stuff of which life is made. How it is used says a great deal about one's stewardship—one's relationship with the Creator. The biblical writers speak to the shortness of time and the necessity of making the most of it. Time is to be used in the development of one's self and in the expression of neighborly love. "Teach us to number our days," says the psalmist (Ps. 90:12), and the wise man exhorts, "Whatever your hand finds to do, do it with your might; for there is no work or thought or knowledge or wisdom in Sheol, to which you are going" (Eccl. 9:10). Paul urges "making the most of the time, because the days are evil" (Eph. 5:16), and he notes that "it is full time now for you to wake from sleep" (Rom. 13:11). Jesus counsels His followers to work while it is day (the time of opportunity), for "night comes, when no one can work" (John 9:4).

F. Children: The Greatest Treasure

Material goods give the Christian steward the means to do ministry in tangible ways. But treasure is not confined to material possessions. Children, "a heritage of the Lord" (Ps. 127:3), are among His most precious gifts. They are placed in the hands of parents, who become responsible for preparing them for service in this life and the world to come, when God will ask, "Where is the flock that was given you, your beautiful flock?" (Jer. 13:20). In parenthood human beings are cocreators. Their offspring are candidates for immortality, who must be gently and firmly moved toward the place where they too can assume full stewardship responsibilities.

Therefore, Christian education—discipline and training—is of great importance. The development of all the faculties is required under the great commandment (Matt. 22:37), and the intentional transmission of values and the culture is critical. The church is an intergenerational community. An excellent example of passing the faith on from generation to generation is that of Eunice and Lois, Timothy's mother and grandmother. "I am reminded of your sincere faith," says Paul to Timothy, "a faith that dwelt first in your grandmother Lois and your mother Eunice and now, I am sure, dwells in you" (2 Tim. 1:5; cf. Deut. 6:7).

Raising children for the Lord is the stewardship duty of parents and indeed of the entire community of faith (Isa. 54:13). Seventh-day Adventists take this stewardship obligation seriously and have developed a system of education, from kindergarten through the university, which is the second largest among Protestant denominations. In addition, Sabbath School, Pathfinder clubs, and a variety of other activities for children and youth are designed to protect and develop this treasure. (See Marriage I. B. 4.)

One official publication sets forth the purpose of Adventist education as follows:

"All children and youth have been entrusted by the church to the education system for spiritual nurture and educational excellence. . . . The education program is predicated on the belief that each student is unique and of inestimable value, and on the importance of the development of the whole per-

son. . . . The total process of Seventh-day Adventist education seeks to renew faith in Christ, to restore in man the image of his Maker, to nurture in man an intelligent dedication to the work of God on earth, and to develop in man a practical preparation for conscientious service to his fellow man" (NAD *Working Policy* 1993-1994, F 05 05, F 05 10).

G. Talents and Abilities

The Scriptures indicate that God endows human beings with gifts and abilities (1 Cor. 12:4-11) that He expects them to use in service to others. This was true also in OT times (Ex. 31:2-6). God gives humans "ability and intelligence, with knowledge and all craftsmanship, to devise artistic designs, . . . for work in every craft" (verses 3-5).

Paul speaks at length about the *charismata*—what is given as a gift. These are skills and abilities that are placed at God's disposal to be used as the Spirit directs. So-called natural gifts and skills become *charismata* only as they are used for the enrichment and upbuilding of the fellowship. The church is described as a community of gifted people—charismatics—who are at the service of the world. Stewardship, therefore, entails ministry, mission, reaching out to meet human need in Christ's name through the exercise of the gifts (1 Peter 4:10, 11; Rom. 12:6-8).

Christians should also make the best possible use of their communication skills. The talent of speech is to be cultivated and used to share the good news of the gospel with all who come into the sphere of their influence. The gift of speech has great potential for good or evil. As all other gifts, it must be used to the glory of God and the blessing of fellow humans.

H. Citizenship

Stewardship also involves support of and respect for properly constituted government. The Department of Public Affairs and Religious Liberty of the Seventh-day Adventist Church provides leadership and counsels the church's members on good citizenship:

"In view of its divinely ordained role, civil government is entitled to humanity's respectful and willing obedience in temporal matters to the extent that civil requirements do not conflict with those of God; in other words, humanity is bound to 'render therefore unto Caesar the things which are Caesar's," to reserve for "God the things that are God's" (Matt. 22:21), to exercise an active, personal interest and concern in matters affecting the public welfare, and to be an exemplary citizen" (NAD *Working Policy* 1993-1994, HC 05 02).

The NT teaches that Christians are "to be subject to rulers and authorities, to be obedient, to be ready to do whatever is good" (Titus 3:1; cf. 1 Peter 2:17; Rom. 13:1). As part of their priestly function Christians are to pray "for kings, and all who are in high positions" (1 Tim. 2:2). Jesus' words imply obligation, duty: "Render therefore unto Caesar the things which are Caesar's, and unto God the things that are God's" (Matt. 22:21, KJV). This is in obedience to the second great commandment, "You shall love your neighbor as yourself" (verse 39). All that is basic to good citizenship can be subsumed under the stewardship motif. Again, faithfulness in these matters is regarded by Heaven as prerequisite to greater responsibilities. In the parable the master says, "Well done, good and faithful servant; you have been faithful over a little, I will set you over much; enter into the joy of your master" (Matt. 25:23; see Lifestyle II. C. 4).

IV. Ellen G. White Comments

A. On the Concept

"By the terms of our stewardship we are placed under obligation, not only to God, but to man. To the infinite love of the Redeemer every human being is indebted for the gifts of life. Food and raiment and shelter, body and mind and soul—all are the purchase of His blood. And by the obligation of gratitude and service thus imposed, Christ has bound us to our fellow men. He bids us, 'By love serve one another' (Gal. 5:13). 'Inasmuch as ye have done it unto one of the least of these my brethren, ye have done it unto me' (Matt. 25:40)" (Ed 139).

"The idea of stewardship should have a practical bearing upon all the people of God. . . . Practical benevolence will give spiritual life to thousands of nominal professors of the truth who now mourn over their darkness. It will transform them from selfish, covetous worshipers of mammon, to earnest, faithful coworkers with Christ in the salvation of sinners" (CS 112, 113).

"The spirit of liberality is the spirit of heaven. The spirit of selfishness is the spirit of Satan. Christ's self-sacrificing love is revealed upon the cross. He gave all that He had, and then gave Himself, that man might be saved. The cross of Christ appeals to the benevolence of every follower of the blessed Saviour. The principle illustrated there is to give, give. This, carried out in actual benevolence and good works, is the true fruit of the Christian life. The principle of worldlings is to get, get, and thus they expect to secure happiness; but, carried out in all its bearings, the fruit is misery and death" (RH Nov. 15, 1906).

"We should never forget that God has placed us on trial in this world, to determine our fitness for the future life. None can enter heaven whose characters are defiled by the foul blot of selfishness. Therefore God tests us here by committing to us temporal possessions, that our use of these may show whether we can be entrusted with eternal riches. It is only as the self-sacrificing life of Christ is reflected in our life that we can be in harmony with heaven, and be fitted to enter there" (2SM 134).

"Evidence of the work of grace in the heart is given when we do good to all men as we have opportunity. The proof of our love is given in a Christlike spirit, a willingness to impart the good things God has given us, a readiness to practice self-denial and self-sacrifice in order to help advance the cause of

God and suffering humanity. Never should we pass by the object that calls for our liberality. We reveal that we have passed from death unto life when we act as faithful stewards of God's grace. God has given us His goods; He has given us His pledged word that if we are faithful in our stewardship, we shall lay up in heaven treasures that are imperishable" (RH May 15, 1900).

"A steward identifies himself with his master. He accepts the responsibilities of a steward, and he must act in his master's stead, doing as his master would do were he presiding. His master's interests become his. The position of a steward is one of dignity because his master trusts him. If in any wise he acts selfishly and turns the advantages gained by trading with his Lord's goods to his own advantage, he has perverted the trust reposed in him" (9T 246).

B. On Creation

"The things of nature, upon which we look today, give us but a faint conception of Eden's beauty and glory; yet the natural world, with unmistakable voice, proclaims the love of God. Even now 'the earth is full of the goodness of the Lord.' It still reveals the working of the great Master Artist. It declares that One omnipotent in power, great in goodness and mercy, has created all things" (AUCR June 1, 1900).

"We were brought into existence because we were needed. How sad the thought that if we stand on the wrong side, in the ranks of the enemy, we are lost to the design of our creation. We are disappointing our Redeemer; the powers He designed for His service are used to oppose His grace and matchless love" (ST Apr. 22, 1903).

"Every faculty of mind and soul reflected the Creator's glory. Endowed with high mental and spiritual gifts Adam and Eve were made but 'little lower than angels' (Heb. 2:7), that they might not only discern the wonders of the visible universe, but comprehend moral responsibilities and obligations" (Ed 20).

"The power of God is manifested in the beating of the heart, in the action of the lungs, and in the living currents that circulate through the thousand different channels of the body. We are indebted to Him for every moment of existence, and for all the comforts of life. The powers and abilities that elevate man above the lower creation are the endowment of the Creator. He loads us with His benefits. We are indebted to Him for the food we eat, the water we drink, the clothes we wear, the air we breathe. Without His special providence, the air would be filled with pestilence and poison. He is a bountiful benefactor and preserver. The sun which shines upon the earth, and glorifies all nature, the weird solemn radiance of the moon, the glories of the firmament, spangled with brilliant stars, the showers that refresh the land, and cause vegetation to flourish, the precious things of nature in all their varied richness, the lofty trees, the shrubs and plants, the waving grain, the blue sky, the green earth, the changes of day and night, the renewing seasons, all speak to man of his Creator's love. He has linked us to Himself by all these tokens in heaven and in earth" (SD 17).

C. On Treasure

"When rightly employed, wealth becomes a golden bond of gratitude and affection between man and his fellow men, and a strong tie to bind his affections to his Redeemer. The infinite gift of God's dear Son calls for tangible expressions of gratitude from the recipients of his grace. He who receives the light of Christ's love is thereby placed under the strongest obligation to shed the blessed light upon other souls in darkness" (RH May 16, 1882).

"There are only two places in the universe where we can place our treasures—in God's storehouse or in Satan's; and all that is not devoted to God's service is counted on Satan's side, and goes to strengthen his cause. The Lord designs that the means entrusted to us shall be used in building up His kingdom. His goods are entrusted to His stewards that they may be carefully traded upon, and bring back a revenue to Him in the saving of souls. These souls in their turn will become stewards of trust, cooperating with Christ to further the interests of God's cause" (CS 35).

"Money is a blessing when those who use it consider that they are the Lord's stewards, that they are handling the Lord's capital, and must one day give account of their stewardship" (OHC 192).

"The special system of tithing was founded upon a principle which is as enduring as the law of God. This system of tithing was a blessing to the Jews, else God would not have given it them. So also will it be a blessing to those who carry it out to the end of time. Our heavenly Father did not originate the plan of systematic benevolence to enrich Himself, but to be a great blessing to man. He saw that this system of beneficence was just what man needed" (3T 404, 405).

"God has a claim on us and all that we have. His claim is paramount to every other. And in acknowledgment of this claim, He bids us render to Him a fixed proportion of all that He gives us. The tithe is this specified portion. By the Lord's direction it was consecrated to Him in the earliest times. The Scriptures mention tithing in connection with the history of Abraham. The father of the faithful paid tithes to Melchisedec, 'priest of the Most High God.' Jacob also recognized the obligation of tithing. When, fleeing from his brother's wrath, he saw in his dream the ladder connecting heaven and earth, the gratitude of his heart found expression in the vow to God: 'If God will be with me, and will keep me in this way that I go, and will give me bread to eat, and raiment to put on, so that I come again to my father's house in peace; then shall the Lord be my God: and this stone, which I have set for a pillar, shall be God's house: and of all that thou shalt give me I will surely give the tenth unto thee' " (RH Dec. 8, 1896).

D. On Talents

"However large, however small the possessions of any individual, let him remember that it is his only in trust. For his strength, skill, time, talents, opportunities, and means, he must render an account to God. This is an individual work; God gives to us, that we may become like Him, generous, noble, beneficent, by giving to others. Those who, forgetful of their divine mission, seek only to save or to spend in the indulgence of pride or selfishness, may secure the gains and pleasures of this world; but in God's sight, estimated by their spiritual attainments, they are poor, wretched, miserable, blind, naked" (ibid. May 16, 1882).

"God has lent men talents—an intellect to originate, a heart to be the place of His throne, affection to flow out in blessings to others, a conscience to convict of sin. Each one has received something from the Master, and each one is to do his part in supplying the needs of God's work. . . . Speech is a talent. Of all the gifts bestowed on the human family, none should be more appreciated than the gift of speech. It is to be used to declare God's wisdom and wondrous love. Thus the treasures of His grace and wisdom are to be communicated" (ibid. Apr. 9, 1901).

"Our first duty toward God and our fellow beings is that of self-development. Every faculty with which the Creator has endowed us should be cultivated to the highest degree of perfection, that we may be able to do the greatest amount of good of which we are capable. Hence that time is spent to good account which is used in the establishment and preservation of physical and mental health. We cannot afford to dwarf or cripple any function of body or mind. As surely as we do this we must suffer the consequences" (CH 107).

"Young friends, the fear of the Lord lies at the very foundation of all progress; it is the beginning of wisdom. Your Heavenly Father has claims upon you; for without solicitation or merit on your part He gives you the bounties of His providence; and more than this, He has given you all heaven in one gift, that of His beloved Son. In return for this infinite gift, He claims of you willing obedience. As you are bought with a price, even the precious blood of the Son of God, He requires that you make a right use of the privileges you enjoy. Your intellectual and moral faculties are God's gifts, talents intrusted to you for wise improvement, and you are not at liberty to let them lie dormant for want of proper cultivation, or be crippled and dwarfed by inaction. It is for you to determine whether or not the weighty responsibilities that rest upon you shall be faithfully met, whether or not your efforts shall be well directed and your best" (FE 85, 86).

E. On Mission

"In commissioning His disciples to go 'into all the world, and preach the gospel to every creature,' Christ assigned to men the work of extending the knowledge of His grace. But while some go forth to preach, He calls upon others to answer His claims upon them for offerings with which to support His cause in the earth. He has placed means in the hands of men, that His divine gifts may flow through human channels in doing the work appointed us in saving our fellow men. This is one of God's ways of exalting man. It is just the work that man needs, for it will stir the deepest sympathies of his heart and call into exercise the highest capabilities of the mind" (9T 255).

"There is a yet deeper significance to the golden rule. Everyone who has been made a steward of the manifold grace of God is called upon to impart to souls in ignorance and darkness, even as, were he in their place, he would desire them to impart to him. The apostle Paul said, "I am debtor both to the Greeks, and to the Barbarians; both to the wise, and to the unwise." By all that you have known of the love of God, by all that you have received of the rich gifts of His grace, above the most benighted and degraded soul upon the earth, are you in debt to that soul to impart these gifts unto him" (Ev 255).

F. On Children as Treasure

"Parents have been entrusted with a most important stewardship, a sacred charge. They are to make their family a symbol of the family in heaven, of which they hope to become members when their day of test and trial here below shall have ended. The influence exerted in the home must be Christlike. This is the most effective ministration in the character-building of the child. The words spoken are to be pleasant. No boisterous, arbitrary, masterful spirit is to be allowed to come into the family. Every member is to be taught that he is to prepare to be a member of the royal family" (10MR 324).

G. On Time

"Time is money, and many are wasting precious time which might be used in useful labor, working with their hands the thing that is good. The Lord will never say, 'Well done, thou good and faithful servant,' to the man who has not taxed the physical powers which have been lent him of God as precious talents by which to gather means, wherewith the needy may be supplied, and offerings may be made to God" (CS 288).

V. Literature

Birch, Bruce C. *Let Justice Roll Down.* Louisville, Ky.: Westminster/John Knox, 1991.

Hall, Douglas John. *The Steward.* Rev. ed. Grand Rapids: Eerdmans; New York: Friendship, 1990.

Landsdell, Henry. *The Sacred Tenth.* London: SPCK, 1906.

Rodríguez, Angel M. *Stewardship Roots: Toward a Theology of Stewardship, Tithe, Offerings.* Silver Spring, Md.: Stewardship Ministries, General Conference of Seventh-day Adventists, 1994.

Thompson, T. K. *Stewardship in Contemporary Theology.* New York: Association, 1960.

Wellman, S. A. *Your Stewardship and Mine.* Washington, D.C.: Review and Herald, 1950.

Christian Lifestyle
and Behavior

Miroslav M. Kiš

Introduction

Human behavior matters to God who created us and who bound Himself to us with love. It matters to the surrounding creation because dominion over the earth is still in human hands. It matters to the human community because our lives are interdependent and closely intertwined. And finally, human behavior matters to each individual because each action, decision, and word is a seed that bears fruit in the character and produces consequences.

Several sciences (psychology, sociology, anthropology) help us to understand and explain the human lifestyle. Christian ethics, however, transcend descriptions of behavior. Drawing on revealed data about the nature, condition, and destiny of human beings, it offers directions for daily life. These define what is good and what is in harmony with optimal humanness (John 10:10).

The foundation of Christian ethics is Christian theology, more particularly, the teachings of the Bible. The task of Christian ethics is to provide guidance by clarifying what is good, what is right, and what is the acceptable way to reach moral excellence (Micah 6:8). Ethical standards challenge social and cultural norms to seek ever-higher goals. The goal of Christian ethics is to help restore the image of God in the human lifestyle, where human finitude and sinfulness are confronted in love and transcended by the power of grace with candor and realism.

Scripture depicts God as a caring and concerned Father whose children continually engage in destructive and self-destructive behavior. In desperate love He uses the most powerful mode of expressions: the imperative (Ex. 20:1-17; Matt. 5; 6; 7); the least ambiguous vocabulary: love, law, forgiveness, judgment (Ps. 119); and the strongest antidote to self-destruction: divine self-sacrifice (John 3:16). This is to say that the biblical orientation is clearly deontological (Gr. *deon*, "duty"). A deontology that has biblical support is neither autonomous (Kant) nor heteronomous (Locke) but rather theonomous (John 6:38, 39).

Teleological concerns, i.e., with consequences (Gr. *telos*, "end"), play a lesser role in Christian biblical ethics. Rewards or punishment should not be the only or even the primary reason for obeying or doing good. Christians obey because they trust and love God; God offers His good gifts because He loves His children. Christians are duty-bound because they are love-bound. Teleological systems, whether the supreme end is pleasure (hedonism), personal self-interest (egoism), social best interest (utilitarianism), or a subjective sense of love (situationism), have no roots in the Word of God. Daniel resolved (Dan. 1:8) and Jesus set His mind (Luke 13:33) prior to the moment of action or temptation. Only when Christians confront the dilemmas of life armed with commitment, prayer, and courage can they avoid following their own bent to sin.

The Bible teaches that Christian life rests on three sovereign acts of God: creation, revelation, and redemption. Through creation humans are endowed with capacities and potentials akin to those of God. In revelation God discloses Himself and His will, inviting humans to a life of communion and discipleship with Jesus Christ. Finally, the act of redemption lifts the fallen human nature and through justification and sanctification restores the original image of God.

In this article we examine the foundations, nature, and practice of the Christian way of life. The first section elaborates the three bases of Christian behavior. The second explores specific standards in the spiritual, physical, social, and personal realms.

I. A Biblical Basis for Christian Ethics

To be a Christian is a vocation, a deep and personal calling to be a special kind of person with a unique mission and purpose in life. Like Abraham and the disciples of Jesus, the Christian hears the call as an imperative. Abraham left his father's home, family, and heritage to go to a land where he could live as God's friend (Gen. 12:1-3). The disciples left their fishing, and forsaking all, followed Jesus of Nazareth, moved by the inner conviction of a divine call to a better life (Mark 1:16-29).

It is not possible to describe the portrait of a Christian in detail here, nor is it conceivable to analyze all the implications of Christian conduct. In this first section we elaborate on the three divine acts on which Christian lifestyle and behavior are based: creation, revelation, and redemption.

A. God's Act of Creation

"Then the Lord God formed man of dust from the ground, and breathed into his nostrils the breath of life; and man became a living being" (Gen. 2:7).

1. Humans as Beings

Scripture affirms that in the realm of God's creation, human beings belong to a unique category of creatures. The conferral of this special status occurred at their creation, on the sixth day of the first week. On this status rest human identity, dignity, and behavior. Regardless of economic or social position, education or gender, the origin and nature of human beings is found in the purposeful and deliberate act of God (Gen. 1:26, 27; 2:7).

"It is he that made us, and we are his" (Ps. 100:3), David exclaims, as if anticipating modern theories of the origin of the human race. When evolution insists that humans and other animals appeared as a result of random mutations, it not only contradicts the historicity of the biblical record but yields a different self-concept and inspires a corresponding lifestyle and behavior. If human dignity and respect are not God-given but earned, then we must fight to preserve them. Human relations, as well as our treatment of ourselves, will follow the evolutionary principle of the survival of the fittest. If humans are children of nature and belong to nature alone, human moral behavior is deprived of one of its basic foundations: responsibility.

Victor F. Frankl commented that the gas chambers of Auschwitz were not to be traced to some ministry of state but to the lecture halls of universities. There "man is defined as nothing but an accumulation of complicated, complex molecules of prothaine, and this complexity runs around some unimportant planet called Earth for about 70 years to dissolve itself afterwards." Small wonder, says this survivor of Auschwitz, that we find gas chambers and other atrocities. When we reject our origin in the divine will, act, and purpose, we are at the mercy of the human will, act, and purpose. Human existence becomes a closed system dominated by the need to maintain homeostasis and inner equilibrium. Conversely, the consciousness by which every human being traces his or her existence to God inspires the sense of belonging and responsibility to Him. It also bestows a dignified and exalted meaning upon human life, and human behavior reflects a sense of self-appreciation and proper deference for other humans.

2. *Imago Dei*

God makes clear that He created humans in His own image (Gen. 1:26, 27). In so doing He granted them the unique privilege of sharing in their limited, creaturely way some of His divine attributes. These reflections of the divine nature, of which we will consider a few, compose the essential dimensions of human beings.

a. God is being Himself. His name is "I AM" (Ex. 3:14). His existence is unborrowed and undetermined, and He consciously and sovereignly holds the universe in His hands. Humans reflect this attribute, albeit partially. Their life is borrowed and dependent, yet they enjoy it in full consciousness and self-consciousness. This gift enables human beings to know themselves, examine and evaluate their own thoughts (Rom. 2:15) and conduct (2 Cor. 13:5) and assess their own condition (Luke 15:17). Unlike animals and plants they are able to perceive distance between themselves and other humans and creatures and to plan the nature of their relationships with them. This dimension, along with reason, turns human conduct into a lifestyle that rests on human responsibility.

b. God is an intelligent being. His intellect is manifested in wisdom, good counsel, and the power to understand (Job 12:13) and know human thoughts (Ps. 94:11). In addition, the whole creation testifies of His rational powers (Ps. 136:5; Prov. 3:19; Jer. 10:12). "His understanding is beyond measure" (Ps. 147:5) and unsearchable by the human intellect (Isa. 40:28). Human beings are able to echo divine intelligence. Reasoning power enables them to discern, compare, understand, and make deliberations, decisions, and choices. This power is indispensable in every aspect of life, particularly in the moral realm (Luke 10:26).

c. God is free. He does what He wants. No one can challenge Him by saying, "What doest thou?" (Job 9:12; Ps. 115:3).

Humans are born with the need for freedom, and Christianity considers it a basic right and reflection of the divine character. Without freedom, humans could not make choices or be responsible for them (Deut. 30:19).

d. God is holy. His holiness implies moral

purity and perfection. As a result, sin cannot coexist with Him (1 John 3:5). Human beings reflect this attribute in their constant yearning for improvement, growth, and innocence. Their destiny and calling are to be perfect as God is perfect (Matt. 5:48).

e. God is eternal. He is not bound by time (Jer. 10:10) nor is He subject to death (1 Tim. 1:17; 6:16). From everlasting to everlasting He is God (Ps. 90:2). At creation, human finiteness reflected God's eternal nature through conditional immortality and infinite potential. After sin, and in spite of death, humans maintain a strong sense of unending existence (Eccl. 3:11). Physically, mentally, and emotionally we all live with eternity in view and fight death with all our energies, will, and means. Human life is most meaningful, enriching, and hopeful when it is shaped and groomed for eternity, promised to all who yield their being and existence to the saving hand of Jesus.

f. God is a person. Scripture presents Him as a unity in thought, will, character, and activity (Num. 23:19). Human beings partially reflect this divine attribute. Inner disharmony or dominance of one aspect of human personhood over the rest (e.g., emotions) produces an unhealthy personality and disturbs normal growth. Humans never achieve complete harmony in their self, but through experiences and divine help they can reach a high potential.

These dimensions of the image of God—identity, reason, freedom, holiness, potential, and personhood—stand as evidence against the existentialist's dismissal of any essential nature, thus favoring total freedom of all individuals to mold themselves. The Bible affirms clearly that humans are definite beings and that their lifestyle must be in harmony with their constitution.

Christian lifestyle depends on, fosters, safeguards, and restores the image of God in humans. When that image is reflected in our nature, our actions will mirror our character just as the fruit corresponds to the tree (Matt. 12:33, 35) and God's image becomes increasingly sharper.

(See Man I. B; Creation I. A. 12; Sin I. A.)

B. God's Act of Revelation

"In the beginning was the Word" (John 1:1). This Word was not just a word of communication or information, as human words are. The Word that broke through the long eons of silence and darkness was the living Word, actively creating and communicating. These two qualities of God's Word have remained closely united ever since Creation. No sooner had Adam and Eve received life than God spoke to them (Gen. 1:28). Through the ages, in visions, dreams, and audible voices, through conscience and events in history, and ultimately through His own Son as the Word incarnate, God has communicated and thus created His will in the human realm (Heb. 1:1, 2; see Revelation/Inspiration II, III).

1. Nature of the Bible

These acts of creation and communication, gathered and recorded under inspiration of the Holy Spirit, make up the Bible. The Bible is thus God's communication and creative word in written form. The Holy Spirit assures that it is not a dead word, a collection of ancient, pious sayings about God, but rather a living and active Word (Heb. 4:12; see Revelation/Inspiration IV).

The Christian lifestyle can have no source other than the Bible. Christian morality and Christian ethics, which are translated into Christian behavior, must be based on that same Word. For several reasons any other foundation or authority cannot yield, account for, or explain the Christlike way of life. First, sinful, human life is dead to good, moral behavior because it follows the "course of this world, . . . the spirit that is now at work in the sons of disobedience" (Eph. 2:2). Any directives proceeding from human wisdom will reflect this death-bound frame of mind and cannot produce happiness. Second, ever since the first lie in the Garden of Eden, the human mind has been confronted with a barrage of false ideas and treacherous systems, competing with God's Word for human allegiance. However, experience and Scripture teach that whatever is out of harmony with God's Word cannot be trusted (Prov. 16:25; Ps. 119:104, 105). Third, both the authority of the church and the credibility of human conscience have proven untrustworthy for moral guidance without Scripture as the ultimate court of appeal.

If the Bible is treated as any other book, no one can expect more help from it than from any other written word. In such a case, God does not speak in its pages and it has no moral or religious authority to be transferred to the individual or some social structure. Without ultimate authority, people do what is good in their own eyes, not caring whether an action is good for others (Judges 21:25).

If the Bible serves as a counselor, educating and nurturing the Christian community with its wealth of God-inspired wisdom, positive results can be expected. Scripture is "profitable for teaching, for reproof, for correction, and for training in righteousness" (2 Tim 3:16). However, authority for interpreting it may be conferred upon the community of faith in such a manner that the pronouncements of its councils and theologians form a corpus of traditions that slowly take precedence over the Bible (Mark 7:7-9). This is dangerous, for human words are bound to conflict, human insight is prone to bias, and human fascination with power (especially when speaking for God) leads to corruption.

On the other hand, some understand the Bible as a trustworthy witness that brings the reader into an encounter with God. In that case the Word of God comes only in the privacy of individual existence, at the moment of encounter, leaving no Word of God in an objective form outside of this "eternal moment." This is a serious conclusion indeed; the Word of God becomes limited to my subjectivity, which may contradict the experience of others and prove to be entirely personal. (See Revelation/Inspiration VI. D.)

2. The Bible as the Word of God

Accepting the Bible as the Word of God means first recognizing that the biblical writers do not expound their own views (2 Peter 1:19-21). It also means acknowledging that the content of the biblical message conveys God's will, since it originates in the inspiration of the Holy Spirit (2 Tim. 3:16), and for that reason is relevant, compelling, and authoritative, independent of human acceptance. It also means following in the footsteps of men and women who trusted Scripture as the Word of God (see Joshua 1:8; Ps. 119; Acts 17:2; Gal. 3:22; 1 Thess. 2:13; 2 Peter 1:20).

The example of Jesus merits special attention. First, Jesus relied on biblical authority in matters of truth (John 10:34-36). He also recognized and affirmed the prophetic nature of the Bible, setting it above ordinary books (Luke 4:21; John 13:18). He affirmed the unique role of Scripture in leading human beings to eternal life (John 5:39). When a rich young ruler inquired about guidance in daily decisions, dilemmas, and actions, Jesus did not suggest expediency (utilitarianism), personal feelings (emotivism), the voice of tradition, or the impact of situation (situationism). He referred him to the Written Word, thus setting all other norms under the authority of God as expressed in the Bible.

Finally, Jesus stood firmly on the biblical Word when confronted with temptation. Reason, human insight, or even personal encounters did not overshadow the Word of Scripture. "It is written," He said, no matter what the consequences (Matt. 4:1-11). Christians follow the example of Christ when they search the Scriptures for guidance in the various decisions of daily life.

3. The Bible and the Christian Lifestyle

Human fallenness and finiteness create a need for strength, guidance, and care to grow in Christlikeness. The Bible responds to this need by presenting standards of behavior within a community of faith where the ministry of divine forgiveness and love fosters growth in grace.

Biblical standards assist the limited and sinful human faculties by (a) providing an authoritative and absolute statement of God's will; (b) helping to distinguish between good and evil; (c) presenting an ethos spanning several millennia and many cultures in which God's standards have functioned; (d) giving examples that motivate, illustrate consequences of conformity or rebellion, indicate the measure of commitment required by a love relationship with God, and explain the reasons for standards; (e) articulating a good number of concrete rules of action.

For the sake of clarity and structure, it is helpful to conceive several categories of standards ranging from general and absolute to particular and relative. We propose three such categories to understand how biblical truth impacts moral life. These are general principles, normative models, and rules of action. In this essay *general principle* stands for an objective, foundational, universal, and often absolute standard of widely acceptable behavior. *Normal model* serves as a guideline from general principle to *rule of action*. The latter is an immediate, direct, often imperative and preventive precept, relative to moral activity in a given context. It is derived from general principles through the help of normative actions.

a. General principles. Most Christians recognize general principles in the Ten Commandments, the Sermon on the Mount, and other places in Scripture. Principles make absolute and authoritative statements of God's will and maintain the distinction between good and evil, right and wrong. The commandment "You shall not commit adultery" is always and universally valid. Even in cultures where such practices may not be prohibited, infidelity and promiscuity hurt the individuals involved, on the physical, moral, or spiritual level. General principles of behavior correspond directly to human nature (Deut. 30:19, 20), and proceed from God's loving concern for our well-being.

However, Scriptures' usefulness does not diminish or disappear totally at the level of concrete situations. Humans are not left to follow their own conscience, reason, or church tradition, unaided by God's Word. Our heavenly Father is too concerned with our happiness and safety, and too distressed when sin and evil ruin our body, mind, and soul, to let His Word grow indifferently silent in our daily lives (Deut. 30:11-14). Thus He gives biblical norms of behavior, which stand between the absolute and universal principles of behavior and the particular and immediate rules of action.

b. Normative models. The Bible narrates real-life stories that have shown the readers of many centuries what is normative within the ethos of God's children. While general principles serve as codes, the biblical normative models in the form of stories illustrate the value system used, the consequences that followed choices, and the measure of commitment manifested in the experiences of those who trusted God (Heb. 12:3, 4). God required recounting or reading the experiences of past generations (Ex. 10:2; Deut. 31:11-13; Ps. 44:1-3) because these stories would put people's frame of mind in harmony with God's mind (1 Cor. 10:11). They confirm that God's will is not arbitrary or impossible.

Instead of being fictitious or inconsistent, all Bible stories fit under one or more general principles. Moreover, there is no contradiction between codes (principles) and cases (biblical normative models). In fact, the general principles are strengthened, whether the case illustrates obedience or disobedience. For example, the principle states clearly "You shall not commit adultery" (Ex. 20:14), and the life story of Joseph sets the norm as if it said, "Do not disobey principle, not even in the context of slavery when your masters force you, not even in the context of singleness, not even when facing prison or possibly death."

Scripture often records negative examples, as in the case of David and Bathsheba (2 Sam. 11:2-27). David sinned without being harassed, in contrast with Joseph in slavery. The way the story is recounted reflects biblical normativeness and enhances the principle of sexual fidelity within marriage (2 Sam. 12:1-25). The norm is valid even for the king, for those in power, and when, according to social norms, the action is not offensive.

While Scripture cannot provide an example for every detail of *our* temptations and dilemmas, through its record we are surrounded with a cloud of witnesses, people like us in whose conduct God has shown the norms, the limits to which He may call us in obedience to Him (Heb. 12:1, 2). A Christian will not be inspired by life stories that reflect the norms of the world, but rather will mold the character in conformity with God's Word and the ethos of His kingdom (Rom. 12:1, 2).

c. Rules of action. Finally, God's Word contains a multitude of direct rules that relate to concrete action in life. At times these rules of action take the form of a command, addressing human behavior in a particular event or situation. Cain was instructed to exercise self-control (Gen. 4:6, 7), Laban to be kind to Jacob (Gen. 31:24), Peter to put his sword into its sheath (John 18:11), and Philemon to take his slave back and treat him as a "beloved brother" (Philemon 15, 16). Obviously, these orders were not given specifically to us. Yet, when today we are tempted to solve our problems by violent means as was Peter, we would do well to heed Christ's injunction.

In addition, the Bible presents indirect objective rules of action suitable for guidance in various circumstances. Thus the principle "Thou shall not commit adultery" finds its norm in the experiences of Joseph and David, and receives an immediate application to relationships with the wife of one's neighbor or with a daughter-in-law in the Mosaic laws (Lev. 20:10-21). Such concrete, objective rules can also be found in Proverbs, Ecclesiastes, the Gospels, and the Epistles. Many of these, especially the rules regulating moral conduct, remain eminently valid today.

The Bible is not, however, an exhaustive catalog of concrete rules of action. Christians are called to think, to pray, and to agonize under the guidance of the Holy Spirit when wrestling with exceptional dilemmas. Yet God's Word can lead us through all perplexities when its principles, normative models, and specific guidelines form our frame of mind.

To be human means to be able to hear God speak. When we are in conformity to His will, hearing the examples of Scripture, we face life with an attitude of trust in God and set our behavior on firm ground (Ps. 112; 119:11).

C. God's Act of Redemption

The divine act of redemption is foundational to the Christian lifestyle. God sent His Son to this planet to transform and recreate human lives in His own image (John 3:16). In the parables of the prodigal son, the lost sheep, and the lost coin, Jesus gives His assessment of the human, sinful condition (Luke 15:3-32). Lost, helpless, and condemned to death, humans waste their energies and talents in anxious wanderings and self-destructive behavior.

At the origin of this lost condition stands a defiant, autonomous act, prompted by a desire for self-affirmation (Gen. 3:1-24). By eating of the forbidden fruit, humans asserted their own will *above* the will of God and placed their own authority *against* that of God. This attitude and action of Adam and Eve plunged the whole of creation under the realm of evil, because evil is the consequence of every sin (Rom. 5:12).

All human efforts at solving this predicament have proven unsuccessful, whether through education (Plato), self-discipline (Buddhism), liberation of the working class (Marx), or through striving for the authenticity of the "man come of age" (humanism). All have proven incapable of changing the cause of evil: human sinfulness and sin. No human sacrifice can atone for the transgression or remove the guilt that destroys the inner harmony of the human soul. Thus, human beings face an unbridgeable gap between themselves and the source of their life (Isa. 59:1, 2).

For that reason Jesus came "in the likeness of sinful flesh" to overcome sin and sinfulness in human nature and behavior, and to open the way of reconciliation with God (Rom. 8:3, 4). Jesus accomplished this with His death and victory on the cross. For it was on the cross that sin displayed its true nature as the cause of evil, and on the cross it became a defeated enemy. By His death, the just requirement of the law found its fulfillment so that now God could call all humanity to Himself, offering a healthy and abundant life. (See Salvation I. E; III.)

1. Call to Repentance and Forgiveness

The crucial step in making the victory on the cross a reality in the life of an individual is the willingness to answer the call to repentance (2 Cor. 5:20, 21). The distance that once separated humans from God must now be set between each sinner and sin. That distance consists of sorrow for the acts committed, an admission of full responsibility for the consequences, and a desire to abandon the old way of life in exchange for a new.

The incentives for such a radical decision are several. To begin, the sinner can count on God. In His love there is nothing He will not give (Rom. 8:32). His power and authority inspire confidence in anyone who will give Him a chance. Next, the sinner has nothing; thus there is nothing to lose. Finally, the testimony of a multitude who, led by the Holy Spirit, have found peace and experienced forgiveness may convince the most reticent soul. But the most encouraging fact is that once sinners turn around, setting distance between themselves and sin, they hear another call, the call to follow Jesus.

2. Call to Discipleship

"And he said to them, 'Follow me, and I will make you fishers of men.' Immediately they left their nets and followed him" (Matt. 4:19, 20). From this call several points emerge. First, a sinner is confronted with the call in the midst of the daily bustle of life. It surprises, intrudes,

and interrupts the normal routine. Second, it is Jesus who calls. Third, the call is actually a command, which allows only two alternatives: a positive or a negative response. To ignore means to disobey, because Jesus refuses to negotiate (Luke 9:59-62). Fourth, the call summons us to walk with Jesus, abandoning whatever security we may have had.

3. Call to Faith and Obedience

One of the four disciples, Andrew, explains why he followed "immediately": he had "found the Messiah" (John 1:41). A Christian believes and therefore obeys. But as Dietrich Bonhoeffer tells us, the reverse is also true. The disciple must obey in order to believe. Unless obedience and faith go hand in hand, the Christian walk will never begin.

"Only the devil has an answer to our moral difficulty, and he says: keep on posing problems, and you will escape the necessity of obedience. . . . Where moral difficulties are taken so seriously, where they torment and enslave man, because they do not leave him open to the freeing activity of obedience, it is there that his total godlessness is revealed. . . . The one thing that matters is practical obedience" (Bonhoeffer 63).

The incentives for obedience and faith are many. Because Jesus, the Messiah and Saviour, calls, no ulterior motives will betray our trust. God knows best what is good for us; He is not limited in time, space, or knowledge as humans are (Prov. 27:1). In addition, He is the Creator. Besides, God is love (1 John 4:8). He cannot remain detached or leave us in ignorance and helplessness. Christian obedience takes place in this loving relationship between heavenly Father and earthly children. Frequently, the lack of willing and spontaneous obedience indicates a need for a deeper and a more loving relationship with God.

4. Call to Holiness

"As obedient children, do not be conformed to the passions of your former ignorance, but as he who called you is holy, be holy yourselves in all your conduct; since it is written, 'You shall be holy, for I am holy' " (1 Peter 1:14-16). Holiness is the ultimate goal of redemption. Two main meanings of the word "holiness" apply to the Christian way of life.

a. Holiness as separateness. God's holiness sets Him apart (Ex. 3:5; 19:18, 24; Hosea 11:9) from other beings, and holds Him independent of, and invulnerable to the rest of His creation. Yet, He is not disconnected from or indifferent to the needs and plight of the human condition (Ps. 14:2; Prov. 15:3; Matt. 10:29-31; Luke 12:6, 7; Acts 14:16, 17).

The call to holiness is an invitation to a life that is separate from passions, fashions, and sinful ways. It is a call to come out, to be separate (Isa. 52:11; 2 Cor. 6:14-18), to escape the influences of the world.

In His prayer Jesus describes the fundamental separateness that must exist between the church and the world by affirming, "They are not of the world, even as I am not of the world" (John 17:16). Christ's disciple is set apart, sanctified by the Word (verse 17) and firmly committed to Him. Certain dimensions in the life and being of a Christian are not negotiable, not relative; on these there can be no compromise. "Be it known to you, O king, that we will not serve your gods," declared Shadrach, Meshach, and Abednego (Dan. 3:18).

The call to holiness is an appeal to be in and yet not of the world. Jesus underscores this fact in speaking of the new identity of His disciples. "You are the light of the world," a light on a hill (Matt. 5:14-16). A light's radiance is not self-serving; neither must Christians serve themselves. Light cannot be overwhelmed by darkness (John 1:5), but rather Christians overcome the night of ignorance and sin by the light of a holy lifestyle.

b. Holiness as moral purity. The Bible declares that God's holiness consists of a total separation from sin. His actions, words, plans, and relationships are all flawless and sinless. There is no profanity or evil in Him (Isa. 5:16; 1 Peter 1:15; 1 John 1:5). He is morally pure.

In His call to holiness, God invites humans to a life of moral purity. "Blessed are the pure in heart," says Jesus (Matt. 5:8). This purity will be manifest both in the essential dimension and existential or behavioral dimension of the human being. The importance of the first dimension is clearly illustrated in the words of Jesus: the kind and quality of fruit depend on the kind and condition of the tree (Matt. 7:16-20). No one can gather grapes from thorns or figs from thistles. The sound, healthy tree will produce quality fruit. Equally, the good life proceeds naturally from the good stored in the heart of men and women (12:35).

But how can one become holy, sound, noble, and pure when, as the psalmist exclaims, humans are brought forth in iniquity and in sin (Ps. 51:5), a condition absolutely incompatible with holiness? How can someone who is accustomed to do evil all at once produce good fruit (Jer. 13:23)? "Apart from me you can do nothing," answers Jesus (John 15:5).

While we cannot elaborate here on the gift of justification, a few key points must be mentioned. (See Salvation III.) The Bible does not teach that transformation of character comes from any natural goodness that needs only to be affirmed and liberated. Whether it comes from liberal optimism about human nature or New-Age fascination with human potential, any method that pretends to permit people to transform themselves contradicts both the Bible and human experience.

Scripture uses many illustrations to show how a sinful being can become holy and how the sinful mind, will, and emotions can become pure. Jesus calls this transformation a new birth (John 3:1-15). Paul refers to it as a "new creation" (2 Cor. 5:17), achieved through death, burial, and resurrection (Col. 2:12-14). The emergence of such a new being is entirely the work of God. In love He breaks through the vicious cycle of sin, offering forgiveness and freedom from guilt and debt. The sinner is detached from previous loyalties, and a new commitment orients all the energies for bearing the fruit of the Spirit (Gal.

5:22, 23). This is the work of justification.

Holiness as moral purity is a dynamic concept in Christianity and, therefore, is not only expressed in the nature of the newborn Christian but also in his or her behavior. Writing to "the exiles of the Dispersion" the apostle Peter confirms that they "have been born anew to a living hope through the resurrection of Jesus Christ from the dead, and to an inheritance which is imperishable, undefiled, and unfading, kept in heaven " (1 Peter 1:1-4). This is a beautiful description of God's work of justification (2 Peter 1:4).

Redemption, however, does not stop here. Justification triggers the onset of the yearning for holiness and the beginning of the process of sanctification. Justification makes us righteous and sets in motion the process of sanctification, growth in grace, until we reach the maturity that measures with that of Jesus (Eph. 4:13, 14). When the early Christians experienced justification, they were called "saints" (Rom. 1:7; 1 Cor. 1:2; Phil. 1:1; Col. 1:2). Paul wrote to the Ephesians that they were chosen to be holy and blameless (Eph. 1:4); he then begged them to lead a life worthy of that calling (Eph. 4:1). God first adopts us as sons and daughters, calls us "saints," and then asks us to reflect this new reality in our conduct. Justification and sanctification cannot be separated. Sanctification incarnates and perpetuates justification.

The apostle Peter quotes Leviticus 11:44: "As he who called you is holy, be holy yourselves." He then adds a small but significant phrase: "in all your conduct" (1 Peter 1:15). The first part refers to justification; the second, to sanctification. A justified, holy life will be noticed not because of a shining halo above the head of a saint, but by the saint's speech, food, activities, entertainment, and associates. All of these will be sanctified, set apart from sinful and profane values and ways, and will reflect the Christian's commitment to God above all.

The same God who calls us to holiness is the One who made us. He knows what we can

and cannot do in our own power; He also knows what is possible with His help. He who began the work in us will finish it (Phil. 1:6). He does not begin a job without considering carefully whether it can be finished (Luke 14:28-32). He also calls us to be the kind of disciples who will make complete renunciation (verse 33) and give Him all the chances He needs. God does not call us to claim our holiness or to boast about our sinlessness, lest we fall while claiming that we stand (1 Cor. 10:12). Paul says, "I do not consider that I have made it my own; but one thing I do, forgetting what lies behind and straining forward to what lies ahead, I press on toward the goal for the prize of the upward call of God in Christ Jesus" (Phil. 3:13, 14).

5. Call to Love and Obedience

Christian behavior transcends the natural, human drive for self-preservation, self-concern, and craving for absolute, personal autonomy because it considers obedience to God and selfless service to others as the main objective of every action (John 14:15; 1 Cor. 13). This kind of lifestyle harmonizes with the biblical definition of love and the central message of the Bible. Quoting from the OT (Lev. 19:18), Jesus describes the life of a Christian in terms of love for God and neighbor (Matt. 22:37-40). Love is not a disposition or sentiment; it is an activity. It motivates and controls all personal, interpersonal, and social relations. On the personal level Christian love inspires humility without sacrificing self-respect and nurtures self-denial which does not lead to self-destruction. A Christian will care for the body, mind, and soul in such a way that personal identity and happiness are preserved and enhanced. In interpersonal and social relations, love requires the same respect of everyone's identity and happiness, regardless of age, race, gender, or status (Gal. 3:28, 29).

Love is the supreme fruit of the Spirit (Col. 3:14; Gal. 5:22), and an ultimate result of God's redeeming act. It finds both its source and its reason in God (1 John 4:10, 11, 19). Therefore, the point of departure for human love is the love of God, which interrupts the vicious human cycle of self-centeredness, endures rejection and hatred, and offers itself in living sacrifice to unlovable humanity. When human beings sense a need to respond in kind, the love of God—the capacity to love—is "poured into our hearts through the Holy Spirit which has been given to us" (Rom. 5:5). The first result is a growing conviction that we can call God *Abba,* "Father" (Rom. 8:15), and that we ought to relate to Him as sons and daughters. At the same time we see our neighbors as brothers and sisters worthy of our loving care and compassion.

Love and obedience meet in the love relationship with God and neighbor. A stranger or an orphan does not have to obey. A slave does not obey either, but submits and complies. But a child who cares about the Father and who is moved by parental love responds with obedience. "If you love me, you will keep my commandments" (John 14:15). Often the love of God is associated with obedience (Deut. 6:4-6; 30:16; Gal. 5:14; 1 John 5:3), because in fact, love enjoys obeying, and obedience incarnates love (Ps. 40:8). The Christian follows God's will without fear of punishment (Rom. 8:15; 1 John 4:18), confident that when His law is transgressed God is ready to forgive repentant sinners. Consequently, only our continual refusal to respond in obedience to God's love can separate us from Him (Matt. 23:37; Rom. 8:35-39).

The Bible describes the lifestyle of a Christian in terms of love as an imperative. Categorically, i.e., unequivocally and explicitly, God defines the nature of love in two ways. In the first place He demonstrates the kind of action (John 3:16), the sort of attitude (John 15:13, 14; Rom. 5:8), and the manner of person (1 John 4:8) that love demands. Second, He sets in writing the standards that lay the foundation of human love in action, attitude, and person (Ex. 20:1-17).

The Bible knows nothing of a love that is hypothetical, indefinite, or distanced from actual human behavior. It is sometimes alleged that Jesus (Matt. 22:40) and Paul (Gal. 5:14) promote this sort of super-ideal by setting a distance between law (God's will) and love (God's activity). The proponents of this view place love first and law in a secondary or auxiliary position: love makes law unnecessary.

It appears, however, that the opposite is true. God's law expresses love in the form of propositions, just as in human history His actions demonstrate His love. We must not assume incongruity between God's loving will (His law) and His loving actions. In fact, when Jesus claims that all the law and prophets depend on love, He counters the assumption that law and love stand in opposition. They are rather two sides of our heavenly Father. One side lovingly but firmly protects from evil by commanding happiness and welfare; the other acts creatively, offering good gifts to His children.

Similarly, in his letter to the Galatians, Paul communicates his understanding of love as the law fulfilled. Instead of conceiving of the two as alternative ways to salvation, or one to the exclusion of the other, Paul affirms law as the prescription for loving relationships, and love as the inner disposition requisite for attaining these relationships.

Love is categorical not only because it is explicitly spelled out in Christ's life and standards of behavior; it is also categorical in the sense of being unconditional and absolute (1 Cor. 13:1-13). Because love is absolute and the nature of God's law is love, His commandments are absolutely binding. On that basis the regenerate heart opts for love and delights in obeying God's law (Ps. 1:2).

As a corollary to being categorical, the biblical *agapē* love is imperative. "You shall love" your God and "your neighbor" are commands and not suggestions. This is so, whether stated in the books of Moses (Lev. 19:18; Deut. 6:5) or restated by Jesus (Matt. 22:39). But unlike human orders, God's commandments are always a supreme expression of love.

Consequently, when Christians in their prayerful study of the Word find themselves faced with foundational principles, with high norms of behavior, or with direct rules of conduct, they do not feel intimidated or humiliated. On the contrary, a deep sense of self-worth and gratitude floods the heart. They realize that it is not a capricious, arbitrary, or senseless authority, but the love of God that calls them to action. With Paul they know that love constrains their sinful tendencies (2 Cor. 5:14).

As the human will becomes identified with God's will and human behavior reflects more and more the loving, divine conduct, the concern for consequences gradually vanishes. The focus of life is expressed in the cry "What shall I do, Lord?" (Acts 22:10). We now turn to the Bible in search of divine guidance for Christian lifestyle.

II. The Call to Live as a Christian

To call oneself Christian means to act as a Christian. Confession and profession of faith must translate into appropriate behavior, as Jesus shows in His parable of the two builders (Matt. 7:24-27). A mere verbal or formal claim of discipleship is as unpredictable and insecure for supporting consistent good behavior as is sand for sustaining a building. The rock, however, symbolizes the solidity of claims that have entered the realm of praxis, on spiritual, physical, social, and personal levels.

In this second section we outline four parts corresponding with the spiritual, physical, social, and personal dimensions of life. The first two will receive limited treatment because other essays in this volume address them in a fuller form. In the first step we identify the foremost concern or issues. The second step consists of hearing God's Word on the issue in terms of biblical standards (general principles, biblical normative models, and rules of action). We cannot venture into further analysis without risk of speculation. In the actual decision process each Christian will have to choose biblical guidance and parameters.

A. Standards of Spiritual Dimension

The most important aspect of Christian lifestyle is its strong spiritual dimension, the relationship with God (Ex. 20:1-11). Humans live in God's presence not only because He is omnipresent (Ps. 139) but also because He desires a close relationship with them (Zech. 2:11). From this spiritual communion with God and a deeply religious lifestyle emerge wholesome relations with other humans and with the rest of creation.

1. Christian Worldview

The existence of God and His continual involvement in the natural order shape a Christian's outlook on life. The Christian worldview is based on biblical principles and norms.

a. General principles. The *principle of the immanence of God* (Gen. 1:1-31; 2:1-25; Jer. 23:23) affirms that the universe is not a closed system (liberalism) and that God is not disconnected from it (deism). On the contrary, the natural world and human history are open to His involvement (Dan. 2), ultimately God controls human affairs (Dan. 4:34-37; see God IV. D). The *principle of transcendence* (Hosea 11:9; Ps. 89:6-8) confirms that God is above His creation. This implies that humans are not His equals. To wait on Him and to trust His leading makes sense all the more since in His transcendence He loves human beings (Matt. 6:25-34; see God III. D). The *principle of the great controversy* (Rev. 12:7-12; Gen. 3:15) places the human reality in the context of a war raging between good and evil, in which humans are inevitably involved. This conflict affects Christian lifestyle because the decisions and actions of men and women affirm their allegiance and bring support either to God and good, or to His challenger the devil and evil (Matt. 6:24). The concept of the great controversy provides a meaning for meaningless suffering, and a hope for hopelessness and death. (See Great Controversy I-VI.)

b. Normative models. Job emerges as a first example of a lifestyle within this biblical worldview. His belief in both the immanence and transcendence of God (Job 9:1-12) gave him the strength not to curse God and die (2:9, 10), but instead to affirm his commitment despite God's apparent distance. The first two chapters of Job shed light on the entire episode, confirming that Job's predicament was a microcosm of the universal conflict of the ages. To know this gives a strength that can overcome the fear of death (Job 13:15, KJV). The final chapters of the book confirm the biblical worldview.

Jesus is the supreme example of a life in God's presence and in constant communion with Him. But His experience leads ever further than that of Job. The extent to which Job suffered stopped short of death (Job 2:6). This was not the case with Jesus (Phil. 2:6-8). Yet, in the hours on the cross, deserted by His earthly companions, forsaken by His Father (Matt. 27:46), Jesus surrendered His life into God's hands (Luke 23:46) and died at peace.

The history of prophets, disciples, and martyrs of the Christian Era confirms that the biblical worldview espoused by Christianity can deal with ultimate questions of life and death as no other worldview can. For this reason the committed Christian can chart new courses, endure incredible challenges (Ps. 23:4), yet remain faithful to the end (Rev. 2:10).

c. Rules of action. Several passages of Scripture enjoin behavior that reflects the Christian worldview. We mention only a few: Psalms 14:1-5; 19:1-14; 23:1-6; 24:1-10; 91:1-16; 104:1-30; 139:1-24; Matthew 6:25-34; Acts 17:22-31.

2. Christian Piety

Consciousness and recognition of God's existence and His nature produce more than a passive fear and a distant rapport. In Christianity, religious life is an intimate relationship with God. Piety is a behavior that expresses deep, personal, and social acts of devotion to God. The first four commandments present several general principles of piety.

a. General principles. The *principle of monotheism* (Ex. 20:1-3) asserts the existence of only one, living, true God, to which the Christian refers for final authority. This same principle prohibits any competition with the only living God, whether in the form of creatures, things, or their representation (verses 4-6). God accepts only exclusive and unadulterated devotion from His creatures. Idolatry and adultery are equally repugnant to God. The *principle of respect for God* (verse 7) prohibits carelessness and triviality in speech or attitude. Calling on the name of God in swearing, joking, cursing, or for any insignificant reason, is sin. The *principle of Sabbath observance* (verses 8-11) extends to humans an invitation to come into God's presence. Sabbath is a special time when Creator and creature are open to each other, not just for a moment, not in some mystical fashion or secluded place, but in the home with the family, in fellowship with other Christians, in worship and prayer, in solitude and praise. This day is uncompromisingly God's day (Isa. 58:13), and Christians keep the seventh day as a sign of their devotion to Him.

b. Normative models. A major portion of the Bible depicts events in which God and humans enter into relationship. From the Garden of Eden (Gen. 3:8), through the patriarchal period (Gen. 5:22-24; 12:7, 8; 13:18), during the time of Israel as a nation (Ex. 25:8; Isa. 57:15), and certainly during the Christian Era, God has sought human fellowship, and many men and women have responded with worship and loyalty. All through millennia since Abel, faithful children of God have endured persecution and death. The three Hebrew young men (Dan. 3:1-30) are representative of those who stood their ground and received deliverance from God. Their friend, the prophet Daniel, had a similar experience (Dan. 6:1-28).

The lifestyle of Jesus fully illustrates genuine Christian piety. His total dependence on God (John 6:38), His habit of worshiping His Father (Mark 1:21; Luke 4:16, 17), His prayer life (Matt. 14:23; Luke 5:16), His respect for the seventh-day Sabbath (Matt. 12:9-12; Mark 2:27), and His all-consuming concern to please God (John 4:34) serve as a model for all to imitate. This example is foundational to the biblical ethos of Christian piety and portrays a biblical norm for behavior.

The episode of the golden calf (Ex. 32) shows human weakness and the tendency of human beings to make their own gods, to find their own center of life. It also illustrates the tragedy that occurs when things such as money, power, beauty, fame, or appetite consume our energies and turn us away from God and our neighbor.

c. Rules of action. We select only a few direct rules from many contained in the Word of God. They confirm the general principles and biblical norms at the level of immediate action: Ecclesiastes 5:1-6; Isaiah 58:13; Matthew 5:33-37; Hebrews 10:25. In the biblical ethos, human life is not only spiritual or religious. Other dimensions of the human being are also of crucial importance. Spirituality is a question of priority. From it the other aspects receive their support and protection from abuse. We turn now to the physical dimension of Christian lifestyle.

B. Standards of Physical Dimension

God, the Creator and Saviour of the whole human being, calls everyone to seek the highest standards of health. According to Scripture, health is a gift and a blessing that we must manage as stewards. We protect our health and, when it is compromised, work toward its restoration (Ex. 15:26; 3 John 2; see Health).

1. Health-preserving Standards

To preserve human health, God expects abstinence from doing, eating, drinking, or thinking what is harmful. He also enjoins temperate use of that which is good (PP 562).

a. General principles. Christian standards of health rest on several general principles. The *principle of life-preservation* (Ex. 20:13) indicates that God is the owner of life and humans must treat it as His own property. Anything that endangers or destroys human life cannot be part of the Christian lifestyle. The *principle of freedom from addictions* (1 Cor. 6:12; 10:23) sounds a warning not to use Christian freedom to satisfy intemperance or a degraded appetite. Slavery to food, drink, tobacco, music, or anything else falls below the Christian standard of life. The *principle of glory to God* (1 Cor. 10:31) orients human life toward its supreme goal. Words, actions, or thoughts that dishonor God's reputation cause harm to human beings and insult God who created them and cares for them. The *principle of total sanctification* (1 Thess. 5:23) emphasizes the developmental, progressive nature of human life. Of equal importance to physical growth is growth in grace and holiness. Every choice and decision can enhance our Godlikeness in terms of holiness and moral strength of character. The *principle of the body as a temple of the Holy Spirit* (1 Cor. 6:19, 20) calls for the rejection of any depreciatory or contemptuous attitude toward the human body. Together with 1 Thessalonians 5:23 it affirms a wholistic view of the human being, where every dimension is equally under the influence of sanctifying grace.

b. Normative models. The Garden of Eden is the example of an ideal environment conducive to human health. Using it as a model, Christians seek to incorporate into their lifestyle wholesome nutrition, rest, clean air, sunshine, work, and useful exercise for muscles and mind. Harmony in the soul is enhanced by a lifestyle in harmony with nature.

In the courts of pagan Babylon four youthful prisoners of war faced the test of faithfulness to health principles treated as normative in the Bible. They purposed in their minds to remain faithful to their convictions. Defying the odds, Daniel and his companions became living proof of the superiority of a biblically prescribed, healthful lifestyle. Daniel and his friends developed a superior physical and spiritual condition that served them well in life-threatening situations. Later, the advisors of King Belshazzar could say, "There is in your kingdom a man in whom is the spirit of the holy gods" (Dan. 5:11). Daniel maintained his body as a temple, the dwelling place of the Holy Spirit.

Such events recorded in Scripture illustrate ways men and women of the past applied or rejected principles of health and bore the consequences that followed. They also orient our actions toward optimum health; thus they counter sinful tendencies toward indulgence (Num. 11:31, 32).

c. Rules of action. In addition to giving principles and concrete illustrations of behavior, the Bible provides even more immediate guidelines for health. The following is a partial list of the precepts relating to various aspects of human health:

Nutrition: Genesis 1:29, 30; Leviticus 11:1-47;
            17:10-15; Proverbs 20:1; 21:17;
            23:20, 30, 31; Ephesians 5:18
Rest: Gen. 2:2, 3; Exodus 20:8-11;
            Psalms 23:1-6; 91:9; Mark 6:31
Stress: Matthew 6:25; Luke 12:29; 1 Peter 5:7

A more subtle form of health abuse involves intemperance in using good things. Excess in work belongs to this category. Given initially as a blessing, work becomes a curse when human sin alters and distorts it to reduce it to a source of evil. Greed and selfishness produce slavery, child labor, indecent wages, inhuman working conditions and practices, sustaining the gap between the rich and the poor. Life becomes work-dependent rather than God-dependent (Ps. 127:1, 2), creating stress and sickness. God's Word encourages temperance and the judicious use of all blessings in order to maintain good health.

2. Health-restoring Standards

Just as the physical dimension is an inseparable constituent of human nature, the ministry of healing is an integral part of God's work of salvation. While health-preserving standards apply to healing as well, certain specifically relevant principles and norms should be stressed.

a. General principles. The *principle of benevolence* (Gal. 6:9) commissions Christians to do good and prevent evil. A passive or indifferent attitude does not confront the aggressiveness of evil. Sickness is an aggressive enemy, and commitment to help those in need is of paramount importance. The *principle of care for others* (Acts 10:38) further challenges Christ's followers to alleviate suffering and pain with gentleness and love. This ministry often involves self-sacrificial effort beyond the ordinary. A judgmental attitude, such as that sometimes shown toward those who have venereal diseases or AIDS, must be replaced by compassionate care. The *principle of responsibility* (John 5:6, 14) calls for the patient to cooperate with the efforts and sacrifices of attending personnel. An atmosphere of mutual trust enhances the process of healing.

b. Normative models. The example of Jesus stands as a matchless norm that inspires men and women throughout the ages (Matt. 4:23, 24; Mark 2:1-12). Following His footsteps, thousands participate in medical missionary work, sometimes at the cost of their own lives. When the church inspires vocations and sponsors medical and educational institutions, it follows the pattern of the Great Physician.

The parable of the good Samaritan (Luke 10:30-37) sets the norm for a caring attitude in the Christian. The suffering person, even the stranger and the outcast, claims human solicitude above religious duty and the pursuit of personal business. A neighbor is not only one who lives in close proximity, but any person needing healing and care.

C. Standards of Social Dimension

Humans are by nature relational beings. The Creator said, "It is not good that the man should be alone" (Gen. 2:18). The immediate establishment of marriage (verses 18-25), daily communion with God (Gen. 3:8, 9), the institution of the family, and the emphasis on the second table of the Decalogue point to the importance of sound relations in the Christian lifestyle. Scripture contains general principles relevant for every context of interhuman associations. Some of these are: "You shall not kill" (Ex. 20:13); "You shall not steal" (verse 15); "You shall not bear false witness" (verse 16); and "You shall not covet" (verse 17). The apostle Paul enumerates a number of such principles in Romans 12 and 13; 1 Corinthians 10:24; and Ephesians 4:25-32. Jesus introduces the "golden rule" as the supreme standard for human relationships (Matt. 7:12; Luke 6:31).

In addition, the Bible contains principles applicable to specific relationships while remembering that the general principles do not cease to be applicable.

1. Christian Marriage and Family

a. Christian marriage. The richest and deepest of all human bonds dates from Creation. In spite of the beauty and harmony of his surroundings, Adam sensed an initial aloneness in the Garden. This God resolved in the creation of Eve. The narrative of Genesis 2 reminds us that by its nature marriage is more than a formal institution defining the rights, duties, and conditions required for a union of two humans of different gender. Primarily, and most important, marriage is an intimate and personal relationship where both adults consent to lower their guard, permitting access to their innermost physical, psychological, and spiritual being. In marriage both are willing to become vulnerable as in no other human association.

Because of this intimate sharing and giving of oneself to the other, the Bible presents

ample provision of standards to guide and guard against abuses. (See Marriage I.)

(1) General principles. The *principle of the marriage triangle* (Gen. 2:18, 22) includes God in marriage. The challenges and risks of life in a close, intimate union can be met with God's help and involvement. Christians trust God in their choice of a life partner. They also refer to His will in relating to each other. The *principle of equality of persons in marriage* (verse 18) is expressed in the words "a helper *fit* for him," not inferior or deficient. The couple fits each other, not only in similarities but even in the differences which can complement and enrich the relationship. This principle rules out any exploitation, subjugation, or elitism. The *principle of exclusivity* (Prov. 5:18) calls for a commitment to only one partner, above any commitments to family and friends. The *principle of unity* (Gen. 2:24) accentuates the willingness of both partners to blend their wills, likes, goals, and means for the emergence of "one flesh." Each spouse watches over the other as over him/herself (Eph. 5:28), each belonging to the other (1 Cor. 7:4). The *principle of faithfulness in marriage* (Matt. 19:6) shelters the unity of the couple from outside attacks, and from frivolity, capriciousness, and unfaithfulness within the marriage (Ex. 20:14). The Christian enters this covenant with total devotion, pledging his or her utmost to love and cherish, in sickness and in health.

The ideals presented in biblical principles manifest God's perfect will for perfect happiness. To inspire men and women to reach for this high standard of married life, God's Word presents several examples that set the norm for Christian marriage.

(2) Normative models. In poetic yet strikingly realistic terms, the Song of Solomon presents the beauty, the pain, the longing, the height, and the depth of married love. The beginning and the deepening of that love between Solomon and the Shulamite maiden, their wedding, a temporary absence and happy reunion, the ripening of an invincible and unquenchable mutual devotion, all of these are

depicted in God's Word as a beautiful model of His will for marriage.

Abigail provides another example worth noting. A woman of good sense and great beauty, she married a man who was "churlish and ill-behaved" (1 Sam. 25:3). No one knows how many times she suffered abuse and shame from her husband, and how often she mediated between her husband and those whom he mistreated. Only her efforts to save her husband from David's indignant wrath are reported, but her example pays a tribute to innumerable spouses who in silence and patience endure heroically, simply because of love.

The experience of Isaac—his readiness to heed his father's advice, his continual prayer and soul-searching that brought him lifelong happiness in marriage (Gen. 24:1-9, 54-67)—presents an example of a proper preparation for marriage. The tragic end of Samson was the result of his impertinence, self-indulgence, and insistence on doing his own will. To him, infatuation was the ultimate and only criterion for happiness (Judges 14-17). Many before and after him have discovered that "without counsel plans go wrong, but with many advisers they succeed" (Prov. 15:22). Unfortunately for many, this discovery comes too late.

(3) Rules of action. In many places Scripture records direct guidance for a happy marriage. Such passages are recorded in Deuteronomy 7:3-5; Ezra 10:10-14; Proverbs 5; Romans 7:2, 3; 1 Corinthians 7:1-39; Ephesians 5:22-31; Colossians 3:18, 19; 1 Timothy 5:14; Hebrews 13:4; and 1 Peter 3:1-7.

Christians strive to maintain high standards in the marriage relation for at least two reasons. First, in embracing God's will, they secure one of the most precious of God-given values: a happy home. This happens in spite of the fact that no marriage is flawless, no spouse is a perfect "helper," and no one always "fits" the other spouse in all respects. Second, Christians keep high standards of marriage because of love, both to God and to the spouse. Faithfulness becomes a gift of love offered exclusively to the spouse, because to do otherwise would hurt and destroy the other. In such an atmosphere the relationship inevitably grows. Another precious value emerges from the healthy and growing marriage love: home becomes a family.

b. Christian family. The Bible attaches great importance to the formation of a human family. Christian family lifestyle reflects this significance in the standards of family life.

(1) General principles. The *principle of childbearing* (Gen. 1:28) assures the propagation of the human race and calls for an adequate home for children. God gave the command to be fruitful and multiply to both Adam and Eve, not only because both were needed for procreation, but also because the best sanctuary for the weak, vulnerable, and totally dependent newborn is the home of a godly couple. Marital harmony must predate the arrival of the child and should be independent of it. When childbearing is considered a means of keeping the marriage together, the children may become victims of tensions between the parents. The *principle of nurturing the child* (Gen. 18:19; Eph. 6:4) encompasses several tasks. First, and most important, is love for every child. Partiality in parent-children relations inflicts deep wounds on those who are neglected and often incapacitates those who are coddled excessively. Based on impartial love parents can engage in education and discipline. The Bible insists that discipline is also an eloquent expression of love when administered appropriately (Prov. 13:24). The *principle of support of children* in financial and physical needs (1 Tim. 5:8) molds the Christian lifestyle. Parents are responsible not only to provide everyday necessities, but when circumstances allow they should furnish education, vacations, cultural activities, and even some inheritance (2 Cor. 12:14).

The *principle of respect for parents* (Ex. 20:12) creates a context in which family responsibilities can be adequately discharged. Parents cannot fulfill the parental duties listed above if they hold no authority over their household. The age, the greater maturity, the education, the experience, are all advantages from which children can and should profit with gratitude. The necessary but unpleasant lessons and tasks may never be learned or accomplished when due respect is wanting. The *principle of care for the elderly* (Lev. 19:32) completes the human life cycle. Christians consider respect and care for elderly parents or grandparents as a Christian duty and privilege. In a civilization where the value of a human being tends to be measured by usefulness, success, and contributions, the weak and elderly are discounted. Often loving parents feel pushed aside, away from the warmth of their children's homes into institutions where infrequent visits by children create inexpressible anguish. The Bible enjoins proper respect for those who are older.

(2) Normative models. The Creation account presents an example for spouses contemplating parenthood. First of all, God planned the creation of man and woman: "Let us make man" (Gen. 1:26). Childbearing must be purposeful and planned, not a thoughtless incident of insignificant consequence. Second, God prepared everything needed for the human creature: air for the lungs, food for the stomach, light for the eyes, work and sleep for the muscles, mysteries and laws of nature for the mind, and the Sabbath for communion with God. A Christian lifestyle beckons modern parents to imitate our heavenly Father in upholding the principles of care and support of the family.

In the household of Isaac and Rebekah there was a serious neglect of the principle of impartial love. Isaac preferred Esau and Rebekah favored Jacob (Gen. 25:28). Sibling rivalry and even hatred tore this family apart. Jacob also showed a preferential bias toward Joseph; identical consequences followed (Gen. 37:3, 4). These two negative examples only support the principle of proper nurture of children, indicating how important it is for parents to be impartial.

Abraham and Isaac stand as a beautiful ex-ample of mutual respect and love. On Mount Moriah the son trusts his father to the point of death because he has learned to trust his father's God (Gen. 22:1-14). A very different example is given by Eli, a father who lost control over his sons, as well as their respect (1 Sam. 2:22-25). Just as Isaac reaped blessings, so the sons of Eli the priest harvested personal ruin and death, and caused national decay and collapse of the moral order.

Finally, many other examples can set norms for family behavior. Among them we mention Hannah and Elkanah (1 Sam. 1; 2), Joseph and Mary (Matt. 1:18-25; 2:1-23), and Lois and Eunice, grandmother and mother of Timothy (2 Tim. 1:5).

(3) Rules of action. For more direct guidelines on family life, a Christian may refer to passages such as Exodus 21:15, 17; Leviticus 19:3; Deuteronomy 27:16; Proverbs 1:8; 6:20; 23:22; Ephesians 6:1-4; 1 Timothy 5:1-8; Titus 2:3-6; and Hebrews 12:7-11.

Many positive values emanate from following Christian standards of family life. Identity, the sense of self, is among the most important. Its basis rests on dialogue with oneself and others (Gen. 2:18). The dialogues may take a form of self-appraisal (Rom. 2:15) or self-encouragement (Ps. 5:11; 116:7). In addition, the need for belonging urges us to dialogue with and imitate those who are important to us. Thus our self-concept receives its social dimension. At birth, humans have no instincts to guide them autonomously as do animals. They need caring, coaching, modeling, forgiving, accepting, and affirming in love. The family is the God-given environment in which humans receive a healthy sense of self-worth and identity.

In the same way, the family provides the context that encourages and facilitates the development of habits and values. The examples that children observe, the opportunities offered to them, the kind of music, books, food, social climate, and religious orientation to which children are exposed, determine in large measure their habits and value preferences.

Ellen G. White writes: "Every one in the family is to be nourished by the lessons of Christ. . . . This is the standard every family should aim to reach. . . .

"Religious instruction means much more than ordinary instruction. It means that you are to pray with your children, teaching them how to approach Jesus and tell Him all their wants. It means that you are to show in your life that Jesus is everything to you, and that His love makes you patient, kind, forbearing, and yet firm in commanding your children after you, as did Abraham" (AH 317).

Experience confirms that religious and spiritual formation cannot be left to the child alone. It takes parental dedication and a loving environment to overcome the pressures that lead humans in the wrong direction. The Christian family seeks to uphold divine standards and thus provides society with men and women who live with integrity and in the fear of God. (See Marriage II. A.)

2. Issues in Marriage and Family

Christians cannot be satisfied with merely describing ideals and identifying shortcomings. The grim reality of troubled and broken marriages and homes cries out for help. Before focusing on the biblical guidelines for dealing with marriage and family problems, it is necessary to highlight briefly the preventive features inherent in the Christian marriage and family lifestyle.

a. Preventive lifestyle. The premarital period is of crucial importance. A Christian lifestyle urges careful self-examination, patient study of the possible marriage partner, sufficient time to know each other before emotional attachments overpower reason, seeking advice from more experienced and trusted people, maintaining a high standard of sexual purity, and most of all constant prayer and searching for God's will. No one can be too prudent and wise for the choice of a marriage partner (5T 106, 107), but the above-mentioned precautions can reduce the risk of serious tragedies.

The Christian lifestyle aims at harmony and permanence in a marriage relationship. For that reason the mutual care and romance from the premarital period should survive the wedding day, the arrival of children, and the coming of the golden years. Both spouses need to nurture their mutual love and work with tenacity to reach their common potential. In a Christian marriage there must be consistent communication of feelings, goals, fears, and hopes to prevent the onset of disillusionment, alienation, and the estrangement that may mar the marriage.

The Christian family lifestyle centers on people within the family. *Togetherness* must be practiced intentionally around games, outings, or in simple cuddling. *Traditions* unique to every family further enhance the sense of identity of each member; these may include special celebrations, vacations, regular spiritual activities, and other creative family customs. *Acceptance* of each member as he or she is will require tolerance of mistakes and affirmation of the personal talents and unique characteristics of each. *Discipline* will protect each member from immediate harm and from the eventual danger of developing harmful habits. And finally, *regular worship* will strengthen the sense of divine presence in the home, bringing a feeling of security to all.

When, in spite of intentional efforts to implement this Christian way of life, troubles set in, the Bible presents guidance for the Christian experiencing problems in marriage and family life.

(1) General principles. The *principle of redemptive confrontation* taught by Jesus in Matthew 18 applies to marital and family problems as well. As soon as a distance in attitude becomes evident, Jesus entreats, "go" and confront, to redeem your "brother." If there is no opening of communication it may be necessary to seek help elsewhere. Sharing the problem with one or more skilled helpers often brings good results. In case such efforts fail, the church that witnessed the marriage vows engages in a healing ministry. The *prin-*

ciple of separation for a period of time may be another redemptive step (1 Cor. 7:5, 10, 11). This might provide time to lessen the tension, think, counsel, and pray through the issues that separate. But Paul cautions that such disassociation might bring temptations to the spouses and advises a short separation for prayer. The *principle of sacredness of marriage* sets the marital union above human touch and beyond vulnerability to the will or desires of any person. The words of Jesus are clear: "What therefore God has joined together, let no man put asunder" (Matt. 19:6). Death is the only inescapable reason for the dissolution of marriage (1 Cor. 7:39). Even adultery, the most serious infraction of marriage law, does not provide automatic cause for divorce. Jesus treats it as an exception to the principle of sacredness or inviolability, not as another rule opposing or alongside the main principle (Matt. 19:9). Malachi speaks of God's rejecting His people "because the Lord was witness to the covenant between you and the wife of your youth, to whom you have been faithless, though she is your companion and your wife by covenant. . . . So take heed to yourselves, and let none be faithless to the wife of his youth. 'For I hate divorce, says the Lord the God of Israel'" (Mal. 2:14-16). A Christian spouse faced with a faithless companion opts for divorce only when there is no possibility for reestablishing communion (1 Cor. 7:15).

(2) Normative models. The experience of the prophet Hosea illustrates the conduct of the husband of an adulterous woman (Hosea 1:2, 3; 3:1-3). The restless spouse runs away but he buys her back, forgives her unfaithfulness, and treats her with respect and love. The prophet's predicament presents only a dim picture of the relationship between God and His people. "They are all adulterers," says God (Hosea 7:4), yet He does not "divorce" them. "How can I give you up! . . . How can I hand you over!" He exclaims (Hosea 11:8), moved by a love that transcends faithlessness. Thus we hear in the Bible the call to faithfulness in

marriage (Mal. 2:14-16), as well as an example of model behavior in the divine example of forgiveness of adultery.

Family problems cannot be totally prevented through faithful conformity to standards alone. Even the home of Adam and Eve faced jealousy between brothers and the insubordinate behavior of Cain. In the parable of the prodigal, Christians can find inspiration for patience and forbearance in dealing with prodigals; they also find encouragement to uphold the principles of redeeming family relations (Luke 15:11-32).

Family problems may result from wrong actions of parents as well. Jonathan sets a worthy example of a son who respected his father, King Saul, but refused to cooperate or submit to his way of life (1 Sam. 19:1-7). Unfortunately, Jacob cooperated with the dishonest scheming of his mother, which resulted in family disturbances for generations (Gen. 27).

(3) Rules of action. Among the biblical passages containing direct rules of action on marriage and family problems we note Deuteronomy 21:15-21; Matthew 5:32; 19:5-9; Mark 10:11, 12; Romans 7:2, 3; and 1 Corinthians 7.

A distressing fact is that good Christians do not always make good marriages and not all Christian families are good families. This may happen because God is not invited or because His will is not discerned aright, not to mention our reluctance to forsake our self-centered ways. Furthermore, since harmonious relationships stand as a bulwark against sin, Satan attacks marriages and families with fury. So we ask, what is the Christian way through fatal relational disintegration?

b. Divorce. Divorce is never a solution, rather a dissolution. It is a dissolution of marriage and a dissemination of its problems. It leaves behind wounded and divided what once was the one-flesh identity. It marks too many innocent people for the rest of their lives. For that reason a Christian will rather be a victim of divorce than cause it, and will seek the strength and counsel needed to save the marriage if possible. Only after all recourses have been exhausted with no improvement may a spouse give in to divorce procedures.

During this painful period, and for a significant time after the divorce is final, the Christian will avoid friendship with individuals of the other gender outside the family. Several reasons demand this. First, the hopes of easy remarriage may be more appealing than persistent efforts at resolving the difficulties of the present marriage. Second, the feeling of failure and deep sense of low self-esteem make for emotional vulnerability, in which necessary caution and discretion become difficult. The relationship may grow too quickly, too deep. Third, when emotional injuries and hurts enter the new relationship they become hidden mines, ready to explode in the face of an unsuspecting partner, causing additional problems. Moreover, the still-hurting individual spends enormous energies on tending to his or her own afflictions, so that little strength remains to confront creatively the needs and deficiencies of the other person. Finally, when minor or dependent children are present, their bruised hearts must witness the attention of their parent turning to a stranger. They are not (often never) "divorced" from the original parent. And when another individual "intrudes" into a shattered home the risks of its collapse become very real.

c. **Remarriage.** Remarriage with a person other than the former spouse does not appear to be a biblical option. The exception may be a person whose spouse has fallen in adultery and broken one-flesh unity in defiance of the covenant of marriage (Matt. 19:9). We say, "may be" because adultery is not an unforgivable sin, and because not all adulteries are the same. Infidelity committed in a context of temptation is not the same as a planned and purposeful adultery of one who tempts others.

But why is adultery such a unique sin? Are not such things as apostasy (breaking the promise of faithfulness to God), abandonment (breaking the promise to care), abuse (breaking the promise to love and cherish), and impure thoughts (also a form of adultery) also a

ground for divorce? In 1 Corinthians 6:16-18 Paul recognizes the unique nature of sexual sin.

1. Physical, mental, and emotional abuse, apostasy, abandonment, and even impure thoughts can occur separately and can be remedied through repentance. The sexual act involves the entire human being, all dimensions of human personality, and affects the very identity of the participant: "He who joins himself to a prostitute becomes one body with her" (1 Cor. 6:16). This does not happen with other sins. They are not against the homogeneity of the body (verse 18).

2. In sexual sin there is another free human being involved. All of that person's dimensions are affected as well, and the repentance of one does not remove or cancel the impact on the other, or on all other people involved.

These two factors, the impact on the unity of the individual who engages in sexual activity and the involvement of the other partner in adultery, make this sin fatal to the marriage union. From that moment on the original marriage is altered and only the miracle of grace can bring reconciliation.

d. **Cohabitation.** By cohabitation is meant living together without legal or church endorsement. It is a private arrangement based on the couple's decision and reflects their own wishes and parameters. Such a way of life is foreign to Christian lifestyle for several reasons:

1. Cohabitation has no biblical support. Any intimate sexual union of two persons of different gender outside of the marriage covenant is termed adultery or fornication.

2. The union of two spouses involves privileges and responsibilities. Experience shows that responsibility *for* someone's happiness is secure only as the responsibility *to* someone is respected. If the husband's responsibility for his wife is based on his responsibility to God and the church, the terms of the covenant are enforced by these authorities (Mal. 2:13-16). But if responsibility for the part-

ner is simply to oneself or to one's partner, a simple decision not to be responsible *to* the partner cancels the duty *for* the other. No one else has a mandate or duty to protect or respect such a union.

3. To commit one's deepest feelings and to make one's self vulnerable with no other guarantee than the promise of human lips, wishes, or desires, is risky and unwise. For that reason the chances for permanency or depth in such relationships are slim. (See Marriage II. B, C.)

3. Issues in Sexuality

a. Human sexuality. A Christian witness regarding appropriate sexual conduct is of enormous importance for contemporary society. Many social and personal problems stem from the inability to effectively restrain and regulate the dynamism of this natural drive. The sexual revolution has only intensified and exacerbated an already difficult situation. As a result, a Christian lives in a civilization that considers sexual expression a key to happiness, extramarital intercourse as normal, and tolerates homosexual practice and certain other sexual perversions as valid alternative lifestyles. To evade clear guidelines in this dimension of human conduct may be as irresponsible as to condone the perversion of intimacy. The Word of God is not silent on, nor indifferent to, sexuality, as a careful reading of Scripture will amply demonstrate.

(1) General principles. The *principle of the goodness of gender difference* appears clearly in Scripture (Gen. 1:27, 28, 31). God intentionally created two persons of different gender. Both men and women are created in the image of God, yet their roles and functions, to say nothing of their minds and bodies, are different. That man and woman are different does not mean that one is inferior to the other. (See Marriage I. E. 1. b.)

The *principle of the goodness of sexuality* affirms that the sexual drive and sexual activities are not in themselves evil or sinful (Gen. 1:28; 2:24, 25; 4:1). The Bible speaks frequently and unabashedly of a man's "knowing" his wife; in so doing Scripture defines the parameters within which sexual conduct remains a good thing. First, intimacy is not only physical in nature; its expression involves and requires emotional, rational, willful, socioeconomic, legal, and spiritual dimensions together with the physical. Second, human sexuality needs the sanctuary of marriage because spiritual communion cannot happen instantly or in a haphazard manner; it requires exclusiveness, genuine emotional rapport, free consent of reason and will, and full assumption of social, economic, and legal responsibilities. Third, because communion and intimacy cannot take place with multiple partners, a Christian lifestyle calls for the lifelong marriage of one man to one woman. Only within these confines can one find enough security, trust, and commitment to lay one's entire being open to another person. Only within these boundaries can sexual relations remain a good thing.

The *principle of sexual purity* stands against all forms of perversions and abuses of human intimacy (1 Cor. 6:15-20). Because of this principle, the Christian will eschew all forms of impurity, even though they may be culturally acceptable.

Prostitution, which consists of selling one's body, stands condemned for several reasons. It isolates the physical aspect of sexuality from the other dimensions of human personality and reduces self-worth to sexual marketability. Besides contributing to the spread of sexually transmitted diseases, prostitution undermines the stability of marriages and the security of social relations. All extramarital sexual relations must be rejected for the same reasons as prostitution, even though the sexual activity may not be subject to remuneration (Deut. 22:22).

Incest is repulsive for additional reasons. It confuses relationships between close relatives and becomes especially traumatic for abused minors or nonconsenting adults. It violates human freedom, cheapens human dignity, and may cause mental and emotional trauma which not infrequently leads to prostitution and sexual imbalance for the rest of life. Rape is forbidden for similar reasons and brings similar consequences. Both are criminal acts; responsible individuals should report their occurrence to the proper authorities.

Christians will abstain from other perverted practices, such as sodomy, transvestism, pedophilia, and voyeurism. Pornography is offensive to the Christian for several reasons. By emphasizing the sensual and provocative, pornography is a powerful instrument in debasing manhood and womanhood to the level of a mere sex object. It stimulates the sexual drive without an interpersonal relationship or mutual respect. Because sexual self-gratification becomes the main goal of sexual activity, the habit of ignoring the other's needs develops easily. Sexuality becomes a matter of fantasy, which quickly degenerates into obsession, and makes for ill-adjusted marriage. Pornography has become a multi-billion-dollar business against which Christians must act and speak decisively.

In order for men and women to understand the biblical view of human sexuality, as well as the duties and privileges of married life, proper instruction is imperative. The family and the church must take responsibility for preparing the young to become strong and virtuous.

(2) Normative models. Scripture frankly records sad episodes of sexual misbehavior and beautiful stories of noble victories over evil. In those events we measure human depravity and consistent divine rejection of sin under all circumstances and situations. Potiphar's wife and her lifestyle are contrasted with Joseph and his lifestyle. In that one event adultery and fornication are rejected unconditionally (Gen. 39:6-23). This story teaches that extramarital sex is off bounds for all: rich and mighty with power to exploit and put to death, or slaves totally deprived of rights.

The outrageous gang rape by some inhabitants of Gibeah demonstrates how low the obsession with sex can bring those who are enslaved by it. The entire nation stood against that city in order to avenge the death of the victim and send a clear message to its citizens that standards of decency and human rights must be honored (Judges 19; 20).

The incestuous rape of his half-sister Tamar perpetrated by the impetuous and undisciplined Amnon (2 Sam. 13:1-20), sends another shocking signal of distress to homes. Amnon was killed by Absalom, but the shame and disgrace could not be removed from Tamar's life. Christian homes must provide opportunities for learning how to manage and control all appetites and drives, including sexuality. They must be the safest place on earth where chastity can be practiced and taught, and where the true outlook on sexuality is presented and discussed without false embarrassment. Parents and children must recognize the need for help and deal aggressively with sexual wrongs. Purity is the norm of Christian behavior. In addition to this, the church has a solemn responsibility to enforce the norms of decency as well (1 Cor. 5:1, 2).

Proverbs 7 relates the story of a young man seduced by a harlot. In the process of attracting his attention she promises emotional fulfillment, a secure and secret place where their love can find its full expression. The sad fact is that she can offer only the physical aspect of sexuality; when the night is over the emptiness, shame, and the feeling of unworthiness persist. By following the lustful appetite of the physical dimension at the expense of the rest of his personality, the young man is left with a discordant inner life and a confused self-image. A thirst for pleasure alone threatens to distort his view of intimacy; mind-body alienation will result.

In contrast, the Song of Solomon depicts the beauty of mutual attraction and intimacy between two lovers who have become husband and wife. There is no trace of impure desires or selfish pursuit of pleasure for pleasure's sake. Instead, self-sacrifice for the happiness of the other brings deep joy to both. This book presents the Christian norm for sexual life.

(3) Rules of action. Scripture contains many direct rules for sexual behavior, still applicable to the Christian. Among these we cite: Exodus 20:14; 22:19; Leviticus 20:11, 12, 17-21; Deuteronomy 22:23-30; Proverbs 5:15-19; 7:25-27; Matthew 5:27, 28, 31, 32; 19:3-9; Mark 10:2-9; 1 Corinthians 5:1, 2; 6:15-19; Galatians 5:19-21; Ephesians 5:3-5, 25; Hebrews 13:4; Revelation 21:8. (See Marriage II. A-D.)

b. The Christian and singleness. Christians may find themselves single, either for a time or on a permanent basis. Life still provides affirmation of their gender qualities, possibilities for contribution to society, and genuine enjoyment of life. In addition, Christianity maintains the possibility of sexual expressions within the parameters of celibacy.

The various human needs that marriage is designed to meet can be satisfied to a great degree without a marital union. The extended family, the church community, work associates, and various social configurations can provide adequate support, both emotionally and spiritually. The sex drive can be sublimated and channeled in various ways. Even bonding does not depend exclusively on sexual intercourse. It may also happen between an individual and his or her calling or mission in life, sometimes to the extent of total commitment. John the Baptist, the apostle Paul, and Jesus Himself are the most recognized examples of bonding between human beings and the mission they live to carry out. Paul is very explicit on this in 1 Corinthians 7:25-35.

Christians who are single, whether by personal choice, or circumstances, may be confident that God, who knows their situation, calls them to a rich and productive life. The secret of Paul's tremendous contribution as a single person did not lie in any energetic or persistent rebellion against his fate. It was found in his willingness to ask the question "What shall I do, Lord?" (Acts 22:10). From then on Paul's life was one with Christ's (Gal. 2:20).

Today's social climate exerts enormous pressure on singles to satisfy their needs for sexual expression in intimacies outside marriage. Yet, the Bible makes no allowance for sexual relations except within marriage. Resistance to temptation is possible through the indwelling Holy Spirit.

A brief word may be appropriate on masturbation as a sexual expression during celibacy. While there is no clear guidance on this in Scripture, because sexual activity is described as occurring exclusively between married persons, those who advocate sexual relief through masturbation would need to give evidence for their position. Masturbation, when practiced repeatedly, may lead to voyeurism, sexual fantasy, or involvement with pornography, which in time produce mental pollution and acts of aggression. This activity may become compulsive. Marriage partners who bring with them the obsession to masturbate often carry a load of guilt and have a low self-image. Their self-control gives way to self-indulgence; the marriage and eventually health are affected.

c. Christians and homosexuality. A Christian's response to homosexuality—here understood as referring to either males or females—must be predicated on biblical principles and norms. In considering the issues, one must make a clear distinction between homosexual orientation and practice. Over the first, the person may have little control; regarding the second, individual choices are decisive. By God's grace, total purity is possible. On the other hand, as Christians relate to the issue, they should remember that people with homosexual tendencies carry a heavy burden and need the love and understanding of Christ's body as they battle temptation. (See Marriage II. B.)

(1) General principles. The *principle of heterosexuality* finds its basis in Creation (Gen. 2:24, 25). Adam and Eve were created male and female so that they might complement and complete each other in the "one flesh" union. The image of God includes not only both genders, but also the femaleness that Adam lacked and the maleness that Eve

found in Adam. This concept has far-reaching implications for homosexuality.

It is evident that homosexuality was not present at Creation but appeared after the Fall. It is a noncreated element of human nature and not an alternative dimension of the image of God. The homosexual orientation must be viewed as a consequence of sin on the human body and psyche. In any case, Paul found homosexuality "unnatural" (Rom. 1:26) or "against nature" (NKJV).

The controversy over the etiology of homosexuality is not resolved. There is some evidence that homosexuality is a learned behavior. However, some studies suggest that homosexuality does not always result from a conscious choice nor is it exclusively based on early influences, but rather that it may be genetic. In any case, the factors that contribute to homosexuality are only partially relevant to the discussion of Christian lifestyle.

Some insist that if homosexuality is genetically determined, it is not merely behavior but rather a unique way in which the gay or lesbian sees him or herself. The homosexual act comes from this unique self-concept. As such it would be natural, and must not be considered illegal or sinful.

To accept this reasoning requires giving up the biblical outlook on homosexuality. The claim that homosexuality is natural, an alternative orientation, is in contradiction with Paul's statement in Romans 1:26, 27. It would also cast a shadow of injustice on God, who sanctioned a death sentence against homosexuals (Lev. 18:22; 20:13).

Furthermore, to consider homosexuality as natural, and its practice as not sinful challenges the Christian view of the power of the gospel. Jesus came to free humans from learned disorders, and from genetic or hereditary tendencies as well. Christians maintain that personal responsibility is not limited to behavior over which we have full choice. We are all born "in sin" (Ps. 51:5), but this sinfulness must not reign in our lives. No one—the homosexual, the alcoholic, the cleptomaniac,

or any other sinner—should remain dead in his or her trespasses, that is, become resigned to this condition. All are invited to yield themselves as instruments to God rather than to wickedness and respond to a call of resurrection with Christ to the newness of life (Rom. 6:1-23).

(2) Normative models. Only two Bible stories suggest homosexual activity. In both cases, homosexual gang rape is threatened but not carried out. In Genesis 19:1-11 the men of Sodom accost the angels who have come to Lot's home. In Judges 19:16-22 the men of Gibeah act in a similar manner. Both stories are told in a way that underlines the wickedness of the men involved.

(3) Rules of action. The following commands set forth clearly the biblical guidance on homosexuality: Leviticus 18:22; 20:13; Romans 1:27; 1 Corinthians 6:9-11; 1 Timothy 1:8-11.

4. Citizenship

The call to live as Christians meets humans in the midst of their professional and social involvement. At times this call means a change in life vocation, but most often the Christian is invited to follow Christ in the same workplace, the same neighborhood, the same family, with the only change being in the way of living. With this, a somewhat paradoxical situation emerges. Jesus summed it up by saying of His followers that they are in the world but not of the world (John 17:14-18).

Throughout history the church has searched for the best way to keep its presence in the world while keeping worldliness out. In a very influential study, H. R. Niebuhr (1951) describes five different relations between Christianity and the world: "Christ against culture," where the church lives in hermetically enclosed enclaves (Tertullian); "Christ of culture," fostering the accommodation of Christianity to fit a given culture (Gnostics); "Christ above culture," searching for a synthesis of Christ and culture (Aquinas); "Christ and culture in paradox," maintaining a dualistic dialectic (Luther); and finally "Christ the transformer of culture," where conversion defines the church's ministry to society (Augustine).

It is evident from Scripture that Christ envisioned the church plunged into the ferment of society, yet free from the evils of the surrounding culture. Three areas of the Christian's daily life must be considered: work relations, civic responsibility, and social responsibility.

a. Work relations. Whatever their work, Christians uphold the standards of Christian behavior. Whatever their position, Christians relate to their superiors, subordinates, or peers in a Christlike manner.

(1) General principles. The *principle of adequate compensation for adequate work* calls the Christian employers and administrators to treat their workers fairly (Luke 10:7; 1 Cor. 9:8-10; James 5:4-6). History testifies to social, economic, and political upheavals fueled by desperate living conditions of workers. Christian employers will watch that greed does not determine the wages and benefits of their employees. Christians should pay fair wages. The *principle of adequate work for adequate compensation* in turn calls Christian employees to work with diligence and constancy (1 Thess. 4:11; 2 Thess. 3:10), resisting the temptation to cheat their employer. Characteristics such as faithfulness, integrity, accountability, creativity, and industry are appropriate to Christians. With loyalty to the employer, the Christian will not exact a higher compensation than the work rendered would warrant. The *principle of equality in Christ* demands that Christians—whether superiors or subordinates—regard and treat each other as equals in Christ (Gal. 3:28). A Christian administrator is a brother or a sister to the employee; neither will seek special privileges because of this relation. Additionally, a Christian employer or administrator may not treat employees differently on the basis of race, gender, nationality, social status, or religion. At the same time, a Christian employee must not expect special treatment on the account of race, gender, nationality, social status, or religion. The wages, promotions, awards, hiring or firing, and demotions must follow the Christian sense of fairness and equality. While important in all areas of life, the *principle of truthfulness* is especially applicable to work relations. Absolute honesty is required of all, whatever their positions. Truthfulness is especially important in the interaction of professionals with clients or patients. At the same time, confidentiality must be kept, even when not explicitly promised, because professional ethics demand it.

(2) Normative models. The Bible reports several instances of bad work relations and clearly discourages such behavior. The case of Laban and Jacob illustrates how a superior can impose manipulation, but it also demonstrates the stratagems the employee is tempted to use to survive the abuse (Gen. 29-31).

The exemplary behavior of Joseph in jail brought him the respect of his fellow prisoners and the chief of guards. As a result he became a trustee and received an incredible promotion from jail to the king's palace (Gen. 39-41).

In the letter to Philemon, Paul describes the relationship between a slave owner and his slave who are brothers in Christ. Obedience to the master still stands, but the requirements and treatment of that slave must become brotherly. In the workplace Philemon is the master, but in human terms they are brothers, and in the church Onesimus the slave might be an elder over his owner.

(3) Rules of action. Several rules apply to Christian work relations: Jeremiah 22:13-19; Ephesians 6:5-9; 1 Thessalonians 4:11, 12; 2 Thessalonians 3:6-12; 2 Timothy 2:6; and James 2:1-9.

b. Civic responsibility. As an integral part of the civic community, a Christian cannot evade responsibility toward society. The following biblical standards relate behavior to public life:

(1) General principles. The *principle of obedience to God first* helps Christians to put

their civic duties in the right perspective (Acts 4:19). The laws of the land at all levels may at times conflict with some of God's commandments. While magistrates bear responsibility for the law, each citizen is accountable to God for the choices he or she makes. In such cases Christians will explain their convictions and appeal to freedom of conscience, which is a God-given right on the basis of creation in His image. If the appeals are rejected, faithfulness to God first may result in fines, persecution, prison sentences, or other sacrifices that Christians in centuries past had to make. The *principle of obedience for the sake of law and order* is also a Christian way of life (Rom. 13:1-7). Loyalty to God first does not entitle anyone to become autonomous and create social disharmony or chaos. Christians pay taxes, participate in civic duties, respect traffic laws and property regulations, and cooperate with civil authorities in curbing or controlling crime and violence. A public officer will receive respect and support from the Christian community. To obey them properly, the Christian will make an effort to know the laws of the land, keep reasonably informed about the events in the community, and participate actively in the life of society. The *principle of social justice* demands that human rights be respected and that Christians lead society in that direction (James 5:1-6). Beginning within the church and expanding to relations in the civic domain, discrimination on the basis of race, gender, or status must never occur without Christian opposition. While the church as an organization cannot resort to immoral or political means it can use all appropriate avenues allowed by the political structure of a country. There should be room within the church for those feeling a call to occupy public office.

(2) Normative models. In the court of Pharaoh, Joseph set a high norm of conduct as an honest, creative, and insightful civil servant. Yet the power he wielded was not used to abuse subordinates, nor did Joseph misappropriate any of the wealth at his disposal (Gen. 41:37-57).

In the court in Babylon and Medo-Persia several Hebrew officials stood their ground whenever obedience to God prevented them from obeying the will of the king. Shadrach, Meshach, and Abednego were thrown into the fiery furnace (Dan. 3); Daniel's faithfulness took him to the lions' den (Dan. 6). As a result, pagan courts and nations witnessed the power of the living God.

In the court of Ahasuerus the Medo-Persian king, Queen Esther remembered her loyalty to God's people. After prayer and fasting she bravely acted and reversed the immoral decree. She risked her life for what was right and good (Esther 4:16) and set a high norm of faithfulness to God first.

Paul was a clear example of an informed citizen who obeyed the laws of the land but did not remain idle when they were abused (Acts 25:8-12). Jesus Himself halted abuse when the soldiers hit Him without a justified reason (John 18:23).

(3) Rules of action. Among many direct commands, we select Proverbs 22:16, 22, 23, 26-29; 23:10, 11; Mark 12:14-17; 1 Timothy 1:8-11; 2 Timothy 1:7-18; and 1 Peter 2:13-20.

c. Social responsibility. By being present in society, Christians expose themselves to the needs, fears, injustices, and suffering of humanity. The lifestyle of a Christian must follow that of Jesus, who went about doing good and bringing relief to those who suffered (Acts 10:38). In addition to living His own example, Jesus attempted by means of parables to instill in the consciousness of His followers the fact that to be His disciple meant to care for others. Seeing suffering or sensing a need mobilizes the will to aid others. This is the frame of mind, the lifestyle, by which Jesus will recognize His own (Matt. 25:31-46).

(1) General principles. The *principle of self-denial* is the first and most difficult step toward a lifestyle of social responsibility (Matt. 16:24). It is possible to turn inward, to tend to one's own legitimate needs, to invest time and means for education and training, to

reach for laudable goals and ideals, or even to keep the commandments and be so preoccupied with one's own salvation that the needs of others pass unnoticed. "Go, sell . . . and give to the poor," says Jesus to the rich young ruler (Matt. 19:21). Jesus affirms that the only way to preserve one's self is through giving one's self up for His sake (Matt. 10:39). The *principle of identification* fills the vacuum created by denying the self (Isa. 53:4-6). The Christian realizes that there is no such thing as poverty; there are humans who are poor. There is no suffering, no hopelessness, no war, no disease in the abstract; there are only suffering humans, homeless people, fighting neighbors, and sick persons. Is not the religious lifestyle chosen by God, "to loose the bonds of wickedness, to undo the thongs of the yoke, to let the oppressed go free, and to break every yoke? Is it not to share your bread with the hungry, and bring the homeless poor into your house; when you see the naked, to cover him" (Isa. 58:6, 7)? This principle causes Christians to see themselves in the helpless person's predicament, just as Jesus placed Himself in the position of the unfortunate (Matt. 25:31-46).

The *principle of sacrifice* ensures that self-denial and empathy do not remain passive (James 1:27). Widows and orphans can profit very little from theories, programs, promises, and prayers. Christians will never find time, means, or motivation to help society in need unless consciously and purposefully they decide to sacrifice their means and their own selves. The *principle of systematic benevolence* makes ministry to those in need more dependable and consistent (1 Cor. 16:1-4). When a disaster strikes, sporadic and haphazardous relief cannot meet the need. A more sustained help and a more involved participation and presence are required. The Christian way of life is systematically benevolent, making provision for such assistance.

(2) Normative models. The entire economy of the people of Israel under the theocracy shows how the poor and unfortunate were cared for. The jubilee system—which mandated the rest of the land, the release of slaves, and the return of property to the original owner—had as its goal the reduction of the gap between rich and poor, fortunate and unfortunate (Lev. 25). The Israelites were taught to be systematically benevolent when they were instructed to leave some of the produce unharvested, so that those in need could find sufficient for survival (Lev. 19:9, 10).

In the story of the good Samaritan, Jesus underlined the danger of religious complacency and religious business which consume our time and energy so that glaring social tragedies remain ignored (Luke 10:30-37). To be a Christian one must act as a neighbor to the person in need. Those who suffer have a claim on the Christian, without detracting from God's claims on humans, because God identifies Himself with those who suffer. To be known and recognized by Christ is not achieved by becoming deeply religious, because religion can be immoral (priest and Levite in the story). The Samaritan, though a stranger to the covenant and an outsider to the promises, becomes a norm for the Christian because of his caring actions.

Dorcas, a member of the church in Joppa, set another norm for Christians. With her acts of benevolence she became an indispensable member of the community. She became the support and hope of the hopeless (Acts 9:36-43). In memory of Dorcas and of the good Samaritan, Christians have raised societies and organized various programs bearing the names of these two people. However, such programs do not accomplish their task unless people such as Dorcas and the good Samaritan become active in benevolence.

(3) Rules of action. God has commanded His people to provide for the needs of those whom He knows as unfortunate and needy. The following is only a sample of biblical references requiring loving care for others: Exodus 22:25; 23:3, 11; Leviticus 25:25-55; Deuteronomy 15:11; 24:12-15; Proverbs 14:31; 17:5; 19:17; 21:13; Isaiah 3:15; 10:1, 2; 61:1-3;

2 Corinthians 8:9; Philippians 2:5-11.

5. Christian Stewardship

God is the Creator, sustainer, and ultimate owner of everything (Ps. 24:1). Even human beings belong to Him (1 Cor. 6:19, 20). As a responsible landlord He has entrusted His property to tenants for management and upkeep (Gen. 1:26). Christians take this assignment very seriously and include in their lifestyle the characteristics of a good steward.

Faithfulness is the basic and overarching principle of stewardship (1 Cor. 4:2). A faithful custodian will have in mind the owner's best interest. His wishes and goals for the property will be decisive in the way the estate is used or managed. Life, nature, and influence are three major goods given by God to humans to guard and develop for Him. (See Stewardship I.)

a. Stewardship of life. Life is the most precious, most mysterious, and most sacred of all the assets that God has shared with humans. Life is also the first thing humans devalued when they fell into sin. For that reason God offered the life of His Son, the highest price ever paid for anything, in order to redeem human life from destruction.

(1) General principles. The *principle of procreation* was the first given in reference to life (Gen. 1:28). This is indeed an awesome responsibility because the word "procreation" means "to create for" or "to create in place of" God. Through this act humans participate in bringing to life new, unique human beings, taking upon themselves the responsibility for birth, development, and education of children. For that reason the Christian stresses the fact that God has given humans the capacity to control their sexual drive and has asked them to use it exclusively within the confines of marriage. The task of bringing life into the world is given by God to parents. The *principle of family planning* urges Christians to take human birth very seriously. "Let us make man," said God as the first human family planning began (Gen. 1:26). No accidents are reported in the Creation week. God never produced any leftover creature or genetic material to waste. Contraception is often used by responsible couples who try to avoid unwanted pregnancies. Two cautions are in order. First, contraceptives should prevent conception, rather than abort fetuses. Second, Christians should never use contraceptives as a shield for extramarital intimacy. Biblical standards promote sexual abstinence outside of marriage.

When an unwanted pregnancy occurs, responsible actions are always painful and risky. Christians should be guided by biblical principles. The *principle of life preservation* (Ex. 20:13) stresses the importance of human life in God's sight (Gen. 9:5, 6), and forbids any action that could endanger it or lower its quality. In addition, this principle prohibits careless or criminal behavior (promiscuity, rape, incest) whether or not it results in conceiving human life. The *principle of sacredness of human life* stands on the fact that human life comes from God (Gen. 1:26, 27; 2:7; Ps. 36:9), that God is the owner of human life (1 Cor. 6:19, 20), and that life is intended for a special purpose (Gen. 1:29, 30; Ps. 8:4-9). This setting apart occurs very early in the process of life (Jer. 1:5; Luke 1:15; Gal. 1:15) and for that reason abortion must not be considered as a method of family planning. Only in extreme situations might this procedure be justifiable. Such cases might be a child pregnancy, pregnancies under criminal circumstances, or abortion to save the mother's life.

(2) Normative model. The divine example of self-sacrifice to save human life sets the highest norm for a Christian lifestyle (John 3:16). Jochebed, the mother of Moses, used skill and courage to preserve her son from certain death; this serves as an example of respect for the human life (Ex. 2:1-10). The midwives' resistance to carry out the order to kill all male newborns challenges Christians to take a stand on this issue (Ex. 1:15-20).

(3) Rules of action. Several direct com-

mands require stewardship of life: Genesis 1:28; 4:15; 9:6; Proverbs 4:23; Ecclesiastes 11:9, 10; 12:1-7; Matthew 6:25-34. (See Marriage II. E. 1; F. 1.)

b. Stewardship of nature. The earth in its beauty and richness of life and resources was entrusted to human dominion (Ps. 8:6-8). The question of what human beings will return to God has become increasingly relevant in view of the depletion of earth's water, atmosphere, flora, and fauna. What assignment does God, the owner, give in His Word to Christians regarding population growth rate, the depletion of natural resources, the threat of nuclear destruction, and the increase of poisonous or radioactive technological waste?

(1) General principles. The *principle of protection of the earth* (Rev. 11:18) is basic. The Christian will refrain from careless destruction of the environment. The *principle of simplicity* can make a significant contribution to the effort of saving the earth's resources. Today's lifestyle is the main culprit for the sad state and bleak future of this planet. The first step toward improvement lies in changing our wasteful way of life.

Adopting a simple lifestyle yields major benefits. Simplicity in eating, especially in the consumption of meat, would save an enormous amount of grain. It has been estimated that a 10 percent reduction in the consumption of meat in North America would save enough grain to feed 60 million people for one year. In addition, controlling food intake and simply not wasting food could save both money and resources. It would also be possible to lower energy consumption by consciously conserving gas, electricity, and water. Finally, simplicity urges rejecting the consumer mentality, buying as need demands, not because something is on sale.

(2) Normative models. Paul gave an example of simplicity and frugality. He earned his livelihood even though he was entitled to remuneration as an apostle (Acts 18:1-3; 1 Cor. 9:12-15). The example of Jesus sets the norm for a Christian's lifestyle today. He owned no house because His life and work did not require it. He wore no extravagant clothes, nor did He attract attention by outlandish or low-quality garments (Matt. 8:20; John 19:23). He did not let anyone dictate to Him what His lifestyle would be.

(3) Rules of action. In their task of keeping this earth for God, Christians are guided by the Bible. It must be kept in mind, however, that large-scale pollution, careless depletion of earth's resources, and overpopulation were not problems in biblical times. For that reason, we find few direct rules; one example is Deuteronomy 23:12-14.

c. Stewardship of wealth. The Bible maintains that God gives ability and opportunity to acquire and accumulate wealth (Eccl. 5:18, 19). This unique talent brings with it both blessings and temptations. Christianity formulates standards that help avoid the pitfalls of wealth and enhance its enjoyment.

(1) General principles. The *principle of gratitude* (Deut. 8:17, 18; 1 Chron. 29:12) reminds us that natural talent and human effort alone cannot produce wealth. While many exploit God-given opportunities, time, and talents for selfish goals and pleasures, Christians know that gratitude to God helps prevent condescending and arrogant attitudes toward the poor and brings humility and caring response to the needs of others. The *principle of honesty* (Ex. 20:15) protects from corrupt and unscrupulous ways of making profits. For a Christian, good ends do not justify evil means; thus, business and religion mix very well. The *principle of generosity* (Prov. 11:24) urges Christians to imitate the great Giver who shares His riches with humankind. To a sinful human heart greed comes subtly. Legitimate wishes are quickly perceived as needs, justified by the ever growing urge for a higher standard of life. To a Christian the presence of the poor is not a nuisance; it is an opportunity to express love. Consequently, decisions that concern one's way of life must always include the plight of the needy. Generosity brings a special joy. At

the same time it protects the giver from avarice (Acts 20:35).

The *principle of dependence on God alone* (Ex. 20:2, 3; cf. Job 22:25, 26) warns against placing our trust and devotion in riches instead of God. Because wealth provides power and a comfortable measure of independence, because it brings respect and consideration, it may alienate the mind and heart from God and shift the focus of life away from His kingdom (Matt. 19:23). The *principle of tithing* (Lev. 27:30) reminds us that everything belongs to God (Ps. 24:1), who systematically and faithfully provides for humans, animals, and every living being. He who owns everything and lacks nothing makes Himself needy and vulnerable in the lives of His servants. He has called pastors to minister full-time, placing them in what would be a very unenviable position of financial dependence if tithe were an offering or a tax. Instead He claims the tithe as His. Any withholding of tithe is done against God (1 Cor. 9:3-14). For that reason Christians return the tithe to its Owner.

(2) Normative models. The Word of God records both positive and negative human stories to inspire obedience to principles of stewardship and to expose the consequences that follow. Abraham was "very rich in cattle, in silver, and in gold" (Gen. 13:2), and yet he contented himself with a simple, nomadic life. For what reason? Because a simple lifestyle did not interfere with his friendship with God and with his yearning for the "city" whose builder and maker is God (Heb. 11:9, 10).

Moses, in line for the power and incredible wealth of the Egyptian throne, opted for a lifestyle of pilgrimage to a promised land. He could not accept all the advantages of kingship because he remained loyal to his poor, exploited, and subjugated nation (verses 24-28).

Although rich and exceedingly powerful, King Solomon realized that earthly treasures, power, and pleasures are but vanity when they become the centerpiece of one's life (Eccl. 5:10, 11). After wandering in an immoral lifestyle, he realized the vanity of it all. Finally, he prayed for neither poverty nor riches so that he might resist the temptation to steal or to disregard God in arrogance (Prov. 30:8, 9).

The tragedy of the rich young ruler consisted in excessive attachment to material wealth and a corresponding separation from God and the needs of his neighbor. Seeing him, Jesus issued a most serious warning to all who cling to material possessions more than to Him (Mark 10:24, 25). The parable of the rich fool underscores the same point (Luke 12:16-21).

The apostle James, along with the prophets before him, calls to account the rich who are unjust and abuse their laborers (James 5:1-6; Isa. 1:16, 17; 3:13-15; Jer. 22:13-17). God, who owns all wealth and who keeps a faithful account of every transaction, will restore what is due, both to the oppressors and the oppressed.

(3) Rules of action. The following verses are only a few examples of direct biblical commands regarding the stewardship of wealth: Leviticus 19:35, 36; Deuteronomy 25:13-16; Psalm 62:9, 10; Proverbs 11:1-4, 18, 19, 28; 22:1-9; 23:1-7, 10, 11; Jeremiah 9:23, 24; Ezekiel 45:9-12; Matthew 6:19-21; 13:22; Mark 10:24, 25.

d. Stewardship of time. Time is another of God's gifts to humanity. During the Creation week, time was divided into 24-hour segments of night and day, during which the Creator accomplished His tasks. While before sin life had only a beginning, after the Fall each creature on earth inherited an end-boundary to life, i.e., death (Acts 17:26). For that reason a Christian is concerned with the proper management of time (Ps. 90:10-12).

(1) General principles. The *principle of trust in God's care* (Matt. 6:25-34) inspires freedom in every Christian. Anxiety over the future and basic necessities can control the use of time more than anything else. The best hours of the day, the best energies of body, mind, and will, are all consumed in earning our living. Jesus was concerned that the struggles for survival and comfort, and even competi-

tion with the neighbors, might overpower the greater need, the need for time with God, with oneself, with family, and with others.

The *principle of rest* (Ex. 20:8-11) indicates that anxiety is not the only factor controlling our time. Time is work as well. To be is to do. Our consciousness is constantly in the working mode, accomplishing and achieving. Were it not for God's call to rest, humans might only work and sleep. God reserved the seventh day for Himself. From sunset Friday to sunset Saturday humans are to stop pursuits and purposes, liberated from the tyranny of earning or spending money, in order to spend time with God, with self, with family, with friends. But this principle also calls us to rest from the temporal and the corruptible, the ever-changing and passing. It helps us to transcend time and think instead of eternity, for which we yearn (Eccl. 3:11). The Sabbath offers a glimpse of life without the fear of death. It is a time when nothing earthly matters much. Abraham Joshua Heschel sums it up well: "In the tempestuous ocean of time and toil there are islands of stillness where man may enter a harbor and reclaim his dignity. The island is the seventh day, the Sabbath, a day of detachment from things, instruments and practical affairs as well as of attachment to the spirit" (29).

The *principle of diligence* (Ex. 20:9) insists on industry and honest work as an integral part of the Christian stewardship of time. Laziness is incompatible with Christian discipleship, for God has given six days for work. Further, rest is a cessation of work, which must necessarily precede the rest. Finally, rest is not passive as is laziness. It is an active mode of focusing on life itself, on its meaning, and on its Creator. The *principle of timeliness* (Eccl. 3:1-8) calls for the careful use of time. Regularity is the basic law of nature; life itself depends on it. Tardiness wastes the time of others involved in an activity. It may also signal an unstable and undependable character.

(2) Normative models. God provides the supreme example of good stewardship of time. He worked during the six days of Creation and

rested on the seventh (Gen. 2:2, 3; Ex. 20:11). He is active in world affairs (Dan. 4:34-37), He sustains the universe and life on earth (Ps. 104:1-30), and it is He who works the miracle of grace that transforms time-bound human life into eternal life (John 4:14). None of His actions came either late or early (Jer. 25:12; Mark 1:15; Gal. 4:4; Eph. 1:10). Yet, He takes time for rest and communion with His children and invites them to do the same. He cares for the land and orders a time for its rest (Lev. 25:4); He created the nighttime so that living things can find repose.

Jesus' lifestyle illustrates a healthy tension between a strong drive to fulfill His mission (John 9:4) and the time set aside for rest, which recreates and refreshes body, mind, and soul (Mark 6:31).

(3) Rules of action. Several direct injunctions express God's will for the stewardship of time: Proverbs 6:6-11; 12:9, 11, 27; 13:4; 20:4; 21:25; 22:13; 24:30-34; 26:13-16; Ecclesiastes 10:18; Ephesians 5:15, 16; 1 Thessalonians 4:10, 11; 2 Thessalonians 3:10-12.

D. Standards of Personal Responsibility

Every action, word, and attitude exerts an impression or a mark; we call this influence. The impact is felt first on the individual and second, on others as well. The Bible urges responsibility in the use of this power, calling Christians to exercise their influence, to inspire good and noble behavior (Rom. 14:19, 20). We will address aspects of Christian lifestyle that cause a powerful impact on self and others. In so doing we seek to identify biblical standards that will render Christian influence a positive force.

1. Standards of Apparel

Creation is not only complex and functional, it is also beautiful. Innumerable forms, colors, and sounds manifested in flowers, birds, animals, plants, mountains, and most completely in human beings point to the greatest artist of all. Human life is destined for beauty and happiness, and hence, the natural human bent to admire and seek beauty (Gen. 2:9).

For millennia apparel has served primarily as a covering and protection. In addition, in affluent circles, it is considered an aesthetic element. Clothing may also be used for display. Christians do not oppose beauty and good taste, but in their lifestyle they seek to avoid enslavement to fashion and display.

(1) General principles. The *principle of frugality* seeks to reduce the waste of money and resources. Good-quality clothes, becoming to the wearer and appropriate for the occasion, are the best investment. Quantity is never more advantageous than quality. The *principle of modesty* (1 Tim. 2:9) calls for moderation in appearance. Christians will not shock or dazzle onlookers, nor will they dress to attract attention. Extremes that display one's body or affluence contradict the Christian sense of decorum and decency. The *principle of inward beauty* (1 Peter 3:3, 4) turns our admiration from colors and styles to the heart. Outward beauty is only skin deep and its attraction only temporary. The inward beauty of character—the beauty of a harmonious, peaceful, and benevolent disposition—is lasting and real beauty. Its influence motivates and inspires moral virtues; its presence creates an atmosphere of trust and love. Christians base their self-image on this inner beauty; for that reason they do not depend on outward appearances for their self-worth (Prov. 31:30).

(2) Normative models. Several examples serve as norms of behavior for the Christian use of apparel. Jesus is an eloquent example of modesty and frugality in dress. However, at the Crucifixion the soldiers found His garments worth dividing among themselves. His seamless tunic was judged to be valuable (John 19:23, 24).

Lucifer, symbolically depicted in the lamentation over the king of Tyre, fell because his heart became proud on account of his beauty (Eze. 28:1-10). Even an angel is not safe from the spell cast by undue attention to beauty. The Christian will recognize here a negative example warning against dependence on outward attractiveness.

The anointing of David as king in the house of his father, Jesse, illustrates the divine norm of beauty. Seven times Samuel failed to recognize the lack of inner beauty because of his fascination with the outward looks of David's brothers (1 Sam. 16:6-13).

(3) Rules of action. Several direct rules enjoining good Christian decorum are found in Scripture. Among these are: 1 Samuel 16:7; Matthew 6:28-33; Romans 12:3; Titus 2:2-7; 1 Peter 3:3-5.

2. Issues in Standards of Apparel

a. Jewelry. The Christian position on personal ornamentation is of particular concern. While most Christians today see little or nothing objectionable in wearing jewelry, biblical instruction leads away from the practice.

(1) General principles. Several biblical principles that govern the Christian's decision regarding personal ornamentation have already been mentioned. Those governing social responsibility—*self-denial, identification,* and *sacrifice* (II. C. 4. c)—apply here also, as do those related to Christian stewardship (II. C. 5). Of prime importance are the principles ruling in matters of apparel (II. D. 1). A Christian is to live a simple life, free from ostentation, unnecessary expense, and any spirit of competition. In the midst of a society that places great importance on outward appearances, the Christian is to cultivate what Peter calls "the imperishable jewel of a gentle and quiet spirit" (1 Peter 3:4).

A Christian's self-esteem is rooted in the fact that human beings are created in the image of God (Gen. 1:26, 27). They need not depend on external embellishments to be worthy. In Psalm 8:4-9 David attributes his self-esteem to Creation. God has given to each person unique gifts and talents (Matt. 25:14-29). But ultimately, and most important, all humans are precious because all are bought at a high price, higher than precious metal or stones (1 Cor. 6:20). Given that we are of such inestimable value that God's Son laid down His own life for us, external ornamentation cannot add to our personal worth.

(2) Normative models. Some claim that in passages such as Psalm 45:9; Isaiah 61:10; Ezekiel 16:11-13; and Revelation 21:2, adornment and jewelry are accepted as biblical norms, and that injunctions in 1 Timothy 2:9 and 1 Peter 3:3, 4 must be considered exceptional. This contention must be explored.

In an effort to understand the use of adornment in the Bible, we must keep in mind the various forms of adornment and the different purposes and intentions that motivated its use. The beautiful vestments of the high priest were heavily adorned and used gold and precious stones. Twelve jewels on his breastplate, for example, symbolized the twelve tribes of Israel, and two stones on his shoulders communicated God's approval or disapproval. A careful study of his attire confirms that symbolic and liturgical purposes took precedence over aesthetics (Ex. 28).

Bridal adornment in the Bible includes jewels and precious metals. To be beautiful for the groom was the all-consuming purpose of this ornamentation. It was not so much a display of riches or a ploy to attract the attention of other men, but an attempt to be pleasing to the beloved. Thus the New Jerusalem in Revelation 21:2 is "adorned for her husband." This kind of embellishment is different in spirit and intention from the modern adorning of gold and jewelry.

In Ezekiel 16:11-13, God Himself adorns the young woman. Several commentators remind us that Scripture uses the thought forms and images of its times to illustrate a point or to teach an important truth, even when that image may not be worthy of imitation or suited to be applied at face value (see Hosea 1:2, 3; Luke 16:19-31). Furthermore, the whole scene is a metaphor. The child that under God's nurture grows up to be a beautiful bride represents Israel, His people, just as the bride in Revelation stands for the New Jerusalem, His church. If the person is symbolic, the

adorning and the jewels bear symbolic meaning as well. The parable represents the miracle of redemption by which the ugliness of sin and the disfiguration of our fallen character is redeemed. We are clothed with fine linen (Rev. 19:8) and decorated with what is precious in God's sight, the gold of Revelation 3:18.

While it is true that the Bible reports several instances of the use of jewelry for which there seems to be no condemnation (Rebekah in Genesis 24:30; Joseph in Genesis 41:42; and the prodigal in Luke 15:22), the use of jewelry is also associated with wicked women (Jezebel in 2 Kings 9:30; the rebellious daughters of Israel in Isaiah 3:16-24; and the harlot of Revelation 17:4). Furthermore, in two clear instances, jewelry was removed at a time of spiritual renewal (see Gen. 35:2, 4; Ex. 33:5, 6). Certainly the inspired counsel of Peter is valuable: "Let not yours be the outward adorning . . . , but let it be . . . the imperishable jewel of a gentle and quiet spirit" (1 Peter 3:3, 4).

(3) Seventh-day Adventist Reasoning. Seventh-day Adventists abstain from display of jewelry because: *We Believe in the Creator-God,* who cares for His creation and is worthy of our trust. We hold that our mission is to demonstrate our total dependency on Him and that even a slight dependence on the valued possessions of perishable ornaments would compromise our witness (Matt. 6:19-21, 25, 26). *We are disciples of the humble, unassuming Master.* We are happy to be like our Master in humility and simplicity (John 15:18-20). *We value inner beauty* and strive to resist the manipulation of advertising and the influence of our society. *We are concerned for the needs of others,* children without proper care, mothers who have no food to offer their children, old people without anyone to love and support them. This concern mandates simplicity of lifestyle (Matt. 25:31-46). "The global outreach of the church cries out for more and more funds. As followers of Jesus, we must do what we can where we are" (Johnsson 10).

b. Fashion. The world of fashion attempts

to dictate what men and women should wear and how they should fix their hair and decorate their faces. With each passing season some change is brought in to make last season's wardrobe obsolete. Furthermore, some of the styles flout biblical principles of *modesty, simplicity,* and *frugality.* Christian discipleship requires total allegiance to Christ, leaving no room for Christians to be enslaved to the dictates of fashion.

3. Standards of Recreation

The human heart and mind are the two centers from which human behavior flows. In Matthew 12:33-35 Jesus indicates that actions and words depend on the heart, while the wise man states, "As he thinketh in his heart, so is he" (Prov. 23:7, KJV). For that reason, David repeatedly prays for God to examine the inventory of his heart and mind (Ps. 26:1-7), to eliminate "any wicked way" (Ps. 139:23, 24).

In view of this, the Christian maintains purity of heart and mind by setting standards that help avoid exposure to evil. Even during hours of leisure and recreation, avenues leading to the heart and mind must be guarded carefully so that nothing that enters the mind or tugs on the heart contradicts God's will (Heb. 8:10).

(1) General principles. The *principle of purity* (Ps. 51:10) rejects any evil thought or desire as unwelcome and dangerous. To linger or waver, to quibble on how much impurity is allowed, how much compromise is permissible, or how close to the danger line one is still safe, contradicts this standard (Ps. 24:4; Matt. 5:8). Christians yearn to be pure as Christ is pure (1 John 3:3). The *principle of total commitment to God* (Matt. 22:37; Phil. 4:8) calls for the whole person to seek God's pleasure above all else. "How can I better reflect His image?" is the query of those who love God more than self. The *principle of self-control* (1 Cor. 9:24-27) directs Christians to put their body, mind, and spirit under the control of the Holy Spirit. Christians are pilgrims in enemy territory where the language is for-

eign, some foods and drinks harmful, values and habits incompatible, and every step requires energy, alertness, and resistance. Peter admonishes us to "make every effort" toward self-control (2 Peter 1:5, 6; see Gal. 2:22, 23). The *principle of recreation* (Isa. 40:31) stresses the spiritual nature of true recreation. When leisure time becomes a time of affirmation, of encouragement, or inspiration for nobler and higher purposes, when it strengthens our sense of belonging to God and our fellow humans, then it truly recreates and renews our heart and mind.

The *principle of God's presence* (Ps. 139:2-12) is both comforting and sobering. Ellen G. White writes, "If we were to cherish an habitual impression that God sees and hears all that we do and say and keeps a faithful record of our words and actions, and that we must meet it all, we would fear to sin. Let the young ever remember that wherever they are, and whatever they do, they are in the presence of God. No part of our conduct escapes observation. . . . The deepest midnight is no cover for the guilty one. He may think himself alone, but to every deed there is an unseen witness" (PP 217, 218).

Yet God's presence is not oppressive or intimidating. His purpose is not to punish, condemn, or destroy. David experienced God's ever-present hand as leading and holding him (Ps. 139:10). By nature God is absolutely incompatible with sin; for that reason a habitual consciousness of His presence in our thoughts and emotions can keep sin at bay.

(2) Normative models. Joseph provides a beautiful example of purity, self-control, and a life lived in the presence of God. He might have thought that his daily tasks and the abusive treatment he received could well earn a moment of pleasure. But Joseph did not weigh the consequences or consider the situation. He faced the incredible temptation with resolute courage. The inner atmosphere of his heart is described by Ellen G. White as "conscious innocence." Sin would take that innocence away, but Joseph was not ready

709

to give it up. Yet, the decisive argument was God's presence. Even when "none of the men of the house was there in the house," Joseph knew and cherished God's company. He asked, "How then can I do this great wickedness, and sin against God?" (Gen. 39:9-11). A sinful course of action would go against the goals of his life, and he preferred to remain close to God.

The Bible records many negative examples of people who spent their time in distractions and unwholesome entertainment. The people of Sodom and Gomorrah reaped destruction for their life of debauchery (Gen. 19:13, 24, 25). Samson's life ended in suicide as a result of his lack of self-control (Judges 16:28-30). But the life of Jesus stands as the supreme example of wholesomeness and purity. The three temptations that followed His baptism (Matt. 4:1-11) and the enticement to give up His mission for kingship and earthly pleasure—all were resisted with vigor and decisiveness. Ultimately His death on the cross became the matchless norm inviting His disciples to follow God's pleasure as a guide for human happiness.

(3) Rules of action. Several concrete rules can serve as guidelines for the Christian's use of leisure time: Psalm 1:1-6; Proverbs 25:28; Ecclesiastes 11:9; 12:1; Romans 1:28; 8:6; Galatians 5:22, 23; Philippians 1:9-11; Colossians 3:2.

4. Issues in Recreation

Christianity is by no means opposed to healthy fun and true recreation. In fact, games, music, reading, listening to the radio, or watching television can be beneficial and uplifting. However, Christians are tempted to participate in unwholesome activities. The infiltration of the values of society coupled with a wish not to appear odd may lead to compromise. The attractiveness of the entertainment with its appeal to the strong urges of body, mind, and heart makes some Christians vulnerable. The lack of creative and purposeful effort of church family and society to provide healthy and wholesome entertainment may create a dangerous vacuum of boredom. Finally, adult examples often orient the youth in a direction that contradicts what they teach and profess. We will briefly touch on several of these issues.

a. Reading. Written materials are strong instruments in communicating ideas, views, and concepts. A skillful writer can paint a picture in the mind of the reader so well that no enactment on screen or stage can match it. Thus the printed page enters the storage rooms of our heart and mind and supplies the inventory from which we draw our actions and reactions. The dangers of improper reading are many. For example, the reading of fiction may separate the reader from reality; the world of fantasy can become an easy refuge when real life demands immediate, hard decisions. Harmful or even sinful values can steal their way into our mind and heart when camouflaged in an exciting style and thrilling plot. Slowly and imperceptibly we become what we read because the mouth speaks from the abundance of the heart.

The choice of reading must be guided by the same biblical principles that govern all of recreation. All reading must glorify God (1 Cor. 10:31) and edify the mind and spirit (Phil. 4:8).

b. Radio and television. Enormous sums are spent to capture radio and television audiences. With rare exceptions, the purpose of these media programs is to sell, either ideas or products. By listening or viewing, one is exposed to constant advertising that brings skillful sales techniques into the privacy of one's home, attempting to create needs that will translate into purchases and a consumer mentality.

The standards of conduct portrayed in many of the programs are not in harmony with the Christian lifestyle that has been described in this article. Sex and violence permeate songs and programs. Disrespect for authority and even God is portrayed routinely. Even news broadcasts and talk shows are generally designed with an agenda foreign to the disciple of Christ.

The quantity of time consumed by television viewing in the average home often far outstrips the amount of time spent in family camaraderie or shared activities. Thus television is becoming the role model and mentor of today's children. Even in Christian homes, family worship is often displaced by television programming. The time spent by many listening to the radio is equally striking.

Although it might be safer not to have a television set, the option is probably unrealistic. However, great care must be exercised in choosing programs to view. Some find it helpful to consult the newspaper or program guide regarding programs to be seen. In any case, carefully considered rules must be implemented and applied, especially in a home where there are children. For the sake of their physical, mental, and spiritual well-being, children should have restricted viewing times. Parents should watch television with their children in order to know what they are seeing and be able to discuss with them the benefits and dangers of such programs. There should be no hesitation to change the channel or turn off the television if a program turns out to be undesirable. Even so, the human brain is so quick to capture ideas, attitudes, and feelings that by the time one realizes the program does not meet Christian standards, it may be too late to prevent some ideas, words, or mental pictures from finding their place in the recesses of the mind and heart. It is important to choose judiciously who will speak, sing, or appear in our home, be it in person or on screen.

c. Theater. Much of what has been said about television programming holds true for movie theaters. In addition, several other issues emerge when films are viewed in the theater. To begin with, the viewer has no control over the film or its scenes. Next, one becomes part of the group of viewers, with personal tastes, values, and preferences overshadowed by the majority. When a Christian has negative feelings about an action presented, the crowd might cheer or laugh; when a Christian feels good or happy about something, the rest might judge the scene the opposite way. The impact of the majority easily weakens one's judgment (Ps. 1:1-3). Besides, the theater is not an ideal place to sense Christ's presence. Finally, having paid the entrance fee, one may feel reluctant to leave.

While some of the problems posed by viewing a film in a theater disappear when one watches a video in the privacy of one's home, the basic issue remains the same. Biblical principles of purity and appropriateness must be followed in choosing what one allows to enter into the mind and heart (Prov. 4:23).

d. Dancing. While dancing for joy and the spontaneous expression of happiness occur in the life of God's people (Ex. 15:21, 22; 2 Sam. 6:14), biblical dance cannot be compared with its modern counterpart. First, the contemporary social dance does not *express* a mood, rather it is programmed to *create* a specific mood chosen by entertainers. The participants in such a dance become vulnerable to influences and values they would not otherwise choose. Experience confirms that the moods expressed in the biblical dance (joy, gratitude, praise) are diametrically different from those created in dancing places (excitement, lust, seduction), which cannot fit the Christian lifestyle. Romantic music and rhythm target the intimate feelings and private emotions in a public context. Inevitably a Christian is faced with unnecessary temptations and incredible challenges to his or her Christian identity. Social dance legitimizes physical closeness that would never be sanctioned in any other situation. Such closeness tends to rouse sexual desire not to be satisfiable outside the marital relation. Finally, dancing is most often accompanied by drinking, drugs, violence, and unrestrained behavior. The sensual apparel, ambiance, and music foster casual contacts, which lead to impure thoughts and unfortunate consequences. Christians must ask themselves if they can be assured of God's presence while visiting such events and places (Ps. 1:1-6).

e. Music. Music is a powerful medium of

communicating ideas and affecting the moods and dispositions of listeners. Several elements combine to exert this strong influence. First, the melody and harmony, which can be pleasing or threatening, mournful or joyful, romantic or cold, reaches the mind and heart, creating a corresponding inner atmosphere. Rhythm and tempo only enhance the effectiveness of the melody and harmony. Lyrics add the poetic expression of words and intensify the overall impact. Because by nature music's influence is mostly subliminal, objective measurement and evaluation are difficult to achieve. Guidelines in this context must rely on the principles of recreation mentioned above.

For example, the combination of religious lyrics with romantic or comical melodies trivializes sacred themes. In a similar way, beautiful harmonies and appealing melodies excite feelings and reduce watchfulness, especially in a group setting. Moreover, very distasteful lyrics can be masterfully concealed in otherwise innocuous music. Finally, music can become a bonding agent that transcends culture and church boundaries, disseminating its good or bad impact on the formulation of ideas or tastes. Generations are divided along these lines and Christian values are strongly affected. Only uncompromising firmness and careful vigilance can provide a measure of security for the inventory of our minds and hearts.

5. Christian Virtues

A Christian lifestyle requires more than conformity to standards, ability to make right decisions, or promptness for good works. Human conduct comprises dimensions and exerts an influence far beyond externally observable behavior. One of its most far-reaching dimensions is the close interdependence between the observable conduct and the inward identity of a moral person. Actions affect personality just as personality affects actions. Repeated behavior forms habits; habitual conduct creates virtues or vices; they in turn carve a pattern unique to each individual human character.

Christianity endeavors to bring into harmony observable conduct with the identity, the image of God. First, God comes into our personal history to deliver us from the vicious cycle of sin and death (John 1:12, 13) and establish a virtuous cycle of righteousness and life (John 3:16). Second, He opens the heavenly treasure house to empower the restoration and growth of His image in us (John 1:14, 16). Finally, His love defines the standards of a Christian lifestyle which incarnates that love within the context of human relationships. We conclude with a brief outline of the Christian virtues that flow from a vibrant, Christian life restored in the image of God.

a. Integrity. From the Latin *integritas,* meaning "whole, untouched, complete." In arithmetic integers are numbers such as 1, 2, 3, 4, which possess several important qualities. First, each is unique and unlike any other. Second, each remains what it is, no matter how it is used: number 5 will be and act as number 5 should, whether in addition, subtraction, division, or multiplication. Third, they cannot admit any tampering. If we add or subtract, no matter how much or how little, the integer will cease to be and will become another number.

The virtue of integrity consists of character, attitudes, actions, and words that stand in complete and immutable harmony with truth and reality. Any divergence by addition or subtraction destroys the completeness and genuineness of truth experienced or expressed.

Integrity of being is the most essential manifestation of truth (John 14:6). A life graced with this virtue acquires the ability to exhibit all other virtues in their fullness. It gains a capacity to grasp, experience, and express reality in the most reliable way. Ellen White describes men and women of integrity as "men who will not be bought or sold, men who in their inmost souls are true and honest, men who do not fear to call sin by its right name, men whose conscience is as true to duty as the needle to the pole, men who will stand for the right though the heavens fall" (Ed 57).

Compromises of principle, hypocrisy, cowardice, dishonesty, dishonor, and the like cannot coexist with integrity. One wrong act or word mars the genuineness and purity of character and only the grace of God can bring healing and recreate lost wholeness. Men and women such as Joseph, Daniel, Esther, and Mary the mother of Jesus stand as examples of sinful men and women who nevertheless developed the virtue of integrity. To be true and pure became a first impulse and a spontaneous but firm choice. A person of integrity, just like an integer, displays authenticity and wholeness under all circumstances and at all times.

Integrity in speech finds its best expression in the counsel of Jesus in Matthew 5:37. Our words must reflect reality. To change the truth or to shortchange it while claiming that it is the whole truth comes from the evil one. A person of integrity loves truthfulness, frankness, candor, and sincerity above any gain or reward. There are no "white lies" or "good deceptions" in the Christian's lifestyle.

Much debate centers on the so-called inevitable lies when life would be in danger if the truth were known. The question is whether someone is "entitled" to know the truth when his or her intentions are to harm the innocent on the basis of that knowledge. In simpler terms, is a person of integrity "entitled" to lie to a person not "entitled" to know the truth? Is an "entitled" lie still a lie? Does the truth change for the "nonentitled" person? A natural urge of the person of integrity is to protect the innocent by withholding the information. In my own experience, I saw several occasions when a simple "I don't know" (if that was true) or "I cannot tell" or "You know enough" or "You must find it another way" prevented the Christian from lying. In those very exceptional situations, the choice was to save innocent lives without losing one's own innocence, and

often at a very high price. After all, my own life is not more precious than that of someone hiding under the protection of my walls and my silence.

Thank God, exceptional circumstances are still exceptional, and He has promised an exceptional measure of grace to match every exceptional need. Thank God also for His mercy that extends to us when we repent from deceitful words and ways, for hearing us when we pray "Lead us not into temptation," and for healing us from evil habits.

b. Prudence. Prudence is the first cardinal virtue of the classical tradition in philosophy (Aristotle) and theology (Augustine, Aquinas). It is defined as the capacity of the moral agent to choose the right means for a specific end. Like integrity, prudence affects all other virtues in that it brings practical wisdom and common sense to their exercise.

A prudent person decides and acts with caution, sagacity, circumspection, and foresight. The Bible underscores the importance of prudence for the Christian lifestyle. In Proverbs the prudent person is portrayed as careful in speech (12:23), ready to avoid evil and its consequences (14:16; 22:3; 27:12), prepared to take reproof and advice (15:5), and willing to ignore an insult (12:16). Jesus demonstrated the need of prudence in everyday life as much as in the spiritual life through several parables (Matt. 7:24-27; 25:1-30; Luke 16:1-9), His personal example (Matt. 16:1-4; John 12:33-36), and in His teachings (Matt. 10:16).

The Christian view of prudence is not self-centered. A prudent decision does not primarily choose for one's own good. Jesus teaches that Christians will act on principle rather than on self-interested prudence whenever there is conflict between duty to God and duty to self (Matt. 5:38-48; 6:19-34; 10:37-39; 16:24-27). The self-sacrificial love of Jesus and the martyrdom of thousands of Christians set an example for Christian lifestyle. Providence functions best under the guidance of the Holy Spirit, the Word of God, and within the context of the Christian community. Christians will weigh the alternatives, pray for wisdom, and seek advice, but ultimately they will trust their prudence to God's provident guidance.

c. Courage. The Bible often describes Christian life in terms of pilgrimage, warfare, and discipleship. Christian lifestyle, therefore, must correspond to the spirit of pioneering, of military valor, and of service to a master. All this requires courage, i.e., the ability to act rationally in the face of danger. Several conditions help to develop courage in the character of a Christian. First, the radical change that occurs on all levels of life at conversion requires courage to face personal habits and evil tendencies (1 Cor. 9:24-27), to resist pressures from society and peers (Dan. 3:16-18; 6:19-23), to accept separation from family members (Matt. 10:34-38), and even to endure persecution and face death (Rev. 2:10; 7:14). Christian commitment also requires courage to remain steadfast in the face of discouragement and hopelessness (Ps. 27:14). Courage grows from the experience of temptations and trials (2 Cor. 4:16-18). Finally, the call to assume a position of leadership develops strength and courage to stand alone with God (Joshua 1:6, 9; 10:25).

Courage as a moral virtue proceeds from faith in a God who rules the universe, cares for the needs of His children, and forgives and heals their infirmities (Rom. 8:31-39). It is not based on physical strength or human qualities alone. It is the kind of moral stamina that enables the disciples to follow the Lord and Master of their lives, in spite of tribulation and pain (Heb. 12:2).

d. Forgiveness. Since the fall into sin, human life has subsisted on forgiveness (Eph. 4:32; Neh. 9:17). The Christian lifestyle must foster this virtue until the consummation of God's kingdom, where forgiveness will become absent because sin will be no more. The Bible insists that God's children must learn to forgive and develop this virtue in their character. This must be so because every human being since Adam (except Jesus) has sinned (Rom. 3:23) and thus brought fatal injury on self and others. The resentment and enmity that result from every sinful act and the distance that sin creates between humans, and between humans and God, are simply unbearable. Forgiveness of sins is the only way to bridge that distance and restore broken relationships. It is achieved by purposely setting aside the resentment caused by a harmful act. Thus, forgiveness plays a crucial role in the process of sanctification.

In all this, the sinful human heart has no resources to produce a sinless holy behavior and thus forestall the future moral injuries. Only God's grace and power can produce forgiveness.

To understand forgiveness, we should say what it is not. Forgiveness is not exoneration or vindication. Rather than proving the nonexistence of a wrongful act, forgiveness affirms it. To ask for forgiveness implies the admission of wrongdoing and is a plea for release from guilt and for a second chance. Neither does forgiving mean excusing a wrong. To excuse means to deny the other's responsibility for a wrongful act, accepting that attenuating circumstances such as ignorance, hardship, or coercion diminish the guilt. A partial admission of guilt can permit only a partial reconciliation. To forgive is to affirm the responsibility, but also to release from guilt, and to restore the relationship. Finally, forgiveness is not an act of rebellion against, or a rejection of, the moral order. The resentment of the offended party signals a breach, a disruption of a regular and orderly state of affairs. Forgiveness seeks to restore order and the respect of rights and privileges.

This view of forgiveness implies that Christians cannot accept the notion of an unconditional pardon for sin. In fact, the Scriptures clearly teach that repentance is the most important prerequisite for the restoration of healthy relationships (Eze. 18:30; Matt. 3:2; Acts 17:30, 31; Rev. 2:5, 16). We can discern three steps in the act of repentance. First is admission or confession of sin (Prov. 28:13;

Eze. 33:14, 15; 1 John 1:9). Hereby the sinner declares the act wrongful and accepts responsibility for it. The moral principles of right and wrong receive reaffirmation from the very individual who transgressed them.

Confession alone may not produce the total separation of the sinner from sin; one who does wrong must be willing to abandon that wrong; this is the second step. A verbal confession must be accompanied by the willingness to change. The Bible never teaches forgiveness *in* sin in the name of love or any other divine act, because God never excuses sin. The Bible insists on the pardon *from* sin, providing the power to escape from the evil one (Luke 1:77; Acts 2:38; Rom. 6:1-4). Ellen G. White states the following:

"Satan deceives many with the plausible theory that God's love for His people is so great that He will excuse sin in them. . . . The unconditional pardon of sin never has been, and never will be. Such pardon would show the abandonment of the principles of righteousness, which are the very foundation of the government of God" (PP 522).

The wrong we do brings damage and loss to others; justice requires a full restitution of this loss. This is the third step in the Christian act of repentance (Num. 5:7). Full restitution is seldom possible. Here the atoning sacrifice of Jesus Christ intervenes. He stands as a substitute, assuming the condition of the guilty one. Forgiveness always happens "in Christ" (Eph. 4:32), so that we forgive our neighbor as Christ forgives us, and for His sake (1 John 2:12).

By repenting, sinners separate themselves from sin. Additionally, repentance sends a message of self-respect, and most of all, respect for the well-being and rights of the other. Thus the relationship is restored. The repentant states: I no longer identify with this wrong and want to be separated from it; I am one with you in condemning it.

But why should there be forgiveness at all? Why is this virtue an absolute requirement for Christian character? Scripture indicates several reasons. The first and most imperative is the absolute truth that God forgives us our sins (Matt. 18:21-25). If we stand at all in relation to God, we stand forgiven (Ps. 130:3, 4). If we live or love or have any hope whatsoever, we owe all our existence—past, present, and future—to the forgiving heart of the Father (Luke 15:11-24).

The second reason is that we ourselves depend on the forgiveness of our fellow human beings (Matt. 5:23-26). In fact, divine pardon is proportionately tied to our forgiveness of our neighbor's sins (Matt. 6:12; Luke 11:4). Because we injure most those whom we love the most and who are the closest to us, we need pardon. The contrition of our heart in seeking pardon is the reason for releasing the contrite heart of our fellow human beings.

Third, forgiveness is a most radical response to the most radical assault on the human soul. It involves both parties, bringing both to a humble recognition of a need for dependence on their Father in heaven. Excuse, weakness, or indifference does not clear the wounded relationship enough to prevent infection and assure healing. Forgiveness reroutes the human relation through Jesus Christ so that the other is treated, understood, and respected as Christ's merits deserve.

Finally, the most encouraging feature of Christian forgiveness is that the offended party must not wait for the offender to repent before proffering pardon. God's forgiveness amply illustrates this (Rom. 5:6-11). The hope of forgiveness motivates the sinner to retrace his steps and repent (Luke 15:17-19), because forgiveness is based on God's pardon alone. The conditionality of repentance refers to the effectiveness of the pardon already given on an unlimited scale (Matt. 18:21, 22). Repentance detaches the offender from the offending attitude and disposition and makes the person receptive to forgiveness. (See Salvation III. A. 1.)

III. Ellen G. White Comments

Christian lifestyle occupies a significant portion of Ellen G. White's writings. From these a few representative statements have been selected.

A. The Moral Nature of Human Life

Unlike the behavior of other creatures, human conduct is moral. Human actions can be categorized as good or bad, right or wrong, because they proceed from an inborn capacity for moral choices (1SM 216, 217; 2T 294; SL 76; PP 48, 49). But human beings are not left alone in their limitations and sinfulness to discern good from evil, and right from wrong (4T 405, 615; 3T 332). "The depths of every heart are open to the inspection of God. Every action, every purpose, every word, is as distinctly marked as though there were only one individual in the whole universe and all the watchfulness and scrutiny of God were employed on his deportment" (5T 627; see also PP 217; SD 309).

This intensity of divine involvement in the human predicament is explained first of all by the fact that God is the Creator of humanity. All life belongs to Him and proceeds from Him (AH 280; Ed 99) and to Him all accounts are ultimately due (3T 523; MM 275; MYP 48, 103; 4T 654; 7T 281, 282). Second, God is a Redeemer who cares for His creatures. He knows how dangerous and tragic human destiny is, and how vulnerable human life becomes without His presence, guidance, and protection. Ellen G. White exclaims: "What a God is our God! He rules over His kingdom with diligence and care, and He has built a hedge—the Ten Commandments—about His subjects to preserve them from the results of transgression. In requiring obedience to the laws of His kingdom, God gives His people health and happiness, peace and joy" (CT 454; see also Ed 76, 77; PK 678). In His love God forbids, withholds, or takes away whatever imperils human life (SD 63; Ed 291).

A Christian lifestyle responds to this divine initiative. It takes the form of willing service to God and neighbor (COL 282), and voluntary sacrifice of self for others (GC 316; 2T 132). Love to God and neighbor is never fully professed in words. It is better expressed in actions that follow God's will and Christ's example (4T 223, 224; LS 80, 81). This is the love which, according to Ellen White, stands as the basis for the deontological/virtue approach to moral life, with obedience and duty as its key expressions (PP 337). She explains, "John did not teach that salvation was to be earned by obedience; but that obedience was the fruit of faith and love. . . . 1 John 3:5, 6. If we abide in Christ, if the love of God dwells in the heart, our feelings, our thoughts, our actions, will be in harmony with the will of God. The sanctified heart is in harmony with the precepts of God's law" (AA 563).

Just as love does not dispense with obedience but rather inspires it, so it is with faith (SC 60, 61; PP 279; 1SM 366; DA 126). The power of grace is given for obedience (PP 370) and through obedience justification is retained (1SM 364, 366). Christ cannot accept partial obedience (DA 523; PP 360, 372; 4T 146) or blind conformity (GC 541) because, Ellen White argues, such attitudes cannot answer Satan's charges about the results of following principle (COL 296).

A Christian will respond promptly to any known duty (PK 219) because the first and most important obligation of love is to do what is pleasing to God, no matter what the immediate consequences (cf. GC 609, 610). "No one can believe with the heart unto righteousness, and obtain justification by faith, while continuing the practice of those things which the Word of God forbids, or while neglecting any known duty" (1SM 396; see also 1SM 366; 4T 145).

However, obedience to Christ does not distract from pleasure and happiness (3T 374; 7BC 989), because it is the result of choice rather than compulsion and because Christian obedience to duty is motivated by an increased awareness of God's love. As the Christian experience grows, conformity to God's will leads to Christ the lawgiver, generating obedience as an expression of love. In this context, Ellen G. White urges us to "remember that a disciple is to do the will of his master. We are not to reason in regard to results; for then we should be kept ever busy, and ever in uncertainty. We must take our stand to acknowledge fully the power and authority of God's word, whether or not it agrees with our preconceived opinions. We have a perfect Guidebook. The Lord has spoken to us; and whatever may be the consequences, we are to receive His word and practice it in daily life, else we shall be choosing our own version of duty and shall be doing exactly the opposite of that which our heavenly Father has appointed us to do" (MM 255, 256; see also GC 460).

Such a response cannot be elicited by fear or coercion. Only love can trust enough to leave the consequences with God, and only a context of love can inspire obedience. Cold, harsh, and judgmental attitudes produce conformity and submission, not obedience. Ellen White reminds us that "Christ does not drive but draws men unto Him. The only compulsion which He employs is the constraint of love" (MB 127). The genius of Christianity is that it incarnates gentleness without compromise of faithfulness to God's will, patience without indifference to eternal happiness, pardon without excusing any sin. In addition, we must "remember that Duty has a twin sister, Love; these united can accomplish almost everything, but separated, neither is capable of good" (4T 62; see also 3T 108, 195).

B. Lifestyle and Scripture

The Bible, the Word of God, authoritatively and infallibly expresses God's will for humans (Ed 260; GC 102; 4T 312, 449; 5T 24). It faithfully presents the standard of right and wrong for all circumstances of moral life (CT 422; 5T 264; GC 521; Te 193). No other book can prove

more effective against temptations (3T 482), for transforming character (COL 60; GC 94), for presenting the rules of holy living (FE 164; CT 138, 139), and for warning and preserving against sin and evil (SW Apr. 23, 1907; Ed 77). Ellen G. White comments: "In the Bible are found the only safe principles of action. It is a transcript of the will of God, an expression of divine wisdom. It opens to man's understanding the great problems of life, and to all who heed its precepts it will prove an unerring guide, keeping them from wasting their lives in misdirected effort" (AA 506).

Ellen G. White also maintains that general principles should be respected in the Christian life as well as specific rules of action (2SM 217; CG 66). Commenting on Daniel's faithfulness to the principle of health by respecting the rule that forbids certain food and drink she says, "There are many among professed Christians today who would decide that Daniel was too particular, and would pronounce him narrow and bigoted. They consider the matter of eating and drinking as of too little consequence to require such a decided stand—one involving the probable sacrifice of every earthly advantage. . . . They will find that what seemed to them unimportant was not so regarded of God. His requirements should be sacredly obeyed. Those who accept and obey one of His precepts because it is convenient to do so, while they reject another because its observance would require a sacrifice, lower the standard of right, and by their example lead others to lightly regard the holy law of God. 'Thus saith the Lord' is to be our rule in all things" (FE 78).

C. Issues in Sexual Relations

Ellen G. White strongly affirms the biblical teaching of chastity before marriage and sexual faithfulness to the marriage partner (AH 58, 59). She insists that sexuality is God's blessing which must be carefully guarded from degenerating into "lower passions" (*ibid.* 124). We submit here several of her practical counsels on Christian sexual behavior.

First, she calls on parents to teach their children the anatomy and physiology of the human body, including the "mysteries of life" (7T 65; CT 126). Second, she advises careful guidance of contacts between boys and girls, in an effort to provide healthy relationships (2T 482, 483; 4T 95, 96). In professional and institutional life she urges "refinement and delicacy"; patients should be seen by physicians of the same sex whenever possible (CH 363-365). All must avoid any appearance of evil (2T 458, 459), any special consideration or undue familiarity (MM 145, 146). Leaders must foster purity of thought among personnel, modesty in dress, and decency in language. "If you have tender, loving words and kindly attentions to bestow, let them be given to him whom you have promised before God and angels to love, respect, and honor while you both shall live" (2T 462).

Just as sexual abstinence is the basic Christian principle for extramarital relations, purity and self-control are essential for the married life. "Passion of just as base a quality may be found in the marriage relation as outside of it" (*ibid.* 473). This happens when animal passions clamor for indulgence, when reason has lost control over lust, and when woman is reduced to an "instrument" for the gratification of "low lustful propensities" (*ibid.* 472-474). Such excesses will result in the loss of love for devotional exercises, limited functioning of the brain, exhausted vitality, and the sacrifice of conscience, dignity, and even the identity of the wife (*ibid.* 476, 477; see also TSB 109-117). Ellen G. White counsels all those "who call themselves Christians to present their bodies 'a living sacrifice, holy, acceptable unto God' " (2T 381).

While the use of the word "homosexuality" cannot be found, Ellen G. White comments on the sins of Sodom and Gomorrah by saying that these cities were destroyed "through the gratification of unnatural appetite" that enslaved them, and "they became so ferocious and bold in their detestable abominations that God would not tolerate them upon the earth" (3T 162; see also TSB 119-121).

Yet her pen has equally strong words of hope and encouragement for whoever seeks to change. "Those who put their trust in Christ are not to be enslaved by any hereditary [genetic] or cultivated [environmental] habit or tendency. . . . Whatever may be our inherited or cultivated tendencies to wrong, we can overcome through the power that He is ready to impart" (MH 175, 176; see also DA 329).

D. Citizenship

"Citizens of heaven will make the best citizens of earth" (MYP 329). This statement summarizes Ellen G. White's outlook on the Christian's life as a citizen. "A correct view of our duty to God leads to clear perceptions of our duty to our fellow man" (*ibid.*). Paul and Barnabas could not be condemned by false statements of their accusers because "they could but acknowledge that the teachings of Paul and Barnabas tended to make men virtuous, law-abiding citizens, and that the morals and order of the city would improve if the truths taught by the apostles were accepted" (AA 178). Christians must be responsible voters (Te 255), and promoters of good relations with governing authorities (6T 394-401; AA 69; 1T 201). But Christ has defined the limits of Christian duty toward civil authorities. When civil requirements conflict with God's will, our choice must be to remain faithful to God first (DA 602, 603; GC 203-205).

E. Stewardship

"We are stewards, entrusted by our absent Lord with the care of His household and His interests, which He came to this world to serve" (8T 37). This is how Christians look upon their lives (see also 9T 246; 7T 176; AH 368). Ellen G. White reminds Christians that property (4T 480; CS 80), learning (6BC 1081), talents (4T 619; 6BC 1081), and energy (2T 432) belong to God. Stewardship of time is of particular importance. Idleness, gossip, and self-gratification are to be removed from the Christian lifestyle (*ibid.* 500; 4T 72, 408; 1T

325; 1SM 86; 9T 48) and replaced by industry, prayer (7T 194; SD 109), culture of the mind (3T 146), physical exercise (ML 144; CT 295), and careful planning (COL 344).

F. Standards of Apparel

Appearance is an important concern for Christians. Ellen G. White penned hundreds of pages on this issue but we will select only a few, referring the reader to the *Index* to her writings under the entries "Clothing," "Dress," "Jewelry," and "Ornamentation."

In reference to dress Ellen White reminds the Christian that "it is our privilege to honor our Creator. He desires our clothing to be not only neat and healthful, but appropriate and becoming" (Ed 248). The book *Child Guidance* presents several basic principles of dress. No one precise style is given as a uniform for the Christian (CG 419), but rather that which is neat, attractive, clean, in good taste, durable, simple, modest, and appropriate for one's age and work (CG 419-431; see also CG 413-418; MH 287-294; 2SM 465-479; 5T 499, 500).

She also wisely warns against the extreme that considers dirty and unkempt clothing an expression of humility, and where neatness is interpreted as pride (4T 142-143; CG 415). Her concern is the avoidance of extremes. She notes, "Many look upon these injunctions as too old-fashioned to be worthy of notice; but He who gave them to His disciples understood the dangers from the love of dress in our time, and sent to us the note of warning" (CG 416).

Ellen G. White also writes about jewelry and adornment. Here she recounts the frustrations of a new convert who gave up wearing "jewelry, gold, silver, or precious stones" and was in the process of selling all of it when some longstanding members exclaimed, " 'Why do you sell it? I would wear it if it was mine.' . . . 'It is not good policy to be singular in our dress; for we cannot exert so much influence.' " Ellen White queries, "Is this in accordance with the teachings of Christ? Are we to follow the Word of God, or the customs of the world?" Approvingly, she reported that the new sister "decided that it was the safest to adhere to the Bible standard" (Ev 270, 271). Seventh-day Adventist Christians abstain from display as a matter of obedience to God's Word, for the sake of modesty (CG 423), because of the needs of the poor (2BC 1012; CH 602), and in order to provide for the preaching of the gospel (6T 441; WM 269).

G. Standards of Recreation

There is a distinction between recreation and amusement, according to Ellen G. White.

"Recreation, when true to its name, recreation, tends to strengthen and build up. Calling us aside from our ordinary cares and occupations, it affords refreshment for mind and body, and thus enables us to return with new vigor to the earnest work of life. Amusement, on the other hand, is sought for the sake of pleasure and is often carried to excess; it absorbs the energies that are required for useful work and thus proves a hindrance to life's true success" (Ed 207; see also AH 513; CT 336; 2T 585-593; 1T 519, 520).

Reading can be beneficial when it does not deter from reality and the reading of Scripture (1T 241, 242; SD 178; FE 92-94). But when reading creates a craving for excitement, physical energies are wasted, disorder in the home routine and neglect of duties cripple normal and harmonious development (4T 497, 498; MH 443-448; CT 120, 122; AH 410-418; 2T 410, 411).

Even though *radio* and *television* were not in use during the time of Ellen G. White, her advice to guard the avenues of the soul, and to "avoid reading, seeing, or hearing that which will suggest impure thoughts" is surprisingly relevant for the modern temptations of the media (PP 460; see also AA 518, 519; 4T 108; AH 406-409).

Theater. While the motion picture appeared only at the onset of the twentieth century, Ellen G. White's counsels can readily apply to the modern film and theater attendance. She claims that "there is no influence in our land more powerful to poison the imagination, to destroy religious impressions, and to blunt the relish for the tranquil pleasures and sober realities of life than theatrical amusements" (4T 653). Several reasons are offered for such a negative appraisal. The theater provides an environment where "vicious habits and sinful propensities are strengthened and confirmed"; moreover, such entertainment is addictive (4T 653). Satan uses the theater to keep "men and women under his influence" (Te 252, 253). The blessing of God cannot be invoked on the time spent at the theater (RH Feb. 28, 1882); "the only safe course is to shun the theater" (MYP 380), for it takes away the desire for heavenly things. Gradually a Christian loses "the spirit of assurance," and love for Bible religion dies out, because no one can serve God with a divided heart (11MR 340).

Dancing. Ellen G. White makes a clear distinction between the dancing at the Red Sea or David's dance, when the ark was returned to Jerusalem, and modern dance. The former "tended to the remembrance of God and exalted His holy name," while the latter weakens "the love for sacred things" and sacrifices "health and morals . . . to pleasure" (PP 707); ballroom dancing produces not even "one virtuous or holy sentiment" (MYP 399). In terms of prevention Ellen White advises that we not educate children to dance (CG 181). "No Christian would wish to meet death in such a place [theatre or dance]. No one would wish to be found there when Christ shall come" (AH 516; MYP 398).

Music is one of the greatest means through which humans can praise God (PP 594) and elevate and ennoble their thoughts (Ed 167). Music rises in heaven to honor God (ST Sept. 16, 1889) and on earth "is as much an act of worship as is prayer" (PP 594). Voice training "is an important feature in education" (PP 594).

Yet, music is also used by Satan as the most attractive means of ensnaring souls (1T 506; 2SM 38). When vocal or instrumental music exalts the performers and not God (MYP 293), when it inspires unholy thoughts and actions (CT 339), when it leads to excitement without imparting strength and courage (1T 497), then the result is "pride, vanity, and folly" (MYP 295). Such music is an instrument of evil.

"Noise is not music. Good singing is like the music of the birds—subdued and melodious" (Ev 510; for further counsels on music, see Ev 496-512).

H. Christian Virtues

Christian character contains wonderful treasures of virtues that "make a man more precious than fine gold" (9T 186). These good, moral habits are not given to us; they must be cultivated (5T 404).

Integrity is an attribute of God (ML 331; MYP 35). It consists of habitual resistance to compromising one's belief, loyalty, and commitment. Neither circumstances (PK 545), emergencies (4T 117), trials and discouragements (MYP 80), vanity, display, or flattery (3T 47), luxury (PP 102), or any gain or worldly advantage (*ibid.* 440) can influence a true Christian to change the course of action away from the known will of God. She urges, "We must have moral backbone, an integrity that cannot be flattered, bribed, or terrified" (MH 498). If anyone "would cling to God more firmly and feel that he should preserve his integrity before God even at the cost of his natural life, he would receive strength from above. . . . He need not think that by seeking to compromise with his friends, who are embittered against our faith, he will make it easier for himself. If he stands with the single purpose to obey God at any cost he will have help and strength" (4T 237).

"Even life itself should not be purchased with the price of falsehood. By a word or a nod the martyrs might have denied the truth and saved their lives. . . . Imprisonment, torture, and death, with a clear conscience, were welcomed by them, rather than deliverance on condition of deception, falsehood, and apostasy" (*ibid.* 336; see also PK 479-490; MYP 27-32; PP 217-233, 309).

Prudence. With particular care Ellen G. White urges her readers to exercise prudence in their daily life. The knowledge of God, commitment to His will, an active prayer and religious life, and even faith cannot dispense with the need for common sense and careful thinking (2T 535). Christians are not religious eccentrics acting irrationally to show their religiosity. God does not condemn the use of prudence in things of this life (CS 159), in family finances (2T 431), in transactions of business, and in economizing with our means. "Religious duty and the highest human prudence in business lines must be co-mingled" (AH 381). She opposes those who by presumption "place themselves in scenes of danger and peril, thus exposing themselves to temptations out of which it would require a miracle of God to bring them unharmed and untainted. . . . We should exercise prudence, caution, and humility, and walk circumspectly toward them that are without" (3T 482). Christian witness becomes a powerful instrument when characterized by practical wisdom and common sense. "How many difficulties we encounter, how often we hinder the working of Providence in our behalf, because prudence, forethought, and painstaking are regarded as having little to do with religion!" (ChS 239; see also PK 633-645).

Courage. Christianity requires stamina and steadfastness. To be a Christian means to stay firm in the midst of growing iniquity, ready to act from principle when under pressure to conform or compromise. Courage is that "stern" virtue (MH 391) needed to face the unbelieving world (1T 287). When obedience to God's commandments (Ev 240) calls for a course of action away from the world's beaten track (GC 597) the Holy Spirit will impart to His servants fortitude necessary for perseverance (PP 657). "Those who would win success must be courageous and hopeful. They should cultivate not only the passive [gentleness, patience, meekness, and kindness] but the active virtues [courage, force, energy, and perseverance]" (MH 497).

But courage, like all other virtues, comes only as a result of purposeful effort and disciplined training (5T 213). Ellen G. White gives valuable advice for those who intend to grow in Christian courage: "We are in no case to become discouraged. Let us keep our eyes off the disagreeable parts of our experience, and let our words be full of good cheer. We can surround ourselves with a sunny atmosphere, or with an atmosphere charged with gloom. Let us educate ourselves to talk courage" (SD 218). Furthermore, she appeals to her fellow Christians to accept the fact that "our only safety is to stand as God's peculiar people. We must not yield one inch to the customs and fashions of this degenerate age, but stand in moral independence, making no compromise with its corrupt and idolatrous practices. It will require courage and independence to rise above the religious standard of the Christian world" (5T 78).

Forgiveness. The concept of forgiveness in the writings of Ellen G. White reflects her systematic integration of several biblical doctrines. First, she affirms that human nature is so permeated by sin that autonomous actions toward God, our neighbor, or oneself become morally offensive without divine assistance (COL 311; SC 18, 19; DA 676). Second, sin is portrayed in her writings as the ultimate and the most intolerable evil in the universe. Sin cannot be excused (DA 811; MH 451; PP 738), forgiven at the expense of His justice, holiness, and truth (7BC 912, 913), justified (4T 370), or treated lightly (SC 33; COL 248; Ed 291). Even God's love does not lead Him to excuse sin (COL 316; PP 522).

Third, "God's hatred of sin is as strong as death" (DA 57), but His love for sinners is stronger than sin in them (SC 54; 5T 633). "Christ always separates the contrite soul from sin. He came to destroy the works of the devil, and He has made provision that the Holy Spirit shall be imparted to every repentant soul, to keep him from sinning" (DA 311). As soon as there was sin there was a Saviour (1BC 1084; DA 210), who by His death assured the destruction (DA 764) and total eradication of sin from the universe (PP 33).

Fourth, forgiveness of sin enters Ellen G.

White's theology at the point of abolishment of sin from human nature. Christ did not save humans *in* their sin but rather *from* their sins (DA 668; 4T 251; MB 114). This He did by paying the penalty for sin so that humans do not continue in sin (TM 161, 162), but that they may be forgiven (3T 372). The experience of forgiveness involves human cooperation as well. While forgiveness *of* sin, and forgiveness *from* sin, cannot be merited (MB 115, 116), bought (GC 84), or secured by self-mortification (5T 635; GC 72) because it is free (DA 745), it is conditional (SC 52; 5T 630) upon our acceptance of it. This acceptance of forgiveness is manifested when sinners come to Christ (MYP 108) with contrition (2TT 94), repentance (7BC 916; SC 26, 27; SD 13; 1SM 393; 2T 293), and confession of sin (2T 293; 1SM 350; SC 37), ready to forsake their sinful ways (MB 127; SC 32), and forgive those who have sinned against them (COL 245-247; MB 113-116; SC 97). Forgiveness proceeds freely from God's unmerited love but becomes effective individually when humans accept this gift

(COL 251). Then the assurance (PK 668), the inexpressible peace, joy, and rest come to the human heart (MH 267).

But the first step is to come to Jesus "just as we are, sinful, helpless, dependent. We may come with all our weakness, our folly, our sinfulness, and fall at His feet in penitence. It is His glory to encircle us in the arms of His love, and to bind up our wounds, to cleanse us from all impurity. Here is where thousands fail: they do not believe that Jesus pardons them personally, individually. They do not take God at His word" (SC 52).

This rich experience of forgiveness teaches humans how to forgive their neighbors. A Christlike, forgiving spirit (2T 566, 567) helps in relieving memories of the painful past (3T 97) and releases the mind and heart for creativity and growth. Compassion and forgiveness restore those who have wronged us and give everyone involved a second chance (2T 566). Christian behavior is a hopeless endeavor without this virtue (MB 21, 22; see also MB 21-24, 113-116; SC 9-56; PP 359-362).

IV. Literature

Atkinson, David J. et al., eds. *New Dictionary of Christian Ethics and Pastoral Theology.* Downers Grove, Ill.: InterVarsity, 1995.

Barclay, Oliver R. *The Intellect and Beyond.* Grand Rapids: Zondervan, 1985.

Bonhoeffer, Dietrich. *The Cost of Discipleship.* London: SCM Press Ltd., 1959.

Childress, James F. and John Macquarrie, eds. *The Westminster Dictionary of Christian Ethics.* Philadelphia: Westminster, 1986.

Davis, John J. *Evangelical Ethics.* Phillipsburg, N.J.: Presbyterian and Reformed Pub. Co., 1985.

Frankl, Victor. "Youth in Search of Meaning," 1973. National Catholic Education Association Convention, New Orleans, Louisiana (Waco, Tex.: Word Cassette Library, 1973 [No. 0205]).

Geisler, Norman L. *Ethics: Alternatives and Issues.* Grand Rapids: Zondervan, 1971.

Henry, C.F.H., ed. *Bakers Dictionary of Christian Ethics.* Grand Rapids: Baker, 1973.

———. *Christian Personal Ethics.* Grand Rapids: Eerdmans, 1975.

Heschel, Abraham Joshua. *The Sabbath.* New York: Farrar, Straus, and Giroux, 1977.

Hess, J. Daniel. *Integrity.* Scottdale, Pa.: Herald Press, 1978.

Johnsson, William G. "On Behalf of Simplicity." *Adventist Review,* Mar. 20, 1986. P. 4.

Kainer, Gordon. *Faith, Hope, and Clarity.* Mountain View, Calif.: Pacific Press, 1977.

Kaye, Bruce, and Gordon Wenham, eds. *Law, Morality, and the Bible.* Downers Grove, Ill.: InterVarsity, 1978.

Lammers, Stephen E., and Allen Verhey, eds. *On Moral Medicine: Theological Perspectives in Medical Ethics.* Grand Rapids: Eerdmans, 1987.

LaRondelle, Hans. *Perfection and Perfectionism.* Berrien Springs, Mich.: Andrews University Press, 1971, 1975.

Lutzer, Erwin W. *How to Say No to a Stubborn Habit.* Wheaton, Ill.: Victor Books, 1985.

McDowell, Josh, and Bob Hostetler. *Right From Wrong.* Dallas: Word, 1994.

Moore, Peter C. *Disarming the Secular Gods.* Downers Grove, Ill.: InterVarsity, 1989.

Mott, S. Charles. *Biblical Ethics and Social Change.* New York: Oxford University Press, 1982.

Niebuhr, H. Richard. *Christ and Culture.* New York: Harper and Brothers, 1951.

Sell, Alan P. *Aspects of Christian Integrity.* Louisville: Westminster/John Knox, 1990.

Shames, Laurence. *The Hunger for More.* New York: Times Books, 1989.

Smedes, Lewis B. *Choices: Making Right Decisions in a Complex World.* San Francisco: Harper and Row, 1986.

———. *Love Within Limits.* Grand Rapids: Eerdmans, 1978.

Smith, Paul. *Managing God's Goods.* Nashville: Southern Pub. Assn., 1973.

Springett, Ronald M. *Homosexuality in History and the Scriptures.* Washington, D.C.: Biblical Research Institute, 1988.

Taylor, Richard S. *The Disciplined Life.* Kansas City, Mo.: Beacon Hill, 1962.

Thielicke, Helmut. *The Ethics of Sex.* Grand Rapids: Baker, 1964.

Marriage and Family

Calvin B. Rock

Introduction

The priority that Scripture places upon marriage and family concerns is seen in the fact that seven of the Ten Commandments—God's moral law—reference its functions. They are: commandment number 2, which relates the actions of parents to the prosperity of their children; number 4, which directs the family to Sabbath obedience; number 5, which mandates respect of children for parents; and number 10, which prohibits coveting anything belonging to another's household. Three of the remaining six, while not specifically naming family members, give explicit guidance for family relations. Number 7 prohibits adultery; number 8 rules against stealing; and number 9 forbids the misrepresentation of one's neighbor.

An additional evidence of divine regard for marriage and family concerns is seen in the fact that Christ, who created the human race (Col. 1:16) and as the great "I AM" provided the moral law as guide for its conduct (John 8:58; Ex. 31:14, 18), utilized the marriage ceremony as the setting for His inaugural miracle (John 2:1-11). Both by precept and example the Scriptures make clear God's concern for the welfare of the home.

Since the family structures of Bible days often were distortions of God's original plan, one cannot take all biblical families as models. It is necessary to differentiate between the absolutes of divine intent and the relative accommodations that devolved after sin. Nevertheless, the individual who prayerfully studies scriptural principles regarding the family will find relevant and effective guidance.

I. Marriage and Family in Biblical Perspective

The counsel that Scripture gives regarding marriage and the family involves a wide range of vital considerations. Of priority among these are the reasons for marriage, the principles that undergird its stability, as well as its roles, relationships, and influences within the family. (See Lifestyle II. C. 1-3.)

A. *An Overview of Marriage in the Bible*

1. The Institution of Marriage

Marriage, along with the Sabbath, was instituted in Eden. God created Eve, gave her to Adam, and joined them in matrimony (Gen. 2:21-24). The description of marriage, "Therefore a man leaves his father and his mother and cleaves to his wife, and they become one flesh," was repeated by Jesus (see Matt. 19:5; Mark 10:7) and by Paul (Eph. 5:31) as normative. Monogamy is here clearly modeled.

According to Genesis 4:1, Adam "knew" Eve, and she conceived a son, Cain: the couple became a family. The Hebrew *yāda'* literally means "to know," but also "to experience," "to understand," "to care about." It is used of sexual relations in the sense of a full knowledge and deep relation between partners.

2. The Regulation of Marriage

The law of Moses provides instruction on marriage. Leviticus 18 lists prohibitions related to marriage: incest, bestiality, and homosexuality (see also Lev. 20:17-21; Deut. 27:20-23). It is even possible to take Leviticus 18:18 as limited counsel against polygamy. Divorce, the termination of marriage, is recognized (Deut. 24:1-4), but not categorically approved. The Levirate marriage, in which the husband's brother married the childless widow of his brother, is included in Deuteronomy 25:5-10.

The NT also speaks about marriage. Jesus took Genesis 2:24 as the basis for teaching that marriage is indissoluble, except in the case of *porneia,* a much discussed term usually taken to mean sexual infidelity (Matt. 19:9). Paul's advice on marriage appears in several Epistles. Because of the trying times Christians faced, he suggested celibacy for some, while recognizing the desirability of marriage for others (1 Cor. 7:1, 8, 9, 28, 29). Divorce, according to Paul, was an option only when an unbelieving spouse refused to live with the believing spouse (7:15).

3. The Celebration of Marriage

While Scriptures nowhere prescribe or even describe a model marriage ceremony, several details can be pieced together to provide a general outline. In early times the groom's family usually chose the bride and arranged for the marriage (Hagar for Ishmael, Gen. 21:21; Judah for Er, Gen. 38:6; Manoah for Samson, Judges 14:2). Gifts were given (for example, those brought to Rebekah, Gen. 24:53) and a betrothal was celebrated, after which the couple were under obligation of total faithfulness to each other (Deut. 22:23-27).

The wedding was accompanied by feasting (Gen. 29:22; Judges 14:12; Matt. 22:1-10;

John 2:1-10), in which the friends of the couple, both male and female, participated (Judges 14:11; Matt. 25:1-13; John 3:29). The festivities might continue for a week (Gen. 29:27). Jesus performed His first miracle to produce drink for such a celebration (John 2:1-11). Music was a recognized part of the marriage festivities (Ps. 45); its absence was a token of disaster (Ps. 78:63; Jer. 7:34).

Special clothes were worn: the bride wore embroidered garments (Ps. 45:13, 14) and jewels (Isa. 61:10); the groom might wear a garland or special turban (verse 10). In the marriage of the Lamb, the bride is beautifully adorned (Rev. 21:2), spotlessly dressed in fine linen (Eph. 5:27; Rev. 19:8).

Sexual intercourse signaled the consummation of the marriage and the conclusion of the festivities. The bride's virginity was proved by a bloodstained garment (Deut. 22:13-21).

4. The Symbolism of Marriage

In Scripture marriage serves as a symbol of the intimate relation between God and His people (Jer. 3; Eze. 16; Hosea 1-3). God woos and weds Israel; the relation is tender and intimate. Israel's apostasy is called adultery. In the NT, marriage is a symbol of the relation between Christ and the church (Eph. 5:22, 23). The consummation of all things is called the "marriage of the Lamb," when Christ takes His "bride," the church, to be with Him (Rev. 19:7-9). Thus, scriptural symbolism teaches that marriage is to be "held in honor" (Heb. 13:4).

B. Reasons for Marriage

1. The Blessings of Companionship

Having made the first human being, God said, "It is not good that the man should be alone" (Gen. 2:18). Humans are social creatures, born with yearnings for interaction with another—the most binding of which finds expression in family life. People can happily live alone; some choose to do so. However, the dominant compulsion is for the fulfillment found in friendship and in the joys of romance and marital relation. The love that undergirds this most sacred of choices is an appreciation for the mental, physical, and spiritual qualities of a member of the opposite sex, together with a conscious decision to cherish and respect that person, so enduring that one wishes to spend the rest of life in matrimony with that individual.

The quality of love that renders marriage the "queen of friendships" finds joyful expression in Adam's view of Eve as "bone of my bones and flesh of my flesh" (Gen. 2:23). It is seen in Jacob's assessment of his lengthy service for Rachel as "but a few days" (29:20) and in Solomon's lyrical praise, "How sweet is your love, my sister, my bride! how much better is your love than wine, and the fragrance of your oils than any spice!" (S. of Sol. 4:10; see Man I. C).

2. The Function of Reproduction

God did not fill the earth with people. He might have done so, but He assigned this task to the wedded pair. His instruction was to "be fruitful and multiply" (Gen. 1:28). Thus, to parents was given the privilege of cooperating with God in the perpetuation of the race. But what is addressed is not simply biological perpetuity. Also included in this responsibility are: (a) the joy of witnessing oneself and one's spouse combined in the offspring, and (b) a renewed reverence and awe for God, whose creative prowess makes life possible.

3. The Fulfillment of the Sexual Urge

Sexual gratification finds its legitimate expression only within the confines of marriage. This arrangement was expressed in both OT and NT times by specific injunctions against fornication and adultery (Ex. 20:14; Prov. 6:24-32; Matt. 5:27-30; Rev. 22:14, 15). God's knowledge of the psychological and physiological frame of humans supports the correctness of this prohibition. Sexual conduct with a person other than one's spouse is not only contrary to God's will; it is problematic to both offending parties and society as well. The

Creator knew that the sexual relation outside of marriage or "alien bonding" would produce a plethora of emotionally dysfunctional responses, i.e., lying, anger, disrespect, jealousy, guilt, and self-depreciation. He also knew that it would spawn a harvest of crippling physical diseases, such as syphilis, gonorrhea, and AIDS. Thus, He lovingly warned His creatures, "You shall not commit adultery" (Ex. 20:14).

Sex outside the marital bond is not biblical; it is a dire and destructive consequence of sin. Sharing one flesh implies that the incompleteness of each life is brought to completness by union with the other. Because Christian love finds in the inner secrets of sex all that it needs for solving the riddle of one's completion, extramarital sex is not only sinful, it is unnecessary.

While God's commands against sexual relations outside the marriage bond are for protection and happiness, so are His provisions for sexual fulfillment within the marital sphere. The fact that our first parents were placed in the Garden "naked and unashamed" not only affirms the innocence of human sexuality; it confirms the propriety of the disclosures of marital intimacy. The terse but positive injunction of Hebrews 13:4, "Let marriage be held in honor among all, and let the marriage bed be undefiled," forcefully declares the same.

The apostle Paul wrote that not being bound by family duties might enhance one's freedom to do God's work (1 Cor. 7:5, 32-34); however, such radical stewardship is not the required or normal path of the Christian life (verse 6). His wise and pointed counsel was, "But because of the temptation to immorality, each man should have his own wife and each woman her own husband" (verse 2).

4. The Socialization of Children

Children are "a heritage from the Lord" (Ps. 127:3), for whom strict accountability is required. This fact is focused in God's judgment-time address to parents: "Where is the flock that was given you, your beautiful flock?" (Jer. 13:20). Society provides a number of institutions helpful for the socialization process, but the primary responsibility lies with the family. Parents are the children's first and foremost teachers. In the home children should be taught to share, respect property, and to observe and respond to the needs of others. It is God's will that these and other such lessons, patiently verbalized and properly modeled, will eventually "translate into virtues such as respect for the common good, self-restraint, helping one's neighbor—in short, into character, which is vital to a society's survival" (Colson 19).

An example of biblical concern in this regard is shown in Nehemiah's response to the cultural contamination suffered by the children of Jewry following their return from the Babylonian captivity. Nehemiah, who saw that because they had foreign mothers, many of the younger generation "spoke the language of Ashdod" and "could not speak the language of Judah," contended severely with their parents and cried out for revival (Neh. 13:24-27).

5. The Sheltering of the Family

A family is a group of persons united by blood, marriage, or adoption who share a common culture and typically live in the same household. The home was created to provide security for its members and is a haven of relief from the threatening forces of outer society. The protection afforded within the ark to Noah, his wife, their three sons, and their wives (Gen. 6:18–7:1) is history's most dramatic illustration of this function. Being of one blood and body, the members of a family are to experience not just physical protection from threatening elements but emotional and psychological security as well. Within the family, there is no need to defend or pretend. Here members are free to communicate hopes and doubts, aspirations and disappointments, with the sure knowledge of full acceptance and without fear of betrayal.

C. Principles of Marriage

1. The Principle of Unity

After reviewing the animals by pairs but finding himself alone, Adam exclaimed upon meeting Eve, "This at last is now bone of my bones and flesh of my flesh" (Gen. 2:23). Such unity involves not only physical but psychological and spiritual fusion also; for "Do two walk together, unless they have made an appointment?" (Amos 3:3). The authors of the *Seventh-day Adventist Manual for Ministers* illustrate the effort that such bonding requires:

"It is no ordinary attainment for two people to become one. Nothing on earth is so delicate and so easily moved as the human heart. If two stringed instruments are to produce a melodious harmony, they must be kept in tune with each other. There must be constant adjustment and regulation. How much more important it is to keep two human hearts, with a thousand strings, in harmony with each other!" (1954, 110).

2. The Principle of Interdependence

Once more, the Scripture is determinative: "Therefore a man leaves his father and his mother and cleaves to his wife" (Gen. 2:24). This principle, repeated by Christ when on earth (Matt. 19:5), establishes the spouse relationship as superseding all others. Christian spouses should not be oblivious to the physical and moral support provided by their outer circle of relatives and friends; however, they are mandated by Scripture to depend most deeply and enduringly upon the encouragement and reassurance that they share with each other.

3. The Principle of Endogamy

Paul enjoins endogamy in 2 Corinthians 6:14, "Do not be mismated with unbelievers. For what partnership have righteousness and iniquity?" or, as stated in the *Modern Language Bible:* "Be not yoked up unequally with unbelievers; for what common ground is there between righteousness and lawlessness, or what association is there between light and darkness?" This is the basis for the Christian preference for endogamy, marrying "within" one's own group. While the mandate of 2 Corinthians 6:14 speaks specifically to the union of Christian with non-Christian, factors such as age, education, class, or culture also affect marriage. All distance occasioned by divergent views of reality and lifestyle increases the challenge to "oneness." Moreover, the impact upon marriage of fundamentally differing religious understandings is especially dysfunctional. When one recalls the strong influence that religious belief and traditions have upon the family, i.e., their role in courtship style, engagement patterns, family finances, diet, dress, recreation, and even beliefs concerning death, burial, and the afterlife, this instruction of Scripture is understandable.

4. The Principle of Monogamy

The Bible portrays polygamy, beginning with Lamech onward (Gen. 4:19), as an act of His creatures' stubbornness. God tolerated it, but it was not His will for their welfare. The pain of Abraham's life with Hagar (16:1-6), the spiritual calamities that Solomon's wives brought upon him (1 Kings 11:1-4), and the bitter results of David's harem arrangements are forceful reminders of the consequences of this deviation from God's will.

In lands where polygamy is lawful, the Christian church often finds it difficult to apply the principle of monogamy. However, even in these countries, monogamy is upheld as the marital ideal.

5. The Principle of Permanence

Marriage is intended to be a lifelong union—a relationship terminated only by the death of one of the partners. The penchant of modern societies to regard this union as a contractual arrangement with easy access and dissolution is contrary to both God's will and society's good. This trend countermands the very reasons for which marriage was instituted and wars against the words of Christ, "What therefore God has joined together, let no man put asunder" (Matt. 19:6).

The popular consensus and libertarian laws of modern society contrast starkly with the biblical teaching of permanence with respect to the marital covenant.

6. The Principle of Privacy

"Leaving" and "cleaving," as instructed by God (Gen. 2:24), mandate another crucial posture for marital partners—privacy. It is God's intention that the wedded pair function without the interference of even well-meaning kin. By this rule, spouses are taught not to share carelessly details of their marital relationship with those outside the sacred circle.

Christians know that there are times when other counsel is needed. However, the "privacy principle" demands extreme caution in such situations, requiring that advice be sought preferably from advisors, i.e., pastors, physicians, and counselors, whose participation avoids emotional involvement and provides a balance of objectivity and personal concern. Marital or family counseling not in harmony with Scripture lacks the needed impress of the Author of family life.

7. The Principle of Exclusivity

Another principle provided in the "leaving and cleaving" injunction appears in J. Stott's definition:

"Marriage is an exclusive heterosexual covenant between one man and one woman, ordained and sealed by God, preceded by a public leaving of parents, consummated in sexual union, issuing in a permanent mutually supported partnership, and normally crowned by the gift of children" (2:163).

The exclusivity intended in this definition is reinforced by the Scripture's imagery of marriage as an alliance or covenant, even a model, of God's faithful relationship with His sometimes unfaithful people (Hosea 3:1). This understanding binds husband and wife by promises to each other and to God in ways

reminiscent of the covenant-making ceremonies witnessed throughout the OT. As in the Exodus covenants, slaves who were "no people" became the exclusive possession of God. As Yahweh is Israel's "spouse" in many prophetic writings (Isa. 50:1; 54:5; Jer. 2; Eze. 16), so in marriage are husband and wife made by their altar promises to be each other's possession in permanent belongingness.

D. Roles in Marriage and Family

1. The Husband/Father

The husband and father fulfills several important roles. He functions as priest, provider, protector, parent, and lover and friend.

a. As priest. The husband's chief function is clearly seen in God's words concerning Abraham, the father of the faithful: "For I have chosen him, that he may charge his children and his household after him" (Gen. 18:19). The husband/father is the family priest and thus assigned to lead its members in spiritual growth and dedication. God's command to Israel, to teach the divine commands to their children (Deut. 6:7-9), is directed to parents, but family leadership in such activities is a role assigned primarily to the husband/father. This is seen in the examples of Noah (Gen. 8:18-20), Abraham (Gen. 12:7; 13:4, 5), and Jacob (Gen. 35:2-7). At the first Passover celebrations, the men were to sacrifice the lamb and sprinkle its blood on the doorposts of their homes (Ex. 12:3-7).

In a practical sense, morning and evening worship offer prime occasions for the father to foster this important function. He is not asked to perform all aspects of the worship exercise himself, but he is chiefly responsible for their conduct and for the general welfare of the family's spirituality.

b. As provider. Scripture also models the father as the chief provider of the family's "daily bread." The mandate "In the sweat of your face you shall eat bread" (Gen. 3:19) was spoken to Adam, not Eve, and places chief responsibility for physical nurture on the husband. Paul repeats this very succinctly: "If any one does not provide for his relatives, and especially for his own family, he has disowned the faith and is worse than an unbeliever" (1 Tim. 5:8). While many women are forced by circumstances to procure their "daily bread," and others choose to participate in the economic endeavor, the Bible points to the male as the partner with major responsibility in the care of family life.

c. As protector. The physical guardianship provided for his mate and offspring in many animal species suggests a third role for the husband/father—that of protector. The Christian husband not only accepts this function but also takes pride in being the defender of his wife and offspring. Jacob's scrupulous care to secure his family from Esau's wrath (Gen. 32:22-24) and his words to his brother demonstrate such protection.

"My lord knows that the children are frail, and that the flocks and herds giving suck are a care to me; and if they are overdriven for one day, all the flocks will die. Let my lord pass on before his servant and I will lead on slowly, according to the pace of the cattle which are before me and according to the pace of the children" (33:13, 14).

The bride in Song of Solomon can rest content sitting in the shadow of her "apple tree" and eat of its fruit, suggesting protection and provision (S. of Sol. 2:3). Paul's statement "Husbands, love your wives, as Christ loved the church and gave himself up for her" (Eph. 5:25) defines ultimate fidelity in this regard.

d. As parent. While child rearing is chiefly the mother's responsibility, the father's participation in this function is emphasized also in Scripture. As witnessed in Paul's command that fathers bring up their children "in the discipline and instruction of the Lord" (6:4), paternal responsibility includes more than provider/protector activities.

Sons are in special need of their father's love and companionship. When mothers struggle alone in rearing sons, these may develop aggressive behavior that leads to delinquency. Seventy percent of imprisoned minors have spent part of their life without a father. E. Cose (61) explains that children reared without fathers are more likely to drop out of high school or to suffer behavioral and emotional problems (Louv 54-56). Fatherlessness is "the most urgent social problem of our generation" (Cose 61).

Likewise, the lack of fatherly attention to daughters is easily funneled into one of a number of dysfunctional attitudes in later life. These include hostility toward men, fear of men, and overanxiety for male affection.

e. As lover and friend. The Bible presents the husband's role of lover and friend as prominent in the marriage relation. The OT is rich in references to the love of the husband for his wife. Isaac "loved" Rebekah and was comforted by her companionship (Gen. 24:67). Later, after Isaac had told the Philistine king that Rebekah was his sister, Abimelech saw Isaac "fondling" her and discovered the real relation between the two (Gen. 26:8). Elkanah asked Hannah, "Am I not more to you than ten sons?" suggesting a relation that provided the wife with support and love (1 Sam. 1:8).

The maiden in the Song of Solomon finds delight in her lover. Using figures appropriate to the times, she calls him a "young stag" (2:9), "radiant and ruddy," his head like "finest gold" (5:10, 11); she compares him to "Lebanon, choice as the cedars" (verse 15). She describes his lovemaking (8:3). "This is," she affirms, "my beloved and this is my friend" (5:16).

Finally, God points to the role of lover and friend by describing His relation to Israel. In a story told through the prophet Ezekiel, God affirms that He has plighted His troth to Israel and she has become His (Eze. 16:8). He gave her garments, jewelry, and food (verses 10-19); the two had sons and daughters (verse 20). When she plays the harlot, He woos her back, offering to remember His covenant with her (verses 60, 62). Hosea's relationship with Gomer is a representation of God's relation to Israel—that of a lover endeavoring to woo his beloved (see Hosea 3:2).

2. The Wife/Mother

The importance of the husband/father role to family welfare is matched in Scripture by portrayal of the exalted role of the wife and mother. For if the home must have a head, it also must have a heart. Nowhere is that posture more graphically outlined than in Proverbs. "A good wife is the crown of her husband" (12:4). "He who finds a wife finds a good thing, and obtains favor from the Lord" (18:22). "A prudent wife is from the Lord" (19:14). A good wife "is far more precious than jewels" (31:10). "A woman who fears the Lord is to be praised" (verse 30).

a. As childbearer and nurturer. As the husband/father's role is amplified in God's reaction to his transgression (Gen. 3:17), so is the wife/mother's role illumined by God's response to her mistake—"in pain you shall bring forth children" (verse 16). The bearing of children, clearly designed by the Creator for the woman, was to become difficult. The childbearing act of a woman results in a bond that benefits the nurture of children. The effects of patient and loving nurture are seen in numerous biblical examples; among them: Hannah's guidance of Samuel (1 Sam. 1:21-28; 2:19, 20), Jochebed's training of Moses (Ex. 2:1-10), and Mary's role in the life of the boy Jesus (Luke 2:40, 51, 52).

b. As homemaker. King Lemuel's account of the activities of the virtuous wife/mother makes it clear that she is indeed the leader in the conduct of home affairs. That emphasis is seen in her attention to the household's sustenance: "She rises while it is yet night and provides food for her household" (Prov. 31:15); to household planning: She rises early to "provide . . . tasks for her maidens" (verse 15); to household investments: "She considers a field and buys it; with the fruit of her hands she plants a vineyard" (verse 16); "She makes linen garments and sells them; she delivers girdles to the merchants" (verse 24); to household clothing: "She puts her hands to the distaff, and her hands hold the spindle" (verse 19); to

household beauty: "She makes herself coverings" and clothing of "fine linen" (verse 22); to household comfort: "She is not afraid of snow for her household, for all her household are clothed in scarlet" (verse 21); to household morale: "She opens her mouth with wisdom, and the teaching of kindness is on her tongue" (verse 26); to general household supervision: "She looks well to the ways of her household" (verse 27).

Most modern families find it difficult to mirror the biblical model from Proverbs 31. By its technological advances, the industrial society has not only revolutionized the processes of family care, radical materialism has also greatly devalued the place of the family in society. Nevertheless, the Christian woman who has not the need, the time, or even the desire to "spin or plant vineyards" is challenged to fulfill within today's society the spirit of these biblical models.

c. As partner. In marriage, the woman is a full partner. She shares with her husband in the tenderness of intimacy and the joy of friendship, as well as the responsibilities of rearing children and keeping a home. The wife shares in decision making and, if need be, in providing for the material needs of the family.

The partnership in administration and homemaking is well described in Proverbs 31:10-31. This virtuous woman supervises her household, sees that everyone's needs are met, and earns money by planting vineyards and selling to the merchants. Especially in single-parent homes, this kind of ideal woman—though difficult to imitate—is needed in modern society.

In the intimacy of marriage, the wife is lover and friend. Proverbs 5:18, 19 points to the wife of one's youth as a delight, one to rejoice with in love and affection. Although the allusions used in the Song of Solomon are not always easy for us to grasp today, the woman is repeatedly described as a source of joy and satisfaction. She has ravished his heart (S. of Sol. 4:9) and her love is sweet (verse 10). He begs of her, "Set me as a seal upon your heart," and affirms that "many waters cannot quench love" (S. of Sol. 8:6, 7). Together, husband and wife are partners in love.

3. The Children

The role of children in the home also has biblical direction. They are not merely dependents, but junior partners in the social circle into which they are born or adopted. That they are dependent is clear. God's Word enjoins, "Children, obey your parents in the Lord" (Eph. 6:1). What is not always as clear is that they are also helpers. The experience of Samuel as Eli's young assistant (1 Sam. 3) and that of the sons the widow sent to gather the vessels she then filled with oil (2 Kings 4:1-7) are but two biblical reminders of this fact.

Children are also teaching partners. It is said of Enoch that he walked with God "after the birth of Methuselah" (Gen. 5:21, 22). Though this statement does not imply that Enoch had been an ungodly individual before the birth of his son, "with the arrival of a son to grace his home he understood through experience the depth of a father's love and the confidence of a helpless baby. As never before he was drawn to God, his own heavenly Father, and eventually qualified for translation" (1BC 246).

Each of these family roles is severely threatened, if not actually altered, in modern society. However, the church boldly declares its allegiance to these role differentiations.

E. Relationships in Marriage

1. Spouse Relationships

The relation between husband and wife, the most fundamental and determinative of the marital bond, is well codified in the Word of God. The operable phrase for this union, "one flesh" (Gen. 2:24; Eph. 5:31), suggests a unity of purpose and thought involving mutual submission and equal status.

a. Mutual submission. While male leadership is indicated in the scriptural injunction "Wives, be subject to your husbands as to the Lord" (Eph. 5:22), male superiority is not intended. The previous verse commands the Ephesian believers to "be subject to one another out of reverence for Christ"; the submission of wives to their husbands is a specific example of what Paul intended. The deference that the woman is told to give to her husband is equaled by the service that he is told to give as her faithful and, if necessary, sacrificial protector and provider.

A passing analogy to this relationship may be found in that of the Trinity itself. Christ's submission to the Father is not a statement of inferior rank, but the implementation of a complementary function in a united endeavor. This concept eliminates the possibility that by the order of creation God intended one sex to command the other. Differences of roles and areas of authority, interpreted by the trinitarian model, support neither the male dominance of traditional understandings, nor the ambiguity of roles promoted by some in recent times. Seen from this perspective the relationship in the Trinity becomes an example of the equality of effort and authority God intended for the pair He created in His likeness.

b. Equal status. The woman's ability to relate to males has been adversely affected by the lesser status afforded her in many societies, both ancient and modern. However, in the words and activities of Christ and Paul we are provided with dynamics that counter those understandings and elevate woman toward the equality provided her at Creation.

Paul's cautions against ignoring certain existing customs (1 Cor. 11:5, 6; 14:34; 1 Tim. 2:11, 12; 5:14) demonstrate his healthy regard for the contemporary social situation. In other writings, however, he transcends existing situations and deposits the seeds of social freedom, which in succeeding generations have borne revolutionary results for male/female relationships. This is seen in his affirming the woman in (a) her sexuality (1 Cor. 7:4), (b) her acceptance by God under grace (11:11, 12), (c) her eligibility for the prophetic gift (verse 5), (d) her privileged place as object of male attention and solicitude (Eph. 5:28, 29), and (e) her categorical equality in Christ Jesus (Gal. 3:28).

The earthly ministry of Christ had an even more dramatic influence on the affirmation of women. He did not proclaim laws that enforced a transformation of spouse relationships. However, in stark contrast with those rabbis who affirmed that "whosoever teaches his daughter Torah teaches her lasciviousness" (Mishnah *Soṭah* 3:4), He pointed the way to equality by granting women new and exalted favor.

This was accomplished by: (a) bringing women to Christian privilege (John 4:1-42), (b) the numerous female characters in His teachings (Luke 15:8; 17:35); (c) His restraints upon the much-abused custom of divorce (Matt. 5:31, 32), (d) His special friendship with Mary and Martha of Bethany (Luke 10:38-42; John 11:1), (e) His making the marriage bond an illustration of the believer's spiritual life with Him (Mark 2:19, 20), and (f) His dying regard for His mother (John 19:26, 27).

Though women were not included in the twelve or the seventy chosen to preach, they were included in His company of workers (Luke 8:1-3), and Mary was honored as the first to herald His resurrection (John 20:10-18).

The biblical words most often used to justify male superiority in marriage are "headship" and "rulership." However, neither expression intends the inequality that they have historically supported. The concept of headship (1 Cor. 11:3) is described after the Fall (Gen. 3:16); Paul speaks of it in the light of Christ's sacrificial regard for His people (Eph. 5:23). If there is to be found significance of function in Adam's primacy in the creation order, it is that of caretaker or servant. He was created first as forerunner or guardian of the being who would follow.

God created humans in His image, male and female (Gen. 1:27). To the man, who was deficient when alone, was added woman—the final and crowning act of God's creation. In other words, to the notion of headship or beginning was added that of fulfillment or completion, each sex being absolutely necessary to the species, each being equal in status, each finding full satisfaction only in the other.

Rulership also characterizes marital relations after sin (Gen. 3:16). It was not a part of God's original plan, and like its corollary, leadership, should be viewed not as privileged superiority but as solemn, sacrificial responsibility.

Not only does the Bible enjoin mutual submission and equal status; it also mandates mutual respect, mutual forbearance, and mutual obligations. The latter involve nurture, comfort, support, and sexual fidelity (Gen. 2:24; Ex. 20:14).

Taken as a whole, the three most effective biblical principles with respect to female dignity are the understandings that: (a) God intended in creation a viable, permanent, monogamous, marital bond; (b) while the Lordship of Christ does not abolish the distinctiveness of social and sexual roles, it does eliminate all differences of personal worth and value; and (c) the understandings of male/female relationships held by biblical authors must be studied in the light of God's original pre-Fall intentions.

2. Parent/Child Relationships

The relationship of children to their parents is likewise addressed in Scripture. Children are to relate to their parents with honor (Ex. 20:12), with gratitude and caring (John 19:26; 1 Tim. 5:4), and in obedience (Eph. 6:1; Col. 3:20). Examples of filial regard in the lives of Samuel (1 Sam. 2:18-21), Isaac (Gen. 22:2-18), Esther (Esther 2:7; 4:4, 12-16), and Christ Himself (Luke 2:51) show how children are to fulfill these mandates.

One of the more comprehensive guides for parental attitudes is the Psalmist's declaration: Children "are a heritage from the Lord" (Ps. 127:3). The concept that informs this declaration is stewardship, and its functional components are patience, kindness, and authority. Each is vital to the parenting process, but authority is most often challenged in today's thought and most often lacking in parental performance. This is especially unfortunate, for if children are to obey (Eph. 6:1), parents must have credible authority over them.

Parents should know and exercise their legal and moral rights. Commonly accepted among these are the right to custody of their children, the right to determine the religious education of their children, the right to discipline their children, and the right to the services of their children who are minors.

What must be remembered, however, is that children also have rights. They have a right to their parents' companionship, a right to their physical support, a right to their proper example, a right to their unselfish love, and the right not to be provoked (verse 4), that is, angered and irritated by oppressive acts or harsh words.

A particularly important lesson derived from the biblical records addresses the destructive force of favoritism within the family circle. Among the saddest of scriptures is the statement, "Isaac loved Esau, because he ate of his game; but Rebekah loved Jacob" (Gen. 25:28). Those parents who repeat the mistakes of Isaac and Rebekah, or of Jacob, who wounded his other sons by giving a costly tunic to Joseph, sow seeds of discord that will reap similar results.

3. Sibling Relationships

Sibling association is also well informed by biblical instruction and example. Many of the examples demonstrate what not to do. Cain and Abel, eldest sons of our eldest parents, become our first teachers in this regard (Gen. 4:2-8). Other negative experiences that instruct us are those of Jacob and Esau (Gen. 27; 28; 32), Joseph and the other sons of Jacob (Gen. 37), the feuding children of David (2 Sam. 13), the greedy and disobedient sons of Eli (1 Sam. 2:12-17, 22-25), and the prodigal son and his elder brother (Luke 15:25-32).

Positive sibling relations also appear in Scripture. Examples are Peter and Andrew, who together followed Christ (Matt. 4:18); James and John who were pillars in service (verses, 21,22), and the daughters of Philip, who prophesied (Acts 21:8, 9). These provide courage for Christian parents.

Throughout Scripture, the words "brother" and "sister" refer to a close and warm relationship. Brothers should not fight (Gen. 13:8, where the Hebrew has "brothers" rather than "kinsmen"; Acts 7:26). A beloved friend is called a "brother" (2 Sam. 1:26). Brothers are "born for adversity," willing to help at all times (Prov. 17:17). A friend who "sticks closer than a brother" is a friend indeed (18:24). In the Song of Songs, the beloved is often called "sister" to show her closeness (S. of Sol. 4:9, 10; 5:1, 2, etc.). Jesus called those who do His will brothers and sisters (Matt. 12:50; Mark 3:35). More than 50 times in the book of Acts the Christians call each other, or are called, "brothers." Paul addresses his readers as "brothers" more than 60 times in his Epistles. Finally, to seal the meaning of true sibling relations, Jesus is the "first-born among many brethren" (Rom. 8:29), made like His human "brethren in every respect" (Heb. 2:17).

F. Family Influences

1. The Family and the Individual

The words of Solomon, "Train up a child in the way he should go, and when he is old he will not depart from it" (Prov. 22:6), are not absolute assurance that proper training guarantees proper adulthood. But it does apply the law of probability to the enduring effect of parental influence upon one's character and happiness. The ingredients of true success—honesty, persistence, self-confidence, hard work, regard for others—are, of course, taught within other institutions, such as church and school. But long before the influences of these institutions touch the individuals, the values honored in the home have indelibly impacted a child's life.

It is no accident that homes that suffer from a moral vacuum are a rich source of immoral and/or psychologically troubled individuals. On the other hand, well-adjusted individuals are much more likely the products of properly directed homes.

2. The Family and Society

The importance of marriage to societal welfare is embodied in the biblical mandate, "Keep your heart with all vigilance; for from it flow the springs of life" (Prov. 4:23). The heart of the community and the nation is the home. The home is the factory whose product, the citizen, builds social communities. When that factory is faulty in its processing, its products are inevitably affected. Such a home produces children who are undisciplined, unscrupulous, and unfazed by rules—whether rules of society, the laws of nature, or the commandments of nature's God.

It is tragic for a family to contribute to society a damaged person or one with misguided values. It is even more tragic that all too often such persons establish their own families and repeat the process of harmful socialization, often leading to disaster in the individual, the family, and society.

Throughout the world families are crippled by the effects of the society in which they live. At the same time, families contribute to the ills of society, whether in affluent suburbs or the slums of developing cities. The social problems of Kathmandu and Harare are of the same character as those of New York and Moscow. The rejection of the ethic of love and the placing of acquisitive lusts before the good of others, learned in the home, are universally debilitating. Moral training is everywhere the basis of good citizenship, and a converted Christian is the "gratuitous gift of the church to secular society."

3. The Family and the Church

By its theological tenets and its religious activities the church has profound influence upon the home. The converse is also true—the family affects the church. The church is comprised of families, and the perceptions, priorities, and practices of these units pervasively determine the strength of the confessing community.

The awareness of the importance of the family to the nation induced ancient Israel's leaders in times of severe challenge to cry out for family reform. Such were Joshua (Joshua 24:15-26), Ezra (Ezra 9:1-4), Nehemiah (Neh. 13:23-27), Malachi (Mal. 4:5, 6).

The primacy of the home is indelibly stamped in the portrayal of the first Passover in Exodus 12:1-13. The redeeming blood was placed, not upon the temple walls or the school doors, but upon the portals of each home, where the Passover lamb was to be eaten (verse 7).

Today, as in Bible times, parents are also guardians of the blood—commissioned to protect and instruct their children in the virtues of Christ's love. The quality of their effort is crucial not only to their family but to the well-being of the church.

II. The Application of Biblical Teaching to the Daily Life

A. *Ideal Marriage*

Marriage was devised by God to meet the needs of His human creatures. The Creator said, "It is not good that the man should be alone" (Gen. 2:18), and remedied Adam's solitude by creating Eve (verses 21-23). Marriage is intended to bring happiness and well-being, not only to the man and woman who choose to be partners for life but to the family and society as well. Ellen White wrote that marriage "was designed to be a blessing to mankind. And it is a blessing wherever the marriage covenant is entered into intelligently, in the fear of God, and with due consideration for its responsibilities" (MH 356, 357).

When husband and wife relate to each other with deference, courtesy, and love, the divine ideal for marriage is most nearly reached. In such a partnership the needs of both husband and wife are met, both submit to each other and neither dominates the other. By following biblical principles for marriage (see I. B), fulfilling the biblical roles in marriage (see I. C), and carrying out the biblically mandated relationships (I. D), Christian couples can make their homes "a little heaven upon earth" (AH 15). In such an atmosphere, spouse abuse—whether verbal, psychological, or physical—cannot exist.

In today's society, intercultural and interracial marriages are somewhat more acceptable than they were. But such marriages routinely face the challenges of bonding disparate backgrounds; often they must deal with negative reactions of family and friends. Theirs is often a difficult task. However, when entered into with proper preparation and resolution, the success of these marriages demonstrates the truth of the biblical statement "Love is strong as death. . . . Many waters cannot quench love, neither can floods drown it" (S. of Sol. 8:6, 7).

On the basis of the scriptural injunction "Do not be mismated with unbelievers" (2 Cor. 6:14), Christians should marry those of like faith. Differences in religious outlook usually spoil the home atmosphere and lead to difficulties, both between partners and with other family members. To one contemplating marriage with an unbeliever, Ellen White wrote: "Unless you would have a home where the shadows are never lifted, do not unite yourself with one who is an enemy of God" (5T 363).

B. Marriage Aberrations

Because marriage is a covenantal relation, blessed by God, it sacredly guards the intimate relations of a husband and wife. Thus, sexual relations outside of marriage are foreign to God's plan for marriage.

Although society condones or even accepts premarital sexual relations and living with a partner to whom one is not married, the biblical framework reserves sexual relations for marriage. Contrary to popular thinking, trial marriages do not result in more stable marriages. In a study of marriages between 1965 and 1985, nonvirgins had a divorce rate of 35 percent, whereas virgins had a divorce rate of 23 percent (Kahn and London 847).

Adultery generally is defined as sexual relations of a spouse with one other than his or her marriage partner. This is specifically prohibited by the seventh commandment: "You shall not commit adultery" (Ex. 20:14). The concept of "adultery," however, includes more than actual sexual intercourse. According to Christ's sermon on the mount, adultery is committed when one "looks at a woman lustfully" (Matt. 5:28). Thus, breaching of the marriage covenant occurs long before actual intercourse, when lustful thoughts are persistently entertained or improper liberties taken with a person of the opposite sex.

In many societies polygamy—one husband with more than one wife—is accepted as a normal and legal form of marriage. For Christians living in most Western countries polygamy is both sinful and illegal. For decades Christian churches have debated what to do with polygamous families who are converted to Christianity. Should the family be broken up? Should church membership be granted to polygamists? The question is only partially resolved. Some observers note that polygamy was also practiced in the Old Testament and argue that it should therefore be accepted as normative today. However, it is clear that polygamy was not the divine intention and that those who practiced it suffered from its effects. The principles of Christianity and the practice of polygamy are mutually exclusive.

Homosexual unions, even though permitted by law in some countries, do not constitute biblical marriage. In the beginning, "male and female he created them" (Gen. 1:27). The biblical model for marriage is given in Genesis 2:24: one man and one woman becoming one flesh. Homosexuality is condemned in both Old and New Testaments (Lev. 18:22; Rom.

1:26, 27; 1 Cor. 6:9). Admittedly, because of the curse of sin, both men and women may be born with homosexual tendencies, just as some are born with a genetic predisposition toward alcoholism. However, in the same way that God's power gives victory to the alcoholic, His loving power also permits the one who has homosexual tendencies to live a life of moral purity. The community of faith must treat both groups with love and compassion. (See Lifestyle II. C. 3. c.)

C. Divorce and Remarriage

According to Jesus, Moses permitted divorce because of the hardness of people's hearts; the willful termination of marriage was not God's plan. However, divorce could be permissible on the grounds of *porneia* (Matt. 5:32; 19:8, 9).

Discussion of the true meaning of *porneia* has filled many volumes. Its core meaning is "sexual immorality" or illicit sexual relations, such as adultery, homosexuality, or bestiality. The RSV correctly translates the word as "unchastity," showing the ambiguity of the term. The interpretation is further complicated by the discussion of the reason for divorce in Deuteronomy 24:1, "some indecency." At the time of Christ, two Jewish schools of thought interpreted this phrase in widely different ways. Shammai affirmed that it referred only to marital infidelity; Hillel taught that the term extended to anything the wife did to displease her husband (Mishnah *Giṭṭin* 9:10).

The sole biblical ground for divorce is adultery—traditionally a consummated sexual union of a spouse with someone other than the marriage partner. More recently, bearing in mind the ambiguity of the term *porneia* and Christ's indictment of lustful thoughts as "adultery," other behavior has been considered as biblical ground for divorce: homosexual practices, sexual perversion, and "persistent indulgence in intimate relationships" that may fall short of coitus (RH Feb. 17, 1977).

However, it remains clear that God hates divorce (Mal. 2:16); His original plan did not include it (Matt. 19:8); and divorce for *porneia* is tolerated, not mandated. Paul echoes Jesus' prohibition of divorce: "the wife should not separate from her husband" (1 Cor. 7:10). "What therefore God has joined together, let no man put asunder" (Matt. 19:6).

Remarriage after a biblically permissible divorce is acceptable. To marry otherwise is to commit "serial polygamy" and to sin before God.

D. Family Abuse

Life in modern times is stressful. Economic pressures, urbanization, family disintegration, loss of roots, health problems—all contribute to the tension that leads to abuse of children, women, and the elderly.

Abuse of children may be physical, psychological, or sexual. The number of battered children and babies admitted to hospitals in the United States has grown dramatically in the past decade. In some instances helpless infants are punished unmercifully at the slightest whim of parents or caretakers. Many children grow up in homes where they are deprived of proper nutrition, hygiene, and care. Some who appear to have the necessities of life are treated in such a way that they become psychologically scarred for life. Since 1986 sexual abuse—ranging from sexual fondling to intercourse—of children by parents or other family members reached an all-time high of 32.8 per 1,000 of all children (Ards and Harrell 337). In 1993 somewhere between 19 and 38 percent of adult women reported being victims of sexual abuse as children (Dubowitz 733). Incest, condemned in Scripture (Lev. 18:6-14; Deut. 27:20-23) and a taboo in most societies, is an evil plague upon an increasingly lawless and promiscuous society.

Women may be abused, both in the home and in society. It is estimated that girls have greater than a one in three risk of sexual abuse by adults, and 40 to 50 percent of women have experienced some form of sexual harassment

(Williams 18). Because of economic and traditional pressures, some societies prefer male children and abort female fetuses or allow female newborns to die. In some areas girls often grow up with less access to education than their male counterparts. In most, they earn less than men in the workplace, and in almost all, an unfortunate percentage suffers as battered wives, berated, beaten, burned, demeaned, and destroyed.

The elderly, instead of being honored by society and their children, often are subjected to abuse. The dramatic increase of longevity stands in stark contrast with the ability of families to care lovingly for the elderly. Whether abandoned in nursing homes or confined to the homes of their children, aged parents often suffer neglect if not physical distress because their children have no time, energy, or desire to care for them. This situation is worse in the more economically advanced nations than in the less-developed world, where the extended family usually continues to respect and care for the elderly.

E. Family Forms and Planning

Families come in different sizes and shapes. They have in common the function of providing warmth, security, and home for those in them. Today, when the family is in danger of losing its identity and vitality, the biblical view proclaims the value of an enduring family.

In developed countries, the nuclear family (parents and offspring) to a large extent has replaced the extended family, which includes other relatives such as grandparents, aunts, and uncles, living together under one roof or in close proximity. Although both family types are legitimate, the nuclear family isolated from the extended family loses many benefits of family solidarity clearly seen in extended families. Granted that today's mobility and the demands of modern life make living in an extended family difficult or impossible, the nuclear family must be encouraged to maintain relations with the extended family, especially with the grandparents. The older generation has much to offer to the socialization of children; likewise, in their older years, they are much in need of the support of the younger generations.

One-parent families, created to a large degree by a rising rate of divorce and the spiraling number of births to unmarried mothers, constitute a large percentage of modern families. The vast majority of these families are headed by women and many of them are poor. Growing up in such a family often has negative aspects. Parental absence—usually of the father—deprives children of proper role models, especially for the child of the same sex as the absent parent. Children of one-parent families are likely to spend a great deal of time without the loving supervision of a parent who must work to provide food and shelter. These children may experience cynicism and bitterness because they feel deprived and cheated of a normal home experience; often they are candidates for dropping out of school and delinquency. To these families society and the church should lend support and encouragement. Perhaps more specifically, individuals who have intact families need to take time to share in the burdens of the one-parent family.

Since so many marriages—for example, one of every two in the United States—end in divorce, and most of these persons remarry, the number of stepfamilies is another reality of our times. Major obstacles face the successful blending of a stepfamily. The pain connected with the dissolution of the original family or families must be overcome. At the same time, relations with, or at least the influence of, the previous family continues. Adjustments must be made to the new and different family members. The number of family interactions increases greatly. Thus, in a family of two parents, two children, four grandparents, and the usual number of extended family members, there is an average of "28 pairs with 247 possible interactions." If one parent is remarried, there are "131,054 possible interactions" and if both are remarried, the "possible interactions leap to an astounding 8,388,584" (Clark 10). These difficulties underline the wisdom of following scriptural instruction regarding divorce. They also constitute a tribute to the step families that succeed in blending and welding into an effective family unit.

Whatever the kind of family, biblical instructions regarding the roles and relations in a family remain in force (see I. D, E). Together, parents and children can, under God's guidance and protection, build a fortress of love that can both protect its inhabitants and radiate warmth and light to its surroundings. (See Lifestyle I. C. 5. a.)

1. Reproduction and Expansion

As already noted, children "are a heritage from the Lord" (Ps. 127:3). Their presence completes the family circle, bringing joy to the parents. Given the circumstances of life today, many couples feel they must limit the number of children they bring into the world. At the same time, other couples take active steps to acquire children, especially when they are unable to procreate naturally.

a. Birth control. Although the practice of birth control is not new, technology now available permits parents to space the birth of children more safely or limit their number. Whether or not to practice birth control is a private decision of the couple. They alone know the limits of their financial and physical strength; they must take responsibility for the education and upbringing of children born into the home. Families that grow beyond the economic capacity of the parents place themselves at a disadvantage that sadly can affect the development of the children. Mothers who have too many children suffer physically and psychologically; their children suffer as well. Thus while respecting the biblical injunction to preserve life, most Christians accept the thesis that failure to prevent the beginning of life can be injurious to the welfare of all participants, effectively countering God's design for our health and prosperity.

Throughout her ministry, Ellen White wrote of the need for parents to consider the welfare of their children before bringing babies into the world (2T 380; RH June 24, 1890). Parents, she wrote, "have no right to bring children into the world to be a burden to others" (2T 380). She wrote to one couple specifically that unless they could discipline their children "from their babyhood . . . it is a sin to increase your family" (5T 323, 324). Furthermore, to improve their missionary possibilities, some couples should remain childless (RH Dec. 8, 1885).

b. Modern technology and adoption. Couples who are unable to procreate may desire to use modern technology or adoption to have children. Many of these arrangements present severe ethical challenges and become a matter of Spirit-guided preference. All demand sober reflection upon the principle of life and the role of Christian stewardship.

Artificial insemination by the father or in-vitro fertilization using sperm and egg of a married couple will produce a child who belongs to both parents. In that sense, there is no moral problem. However, parents may wish to consider the stewardship of means involved in these usually expensive procedures. They may also consider whether overcoming infertility could be contravening God's will for them as individuals.

Artificial insemination by a donor poses a number of difficult questions. Regardless of the care of the sperm bank in selecting donors, the father may pass on to the child undesirable traits. A child who finds that its father was an unknown donor may spend a lifetime wondering and worrying about the absent parent. On the other hand, if the father were known, either the child or the father could choose to destroy the bond linking the child to the family in which he or she was reared. The problems raised by using a donor egg and the father's sperm would be similar.

Adoption is an age-old means of family expansion and fulfillment. Abraham considered adopting Eliezer to make him his heir (Gen.

739

15:2, 3). Pharaoh's daughter adopted Moses (Ex. 2:10). Mordecai raised Esther as his own child (Esther 2:7), and Joseph took responsibility for the child Jesus (Luke 2:41-52).

Most adoptions take place for two reasons. Infertile couples with a great desire to have children may choose to adopt a baby. Couples or families who see a child in need may decide to open their home to that little one. Whatever the reason, adoptive parents commit themselves to their adopted children for life.

That adoption may pose dilemmas cannot be denied. Children may carry with them genetic predispositions or results of early mistreatment that are difficult for the adoptive parents to understand or accept. Interracial or intercultural adoptions may also require a great deal of wisdom and an exceptional amount of love.

When undertaken out of altruistic motives, adoption is a beautiful Christian gesture. It provides for the child a loving home to meet inborn physical and psychosocial needs. It also allows the couple to reap the benefits of parenthood.

One of the beauties of Christian adoptive families is that they mirror the love and care God has for His children. In this regard, Paul said that Christians were adopted by God, thereby becoming children of God (Rom. 8:15, 16; 9:4).

2. Wills and Trusts

Christians are to trust in God. They are also to make provision for the future by preparing in times of ability for days of crisis (Prov. 6:6-11). The use of wills and trusts to ensure proper care of children who may be orphaned and to distribute appropriately the estate is one way in which wisdom is applied. Emphasis should be placed on including the church in the disposition of one's estate.

Among legal documents now commonly used are the prenuptial agreement and the living will. The first agrees on the distribution of assets should the marriage be dissolved. This agreement is often helpful to protect the interests of children of prior marriages. While perfectly legal, the prenuptial agreement raises questions. Does preplanned dissolution of marriage prove inimical to the principles of family unity and forgiveness so fundamental to marital success? Does marrying with an escape clause somehow weaken the "foreverness" of the marriage covenant?

A living will dictates the nature and extent of treatment in the event of terminal illness, including the measures that medical personnel are to take to prolong or maintain life and, in case of death, the use of organs for transplant or research. Before signing such a will, a person should consult with family members who may view the arrangements mandated in a different light, and discuss his or her own wishes with those who will need to make medical decisions.

F. Family Dilemmas

1. Abortion

Whereas birth control usually is understood as preventing life from occurring, abortion involves the termination of life and becomes a theological issue.

God is the source and giver of life (Acts 17:25, 28). Human life has unique value because human beings are created in the image of God (Gen. 1:27). God calls for the protection of human life (Ex. 20:13) and holds human beings accountable for its destruction (Gen. 9:5, 6). God is especially concerned for the protection of the defenseless (Prov. 24:11, 12; James 1:27). On the other hand, God gives to human beings the freedom of choice (Deut. 30:19, 20; Gal. 5:13) and calls us individually to make moral decisions on the basis of biblical principles (Acts 17:11), always attempting to do the will of God (Rom. 12:2).

The life of an unborn child is to be respected because of the sanctity of all human life. Abortion is never an action devoid of moral consequences and should never be taken lightly. However, decisions about abortion must be made in the context of a sinful world, not by outsiders, but within the setting of a caring, supportive family, guided by biblical principles. Few Christians would argue that all abortions are right or that it is never an option to be considered. When consideration is given, however, it almost always concerns incest, rape, or a radical threat to the life of the mother.

Whatever their convictions on the matter, Christians should not display attitudes of condemnation for those who have gone through the trauma of abortion. Compassion and support should be offered by the church to those facing the dilemma of unwanted pregnancy.

2. Euthanasia

Two kinds of mercy killings are gaining acceptance in today's society. Passive euthanasia is the denial of nourishment or life-support systems to the terminally ill. Active euthanasia refers to taking a person's life in order to prevent further pain.

Several questions face the person involved, as well as the family. When is a person dead? When the brain ceases to function? When the heart stops beating? Is it morally right to keep a person mechanically alive when the body systems have failed? Is it murder to assist a person to die? Should the family honor the wishes of one whose living will states the desire not to be maintained by mechanical means?

Those who categorically oppose euthanasia believe it to be a breach of the command "Thou shalt not kill." On the other hand, those who accept it as correct remind us that the Hebrew of Exodus 20:13 reads "Thou shalt not murder," and consider that passive euthanasia is not taking life but lessening the trauma of dying.

Predicated on the law of love, the respect for life, and the principles of justice, these aberrations within the family cannot be accepted. While recognizing that we live in a sinful world, where sin, disease, and pain abound, as Christians we are obligated to pursue the divine ideal for family life.

3. Cloning

Since human replication (cloning) is not yet a reality, its consequences have not been demonstrated, but there are some effects, both positive and negative, that are quite predictable.

Among the negative consequences are: the muting of such vital human emotions as affection, respect, and love because of feelings of infinite replaceability; the devaluation of life as a result of reproducing humans via an industrial or "factorylike" methodology; the further denigration of marital intimacy because of the disengagement of sexuality from human reproduction; the weakening of the family system because of the creation of a human class that has neither father nor mother; and the ratification of self-centeredness and elitism in consequence of the selectivity that decides who is worthy to be cloned and who is not.

Among the positive consequences envisioned are the enhancement of life that would result from the use of the body parts such as bone marrow or a kidney, and the perpetuation within society of the genius of an Elizabeth Barrett Browning, an Albert Einstein, or a George Washington Carver.

When we add to cloning's probable negative consequences the fact that the replication of genius does not guarantee its development or use to the same degree or for the same purposes as seen in the original, it is clear that Christians are justified in viewing with great caution this exciting but radical advance that God has permitted into the secret of life.

4. Nonnatural Conception

The two most common nonnatural methods of conception are in-vitro fertilization and artificial insemination. In-vitro fertilization is conception outside the mother's womb. In this process eggs are surgically removed from the female and mated with the male sperm in a small glass laboratory dish. After a short incubation period, several (three or four) of the developing embryos are implanted within the womb with the hope that at least one will survive.

The other, and better-known process, artificial insemination, is a procedure whereby the semen of either the husband or a donor male is deposited into the womb by use of a syringe. Births by this process number annually in the hundreds of thousands around the world.

Questions arising from the processing of in-vitro fertilization include:

a. When does life begin? In other words, are the developing embryos human? If so, is it right to start several lives, even artificially, knowing that most of them will die?

b. While children of in-vitro fertilization involving husband and wife may appear quite natural in their development, what will happen when this method involves a donor male other than the husband?

c. Should the mother and child be identified to the donor?

d. What rights and/or responsibilities does the natural father have in such a case?

e. What psychological negatives are likely to affect a father for hire or a child of such a process?

Artificial insemination involving husband and wife carries fewer legal ethical questions. However, when someone other than the husband acts as donor, all of the questions above regarding the donor male's rights and responsibilities become intensified as do questions about the psychological welfare of the child if he or she is informed of having been so conceived. This includes the question of whether or not he or she should be informed.

A parallel dilemma in this regard is for-profit surrogate motherhood, or, as some have termed it, "renting a womb."

Among the more disturbing questions concerning this method of childbearing are:

a. The effects upon society of commercializing the childbearing process.

b. The effects upon the biological mother and the child of forced separation.

c. The confusion and tension often encountered in disputes over parentage and visitation rights. The example of Abraham and Sarah's use of Hagar's womb has illumined these issues for centuries (Gen. 16:1-16).

It is possible for sincere Christians to view the above options differently. However, none who seek to do the will of God and thus function for the good of family and society view them lightly.

III. Marriage and Family in Historical Perspective

A. Judaism

The biblical record gives information on marriage and family in early Judaism. Among the oldest extrabiblical Jewish references to marriage is a marriage contract found among the Elephantine papyri and the story of the wedding of Sarah and Tobias in Tobit 7 and 8, which describes the feast, as well as the marriage contract.

In rabbinic Judaism, marriage was considered a great blessing: "He who has no wife is not a proper man" (Babylonian Talmud *Yebamoth* 63a); he "lives without joy, without blessing, and without goodness" (Babylonian Talmud *Yebamoth* 62b). Polygamy was pos-

sible, but practically unknown in Talmudic times. Procreation was a duty (Mishnah *Yebamoth* 6:6). After 10 years of barrenness, a wife was to be divorced.

The father's duty was to teach his son Torah and a means of livelihood (Babylonian Talmud *Ḳiddushin* 29b). It was strictly forbidden for a parent to show favoritism to any child (Babylonian Talmud *Shabbath* 10b). "A man should spend less than his means on food, up to his means on clothes, beyond his means in honoring wife and children" (Babylonian Talmud *Ḥullin* 84b).

The home was the center of religious practice. Outstanding among its festivities were the Sabbath and the Passover. In addition, families celebrated the Feast of Tabernacles and daily table rituals, which strengthened the bonds uniting them.

To this day marriage is practically mandatory among religious Jews. The Jewish family continues to be the place where religious instruction takes place most effectively.

B. Early Christianity

Marriage and family in early Christianity were influenced by Jewish tradition, but even more so by NT injunctions, which detailed the duties of family members (Eph. 5:21–6:4; Col. 3:18-21; 1 Peter 3:1-8).

Among Christians, marriage normally was accompanied by religious ceremonies. Ignatius affirmed that Christian marriage should take place with the knowledge of the bishop, suggesting that the advice and approval of the congregation was necessary (*To Polycarp* 5 [ANF 1:100]). Clement of Alexandria speaks of "marriage consummated according to the word" as being sanctified (*Stromata* 4. 20 [ANF 2:432]). From the fourth century onward a priest or bishop officiated.

From the third century onward, some Christians began to consider celibacy as preferred over marriage, especially for the clergy, who by the end of the fourth century were required in the West to be celibate. The Gnostics already had taught that conjugal union was sinful. Jerome (c. 340-420) so praised virginity as to suggest that marriage was not ideal. Augustine's (354-430) views were more moderate than those of Jerome, for he taught the three goods of marriage: fidelity, offspring, and the sacrament (*The Good of Marriage* 32 [NPNF-1 3:412]). Carnal concupiscence was turned into good by having children (*ibid.* 6 [NPNF-1 3:401]). However, he still held that sexual intercourse for any purpose other than procreation was sinful. He also upheld the superior worth of celibacy. In spite of all, he could see marriage as participation in the sign of union of Christ and His church.

The dissolution of marriage was forbidden by the church, except for adultery. By the third century, remarriage, even of the innocent party, was frowned on. In the East, there was more tolerance; for example, Basil (330-379) did not approve, but refused to condemn, the second marriage. At that time, according to Roman law, either husband or wife could obtain a divorce on any of numerous grounds and freely remarry.

Mixed marriages, those of Christians with non-Christians, were not considered proper. The Council of Elvira (306) prohibited the marriage of Christians to Jews, heretics, and heathen. Ambrose (c. 339-397) condemned as sacrilege the marriage of believers with unbelievers (*Epistle* 19. 7). The Theodosian Code (438) made mixed marriages a capital offense.

C. Middle Ages

During the Middle Ages the church was the principal authority and legislator on marriage and family. Charlemagne (742-814) prohibited marriage without benediction (Capitulary 7. 363). In 895 Leo VI, the Philosopher, emperor in Constantinople, decreed that marriage of free persons contracted without the nuptial blessing was invalid. In the West, the nuptial mass was instituted by the tenth century. Ecclesiastical regulations on who could marry whom were enforced, except when the persons involved were influential and might secure papal dispensation for their actions. Finally the Council of Trent (1545-1563) decreed that no marriage should be considered valid unless celebrated by a priest in the presence of two witnesses.

Scholars and churchmen discussed at length the purpose of marriage and what made it valid. Around 1140 Gratian published his *Concordance of Discordant Canons,* in which he attempted to harmonize major texts on marriage. He concluded that consent validated a marriage and intercourse simply completed it. On the purpose of marriage, Peter Lombard, twelfth-century bishop of Paris, affirmed that the primary goal was procreation, while the secondary was refuge from fornication. The same idea is clearly expressed in Canon 1013:

"The primary end of marriage is the procreation and nurture of children; its secondary end is mutual help and the remedying of concupiscence."

Thomas Aquinas (1225-1274) regarded marriage as natural and created by God. Since sexual intercourse was needed to keep God's creation alive, the carnal relation was good. Furthermore, friendship in marriage was also good. However, in the sixteenth century the Council of Trent condemned those who taught that the conjugal state was equal to or superior to celibacy.

Differences of opinion on divorce and remarriage prevailed. Church law early prohibited divorce and consequent remarriage in the West. In the East both were permitted, not only for adultery but for other serious causes, but only once in a lifetime. Even today most Catholic countries conform to the ecclesiastical ruling of the Council of Trent, which denies the right to divorce but permits annulment on certain grounds.

D. Reformation

The Protestant Reformation refuted, but did not completely erase, the mechanistic image of marriage so ingrained in Medieval thinking. The Reformers rejected the sacramental theory of marriage, thus freeing it from bondage to celibacy and asceticism. Marriage became acceptable, but more an aid to continence than a covenant of partners. In his comment on the commandments in the *Large Catechism* Luther wrote:

"Where nature takes its course, as God planted it in us, there's no way we can remain pure outside of marriage, for flesh and blood remain flesh and blood, and our natural instincts and stirrings take their course unhindered, as everyone sees and feels. To make it easier for us to avoid sexual immorality up to a point, God has set up the estate of marriage, so that each person can have his fair share and be satisfied with it—although, of course, God still has to add his grace so that our hearts are pure, too" (*Large Catechism,* on the sixth commandment).

On the other hand, Luther felt that a good wife was a gift of God. The religious education of children was a valuable ethical task. Inasmuch as marriage calls for sympathy, sacrifice, and patience, it offers an opportunity to obtain a higher spiritual plane.

The Reformers pointed out that if divorce is always wrong, it would not have been permitted by God. Therefore, divorce for adultery or desertion was permissible and those who divorced for these causes could remarry. At the same time Luther affirmed that those "who want to be good Christians are not to be divorced . . . although he or she may be strange, peculiar and faulty; or, if there be a divorce, that the parties remain unmarried" (*Commentary on the Sermon on the Mount,* Matt. 5:31, 32). Yet he could say, "As to divorce it is still a moot question whether it be allowable. For my part I so greatly detest divorce that I should prefer bigamy to it, but whether it be allowable, I do not venture to decide" (*The Babylonian Captivity of the Church*). John Milton carried the Reformers' argument even further, affirming that marriage was indissoluble only when there was complete and perfect unity of heart between the partners.

Calvin was more positive about marriage than Luther in that he saw marriage as a pure and positive gift of God. However, he too failed to overcome the uneasiness about the pleasurable elements of sexual intimacy that had plagued the church since the time of the early Fathers.

In Great Britain, under Edward VI, an attempt was made to alter the ecclesiastical laws and permit remarriage after divorce. Although it did not succeed and judicial separation without remarriage could be granted by the ecclesiastical courts according to the 1604 canons, remarriage was permissible by a special Act of Parliament. The Lambeth Conference of 1888 concluded that the innocent party of a divorce for adultery might remarry but that the marriage should not receive the blessing of the church.

E. Adventist Understanding

Throughout their history Adventists have attached great importance to marriage and the family. These institutions are seen as having divine origin and being God's gifts to the human race, along with the seventh-day Sabbath.

1. The Sabbath

Particularly important to Adventist family stability is the observance of the seventh-day Sabbath. This day, dedicated to God, provides time for the family to worship and fellowship together. The preparation for it also affords opportunity for physical and spiritual cleanness—home, body, and clothing, as well as spirit and mind, are prepared for this special 24-hour spiritual high day. During the Sabbath hours, families are encouraged to attend church services, have fellowship with fellow believers, explore and study nature, and serve others. God rewards families, as well as individuals (Isa. 58:13, 14), for observing the fourth commandment (Ex. 20:8-11).

2. Books and Publications

Adventists early displayed concern for the family. In 1865 Ellen G. White wrote six articles on health and published them with articles by other authors in a series of pamphlets titled *How to Live* (reprinted several times, most recently in *Selected Messages,* book 2, 1958). Of these, the second deals with marriage and family within the context of health and disease. Ellen White describes marriage as an institution "designed of Heaven to be a blessing to man" (2SM 421). She counsels couples to seek each other's happiness (*ibid.* 430) and the welfare of their children, who should be brought up in harmony with the laws of health and virtue. Godly parents "will feel that their children are precious jewels committed to their keeping by God." Christian families will make the world "better for their having lived in it" and will be "finally fitted for the higher life, the better world" (*ibid.* 440).

Numerous articles addressing home and family are found among Ellen White's articles and testimonies. Her book *The Ministry of Healing* (1905) contains major sections on the topic. Two major compilations of Ellen White's writings on marriage and family have been made: *The Adventist Home* (1952) and *Child Guidance* (1954).

Through the decades many Adventist authors have addressed issues related to home and family. Arthur W. Spalding (1877-1953), well known for his history of the Adventist Church, also wrote on matters pertaining to the church's children and youth. His book *Makers of the Home* (1928) was considered a church classic. Belle Wood Comstock (1880-1961), a physician and professor of endocrinology, cooperated with Spalding in writing *The Days of Youth* (1932), *Growing Boys and Girls* (1931), and *Through Early Childhood* (1930). In addition she wrote many articles for health magazines and other books, such as *All About the Baby* (1930). Harold Shryock (1906-), physician and professor of medicine, wrote several books about marriage and family, of which the best known are *Happiness for Husbands and Wives* (1949), *On Becoming a Man* (1951), and *On Becoming a Woman* (1951). These books were translated into several languages and distributed extensively.

3. Church Structures and Pronouncements

Concern for the family is evident in the church organization at all levels, from the General Conference to the local church. In 1922 Spalding founded the Home Commission of the General Conference. Until 1941 he prepared materials for the use of the church on topics related to marriage and family. The commission was integrated with the Department of Education from the end of Spalding's tenure until 1975. At that time, the Home and Family Service (later renamed Family Life Ministries) was created to oversee the preparation of materials and presentation of workshops on marriage, singles, parenting, and several aspects of family. A church-sponsored Family Life International workshop has convened annually since 1975, offering family life certification for church educators. Several expressions of Adventist concern for the marriage partnership are part of the family life movement. The achievements of the past 20 years have been the curricularization of family life materials and the internationalization of activities and personnel.

The Seventh-day Adventist Church has voted and published various documents on matters concerning home and family. The following show the trend of Adventist thinking.

The official church policy on divorce and remarriage, voted in 1958 by the General Conference in session, appears in the *Church Manual* (1990, 172-174). It considers divorce and remarriage permissible only in cases of "fornication," which is defined as "unfaithfulness to the marriage vow." The 1976 Annual Council reaffirmed the policy and voted guidelines for its implementation. These include procedures to be followed for discipline of persons divorcing for reasons other than clear adultery and a broader interpretation of the word "fornication," which may include the following:

"a. Perversions of, and deviations from, a normal sex life, which either do not disappear with treatment or for which no therapy is sought. . . .

"b. Homosexual practices are recognized as a misuse of sexual powers, and disapproved in Scripture. As a violation of the divine intention in marriage, they thus become just cause for divorce.

"c. Persistent indulgence in intimate relationships with a partner of the opposite sex other than the spouse, even though falling short of coitus, is a form of unfaithfulness, bordering on actual adultery, and may be contributory to divorce" (AR Feb. 17, 1977).

Because of the biblical injunction not to be "mismated with unbelievers" (2 Cor. 6:14), Seventh-day Adventist pastors are instructed not to perform a wedding ceremony uniting in matrimony a church member with one who is not (*Seventh-day Adventist Minister's Manual* 1992, 246).

At the 1980 session of the General Conference, 27 statements of fundamental beliefs were approved. Statement 22 deals with marriage and family.

"Marriage was divinely established in Eden and affirmed by Jesus to be a lifelong union between a man and a woman in loving companionship. For the Christian a marriage commitment is to God as well as to the spouse, and should be entered into only between partners who share a common faith. Mutual love, honor, respect, and responsibility are the fabric of this relationship, which is to reflect the love, sanctity, closeness, and permanence of the relationship between Christ and His church. Regarding divorce, Jesus taught that the person who divorces a spouse, except for fornication, and marries another, commits adultery. Although some family relationships may fall short of the ideal, marriage partners who fully commit themselves to each other in Christ may achieve loving unity through the guidance of the Spirit and the nurture of the church. God blesses the family and intends that its members shall assist each other toward complete maturity. Parents are to bring up their children to love and obey the Lord. By their example and their words they are to teach them that Christ is a loving disciplinarian, ever tender and caring, who wants them to become members of His body, the family of God. Increasing family closeness is one of the earmarks of the final gospel message. (Gen. 2:18-25; Matt. 19:3-9; John 2:1-11; 2 Cor. 6:14; Eph. 5:21-33; Matt. 5:31, 32; Mark 10:11, 12; Luke 16:18; 1 Cor. 7:10, 11; Ex. 20:12; Eph. 6:1-4; Deut. 6:5-9; Prov. 22:6; Mal. 4:5, 6.)"

After repeated meetings, a special committee adopted a statement on abortion that was approved by the Annual Council of 1992 and published in the *Adventist Review* on December 31 of the same year. The statement reads, in part:

"1. Prenatal human life is a magnificent gift of God. God's ideal for human beings affirms the sanctity of human life, in God's image, and requires respect for prenatal life. However, decisions about life must be made in the context of a fallen world. Abortion is never an action of little moral consequence. Thus prenatal life must not be thoughtlessly destroyed. Abortion should be performed only for the most serious reasons.

"2. Abortion is one of the tragic dilemmas of human fallenness. The church should offer gracious support to those who personally face the decision concerning an abortion. Attitudes of condemnation are inappropriate in those who have accepted the gospel. . . .

"3. In practical, tangible ways the church as a supportive community should express its commitment to the value of human life. These ways should include: (a) strengthening family relationships, (b) educating both genders concerning Christian principles of human sexuality, (c) emphasizing responsibility of both male and female for family planning, (d) calling both to be responsible for the consequences of behaviors that are inconsistent with Christian principles, (e) creating a safe climate for ongoing discussion of the moral questions associated with abortion, (f) offering support and assistance to women who choose to complete crisis pregnancies, and (g) encouraging and assisting fathers to participate responsibly in the parenting of their children. . . .

"4. The church does not serve as conscience for individuals; however, it should provide moral guidance. Abortions for reasons of birth control, gender selection, or convenience are not condoned by the church. Women at times, however, may face exceptional circumstances that present serious moral or medical dilemmas, such as significant threats to the pregnant woman's life, serious jeopardy to her health, severe congenital defects carefully diagnosed in the fetus, and pregnancy resulting from rape or incest. The final decision whether to terminate the pregnancy or not should be made by the pregnant woman after appropriate consultation. She should be aided in her decision by accurate information, biblical principles, and the guidance of the

Holy Spirit. Moreover, these decisions are best made within the context of healthy family relationships" (AR Dec. 31, 1992).

At the same 1992 Annual Council, the statement "Care for the Dying" was approved. In part it reads as follows:

"God has given human beings freedom of choice and asks them to use their freedom responsibly. Seventh-day Adventists believe that this freedom extends to decisions about medical care. After seeking divine guidance and considering the interests of those affected by the decision (Rom. 14:7), as well as medical advice, a person who is capable of deciding should determine whether to accept or reject life-extending medical interventions. Such persons should not be forced to submit to medical treatment that they find unacceptable. . . .

"When a dying person is unable to give consent or express preferences regarding medical intervention, such decisions should be made by someone chosen by the dying person. If no one has been chosen, someone close to the dying person should make the determination. Except in extraordinary circumstances, medical or legal professionals should defer decisions about medical interventions for a dying person to those closest to that individual. Wishes or decisions of the individual are best made in writing and should be in agreement with existing legal requirements. . . .

"While Christian love may lead to the withholding or withdrawing of medical interventions that only increase suffering or prolong dying, Seventh-day Adventists do not practice "mercy killing" or assist in suicide (Gen. 9:5, 6; Ex. 20:13; 23:7). They are opposed to active euthanasia, the intentional taking of the life of a suffering or dying person" (ibid.).

In its 1988 assembly in Nairobi, Kenya, the Annual Council of the General Conference took an action against sexual misconduct by employees or volunteers working for the denomination. In all activities they are to "exemplify the Christlike life" and "avoid all appearance of wrongdoing." The church organization will not condone any type of sexual harassment. The document voted includes guiding principles and definitions and outlines the process to follow in doing justice to situations that may occur (*ibid.* Feb. 23, 1989).

IV. Ellen G. White Comments

A. *The Sanctity of Marriage*

"Polygamy had been early introduced, contrary to the divine arrangement at the beginning. The Lord gave to Adam one wife, showing His order in that respect. But after the Fall, men chose to follow their own sinful desires; and as the result, crime and wretchedness rapidly increased.

"It was Satan's studied effort to pervert the marriage institution, to weaken its obligations and lessen its sacredness; for in no surer way could he deface the image of God in man and open the door to misery and vice" (PP 91, 92, 338).

"God celebrated the first marriage. Thus the institution has for its originator the Creator of the universe. 'Marriage is honorable' (Heb. 13:4); it was one of the first gifts of God to man, and it is one of the two institutions that, after the Fall, Adam brought with him beyond the gates of Paradise.

"When the divine principles are recognized and obeyed in this relation, marriage is a blessing; it guards the purity and happiness of the race, it provides for man's social needs, it elevates the physical, the intellectual, and the moral nature" (*ibid.* 46).

"Never should God's people venture upon forbidden ground. Marriage between believers and unbelievers is forbidden by God. . . .

"The unbelieving may possess an excellent moral character, but the fact that he or she has not answered to the claims of God and has neglected so great salvation is sufficient reason why such a union should not be consummated" (AH 63).

B. *Marital Relations*

"The Lord has constituted the husband the head of the wife to be her protector; he is the house-band of the family, binding the members together, even as Christ is the head of the church and the Saviour of the mystical body" (*ibid.* 215).

"The king upon his throne has no higher work than has the mother. The mother is queen of her household. She has in her power the molding of her children's characters, that they may be fitted for the higher, immortal life. An angel could not ask for a higher mission; for in doing this work she is doing service for God. Let her only realize the high character of her task, and it will inspire her with courage" (*ibid.* 231).

"Neither the husband nor the wife should attempt to exercise over the other an arbitrary control. Do not try to compel each other to yield to your wishes. You cannot do this and retain each other's love. Be kind, patient, and forbearing, considerate, and courteous. By the grace of God you can succeed in making each other happy, as in your marriage vow you promised to do" (*ibid.* 118).

C. *Marital Influences*

"In the home the foundation is laid for the prosperity of the church. The influences that rule in the home life are carried into the church life; therefore church duties should first begin in the home" (*ibid.* 318).

"If religion is to influence society, it must first influence the home circle. If children were trained to love and fear God at home, when they go forth into the world, they would be prepared to train their own families for God, and thus the principles of truth would become implanted in society and would exert a telling influence in the world" (*ibid.*).

"A well-ordered Christian household is a powerful argument in favor of the reality of the Christian religion—an argument that the infidel cannot gainsay" (*ibid.* 36).

"The first work of Christians is to be united in the family. Then the work is to extend to their neighbors nigh and afar off. Those who have received light are to let the light shine forth in clear rays. Their words, fragrant with the love of Christ, are to be a savor of life unto life" (*ibid.* 37).

D. Child Care

"Many seem to think that the declension in the church, the growing love of pleasure, is due to want of pastoral work. . . . But ministers may do their work faithfully and well, yet it will amount to very little if parents neglect their work. It is to a lack of Christianity in the home life that the lack of power in the church is due" (CG 550).

"Parents flock with their families to the cities because they fancy it easier to obtain a livelihood there than in the country. The children, having nothing to do when not in school, obtain a street education. From evil associates they acquire habits of vice and dissipation. The parents see all this; but it will require a sacrifice to correct their error, and they stay where they are until Satan gains full control of their children" (5T 232).

"Even before the birth of the child, the preparation should begin that will enable it to fight successfully the battle against evil.

"If before the birth of her child she is self-indulgent, if she is selfish, impatient, and exacting, these traits will be reflected in the disposition of the child. Thus many children have received as a birthright almost unconquerable tendencies to evil" (AH 256).

E. General Counsel

"It is not the purpose of God that His people should colonize, or settle together in large communities. The disciples of Christ are His representatives upon the earth, and God designs that they shall be scattered all over the country, in the towns, cities, and villages, as lights amidst the darkness of the world. They are to be missionaries for God, by their faith and works testifying to the near approach of the coming Saviour" (CL 22).

"Death will not come one day sooner, brethren, because you have made your will. In dis-

posing of your property by will to your relatives, be sure that you do not forget God's cause. You are His agents, holding His property; and His claims should have your first consideration. Your wife and children, of course, should not be left destitute; provision should be made for them if they are needy. But do not, simply because it is customary, bring into your will a long line of relatives who are not needy" (AH 397).

"Parents should not increase their families any faster than they know that their children can be well cared for and educated" (*ibid.* 163).

"It is not best to establish institutions for the care of the aged, that they may be in a company together. Nor should they be sent away from home to receive care. Let the members of every family minister to their own relatives. When this is not possible, the work belongs to the church, and it should be accepted both as a duty and a privilege" (*ibid.* 363).

"The highest duty that devolves upon youth is in their own homes, blessing father and mother, brothers and sisters, by affection and true interest. Here they can show self-denial and self-forgetfulness in caring and doing for others" (*ibid.* 35).

"Those who break the seventh commandment should be suspended from the church, and not have its fellowship nor the privileges of the house of God. Said the angel, 'This is not a sin of ignorance. It is a knowing sin and will receive the awful visitation of God, whether he who commits it be old or young'" (TSB 248, 249).

"The Sabbath and the family were alike instituted in Eden, and in God's purpose they are indissolubly linked together. On this day more than on any other, it is possible for us to live the life of Eden. It was God's plan for the members of the family to be associated in work and study, in worship and recreation, the father as priest of his household, and both father and mother as teachers and companions of their children" (CG 535).

"These and other cases of Bible history

illustrate the critical nature of the mother's relationship with the child and provide the basis for Ellen White's conclusion: "The mother's work is given her of God, to bring up her children in the nurture and admonition of the Lord" (AH 233); these "distinctive duties of woman are more sacred, more holy, than those of man" (*ibid.* 231).

V. Literature

Ards, Sheila, and Adele Harrell. "Reporting of Child Maltreatment: A Secondary Analysis of the National Incidence Surveys." *Child Abuse and Neglect* 17 (May-June 1993): 337, 344.

Bacchiocchi, Samuele. *The Marriage Covenant.* Berrien Springs, Mich.: Biblical Perspectives, 1991.

Canfield, Ken. *The Seven Secrets of Effective Fathers.* Wheaton, Ill.: Tyndale, 1992.

Clark, Harriett. "Another Look at Stepfamilies." *The Harding Journal of Religion and Psychiatry* 8 (1989): 10.

Colson, Charles. "Barbarians in the Parlor." *Signs of the Times,* February 1989.

Cose, Ellis. "The Year of the Father." *Newsweek,* Oct. 31, 1994.

Dubowitz, Howard, and others. "A Follow-up of Behavior Problems Associated With Child Sexual Abuse." *Child Abuse and Neglect* 17 (November-December 1993): 743-754.

Du Preez, Ronald. "Polygamy in the Bible With Implications for Seventh-day Adventist Missiology." D.Min. Project Report, Andrews University, 1993.

Garrett, Thomas M., Harold W. Baillie, Rosellen M. Garrett, *Health Care Ethics: Principles & Problems.* Englewood Cliffs, N.Y.: Prentice Hall, 1989.

Kahn, Joan R., and Kathryn A. London. "Premarital Sex and the Risk of Divorce." *Journal of Marriage and the Family* 53 (November 1991): 845-855.

Keener, Craig. *And Marries Another: Divorce and Remarriage in the Teaching of the New Testament.* Peabody, Mass.: Hendrickson, 1993.

Koop, Charles Everett, and Timothy Johnson. *Let's Talk: An Honest Conversation on Critical Issues.* Grand Rapids: Zondervan, 1992.

Kuzma, Kay. *To Understand Your Child.* Redlands, Calif.: Parent Scene, 1985.

———. *Working Mothers and Guilt.* Boise, Idaho: Pacific Press, 1987.

Larson, David R., ed. *Abortion: Ethical Issues and Options.* Loma Linda, Calif.: Loma Linda University Center for Christian Bioethics, 1992.

Londis, James. *Abortion: Mercy or Murder?* Nashville: Southern Pub. Assn., 1980.

Louv, Richard. "The Crisis of the Absent Father." *Parents' Magazine,* July 1993.

Luther, Martin. *Luther's Large Catechism.* Trans. Friedemann Hebart. Adelaide: Lutheran Pub. House, 1983.

McMillan, Len D. *Parentwise.* Hagerstown, Md.: Review and Herald, 1993.

Shannon, Thomas, and James Walter, eds. *Quality of Life: The New Medical Dilemma.* New York: Paulist, 1990.

Small, Dwight Hervey. *Remarriage and God's Renewing Grace.* Grand Rapids: Baker, 1986.

Springett, Ronald M. *Homosexuality in History and the Scriptures.* Washington, D.C.: Biblical Research Institute, 1988.

Stott, John. *Involvement: Social and Sexual Relationships in the Modern World.* 2 vols. Old Tappan, N.J.: Fleming H. Revell, 1985.

Van Leeuwen, Mary Stewart. *Gender and Grace: Love, Work, and Parenting in a Changing World.* Downers Grove, Ill.: InterVarsity, 1990.

Van Pelt, Nancy. *The Compleat Parent.* Hagerstown, Md.: Review and Herald, 1985.

———. *Train Up a Child.* Hagerstown, Md.: Review and Herald, 1984.

Williams, David R. "Why Does Sexual Abuse Occur?" *Adventist Review,* Sept. 2, 1993.

Health and Healing

George W. Reid

Introduction

The biblical degree of interest in health and healing is underrepresented in contemporary theological and biblical studies. An adequate grasp of the subject rests on broad theological truths about God's character as expressed in creation, His dealings with humanity, His plan of salvation, and His ultimate restoration of all things. Our understanding incorporates the uniqueness of creation in God's image, the impact and consequences of sin, and how God in Christ addressed the problem of suffering, pain, and death. In a world of widespread illness and universal death, we would expect the Scriptures to address suffering and pain. As consequences of sin, both sickness and death represent anomalies in God's universe, to be coped with for the present, but destined to end in the coming triumph of Christ's kingdom.

The Scriptures present no systematic discussion of issues in health and healing, although many examples of illness and healings appear there. Especially in the ministry of Jesus we encounter repeated confrontations with sickness and demon possession. These He used as opportunities to teach lessons about God's character and purpose as well as to bring relief from suffering and demonic oppression. His ministry presents the ultimately compassionate approach to humanitarian concern, but it is more, for it opens penetrating insights into the character of both God and man. This brief article begins with Creation, tracing the biblical picture of health and healing to its summit in the work of Jesus, and concludes with His final triumph over evil, suffering, and death.

I. Creation the Basis of Well-being

A. *Origin in Creation*

1. Very Good

Although several biblical passages discuss creation in some detail, the foundational account occurs in Genesis 1 and 2. The sweeping narrative of the first chapter is followed by more specific detail in the second, where the focus turns to God and humans. (See Creation I. B.) Beginning with the separation of land from water, the Creator makes a value judgment that becomes a refrain, "It was good," culminating in the summary notation "Behold, it was very good" (Gen. 1:10, 12, 18, 21, 25, 31). God's statement is absolute, not comparative. The Scriptures present Him as by nature fully good (Ps. 100:5; 119:68), with Himself as the standard of absolute holiness (Lev. 19:2).

Today the implications of primal, complete goodness are difficult to assess because of our experience in an environment corrupted by sin. But the model of original goodness underlies the whole of biblical theology, with substantial consequences that guide Christian understanding of the world and its functions. The Scriptures present a first condition in which the entire creation resonated with God. Into an environment free from disjunction, conflict, predation, or any element alien to His purpose, the Creator introduced humans, creatures uniquely capable of intimate association with Him. His world was a planet of great complexity, organized in an integrated harmony in which humans and all nature united to achieve divine ideals. Any reasoned assessment of biblical teachings about health and healing must be seen against this backdrop.

2. *Imago Dei*

The forming of humans was God's crowning creative act. Of all earthly creatures, only they were designated as "in our image, after our likeness" (Gen. 1:26). "So God created man in his own image, in the image of God he created him, male and female he created them" (verse 27). By using "image" and "likeness" in parallel, the writer conveys both outward physical resemblance and inward character, a literary form found also in Genesis 5:1-3, where we are told of Adam, "He became the father of a son in his own likeness, after his image, and named him Seth."

What does it mean to be in the image and likeness of God? Because of its impact on many areas of theology, this question has been long debated. At the very least it describes a high-level correlation between God and man, paralleled dimly in human terms by the relationship between parents and their children. Being created in the image of God means that humans share vital qualities granted them in a gift from God, without compromising, however, the distinction between Creator and creation. Foremost among them are an ability to relate to God and His purposes, freedom to make moral choices, the capacity to make abstractions, and an advanced intellect strikingly superior to that of the animals, all set in a balance where each component functions well. The biblical narrative assures us that in its original state mankind stood in harmony with the character of God, sharing an identity later lost with the entrance of sin.

3. Specific Provisions

The Genesis creation account intrigues us with its blend of sweeping general statements in combination with specific details. In deliberate steps God forms Adam and breathes into his nostrils the breath of life (Gen. 2:7). Immediately God makes specific assignments, formulating a structure of exact duties as He inaugurates human custody over His world. A specific social relationship is established in which the man will leave his parental home to join in one-flesh unity with his wife, creating new families designed to extend and populate the earth. The seventh day is set aside as recurring dedicated time, a perpetual tribute to and reminder of God and His work as Creator. A profound sense of intimacy exists between Creator and creature. Among His first instructions, God institutes a specific vegetarian diet limited to the products of seed-bearing plants and trees, to which are added immediately after the fall of Adam and Eve the plants themselves (Gen. 1:29; 3:18). Although not specifically labeled as such, these provisions initiated a stable and ideal spiritual, social, mental, and physical environment as a pattern for the future. No provision was needed for what today are called health issues.

The Creation narrative introduces us to a manner of teaching common to the Scriptures, illustration and example rather than definition and argument. Success and failure, both physical and moral, appear in episodes from the lives of real people, seen from an inspired perspective. God reveals Himself in terms that recognize and accept both the physical and spiritual. Humans are uniquely related to God, their person being expressed in spiritual,

physical, mental, and social modes. The original world comes into existence with optimum goodness in all these modes. By divine design, both God and humans function freely in the economy of a pristine new planet.

B. The Impact of Sin

By exercising their ability to violate directly God's instructions, the man and woman not only acted in a self-driven way, but plunged themselves and their world into cataclysm, radically altering both their persons and their environment as their full harmony with the Creator ended. (See Sin III. B.)

The Scriptures teach that sin originated outside the plan of God (Eze. 28:14-16). By vesting creatures with freedom God introduced an element of risk. However, through this means He made it possible for humans to return an intelligent loving response to Him. In no sense can the misuse of the power of choice, by either angels or humans, be interpreted as divine approval of their decisions.

In the Bible sin is treated as a distorting state of violation against God, destined to be finally removed. Satan is the promoter of sin (2 Cor. 2:11), which by sly deception he introduced into the human family. Both sin and he as its originator will perish together (Matt. 25:41; Rev. 20:10, 14). These core parts of biblical cosmology explain the presence of suffering, sickness, pain, and death in the world. The devastating impact of sin damaged the original harmony, not only between God and man, but among humans themselves, both internally and interpersonally, and indeed in all nature (Rom. 8:22-25). Its consequence would be a tragic fall, the entire world slipping into a mixed existence in which even the remains of the good and pleasureful would be clouded by decline and decay, plagued by pain, grief, sickness, and suffering, and finally, consumed in universal death and disintegration.

With the coming of sin, its consequences appeared immediately. Former innocence and trust fell away. In poignant simplicity the text observes, "Then the eyes of both were opened" (Gen. 3:7). Nakedness produced embarrassment, and fear of facing God in the light of their deed led them to hide from Him (verse 8). And they offered defensive excuses (verses 12, 13). The original relationship was broken. In a series of judgments the Lord God outlined a new order, first the curse upon the serpent as the pawn of Satan, then judgments on the woman and man. For the first time pain appears in the biblical text, at childbirth, from the very beginning of every new human.

The relationship between husband and wife changed, with the benign standing conferred by primacy upon Adam (1 Tim. 2:13) taking on a new form. In a world now hazardous, inhospitable, and often adversarial, humans must wrest their livelihood from a hostile, toil-ridden ground. God assigned new responsibilities to Adam as provider, protector, advocate, and self-sacrificing leader of the family (Gen. 3:16-19; Eph. 5:25, 28). To the errant man the Lord God pronounced his fate: "In the sweat of your face you shall eat bread till you return to the ground, for out of it you were taken; you are dust, and to dust you shall return" (Gen. 3:19). God's warning that sin would result in death (Gen. 2:17), although by grace deferred in time, came into effect.

From this point forward vast changes would invade the world and consequently the human experience. Among them would come a plethora of disastrous consequences, beginning with spiritual separation from God, bringing dissatisfaction, fear, loss of meaning, loneliness, and despair, coupled with physical decline and sickness. Social alienation appeared among persons and groups, soon to lead to fratricide (Gen. 4), mistrust, inward stress and malaise of spirit, physical pain, suffering, sickness, and in the end, death. Each became a sickness to cry out for healing.

Lest the magnitude of such sorrows wholly overwhelm the man and woman, God followed condemnation of the serpent (and the evil one who manipulated it) with the first promise of human redemption (Gen. 3:15). From among the descendants of the woman would come a deliverer who, although Himself suffering the consequences of sin, would deal the fatal blow to end the career of the deceiver, Satan, who instigated it. At sin's first appearance in Eden the Lord God provided to the grieving couple the gospel's assurance of His healing presence and salvation to come.

C. The Nature of Health: The Biblical Foundation

1. Biblical Terminology

The reason modern translations of the Bible seldom use the word "health" (the RSV uses it only six times) can be ascribed not to its absence from the Scriptures but to wide differences between ancient and modern understandings of what is meant by "health," which led to the choice of other words. Although biblical Hebrew has names for more than 80 body parts, it lacks a clear term for body. Nearest to the modern sense is *gĕvîyah,* which occurs 13 times in the Hebrew Bible, almost always with extended meanings. It refers to dead bodies (eight times) or figures in dreams (three times). The Hebrew mind did not think of the human being as a purely physical object, nor could health be characterized primarily as a physical condition. Material from which the body is made is expressed in the word *bāsār,* the physical substance of the human body and commonly translated as "flesh" (Num. 8:7 [KJV]; 1 Kings 21:27; Job 4:15), but the word refers to components, not the total body itself.

Modern translations render several Hebrew words with the English word "health," often mingled with the idea of healing, and typically in ways that appear to the modern reader to carry a poetic sense, such as the Isaiah 58:8 promise to repentant Israel, "Your healing shall spring up speedily," and "Why then has the health of the daughter of my people not been restored?" (Jer. 8:22). Other Hebrew words occasionally translated "health" are *yĕšû'āh,* which carries the thought of safety or security, *'arûkāh,* with its sense of lengthening or prolongation, *marpē',* with the root meaning of healing, and *šālôm,* which will be treated below. Greek words include *hugiainō,* "to be in good health" (3 John 2) and *sōtēria,* usually translated in the NT by other words such as safety, deliverance, or salvation.

2. Biblical Concepts of Health

In modern times health is described largely in physical terms relating to the body, although it may be broadened somewhat in a term such as mental health or used occasionally in a figurative sense. Even mental health or mental illness increasingly is described in terms of response to biochemical functions within the body. Such reductive confinement to the physical alone is alien to the biblical understanding of health.

In general, contemporary society thinks of health and its care as the domain of science, concentrated in the physical, described and, where necessary, treated as a function of nature. Methods shown to be effective in science are applied to the human body in a way that, conforming to the canons of modern science, usually excludes the supernatural from consideration. Current practice acknowledges that emotional and social environments affect human health, but the primary concerns are physical and natural, with solutions to problems addressed largely through laboratory and pharmaceuticals. In contrast, the biblical approach not only acknowledges divine involvement beyond nature, but makes that involvement central.

As defined by the World Health Organization, health is "a state of complete physical, mental, and social well-being, and not merely the absence of disease or infirmity." Although it allows for certain breadth, as a secular statement it fails to approach the global inclusiveness that characterizes the biblical picture, and omits the central role of God.

The Bible understands health as full integration. From its point of view health reaches beyond the physical into every aspect of life, being the harmonious function of the person—bodily, emotionally, spiritually, and socially. Physically, such a definition does not require total freedom from disease in every part, or deny the normal aging that weakens stamina. But it requires inclusiveness.

Health in the Bible, particularly as developed in the Hebrew Scriptures, takes its identity first from the continuing relationship between God and fallen humankind. The effects of humanity's fall are severe, not only in physical separation from God, but in altering the basic motives of humans to render them self-centered and by nature oriented toward evil. "The heart is deceitful above all things, and desperately corrupt; who can understand it?" (Jer. 17:9). "Also the hearts of men are full of evil" (Eccl. 9:3). Paul's struggle against the evil within him provides an example of sin's impact on both judgment and moral values, even in a committed Christian (Rom. 7:15-20).

Health in the OT falls into four broad categories, (1) a state of wholeness and fulfillment, (2) integrated harmony with God and His law, (3) as righteousness—including a right relationship with God and neighbor, and (4) physically in the sense of strength, the ability to achieve, fulfilled in long life. The first will be addressed in a succeeding section. (See I. E.) In some passages the OT describes health in terms of a condition of harmony with God's will, particularly as expressed in His law *(torah).* Active loyalty to and conformity with the law means health (Ps. 119:165; Jer. 7:23). Harmony with God's law brings protection from disease (Ex. 15:26; 23:20-26; Deut. 7:12-15; Prov. 3:7, 8). In contrast, disobedience brings judgment (Lev. 26:14-16; Deut. 28:59), as in the experience with serpents (Num. 21:4-8) and the cases of Miriam (Num. 12:1-15) and Gehazi (2 Kings 5:27). In other places the Bible equates health with righteousness (Heb. *ṣedeq* or *ṣedāqāh*), in the sense of conformity to divine norms. The basic norm is God's character, therefore a right relationship to God's character produces *šālôm* (Isa. 32:17). Yet another OT concept equates health with strength and well-being. David is the man of valor, the very demonstration of good health. Moses dies with his faculties intact (Deut. 34:7), and Joseph lives to 110 years of age (Gen. 50:26), all cited examples of robust health. The texts have in mind more than physical vigor, but a completely integrated being that springs from faithfulness to God. Alongside strength, the OT describes health in terms of longevity, particularly in reference to the patriarchs (Gen. 5). Strength is the gift of God (Ps. 29:7-9), but the meaning extends beyond the physical to include all aspects of life. Long life is promised to the obedient, personally and collectively (Deut. 6:2; 30:20; 1 Kings 3:14; Ps. 34:12-14). As could be expected, poor health is weakness, which becomes a term for sickness and disease.

D. Shalom

The Bible treats essence and form as inseparable. Life is a matter of the whole person, undivided, characterized by the Hebrew word *šālôm*. Although popularly limited today to a word for peace, its use in the Bible is much broader, conveying the foundational meaning of total personal well-being. Along with its related term, *šālēm,* it conveys a sense of "healthy," or whole. *Šālôm* appears nearly 240 times in the Bible (with its derivatives, more than 350 times). It is especially common in the Psalms, Isaiah, and Jeremiah. Of its many occurrences, only 38 times is it used for peace as contrasted to war.

Lexicographers' definitions include completeness, soundness, good welfare, prosperity, well-being, harmony between or among parties, and harmony within oneself. At its root lies the idea of wholeness, completeness, or integrated well-being. Its orientation is captured in the expression "may you be well," taken in the broad sense of "may everything in your experience be satisfying." Inherent in this word is the idea of integration, wholeness, and organized sufficiency, a dynamic condition of well-being, including but surpass-

ing the modern idea of "health." In the Scriptures *šālôm* incorporates every aspect of life, including the physical, mental, spiritual, and social, whether individually, collectively, or nationally (Gen. 29:6; 43:27, 28).

In contrast to the modern idea of "peace" as a state of passive inactivity—a lack of movement, in Hebrew usage *šālôm* carries a sense of active, dynamic wholeness and satisfaction that displaces its negative opposites. *Šālôm* may express an untroubled state of mind, a tranquillity that stems from acceptance with God (Lev. 26:6), but that peace is not achieved easily, for it strikes at the heart of the human a natural inclination to compromise with wrong. Ultimately *šālôm* comes to a cosmic fulfillment, an ultimate unity of all things in perfect harmony with the Creator.

The physical side of man is included. The earliest use of *šālôm* in the Bible occurs in a health-oriented setting where Jacob inquires about the *šālôm* of Laban, the grandson of Abraham's brother, Nahor (Gen. 29:5, 6). It appears in connection with Hezekiah's illness and healing (Isa. 38:17), and in Proverbs 3:2 obedience to God's law is associated with long life and *šālôm*. On the basis of *šālôm*'s breadth of meaning, the biblical idea of health, while including the physical state, extends through every aspect of human experience. God alone can provide *šālôm,* harking back to His original provision of total well-being in Creation. Despite the intrusion of sin, to those who serve Him He offers a covenant of *šālôm* (Num. 25:12; Isa. 54:10; Jer. 32:40; Eze. 34:25). But there can be no *šālôm* for the wicked, for that person is at odds with God (Isa. 48:22; 57:21; 59:8).

Drawing from its OT roots, the message of *šālôm* became foundational in the Christian faith, with its enhanced emphasis on Christ's reconciling us to God as the basis of true peace. As Jesus said, "Peace I leave with you; my peace I give to you; not as the world gives do I give to you" (John 14:27). Paul joins in the theme, "Therefore, since we are justified by faith, we have peace with God through our

Lord Jesus Christ" (Rom. 5:1). "For he is our peace" (Eph. 2:14). Defined in the sense of *šālôm,* health becomes a full, integrated state in which all elements of a person are in harmony with one another. Inner contentment, stemming from peace with God, other persons, and one's environment, combines with cooperating physical functions to produce true wellness.

E. Wholeness

The biblical message presents all reality as bound together in a single multifaceted unity centered on God. Therefore there can be no secular, fragmentary cosmology. Despite rebellion against Him by some of His creatures, the Bible knows of no element or entity apart from or not responsible to the Creator. Elements may be sacred or profane, but never secular. Within this setting, at creation humanity emerges from the hand of God as a new, distinct order, different and separate from the animals (Gen. 1:26, 27, 31). From that point throughout biblical history humans both are and are treated as unified, fully integrated persons (Gen. 5:1, 2; Ps. 8:3-5; 139:13-17; 1 Cor. 6:15; 3 John 2; 2 Peter 1:3, 4).

Such unity is manifested in the form and function of the human body, with its intricate structure and physiological action that, when operating properly, sustains health. Such wholeness is important to both health and healing, providing a biblically oriented ground for preserving good physical health and a basis for restorative therapeutics. A person consists of elements that include but reach beyond the physical body. Both the emotional and spiritual elements interact with the physical to produce the whole. Seeing each person in this broad sense not only is in harmony with the biblical understanding but establishes a unique Christian approach to healing, distinguished from the kind of health care limited to the physical body. Throughout the Scriptures a person is dealt with in terms of unity, free from the body versus soul duality.

F. Etiology of Illness

1. The Incidence of Sickness

The OT begins with an original high quality of life conferred by the Creator, which sets forth the kind of abundant wellness He intended human beings to enjoy. Possibly a residual benefit lingering from that initial condition is reflected in the fact that the OT deals more with health, the NT more with healing. Jesus and the apostles lived among people upon whom some thousands of years had taken their toll.

Biblical records of the early patriarchs are biographical, capsulized reports of the lives of people who lived in the period between the fall into sin and the Exodus. Although the narrative includes hundreds of details, there is no report of illness among the antediluvians and precious few prior to the Exodus. Repeatedly the narrator uses the formula "All the days of this or that person were . . . and he died." These reports, admittedly condensed, include few reports of final illness or physical incapacity, which suggests that either the narrator was wholly uninterested in such things or the problem of severe and extended illness was not yet a pressing one. While such evidence may not be conclusive, it is compatible with the premise that the stamina of the original humans was transmitted in a declining pattern from generation to generation. The pattern of ages at death among the patriarchs supports this suggestion.

What kinds of physical sickness are included in the OT reports? The most common include opthalmic, especially blindness, of which there are several reports. Blindness may come as a divine visitation (Ex. 4:11; 2 Kings 6:18) but in other instances not so. Interestingly, there are no specific Pentateuchal hygienic enactments for the eyes, although general hygienic provisions would have offered certain protections. Following the Exodus there are occasional reports of sicknesses and disabilities of hearing or speech. Curiously, at the time of Israel's settlement in Palestine lefthandedness appears to have been regarded as a crippling disorder (Judges 3:15; 20:16; LXX *amphoterodeios*), bypassed, however, by God to deliver Israel from Moab (Judges 3:15-30).

Cutaneous problems are reported, including itch (Lev. 13:30, 39), boils (Ex. 9:9-11), scurvy (Lev. 21:20; Deut. 28:27), and leprosy (Lev. 13), which today is thought not to have been Hansen's disease. Several reports speak of plagues (Heb. *maggephāh*, LXX *sunantēma*) such as those in Egypt (Ex. 9:14), and among the Philistines (1 Sam. 6:4); however, the generalized meaning of the term broadens its application.

Extra-biblical sources, such as the Ebers papyrus (66 feet [20 meters] long with 877 sections in 10 columns), provide us with substantial reports of diseases and treatment in Egypt, both before and during the time of Moses. In fact, Western rational medicine can trace much of its current methodology to Egyptian practices dating as early as the third millennium B.C., which, especially in the Ptolemaic period, became incorporated into Greek healing praxis. In an early promise to His people, the Lord pledged to deliver them from the diseases of Egypt if they were obedient (Ex. 15:26), but threatened to place disease upon the people if disobedient (Deut. 28:60).

As they report the activities of Jesus the Gospels present a wide array of illnesses. Blindness (Mark 8:22-26; 10:46-52), leprosy (Matt. 8:2, 3; Mark 1:40; Luke 4:27), paralysis (Matt. 9:2; Mark 2:3; Luke 5:18, *paralelumenos,* perhaps a paraplegic condition), and repeated cases of demonic activity are among the best known. (See II. D.) A major portion of Jesus' ministry dealt with sickness.

Across the ancient pagan world disease was attributed to supernatural causes, which normally were combated with sorcery and magic. By contrast, in the Scriptures sickness is described as from only a few basic sources: (1) divine visitation (Deut. 28:27-29), (2) an adversarial devil (Job 2:7; Mark 9:17), (3) decline accompanying age (Gen. 27:1; 1 Sam. 3:2;

4:15), and (4) accident (2 Sam. 4:4; 2 Kings 1:2; 4:18-20).

The Bible does not encourage a purely naturalistic theory of disease. Because health and illness impact the whole person, not merely the physical component, the biblical understanding acknowledges a spiritual element in what today are defined as pathological causes of disease. God is the great physician-restorer (Deut. 32:39). Recovery is to be found in Him; therefore cooperation with Him tends toward prosperity of body and spirit (Ex. 15:26).

In harmony with widespread ancient practice, specific functions were symbolically assigned to specific organs, e.g., the heart as the seat of feelings and value judgments. Therefore the Lord speaks of full-spectrum healing in terms of providing a "new heart" (Eze. 18:31). In the Scriptures, however, the Egyptian/Greek classical humoral theory of cause and diagnosis is notably absent. Although we hear of the head and the mind, the brain as an organ never is mentioned in the Scriptures, despite the fact that Egyptian medicine was well acquainted with it. Infantile disease is only nominally noticed in the Scriptures, although exceptions may be found (2 Sam. 12:15; 1 Kings 17:17; 2 Kings 4:18-37). The most systematic description of disease and treatment to be found in the Bible appears in Leviticus 13.

2. God as Cause of Sickness

Repeatedly the Scriptures describe God as the cause of sickness (Lev. 26:14-16; Num. 12:9-15; Deut. 28:20-22, 27, 29, 35, 59-61; 1 Sam. 5:6-12; 25:37, 38; 2 Sam. 12:15; 1 Kings 13:4; 2 Kings 5:27; Job 5:17, 18; Ps. 38:1-8; 106:15; Isa. 10:16; 30:26; Jer. 16:3, 4; Hosea 5:13–6:2). Since this article attributes sickness to a consequence of sin (see I. B), the result confronts the reader with difficulty. The problem appears in a new light, however, by recognizing that in the Scriptures no event ever takes place in God's absence. From this viewpoint whatever happens to persons, nature, or otherwise, is seen in the light of God's presence, although by no means does this imply His initiation.

From this perspective Bible writers can attribute to God things that happen within His domain, even when those events represent the activities of devils who He allows to continue until the final judgment (Rev. 20:7-10). To say God permits such activities or releases forces that bring evil may be helpful but fails to address all the elements involved. Without compromising God's sovereignty, Bible writers proceed also to assign all manner of evils to their originators, Satan and his fallen angels. In the case of Job, for example, God clearly holds the dominant role, but Satan acts also within the limits of what God permits (Job 1:6-12; 2:1-7).

3. Personal Sin as Cause of Illness

While in overall terms sickness is the result of sin, which was introduced in Eden, it is clear that sickness may follow as a consequence of personal or corporate sin (Lev. 26:14-16; Ps. 41:3, 4; 107:17-20). Biblical examples include the case of Miriam (Num. 12), and David's anguished cry in Psalm 38, where he laments, "There is no soundness in my flesh because of thy indignation; there is no health in my bones because of my sin" (verse 3).

Although the background reason always is the presence of sin in the world, the Bible requires no inevitable tie between personal sin and sickness. At times sickness comes upon the "blameless and upright," which are the words God used in His character description of Job (Job 1:8). Theologically, Job's experience challenges the premise that suffering can be interpreted uniformly as the result of personal sin. A second report is that of Hezekiah's grave illness, which the text does not attribute to any wrong he had done (2 Kings 20). Jesus' disciples wrestled with this question in a discussion about a man blind from birth, to which Jesus responded in essence, neither his nor his parents' sins had caused his blindness (John 9:1-3).

In the background of Jesus' healing ministry was the rabbinical assertion that sickness is evidence of sin. As an idea that grew in the postexilic period, its rigor was mollified by Ben Sirach's acceptance of intervention by physicians (Ecclesiasticus 38:1-15). By the time of Jesus the concept had been elaborated in a series of cause-and-consequence teachings. Sickness and sin came to be thought of in virtually interchangeable terms. Religious leaders connected certain sins with specific outcomes: immorality and licentiousness produced ulcers and dropsy; neglect of tithes produced quinsy (inflammation of the throat). Blasphemy, bloodshed, and perjury could induce the dreaded leprosy, and epilepsy could be evidence of marital infidelity, either of the person or an ancestor. In an extreme, some held that the sins of children yet in utero could result in specific conditions or sicknesses.

While acknowledging the cause and effect principle, Jesus refused to apply it in all cases (John 9:1-3; Luke 13:1-5). One's behavior may in fact bring destructive illness to the person; however, the existence of such conditions is not necessarily evidence of a specific sin. These principles, while discussed here in terms of the person, apply also in a collective sense to groups, even nations. A people that chooses to depart from God can expect to suffer dire consequences, whether in distress of soul, invasion by enemies, devastating disease, famine, or other aftereffects. This theme, explicit in Deuteronomy (28:25-29), is echoed among the prophets in their appeals for Israel to return to God alone.

4. Magic and Disease

Although some scholars argue that the biblical belief in angels and demons and their involvement in sickness or recovery represents a form of magic, the argument is seriously flawed. Angels and demons appear widely in the Scriptures where no sort of magical situation is implied. The apocalyptic worldview of the Bible differs markedly from a magical view in which the gods and all other powers are forces to be manipulated and exploited for present benefit or to hinder enemies. There is no evidence of such in either the Old or New Testaments.

Because in the ancient pagan world demonic activity was believed to be the cause of accidents and disease, the remedy of choice was a preventive resort to magical means, or if stricken, a magical cure. Among the Hebrews the practice of magic was discounted and, with the establishment of the nation of Israel, strictly forbidden (Gen. 41:1-8; Ex. 7–9; Lev. 19:26-28; Num. 22; 1 Sam. 28; 2 Kings 21:6; Isa. 2:6; Jer. 14:14; 27:9; Eze. 13:17, 18). In the Scriptures magicians are enemies, at times peppered with ironic taunts about their inabilities. In the Bible only a few incidents seem to approach the magical, such as the incident with the bones of Elisha (2 Kings 13:21). Certain scholars have identified the sudden deaths of Ananias and Sapphira (Acts 5:5-10) as quasimagical, but the text bears no suggestion of magic; the two die by immediate judgments of God. More problematic are reports of healing by means of Peter's shadow (Acts 5:15) and the employment of pieces of cloth in Paul's ministry (Acts 19:12). These are presented, however, not as works of magic, but as the employment of symbolic means to vindicate the work of the prophet or apostle, and to confirm faith. Given the prevalence of magic in the ancient Near East, the Bible is unique in rejecting it as a prevention or cure for sickness and disease.

II. Healing in the Scriptures

A. Biblical Terms for Healing

Contrary to modern usage, which confines healing largely to the physical, the wholistic sense that pervades both the OT and NT requires that all aspects of the human experience are subject to healing, not the body alone. This breadth is illustrated in several Hebrew and Greek terms translated "heal" or "healing." The most common Hebrew term, *rāphā'* (36 times), means to heal or repair, often in the broader sense of relief from inner tensions, or reconciliation and restoration.

G. In Retrospect

In the exploration of the biblical narrative relating to primal health and its loss in the fall of humanity, several basic principles emerge. First is that the elements of health relate to the Creator, and harmony with His plan underlies human well-being. The decline of health and its bitter end in death follow as direct consequences of sin.

Two additional principles become clear, the first relating to the nature of humanity. The human is a creature of remarkable complexity, yet expressed in unity, and is treated as such in the Scriptures. Powerful ties bind physical, emotional, spiritual, intellectual, and social characteristics into one interactive whole. Diversity functions as one. Both elements play fundamental roles in maintenance of ideal health. While the contemporary tendency toward specialization underscores diversity, the biblical emphasis on the wholeness of the healthy person contributes to a Christian understanding of health.

An additional observation is of interest, to note the close affinity between maintenance of health and the divine presence. At times the two coalesce in scriptural passages in language so nearly identical that the passages may refer either to health or to God's acceptance of us.

'Arûkāh brings the concept of healing in the sense of lengthening, or prolongation, as in contrast to shortening life. *Yᵉšû'āh* implies the safety aspect of God's care, and *marpē'* often means healing in the sense of bringing satisfaction where there has been distress. *Tᵉ'ālāh* suggests strength in contrast to *ḥālāh,* weakness. And *šālôm* often bears the sense of wholistic health, as "Art thou in health, my brother?" (2 Sam. 20:9, KJV).

At times the NT Greek terms parallel nuances from the Hebrew Scriptures, however with certain differences. Most common are *therapeuō,* whose earlier meaning of caring for another developed in Koine Greek, to "cure," usually in a physical sense. It is used commonly in the Synoptics and the book of Acts for miraculous healings. *Iaomai,* to cure or restore, is similar to *therapeuō;* however, it had both medical and figurative uses as early as Homer. *Hygiainō,* basis of the English word "hygiene" carried the sense of shrewd, capable, of sound mind, and good functioning order in the general state of one's being. Frequently the LXX used this word for *šālôm.* Used especially in the Gospels and Pastoral Epistles, *hygiainō* has a broad meaning that refers to the profound healing of the whole person. The participle, *hygiainōn,* tells us that the father received his returning prodigal son "safe and sound" (Luke 15:27). The Greek verb, *sōzō,* brings the idea of save, preserve, or rescue. From the same root comes *sōteria,* often translated as salvation, deliverance, or preservation. Sixteen times *sōteria* occurs in the Gospels with a sense of deliverance in order to heal the whole being. It is used for both healing and salvation (Luke 19:9; Acts 27:34).

B. God the Healer

Repeatedly the Bible attributes healing to God alone (Ex. 15:26; Deut. 7:15; 32:39; 1 Kings 13:6; Job 5:17,18; Ps. 41:3, 4; 107:17-20; 147:3; Isa. 30:26; Jer. 30:17; 33:6; Hosea 5:13–6:2), not remotely, but in an highly personal sense. Thus, immediately after crossing the Red Sea, Yahweh makes with His people a special covenant commitment, "If you will diligently hearken to the voice of the Lord your God, and do that which is right in his eyes, and give heed to his commandments and keep all his statutes, I will put none of the diseases upon you which I put upon the Egyptians, for I am the Lord, your healer" (Ex. 15:26).

Six centuries later He spoke with passion to His covenanted people, reminding them of His deliverance and pledge:

"When Israel was a child, I loved him, and out of Egypt I called my son. The more I called them, the more they went from me. . . .Yet it was I who taught Ephraim to walk, I took them up in my arms; but they did not know that I healed them; I led them with cords of compassion, with the bands of love, and I became to them as one who eases the yoke on their jaws, and I bent down to them and fed them" (Hosea 11:1-4).

Prior to the Exile the Lord pleaded with His straying people to return and be healed (Jer. 3:22), promising restoration (Jer. 30:17-22). These texts, as so many others, treat healing in its broad sense of full reconciliation to God, as does Malachi when he foresees the day of the Lord as a time of healing (Mal. 4:1-3).

Although the Bible's first concern lies with the people of the covenant, Israel, it harbors also a persistent strand of universal care. The sojourner who elects to join with Israel in serving God is to receive circumcision as a covenantal sign and join in the community with the Hebrew (Ex. 12:48, 49). The sojourner is specifically included in the Sabbath commandment (Ex. 20:8), and explicitly included in the law (Lev. 24:22; Num. 9:14), welcomed to participate in offerings before the Lord (Num. 15:14; Isa. 56:6-8), and although with certain distinctions, to participate in the advantages provided by God. The covenant healing becomes theirs as well. All humanity, His children by creation, may receive His acceptance and healing power. Even Egypt, that pariah judged of God, can be healed of its past and welcomed in the worship of God (Isa. 19:19).

1. The Psalms of Sickness and Healing

As observed, the Scriptures present God alone as healer. Decline and sickness are defined broadly, not merely as a product of but in the sense of alienation from God, hence the solution is reconciliation with Him as the originator and sole continuing source of well-being. Recovery, then follows repentance, forgiveness, and an outreach by the hand of God, certainly in physical terms but also in the spiritual and relational. He presents Himself to His people Israel in a statement, "I am the Lord, your healer" (Ex. 15:26). While including physical healing, the broader meaning is obvious.

The psalms of sickness and healing bring a picture of repentance and healing forgiveness. Psalms 6, 38, 41, 88, and 102 deal almost wholly with the healing theme, and others, including 31, 32, 71, and 91, include such passages. Isaiah 38 presents the confession psalm of Hezekiah. Through confessions, laments, appeals, and expressions of confidence they look beyond human help to the Creator for succor. In these psalms the afflicted persons confess their wrongs, acknowledging that God is disciplining them. Therefore their appeals reach out not only for physical recovery, but for vindication, deliverance that bursts into thanksgiving and joy, lifting up a living testimony to what God will do for those who come to Him.

2. Creation and Healing

Healing is best thought of in terms of restoration to that original good condition. Any human act that enhances return to original goodness is then in harmony with the purpose of God. The English words "heal" and "whole" share a common etymology, just as *salvus,* the Latin word for salvation, appears again in the English word "salve." The Creator has priority, the creature being always in a derivative and dependent status. As such the human is always a steward, and self-sufficiency becomes primal sin. This concept permeates the biblical record. In presenting Himself as the healer, God then is true to His original purpose in creating the world. (See I. A. 1.)

3. Healing in Nature

The healing capacity in nature is clearly evident. It is an intrinsic function implanted by the Creator, a kind of residual "wisdom" in nature through which He brings repair and relief to a sin-damaged creation. This healing capacity is an expression of God's activity, although naturalistic philosophy assigns it to purely natural function. Ambrose Pare's pithy saying "I dress the wound, God heals it" describes accurately the biblical understanding of recovery shared by God and humans.

Based on the premise that the Creator functions in an orderly way, natural laws are drawn up, based on observations about how God works throughout all nature. Natural laws, then, are descriptive, not causative. Properly understood, natural laws provide normative guidelines by which God's healing power can be applied. This principle means that by respecting natural laws the believer cooperates with God in the prevention of disease and in recovery from it. In that sense, natural laws, become a kind of divinely appointed law that, along with moral laws, expresses His will. Since He is the healer, recovery brought about through the function of natural law is an expression of His healing power. The inward capacity to regenerate and to resist invasive organisms becomes a part of His plan for healing and restoration. Scientific discoveries and a developing pharmacopia therefore are legitimate parts of God's healing. The Bible accepts the function of God's natural laws and encourages cooperation with them (Ps. 19; Rom. 1:19, 20; Heb 1:1, 2).

C. Kinds of Healings in the Scriptures

The OT reports comparatively few instances of physical healings, although all through its books the Lord reminds His people of His healing grace in the wider sphere. For the repentant He heals the sin that separates man from God (Ps. 107:17-22), as well as sorrows, bitterness, regrets, loneliness, distrust, alienation from Him and from one another, despair, lost sense of self-value, in fact the entire range of problems common to our fallen state. His healing applies to nations as well (Ex. 23:22-25; Lev. 26:14-21; Deut. 7:15).

The first recorded physical healing is that of God's restoration of Abimelech's wives after he returned Sarah to Abraham (Gen. 20:18). Others follow in a variety of circumstances. When Saul was deposed for his failure to follow God, the Spirit of God was withdrawn and replaced with an evil spirit from Yahweh

(1 Sam. 16:14), for which David's music on the lyre became therapeutic (verse 23). Through Elijah God healed the widow's son (1 Kings 17). Through Elisha the Lord resurrected the Shunammite's son (2 Kings 4), and Naaman the Syrian was healed of leprosy (2 Kings 5). The case of Hezekiah's recovery involved the use of a therapeutic measure in the form of a poultice (Isa. 38:16-21). These few instances virtually exhaust the historical reports of miraculous healings in the OT, which stands in contrast with the numerous reports in the Gospels.

In the OT God's healings and judgments provide evidence of His control of history. Frequent divine interventions are reported, the nearest to a healing in the NT sense being deliverance in Daniel (Dan. 3:1-25; 6:27) and Nebuchadnezzar's recovery (Dan. 4:34-36). Signs and wonders in the OT concentrate on the destiny of God's covenant people, but Messianic passages in Isaiah (Isa. 35:3-6; 53; 61:1-3; 63:1) and other books foresee the ministry of healing to come in the Messiah. Bodily healings become a prominent feature of the NT, particularly in the ministry of Jesus, but continuing in the apostolic church.

D. Jesus' Healing Ministry

Healings by Jesus constitute by far the largest direct discussion of the subject found in the Scriptures. While preserving the broader OT emphasis on healing as forgiveness and reconciliation, in the NT Jesus enters into direct confrontation with sickness and suffering, and the evil powers behind them, repeatedly triumphing over them. Jesus' ministry reflects a broader healing, delivering persons physically, and also from sin and guilt. In the NT a stronger emphasis on physical healing appears. Suffering, often seen as oppression rather than punishment, is no longer to be endured as a consequence of humanity's fall, but something to be rebuked. Jesus' intervention is intentional, intrusive, and potent.

1. Reports of His Healings

Roughly calculated, approximately 20 percent of the Gospels is dedicated to healings and their consequences. If we should classify the material of the Gospels as narrative or discourse, the reports dealing with healing being narrative, a surprising one third deals with healings. Although in some cases duplication occurs, the four Gospels report 41 accounts of specific healings, alongside general reports, such as "And he went about all Galilee, teaching in their synagogues and preaching the gospel of the kingdom and healing every disease and every infirmity among the people" (Matt. 4:23). On this basis Jesus could be thought of as principally an itinerant healer, but His joint teaching and healing renders such a description oversimplified. All four Gospels portray Him as a healer, usually in conformity with a pattern. First, the need is described; then Jesus intervenes, often with dialogue with the seeker or opponents; third, the healing occurs, followed by acclamation by onlookers, especially in Luke.

All four Gospels place Jesus' work in the setting of a cosmic war against Satan, being from the beginning of His ministry an engagement in personal struggle to the death. At its end Satan enters into Judas Iscariot, through whom he brings to a climax his contest with Jesus. Jesus characterized his opponent as "the ruler of this world" (John 14:30), and the evil one to be cast out (John 12:31). In fact, the gospel story makes little sense apart from this cosmic struggle.

The record of Jesus' healings varies according to the special focus of each book. Mark, for example, reports four castings out of demons (Mark 1:23-28; 5:1-20; 7:24-30; 9:14-29), eight healings: fever (1:29-31); leper (1:40-45); paralytic (2:1-12); withered hand (3:1-6); hemorrhage (5:25-34); deaf mute (7:31-37); blindness (8:22-26; 10:46-52), and in a special category, the resurrection of a girl (5:21-24, 35-43). He withstands charges of blasphemy (2:7); Sabbathbreaking (3:1-6); and reliance on demonic power (3:22). With characteristic vigor, Mark reports Jesus' assaults on the dominion of Satan, arriving at a triumphal climax in the cross and Resurrection. In reporting healings Mark gives minimal attention to health-related side issues, being more concerned with answering the question Who is Jesus? If He is the Messiah, then what kind of Messiah? Repeatedly, Jesus requests those He heals not to publicize their deliverance, apparently to forestall untimely conflict with the authorities.

Mark's Gospel gives special attention to conflict with demons and displays sympathy with victims of possession. He also includes an element of delay associated with miracles. Demons argue with Jesus (5:6-12), delaying their expulsion, the incident of the woman healed from a hemorrhage of 12 years' standing delays Jesus so long that Jairus' daughter dies during the interim (verses 27-43), and the casting of demons from a boy is delayed until Jesus descends from the Mount of Transfiguration (9:22-29).

Matthew's Gospel retells almost all the healings reported by Mark, however with increased dialogue between Jesus and others. He gives special prominence to Jesus' motive of compassion (Matt. 9:35, 36; 14:14; 20:34; 9:27; 15:22). Matthew especially calls attention to OT prophecies fulfilled in Jesus' work, particularly His servanthood role (8:17 [from Isa. 53:4]; 12:15-21 [from Isa. 42:1-4]). Matthew takes special note of how Jesus' healings in the Temple late in His ministry deeply offended the priests (21:14).

Luke's report contains 16 healings, more than any other Gospel (Luke 4:31-39; 4:38, 39; 5:12-26; 6:6-11; 7:1-17; 8:26-56; 9:37-43; 11:14-16; 13:10-17; 14:1-6; 17:11-19; 18:35-43; and 22:50, 51). When we consider Luke's training as a physician (Col. 4:14), this need not surprise us. He traces Jesus' ministry as a healer from His sermon in the synagogue at Nazareth (Luke 4:16-21). There Jesus reads an acknowledged Messianic passage from Isaiah 61:1, 2: "The Spirit of the Lord is upon me, because

he has anointed me to preach good news to the poor. He has sent me to proclaim release to the captives and recovering of sight to the blind, to set at liberty those who are oppressed, to proclaim the acceptable year of the Lord." By applying this prophecy to Himself, Jesus was legitimizing His ministry with a claim to fulfill this Messianic passage. Luke's Gospel also includes seven summary statements reporting that Jesus healed additional large numbers of people from their diseases and cast out many demons (Luke 4:40, 41; 6:17-19; 7:18-23; 9:10, 11; 10:13-15; 13:31-33; 24:19-21). The reports carry a strong liberation theme, liberation from demons, sin, and social boundaries. Luke also features stories of faith on the part of non-Jews and outcasts, as in the cases of the soldier's servant (7:1-10), the woman made an outcast by long hemorrhage (8:43-48), and the faith of the Samaritan leper, who, alone of 10 healed, returns to express his gratitude (17:11-19). Luke presents healing as a direct part of Jesus' mission as Saviour (4:40, 41; 6:17-19; 9:11). Even His disciples become healers (9:1, 2; 10:9, 17). Also, in unusual detail he describes the reactions of those healed.

Jesus' sympathy with sufferers is especially prominent in Luke, expressed in connection with such healings as the raising of the son of the widow of Nain (7:11-17) and three Sabbath miracles, the man with the withered hand (6:6-11), the woman bent for 18 years (13:10-17), and the man with dropsy (14:1-6). Luke's abundant health and healing reports seem to emphasize the high sense of satisfaction found among those healed by Jesus.

John's Gospel is more selective, including only seven miracles. He labels them "works" ('erga), or "signs" (semeia), literally acts of God (John 5:17, 19-21). Only three healings are reported, each set in long discourses. They are the official's son (4:46-54), the man lame for 38 years but healed at the Pool of Bethesda (5:1-15), and the man blind from birth (9:1-34). Two occurred on the Sabbath, precipitating conflict with the religious authorities. There is one resurrection, that of Lazarus, where

Jesus is presented as the source of life. "I am the resurrection and the life; he who believes in me, though he die, yet shall he live, and whoever lives and believes in me shall never die" (11:25, 26). Faith holds a prominent place in John's Gospel, not a faith based on signs, but on Him as a person, the life-giver (20:24-29). Not only is Jesus the source of health, but in Him is found the sum of all health— eternal life. The Gospel of John includes no reports of demon possession, and the struggle between Christ and the devil, while present, is more subtle.

2. Kinds and Methods of Healings

The striking contrast between Hellenistic healings and those of Jesus draws strong lines of distinction between divine healing and others. Contrary to most Greek healers, Jesus' work was not in seclusion, but often among large crowds. He cast no spells, called upon no external power sources for authority, induced no hypnotic trances, and pronounced no incantations. His method was simple, a few words and a touch. The cases Jesus healed were ones of serious illness, often of long standing. His ministry was like no other.

As noted earlier, Jesus dealt with a wide range of conditions, the majority described in physical terms. With a simple movement He reattached a severed ear (Luke 22:51), with a touch cleansed a leper (e.g., Luke 5:12-16), and restored vision to the blind, at times without, at other times with, physical means (John 9:7, 11).

His most common method of healing was by word, briefly spoken, and immediately the sick person was well. At other times He chose indirect means, such as healing in stages or by delayed completion (Mark 8:22-26; John 9:1-11). All Jesus' exorcisms were by word, for in the Gospels there is no case in which He touched a victim of devil possession. The demons knew who He was (Mark 1:24; 5:7). Even when the contest with demons was most heated, His order was authoritative. In three parallel accounts the Gospels report Jesus'

exact words, which in each case were direct commands to the demons (Mark 1:25; 5:8; 9:25; Luke 4:35). In only one instance does He pray or call on the name of God in performing His miracles, and there it is explained as done for the benefit of onlookers (John 11:41, 42).

At times Jesus' miracles were performed close at hand, at other times at a distance (Matt. 8:5-13; Mark 7:24-37). Often Jesus responded to an appeal by the sufferer (Matt. 9:27; Luke 17:13; Mark 10:47), at other times to requests on their behalf by another person (Mark 1:30; 2:3; 7:26; 9:17; Matt. 8:5; John 4:47; 9:2). On occasion Jesus initiated the question of healing with no appeal from the sufferer (John 5:6-9; Luke 7:14; 13:12; 22:51).

Several observations help define Jesus' ministry of healing. For Him disease was alien to divine order, being the work of the devil, whom He came to combat and defeat (Luke 13:16). He accepted the weak and sick, not in a contemptuous manner, but compassionately as victims. His approach was never distantly clinical, rather always in the setting of dealing with a respected person, for Jesus understood persons in the wholistic manner taught in the OT Scriptures. He sought to reestablish a profound connection between man and God (Luke 7:11, 21), and to achieve that goal divine love must be accepted by faith, a faith resting in the person of God.

3. Purposes of Healing

The mandate of Isaiah 61:1, 2 described five assignments: (1) preach the good news, (2) proclaim release to captives, (3) physical healing, such as restoring sight to the blind, (4) liberate those oppressed by sin or direct demonic power, and (5) proclaim the kingdom of God. Matthew reports that "He went about all Galilee, teaching in their synagogues and preaching the gospel of the kingdom and healing every disease and every infirmity among the people" (Matt. 4:23). A similar statement occurs in Matthew 9:35, where He gave His mission charge to the 12.

It seems clear that Jesus saw His first task not simply in performing physical healings, but in proclaiming the grand news of God's new and unique intervention in human affairs, deliverance, forgiveness, reconciliation, rescue, and salvation, elements including but far surpassing physical relief. He was summoning people to a new mode of life wholly committed to God in a setting of repentance, a conscious and continuing dedication, lest seven demons return to occupy the house (Luke 11:20-26). Typically His healings were coupled with forgiveness. Physical healings held a place in a larger ministry that alone can restore šālôm, healing in every category of human existence, re-creating the original meaning of health as bestowed in the Creation. He who had created the world and all that is in it (Col. 1:16-20; Heb. 1:2; John 1:3) appears now among us in human form to bring restoration of all that had been lost by sin. He was the deliverer promised to Adam and Eve in Eden (Gen. 3:15). He was more than a prophet serving as the vehicle for God's work. While participating fully in a world disrupted by sin, He stood above its moral impurity (Heb. 2:17, 18; 4:15). His healing ministry clearly was divine power at work.

Careful study of Jesus' ministry confirms this evaluation. His primary task was to proclaim that God is receiving His sinful, suffering creatures in a sweeping act of grace and love. In His work the kingdom of God had an already-now presence, with total deliverance to come. What occurred was evidence of final deliverance from a world of sin. He had come to deliver, to seek and to save, to forgive, to proclaim the day of God's mercy, to confer life everlasting, to be the restorer of all that was lost. He was first of all the Saviour, and physical healings were evidences, signs of His authority.

Without question, spectacular healings and deliverances from demons attracted crowds and confirmed Jesus' miraculous power, creating a willingness to listen to His teachings. He was challenged by a problem that contin-

ues to plague those who bring the benefits of the gospel; how to ground followers in God rather than in the prosperity that comes from serving Him. It was not Jesus' purpose to attract followers on the grounds of the miracles, and He said as much to the self-serving beneficiaries of His miracle of loaves and fishes (John 6:26). The miracle healings of Jesus had clear boundaries. For example, the Gospels record no visit by Jesus to Tiberias, by far the largest city in Galilee. It seems that few if any of the sick in Tiberias were healed. The same could be said of numerous other towns and cities of Palestine. We must clearly understand, however, that while the utilitarian aspect of Jesus' healings as part of His larger ministry has its place, at the same time His healings and deliverances were indeed expressions of merciful compassion. Physical healings are an earnest of the fullness of the kingdom of God.

4. Healings and Faith

In many instances faith is intimately involved with Jesus' healings, in fact treated as a prerequisite to the healing itself (Matt. 9:2, 22, 29; 8:13; 15:28). Disbelief was a deterrent, as in the case of Nazareth (Mark 6:5, 6; Matt. 13:58). In one case when the disciples were unable to perform a healing, Jesus told them the reason was their lack of faith (Matt. 17:20). At times faith is present in the person being healed, on other occasions in a sponsor acting in another's behalf. Normally faith is expected as a condition for healing (Matt. 9:29; Luke 17:19; 18:42). Many examples can be cited in which faith is of primary importance, especially in the Gospels and the book of Acts.

This fact has led many Christians to a conclusion, superficially attractive but not logically necessary, that if an attempt of prayer for healing fails, the fault lies in a lack of faith. The assumption may be that if sufficient faith is present, its very presence would move God to respond, or at least conditions would be present to enable the healing to occur. For some, faith assumes the role of a magic bullet that in itself heals or releases God's power, based on a misreading of the woman who touched the hem of Jesus' garment (Matt. 9:22).

While the necessity for faith is important to Christ's healings, another theme also appears in the same Gospel accounts, that healings may occur where there is little or no faith expressed. These miracles are designed to generate faith in Jesus as the Son of God. In the case of the paralytic, persons of faith bring the man to Jesus, but the text records no faith on his part, yet Christ heals him because of the faith of those who brought him (Matt. 9:1-8). The man with the withered hand receives healing in the absence of any expressed faith, neither his own nor that of any sponsor. Apparently it was to demonstrate to the religious leaders that Jesus had power to heal (Matt. 12:9-13). The woman bent for 18 years is addressed by Jesus and healed, where there is no recorded expression of faith (Luke 13:11-13). The man with dropsy was healed in the absence of any expressed faith, as Jesus was using his case to demonstrate that healing is appropriate on the Sabbath (Luke 14:4). The case of the servant of the high priest, his right ear severed from his head by Peter's sword in Gethsemane, provides another healing in the absence of expressed faith (Luke 22:51). These accounts seem to be cited not to diminish the importance of faith, but as evidence that expressed faith may or may not be the essential element in Christ's healings. Given Jesus' evaluation of those who demand signs before believing (John 4:48; 20:29), these texts suggest that in the presence of developed faith healings may be less necessary.

One more observation may be helpful in defining faith. Throughout the Scriptures faith (Heb. 'emunah; Gr. pistis) refers to a confidence of heart and mind in God, leading to trust in His sovereign will (Ps. 31:23; 2 Cor. 5:7; Heb. 11:8). It is not a blind, uninformed "leap in the dark," but rests on evidence. It represents a conscious, intelligent commitment, not credulity or sensory feelings. Faith

plays a vital role in biblical teaching and experience. By faith sinners are justified in Christ Jesus (Rom. 3:28; 5:1; Gal. 2:16; 3:8), and God's redeemed people are those who have the faith of Jesus (Rev. 14:12).

5. Sabbath Healings

Without apology Jesus healed on the Sabbath. While such activity violated no biblical statute with respect to proper Sabbath observance, His actions conflicted with at least elements of the corpus of traditional rules governing Sabbathkeeping. The Gospels report seven different incidents of Jesus' healing on the Sabbath, often in the setting of controversy with the religious authorities. Of the Synoptic Gospels Luke records five: the fever of Peter's wife's mother (4:38, 39), a demon-possessed man (verses 31-35), both on the same Sabbath, the man in the synagogue with the withered hand (6:6-10), the woman in the synagogue with a spinal deformity (13:10-17), and the man healed of dropsy at the house of a Pharisee (14:1-6). Matthew includes two of the incidents, Mark three.

John records two more Sabbath healings, both developed at some length: the paralytic healed at Bethesda (John 5:2-18) and the man born blind, whose story fills the entire ninth chapter of his Gospel (verses 1-41).

A careful reading of Jesus' Sabbath activities confirms that while Jesus honored and respected the Sabbath as taught in the Scriptures, at the same time He disregarded the traditional regulations that had been added. That disregard was capitalized upon by His enemies to accuse Him of Sabbath desecration, a charge that He countered by redefining the purpose of the Sabbath and appealing to higher authority by citing biblical precedents. The fullest of His responses are recounted by John, in relation to the paralytic at Bethesda and the man born blind. Neither of the healed people was sure who Jesus was, nor were they concerned with the leaders' inquiries about Jesus' specific identity as a righteous person or sinner. Jesus' response to His critics focused on the fact that His Father continually works, even on Sabbaths, to sustain the functions of all nature, including the healing process, and that extending compassion transcends ritual regulations governing Sabbath observance. It is notable that on the Sabbath Jesus healed both acute and chronic cases without apparent distinction. The releasing power of God brings freedom to those who suffer, regardless of time. In His Sabbath activities Jesus demonstrated how two principles may be sustained in certain tension, respect for Sabbath sanctity and compassion for those who suffer. Among all Jesus' disputes with religious leaders of the day, the issue of what is legitimate activity for the Sabbath was one of the sharpest.

Rather than acting as a barrier, the Sabbath should serve as a bridge toward the initial intimacy that once existed between God the Creator and just-created humans. Even its Hebrew name, *šabbāt,* meaning "rest," and the wider description of its purpose in the fourth commandment emphasize rest from human activities as God rested from His Creation work. The healing power in the Sabbath springs from the way it uniquely disconnects the person from the stress of everyday concerns and restores human interests toward the things of God. Physical and emotional release allows for recovery from the stress that accompanies life.

The benefits of the Sabbath are universal. The fourth commandment defines its universality, its benefits extending to family members, employees, and even to beasts of burden and the sojourning foreigner (Ex. 20:8-11; cf. Isa. 56:6-8). Sabbath services for worship and study bring believers together in a community where mutual care and concern are shared among all and worshipers' attention is deflected from the ordinary through adoration of God. The Sabbath points forward to a future time when every unresolved problem, whether physical, emotional, or spiritual, will be healed in the coming kingdom. "So then, there remains a sabbath rest for the people of God" (Heb. 4:9). In the presence of God every wound of suffering humanity finds healing.

6. Healing as Restoration

The restoration theme permeates the Scriptures, providing a solid foundation for hope (Gen. 3:15; Rom. 6:4, 9-11; Col. 1:20, 21; 3:8-10; 2 Cor. 5:18-20; 1 Cor. 15:51-57; 1 John 3:2). Healing and restoration often are identified, for as sickness separates from God, healing restores relationships. God's promises to restore Israel spill forth in language filled with healing and curative terms (Jer. 30:12-17; 33:6; 46:11; Eze. 47:12; Mal. 4:2). So clear is the affinity in the NT that one of its principal words for healing *(soteria)* may be translated as either healing or salvation. Salvation, then, may include not only rescue from sin and its consequences, but also restoration, healing of the whole person.

All biblical teachings are predicated on the basis that in the end, what was lost when sin entered will be restored when He who created becomes the One who restores His creation. Having healed our wounds and vicariously borne our transgressions at Calvary, He appears at last in the Apocalypse as *Christus Victor,* in triumph over Satan and the forces of evil (Rev. 20:14; 21:8). Those who love and serve God will be restored to the perfect condition that once was, while all that is evil will be destroyed never to rise again. In both OT and NT prophecies this new earth is foreseen as free from sickness, pain, and death (Isa. 33:24; Rev. 21:4). The apostle Paul rejoices in Christ's resurrection as proof that He is victor over all these evil forces. Christ's victory has become our victory (1 Thess. 4:14-17).

E. Healing in the Pauline Writings

1. Distinguishing Features

In comparison with the Gospels, Paul's ministry gives less attention to healings, although they occur. The Epistles include little direct discussion of healing in the modern sense, but provide guiding principles. As in the remainder of the Scriptures, Paul's understanding of humanity is wholistic: man is a unified person capable of sin and restoration (1 Thess. 5:23). On this basis the apostle values the body, a gift from God to be presented to Him as a living sacrifice (Rom. 12:1). From Paul's perspective the loss in Eden is restored in Christ through His resurrection, it being evidence of our coming eternal life with God. Restoration comes only by the act of God, *sola gratia* (Rom. 3:28; Gal. 2:16). Works never can be a means of restoration; even Abraham was justified by faith, *sola fide,* prior to receiving circumcision (Rom. 4:9-11). The redeemed are to live in the Spirit (Rom. 8:1-4), through whom new covenant harmony is restored (Heb. 8:10, 11).

In Paul's writings the miraculous is affirmed (1 Cor. 12:8, 28), as well as the natural (1 Tim. 5:23). However he seldom speaks of health in the physical sense. For him health or healthy *(hugiēs)* means a balanced function of order in the whole. He always uses the term metaphorically in this sense.

Paul has considerable interest in what the KJV translates as " temperance," but in recent translations often is rendered more broadly as "self-control." Although the word's meaning is broader than simple avoidance of alcohol, several times the apostle returns to that theme (Rom. 14:21; Eph. 5:18; 1 Tim. 3:8; 5:23; Titus 2:3; and indirectly in 1 Cor. 6:10). In these passages the evidence is not conclusive that Paul teaches full abstinence; however, it would be in harmony with his understanding of the body temple (Prov. 20:1; Rom. 12:1, 2). His message against intoxication is unmistakable (1 Tim. 3:2, 3; Titus 1:7; 2:2-6, 12; Rom. 12:3; 2 Cor. 5:13).

Although miracles take place in Paul's ministry, he attributes them to the work of God, never to himself, which echoes the OT theme (Ex. 7:3; Deut. 6:22). The Spirit is the immediate source of miracles (Gal. 3:5), a comment not recorded of Jesus. The coming of the gospel brings "signs and wonders" (Rom. 15:18, 19; 2 Cor. 12:12; 2 Thess. 2:9), a stereotyped expression that includes physical healings.

While "signs and wonders" serve to authenticate the message he proclaims, for Paul they represent also deliverance from the suffering imposed by sin, from which the whole world groans for release (Rom. 8:19-23).

In carrying the gospel to the heart of the Hellenistic world the apostle moved from the wholistic, God-centered understanding of health and healing common to the Scriptures to a different mode. In Greece health was directly expressed in athletic prowess (in fact, virtually defined in physical development). By contrast, the Hebrews gave sparse attention to games, competitions, or athletic prowess, for physical activity was expressed largely in productive work. Personal reward came in the satisfaction of a job well done.

2. Gifts of Healings

Healings *(charismata iamatōn)* appear among the gifts of the Spirit listed by Paul, where always they are separated from miracles and are listed in the plural (1 Cor. 12:4-11, 27, 28), although they are absent from shorter lists of gifts (Eph. 4:11, 12; Rom. 12:6-8). Such healings are treated as gifts of God, not familiar human abilities. Expression of the gifts of healings does not hold a high profile in the records of the apostolic church; however, it is clear they existed. Gifts of healing evidently were intended to function through individual believers, as suggested by the use of *allos* [another, singular] (1 Cor. 12:8-10) and the gifts of healings [plural] (verses 28, 30). This structure suggests strongly that the apostle does not refer to gifts carried among the churches by itinerant healers, but gifts exercised by individuals on specific occasions.

3. Three Nonhealings

Paul's somewhat cryptic metaphorical reference to his "thorn in the flesh" (2 Cor. 12:7-9, KJV) requires us to face the fact that even among faithful Christians, God may not see fit to bring physical healing. This first conclusion humbles us, requiring us to admit that we may be incapable even of identifying the elements involved, and that failure to heal is no final proof of lack of faith, rejection by God, or some disqualifying moral defect. Ultimate trust must rest in God, whose benevolent character we know and can rely upon as in our best benefit.

The exact nature of Paul's problem has generated speculation from the time of the Church Fathers to today, the answer remaining elusive. Most widely accepted is the suggestion that it was physical and probably involved a visual difficulty, an argument buttressed by Paul's use of a writer to record letters (Rom. 16:22), and his writing final greetings with his own hand in certain Epistles, the implication being that the remainder was by another person (1 Cor. 16:21; 2 Thess. 3:17; Gal. 6:11). A historical factor cited is his three days' blindness following his encounter with Christ at Damascus, reported to be healed (Acts 9:18) and his passing reference to another problem, either the same or another condition (Gal. 4:14).

Of greater significance is what the condition meant to Paul. It was not accidental, but something intentionally placed. Although given by God, it appeared to Paul to do the work of Satan, harassing him (*kolaphizō*, 2 Cor. 12:7) lest he become elated with his privileges. Seen as a limiting, recurring problem, Paul's three prayer appeals for its removal were met with refusal, turning him from physical concerns to the larger purpose and sustaining power of God. Paul's response: "I will all the more gladly boast of my weaknesses, that the power of Christ may rest upon me" (verse 9).

Paul's experience assures us that sickness may have a meaning beyond the physical and pathological. With its intrusive physical presence, bodily sickness threatens to displace the broader understanding of healing as harmony with God. Above every human experience He stands, one God, blocked from our vision by sin but touched by human suffering and filled with compassion. Although the word "providence" does not occur in the Bible, what it signifies stands out on every page.

Second is the case of Timothy. Although a young man, Timothy seems to have been plagued by stomach problems. To deal with these Paul gave his only medical counsel, advising "a little wine for the sake of your stomach and your frequent ailments" (1 Tim. 5:23). Timothy's practice had been to drink only water (verse 23) but now as a medical treatment he is advised differently, the implication being that medication would cease with recovery. Despite Timothy's personal commitment to Christ, the physical difficulty continued, and Paul turned to a medical application for it. This experience validates the truth that use of medical treatments is compatible with prayer to God for healing.

A third instance is that of Trophimus, a close associate of Paul. While accompanying him on his third missionary journey, Trophimus became ill and was left in Miletus to recover from his illness (2 Tim. 4:20). Neither in this case nor in the two previous ones cited were the gifts of healing applied for recovery. These cases remind us that an ideal state of health in the full sense described in the Bible is not possible in this life. Living under the universal consequences of sin, all will suffer, and death is the last end of every person. In the Scriptures we find not only the answer to the question Why suffering? but also the good news of its coming end in the return of Jesus. His triumph over Satan, sin, and all its consequences was wrought at Calvary and evidenced by the empty tomb. Full healing in every sense will be accomplished with the return of Jesus.

F. Healing in the Apostolic Church

Midway through His ministry Jesus gathered around Him the twelve and granted them power *(exousia)* to cast out demons, heal every disease, and every infirmity (Matt. 10:1). The record indicates that their use of this gift was at times effective and at other times not (Matt. 17:16); however, the potential remained. At His ascension Jesus' assignment was to bear witness to Him, ultimately to the end of the world, but first the Spirit would come. From the time of the Spirit's coming (Acts 2:1-4, 43), the fledgling church witnessed a remarkable series of healings.

Much of the history of the apostolic church is concentrated in the book of Acts, which makes its reports of healings of special interest in that the author was a physician. Beginning with the healing by Peter of a lame man at the gate of the Temple (Acts 3:1-10), the record provides healings or exorcisms of seven additional persons and several groups, ending on Malta with Paul's delivery from death by snakebite and the healing of an island official (Acts 28:3-6, 8). Additional wonders and signs are reported, both in Jerusalem and elsewhere (Acts 5:12-16; 8:5-8), and the diseases and conditions healed included both acute and longstanding cases. Yet in terms of verses the healings in Acts constitute less than one twentieth of the text.

Occasional comments suggest that many healings occurred that were not included in the record (Acts 5:16). While important, the miracles in Acts seem more incidental than those reported in the Gospels. In both the work of Paul and the historical reports in Acts, healings occur, are accepted in the plan of God's work, and bring physical restoration to certain persons, but the core evangelistic methodology of the apostolic church rests more on proclamation than physical healings.

G. Prayer and Healing in James

The Epistle of James presents the only NT example of how healing seems to have been integrated into the functioning of early Christian congregations. The passage is found in James 5:13-16, whose principal theme actually is prayer. Prayer was warmly commended by Jesus (Luke 18:1), and permeated His life, playing a significant part in His teaching ministry (Matt. 21:22; Luke 11:9, 10; 22:42); however, healing and prayer are not uniformly connected in the Bible. In connection with Jesus' healings prayer is hardly mentioned, although often He had spent previous long hours in private communion with the Father and had strongly commended prayer to His disciples. Even where not mentioned, in those cases in which the person appealed to Jesus, a certain sense of prayer was present.

In James, however, healing occurs not only in conjunction with but actually as a function of prayer. The passage addresses prayer by naming three classes of believers, first those in trouble, difficulty, afflicted, even downhearted or unhappy (*kakopatheō*), who are to pray (present imperative), a repeated practice. They have no assurance that the trouble will be removed, but will be enabled to cope with it as needed. Second are those who are cheerful, for whom problems are overcome in faith and through a cheerful attitude. To them, James advises singing praises (James 5:13). Then he addresses the sick. They are told to call for the elders to pray, anoint with oil in the name of the Lord, and the prayer of faith will save.

Because these steps describe a single procedure, certain questions are appropriate. Why the elders? The answer seems clear, because they represent the community of believers and their participation involves the entire church. No priestly role is assigned them, and while they are to be respected (1 Tim. 5:17-20), nowhere else in the NT are elders assigned the specific task of healing. The gifts are distributed throughout the membership as the Spirit sees fit. James makes this point in James 5:16, where confession of sins is assigned to the entire congregation, not specific officers of the church.

Along with prayer the elders will anoint the sick person with oil. The only parallel use of anointing with oil is found in Mark 6:13, where it was used by the disciples in healing. Was the anointing a medical procedure or a religious act? Using olive oil as an emollient was well known in the NT world. The word "anoint" (*'aleiphō*) appears eight other times in the NT, always in a nonreligious context. The claim that the oil itself conveys merit is not biblical, but took form in medieval Europe. Neither does the text suggest a rite provided for those nearing death; it is applicable to any sickness.

The text locates healing power in the prayer of faith itself, particularly of the elders, righteous men (James 5:16), whose prayers will have profound effect. Although the Greek words are ambiguous, three outcomes are to be expected, first that the Lord will save the sick, raise them up, and if they have sins they will be forgiven. James expresses the promises as absolutes, although it would be in harmony with the remainder of the NT to place such an outcome within the will of God.

From this brief survey of the passage, several important truths relating to prayer emerge: 1. Effective prayer is based on faith and arises from faith. 2. Intercessory prayer must come from a dedicated Christian, one whose motives and actions are in harmony with the will of God. 3. The prayer is not to be general, but directed to God on behalf of the specific sick person. 4. Its outcome is tied to the faith of the elders. 5. Healing and/or salvation is expected to occur.

Anointing with oil is combined with prayer by the elders. This simple, faith-laden service commended by James to the apostolic church provides a healing model for Christian churches in all ages. With respect to healing and the church, the passage shows: 1. The church is directly concerned with sickness among its members, that healing is a part of the work of Christ's people. 2. Healing is based in the Christian community. Only in recent times has healing become a secular enterprise of repairing bodies, which represents a truncated view of healing alien to the Scriptures. 3. Physical and spiritual methods merge in God's healing process, His own healing power exerted through both channels. 4. Sickness and healing involve more than the physical, they involve the wider being of the whole person. 5. Release from sins in this setting knits together redemption and healing in one great act of God's grace.

H. Observations on Healing

The Scriptures devote much greater attention to healing than health, which illustrates the fact that present problems command more urgency than those in solution. Jesus' observation that "those who are well have no need of a physician, but those who are sick" (Matt. 9:12) illustrated His intention as the Master Physician to turn suffering into health.

In the Scriptures Jesus is easily the central figure in healing the sick. Despite the fact that many non-Jews lived in Galilee and that Capernaum, a major center of His work, was at least half non-Jewish, His approach to healing never gave a hint of the pervasive magical approach of the Gentile community. His frequent assignment of illness to observable causes, met by the healing power of God, demonstrated how sickness and healing are to be met on rational terms that relate to cause and effect. This perspective has contributed in a major way to the development of modern rational health care.

It is clear that Jesus intended His healing ministry to be continued by His disciples and the church. His assignment of this task to the disciples and its manifestation in the apostolic church give evidence that healings continued both for signs and to bring relief to suffering humans. It is reasonable to expect this same ministry to be found in the ministry of the believers in the last days. According to the biblical teaching, healing is uniformly of God, whether in immediate manifestation or the action of restorative powers under His guidance. However, the character of Christian healing is marked by the intimate connection between bodily restoration and reconciliation of the sufferer to God.

III. Health and Holiness

Integral connection between health and holiness is an inevitable corollary to close ties between God and His human creatures. Although distorted temporarily by sin, the intense Creator-creature bond remains permanent, guaranteeing that whatever impacts upon humans is of direct concern to God. So elemental is this truth that the apostle Paul incorporated it into his address to pagans in Athens, "He himself [God] gives to all men life and breath and everything. . . . He is not far from each one of us, for 'in him we live and move and have our being'" (Acts 17:25-28).

The fact of Creation places humans in a position of dependency and responsibility to the Creator. However, because God is benevolent, His plans always favor the long-term welfare of His creatures. These faith statements form the framework of the biblical worldview and demonstrate why human life and self-understanding must be essentially religious.

A. The Moral Factor

If humanity owes its origin and daily sustenance to God, the matter is automatically religious. God is holy in the absolute sense (1 Sam. 2:2; Ps. 99:9; Isa. 6:3; Rev. 15:4), and humans, made in His image, are designed to reflect in their persons and lives the holiness of their Creator (Lev. 9:2; 11: 44, 45; 20:7; 21:8). Hence the original creation, including humans, was good because it was in total harmony with Him. This kind of goodness included all elements of existence, the spiritual, physical, emotional, social, and every other quality of being. It was in fact "very good" (Gen. 1:31). Such unity grounds the wholistic understanding of man found throughout the Bible.

"Holy" and "holiness" are derived from several near synonyms in Hebrew and Greek that share a common sense of separateness for a purpose. Holiness may mean sacred or set apart from the common (Heb. *qādōš, qōdes*), a separation from what defiles, or dedication to religious use (Ex. 19:6; 30:31, 32). In the NT the Greek word *hagios* applies the same to the church. Peter writes, "But you are a chosen race, a royal priesthood, a holy nation, God's own people, that you may declare the wonderful deeds of him who called you out of darkness into his marvelous light" (1 Peter 2:9). The theme is common in the NT (1 Peter 1:15, 16; Rom. 12:1; 1 Cor. 3:17; Eph.

1:4; 5:27; Col. 1:22; 3:12).

The Ten Commandments were given to provide humanity with an infallible guide to the character of God, expressed in terms understandable to people. To honor them brings people toward harmony with God. Hence they constitute the basic moral code. (See Law.)

1. The Levitical Code

Brief attention is given in this section to additional statutes provided by God in covenant to govern many elements of daily life, often called the Mosaic code. Its name is taken from the fact its fullest expression appears in Leviticus (19-27), although similar passages occur in Deuteronomy (22-26). The fact that these laws may adjoin laws governing worship and ritual matters has led many to overlook their value, many of which had an impact on mental and physical health. Although oriented to the situation of ancient Israel, these laws sought to restore, within the limits imposed by sin, what is possible of the original unity. They addressed a broad cross section of human experience, from diet to interpersonal relationships, hygiene, sexual mores, service to God, and other issues.

Why should the people adopt this body of laws? The appeal to obey God to obtain the benefits of obedience is secondary. Instead, the reason given is a moral one, "You shall be holy for I the Lord your God am holy" (Lev. 19:2). On the other hand, the Levitical code was established as a covenant between God and His people. Scholarly debate continues about whether these laws were given on a health or ritual basis; however, even if ritual, they carried many benefits. The laws' sexual and marriage provisions, if observed, would have virtually eliminated the spread of sexually transmitted diseases. Public health would have been enhanced, with clean food, water, air, clothing, dwellings, disposal of sewage, burial of the dead, also isolation and observation in quarantine of those with communicable diseases. The code provided an organized group of priests to enforce the regulations.

The covenant promise had been to inflict on Israel "none of the diseases" that prevailed in Egypt (Ex. 15:26), a promise that far exceeded the impact of the regulations. However, the immunity promised was conditional (Deut. 28:56-61). From modern scientific knowledge it is clear that the implementation of the Levitical code would have placed Israel far in advance of all other countries of their time, attaining a level of benefits not equaled until the eighteenth century A.D. The holiness motif resident in these laws had the effect of elevating the value of the person's body to establish a vital connection between the body and service to God.

2. The Body Temple

In Paul's teaching about the body as God's dwelling place the apostle draws from OT teachings to show that physical care is a matter of concern to God. It is a moral issue. "I appeal to you therefore, brethren, by the mercies of God, to present your bodies as a living sacrifice, holy and acceptable to God, which is your spiritual worship" (Rom. 12:1). The sacrificial language of this verse suggests that Paul had in mind the physical body, and more. He draws directly from the covenant promise with Israel, "And I will walk among you, and will be your God, and you shall be my people" (Lev. 26:12). In a theme often repeated, God promised to dwell among His people (Ex. 25:8; Num. 35:34; 1 Kings 6:13; Joel 3:17; Zech. 2:10, 11).

As a sacrifice, the whole person would be set apart, consecrated solely to God. For Paul the believer becomes a divine dwelling place. He writes to the Corinthians, "Do you not know that your body is a temple of the Holy Spirit within you, which you have from God? You are not your own; you were bought with a price. So glorify God in your body" (1 Cor. 6:19, 20). A few lines earlier he had written, perhaps in a collective sense, "Do you not know that you are God's temple and that God's Spirit dwells in you? If any one destroys God's temple, God will destroy him. For God's temple

is holy, and that temple you are" (1 Cor. 3:16, 17). Paul's intense language shows that he regards this as important truth.

In these three passages the body is explicitly cited four times. In part his appeal is to sexual purity, but two core themes are clear: (1) by both creation and redemption, the body belongs to God and is important, and (2) keeping the body pure for the Spirit's dwelling is a Christian responsibility. Care for the body has strong moral ties and is a solid, if neglected, part of the Christian life.

Although the Scriptures are clear that humans belong to God by creation and redemption, and that as stewards they have the responsibility of caring for themselves, no systematic charter of how to do so is provided. Those that come nearest are the health components of the Levitical code, however they are couched in social settings, and seldom given directly to govern personal choices. Basic goals are God-given, but the exact measures to be taken remain to be discovered through study of how body and mind function in the larger natural setting. Maintaining optimum health therefore is a cooperative venture between the Creator and His creature. (See IV. A.)

A striking exception to this general observation deals with food. This fact alone justifies special attention to diet as the one major health factor dealt with at some length in the Scriptures.

B. Diet in the Bible

God's concern with what people eat begins with the first chapter of Genesis, where He prescribed the original diet. It resurfaces with surprising frequency throughout the Scriptures, having applications that involve both physical health and one's service to God. The original diet was vegetarian, given in exact detail. "And God said, 'Behold, I have given you every plant yielding seed which is upon the face of all the earth, and every tree with seed in its fruit, you shall have them for food' " (Gen. 1:29). Specific mention is made of an abundance of trees in Eden, including the tree of life, to all of which the first couple had access, with exception of a single fruit-bearing tree that God had reserved (Gen. 2:9). Of it, He told them, "You shall not eat." Their disobedience in this point constituted the first sin. We note the connection between food and a moral issue.

Following the entrance of sin the original diet was expanded to include herbaceous plants as well as fruits and nuts; however, it remained vegetarian. Modern scientific studies continue to demonstrate both the adequacy and unique health advantages to be gained by following a balanced vegetarian regimen. Only after the Flood diminished the earth's food-producing capacity was permission given to use animal flesh as food, and that with restriction against use of flesh with blood (Gen. 9:3, 4), and later fat (Lev. 3:17). Already God had introduced a distinction among animals, clean or unclean (Gen. 7:2; 8:20). As the patriarchal narratives make clear, humans adopted the use of flesh in their diets, a practice particularly suited to a nomadic life in an arid climate. The book of Daniel, written in Mesopotamia, narrates an incident involving food dating to the arrival of Daniel and his companions at the court of the Babylonian king, Nebuchadnezzar II (605-562 B.C.). Their choice of a simple vegetarian diet in contrast to the king's stimulating cuisine is linked to increased clarity of mind, the issue serving as a test of Daniel's commitment to God in an alien setting (Dan. 1:8-16). Given the limited sources of food available to common people in ancient times, a return to the Edenic vegetarian diet is not an issue in the Scriptures; however, it remains as the ideal, and as noted above, is increasingly supported by current scientific research.

Luke's particular interest in matters of food has been noted also by commentators. Almost every chapter makes reference to food. Food is connected with joyful occasions such as weddings and feasts (Luke 5:33-35; 6:21-25; 15:3-32) and in his foreshadowing of the banquet at Christ's table in the world to come (Luke 13:29, 30; 22:28-30). Sharing food and possessions with the poor becomes an obligation of Christ's followers (Luke 3:11; 14:7-24). As in none of the other Gospels, Luke associates one's attitude toward food with morality. The believer is to avoid a self-satisfying obsession with food and drink, these being sins that led to judgment in the days of Noah and Lot (Luke 17:20-37).

Exact characteristics to distinguish between clean and unclean animals were not included in the Flood narrative (Gen. 7-9), but are detailed in Leviticus 11 and Deuteronomy 14. Clear instructions required clean animals to be those that chewed the cud and had cloven hooves. Others were unclean. Clean marine animals were required to possess both fins and scales (Lev. 11:2-23). In general, birds of prey and scavengers were designated as unclean. Were the distinctions intended as health measures or for ritual purposes? Particularly in Deuteronomy, the listing seems connected with eating rather than with things sacrificial (Deut. 14:3-21). Are the distinctions temporary, to be discontinued in the NT? The distinction among animals can be traced to Noah, who becomes patriarch of the entire human race, explicitly defined at Mount Sinai, and continued through the biblical narrative. Hosea, Isaiah, and Ezekiel maintained the distinction between clean and unclean (Isa. 66:17; Hosea 9:3; Eze. 22:26; 44:23). As practicing Jews Jesus and the apostles undoubtedly respected it, and no issue over it appears among their enemies. Does the NT invalidate it? While Jesus disregarded traditional ceremonial distinctions (Mark 7:15-23), no NT text erases the basic distinction, and it hardly could have been discontinued at the cross, for the Jerusalem Council of Acts 15 (c. A.D. 49) applies specific dietary laws to Christians. Peter's personal practice was to avoid unclean foods (Acts 10:14). Discussions of foods offered to idols (1 Cor. 8 and Rom. 14) deal with issues other than the clean/unclean distinction. Although he is addressing other moral matters, the writer of the Apocalypse draws from familiar OT distinctions by noting that in the New Jerusalem "nothing unclean shall enter it" (Rev. 21:27; Isa. 35:8).

Other evidence supports the distinction between clean and unclean as noncultic. Cultic uncleanness could be removed by cleansing; however, the uncleanness of animals was permanent, with no ritual available for its removal. Furthermore, Israelites could come into contact with unclean animals without themselves becoming unclean. Application of the regulation was universal, the obligation applying even to aliens in Israel (Lev. 17:12-15). Given the evidence cited, the biblical testimony supports the distinction between clean and unclean as applicable from at least the time of Noah to the present.

C. Health and Obedience

While treasuring the grace by which God in Christ provides salvation-healing, Christians acknowledge that the evidence of redemption will appear in genuine, heartfelt obedience to God (Rom. 6:17). Healing of the whole person in all its aspects requires cooperation with God. As sin entered the world by an act of disobedience, plunging humanity and the planet into a comprehensive sickness with spiritual, social, emotional, and physical distortion, so in Christ

came the restoration (Rom. 5:15).

The eschatalogical biblical picture foresees a special remnant people at the end of the career of sin, covenant people wholly committed to God, who living in a distorted world still choose righteousness at great personal cost. They take seriously Jesus' warning that those approaching the eschaton must live sober, committed lives (Matt. 24:36-51; 25:1-13; Luke 12:13-21; 35-48; Mark 13:32-37). John the revelator describes them as the saints, "those who keep the commandments of God and the faith of Jesus" (Rev. 14:12). For these and the multitude of resurrected saints from throughout the ages, Christ comes with full healing and an end to sin and its consequences. "And the sea gave up the dead in it, Death and Hades gave up the dead in them, and all were judged by what they had done. Then Death and Hades were thrown into the lake of fire" (Rev. 20:13, 14). (See Millennium.) "And I heard a great [KJV] voice from the throne saying, 'Behold, the dwelling of God is with men. He will dwell with them, and they shall be his people, and God himself will be with them; he will wipe away every tear from their eyes, and death shall be no more, neither shall there be mourning nor crying nor pain any more, for the former things have passed away' " (Rev. 21:3, 4). All that was lost in Eden is restored. (See Great Controversy.)

IV. Prevention of Disease and Recovery

Although all healing is from God, the Scriptures reject any form of deterministic fatalism. Humans made in His image may not only provoke illness, but may share in mediating its effects. God's continuing outreach to humans assures them that all is not lost, as it invites them to participate not only in the adventure of His gift of life, but also its restoration.

A. God and Nature's Laws

Both the Bible and human observation confirm that healing occurs at two levels, in nature and what is called divine healing, a more direct intervention by God. In nature, healing

is continuous, making the remarkable so common that its process is often attributed to nature itself, the connection with God being forgotten. Healing in nature may take place at all levels of dysfunction. The healing "wisdom" planted by God as He created the organism begins its healing immediately when damage occurs. Physically, a broken bone quickly begins to knit on the way to recovery. Mentally and emotionally, as Shakespeare observed, it is sleep that "knits up the raveled sleave of care." The merciful ability to forget eases the pain of tragedy. Spiritually, the heart is created with an inward longing for God, and socially, despite the presence of conflict, a longing for peace is near universal.

The basic laws observed in nature stem from God's creative provision. Functioning in a sin-distorted world, they may yield outcomes good or bad, but if they function in a positive manner they may go far toward alleviating human problems. Just as with the moral precepts of the Ten Commandments and the Sermon on the Mount, the laws implanted in nature, although serving a different purpose, are His laws. This fact both encourages exploration of nature and validates the use of procedures and therapeutics to enhance recovery. Hence the valid use of such means promotes the healing effect of the organism and lies within God's intent for healing. Because God's natural laws may be abused as well as rightfully used, intensive investigation is needed in order to make sure they are properly understood and applied. Methods of care and treatment will change with increased understanding of natural laws, but the healing impulse is of God. In this understanding, the physician becomes an agent of God.

Affirming the legitimacy of the physician's ministry calls attention to the unexpectedly low profile physicians occupy in the Scriptures. It is possible that this phenomenon relates to the character of traditional medicine in the ancient world, whose practice usually accepted irrational approaches to sickness, healing, and therapeutics. The OT contains only four references to physicians, with but one being favorable, Joseph's commission of Egyptian physicians to embalm the body of his father, Jacob (Gen. 50:2). The other instances are negative, one noting Asa's refusal to consult the Lord regarding his severe illness, turning instead to physicians (2 Chron. 16:12); Job's likening of his counselors to "worthless physicians" (Job 13:4); and Jeremiah's ironic comment about there being no balm or physicians in Gilead (Jer. 8:22). The same pattern prevails in the NT, where in six places physicians are mentioned in somewhat negative terms (Matt. 9:12; Mark 2:17; 5:26;

Luke 4:23; 5:31; 8:43). The seventh and the exception is Paul's reference to Luke as "the beloved physician" (Col. 4:14), which is unquestionably favorable.

At the same time, Jesus' healing ministry provides a positive model of Christian care applicable to either physicians or associates in health care. Christ's work of compassion and deliverance, of whole-person concern above merely pecuniary interest, demonstrates how skills that in modern times are divided into wholly separate professions can be merged in the ministry of a single trained believer. Today's Christian physicians carry their patients to God in prayer while at once ministering God's healing power through discoveries found in nature. Through both means the physician brings alleviation to suffering and restores to health in ways harmonious with biblical patterns.

B. Health and Healing in Daily Life

What is finally important depends on whether practical biblical principles become adopted as guides to Christian life. As with other matters, biblical teachings and their cited examples relating to health and healing are meant to direct believers to an accurate understanding of God and show them how to relate effectively to the world in which they live. Such truths are more than informative intellectual exercises; they provide the foundation of a practical model for living. In fact, these matters deal with life and death.

Several basic but important principles serve as guides to good health. The Bible endorses the value of the physical body and wholesome activities that occur there. Therefore the believer should seek to understand and intentionally put into practice measures that enhance health. These actions are not pursued merely for pragmatic reasons, but in honor of God as Creator and Lord. Care for one's health is a moral matter, not simply an option. It is evidence of loyalty and responsible service to Him. At the practical level, the condition of one's health largely determines whether a person can carry out effective service to Him.

Because the body with its mental function serves as sole conduit for communication with God, how they are treated is of utmost importance, for there spiritual growth takes place. One's ability to respond to the Holy Spirit's appeals is affected. Although the foundational goals and values of Christian living are conveyed through God's Word, the exact means of achieving them advances through a process of discovery. It is science that largely has identified the specific ways to enhance and preserve wellness. Far from opposing each other, divine healing and scientific discovery both are channels through which God works to preserve and restore health.

Care of one's health is eminently important.

To neglect it is to discard basic principles relating to Christian living. Responsible stewardship calls every believer to acquire a knowledge of those things that either build or threaten good health, to choose the one and avoid the other. Health-building activities, including exercise, wholesome diet, proper systematic rest, practical satisfying work, avoidance of damaging substances or practices, good habits of cleanliness, a consciously structured life, cultivated efforts to live in peace with and help others, and a profound trust in God make the best possible use of the life God has shared with us. The apostle John's wish for Gaius reveals God's ideal for all. "I pray that all may go well with you and that you may be in health; I know that it is well with your soul" (3 John 2).

V. Illness and Healing in Christian History: An Overview

Christ's healing ministry was continued in His disciples' ministries (Mark 6:7-13; Matt. 10:1-5; Luke 9:1-6; Luke 10:1-9) as well as in the apostolic church. It is described as yet present in the church by many of the Church Fathers, e.g., Irenaeus (c. 130-c. 200), Origen (c. 185-c. 254), Justin Martyr (d. c. 165), Tertullian (c. 160-c. 220), and Augustine (354-430), but usually defined in physical terms. Despite a fleeting revival among the Montanists, it declined.

Four factors contributed to the subsidence of Christian healing ministry: 1. The intrusion of Gnostic theories depreciated the value of the human body, compounded by tangential adoption of allegorical and fanciful interpretations of the Scriptures. 2. The increasing acceptance of the Greek dualistic view of the person, replacing biblical wholism with a clear-cut separation of the physical body from the immortal soul. The soul was the eternal and spiritual center, the body denigrated to a temporary and often unruly trapping. 3. The legitimization of suffering as God's discipline. As enemies of the soul, passions of body and mind offered only evil and temptation, to be suppressed by ascetic torment of the body.

Hundreds of thousands of Christians turned to hermitage to battle the flesh by rigorous deprivations, establishing a tradition continued in monasteries and convents. 4. Growth of sacramentalism and sacerdotalism in an institutional, liturgical church set aside the idea of healing, with its uncertain outcomes. Virtue was vested in the sacraments, leaving the physical largely unattended.

Especially in the east, humanitarian relief continued for a time as a Christian benevolence. Basil the Great, bishop of Caesarea in Cappadocia (329-379), established a large hospital on the outskirts of his city, where there were reports of certain miracles (Theodoret *Church History* 4. 19. 1-13). Augustine (354-430) argued that miracles ceased with the apostolic period; however, he found a limited place for them in his later writings (cf. *On the Profit of Believing* 1. 34; *Retract* b. i. c. 14. 5).

In the sixth century Justinian, powerful Byzantine emperor (483-565), closed the medical schools of Athens and Alexandria. However, a limited knowledge of medicine retained by Arab physicians kept alive many procedures that made Moorish Spain a center of health care in the later Middle Ages. Through the Middle Ages certain churches and monasteries maintained primitive hostels for the sick and dying, and smaller groups ostracized as heretical gave attention to healing.

By the twelfth century, however, a series of church decrees severed the church from medicine, and in 1163 the Council of Tours prohibited church personnel from working as surgeons. The sick were referred to devotions based on claims for meritorious powers of relics and of the saints, for which medical attention was seen as competition. By 1566 canon law required physicians to discontinue treatment of any patient not confessing his sins by the third day of illness. Dissection of bodies was strictly prohibited, hampering the knowledge of both anatomy and physiology. The famed case of Servetus (1511-1553) stemmed in part from his violation of church law prohibiting dissection, although his discoveries preceded those of Harvey (1578-1657) in identifying the circulation of blood in the body.

Calvin (1509-1564) and Luther (1483-1546) followed the traditional premise that assigned healing miracles to the apostolic era, although the latter was impressed by a recovery of Melanchthon in response to prayer. Wesley's *Primitive Physick* ran many editions and was popular as a guide to healing. With the development of modern science in the late eighteenth century and onward, health care migrated gradually into secular circles, the transition largely complete by the 1850s.

Seventh-day Adventists became interested in health in the late 1850s and early 1860s, largely through the influence of Ellen G. White, who in 1863 made an appeal for the fledgling church to give serious attention to health as a religious ministry. Under the influence of a vigorous health reform movement in North America, Adventists adopted reforms that included rejection of the then-popular treatments with heavy metals and powerful herbal substances as well as the use of tobacco and alcohol. These were joined with promotion of a vegetarian reform diet and reliance upon natural remedies, particularly hydrotherapy. The Adventist theology of health accepts scientific advance as part of God's plan of healing, and the church is widely known for its health care ministry focused on wholistic principles.

To a degree unique in the Christian community Seventh-day Adventists, while relying on prayer and divine intervention in healing, include among God's healing agencies the understanding of an application of natural laws. In nature God has provided many features that may be used in preventive and curative ways to reduce suffering. Physical health is promoted by interaction with the cleansing and curative basics of nature. Therefore, prevention calls for attention to the positive effects of fresh air; pure water; a balanced, wholesome diet; access to sufficient sunshine; exercise and work; adequate rest; and in all, trust in God. At the same time, every proven therapy is to be applied in coping with disease and disability. Restoration of the whole person is the ultimate goal of health care, much of which can be achieved by a conscious return as nearly as possible to God's original plan for living.

This wholistic view of the person means that humans have no reality or existence apart from the body. A person is a complex, interactive unity, able to comprehend only through the function of the mind in intimate interaction with the physical body; hence care for all aspects of health is important, for it is service to God.

VI. Ellen G. White Comments

A. Introduction

As early as the 1860s Ellen White grasped the importance of the interactive unity among the physical, spiritual, and emotional, and began to write about ways in which treatment of the physical impacts the others. Over the course of the next 50 years her appeals for reform of health practices developed into a major theme, reaching its written climax in her book *The Ministry of Healing* (1905). Her basis rested on acknowledgment that the Scriptures and the laws of nature function jointly as agencies of God for the promotion of human wellness in all its dimensions. The healing ministry of Jesus provides the model of integrated healing for all aspects of the person.

Largely at Ellen White's instigation, the Seventh-day Adventist Church developed a network of health care institutions now to be found in most parts of the world, coupled with high-level offerings in professional health education and a major ministry in applied health education for the public. Health and healing from this perspective rest on a fusion of Christian biblical principles with an advanced understanding of therapeutics founded on natural law. The selections included below represent but a tiny fraction from her extensive writings on health and healing.

B. God Active in the World

"God is constantly employed in upholding and using as His servants the things that He has made. He works through the laws of nature, using them as His instruments. They are not self-acting. Nature in her work testifies of the intelligent presence and active agency of a Being who moves in all things according to His will. . . .

"The mechanism of the human body cannot be fully understood; it presents mysteries that baffle the most intelligent. It is not as the result of a mechanism, which, once set in motion, continues its work, that the pulse beats and breath follows breath. In God we live and move and have our being. The beating heart, the throbbing pulse, every nerve and muscle in the living organism is kept in order and activity by the power of an ever-present God" (MH 416, 417).

"In dwelling upon the laws of matter and the laws of nature, many lose sight of, if they do not deny, the continual and direct agency of God. They convey the idea that nature acts independently of God, having in and of itself its own limits and its own powers wherewith to work. In their minds there is a marked distinction between the natural and the supernatural. The natural is ascribed to ordinary causes, unconnected with the power of God. Vital power is attributed to matter, and nature is made a deity. It is supposed that matter is placed in certain relations and left to act from fixed laws with which God Himself cannot interfere; that nature is endowed with certain properties and placed subject to laws, and is then left to itself to obey these laws and perform the work originally commanded.

"This is false science; there is nothing in the Word of God to sustain it" (8T 259).

C. Nature's Laws as God's Laws

"The same power that upholds nature is working also in man. The same great laws that guide alike the star and the atom control human life. The laws that govern the heart's action, regulating the flow of the current of life to the body, are the laws of the mighty Intelligence that has the jurisdiction of the soul. From Him all life proceeds. Only in harmony with Him can be found its true sphere of action. For all the objects of His creation the condition is the same—a life sustained by receiving the life of God, a life exercised in harmony with the Creator's will. To transgress His law, physical, mental, or moral, is to place oneself out of harmony with the universe, to introduce discord, anarchy, ruin" (Ed 99, 100).

"Since the laws of nature are the laws of God, it is plainly our duty to give these laws careful study. We should study their requirements in regard to our own bodies and conform to them" (6T 369).

"God has formed laws which govern our constitutions, and these laws which He has placed in our being are divine, and for every transgression there is affixed a penalty, which must sooner or later be realized. The majority of diseases which the human family have been and still are suffering under, they have created by ignorance of their own organic laws" (*Health Reformer,* October 1866).

"God is as truly the author of physical laws as He is the author of the moral law. His law is written with His own finger upon every nerve, every muscle, every faculty, which has been entrusted to man" (COL 347, 348).

"It is as truly a sin to violate the laws of our being as it is to break the ten commandments. To do either is to break God's laws. Those who transgress the law of God in their physical organism, will be inclined to violate the law of God spoken from Sinai" (CDF 17).

D. Objectives for Practical Living

"Our first duty toward God and our fellow beings is that of self-development. Every faculty with which the Creator has endowed us should be cultivated to the highest degree of perfection, that we may be able to do the greatest amount of good of which we are capable. Hence that time is spent to good account which is directed to the establishment and preservation of sound physical and mental health. We cannot afford to dwarf or cripple a single function of mind or body by overwork or by abuse of any part of the living machinery" (Te 137).

"Let it ever be kept before the mind that the great object of hygienic reform is to secure the highest possible development of mind and soul and body. All the laws of nature—which are the laws of God—are designed for our good. Obedience to them will promote our happiness in this life, and will aid us in a preparation for the life to come" (CDF 23).

E. Healthful Living and Moral Decision-making

"These [our natural inclinations and appetites] were divinely appointed, and when given to man, were pure and holy. It was God's design that reason should rule the appetites, and that they should minister to our happiness. And when they are regulated and controlled by a sanctified reason, they are holiness unto the Lord" (Ms. 47, 1896).

"The brain nerves which communicate with the entire system are the only medium through which Heaven can communicate to man and affect his inmost life. Whatever disturbs the circulation of the electric currents in the nervous system lessens the strength of the vital powers, and the result is a deadening of the sensibilities of the mind" (2T 347).

"Our physical health is maintained by that which we eat; if our appetites are not under the control of a sanctified mind, if we are not temperate in all our eating and drinking, we shall not be in a state of mental and physical soundness to study the word with a purpose to learn what saith the Scripture—what shall I do to inherit eternal life?" (Te 15).

F. All Healing Is From God

"Through the agencies of nature, God is working, day by day, hour by hour, moment by moment, to keep us alive, to build up and restore us. When any part of the body sustains injury, a healing process is at once begun; nature's agencies are set at work to restore soundness. But the power working through these agencies is the power of God. All life-giving power is from Him. When one recovers from disease, it is God who restores him" (MH 112, 113).

"The love which Christ diffuses through the whole being is a vitalizing power. Every vital part—the brain, the heart, the nerves—it touches with healing. By it the highest energies of the being are roused to activity. It frees the soul from the guilt and sorrow, the anxiety and care, that crush the life forces. With it come serenity and composure. It implants in the soul, joy that nothing earthly can destroy—joy in the Holy Spirit—health-giving joy" (ibid. 115).

G. Mind and Body

"The sympathy which exists between the mind and the body is very great. When one is affected, the other responds. The condition of the mind has much to do with the health of the physical system. If the mind is free and happy, under a consciousness of rightdoing and a sense of satisfaction in causing happiness to others, it will create a cheerfulness that will react upon the whole system, causing a freer circulation of the blood and a toning up of the entire body" (4T 60).

H. The Christian Physician

"Every medical practitioner, whether he acknowledges it or not, is responsible for the souls as well as the bodies of his patients. The Lord expects of us much more than we often do for Him. Every physician should be a devoted, intelligent gospel medical missionary, familiar with Heaven's remedy for the sin-sick soul as well as with the science of healing bodily disease. . . .

"The physician should not only give as much physical relief as possible to those who are soon to lie in the grave, but he should also relieve their burdened souls. Present before them the uplifted Saviour. Let them behold the Lamb of God, who taketh away the sin of the world" (MM 31).

"In the ministry of healing the physician is to be a coworker with Christ. The Saviour ministered to both the soul and the body. The gospel which He taught was a message of spiritual life and of physical restoration. Deliverance from sin and the healing of disease were linked together. The same ministry is committed to the Christian physician" (MH 111).

I. Faith, Healing, and Prayer

"There are cases where God works decidedly by His divine power in the restoration of health. But not all the sick are healed. Many are laid away to sleep in Jesus. John on the Isle of Patmos was bidden to write: 'Blessed are the dead which die in the Lord from henceforth: Yea, saith the Spirit, that they may rest from their labors; and their works do follow them' (Rev. 14:13). From this we see that if persons are not raised to health, they should not on this account be judged as wanting in faith.

"We all desire immediate and direct answers to our prayers, and are tempted to become discouraged when the answer is delayed or comes in an unlooked-for form. But God is too wise and good to answer our prayers always at just the time and in just the manner we desire. He will do more and better for us than to accomplish all our wishes. And because we can trust His wisdom and love, we should not ask Him to concede to our will, but should seek to enter into and accomplish His purpose" (ibid. 230, 231).

J. Use of Remedies and Faith

"Those who seek healing by prayer should not neglect to make use of the remedial agencies within their reach. It is not a denial of faith to use such remedies as God has provided to alleviate pain and to aid nature in her work of restoration. It is no denial of faith to cooperate with God, and to place themselves in the condition most favorable to recovery. God has put it in our power to obtain a knowledge of the laws of life. This knowledge has been placed within our reach for use. We should employ every facility for the restoration of health, taking every advantage possible, working in harmony with natural laws. When we have prayed for the recovery of the sick, we can work with all the more energy, thanking God that we have the privilege of cooperating with Him, and asking His blessing on the means which He Himself has provided" (ibid. 231, 232).

"When the Israel of today humble themselves before Him, and cleanse the soul temple from all defilement, He will hear their prayers in behalf of the sick and will bless in the use of His remedies for disease. When in faith the human agent does all he can to combat disease, using the simple methods of treatment that God has provided, his efforts will be blessed of God" (9T 164).

K. Importance of Health Reform

"The health reform is one branch of the great work which is to fit a people for the coming of the Lord. It is as closely connected with the third angel's message as the hand is with the body" (CH 20, 21).

VII. Literature

Bacchiocchi, Samuele. *Wine in the Bible.* Berrien Springs, Mich.: Biblical Perspectives, 1989.

Brown, Michael L. *Israel's Divine Healer.* Grand Rapids: Zondervan Publishing House, 1995.

Brunt, John. *A Day for Healing: The Meaning of Jesus' Sabbath Miracles.* Washington, D.C.: Review and Herald, 1981.

Frost, Evelyn. *Christian Healing.* London: Mobrays, 1940.

Grmek, Mirko D. *Diseases in the Ancient Greek World.* Baltimore: Johns Hopkins University, 1989.

Gustafson, James M. *The Contribution of Theology to Medical Ethics.* Milwaukee: Marquette University Press, 1975.

Harrison, R. K. "Healing, Health" in *Interpreter's Dictionary of the Bible.* New York and Nashville: Abingdon Press, 1962. Vol. 2.

Hogan, Larry P. *Healing in the Second Tempel [sic] Period.* Göttingen: Vandenhoeck & Ruprecht, 1992.

Kee, Howard Clark. *Medicine, Miracle, and Magic in New Testament Times.* Cambridge: Cambridge University Press, 1986.

Kelsey, Morton T. *Healing and Christianity.* London: SCM Press, 1973.

Lindström, Fredrik. *Suffering and Sin: Interpretations of Illness in the Individual Complaint Psalms.* Stockholm: Almquist and Wiksell International, 1994.

Marty, Martin E. *Health and Medicine in the Lutheran Tradition: Being Well.* New York: Crossroad Publishing Co., 1986.

Murray, Andrew. *Divine Healing.* Springdale, Pa.: Whitaker House, 1982.

Palmer, Bernard, ed. *Medicine and the Bible.* Exeter: Paternoster Press, 1986.

Pilch, John J. "Sickness and Healing in Luke-Acts" in *The Social World of Luke-Acts: Models for Interpretation,* ed. Jerome H. Neyrey. Peabody, Mass.: Hendrickson, 1991.

Proctor, Stoy, et al., eds. *Health 2000 and Beyond.* Silver Spring, Md.: General Conference of Seventh-day Adventists, Health and Temperance Department, 1994.

Seybold, Klaus, and Ulrich Mueller. *Sickness and Healing.* Nashville: Abingdon Press, 1981.

Short, A. R. *The Bible and Modern Medicine.* Exeter: Paternoster Press, 1953.

Smith, C. R. *The Physician Examines the Bible.* New York: Philosophical Library, 1950.

Stockmayer, Otto. *Sickness and the Gospel.* London: Bemrose & Sons, 1887.

Tillich, Paul. "The Meaning of Health," in *On Moral Medicine: Theological Perspectives in Medical Ethics.* ed. Stephen E. Lammers and Allen Verhey. Grand Rapids: William B. Eerdmans Pub. Co., 1987.

Torrey, R. A. *Divine Healing: Does God Perform Miracles Today?* New York, Chicago: Fleming H. Revell Co., 1974.

Vermes, Geza. *Jesus the Jew.* New York: Macmillan, 1973.

Warfield, Benjamin B. *Counterfeit Miracles.* 1918. Republished as *Miracles: Yesterday and Today, True and False.* Grand Rapids: Eerdmans, 1965.

Weatherhead, Leslie. *Psychology, Religion, and Healing.* New York: Abingdon, 1951.

Wilkinson, John. *Health and Healing: Studies in New Testament Principles and Practice.* Edinburgh: Handsel Press, Ltd., 1980.

World Health Organization. *WHO Basic Document.* Geneva, 1948.

Biblical Apocalyptic

William G. Johnsson*

Introduction

Anyone who takes the Bible seriously must seek to understand its apocalyptic element. This element is significant for both its quantity and its role. Two books of the Bible are almost entirely apocalyptic in nature—Daniel in the Old Testament and Revelation in the New. Apart from these, several portions of other books in both Testaments consist of apocalyptic. Further, we find apocalyptic scattered among the prophetic writings of the OT and assigned in the NT to Jesus Himself, as well as to the apostles.

Throughout the twentieth century apocalyptic has generated considerable scholarly interest and investigation. Attempts to engage the biblical element often have led students of the Scriptures on wider quests; they have sought to understand biblical apocalyptic by attempting to trace its roots in extrabiblical sources. Thus the study that began with biblical apocalyptic usually has become an investigation of apocalyptic per se—apocalyptic as a literary genre.

Despite considerable effort on the part of many scholars, no clear consensus regarding the meaning and interpretation of apocalyptic has emerged. Even a definition of apocalyptic eludes universal acceptance.

This article has been prepared from the conviction that a study of biblical apocalyptic is both necessary and possible—necessary because of the importance of the apocalyptic element in the Bible itself, and possible if presuppositions of interpretation are subjected to close scrutiny and the biblical text is made the focus of effort. Thus while this essay is written from an awareness of scholarly efforts to understand apocalyptic as a genre, it concentrates on the biblical text itself rather than on supposed extrabiblical sources of apocalyptic.

---

*This article, particularly in the section dealing with the historical overview of apocalyptic, draws upon an unpublished paper on biblical apocalyptic by the late Arthur J. Ferch.

I. The Definition and Characteristics of Biblical Apocalyptic

A. Definition

The word "apocalyptic" comes from the Greek word *apokalypsis*, which means "revelation" or "disclosure." Although apocalyptic is an adjective, in modern times it has come to function as a noun to describe revelatory literature. Nouns deriving from *apokalypsis* are apocalypse (the revelation itself), apocalypticism (the study of such revelations), and apocalypticist (the seer of the revelation).

The first attested use of the word *apokalypsis* is in Revelation 1:1: "The revelation [*apokalypsis*] of Jesus Christ, which God gave him to show to his servants what must soon take place; and he made it known by sending his angel to his servant John." Here the term appears to be a title for a specific type of composition; hence the last book of the Bible is frequently called the Apocalypse.

Other writings of the Bible resemble the Apocalypse, in both manner of presentation and message. In particular, the OT book of Daniel shows marked similarities with the revelation given to John: common symbolism, common time periods, and a common concentration on last-day events. On the face of it Daniel and Revelation are twin books that invite the student of Scripture to study them together.

While Daniel and Revelation provide the clearest profiles of biblical apocalyptic books, apocalyptic writings occur in several other places as portions of biblical books. Thus in the OT, Isaiah 24-27; Ezekiel 38; 39; Joel 2; 3; and Zechariah 9-14 resemble the content of Daniel and Revelation, as do Matthew 24; Mark 13; Luke 17; 21; 1 Thessalonians 4; and 2 Thessalonians 1; 2 in the NT.

By biblical apocalyptic, therefore, we mean the books of Daniel and Revelation and these sections of other biblical works. All these materials exhibit common features that at once resemble one another and set them apart from the other literature of the Bible. This article addresses principally these materials, especially Daniel and Revelation—their characteristics, interpretation, and theological significance.

To grasp the significance of this definition, we note two other understandings of apocalyptic in vogue. One concerns apocalyptic as a literary genre; the other, apocalyptic as a worldview.

Although *apokalypsis* comes from the Bible, this term has been applied in antiquity and in modern scholarship to other writings that seem to resemble the Apocalypse of John. Especially since 1832 (see IV. D. 2) noncanonical writings from both Jewish and Christian sources have been brought together with biblical apocalyptic to form a corpus of works believed to be more or less distinct from other forms of literature and labeled simply "apocalyptic."

This approach has led to an extraordinary result: instead of biblical apocalyptic shaping the definition of apocalyptic, the larger body of literature now is used to shape the understanding of biblical apocalyptic! For example, several of the nonbiblical apocalypses are obviously pseudonymous; in consequence, many scholars today call into question the authorship of both Daniel and the Revelation. Thus we find the primary meaning of "apocalypse" in *Webster's New World Dictionary* as "any of various Jewish and Christian pseudonymous writings (c. 200 B.C.- c. A.D. 300) depicting symbolically the ultimate destruction of evil and triumph of good."

Although the focus of this article is biblical apocalyptic, we are aware of the larger corpus of literature dubbed "apocalyptic" (although scholars struggle to define its limits and to reduce it all to a common definition). We believe, however, that the biblical material stands apart. It alone holds a place in the Sacred Canon, accepted as God-breathed like the rest of Scripture.

Another popular use of apocalyptic involves a particular worldview. Both apocalypse and apocalyptic have been applied as metaphors for the contemporary human condition, which considers life as a battleground. A broken planet, ravaged by opposing forces and engulfed by wars and threats of wars, abandoned the idealism generated by idealistic philosophers and liberal theologians of the eighteenth and nineteenth centuries to discover in its own agonies a portrait of the contending forces reflected in the biblical literature. This trend is evidenced in a spate of articles, books, and motion pictures that describe our chaotic and anxiety-ridden age moving toward a cosmic holocaust.

This current use of apocalyptic terminology cannot control our understanding of the scriptural material. Biblical apocalyptic must disclose itself to us on its own terms.

B. Characteristics

Only the last book of the Bible is called an apocalypse; nevertheless Daniel and the other portions of Scripture we identified above share significant and recurrent features with the Apocalypse.

1. Revelatory Literature

First and foremost, biblical apocalyptic is revelatory literature. It discloses that which has been hidden from human sight and knowledge. The curtain that presently hides the heavenly world and future realities from our view is drawn aside to provide a glimpse of the divine world and its involvement in the affairs of our planet.

2. Circumstances and Manner of Revelation

The literary forms of both Daniel and Revelation, though complex, spell out the circumstances. Thus the narrative framework of the book of Daniel (the apocalyptic visions are limited to chapters 2; 7-12) consists of stories about Daniel and his three companions, their capture, life in exile, and relationship to foreign kings (Dan. 1; 3-6). It tells us when the various recorded events or visions occurred (e.g., Dan. 1:1; 2:1; 5:30; 7:1; 8:1; 9:1; 10:1). It also provides information about the seer's disposition (e.g., Dan. 7:1, 15, 16, 19, 28; 8:1, 2, 15-18, 27; 12:5-13).

Similarly, the framework of the book of Revelation, largely in the form of a circular letter (Rev. 2; 3; 22:7, 16-19), informs the reader that John was in exile on Patmos when the revelation was given (Rev. 1:9, 10).

The apocalyptic sections of Isaiah, Ezekiel, Joel, and Zechariah come in the midst of prophecies. Ezekiel prefaces his apocalypse with "The word of the Lord came to me" (Eze. 38:1). Our Lord's apocalypse was given on the Mount of Olives shortly before the Passover (Matt. 24:1-3), while Paul's came in the middle of a letter (2 Thess. 1:1).

The manner of revelation is expressed in

terms of visions and dreams in Daniel and Revelation (e.g., Dan. 2:19; 7:1, 2; 8:1, 2; 10:5, 7, 8; Rev. 6:1-12; 8:2; 10; 12:1–15:7). Some of the visions are supplemented by auditions (e.g., Dan. 8:23-25; Rev. 12:10; 14:13; 16:1; 22:8). However, apocalyptic messages elsewhere come by conversation (Jesus), letter (Paul), or prophetic utterance (Isaiah, Ezekiel, Joel, Zechariah).

Although the *content* of biblical apocalyptic may appear mysterious, there is nothing mysterious as to how the messages were *conveyed* to humanity. Biblical apocalyptic is not secret literature generated in time and place unknown to us. Christ Himself brings the apocalyptic word in both the Gospels and Revelation.

3. Heavenly Beings

Though the ultimate source of the revelations is God, heavenly beings may mediate the messages (Dan. 7:16; 8:15; 9:22; Rev. 1:1; 7:13-17; 10; 17; 19:9, 10; 21:9–22:12, 16).

Heavenly beings feature prominently in Daniel and Revelation. In Daniel, Gabriel and Michael not only mediate the divine communications but also struggle with evil supernatural powers that represent the interests of Persia and Greece (Dan. 10:13-21). Michael arises at the end of time to defend God's people (Dan. 12:1). A heavenly messenger protects Daniel in the lions' den, and Nebuchadnezzar recognizes that an angel delivers Daniel's companions from death in the fiery furnace (Dan. 6:22; 3:28). In Revelation angels deliver messages, stand at the four corners of the earth, surround the throne of God, sound trumpets, pour out the bowls of God's wrath, and minister to John (Rev. 5:2; 7:1; 8:2; 10:1; 12:7-10; 14:6-10).

4. Times of Crisis or National Tragedy

This setting applies particularly to Daniel and Revelation. Daniel received his messages while in exile. Jerusalem and the Temple lay in ruins, and most of the people of Judah had been deported to Babylon. John had also been forced into exile. Despair, crisis, and persecution are the backdrop to both books. The purpose of the messages given to both visionaries under such circumstances was to assure them that, contrary to all appearances, God was still in control of history. Ultimately the divine purpose would triumph, God's people would be vindicated, and the divine kingdom established. In a setting of suffering, God's messages provided comfort and hope.

Likewise, Ezekiel wrote while in exile, and Joel's apocalyptic was given at a time of devastation (Joel 1). On the other hand, Zechariah wrote after the Jews returned from exile. Nor is it clear that crisis furnished the occasion for Matthew 24/Mark 13/Luke 21 or Paul's apocalypse. Rather, Jesus' words were occasioned by incidental remarks of the disciples (Matt. 24), and Paul's by false ideas that were current among believers (2 Thess. 2:1, 2).

Therefore, we cannot state that biblical apocalyptic always arises out of times of crisis and national tragedy, although it does for Daniel and Revelation.

5. Striking Contrasts

Biblical apocalyptic is marked by striking contrasts. The writers make unmistakable distinctions between good and evil, the present and the future, that which is above and that which is below.

Daniel distinguishes sharply between the present transitory kingdoms of this world and the future eternal kingdom of God (e.g., Dan. 2:21, 44; 4:3, 34, 35; 6:26; 7:14, 27). He draws contrasts between the little horn power and the manlike being, the persecutor and the persecuted (Dan. 7). The revelator differentiates between the seal of God and the mark of the beast, between the deceptive serpent and the faithful witness, the pure woman and the gaudy harlot, the armies of heaven and the forces of earth, Jerusalem and Babylon (Rev. 7:2; 9:11-19; 12:1; 13:16; 17:1; 18; 21:2).

Nowhere in the Bible are heaven and earth in such close touch as in Revelation. This relationship between the realms above and realms below has been labeled a vertical continuity. But Daniel also portrays heavenly settings in connection with descriptions of activities taking place on earth. The prophet beholds events occurring in heaven that are contemporaneous with events transpiring on earth (e.g., Dan. 7:8-14). The great controversy between the angelic beings finds its counterpart in the struggles on earth below (e.g., 10:12-20). The meaning of the cross of Christ is given a cosmic perspective in Revelation 12, manifesting its significance for both past and future, as well as for the realms above and below.

6. Vivid Imagery

Apocalyptic writings are heavy with imagery. Indeed, the symbols in apocalyptic compositions are often heightened and composite in nature. Whereas the prophet might refer to ordinary beasts, the apocalyptic author sees a beast with ten horns and seven heads, resembling a leopard, with feet like those of a bear, and a mouth like that of a lion (Rev. 13:1, 2).

Composite, vivid, and extensive imagery is woven into the tapestry of the messages of both Daniel and the revelator. We see winged lions and leopards; a little horn with eyes and mouth; one like a son of man with hair white like wool, eyes like blazing fire, feet like bronze glowing in a furnace, a voice sounding like rushing waters; locusts that have the appearance of horses with faces like human faces, hair like women's hair, and teeth like lions' teeth (Dan. 7:4, 6; Rev. 1:12-16; 9:7-9).

In biblical apocalyptic apart from Daniel and Revelation we do not find such heavy use of symbolism. However, the language is vivid, with graphic word pictures and strong contrasts.

7. The End of History

Biblical apocalyptic discloses God's long-range plans for history. Predictions of the rise and fall of kings and kingdoms assert God's control of history. In Daniel, for instance, God preordained events in Nebuchadnezzar's Babylon, which gives way to Medo-Persia and Greece (Dan. 2:38; 8:20, 21). Other powers would succeed until finally the indestructible and triumphant kingdom of God would supersede all human authorities (2:44; 7:18, 27). Similarly, Revelation 12-14 describes a series of events that take the reader from the conflict in heaven to the death of Jesus on the cross, through a "time, and times, and half a time" on to the harvest of the earth at the second coming of Christ.

The dawn of the new age is heralded by physical, political, and moral woes. Signs of the end consist of an unprecedented time of trouble, earthquakes, war, and bloodshed (Dan. 12:1). Cosmic disturbances will affect the sun, moon, and stars (Mark 13:24, 25; Rev. 6:12, 13). To herald the end of the present age, the sky will vanish like a scroll, and mountains and islands will be removed from their place (Rev. 6:14).

Daniel is convinced that "what is determined shall be done" (Dan. 11:36). "Seventy weeks of years are decreed concerning" Daniel's people and Jerusalem (9:24). The visions in both Daniel and Revelation reveal what God has determined shall occur. No conditions are listed in the dream visions through which humans can alter the divinely ordained course of events. The course of the universe has been decided, and nothing the hearers or readers of the biblical apocalypses can do will change this plan.

Daniel foresees a judgment preceding the eschaton. The end will come in an unprecedented time of trouble from which God's people, "whose name shall be found written in the book," shall be delivered. The seer is assured that many of those who sleep in the dust of the earth shall awake and "those who are wise shall shine like the brightness of the firmament; and those who turn many to righteousness, like the stars for ever and ever" (12:1-3; cf. 7:9-14).

The eschatological scenario in Revelation includes cosmic disturbances and eschatological upheavals (Rev. 6:12, 13; 16); Christ in the role of a heavenly warrior pressing the battle against the beast, false prophet, and the kings of the earth and their armies (Rev. 19:11-21); Satan's confinement for 1,000 years and subsequent release when he marshals his evil troops against the camp of the saints (Rev. 20); the destruction of the devil, death, and hades; the resurrection of the righteous and their rule with Christ; the final judgment (Rev. 20); the creation of a new heaven and a new earth; and the establishment of the Holy City (Rev. 21; 22).

In the other biblical apocalyptic materials we do not find the wealth of detail that Daniel and Revelation provide. This is not surprising, since these materials are less extensive. However, like Daniel and Revelation we find in all of them a concentration on the end of human history as God brings about closure to the present world order and ushers in His reign.

C. Relation to Classical Prophecy

Biblical apocalyptic should be viewed as part of biblical prophecy. The apocalyptic portions of Isaiah, Ezekiel, Joel, and Zechariah that we have identified occur in the midst of prophetic messages. The book of Daniel originally found its place in the Hebrew canon among the prophetic works (Hasel in Holbrook 1986, 2:150), while Jesus referred to its writer as "the prophet Daniel" (Matt. 24:15). And the final book of the Bible itself, the one that gave rise to the word "apocalypse," is designated as "the book of this prophecy" (Rev. 22:19).

Excluding the book of Daniel, the literary works that run from Isaiah to Malachi commonly are termed classical prophecy. They were produced by an extraordinary line of Hebrew figures—the prophets.

The prophet (nābî') was a messenger of Yahweh. He or she was raised up, set apart, and empowered by Yahweh to bring "the word of the Lord" to His people and sometimes to the surrounding nations. The prophet spoke for Yahweh, proclaiming boldly and often at risk of life the messages that the Lord revealed.

"The word of the Lord," declaring the divine will, covered a wide range of topics. Many prophecies dealt with the here and now, rebuking sins such as drunkenness, idolatry and imitation of their neighbors' pagan practices, oppression of the poor, injustice, bribery, immorality, and spiritual torpor, thereby calling individuals or the nation to repentance. Such messages were *forth*telling, not *fore*telling, and they account for much of classical prophecy.

Other prophecies, however, were predictive in nature. They foretold the rise and fall of kings and priests, or calamities that the Lord would bring upon a city or the nation. Sometimes they proclaimed Yahweh's judgment on other nations or cities outside Israel. The time involved in the prediction might be short (40 days, Jonah 3:4), a specific number of years (40 years, Eze. 4:6), or stretch into the indefinite future.

A term of particular significance in predictive prophecy is "the day of the Lord." It describes Yahweh's visitation in wrath on a city, His people, a foreign nation, or the whole earth (e.g., Isa. 2:12; 13:6; Eze. 30:3; Amos 5:18; Zeph. 1:14).

Not all predictions carried messages of doom. The Hebrew prophets foretold not only the captivity of Jerusalem or exile of the nation but also the subsequent return from exile and restoration of the land, as well as Yahweh's punishment of Israel's enemies.

The NT has nothing comparable to classical prophecy. However, Jesus of Nazareth proclaimed, taught, and lived in the prophetic mode. Many of the people of His time saw Him as a prophet or even as one of the ancient prophets raised to life. Jesus may rightly be seen as the climax and culmination of the OT prophets. Among His messages we also find predictions. In the NT church, prophecy continued as one of the gifts of the Spirit (1 Cor. 12:10; Eph. 4:11); however, with the church rather than the nation as the recipient of divine messages, the role of the prophet inevitably changed. (See Gifts IV. A-C; VIII. A, B.)

We must place apocalyptic within this fairly

large framework of biblical prophecy. Biblical apocalyptic belongs among the predictive material of biblical prophecy, not as the sum total of this material but as an important and distinctive part.

As we noticed above, the distinguishing characteristics of biblical apocalyptic in part overlap classical prophecy, but taken together they establish a profile that warrants separate classification. When we read Daniel and Revelation, we at once sense that we have encountered different material, both in form and in content. The same happens with Isaiah 24, Ezekiel 38, Joel 2, Zechariah 9, Matthew 24, or 2 Thessalonians 2. It is not as though we had a new writer, but the mode of communication has shifted. A rough comparison would be the shift that the reader feels before a change from prose to poetry within the same book, or even a change from words to pictures.

At the same time, however, no hard and fast line of demarcation between classical prophecy and biblical apocalyptic can be drawn. We see interconnections on various levels. Thus the visions of dreams that so characterize Daniel and Revelation also appear to some degree in prophecy: Amos reports symbolic visions (Amos 7:7-9; 8:1-3). Again, Ezekiel, a contemporary of Daniel, is accompanied by a transcendent person (Eze. 40:3). In Zechariah 4 an angel appears, dialogues with the prophet, and provides the interpretation of the vision.

The point at issue, however, is not whether some of the features of apocalyptic may be found in classical prophecy, but rather the *predominance* of these features in biblical apocalyptic. And beyond these overlapping features we discern clear discontinuities between classical and apocalyptic prophecy in terms of the predictive element itself.

Prophecy contains predictions that are primarily local and contemporary. In some cases, these prophecies expand to find a broader fulfillment at the end of the age. Apocalyptic, on the other hand, has a continuous perspective that unfolds through time and encompasses the whole of history.

Another fundamental difference lies in the character of the respective predictions. The nonapocalyptic predictions tend to expect a future that will arise out of the present, whereas biblical apocalyptic by and large predicts a future that will break into the present.

The manner in which conditionality impacts predictions in nonapocalyptic and apocalyptic also differs (see II. B).

D. Apocalyptic in the Biblical Pattern

The relationship between classical prophecy and biblical apocalyptic that we have described here—apocalyptic as part of biblical prophecy, but with distinctive features—differs profoundly from the view held by historico-critical scholars. Because they have tried to establish a genre of apocalyptic, drawing together many noncanonical materials, biblical apocalyptic has ceased to exist in its own right. Rather, it has emerged as something imported into the Scriptures, probably from unknown writers who took the name of biblical characters to try to obtain credibility for their material. According to this scenario, Daniel was not written by Daniel but by someone in the second century B.C.; Jesus did not give the apocalyptic prediction of Matthew 24/Mark 13/Luke 21; Paul borrowed from a Jewish apocalypse when he wrote 2 Thessalonians; and the apostle John did not write Revelation. (See Interpretation IV. F. 1-4.)

When we study biblical apocalyptic in its own right, however, we see a radically different picture. We see apocalyptic arising within biblical prophecy in preexilic times. During the Exile the development of apocalyptic goes further, as Daniel presents much of the material of his book in this mode. Finally, in the NT an entire book—fittingly the final one of the biblical canon in that apocalyptic focuses on the end-time—is written as an apocalypse.

All attempts to trace the origins of biblical apocalyptic to a noncanonical genre of apocalyptic literature have failed. Instead of the attribution of biblical apocalyptic to non-canonical sources, the more reasonable case is that the nonbiblical was written in imitation of, or influenced by, biblical apocalyptic.

II. The Interpretation of Biblical Apocalyptic

Biblical apocalyptic manifests distinctive features that call for its own principles of interpretation. At the same time, however, biblical apocalyptic is part of the larger literature of predictive prophecy, which calls attention to how apocalyptic predictions compare and contrast with nonapocalyptic ones. We shall confine our discussion to the principles for interpreting Daniel and Revelation, the two major works of biblical apocalyptic. (See Interpretation III. E. 3.)

A. Presuppositions

How the interpreter relates to the element of prediction in the Bible becomes a crucial hermeneutical issue.

The Bible writers unabashedly assert that Yahweh knows the future. Indeed, His ability to foretell events sets Him apart from other gods. "Set forth your case, says the Lord; bring your proofs, says the King of Jacob. Let them bring them, and tell us what is to happen. Tell us the former things, what they are, that we may consider them, that we may know their outcome; or declare to us the things to come. Tell us what is to come hereafter, that we may know that you are gods" (Isa. 41:21-23; see also verse 26; 43:9; 44:7; 45:21; 48:14). In the NT Jesus utters predictions as do other prophets, while the Apocalypse claims to show "what must soon take place" (Rev. 1:1) and "what is to take place hereafter" (verse 19).

The presuppositions from which interpretation of biblical apocalyptic proceeds are, therefore, that God knows the future and that He has revealed it in His Word. All the predictions of Scripture—including biblical apocalyptic—must be taken seriously as a portrayal of the future that God has chosen to make known to humanity.

Therefore, the predictions cited in biblical apocalyptic are not, as some scholars assert, historical accounts given in the guise of prophecy (the term used is *vaticinia ex eventu,* "prophecies after the event"). Daniel, for instance, need not be dated to the second century B.C. on the assumption that the book mentions historical events in the reign of Antiochus IV Epiphanes (Dan. 11:31). It is rather a series of predictions that reach, not only from Daniel's day through the second century B.C., but to the climax of history at the last day. (See Interpretation IV. F. 3.)

Jesus Christ so understood Daniel. Referring to Daniel (Dan. 8:9-14; 9:27; 11:31), He stated, "So when you see the desolating sacrilege spoken of by the prophet Daniel, standing in the holy place (let the reader understand), then let those who are in Judea flee to the mountains" (Matt. 24:15, 16). Obviously Jesus viewed this prediction as still future in His day—He presupposed the veracity of biblical predictions. We too approach biblical apocalyptic with the same presuppositions.

B. Apocalyptic and Nonapocalyptic Predictions

Some Bible students assert that all Bible prophecy, both classical and apocalyptic, is conditional. They see apocalyptic prophecy as a statement of God's *purpose* for the future. God depends on agencies such as the nation of Israel for the accomplishment of His plans. If Israel fails, the prophecy is moot. According to this view, the prophecies of the book of Daniel collapsed because of Israel's national and spiritual disobedience.

In contrast, other Bible students hold that apocalyptic prophecy is a statement of God's *foreknowledge.* Because God sees the future unerringly, these predictions are absolutely certain—not conditional upon a particular human response.

This critical issue of interpretation can be adjudicated only by a careful study of the various types of predictive prophecy in Scripture.

1. Nonapocalyptic Predictions

There are at least four groups of predictions in the nonapocalyptic biblical literature.

a. Predictions to Israel that arise out of a covenant context. Probably the large majority of predictions in nonapocalyptic literature belong here. The eighth- and seventh-century B.C. prophets rebuke the people of Israel for their sins, calling them back to Yahweh, warning them of impending doom because of their unfaithfulness to the covenant.

Isaiah 1 provides a classic illustration. Israel is arraigned before God, who calls heaven and earth to witness (verse 2). Yahweh's complaint is that His people are guilty of gross stupidity. Although He has nurtured them tenderly, they do not display even the elemental gratitude of an ox or an ass (verses 2, 3). Their failure to live within the covenant is demonstrated in unethical practices (verses 4, 15, 17, 21-23) and religious observances that are merely formal (verses 11-14). Because of Israel's sins the land has been devastated (verses 5-9) as Yahweh has punished national transgression. Yet He has not cast them off utterly. He has left a remnant (verse 9). Now He calls them back to the covenant: "Come now, let us reason together" (verse 18). Because Yahweh is a covenant-keeping God, one who remains faithful despite humankind's unfaithfulness, because His lovingkindness (*hesed*) is at the heart of the covenant, there is hope for Israel—forgiveness and restoration (verses 25-27).

Israel's history through the OT exhibits an oscillatory pattern. Prosperity, apostasy, decline, repentance, restoration—this is the cycle in Judges, Kings, and Chronicles. The principle governing the pattern is "If you are willing and obedient, you shall eat the good of the land; but if you refuse and rebel, you shall be devoured by the sword; for the mouth of the Lord has spoken" (Isa. 1:19, 20).

Israel's history in its various fortunes demonstrates the truth of Deuteronomy 28. This passage sets out the two ways that lie before the young nation. If the people will "obey the voice of the Lord [their] God, being careful to do all his commandments," they will be blessed richly—materially, nationally, spiritually (verses 1-14). If, however, they are unfaithful to the covenant provisions, terrible curses will come upon them until Israel is a byword among the nations (verses 15-68).

Repeatedly the prophets speak to a sinful nation in terms of these blessings and curses. Are their words, however, to be considered predictive prophecy?

The element of conditionality is self-evident: the people's response determines the outcome. That the words are "prophecy," in the sense of a message from Yahweh, is also true—the prophets are conscious of a divine impelling. But we should not consider such messages *predictive* prophecy in the sense of disclosing a future otherwise unknown. Rather, they are applying the "law" of the covenant, something as fixed as Yahweh Himself.

The element of prediction here is no stronger than an NT parallel: "He who believes in him is not condemned; he who does not believe is condemned already, because he has not believed in the name of the only Son of God" (John 3:18). We are dealing with certainties, with the very plan of God for humankind. It is laid down by Him and cannot be negotiated.

Predictions in this first class are covenant promises or threats rather than "conditional" prophecy. These remarks also apply to the provisions of the Abrahamic covenant. Like the promises of Deuteronomy 28, they presuppose an obedient response (cf. Gen. 12:1-3; 13:14-18; 15; 17; 18:17-19; 21:1-13; 22:1-18).

b. Short-term predictions. Many short-term OT predictions do not come within the promises/threats of the covenant relationship. They involve surrounding nations and, in some cases, individuals.

Although Yahweh has entered into covenant relation with one nation—Israel—He is nonetheless Lord of the world. He does not condemn wickedness among His special people only to wink at it among the surrounding nations. Therefore, they too come under judgment (e.g., Isa. 13; Jer. 46-51; Eze. 25-32; Amos 1; 2).

Predictions concerning Israel's neighbors are not as clear-cut in interpretation as the covenant promises/threats to Israel, however. Conditionality stands in a certain tension with divine sovereignty.

In some cases God's promises or judgments are linked directly to human decisions.

"If at any time I declare concerning a nation or a kingdom, that I will pluck up and break down and destroy it, and if that nation, concerning which I have spoken, turns from its evil, I will repent of the evil that I intended to do to it. And if at any time I declare concerning a nation or a kingdom that I will build and plant it, and if it does evil in my sight, not listening to my voice, then I will repent of the good which I had intended to do to it" (Jer. 18:7-10).

Omitting mention of a condition does not necessarily negate conditionality. If the prophecy grows out of the covenant, if it is related to a blessing or a curse where a human response is involved, then it is conditional, even if not so declared (e.g., Jer. 31:35-37).

The Jonah case provides the sharpest example of conditionality. Change in the people leads to a change in the divine plan (Jonah 3:9, 10). The final verse of the book underscores Yahweh's character, which ensures both justice and mercy in all His dealings. "And should not I pity Nineveh, that great city, in which there are more than a hundred and twenty thousand persons who do not know their right hand from their left, and also much cattle?" (Jonah 4:11).

Yahweh does not destroy capriciously. Although Israel's neighbors are outside the covenant, the God of all the earth will deal justly in whatever He brings upon them. We may be sure that when a nation goes down to ruin, ultimately it is because of its gross wickedness. We should note that Jonah's prophecy concerning Nineveh is but one of a series

delivered against the city by messengers of Yahweh. Nahum predicts in graphic detail the final end of Nineveh (cf, Zeph. 2:13-15).

The example of Nineveh is not typical of the prophecies concerning the nations. From Isaiah to Malachi there is no instance of a prophet's being sent to deliver in person the word of doom. How the nations heard the divine threatenings (perhaps through ambassadors at times; cf. Isa. 21; Jer. 27) or whether they always heard, we are not told. These dire predictions come in the setting of divine certainty; Yahweh has determined that retribution cannot be delayed.

Consider two striking examples from Isaiah's predictions about the nations. In chapter 10 we meet the dramatic "Ah, Assyria, the rod of my anger, the staff of my fury!" (verse 5). Here Assyria is God's appointed instrument to chastise Israel. But haughty Assyria itself will come to an end after the divine purpose is fulfilled (verses 12-19). With this prediction we have gone beyond conditionality into the realm of divine sovereignty.

The second example is that of Cyrus (Isa. 44:28; 45:1-6). Here a heathen king is called by name (Isa. 45:4) before his birth so that Yahweh's plan to restore Israel from Babylonian captivity may come to fruition. This is not a conditional prophecy; it is rather to be interpreted in terms of God's foreknowledge and sovereignty.

There are not as many short-term predictions in the NT, but some occur. Agabus foretells the famine (Acts 11:28); the friends of Paul foresee by the Spirit the bonds that await him in Jerusalem (Acts 20:23; 21:10, 11). The most significant short-term prediction, however, concerns the fall of Jerusalem and the destruction of the Temple (Matt. 24; Mark 13; Luke 21). Conditionality is mentioned in none of these. With Paul, the only "if" lies in the decision to go or not to go to Jerusalem. There is no hint that the impending fall of Jerusalem is conditional. The question is only "When will this be?" (Matt. 24:3).

It is obvious, therefore, that when interpreting short-term predictions outside the covenant provisions, the prophecy may or may not be conditioned on human response. Divine sovereignty and human decisions intersect and interact.

c. Long-term predictions. Occasionally we find long-term predictions—those that have to do with the very end of time. The expression "the day of the Lord" is a case in point. This term signifies God's judgment on a city or nation; it is the day of retribution when justice can no longer be withheld. While "the day of the Lord" usually refers to impending doom for the nation of Israel, it gradually takes on a wider aspect. In some prophecies it comes to indicate the end of all things as Israel's punishment is extended on a cosmic scale (Joel 1:15; 2:1; 3:14; Isa. 2:2, 12; 34:8; Amos 5:18-20; Eze. 7:19; Zeph. 1:7, 14, 18; 2:2; 2 Peter 3:7-12).

Out of such considerations some prophetic passages may seem to have double focus. While in the original context their messages addressed the people of Israel, they also apply to conditions at the close of human time when the judgments on Israel are painted on a worldwide canvas.

The NT contains many apparently long-term predictions. It is difficult to know how long is the period envisaged by NT writers, since the NT embodies such a strong note of imminence (e.g., Matt. 24:34; Rom. 13:11, 12; 1 Thess. 4:15; Heb. 10:37; Rev. 1:3; 22:20). The questions raised by an awareness of NT imminence have given rise to much discussion among Christians of all persuasions. (See Second Coming II. D.)

Leaving aside Mark 13 (Matt. 24; Luke 21) and Revelation, we see clearly that the NT predicts developments that will affect the church. For example, the "man of lawlessness" is to arise before the Second Coming (2 Thess. 2:3); there is to be a rebellion (Acts 20:29, 30); "times of stress" are to arise (2 Tim. 3:1-9); persecutions will increase (1 Peter 4:12). And the supreme happening, the event of all events, is the return of Jesus in the clouds (Acts 1:9-11; John 14:1-3; 1 Thess. 4:14-18). This event per-

meates the entire NT, not merely its apocalyptic parts, imbuing its messages with hope and expectation.

The conditionality principle is nowhere in evidence in these long-term predictions. These prophecies come with the ring of the divine foreknowledge; as such they are presented as inevitable. Although none but the Father knows the precise date of the Parousia, the event is fixed, altogether sure.

d. Predictions of the first advent of Christ. Paul wrote to the Galatians, "When the time had fully come, God sent forth his Son" (Gal. 4:4). Thus, the first coming of Christ, the Incarnation, was not by chance. Rather, it occurred according to God's own wisdom. Even though sincere followers of God had awaited Messiah's appearance for centuries, God had His own timetable; when the time had come fully, He appeared. Church historians often have drawn attention to the way "the world" had been prepared for the birth of Jesus; beyond this, however, we should recognize the divine outworking of the plan of salvation.

The coming of the Messiah, the seed of Abraham in whom all nations of the earth would be blessed (Gen. 12:3), is clearly part of the covenant promises made to Israel. Yet it transcends the covenant, since the Messiah is for all nations, not Israel alone. In that transcending, the conditionality principle ruling the covenant promises and threatenings is subjugated. Was the Messiah's coming delayed because Israel had not prepared the world for Him? We have no hint of it. Surely such preparation as they had made was feeble, but the Messiah came. He had to come! In the fullness of the time God sent Him forth.

It seems impossible to apply the conditionality principle to the prophecies of the Messiah. That He would come of the line of Judah (Gen. 49:10), that He would be the son of David (Isa. 11:1), that He would be born in Bethlehem (Micah 5:2), that He would be the Saviour, the substitute for our sins (Isa. 53)—we cannot speak of conditionality in these predictions. Repeatedly Matthew quotes the OT with the formula "to fulfil what the Lord had spoken by the prophet" (e.g., Matt. 1:22; 2:15, 17, 23; 4:14; 8:17). Even His name is told to Mary before His birth (Matt. 1:21)—surely a microcosm of the divine foreordering of the Messiah's first coming! Beyond the specific prophecies that may be labeled Messianic, the entire OT looks to Him. It is a work of expectation, moving forward and narrowing in upon the birth that is celebrated in the NT. (In some OT prophecies of the Messiah the two advents merge [e.g., Isa. 11:1-9].)

e. Conclusions. Classification of the non-apocalyptic portions of biblical prophecy reveals the complexity of the data. Conditionality emerges as an important principle of classical prophecy. It applies to large portions of the OT that in effect repeat the promises and threats of the covenant; it also applies to portions of the prophecies about the nations surrounding Israel. However, not all non-apocalyptic prophecy is conditional: among both short- and long-term predictions we find certainty of fulfillment regardless of the human response.

2. Predictions in Daniel and Revelation

To examine biblical apocalyptic is to enter another sphere. Although apocalyptic arises in Israel or Asia Minor, it bursts the confines of Israel or Asia Minor. Whether it first speaks a message of God to a nation in captivity (Daniel) or to churches undergoing persecution (Revelation), it transcends the immediate setting in which it came to birth. Apocalyptic has a cosmic sweep, rushing down the continuum of world history to focus on the end-time.

a. Daniel. Between the prophecies of Daniel 2; 7; 8; and 12, and those of Isaiah, Jeremiah, or Ezekiel, stands a marked contrast. In Daniel, the place of Israel has receded, as has the element of threatenings. In its place is a panorama, a march of the kingdoms leading on to the eschaton. We have become spectators to events on a world stage; divine foreknowledge unfolds the course of the future.

Yahweh "changes times and seasons," removing kings and setting up kings; He "reveals deep and mysterious things" (Dan. 2:20-22). He unveils mysteries, making known what is to be (verses 28, 29). He "does according to his will in the host of heaven and among the inhabitants of the earth," and none can thwart His plan (Dan. 4:35). He "rules the kingdom of men, and sets over it whom he will" (Dan. 5:21).

These ideas center in divine sovereignty and divine foreknowledge. In this presentation, the human side of history, while portrayed in the ebb and flow of the fortunes of the people of God, is gathered up within the ruling conception of Yahweh as Lord of history. We search in vain for the element of conditionality.

The prophetic time periods are laid out before us. They are long ones. In keeping with the panoramic scope of history in which they are given, they must be such. We hear of 1260 days for the reign of the blasphemous "little horn" power (Dan. 7:25) and of 2300 evenings and mornings until the sanctuary shall be vindicated after the evil work of the little horn (Dan. 8:14). Given the setting, these time predictions cannot be meant literally.

Since our studies of classical prophecy showed the importance of identifying any covenant setting, we need to take note of this motif in the book of Daniel. The covenant idea in fact occurs in two lines of prophecy—chapters 9 and 11. But these occurrences do not suggest that conditionality is in any sense a hidden agenda of the book.

We need, first, to distinguish clearly between Daniel's own hopes and understanding and the unfolding of the future that Yahweh, Lord of history, communicates to him. Daniel, though prominent in public life, is a captive—along with his people. Jerusalem is in ruins; the sanctuary is desolate. Out of this situation Daniel prays for the restoration of his people, his city, his sanctuary (Dan. 9:1-19). His prayer is based on the covenant: the desolations have come in fulfillment of the threats "written in the law of Moses" (verse 13); likewise that law provides hope of Yahweh's mercy.

But predictions given to Daniel far outstripped the history of Israel. Indeed, Daniel could not comprehend the vision of chapter 8, with its sanctuary references (verse 27). Likewise, the reply to his prayer went far beyond the restoration of city and Temple, reaching to the Messiah (Dan. 9:24-27).

Israel and covenant are mentioned also in the prophecy of chapter 11 (verses 22, 28, 30-35). It may be significant that, as in Daniel 9:24-27, the apocalyptic nature of chapter 11 is much less evident than in chapters 2, 7, and 8. Even if we include chapter 11 under apocalyptic, however, two observations are valid: the fortunes of Israel are treated in a relatively minor manner—the concern is with the conflict between "the king of the north" and "the king of the south," and we find no hint of conditionality. Indeed, the very nature of the prophecy, detailed as it is and linked through many generations, speaks strongly against conditionality as a factor in interpretation.

b. Revelation. The book of Revelation is similar to Daniel. John is told to write "the things which are, and the things which shall be [not may be] hereafter" (Rev. 1:19, KJV). He sees the struggles of the people of God, the final judgment scene (Rev. 20), and a remnant people at the end of all things who stand faithful and loyal to God—"those who keep the commandments of God and the faith of Jesus" (Rev. 14:12). As the world order comes to a total halt in the final outworking of the confederacy of evil and in the divine intervention of punishment, God's people stand secure in Him. Beyond the turmoil, after the nightmare happenings preceding the Second Advent, the "new heavens and a new earth," where righteousness dwells, emerge at last.

So the great controversy, the age-long conflict between Christ and Satan, is ended. It is ended because God has ended it. Its end is as sure as the lordship of God over time and space. (See Great Controversy I-V.)

c. Conclusion. We conclude, therefore, that except in those passages where the covenant with Israel is the leading concern, apocalyptic predictions in Daniel and Revelation do not hinge on conditionality. Divine sovereignty and foreknowledge are the leading ideas.

C. Historicism

According to its self-witness the prophetic messages of the book of Daniel are predictions given during the Babylonian exile. The terminus of these prophetic forecasts is the establishment of God's kingdom. A first-century-A.D. origin of the book of Revelation is a generally accepted datum. The end point of the NT Apocalypse is the second coming of Christ, the subsequent millennium, and the setting up of a new heaven and a new earth.

The two apocalypses are clearly interrelated. The revelator selects certain Danielic motifs, amplifies them in his own Christian context (e.g., cf. Dan. 3 with Rev. 13; Dan. 7:13, 14 with Rev. 4; 5; and 13:1, 2), and parallels much of the history that Daniel describes. Both books end with the consummation of God's purpose, although the revelator expands Daniel's description of the eschaton.

In contrast with the local and contemporary messages of the prophetic writers, the visions of both Daniel and the Revelation offer outlines of history that have a universal sweep. Hence, interpretation of the apocalyptic visions must respect the cosmic range that begins in the writers' own day and takes the reader down to the end. There is no narrow concentration on the years of Jewish persecution by Antiochus IV Epiphanes. The focus of John is not merely on the harassment of the Christian church by a first-century Roman emperor. Nor do we find in these books an exclusive attention to the end of time.

Modes of interpretation that place the fulfillment of these chapters totally in the past (e.g., the historico-critical perspective) or entirely or primarily in the future (e.g., futurism), or that make their fulfillment no more than the eternal confrontation between the forces of good and evil (e.g., idealism) or the presentation of the Christian Age (e.g., amillennialism) fail to do justice to the intent of these compositions.

A historical continuum in the apocalyptic visions is suggested by temporal indicators such as numerical adjectives or words such as "after," "next," and "another." Daniel says to Nebuchadnezzar, *"After* you shall arise *another* kingdom inferior to you, and yet a *third* kingdom. . . . And there shall be a *fourth* kingdom" (Dan. 2:39, 40). In relating the dream of chapter 7, the prophet sees a *first* animal like a lion, then *"another* beast, a second one, like a bear" (verses 4, 5). *"After* this" Daniel saw a leopardlike beast and a *"fourth* beast" (verses 6, 7; cf. Dan. 8:17, 19, 23, 26; 9:24-27; 11:2, 6, 35, 40; 12:1, 4).

Sequential development is also noticeable in the struggles described in Revelation 12-14. In chapter 12 the woman is pregnant; she gives birth; the child is snatched away; the woman flees to the desert; she finds protection in the wilderness for 1260 days; the dragon makes war with the rest of her offspring.

In chapter 13 we see a parade of monsters—dragon, sea beast, land beast—the latter two deriving their existence from the dragon. The dragon, having failed to destroy the holy Child, pursues the "seed" (KJV) of the woman (Rev. 12:13, 17); in seeking to accomplish this purpose he gives "his power and his throne and great authority" to the sea beast (Rev. 13:2). The sea beast receives a mortal stroke, but is healed (verse 3). The sea beast's supremacy lasts for "forty-two months" (verse 5).

Chapter 14 forms the counterpart of chapter 13. Here the three angels of Revelation 14:6-12 sound a proclamation couched in the setting of the deception of the land beast; their work is consummated by the Second Coming (verse 14).

Thus the very form of the vision compels us to understand some sort of historicist fulfillment. Revelation 12-14 focuses on the period between the first and second advents of Christ.

Numerical adjectives recur in the seals and trumpets. Revelation 17:10 interprets the seven heads of the beast as a reference to *"seven* kings *five* of whom have fallen, *one* is, the *other* has not yet come, and *when* he comes he must remain only a little while."

In contrast with other modes of exposition, historicism—though sometimes marred by diverse, sensational, speculative, and contradictory approaches—appears as the most valid hermeneutical approach to the biblical apocalypses. The temporal markers guide the reader like signposts on a journey that commences in the writer's own day and ends in God's eternal kingdom. The path historicism takes does not disappear after a few short footsteps (as historico-critical interpretation would suggest), nor does it appear out of nothing (as futurism would argue). Rather, it advances in a continuous line, sometimes winding, and to all appearances backtracking, but always heading toward the eschaton.

D. The Day-for-a-Year Principle

The symbolic visions include time elements that are cast in figurative language. According to Daniel 7:25 the little horn will oppress the saints of the Most High for "a time, two times, and half a time." In the audition of the following chapter one angel tells another that the sanctuary will be restored after "two thousand and three hundred evenings and mornings" (Dan. 8:14).

John writes that the woman who had given birth to the male child fled into the wilderness, where she was nourished for "one thousand two hundred and sixty days" (Rev. 12:6). Later in the same chapter the woman is once again pictured as being in the wilderness, where she is taken care of for "a time, and times, and half a time" (verse 14). In the following chapter the beast that derived its power from the dragon exercises its authority for "forty-two months" (Rev. 13:5).

Since several of these temporal references

occur in identical settings, namely, in descriptions of the oppression of God's people, it seems evident that the phrases "a time, and times, and half a time," "one thousand two hundred and sixty days," and "forty-two months" refer to the same period. Both Daniel and John are speaking about the same time interval. What then do these symbolic time references signify?

At the outset it is important to recognize that these temporal references occur in symbolic contexts. Hermeneutical consistency, therefore, demands that the time elements be treated in the same way as the rest of the symbolic imagery. The interpreting angel indicated that the ram with the two horns was symbolic of the kings of Media and Persia (Dan. 8:20). The he-goat signified the king (kingdom) of Greece (verse 21). In the symbolism of Revelation 12 the great dragon represents Satan, and the woman symbolizes God's people.

Clearly the imagery is symbolic. The beast, the woman, and the time references should not be understood literally. It is most reasonable, therefore, to assume that just as the short-lived creatures symbolize entities whose existence or dominion in history extended over long periods of time, so also the time elements associated with these symbolic creatures must signify extensive time intervals.

Daniel 9 provides a key to the nature and meaning of these expressions. The vision of Daniel 9:24-27 begins with a time period that literally reads "seventy sevens" or "seventy weeks." The "seventy sevens" commence with the going forth of the decree to restore and rebuild Jerusalem and continue until the coming of an Anointed One, His death, and the destruction of the city and sanctuary.

Both historico-critical and conservative scholars believe that the period of "seventy sevens" must be understood in terms of years in order to allow sufficient time for the fulfillment of the various aspects specified in verses 24-27. The unfolding of events detailed in this passage requires more time than the one year, four months, and 10 days that a reading of "seventy sevens" in terms of *days* (i.e., 490 *days*) would allow. It is for this reason that commentators generally and some Bibles (e.g., the RSV) supply the word "years" after "seventy sevens" and read "seventy weeks of years."

This interpretation of the "seventy sevens" or "seventy weeks" receives support from the larger context. From Daniel 9:2, verse 24 takes up the concept of "seventy years" that Jeremiah predicted Israel would spend in Babylon (cf. Jer. 25:11, 12; 29:10). In effect, Daniel says that the time allocated to the events mentioned in Daniel 9:24-27 would amount to *seven times* "seventy years," of which Jeremiah spoke. The reference to "seventy years" in Daniel 9:2 therefore suggests that the word "seventy" in verse 24 should also be understood in terms of years.

Given the interrelationships between the various time references in the visions and the parallel nature of the visions, it is reasonable to assume with historicist interpreters of the past that in the apocalyptic chapters of Daniel and Revelation a symbolic day signifies a literal year.

William H. Shea carefully examined the day-for-a-year principle. He advanced 23 biblical reasons validating the application of this principle to the time periods in the apocalyptic prophecies of Daniel and Revelation. He also established that the year-day principle was known and applied by Jewish interpreters during the second century B.C. and down to the post-Qumran period (Shea 56-92; for additional detail on Daniel's three major time periods, see Judgment III. B. 1. a. (2).)

E. Symbolism

The long-range predictions of Daniel and Revelation are replete with symbols which, although at times perplexing, are not unintelligible. The interpretations provided in Scripture neither stress nor attempt to explain every detail, but clarify the thrust of the messages. Thus the manlike image of Daniel 2 signifies a succession of empires and rulers without attempting to spell out the significance of the number of toes of the image or their precise identity.

Similarly, John does not dwell upon all the details associated with the symbolic imagery he uses. The evocative power of these details is utilized but not fully explored. It would be presumptuous and probably unproductive—if not counterproductive—for modern interpreters to advance meanings that have not been revealed. In fact, fanciful interpretations often have attracted—occasionally justifiably—the opprobrium of scholars who reject the historicist approach.

The interpretation of apocalyptic symbols should be sought primarily within Scripture itself. Sometimes interpretations are given within the very passage, as when Daniel is told the meaning of the ram and of the goat he has seen in vision (Dan. 8:3-5, 20, 21), or John learns that the "waters" on which the great prostitute sits are "peoples and multitudes and nations and languages" (Rev. 17:1, 15, NRSV). Beyond such specific explanations, apocalyptic draws heavily upon biblical imagery, which may be explored for its meaning. Thus Revelation echoes the symbolism of Daniel; it also pulls in symbols and allusions from classical prophecy. The historical background of Daniel and Revelation also may help in the interpretation of apocalyptic symbols; however, meaning should first be sought within the Bible.

F. Recapitulation

Both Daniel and John juxtapose their visions. At the same time the visions recapitulate and expand the subject matter already given. Thus Daniel 7 goes over the ground covered by Daniel 2 but adds details not present in the previous account. Similarly, the structure of the book of Revelation suggests that sequences like the seven seals and seven trumpets are parallel and take the reader from apostolic times to the second advent of Christ. This recapitulatory nature of the various sequences precludes a continuous or straight-line reading of the chapters as if the events of Daniel 8 followed chronologically those of Daniel 7 or the seven trumpets of Revelation succeeded the seven seals.

Occasionally the visionary either repeats himself or rushes ahead of his subject matter (e.g., Rev. 14:1-5; 20:9). He does not pretend to give a comprehensive account in which he details every feature of history. Rather, he selects events that best serve his purpose. None of these practices, also characteristic of other biblical writers, invalidates the sequential historical process.

III. The Theological Significance of Biblical Apocalyptic

Biblical apocalyptic reveals a universe in which heaven and earth are in close touch with each other. The cosmos is suffused with a sense of the divine. Humanity is not left ignorant of the transcendent, for the Sovereign of the universe communicates with us. Because it is God who speaks to humanity, His messages have a supernatural authority. Thus apocalyptic not only discloses the divine superintendence of history but suggests implications for daily life in the here and now.

A. The Divine Superintendence of History

These divine revelations lift the curtain that limits our view of reality. They disclose a heavenly world that constantly intersects with the world of humankind. The revelations portray a vision of God, whose existence and dominion are eternal, whose wisdom is unfathomable, whose power is absolute, whose grace is matchless, and whose purposes are for the best good of humanity. Because He knows the end from the beginning, He can be trusted for the present and the future. The God of the apocalypses is not some absent, unpredictable landlord of the hoary past or distant future; rather, He is Lord of *present* history. Believers can rest assured that God is in control of life today.

Biblical apocalyptic exposes the world of heavenly beings. Angels are sent to further the divine plan, to instruct, and to protect humanity. But demons also are intent on frustrating God's purpose.

Biblical apocalyptic affirms God's control of the course of events. The orderly sequence in the rise and fall of human powers portends that this is, after all, a managed universe. Apocalyptic history is not limited geographically, nationally, or racially, for God's purposes encompass the totality of human history and embrace both the world above and the world below.

Biblical apocalyptic traces a sequence of sacred history that focuses particularly on the last days. It reveals that the course of this world is preordained and, therefore, under divine management. God's hand is in all, and nothing can frustrate the outworking of His ultimate will.

History has been measured out, and therefore hearers and readers of the Apocalypse can locate their generation in the stream of time. Since few events remain to be fulfilled, the modern reader is reminded that time has almost run out. In this respect biblical apocalyptic represents a path between the past and the eschaton, along which the devout travel to the kingdom. They are sure that the path will take them to their destination because of the landmarks they have already passed.

Biblical apocalyptic provides a meaning that transcends the pain and agony of this world. Though the hues of conflict and persecution deepen as time progresses, the apocalypses relativize the power of pagan rule. In spite of all appearances, the pilgrims are left neither to the whims of their fellows nor to the accidental forces of chance. Hope alternates with despair and oppression, and the divine purpose of peace and joy triumphs in the end. The assurance of God's control in history proscribes the cause of evil. Though the blight of evil seems to be ubiquitous, it will be removed inexorably.

Biblical apocalyptic accepts the legitimacy of human governments. Kings and kingdoms come and go, and so do their threats and their victories. They rise and fall at their appointed times. Ultimately, however, they must give way to the kingdom of God. God overrules and judges in the affairs of men. Rather than rejecting human powers, the apocalypses subsume them under the providence of God. Interestingly enough, apocalyptic also teaches that faithfulness to God is not incompatible with service to the king. Indeed, it is fidelity to the divine Lord that becomes the ground for success in the service of human lords.

Biblical apocalyptic proclaims that humanity lives under judgment. No one can escape the moment of individual accountability. When Jesus returns, He will bring His recompense with Him and "repay every one for what he has done" (Rev. 22:12). Though individuals may not change the course of history that divine grace has preordained, they can choose to be members of His kingdom in the present and triumph with the kingdom in the future. The judgment both clarifies moral values now and reveals human choices and destinies then.

Biblical apocalyptic confirms Jesus' prediction that the gates of hell will not prevail against His church. The revelator declares that in the death of Christ God has already attained the victory (Rev. 12:10, 11). Presently God's people await the visible appearance of the King and their own ultimate vindication.

Though only God knows the day and hour of the consummation, signs of the end herald the impending denouement. In the face of end-time pressures, the test of last-day loyalty will be close. Yet God's people responding to divine grace will remain true and upright in their inmost souls. Buoyed up by the apocalyptic promises, admonitions, and consolations, they anticipate the divine intervention into human history, through which the world will be changed forever. They have no faith in the present to beget the future.

God's ultimate triumph begins with Jesus' return, the resurrection of the dead in Christ, and the translation of the righteous living. The millennium demonstrates unquestionably the true motives of God's enemies and ends with the removal of all evil. The apocalyptic visions close with the ushering in of a new heaven and a new earth, in which God's people will dwell in the presence of God forever (cf. Rev. 21:1-4).

B. Implications for Daily Life

Although biblical apocalyptic lifts our sights to the realm of God, where angels sing in worship, it impacts life on this earth. Although it carries us away to the consummation of all things, it affects how we live and work now.

Biblical apocalyptic is not literature of withdrawal from the world. It does not deny the world; rather, it shows how God's followers are to live in the world.

The book of Daniel provides a striking illustration of this truth. Half the book is apocalyptic on a grand scale: the rise and fall of nations, the sufferings of the saints, the reign of evil powers, cruelty, deception, and God's intervention at last to vindicate His people and His rule as He overthrows the forces of evil and brings in everlasting righteousness. The other half tells the story of Daniel himself—his tests, service in the court of kings, and counsel and wisdom. The message is this: apocalyptic goes hand in hand with service to God and humanity.

Although Daniel shows most clearly the interplay of apocalyptic with life in the here and now, the other biblical apocalyptic writings make the same point. Isaiah 24-27 falls in the midst of a series of prophecies against the nations surrounding Israel. The apocalyptic interlude, while it sweeps beyond national boundaries to describe the desolation of the whole earth, is nonetheless rooted in the practical concerns that shape the entire book. Ezekiel 38, 39 likewise are tied to the restoration of Israel: when Yahweh destroys their enemies, "the house of Israel shall know that I am the Lord their God, from that day forward" (Eze. 39:22). In Joel 2, 3 we also find the prediction of doom impacting daily life as the prophet calls for national repentance (Joel 2:12-17). And Zechariah 9-14 comes as a message of hope to the Jews who, returned from exile, struggle against enemies and discouragement as they try to rebuild the Temple and restore society.

In the NT, Matthew 24/Mark 13/Luke 21 dovetail with daily life. In Matthew Jesus immediately follows the apocalyptic prediction of the end of the age with instructions on how His followers are to live during the waiting time (Matt. 25). We do not find them withdrawing from the world; rather, they are to be busy, improving every talent and opportunity, and manifesting the grace of Jesus in unstudied deeds of mercy and compassion. Again, Paul's apocalypse (2 Thess. 2) is preceded and followed by practical concerns. Finally, the Apocalypse is cast in letter form and brings specific, practical counsel to seven actual churches of Asia Minor.

If biblical apocalyptic is otherworldly, then its implications are altogether this-worldly. It reassures, encourages, and warns God's people as they go about their tasks in this life. In many respects they seem to be just like other people, but they are not, because they have the confidence that God is in control of the flow of history and of their lives.

IV. Historical Overview

Limits of space permit only a brief and selective survey. Throughout the Christian Era biblical apocalyptic has continued to be an unending source of inspiration to a wide variety of believers. Intervals of vigorous interest in and study of biblical apocalyptic include the early period of the Christian church, the later Middle Ages, the Reformation Era, the nineteenth century, and the contemporary period since the 1960s.

A. The Period of the Early Church

1. Historicism

During the first centuries of the Christian church the abiding influence of biblical apocalyptic is found in the works of Papias (c. 60-c. 130), Justin Martyr (c. 100-c. 165), Irenaeus (c. 115-c. 202), Tertullian (c. 160-c. 225), Hippolytus (c. 170-c. 236), Commodius (third century), Victorinus (d. 304), Methodius (d. c. 311), and Lactantius (c. 250-c. 325).

Chiliasm, or millenarianism, though varied in interpretation, was prominent in the eschatological conceptions of the postapostolic church. Papias taught that during the millennium, following the resurrection from the dead, Christ would reign with His saints on earth. Justin Martyr took a similar premillennial stance and taught that the climax of prophecy was the literal Second Advent, at which the resurrection would occur. This would be followed by the 1,000 years of Revelation 20 and the subsequent judgment of all humankind.

Irenaeus appealed to the prophecies of the Bible to demonstrate the truthfulness of Christianity. He believed that the events predicted in Daniel 2 and 7 were closely related. In his view the Roman Empire was the fourth kingdom, which would break into 10 divisions as predicted in the symbols of the 10 horns of Daniel 7 and Revelation 17. Irenaeus identified the antichrist with Daniel's little horn, Paul's "man of sin" (KJV), and the first beast of Revelation 13.

During the second Christian century highly propagandist works resembling the historical apocalypses came to be popularly used by Christians. Known as the Sibylline Oracles, the documents consisted of a conglomerate of writings composed in imitation of the pagan sibyls (aged prophets credited to different parts of the world, especially ancient Greece and Rome). Both Jews and Christians composed writings in imitation of the heathen sibyls and pressed these curious composites of pagan, Jewish, and Christian writings into the service of propagating their faiths, especially their eschatological hopes.

The most significant analogy between these oracles and apocalyptic literature lies in their division of history into generations and named successive kingdoms. The sequences are followed by the destruction of the earth, the resurrection, the judgment, and the blessed state of the new earth. The Sibylline Oracles continued to be consulted down through the Middle Ages and exerted a powerful influence on millenarian thinking.

Tertullian commented on both the books of Daniel and Revelation. He believed that the Roman state delayed the appearance of antichrist as predicted by Paul (i.e., Rome was the restrainer of 2 Thessalonians 2:6, 7). At the beginning of the third century Tertullian espoused Montanism, a movement also characterized by chiliastic beliefs and extremes that brought discredit to millennial interpretation.

Hippolytus wrote the earliest complete Christian commentary on the book of Daniel to come down to us so far. According to Jerome and other sources, Hippolytus also authored a treatise on the book of Revelation. He regarded the prophecies as a sacred calendar of the future. For him the fourth empire in both Daniel 2 and 7 was Rome. In harmony with prophecy he expected the dissolution of Rome into 10 kingdoms. Antichrist would appear among these divisions, but his reign would be terminated by the Second Advent, which he considered to be the goal of prophecy. Hippolytus identified the concluding events of Daniel and Revelation and applied them to the Second Coming.

Hippolytus seems to have been the first to develop the theory that the 69 weeks of Daniel 9:24-27 led up to the First Advent, while the seventieth week of the same prophecy ushers in the Second Coming. Also, it would appear that he succumbed to the temptation of setting a date for our Lord's return.

In his expositions of Revelation 12 Hippolytus applied the symbol of the woman to the church and that of the man-child to Christ. He identified the fourth kingdom of Daniel 7 with the first beast of Revelation 13, while he claimed that the second beast typified the kingdom of antichrist.

Theologically the Latin poet Commodius was a chiliast. He also wrote about antichrist. Victorinus, who died a martyr under the emperor Diocletian, is the author of the oldest preserved commentary on Revelation. Jerome classified him as a millenarian. Victorinus established the principle that the Apocalypse is not to be read as one continuous and progressive line of prophecy, but rather that its various parts return and repeat the ground already covered.

Methodius, although influenced by Origen's allegorical interpretations of Scripture, contended against Origen for the resurrection and identified the woman and the child of Revelation 12 with the church and the saints respectively. Lactantius, tutor of the emperor Constantine's son, was a zealous and sometimes fanciful chiliast who made use of the Sibylline Oracles.

Although Jerome (c. 340-420) was a militant antimillenarian and warned that the Apocalypse was a book of mysteries, he wrote a significant commentary on the book of Daniel. In this volume he sought to counter the criticisms of the book by the third-century-A.D. Neoplatonist philosopher Porphyry. Jerome identified the Roman state with the fourth empire in Daniel 2 and 7 and claimed that Christ represented the stone that smote the image of Daniel 2. In his view the Second Advent would occur after antichrist, who was identical with Daniel's little horn, had appeared.

2. New Directions

Several forces began to undermine the dominant prophetic understanding of the early church and to suggest new directions in apocalyptic interpretation. One of these was the spiritualizing and allegorizing of Scripture by Origen (c. 185-c. 254). Having stressed the manifestation of God's kingdom in the believer's soul rather than in the real world,

he shifted attention from the historical toward the spiritual. As a result, Origen undermined the early church's belief in the doctrines of a personal coming of Christ, the resurrection, and a literal millennium.

Another factor contributing to a shift in exposition of biblical apocalyptic was the conversion of the emperor Constantine (d. 337). Whereas prior to Constantine, Christians had entertained negative views toward the Roman Empire, Christianity now became the main religion of the empire. With this new policy of toleration and imperial favor Christianity developed an "imperial theology."

However, the most profound influence to eclipse the prophetic and historic understanding of the early church must be attributed to Augustine (354-430). Augustine and subsequent medieval exegesis followed the hermeneutical principles of Tyconius (d. c. 400). According to subsequent medieval authors, Tyconius wrote on the Apocalypse, producing a commentary that assigned fulfillment of the book's prophecies to subjective spiritual development rather than historical events.

Tyconius claimed that the first resurrection, mentioned in Revelation 20:6 in connection with the millennium, was spiritual (that of the soul when awakened from the death of sin), while the second resurrection was the general resurrection of all. In his view the millennium was not the reign of the righteous on earth for 1,000 years after the resurrection. Rather, Tyconius identified it with the Christian dispensation beginning at the first advent of Christ. For Tyconius the book of Revelation does not speak so much about coming historical events as it depicts the spiritual controversy between the diabolical powers and the kingdom of God.

This mystical, spiritual, and nonhistorical approach to the Apocalypse is reflected and developed in the allegorical interpretations of Augustine. For the bishop of Hippo the millennium was a round number designating an indeterminable time interval spanning the period between the ministry of Christ on earth and the end of the world. Augustine reacted particularly to the extremes and carnal expectations of millenarians, some of which he himself had once shared.

For Augustine the first resurrection was spiritual and allegorical and occurred as the soul dead in trespasses arose to the life of righteousness. The second resurrection was that of the body at the end of the world. Between these two events the kingdom of heaven was identical with the church on earth. The church was the kingdom of Christ reigning with her Lord in the present. Those sitting on the thrones of judgment in Revelation 20:4 were the prelates of the church.

Whereas many historical interpreters had identified the first beast of Revelation 13 with the Roman state, Augustine interpreted it as the wicked world. In this way Augustine disallowed any attempt to find in the canonical apocalypses information about contemporary historical events.

Although Augustine held to belief in the second coming of Christ, his system relegated the Advent hope to the distant future and thus undermined the imminent expectation of the end. Augustine profoundly affected the life of the church and the cause of prophetic interpretation. His revolutionary philosophy of the millennium as the reign of the church in the present made a deep impact on the thinking of subsequent church history. In fact, Augustine's spiritual and allegorical interpretation of the biblical apocalypses became the doctrine of the official church throughout the Middle Ages.

B. The Middle Ages

As long as Augustine's symbolic view remained dominant during the next 1,000 years, the prophetic and premillennial notions that characterized the period of the early church remained dormant and were only occasionally revived by chiliastic groups.

In the twelfth century Joachim, of Fiore (c. 1135-1202), became one of the most significant apocalyptic authors of the Middle Ages.

Historians suggest that Joachim and his followers pioneered a new stage in the history of apocalyptic tradition.

Joachim, abbot of Fiore, used allegorism freely, and his exegesis was amazingly imaginative and original. Using the Trinity as a model, he divided history into three great ages that flow into one another. The age of God the Father, largely coincidental with the period of the OT, was the interval during which men lived according to the flesh. The age dominated by God the Son was an era when carnal and spiritual things were interwoven. Characterized by the ecclesiastical hierarchy, the second age spanned a period of 42 generations of approximately 30 years each, beginning with the rise of Christianity. Joachim expected the age of God the Holy Spirit to begin shortly, possibly even in his own day. The last would be a new age led by a new monastic order and a new society without prelates and clerics.

Joachim commented on both Daniel and the Revelation, offering certain fantastic expositions. He combated the chiliastic ideas of an earthly kingdom of 1,000 years and identified the millennium of Revelation 20 with the age of the Spirit.

The abbot appears to have been the first Christian to interpret the period of the 1260 days of Revelation 12 as 1260 years, although three centuries earlier Jewish expositors had already considered the 1290 days of Daniel 12 as years. By comparing letter with letter in both Testaments, Joachim found events in the past, present, and future clearly revealed in Scripture.

During the following centuries Joachim's ideas captured the imagination of individuals and groups, some of whom, however, carried his notions to revolutionary conclusions (e.g., the Spiritual Franciscans).

Subsequent to Joachim, concern with biblical apocalyptic appeared across Europe but was particularly evident in Britain (e.g., John Wycliffe, c. 1320-1384, and his friend John Purvey, c. 1353-c. 1428), as well as in Bohemia (e.g., John Milic, d. 1374; his disciple

Matthias, of Janow, d. 1394; and later John Huss, c. 1372-1415).

C. The Reformation

1. Reformers' Historicism

The Reformation's stress on the Bible was accompanied by a revival of interest in apocalyptic interpretation. Among the publications produced in the sixteenth century was a large volume of polemical literature written in forthright, and to twentieth-century ears, often crude and vulgar language. Many of the tracts and commentaries were illustrated with powerful cartoons and satire. Political and social frustrations injected themselves into the volatile religious atmosphere and caused outbursts of violence beyond the control of the religious Reformers. The direction Protestantism took in one geographical region was often very different from the course it took in another.

While the views of Augustine continued—even if in modified form—in the interpretations of some writers (e.g., John Calvin), the historical interpretation of and literal approaches to biblical apocalyptic became dominant during the Reformation. The application of the time prophecies of Daniel 2 and 7 to the four kingdoms of Babylon, Medo-Persia, Greece, and Rome, followed by the breakup of Rome, continued to lend weight to the long-held view of the historical fulfillment of the prophecies. Similarly, the application of the literal-year-for-a-prophetic-day principle in apocalyptic was widely applied during this period, particularly to the 1260 prophetic days, three and one half prophetic times, and 42 prophetic months. The prophecies of Daniel and Revelation were held by many to be a panorama of the Christian Era.

While exposition was not uniform, there was widespread agreement among the Reformers on identifying the predicted antichrist with the Papacy, in some cases with the Turk, and by still others with both. The antichrist was identified with the little horn of Daniel, the "abomination of desolation" of Matthew 24 (KJV), the "man of sin" of Paul (KJV), the beast, Babylon, and the harlot of Revelation. These identifications with the Papacy contributed largely to a widespread exit from the church of Rome during this period.

Even though Martin Luther and Ulrich Zwingli depreciated the Apocalypse and John Calvin remained uncertain about the identity of many of the apocalyptic symbols, none of them hesitated to identify the Papacy or the Turk with the apostate and oppressive system referred to in Daniel and Revelation.

The end was believed to be drawing near. Though Reformers like Luther and Zwingli were suspicious of millennial speculations, several violent outbreaks, such as the ones among the radical Reformers in Münster and the Fifth Monarchy men during the Puritan Revolt, could not be prevented.

2. Counterinterpretations

During the second half of the sixteenth and the first half of the seventeenth century, Catholic counterinterpretations intended to meet the Protestant exposition of biblical apocalyptic were developed. Three learned Jesuits spearheaded Rome's attack on the historical approach, with the book of Revelation as the main focus.

The first of the alternative expositions was developed by Francisco Ribera (1537-1591). Ribera related the first few chapters of the Apocalypse to Rome in John's own time and applied the remaining chapters to a future three-and-a-half-year reign of an infidel antichrist at the end of the Christian dispensation. Subsequent commentators suggest that Ribera was the founder of the modern futurist system of interpretation, which later was developed by writers such as Samuel R. Maitland (1792-1866) and John N. Darby (1800-1882).

Robert Bellarmine (1542-1621), brilliant theologian and controversialist, augmented the work of Ribera, attacking particularly the prophetic day-for-a-year principle. Bellarmine sought especially to exploit the differences in the interpretations among his Protestant adversaries.

The second challenge was mounted by Luis de Alcazar (1554-c. 1613). Alcazar proposed that the book of Revelation addressed the victorious war of the church in the early centuries against the Jews and Roman paganism. Since Alcazar's method applied the entire book of Revelation to the past, his system of interpretation has been labeled preterism.

Though Alcazar probably was the first to apply a preterist approach to the whole of Revelation, the third-century adversary of Christianity, Porphyry, already had subjected the book of Daniel to a preterist approach, limiting it to the period of Antiochus IV Epiphanes. In a sense, therefore, Porphyry and Alcazar became forerunners of the present mode of historico-critical interpretation, which limits the meaning and significance of the biblical apocalypses to the past.

The proposals of Ribera and Alcazar diverted support from the Protestant application of the antichrist to the Papacy. The first consigned antichrist to the distant future; the second, to the remote past. Although these approaches were mutually exclusive, they deflected attention from the historical period of papal dominion.

3. The Seventeenth and Eighteenth Centuries

Despite these counterinterpretations the historical application of apocalyptic continued in the seventeenth and eighteenth centuries as hundreds of commentaries appeared in Britain, Europe, and the New World. Expositors of note during this period include Joseph Mede (1586-1638), Isaac Newton (1642-1727), and Johann A. Bengel (1687-1752). Though varying in detail, clarity, and understanding, these expositors basically continued their application of biblical apocalyptic to fulfillment in the course of history.

The chiliastic views of this period were challenged by a new millennial theory formulated by Daniel Whitby (1638-1726). Whitby placed a spiritual millennium, consisting of the universal triumph of the gospel and the conversion of all nations, in the 1,000 years of Revelation 20 *before* the coming of Christ.

Whitby envisioned a society in which Judeo-Christian values would be the predominant influence. He believed the millennium to be a "golden age" of paradisiacal righteousness and peace, during which the nations would be converted to Christianity prior to Christ's return. Unfortunately, such postponement of Christ's advent into the distant future beyond the millennium tended to dilute the sense of the imminent coming of our Lord and lull people into a false security.

D. The Modern Period

1. Revival of Interest in Prophecy

The violent uprooting of social and political institutions in Europe during the French Revolution aroused an unprecedented concern with biblical apocalyptic. A new epoch in the study of the books of Daniel and Revelation opened on both sides of the Atlantic. Expositors and expositions of apocalyptic seemed to multiply on an unparalleled scale.

Some writers began to call this period the time of the end and regarded the period as the fulfillment of events predicted in the apocalypses. There was intense expectation, especially among groups such as the Millerites, of the second advent of Christ and the subsequent commencement of the millennium.

Insistence on the letter of Scripture and eagerness to vindicate the OT prophecies about Israel led some premillennialists to extremes of literalism, introducing a Judaizing chiliasm. This tendency, which grew in popularity and continues until today as the dominant form of premillennialism, came to be known as dispensationalism.

In contrast with premillennial expositions of Scripture, throughout the remainder of the nineteenth century, postmillennialists continued to proclaim their doctrine of universal improvement and world conversion before the second coming of Jesus.

In a parallel development the rationalist views of prophecy mediated initially by Porphyry and Alcazar became popularized by Hugh Broughton (1549-1612), Hugo Grotius (1583-1645), Henry Hammond (1605-1660), and the German rationalists. The latter approach relegated biblical apocalyptic to the distant past, depriving it of its predictive elements and cosmic sweep.

This form of preterism is better known today as the historico-critical school. Apart from occasional writers who continue to regard the apocalyptic predictions as panoramic forecasts of events, the historico-critical approach has come to dominate apocalyptic exposition into the present. It soon broke down the distinction between biblical and nonbiblical apocalypses and began to study the apocalyptic documents merely as historical phenomena.

2. Historico-Critical Study of Apocalyptic

The first comprehensive description of Jewish and Christian apocalyptic was published by Friedrich Lücke in 1832. He began his study with an investigation of the book of Revelation and then turned to other apocalyptic compositions. The subtitle of the work is significant: *An Attempt at a Comprehensive Introduction to the Revelation of John and to the Complete Apocalyptic Literature.*

Lücke believed that Jewish apocalyptic was best represented in the book of Daniel (though he dated it to the second century B.C. with other critics of his day) and Christian apocalyptic in the book of Revelation. Throughout, he still sought to preserve the uniqueness of revealed religion by distinguishing between canonical and noncanonical apocalypses. He concluded that apocalyptic is essentially prophetic, though he recognized that not all prophecy in Scripture is apocalyptic. In his view the essence of apocalyptic was its universal conception of history.

In a brief article published in 1843 Eduard Reuss proceeded from the conviction that the Apocalypse of John should be considered part of apocalyptic literature. Unlike Lücke, however, Reuss abandoned the distinction between the canonical Apocalypse of John and other apocalypses, which has since become the accepted norm in historico-critical study. Reuss decided to examine the compositions from a rationalistic standpoint, studying them as they made their appearance in history.

The first monograph dealing specifically with Jewish apocalyptic was published by Adolf Hilgenfeld in 1857. Hilgenfeld attempted to discover the nature of apocalyptic through a study of its historical development. He sought to displace Lücke's distinction between inspired and noninspired writings and applied Hegelian constructs as he traced the development of apocalyptic.

Apart from occasional signs of interest, the study of apocalyptic declined for almost a century after Hilgenfeld. Historians trace this change to the powerful influence of Julius Wellhausen's monumental reconstruction of Israelite religion published in 1878.

Wellhausen and his students denied any authentic prophetic spirit in the apocalyptic works, considering their authors to be imitators of the preexilic prophets and borrowers of foreign, especially Persian, materials. Whereas previous scholars had regarded the apocalyptic works as links between prophecy and New Testament Christianity, Wellhausen claimed that the classical prophets were the spiritual predecessors of Jesus. This notion gave rise to the "prophetic connection" theory. Accordingly, any link between prophecy and apocalyptic was denied, and little value was placed on the apocalyptic writings.

Among the notable exceptions was British scholar Robert H. Charles. At the beginning of the twentieth century he developed an absorbing fascination with apocalyptic. Although Charles used the tools that Wellhausen had developed, he devoted a lifetime to collecting apocalyptic and apocryphal texts. He prepared critical editions and translations of these works and endeavored to discover the intrinsic qualities of apocalypticism. Among his many publications is the monumental two-volume work *The Apocrypha and Pseudepigrapha of the Old Testament,* an indispensable tool to scholars for 70 years.

Like Wellhausen, Charles followed literary and source-critical principles that presupposed standards of coherence, consistency, and Aristotelian logic largely foreign to the apocalyptic and biblical materials. Expecting a consistent point of view and uniformity in content and style, Charles was intolerant of the inconsistency and repetition noticeable in apocalyptic. His dating of apocalyptic documents was greatly influenced by his evolutionary perspective. The Hegelian "rational spirit" clearly lives on in his historical reconstruction of apocalyptic.

Unlike Wellhausen, Charles saw an organic connection between prophecy and apocalyptic. He thus countered the prophetic connection theory proposed by Wellhausen and resolutely stood for a close relationship between apocalyptic and NT Christianity.

The continuity between prophecy and apocalyptic proposed by Lücke, Reuss, Hilgenfeld, Charles, and others was maintained in the writings of Harold H. Rowley (*The Relevance of Apocalyptic,* 1944), David S. Russell (*The Method and Message of Jewish Apocalyptic,* 1964), Peter von der Osten-Sacken (*Die Apokalyptik in ihrem Verhältnis zu Prophetie und Weisheit* [Apocalyptic in Its Relationship to Prophecy and Wisdom], 1969), and more recently in Paul D. Hanson (*The Dawn of Apocalyptic,* 1975), and Joyce G. Baldwin (*Daniel,* 1978).

At the turn of the century another historico-critical approach to apocalyptic was pioneered by Hermann Gunkel (*Schöpfung und Chaos in Urzeit und Endzeit,* 1895). Gunkel attempted to isolate what he believed were mythic fragments embedded in apocalyptic. Since, according to Gunkel, these fragments could not be identified with historical events, he sought to discover their significance in the larger pattern of ancient Near Eastern mythology.

While Gunkel turned to Babylonian mythology, more recent studies typifying this approach have tended to focus particularly on Canaanite literature. Historians of religion suggest that the royal cult in Jerusalem absorbed Canaanite motifs and concepts into the religion of Israel until they reemerged in the apocalyptic writings.

The methodology and comparative approach suggested by Gunkel were further developed by writers such as Sigmund Mowinckel (*He That Cometh,* 1954), Frank M. Cross (*Canaanite Myth and Hebrew Epic,* 1973), and John J. Collins (*The Apocalyptic Imagination,* 1984). Rather than searching for historical identifications in apocalyptic, this approach prefers to investigate the alleged mythological roots of apocalyptic imagery and then give them symbolic and allusive meanings.

A third direction in contemporary apocalyptic research is to understand the literature in the context of Hellenistic and Eastern religious syncretistic writings.

The lively current interest in apocalyptic had its beginning in a programmatic essay by Ernst Käsemann written in 1960, in which he made the claim that "apocalyptic was the mother of Christian theology."

Systematic theologians like Wolfgang Pannenberg (*Revelation as History,* 1968) and Jürgen Moltmann (*Theology of Hope,* 1967) also drew attention to the importance of apocalyptic literature for the early stages of Christian theology. This link between apocalyptic and Christianity is particularly startling in view of previous scholarly rejection of a bond between apocalyptic and early Christianity. For an increasing number of contemporary scholars, Jewish apocalyptic is essential for an understanding of early Christianity and Christian theology.

3. Contemporary Approaches to Biblical Apocalyptic

Approaches to biblical apocalyptic in the

second half of the twentieth century, though diverse and complex, may be grouped into two broad categories—spiritual and allegorical approaches, and literal and historical interpretations.

Postmillennialism (i.e., the notion that Christ's second advent takes place after the millennium), stemming from the writings of Daniel Whitby, dominated eschatological thought among conservative Protestants during much of the nineteenth century. It has now lost popularity. Worsening social conditions throughout the world today have robbed postmillennialism of its former strength. Apart from the increasing precariousness of our times, Scripture also militates against the postmillennial stance, for contrary to Whitby's position, the revelator clearly positions the Second Advent *before* rather than after the millennium (Rev. 19:11–20:10).

a. Spiritual or allegorical approaches. Applying the historico-critical method to biblical apocalyptic, many scholars see Daniel and Revelation, not as forecasts of what is to be, but as suggestions of the inner meaning of the universe and of human experience.

Though this position on biblical apocalyptic is increasing in popularity, particularly among scholars who trace apocalyptic imagery back to ancient Near Eastern mythology, it is not shared by all historical critics. The tendency to view apocalyptic imagery as code words for historical entities (even though these entities are limited to the past) has been and still is widely accepted among historico-critical scholars.

Another form of the allegorical or spiritual interpretation of biblical apocalyptic is found particularly in the amillennial understanding of Revelation 20:1-10. Amillennialists do not all share the presuppositions of historico-critical scholarship; however, they do agree that the 1,000 years of Revelation 20 are a symbolic representation of the Christian Era between the first and second coming of our Lord. Accordingly, we are now in the millennium, for the kingdom of God began with Christ's birth and will end at His second advent.

Amillennialism, first articulated by Augustine, is suspect, because it is hermeneutically inconsistent and because it defies the position of the millennial period in the book of Revelation. For this approach there is no consistency in the application of hermeneutic principles to Revelation 20 and to other parts of Scripture.

The literary structure of John's Apocalypse divides into two major sections. The first half of the book deals with *historical sequences* from apostolic times to Christ's second advent. The second division of the book portrays the *eschatological consummation.* If the amillennial view were correct, the millennium should have been placed in the first rather than second division of the book. By positioning the 1,000 years in the second, or eschatological, section, John placed the millennium in the future and anchored Revelation 20:1-10 firmly to the series of events that constitute God's final and ultimate activity.

b. Literal interpretations. The second dominant contemporary approach to biblical apocalyptic is typified in premillennialism (the notion that Christ's second coming will occur before the 1,000-year period of Revelation 20). Premillennial interpretation has roots in the first few centuries of the Christian church. After Augustinian amillennialism became official church doctrine at the beginning of the Middle Ages, premillennialism remained dormant and revived periodically through the past 20 centuries, particularly after the decline of postmillennialism at the beginning of the twentieth century.

Premillennialism, like historicist interpretations of apocalyptic prophecy, is characterized by a wide variety of views, although all premillennialists agree that the second advent of Christ precedes the 1,000 years of Revelation 20.

For the most part, premillennialists view the biblical apocalypses as forecasts. The sequences of events in Daniel and Revelation lead up to the end and form part of a long, sacred history that God has predetermined. This sacred history may be known to those who study the books of Daniel and Revelation. The biblical apocalypses complement each other, and their messages may be understood on the principle of the unity of Scripture. The images of the visions stand for real things, and the sequences of events correspond to historical happenings.

Historic premillennialism was modified with the rise of dispensationalism in the nineteenth century, and presently dispensational premillennialism is numerically dominant among premillennialists. Edward Irving, John N. Darby, Lewis S. Chafer, and C. I. Scofield (particularly the *Scofield Reference Bible*) all contributed to the shape of present dispensationalism, which represents a number of schools rather than a movement.

Though contemporary dispensational premillennialism is far from uniform, many still agree with Darby that Christ's second coming consists of two stages. The first involves a secret rapture when all Christian saints will be "caught up" to be with Christ, and the second focuses on Christ's return seven years later to rule on earth for 1,000 years.

Darby believed that during the future seven years, or "age to come," mass conversions would occur, even though the gospel age would have come to an end and the Holy Spirit would have been withdrawn. During the subsequent millennium Jewish Temple worship would be reestablished in Jerusalem, and the OT kingdom prophecies would be finally fulfilled. This insistence on a *literal fulfillment* of the OT kingdom prophecies in a restored Jewish nation has led to a Judaizing form of chiliasm. (See Millennium III. B. 7.)

E. Seventh-day Adventist Interpretation

Seventh-day Adventists also are premillennialists, but like most premillennialists of the early nineteenth century, not dispensational. Given their historicist understanding of biblical apocalyptic, Adventists believe that history has run most of its course and that the second coming of Christ is imminent.

Whereas Adventists understand Scripture to teach a cataclysmic return of our Lord prior to the millennium, they see no biblical support for the bifurcation of the Second Advent into a "rapture" and an "appearing." The scriptural vocabulary used to describe our Lord's return suggests that the Second Coming will be an indivisible, single, literal, audible, and visible event. (See Second Coming I. E. 1-5.)

At the second advent of Christ believers will meet the Lord in the air and follow Him back to the heavenly places prepared for them, while the impenitent are slain (cf. John 14:2, 3; 1 Thess. 4:16, 17; Rev. 19:11-21). The millennium therefore begins with a depopulated earth. Inability to continue his nefarious activity because of the depopulation of the earth causes Satan's binding (Rev. 20:1-3, 7, 8; see Millennium).

Since Revelation 20 is the only passage in Scripture that explicitly depicts the 1,000-year period, any valid description of the millennium must be derived from or be in accord with this passage. There is therefore no reason to read into it the unfulfilled OT kingdom prophecies, which originally applied to the Jewish nation. Neither is there evidence that conversions will occur after the coming of Christ, for all destinies have been sealed with the return of our Lord. Likewise, the idea that the Temple ritual will operate once more, even if only in the sense of memorial services and sacrifices, is misguided in the light of the efficacy and nonrepeatable nature of the death of our Saviour.

At the end of the 1,000-year reign of Christ with His saints in heaven, the impenitent on earth are revived, Satan is able to resume his activity of deception, the final judgment takes place, all evil is eliminated, and a new heaven and a new earth are established (Rev. 20:7–21:4; see Judgment III. B. 3; Millennium I. C. 3).

Seventh-day Adventists, therefore, stand in continuity with the historical and premillennial interpretation of biblical apocalyptic, believing that the fulfillment of the predictions covers the entire history of pagan empires from Daniel's day down to the final setting up of God's kingdom. Adventists do not accept the total application of the apocalyptic visions of Daniel and Revelation to the past. They also avoid the "spiritualizing" tendency of postmillennialism or amillennialism and the "overliteralizing" that has led dispensational premillennialists to a Judaizing form of chiliasm.

The Adventist vision of the imminence of Christ's return and the finality this event brings to the offer of salvation challenges the notions of a "golden age" and an "age to come." Adventist prophetic interpretation also steers clear of the pitfalls of speculation and sensationalism so popular among premillennialists.

Adventists long for a new world yet endeavor to take seriously the social, cultural, and ecological responsibility to the present world. Nevertheless, their prayer at all times is "Amen. Come Lord Jesus!"

V. Ellen G. White Comments

Ellen White's extensive writings reveal a person who was profoundly influenced by, and had the highest regard for, biblical apocalyptic, especially the books of Daniel and Revelation. She saw these books as having particular import and value for God's people in the last days and recommended their careful study. As an interpreter, she remained a consistent advocate of the historicist approach, understanding the visions of Daniel and Revelation as unfolding the successive stages of history, which is to climax in the second coming of Jesus and the restoration of all things.

Because of the diffuse nature of her use of Scripture, it is impossible to quantify Ellen White's references to biblical apocalyptic. She wrote no book specifically on Daniel or Revelation, nor an eschatology per se. But we may gauge something of the profound influence of apocalyptic on her thinking by two measures. First, the *Comprehensive Index to the Writings of Ellen G. White* lists the biblical references in her main works. Each page of this listing gives several hundred references, and for the book of Daniel the *Index* covers more than two full pages, while for Revelation it stretches to eight complete pages. Second, a compilation of Ellen White's writings relative to the end-time was published in 1992 under the title *Last Day Events*. It runs 330 pages.

The following citations are typical of the many that might be brought to bear from Ellen White's writings.

A. The Call to Study Daniel and Revelation

"Read the book of Daniel," she counseled. "Call up, point by point, the history of the kingdoms there represented. . . . The light that Daniel received direct from God was given especially for these last days" (4BC 1166). "The book of Revelation opens to the world what has been, what is, and what is to come; it is for our instruction upon whom the ends of the world are come. It should be studied with reverential awe. We are privileged in knowing what is for our learning" (RH Aug. 31, 1897).

To ministers she advised: "Ministers should present the sure word of prophecy as the foundation of the faith of Seventh-day Adventists. The prophecies of Daniel and the Revelation should be carefully studied, and in connection with them the words, 'Behold the Lamb of God, which taketh away the sin of the world'" (GW 148).

B. The Interpretation of Biblical Apocalyptic

Ellen White nowhere uses the word "apocalyptic," nor does she evince any interest in the speculations of historico-critical scholarship regarding the relation of biblical apocalyptic to apocalyptic literature in general. Her focus is on Daniel and Revelation and to a lesser extent on other apocalyptic chapters such as Matthew 24.

She identifies Daniel, the Hebrew captive taken to Babylon, as the author of the book by that name (PK 553, 554; 7T 161). Further, she states that he wrote about 500 years before Christ, thus implicitly rejecting the second-century-B.C. date for the book (DA 98). For Revelation she identifies John the beloved, one of the original 12 apostles, as the author and places the writing of the book late in his life during the reign of the emperor Domitian, who banished John to the island of Patmos (AA 568-571).

Ellen White called for Revelation to be studied in connection with Daniel. In 1902 she wrote, "It was my idea to have the two books bound together, Revelation following Daniel, as giving fuller light on the subjects dealt with in Daniel. The object is to bring these books together, showing that they both relate to the same subjects" (TM 117).

Her many references to Daniel and Revelation reveal a consistently historicist hermeneutic, although she never uses the term. For her the prophecies of these books unroll in historical panorama from the days of Daniel and John until the establishment of the eternal kingdom of God. Just as she knows nothing of a second-century-B.C. date for the writing of Daniel, so she knows nothing of a preterist interpretation of Revelation. Nor is she an idealist or a futurist: those parts of biblical apocalyptic whose fulfillment lies in the future are only the conclusion of the unfolding course of history that God has predicted through vision and symbol.

The following statements reveal Ellen White's understanding of the sequential fulfillment of the prophecies of these books:

"In the Revelation are portrayed the deep things of God. . . . Its truths are addressed to those living in the last days of this earth's history, as well as to those living in the days of John. Some of the scenes depicted in this prophecy are in the past, some are now taking place; some bring to view the close of the great conflict between the powers of darkness and the Prince of heaven, and some reveal the triumphs and joys of the redeemed in the earth made new" (AA 584).

"The book of Revelation opens to the world what has been, what is, and what is to come; it is for our instruction upon whom the ends of the world are come" (7BC 954).

Although some have endeavored to find support for a double fulfillment of prophecy from a few of her statements, the weight of evidence militates against this viewpoint. Warning against such approaches, she wrote, "Events in the train of prophecy that had their fulfillment away in the past are made future, and thus by these theories the faith of some is undermined" (2SM 102). Ellen White speaks of the prophetic chain running through history, with God revealing history "from eternity in the past to eternity in the future" (PK 536). She states, "The prophecies present a succession of events leading down to the opening of the judgment. This is especially true of the book of Daniel" (GC 356). Rather than suggesting that Ellen White indicated that prophecy should be repeated, we can conclude that *history* will be repeated (Rice 145-161).

C. Comprehensive Presentations

Not only do Ellen White's writings give evidence of an abiding interest in biblical apocalyptic, but also in some places she elaborates apocalyptic, fleshing out indications in the book of Revelation to paint a scenario of events just prior to the Second Coming and beyond. Thus the entire second half of her important work *The Great Controversy Between Christ and Satan* focuses on the period from the Advent awakening of the early nineteenth century through the Second Coming and on to the final restoration of all things. The first chapter of this section (chapter 18) deals with William Miller, who, she wrote, was called like Elisha "to leave his plow and open to the people the mysteries of the kingdom of God" (GC 331). The final chapters in this presentation deal with events that are still future.

In this comprehensive presentation Ellen White gives a clear interpretation of the little horn of Daniel 7, the dragon of Revelation 12, the leopard beast of Revelation 13, and the two-horned beast of Revelation 13. She presents the 1260 days of prophetic time in Daniel and Revelation as being the same as the three and one-half years and the 42 months, and as fulfilled in 1260 years of papal supremacy (538-1798). Looking beyond her day, she foresaw the final conflict over the Sabbath and God's law, symbolized by the enforcement of the "mark of the beast" by the "image of the beast."

D. The Divine Superintendence of History

For Ellen White the great message of biblical apocalyptic was the divine superintendence of history. The God of Daniel and Revelation, the God of the entire Scriptures, is Lord of time and space. He sees all, He knows all, He controls all. He does not coerce the human will—essential freedom is a reality—but ultimately He works all things to accomplish His eternal purpose. Chaotic and meaningless though life may seem to humanity, God is in charge, and ultimately He will resolve all and restore the world to perfect peace and harmony.

Speaking of the first coming of Jesus, Ellen White wrote: "But like the stars in the vast circuit of their appointed path, God's purposes know no haste and no delay. . . . So in heaven's council the hour for the coming of Christ had

been determined. When the great clock of time pointed to that hour, Jesus was born in Bethlehem" (DA 32).

That focuses her understanding of the course of divine history: ultimately God retains control. Although humans cooperate and interact with the divine plan, they cannot frustrate it.

She pictures the calm, controlled, divine superintendence of history: "In the annals of human history, the growth of nations, the rise and fall of empires, appear as if dependent on the will and prowess of man; the shaping of events seems, to a great degree, to be determined by his power, ambition, or caprice. But in the Word of God the curtain is drawn aside, and we behold, above, behind, and through all the play and counterplay of human interest and power and passions, the agencies of the All-merciful One, silently, patiently working out the counsels of His own will" (PK 499, 500).

This, of course, is the portrayal of history that biblical apocalyptic presents. In Daniel Yahweh sets up kings and removes kings; in Revelation He watches over the apple of His eye, the church.

And, at last, He makes a new heaven and a new earth, wherein righteousness dwells.

"The great controversy is ended. Sin and sinners are no more. The entire universe is clean. One pulse of harmony and gladness beats through the vast creation. From Him who created all, flow life and light and gladness, throughout the realms of illimitable space. From the minutest atom to the greatest world, all things, animate and inanimate, in their unshadowed beauty and perfect joy, declare that God is love" (GC 678).

VI. Literature

Charlesworth, James H., ed. *The Old Testament Pseudepigrapha*. 2 vols. Garden City, N.Y.: Doubleday, 1983-1985.

Collins, John J. *The Apocalyptic Imagination: An Introduction to the Jewish Matrix of Christianity*. New York: Crossroad,

1984.

Froom, LeRoy E. *The Prophetic Faith of Our Fathers*. 4 vols. Washington, D.C.: Review and Herald, 1946-1954.

Holbrook, Frank B., ed. *The Seventy Weeks, Leviticus, and the Nature of Prophecy*.

Daniel and Revelation Committee Series. Vol. 3. Washington, D.C.: Biblical Research Institute, 1986.

————. *Symposium on Daniel*. Daniel and Revelation Committee Series. Vol. 2. Washington, D.C.: Biblical Research Institute, 1986.

————. *Symposium on Revelation—Book 1*. Daniel and Revelation Committee Series. Vol. 6. Silver Spring, Md.: Biblical Research Institute, 1992.

————. *Symposium on Revelation—Book 2*. Daniel and Revelation Committee Series. Vol. 7. Silver Spring, Md.: Biblical Research Institute, 1992.

Koch, Klaus. *The Rediscovery of Apocalyptic*. Studies in Biblical Theology, second series. No. 22. London: SCM, 1972.

McGinn, Bernard. *Visions of the End: Apocalyptic Traditions in the Middle Ages*. New York: Columbia University Press, 1979.

Rice, George E. "Ellen G. White's Use of Daniel and Revelation." In *Symposium on Revelation—Book 1*. Ed. Frank B. Holbrook, Daniel and Revelation Committee Series. Vol. 6. Silver Spring, Md.: Biblical Research Institute, 1992.

"The Role of Israel in Old Testament Prophecy." In *The SDA Bible Commentary*. Washington, D.C.: Review and Herald, 1955. Vol. 4, pp. 25-38.

Rowland, Christopher. *The Open Heaven: The Study of Apocalyptic in Judaism and Early Christianity*. New York: Crossroad, 1982.

Shea, William H. *Selected Studies on Prophetic Interpretation*. Daniel and Revelation Committee Series. Vol. 1. Washington, D.C.: Biblical Research Institute, 1982.

Divine Judgment

Gerhard F. Hasel

Introduction

The judgment theme is as pervasive in the Bible as the theme of salvation. Judgment and salvation are the twin topics that weave themselves like threads from Genesis to Revelation. This is because salvation and judgment reflect the twin characteristics of mercy and justice in the nature of God. Therefore, the double themes of salvation and judgment, reflecting divine mercy and justice, cannot and must not be separated; otherwise both lose their fullness and mutual complementarity.

Judgment deserves careful attention, since it is involved in the issues of (a) divine justice in an unjust world (theodicy), (b) retribution for wrong done, (c) the suffering of the innocent, (d) the resolution of the conflict of good and evil, and (e) the end of sin and suffering. But above all, final judgment vindicates the Creator—His character, law, and governance—in the minds of all created intelligences, whether loyal or lost, thereby obtaining eternal security and peace for the universe. Judgment is thus portrayed in Scripture as an essential part of the "eternal gospel" (Rev. 14:6, 7).

I. The Language of Judgment

The specific language of judgment in the Bible is rich and multifaceted. Yet the judgment theme is present in Scripture in a number of places without the usage of typical judgment terminology. However, it is illuminating to investigate the explicit language of judgment in both the OT and NT.

A. *Judgment Language in the OT*

1. The Hebrew Root *Špṭ* and Derivatives

The Hebrew root špṭ is used a total of 642 times in the OT in both verbal and nominal forms. These refer to an action that restores an impaired or disturbed relationship.

The Hebrew šōpēṭ is used 58 times to refer to a person who tests the guilt or innocence of a defendant, subsequently rendering a verdict for or against that person (Deut. 1:16; 1 Sam. 7:15-17. However, a "judge" is also a "helper," "saviour," or "deliverer" (Judges 3:9, 15; 2 Kings 13:5; Isa. 19:20; Neh. 9:27). The goal of the "judge" is to bring about well-being and peace (Heb. šālôm). The judging provides deliverance, vindication, and salvation, or condemnation and punishment.

The noun "judgment" or "justice" (Heb. mišpāṭ) is used 424 times. Among its various meanings the following are relevant: (1) A judicial decision (c. 200 times; 1 Kings 20:40), (2) a court case (Isa. 3:14), (3) authority, right, or justice, as a human activity (Ps. 106:3; Prov. 12:5), but especially (4) as an attribute of God (Deut. 1:17; 32:4; Ps. 119:149). God executes judgments (plural, šepāṭîm) against the Egyptian gods and the firstborn of Egypt (Ex. 12:12; Num. 33:4), redeeming Israel "with an outstretched arm and with great acts of judgment" (Ex. 6:6).

Israel also experiences divine judgments (Eze. 5:10, 15). God can bring these by means of military ("sword," Isa. 3:25; Jer. 9:16) and/or natural disasters as in Ezekiel 14:21: "acts of judgment, sword, famine, evil beasts, and pestilence." A covenant-breaking, unfaithful, rebellious Israel is treated with punitive judgments in the same way in which God executes "judgments" on pagan nations such as Moab (Eze. 25:11) and Egypt (Eze. 30:19). Yet survivors will escape, and the Lord will restore them (Amos 9:11-15). This faithful remnant will be protected from enemies and oppressors by God Himself, who will "execute judgments" on those "who have treated them with contempt" (Eze. 28:26).

The verbal form of the Hebrew root špṭ, "to judge," often expresses the idea of judging between two persons (Gen. 16:5) or two groups of people (Judges 11:27) whose relationship has been interrupted. They are thus reconciled and returned to a state of "peace" (Heb. šālôm) by means of the third party's judgment.

The judging activity can terminate in a negative decision, a condemnation (Eze. 23:45) or a positive decision, a vindication of the accused (Ps. 10:18, with God as subject; Isa. 11:4; Ps. 82:3, with people as subject). This is illustrated in Deuteronomy 25:1 where "there is a dispute [rîb] between men, and they come into court [mišpāṭ], and the judges decide between them [špṭ], acquitting the innocent and condemning the guilty."

The oppressed call out, "judge me" or "vindicate me" (Ps. 7:8; 35:24; 43:1). The appeal is made to Yahweh, who is called upon to "judge" or "vindicate" the oppressed one and is expected to save and deliver. God alone can bring about just judgment and final vindication.

From the various usages of the Hebrew root špṭ, it is evident that in both divine or human judgment activities the dual aspect of condemnation/punishment and vindication/deliverance play key roles. Various forms can be used either in the positive or in the negative sense. Judgment is not negative per se.

2. The Hebrew Root *Dîn* and Derivatives

Although the basic meaning is "judge," *dîn* more narrowly expresses an authoritative, binding decision in a legal case. Often verbal forms of *dîn* are used in parallelism with a form of the verb *špṭ* (Ps. 9:8 [9]; 140:13 [12]; Prov. 31:9; Isa. 10:2), indicating a closely related meaning.

Yahweh "will vindicate *[špṭ]* his people" (Deut. 32:36) and "judges the peoples" (Ps. 7:9 [8]) by coming to their rescue to exonerate them. The Messianic king will "judge thy people with righteousness" (72:2). On the negative side He will "bring judgment on the nation which they [Israel] serve" (Gen. 15:14) and He will "judge his people" of Israel (Isa. 3:13) who have done wrong.

The Hebrew noun *dîn* (used 19 times) has meanings such as "legal right" (Deut. 17:8; Jer. 5:28; Ps. 9:4 [5]; Prov. 29:7) and "lawsuit" or "case" (Job 35:14; Esther 1:13). It can also refer to the "judgment" or "verdict" (Ps. 76:8 [9]) that God gives from heaven.

The noun *dayyān*, "judge" or "protector," appears in 1 Samuel 24:15; and Psalm 68:5 [6] as a designation for deity. God is the judge. Daniel's name, based on *dîn*, means "God is my judge."

The Aramaic noun *dîn* is ascribed to the King of heaven in Daniel 4:37 [34], with the meaning of "justice." The same noun is used in the heavenly judgment scene in Daniel 7 in the sense of "court" of judgment (Dan. 7:10) and "judgment" rendered by the Most High for His saints (verse 22).

3. The Hebrew Root *Rîb* and Derivatives

The basic meaning of *rîb* is "to dispute, quarrel, strive, contend" (Gen. 26:20-22; Num. 20:3; Deut. 33:7, 8) or "to conduct a legal case, engage in a lawsuit" (Isa. 3:13; Jer. 2:9; Hosea 4:4; Ps. 74:22).

The noun *rîb* (62 usages) refers to a dis-

pute between persons or groups (Gen. 13:7; Deut. 25:1; Isa. 58:4). However, of greatest interest for our subject is its use in the sense of a covenant lawsuit (Ps. 35:23). God is depicted as coming to the legal assistance of an individual or a group (1 Sam. 25:39; 2 Sam. 22:44; Ps. 35:1, 23; Lam. 3:58). Yahweh contends in a controversy (or legal case) against the nations (Jer. 25:31; 51:36). He also contends in a covenant "lawsuit" against His own people Israel (Hosea 4:1; Micah 6:2; Jer. 2:9) and also fights for them (Jer. 50:34; 51:36). Yahweh is both judge and defender; He takes on the role of prosecutor and defender at the same time.

B. Judgment Language in the NT

The Koine Greek language of the NT has a cluster of words that are used to express various ideas of judgment. Their precise meaning depends on the context as much as on the word itself.

1. The Word Grouping of *Krinō*

The Greek verb *krinō*—meaning to separate, distinguish, discriminate, divide, judge— is used as a technical legal term in human judgment settings with the idea of judging, deciding a case, or bringing to a court (for example, Luke 19:22; John 7:51; Acts 25:9, 10). It is employed also for judgment in which either Christ or God is the agent (John 5:30; 8:16; 1 Cor. 5:13; 2 Tim. 4:1; James 2:12; 1 Peter 4:5; Rev. 6:10).

The meanings "to condemn" or "to punish" are sometimes more appropriate than "to judge." For example, the Father did not send Christ to "condemn" (rather than "judge") the world (John 3:17, 18). Those who know the law will be "condemned" (rather than "judged") by the law (Rom. 2:12). "The Lord will judge, [or punish,] his people" (Heb. 10:30).

2. The Noun *Krisis*

This noun is rendered by such words as "judgment," "condemnation," "punishment." It expresses mostly penal judgment, in the sense of "condemnation" and the "punishment" that follows. In 2 Peter 2:4, 11 *krisis* is used for a judgment that brings condemnation. The "day of judgment" is the day of condemnation by the divine Judge (verse 9).

The Gospel of John contains a number of words with which Jesus refers to a judgment in the present. John 12:31 refers to the judgment of Satan: "Now is the judgment *[krisis]* of this world, now shall the ruler of this world be cast out." In John 16:11 the Comforter teaches about "judgment *[krisis]*, because the ruler of this world is judged" ("has been condemned," NRSV).

The judgment of Satan refers to the limitation of his sphere of activity. His condemnation is the restriction of activity to this world, which "is in the power of the evil one" (1 John 5:19).

In Jesus' teaching the believer who abides in Him has eternal life now: "He who believes in the Son has eternal life" (John 3:36). Believers who already possess eternal life will still die, but Christ will raise them up "at the last day" (John 6:40). They will still enter into judgment, even though they are not under condemnation. John 5:24 explains, "Truly, truly, I say to you, he who hears my word and believes him who sent me, has eternal life; he does not come into judgment, but has passed from death to life." This word of Jesus does not teach that there is no longer any judgment for the believer. John 5:24 is an integral part of verses 19-30. That context shows that the Father "has given all judgment *[krisis]* to the Son" (verse 22), indicating that a present judgment does not rule out a future judgment.

The conditions that lead to eternal life now consist of hearing the word of Jesus and believing that the Father has sent Him (verse 24). Both terms are present active participles, indicating that believers remain in a state of hearing and believing for eternal life to be a continuing reality in their experience. Eternal life is not a state or condition that can never be lost; again it is a reality of faith in the present only for those who remain in Christ. For the believer who apostatizes, eternal life is lost and judgment determines his or her fate.

The believer who remains faithful "does not come into judgment" *(krisis),* which also means "condemnation" or "punishment." Thus, believers do "not come under condemnation" (NAB); "will not be condemned" (NIV). The *Modern Language Bible* reads, "he comes under no sentence," that is, a "sentence" of condemnation.

John 3:19 states that "this is the judgment *[krisis],* that the light has come into the world, and men loved darkness rather than light, because their deeds were evil." The clear emphasis here is on "separation" and "division." People who are confronted with Christ separate themselves into followers (lovers of light) or opponents (lovers of darkness). Into the lives of those who meet Him Christ brings a "crisis" *(krisis)* that forces them to make a decision for or against Him. Those who decide for Him will not face future condemnation in the final judgment, but those who reject Him will at that time face both condemnation and punishment.

3. The Noun *Krima*

While *krima* is traditionally rendered "judgment," it often has the connotation of "decision" or "judicial verdict." Often *krima* is employed in an unfavorable sense, as condemnation resulting from a negative decision in God's judgment (2 Peter 2:3; Jude 4; Rev. 17:1). This meaning seems appropriate in a number of instances where the verdict or decision is unfavorable (Mark 12:40; Rom. 13:2; Gal. 5:10; 1 Tim. 5:12; James 3:1).

In some contexts both positive and negative aspects are present in *krima.* There is a divine "verdict" *[krima]* for the saints "against her [Babylon]" (Rev. 18:20). In this passage *krima* clearly involves a judgment with a decision by God for His loyal ones and against Babylon.

The context of Revelation 20:4 reveals that *krima* has to mean "judgment." In the millennial judgment the term is employed for the activity of the saints, now vindicated and seated upon thrones, to sit in judgment, with authority to judge the wicked in anticipation of rendering a negative verdict (note the similar picture in Daniel 7:10, 22, where God is seated and the saints come into judgment). This noun seems to be used here because of its typically negative connotation of condemnation (cf. Rev. 17:1; 18:20). The work of judgment referred to here is that mentioned by Paul: "Do you not know that the saints will judge the world? . . . Do you not know that we are to judge angels? (1 Cor. 6:2, 3). This work will involve a careful investigation in heaven of the records of the wicked (cf. Rev. 20:12-15, where the punishment is meted out).

4. The Noun *Kritēs*

This noun is rendered "judge," either for human beings (Matt. 5:25; Luke 18:2, 6; Acts 24:10) or for God. In Hebrews 12:23 reference is made to "a judge who is God of all." James 4:12 speaks of Christ as judge: "he who is able to save and to destroy." He is depicted as "the righteous judge" (2 Tim. 4:8), the "judge of the living and the dead" (Acts 10:42), and the "Judge [who] is standing at the doors" (James 5:9).

II. Divine Judgment Within the Process of History

Why is judgment needed in the historical process, not to speak of the end of the age? What calls for judgment? Would not the love of God be sufficient? Will divine love overrule divine judgment?

A. Divine Judgment and Grace in Genesis

From the beginning of the Bible there is a profound relationship among sin, judgment, and grace. This correlation is present not only in Genesis, but is seen as well in the historical books of the OT. It plays a significant role in the prophetic writings and in other parts of the Bible as well.

1. Sin, Fall, Divine Judgment, and Grace

The tempter succeeded in bringing sin into the world, changing both humanity and the world itself. Immediately God entered into the picture with the divine call, "Where are you?" (Gen. 3:9). This call is not to be perceived as condemnation but as an invitation to turn back to God and away from Satan and the bondage to sin he has brought into the world. The Creator presents Himself as Saviour with a call that offers grace. The gracious Creator is also judge. His judgment activity involves the curse on the serpent (Gen. 3:14). In this act judgment is pronounced and executed. God also judges Eve (verse 16) and Adam (verses 17-19).

At the beginning of human history a relationship between sin, judgment, and grace emerges and sets the tone for the rest of the Bible. God, after having given the first messianic promise, thereby establishing enmity between the serpent and the woman and announcing that a "seed" would crush the serpent's head (Gen. 3:15), pronounces a judgment upon the woman. It related to pain in childbirth and to her clinging to her husband (verse 16). This judgment was both remedial and restraining in purpose, revealing divine grace. It was to reestablish broken relationships, to safeguard the husband-wife relationship, and to maintain a new relationship with the Creator-Saviour. It also had the purpose of restraining the growth of sin and wickedness.

The judgment upon Adam was also remedial and restraining. Adam was to toil for food in the sweat of his face (verse 19). This too was part of God's larger redemptive plan that would restrain the effects of sin. Work was to be a beneficial antidote to wasteful idleness, providing happiness and the joy of accomplishment.

A number of basic patterns in the biblical concept of judgment emerge: 1. Judgment may be remedial and restraining in nature. God remains in control over sin by setting new orders, establishing new relationships, and curtailing sin's growth. 2. Sin is disobedience to God's specific commandment, which was given to protect the first pair from doing wrong and from bringing misery upon themselves and the world; thus judgment is the result of the infringement of the divine will as expressed in God's laws. 3. The remedial aspect in judgment is (when present) intended to bring about renewal and restoration; it aims at holding sin in check and providing ways for humankind to remain loyal to the Creator-Redeemer.

2. Sin, Divine Judgment, and Grace for Cain

The narrative of Cain and Abel shows sin growing to new proportions. Sin leads to the murder of a brother over the issue of proper worship (Gen. 4:1-16). Cain is directly confronted by God with two questions, "Why are you angry?" (verse 6) and "Where is Abel your brother?" (verse 9). Cain is judged (verses 10-12) and goes out "from the presence of the Lord" to settle "in the land of Nod, east of Eden" (verse 16).

The sequence of events in the story of Cain and Abel can be sketched as follows: human sin (verses 3-8), divine intervention with judgment (verses 9-12), forgiving grace for protection (verses 13-15), and punishment experienced (verse 16). It is striking that God takes a decisive role not only in judgment and punishment, but also in providing gracious protection from future threat.

Judgment seems to be both punitive (retributive) and remedial in nature; it controls sin, restrains the results of the punishment, and protects Cain from the treatment of an eye for an eye and a tooth for a tooth (Ex. 21:23).

3. Sin, Divine Judgment, and Grace for the World

The narrative of the "sons of God" (Sethites) who married the "daughters of men" (Cainites) in Genesis 6:1-4 provides a background for the deterioration of human nature, which resulted in the universal flood,

bringing the antediluvian world to an end (Gen. 6-9).

By the time of Noah, "the Lord saw that the wickedness of man was great in the earth, and that every imagination of the thoughts of his heart was only evil continually" (6:5). The earth "was corrupt" and "filled with violence" (verse 11) and "all flesh had corrupted their way upon the earth" (verse 12). This universal corruption included human thinking and doing, and provided the moral motivation that caused God to bring retributive (punitive) judgment in the form of a destructive flood.

The moral motivation of Scripture is unique in the ancient world. None of the flood stories known from the ancient Near East, whether Sumerian or Akkadian, provided a moral motivation for divine judgment. The nonbiblical flood stories have the gods act capriciously in sending a flood without any moral cause that would justify such severe action. The Atrahasis Epic reports that the flood was sent by the gods because the noise of men in their nightly feasting disturbed the gods in their sleep.

The biblical narrative, on the other hand, reveals a God who brings judgment because of the unprecedented growth of sin caused by the utter moral corruption of humankind. The divine judgment of the Flood narrative reveals that judgment is retributive in nature, bringing upon sinners their deserved rewards, based on their unrelentingly wicked deeds. It also indicates that judgment has a restraining purpose, holding sin in check. While God announces the blotting out of life from the face of the earth (verses 7, 13), He graciously reveals His design to save those who would turn to Him (verses 14-22). Divine punishment in the Genesis narrative is neither indiscriminate nor capricious.

Divine grace was also at work. A period of 120 years of probationary time was announced, during which sinful humanity was invited to turn to God and be saved. Grace was also shown by providing a way of escape from a doomed world: An ark was to be built and readied by a faithful remnant (verses 17, 18).

In the record of the Flood there is again a specific sequence: (1) growth of sin [verses 1-5, 11, 12], (2) divine announcement of judgment because of sin [verses 6, 7, 13], (3) forgiving grace to save [verses 14-22; 7:1-5], and (4) punishment meted out and a remnant of faith saved [Gen. 7:1–8:22].

4. Sin, Divine Judgment, and Grace for Sodom and Gomorrah

The narrative of Genesis 19 reveals again the interplay between judgment and salvation. It again shows God acting directly, without involving any human agency, to bring retributive judgment on the wicked cities of the plain. Two messengers (RSV "angels") come to the city, and Lot invites them to spend the night in his house (Gen. 19:1-3). Some of the men of the city wish to engage the strangers in sexually aberrant acts (verses 4-6). This outrageous behavior fills their cup of iniquity, and the heavenly guests inform Lot that he and his family must leave, lest they "be consumed in the punishment of the city" (verse 15).

The conclusion of the narrative records that God "overthrew the cities in which Lot dwelt" (verse 29). According to verse 24, "the Lord rained on Sodom and Gomorrah brimstone and fire from the Lord out of heaven." The direct and unmediated agent of destruction of the wicked cities was Yahweh. He used elements of nature to bring about the deserved retributive judgment.

Here, as in the universal flood, is no divine abandoning of the cities, in which God withdraws so that humanity can destroy itself. God Himself stops their wickedness. He is judge and destroyer of the wicked, while He is Saviour of the faithful remnant. Judgment, grace, and salvation interact.

The judgments recounted in Genesis set the tone and provide the pattern for the salvation-judgment correlation of the remainder of Scripture. A perfect creation is permanently impacted by sin, which continues to grow to horrendous proportions. Divine judgment is called for at the various junctures of human history. Repeatedly the grace of God is at work with repeated invitations to repent and return to a loving and benevolent God whose purpose it is to save any who wish to be saved. The movement from the unlawful eating of fruit to murder, to reckless killing, to complete corruption and violence with intense sexual immorality, is met by judgments appropriate to the respective situations. The divine judgments are remedial in purpose for repentant sinners, retributive (punitive) in nature for those who remain obstinate, and designed to restrain the growth of sin.

The record also reveals that God remains the final and unique judge. He is both a just and righteous judge, and He is also a God manifesting grace. Divine justice is not separated from divine grace and mercy. Adam and Eve are justly judged, but God's grace also holds back the threatened penalty of death. Cain is driven out, but a sign of grace is put on him for protection. The universal deluge destroys all life on earth, but only after God graciously offers salvation to all repentant humanity. Divine judgment is not indiscriminate, capricious, or arbitrary. Divine justice is applied appropriately and with restraint. Grace and mercy are available to those who desire them.

B. Sin, Divine Judgment, and Grace for the Nations and Israel

The Bible, particularly the OT, contains numerous passages in which nations are the recipients of divine judgment. This topic is surveyed first in relation to the Canaanites and pagan nations. After that, the question of God's dealings in judgment and grace with ancient Israel is addressed.

1. Divine Judgment and Grace for the Canaanites

Within the context of God's covenant with Abraham, the Lord's covenant promise was to provide a land for the descendants of Abraham (Gen. 12:7; 17:8). The pre-Israelite inhabitants who occupied this land were to have an opportunity to know the true God and to follow Him.

Abraham's descendants would be enslaved and "oppressed for four hundred years" (Gen. 15:13). After that, God would "bring judgment on the nation which they serve" (verse 14). He was speaking about Egypt as the oppressor of Israel. Then in "the fourth generation [Heb. *dôr*, "life-span"]," they would return to Canaan, "for the iniquity of the Amorites is not yet complete" (verse 16). More time of grace and mercy was to be provided so that these pre-Israelite inhabitants might know the true God and turn to Him.

The collective designation "Amorites" in Genesis 15:16 appears to include the tribes or peoples enumerated in verses 19-21. These same tribes appear in the listing of peoples displaced by the Israelites when they occupied Canaan (Ex. 13:5; Joshua 3:10). Extrabiblical information on the inhabitants of Canaan, together with biblical data, show something of the character of these people.

The Canaanites practiced immoral activities, particularly as part of their religious worship. The Canaanite religion was polytheistic, with El as chief deity and Baal as the most active of gods. Athirat was the consort of El, and her cult symbol was the Asherah. The consort of Baal was the goddess Anat. The death of the god Mot at the hands of Anat is depicted in most gruesome terms. Among the sacrifices brought to the various gods of the Canaanites was also that of humans, especially children, for the god Molech. Sacred prostitution, with gross immoral practices, was part of the fertility cult of the Canaanites. Divination was practiced as well.

In the time of Abraham God pronounced that the cup of iniquity of the Amorites (Canaanites) was not yet full (Gen. 15:16). They deserved a time of grace and probation, a time of additional mercy. They were to have the opportunity of finding the true God and turning to Him. Abraham and his descendants were placed in their midst, in order that they

might find God and the true way of salvation.

Shortly after the Exodus the Israelites encountered the Amalekites, descendants of Esau and his Hittite wife (Gen. 36:2, 10-12). At Rephidim the Amalekites attacked the Israelites (Ex. 17:8-13) from the rear (Deut. 25:17, 18). A revealing statement notes that the Amalekites "did not fear God" (verse 18). While they must have known from their ancestor Esau about the true God, heard what God had done to the Egyptians, and seen how His power was manifested in the Exodus, they chose defiance. The despicable treachery of Amalek filled their cup of iniquity, and God's retributive (punitive) judgment came upon them: "I will utterly blot out the remembrance of Amalek from under heaven" (Ex. 17:14). God used the Israelites to defeat the attacking Amalekites (verses 6-16). Love, no less than justice, demanded that the Amalekites experience retributive (punitive) judgment.

When Israel came to the territory of Sihon, king of Heshbon, Israel asked to pass through his territory, offering to pay for food and water (Deut. 2:27-29). Sihon refused, for his heart had been hardened and his spirit had become obstinate (verse 30). This suggests that Sihon had the opportunity to know and follow the ways of the true God, but like Pharaoh, he hardened his heart and set his spirit against God. His cup of iniquity was now filled by this defiant obstinacy. God would judge him by His power (verses 32-36). This was retributive and punitive judgment. Subsequently, Og, the king of Bashan, was also defeated (Deut. 3:1-11). "So we took the land at that time out of the hand of the two kings of the Amorites who were beyond the Jordan" (verse 8).

The fall of Jericho, an ancient and famed city, came about by a miraculous act of Yahweh. The city was well fortified, but God Himself brought down the walls of Jericho (Joshua 6:1-24). The narrative of the battle of Jericho reveals that God was the leader. As judge, He brought judgment by natural human means. This story is representative of all wars of conquest reported in the OT. Yahweh led Israel in the wars of conquest. When the Israelites took leadership in their own hands, they failed utterly, as the narrative of the conquest of Ai reveals (Joshua 7:1-5). Israel was called upon by God to function as an instrument of judgment, thus showing a total reorientation of warfare and political power in Israel. It was the purpose of God that in His theocratic nation He would exercise His power and leadership. They were not to act on their own. Unfortunately, they did not long follow God's plan.

God is the one who judges the nations. This concept puts the wars of conquest into a category of their own. Human instruments can be used as He commands. In using Israel He teaches the lesson of the dire consequences of sin, idolatry, and rebellion. Israel learns what befalls those who follow the way of the pagan nations.

God also uses instruments of nature, such as hailstones (Joshua 10:11), hornets (Joshua 24:12), plague (Ex. 32:35), or famine (Jer. 11:22). In Noah's day judgment came by water (Gen. 6-8); in the destruction of Sodom and Gomorrah God used "brimstone and fire" (Gen. 19:24). God's method of executing judgment can be by direct supernatural agents (Ex. 33:2, "I will send an angel before you, and I will drive out the Canaanites"), direct natural agents (water, fire, famine, pestilence, plague, hail, hornets), or indirect through human agents (Israel, and later Assyria, Babylon).

The destruction of the Canaanites, as depicted in the OT, was to follow the express command of God, "You must utterly destroy them; you shall make no covenant with them, and show no mercy to them" (Deut. 7:2).

The destruction of the ancient Canaanites is perceived by some to be out of harmony with the spirit of divine love and mercy known from the Bible. We have already seen that the destruction of the Canaanites was part of a larger context, because of their wickedness, their immoral practices, their refusal to turn to God during their time of probation, and the rebellious defiance with which they met Israel. Evidently the 400 years of probationary time had no effect upon them. They, and their descendants after them, remained rebellious and licentious, as the Canaanite religion and cult practices indicate.

The biblical picture reveals that these peoples had ample opportunity to learn of the true God. Abraham lived among the Canaanites a full century; Isaac, his son, an entire lifetime, 180 years. The Edomites had Esau as their forefather; yet they did not turn to the true God. They were the first who turned on the Israelites in outright defiance against God and the needs of a sojourning people. The Canaanites had witnessed what God had done to the Egyptians and how He had miraculously protected and cared for those who followed Him. The Canaanites persisted in their rebellion and defiant idolatry, attacking and mistreating God's people. Both divine justice and love demanded that they would be judged and experience the results of their own deeds as God would direct and act.

2. Divine Judgment and Grace for the Nations

The prophetic books of the OT contain numerous oracles of God's judgment upon the nations. The first major unit of such oracles is presented in the opening part of the book of Amos (1:3–2:16). The nations referred to are Syria (verses 3-5), Philistia (verses 6-8), Tyre (verses 9, 10), Edom (verses 11, 12), Ammon (verses 13-15), Moab (2:1-3), and also Judah (verses 4, 5) and Israel (verses 6-16).

Each of these prophecies begins with the introductory phrase "Thus says the Lord," revealing that the judgment comes from Yahweh. In each of the prophecies the same "I" statement of Yahweh is used in the phrase "For three transgressions . . . and for four, I will not revoke the punishment." This continues to emphasize that Yahweh is actively engaged in retributive judgment for transgressions committed that filled the cup of iniquity of each nation. God holds each nation responsible for what it has done.

Retributive judgment is not based on an automatic or mechanical deed-consequence relationship in which God is inactive and the consequences follow automatically upon the deed committed. Yahweh is depicted time and again as being actively engaged in the judgment process within the flow of history. There is a divine moral standard by which the nations are to live.

Other minor prophets also contain oracles against the nations. They are present in Joel (3:9-17), Zephaniah (2:4-15), Obadiah (verses 1-6), and Zechariah (9:1-6). The entire book of Jonah speaks about judgment and mercy for the Assyrians (and Jonah himself).

The book of Isaiah contains a series of judgment prophecies: against Babylon (13:1-22), Assyria (14:24-27), Philistia (verses 29-32), Moab (15:1–16:14), Syria (17:1-14), Ethiopia (18:1-7), Egypt (19:1-17; 20:3-6), Edom and Arabia (21:11-17), and Tyre (23:1-18). Jeremiah 46-51 and Ezekiel 25-32 contain further oracles against the nations. These judgment prophecies against the nations show that God is truly judge over all nations and that His sphere of judgment activity is as comprehensive as is the sin and guilt of the nations (cf. Jer. 51:2-23, 25, 26).

The expression "day of the Lord" is used for the day of judgment against foreign nations (Isa. 13:9; Jer. 46:10) and against Israel (Amos 5:18-20).

The book of Daniel also speaks of the judgment of the nations before the end-time judgment. While the major thrust of the book is on apocalyptic eschatology, there is a continuous historical connection from the time of the kingdom of Babylon (2:28) through the historical periods of Medo-Persia (8:20), Greece (verse 21), and Rome with the "little horn" (verses 9, 23-25) and into the "time of the end" (verses 17, 19; 11:40; 12:1). Each of the four world empires is judged and comes to an end (7:11, 12). God not only has foreknowledge of the historical sequence of the nations, revealing in advance their arrival, activity, and fall, but He is actively involved in shaping history. "He removes kings and sets up kings" (2:21). He is the great judge of the nations and the history of the world.

3. Divine Judgment and Grace for Ancient Israel

Israel was established as a nation by divine intervention in history. On Mount Sinai God graciously provided a covenant to the wilderness generation (Ex. 19-24). The Exodus generation had experienced redemption, salvation, and liberation from spiritual and physical bondage (Ex. 1-18). The Sinai covenant established a profound relationship with God (Ex. 19:1-6).

God incorporated in His covenant with them His universal moral law as a way for them to live a successful life. It would regulate their relationship of love to God (the first four commandments of the Decalogue) and their relationship with fellow human beings (the remaining six commandments). Thus, the Decalogue would provide the comprehensive norms intended to govern all God-human and human-human relationships.

The ceremonial law given to ancient Israel was to make it possible for those who fell into sin to be forgiven, for sin to be atoned for by a substitutionary sacrifice, and for the sinner to be restored to full covenantal fellowship with the holy God. The ceremonial law was intended to take care of Israel's sins until the one true Sacrifice of the future Messiah would fulfill it. The dietary law (Lev. 11:2-23, 41-45; Deut. 14:3-21) reaches back to pre-Israelite times (Gen. 9:2-4) and continues to function after Israelite times (Acts 15; cf. Hasel 1991; see Sanctuary I. B, C).

All these laws—different in origin, design, and function—were basic to God's plan for ancient Israel. "In Israel, then, all law is referred to Yahweh as Lord and Judge. Herein is the distinctiveness of the OT relationship to God. The theological use of legal terms is possible only when faith in nature gods is vanquished by faith in the personal God who has established a historical relationship with the people which worships Him" (TDNT 3:925). The covenantal relationship, which includes universal and time-restricted laws, is the basis of and rationale for God to judge Israel when the nation breaks the covenant.

Judgment upon Israel is connected with the covenant blessings and curses. At the end of the long recitation of the covenantal laws, statutes, and ordinances (Deut. 5-26) the covenant blessings and curses appear (Deut. 27; 28). In Deuteronomy 30 Moses admonishes Israel to choose "life and good" (verse 15) and "blessing" (verse 19) over "evil," "death" (verse 15), and "curse" (verse 19) by remaining loyal to the covenant God. The book of Leviticus also contrasts covenant blessings (Lev. 26:3-13) and curses (verses 14-39). Israel's history is the fulfillment of these blessings and curses.

Tragically Israel rebelled time and again against her beneficent covenant God and His laws. In order to bring Israel back into the right covenantal relationship, God sent His prophets with calls to repentance and warnings of the dire consequences of their actions. Yahweh repeatedly brought against them the "covenant lawsuit" (Heb. *rîb;* Hosea 4:1-3; Micah 6:1-8).

The "covenant lawsuit" of Yahweh against His people is presented in detail in Micah 6:1-8. First comes the summons for Israel to listen (verse 1), for Yahweh has a "lawsuit" (*rîb*) with His people (verse 2). He pleads His case before the mountains, hills, and the foundations of the earth (verses 1, 2). He directs His questions to the accused and pleads for a defense (verse 3). He states what kind of care He has bestowed on Israel and affirms why He has a claim on them (verses 4, 5). Israel responds by asking what sacrifice would be adequate to repair the estrangement from Yahweh (verses 6, 7). The appropriate response is that it should be not empty animal sacrifices but a life of faith in submission to God: "He has showed you, O man, what is good; and what does the Lord require of you, but to do justice [*mišpāṭ*], and to love kindness

[*hesed*], and to walk humbly with your God?" (verse 8). Israel should live up to the beneficent covenant obligations, its norms and laws. The answer does call for sacrifice, but external animal sacrifices have meaning only if there is first an internal sacrifice of self, manifested in a genuine turning to God.

The expression "the day of the Lord" appears for the first time in Amos 5:18-20. This phrase occurs 16 times in six different prophetic books. But if we consider such expression as "Yahweh has a day," "the day of the anger of the Lord," "that day," "the day of," and "the day when," we find over two hundred usages, primarily in the prophetic books of the OT. There is ample evidence in the OT demonstrating that the expression "the day of the Lord" often expresses a day of judgment against His people Israel.

The popular conception of many Israelites in Amos's time was that "the day of the Lord" would be a day of vindication for Israel, because Yahweh would come to their rescue when they were threatened by enemies. However, Amos proclaimed, "Woe to you who desire the day of the Lord! Why would you have the day of the Lord? It is darkness, and not light; as if a man fled from a lion, and a bear met him; or went into the house and leaned with his hand against the wall, and a serpent bit him. Is not the day of the Lord darkness, and not light, and gloom with no brightness in it?" (Amos 5:18-20). This reversal of what was popularly believed was intended to shake Israel out of its false sense of security and to cause Israel to consider seriously their intense rebellion. Its aim was to announce what would come upon them and thus to turn them back to the Lord before it was too late. If they insisted in their wickedness, God would judge His people and bring deserved punishment because they had broken the covenant with Him.

The purpose of divine judgment was to confront Israel with the reality of the path of death, which they had chosen as they departed from His beneficent covenant. If they continued on this path, they must know that it would mean separation from life and the God who gave them life, leading to destruction and death, which their own God would bring them. It would also serve to purify Israel and graciously reclaim His people. Judgment is used by God to function as a refiner's fire that smelts away the dross and removes the alloy (Isa. 1:22-25). Judgment would bring about just and appropriate rewards for their evil deeds. Their sins, transgressions, and evil cried out for justice; wrong had to be righted.

Israel continued in the path of rebellion and experienced judgment. The tribes of the Northern Kingdom, after many warnings and messages to return to God, finally went into Assyrian exile in 722 B.C. The Southern Kingdom of Judah came to its avoidable and tragic end in 586 B.C., again after the people had rejected many voices of prophetic warning and counsel.

Daniel's famous prayer (Dan. 9:4-19), speaks of God, who keeps His "covenant and steadfast love with those who love him and keep his commandments" (verse 4) and the "treachery" which Israel has committed against God (verse 7). It also recognizes that they did not obey the teachings of "his servants the prophets" (verse 10). Daniel speaks of the covenant curse "in the law of Moses . . . poured out upon us" (verse 11) and appeals to God's "great mercy" (verse 18), confessing all the sins and pleading for forgiveness (verses 9, 19). Divine compassion, mercy, and grace are shown to Israel by their God in that they are permitted to return to rebuild the Temple and Jerusalem (Ezra 1:2-4; 6:6-12; 7:11-26; Neh. 1, 2). A period of "seventy weeks," or 490 years (III. B. 1. a. [2]) of special probationary time of grace is granted to Israel, at the end of which the coming Messiah would die and do away with "sacrifice and offering" (Dan. 9:24-27). In all of these experiences God showed Himself to be in control of history. He directed His people whenever they wished to listen. He is in ultimate control of the affairs of the world in His own mysterious ways. Today's popular belief that God is a sentimental and loving godling who winks at evil and loves humans regardless of what they do does not agree with the picture of God in Scripture.

C. Divine Judgeship

The consistent testimony of Scripture is that the divine Judge holds human beings, as well as Satan and his angels, responsible for what they have done. This part of our study refers to major passages that speak of the judgeship of God or Christ.

Abraham raises the question "Shall not the Judge *[šōpēt]* of all the earth do right *[mišpāṭ]?*" (Gen. 18:25). This ringing affirmation that God is "the Judge of all the earth" is linked to the resounding affirmation that He will judge with "justice."

The divine self-revelation granted to Moses affirmed that the Lord God is "merciful and gracious, slow to anger, and abounding in steadfast love and faithfulness, keeping steadfast love for thousands, forgiving iniquity and transgression and sin, but who will by no means clear the guilty, visiting the iniquity of the fathers upon the children and the children's children, to the third and fourth generation" (Ex. 34:6, 7). In this self-revelation God correlates grace and judgment, love and punishment. He also affirms that the gracious and merciful God is a righteous judge who does not leave the guilty unpunished. These divine words are cited throughout Scripture (Num. 14:18; Deut. 5:10; Ps. 86:15; Joel 2:13; Jonah 4:2; Nahum 1:3).

The second commandment makes it clear that God will visit "the iniquity of the fathers upon the children to the third and the fourth generation of those who hate me" (Ex. 20:5). God is judge, and He judges with love and compassion; only "those who hate me" (Ps. 69:4), who refuse to live in harmony with His will, experience this divine judgment.

The psalmists have much to say about divine judgeship. "But the Lord sits enthroned for ever, he has established his throne for judgment; and he judges the world with righteousness, he judges the peoples with equity"

(Ps. 9:7, 8). He judges the earth "with equity [mišpāṭ]" and "in righteousness" (ṣedeq) because He is "a righteous judge" (Ps. 7:11); the foundation of His throne is "righteousness and justice" (Ps. 89:14; cf. 97:2). In fact, "the heavens declare his righteousness, for God himself is judge" (Ps. 50:6). The Lord "comes to judge the earth. He will judge the world with righteousness, and the peoples with his truth" (Ps. 96:13). The psalmist prays, "Arise, O God, judge the earth; for to thee belong all the nations!" (Ps. 82:8).

The prophet Isaiah states, "For the Lord is our judge, the Lord is our ruler, the Lord is our king; he will save us" (Ps. 33:22). The sequence of Judge-Lawgiver-King-Saviour is overwhelming in its comprehensiveness and sublime brevity.

The heavenly Judge can see what humans do not, because He looks into the heart. God understands all motives and motivations for human action. He has the ability to see and understand all aspects of the evidence on the inner human level, all social dimensions, motivational perspectives, and inherited tendencies that are part of humanity. The psalmist affirms, "He knows the secrets of the heart" (Ps. 44:21). The Lord states to Samuel, "The Lord sees not as man sees; man looks on the outward appearance, but the Lord looks on the heart" (1 Sam. 16:7). God vindicates those who are subjugated and persecuted, the orphan and oppressed (Ps. 10:18; 35:24). David, after sparing the life of King Saul, says to him, "May the Lord judge between me and you, may the Lord avenge me upon you; but my hand shall not be against you" (1 Sam. 24:12). He then added, "May the Lord therefore be judge, and give sentence between me and you, and see to it, and plead my cause, and deliver me from your hand" (verse 15).

The Messianic "righteous Branch" (Jer. 23:5) will be called "the Lord . . . our righteousness" (verse 6). The Messiah brings salvation and righteousness to His people. Both salvation and judgment are grounded in His righteousness. Divine righteousness is "like an everflowing stream" (Amos 5:24).

Divine justice is the other essential aspect of the nature of God that manifests itself in His judgment. The Hebrew term mišpāṭ in Psalms 89:14 and 97:2 should be understood as the justice which issues out of divine judgment. Here "justice" has a positive connotation. The divine judgment for the guiltless shows that they are just and brings with it vindication. The faithful look for justice from God and rejoice in it (Ps. 48:11; 97:8). The "righteous" eagerly wait for divine "judgments/justices" (Isa. 26:8) in the final judgment.

The NT continues the theme of the divine judgeship already revealed in the OT. God is "the Judge of all" (Heb. 12:23, NASB). The apostle Paul speaks of the "righteous judgment" (Rom. 2:5), which will be revealed on the day of wrath (cf. verse 3) and affirms that God will judge the world (Rom. 3:6).

As noted before, God the Father has handed judgment to His Son. "The Father judges no one, but has given all judgment to the Son" (John 5:22). Jesus Christ further stated, He "has given him authority to execute judgment, because He is the Son of man" (verse 27). Peter and Paul teach the same. Peter maintains that Jesus Christ "is the one ordained by God to be judge of the living and the dead" (Acts 10:42). Paul affirms that God "has fixed a day on which he will judge the world in righteousness by a man whom he has appointed, and of this he has given assurance to all men by raising him from the dead" (Acts 17:31). Paul further states that while God is the judge, He "judges the secrets of men by Christ Jesus" (Rom. 2:16). Because the Father judges by the agency of the Son, "God's righteous judgment" (verse 5) and "the judgment seat of Christ" (2 Cor. 5:10) are equivalent.

In some 20 passages in the OT judgment issues from the sanctuary/temple, either in heaven or on earth. More than two thirds of them deal with divine judgment of two groups of God's professed people, the faithful and the unfaithful; the remaining passages deal with the judgment of the nations (Shea 1992,

1-29). In all these texts God or Christ judges from the sanctuary/temple.

D. Divine Judgment According to Works

The idea of judgment according to works permeates the teaching of the OT and is taken up by Jesus (Matt. 7:17, 18; 25:31-46; John 15:1-11) and Paul (Rom. 2:13; 1 Cor. 3:8, 13-15). The same refrain is presented in the Apocalypse (20:12; 22:12).

The believer's life of faith produces the fruit of faith through the "work of faith and labor of love" (1 Thess. 1:3). The "work of faith" of the justified believer is the fruit of justification and the expression of a life guided by the Holy Spirit in sanctification. Human works do not contribute in any way to the salvation of the believer. Human works are the fruit of salvation but not the means to gain salvation.

Some people have observed an apparent tension between the affirmation that justification is attained by faith aside from works and the equally strong affirmation that divine judgment is according to works. Some passages, if read in isolation or out of context, can create confusion. Leviticus 18:5 states, "You shall therefore keep my statutes and my ordinances, by which a man shall live: I am the Lord." The essence of this text is referred to in Luke 10:27, 28; Romans 10:5; and Galatians 3:12.

The context of the Leviticus passage shows that this statement is made within the larger framework of God's giving ancient Israel the covenant. Israel accepted the life God had granted to them in their redemption from Egyptian slavery and promised to live within the covenant norms which God had detailed. There is no indication that Israel would ever be saved on the basis of their works. If Israel stayed within the covenant framework and its gracious provisions, their works would reveal that they lived on the basis of their faith relationship with God. By the enabling power provided by God, it would be possible for them to do what is right, and they might live.

There is no hint in Leviticus 18:5 regarding earning salvation. Salvation was Israel's already; now God told them how they could continue in that state of salvation. The salvation granted continued to be theirs if they manifested by good works that this state of salvation had not been permanently interrupted by rebellious deeds. They may live by grace within the horizon of God's continuing empowerment.

Israel was expected to keep God's law as a loving response to the gracious redemption provided by God (verse 30; 19:3, 4, 10, 25, 31; 23:22; 24:22; 25:17; 26:1). For redeemed Israel the law was the way of life but not the means to gain life and redemption. The law was to be kept, but not to achieve life in the here-and-now or eternal life in the future. It was to be kept by saved believers as a way of life.

Furthermore, the "if" in Leviticus 18:5 (KJV) is conditional in nature. The condition was not "in order to" establish life now or eternal life later by commandment keeping, but the condition related to the enjoyment of the full covenantal benefits of the new life, redeemed from Egyptian slavery. The purpose was not that new life in God would be established, but that the life of faith begun might be experienced fully by grace on a continuing basis (Deut. 5:33). The keeping of the law was the condition for keeping alive the covenant blessings. If the believer departed from the way of life and entered the ways of the rebellious, the Lord would not provide the full blessings of the covenant.

The context of Leviticus 18 reveals that this instruction pertains to the life of the sanctified and not to the process of justification or the gaining of salvation. The Israelite who remained in the covenant was to stay away from the abominable practices and idolatries of pagan neighbors (verses 3, 30). This instruction was meant not to be a matter of salvation by works but a matter of salvation that works, a salvation that manifests itself by deeds and acts in harmony with a holy God who made them a holy people by separating them from the world. It is a matter of the sanctified life and how it functions.

Finally, a better translation of the phrase "by doing which a man shall live" is "he will live through them" (Lev. 18:5). In Romans 10:5 and Galatians 3:12 the Greek preposition used is *en,* typically translated "by them," reflecting an instrumental meaning of *en* in the sense of "by means of them." However, it seems better if the Greek preposition *en* is taken here with a locative force. In this case it might be rendered "in the sphere of them." If the locative force is intended in this instance, the keeping of the law is not the means of salvation but the sphere, horizon, or context of salvation in which the life of the believer is to be lived. In summary, the alleged tensions between justification by faith and judgment by works do not exist in reality. "But now that you have been set free from sin and have become slaves of God, the return you get is sanctification and its end *[telos],* eternal life" (Rom. 6:22). The movement is from justification by grace through faith at conversion to a life of faith lived within the horizon, sphere, and context of sanctification in the sense of obedience by "faith working through love"; it finishes with the end result (Gr. *telos*) of "eternal life" experienced in full when Christ returns. This sequential experience proceeds from the past (justification by grace through faith), through the present (sanctification by faith manifested in "good works"), and climaxes in the future (full eternal life; see Salvation III. B. 3).

E. Retributive Judgment and Natural Consequences of Human Deeds

Some people have suggested that God does not engage in retributive (punitive) judgment. This view is based on an understanding of God that takes only a part of the biblical picture at face value and considers other parts as outdated and/or primitive and belonging to another era and/or culture, with no connection to our own. They claim that judgment and punishment are not determined by divine norms or laws. Instead, "the concept of ac-

tions with built-in consequences is at work" (Koch 68). Thus, judgment and punishment issue in a natural way from the sin or crime itself. In this understanding, punishment is the natural, not divinely caused, consequence of evil. Judgment and punishment are automatic results or "built-in consequences of an action" (*ibid.* 82). They are not the result of a divine reaction to previously established norms and laws. In this sense, fate is created by the action of the human agent without any participation of God, either directly or indirectly.

The Bible affirms time and again that sin is the transgression of divine norms and laws. Divine judgment of sin and sinners is not independent of these laws. There is, therefore, divine retribution, and it is not a natural retribution of a fate-determining sphere of action. We have noted above that divine judgment/punishment is always appropriate to the sin or evil committed. Punishment is the result of appropriate divine judgment.

Retribution means appropriate and just rewards or punishments meted out to individuals, communities, peoples, or nations, and finally to the whole world. Divine retribution is the appropriate payment for actions accomplished. Divine retribution means the divine reward or punishment according to good or evil deeds done. This is the consistent emphasis manifested in the judgment passages recorded from Genesis to Revelation.

Humanity is not abandoned by God and left to itself, as is suggested by deism with its picture of a God who is no longer involved in the processes of history. A theology of an absent god *(deus absconditus)* is not portrayed in Scripture. God Himself was engaged, actively and directly, in bringing on the Flood (Gen. 6-9) and the destruction of the cities of the plain (Gen. 19:24, 25). Human agents do not manipulate nature to bring about their own final destruction. God Himself enters the scene of history and at times even changes the laws of nature that have prevailed in order to bring about the deserved punishment. At the same time He is active in bringing salvation to those

829

who choose to remain loyal to Him. A remnant of faith experiences time and again salvation from certain death because of God's decisive salvific intervention (Hasel 1980a). A final faithful remnant will see Christ come in the clouds of heaven, and He will take them with those raised in the first resurrection to be with Him forever.

The consistent biblical picture of judgment within the flow of history contradicts a non-retributive theology which claims that God simply abandons human beings by withdrawing from the affairs of humanity, allowing them to bring on themselves their own destruction. It also argues against any view claiming that an automatic fate produced by human deeds will bring about punishment independent of any ultimate involvement of God. This consistent biblical picture is further supported by the scriptural evidence regarding the last judgment, to which attention is given in the next section.

III. Divine Judgment at the End of History: The Last Judgment

A divine judgment at the end of history is a climactic aspect of the total judgment theme of the Bible. The discussion above revealed repeated divine judgments. The topic of divine judgment in Scripture demands careful attention to judgment at the end of history, even reaching beyond history as we know it. This part of the study presents, from the perspectives presented in Scripture, what in Christian theology has been called the "last judgment" or the "final judgment." Scripture reveals three major phases to the final judgment, each of which deserves attention. A study of major judgment passages that speak of the final judgment in a summarizing or telescoping way is presented first. Then attention is given to those passages that detail the three phases of the final judgment.

A. Summary of the Universal Last Judgment

1. Universal Last Judgment in OT Prophets

The prophet Joel speaks of "the day of the Lord" (1:15) in which God will "judge all the nations round about" (3:12) in "the valley of decision" (verse 14). At that time God's people have nothing to fear, since they are His (verse 16).

The prophet Isaiah provides major passages that deal with an end-time universal judgment. Isaiah 2:6-22 moves in majestic lines from a picture of the judgment of Israel (verses 6-11) to a universal judgment against "all that is proud and lofty, against all that is lifted up" (verse 12; cf. verse 17). It will take place at the "day of reckoning" (verse 12, NASB). The movement from the local judgment on Israel to a universal judgment reveals that God's judgments within the flow of history are signs of the universal judgment at the end of history. This universal judgment involves an earthquake (Isa. 5:25) and humans attempt to hide in "the caverns of the rocks and the clefts of the cliffs" (Isa. 2:21; cf. Rev. 6:15, 16).

"The day of the Lord" in Isaiah 13:6, 9 is described in global terms. This day of judgment will come "as destruction from the Almighty" (verse 6), "with wrath and fierce anger" (verse 9). The word "Babylon" in verse 1 may be taken as a symbol for all the powers of evil, as is often the case in the Bible, for the Lord "will punish the world for its evil" (verse 11). The Lord will destroy "the whole earth" (verse 5). As a result, the earth will be desolate, and sinners will be exterminated (verse 9). On that judgment day God "will make the heavens tremble, and the earth will be shaken out of its place" (verse 13).

Isaiah 24-27, the so-called "Isaiah apocalypse," describes an apocalyptic end-time judgment. God's judgment involves all creation (Isa. 24:1). "The earth shall be utterly laid waste and utterly despoiled; for the Lord has spoken this word" (verse 3). The earth's pollution comes as a result of transgression of "laws," violation of "statutes," and the breaking of "the everlasting covenant" (verse 5).

But there is also hope in these chapters. A remnant will be left. It will consist of those whose desire is the name of the Lord (Isa. 26:8) and who confess His name (verse 13). The remnant will possess a "strong city" (verse 1), seemingly the city of God, a concept that is all-inclusive. All the faithful are citizens of this city. The NT speaks of such a city as "the heavenly Jerusalem" (Heb. 12:22; cf. 11:16) and of the faithful enrolled in that city (Heb. 12:23).

The "Isaiah apocalypse" provides the first reference to the resurrection from the dead in apocalyptic literature (Hasel 1980b, 267-276): "Thy dead shall live, their bodies shall rise. O dwellers in the dust, awake and sing for joy!" (Isa. 26:19). The verbs "to live," "to rise," and "to awake" are technical terms for the resurrection. The "dwellers in the dust" (cf. Job 7:21; 20:11; 21:26) are the "dead" who rest in the grave. The "Isaiah apocalypse" not only presents penal judgment of the wicked, but it climaxes in the physical resurrection of the righteous.

The resurrection appears in even more explicit ways in Daniel 12:1-3. Here again it is connected with a universal judgment. Those who repent and belong to God will be resurrected (Dan. 12:2; see Hasel 1980b, 276-281).

2. Universal Last Judgment in the Teaching of Jesus

Jesus' announcement, "For with the judgment you pronounce you will be judged" (Matt. 7:2), usually is taken to refer to the final judgment.

The parable of the net (Matt. 13:47-50) depicts the final judgment. Every kind of fish is caught; the good "fish" are kept, and the "bad" ones are thrown away (verse 48). "So it will be at the close of the age. The angels will come out and separate the evil from the righteous, and throw them into the furnace of fire; there men will weep and gnash their teeth" (verses 49, 50).

Another judgment parable is that of the wheat and the tares (Matt. 13:24-30, 37-43). This parable climaxes with the picture of the harvest: "Let both grow together until the harvest; and at harvest time I will tell the reapers, Gather the weeds first and bind them in bundles to be burned, but gather the wheat into my barn" (verse 30).

Several observations are in order regarding the parables of the net and the tares and the wheat. First, patience is called for on the part of believers. Both good and bad fish are caught together; both tares and wheat grow together. Human beings are not equipped to carry out an efficient separation (verse 29). This work is assigned to angels. It is not the work of humans.

Second, God fixes the time of separation. It will be at the time of the end of the world (Matt. 13:39, 49). That time is not yet; thus repentance is still available (Luke 13:6-9).

Third, these parables speak of the last judgment in general terms. The tares and the bad fish are gathered by the angels for permanent destruction (Matt. 13:41, 42, 50). The righteous, however, "will shine like the sun in the kingdom of their Father" (verse 43).

The parable of the wedding garment (Matt. 22:1-14) has the king inspect "both bad and good" wedding guests invited to the feast. The inspection before the wedding feast touches on the investigative facet of the final judgment. Upon investigation the king casts the one who is improperly attired into "outer darkness," where "men will weep and gnash their teeth" (verse 13). Here investigation and a verdict precede the subsequent execution of the judgment.

The parable of the ten virgins (Matt. 25:1-13) suggests a delay in the coming of Jesus Christ (verse 5) even as it maintains the certainty of His coming (verse 6). It reveals that not all who claim to be followers of Christ are prepared for the delay. The bridegroom had to declare to the foolish virgins, "Truly, I say to you, I do not know you" (verse 12). This sentence of judgment reveals that not all who claim to belong to Him do so in reality.

The parable of the sheep and goats (verses 31-46) has a significant place within the context of Matthew 24, 25, the time of the end and the advent of Christ. It begins with the coming of the Son of man in glory (Matt. 25:31). All the nations will be gathered, and the sheep and the goats will be separated (verse 32). The sheep are the "righteous" (verses 33, 37) and the goats are the unrighteous (verses 33, 41-45). The King will judge the inhabitants of the nations by dividing them on the basis of how they treated "these my brethren" (verse 40), His followers. Those who did not support Christ's brothers and sisters will be consigned to "the eternal fire prepared for the devil and his angels" (verse 41). It serves as an "eternal punishment." But the righteous will go away "into eternal life" (verse 46).

This parable represents the Second Coming and the subsequent judgment of the nations by the Son of man who is seated on His glorious throne (verses 31, 32) and concludes with the executive phase of the judgment, when the wicked will "go away into eternal punishment" (verse 46).

In John 12:47, 48 Jesus states, "If any one hears my sayings and does not keep them, I do not judge [krinō, "condemn"] him; for I did not come to judge [krinō, "condemn"] the world, but to save the world. He who rejects me and does not receive my sayings has a judge [krinonta]; the word that I have spoken will be his judge [krinei, "will condemn"] on the last day." The "last day" is the day of the eschatological judgment. The decision reached at that time is dependent on the decision of people for or against Christ in their lifetime.

Jesus Christ taught that there is a "resurrection of life" and a "resurrection of judgment [krisis]" (John 5:29). He expanded what was written in the books of Isaiah and Daniel. Those who are raised in the "resurrection of judgment" are the wicked; they will experience "condemnation [krisis]." The others will be raised in the first "resurrection of life." The believer who abides in Christ (6:39, 40) has nothing to fear from the future judgment because he will be vindicated.

The "day of judgment [krisis]" is a day when men will have to give an account of every careless word. "By your words you will be justified, and by your words you will be condemned" (Matt. 12:36, 37). John affirms emphatically "that we may have confidence for the day of judgment [krisis]" (1 John 4:17). The day of judgment is a day of condemnation for the wicked, but for the faithful it is a day of vindication because of Christ, their Lord and Saviour.

3. Universal Last Judgment in the Teaching of the Apostles

Peter affirms that Jesus Christ is "the one ordained by God to be the judge of the living and the dead" (Acts 10:42). The Gentiles are to be ready to "give account to him who is ready to judge the living and the dead" (1 Peter 4:5).

In 2 Peter 3:9-13 we find a blended description of "the day of the Lord" (verse 10) and "the day of God" (verse 12), when the heavens will melt and the earth with its works will be burned up. Finally, the promise of "new heavens and a new earth in which righteousness dwells" (verse 13), becomes a reality. This passage reveals that "the day of the Lord" will come unexpectedly, "like a thief" (verse 10), at the end of the world when "the heavens will pass away . . . , the elements will be dissolved with fire, and the earth and the works that are upon it will be burned up" (verse 10).

Paul has believers appear before the "judgment seat [bēma] of Christ" (2 Cor. 5:10). Various other Pauline passages on judgment were mentioned previously (Rom. 2:16; 1 Cor. 3:13; Gal. 6:7, 8; 2 Thess. 1:9).

4. Universal Last Judgment Placed at the End of the World

The universal last judgment did not take place when Christ died on the cross. Jesus stressed that the judgment would take place "at the close of the age" (Matt. 13:40, 49).

In his famous Mars Hill speech (Acts 17:22-

32) Paul insisted that God "has fixed a day on which he will judge the world in righteousness by a man whom he has appointed, and of this he has given assurance to all men by raising him from the dead" (verse 31). Paul clearly holds to a future eschatological judgment, one that did not begin when sin entered into the world.

In his defense before Felix, Paul spoke of "future judgment [krima]" (Acts 24:25). Emphasis is placed on the fact that humans must face divine future judgment, in which a verdict will be rendered based on ethical decisions made in this life.

In 2 Peter 3:9-13 the judgment is placed into the future, when the world will be totally destroyed. At that time "the day of the Lord" will be manifested.

Paul also argues that "the day of the Lord" has not yet arrived (2 Thess. 2:1-12), because first "the man of lawlessness" is to be revealed (verse 3). "The lawless one . . . the Lord Jesus will slay . . . and destroy him by his appearing and his coming" (verse 8). Before this day all kinds of deluding influences will be brought about by "the activity of Satan . . . with all power and with pretended signs and wonders" (verse 9).

B. Detailed Presentations of the Universal Last Judgment

This part of our study focuses on parts of Scripture that provide detailed descriptions of three sequential phases of the last judgment and their larger connections in Scripture. The first phase is the pre-Advent investigative judgment; the second is subsequent to the return of Jesus Christ in the clouds of heaven and may be referred to as the post-Advent millennial judgment; the last and final phase is the postmillennial executive judgment. Each of these phases of the universal last judgment will now receive attention.

1. The Pre-Advent Investigative Judgment

The word "pre-Advent" in the designation for this judgment phase reveals something about the timing of this judgment. It takes place before the second advent of our Lord Jesus Christ. To be precise, it pertains to the last period in history, called "the time of the end." The word "investigative" applied to this judgment phase describes the nature of this judgment. The investigative judgment is a divine investigation of records in the presence of heavenly beings (Dan. 7:9, 10). Thus, the designation of this judgment phase with both the timing ("pre-Advent") and the nature ("investigative") is deliberate.

a. The timing of the pre-Advent investigative judgment phase. The timing of this first phase of the universal last judgment can be established on the basis of explicit statements in the books of Daniel and Revelation, as well as on the basis of the relationship of the Day of Atonement and its typology to the final judgment. (See Sanctuary I. C. 3. b; III. C.)

(1) The Timing according to Revelation. In the Apocalypse the angelic messenger announces that "the hour of his judgment has come" (Rev. 14:7). This "hour of his judgment" is placed in the apocalyptic end-time. Within the sequential flow of recapitulated events presented in the Apocalypse, the three angels' messages appear (verses 6-12). The first angel flies in midheaven "with an eternal gospel" for all humankind with the call "Fear God and give him glory, for the hour of his judgment has come" (verse 7). The reason for this final call of the "eternal gospel" to all humankind is given with a causal clause, "because [hoti] the hour of his judgment has come" (NIV).

The reference here is to a time before the return of Jesus Christ, as Revelation 14:14 clearly indicates. "The hour of his judgment" refers to the final period before the return of Jesus Christ in glory. The "hour" is not a single moment or literal hour in time. "The hour of his judgment" precedes "the hour to reap" (verse 15). "The hour to reap" is the time when the harvest is brought in at the second coming of Christ. But before the harvest is brought in, there must be "the hour of his judgment," a time when decisions are made as to who will be gathered in the subsequent harvest at "the hour to reap." Before the harvest is reaped, a judgment must take place in which to decide who among God's professed children can be reaped and taken into the eternal kingdom.

The judgment (krisis) in this end-time is the divine judgment in which God the Father is judge. He will judge between those who have remained loyal and those who have fallen away. Since this judgment precedes the harvest at the Second Advent, it is a pre-Advent judgment, which has to be investigative in nature to accomplish its purpose.

The judgment, which according to Revelation 14:7 has arrived, can be located neither at Christ's return nor after Christ's return during the millennium. Neither can it be located at Christ's death on the cross nor at Creation, when Adam and Eve fell first into sin. The text in Revelation does not support these hypotheses. The arrival of the judgment time is part of the arrival of the time of the end, a time before the end of the world when humankind has still the opportunity to accept the "eternal gospel." (See Remnant/Three Angels V. B.)

(2) The timing according to Daniel. Daniel 7-9 also presents the timing of the pre-Advent investigative judgment. Daniel 7 provides a comprehensive vision of the flow of history presented by four sequential beasts arising out of the sea of humanity, representing four world empires. The last beast has ten horns; a "little one" arises after the appearance of the ten (verses 3-8). This portrayal of events on earth is followed by poetic speech moving into the realm of heaven and depicts the heavenly judgment scene (verses 9, 10, 13, 14, 21, 22). It concludes with the coming of the everlasting kingdom (verse 27).

This comprehensive vision of Daniel 7 outlines the course of history from the Babylonian empire (lion, verse 4), through the empires of Medo-Persia (bear, verse 5), Greece (leopard, verse 6), and Rome (dreadful beast, verse 7), and the period of the "little horn" (verse 8) to the end of the world (verses 11, 27), when the kingdom of God will be given the faithful, who are called "the saints of the Most High" (verses 18, 27).

After the little horn's war against the saints (verses 8, 21), the heavenly judgment commences (verses 9, 10, 22). The Ancient of days is seated on a throne (verse 9), surrounded by innumerable heavenly beings, and "the books were opened" (verse 10).

The time of the judgment is explicitly provided with unusual detail in verses 21, 22: "As I looked, this horn made war with the saints, and prevailed over them, until the Ancient of Days came, and judgment was given for the saints of the Most High, and the time came when the saints received the kingdom."

This passage provides a temporal progression with three chronological-sequential events separated by two explicit time markers. The first time marker is the word "until" (Aramaic 'ad), which is a temporal preposition. The second time marker is the phrase "the time came." These two time markers separate the three phases of activity indicated in Daniel 7:21, 22 as follows: (a) Phase I is the war of the little horn against the saints of the Most High; (b) Phase II is separated from Phase I by the word "until," indicating that a new situation commences, which is temporally separated from the previous phase; Phase II consists of the heavenly judgment on the part of the Ancient of days "in behalf of" (or "in favor of" [NASB, REB, NIV], "for" [RSV]) the saints of the Most High; (c) Phase III is separated from the previous divine judgment phase and is subsequent to it, as is indicated by the expression "and the time came." After the divine judgment by the Ancient of days "the time came when the saints received the kingdom" (verse 22).

These three chronological sequences, with their specific time markers, demonstrate that the divine heavenly judgment of the Ancient of days takes place after the war of the little horn against the saints of the Most

High and *before* the saints of the Most High receive the eternal kingdom. These three explicit temporal sequences of events manifest conclusively that the divine heavenly judgment of the Ancient of days is a pre-reception-of-the-kingdom judgment. It is a divine judgment, which must precede the time when the saints receive the kingdom. This sequencing shows that this judgment comes after the little-horn war before the Second Advent (Shea 1992, 135-143).

If it is possible to pinpoint the timing of the war of the little horn against the saints, then we can have a still clearer indication of the time for the judgment to commence. The war against the saints of the Most High is limited to a specific time period, referred to in Daniel 7:25: "and they shall be given into his [little horn's] hand for a time, two times, and half a time." These three and a half symbolic times (Aramaic *'iddān*) need to be translated into literal, historical time. The same Aramaic word appears in Daniel 4:16, 23, 25, 32 with regard to the "seven times" of the madness of Nebuchadnezzar. The word "times" in Daniel 4 refers to "years" in literal, historical time within the life of Nebuchadnezzar. The LXX translation of Daniel 4 actually reads "years." This internal key to the meaning of "times" in the three and a half times of Daniel 7:25 is crucial. The symbolic "times" are meant to be "years" in literal time.

Each of these years consists of 360 days each, as the parallel passages in Revelation 12 and 13 indicate. The parallel prophecy in Revelation 12:14 employs the same wording of "a time, and times, and half a time." This period is referred to earlier as "one thousand two hundred and sixty days" (verse 6). Earlier still the 1260 days are equated with "forty-two months" (Rev. 11:2), indicating a prophetic year of 360 "days." Thus three and a half times are equal with 42 months, or 1260 prophetic "days." Based on the year-day principle, as illustrated in Ezekiel 4:6 and Numbers 14:34, a symbolic day in prophecy stands for a literal year in historical time. This means that the 1260 symbolic days in apocalyptic prophecy are 1260 years of literal, historical time. (See Apocalyptic II. D.)

The 1260 years of Daniel 7:25 began in A.D. 538 when the Ostrogoths abandoned the siege of Rome, and the little-horn power, the bishop of Rome, who had been freed from Arian control, was able to increase his authority, based on the decree of the Roman emperor Justinian in 533. A period of papal power began, which led to extensive persecutions, including the Inquisition with its cruel torture (Maxwell 121-129). Exactly 1260 years later, in 1798, this long prophetic time period concluded with the climactic taking of Pope Pius VI prisoner by General L. A. Berthier, under the authority and direction of the military government of France. The arrest and exile of the pope decisively curtailed the power of Roman Catholicism at the time. Without detailing the prophetic fulfillment of historical events any further, we note that the divine heavenly judgment by the Ancient of days takes place *after* 1798, after the end of the war of the little horn against the saints (Dan. 7:21), and *before* the saints of the Most High receive the eternal kingdom (verse 22) at the second coming of Jesus Christ. When the symbolic prophetic time sequence of three and a half times is rendered into literal historical time on the basis of biblical data (see Shea 1992, 67-104), it provides the temporal key for the timing of the divine judgment. This makes it a judgment by God, the Ancient of days, in the heavenly realm, in the time of the end before the saints receive the eternal kingdom. According to this evidence the heavenly pre-Advent investigative judgment of the saints takes place between 1798 and the Second Advent. It is located in the time of the end.

Daniel 8 and 9 provide even greater precision and enlarge upon the vision of Daniel 7. These chapters contain two prophetic time-tables, the 2300 evening[s]-morning[s] and the "seventy weeks." These are highly significant in pinpointing the exact beginning of the time of the first phase of the last judgment, the pre-Advent investigative judgment.

The prophetic unit of Daniel 8 and 9 speaks also of a cleansing of the sanctuary (Dan. 8:14), an activity which corresponds typologically to the ritual, yearly Day of Atonement in the earthly sanctuary services. In chapter 8 the sanctuary is the heavenly one, and the cleansing takes place at "the time of the end" (verses 17, 19) after the 2300-evening[s]-morning[s] period of history is concluded. Daniel 8 reveals internally that the 2300 evening[s]-morning[s] are 2300 years, which begin during the period of Medo-Persia and conclude in "the time of the end." Daniel 9:24-27 provides the precise beginning date within the period of Medo-Persia.

Daniel 8 gives the flow of historical events and the beginning and conclusion of the 2300 evening[s]-morning[s]. Here we find the third sequential prophetic outline vision in the book of Daniel, enlarging and complementing the visions of Daniel 2 and 7. The sequence involves the ram (Dan. 8:3, 4) and the he-goat with its four horns (verses 5-8) and finally the "little horn" (verses 9-12), which reaches up to the very presence of the heavenly Prince of the host (verse 11), removes from Him the continual ministry (verse 11), and overthrows the place of His sanctuary (verse 11). This is the background of the auditory revelation of the heavenly beings (verses 13, 14).

The question raised by one of the heavenly beings is of temporal significance. "How long," or literally, "until when," will be the "vision" (Heb. $h\bar{a}z\hat{o}n$)? The question "until when" points forward to the end point of the time period, its termination. Whereas the focus of the question is on the point of termination of the time period, the issue is whether the time period includes the entire historical period of the vision from its beginning or whether it begins at some later point during this historical period. What precisely is included in the time period that comes to an end with the 2300 evening[s]-morning[s]? If we can determine when the time period concludes, then we can determine when the beginning of the period

commences and how far from that point it extends into the future.

Answers to these issues demand an investigation of the question of Daniel 8:13, "Until when is [shall be] the vision ($h\bar{a}z\hat{o}n$)?" The word "vision" is of essential importance for the question; this term is employed for the first time in Daniel 8:1, 2. The word thus includes the entire "vision" from the ram period forward. The word "vision" reappears in verse 13, where the question about its point of termination is asked. This reveals that the "vision" includes the historical periods of the ram, goat, and little horn to "the time of the end" (verses 17, 19). Thus the question is meant to say, "Until when will be the vision which begins during the ram (Medo-Persia) period, moves through the period of the goat (Greece), the period of the four horns (the *diadochoi*), and far into the time period of the little horn (pagan and papal Rome), including the matters depicted in the last part of verse 13 that pertain to the latter part of the 'little horn' period?" In short, the question is inclusive of the "vision" from the period of Medo-Persia to "the time of the end."

The time frame encompassed within this question is of utmost significance for the meaning of the question itself. The angelic answer is "For [lit. "until"] two thousand three hundred days [lit. "evenings-mornings"]; then the sanctuary shall be cleansed" (NKJV). This answer provides a clearly stated time period of 2300 "evening[s]-morning[s]" that must transpire before the commencement of the cleansing of the sanctuary. The "sanctuary" cleansing will begin when 2300 "evening[s]-morning[s]" have come to an end.

The question asked in verse 13 is, "Until when shall be the vision?" The "vision" ($h\bar{a}z\hat{o}n$) began in the ram period, of "the kings of Media and Persia" (verse 20). This would be at some point after Babylon had come to an end in 539 B.C.

The vision also includes the period of the goat with its first large horn and the four subsequent horns (verses 5-8). Thus it also covers the historical time of the kingdom of "Greece; and . . . the first king" and the "four kingdoms [which] shall arise from his nation" (verses 21, 22). This historical period of time of Greece reaches from 331 B.C. down to 168 B.C. The historical period covered by the vision also includes that of the little horn, which begins at 168 B.C. and reaches through the period of pagan Rome (ending in A.D. 476, when the last emperor of the Western Roman Empire, Romulus Augustulus, was deposed by Odoacer and his barbarian Germanic mercenaries) into the subsequent period of papal Rome, indeed to "the time of the end" (verses 17, 19).

One angelic being raises the question "until when"; another provides the answer. He states in unambiguous words: "The vision [ḥāzôn] . . . [reaches] to the time of the end" (verse 17, NKJV). "The time of the end" is the time before this world comes to a complete end at the eschaton (Pfandl 316). This means that the symbolic evening[s]-morning[s] cannot refer to anything but years in historical time. Thus, Daniel 8 informs us internally and contextually that an evening-morning, or a day of prophetic time, equals a year of historical time. This chapter provides its internal year-for-a-day equation; it teaches the year-day principle known also from Daniel 7, 9; Revelation 11-13; as well as Ezekiel 4:6; and Numbers 14:34.

A determination of the precise year for the beginning of the 2300 years would also permit us to fix in history the year for the termination of this prophetic time period within the time of the end. This very year would then be the year for the beginning of the cleansing of the heavenly sanctuary.

The correlation between Daniel 8 and 9 is of decisive importance to answer these issues. These chapters consist of one large prophetic unit.

Major linkages must be considered: a. Common terminology. Verbal forms of the Hebrew root bîn, "understand," are used in Daniel 8:15-17, 23, 27 and again in Daniel 9:2, 22, 23 in key positions regarding the interpretation of the vision (Dan. 8:17; 9:23). Understanding is not complete until all elements, including the time element, is understood. The vision of Daniel 8 is not understood until further explanations are provided in Daniel 9:24-27. b. Cultic perspective. Daniel 8:13, 14 emphasizes cultic issues ("transgression," "sanctuary," "cleansed" [JKV]) as do verses 11, 12 ("sanctuary," "transgression," "truth"). Daniel 9:24-27 are filled with rich cultic perspectives, such as "transgression," "atone," "anoint," cessation of "sacrifice and offering." Each of these chapters depends on the other from a cultic perspective and complement each other. c. Same angel-interpreter. In Daniel 8:16 Gabriel appears for the first time in the book. He is sent to interpret the vision (verses 17, 19). He reappears in Daniel 9:21-23 to complete the interpretation of what had remained unexplained in Daniel 8:26, 27. Daniel describes the situation as follows, "Gabriel, whom I had seen in the vision at the first, came to me. . . . He said to me, . . . 'Understand the vision [Heb. mar'eh]' " (Dan. 9:21-23). This links the explanation with the mar'eh aspect of the vision left unexplained in Daniel 8:26, 27. d. Auditory-revelation. Daniel 8:13, 14 contains the auditory part of the vision (verses 2-8) with the timetable. Daniel 9:24-27 is another auditory revelation in which a timetable figures prominently. Gabriel informs Daniel that he has come to give him understanding of the vision, [the mar'eh, verse 23] that is, the very element of the unexplained timetable of Daniel 8. The angel interpreter did so by giving a time table, which "cut off" a time period from that of Daniel 8. e. Conceptual link. The grand climax of the work of the Messiah is the anointing of the sanctuary (verse 24, Heb. qōdeš qodāšîm). This takes place at the beginning of the heavenly ministry of Jesus Christ, after He was "cut off," that is, died on Calvary. The grand climax of the vision of Daniel 8 is the cleansing of the sanctuary in "the time of the end," once the 2300 "evening[s]-morning[s]" are finished (verse 14). The auditory revelation of Daniel 8:13, 14 points to the end of the long period of the 2300 "evening[s]-morning[s]" with the cleansing work that was to begin in "the time of the end" (verses 17, 19). The auditory revelation of Daniel 9:24-27 provides the starting point of the sanctuary work with its anointing (verse 24). Thus, the beginning (anointing of the sanctuary) and the end (cleansing of the sanctuary) belong to the grand climactic events in the heavenly cultus. Each aspect is prophetically predicted to take place according to its own timetable. These major linkages join Daniel 8 and 9 into a unitary vision (Dan. 8:1-12) with audition (verses 13, 14) and interpretation (Dan. 8:15-26; 9:24-27), with particular interest in the time elements.

Daniel 9:24-27 reveals that Israel's probationary time period would extend for "seventy weeks," or 490 years. This seventy-week prophecy contains an uninterrupted, sequential, three-part chronology based on sequences of "weeks," divided into "seven weeks," with 49 years; "sixty-two weeks," with 434 years; and "one week" with seven years (Hasel 1993, 118).

In the "middle of the [last] week" the Messiah will "put a stop to sacrifice and grain offering" (Dan. 9:27, NASB) because He is "cut off" (verse 26), being violently put to death. The sacrifice of the Messiah rendered the animal sacrifices of the Jerusalem temple obsolete; thereby the ceremonial laws of the OT found their fulfillment. This messianic sacrifice took place through Jesus Christ in A.D. 31, exactly as the prophetic timetable had indicated. After His resurrection and ascension He did "anoint a most holy place" (verse 24), that is, the heavenly sanctuary. This marks the beginning of His heavenly ministry, the daily ministry of Christ.

Daniel 9:24 states that "seventy weeks of years are decreed," or "cut off," for "your people [Israel] and your holy city [Jerusalem]" (Owusu-Antwi 121-123). Since no other time period is in the prophetic unit of Daniel 8, 9, this can be only the 2300 evening[s]-morning[s], or years, from which the time period of

"seventy weeks," or 490 years, are "cut off." Both time periods in Daniel 8, 9, the 2300 evening[s]-morning[s], or years, and the "seventy weeks of years" begin in the same period of Medo-Persia, which means that the 490 years have to be cut off from the beginning of the 2300 evening[s]-morning[s].

If the exact year of the beginning of the 490 years can be determined, the exact year of the beginning of the 2300 years is also indicated. Daniel 9:25 makes it clear that the 490 years begin "from the going forth of the word to restore and build Jerusalem." The restoration and rebuilding of Jerusalem refer to two separate but related aspects, namely the restoration of its religiopolitical autonomy and self-governance and the physical rebuilding of Jerusalem (Owusu-Antwi 378-382). The decree called for in Daniel 9:25 has to contain both of these aspects.

The decree of Cyrus, which mandated the rebuilding of the Temple (Ezra 1:2-4), does not qualify. This is true also of the decree of Darius I (6:1-12), which is a reiteration of the decree of Cyrus. Both of these decrees deal with the rebuilding of the Temple but not with the specifications of Daniel 9:25.

The next major decree known from Scripture is the one given in the seventh year of Artaxerxes I and recorded in Ezra 7:12-26. This decree qualifies as the fulfillment of the one mentioned in Daniel 9:25, because it speaks of both the rebuilding and the restoration of Jerusalem. The king's command restored Jerusalem's religiopolitical autonomy and self-governance in that it gave privileges to pay for and to offer sacrifices (Ezra 7:17) and to appoint magistrates and judges who would judge according to "the laws of your God" (verse 25). It even provided for full authority of judicial penalty, including imprisonment, confiscation of goods, banishment, and death (verse 26). It applied both to Jews and non-Jews "in the province Beyond the River" (verse 25). The decree of Artaxerxes I, given in his seventh year, also qualifies because it fulfills the "building" aspect of Jerusalem, that is, the physical rebuilding of Jerusalem (see Ezra 4:7, 11-16).

The "decree" given by Artaxerxes is the only one which meets the two qualifications of Daniel 9:25, the restoration and rebuilding of Jerusalem. Based on classical historical sources, an Egyptian astronomical source, a Babylonian astronomical source, Egypto-Jewish historical sources, and Babylonian historical sources, the decree and the return are dated to 457 B.C. (Shea 1991, 121-126). The year 457 B.C. is the beginning of the 490 years of Daniel 9 and likewise the beginning of the 2300 years of Daniel 8, from which the 490 years are "cut off."

Based on Daniel 9:24, 25, where it is stated that the "seventy weeks" or 490 years began in 457 B.C. and were "cut off" from the 2300 years, it follows that the 2300 years also commence in 457 B.C. They conclude in "the time of the end," in A.D. 1844. Thus, the expression "evening[s]-morning[s]," which in the Hebrew text has no plural and no conjunction, is meant to refer to "years" in historical time. The 2300 "evening[s]-morning[s]" are 2300 literal years. They begin in 457 B.C. and conclude in A.D. 1844. Thus 1844 is the year in which the cleansing of the heavenly sanctuary begins.

Daniel 7 revealed that the divine heavenly judgment must commence after 1798 and that it must be completed when the saints of the Most High, the faithful followers of God, receive the eternal kingdom at the second coming of Christ. In other words, the heavenly assize takes place during the time of the end, as Daniel 7 clearly shows. Daniel 8 and 9 reveal the precise date of the beginning of this judgment, which is referred to as the restoration, or cleansing, of the heavenly sanctuary (verse 14). In 1844 the heavenly pre-Advent investigative judgment began. This is during "the time of the end" (verses 17, 19) and is in harmony with "the hour of his judgment" of Revelation 14:7.

(3) The timing in the typology of the earthly sanctuary services. In addition to evidence from apocalyptic literature, which reveals that the pre-Advent investigative judgment began in 1844, in "the time of the end," the ancient Israelite sanctuary service provides additional typological support for the timing of the first phase of the last judgment.

The activity in the earthly sanctuary was divided into daily and yearly services. The latter came at the end of the ritual year, on the Day of Atonement (Lev. 16; 23:26-32; Num. 29:7-11; see Hasel 1981). The Hebrew name of the Day of Atonement is *yôm kippur,* also translated as "Day of Purgation," indicating the purification and cleansing (Lev. 16:19, 30) that this final day of the ritual cycle of the year includes. This corresponds typologically to the cleansing of the heavenly sanctuary, to which Daniel 8:14 refers. The linkage between Daniel 8:14 and Leviticus 16 consists in this conceptual connection as well as in the term "sanctuary" (Heb. *qōdeš*), used consistently for the "sanctuary" and the Day of Atonement activities in Leviticus 16.

In harmony with the antitypical role of Jesus Christ as heavenly Priest (Heb. 6:20; 7:3, 15-17) and upon the anointing of the heavenly sanctuary (Dan. 9:24), our Lord began His daily ministry of intercession and mediation (Rom. 8:34; 1 Tim. 2:5; Heb. 7:25). He provides for all believers "access" to God (Rom. 5:2; Eph. 2:18) through His better ministry (Heb. 8:6) based on a "better covenant" (Heb. 7:22), providing a "new and living way" (Heb. 10:20), through which we can "draw near to the throne of grace" (Heb. 4:16). Christ's own blood shed on Calvary at the right time in God's timetable (Dan. 9:26, 27) assures our entrance into the sanctuary (Heb. 10:19), where we find forgiveness for our confessed sins (1 John 2:1, 2), which are transferred to the heavenly sanctuary.

The ministry which Christ began after His inauguration as heavenly High Priest corresponds typologically to the daily service of the earthly priests during the cultic year, before the climactic Day of Atonement work took place. Christ also fulfills, typologically the high priestly ministry of the Day of Atonement, the day of judgment and cleansing of the sanctuary.

The Day of Atonement was a day of judgment (Lev. 23:29). The predominant aspect was the vindication of the faithful and loyal Israelites who had utilized all the provisions given by God to be restored during the daily services of the ritual year. The Israelites were to utilize by faith the appropriate substitutionary sacrifices in the daily services, which consisted of the first phase of the ritual year and thus be able to stand in the presence of God on the Day of Atonement. For them the Day of Atonement was a day of vindicative judgment. They had followed God's redemptive plan and were able to reap the benefits of this plan through God's grace.

Another aspect of the Day of Atonement, or day of judgment, was retributive, penal judgment. Unfaithful Israelites who did not humble themselves on this special day (verse 29) would "be cut off from" their people. The expression "cut off" is a technical term for the loss of life either by direct intervention of God or by capital punishment. Thus, the Day of Atonement would bring to all Israelites either vindication and life or condemnation and death, depending on their willingness to remain faithful to God or to remain in their state of rebellion and unfaithfulness. Only Israelites came into judgment. Non-Israelites had no part in the Day of Atonement experience.

The timing of this grand ritual day at the end of the ritual year is analogous to the timing of the heavenly antitypical day of atonement in "the time of the end." Thus the pre-Advent judgment corresponds antitypically to the Day of Atonement of the earthly sanctuary services. (See Sanctuary II, III.)

These major lines of evidence provided in Scripture give the Bible student a clear and definitive understanding of the timing of the heavenly pre-Advent investigative judgment, the first phase of the universal last judgment. It began in A.D. 1844 and will conclude before the return of Jesus Christ, when the time of probation for the world comes to an end.

b. The Judge of the pre-Advent investigative judgment. The first phase of the last judgment has God the Father as its judge. Daniel 7:9 identifies the divine Judge as "the ancient of days" (cf. verses 13, 22), a designation unique in the OT. It communicates that God is august and venerable, respected and wise. It distinguishes God from the "son of man" who comes to the Ancient of days "with the clouds of heaven" (verse 13).

The picture of the apocalypse again harmonizes with the judgment figure of Daniel 7. In Revelation 14:7 we read that "the hour of his judgment has come." This is the judgment of the One mentioned in the previous call, "Fear God." God the Father is the judge in the pre-Advent investigative judgment.

Christ does not judge at that time. But Jesus Christ, the risen Saviour, is present at this judgment (Dan. 7:13, 14), taking the role of support for those whose names come up for judgment. He receives the kingdom from the Father (verse 14) and later gives it to the saints (verse 18).

That God is judge seems to communicate that the Father is vitally interested in the welfare of those who come up before Him in a judgment which can be either vindicative or penal, depending on the deeds and lives of the professed people of God whose cases are reviewed. (See II. D.)

The Father is seen as having an active role in the plan of salvation. The Gospel of John affirms that "God so loved the world that he gave his only Son, that whoever believes in him should not perish but have eternal life" (John 3:16). The following verses (17-21) reveal the context of judgment and the possibility of condemnation. Christ was sent by the Father to bring about a decision for or against Christ. All who believe in the Son have eternal life. In the judgment over which the Father presides the cases are reviewed of those who have been touched by the Father's attempts to bring salvation to humanity.

c. The recipients of judgment in the pre-

Advent investigative judgment. In determining who are judged in the pre-Advent judgment, the typology of the Day of Atonement experience is essential. At that time only Israelites came into judgment, indicating that only professed people of God enter into judgment.

The apostle Peter affirms that judgment must "begin with the household of God; and if it begins with us, what will be the end of those who do not obey the gospel of God?" (1 Peter 4:17). "Those who do not obey the gospel of God" may be those who had the opportunity to obey it at one time or another.

The books of Daniel and Revelation are explicit on this subject. It has been claimed that the "little horn" of Daniel 8 has defiled the sanctuary and therefore should enter into judgment, which typifies the cleansing of the sanctuary. Careful study of the cultic language of verses 9-14 shows that the cleansing, vindication, and restoration of the sanctuary in verse 14 are not a response required by the activity of the "little horn." It attacks the "Prince of the host," but it does not contaminate the sanctuary (Rodríguez 529). Therefore, it follows that Daniel 8 does not claim that the "little horn" is included in the cleansing of the sanctuary.

The first judgment scene in the vision of Daniel 7 concludes with the decisive sentence "the court sat in judgment, and the books were opened" (verse 10). The word "judgment" *(dîn)* implies that there will be a judgment of certain people, but the text does not mention whom. It does, however, provide a vital piece of evidence that calls for consideration.

References to books in heaven usually point to books pertaining to human beings. Thus, human beings will come up in judgment. This is another reason to understand that "the saints of the Most High" are godly human beings, and not angels (Hasel 1975, 190-192). The books are obviously not opened for God, who is all-knowing. These books under investigation are expected to give us insight into the question of the recipients of the judgment.

Daniel 12:1 provides basic information on the comments of these books. At the end of the "time of trouble" "every one whose name shall be found written in the book" will be saved. It is clear from this text that the "book," or "books," contains the names of those who are God's people.

Other references in the OT speak of heavenly records in the form of a "book." When Israel rebels at Sinai and God makes it known that He will destroy them, Moses pleads with God: "Blot me, I pray thee, out of thy book which thou hast written" (Ex. 32:32). The Lord responds to Moses by saying, "Whoever has sinned against me, him will I blot out of my book" (verse 33). This first mention in the OT of a heavenly book reveals that it contains the names of professed people of God. The same picture is portrayed in other OT passages that speak of a book of God in heaven (see Ps. 69:28; Mal. 3:16). The following conclusion is sound: "Thus every reference in the OT to a book of God in heaven is connected in one way or another with God's people rather than with His enemies" (Shea 1992, 148).

Briefly stated, the evidence from the book of Daniel and elsewhere points uniquely in the direction that God's professed people, both true and false believers, will come into judgment in this first phase of the investigative pre-Advent judgment.

Of key importance in confirming this conclusion is Daniel 7:22: "The Ancient of Days came, and judgment was given for the saints of the Most High." Other versions (NKJV, NASB) translate "in favor of" the holy ones. These recent versions put into contemporary English the meaning of the Aramaic preposition *"l"* which had been rendered in the KJV "to the saints." Daniel 7:22 teaches explicitly that "the saints of the Most High," God's people, are under consideration as the books are opened in the heavenly assize.

"The saints of the Most High" were under heavy attack by the "little horn," which persecuted them for a long time and killed many of them (verses 21, 25). God takes up their case in the pre-Advent judgment. He opens

HOSDAT-28

841

the books in the view of all assembled heavenly beings, and the recorded deeds and faith of the saints are open for investigation. This investigative judgment with the open books will vindicate God's true saints before the intelligences of the universe by pronouncing them ready to receive the eternal kingdom from the Son of man (verse 18). The myriads of heavenly beings who attend this first phase of the judgment (verse 10) need to know who among those who ever professed to be followers of God deserve to inherit and live in the eternal kingdom of God. All who remain loyal in faith to the end will be vindicated in the pre-Advent judgment. Their sins will be blotted out because Christ took care of them.

The names of the professed followers who did not remain loyal and faithful will be blotted out of the heavenly record (cf. Ex. 32:32, 33). The pre-Advent investigative judgment will not vindicate them. Their deeds and lack of faith will speak against them, and their names will be erased from the book of life.

In this pre-Advent investigative judgment God presents the cases of His people in the heavenly assize. It is a judgment of vindication for the faithful ones of His people; it is in favor of "the saints of the Most High" (Dan. 7:22). The Ancient of days who judges them is not their enemy. He is the righteous judge, who judges "for" them because He has made all the provisions through His Son Jesus Christ so that all their sins can be forgiven and they can possess the eternal kingdom.

There is also a threatening aspect in this pre-Advent investigative judgment. It is possible that a person, once a follower of God, will again decide to go his or her own way. Those who persist in sin will have their names blotted out of the book (see Ex. 32:33). While this aspect of judgment remains, it is not the predominant theme of the pre-Advent investigative judgment.

The dominant theme of the pre-Advent investigative judgment is judgment pronounced in favor of the saints (Dan. 7:22). God is on the side of His people. In the "time of trouble"

Michael Himself will stand up to do battle for His own and come to their rescue (Dan. 12:1). All faithful ones who have died before He comes in the clouds of heaven will then be raised to "everlasting life" (verse 2). God is Judge and Saviour. Christ's death on the cross makes Him a victorious deliverer and able sustainer of all who trust Him in faith until He comes.

d. The place of the pre-Advent investigative judgment. Daniel 7 reveals a cosmic dimension with an interplay between scenes on earth and heaven, revealing an ABAB literary pattern (earth [verses 2-8]; heaven [verses 9, 10]; earth [verses 11, 12]; heaven [verses 13, 14]). This pattern is emphasized by the alternation of prose (the A parts) with poetry (the B parts). The poetic parts transport the reader to the heavenly assize. This is supported by the vision's emphasis on "thrones" (verse 9). Throughout the Bible a throne connected with deity—here the Ancient of days—is always a throne in the heavenly realm. Thus, Daniel 7 reveals that the judgment takes place in heaven.

Daniel 8 provides further details. In this chapter we have once more an interplay of earthly and heavenly dimensions. The vision moves from a purely earthly scene, with two animals symbolizing earthly powers (verses 3-8) to a "little horn," which at first expands itself horizontally (verse 9; possibly verse 10) and then vertically (possibly verse 10; surely verses 11, 12) to reach into the realm of "the Prince of the host" and His heavenly sanctuary (verse 11). The auditory part of the vision (verses 13, 14) places the reader squarely into the heavenly realm, with heavenly beings engaged in dialogue. "The climax of the vision is its focus on the conflict between the Prince and the little horn" over the heavenly "sanctuary and its ministration" (Shea 1986, 513).

Within this context the "sanctuary" of verses 11 and 14 cannot be other than the heavenly sanctuary, as the timing in the flow of the chapter indicates. The cleansing of the heavenly sanctuary (verse 14, KJV) involves a judgment work of God, which is located within the heavenly sanctuary itself. Once more, Daniel 8 adds details to Daniel 7.

The reality of the heavenly sanctuary is so well known from the OT and NT that only a brief statement is needed, since some interpreters claim there is no sanctuary in heaven. The vertical heavenly-earthly dimension of the sanctuary is outlined in Exodus 25:8 [9] where the "pattern" (Heb. *tabnît*) of the earthly sanctuary was shown to Moses on the mountain. The term used in the OT for what was shown to Moses on Mount Sinai is referred to in the NT as the "type" (Gk. *typos;* see Acts 7:44; Heb. 8:5). The earthly sanctuary was but a "copy and shadow" of the heavenly reality (Davidson 367, 368). In this sense the heavenly original sanctuary is copied by the earthly counterpart.

Numerous texts in the Psalms (including 11:4; 18:6 [7]; 29:9; 68:35 [36]; 96:6; 150:1) and in the prophetic writings of the OT refer to God's heavenly sanctuary (Isa. 6:1; Jonah 2:7 [8]; Micah 1:2; Hab. 2:20). F. Delitzsch stated correctly, "At an infinite distance above the earth, . . . is a *hêkal qōdeš* [holy temple]. . . . And this temple, this palace in the heavens, is the place whence issues the final decision of all earthly matters, Hab. 2:20; Micah 1:2. For His throne above is also the superterrestrial judgment-seat" (Delitzsch 1:189).

The reality of the heavenly sanctuary is affirmed with equal vigor in the NT. The letter to the Hebrews affirms in its central part (8:1–10:25) that Jesus is high priest and "minister in the sanctuary and the true tent which is set up not by man but by the Lord" (Heb. 8:2). The "sanctuary" (Gr. *hagia*) referred to here is the heavenly one. It is called also the "true tent." The Greek term for "true" is *alēthinos,* "real," as opposed to "apparent." The same term is used of the reality of God (John 17:3). The heavenly sanctuary is real as God Himself is real.

In Hebrews 9:1-5 the "earthly sanctuary" consists of an outer tent, the first compartment of the earthly sanctuary, which is usu-

ally called "Holy Place," and the second tent, which is called "Holy of Holies" or "Most Holy Place." Beginning in verse 8 the sanctuary is related to the heavenly realities under the new covenant. The first, or outer, tent of Hebrews 9:8 (*protos* in the sense of former) refers to the whole earthly sanctuary. The "sanctuary" in heaven cannot have any standing while the "first" or "former tent," that is, the earthly sanctuary still functions for the believer. "The first tent becomes the old, earthly tent in its entirety, including both the Holies and Holy of Holies, and the second tent, 'the better and more perfect tent' of verse 11, becomes the celestial sanctuary" (Cody 147, 148; cf. 7BC 450). There is a heavenly sanctuary with two compartments (or areas), vastly more glorious than the earthly sanctuary.

The emphasis of Hebrews 9:23, 24 supports this picture. The text reads "Thus it was necessary for the copies of the heavenly things to be purified with these rites, but the heavenly things themselves with better sacrifices than these. For Christ has entered, not into a sanctuary made with hands, a copy of the true one, but into heaven itself, now to appear in the presence of God on our behalf." The "heavenly things" are the heavenly sanctuary, where Christ has entered to engage in His high priestly ministry on behalf of the human race.

Jesus Christ is the great high priest serving in a special ministry in this heavenly sanctuary. After His ascension He began his first phase of His heavenly sanctuary ministry, His "daily" ministry, in the first compartment/area of the two-part heavenly sanctuary; in 1844 He began His second phase of ministry, the "yearly" or antitypical day of atonement ministry, in the second compartment/area of the heavenly sanctuary.

The book of Revelation makes a clear distinction between heaven as such and the sanctuary/temple in heaven, as is seen in Revelation 11:19: "Then God's temple in heaven was opened, and the ark of his covenant was seen within his temple." The Greek reads "the temple of God, the one which is in heaven, was opened." Heaven indeed does have a temple, or sanctuary. The angels coming out of the temple indicate this (Rev. 14:15, 17; 16:17). This emphasis is seen also in Revelation 15:5: "After this I looked, and the temple of the tent of witness in heaven was opened." In this two-part heavenly sanctuary, or temple, divine judgment takes place and from it divine judgments go forth (Rev. 7:15; 16:17). The heavenly sanctuary is God's command center of the universe, for the throne of God is there.

Based on this evidence from both the OT and NT, the pre-Advent investigative judgment takes place in the Most Holy Place of the heavenly sanctuary. The first phase of the final judgment takes place in analogy with the earthly Day of Atonement activity. As the old covenant had an earthly sanctuary with daily and yearly services, so the new and better covenant has a heavenly sanctuary in which Christ as high priest engages in a daily ministry and since 1844 has been involved in a new and final ministry in the presence of the Father, who is judge of the professed people of God of all ages. Christ's is a ministry of intercession in the presence of the Ancient of days for those who have claimed Him as Lord and Saviour. Both Father and Son are involved in the salvific judgment process, each taking His respective role for the salvation of the faithful of humankind. (See Sanctuary II. B. 2.)

e. The purpose of the pre-Advent investigative judgment. The pre-Advent judgment is both investigative and evaluative in regard to all who have made a profession to be believers. One of the accomplishments of the pre-Advent judgment is the determination of those among the professed people who will inherit the kingdom.

Students of Scripture have recognized that there must be what has been called a "pre-judgment" (Düsterwald 177), here referred to as the pre-Advent judgment. The resurrection and translation of the saints come as the result of a judgment prior to the judgment of the

nations of nonbelieving humanity. "When Paul writes that 'the saints will judge the world' (1 Cor. 6:2; cf. Matt. 19:28) one has to draw the conclusion that the judgment of the community of the 'saints' and the judgment of the 'world' cannot be one and the same judgment activity. Just as the resurrection of those who belong to Christ precedes the general resurrection of the [wicked] dead, so the judgment of the believers precedes in time the judgment of the 'nations' (heathen) . . ." (Lamparter 161).

A second major factor of the pre-Advent investigative judgment is the vindication of the saints. We have noted already that Daniel 7 reports how the "saints of the Most High," that is, the saints who belong to God, are under attack by the "little horn," that is, the agents of satanic forces which are marshalled against God's people (verses 21, 25). The saints of God are falsely accused, persecuted, and misjudged. God opens the records of heaven in the pre-Advent judgment so that all heavenly intelligences can look into their records. God will come to the rescue of those who are thus mistreated and misjudged. He vindicates them before the universe in this grand assize.

A third major aspect of the pre-Advent judgment is that God's character is also vindicated. God has been misrepresented as being capricious, vindictive, and judgmental. He has been portrayed as distant and noncaring. He has been depicted as vengeful and malevolent. Doubts have been cast on His character and His being. The pre-Advent judgment shows God the Father as He really is. He comes to the rescue of His children; He takes up their case in the presence of all the heavenly beings, who can see His justice and righteousness, the very foundation of His judgment seat, His throne (Ps. 89:14; 97:2). God Himself will stand vindicated in this judgment.

A fourth major aspect of the pre-Advent judgment relates to the cleansing of the sanctuary (Dan. 8:14; Heb. 9:23). The "heavenly things" (Heb. 9:23), the heavenly sanctuary (Johnsson 94-98), stand in need of cleansing from the accumulated sins of the saints of all times. The earthly sanctuary was cleansed (Lev. 16:19, 30; Heb. *ṭāhēr*) on the Day of Atonement. This idea is underlined with the term "atoned" (Heb. *kāpar*, "to cover"), which in many contexts carries strong connotations of cleansing.

In Daniel 8:14 "the sanctuary shall be cleansed" (KJV; cf. NKJV, NAB), is a rendering that reaches back to pre-Christian times, as the LXX shows. The word "cleansed" translates the Hebrew *niṣdaq,* which carries rich semantic connotations (Andreasen 495, 496), including the ideas of cleansing, justifying, vindicating, and setting right (Hasel 1986, 448-458). The antitypical heavenly day of atonement, which began in 1844, needed the larger view expressed in *niṣdaq.* The language of Daniel 8:14 links this verse with the Day of Atonement, as is evidenced particularly by the usage of the word "sanctuary" (Heb. *qōdeš*), the term used for the "sanctuary" throughout Leviticus 16. In short, the language used for the "cleansing" of the heavenly sanctuary evokes associations with the Day of Atonement, that is, the day of cleansing, purgation, and judgment. The heavenly activity involves cleansing, setting right, justifying, and vindicating. These concepts relate to the sanctuary, the people, and to God Himself as the final work in heaven goes on. Regarding the professed people of God, this work is judicial, yet redemptive, revealing that the atonement process begun with the death of Christ at the cross comes to an end at the conclusion of the pre-Advent investigative judgment in the heavenly sanctuary. When the pre-Advent judgment is concluded, the atonement process of God and Christ is completed.

The earthly Day of Atonement cleansing meant the blotting out of sin. The Hebrew term rendered "atone" *(kāpar)* is employed parallel to the term "to blot out" (Heb. *maḥāh*), as seen in Jeremiah 18:23 and Nehemiah 4:5. The heavenly cleansing (Heb. 9:23, 24) involves a blotting out of sin from the heavenly records. Subjectively, the sinner receives personal forgiveness upon daily repentance and confession of sins, being saved in the Lord; objectively, the recorded and forgiven sins in heaven are blotted out once the case of each professed follower has been presented in the pre-Advent judgment. All faithful ones remain saved in the hands of Christ and the hands of the Father, who gave Christ to save the human race. However, believers continue to have the freedom of choice; they continue to have the power to separate themselves from God if they so desire.

These major purposes of the pre-Advent investigative judgment reveal who has ultimate power over the saints of God, who from among all human beings throughout time have ever made a profession of faith and remained on God's side; who deserves to inherit the kingdom that Christ brings with Him; and who is on the side of the saints in the judgment. God's righteousness and justice will shine forth in full brilliance and will manifest the essence of judgment in a most unique way. His divine character will be revealed in its ultimate glory as never before. All heavenly intelligences will recognize more than at any other time that God is Lord of lords and King of kings. All will see that He is a judge who judges justly and with fairness, taking all motivations and issues of the human heart into consideration. He will be seen as the one who understands all inherited tendencies and deformities of mind, soul, and body. Nothing escapes Him or is beyond His grasp as He renders judgment in behalf of the saints (Dan. 7:22). He gave His only begotten Son as a substitute for lost humanity, so that everyone who trusts by faith in the Lord Jesus Christ can be saved by His merits, which the Father will reckon to each believer as righteousness. Love and justice meet in God to the benefit of all those who are His own.

f. Summary. In conclusion, the pre-Advent investigative judgment is a vital heavenly sanctuary activity of God that began in 1844. It is a major turning point in the plan of salvation that is about to end. This first phase of the final judgment is decisive for all professed followers of Christ. It focuses on God the Father as the benevolent judge, on those who belong to Him through Jesus Christ, and on the merits He has achieved for them and credited to them.

The present "hour of His judgment" involves a call to remain faithful or to return to the Lord of life in preparation for the imminent Second Coming. The destiny of all professed believers is at stake, and the destiny of unbelievers is also involved. The former need to stay loyal to the "eternal gospel," and the latter need to hear its powerful proclamation. The commission to preach the "good news" in all the world as a powerful witness is seen in a new light in connection with the pre-Advent investigative judgment.

The character of God is also seen in this judgment phase in a new and positive light. He is vindicated in His just and righteous judgment in the presence of all loyal heavenly beings.

All followers of God and Christ are challenged to maintain their biblical ethics with the power of the Holy Spirit. Since judgment is based on works accomplished by faith, there is an implied emphasis on faithfulness in the keeping of the commandments of God. Since God is presently engaged in the first phase of the final judgment, which is at the same time the second phase and final phase of Christ's heavenly sanctuary ministry, all believers are challenged to live holy lives. As the end of this world approaches, divine agents above and human saints below are at work, all in their respective spheres and assigned tasks, toward the full realization of the eternal plan of redemption for God's glory and honor.

2. The Post-Advent Millennial Judgment

The post-Advent judgment takes place during the millennium and is the second major phase of the universal, final judgment (Rev. 20:4; see Millennium I. C. 2).

a. The timing of the post-Advent millennial judgment. As noted above, the judg-ment begins with "the household of God" (1 Peter 4:17; cf. Eze. 9:6). The second phase of judgment moves to the remaining part of humanity, those who do not belong to "the household of God." This judgment takes place during the millennium, after the second coming of Christ, when He takes to Himself those who belong to Him (John 14:1-3).

b. The judges of the post-Advent millennial judgment. In the millennial phase of the last judgment Christ and the saints are the judges. This occurs in their "reign with him" (Rev. 20:4, 6). "I saw thrones, and seated on them were those to whom judgment was committed" (verse 4). "Do you not know that the saints will judge the world?" (1 Cor. 6:2).

c. The recipients of the post-Advent millennial judgment. The prophet Isaiah declared that "after many days they [the fallen host of heaven and the wicked on earth] will be punished" (Isa. 24:22). Paul used the general term "the world" for the recipients of this judgment (1 Cor. 6:2; cf. Rom. 2:2-16; Jude 14, 15).

Jesus spoke of the judgment of the sheep and goats (Matt. 25:32). While the sheep inherit the kingdom (verse 34), the goats receive their reward according to their evil deeds. Theirs will be an "eternal punishment" (verse 46) in "the eternal fire" (verse 41).

The millennial judgment, however, goes beyond judging human beings. It judges also "the angels" (Jude 6; 1 Cor. 6:3). These are the fallen angels who were thrown down to earth with Satan (Rev. 12:9).

The judgment is based on "the law" (Rom. 2:12-16) and "works" (Rev. 20:13) inasmuch as all judgment is based on what is done (Matt. 24:45-51; 25:41-46; John 5:28, 29; Rom. 2:1-10; 2 Cor. 5:10; Rev. 20:12).

d. The purpose of the post-Advent millennial judgment. The purpose of this judgment is to determine punishment deserved, according to the works done. According to Revelation 20:11-15 the cases of "the dead, great and small," came up in the judgment. They were judged "by what was written in the books, by what they had done" (verse 12).

Another purpose is to determine why the names of the lost are not in "the book of life" (verse 15). In the pre-Advent investigative judgment, myriads of heavenly beings look into the records of the saints, to see on what basis "the saints of the Most High" may inherit the eternal kingdom. In the same manner during this millennial judgment, the saints will have an opportunity to look into the records of the lost, where their works are recorded, to see why they could not inherit the kingdom of God. Here again the idea of the vindication of God's character as manifested in His righteousness and justice is an issue. All the saints have the opportunity to answer the question for themselves why the lost are indeed lost. The redeemed in heaven will see what choices the lost made and why they persisted in a life of separation from God with the fatal consequences of eternal separation from Him.

3. The Postmillennial Executive Judgment

The postmillennial executive judgment is the final phase of the universal last judgment. It is the final result of sin and separation from God. It involves eradication of sin and sinners from the universe so that sin will never rise again. (See Millennium I. C. 3.)

a. The timing of the postmillennial executive judgment. The executive judgment takes place after the thousand years of the millennium are completed (verses 1-3, 5). "And when the thousand years are ended, Satan will be loosed from his prison and will come out to deceive the nations which are at the four corners of the earth" (verses 7, 8). Also after the millennium, "the rest of the dead" (verse 5), who had no part in the first resurrection of the saints when Christ appeared in the clouds of heaven, will be raised at the "resurrection of judgment" (John 5:29), the resurrection of "the unjust" (Acts 24:15), also called the second resurrection.

The NT depicts those who have rejected Christ, as numerous as "the sand of the sea"

(Rev. 20:8), marching in battle, led by the archdeceiver, against "the camp of the saints and the beloved city" (verse 9). At this time, after the millennium is concluded, their final destruction takes place in the divine executive judgment.

b. The judges of the postmillennial executive judgment. In Matthew 25:40 Jesus describes Himself as "the King," who will say to the wicked, "Depart from me, you accursed, into the eternal fire prepared for the devil and his angels" (verse 41). The cursed ones are "the goats," who did not assist the hungry, the thirsty, the stranger, the naked, the sick, or those in prison (verse 44).

God the Father will also be part of this final event (Isa. 34:8; Mal. 4:1). Throughout the book of Revelation He is depicted as a judge seated on the throne (Rev. 4:2, 8, 9; 5:1, 7, 13; 6:16; 7:10, 15; 19:4). In the eradication of Satan, the originator of sin, and his followers, both Father and Son are judges together.

c. The recipients of judgment in the postmillennial executive judgment. In this final phase of judgment the recipients are the wicked. These are "the devil and his angels" (Matt. 25:41)—all those who followed Satan and who were judged in the millennial judgment.

d. The purpose of the postmillennial executive judgment. The purpose of this final executive phase of judgment is the utter and final destruction of the originator of sin, Satan, who carries the responsibility for sin. "His angels" (Matt. 25:41) will share his end in "the lake of fire and sulphur" (Rev. 20:10; cf. verses 14, 15); likewise, "if any one's name was not found written in the book of life, he was thrown into the lake of fire" (verse 15). This is "the second death" (verse 14), which makes it impossible for anyone to suffer eternal torture in hellfire.

"The lake of fire" refers to the burning surface of the earth after the millennium. It is, therefore, not hell in the traditional sense of an eternally burning place of torment of the wicked dead, nor is it some kind of underground terrestrial eternal fire in which the wicked suffer eternally. These ideas are present in Greek philosophy and became incorporated in extrabiblical Jewish literature. They are not part of the Bible. The biblical "lake of fire" is the burning surface of this planet when the final judgment takes place. "For behold, the day comes, burning like an oven, when all the arrogant and all evildoers will be stubble; the day that comes will burn them up, says the Lord of hosts" (Mal. 4:1).

Through the executive judgment, God brings about the final destruction of the wicked. The biblical picture is not one of divine withdrawal from the wicked, who then destroy themselves as they are left without the presence of God. Those who wish to exclude God and Christ from the final victory over sin and its originator deprive the scriptural witness of an essential element of final eschatology.

After this final destruction of the wicked God will create "new heavens and a new earth in which righteousness dwells" (2 Peter 3:13; cf. Rev. 21:1; Isa. 65:17). This will be the eternal abode of all the redeemed.

IV. Judgment and the Christian Life

The biblical teaching on judgment is by no means peripheral in biblical thought. It is an integral part of the outworking of the plan of salvation and connected in an inseparable way with both redemption and salvation.

Judgment guarantees human freedom, the freedom to choose, with a full range of consequences. It involves the ethical dimension of human responsibility. Judgment also communicates that sin does not run a never-ending course. God ultimately remains in control of sin. Judgment limits sin and its sphere, bringing it finally to an end. God is the decisive actor in this matter. His judgments guarantee divine righteousness and justice. His judgment finally and ultimately demonstrates His love. "The judgment of God is understood in the final analysis as an expression of his love. For the only really radical judgment of sin is that of pure love" (Aulen 146). Or expressed differently: "Judgment protects the idea of the triumph of God and of good. It is unthinkable that the present conflict between good and evil should last throughout eternity. Judgment means that evil will be disposed of authoritatively, decisively, finally" (Morris 72). Judgment is made necessary because sin exists; it is called for by human rebellion, but not by vindictiveness in God's nature. God's love and justice, His grace and righteousness, meet in divine judgment.

As believers, we may face each aspect of the judgment with confidence. With Paul we affirm, "It is God who justifies; who is to condemn?" (Rom. 8:33, 34). Our security of salvation and faith rests in the God who is both Saviour and Judge. With the author of Hebrews we say that "God is not so unjust as to overlook your work and the love which you showed for his sake" (Rom. 6:10). Divine justice is what we need and can count on.

John speaks of "love perfected with us, that we may have confidence for the day of judgment" (1 John 4:17). This means trusting in the forgiving love of our Lord Jesus Christ and in the justice and righteousness of God the Father. The faithful are saved in the Lord, who graciously forgives their sins (1 John 1:9), our heavenly Mediator (1 Tim. 2:5; Heb. 9:15; 12:24), who stands good for our debt (Heb. 10:12-14), and in whose merits we can face the judgment with confidence. Through our Lord Jesus Christ we can "with confidence draw near to the throne of grace" (Heb. 4:16), because He is our "advocate with the Father" (1 John 2:1). Our relationship with our Mediator, Advocate, and High Priest makes us confident in the day of judgment.

The same confidence is ours regarding our Father, who Himself "so loved the world that he gave his only Son, that whoever believes in him should not perish but have eternal life" (John 3:16). God the Father "saved us, not because of deeds done by us in righteousness, but in virtue of his own mercy"; He also gave the Holy Spirit, "through Jesus Christ our Savior, so that we might be justified by his grace and become heirs in hope of eternal life" (Titus 3:5-7).

The fruit of this confidence of being saved through God the Father and Jesus Christ His Son makes us "careful" to practice "good deeds" (verse 8). The one who does not manifest "good deeds" by the enabling power of Jesus Christ through the Holy Spirit is called "unfruitful" (verse 14). The faith of such a one is empty, because it is not a faith that works. Based on Christ's empowerment, God's people engage in works of faith that make them fruitful. The believer is to have full confidence and complete joy from now until the day of Christ's triumphant return in the clouds of heaven, experiencing even in this life a most joyous union with the Lord. The time will soon be here when our Lord appears, and the faithful will join Him face-to-face.

V. Historical Overview

Over the centuries Christian thought about divine judgment has varied. Ecclesiological, theological, and sociocultural considerations have often influenced the form of the teaching rather than the Scriptures.

A. Divine Judgment
From the Early Church to the Age
of the Enlightenment

The Apostolic Fathers assumed that there would be a last judgment at the end of time. Consistently Jesus Christ is designated as the one who comes as a judge of the living and the dead (Polycarp, *To the Philippians* 2 [ANF 1:33]). Clement speaks of a "judgment to come" (*1 Clement* 27, 28 [ANF 1:12]).

Second-century apologists such as Justin Martyr, Aristides, Athenagoras, Theophilus of Antioch, and Tatian also spoke of Christ as the judge of the living and the dead. Some of these, however, conceived a judgment immediately after death.

In fighting Gnosticism and the Marcionite heresy, Irenaeus (c. 115-c. 202) pointed out that, according to Scripture, judgment is a necessary aspect of the return of Christ (*Against Heresies* 5. 27 [ANF 1:556]). The standard of Christ's judgment is the keeping of the commandments (*Against Heresies* 1. 10. 1; 3. 5. 3; 4. 37. 1 [ANF 1:330, 418, 518]).

The idea of the judgment is a key theme of the theology of Tertullian (c. 160-c. 240, *Testimony of the Soul* 2; cf. *Apology* 17, 18, 45 [ANF 3:176, 32, 50]). He points out that Christians will participate in the judgment of the wicked people, Satan, and his angels (*On Repentance,* 7; *Flight in Time of Persecution,* 10. 2; *On the Apparel of Women,* 1. 2. 4 [ANF 3:662, 663; 4:15, 122]).

Origen (c. 185-c. 254) interpreted the judgment in allegorical fashion. He said that the saints go immediately after death to paradise which he called the "school of the souls," while the wicked enter an immaterial fire of judgment fed by sins, serving to purify sinners (*Against Celsus* 5. 15-17; 6. 26 [ANF 4:549, 550, 585]). His influence is left on various later spiritualizing interpretations of judgment (so Basil of Caesarea [c. 330-379], Gregory of Nazianzus [c. 329-390], and Gregory of Nyssa [c. 330-c. 395]).

Cyprian (c. 200-258), bishop of Carthage, developed the idea of judgment as an incentive for Christians to do good, profoundly influencing the development of the doctrine of merit in later Catholicism. The righteous and the martyrs go immediately into heaven (*On Mortality* 20, 26 [ANF 5:474, 475]), but the wicked burn eternally in hell (*Letters* 30. 7; 55. 10 [ANF 5:311, 350]).

The Latin apologist Lactantius (c. 250-c. 325) taught that at the beginning of the millennium the righteous would be raised and enter into judgment (*Divine Institutes* 7. 20; 22-24 [ANF 7:216-219]). Satan and his angels, along with the wicked, would burn forever, beginning after the millennium (*Institutes* 7. 26 [ANF 7:220, 221]).

Augustine of Hippo (354-430) fully developed the teaching of judgment in his *City of God* (books 20 and 21 [NPNF-1 2:421-478]). Judgment is based on the righteousness of God (20. 1-3). The judgment in John 5:22-24 is understood as condemnation (20. 5). Satan, evil angels, and the wicked will burn in hell eternally (21. 1-9) but with some gradation of punishment (20. 16). The prayers of the faithful and the intercession of the saints will assist the righteous in their purgatorial torment (21. 27), which will purify some of them (21. 13).

The scholastic Thomas Aquinas (1225-1274) developed for the first time a detailed concept of the double judgment. The first (or particular) judgment occurs immediately after physical death. The final or general judgment comes at the general resurrection when souls and bodies are reunited (*Summa Theologiae* 3a. 59. 5). This teaching was subsequently supported by Pope Benedict XII (1285-1342). A striking phenomenon of medieval theology is the picture of Christ as a stern and exacting judge, feared to the extreme. The judgment motif was thus used extensively as an incentive to good, moral life.

Martin Luther was deeply influenced by this medieval picture of Christ, which produced fear and anxiety in him (*Weimar Ausgabe* 38. 148. 11, 12; 40. 1; 298. 9; 41. 197. 5, 6). He was taught that the cross had taken care of original sin only and that individual sins call for penance with pilgrimages and good works (*ibid.* 47. 310. 7-17; 47. 344. 39-42). Luther changed this picture of Christ by presenting Him as "Saviour, Mediator, Brother, and Friend," the one who tells us to leave aside our works righteousness and encourages us to abide in Him by faith (*ibid.* 33. 85. 7-22). God is now presented as the stern judge in the final judgment, but Christ as our major glory (*ibid.* 36. 450. 4-6).

The Swiss Reformer Ulrich Zwingli held to the medieval doctrine of double judgment. The final judgment simply announces the decision for rewards and punishment to be experienced by humans whose soul and body are reunited (*Exposition and Basis of the Conclusions*, art. 57).

John Calvin produced the most developed judgment theology of the major Reformers. He also held to the medieval double judgment.

The souls of the righteous experience immediately after death an initial form of eternal salvation, but the souls of the wicked experience torment and torture (*Institutes* 3. 25. 6, 9). The final judgment will mete out eternal bliss or eternal punishment to the reunited bodies and souls (*ibid.* 3. 25. 10, 12).

Roman Catholicism responded to the Reformation challenge with the declarations of the Council of Trent. "Good works," it affirmed, are meritorious and play an important role in the final judgment, in addition to the merits of Christ.

The picture of the doctrine of judgment from Protestant orthodoxy to the Age of the Enlightenment is diverse. On the whole, there is a trend away from a literal future judgment, conditioned by various rationalistic innovations which reinterpreted God as an impersonal reality. Such changes demanded adjustments in the doctrine of judgment.

B. Divine Judgment From the Age of the Enlightenment to the Present

1. Trends in Liberal Theology

The removal of transcendent dimensions in modernity caused the idea of a divine judgment to be pushed aside. It hardly enters into theological systems in liberal theology (see, for instance, Paul Tillich, Jürgen Moltmann, Wolfhart Pannenberg, Gerhard Ebeling).

Today's liberal theologians speak of cultural revolutions of modernity as manifested since the eighteenth century, culminating in the French Revolution, the subsequent industrial revolution, and the two world wars, as well as the present man-made ecological crisis, as judgments which humanity has produced for itself (so Karl Holl, M. Greschat, Moltmann, Pannenberg). In this sense, judgment is nothing more or less than present human experience, determined by the immanent forces of culture. In liberal theology, therefore, there is no substance to a future divine judgment. Judgment basically happens here and now as the product of humanity itself. R. Bultmann reinterpreted the biblical message of judgment as an existential "crisis of decision."

Some modern minds perceive the theme of divine judgment as primitive, mythical, and outdated. Others wish to criticize it as unethical and outmoded from the point of view of modern universalism. We need to consider briefly two of these major points of view.

a. Divine love and divine judgment. Some modern thinkers have pitted divine love against divine judgment. This alleged dichotomy between love and judgment was expressed already by the Christian heretic Marcion in the second century A.D.

The modern position holds that God is primarily a God who loves and saves. Hence, any eschatological, end-time statement of a divine future judgment must take into account the inadequacy of the ancient context. A unique modern emphasis on God's all-pervasive love leads some to new conclusions, which include the idea that a God of love will not destroy sinners. Some theologians say that a loving God cannot destroy, because love is an all-embracing and predominant force within the nature of God.

In harmony with the overemphasis on the love of God, judgment is reinterpreted as a divine withdrawal from those who have rebelled against Him. The human race, which has withdrawn from God, is left to deteriorate and finally destroy itself. God's withdrawal is the judgment. A God of love, it is claimed, will not condemn, punish, or destroy the wicked. This modernistic theological view sees an opposition between the love of God and the justice and righteousness of God, which are manifested in divine judgment. This view denies, at least in part, the seriousness of God's opposition to sin and its resultant evil. It denies the moral relationship of human activity with its consequences, which call for divine judgment. It denies the need of the death of Christ in behalf of and in place of sinners; Christ has not paid for human sin on the cross, He is a representative man and not our Sub-

stitute. This teaching also denies that sinners are held responsible by God for their actions and that God will deal with the consequences of sin in judgment. These denials cut to the very core of the understanding of biblical revelation, the nature of sin and judgment, the nature of Christ's death on the cross, and the nature of biblical eschatology.

Divine love is taken as the supreme guiding principle and highest norm, separating it from other qualities in the nature of God. Love is thus stretched into an all-encompassing umbrella that can cover any kind of human deed, regardless of its ugliness or impact on the individual and society. This view of divine love separates it from its biblical context. Love becomes an abstract principle dependent on and informed by philosophical notions of modern thought. In other words, love is defined as a "canon within the canon," that is, a superior norm on the basis of which other parts of Scripture are either considered antiquated, primitive, and inferior or reinterpreted to say something that fits a modernistic way of thinking. The final result of such a procedure is a picture of the love of God that is very distant and rather unrelated to the full revelation of the Bible.

In Scripture, divine love, divine justice, divine righteousness, divine judgment, and divine retribution are all held together in a dynamic correlation without sacrificing any of these. The Bible shows itself much richer and more profound than modernistic notions that limit God and His activity in the resolution of the great controversy between Christ and Satan.

The full revelation of the Word of God includes all aspects of divine love and divine judgment, with both condemnation for the wicked and vindication of the righteous. God is and remains the judge of all, even of our own imaginative constructs about His judgment and His being.

b. Universalism and divine judgment. Both past and present thinkers have held to universalism, that is universal salvation of all human beings. Some of them claim that the Bible itself moves in the direction of the salvation of every human being. It is often supposed that God's saving purpose is greater than the literal requirements of His justice and righteousness as manifested in divine judgment. Therefore, it is assumed that God is not bound to give a just payment to those who have remained rebellious sinners.

Historically, universalism, the teaching that all human beings will in the end be saved in some way or another, is known as *apokatastasis*, final salvation. This theory was supported in post-NT times by Gregory of Nyssa and Scotus Erigena; in the Radical Reformation by Hans Denck; and in modern theology by F. Schleiermacher, Clarence Skinner, Karl Barth, and others.

Universalism, the final salvation of all human beings, is based on the misapplication or misinterpretation of several Scripture passages (Rom. 5:18, 19; 1 Cor. 15:22; Eph. 1:9, 10). Accordingly, universalism is engaged in several denials of what Scripture holds. It denies the final judgment of the wicked and, of course, divine retribution. It denies the reality of eternal death of unrepentant sinners. It denies that in the end there will be two groups of persons, the saved and the unsaved. Finally, it denies the "second death."

Universalism demands a departure from the truth of biblical revelation. It is unable to encompass all of Scripture. Universalism, with its seemingly attractive features, is another form of reductionism of biblical truth. It can function only if an unbiblical view of progressive revelation is superimposed on Scripture and the parts of the Bible that do not agree with a modern theological position are relegated to what is said to be an outdated view of Scripture.

These trends in theology, informed by the spirit of modernity, are inadequate with regard to the biblical evidence itself. The biblical teaching on judgment shows that it is neither capricious nor emotional; it is neither primitive nor mythological. Judgment is a reality of biblical faith, and as we have seen, it is no peripheral theme in the Bible. It is profoundly linked to the sin problem and its resolution, to divine justice and righteousness, to the correlation of love and judgment, to the matter of the suffering of the innocent, to the issue of salvation, and so on. It cannot be moved to the side as something that is marginal or insignificant, outdated or primitive, or whatever else may be said against it. Judgment belongs to salvation as salvation is emptied without judgment.

In view of the moral decadence of our own time, the judgment theme of the Bible is highly relevant. Will the wicked ever receive their just recompense? Will the mass murderers and today's serial murderers ever come to full justice? In view of the limitation of human justice, will there ever be a complete, just, and comprehensive judgment where all aspects and sides come into view? These and many similar questions are raised by many today, and rightly so.

The fact is that the issue of theodicy, the justice of God in a world permeated by injustice, is a cause of great offense to modern thinkers, and it is among the key reasons cited for the tendency toward agnosticism and atheism. Divine judgment is a key element in the unraveling of the matter of injustice in the world. It remains an essential part of the "eternal gospel" (Rev. 14:6).

The final call to worship the Creator with the command, "worship him who made heaven and earth, the sea and the fountains of water" (verse 7), demands the proclamation that the end-time "hour of His judgment has come." Judgment is part of the "eternal gospel" (verse 6) and is in full harmony with the message of righteousness by faith, which it is in verity and which is to be proclaimed with power to those who dwell on earth, to every nation, tribe, tongue, and people. God is love, and the proclamation of the love of God demands the proclamation of His justice. Divine love calls for divine justice in judgment. The "proclamation of the love of God always presupposes that all men are moving toward God's judgment and are hopelessly exposed to it" (Büchsel 941).

2. Trends in Evangelical Theology

Evangelical Christianity has not given up the divine judgment. Dispensationalists have developed the last judgment along the lines of their own apocalyptic eschatology with various pretribulation, midtribulation, and posttribulation rapture theories. Depending on each one of these theories the judgment of Christ, the judgment on Israel, the judgment on the nations, the judgments of the tribulation, the judgment associated with the Second Advent, the "great white throne" judgment, and the final judgment on Satan, his angels, and sinners receive their respective interpretations (see Pentecost 156-218; 412-426).

Nondispensational evangelicals generally hold to a final judgment that is largely undifferentiated, depending on whether they are amillennialists (e.g., König 128-137) or premillennialists (e.g., Ladd 87-102; Martin 1977, 187-205). Because amillennialists do not hold to a literal millennium in the future, all judgment merges together around the second coming of Christ. Premillennialists, on the other hand, support a divine judgment in connection with the Second Coming and the "great white throne" judgment at the end of the millennium, with the verdict of eternal punishment of the wicked.

C. Adventist Understanding

Seventh-day Adventist teaching on the final judgment is closely entwined with their understanding of Christ's high-priestly ministry in the heavenly sanctuary. For a brief sketch of the early historical development of both beliefs, see Sanctuary V. D.

VI. Ellen G. White Comments

Ellen G. White wrote extensively on many subjects, including the judgment. She spoke of several aspects of judgment, including its nearness (2T 355), its certainty (RH Nov. 22, 1898), its basis (the law of God, COL 314), the evidence to be examined (human actions as recorded in the heavenly books, 4T 481), as well as the results of the judgment (eternal life for the righteous and eternal death for the wicked, GC 673, 674). Yet perhaps her greatest contribution to the topic was her placement of divine judgment within the setting of the great controversy between good and evil, and closely related to God's love for His creatures (*ibid.* 541, 543, 670, 671; 4T 165; PK 292). Obviously, space is insufficient to quote more than a few paragraphs and refer the reader to others. Given the emphasis of the article, quotations and references are divided according to the three phases of the judgment.

A. Pre-Advent Investigative Judgment

Ellen White had no doubt about a pre-Advent investigative judgment of God's professed people. This, the first phase of the final judgment, had begun in 1844, in harmony with the prophecies of Daniel and Revelation and the typologies of Leviticus and Hebrews (GC 479-491; PP 357, 358).

Within the heavenly sanctuary and in the presence of angels as ministers of God and witnesses (GC 479), God the Father judges His people, with Christ as Advocate and Satan as the accuser. Christ intercedes for them, showing "their penitence and faith, and, claiming for them forgiveness" (*ibid.* 484), pleading "His blood in behalf of penitent believers" (PP 357).

Those who have once accepted Jesus' sacrifice and merits are investigated, beginning with the righteous dead and continuing with the righteous living (4T 384; EW 280). Their good deeds, as well as their sins—whether of omissions or commission, are examined in the heavenly books against the standard of God's law (LS 241; COL 310; GC 482). "Then by virtue of the atoning blood of Christ, the sins of all the truly penitent will be blotted from the books of heaven. Thus the sanctuary will be freed, or cleansed, from the record of sin" (PP 357, 358; cf. GC 425). The names of the faithful remain in the book of life. The names of those who never accepted Christ do not come up in this judgment (GC 480). On the other hand, those who once accepted Christ but have given up their relationship with Him have their names blotted out of the book of life (*ibid.* 483).

At the same time, "while the investigative judgment is going forward in heaven, while the sins of penitent believers are being removed from the sanctuary, there is to be a special work of purification, of putting away of sin, among God's people upon earth" (*ibid.* 425). At the end of the pre-Advent judgment in heaven, "the destiny of all will have been decided for life or death." God's people living on earth will be ready to meet their Lord, and the Second Coming will take place (*ibid.* 490, 491).

B. Post-Advent Millennial Judgment

After Christ takes His saints to heaven, the millennial judgment will sit. This is a judgment totally separate from the pre-Advent judgment (*ibid.* 479-491). In it, Christ as judge (DA 210), together with the redeemed, will investigate the deeds of the wicked, including Satan and the fallen angels (EW 290, 291; GC 661). Again, evidence is provided by the books of heaven, especially "the book of death," which "contains the evil deeds of the wicked." The Bible is used as "the statute book" (EW 52, 291).

In addition to ascertaining that the wicked have, indeed, rejected Jesus' salvation, this judgment determines the punishment to be received by each one (*ibid.* 291; GC 661). The millennial judgment ends with the 1,000 years, just before the second resurrection and the descent of the Holy City (SR 416, 417).

C. Postmillennial Executive Judgment

At the end of the millennium the second resurrection, that of the wicked, takes place. Christ returns to earth with His redeemed saints. At the same time, Satan prepares a mighty attack against the saints and the New Jerusalem as it comes down from heaven. At this time, in the presence of all those who have ever lived on earth, both redeemed and impenitent, as well as Satan and his evil angels, Christ is crowned. "And now, invested with supreme majesty and power, the King of kings pronounces sentence upon the rebels against His government and executes justice upon those who have transgressed His law and oppressed His people" (GC 666).

"As soon as the books of record are opened, and the eye of Jesus looks upon the wicked, they are conscious of every sin which they have ever committed" (*ibid.*). "The whole wicked world stand arraigned at the bar of God on the charge of high treason against the government of heaven. They have none to plead their cause; they are without excuse; and the sentence of eternal death is pronounced against them" (*ibid.* 668).

Satan's machinations stand exposed (*ibid.* 672). Manifestly, it is clear that "the wages of sin is not noble independence and eternal life, but slavery, ruin, and death" (*ibid.* 668). Also abundantly clear is the fact that "no cause for sin exists" (*ibid.* 503). The impenitent, aware of these realities, prostrate themselves in worship, while "Satan bows down and confesses the justice of his sentence" (*ibid.* 670). At last "God's wisdom, His justice, and His goodness stand fully vindicated" (*ibid.*). Along with God's government, the law is also vindicated (7BC 986; DA 58; PP 338-340).

Fire then "comes down from God out of heaven. The earth is broken up. The weapons concealed in its depths are drawn forth. Devouring flames burst from every yawning chasm. The very rocks are on fire" (GC 672). In this fiery conflagration the wicked are as straw. "All are punished 'according to their deeds.' The sins of the righteous having been transferred to Satan, he is made to suffer not only for his own rebellion, but for all the sins which he has caused God's people to commit. His punishment is to be far greater than that of those whom he has deceived. . . . In the cleansing flames the wicked are at last destroyed, root and branch. . . . The full penalty of the law has been visited; the demands of justice have been met; and heaven and earth, beholding, declare the righteousness of Jehovah. Satan's work of ruin is forever ended" (*ibid.* 673).

VII. Literature

Andreasen, Niels-Erik. "Translation of Niṣdaq/Katharisthēsetai in Daniel 8:14." In *Symposium on Daniel.* Ed. Frank B. Holbrook. Daniel and Revelation Committee Series. Washington, D.C.: Biblical Research Institute, 1986. Pp. 475-496.

Aulen, Gustaf. *Christus Victor.* New York: Macmillan, 1969.

Büchsel, F. *"krino ktl."* In *Theological Dictionary of the New Testament.* Ed. G. Kittel. Grand Rapids: Eerdmans, 1965. Vol. 3, pp. 933-954.

Cody, Aelred. *Heavenly Sanctuary and Liturgy in the Epistle to the Hebrews. The Achievement of Salvation in the Epistle to the Hebrews: The Achievement of Salvation in the Epistle's Perspectives.* St. Meinrad, Ind.: Grail, 1960.

Davidson, Richard M. *Typology in Scripture. A Study of Hermeneutical Typos Structures.* Andrews University Seminary Doctoral Dissertation Series. Vol. 2. Berrien Springs, Mich.: Andrews University Press, 1981.

Delitzsch, F. *Psalms.* 3 vols. *Commentaries on the Old Testament.* Grand Rapids: Eerdmans, 1990.

Düsterwald, Franz. *Die Weltreiche und das Gottesreich nach den Weissagungen des Propheten Daniel.* Freiburg: Herder, 1890.

Hasel, Gerhard F. "The Distinction Between Clean and Unclean Animals in Leviticus 11: Still Relevant?" *Journal of the Adventist Theological Society* 2 (1991): 91-125.

———. "The Hebrew Masculine Plural for 'Weeks' in the Expression 'Seventy Weeks' in Daniel 9:24." *Andrews University Seminary Studies* 31 (1993): 105-118.

———. "The Identity of 'The Saints of the Most High' in Daniel 7." *Biblica* 56 (1975): 173-192.

———. "The 'Little Horn,' the Heavenly Sanctuary and the Time of the End: A Study of Daniel 8:9-14." In *Symposium on Daniel.* Ed. Frank B. Holbrook. Daniel and Revelation Committee Series. Washington, D.C.: Biblical Research Institute, 1986. Pp. 378-461.

———. *The Remnant. The History and Theology of the Remnant Idea From Genesis to Isaiah.* Rev. ed. Andrews University Monographs: Studies in Religion. Vol. 1. Berrien Springs, Mich.: Andrews University Press, 1980.

———. "Resurrection in the Theology of Old Testament Apocalyptic." *Zeitschrift für die alttestamentliche Wissenschaft* 92 (1980): 267-284.

———. "Studies in Biblical Atonement II: The Day of Atonement." *The Sanctuary and the Atonement: Biblical, Historical, and Theological Studies.* Ed. A. V. Wallenkampf and W. Richard Lesher. Washington, D.C.: General Conference of Seventh-day Adventists (1981): 115-133.

Herntrich, Volkmar. "The OT Term *mišpāṭ.*" *Theological Dictionary of the New Testament.* Ed. G. Kittel. Grand Rapids: Eerdmans, 1965. Vol. 3, pp. 923-933.

Holbrook, Frank B., ed. *Symposium on Daniel: Introductory and Exegetical Studies.* Daniel and Revelation Committee Series, vol. 2. Washington, D.C.: Biblical Research Institute, 1986.

Johnsson, William G. "Defilement/Purification and Hebrews 9:23." *Issues in the Book of Hebrews.* Ed. Frank B. Holbrook. Daniel and Revelation Committee Series. Silver Spring, Md.: Biblical Research Institute, 1989. Pp. 79-103.

Koch, Klaus. "Is There a Doctrine of Divine Retribution?" *Theodicy in the Old Testament.* Ed. James Crenshaw. Philadelphia: Fortress, 1983. Pp. 57-87.

König, Adrio. *The Eclipse of Christ in Eschatology.* Grand Rapids: Eerdmans, 1989.

Ladd, George Eldon. *The Last Things*. Grand Rapids: Eerdmans, 1978.

Lamparter, Helmut. *Die Hoffnung der Christen*. Stuttgart: Quell, 1967.

Martin, J. P. "The Last Judgment." In *Dreams, Visions and Oracles*. Ed. Carl E. Amerding and W. Ward Gasque. Grand Rapids: Baker, 1977. Pp. 187-205.

─────. *The Last Judgment in Protestant Orthodoxy to Ritschl*. Grand Rapids: Eerdmans, 1963.

Maxwell, C. Mervyn. *God Cares*. Vol. 1. Mountain View, Calif.: Pacific Press, 1981.

Morris, Leon. *The Biblical Doctrine of Judgment*. Grand Rapids: Eerdmans, 1960.

Owusu-Antwi, Brempong. *An Investigation of the Chronology of Daniel 9:24-27*. Ph.D. dissertation, Andrews University, 1993. Now published as *The Chronology of Daniel 9:24-27*. Adventist Theological Society Dissertation Series. Vol. 2. Berrien Springs, Mich.: Adventist Theological Society Publications, 1995.

Pentecost, J. Dwight. *Things to Come: A Study in Biblical Eschatology*. Grand Rapids: Zondervan, 1958.

Pfandl, Gerhard. *The Time of the End in the Book of Daniel*. Adventist Theological Society Dissertation Series. Vol. 1. Berrien Springs, Mich.: Adventist Theological Society Publications, 1992.

Rodríguez, Angel M. "Significance of the Cultic Language in Daniel 8:9-14." In *Symposium on Daniel*. Ed. Frank B. Holbrook. Washington, D.C.: Biblical Research Institute, 1986. Pp. 527-549.

Schneider, Johannes. *The Letter to the Hebrews*. Grand Rapids: Eerdmans, 1957.

Schwarz, Reinhard. "Die spätmittelalterliche Vorstellung vom richtenden Christus—ein Ausdruck religiöser Mentalität." *Geschichte in Wissenschaft und Unterricht* 32 (1981): 526-553.

Shea, William H. "The Investigative Judgment of Judah, Ezekiel 1-10." *The Sanctuary and the Atonement: Biblical, Historical, and Theological Studies*. Ed. A. V. Wallenkampf and W. Richard Lesher. Washington, D.C.: General Conference of Seventh-day Adventists, 1981. Pp. 283-291.

─────. *Selected Studies on Prophetic Interpretation*. Rev. ed. Daniel and Revelation Committee Series. Vol. 1. Washington, D.C.: Biblical Research Institute, 1992.

─────. "Spatial Dimensions in the Vision of Daniel 8." *Symposium on Daniel: Introductory and Exegetical Studies*. Ed. Frank B. Holbrook. Washington, D.C.: Biblical Research Institute, 1986. Pp. 497-526.

─────. "When Did the Seventy Weeks of Daniel 9:24-27 Begin?" *Journal of the Adventist Theological Society* 2, No. 1 (1991): 115-138.

The Remnant and the Three Angels' Messages

Hans K. LaRondelle

Introduction

The ultimate focus of all Bible prophecy and salvation history is the establishment of the kingdom of God on earth. Holy Scripture begins with Paradise created and lost (Gen. 1-3) and ends in the NT with Paradise restored (Rev. 21; 22). The election of Israel as the chosen covenant people of God was not an end in itself but God's appointed way to establish a visible sign before the nations of the justice and peace of the coming kingdom of God. Christ Jesus taught the New Covenant people, His church, to pray, "Thy kingdom come, thy will be done, on earth as it is in heaven" (Matt. 6:10). Thus the apostolic gospel message received its apocalyptic perspective in fundamental continuity with God's covenant with ancient Israel.

The humble coming of Jesus of Nazareth as the Messiah of prophecy brought the decisive turning point in Israel's redemption history, the crucial and final test of the nation's faith and loyalty to the covenant God. While the four Gospels concentrate on the Messiah's life, death, and resurrection, John's Apocalypse centers on the consummation of His mission as judge and restorer in the time of the end. In the last Bible book all the other books of Scripture meet and find their ultimate glorious fulfillment. A true understanding of the prophecies concerning the church and the world in the end-time must be based, therefore, on a responsible exegesis of the theological core and literary center of John's Apocalypse: Revelation 12-14. In this unbreakable unit of apocalyptic revelation both the Millerite movement and subsequent Seventh-day Adventist Church found their theological roots and mandate.

The focus in the Advent awakening, both before and after 1844, was on the end-time prophecies of Daniel and Revelation. It was in the light of these prophecies that the SDA pioneers began to develop their theological self-understanding as a new movement in Christian history. Believing they were a specially chosen people, they employed for themselves such designations as "the remnant church," "the remnant people of God," or simply "the remnant." Through these designations they gave evidence of their belief that they were indeed the final segment of the church foreseen in Revelation 12.

857

I. The Remnant Concept in the OT

A remnant cannot be understood apart from a clear depiction of the body to which the remnant belongs. Thus, this section must begin with a study of the special role and function of Israel as shown in the OT.

A. The Role of Israel

The role of Israel is determined by the religious nature and the theological meaning of the name "Israel" in the OT. The name Israel is used in a twofold manner: On the one hand it stands for a people or nation, and on the other it refers to the people of Yahweh as a religious congregation. From the outset the name Israel in the OT presents a religious explanation, given by God to the patriarch Jacob after he had persistently entreated the Lord for His blessing: "Your name shall no more be called Jacob, but Israel, for you have striven with God and with men, and have prevailed" (Gen. 32:28; cf. 35:9, 10; Hosea 12:3, 4). Thus the name Israel is revealed as being of divine origin. It symbolizes Jacob's new spiritual relation to Yahweh and represents Jacob as reconciled to God through His forgiving grace. Having been forgiven, Jacob's name "was changed from one that was a reminder of his sin, to one that commemorated his victory" (PP 198). In short, from the very beginning the name Israel symbolizes a personal relation of reconciliation with God.

The OT maintains throughout this sacred origin of the name as representing its higher calling. Through the prophet Hosea, God pointed to Jacob's wrestling with Yahweh as an example to be imitated by the apostate tribes of Israel, who were trusting more in the war horses of Assyria and Egypt: "So you, by the help of your God, return, hold fast to love and justice, and wait continually for your God" (Hosea 12:6; see verses 3-6; 14:1-3). In other words, all Israelites must seek basically the same religious encounter with God and its transforming experience as Jacob had, in order to be the light of the world and to receive the covenant blessings.

God's purpose for Israel was expressed in essence by Moses when he said to Pharaoh, "Thus says the Lord, Israel is my first-born son, and I say to you, 'Let my son go that he may serve me ["worship me," NIV]'" (Ex. 4:23). The tribes of Israel were called to worship the Lord God according to His revealed will. Israel was different from all other nations, not because of any ethnic, moral, or political quality, but because Israel was chosen by God to receive His promises, which He had made to the patriarchs (Deut. 7:6-9). God redeemed Israel from its bondage to Egypt in order to bind Israel exclusively to Himself: "You have seen what I did to the Egyptians, and how I bore you on eagles' wings and brought you to myself. Now therefore, if you will obey my voice and keep my covenant, you shall be my own possession among all peoples; for all the earth is mine, and you shall be to me a kingdom of priests and a holy nation" (Ex. 19:4-6).

Israel was chosen and redeemed by God's grace at the Exodus in order to be a holy people, that is, set apart to keep God's covenant and to be priests or mediators between God and the Gentile nations. Israel was saved by grace *from* a deadly enemy, but at the same time saved *for* God's glory and *for* the salvation of the other nations. The book of Deuteronomy teaches that the purpose of Israel's election was a deeply religious mission. They had to respond to God's redemptive act as "the sons of the Lord your God" (Deut. 14:1) by loving their covenant God with total commitment of heart (Deut. 6:5), by obeying Him willingly (verses 6-9, 18), and by worshiping Him exclusively (verses 13-15). In this religious sense Israel was called to be free from idolatry, that is, "blameless *[tāmîm]* before the Lord your God" (Deut. 18:13; also 13:1-5; Ex. 20:1-3). Of fundamental importance for understanding Israel's election is the priority of divine grace before moral obedience. Moses explained, "Keep silence and hear, O Israel: this day *you have become the people of the Lord your God.* You shall *therefore obey* the voice of the Lord your God, keeping his commandments and his statutes, which I command you this day" (Deut. 27:9, 10).

From the Exodus onward, Israel was more than an ethnic entity; it was primarily a redeemed people, a religious community that found its unity and mission in the divine revelation of Yahweh embodied in the Torah. God's own word and act had elevated Israel into a worshiping congregation or assembly *(qāhāl)* in order to share its saving and sanctifying knowledge with the rest of humanity.

At Shechem Joshua renewed Israel's commitment to the exclusive worship of Yahweh for later generations. In this renewal of the covenant, Israel pledged to revive their hearts and to reform their lives in accord with the revealed will of their Redeemer-God: "And the people said to Joshua, 'The Lord our God we will serve, and his voice we will obey' " (Joshua 24:24). Israel renewed its covenant with God continually in the sacred liturgies of the annual festivals centered in the sanctuary of God. Thus the worship feasts called Israel back constantly to a covenant relationship with God in order to revitalize its participation in the Exodus redemption and freedom.

The book of Psalms uses the name Israel more than 50 times to refer to an assembly that worships Yahweh in the Temple at Jerusalem (Ps. 147:19, 20; 148:14; 149:2). The Psalms show that Israel's religion is based on the Torah of Moses. These songs not only commemorate God's redemptive acts of the past, but also teach Israel that to praise the Lord for all His benefits is the essence of Israel's calling and election (Ps. 103). The psalmists were not glorifying Jerusalem or David or Israel, but the God of Israel as the Creator of all and the Redeemer of Israel. He had selected Mount Zion as the earthly center for His universal kingdom (Ps. 2; 87).

Ezekiel states, "Thus says the Lord God: This is Jerusalem; I have set her in the center of the nations, with countries round about her" (Eze. 5:5). Israel's worship was basically inspired by its hope of the Messiah, or King-Priest, who would fulfill God's promises to Abraham and his sons for the salvation of the world: "By you all the families of the earth shall bless themselves [shall be blessed, NKJV]" (Gen. 12:3; cf. Gal. 3:8).

The ultimate aspiration of Israel's psalms is that all humanity shall acknowledge Yahweh's sovereign rulership: "Let everything that breathes praise the Lord! Praise the Lord!" (Ps. 150:6). The great historical psalms (77; 78; 105; 106; 107) taught Israel that its history was largely a record of failure to respond adequately to God's saving initiatives. Ezekiel holds up before an apostate Jerusalem the mirror of Israel's history of rebellion and defilement of God's sanctuary (Eze. 16; 23). The prophet generally perceived Israel as rebellious and disobedient. Nevertheless, there still remained a faithful remnant who constituted the true people of God and hence were the particular object of God's care.

God's plan to bless the nations through Israel will be fulfilled, but in God's own innovative way: by means of Israel's faithful remnant. A divinely chosen remnant will inherit the covenant promises and responsibilities to enlighten the world. God's eternal purpose will stand and be fulfilled. The prophetic forecasts of Israel's restoration after the Assyrian and Babylonian exiles focus on God's concern with Israel as a restored theocracy, as a spiritually cleansed and worshiping people of God (Isa. 56; Eze. 36; Jer. 31), not as a secular, political state (Eze. 20:32-38).

Postexilic Israel was a religious community centered around the rebuilt Temple, not around a royal throne. Malachi emphasized that only those Israelites who "fear Yahweh" are the people of God and that only those "who serve God" are recognized as God's own treasured possession in the final judgment (Mal. 3:16–4:3). The purpose of the OT promise of a future remnant is to assure that Israel's covenant blessings will be realized, but *not* in unbelieving national Israel, only in that chosen Israel that is faithful to Yahweh and trusts in Israel's Messiah. The fundamental purpose of Israel's mission reaches its greatest clarity in Isaiah's four prophetic "Songs concerning the Servant of Yahweh" (Isa. 42:1-4; 49:1-6; 50:4-10; 52:13–53:12). The Servant here stands for the faithful Messiah of Israel, the representative Israelite who embodied the people. Israel as a whole was called to be a missionary community, but ultimately only One would fulfill the mission outlined by Isaiah. The chosen Servant would serve the Lord, not only in spreading the knowledge of the true God to the ends of the earth (Isa. 42:1-4), but also in gathering Israel's faithful remnant back to God (Isa. 49:5, 6). Isaiah distinguished between an Israel that was a "blind" and "deaf" servant of Yahweh (Isa. 42:19, 20), and a suffering Servant obedient to Yahweh (verses 1-4; 49:1-6; 50:4-10;

52:13–53:12). As F. F. Bruce (86) observed: "But while the Servant is in some sense the representative or embodiment of Israel, he is distinguished from the nation as a whole, to which indeed his mission is first directed, as well as (thereafter) to the Gentile world." The individual Servant is strengthened by God for His mission and is vindicated against false charges from either Jewish or Gentile opposition (Isa. 50:4-9). The fourth Song of Yahweh's Servant, Isaiah 52:13–53:12, describes the Servant in detail: He would accept not only suffering and contempt, but also death as the crowning act of obedience, by which act He would fulfill God's purpose and secure blessing and liberation for multitudes. "For he was cut off from the land of the living; for the transgression of my people he was stricken. . . . Yet it was the Lord's will to crush him and cause him to suffer, and though the Lord makes his life a guilt offering, he will see his offspring and prolong his days, and the will of the Lord will prosper in his hand" (Isa. 53:8-10, NIV). God's plan with Israel on behalf of the Gentiles was, therefore, not thwarted or postponed, but prospered instead in the Messiah (Isa. 53:10).

B. The Remnant of Israel

The OT uses the word "remnant" (*šᵉˀār, šᵉˀērît*) to describe three types of people: (1) a *historical* remnant, survivors of a catastrophe; (2) a *faithful* remnant that maintains an active covenant relationship with God and carries the divine election promises; (3) an *eschatological* remnant consisting of those future faithful believers in the Messiah, who persevere till the end of the church era and ultimately emerge victorious. The remnant motif in Holy Scripture reaches from Genesis to Revelation and is found in every OT book. Its terminology is used more than 540 times in the OT alone.

1. Historical Remnant

Often the "remnant" refers to the historical survivors of Israel (or Judah) who were left alive after a certain national catastrophe (2 Kings 19:31; 25:11; 2 Chron. 34:21; Jer. 24:8; 52:15; Eze. 9:8; 11:13). When Jerusalem's remnant was deported to Babylon in 586 B.C., only few were left behind in the land of Judah (2 Kings 25:22; Jer. 40-44). When this final remnant fled to Egypt, Jeremiah predicted that those would have "no remnant or survivor from the evil" (Jer. 42:17; 44:7). The Jews or Israelites who later returned from Babylon to Palestine under Zerubbabel were described by the postexilic prophets as the remnant people of God (Haggai 1:12, 14; 2:2; Zech. 8:6, 11, 12). In these passages "remnant" refers primarily to the survivors of Israel's national catastrophes. To that remnant the God of Israel offers a new covenant fellowship, so that "Jerusalem shall be called the faithful city" (Zech. 8:3).

2. Faithful Remnant

The remnant idea takes on an explicitly theological characteristic in the prophetic writings. An example of the theological use of the remnant motif by the prophets is God's promise to Elijah, who thought no one was loyal to Yahweh except himself: "Yet I will leave seven thousand in Israel, all the knees that have not bowed to Baal, and every mouth that has not kissed him" (1 Kings 19:18). Israel as a political nation or ethnic people, therefore, could not automatically equate itself with the faithful remnant. Only those who worshiped God according to His covenant were the faithful remnant within Israel. It is further significant that the remnant people of God who survived God's judgments in the OT were to return with their whole hearts to their covenant God or they would also fall under the punishing judgment of God (Deut. 30:1-3; 2 Kings 21:14, 15; 2 Chron. 30:6). Representative is Zechariah's appeal to the remnant of his time: "Return to me, says the Lord of hosts, and I will return to you" (Zech. 1:3). The response of God is pictured in His act of divine justification of the repentant high priest Joshua (Zech. 3:3-5). Ezra expresses the genuine repentant attitude of the postexilic remnant: "O Lord the God of Israel, thou art just, for we are left a remnant that has escaped, as at this day. Behold, we are before thee in our guilt, for none can stand before thee because of this" (Ezra 9:15).

Ezra's supplication indicates the abiding need of a humble and repentant attitude of the remnant people of God. Such a remnant carries both the covenant promises and responsibilities. All the writing prophets distinguish between an apostate Israel and a faithful remnant within national Israel. Amos and Isaiah, both writing in the eighth century B.C., developed a specific remnant theology within their judgment proclamation for Israel and Judah. While Amos announced the end of the northern kingdom (Israel) as a nation in the imminent day of Yahweh, at the same time he held out the hope that God might be "gracious to the remnant of Joseph" (Amos 5:15), if they sought Him and the good (verses 4, 6, 14). Thus, Amos broke with the popular opinion that Israel as a whole was automatically sure of the covenant blessings and exempted from divine judgment (verses 18-27). He rejected Israel's misuse of the divine election as the chosen people, and he exposed the false idea that God's promises were unconditional (Amos 3:2; 9:7-10).

The surprising new elements of Amos' message were: (1) God will raise up a faithful remnant from the house of David after the Assyrian crisis; (2) in addition, non-Israelite nations such as Edom will have faithful remnants that will unite with Israel (Amos 9:11, 12). Amos' judgment message thus intended to raise up a faithful remnant of God-seekers in the end-time of Northern Israel. His promise of restoration of Israel's true worship (verses 11, 12) was only partially fulfilled following the Babylonian exile. Its Messianic fulfillment would be declared by the Christian apostles in Jerusalem (Acts 15:13-18).

The prophetic-remnant promise has an initial historical fulfillment within the OT (after the Assyrian-Babylonian exile), but it receives an eschatological fulfillment in the Messianic age. This dual realization is owing to the typological perspective in which the prophets place the coming day of the Lord: that day has an imminent, local realization in Israel's national judgment by means of Assyria and Babylon, but will ultimately find a more complete and universal fulfillment in the new covenant people of the Messiah and in His cosmic judgment day.

The context of both Testaments must determine in what sense or measure an OT prophecy about the future remnant people of God has received a past historical fulfillment within the old dispensation and whether it has a further eschatological fulfillment in the NT. The basic continuity between the OT and the NT remnant peoples and remnant theology is guaranteed by the Messiah of Israel, Christ Jesus.

3. Eschatological Remnant

Isaiah, more than the other prophets, unites Messianic prophecies with a specific remnant theology. In doing this he transcends all historical fulfillments of a remnant within OT times. Isaiah predicts that the Messiah as the "branch of the Lord" (Isa. 4:2) shall preserve a "holy" remnant or "holy seed" (Isa. 6:13) in Zion amid the fire of judgment: "And he who is left in Zion and remains in Jerusalem will be called holy, every one who has been recorded for life in Jerusalem, when the Lord shall have washed away the filth of the daughters of Zion and cleansed the bloodstains of Jerusalem from its midst by a spirit of judgment and by a spirit of burning" (Isa. 4:3, 4).

This remnant people will "lean upon the Lord, the Holy One of Israel, in truth. A remnant will return, the remnant of Jacob, to the mighty God" (Isa. 10:20, 21; cf. 30:15). This "mighty God" (*'ēl gibbôr*) is a name given the Messiah (Isa. 9:6). Isaiah also makes the Messiah the foundation stone on which the new Israel will be built (Isa. 28:16; cf. Rom. 9:33; 10:11). Not all who belong to ethnic Israel are the true Israel: "For though your people Israel be as the sand of the sea, only a remnant of them will return" (Isa. 10:22).

For Isaiah, the spiritual characteristics of the faithful remnant are faith, trust, and willing obedience to God and His Messiah (Isa. 1:18, 19; 7:9; 53). Isaiah experienced this personally in his call vision (Isa. 6:1-8). "The prophet himself may be considered the proleptic of the future remnant because he was confronted by Yahweh's holiness and emerged as a cleansed and purified individual" (Hasel 243). The prophet even gave his son the symbolic name Shearjashub, "a *remnant* shall return," to summarize one essential aspect of his prophetic proclamation.

Isaiah makes even more explicit the remnant concept of Amos by stressing that the eschatological or Messianic remnant people also will include non-Israelites, specifically those Gentiles who choose to worship the covenant God of Israel and who seek His Messiah as the "ensign to the peoples" (Isa. 11:10, 11; 56:3-8). Those survivors of the nations will be sent out again *to* the nations in order to declare God's "glory among the nations" (Isa. 66:19; cf. Zech. 14:16). The eschatological remnant will be a Messianic people who engage in a worldwide missionary outreach to gather all who will accept God's message into a united community of faith and worship. Many Gentiles will recognize Zion as the true city of God (Isa. 2:1-4; Micah 4:1-5). Isaiah pointed out that one particular characteristic of the revival and reformation of the faithful remnant would be a restored Sabbath worship (Isa. 56; 58).

Micah also unites the promise of the coming King-Messiah with the picture of Israel as His flock (Micah 2:12, 13; 5:2-4), whose transgressions have been graciously forgiven (Micah 7:18, 19). Joel and Zephaniah specifically emphasize the promise of a final remnant people who worship the Lord in the Spirit and in truth in His temple (Joel 2:32) and in genuine humility and purity of heart and lips (Zeph. 3:9, 12, 13).

Jeremiah and Ezekiel announced God's imminent historical judgment on Jerusalem and Judah by means of the Babylonian king, because of the people's refusal to repent of religious and moral apostasy (Jer. 5:1-3; 6:9; 8:3,

5; 21:8-10; Eze. 5:12; 8:6-18; 9:8). Neverthe-less, after this historical catastrophe God would gather a faithful remnant who mani-fested a cleansed heart and a new spirit and lived out the power of God's "new covenant" (Jer. 31:31-34; Eze. 36:24-27). They would be bound together as a religious, rather than po-litical, community by their common commit-ment to the promised King-Messiah (Jer. 23:5, 6; 33:14-16; Eze. 34:23, 24; 37:24-27). Here again the eschatological remnant is connected inex-tricably with the coming Messiah. The rem-nant would be the people of the Messiah.

Daniel's apocalyptic book contributes to the prophetic forecast by placing the escha-tological remnant within the progressive cal-endar of Messianic times. Daniel not only foresees the future saints of God as the perse-cuted people of God within the three and a half times or 1260 years following the collapse of the Roman Empire (Dan. 7:25; cf. Rev. 12:6, 14), but also predicts a time of distress for a *final* remnant that will be delivered from the apocalyptic woes of the day of judgment by Michael as the Son of man (Dan. 12:1-4).

In summary, the OT always portrays the future remnant of Israel as a faithful religious community that worships God with a new heart created by the Spirit of God, on the basis of the new covenant. The prophets Isaiah, Micah, Jeremiah, and Ezekiel center the eschatologi-cal remnant of Israel and the nations around the Messiah, the Servant of Yahweh par excel-lence (Isa. 42:1-7; 49:6).

II. NT Concept of the Remnant: The New Israel

The coming of Christ Jesus to Israel was the ultimate test for the Jewish people as a theocracy or God-ruled nation. As Messiah, Jesus of Nazareth was the "stumbling stone," the "rock that will make them fall" (Rom. 9:32, 33; 1 Peter 2:4-8).

Israel's relationship with Yahweh was de-termined by its response to the advent of Christ and His atoning self-sacrifice. For Jesus, the true descendants of Abraham were de-fined, not by the blood of Abraham, but by the faith of Abraham. Sonship and fatherhood are primarily determined not by a physical but by a spiritual relationship (Matt. 12:48-50). Christ claimed that all Israel should come to *Him* to receive the rest of God or they would stand judged: "Come to me, all who labor and are heavy laden, and I will give you rest" (Matt. 11:28; see Isa. 45:22); and "he who is not with me is against me, and he who does not gather with me scatters" (Matt. 12:30).

Christ was sent by God first of all to gather "the lost sheep of the house of Israel" to Him-self as the promised Messiah, just as the prophets had predicted (Matt. 10:5, 6; 15:24; see Jer. 23:3-5; Eze. 34:15, 16, 23, 24). But Christ also proclaimed that His mission—to suffer death under God's will and judgment—was intended to benefit all peoples of the earth: "And I, when I am lifted up from the earth, will draw all men to myself" (John 12:32).

Referring to Isaiah's prophecy of a future gathering of Gentiles to the temple of God, Christ declared, "And I have other sheep, that are not of this fold; I must bring them also, and they will heed my voice. So there shall be one flock, one shepherd" (John 10:16; see Isa. 56:8). This claim called for a decision of faith in Him as the Messiah of Israel. To fulfill His universal mission, Jesus called from Israel His 12 apostles, who in their chosen number clearly represent the 12 tribes of Israel. Begin-ning with the 12 disciples, whom He called to Himself and commissioned as apostles (Mark 3:14, 15), Christ formed a new Israel, the Mes-sianic remnant people of Israel, and called them "my church *[ekklēsia]*" (Matt. 16:18). To this new organism, with its own structure and authority, He gave "the keys of the king-dom of heaven" (verse 19; see 18:17).

Christ's final decision regarding the Jew-ish nation came at the end of His ministry, when the Jewish leaders had determined to reject His claim of being Israel's Messiah. Christ's words reveal that Israel's guilt before God had reached its completion (Matt. 23:32).

His verdict was: "The kingdom of God will be taken away from you and given to a nation producing the fruits of it" (Matt. 21:43). This solemn decision implies that Israel would no longer be the people ruled by God and would be *replaced* by a people that would accept the Messiah and His message of the kingdom of God.

Christ did not promise the kingdom of God—the theocracy—to another "generation" of Jews in the distant future, as dispensational writers favor, but to Christ-believing people from all races and nations, "from east and west" (Matt. 8:11, 12). In short, His church ("my church," Matt. 16:18) would replace the Christ-rejecting nation.

Jesus Himself identified the "people" whom God had chosen. To His disciples He said, "Fear not, little flock, for it is your Father's good pleasure to give you the kingdom" (Luke 12:32; cf. 22:29). That Christ unmistakably identified His disciples as the true Israel is strengthened by the fact that the Israel of God was called the flock or sheep of God by Israel's prophets (Isa. 40:11; Jer. 31:10; Eze. 34:12-14).

By calling the disciples to form the little flock who would receive the kingdom, Christ formed the nucleus of the new Israel (Luke 12:32). Christ created His church, not *besides* Israel, but *as* the faithful remnant of Israel that inherits the covenant promises and responsibilities. Christ's church is not separated from the Israel of God, only from the Christ-rejecting Jewish nation as a whole. The immediate consequence of Christ's taking the theocracy away from the nation of Israel was the imposition of the covenant curse, as specified by Moses in Leviticus 26 and Deuteronomy 28.

Christ expressed His longing for Jerusalem under the figure of a mother hen who tenderly cares for her chicks. They had not been willing; therefore, He affirmed, "your house is forsaken and desolate" (Matt. 23:37, 38). Weeping intensely over the city's horrible future under God's curse, Christ described the destruction it would suffer at the hands of its enemies because they had not recognized the day of their "visitation" (Luke 19:42-44).

For Israel, Christ's coming to Jerusalem had been that "day of visitation." The consequences of the Messiah's withdrawal were immense for the Jewish nation. The loss of God's protective theocracy will reach till the very end of time (Luke 21:24; 1 Thess. 2:16). Christ emphatically urged His little flock, the faithful remnant of Israel, to flee out of the doomed city (Matt. 24:15-20; Mark 13:14; Luke 21:20-24).

Only in Christ could Israel as a nation have remained the true covenant people of God. In rejecting Jesus as God's Messianic king, the leaders of the Jewish nation failed the decisive test of fulfilling God's purpose for the Gentiles. Christ, however, renewed God's covenant with His 12 apostles. He bestowed the divine calling of ancient Israel on His Messianic flock, to be the light of the world (Matt. 5:14) and to "make disciples of all nations, baptizing them in the name of the Father and of the Son and of the Holy Spirit" (Matt. 28:19). God was not dependent on the Jewish nation for the fulfillment of His divine purpose for all men. His plan could not be thwarted or delayed by Israel's rejection of the Messiah.

Peter's interpretation of the outpouring of the Spirit as the direct fulfillment of Joel's prophecy for the last days (Acts 2:16-21) confirms that the church was *not* an unforeseen, unpredicted entity in the OT. Rather it was the surprising fulfillment of Joel's remnant prophecy. Thus the church is not an afterthought or interruption of God's plan with Israel for the world, but the divine progress and realization of the new, Messianic Israel.

Shortly after the outpouring of God's Spirit on the church, Peter stated categorically, "And all the prophets who have spoken, from Samuel and those who came afterwards, also proclaimed these days" (Acts 3:24). In other words, since Pentecost the OT prophecies concerning the remnant of Israel had received their fulfillment in the formation of the apostolic church. More than that, the faithful church of Christ down through the ages, especially in its fully restored apostolic faith in the time of the end, fulfills the remnant promises of the OT.

Peter addressed the Christian churches of his time, scattered throughout Asia Minor (1 Peter 1:1), with the honorable titles of Israel: "But you are a chosen race, a royal priesthood, a holy nation, God's own people, that you may declare the wonderful deeds of him who called you out of darkness into his wonderful light" (1 Peter 2:9; cf. Ex. 19:5, 6). Although the apostle does not use the name "Israel," all that Israel stood for as the covenant people of God he now applies to the church. This is Peter's ecclesiological interpretation of God's covenant with Israel (Ex. 19:5, 6). This application is the outgrowth of the Christological interpretation of the Messianic prophecies. The ecclesiological application is only the organic extension of the Christological fulfillment. As the body is organically connected to the head, so is the church to the Messiah. The ecclesiological interpretation completely removes the ethnic and national restrictions of Israel's old covenant. The new covenant people is no longer characterized by the bonds of race or country but exclusively by faith in Christ. This people Peter called spiritual Israel, a "holy nation."

Paul actually calls the churches in Galatia, in Gentile territory, "the Israel of God" (Gal. 6:16). Although some commentators have interpreted this phrase to mean the Jewish members of the churches, the historical context of this Epistle indicates that Paul was vehemently rejecting any status or claim of the Jewish Christians different from or above that of Gentile Christians before God. Baptized Jews and Gentiles are all one in Christ, "all sons of God, through faith" in Christ Jesus. Consequently, "there is neither Jew nor Greek" in Christ (Gal. 3:26-28). Paul's expression "the Israel of God" (Gal. 6:16) is a synonym of his earlier description of all Christian believers: "And if you are Christ's, then you are Abraham's offspring, heirs according to promise" (Gal. 3:29).

The apostle emphatically confirms this theological understanding of the church in his letter to the Ephesians. Through the gospel, Christians have received "citizenship in Israel" and rejoice in the same hope as Israel (Eph. 2:12, 13, NIV). "So then you are no longer strangers and sojourners, but you are fellow citizens with the saints and members of the household of God, built upon the foundation of the apostles and prophets, Christ Jesus himself being the cornerstone" (verses 19, 20).

Through the cross Christ reconciled both Jews and Gentiles "to God" (verse 16). He thereby destroyed also the barrier, "the dividing wall of hostility" between Jews and Gentiles, "by abolishing in his flesh the law of commandments and ordinances" (verses 14, 15). This is an apparent reference to Christ's abrogation of the Mosaic law. Christ's mission was the formation of a Messianic Israel made up from all believers in Christ. His purpose was to "create in himself one new man in place of the two [Jews and Gentiles], so making peace" (verse 15). This purpose was realized through the cross of Christ (verse 16) and made known to God's holy "apostles and prophets" (verse 19). "This mystery is that through the gospel the Gentiles are heirs *together* with Israel, members *together* of one body, and sharers *together* in the promise in Christ Jesus" (Eph. 3:6, NIV). With the word "together" Paul stresses three times that Jewish and Gentile Christians are totally equal within the Israel of God and the covenant promise. No one is justified, therefore, in rebuilding the dividing wall between Israel and the church.

In the church at Rome, Paul was faced with an emerging hostile attitude among Gentile Christians toward Jewish Christians and Jews. Such an anti-Judaism he rejected. Paul warns the Jewish and Gentile factions within the church at Rome not to boast about some alleged superiority or prerogative (Rom. 11:18, 25; 12:3). In Romans 9-11 Paul reaches the climax of his Epistle in the exposition of how believing Gentiles relate to the Israel of God. He portrays the conversion of Gentiles to Christ as the ingrafting of wild olive branches into the one olive tree of the Israel of God (Rom. 11:17-24). In this way Paul visualizes the spiritual unity and continuity of God's covenant with Israel and His new covenant with the church of Christ. Through faith in Christ Gentiles are legally incorporated into the olive tree, the covenant people of God, and share in the root of Abraham (verse 18). The lesson of the parable of the cultivated olive tree in Romans 11 is that the church lives from the root and trunk of the OT Israel (verses 17, 18). Paul's specific burden in Romans 11 is the revelation of a divine "mystery" concerning ethnic Israel: "A hardening has come upon part of Israel, until the full number [the *plērōma*] of the Gentiles come in, and so [*houtōs*, in this way] all Israel will be saved; as it is written" (verses 25, 26).

Paul does not suggest an order of successive dispensations. He sees *many* Jews responding favorably to the salvation of *many* Gentiles who rejoice in God's mercy through Christ. And he sees it happening "now."

"Just as you [Gentile Christians] were once disobedient to God but now have received mercy because of their disobedience [Jewish rejection of Christ], so they have now been disobedient in order that by the mercy shown to you they also may ["now," NIV] receive mercy. For God has consigned all men to disobedience, that he may have mercy upon all" (verses 30-32).

Paul allows no other way for Jews to be saved than the way all the Gentiles are saved: by faith in Christ, by the confession from the heart that Jesus is the risen Lord of Israel (Rom. 10:9, 10). He explicitly states God's condition for Israel's salvation: "If they do not persist in their unbelief, [they] will be grafted in, for God has the power to graft them in again" (Rom. 11:23). Ethnic Israel had largely come to claim God's covenant promises by trusting in its blood relation to Father Abraham and thus to expect God's eschatological blessings as an *unconditional* guarantee (see Matt. 3:7-9; John 8:33, 34). Against this attitude of boasting in Israel's ethnic advantage (see Rom. 2:25-29), the apostle proclaims, "For there is no distinction between Jew and Greek; the same Lord is Lord of all and bestows his riches upon all who call upon him. For, 'every one who calls upon the name of the Lord will be saved'" (Rom. 10:12, 13).

The church now fulfills the mission of ethnic Israel, the lopped-off branches in Rom. 11:17, and is therefore endowed with Israel's covenant, blessings, and responsibilities, as well as curses if apostasy occurs. The spiritual blessing of God's presence among His people is intended to arouse the jealousy of natural Israel, because God's redemptive calling of Israel is irrevocable (verse 29). Though as a nation and God's agent, Israel of old has lost its special status, the door of salvation remains open to the individual Jewish people if, as individuals, they repent and respond to the call.

III. Apostasy of the Church in Prophecy

The apostle Paul's prophetic outline of church history (2 Thess. 2) forms an important and illuminating link between Daniel and Revelation. To meet the unjustified expectation of Christ's coming in his time, Paul warns against the religious apostasy of the "man of lawlessness" within the NT temple of God on earth, within the church as an institution, an apostasy that will continue until the glorious return of Christ: "Let no one deceive you in any way; for that day will not come, unless the rebellion *[hē apostasia]* comes first, and the man of lawlessness is revealed, the son of perdition, who opposes and exalts himself against every so-called god or object of worship, so that he takes his seat in the temple of God, proclaiming himself to be God" (2 Thess. 2:3, 4).

Two features characterize Paul's prophetic outline of uninterrupted church history from his time until Christ's return: (1) the chronological development, that is, the historical timing of the emergence of the "man of lawlessness" (or antichrist) within church history; (2) the religious nature of his blasphemous Messianic claims. It is evident that Paul's antichrist description blends three OT revelations concerning anti-God powers: (1) the historical timing of the rise of the anti-Messiah in Daniel 7, 8, and 11; (2) the religious self-deification by the kings of Tyre and Babylon in Ezekiel 28 and Isaiah 14; (3) the final destruction of the wicked one by the glorious appearance of the King-Messiah in Isaiah 11.

The literary and thematic allusions to the OT prophecies in 2 Thessalonians 2:4 become apparent in the following survey:

A. Paul's Historical Timing of the Antichrist

Paul's specific pastoral burden in 2 Thessalonians 2 is to correct the false view among the Thessalonian Christians that the day of the Lord has begun already (2 Thess. 2:3). He reminds them of his explicit oral teachings that "first" the predicted rebellion [hē apostasia] must arise within the "temple of God." Only after this development will the day of Christ break in and destroy "the lawless one" by "his appearing" (verses 3-8). In Paul's view, true knowledge of the sequential order of these major events was essential to cure the Thessalonians' apocalyptic fervor. He introduced, however, the element of retardation of the coming antichrist, because of the presence of a restraining power: "And you know what is restraining him now" (verse 6). The apostolic church apparently had no question about the identity of this "restraining" power. They knew what it was. Most of the early fathers in the postapostolic church taught that the civil order of the Roman Empire, with the emperor at its head, was the hindering power Paul referred to in verses 6, 7 (Forestell 2:234). In spite of various new theories, several leading scholars today maintain that "the classical interpretation . . . is quite satisfying" (Ladd 68).

The implication of Paul's message in 2 Thessalonians 2 is unmistakable: When the empire of the city of Rome will have fallen, the rise of the antichrist will no longer be restrained. Consequently the antichrist must be revealed without delay in the subsequent age, commonly called the Middle Ages. This prolonged age was described by Daniel as the time of the three and one-half times of oppression of the true saints, or faithful remnant (Dan. 7:25; 12:7).

Daniel's time period (Dan. 7:25; 12:7) reappears in Revelation in different forms: three and one-half times (Rev. 12:14), 42 months (11:2; 13:5), and 1260 days (11:3; 12:6). On the basis of the continuous-historical fulfillment of prophecies, the symbolic "days" stand for literal years (Shea 1982, 56-88; see Apocalyptic II. D). This means that after the breakup of the Roman Empire, 1260 literal years of apostasy would prevail. In connection with the significant events in church history regarding the rise and fall of the papal power, the dates of this period have been recognized by many Bible expositors in Europe and America as going from 533/538 to 1793/1798 (PFOF 2:765-782; 3:743, 744). During that medieval time Paul locates the apostasy that would arise "in temple of God." Anglican bishop Christopher Wordsworth (15) has drawn the logical conclusion: "Since, also, the Man of Sin is described here by St. Paul as *continuing* in the world *from the time of the removal* of the restraining Power even to the *Second Advent of Christ* (verse 8), therefore the Power here personified in the 'Man of Sin' must be one that has continued in the world *for many centuries,* and continues *to the present time.* Also, since it has this long continuance assigned to it in the prophecy—a continuance very far exceeding the life of any *one individual,* therefore the 'Man of Sin' *cannot be a single person.*"

B. The Religious Nature of Paul's Antichrist

Paul describes the coming "apostasy" as a revelation of the "son of lawlessness," who will deny both true Christian worship and all heathen worship: He "opposes . . . every so-called god or object of worship" (2 Thess. 2:4). He will exalt himself to the point of self-deification within the NT temple of God "so that he takes his seat in the temple of God, proclaiming himself to be God" (verse 4). Paul's use of the word "temple" *(naos)* in his other writings (1 Cor. 3:16, 17; 2 Cor. 6:19; Eph. 2:21) reveals that Paul meant not the material shrine in Jerusalem but the *church* as the spiritual temple of God.

Specifically significant is Paul's statement that the apostate one will "take his seat" in this temple of God. This provocative image reminds us of Daniel's vision in which the Ancient of days "took his seat" to judge the self-deifying powers on earth. In the light of this Danielic background of the judgment seat, Paul's typecasting of the archadversary becomes even more pronounced: "The Rebel would set himself up as teacher or judge in the church" (Giblin 80). The horrifying apostasy predicted in Daniel 7, 8, and 11 would arise *within* the new covenant people or the Messianic community, as the scheme of a false dogmatic teacher, as the deception of a false christ and the religious-cultic worship of himself.

Paul refers to the hidden activity of evil: "For the mystery of lawlessness is already at work" (2 Thess. 2:7). In Paul's writing, the word "mystery" carries the basic concept of the truth of redemption, once kept secret by God but now disclosed to the saints in the gospel of Christ (see Rom. 16:25, 26; 1 Cor. 2:7; Eph. 1:9, 10; Col. 1:26, 27). When Paul, however, speaks of "the mystery of lawlessness" he apparently has in mind the very opposite of the revealed truth of God in Christ: a mystery characterized by lawlessness.

From Paul's teachings, then, we derive the following points of instruction concerning the antichrist: 1. This "mystery" is not simply a matter of the apostolic age but rather will be continuously operative from Paul's time down to the end of time. Consequently, the incessant satanic activity does not permit us to locate "the mystery of lawlessness" exclusively in a single isolated historical period in the past or in the future, as the theories of preterism or futurism postulate. The very opposite is taught by Paul: After the fall of Rome this mystery of rebellion will be active without restraint (2 Thess. 2:7). 2. This satanic secret is, however, known to the true elect of Christ, because they "are not ignorant of his designs" (2 Cor. 2:11). Enlightened by the divine wisdom coming from the book of Daniel (see Dan. 11:33; 12:10), they know that Satan's attack is aimed at God's kingship and His plan of redemption, centered in the sanctuary with its sacred law and gospel. 3. By analogy with the "mystery of godliness," God's plan of disclosing His humility in Jesus and His gospel of salvation through union with Christ, the "mystery of lawlessness" indicates Satan's malicious plan to oppose and frustrate God's plan by means of a diabolical counterplan and countercultus that exalt the false priest-messiah.

In short, the apostle alerts the church to be on guard against the deception of a false teacher of Christendom who will claim to speak in Christ's stead. Paul warns against a coming counterfeit gospel and cultic worship. Above all, Paul points to the cosmic source of this master deception: It is Satan's scheme and achievement. In this perspective, Paul further develops Daniel's apocalyptic outlook.

In summary Paul's theological interpretation and historical application of Daniel's antichrist form an essential interpretive link between Daniel and Revelation. Paul's further unfolding of Daniel in 2 Thessalonians 2 provides an apostolic confirmation of the continuous-historical approach of Daniel's prophecies. The apostle characterizes the coming Christian apostasy as a counterfeit cultic worship, authorized by a rival messiah, who will rise within the Christian church soon after the fall of pagan Rome. Only the Papacy fulfills this prophetic forecast accurately.

IV. The End-time Remnant

A. OT Prediction and NT Fulfillment

Several OT prophets describe the mission and religious character of God's people in the time of the end; specifically Joel, Ezekiel, Daniel, Zephaniah, and Malachi. In order to understand their end-time prophecies adequately, we need to establish *how* their apocalyptic perspectives converge and culminate in the book of Revelation.

The interpretive principle of the gospel requires that the covenant promises and their ethnic imagery be understood in their Christological essence. The NT introduces Christ as the central key to interpret the basic meaning of all OT eschatological prophecies. The decisive test of faith is, therefore, the acceptance of Jesus of Nazareth as the Messiah of prophecy, as the divine "son of man" of Daniel's apocalyptic forecast (Dan. 7:13, 14; John 5:22-27; 9:35-39).

In the fourth Gospel the judgment of God through the Son of man is *both* present and future (John 3:19, 36; 12:48). The emphasis is on the shocking, new reality that the apocalyptic Son of man has already descended from heaven as the bread that "gives life to the world" and assurance for the apocalyptic "last day" (John 6:27, 33, 37, 40, 53). The gospel of Christ redefines and restructures OT eschatology in the light of its salvation-historical fulfillment and, therefore, creates a twofold eschatological application: a present gospel fulfillment and a future apocalyptic consummation.

The Apocalypse of John functions as the complement of John's Gospel in that it concentrates rather on the *future* joys and the *coming* inheritance of those who have been faithful until the end and who have overcome the evil one by the blood of the Lamb and the word of their testimony (Rev. 12:11). The four Gospels focus on the initial fulfillment of prophecy in Christ and His Messianic people. The book of Revelation focuses its message of hope on the ongoing and final fulfillments in the Christian church.

Joel 2:28-32 predicts that the coming age will be characterized by the outpouring of the Spirit of God on all people "before the great and terrible day of the Lord" (verses 31, 32). The true remnant people are described as those who call on the name of the Lord, "for in Mount Zion and in Jerusalem there shall be those who escape" (verse 32). Both Peter and Paul quote Joel 2:32 and proclaim its initial fulfillment in the universal church of Christ (Acts 2:21; Rom. 10:13). This gospel fulfillment of Joel 2 does not rule out a special end-time fulfillment at the conclusion of the church era. The book of Revelation focuses specifically on the ultimate consummation of Joel's remnant promise. The central part of John's Apocalypse, Revelation 12-14, concerns itself with the worldwide completion of the gospel mission of the church of Jesus Christ.

Employing the traditional imagery of the bride of Yahweh in the classical prophecies (Isa. 54, Eze. 16, Hosea 2), John paints the future of Christ's church as a persecuted woman who flees "into the wilderness," where God nourishes her for "one thousand two hundred and sixty days" (Rev. 12:6), or three and one-half "times" (verse 14). These prophetic periods suggest a particular eschatological application of Daniel's prediction of the persecution of the faithful saints in Daniel 7:25 to those Christian saints who were outlawed and executed during the reign of the papal state-church. John then continues to describe the final conflict of the remnant church after the 1260 years of the Middle Ages: "Then the dragon was angry with the woman, and went off to make war on the rest of her offspring, on those who keep the commandments of God and bear testimony to Jesus" (or Gr., "have the testimony of Jesus," Rev. 12:17).

John furthermore portrays the ultimate triumph of the faithful remnant on Mount Zion: "Then I looked, and lo, on Mount Zion stood the Lamb, and with him a hundred and forty-four thousand who had his name and his Father's name written on their foreheads" (Rev. 14:1). Revelation 12:17 and 14:1 together portray the fulfillment of Joel's remnant promise (Joel 2:28-32) for the end of the church age. Joel's remnant people who "call upon the name of the Lord" on Mount Zion (verse 32) are described in their end-time fulfillment: "Here is a call for the endurance of the saints, those who keep the commandments of God and the faith of Jesus" (Rev. 14:12; cf. 12:17). The three-fold message of Revelation 14 will produce the 144,000 spiritual Israelites (verse 1) who have been called out of Babylon in order to be gathered on Mount Zion, where the Lamb offers them eternal safety. In this way Revelation strongly suggests that Joel's prophecies, which were fulfilled as "the early rain" at the beginning of the church age, apply once more at its close on a global scale.

The apostolic church saw thousands of new believers added to its numbers (Acts 2:47; 4:4). So shall the remnant church witness the predicted influx of "believing remnants" of many peoples, who want to be instructed and saved on "Mount Zion" (Isa. 2:1-3; Micah 4:1, 2). After the final witness, all the followers of Christ will be part of the faithful "Israelites." Not one of them will be part of Babylon any longer (Rev. 14:4; 17:5). These companions of the Lamb are described as His "called and chosen and faithful" followers (Rev. 17:14).

In summary, the Apocalypse projects two opposing parties in the final conflict before God: Babylon and the Israel of God and Christ. Both are represented as worshiping communities and are, therefore, identified in terms of worship before God (Rev. 14:9-11). The true remnant people "obey God's commandments and hold to the testimony of Jesus" (Rev. 12:17, NIV). The importance of this recurring combination of "the word of God" and the "testimony of Jesus," in the Apocalypse (1:2, 9; 6:9; 12:17; 20:4) establishes it as a central theological theme in the book, even as the line of demarcation between Babylon and the Messianic Israel. As Kenneth A. Strand (133) concludes: "In the book of Revelation, faithfulness to the 'word of God' and to the 'testimony of Jesus Christ' separates the faithful from the faithless, and it brings about persecution that includes John's own exile and the martyrdom of other believers (cf. Rev. 1:9; 6:9; 12:17; 20:4; etc.)."

John's theology of the remnant is rooted in Ezekiel's vision of the deliverance of a repentant remnant among an idolatrous Israel in Jerusalem (Eze. 8; 9). Ezekiel saw six angels, appointed executioners of God's wrath, approach the apostate city of Jerusalem. Starting at the sanctuary of God, they were ordered to slaughter without pity or compassion all men, women, and children who did not have a specified mark on their forehead, placed there by a special angel who went in advance of the executioners, with a writing kit at his side. Fearing the destruction of all Israelites in God's retributive judgment, Ezekiel cried out, "Ah Lord God! wilt thou destroy all that remains of Israel in the outpouring of thy wrath upon Jerusalem?" (Eze. 9:8; cf. 11:13).

God's mercy is revealed, however, in His provision that through the discriminating judgment of a priestly man, "clothed in linen" (Eze. 9:2; cf. Rev. 1:13), the truly repentant ones will be exempted from divine wrath: "Go through the city . . . and put a mark upon the foreheads of the men who sigh and groan over all the abominations that are committed in it" (Eze. 9:4).

Revelation 7 applies Ezekiel's sealing vision to its end-time fulfillment. John hears in a vision that 144,000 Israelites (12,000 from each of 12 tribes) will be sealed on their foreheads with the "seal of the living God" by angels of God as the sign of divine approval and protection against the last destructive winds (verses 1-8). This revelation was the immediate reply to the anxious cry of those experiencing the terrors of the wrath of God and of the Lamb under the sixth seal: "The great day of their wrath has come, and who can stand before it?" (Rev. 6:17).

John's vision of the "sealing" of the "Israelites" or "servants of our God" (Rev. 7:3) before the final tribulation of the four destructive "winds" brings the comforting assurance that God will protect His faithful ones all over the world during the last tribulation. A faithful remnant people shall stand safe and secure from the destructive force of the seven last plagues (Rev. 16:1, 2). The righteous character of the true saints will be made evident when they choose to follow the Lamb and refuse to compromise with the antichrist powers in rejecting the "mark" of allegiance to the "beast" (Rev. 13:15-17; 14:1, 4; 22:11). Symbolically the 144,000 Israelites are spiritual "virgins" *(parthênoi)* "who have not defiled themselves with women" (Rev. 14:4). These "women" are further defined as the harlot Babylon and her daughters (verse 8; 17:4, 5), and represent apostate religion. The 144,000 true Israelites all follow the Lamb so that "in their mouth no lie was found, for they are spotless" (Rev. 14:5). In this respect the 144,000 function also as the end-time fulfillment of Zephaniah's promise of a faithful remnant: "For I will leave in the midst of you a people humble and lowly. They shall seek refuge in the name of the Lord, those who are left in Israel; they shall do no wrong and utter no lies, nor shall there be found in their mouth a deceitful tongue. For they shall pasture and lie down, and none shall make them afraid" (Zeph. 3:12, 13).

In direct contrast with those who have accepted the mark of the beast, the true Israel will receive the sign of divine approval on their foreheads (Rev. 14:1). They have the courage to confess Christ as the Lord of their thinking and acting. Their victory over the antichrist comes only because of their union with Christ in His death and resurrection. As overcomers of the antichrist, they will be rewarded with eternal honors around the throne of God, and they will sing the Song of Moses and the Lamb (verse 3; 15:2, 3).

B. Daniel's Time of the End

The apocalyptic phrase "time of the end" in the book of Daniel needs careful attention. This expression is found only in Daniel's visions concerning the "distant future" (five times in Daniel 8-12). It is not completely identical with the familiar phrase "the last days" or "days to come," as used 14 times by the OT prophets. While the classical prophets combine God's judgments in their own time *directly* with the final judgment, Daniel leads his readers from his own time down through the ages of redemptive history. His time frame extends beyond the violent death of the Messiah (Dan. 9:26) to the emergence of the anti-Messiah or antichrist (Dan. 7:8, 24, 25). He also predicts God's judgment upon that evil power. Daniel's sacred forecast covers the history of God's people from the OT to the end of time.

One unique characteristic of Daniel's prophecy is the clear determination of the time period allotted to the antichrist's rulership (7:25; 8:14, 17; 12:7). Daniel uses the phrase "the time of the end" to designate not the end of time but rather a certain time span that precedes the final judgment and the resurrection of the dead (Dan. 11:40; 12:1, 2). This apocalyptic "time of the end" will begin at a fixed time, at its appointed time (Dan. 11:35; cf. 8:19). This time seems to coincide with the completion of the 1260 years of papal church-state union in 1798 (Dan. 7:25), and with the subsequent restoration (in 1844) of the downtrodden sanctuary truth of Christ's high-priestly ministry (Dan. 8:14, 17; see Sanctuary III. C. 2. a, b).

Daniel's symbolic visions were not fully understood by the prophet himself (Dan. 8:27; 12:8). In fact, they could not be comprehended before the "time of the end" had arrived, because the interpreting angel announced, "But you, Daniel, shut up the words, and seal the book, until the time of the end. Many shall run to and fro, and knowledge shall increase" (Dan. 12:4). If the prophetic visions of Daniel point to the period immediately preceding the second advent of Christ, then the divine unsealing of Daniel's prophecies must produce practical results in the end-time. The increase of the knowledge of Daniel's book resulted in an interdenominational revival of apocalyptic studies and in a renewed hope of the nearness of the second advent of Christ. This led LeRoy E. Froom (PFOF 4:1209) to the conclusion, "It [Dan. 12:4] obviously is a forecast of the great revival in prophetic exposition that came under the simultaneous awakening in the nineteenth century, in both the Old World and the New." James White rightly warned that the promised "increase of knowledge" in Daniel 12:4, 10 does "not refer to the progress in scientific discoveries, but to the subject of the end" (ST July 22, 1880). He explained that "the truly wise, the children of God, understand the subject upon which knowledge increases in the time of the end, while the wicked, however scientific, do not understand. The facts in the case are decidedly against the position that the prophetic statement relative to the increase of knowledge in the time of the end has reference to the discoveries of the scientists" (ibid.).

The promise of Daniel 12:4 points to the providential rise of a worldwide awakening regarding apocalyptic prophecy in Holy Scripture. The significance of Daniel and Revelation dawned upon the Christian consciousness fully only in the mid-nineteenth century. Only then did the investigation focus on the meaning of Daniel 8 and of the reformation message of Revelation 14.

V. The Three Angels' Messages: God's End-time Message

The three angels' messages of Revelation 14:6-12 express heaven's final appeal to all people on earth to renounce every form of idolatry and falsehood, to worship the Creator and accept His everlasting gospel. In face of the final threat of the antichrist, God requires a twofold fidelity: faithfulness to Jesus' testimony and obedience to God's commandments (Rev. 14:12).

These angels are symbolic of Christian religious movements. Their location in time is quite obvious: The first angel announces that the final judgment has come (verses 6, 7), a message that ties in with Daniel 7:9-14; 8:14; this judgment started in 1844. (See Judgment III. B. 1.) The third one is immediately followed by the Lord's return (Rev. 14:14-16). Hence all are proclaimed between 1844 and Jesus' second coming. They constitute God's last appeal to humankind.

These three messages eventually merge into one threefold message. The first, which begins at a specific point in time, proclaims the everlasting gospel, which will be preached until the end of time (Matt. 28:18-20). At some point later the second angel (Rev. 14:8) proclaims a specific message about Babylon, a message that evidently will continue to the end, since Babylon is described as growing progressively worse and the same message is repeated until the seven last plagues come down upon her (Rev. 17:1-6; 18:2, 4, 8). In effect, the second message merges with the first. At a still later time the third angel follows "them" with the warning regarding the mark of the beast and the ultimate destruction of those who worship it and receive its mark (Rev. 14:9). Since the wrath of God (verse 10) likewise appears in the last seven plagues (Rev. 16:1-17), it is evident that this message continues to the end of time. Since it joins the other two, it is likewise obvious that to a certain degree the three messages coalesce to form one proclamation: the everlasting gospel with a certain end-time emphasis.

It is the role of the end-time people of God to preach this end-time threefold message (Rev. 14:12). They are the people described in the same chapter as keeping "the commandments of God and the faith of Jesus" (verse 12) and in Revelation 12:17 as a remnant that "keep the commandments of God and bear testimony to Jesus," or, more accurately translated, "who have the testimony of Jesus."

A. The Dramatic End-time Setting of Revelation 10

The meaning of the three angels' messages in Revelation 14 can be better understood if that segment of the prophecy is related to the vision of the "mighty angel" of Revelation 10. The angel who appears before the seventh trumpet sounds (verse 7) is "wrapped in a cloud, with a rainbow over his head, and his face was like the sun, and his legs like pillars of fire" (verse 1). This picture recalls the vision of the Son of man in Revelation 1:12-16 and Daniel's description of a majestic being in Daniel 10:5, 6 and 12:5-7. Revelation 10 introduces Christ's authoritative end-time message as the unsealing of Daniel's prophecies for the time of the end (Dan. 8-12). The subject of Revelation 10 is the creation of a new prophetic commission, similar to the one Ezekiel received when he became a prophet (Eze. 3:1-3). It is based on the "little scroll," open in the angel's hand (Rev. 10:2). He stands with both feet on sea and land, bringing a universal message for the end-time. With an uplifted right hand he swears with a solemn oath to the Creator that there will "be no more delay [*chronos,* time]" (verse 6), and that the seventh trumpet will soon sound and "the mystery of God" will be accomplished in fulfillment of prophecy (verse 7).

The angel of the seventh trumpet announces the joyful fulfillment of the Creator's purpose of all salvation history: "The kingdom of the world has become the kingdom of our Lord and of his Christ, and he shall reign for ever and ever" (Rev. 11:15). However, a more specific meaning is implied in the heavenly oath that "time" shall be no more, if one is willing to consider its root connection with Daniel's prophecies. Daniel predicted that the antichrist would be allowed to rule for three and a half times (Dan. 7:25; 12:7). When the mighty angel of Revelation 10 announces that all prophetic time periods (including those of

Daniel 8:14; 12:11, 12) have expired, there will be no more delay in the accomplishment of God's purpose (MS 59, 1900, in 7BC 971; Shea 1992, 302-316).

The command of the mighty angel is significant; it clearly calls on the end-time people of God (before the seventh trumpet sounds, Rev. 10:7), to "take the scroll which is open in the hand of the angel who is standing on the sea and on the land" and to "eat" it (verses 8, 9). This imagery was used by the OT prophets when they were called to assimilate a prophetic message from God (Jer. 15:16; Eze. 3:1-3). The end-time church—the remnant—must make the apocalyptic message of the scroll its own mission and mandate.

Daniel states explicitly that the end-time prophecies had been sealed up (Dan. 12:4). But that message would finally be *unsealed* or "opened" by God, according to Revelation 10:8; 22:10. The sacred promise of the divine angel of Revelation 10 reflects the same oath regarding prophetic times in Daniel 12:7 and assures of the joyful tiding that the prophetic time periods have expired and that the time is at hand for the dead to be judged and for the saints to be rewarded (Rev. 11:18). As William H. Shea (1992, 299) concludes: "In one case (Dan. 12:4), we have a scroll that is sealed until 'the time of the end.' In the other case (Rev. 10:2, 5-7), we have a scroll that has been opened in the end of time."

The emphatic elaboration of the angel's oath by the Creator of heaven, earth, and sea (Rev. 10:6) is remarkable. It forms a specific link with the first angel's message in Revelation 14:6, 7, which also calls for worship of God as the Creator. Both the theme and wording come directly from the fourth commandment of the Decalogue (Ex. 20:8-11). But the sweet hope of God's words (Ps. 119:103) will be experienced by God's servants with an unexpected bitterness (Rev. 10:9, 10). When the people of God announce the imminent advent of Christ, they will experience a bitter disappointment when their expectation is not realized as they had hoped. As the proverb says:

"Hope deferred makes the heart sick" (Prov. 13:12).

The resurgence of the antichrist, accompanied by the final test of faith and the outpouring of God's wrath still had to be accomplished (Rev. 15-18). However, the bitter disappointment experience was not in vain. It served a purpose in divine providence: to prepare a people to meet their God (Amos 4:12); to prepare the final Elijah movement that would bring the whole world to the final decision between Christ and the antichrist (Mal. 4:5, 6; Rev. 14:6-12). This commission is embedded in the heavenly command "You must again prophesy about many peoples and nations and tongues and kings" (Rev. 10:11). This mandate of the mighty angel (verse 11) is unfolded still further in the threefold angels' message of Revelation 14. The angels of Revelation 10 and 14 are intimately related, both representing the dramatic origin of the end-time remnant of God's people, who have a universal mission and divine credentials to proclaim a message of judgment based on the book of Daniel and its prophetic times.

B. The First Angel's Message (Rev. 14:6, 7)

"Then I saw another angel flying in midheaven, with an eternal gospel to proclaim to those who dwell on earth, to every nation and tribe and tongue and people; and he said with a loud voice, 'Fear God and give him glory, for the hour of his judgment has come; and worship him who made heaven and earth, the sea and the fountains of water' " (Rev. 14:6, 7).

The focal point of the book of Revelation is formally and substantially chapter 14. It is the specific chapter that deals with God's judgment (verses 7, 14-20). It follows after the antichrist (the sea beast) and his ally (the land beast) have accomplished their apostasy and persecution of the saints (Rev. 13). These chapters (Rev. 13; 14) constitute the detailed outworking of Daniel 7.

The parallelism of the alternate movements of the prophetic beacon light between heaven and earth in both Daniel 7 and Revelation 13, 14 is particularly important. Daniel 7:2-8 provides a historic outline of worldly empires, followed by the "little horn" power. This outline represents an earthly scene that is succeeded historically by a judgment scene in heaven (Dan. 7:9, 10). Daniel 7:11, 12, however, reverts to the earth to pursue the action of the little horn, as well as its destiny. Verses 13 and 14 focus on the heavenly scene of the coming of Christ in judgment. This sequence of events in Daniel 7 is followed and expanded in Revelation 13; 14: on earth (Rev. 13; cf. Dan. 7:2-8), in heaven (Rev. 14:1-5; cf. Dan. 7:9, 10), on earth (Rev. 14:6-13; cf. Dan. 7:11, 12), in heaven (Rev. 14:14-20; cf. Dan. 7:13, 14). In this connection it is significant that Daniel's phrase "one like a son of man" (Dan. 7:13) is repeated in Revelation 14:14. This supports Jacques B. Doukhan's conclusion (133): "The text of Daniel 7 seems, therefore, to be more than any other text in the mind of the author of Revelation 14." Comparing the progression of prophetic events in both Daniel 7 and Revelation 13; 14, Doukhan observes, "The judgment of heaven predicted in Daniel 7 and the shout of the three messengers of Revelation 14 coincide" (60).

The theological implication of this parallel situation of the heavenly court session in Daniel 7 ("the court sat in judgment, and the books were opened" [verse 10]) and the first angel's message, "Fear God and give him glory, for the hour of his judgment has come" (Rev. 14:7), is clear. The angel's announcement refers directly to the beginning of the heavenly court session of Daniel 7:9, 10. It announces to the whole family of earth that the final judgment in heaven has begun.

This heavenly tribunal begins only after the antichrist ("the little horn" of Daniel 7) has risen and ruled over the nations for three and a half prophetic times, or 1260 prophetic days (Dan. 7:25; Rev. 12:6, 14). This implies that the hour of God's investigative judgment in heaven would begin sometime after the 1260 years of religious intolerance and persecution had ended in A.D. 1798.

The first angel's appeal to "fear God" and to "worship Him" as the Creator of heaven and earth in the hour of heavenly judgment associates judgment with Creation: "And worship him who made heaven and earth, the sea and the fountains of water" (Rev. 14:7).

The Creator as the judge and Saviour of His own covenant people appears repeatedly in the writings of Moses, the prophets, and a number of psalms. Specifically, Israel's annual rituals of the Day of Atonement (Lev. 16) highlighted the judgment work of Yahweh as one who separates the truly repentant worshipers of the Creator from the impenitent worshipers on that annual "sabbath of solemn rest" (Lev. 23:27-32). The cleansing rituals of the Day of Atonement thus pointed to God's judgment of Israel as His professed covenant people, the great day of the Lord.

In the book of Daniel the vision "for the time of the end" (Dan. 8:17), or for "the appointed time of the end" (verse 19), culminates in the prediction "For two thousand and three hundred evenings and mornings; then the sanctuary shall be restored to its rightful state [literally, "shall be justified" or "vindicated"]" (Dan. 8:14). The LXX translates, "shall be cleansed."

On the basis of the parallelism between Daniel 7 and 8, the event of the end-time "vindication" of the sanctuary of God of Daniel 8:14 equals the heavenly court session of Daniel 7:9, 10. The appointed time for this judgment to begin is the end of the 2300 prophetic days or literal years according to the year-day principle. This period is initiated in 457 B.C., according to the angel's own elaboration of the Daniel 8 vision (Dan. 9:24-27). The period of 2300 literal years expires in A.D. 1844. (See Sanctuary III. C. 2. a. [2].) This year marks the beginning of God's judgment session in the heavenly sanctuary (Dan. 7:9, 10; 8:14, 17, 19). This fact the first angel announces: God's judgment has come. In itself such knowledge has no sanctifying value unless it is integrated in the urgency of the first angel's message:

"Fear God and give him glory, . . . and worship him" (Rev. 14:7).

These heavenly appeals are expressed in terms typical of the OT, which must be understood, therefore, in their setting in God's covenant of grace with ancient Israel. Moses often used the verb "to fear God" in connection with obeying God's commandments from a heart full of love for God and His work of deliverance (Deut. 5:29; 6:2; 8:6; 13:4). The Hebrew phrase "fear God" refers to a trembling reverence for God, expressed in loving obedience (see Deut. 10:12, 13; Eccl. 12:13). On the basis of God's gracious Exodus deliverance, Moses' appeal to Israel was: "You shall fear the Lord your God; you shall serve him and cleave to him, and by his name you shall swear." "You shall therefore love the Lord your God, and keep his charge, his statutes, his ordinances, and his commandments always" (Deut. 10:20; 11:1).

In this light the call of the first angel of Revelation 14 to "fear God and give him glory" is also an appeal to the Christian church to respond to Christ's atoning sacrifice with loving obedience to God's commandments. The angel's stress on worshiping God as the Creator of heaven and earth (verse 7) points unmistakably to the neglected fourth commandment of the law of God, the seventh-day Sabbath precept (Ex. 20:8-11). The purpose of the angel's call for the restoration of true worship is to prepare the inhabitants of the earth for the second coming of Christ. (See Sabbath III. E.)

C. The Second Angel's Message
(Rev. 14:8)

"Another angel, a second, followed, saying, 'Fallen, fallen is Babylon the great, she who made all nations drink the wine of her impure passion'" (Rev. 14:8). To understand the meaning of "Babylon" and her fall, it is mandatory to discern the typological connection of end-time Babylon with ancient Babylon in the history of Israel. The phrases used by the second angel are a conflation of doom oracles against ancient Babylon by Isaiah and Jeremiah: "Fallen, fallen is Babylon; and all the images of her gods he has shattered to the ground" (Isa. 21:9). "Flee from the midst of Babylon, let every man save his life! Be not cut off in her punishment, for this is the time of the Lord's vengeance, the requital he is rendering her. Babylon was a golden cup in the Lord's hand, making all the earth drunken; the nations drank of her wine, therefore the nations went mad" (Jer. 51:6, 7).

The literary and thematic correspondences between Revelation 14:8 (and 18:2-5) and OT prophecy establish the underlying structure of a Christian typology (LaRondelle 1983, 35-59). The *theological* characteristic of ancient Babylon is apparent in the OT: It was the archenemy of both Israel and her covenant God. It oppressed the people of God, took them into captivity to Babylon, blasphemed the God of Israel, and trampled the Temple of God underfoot from Nebuchadnezzar until Belshazzar. Babylon thus was at war on two fronts: against Yahweh, the God of Israel, and against the Israel of God. God's verdict of retribution was caused by the evil that Babylon had committed against Zion (Jer. 51:24) and against God's Temple (verse 11). Babylon was thus the antithesis of Zion, the Israel of God. Given the theological relationship between the Israel of old and the end-time people of God, the final remnant people represent the consummation of Israel's salvation history. Thus the same enmity exists between spiritual Babylon and the new covenant remnant.

The new covenant fulfillment of the final conflict between Israel (or Zion) and Babylon during the church age has no ethnic or geographic restrictions. Israel and Babylon in the Apocalypse must be defined theologically and Christologically, that is, in their relation to Messiah Jesus. The OT national terms are applied in Revelation on a universal scale, in relation to the worldwide church of Christ. As ancient Babylon invaded the land of Israel, destroyed its Temple, and carried away its people into captivity, so end-time Babylon attacks and enslaves the universal church of Christ, blasphemes the new covenant temple in heaven, and replaces Christ's divine intercession with a counterfeit system of mediation and worship (Rev. 13 and 17). Babylon is the archenemy of Christ's faithful followers (Rev. 17:6).

The symbolic portrayal of Babylon in Revelation 17 as the great "prostitute" is covenantal language borrowed from the OT prophets. Israel's prophets had portrayed the apostate covenant people repeatedly as the "wife" of Yahweh who had become in their time the greatest "prostitute" on earth (Isa. 1:21; Jer. 3:1-3, 8, 9; Eze. 16:15-34; Hosea 2:2, 4). Israel would not, therefore, escape its judgment, the covenant wrath of God. The OT story of Queen Jezebel and her cruel religious rule over the northern kingdom of Israel constitutes, in particular, the chosen model or type of the apostasy that would develop *within* the Christian church in the book of Revelation. This is the same apostasy that Paul foretold in 2 Thessalonians. Specifically, the church of Thyatira is charged with tolerating "the woman Jezebel" and her deceptive teachings and false worship (Rev. 2:20-23). Revelation 17 pictures the new Babylon as a murderous prostitute queen (verses 3-6) in exact antithesis to the pure woman of God whose children are persecuted and murdered (Rev. 12). In the Apocalypse Christ thus correlates Babylon with an unfaithful, fallen *church* rather than with the Roman Empire.

While the woman of Revelation 12 is rescued, the woman of Revelation 17 is destroyed by her former lovers (verse 16). The prophetic drama in Revelation 12 and 17 suggests a basic repetition of the history of Jezebel for the new covenant people of God. (See LaRondelle 1992, 157-163.) Since the prostitute was "sitting on a scarlet beast" (Rev. 17:3) in her war against the followers of Christ (verse 6), in its wider sense Babylon seems to include church and state on a world scale. It is said that "the kings of the earth have committed fornication" with the great harlot Babylon (verses 1, 2).

Apocalyptic Babylon as apostate Christianity culminates in an alliance of ecclesiastical and civil-political powers, "in order to consolidate religious control over public policy" (7BC 851). The result will be the death of many saints (Rev. 17:6).

In God's last warning message to the world, the first angel calls for a restoration of pure, apostolic worship (Rev. 14:6, 7). This appeal creates a new spiritual Israel of God in the end-time. Those who reject and oppose the revival of the eternal gospel by promulgating a counterfeit gospel and religious cultus are addressed by the second angel as fallen Babylon (verse 8). This divine sentence on Babylon thus follows the proclamation of the angel who creates the true Israel of the end-time.

The angel's verdict, "Fallen, fallen is Babylon the great" (verse 8), pronounces a divine court sentence and relates, therefore, primarily to the moral fall of Babylon. This verdict can be compared to the angel's writing on the palace wall of ancient Babylon, which only Daniel could understand. His explanation to Belshazzar was "You have been weighed in the balances and found wanting; . . . your kingdom is divided and given to the Medes and Persians" (Dan. 5:27, 28).

The historical fall of Babylon took place shortly after its moral fall was announced (Dan. 5:30, 31). Revelation likewise distinguishes between the end-time *verdict* of the fall of Babylon (Rev. 14:8; 18:2-8) and the actual *destruction* of Babylon under the seventh plague when probationary time has closed (Rev. 16:17-21; 18:20; 19:2). The second angel calls God's people to come out of fallen Babylon so they can escape participation in her culpability and judgment (Rev. 18:1-5).

D. The Third Angel's Message
(Rev. 14:9-11)

The third angel is said to "follow" the first two. At the same time, his message forms an unbreakable unit with the first and second angels' messages. While we have here an irreversible sequential order, all three continue in flight as one unified threefold message (see V. A).

"And another angel, a third, followed them, saying with a loud voice, 'If any one worships the beast and its image, and receives a mark on his forehead or on his hand, he also shall drink the wine of God's wrath, poured unmixed into the cup of his anger, and he shall be tormented with fire and sulphur in the presence of the holy angels and in the presence of the Lamb. And the smoke of their torment goes up for ever and ever; and they have no rest, day or night, these worshipers of the beast and its image, and whoever receives the mark of its name' " (Rev. 14:9-11).

The solemn warning of the third angel in Revelation 14 constitutes a specific mandate for the end-time church. It allows the church to face the totalitarian claims of the antichrist (the "beast" of Rev. 13) and to warn against the imposition of the mark of the "beast" on all the inhabitants of the earth. The warning message alerts true believers to the inescapable consequences of drinking the "wine" of Babylon. Whoever does, it says, "shall drink the wine of God's wrath, poured unmixed into the cup of his anger" (Rev. 14:10). The warning concerning the "unmixed" wrath of God (verse 10) suggests that God's judgment shall no longer contain His mitigating mercy, as in the past (Hab. 3:2; Dan. 9:11, 12, 16-18). The third angel announces the judgment, the seven last plagues, as the outpouring of God's wrath on Babylon (Rev. 15:1; 16).

The third angel sounds the most fearful threat ever addressed to mortals. As an indissolubly united message, the clear purpose of the threefold warning of Revelation 14:6-12 is to prepare the inhabitants of the earth for the second advent of Christ (see verses 14-20). The central theme of the message is expressed in Revelation 14:12: "Here is a call for the endurance of the saints, those who keep the commandments of God and the faith of Jesus." This text describes the result of the threefold warning message (verses 6-11). In spite of fierce opposition by the anti-Christian powers of the beast and its image, in spite of their threat against those who refuse to accept the mark of the beast, the saints of God persevere or endure in worshiping Him in "the fear of the Lord." The divine appeal to "fear God and give him glory" (verse 7) will be effective in that all over the world a faithful remnant of true worshipers endures (verse 12). The "fear of God" recalls the keeping of God's sacred commandments (Deut. 5:29; 8:6; 10:12, 13; Eccl. 12:13), which present a revelation of God's will and character.

The angel's appeal to worship God as the Creator of heaven and earth (Rev. 14:7) points directly to the Sabbath as the memorial of God's work of creation (Gen. 2:1-3). The remnant people of God are characterized not only by their obedience to God's covenant law, but also by keeping the "faith of Jesus" (Rev. 14:12). Such faith excludes the attitude of legalism or works-righteousness. This "faith of Jesus" means in the NT the faith that has Jesus and His teachings as its object: exercising faith in Jesus as God's Son and Messiah (John 6:29; James 2:1). In this sense Christ commended the church of Pergamum for keeping faith in His name and teachings to the point of martyrdom: "You hold fast my name and you did not deny my faith" (Rev. 2:13).

In Revelation 14:13 a voice from heaven blesses those "who die in the Lord henceforth," that is, during the final conflict with the rule of the beast. They are assured that "their deeds follow them!" which means that their fidelity to God's commandments and their living faith in Jesus in the end-time persecutions accompany the saints to the judgment and bring them the reward of divine approval. Eternal destinies are at stake in the final clash between Christ and the antichrist, the last great test of faith in Jesus.

The faithful ones in Revelation 14:12 are the same group of believers as "the remnant" of the woman's seed in Revelation 12:17 (KJV). Both Scripture passages stress the point that the end-time people of Jesus are keeping God's commandments through a living faith in Jesus and in His testimony to them (Rev. 19:10). They hold on to or maintain the apostolic gospel message that unites God's saving grace with His sacred law as the standard of character in the judgment (Rom. 2:12-16). For this sacred testimony of Jesus or "spirit of prophecy" the apostles and their followers had suffered persecution (Rev. 1:9; 6:9; 19:10). The end-time church of Christ will be loyal both to the commandments of God and to the testimony of Jesus (Rev. 12:17).

The third angel warns against the dreadful consequences of worshiping the beast and its image, and of receiving the mark of the beast either on the forehead or on the right hand (Rev. 14:9, 10). This conflict recalls Revelation 13:15-17, where the worldwide imposition of the mark of the beast on all peoples is portrayed. The end crisis is clearly of universal importance because ultimately it concerns the matter of true or idolatrous worship (verse 15; 14:9, 11; 16:2; 19:20). Therefore the mark is given in the context of religious cultus. A second beast, with two lamblike horns, also called the "false prophet," is able to force all to worship the sea beast through the deception of miraculous signs (Rev. 13:13, 14; 19:20).

Eventually, obedience to the cult of the sea beast is forced by the political enactment of the death sentence on all who refuse to worship the beast's image (Rev. 13:15). Finally, an economic boycott is implemented on those who have not received the mark of the beast (verses 16, 17). As a result, the acceptance of the mark signifies a public confession of faith in the allegiance to the authority of the anti-God forces, either by consent ("on the forehead") or by the mere act of compliance ("on the right hand"). The third angel's warning, on the other hand, announces that the possessors of the mark of the beast will incur the unmixed wrath of God, to be poured out in the seven last plagues. God's sign of approval and protection is called "the seal of the living God," which His angels place on the foreheads of all who reject the mark of the beast (Rev. 7:2, 3).

Just as the mark of the beast reflects the "name" or character of the antichrist (Rev. 13:17), so the sealing of God's servants in Revelation 7 reflects the confirmation of their Godlike moral character. This can be derived from the fact that God's seal is also called the Lamb's *name* and His Father's *name* (Rev. 14:1; cf. 22:4). The mark or seal indicates a relationship of belonging either to Christ the Lamb or to antichrist the beast. John deliberately portrays this antithesis. God has made rejection of the mark of the beast an essential qualification of the conquerors (Rev. 15:2; 20:4). The mark is totally antithetical to the seal placed on the followers of the Lamb. It represents the mentality of the antichrist, the disposition of self-exaltation and rebellion. Because the end-time seal of God represents the divine recognition of the obedience of faith to God's commandments (Rev. 12:17; 14:12), the mark of the beast represents a cultic sign of disobedience to one or more of God's commandments (see VI. H. 3).

E. The Promise of a Universal Pentecost (Rev. 18:1-8)

"After this I saw another angel coming down from heaven, having great authority; and the earth was made bright with his splendor" (Rev. 18:1). Revelation 18 is intimately related to Revelation 17. Both chapters deal with the same end-time Babylon and her consummation by fire (17:16, 17; 18:8). Revelation 17 portrays Babylon as the fallen woman, "the great harlot" (verse 1), while Revelation 18 describes Babylon more as a commercial empire, as the "great city" (verses 10, 16, 19). However, the oneness of the harlot and the city is explicit in Revelation 17:18. Revelation 18 also speaks of Babylon as a harlot queen (verses 3, 7); the clothing and adornments are the same (Rev. 17:4; 18:16), and in both chapters Babylon holds a cup (17:4; 18:6). More important, the actions of Babylon in chapters 17 and 18 are identical: an immoral relationship with the kings of the earth (17:2; 18:3), causing the intoxication of all earth dwellers, and more serious yet, the persecution unto death of God's faithful remnant who stand in opposition to Babylon (17:6; 18:24).

Both chapters contain God's timely response to Satan's final grasp for world dominion. The angel who is "coming down from heaven" (Rev. 18:1) is placed in deliberate contrast with the beast that "is to ascend from the bottomless pit and go to perdition" (Rev. 17:8). L. F. Were (151) distinguished between the two powers in Revelation 17, 18: "One presents the power of evil, particularly of religious persecution, rising in strength until the whole world is taken in the snare; the other represents special power which heaven will pour upon the remnant church in order to meet the rising power of evil."

The powerful angel of Revelation 18 meets the end crisis with a "loud cry" and added power to reinforce the second angel's message. The fall of Babylon is now worldwide and its rebellion against the eternal gospel is complete. "And he called out with a mighty voice, 'Fallen, fallen is Babylon the great! It has become a dwelling place of demons, a haunt of every foul spirit, a haunt of every foul and hateful bird'" (Rev. 18:2).

This "loud cry" constitutes the final call for God's people to separate from communion with Babylon and is the last warning against the renewed union of church and state as portrayed in Revelation 17. It is the ultimate plea of heaven to escape the impending outpouring of the seven last plagues. In the final conflict between the followers of the Lamb and the followers of the beast, Christ will be exalted with renewed Pentecostal power and glory (Rev. 18:1). Every individual will have to take sides. No one can remain neutral to the claims of Christ.

Ultimately the situation will become as in Jerusalem of old. As Jesus warned His disciples that when the time of Jerusalem's decreed destruction would come because of her definitive rejection of Him as the King-Messiah, they should flee from the doomed city before her judgment would strike (Matt.

24:15-20; Mark 13:14-18; Luke 21:20-24), so it will be at the end of time. The apocalyptic summons of Christ to His remnant people for the final exodus from the new Babylon comes as an integral part of the revived gospel message: "Come out of her, my people, lest you take part in her sins, lest you share in her plagues; for her sins are heaped high as heaven, and God has remembered her iniquities" (Rev. 18:4, 5). Babylon functions here precisely as the fallen and rebellious Jerusalem of Jesus' days: her sins have fi-nally "filled up" the measure of the guilt of her forebears, from the blood of the righteous Abel onward (Matt. 23:32, 35). As Jerusalem received her judgment only after rejecting the Pentecostal appeal of the risen Christ, so end-time Babylon will receive her judgment only *after* the last Pentecostal appeal of Christ. The final call to exit from degenerated Christendom forms the most dramatic antitype of all the previous commands to flee (Gen. 19:14-17; Jer. 51:6, 45; Matt. 24:15, 16).

VI. Historical Overview

Throughout Christian history different groups have arisen, in a sense remnant groups, with a burden to draw Christians of their day back to a more scriptural faith. While some have insisted that their faith was not entirely new, they held the Bible as their prime authority and longed to call the believers back to it. Although Seventh-day Adventists differ from these groups in various respects regarding doctrine and practice, they have in common with them the image of the remnant in the sense of bringing their contemporaries to a faith closer to the Scriptures.

A. Waldenses and Pre-Reformers

The Waldensian movement, commonly identified with Peter Waldo in the twelfth century, officially stressed the need for a return to the apostolic life of poverty and witnessing to the gospel. There is ample scholarly evidence to suggest that this movement may have predated Waldo himself.

Showing the same concern, others in the fourteenth and fifteenth centuries paved the way for the teachings of the Reformation. Among them were John Wycliffe (c. 1329-1384), John Huss (1369-1415), and Jerome (c. 1370-1416). While working independently, the three were united in open dissent from the established church's ritual and doctrinal teachings.

Setting the pace in the pre-Reformation development, John Wycliffe, in his sermons and writings upheld the supreme authority of the Bible for both clergy and laypeople. The many issues on which he disagreed with the Roman Catholic Church may be summarized under five main points: (1) the nature of the church, (2) the role and authority of the Roman pontiff, (3) the priesthood, (4) the doctrine of reconciliation, and (5) the use and authority of Scripture. On all these issues, Wycliffe's teachings were based on the literal sense and plain meaning of the Bible to which he wanted the church and his countrymen to return. Wycliffe's views were subsequently espoused by Huss of Bohemia and the latter's friend, Jerome, both of whom suffered martyrdom for their faith.

B. Luther, Calvin, and Zwingli

In the sixteenth century Luther (1483-1546), Zwingli (1484-1531), and Calvin (1509-1564) directed their protests against more than the dissolute life of church officials or the abuse of church practices. They aimed to radically reform doctrine concerned with the essence of the church, its structure, order, sacraments, and its message of salvation. Their protest was theological. Like their predecessors, they called for a fundamental return to the apostles' teachings on church policies and redemption, based on the Bible alone *(sola scriptura)*.

Martin Luther's ecclesiology included restoration of the biblical teaching of the priesthood of all believers and their responsibility to exercise personal faith in and obedience to the Word of God. On the basis of the Scriptures he identified as specific forms of the apostasy of the medieval church the dogma of transubstantiation, the sacrifice of the Mass as a renewal of Christ's sacrifice on the cross, and the mediatorial function of the church. This made his break with the Roman Catholic Church final and definitive. In his view, where the gospel as found in the Bible is proclaimed, there are Christ and His church, however weak and sinful it may be. He clearly restricted the true church to a remnant of faithful believers in the gospel of Jesus Christ.

Ulrich Zwingli, the Swiss Reformer, freely agreed with Luther's teaching on justification by faith, which he insisted that he also had received from the biblical authors themselves. His efforts to restore the Bible and the Bible alone as the supreme authority in the midst of the nominal Christian society of Zurich and Bern led in some ways to a more radical reformation than Luther attained. To restore a true people of God he rejected everything except that which could be proven by Scripture.

John Calvin, the French theologian, won Luther's respect with his famous *Reply to Cardinal Sadoleto* (1539), in which he discussed the relation of the authority of Scripture to that of the Church Fathers and councils. Along with the German Reformer he agreed that, contrary to widespread accusations, Protestants were not disrupting the harmony and peace of the church but restoring the ancient teaching of the apostles as understood by the early Church Fathers, as against later innovations introduced by the medieval Roman Catholic Church. Like Luther and Zwingli, Calvin professed that, although insignificant in number, the true church of the apostles is gathered and led only where the biblical word is faithfully preached. His theological insights, his skillful exegesis, his clear and precise language, along with his systematic presentations, make him one of the most influential writers among the Reformers, all of whom believed they had received the mission to restore the Christian church to its biblical purity.

C. The Anabaptists

The sixteenth-century Anabaptists, whose refusal to accept infant baptism led to their descriptive title, reinstituted the biblical baptism of believers and insisted on a faithful return to all scriptural teachings. Their various groups on the European continent, including Swiss Brethren, South German Brethren, Hutterites, and Dutch Mennonites, also taught pacifism and nonresistance. Often persecuted by both Roman Catholics and Protestants for their opposition to church-state unions and their staunch defense of religious tolerance and liberty, Anabaptists sought restoration of primitive Christianity with its apostolic concept of the church as presented in the NT. They urged all true Christians to leave Babylon. "Apostolic" was only that which was laid down in the teachings of Jesus Christ and the apostles. While most of them observed Sunday as their day of worship, some Anabaptist groups in Moravia and Silesia kept the seventh-day Sabbath holy as a Creation ordinance (Hasel 1967, 101-121; 1968, 19-28; Müller 110-130).

D. The Puritans

Eager to purify the Anglican Church from unscriptural and corrupt forms, sixteenth-century Puritans demanded express biblical warrant for all the details of church government and public worship. T. Cartwright, R. Field, and W. Travers denounced the institution of episcopacy itself, advocating a Presbyterian polity. In the seventeenth century, an increasing number of Puritans, even among Presbyterians and Congregationalists, expressed further concern for doctrinal purity and holiness of life.

Baptist Puritans, such as Thomas Helwys, associated infant baptism with the apostasy of the antichrist and condemned its practice as evidence that the Reformation was incomplete among the Protestant churches that retained it. Others advocated a return to the Christian observance of the seventh day of the week, insisting, with Edward Stennett, for instance, that the seventh-day Sabbath should be restored in the last days (Müller 167). By the mid-1650s many Seventh Day Baptist churches were established in England.

Equally noteworthy, some Puritans emphasized the study of biblical prophecy, especially the books of Daniel and Revelation. Joseph Mede, William Hicks, John Napier, and others stressed the crucial importance of interpreting these two books, maintaining that their visions form an organic and related whole in the chronological sequence (Ball 193-212).

The Puritans were convinced that the ultimate issue was that of authority in matters of faith and practice. They identified the papal system with the antichrist—in the sense of "counter-Christ"—and exhorted their contemporaries to come out of the Roman Catholic Church, continuing the interpretation of the Reformation.

E. The German Pietist Movement

One of the founders of German Pietism, seventeenth-century Philipp Jacob Spener, sought to inspire new vigor in the lifeless official Protestantism of his time. Spener and August Hermann Francke, his disciple, were convinced that by exclusive stress on dogmatic orthodoxy, Lutheranism in Germany had ceased to be a living faith.

Like the Anabaptists, Spener and Francke desired to carry the Reformation to its logical conclusion, i.e., restoration of the teachings and lifestyle of the early church as described in the Scriptures, as well as recovery of the ethical motif of imitating Christ. Their independent outlook, along with an effort to give to the laity a genuine part in church life, met with increasing opposition from Lutheran orthodoxy. Spener and Francke's enthusiasm for reform of the Lutheran Church, together with their insistence on the inner religious life of individual believers, deeply influenced European Protestantism.

F. The Methodist Movement

As the spiritual fire of English Puritanism waned and the English nation fell prey to lifeless deism, the Methodists initiated a revival of the gospel stressing the experience of deliverance from sin. Launched by John and Charles Wesley, this revival movement in the Anglican Church started in 1738. At first the Wesleys had no thought of seceding from the Anglican Church. Their aim was to make contact with the indifferent masses, clergy, or laypersons, to meet them in their own environment. Finding the church increasingly closed to them, they adopted a new method of preaching that spoke directly to laypeople, called them to accept justification by faith alone, and to reform their lifestyles according to the Scriptures. Lay preaching, open-air services, and a personal experience of justification and salvation were the hallmarks of this reform movement.

G. The Millerite Revival
of the Advent Hope

William Miller (1782-1849), a farmer and Baptist lay preacher, proclaimed the imminent return of Christ in glory. He based his message on the book of Daniel and at first calculated that Christ's coming would take place about 1843.

Taking the Bible as its own interpreter, Miller rejected the popular views of contemporary revivalists such as Charles G. Finney, that Christ would return spiritually in a temporal millennium prior to the end of the world and that the Jews would return to Palestine to restore a theocracy. Miller was a vigorous premillennialist who taught that Christ would come in glory *before* the millennium. He exhorted his contemporaries to prepare for Christ's imminent return.

By 1840 Miller's message received a new impetus when his revival broadened nationwide. At the same time, it became an interdenominational movement including the Methodist minister Josiah Litch, the Presbyterian-Congregationalist pastor/rectors Charles Fitch and Henry Jones, Joshua V. Himes from the Christian Connection, and Episcopalian Henry Dana Ward.

The common purpose of their crusade was not to create a new church or denomination but to save sinners from death and to prepare a people ready for the imminent coming of the Lord. In the 1840s, when a firm date was set for the Advent, opposition arose from various Protestant churches. Their objection was not only to the prophetic time calculations but also to the premillennial advent of Christ.

Even among prominent Millerite lecturers there was disagreement on the question of time setting. By mid-1842 the Millerites sharpened their position on the time (between March 21, 1843, and March 21, 1844), premillennialism, and on rejection of a new Jewish theocracy in Palestine. This development led Henry Ward and Henry Jones to leave them. Church doors once open now were closed and Millerism's relationship with the various churches became cold.

Although Miller himself never advised Adventists to separate from their respective churches, in July 1843 Charles Fitch began to preach a call based on Revelation 18 to come out of Babylon. He equated the fall of apocalyptic Babylon with the fall of all Christendom. For him and those who followed him, Babylon as the antichrist included all the churches in Protestant and Catholic Christendom. His appeal was clear: "If you are a Christian, *come out of Babylon!* If you intend to be found a Christian when Christ appears, *come out of Babylon,* come out Now!" (19).

H. The Adventist Understanding

While the majority of the Millerite Adventists interpreted the great disappointment of 1844 as a failure of their time calculation, a minority group held that the mistake was not related to the time-setting but to a misunderstanding of the nature of the event that took place on October 22, 1844. Hiram Edson interpreted the Disappointment as a fulfillment

of John's sweet and bitter experience in his prophetic vision of Revelation 10:8-10. He explained the actual fulfillment of the cleansing of the sanctuary of Daniel 8:14 as the beginning of the final phase of Christ's heavenly ministry in the sanctuary above. "This group," according to Froom (PFOF 4:840, 841), while "holding to the validity of the 1844 movement as a fulfillment of prophecy, saw in the Disappointment a test of those who were willing to make every sacrifice to be ready to meet their Lord, and then to hold their faith in the face of bitter disappointment." They gradually came to believe that Christ's final cleansing ministry had only opened a new door to a worldwide proclamation of the everlasting gospel (Rev. 3:8; 10:9-11; EW 42, 43; GC 428, 429).

In 1837 a former Methodist, Rachel Oakes, became a Seventh Day Baptist in the state of New York. Joining the Millerites in 1843 in New Hampshire, she led a former Methodist pastor, Frederick Wheeler, to accept the biblical Sabbath in March 1844. He created the first nucleus of Sabbatarian Adventists in Washington, New Hampshire. A few months later the Millerite preacher T. M. Preble, a former Baptist pastor, accepted the Sabbath and through his pamphlet (1845) a prominent Millerite, Joseph Bates, became convinced of the Sabbath. In 1846 Bates wrote the first comprehensive Adventist treatment of the Sabbath: *The Seventh Day Sabbath; A Perpetual Sign From the Beginning to the Entering Into the Gates of the Holy City, According to the Commandment.* This 48-page booklet led James and Ellen White to accept the Sabbath truth in the winter of 1846.

Three key teachings, each developed independently, merged into one message that began to characterize the movement of the Sabbatarian Adventists: Christ's final ministry in the sanctuary, the Sabbath as a sign of obedience to God's commandments, and the application of the phrase "testimony of Jesus" to a new manifestation of the prophetic gift through Ellen G. White (1827-1915) in the "remnant" church (Rev. 12:17; 14:12; 19:10). These distinctive concepts began to be integrated into a unified body of belief during six Bible conferences held in the northeastern United States in 1848. The participants held in common a belief that in the post-1844 period all biblical truth had to be restored among God's remnant people before the Second Advent would take place. They agreed on seven principal points, which came to be called the "landmarks" or fundamentals. These formed the "firm platform" of present truth on which the emerging Seventh-day Adventist Church was built. Specifically, they were (1) the imminent Second Advent, (2) the continuous historical interpretation of the major time prophecies of Daniel and Revelation, (3) the conditional immortality of human beings, (4) Christ's beginning of His final ministry in the heavenly sanctuary in 1844, (5) the seventh-day Sabbath, (6) the renewed manifestation of the Spirit of Prophecy, and (7) the historical fulfillment of the three angels' messages of Revelation 14 in the revivals of the Millerites and the new Sabbathkeeping Advent movement (PFOF 4:1030, 1031; CW 30, 31; A. L. White 38-40).

It is apparent from this new platform of "present truth" that the Sabbatarian Adventists were bound together by their continuing confidence in the imminent return of Christ. They based their new mission on the third angel's message of Revelation 14:9-12, specifically on Revelation 14:12: "Here is the patience of the saints: here are they that keep the commandments of God, and the faith of Jesus" (KJV). They applied Revelation 14:12 to the "patient waiting time" *after* the 1844 disappointment. In this way they integrated the Sabbath doctrine into their Advent experience, endorsing the moral law as kept in the heavenly sanctuary (Rev. 11:19). The gathering of Sabbathkeeping Adventists was the reunion of those Adventists who had been looking for Christ in 1844 and were now designated as the "remnant" (EW 38, 66, 70, 74, 86, 114, 255).

1. The First Angel's Message

The first of the three angels' messages (Rev. 14:6-11) was accepted by William Miller and his followers (1831-1844) as God's endtime call for reform in worship and true preparation for the second coming of Christ. He identified the phrase "the hour of his judgment has come" (Rev. 14:7) with the judgment scene of Daniel 7:9, 10 and applied "the hour" of God's judgment to the Papacy under the French Revolution (Damsteegt 45). In 1843, however, he began to interpret the phrase as a warning of the day of judgment soon to come, the second coming of Christ (*ibid.*; GC 375). Ellen G. White endorsed this interpretation of Revelation 14:7 as the right message at the right time, stating, "The first of these warnings [in Revelation 14] announces the approaching judgment" (GC 311; cf. 1SG 133-140; GC 379). She declared, "It was here [in America during the Millerite movement] that the prophecy of the first angel's message had its most direct fulfillment" (GC 368). The first angel's message of Revelation 14:7 was thus treated "as a symbolic representation of the Millerite missionary experience" (Damsteegt 46).

Following the great disappointment of 1844, a small group of Millerites restudied the apocalyptic prophecies of Daniel and Revelation. They reinterpreted the "cleansing of the sanctuary" in Daniel 8:14 to indicate the closing judgment work of Christ's ministry in the Most Holy Place of the heavenly sanctuary, not the cleansing of the church or the earth at Christ's second coming. They applied the phrase of the first angel, "the hour of his judgment has come" (Rev. 14:7) to the beginning of the heavenly work of judgment by Christ in A.D. 1844 (Dan. 7:9, 10), which will last until the close of human probation. This interpretation of Revelation 14:7 became the impetus for preparing a people for the final judgment. At its center was a worshipful, sanctified life in harmony with the moral law of God, as described in Revelation 14:12. This clearer understanding of the first angel's message of Revelation 14 revealed new duties and played an important role in the formation of the Seventh-day Adventist Church.

2. The Second Angel's Message

As with the first angel, the Millerites applied the second angel's message to their own historical situation. Before 1843 they held the general Protestant viewpoint that the Roman Catholic Church was Babylon. Its fall (Rev. 14:8) was seen as the fall of Rome to French civil domination in 1798 (Damsteegt 47).

When leading Protestant churches began to reject Millerite enthusiasm about the imminent return of Christ in 1843, Miller began to apply Christ's message for the Laodicean church in Revelation 3:14-22 to the Protestant churches. Charles Fitch applied "Babylon" to the Protestant churches because of their sectarianism, heresies, and thirst for power (*ibid.* 79, 80). By the summer of 1844 some Millerite leaders began to call for separation from all churches. The separation was supported with the theological argument that Babylon was "the mother of harlots and abominations of the earth," according to Revelation 17:5. The implied "daughters" were viewed as symbolizing the petrified Protestant denominations. Their different creeds were presented as the confusion of "Babylon" (*ibid.* 82, 83). Consequently, the heavenly call of Revelation 18:2, 4, to "come out of her, my people," was interpreted as God's call to leave all organized religion in 1844.

As the Seventh-day Adventist Church developed, the word "Babylon" came to be applied to both the Protestant and Catholic churches who had formed unlawful alliances with secular governments. The "fall" of Babylon (Rev. 14:8) and the heavenly call to "come out of her" (Rev. 18:4) were now applied specifically to the spiritual fall of the Protestant churches after their rejection of the first angel's appeal for severance from a sinful union with the world (GC 383). The great sin charged against Babylon by the second angel is that she "made all nations drink the wine of her impure passion" (Rev. 14:8). This intoxicating "wine" was interpreted as "the false doctrines" that are "opposed to the plainest statements of Holy Writ" (*ibid.* 388).

Representing the Sabbatarian Adventists, J. N. Andrews (51-53; 68, 69) pointed to several essential errors that had turned the various factions of Christendom into Babylon: (1) the doctrine of infant baptism; (2) the unlawful and criminal union of the church with the civil power of the state, causing the pure church to become the intolerant and persecuting prostitute of Revelation 17; (3) the doctrine of a millennium of peace and prosperity on earth before the advent of Christ; (4) the change of the fourth commandment into a demand for the Sunday-Sabbath; (5) the doctrine of the natural immortality of the soul, derived from pagan mythology; (6) the spiritualizing of the second advent of Christ.

At first the appellation "Babylon" was believed to have "a more direct application to the churches of the United States" (GC 389), because of their rejection of the judgment messages by the Millerites. Consequently, the moral fall of Babylon "did not reach its complete fulfillment in 1844" (*ibid.*). Babylon had not yet intoxicated all nations. The union of the church with the world had not yet reached its culmination.

Hence the moral fall of Babylon was interpreted as an ongoing, increasing, universal process. Ellen G. White stated, "The change is a progressive one, and the perfect fulfillment of Revelation 14:8 is yet future" (*ibid.* 390). This would be the result of rejecting the threefold warning of Revelation 14 and was foretold in 2 Thessalonians 2:9-12. Such resistance justified a final call to come out of the fallen churches, the final "loud cry" of Revelation 18:1-5. Consequently, the Adventist pioneers acknowledged that many of God's people, including ministers of the gospel, still remained in the fallen churches.

The second angel's message is valid only if it follows and accompanies the authentic proclamation of the apostolic gospel of the first angel (Rev. 14:6, 7). False worship is unmasked most fully by a demonstration of true worship.

3. The Third Angel's Message

A theological understanding of the third angel's message finally emerged among Sabbatarian Adventists during a series of Bible conferences in 1848. As their sanctuary theology developed, they followed Christ by faith into the Most Holy Place. From Revelation 11:19 they derived the abiding validity of God's covenant, with its sacred ark containing the Decalogue. Considering Revelation 14:12 as the central truth of the third angel's message, they identified the commandments of God with the Ten Commandments. In 1846 Joseph Bates convinced James and Ellen White that the fourth commandment should be restored in the true worship of God.

E. G. White viewed the seventh-day Sabbath as "the separating wall between the true Israel of God and unbelievers" (EW 33), although she acknowledged at the same time that "God had children who do not see and keep the Sabbath" *(ibid.)*. This concept elevated the Sabbath truth to the status of a sealing message (Rev. 7:2) or testing truth for standing with the remnant church of Revelation 14:12. "The faith of Jesus" (verse 12) was interpreted as *"all* the teachings of Jesus in the New Testament" (Damsteegt 194) or "the precepts and doctrines of the gospel" (Andrews 135).

Although for several years the phrase "the testimony of Jesus" (Rev. 12:17, KJV) was used as a synonym for "the faith of Jesus," a new interpretation emerged in the 1850s. Now "the testimony of Jesus" was linked with the prophetic gift manifested in the ministry and writings of Ellen G. White (cf. Rev. 19:10). This interpretation became an identifying sign of the remnant church of Revelation 12:17 and was integrated into the missionary proclamation of the Seventh-day Adventist Church.

The interpretation of "the beast and its image" (Rev. 14:9-11) came to be of vital impor-

tance for the understanding of the third angel's message. In 1851 J. N. Andrews identified the beast of Revelation 14:9-11 with the beast of Revelation 13:1-10, which was a prophetic development of the fourth beast of Daniel 7. Both symbolic beasts (Dan. 7 and Rev. 13) ascend out of the sea. After listing five other points of similarity, Andrews concluded (76), "The beast is evidently the papal form of the fourth empire; for it receives its power and seat from the dragon, imperial Rome. Verse 2." As the medieval state church, it would rule over the saints for 42 months (Dan. 7:23-26; Rev. 13:5-8). This period ended in 1798 with the "deadly wound" (Rev. 13:3), from which the beast was to recover. Andrews concluded that "an image to the beast, then, must be another ecclesiastical body clothed with power and authority to put the saints to death. This can refer to nothing else but the corrupt and fallen Protestant Church" (105).

Both Andrews and Bates agreed on the imposition of the mark of the beast as an "institution of the Papacy enforced by Protestantism" (PFOF 4:1101). Andrews interpreted the "mark" as Sunday enforcement, in opposition to the saints who are engaged in keeping the commandments of God: "Notwithstanding the fourth commandment in the plainest terms enjoins the observance of the sanctified rest day of the Lord, almost all the world now wonders after the beast, and observes the pagan festival of Sunday, which the great apostasy has substituted for the holy Sabbath" (108). He noted, however, that "Sundaykeeping is not yet the mark of the beast, and will not be until the decree goes forth causing men to worship this idol sabbath. The time will come when this day will be the test, but that time has not come yet" (MS 118, 1899).

With this understanding of the three angels' messages as the last warning message, Seventh-day Adventists came to believe they stood on "a solid, immovable platform" (1SG 169); the sanctuary theology and the Sabbath truth united to comprise "present truth." The timeliness of the third angel's message, which calls for restoration of the apostolic gospel and worship, stands out more fully against the rise of modern liberal theology and evolutionism, which spiritualize away the Creation accounts of Genesis 1; 2. A major feature of the Seventh-day Adventist message lies in the fact that it "directly meets the key heresy of our age, the evolution theory, and calls on all who wish to come out of Babylon, out of apostasy, to accept the true sign of allegiance to the living God, the Creator" (Nichol 709).

Ellen White stressed the inextricable union of the Sabbath and the messages of the three angels as follows: "Separate the Sabbath from the messages, and it loses its power; but when connected with the message of the third angel, a power attends it which convicts unbelievers and infidels, and brings them out with strength to stand, to live, grow, and flourish in the Lord" (1T 337).

Hence, according to Seventh-day Adventist theology, accepting the seventh-day Sabbath implies acceptance of the eschatology of the threefold message of Revelation 14. Above every reform of worship, however, the three angels convey the urgent call to choose Jesus as personal Lord and Saviour and to remain loyal to Him through the final crisis (Rev. 14:1-5).

VII. Seventh-day Adventists and the Remnant Church

According to article 12 of their 1980 Statement of Fundamental Beliefs, Seventh-day Adventists believe that "the universal church is composed of all who truly believe in Christ, but in the last days, a time of widespread apostasy, a remnant has been called out to keep the commandments of God and the faith of Jesus. This remnant announces the arrival of the judgment hour, proclaims salvation through Christ, and heralds the approach of His second advent. This proclamation is symbolized by the three angels of Revelation 14" (*SDA Yearbook* 1981, 6).

Adventists see themselves as a fulfillment of apocalyptic prophecy, a prophetic movement called to prepare a people in all parts of the earth to be ready for Christ's appearance. They consider themselves collectively to be the fulfillment of the promised Elijah in Malachi 4:5, 6, sent by God "to restore all things" (Matt. 17:11). Therefore, they are committed to restoring all the neglected Bible truths of the new covenant. They see their message as the ultimate fulfillment of Isaiah 58:12-14, combining ideas of restoration and preparation.

They emphasize certain truths revealed in the end-time prophecies as testing truths, which reflect their understanding and historical applications of the three angels' messages.

They emphasize the restored gospel truths of justification by faith in Christ Jesus and sanctification in willing obedience from a redeemed heart to the covenant law of God, the law by which God will judge His covenant people (James 2:12; Rom. 2:13; 2 Cor. 5:10). They believe that the seventh-day Sabbath of the fourth commandment, altered into the Sunday-Sabbath by the postapostolic church, now should be restored as the appointed sign of worshiping the Creator in truth and in the Spirit (Isa. 56; 58; Dan. 7:25; Mal. 4:5, 6). They view the restored Sabbath as a providential testing truth to counteract the modern dogma of evolution, one of the key heresies of the end-time. To them the Sabbath celebration is not an isolated test of the correct day of the week, but an appointed sign of true worship of the Creator by a redeemed and sanctified people. They honor the biblical teaching that professed believers are saved by grace and judged by the works produced by their relation with Christ.

Seventh-day Adventists believe it their appointed role as the remnant church to restore revealed truth in worshiping God as Creator-Redeemer by restoring the seventh-day Sabbath as the memorial of His creation and the sign of giving Him glory. Based on the urgency of this message, they summon God's children in all churches to flee from the historic apostasy to escape punishment for Babylon's sins under the seven last plagues, and instead, to receive the fullness of God's Spirit and be ready to meet Christ in His glory (Rev. 18:1-5).

The summons of the first angel to give "glory" to God as the Creator (Rev. 14:7) led Adventists to take more seriously their accountability for the well-being of the human body and mind as the soul temple of God's Spirit (1 Cor. 6:19, 20). From their beginnings Seventh-day Adventists have promoted a style of healthful living and abstinence from all harmful habits (1 Cor. 10:31) as part of letting their light shine before men (Matt. 5:14-16).

Another specific application of Bible prophecy became a prominent characteristic of the Seventh-day Adventist Church. In Revelation 12:17 the remnant community is described as "those who keep the commandments of God and bear testimony to Jesus" (lit. "have the testimony of Jesus").

Adventist pioneers identified "the testimony of Jesus" not only with the testimony that Christians bear when they witness for their Saviour but more specifically the testimony of Jesus Himself, the witness He bore in His own life while on earth and continues to bear through the centuries in and through His servants the prophets.

They found their understanding corroborated by John who, when relating the words of the angel, explains that "the testimony of Jesus is the spirit of prophecy." The angel had just told him that he was "a fellow servant with you and your brethren who hold [lit. "have"] the testimony of Jesus" (Rev. 19:10). Later he repeated the expression in almost identical terms, "I am a fellow servant with you and your brethren the prophets" (Rev. 22:9). In the first instance he refers to "your brethren who hold [lit. "have"] the testimony of Jesus"; in the second, the text reads "your brethren the prophets." Therefore, those who have the testimony of Jesus are the prophets, recipients of the spirit of prophecy, who mani-

fest the spiritual gift granted to the church until the end of time.

When in Revelation 12:17 the Scriptures describe the remnant church as having the testimony of Jesus, they characterize it as having the gift of the spirit of prophecy, a gift that in the Bible is exercised through the prophets. Through the years Seventh-day Adventists have believed that the gift of prophecy has been manifest among them in the work of Ellen G. White. For seven decades, as God's messenger to the Advent people she gave messages of counsel and warning received as truly from God as messages of the prophets in days of old. These messages were, however, noncanonical. (See Gifts XI. A-E.)

Such an identification with the remnant church of prophecy (Rev. 12:17; 14:6-12) offers no ground for a spirit of exclusivism or triumphalism. Instead, Seventh-day Adventists understand their mission as the antitype of the ancient exodus movements of Israel from Egypt and Babylon. Such a comparison serves to heighten a sense of responsibility and self-criticism. In 1867 Ellen G. White wrote, "Modern Israel are in greater danger of forgetting God and being led into idolatry than were His ancient people. Many idols are worshiped, even by professed Sabbathkeepers" (1T 609). This self-evaluation holds the remnant church fully accountable to Christ. Those who are the final remnant people of God in history will be a spiritual people who "will include every true and faithful follower of Christ" (QOD 194) among many denominations and religions.

When in the future the Holy Spirit descends with Pentecostal power on the remnant church all over the world (Rev. 18:1), the issues in the conflict between Christ and Satan will be made fully clear to all (verses 2-8). The purified remnant church then will become the nucleus around which all the genuine people of God will cluster. Only during the final outpouring of God's Spirit will the gospel in its fullness separate all people into two visible camps as

"Babylon" and "the Israel of God." The impact of this apocalyptic perspective on Christian believers is to choose *now* wholeheartedly for Christ as Lord and Saviour, to uplift Christ and His redemptive work before the world, and to demonstrate by a Christian lifestyle that Jesus lives within their hearts and is their pattern of holiness.

VIII. Ellen G. White Comments

"The fourteenth chapter of Revelation is a chapter of the deepest interest. This scripture will soon be understood in all its bearings, and the messages given to John the revelator will be repeated with distinct utterance" (RH Oct. 13, 1904).

"Christ is coming the second time, with power unto salvation. To prepare human beings for this event, He has sent the first, second, and third angels' messages. These angels represent those who receive the truth, and with power open the gospel to the world" (7BC 978, 979).

"It is for the interest of all to understand what the mark of the beast is, and how they may escape the dread threatenings of God. Why are men not interested to know what constitutes the mark of the beast and his image? It is in direct contrast with the mark of God. [Ex. 31:12-17 quoted.]

"The Sabbath question will be the issue in the great conflict in which all the world will act a part. [Rev. 13:4-8, 10 quoted.] This entire chapter is a revelation of what will surely take place [Rev. 13:11, 15-17 quoted]" (*ibid.* 979).

"John was called to behold a people distinct from those who worship the beast and his image by keeping the first day of the week. The observance of this day is the mark of the beast" (*ibid.*).

"The third angel's message has been sent forth to the world, warning men against receiving the mark of the beast or of his image in their foreheads or in their hands. To receive this mark means to come to the same decision as the beast has done, and to advocate the same ideas, in direct opposition to the Word of God" (*ibid.*).

"Religious powers, allied to heaven by profession and claiming to have the characteristics of a lamb, will show by their acts that they have the heart of a dragon, and that they are instigated and controlled by Satan. The time is coming when God's people will feel the hand of persecution because they keep holy the seventh day. Satan has caused the change of the Sabbath in the hope of carrying out his purpose for the defeat of God's plans. He seeks to make the commands of God of less force in the world than human laws.

"The man of sin, who thought to change times and laws, and who has always oppressed the people of God, will cause laws to be made enforcing the observance of the first day of the week. But God's people are to stand firm for Him. And the Lord will work in their behalf, showing plainly that He is the God of gods" (*ibid.* 975).

"The Word of God plainly declares that His law is to be scorned, trampled upon, by the world; there will be an extraordinary prevalence of iniquity. The professed Protestant world will form a confederacy with the man of sin, and the church and the world will be in corrupt harmony.

"Here the great crisis is coming upon the world. The Scriptures teach that popery is to regain its lost supremacy, and that the fires of persecution will be rekindled through the timeserving concessions of the so-called Protestant world" (*ibid.* 975).

"The time is at hand when Satan will work miracles to confirm minds in the belief that he is God. All the people of God are now to stand on the platform of truth as it has been given in the third angel's message. All the pleasant pictures, all the miracles wrought, will be presented in order that, if possible, the very elect will be deceived. The only hope for anyone is to hold fast the evidences that have confirmed the truth in righteousness" (RH Aug. 9, 1906).

"Those who love and keep the commandments of God are most obnoxious to the synagogue of Satan, and the powers of evil will manifest their hatred toward them to the fullest extent possible. John foresaw the conflict between the remnant church and the power of evil, and said, 'The dragon was wroth with the woman, and went to make war with the remnant of her seed, which keep the commandments of God, and have the testimony of Jesus Christ.'

"The forces of darkness will unite with human agents who have given themselves into the control of Satan, and the same scenes that were exhibited at the trial, rejection, and crucifixion of Christ will be revived. Through yielding to satanic influences, men will be transformed into fiends; and those who were created in the image of God, who were formed to honor and glorify their Creator, will become the habitation of dragons, and Satan will see in an apostate race his masterpiece of evil— men who reflect his own image" (*ibid.* Apr. 14, 1896).

"There are only two parties upon this earth—those who stand under the blood-stained banner of Jesus Christ and those who stand under the black banner of rebellion. In the twelfth chapter of Revelation is represented the great conflict between the obedient and the disobedient [Rev. 12:17; 13:11-17 quoted]" (7BC 974).

"We are living in a momentous period of this earth's history. The great conflict is just before us. We see the world corrupted under the inhabitants thereof. The man of sin has worked with a marvelous perseverance to exalt the spurious sabbath, and the disloyal Protestant world has wondered after the beast, and has called obedience to the Sabbath instituted by Jehovah disloyalty to the laws of the nations. Kingdoms have confederated to sustain a false sabbath institution, which has not a word of authority in the oracles of God" (RH Feb. 6, 1900).

"The Sabbath question is to be the issue in the great final conflict, in which all the world will act a part. Men have honored Satan's principles above the principles that rule in the heavens. They have accepted the spurious sabbath, which Satan has exalted as the sign of his authority. But God has set His seal upon His royal requirement. Each Sabbath institution, both true and false, bears the name of its author, an ineffaceable mark that shows the authority of each.

"The great decision now to be made by every one is, whether he will receive the mark of the beast and his image, or the seal of the living and true God" (ST Mar. 22, 1910).

"Sundaykeeping is not yet the mark of the beast, and will not be until the decree goes forth causing men to worship this idol sabbath. The time will come when this day will be the test, but that time has not come yet" (7BC 977).

"The Lord has shown me clearly that the image of the beast will be formed before probation closes; for it is to be the great test for the people of God, by which their eternal destiny will be decided. [Rev. 13:11-17 quoted.] . . .

"This is the test that the people of God must have before they are sealed. All who prove their loyalty to God by observing His law, and refusing to accept a spurious sabbath, will rank under the banner of the Lord God Jehovah, and will receive the seal of the living God. Those who yield the truth of heavenly origin and accept the Sunday sabbath will receive the mark of the beast" (*ibid.* 976).

"When the Protestant churches shall unite with the secular power to sustain a false religion, for opposing which their ancestors endured the fiercest persecution; when the state shall use its power to enforce the decrees and sustain the institutions of the church—then will Protestant America have formed an image to the Papacy, and there will be a national apostasy which will end only in national ruin" (ST Mar. 22, 1910).

"There are many who have never had the light. They are deceived by their teachers, and they have not received the mark of the beast.

The Lord is working with them; He has not left them to their own ways. Until they shall be convicted of the truth, and trample upon the evidence given to enlighten them, the Lord will not withdraw His grace from them" (7BC 976).

"Those who have in their foreheads the seal of the infinite God will regard the world and its attractions as subordinate to eternal interests" (RH July 13, 1897).

"Christ says that there will be those in the church who will present fables and suppositions, when God has given grand, elevating, ennobling truths, which should ever be kept in the treasure house of the mind. When men pick up this theory and that theory, when they are curious to know something it is not necessary for them to know, God is not leading them. It is not His plan that His people shall present something which they have to suppose, which is not taught in the Word. It is not His will that they shall get into controversy over questions which will not help them spiritually, such as, Who is to compose the hundred and forty-four thousand. This those who are the elect of God will in a short time know without question.

"My brethren and sisters, appreciate and study the truths God has given for you and your children. Spend not your time in seeking to know that which will be no spiritual help. 'What shall I do to inherit eternal life?' This is the all-important question, and it has been clearly answered. 'What is written in the law? how readest thou?' " (7BC 978).

"We need not wait till we are translated to follow Christ. God's people may do this here below. We shall follow the Lamb of God in the courts above only if we follow Him here. Following Him in heaven depends on our keeping His commandments now. We are not to follow Christ fitfully or capriciously, only when it is for our advantage.

"We must choose to follow Him. In daily life we must follow His example, as a flock trustfully follows its shepherd. We are to follow Him by suffering for His sake, saying, at every step, 'Though he slay me, yet will I trust in him.' His life practice must be our life practice. And as we thus seek to be like Him, and to bring our wills into conformity to His will, we shall reveal Him" (RH Apr. 12, 1898).

IX. Literature

Andrews, J. N. *The Three Messages of Revelation XIV, 6-12.* 5th ed. rev. Battle Creek, Mich.: Review and Herald, 1892.

Ball, Bryan W. *The English Connection. The Puritan Roots of Seventh-day Adventist Belief.* Cambridge: James Clarke, 1981.

Beale, G. K. *The Use of Daniel in Jewish Apocalyptic Literature and the Revelation of St. John.* Lanham, Md.: University Press of America, 1984.

Bruce, F. F. *New Testament Development of Old Testament Themes.* Grand Rapids: Eerdmans, 1970.

Charles, R. H. *Eschatology.* New York: Schocken, 1963.

————. *A Critical and Exegetical Commentary on the Revelation of St. John.* 2 vols. ICC. Edinburgh: T. & T. Clark, 1920.

Damsteegt, P. G. *Foundations of the Seventh-day Adventist Message and Mission.* Grand Rapids: Eerdmans, 1977.

Daniels, A. G. *The Abiding Gift of Prophecy.* Mountain View, Calif.: Pacific Press, 1936.

Doukhan, J. B. *Daniel: The Vision of the End.* Berrien Springs, Mich.: Andrews University Press, 1987.

Emmerson, W. L. *The Reformation and the Advent Movement.* Hagerstown, Md.: Review and Herald, 1983.

Fitch, Charles. *Come Out of Her, My People.* Rochester, N.Y.: J. V. Himes, 1843.

Forestell, J. T. "The Letters to the Thessalonians." *The Jerome Biblical Commentary.* Ed. R. E. Brown and others. Englewood Cliffs, N.J.: Prentice Hall, 1968.

Froom, LeRoy. *The Prophetic Faith of Our Fathers.* 4 vols. Washington, D.C.: Review and Herald, 1950-1954.

Giblin, C. H. *The Threat to Faith: An Exegetical and Theological Re-examination of*

2 Thessalonians 2. Analecta Biblica 31. Rome: Pontifical Biblical Institute, 1967.

Hasel, Gerhard F. "Sabbatarian Anabaptists of the Sixteenth Century." *Andrews University Seminary Studies* 5 (1967): 101-121; 6 (1968): 19-28.

————. *The Remnant: The History and Theology of the Remnant Idea From Genesis to Isaiah*. 3rd ed. Berrien Springs, Mich.: Andrews University Press, 1980.

Ladd, G. E. *The Last Things: An Eschatology for Laymen*. Grand Rapids: Eerdmans, 1978.

LaRondelle, H. K. *The Israel of God in Prophecy: Principles of Prophetic Interpretation*. Berrien Springs, Mich.: Andrews University Press, 1983.

————. *Chariots of Salvation: The Biblical Drama of Armageddon*. Washington, D.C.: Review and Herald, 1987.

————. "Babylon: Anti-Christian Empire." In *Symposium on Revelation*. Ed. Frank B. Holbrook. Silver Spring, Md.: Biblical Research Institute, 1992. Vol. 2, pp. 151-176.

Müller, Richard. *Adventisten, Sabbat, Reformation*. Studia Theologica Lundensia. Lund: CWK Gleerup, 1979. P. 38.

Nichol, F. D. *Answers to Objections*. Washington, D.C.: Review and Herald, 1952.

Shea, W. H. *Selected Studies on Prophetic Interpretation*. Silver Spring, Md.: Biblical Research Institute, 1982.

————. "The Mighty Angel and His Message." In *Symposium on Revelation*. Ed. Frank B. Holbrook. Silver Spring, Md.: Biblical Research Institute, 1992. Vol. 1, pp. 279-326.

Smith, U. *The Prophecies of Daniel and the Revelation*. 2 vols. Rev. ed. Washington, D.C.: Review and Herald, 1944.

Strand, K. A. "The Two Witnesses of Rev. 11:3-12," *Andrews University Seminary Studies* 19 (1981): 127-135.

Walther, Daniel. "Were the Albigenses and Waldenses Forerunners of the Reformation?" *Andrews University Seminary Studies* 6 (1968): 178-202.

Were, L. F. *The Woman and the Beast in the Book of Revelation*. Berrien Springs, Mich.: First Impressions, 1983.

Wesley, John. *The Works of John Wesley*. 14 vols. London: Wesleyan Methodist Book Room, 1831.

White, Arthur L. *Ellen G. White: Messenger to the Remnant*. Washington, D.C.: Ellen G. White Estate, 1954.

White, James. *Bible Adventism*. Battle Creek, Mich.: Seventh-day Adventist Pub. Assn., 1877; reprinted Nashville: Southern Pub. Assn., 1972.

Wilcox, F. M. *The Testimony of Jesus*. Washington, D.C.: Review and Herald, 1944.

Williams, George H. *The Radical Reformation*. Philadelphia: Westminster, 1962.

Wordsworth, Christopher. *Is the Papacy Predicted by St. Paul? An Inquiry*. Cambridge: Harrison Trust, 1985.

The Second Coming of Jesus

Richard P. Lehmann

Introduction

The second coming of Jesus is a cardinal doctrine of Scripture, appearing already in the OT. The "day of the Lord" was to be a dark day for the wicked, but a day of joy for those who love His appearing (Isa. 35:4). However, a full understanding of the Second Advent would only follow Christ's first advent.

Jesus Himself foretold His return (Luke 21:27; John 14:1-4) and this promise was confirmed by the angels who ministered to the sorrowing disciples as Christ ascended to heaven (Acts 1:11). That Christ would "appear a second time . . . to save those who are eagerly waiting for him" (Heb. 9:28) was the "blessed hope" of Paul and early Christian believers (Titus 2:13).

Although the precise moment of the Advent is not known (Matt. 24:36), Christ set forth signs that point to His coming (verses 3-33). In preparation for this climactic event, when Christ shall "repay every one for what he has done" (Rev. 22:12), Christians are advised to watch and pray that they may be able "to stand before the Son of man" in that day (Luke 21:36).

The Second Coming finds its place in the name "Seventh-day Adventist." The pioneers felt that belief in Christ's second coming was sufficiently important to warrant a place in the name of the "little flock" when it became a church in 1860. Today God's people on earth eagerly await Jesus' return to earth, along with prophets and apostles and many faithful throughout the centuries.

I. The Second Coming in Scripture
A. OT Terminology
   1. The Day of Yahweh
   2. The Choice of a Remnant
   3. The Establishment of a Kingdom
   4. The Return to Paradise
   5. Apocalypticism
B. NT Terminology
   1. The Parousia
   2. The Epiphany
   3. The Apocalypse
C. The Center of Hope
   1. The Hope
   2. Maranatha
   3. Thanksgivings
   4. The Son of Man
D. The Kingdom of God
   1. A Transcendental Kingdom

   2. A Mysterious Kingdom
   3. A Spiritual Kingdom
   4. A Future Kingdom
E. Manner of His Coming
   1. Personal and Literal
   2. Visible and Audible
   3. Glorious and Triumphant
   4. Cataclysmic
   5. Sudden
F. The Signs of the Second Coming
   1. Some Difficult Texts
   2. Signs in the Natural World
   3. Signs in the Moral World
   4. Signs in the Religious World
   5. False Signs
   6. A Mistakenly Interpreted Sign
G. The Reasons for Jesus' Second Coming
   1. To Gather the Chosen

I. The Second Coming in Scripture

The theme of Christ's second coming recurs in both the Old and New Testaments.

A. OT Terminology

For OT authors, just as God delivered His people from Egypt, He would set them free from this world's bondage on the "day of the Lord" (Isa. 13:6, 9; Eze. 13:5).

1. The Day of Yahweh

The central theme of OT eschatology (doctrine of the *eschaton,* "the end") is the coming of Yahweh (Andreasen 31-45). The prophets frequently speak of "that day" (Zech. 14:9), about "those days" (Joel 2:29), or, like Daniel, about a "time" when salvation would take place (Dan. 12:1). The "day of Yahweh" is awaited as a decisive event of history, with changes on both the sociopolitical and cosmic level. The coming of Yahweh would initiate a new creation. Because He is the Creator, Yahweh is also the master of history, and the One who will bring it to its end (Amos 4:13; cf. Rev. 14:6, 7).

The disasters that follow one another and the deplorable moral condition of Israel and the nations call for God's intervention. But the end does not come as a consequence of political, social, or moral evil. It occurs because God comes. The tragedy lies in the apathy of the nations, which continue in their ways, not taking this coming into account. The prophets urge Israel and the nations to "seek the Lord" (Zeph. 2:1-3), for without preparation they would not be able to stand in the presence of the holiness of Yahweh. Amos summarizes the prophets' cry when he says, "prepare to meet your God, O Israel" (Amos 4:12).

a. A historical event. The coming of Yahweh cannot be separated from history. It is not a coming beyond time, but an irruption of God in history. The present historical events convey meaning, announcing a great theophany (manifestation of God). This can be compared with the enthronement of a sovereign who has vanquished his enemies.

This coming is already perceptible as God

comes close to His children when they worship Him (Ex. 20:24). He enters His holy temple and His worshipers celebrate His presence (Ps. 24:7-10).

God also comes in the events of history in order to deliver or to punish His people. This coming is both happy (Isa. 35:4) and terrible (Amos 5:18-20).

God can also come through His anointed Shiloh (Gen. 49:10, KJV), "the Prince of Peace" (Isa. 9:6), the One who bears the Spirit in His fullness (11:2), and who will rule with Yahweh's majesty and strength (Micah 5:1-3).

God comes finally to accomplish the promise of the eschaton. All the other comings are guarantees of the ultimate Advent. He comes at "the end of the days" (*bᵉʾaḥᵃrît hayyāmîm*) in order to show His royalty with power and to renew all things for the happiness of those who have expected Him (Isa. 2:1-4; Hosea 3:5; Micah 4:1-4).

b. A climactic event. The ultimate coming of Yahweh is announced as climactic and without appeal. The prophets present it as "a day of darkness and gloom" (Joel 2:2; Amos 5:18; Zeph. 1:15), a day of anger and wrath (Zeph. 1:18; 2:2), "a day of distress and anguish" (1:15), a "day of vengeance" (Isa. 34:8; Jer. 46:10), of retribution (Hosea 9:7), and of punishment (Isa. 10:3).

The disasters experienced by Israel and the nations are summarized in Jeremiah's trilogy as sword, famine, and pestilence (Jer. 14:12), interim tokens of the final judgment, anticipating the final day of Yahweh, which will burn like an oven (Mal. 4:1-3). The final day is not a local event from which one may escape, because the whole earth is affected by the coming of Yahweh (Isa. 2:12-19; Zeph. 3:8; Mal. 4:1). Every person must face God's judgment (Amos 5:18-20).

c. A judgment day. The prophets stress the ethical content of Yahweh's coming. The Lord Almighty comes to judge His people and the nations. He comes to condemn unfaithfulness toward His law, which has been treated with contempt, and to reestablish justice. Adultery, rape, oppression, lies, and violence deserve their penalty (Amos 2:7; Mal. 3:5). Even in the practice of religion, scorn and pride appear (Mal. 1:6-14; 3:7-9). God will repay all according to their deeds (Isa. 59:18), and all the evildoers will burn like stubble on the coming day (Mal. 4:1).

But if Yahweh is the holy God who punishes sin, He is also the God of mercy who forgives and saves (Ex. 20:5, 6; Isa. 6:6, 7). Those who have repented and entered into His covenant (Jer. 31:31-34) will receive salvation (Isa. 59:20; Jer. 26:13; Eze. 18:31, 32). A remnant will be saved.

2. The Choice of a Remnant

The idea of a remnant suggests terrifying events that destroy everything, leaving only a residue. Amos describes the remnant as "two legs" and "a piece of an ear" rescued "from the mouth of the lion" (3:12), "a brand plucked out of the burning" (4:11). For Isaiah, there are only two or three berries on the olive tree after it has been shaken (17:5, 6). Gerhard Hasel has shown that this theme is linked to the account of the Flood (1980: 374, 375). The remnant is found again in Jesus' eschatological speech (Matt. 24:37-41) in connection with the Flood and with the end of the world.

From this small remnant, from the stump of the felled tree (Isa. 6:13) a new humanity will appear. By giving his son the name of Shearjashub, Isaiah expresses the notion that *only* a remnant will be saved, those who remain faithful to Yahweh's covenant (7:3; 10:21).

The prophets emphasize that the remnant will be formed only in part by Israel (Amos 9:12). It will also include other nations (Isa. 56:6, 7). The election of the remnant lies not so much in its own righteousness as in God's faithfulness. God's grace produces a new community through His covenant. It is not the result of a long historical ripening process, but of God's breaking into history (Hasel 1980:396; see Remnant/Three Angels I-IV).

3. The Establishment of a Kingdom

The eschatological hope of Israel focused upon the restoration of a kingdom which would stand forever and never be destroyed (Dan. 2:44). This would be the kingdom of the Davidic Messiah according to the promise (2 Sam. 7:12-16).

This kingdom is presented in two contrasting ways. On one hand it rises modestly, as the charismatic kings whose common features are enhanced by an almost unexpected birth, but who then go on to obtain a great victory through faith. Isaac, Jacob, Joseph, Samson, and Samuel received the fruits of faith by experiencing victory over weakness through faith. Cases of obscure and modest origin appear in the stories of Gideon, Jephthah, Saul, and even David (Micah 5:1, 2) all born of families of little influence. Power came to these saints not because of their own personal might but because God's spirit rested upon them (Zech. 4:6). This was to be the fate of the shoot that came forth from the dry stump, as announced in Isaiah 11:1, 2 and 53:2.

Beyond the kingdoms foretold we come to the reign of the Son of man. Of a radically superior nature, this kingdom already is suggested in Daniel 2:44, 45, but clearly defined in Daniel 7:13. The one coming with the clouds of heaven is none other than a divine figure (cf. Eze. 1:4; 10:3, 4). Jewish nationalism is surpassed by a universal and transcendental perspective. The kingdom comes from above, together with the one riding upon the clouds of heaven.

4. The Return to Paradise

After the Babylonian captivity, the culmination of alienation, would come a great return, both of God and of His people. It is presented as almost Paradise, when communion with God would be perfect.

Isaiah and Ezekiel clearly announce a reestablishment of Edenic conditions (Isa. 51:3; Eze. 36:35). Showers will fall in season (Eze. 34:26; Joel 2:23), and the fields will produce abundantly (Isa. 30:23; Eze. 34:27; Joel 3:18; Amos 9:13; Zech. 8:12). Life expectancy will be uncommonly long (Isa. 65:20), and there will be peace among animals (Isa. 11:6-8) and humans (Isa. 2:4; Micah 4:3, 4). God Himself, like a shepherd, will care for His flock (Isa. 40:11) and reign over Zion (Isa. 52:7). Evil will disappear. Prompted by a new spirit, the people of God faithfully will follow divine instruction (Eze. 36:25-27). The first love will be reestablished (Hosea 2:16-20).

5. Apocalypticism

This new age does not grow out of the old. It is a new creation. The present age is under the control of evil; salvation must come from outside.

Thus, the prophet Daniel describes history from God's point of view (Dan. 2). Interpreting Nebuchadnezzar's dream of the metal image, he announces the succession of world empires and the cataclysmic manner in which the end will come. Beginning with the neo-Babylonian Empire (605-539 B.C.), he foresees the Medo-Persian (539-331 B.C.), the Hellenistic (331-168 B.C.), and the Roman Empires (168 B.C.-A.D. 476) that follow one another. No other empire succeeds Rome, but different nations occupy its territory. Finally, after the period of the divided nations, a kingdom represented by a stone is set up by God. It pulverizes all the former kingdoms, and stands forever (Dan. 2:36-45). Jesus Christ identified this stone with Himself (Luke 20:17, 18).

Anxious about the spiritual implications of such a narrative, the prophet was informed that evil would abound. In related visions in Daniel 7 and 8, the same world empires are represented by terrible animals, which devour, break in pieces, and speak great things (Dan. 7:4-8). An ultimate outgrowth of the last animal, a horn, extends its action over the religious world, oppressing the saints and thinking to change times and laws (verses 23-25). It casts truth down to the ground (Dan. 8:9-12). Here Daniel foretells the way the Papacy, spiritual Rome, would take up political power and act through the centuries.

Such oppression calls for a judgment (Dan. 7), which is pronounced against the arrogant horn. So the universal authority of the Son of man is established.

The starting point of this judgment is given: after 2300 days. According to the year-day principle, this would be after 2300 years (Shea 56-88; Schwantes 462-474). The terminal point seems far away, but it is in harmony with the visions of chapters 2 and 7, which locate God's intervention as following the evil activities of the last power. A careful study of the links between this prophecy and the 70 weeks of Daniel 9 leads to the establishment of the date of 1844 as the starting point for the pre-Advent judgment. (See Hasel 1986:378-461; see Judgment III. B. 1. a; Sanctuary III. C. 2. a; Remnant/Three Angels V. B.)

This pre-Advent judgment is implicit in Jesus' statements about the end of the world. When the end comes, the sheep and the goats already have been identified (Matt. 25:32, 33); so have the tares and the wheat (13:30). In the OT, as in the New, there is no final decision without careful inquiry (Job 10:6; cf. Gen. 6:5, 12; Deut. 17:4; 19:18).

These are, in brief summary, the trends in OT thought about the eschatological expectation. They shape the framework for hope in the NT.

B. NT Terminology

The NT has retained various forms of OT statements concerning the "day of the Lord," applied in particular to the second coming of Christ. For this reason Jesus refers to His return using terms such as "on that day" (Matt. 7:22) and "of those days" (24:19). It will be "the last day" (John 6:39) and a "day of judgment" (Matt. 10:15). The apostle Paul recognizes it as "the day of wrath" (Rom. 2:5) and "the day of our Lord Jesus Christ" (1 Cor. 1:8). The apostle Peter calls it "the day of God" (2 Peter 3:12).

The vocabulary of the NT on this topic is more varied than that of the OT. In order to speak about the last day of history, the day when Christ will come, the NT employs the Greek words *parousia, epiphaneia,* and *apokalypsis.* These words underline the transcendental aspect of the Messiah's second coming. (See Fagal 46-64.)

1. The Parousia

In the Hellenistic world, *parousia* had a double connotation. It meant both a presence and an arrival which filled up an absence. The word was also used for the epiphany of a god. Christians appropriated the term and filled it with fresh meaning.

The NT characterizes the advent of Christ in various ways. Paul uses the expression "the day of the Lord" as equivalent to parousia (1 Thess. 4:15; 5:2). Peter uses both terms together when he speaks about "the parousia of the day of the Lord" (2 Peter 3:12). Thus, parousia becomes an eschatological term linked to the "day of Yahweh" in the OT.

Parousia also evokes the royal character of the event. The emphatic use of the title *Kyrios* (Lord), in connection with the Parousia, belongs to the imperial protocol (1 Thess. 4:16, 17). In that connection one finds references to the crown, to the joy (2:19), and to the gathering of the faithful, who go out to meet the royal procession (4:17). The royal connotation of this word continues in the NT: the Parousia will destroy all principalities and hostile powers, including Satan, the evil one, and death itself. After all enemies are annihilated, all things will be submitted to Christ (1 Cor. 15:24-26). In the NT the Parousia is a glorious and regal manifestation of Christ.

2. The Epiphany

The verb *epiphainō* (to show, to appear) and its related noun *epiphaneia* (appearance, revelation) occur infrequently in the NT. They have rich meanings, which help us to understand how the first Christians viewed the second coming of Christ. Two of the four uses of the verb refer to light shining in darkness (Luke 1:79; Acts 27:20). The other two underline the visible, perceptible character of God's grace and love in the person of Jesus Christ at the time of His first coming (Titus 2:11; 3:4).

The noun is employed in the Pastoral Epistles to characterize both the appearances of Christ before Pentecost (2 Tim. 1:10), and at His second coming at the end of time (1 Tim. 6:14). Thus, these words speak of Christ's incarnation, of His appearance at the resurrection, and of the Second Coming. This threefold use focused the faith of the early church upon the visible nature of Christ's second coming.

The context of the use of *epiphaneia* in 2 Timothy 4:1, 8, underlines the imminent eschatological character of the expectation. In the form of a confession of faith, Christ's appearance is coupled with the last judgment. The association of *elpis* (hope), *epiphaneia* (manifestation), and *doxa* (glory) in Titus 2:13 emphasizes the expectation of a visible event. When the announcement of the appearance of the lawless one just before Christ's second coming (2 Thess. 2:8) is added to these testimonies, the word *epiphaneia* is seen as stressing the visible nature of the appearance of Christ at the end of time.

3. The Apocalypse

The term *apocalypsis* (revelation, apocalypse) is employed in the NT to show that something that was previously hidden now is revealed. The word is used for the mystery of salvation (Rom. 16:25), the gospel (Gal. 1:12), and a plan to be followed (2:2).

The term refers also to a manifestation. This sense is evident wherever the word designates the glorious second advent of Jesus Christ from heaven. Christ's glory is still hidden (Luke 17:30). It is perceived only by the eyes of faith (Eph. 1:17, 19), but it will be manifested one day (Acts 3:21). The One who is to come will return. He will descend from heaven in His glory (2 Thess. 1:7; 1 Peter 4:13). Believers live in expectation of that day (1 Cor. 1:7; 1 Peter 1:7).

C. The Center of Hope

This examination of the vocabulary and major themes of the Old and New Testaments concerning the end of the world has shown that the hope of God's coming in the OT and of Jesus Christ's return in the NT represent the culmination of all biblical eschatology.

1. The Hope

A deep yearning for the second coming of Jesus is present everywhere in the NT. It is related to hope for righteousness (Gal. 5:5), glory (Col. 1:27), resurrection (Acts 24:15), salvation (1 Thess. 5:8), and eternal life (Titus 1:2). It is based on God Himself (1 Tim. 4:10). Jesus promises to come again (John 14:3, 28). He announces His glory (Matt. 24:30) and pledges not to be the unrighteous judge who ignores those who cry to Him day and night (Luke 18:6-8). The endurance of those who trust Him to the end will not be in vain (Matt. 10:22).

However, the "blessed hope, the appearing of the glory of our great God and Savior Jesus Christ" (Titus 2:13) should not be confused with ordinary human hope. Hope, in the common sense of the word, is an aspiration, a wish for the future. It desires something not presently in hand, of uncertain possession.

Biblical hope, on the other hand, has a sure anchor (Heb. 6:19). It lies in the mighty deeds of God in the past: God has delivered His people from Egypt; Jesus Christ "came to his own" (John 1:11), died for our sins and was resurrected for our justification (Rom. 4:25). Biblical hope stands on this rock, which is the power of God "accomplished in Christ when he raised him from the dead and made him sit at his right hand in the heavenly places," above all earthly powers (Eph. 1:20, 21). This is a living hope based upon the present sovereignty of Jesus, who has been made Lord and Christ (Acts 2:36). He has become "a forerunner on our behalf" in the heavenly sanctuary (Heb. 6:19, 20).

Christian hope is based upon something

already accomplished, to which Christ Himself witnesses (1 Cor. 15:19, 20). Through the Holy Spirit (Rom. 5:5) the God of hope calls the chosen (Eph. 1:18) and fills their hearts with hope (Col. 1:27). Without God there would be nothing for which to hope (Eph. 2:12); with God, hope strengthens faith and mobilizes love (Col. 1:4, 5).

2. Maranatha

Eschatological hope always has been dear to the heart of Christians. The persistence of the ancient Aramaic formula *marana tha* (1 Cor. 16:22) in church tradition testifies to this fact. This prayer that "our Lord will come" has been kept in its original form, like the prayer pronounced in Aramaic by Jesus (*abba,* "Father," Mark 14:35). *Marana tha* is translated into Greek in Revelation 22:20.

The importance of this prayer in the early church worship service shows how much the church lived in expectation of the Second Coming. That return was also anticipated in the Communion service: the apostle Paul said that partaking of the Communion bread and cup constituted a proclamation of faith in the coming of the Lord (1 Cor. 11:26). In both expectation and announcement the Second Advent found its place at the very heart of the early church liturgy.

3. Thanksgivings

Thanksgiving also occupied an important place in the early church liturgy, particularly the Communion service. The apostle Paul used thanksgivings as introductions to his letters to the churches. A thanksgiving contained the elements of faith common to all those who pronounced it. When the apostle appealed to the churches, he wrote about the giving of thanks, to which his readers could say "Amen."

Most thanksgivings end with a reference to the Second Advent (1 Cor. 1:7; Eph. 1:10; Phil. 1:6; 1 Thess. 1:10; 2 Thess. 1:7-10; cf. also 1 Peter 1:5). The reference to the Second Coming in the thanksgiving formula demonstrates how the hope of the Second Advent lay at the very heart of faith and worship in the apostolic church. For the church, the present "coming" of Jesus to His own through His Holy Spirit constituted the pledge of the heritage to come (Eph. 1:13, 14). The coming of the Spirit was not the final promise; the Son of man was still to come in the clouds of heaven.

4. The Son of Man

Jesus often applied the title "Son of man" to Himself. The term is derived from Daniel 7:13, where the Son of man appears as an eschatological being, endowed with the divine attributes and fulfilling royal Messianic power (Ferch 174). This is confirmed by mention of the cloud upon which He travels and the power to judge attributed to Him (Dan. 7:13, 14).

The title "Son of man," which Jesus adopted for Himself, helps explain the Parousia. By employing this title, Jesus announced His identity; the formula expresses a concrete aspect of His earthly existence. In the same way He clearly indicated how and why He will return. First, the One who must come is the One who has come; the resurrected Christ is recognized by His human characteristics (Luke 24:30, 31, 41-43; John 20:20, 27). Second, He was carried up into glory by a cloud (Acts 1:9), and on a glorious cloud He will return (Rev. 1:7). Fulfilling the functions mentioned in Daniel 7, He is coming to judge the world (Matt. 25:31-33). Finally, because of well-recognized links between Daniel 2 and 7, His coming must occur at the end of this world's history. Jesus identified Himself as the stone that causes the symbolic image of this world's kingdoms to be shattered (Dan. 2:34; Luke 20:18). With the coming of the Son of man in glory the kingdom of God is finally and forever established (Matt. 25:31).

D. The Kingdom of God

The announcement of the kingdom of God deserves a special place, for the hope of the kingdom occupies a central place in OT eschatology. If Yahweh is the One who rules over the earth and the nations (Ps. 29; 47; 74; 89; 93; 96-99), His eternal kingdom is also expected (Dan. 2:34, 44), and it will be established on Yahweh's great day (Zech. 14:9; Obadiah 15, 21; Isa. 2:12-21; 24:21-23). Long before the Davidic monarchy, the kingdom of God was celebrated in song (Ex. 15:1-18; Num. 23:21, 22; Deut. 33:5). In Jesus' teaching the NT gives to the kingdom an even more important role.

1. A Transcendental Kingdom

The Gospel writers mention more than 100 references to the kingdom in Jesus' teaching (see, for example, Mark 1:15; Luke 9:60; 22:18). In Matthew Jesus spoke especially about the kingdom of *heaven* (32 times; cf. Matt. 3:2; 7:21; 8:11). This special feature of Matthew has sometimes been ascribed to the writer's concern for the sensitivities of his Jewish readers, who may have been shocked by the frequent use of God's name. However, Matthew's preference for the term seems to be based more upon theological than psychological concerns.

In Jesus' time the Jews were expecting a Messiah and an earthly kingdom. Even after the resurrection, the apostles were still waiting for the reestablishment of earthly Israel (Acts 1:6). By way of contrast, Matthew's emphasis upon the kingdom of heaven stresses its transcendental nature, its heavenly—rather than earthly—origin. John goes even further than Matthew and Mark by giving an account of Jesus' words before Pilate: "My kingship is not of this world" (John 18:36).

Jesus does not announce a kingdom to be established progressively as a result of human efforts, even those sanctified by the Spirit. His kingdom is of a nature different from the kingdoms of this world: it is a future kingdom, to be established when the Son of man comes at the Parousia (2 Tim. 4:1). This is what Jesus teaches in the parable of the sower. The kingdom of heaven, He says, may

be compared to a man who sowed good seed. This sower is the Son of man and this kingdom is the kingdom of God (Matt. 13:24-30). The Son of man must come from heaven with His kingdom (16:28). For this reason Jesus invited His disciples to pray, "Thy kingdom come" (6:10).

2. A Mysterious Kingdom

Jesus pointed out that the kingdom was already present in the midst of the disciples (Luke 17:20, 21). Where Jesus is, there His kingdom is as well (Matt. 12:28). Those who are born anew can see it (John 3:3). It is a mystery revealed only to believers (Mark 4:11). It is not the kingdom of glory, but the kingdom of grace, seen now only by faith. In the parable of the mustard seed the kingdom of heaven is minute, no larger than a grain of mustard (Matt. 13:31, 32).

Some, following the Church Fathers, have used this parable to describe the growth of the church, understood as the kingdom of God. But Jesus is not speaking about growth here. He is contrasting two stages of the kingdom: the seed and the tree. Tiny, weak, and fragile as the kingdom of Christ appears now, one day it will be powerful and glorious. The glory of the righteous will appear then, in the kingdom of the Father (verse 43).

More than any other biblical writer, the apostle Paul emphasized the coming kingdom of glory. Those who enter it experience suffering (Rom. 8:17; 2 Thess. 1:5; see also 2 Tim. 4:17, 18). With irony Paul reproved the Corinthians who imagined that through their charismatic experiences they were already in the kingdom of glory, pointing out, instead, the difficulties he still suffered in this world (1 Cor. 4:8, 9).

For Paul the kingdom presents a paradox. It is a glorious kingdom (Eph. 1:20-22), but one enters it through tribulations (Acts 14:22; 2 Thess. 1:4, 5). The chosen already have been transferred into that kingdom and are sitting in heavenly places with Jesus Christ (Col. 1:13; Eph. 2:6). Their lives, however, like the glory of the kingdom, remain hidden. They will not be revealed until Christ appears in His glory (2 Thess. 1:7; Col. 3:3, 4).

Here below, the citizens of the kingdom are not recognized by their enfolding glory, by their oratorical gifts (1 Cor. 2:1, 4), or by the way they eat and drink, but by their righteousness, peace, and joy, all produced by the Spirit (Rom. 14:17). In this sense one may speak of a spiritual kingdom that exists when each believer is led by the Spirit.

3. A Spiritual Kingdom

For Paul, the heirs of the kingdom do not practice unrighteousness (1 Cor. 6:9, 10), but submit themselves to the law of God, of which love is the supreme expression (Gal. 5:16-23).

Jesus affirmed that in order to enter the kingdom one had to be born of the Spirit (John 3:5). Those who have been converted, who have received the baptism of water and the Spirit, are welcome in the kingdom of God. Hence the kingdom is within reach of the poor in Spirit (Matt. 5:3), those who, like children, are ready to be instructed about the kingdom (Mark 10:14). Like the tax collectors and the harlots, they have repented and believed in Jesus (Matt. 21:31, 32).

Not all who call Jesus Lord will enter the kingdom of God, but only those who do the Father's will (Matt. 7:21-23). The kingdom is ruled by God's law (Matt. 5:17-20), and in order to enter life the observance of the commandments is indispensable (verses 21-43; 19:17).

Access to the kingdom is by grace, which is accorded to all (John 3:16), as is the wedding garment (Matt. 22:11). But the guests who refuse the festal garment show that they do not deserve the kingdom (verses 13, 14). On the other hand, those who experience God's grace cannot but show this same grace, this same love, toward others (Matt. 25:31-46; 18:21-35). When the Son of man comes, He will repay each one according to deeds committed (Matt. 16:27; see Salvation III. C. 1, 2).

4. A Future Kingdom

As Jesus approached Jerusalem one day He gave a parable to certain people who were expecting the soon coming of the kingdom of God. A nobleman had gone to a foreign country in order to receive royal authority, after which he would return (Luke 19:11, 12). With this story Jesus was leading them to understand that the kingdom was not to come immediately. Like this king, He also had to leave for a faraway place and come back afterward.

Certain theologians have concluded from this that Jesus' appearances after the Resurrection constituted His second coming. When Jesus left for heaven, however, angels announced to the disciples that they should await His second coming (Acts 1:7-11). Thus the appearance of Christ after His resurrection could not be His second advent.

Since the first century the church has waited for a kingdom to come. As long as death continues to occur, Christ's reign will not be completely established (1 Cor. 15:24-26). According to Peter, unbelievers are wrong in thinking that the promise of the advent of the kingdom is in vain. As certainly as the antediluvian world was annihilated by water, the postdiluvian world will be destroyed by fire when the Lord comes. Then will be established a new heaven and a new earth, where justice dwells (2 Peter 3:3-13). John recorded the beautiful promise of Jesus: "Let not your hearts be troubled; believe in God, believe also in me. . . . And when I go and prepare a place for you, I will come again and will take you to myself, that where I am you may be also" (John 14:1-3). Only ultimate and total communion with God will put an end to the misery of this world (Rev. 21:1-5).

E. Manner of His Coming

Because the death and resurrection of Jesus guarantee final victory, the authors of the NT declare that we are living at the end of time (Heb. 1:2; 9:26; 1 Cor. 10:11; James 5:3; 1 Peter

1:20). Such statements have led certain scholars to believe that the second coming of Jesus would not take place literally but through the presence of His Spirit in the church. Then the coming of Christ's kingdom would be accomplished through the victory of the moral principles of Christianity.

Christ's resurrection introduces a new era—the "last days" (Acts 2:17; Heb. 1:2). The end has come near because Christ has inaugurated the last period of this world's history. No longer does time signify delay, but anticipation (2 Peter 3:9); it journeys forward toward the glorious explosion of the Parousia (Rom. 13:11, 12). Therefore the believer can wait in confidence to be admitted to the promised heavenly dwelling (2 Cor. 5:1-5; John 14:1-3).

In this way the NT can affirm in a logical and coherent chain of thought that the second coming of Christ will be:

1. Personal and Literal

The Gospels insist that the Crucified One Himself appeared to the disciples after the Resurrection. Jesus of Nazareth presented Himself to them (Mark 16:9; Luke 24:25-43). He invited Thomas, who doubted, to touch His wounds (John 20:26, 27). Jesus was taken into glory after having proved to His disciples over 40 days that He was actually alive (Acts 1:3).

To the disciples, upset by this new separation, angels announced that *this Jesus* would come back in the same way He had gone to heaven (verse 11). The Son of man had left on a cloud; He would return on the clouds of heaven, with power and great glory, according to His promise (Matt. 26:64; Mark 13:26; Rev. 1:7).

According to the apostle Paul, "the Lord himself will descend from heaven" (1 Thess. 4:16). The Lord, "who is our life," will appear (Col. 3:4) in order to give us "the crown of righteousness" (2 Tim. 4:8). We are waiting for Jesus, the Son of God, raised from the dead by His Father, to come from heaven (1 Thess. 1:10). He who offered Himself once "to bear the sins of many" will bring salvation to those who await His coming (Heb. 9:28).

2. Visible and Audible

If the Second Coming is personal, it cannot but be visible. The terms *apokalypsis, epiphaneia,* and *parousia,* employed by the NT to describe His return, testify to what Jesus Himself announced: All nations of the earth will see Him (Matt. 24:30). John is more specific: "Every eye will see him" (Rev. 1:7). His return will be accompanied by terrifying cosmic signs impossible to ignore (Luke 21:25-27). Jesus warned His disciples about false prophets who would try to lead them to believe that the Second Coming would be hidden, veiled, mysterious, whereas it will be visible from all points of view. It will be like a flash of lightning rending the clouds (Matt. 24:26, 27).

Jesus is coming to manifest His glory (Titus 2:13), to be admired by His saints (2 Thess. 1:10). He will appear in a flaming fire, to slay those who do not know God (verses 7, 8). Any attempt to reduce the second advent of Jesus to an invisible and mysterious event is contrary to the testimony of the whole NT. Jesus' coming will be public, announced by a loud trumpet, as was the arrival of ancient kings (1 Thess. 4:16; Matt. 24:31). There is no secrecy here.

3. Glorious and Triumphant

If the First Coming was one of humiliation, the Second Coming, on the contrary, will take place in glory. Christ will come in the clouds of heaven, with power and glory (Matt. 24:30), accompanied by angels (2 Thess. 1:7). He will return as King of kings and Lord of lords (Rev. 19:16), victorious over all His enemies (1 Cor. 15:25).

The world lives in anguish from uncertainty about the present and future. Theology cannot appease this uneasiness by reducing eschatology to survival after death. Beyond the end of each individual, Scripture has answered the question on the future of history by announcing the second advent of Christ in glory. The Christian's future is enhanced by the glorious prospect of the Saviour's second coming, the hope of all Christians (1 Tim. 1:1).

4. Cataclysmic

The end of this world had already been announced in the OT. The NT associates this end with Christ's second coming (Matt. 13:40, 41). According to Daniel, the stone cut from the mountain will reduce all the kingdoms of the world to nothing (Dan. 2:44). In the same way that the Flood annihilated the antediluvian world, so the coming of Christ will cause the heavens to "pass away with a loud noise" and the earth to be burned up (2 Peter 3:10). Because God wants to establish "a new heaven and a new earth" (Rev. 21:1), the end of this world as we now know it is not only a worldwide phenomenon, it has cosmic dimensions.

5. Sudden

The transcendental character of the Second Coming is underlined again by its suddenness. Men and women will be taken by surprise. Jesus employed several metaphors to warn the disciples about this: the thief in the night (Matt. 24:42-44; Luke 12:40; cf. 1 Thess. 5:2, 4; 2 Peter 3:10), the bridegroom and the 10 virgins (Matt. 25:1-13), the Flood and the pre-Flood world (24:38, 39). The apostle Paul adds to this the figure of labor pains coming upon a pregnant woman (1 Thess. 5:3).

Far from suggesting a secret or invisible Second Coming, these images announce it as breaking upon the scene of action in a sudden and unexpected way. For this reason the disciples were called upon to be watchful (Matt. 25:13; 24:42). "You also must be ready," said Jesus, "for the Son of man is coming at an hour you do not expect" (24:44).

The figures employed by Jesus and Paul do not even mention the time when the Advent will take place: The master of the house does not know when the thief will come; the virgins do not know when the bridegroom will arrive; the woman wonders when the pain will start. No one knows the moment, neither the angels, nor even the Son (Matt. 24:36), but only the Father (Mark 13:32). The disciples are not informed about the precise time (Acts 1:6, 7; RH Aug. 16, 1887; 1T 72).

However, Jesus has provided signs to herald His coming, not to allow a calculation of the date of the coming, but to sustain the disciples' attention, to keep them awake (1 Thess. 5:4-6). Nobody knows if the master will come in the evening, at midnight, at cock-crow, or in the morning; however, no one should be sleeping when He arrives suddenly (Mark 13:35, 36) because important events have already announced His coming (Mark 13:28, 29). It is important to be attentive to these signs.

F. The Signs of the Second Coming

In his study of the Advent hope, Samuele Bacchiocchi has dedicated many pages to the signs of the second coming of Christ (113-262). This is in harmony with the emphasis Christ Himself gave to the signs in His Olivet discourse (Matt. 24; Mark 13; Luke 21). The believer waiting for the Second Coming finds hope in the signs. As the prophecies were given to strengthen the faith of the disciples (John 13:19; 14:29), the signs energize the believers, who recognize with Paul that "salvation is nearer to us now than when we first believed; the night is far gone, the day is at hand" (Rom. 13:11, 12).

The signs were to take place in nature, among nations, and in the hearts of human beings. However, before addressing the signs, certain puzzling verses that have been used to set a time for the Second Coming should be examined.

1. Some Difficult Texts

The misunderstanding of three texts in Matthew has caused some to suggest that Jesus expected a very early time for the Second Coming. Since the Advent did not occur then, the reliability of Scripture is negated.

An examination of these passages should clarify the true meaning of the signs in these verses.

a. Matthew 10:23. "When they persecute you in one town, flee to the next; for truly, I say to you, you will not have gone through all of the towns of Israel, before the Son of man comes."

This text would seem to indicate that only a short time would elapse before Christ's return. In an attempt to relate this saying to the delay of nearly 2,000 years, some have suggested that the coming of the Son of man was in reality the resurrection or the outpouring of the Holy Spirit. Others have taken this as an expression of the wishes of Matthew's Christian community.

In Matthew 24 Christ blends the prophecy of the destruction of Jerusalem with the prediction of the end of the world. This apparent merging of the particular with the general is characteristic of many eschatological prophecies. Just as the judgment of the world in the OT is considered against the background of judgments pronounced on Edom (Isa. 34:5-15; Jer. 49:7-22) or Assyria (Nahum 3:18, 19), so in this chapter, the judgment of this world is apparently merged with the judgment of Jerusalem.

In this passage the term Israel seems to have been used not in either a geographical or political sense but rather with reference to people. This passage can be interpreted as a double prediction: the spread of the gospel would take place until the very end of time, and it would be accompanied at times by trouble and persecution. Thus, if Israel is taken as a broad term and disciples are understood as all believers, the process of preaching goes on until the Second Coming, regardless of its date.

b. Matthew 16:28. "Truly, I say to you, there are some standing here who will not taste death before they see the Son of man coming in his kingdom."

For the Church Fathers and many scholars through the centuries, Jesus was referring here to the Transfiguration, as indicated by Matthew 17:1. In Matthew 16:21-28, Jesus announces His death and sets forth the cost of discipleship for His followers. He then encourages them by affirming the certainty of His glorious victory: some would see His glory in their lifetime. Immediately Matthew notes that the Transfiguration took place only six days later.

That the disciples were eyewitnesses to His majesty is corroborated in 2 Peter 1:16-18. Certainly the Transfiguration shares certain features with the Second Coming: it occurs in a high place and is accompanied by a bright cloud (Matt. 17:1, 5; 26:64; cf. Dan. 7:13).

c. Matthew 24:34. "Truly, I say to you, this generation will not pass away till all these things take place."

The misunderstanding regarding the time of the Second Coming derives from the interpretation of the word "generation." The word *genea* can refer to descent or the time between the birth of a father and his son. It also refers to an age, a time period. The Greek word corresponds to the Hebrew *dôr*, which is often used to designate a group or class of people: "a stubborn and rebellious generation" (Ps. 78:8) is not limited to one age group. In Proverbs 30:11-14 (KJV) the beginning word of each verse is *dôr*, "generation"; the RSV correctly translates "there are those who," for here "generation" refers to a kind of people, not an age group.

In harmony with this OT usage, Jesus would have used the term "this generation" without a temporal meaning, to refer to a class of people. The evil generation would include all who share evil characteristics (Matt. 12:39; 16:4; Mark 8:38).

If the word "generation" is given a temporal meaning in this passage, care should be taken to respect the time frame given in the context. In Matthew 24:34 Jesus is speaking of final events. Thus, the temporal generation would be that of those living at the end-time, not the one to which Jesus was speaking.

Jesus Himself made it clear that His words were not to be taken as setting a time for His coming. He said, "But of that day and hour no one knows, not even the angels of heaven, nor the Son, but the Father only" (Matt. 24:36). This would not fit with the claim of some that although the day or the hour cannot be known, the year may be ascertained. Nowhere did Jesus suggest a time for His coming, either in His time or in the distant future.

In Mark's version of Jesus' prophetic sermon (Mark 13) it is clear that Christ did not expect that all of the prophecy would be fulfilled during the time of the apostles. Jesus said: "The end is not yet" (verse 7); "This is but the beginning of the birth-pangs" (verse 8); "The gospel must first be preached to all nations" (verse 10); "He who endures to the end will be saved" (verse 13). Finally, the elect would be gathered "from the ends of the earth to the ends of heaven" (verse 27), suggesting the results of worldwide evangelism.

None of these three texts can be used as a basis for setting the time of the second coming of Christ. Neither can they be considered as evidence that the signs of the Second Coming are not valid. The signs serve as landmarks, assuring us that the historical process is moving toward its intended goal, without a specific calendar for the end. The believer is filled with hope as the signs are fulfilled.

The prophetic signs were given to strengthen the faith of the disciples (John 13:19; 14:29), to keep them awake to the importance of the times. Likewise, they keep us alert and aid us in understanding that the end "is nearer to us now than when we first believed" (Rom. 13:11).

2. Signs in the Natural World

"And there will be signs in sun and moon and stars," Jesus foretold (Luke 21:25); He further specified, "the sun will be darkened, and the moon will not give its light, and the stars will be falling from heaven, and the powers in the heavens will be shaken" (Mark 13:24, 25).

Jesus was not merely announcing future eclipses of the sun and moon. These would not have made good signs because they occur regularly and do not constitute exceptional phenomena. Furthermore, the place these signs occupy in the Olivet sermon should be considered: just after a great tribulation, and just before the appearing of Christ (Mark 13:24-26; Matt. 24:29, 30). These signs were specific, marking the end of the 42 months of persecution, as described in Revelation 12:13-17 and 13:1-10.

In Revelation 12 and 13 John is referring to Daniel 7-9, where the prophet sees a horn, a power, coming out from the Roman Empire and speaking against God and His saints. Following a large body of historicist interpreters, Seventh-day Adventists have recognized the Papacy in this political and religious power (4BC 49-54). This power grew slowly from the ruins of the Roman Empire, and received a great impetus about 538, when the siege of Rome was lifted, and the Ostrogoths were subsequently defeated (ibid. 834-838). During 12 centuries the pretensions of papal Rome were such that this power persecuted those who disagreed with it. The prophecy of Daniel 7:25, interpreted by John in Revelation 12:6, 14 as 1260 prophetic days or 1260 years according to the year-day principle (Shea 56-92), locates the end of the prophetic period in 1798. At that time the effects of the French Revolution resulted in a disruption of the power of the Roman Catholic Church, when General L. A. Berthier took Pope Pius VI into exile. (See PFOF 2:749-782.)

It is understandable, therefore, that those events revived eschatological hope around the world. Three times Daniel places the last judgment immediately after the evil doings of the beast (7:13, 14, 21, 22, 26). Out of the political and religious upheavals that shook Europe at the end of the eighteenth century, a great awakening arose, and the attention of believers was directed to the signs of the times prophesied. The end of the world seemed to be near, and the signs preceding that event were recognizable.

The appearance of heavenly phenomena would be preceded, according to John, by a great earthquake (Rev. 6:12). The book of Revelation regularly associates earthquakes with the final events (8:5; 11:13, 19; 16:18), as if the earth itself were sharing in the anguish of human beings who face the fearful prospect of coming events (Luke 21:25, 26).

a. Lisbon earthquake. The Lisbon earthquake, which occurred on November 1, 1755, was one of the strongest in recorded history. It was felt in North Africa and several parts of Europe. Combined with a tidal wave, it caused the death of tens of thousands of people. It was recognized at the time as a portent of the end (Smith 439-441).

b. Darkening of the sun. On May 19, 1780, thick darkness covered the northeastern part of the North American continent, remaining until the next morning. Many people believed that the time of judgment had come. Following the dark day, the moon rose blood red. These phenomena can be associated with the celestial signs to accompany John's earthquake: "The sun became black as sackcloth, the full moon became like blood" (Rev. 6:12; Smith 441-445).

c. Falling of the stars. In addition to the signs just described, John notes that "the stars of the sky fell to the earth as the fig tree sheds its winter fruit when shaken by a gale" (Rev. 6:13). This part of John's prophecy was fulfilled on November 13, 1833. That night the sky was crossed by an estimated 60,000 meteors an hour. From Canada to Mexico, from the Atlantic to the Pacific Ocean, the whole of North America was witness to this extraordinary demonstration. Many wondered about the meaning of such an event (PFOF 4:289-300; Smith 439-448).

In and of itself an earthquake or meteor shower may have no more religious meaning than a storm or blizzard. But when these phenomena are notable and occur according to the biblical sequence, at the time foreseen by prophecy, one should heed Jesus' words: "When these things begin to take place, . . . your redemption is drawing near" (Luke 21:28).

Seventh-day Adventists have traditionally given particular importance to these signs which appeared in areas where people were studying the Scriptures, more particularly biblical prophecy. Already at that time these portents were taken as God's signs.

d. Famines. Without including them in a precise chronological order, Jesus also announced that before His coming there would be famines in various places (Matt. 24:7). It may be difficult to recognize famine as a sign because today hunger is so widespread. Famines have always existed. However, the scale of hunger in the late twentieth century is unprecedented. Furthermore, famines are evidence of our inability to solve our problems in spite of our extraordinary scientific achievements. They also attest the egotism and violence that are the roots of most endemic famines.

In the OT famines were considered as God's judgments upon His people, or upon the heathen nations, because of their rebellion (2 Sam. 24:13; Jer. 29:17, 18; Eze. 5:11, 12). Today we do not judge as guilty the famished populations of the earth. But the hosts of starving people testify that the day of the One who will judge the world is near.

e. Other natural disasters. Jesus did not announce only one earthquake; He foretold many (Matt. 24:7). Famines and earthquakes are only one aspect of the imbalance of our planet. The ecological movement around the world today emphasizes the increasing problems created by human carelessness and greed. It is time for God to judge "the destroyers of the earth" (Rev. 11:18).

3. Signs in the Moral World

The evils of this world are not simply a consequence of natural phenomena. People share an important part in them. Jesus foretold the moral debasement of the human race in His sermon on Olivet, comparing the time of the end with the situation preceding the Flood (Matt. 24:37-39), when "the wickedness of man was great in the earth" (Gen. 6:5). He also compared the end-time with the condition of

Sodom prior to its destruction (Luke 17:28-30). Paul describes in detail the moral pollution of the world at the time of the end (2 Tim. 3:1-5). Statistics on the abundance of crime confirm his predictions.

Jesus used two key words to describe the moral state of the world at the eve of His second coming. He said that "because *wickedness* is multiplied, most men's *love* will grow cold" (Matt. 24:12). "Wickedness" comes from the Greek *anomia,* which more specifically refers to the absence of law, the refusal to recognize the authority of any law and thus to live by one's own desires and passions. From this lawlessness spring all the deviations in matters of sexuality, food, entertainment, or leisure, which modern people practice in the name of freedom. In contrast, Revelation praises those who in the end-time "keep the commandments of God" (Rev. 12:17; 14:12).

The second term used by Jesus in Matthew 24:12 is *agapē,* "love." Paul gives this word an extended definition in 1 Corinthians 13. *Agapē* presides over relations with others. Its absence results in family conflicts such as divorce, conflicts between nations (Matt. 24:7), the disruption of societies through exploitation, revolutions, and strikes, as well as the loss of respect for human beings (10:21). A lack of love can take on criminal forms, such as rape, murder, theft, or use of drugs; it also leads to the various ways in which humans exploit one another (cf. James 5:1-6; 2T 252; FE 101).

4. Signs in the Religious World

From a religious perspective the time of the end is paradoxical. On one hand the gospel is announced to the whole world (Matt. 24:14). Already in their time, the apostles had pressed toward this goal (Col. 1:6). Now, in the end-time, the gospel proclamation is symbolized by an angel who cries with a loud voice, "Fear God and give him glory, for the hour of his judgment has come" (Rev. 14:6, 7; see Remnant/Three Angels V. A-E). On the other hand, people will attempt to quench their thirst for

God's Word from broken cisterns (Amos 8:13, 14; Jer. 2:13). Jesus pointed out that false christs and false prophets would appear in the end-time (Matt. 24:5, 11; 1SM 15). Among those whom John denounces in special terms is the one called antichrist (1 John 2:18; 4:3; 2 John 7); that is to say, the one who is opposed to Christ or who takes Christ's place. In John's time the antichrist spirit already was recognizable by its rejection of Jesus' incarnation and divinity (1 John 2:22). This same spirit of falsehood will reappear in the beast of Revelation 13:11-17. With it, an extreme form of religious oppression and fanaticism will develop, which will put an end to religious freedom by imposing a new idolatry (Rev. 13:14-17) akin to that mandated by Nebuchadnezzar, king of Babylon (Dan. 3).

The challenge during this period of trouble and delusion is to persevere until the end in order to be saved (Matt. 10:22; Rev. 13:10; 14:12). For this reason it is important for all believers to be acquainted with both the true and false signs of Christ's coming. (See Great Controversy V. A-C.)

5. False Signs

Jesus cautioned His disciples that some would perform miracles in His name even though He did not recognize or accept them (Matt. 7:21-23). In His eschatological speech, He warned about the false nature of those miracles and their purpose: "to lead astray, if possible, even the elect" (Matt. 24:24). The apostle Paul indicated that the "man of lawlessness" would appear with "all power, and with pretended signs and wonders" (2 Thess. 2:3-9). Paul describes the coming of the "lawless one" in the same terms used to describe Jesus' advent: *apokalypsis* (verses 3, 6, 8) and *parousia* (verses 8, 9).

The prophet Elijah called fire from the Lord down upon the altar at Mount Carmel to demonstrate the identity of the true God (1 Kings 18:24, 38). In the end-time the same miracle will be performed by the power with two horns that look like those of a lamb, but that speaks like a dragon (Rev. 13:11, 13; GC 624). The only means by which to escape such seduction is the love of truth (2 Thess. 2:10; RH Sept. 5, 1899).

6. A Mistakenly Interpreted Sign

The dispensationalist school of thought applies the vision of Ezekiel 37 to the state of Israel. Accordingly, the return of Israel to Palestine, its conversion to Jesus Christ, the re-establishment of the Davidic monarchy, and the rebuilding of the Temple serve as signs of the end for this school of thought (Pache 317-350). The secret rapture of the church becomes an important part of this scheme.

This unscriptural teaching about the massive conversion of the people of Israel is most frequently supported by an interpretation of Romans 11:12, 26. However, this important chapter is not a prophecy regarding the end-time. Having shown that there is no difference between Jews and Greeks concerning salvation, for all are under the power of sin (Rom. 3:9), Paul expresses his wish for all Israel to be saved. While all, Jews and Greeks alike, are consigned to disobedience, all have equal access to God's mercy (Rom. 11:32). Paul does not discuss the time of the conversion of the people of Israel; he teaches rather the manner of their gathering: the heathen will come together with the converted Jews, the Israel of God (verse 26; cf. Berkouwer 323-358).

It is clear, both in Jesus' statements (Matt. 24:6-13) and in Revelation 12-14, that the time preceding the Second Coming will not be a golden age. Rather, it will be a period of trouble and anguish (Luke 21:25, 26). Because of the wickedness of human beings, true faith will become uncommon (18:8). Moreover, Jesus did not talk about several returns or of several occasions of conversion. He described only one visible, glorious, and mighty coming. At that time the living saints, together with those resurrected, will be taken up in the clouds of heaven to receive their Saviour (1 Thess. 4:16, 17).

G. The Reasons for Jesus' Second Coming

"The final triumph of God is a theological necessity" (Pidoux 53). He is the Almighty, the master of history. He has demonstrated this fully through Jesus Christ. It would be contrary to His very nature not to accomplish His promise to manifest His glory both to the living and to the dead. Our Lord Jesus comes, therefore, in order to finish the work of redemption of which His resurrection was a guarantee.

His second coming accomplishes seven great purposes:

1. To Gather the Chosen

As the priests blew the trumpet at the time of the great convocations (Num. 10:2), so "with a loud trumpet call" powerful angels assemble the elect from the four winds (Matt. 24:31; Mark 13:27). The "gathering" reflects Israelite hope of seeing the Jews of the diaspora gathered again by God, according to His promises (e.g., Deut. 30:3; Isa. 43:3-5; Eze. 39:27). Having been scattered all over the world in order to witness to Jesus Christ (Acts 1:8), the disciples are once more gathered together.

2. To Resurrect the Dead

Believers who have lost their lives have the glorious privilege of becoming partakers in Jesus' resurrection (Rom. 6:5; Phil. 3:10). His resurrection provides the basis for our hope (1 Peter 1:3; 1 Thess. 4:14), it guarantees His promise (John 6:40). If Jesus does not bring the dead to life, the gospel is meaningless and our hope is in vain (1 Cor. 15:14-19). Contrary to popular thinking about spirit-life after death, God's plan for those who have died in Christ is not complete until the glorious day of the resurrection. Until then, believers rest in unconscious sleep, waiting for the resurrection when they will receive their reward. So Oscar Cullmann could write that "the biblical hope of resurrection does not see the individual's destiny except as a result of the total work of

Christ. That is why the resurrection of our 'mortal bodies' (Rom. 8:11) will take place only at the end," not at each individual's death (1945, 20).

The trumpet that assembles the elect also wakes the dead (1 Thess. 4:16). They will come out of their graves in a glorious, energized, imperishable condition (1 Cor. 15:42-44, 53). Then they will exclaim with the apostle, "O death, where is thy victory? O death, where is thy sting?" (verse 55). The righteous dead will come to life as witnesses of God's might (6:14; see Resurrection I, II).

3. To Transform and Receive All the Saints

The living righteous will retain a physical human body, although not in its present state. They will be transformed (Phil. 3:21), in the twinkling of an eye (1 Cor. 15:51, 52), because the perishable cannot inherit the imperishable (verse 50). God wants to save His faithful people of all time. Together with those who are alive, the resurrected saints will be caught up in the air to form a joyous procession to acclaim their Lord (1 Thess. 4:17).

4. To Destroy the Evil Powers and the Wicked

Jesus will also come to put an end to this world's suffering by destroying those who cause it. Thus, He answers the prayer of the martyrs who exclaimed, "O Sovereign Lord, holy and true, how long before thou wilt judge and avenge our blood?" (Rev. 6:10).

The wicked will not be able to endure His dazzling presence. They pronounce their own condemnation (verse 16). All the evil powers are destroyed: the wicked (2 Thess. 2:8), those symbolically called Babylon (Rev. 18:8; 19:2), the beast and the false prophet (verse 20), and all those who accompany them (verse 21). Following the millennium Satan himself will be consumed (Rev. 20:10; see Millennium I. C. 1, 3).

5. To Vindicate God

The problem of evil is not completely re-solved with the destruction of its author. Throughout history, God's love has been questioned, hence the need for His vindication. At Christ's second coming, however, the wicked were destroyed by the brightness of His presence. This suggests that the post-millennial judgment does not aim at establishing the innocence of some and the guilt of others (Rev. 20:4-6, 11-15). Rather it vindicates God and His dealings with humanity (Eph. 3:10, 11). This vindication consists in God's reconciling the world to Himself through Christ (2 Cor. 5:19). Because all things proceed from Him, the glory belongs to Him. It is to demonstrate finally God's love, mercy, justice, and vindication to the whole universe that the wicked are resurrected after the millennium. (See Judgment III. B. 3.)

6. To Restore the Earth

Nature has been subjected to the curse of sin and longs for renewal (Rom. 8:19-21). The elect will not need to restore the ruins or erase the traces of a corrupt civilization. According to His promises, God will create a new heaven and a new earth (Isa. 65:17; 66:22; 2 Peter 3:13; Rev. 21:1). In that ideal setting the redeemed will acknowledge the grand accomplishments of the entire plan of salvation. (See New Earth I-III.)

7. To Reestablish Communion With God

Nothing is dearer to the heart of God than to reconcile all things to Himself through Jesus Christ (Col. 1:19, 20; 2 Cor. 5:20; Eph. 1:9, 10). Now communion between God and man has been interrupted by sin (Isa. 59:2). Then God will be able to dwell with His own (Rev. 21:3), and the redeemed will be with the Lord forever (1 Thess. 4:17).

All these reasons for Jesus' second coming imply a preliminary judgment that has taken place before that coming (Dan. 7:9-14). Many NT references concerning the end of time indicate that Jesus will return to pass sentence, not to initiate court hearings (Matt. 3:12; 8:11, 12; 13:30; 24:37-41).

This is particularly clear in the parables of Matthew 25, which presuppose a time of preliminary inquiry into the way human beings have employed their waiting time. At Jesus' second coming the apostle Paul expects his reward, not an examination of his case. At that time he will receive "the crown of righteousness" (2 Tim. 4:8). "Behold, I am coming soon, bringing my recompense, to repay every one for what he has done" says Jesus (Rev. 22:12; see Judgment III. B. 1).

II. Implications of the Doctrine

Belief in the Second Coming influences Christians' lives in many ways. Not only does one's way of daily life reflect a belief, but motivation for witnessing and making spiritual preparation for that day, regardless of the apparent delay. of the Second Coming, a believer's life shows specific ethical characteristics. Among these are hope, love, humility, and holiness.

A. Effects on the Believer's Daily Life

Eschatological expectation often is considered by its detractors as immobilizing, leading Christians to pessimism about the world, uninterested in the affairs of life. It is true that setting a date for the Second Coming has led to extreme attitudes. Apparently, in the time of the apostle Paul, certain people had given up work because of this (1 Thess. 4:11; 2 Thess. 3:10-12). Others had given up conjugal relations to devote themselves to prayer (1 Cor. 7:3-5) or thought of divorcing a spouse, better to prepare for the Parousia (verse 10).

However, far from reducing Christians to isolated islands, the hope of the Second Advent actually reminds them of their mission as salt of the earth and light of the world (Matt. 5:13-16). When the Master returns, He will find His faithful servants giving His people their needed nourishment (Matt. 24:45, 46). Even in the management of wealth they will glorify their Lord (Luke 16:11). Each passing day is a time of grace from which the Lord expects fruit (13:6-9). This teaching is especially illustrated by the parable of the talents (19:13-26; Matt. 25:14-30). While waiting for his or her Master, each servant of God is called to bear fruit through the gifts given. Paul understood this well, as shown by his urging the believers to walk faithfully according to the call they had received (1 Cor. 7:17-24). Furthermore, in view

1. Hope

To serve the God of hope means to enter a way of thought filled with joy, peace, and faith in the future reign (Rom. 15:13). No situation appears desperate, since the presence of the Holy Spirit guarantees the promise of the future. Hope is an anchor of the soul that keeps the ship of faith solidly anchored to the very sanctuary of God (Heb. 6:19, 20). Hope banishes worry, fear, and anguish, allowing people to lift up their heads (Luke 21:28). All things in the world can be evaluated at their true worth in this light.

2. Love

Jesus has not called His people to love more earnestly because of the nearness of His second coming, but the Second Advent gives love consistency. The apostle Paul placed love between faith and hope, between the certainty of what Jesus has done for us and what He will still do for us at His second coming (Gal. 5:5, 6). Christians are called to live in a world that opposes their faith. The victory of the wicked, the outburst of hostile powers, and Christians' own weaknesses could lead to doubt; but faith, carried by the wings of hope, allows the Christian to testify in this world that love will never perish (1 Cor. 13:8).

In person, God will come to put an end to all suffering (Rev. 21:4). For this reason the believer's sufferings become a participation in the suffering of Christ and a pledge of the comfort to come (2 Cor. 1:5-7). Whatever the weight of suffering, it cannot compare with the glory to come (Rom. 8:18). Christians may look at their present situation with confidence because the God of love will soon make His victory manifest. Faith, acting through love, testifies to the reality of hope.

3. Humility

To know that the present time will end leads to a proper evaluation of this world's riches. Wealth in itself is not to be condemned, but to think only of earthly matters is enmity to the cross (Phil. 3:18, 19). The one who awaits the Lord Jesus as Redeemer is a citizen of heaven (verses 18-20; John 14:2, 3). The Christian's manner of dealing with the world is predicated upon the knowledge that it is passing away (1 Cor. 7:30, 31). Riches are to be measured by the standard of the future (1 Tim. 6:17-19), and the goods of this world by the norm of God's kingdom (Matt. 13:44-46). By seeking first the kingdom and God's righteousness, the believer lays up treasures in heaven (6:19, 20, 33).

The Christian is an heir of God and a fellow heir with Christ (Rom. 8:17). Enlightened by the Spirit, the believer discovers the hope that is linked to one's call and the riches of the glory of God's inheritance reserved for the saints (Eph. 1:18). All other matters and objects are transitory and relative. With a renewed mind, one can discern what is good, acceptable, and perfect, bringing eternal dimensions to temporal choices (Rom. 12:2).

4. Holiness

The ethical implications of the Second Coming cannot be overemphasized. To await the last judgment calls for godly living (2 Peter 3:11). To believe in the resurrection brings with it a respect for all mankind and leads to an appreciation of the value of time (1 Cor. 15:32-34). Christians do not live in terror of the judgment, for they know that they are free from condemnation in Jesus Christ (Rom. 8:1). But they must live as redeemed persons, ordering their lives according to faith (Phil. 2:12, 13). Without sanctification or holiness, no one will see the Lord (Heb. 12:14).

Growth in holiness does not entail a retreat into oneself, a search for one's own salvation apart from others. The hope of the Second Advent mobilizes social values (Heb. 10:25); it develops the sense of justice, goodness, beauty, and truth (Phil. 4:8); it improves the moral character of believers (AH 16). Christians are particularly capable of fighting injustice, not by anger (James 1:20) but with the spiritual weapons God has given them (Eph. 6:10-18). God's servants cannot be insensitive to this world's matters (1 Cor. 6:2, 3), while being confident that He will soon vindicate those who cry out to Him (Luke 18:7, 8; see Lifestyle II. C. 4).

B. Motivation for Evangelization

Not only does the conviction of a soon-coming return of Jesus affect the quality of the believer's daily life, but it also provides strong motivation for evangelization. The waiting time provides opportunity for the Holy Spirit to act on believers, imbuing them with a sense of urgency to employ their gifts in sharing the message of grace.

1. The Time of the Holy Spirit

As an answer to the question of the disciples regarding the date of His advent, Jesus promised to send them the Holy Spirit to make them witnesses to the ends of the earth (Acts 1:8). The good news must be preached in the whole world before the end comes (Matt. 24:14), but Jesus does not make His return dependent upon the proclamation of the gospel. Still, He does want His followers to take part in His plan for the salvation of the world (Matt. 9:36-38). The same feelings of compassion that motivated Jesus will move all those who live in Christ.

The time of expectation is not, therefore, an intermediate time, an emptiness through which one must try to pass as quickly as possible with eyes fixed on the end. The waiting time belongs to the Holy Spirit, who gathers the believers to establish the eschatological community. He desires them to come into communion with the living Christ and announce to the world that the same grace is offered to all (ST Sept. 15, 1887; RH Aug. 16, 1887).

2. The Time of Grace

"The NT is clear that the present ('now') is *the* opportunity which men have to repent and believe (Mark 1:15; cf. Acts 3:19, 20) and that the End delays only for this purpose—and not indefinitely." "It is man's final chance," writes A. L. Moore (209). The apostle Peter calls our time the time of God's patience (1 Peter 3:9, 15).

The end of the world is not a question for tomorrow but a call for today (Heb. 4:7). At Jesus' return "one is taken and one is left" (Matt. 24:40, 41). Not to warn the world means to be guilty of nonassistance to people in danger. The time of grace will soon be over, and the closer the end comes, the more urgent it is to take a stand for God. As Hebrews 4:1 states: "Therefore, while the promise of entering his rest remains, let us fear lest any of you be judged to have failed to reach it."

3. The Time of Urgency

Living in the expectation of Jesus' return conveys a sense of urgency (YI Apr. 28, 1908). Jesus Himself traveled the highways and byways of Palestine with the conviction that His time was short (John 9:4). The apostle Paul was inspired by this conviction (1 Cor. 7:29); for this reason he urged believers to make the best possible use of their time (Eph. 5:16; Col. 4:5). They were to take every opportunity to testify honestly, because as time went by it would become increasingly difficult to find sympathetic and attentive listeners (2 Tim. 4:2-4).

If the devil is particularly zealous "because he knows that his time is short" (Rev. 12:12), how much more should the believers be awake, especially because "salvation is nearer to us now than when we first believed" (Rom. 13:11; cf. ST Sept. 15, 1887; RH Aug. 16, 1887).

4. The Time of Spiritual Gifts

The book of Acts shows that the waiting time gives opportunity for the evangelization of the world. The Holy Spirit calls people to this work (Acts 13:1, 2). He imparts His gifts for the edification and the growth of the church (Eph. 4:11-13). Among the gifts, prophecy was particularly favored as best suited for the building up of the body of Christ and the conversion of unbelievers (1 Cor. 14:1, 3, 24, 25).

Spiritual gifts are bestowed so that the disciples may be the salt and light of the earth, to flavor and illumine the world (Matt. 5:13-16). Christians cannot shirk the duty of testifying, especially as that day approaches. (See Spiritual Gifts II.)

C. Spiritual Preparation for His Return

Faith in the second coming of Jesus affects our value system, creating a motivation for witnessing and evangelization. Of necessity it also presupposes a spiritual preparation. After exhorting His disciples to be ready for the coming of the Son of man (Matt. 24:44), Jesus presented the parable of the 10 virgins (Matt. 25:1-13). Five were depicted as foolish because, even though they were convinced that the bridegroom would arrive in a short time, they did not make any provision for the future. The other five were called wise because they kept on hand a supply of oil, suggesting that they thought the bridegroom might be delayed. Both groups were surprised at the announcement of the bridegroom's arrival, but only the wise ones were able successfully to pass the test of the waiting time between the announcement and the arrival of the bridegroom. Only those who have a personal relationship with Jesus will be able to face every difficulty.

The parable of Matthew 25:1-13, like the preceding one about the two servants (Matt. 24:45-51), emphasizes the importance of spiritual life and faithful service in relation to Jesus' second coming. Christians should be thankful for the opportunities given every day to repent and grow in sanctification (Heb. 12:14). They know that they will soon experience glorious renewal as the culmination of a process begun with baptism and the gift of the Holy Spirit (John 3:5).

To live forever under God's authority we must first live now in submission to His laws. For this reason the apostle Paul denounced those sins typical of people who will be lost (1 Cor. 6:9, 10). John reinforces this point (Rev. 21:8; 22:15). As the prophet Amos writes: "Woe to you who desire the day of the Lord!" but do not "let justice roll down like waters, and righteousness like an everflowing stream" (Amos 5:18, 24). In contrast, all those who keep the commandments of God and bear the testimony of Jesus are praised (Rev. 12:17; 14:12). Holiness of behavior and piety are the natural effects of awaiting the Second Coming (2 Peter 3:11; cf. 4T 309; see Great Controversy VI. E).

D. An Apparent Delay

Christ has not yet come. After 2,000 years of expectation, Christians long for the Advent. Could the second coming of Jesus be deferred, delayed, or even worse, cancelled? Many a believer wonders about these possibilities.

In the NT there is a tension between the nearness and the distance of the Second Coming. For Paul, James, and Peter, the day is "at hand" (Rom. 13:12; James 5:8; 1 Peter 4:7). Jesus Himself assures, "Surely I am coming soon" (Rev. 22:20). But other passages place the Second Coming well into the future. To dispell the notion that the kingdom of God was to appear immediately, Jesus taught the parable about the nobleman who went into a far country (Luke 19:11-27). For Matthew the Master will come back *after a long time* (Matt. 25:19). In other parables Jesus also alludes to an apparent delay (24:48; 25:5).

The same tension can be found in the OT. The day of the Lord is both far and near (Hab. 2:3; Isa. 2:2, 20; 13:6; Zeph. 1:14; 3:8).

The tension between "now" and "not yet" excludes any possibility to establish even the year of Jesus' return (10MR 270). The disciples were to be ready at any time (Matt. 24:36-51). The delay, according to Peter, is an expression of the forbearance of the Lord, who is not willing that any should perish (2 Peter 3:9).

God is not slow about His promise. As G. C. Berkouwer rightly states: "Were, now, the return of Christ to be cancelled, the result would not merely be disappointment or disillusionment but a crisis of faith in the veracity and dependability of God" (66, 67). The Bible never suggests any possibility of default on the promise (2 Peter 3:9; Heb. 10:39). To the contrary, the surety of the Second Coming is amply confirmed.

God Himself confirms the promise of the Second Coming. His Word is sure. To change what has come out of His mouth would violate His covenant (Ps. 89:35); God does not lie (Num. 23:19; 1 Sam. 15:29; Heb. 6:13, 18). In spite of our unfaithfulness, He remains faithful (2 Tim. 2:13); thus we may hold fast the confession of our hope (Heb. 10:23).

Through His first coming Christ confirmed the surety of the Second Advent. The cross, through which justification was provided, was evidence of His intention to complete the salvation of the believers (Rom. 5:8-10). "He who did not spare his own Son, but gave him up for us all, will he not also give us all things with him?" (8:32) echoes this certainty. Christ's resurrection and ascension clearly point toward His return (John 14:1-3).

The Holy Spirit also confirms the assurance of Jesus' return. His very presence in the heart of the believer and the gifts He gives certify the promise (2 Cor. 1:18-22; Heb. 2:4).

The preaching of the gospel, commissioned by Christ, finds its meaning and strength in the hope of life to come. God would not raise up preachers of a message and then not be faithful to that message (Titus 1:2, 3; Heb. 2:1-3).

Human reactions to the delay are exemplified

in the parable of the faithful and unfaithful servants of Matthew 24. The unfaithful servant thinks his master delays, for he is not interested in the task he has been given (verse 48). The faithful servant, on the other hand, is totally absorbed by the trust his master has put in him (verses 45, 46). He looks for the coming of his Lord, but he is thankful for the time of grace he is allowed to live and serve (2 Peter 3:9). He rejoices that the coming of Christ is announced and that the gospel is growing all over the world (Phil. 1:8; Col. 1:6). Time seems to be short in view of the magnitude of the task still to be performed, both in the world and in his own heart (2 Cor. 7:1; Matt. 9:36-38).

The "delay" of Jesus is not a problem for the believer. It gives meaning to the suffering each believer experiences. Each day brings the joy of seeing more souls added to God's people (Rev. 6:11).

E. Conclusion

The second coming of Christ gives deep meaning to the history of nations and individuals. A history that consists only of the aimless piling up of facts would lack meaning and order. History without an end or goal becomes senseless.

The Bible invests history with a transcendental character. It has a beginning, and it will have an end, but not just any end. It will not end with a catastrophe produced by human selfishness and pride, nor with that glorious end promised in all humanist utopias. It will be brought to a full stop by God Himself (Ps. 46:9-11).

In a similar manner, life in the Spirit is linked to a destiny. Such a life may be sown in tears, but it will harvest in joy (Ps. 126:4-6). The ethical choices of Christians have meaning. They spread love, trusting in the promise of God. Jesus is coming. The One who came to Judea to teach mercy and forgiveness is coming to establish His kingdom of love. "For yet a little while, and the coming one shall come and shall not tarry" (Heb. 10:37).

Soon the great controversy between God and Satan will come to an end. God's justice will be established over the world through Jesus Christ: not only on the earth, but also in heaven, where the battle began. The whole universe will be reconciled with God (Col. 1:20; 1 Cor. 15:28).

Jesus is coming back soon. What a comfort, what certainty, what peace! The last book of the Bible closes emphasizing confidence in the second coming of Jesus. "Behold, I am coming soon, bringing my recompense, to repay every one for what he has done" (Rev. 22:12). In response, "the Spirit and the Bride say, 'Come.' And let him who hears say, 'Come'" (verse 17). No believer can help but respond to the invitation of the Spirit and the Bride saying, "Amen, Come Lord Jesus!" (verse 20).

III. Historical Overview

A. The Apostolic Period

Historians are unanimous in recognizing that the hope of Jesus' return remained alive in the early church. The very terms of one of the earliest NT documents testify to that effect: 1 Thessalonians 4:16, 17. The thanksgivings that introduce Paul's Epistles demonstrate that faith in the Parousia constituted a fundamental belief of the early church. Later Epistles still retain a strong eschatological expectation (2 Peter 3:8-13). The Revelation of John, written in a period of crisis at the end of the first century, sustains the believers' faith through to the glorious visions of the last judgment.

But even in the first century false teachings infiltrated the church, threatening its faith. Some gave up their belief in the resurrection of the dead (1 Cor. 15:12). The certainty of the second advent of Christ was questioned by others (2 Peter 3:4), along with His incarnation (1 John 4:1-3). NT writers wrestled against such tendencies, seeing in them a sign of the approaching end (2:18, 28; 2 Peter 3:3).

B. The Ante-Nicene Period

Some scholars hold that the decline in the church's fervor toward the Parousia began in the NT period. The evidence cited is the scarcity of eschatological references in several NT Epistles.

Such opinions, however, are disproved by the testimony of second-century writers (Landa 65-95). The expectation of the Parousia remained strong. Thus, Clement of Rome reminded the Corinthians that the Lord must come back soon (*1 Clement* 23); the *Didache* is rich with the eschatological vocabulary of Paul's First Epistle to the Thessalonians (16:3-8); and Ignatius of Antioch wrote that "the last times are come upon us" (*Ephesians* 11), because of which Christians were to "weigh carefully the times" (*Polycarp* 3). *The Epistle of Barnabas* points out that "the day is at hand on which all things shall perish with the evil [one]. The Lord is near, and His reward" (21. 3). The *Shepherd of Hermas* trusts in the promise of His coming (*Vision* 3. 8, 9). Polycarp of Smyrna (*Philippians* 5) and Papias (as quoted in Eusebius *Ecclesiastical History* 3. 39) wrote of the resurrection of the dead and Christ's personal return to earth.

The apologists followed the lead of their predecessors. Justin Martyr noted that the prophets proclaimed two advents. In the second, Christ would "come from heaven with glory, accompanied by His angelic host, when also He shall raise the bodies of all men who have lived" (*Apology* 1. 52). In his refutation of Gnosticism, Irenaeus applied the prophecy of Daniel 2, including the stone signifying the reign of Jesus, to his day (*Against Heresies* 5. 26). At the beginning of the third century Tertullian anticipated the final coming of Christ (*On the Resurrection of the Flesh* 22). In his *Treatise on Christ and Antichrist*, Hippolytus reviewed the prophecies of Daniel and Revelation, concluding with the Second Coming as described in the words of Paul in 1 Thessalonians 4:13-17.

In a number of writings of that period, however, belief in the immortality of the soul already was relegating eschatology to a secondary role. With their adoption of Greek philosophical thinking, Christian writers no longer felt a great need for Christ's return in glory because, as noted by Ignatius of Antioch, through death Christians attain to God (*Romans* 1, 2, 6).

Origen spiritualized away the events of the end through the allegorical method of interpretation of Scripture. He affirmed that the Parousia of the Lord on the clouds took place every day in the soul of believers (*Series Commentary on Matthew* 50; cf. PFOF 1:317-320).

At the beginning of the third century the problem of the end of the world was an important question among Christians, particularly at Rome. Political and economic instability, together with persecution, oriented speculation on prophecy toward the coming of the antichrist, believed to be near. Still much influenced by the ordeal of persecution, the Council of Nicea (325) held that "the divine Logos . . . will come to judge the living and the dead" and that "the Holy Scriptures teach us to believe also in . . . the resurrection of the dead and a judgment of requital" (Kelly 210).

C. The Post-Nicene Period to the Reformation

Soon after Constantine's death "the idea developed that the earth in its present state" was "the *territory of the prophesied kingdom;* that the present dispensation" was "the *time of its realization;* and that the establishment of the earthly church by human hands" was "the *mode of fulfillment.* Thus it came to be held that the hierarchical rule of the church was actually the predicted kingdom of Christ on earth" (PFOF 1:373).

Several factors contributed to this new trend of thought. Paramount was the church's new legal status and the support brought to the church by the empire. In harmony with this spirit, Eusebius of Caesarea (d. c. 340), having formerly taught that the Second Coming would usher in the divine kingdom (*Proof of the Gos-*

pel 4. 16; 9. 17), now demonstrated the extent to which the Christian empire fulfilled the OT prophecies concerning the covenant (*Commentary on Isaiah* 19. 18). At the same time he showered Constantine with praises, taking him to be the fulfillment of the Christian hope (*Life of Constantine* 2. 28; 3. 1).

No one denied that the ultimate goal of the history of salvation was the advent hope. In fact the Second Coming was mentioned repeatedly in sermons and treatises. Cyril of Jerusalem was even convinced that "the end of the world . . . [was] imminent" (*Catechetical Lectures* 15. 12). However, the urgency of the Parousia was no longer as important to Christians as theological disputes on other doctrines.

Influenced by Alexandrian allegorical interpretation of the Bible, Tyconius (fourth century) propounded the idea that the seventh millennium should be counted, not from the Second Coming, but from the Christian Era (Landa 86). Augustine of Hippo (354-430), using Tyconius as his basis, identified the church with the kingdom of God and affirmed that Christ comes to it every day, and the thousand years of the church's reign on earth had begun with Jesus Himself (*City of God* 20. 5-9). At the same time, Augustine could affirm that "the whole church of the true God holds and professes as its creed, that Christ shall come from heaven to judge quick and dead; this is what we call the last day, or last time, of the divine judgment" (*ibid.* 20.1).

Throughout the Middle Ages most Christian theologians followed Augustine's scheme. They believed in an eventual Second Coming while affirming that the church was the kingdom of God. At the same time, many commentators wrote on the book of Revelation. The coming of the antichrist and divine judgment became a prominent yet painful, part of common thought. The flagellants in Italy (thirteenth century) and *The Divine Comedy* of Dante demonstrate to what extent the fear of hell dominated medieval thinking. The belief grew that "the man of sin," or the antichrist, whose coming was an important sign of the end, was not an emperor or a prophet, but rather the visible head of the Christian church. This preoccupation provided leaven for reformation.

D. Reformation

Since Augustine (fifth century), eschatological expectation had been applied to the victory of the church over the world. However, the failure of the church and the Augustinian thesis called for a reformation.

For Luther, the antichrist, whose coming was to precede the end of the world, had already become reality in the Papacy. In view of the "words and signs of Christ," he stated in 1522 that the Second Coming was not far away (*Weimar Ausgabe* 10/1, 2:95); in a 1532 Table Talk, he affirmed that it was "at the door" (*Tischreden* 1291). This expectation was a deep and abiding part of his faith. Far from seeing the Second Coming as a manifestation of God's wrath, Luther considered it a happy occasion, one that could be expected with confidence, for the doctrine of justification by faith gave it new meaning. He prayed for that day to come so that Christians might be delivered from suffering and obtain bodies freed from physical distress (WA 41:37). In a 1537 sermon on Matthew 25 Luther gave the following picture: "He will return on the last day with great power, and glorious majesty, and with him the full army of angels. . . . It will be a glorious judgment and an unspeakable majesty with all the angels present and he in their midst" (*ibid.* 45:325).

Luther's hope was kept alive in the German reformation. His followers, among them Melanchthon and Nikolaus Herman, believed ardently in the Second Coming. His hymns, sung in the congregations, spoke of the glorious expectation.

Similarly, John Calvin admonished his followers to "desire the advent of the Lord" as the "most propitious of all events," when Christ should come "as a Redeemer to deliver" from "evil and misery, and lead us to the blessed inheritance of his life and glory" (*Institutes* 3. 9. 5). In 1545 Calvin affirmed that the hope of the Second Coming and its accompanying judgment brought happiness to the believer (*Catechism of the Church of Geneva*). In 1560 he dedicated two paragraphs of his *Institutes* to the favorable judgment that Christ would pronounce over His people at His coming (2. 16. 18). Calvin linked the promise of the resurrection to the Second Coming (3. 25. 1-4).

Both Luther and Calvin saw the Protestant Reformation as a fulfillment of Christ's words in Matthew 24:14. The study of the Bible and the preaching of a gospel purer than that of the times of Augustine and Jerome would make way for the coming of God's heavenly kingdom. Neither expected the conversion of the whole world, but Luther affirmed, "I believe that the last day is not far off, for the gospel is now making its last effort" (*Tischreden* 5488).

E. From the Reformation to the Nineteenth Century

Following the Reformation, two different eschatological understandings developed on the continent. The radical reformation maintained a live interest in eschatology, sometimes with extreme views regarding an earthly millennium. Menno Simons, as well as later Mennonite confessions, sustained belief in a soon-to-return Saviour. On the other hand, in German Lutheranism, Pietists insisted that for the believer, the greatest challenge was being certain of one's own salvation. Intense personal religious experience was the hallmark of their experience.

In the British Isles, the hope of Christ's second coming "appears as one of the most important outcomes of Puritanism's rediscovery of the essential Biblical message" (Ball, *Advent Hope* 132). Although they held variant interpretations of the millennium, Anglican, Presbyterian, and Congregationalist theologians wrote and preached that the Second Coming was at hand. The effect of this hope on the believers should be, they pro-

claimed, to live in readiness for that great day (*ibid.* 146-149).

The French Revolution and the wars that followed it produced social, political, and religious consequences, which, in turn, fostered increased eschatological expectations. A widespread revival of the study of prophecy developed throughout the world. For example, Chilean-born Jesuit Manuel Lacunza published anonymously in 1790 a work entitled *The Coming of the Messiah in Glory and Majesty*, widely translated from its original Spanish. In London, Edward Irving (1792-1834) appended it to the report of the first Albury Prophetic Conference in 1826. To these conferences, held yearly from 1826 to 1830, came clergy from different churches and communions to study the nearness of the Second Advent, the prophecies of Daniel and Revelation, and "the duties of the church arising from these questions" (PFOF 3:276). Joseph Wolff, one of the 20 who attended the 1826 conference, traveled extensively throughout Western and Central Asia, teaching that Christ would come about 1847 to establish a millennial rule in Jerusalem. In Switzerland, François Gaussen presented, beginning in 1837, a series of Sunday school lectures on the prophecies of Daniel. In these he showed that Daniel and Revelation portrayed the history of the world, which would soon come to a close.

Early in the nineteenth century, Christ's second coming was proclaimed by numerous voices, from scholars in England to young children in Sweden. Many, including Lacunza, showed how the prophecies of Daniel and Revelation clearly pointed to the end of the world by the mid-1900s. In the United States "prophecy was the motivating force in much of the religious thought and activity" of the period (*ibid.* 4:85). Sermons, pamphlets, and books proclaimed that events occurring in the world could only be a prelude to the millennium. Best known of the American preachers was William Miller, who in 1831 began writing and teaching that Jesus would come in 1843. (On William Miller and the Millerite movement, see Adventists I. A-C; Remnant/Three Angels VI. G.)

These movements did not receive a universal welcome from traditional theologians. Catholic theology, born of scholasticism, offered a nontemporal eschatology, mostly interested in death and judgment, heaven and hell (Rast 501-503). Protestant theology was deeply influenced by the development of rationalism and saw the kingdom of God being established on earth by means of the conquest of science and reason. Thus, in the last half of the nineteenth century, the expectation of the nearness of Christ's coming very nearly disappeared.

F. The Modern Era

After the great disappointment in 1844, believers in the Second Advent had to confront the problem of the delay of the Parousia. This problem has become central to theology today. It has become necessary to explain why the second coming of Christ, so clearly announced in Scripture, has not taken place.

The most prominent scholar to address this question was Albert Schweitzer, who made a distinction between the thinking faith that wonders if one has already entered a supernatural era and the simple faith that lives in the expectation of the Messianic kingdom (75, 90, 99). For Schweitzer the event of the cross is already an eschatological catastrophe, which puts to an end any apocalyptic expectation.

Karl Barth and Paul Althaus' dialectic theology, recaptured by E. Brunner, ends in transcendental eschatology. These authors had no place for the consummation of concrete history in a universal drama. God transcends time, and His "coming" takes place at all times.

Rudolph Bultmann took yet another step in demythologizing eschatology and history. He elaborated an existential eschatology, according to which the return of Christ takes place in the proclamation of the essence of the gospel, which forces the listener to make a decision of faith.

In the realized eschatology of C. H. Dodd, the final event already has taken place in Jesus' life and preaching. Thus God's eschatological intervention already has been accomplished.

On a differing note, Jürgen Moltmann offers a theology of hope. The future rests upon God's promises, the fulfillment of which we can see in the political, social, and ecological involvement of believers in the world. Thus Moltmann proposes a new humanistic perspective of history. The foremost proponent of the "theology of hope" in the late twentieth century is Wolfhart Pannenberg, whose eschatology is based on the "final future," which determines the ultimate significance of history as a whole and of every individual life. However, the specific content of this "final future" can be referred to only metaphorically and cannot be predicted. The distinction between present and future seems to collapse in the eternal concurrence of all events (Pannenberg 81) and suggests that to some extent Pannenberg shares Moltmann's perspective.

Oscar Cullmann has restored to the history of salvation the central focus of Scripture. History develops objectively in past, present, and future. The church is between the "already" and the "not yet"; this is the time of expectation and proclamation of the gospel. For Cullmann the resurrection of Christ is the foundation of the waiting process. The believer is to live in the "not yet," expecting something that must come. To reduce eschatology to a personal encounter of faith is an impoverishment of faith. Bible eschatology rests not only upon the resurrection of the body but also on the renewal of all things.

G. Seventh-day Adventists

Shortly after the great disappointment of 1844, believers in the Advent still affirmed the correctness of the date, but recognized their mistaken identification of the event. Christ's coming was still future; they were in the tarrying time and must be found "watching" for that day (see Luke 12:36, 37). Although doctrinal disputes on several issues created factions, there was no serious division on the certainty of a soon-to-return Saviour.

In 1850 James White published four issues of the *Advent Review*. The next year a new journal was begun: *Second Advent Review and Sabbath Herald*. The titles gave evidence of the hope and conviction of the pioneers. In 1851 Ellen White wrote that time could "last but a very little longer" (EW 58).

When the fledgling church adopted a name in 1860, the choice clearly reflected the believers' confidence. "The name Seventh-day Adventist," wrote Ellen White, "carries the true features of our faith in front" (1T 224). Early leaders among Seventh-day Adventists were united in the strong conviction that the Second Coming stood near the heart of their message.

The *Seventh-day Adventist Yearbook* of 1889 stated that "the second coming of Christ is to precede, not follow, the millennium." Furthermore, the prophetic period of 2300 days of Daniel 8:14 terminated in 1844, and no other "prophetic period is given to reach to the second advent." In addition, the work of preaching the "approach of the second advent" was symbolized by the three messages of Revelation 14 (148-150).

The basic Adventist understanding of the Second Coming has varied little through the decades. The statement of beliefs that appeared from 1932 onward in the *Seventh-day Adventist Yearbook* clearly reaffirmed the importance of the Second Coming as "the great hope of the church and the grand climax of the gospel and plan of salvation" (*SDA Yearbook* 1932:382).

On the other hand, discussion has occurred on some issues related to the Advent. For example, among Adventists as late as 1874, the "generation" of Matthew 24:34 was held to be the generation of those who had seen the darkening of the sun and the falling of the stars. Therefore, Jesus' coming had to occur soon. The importance attached to the

signs has also varied. In the late nineteenth century the fate of the Turkish empire was interpreted as a critical sign. Toward the end of the twentieth century, more emphasis has been placed on the earth's inability to sustain life as an indication of the imminence of Christ's coming.

Since 1883, when Ellen White's earlier expressions of belief in a soon-coming Saviour were challenged, Seventh-day Adventists have displayed interest in the question of the delay: Why has Christ not returned? Authors such as L. E. Froom, Herbert Douglass, and Jack Provonsha have attempted to respond. Much has been made of "conditional prophecy" in this respect (Pease 177-182). However, the certainty of the Coming has been repeatedly affirmed, as by Sakae Kubo in 1978: "The cross, the resurrection, and the ascension of Jesus make the coming of Christ an absolute certainty" (99).

In 1987 the Review and Herald Publishing Association published a book written by a group of Seventh-day Adventist scholars: *The Advent Hope in Scripture and History*. In 11 chapters the history and theology of the Second Coming are traced from the OT through the twentieth century, showing the centrality of this teaching for Christians, and especially for Seventh-day Adventists.

The 1980 General Conference session of Seventh-day Adventists adopted 27 "fundamental beliefs." Number 24 expresses the conviction held by the church and shows continuity with the belief of early Adventists.

"The second coming of Christ is the blessed hope of the church, the grand climax of the gospel. The Saviour's coming will be literal, personal, visible, and worldwide. When He returns, the righteous dead will be resurrected, and together with the righteous living will be glorified and taken to heaven, but the unrighteous will die. The almost complete fulfillment of most lines of prophecy, together with the present condition of the world, indicates that Christ's coming is imminent. The time of that event has not been revealed, and we are therefore exhorted to be ready at all times" (*SDA Yearbook* 1981:8).

Such a view is strongly supported by the Scriptures, as the preceding exposition demonstrates.

IV. Ellen G. White Comments

"The doctrine of the second advent is the very keynote of the Sacred Scriptures" (GC 299).

A. The Second Coming in the Scriptures

1. The Center of Hope

"The communion service points to Christ's second coming. It was designed to keep this hope vivid in the minds of the disciples. Whenever they met together to commemorate His death, they recounted how 'He took the cup, and gave thanks, and gave it to them, saying, Drink ye all of it; for this is my blood of the new testament, which is shed for many for the remission of sins. But I say unto you, I will not drink henceforth of this fruit of the vine, until that day when I drink it new with you in my Father's kingdom.' In their tribulation they found comfort in the hope of their Lord's return. Unspeakably precious to them was the thought, 'As often as ye eat this bread, and drink this cup, ye do show the Lord's death till He come' (1 Cor. 11:26)" (DA 659).

2. The Kingdom of God

"And the 'kingdom of God' which they had declared to be at hand was established by the death of Christ. This kingdom was not, as they had been taught to believe, an earthly empire. Nor was it that future, immortal kingdom which shall be set up when 'the kingdom and dominion, and the greatness of the kingdom under the whole heaven, shall be given to the people of the saints of the Most High'; that everlasting kingdom, in which 'all dominions shall serve and obey him' (Dan. 7:27). As used in the Bible, the expression 'kingdom of God' is employed to designate both the kingdom of grace and the kingdom of glory. The kingdom of grace is brought to view by Paul in the Epistle to the Hebrews. After pointing to Christ, the compassionate intercessor who is 'touched with the feeling of our infirmities,' the apostle says: 'Let us therefore come boldly unto *the throne of grace,* that we may obtain mercy, and find grace' (Heb. 4:15, 16). The throne of grace represents the kingdom of grace; for the existence of a throne implies the existence of a kingdom. In many of His parables Christ uses the expression 'the kingdom of heaven' to designate the work of divine grace upon the hearts of men.

"So the throne of glory represents the kingdom of glory; and this kingdom is referred to in the Saviour's words: 'When the Son of man shall come in his glory, and all the holy angels with him, then shall he sit upon the throne of his glory: and before Him shall be gathered all nations' (Matt. 25:31, 32). This kingdom is yet future. It is not to be set up until the second advent of Christ" (GC 347).

3. Manner of His Coming

"Between the first and the second advent of Christ a wonderful contrast will be seen. No human language can portray the scenes of the second coming of the Son of man in the clouds of heaven. He is to come with His own glory, and with the glory of the Father and of the holy angels. He will come clad in the robe of light, which He has worn from the days of eternity. Angels will accompany Him. Ten thousand times ten thousand will escort Him on His way. The sound of the trumpet will be heard, calling the sleeping dead from the grave" (RH Sept. 5, 1899).

"As the crowning act in the great drama of deception, Satan himself will personate Christ. The church has long professed to look to the Saviour's advent as the consummation of her hopes. Now the great deceiver will make it appear that Christ has come. In different parts of the earth, Satan will manifest himself among men as a majestic being of dazzling brightness, resembling the description of the Son of God given by John in the Revelation (Rev. 1:13-15). The glory that surrounds him is unsurpassed by anything that mortal eyes have yet beheld. The shout of triumph rings out upon the air: 'Christ has come! Christ has come!' The people prostrate themselves in adoration before him, while he lifts up his hands and pronounces a blessing upon them, as Christ blessed His disciples when He was upon the earth. His voice is soft and subdued, yet full of melody. In gentle, compassionate tones he presents some of the same gracious, heavenly truths which the Saviour uttered; he heals the diseases of the people, and then, in his assumed character of Christ, he claims to have changed the Sabbath to Sunday, and commands all to hallow the day which he has blessed. He declares that those who persist in keeping holy the seventh day are blaspheming his name by refusing to listen to his angels sent to them with light and truth. This is the strong, almost overmastering delusion" (GC 624).

"Satan has come down with great power, working with all deceivableness of unrighteousness in them that perish; but it is not necessary for any to be deceived; and we shall not be if we have fully taken our stand with Christ to follow Him through evil as well as through good report. The serpent's head will soon be bruised and crushed" (RH Sept. 5, 1899).

4. Signs of the Second Coming

"The revelator thus describes the first of the signs to precede the second advent: 'There was a great earthquake; and the sun became black as sackcloth of hair, and the moon became as blood' (Rev. 6:12).

"These signs were witnessed before the opening of the nineteenth century. In fulfillment of this prophecy there occurred, in the year 1755, the most terrible earthquake that has ever been recorded. Though commonly known as the earthquake of Lisbon, it extended to the greater part of Europe, Africa, and America" (GC 304).

"The marriage relation is holy, but in this degenerate age it covers vileness of every description. It is abused, and has become a crime which now constitutes one of the signs of the last days" (2T 252).

"One of the signs that we are living in the last days is that children are disobedient to parents, unthankful, unholy" (FE 101).

"Spiritual darkness has covered the earth and gross darkness the people. There are in many churches skepticism and infidelity in the interpretation of the Scriptures. Many, very many, are questioning the verity and truth of the Scriptures. Human reasoning and the imaginings of the human heart are undermining the inspiration of the Word of God, and that which should be received as granted, is surrounded with a cloud of mysticism. Nothing stands out in clear and distinct lines, upon rock bottom. This is one of the marked signs of the last days" (1SM 15).

"The spirit of intense worldliness that now exists, the disposition to acknowledge no higher claim than that of self-gratification, constitutes one of the signs of the last days" (5T 365).

5. Reasons for Jesus' Second Coming

"Christ has declared that He will come the second time to gather His faithful ones to Himself" (GC 37).

"No literal devil, and probation after the coming of Christ, are fast becoming popular fables. The Scriptures plainly declare that every person's destiny is forever fixed at the coming of the Lord (Rev. 22:11)" (1T 342, 343).

"The work of the investigative judgment and the blotting out of sins is to be accomplished before the second advent of the Lord. Since the dead are to be judged out of the things written in the books, it is impossible that the sins of men should be blotted out until after the judgment at which their cases are to be investigated. But the apostle Peter distinctly states that the sins of believers will be blotted out 'when the time of refreshing shall come from the presence of the Lord; and he shall send Jesus Christ' (Acts 3:19, 20). When the investigative judgment closes, Christ will come, and His reward will be with Him to give to every man as his work shall be" (GC 485).

"When the work of the investigative judgment closes, the destiny of all will have been decided for life or death. Probation is ended a short time before the appearing of the Lord in the clouds of heaven" (*ibid.* 490).

" 'Even so them also which sleep in Jesus will God bring with him,' Paul wrote. Many interpret this passage to mean that the sleeping ones will be brought with Christ from heaven; but Paul meant that as Christ was raised from the dead, so God will call the sleeping saints from their graves, and take them with Him to heaven" (AA 259).

"So was the faith of this woman rewarded. Christ, the great Life-giver, restored her son to her. In like manner will His faithful ones be rewarded, when, at His coming, death loses its sting and the grave is robbed of the victory it has claimed. Then will He restore to His servants the children that have been taken from them by death" (PK 239).

B. *Implications of the Doctrine*

1. Effects on the Believer's Daily Life

"If you have become estranged and have failed to be Bible Christians, be converted; for the character you bear in probationary time will be the character you will have at the coming of Christ. If you would be a saint in heaven, you must first be a saint on earth. The traits of character you cherish in life will not be changed by death or by the resurrection. You will come up from the grave with the same disposition you manifested in your home and in society. Jesus does not change the character at His coming. The work of transformation must be done now. Our daily lives are determining our destiny" (AH 16).

"Belief in the near coming of the Son of man in the clouds of heaven will not cause the true Christian to become neglectful and careless of the ordinary business of life. The waiting ones who look for the soon appearing of Christ will not be idle, but diligent in business. Their work will not be done carelessly and dishonestly, but with fidelity, promptness, and thoroughness. Those who flatter themselves that careless inattention to the things of this life is an evidence of their spirituality and of their separation from the world are under a great deception. Their veracity, faithfulness, and integrity are tested and proved in temporal things. If they are faithful in that which is least they will be faithful in much" (4T 309).

2. Motivation for Evangelization

"Upon those to whom God has given great light, rests the solemn responsibility of calling the attention of others to the significance of the increase of drunkenness and crime. They should also bring before the minds of others the Scriptures that plainly portray the conditions which will exist just prior to the second coming of Christ" (Te 27).

"There is not one of you that will enter in through the gates into the city alone. If you give back to God in willing service the powers He has given you, not only will you save your own soul, but your influence will be to gather others. Everyone who takes his position steadfastly for the truth is bringing other souls to the same decision and to Heaven" (ST Sept. 15, 1887).

"This is God's plan: that men and women who are partakers of this great salvation through Jesus Christ should be His missionaries, bodies of light throughout the world, to be as signs to the people—living epistles, known and read of all men; their faith and works testifying to the near approach of the coming Saviour, and that they have not received the grace of God in vain. The people must be warned to prepare for the coming judgment" (RH Aug. 16, 1887).

3. Spiritual Preparation for His Return

"The judgments of God are about to fall upon the world, and we need to be preparing for that great day.

"Our time is precious. We have but few, very few, days of probation in which to make ready for the future, immortal life. We have no time to spend in haphazard movements. We should fear to skim the surface of the word of God" (6T 407).

"They were to pray for its coming as an event yet future. But this petition was also an assurance to them. While they were not to behold the coming of the kingdom in their day, the fact that Jesus bade them pray for it is evidence that in God's own time it will surely come" (MB 108).

4. Apparent Delay

"Many who have called themselves Adventists have been time-setters. Time after time has been set for Christ to come, but repeated failures have been the result. The definite time of our Lord's coming is declared to be beyond the ken of mortals" (RH Aug. 16, 1887).

"Different times were set for the Lord to come, and were urged upon the brethren. But the Lord showed me that they would pass by, for the time of trouble must take place before the coming of Christ, and that every time that was set, and passed, would weaken the faith of God's people" (1T 72).

"Our position has been one of waiting and watching, with no time-proclamation to intervene between the close of the prophetic periods in 1844 and the time of our Lord's coming. We do not know the day nor the hour, or when the definite time is, and yet the prophetic reckoning shows us that Christ is at the door" (10MR 270).

"Those who think they must preach definite time in order to make an impression upon the people, do not work from the right standpoint. The feelings of the people may be stirred, and their fears aroused; but they do not move from principle. An excitement is cre-ated, but when the time passes, as it has done repeatedly, those who moved out upon time fall back into coldness and darkness and sin, and it is almost impossible to arouse their consciences without some great excitement" (RH Aug. 16, 1887).

"In consideration to the shortness of time, we as a people should watch and pray, and in no case allow ourselves to be diverted from the solemn work of preparation for the great event before us. Because the time is apparently extended, many have become careless and indifferent in regard to their words and actions. They do not realize their danger, and do not see and understand the mercy of our God in lengthening their probation, that they may have time to form characters for the future immortal life" *(ibid.)*.

C. Historical Overview

1. The Apostolic Period

"The coming of the Lord has been in all ages the hope of His true followers. The Saviour's parting promise upon Olivet, that He would come again, lighted up the future for His disciples, filling their hearts with joy and hope that sorrow could not quench nor trials dim. Amid suffering and persecution, the 'appearing of the great God and our Saviour Jesus Christ' was the 'blessed hope'" (GC 302).

2. The Post-Nicene Period Until Reformation

"The Waldenses cherished the same faith" *(ibid.* 303).

"Wycliffe looked forward to the Redeemer's appearing as the hope of the church" *(ibid.)*.

3. The Reformation

"Luther declared: 'I persuade myself verily, that the day of judgment will not be absent full three hundred years. God will not, cannot, suffer this wicked world much longer'" *(ibid.)*.

"'This aged world is not far from its end,' said Melanchthon" *(ibid.)*.

"Calvin bids Christians 'not to hesitate, ardently desiring the day of Christ's coming as of all events most auspicious'; and declares that 'the whole family of the faithful will keep in view that day'" (*ibid.*).

"'Has not the Lord Jesus carried up our flesh into heaven?' said Knox, the Scotch Reformer, 'and shall He not return? We know that He shall return, and that with expedition'" (*ibid.*).

"Ridley and Latimer, who laid down their lives for the truth, looked in faith for the Lord's coming" (*ibid.*).

"'The thoughts of the coming of the Lord,' said Baxter, 'are most sweet and joyful to me'" (*ibid.*).

"Such was the hope of the apostolic church, of the 'church in the wilderness,' and of the Reformers" (*ibid.* 304).

4. From the Reformation to the Nineteenth Century

"But as the spirit of humility and devotion in the church had given place to pride and formalism, love for Christ and faith in His coming had grown cold. . . . The doctrine of the second advent had been neglected; the scriptures relating to it were obscured by misinterpretation, until it was, to a great extent, ignored and forgotten. Especially was this the case in the churches of America" (*ibid.* 309).

"It was not the scholarly theologians who had an understanding of this truth, and engaged in its proclamation. Had these been faithful watchmen, diligently and prayerfully searching the Scriptures, they would have known the time of night; the prophecies would have opened to them the events about to take place. But they did not occupy this position, and the message was given by humbler men" (*ibid.* 312).

"Like the great Reformation of the sixteenth century, the advent movement appeared in different countries of Christendom at the same time. In both Europe and America men of faith and prayer were led to the study of the prophecies, and, tracing down the inspired record, they saw convincing evidence that the end of all things was at hand" (*ibid.* 357).

"In South America, . . . Lacunza, a Spaniard and a Jesuit, found his way to the Scriptures and thus received the truth of Christ's speedy return. . . . Lacunza lived in the eighteenth century, but it was about 1825 that his book, having found its way to London, was translated into the English language. Its publication served to deepen the interest already awakening in England in the subject of the second advent" (*ibid.* 363).

"In Germany the doctrine had been taught in the eighteenth century by Bengel, a minister in the Lutheran Church and a celebrated Biblical scholar and critic" (*ibid.* 363).

"Bengel's writings have been spread throughout Christendom. His views of prophecy were quite generally received in his own state of Württemberg, and to some extent in other parts of Germany" (*ibid.* 364).

"The light shone also in France and Switzerland. At Geneva where Farel and Calvin had spread the truth of the Reformation, Gaussen preached the message of the second advent" (*ibid.* 364).

"In Scandinavia also the advent message was proclaimed, and a widespread interest was kindled. . . . But the clergy of the state church opposed the movement. . . . In many places where the preachers of the Lord's soon coming were thus silenced, God was pleased to send the message, in a miraculous manner, through little children" (*ibid.* 366).

"In 1821, three years after Miller had arrived at his exposition of the prophecies pointing to the time of the judgment, Dr. Joseph Wolff, 'the missionary to the world,' began to proclaim the Lord's soon coming" (*ibid.* 357).

"As early as 1826 the advent message began to be preached in England" (*ibid.* 362).

V. Literature

Althaus, Paul. *The Theology of Martin Luther.* Trans. Robert C. Schultz. Philadelphia: Fortress, 1966.

Andreasen, Niels-Erik. "The Advent Hope in the Old Testament." In *The Advent Hope in Scripture and History.* Ed. V. Norskov Olsen. Hagerstown, Md.: Review and Herald, 1987. Pp. 15-30.

Bacchiocchi, Samuele. *The Advent Hope for Human Hopelessness.* Berrien Springs, Mich.: Biblical Perspectives, 1986.

Ball, Bryan W. "Eschatological Hope in Puritan England." In *The Advent Hope in Scripture and History.* Ed. V. Norskov Olsen. Washington, D.C.: Review and Herald, 1987. Pp. 132-151.

————. *A Great Expectation: Eschatological Thought in English Protestantism to 1660.* Leiden: Brill, 1975.

Berkhof, Louis. *The Second Coming of Christ.* Grand Rapids: Eerdmans, 1953.

Berkouwer, Gerrit Cornelius. *The Return of Christ.* Studies in Dogmatics. Grand Rapids: Eerdmans, 1972.

Causse, Antonin. *L'évolution de l'espérance messianique dans le christianisme primitif.* Paris: Fichtbacher, 1908.

Cohn, Norman R. C. *The Pursuit of the Millennium: Revolutionary Millenarians and Mystical Anarchists of the Middle Ages.* New York: Oxford University Press, 1970.

Cullmann, Oscar. *Christ et le temps: temps et histoire dans le christianisme primitif.* Neuchâtel: Delachaux et Niestlé, 1957.

————. *Le retour du Christ: espérance de l'église selon le Nouveau Testament.* Cahiers théologiques de l'actualité protestante, 1. Neuchâtel: Delachaux et Niestlé, 1945.

Emmerson, Richard K. *Antichrist in the Middle Ages: A Study of Medieval Apocalypticism, Art, and Literature.* Seattle: University of Washington Press, 1981.

Fagal, Harold E. "The Advent Hope in the New Testament." In *The Advent Hope in Scripture and History.* Ed. V. Norskov Olsen. Hagerstown, Md.: Review and Herald, 1987. Pp. 46-64.

Ferch, Arthur J. *The Son of Man in Daniel Seven.* Andrews University Seminary Doctoral Dissertation Series. No. 6. Berrien Springs, Mich.: Andrews University Press, 1979.

Froom, LeRoy. *The Prophetic Faith of Our Fathers.* 4 vols. Washington, D.C.: Review and Herald, 1950-1954.

Hasel, Gerhard F. "The 'Little Horn,' the Heavenly Sanctuary, and the Time of the End: A Study of Daniel 8:9-14." In *Symposium on Daniel.* Ed. Frank B. Holbrook. Washington, D.C.: Biblical Research Institute, 1986. Pp. 378-461.

————. *The Remnant: The History and Theology of the Remnant Idea From Genesis to Isaiah.* Berrien Springs, Mich.: Andrews University Press, 1980.

Holbrook, Frank B., ed. *Seventy Weeks, Leviticus, and the Nature of Prophecy.* Daniel and Revelation Committee Series. Vol. 2. Washington, D.C.: Biblical Research Institute, 1986.

————. *Symposium on Daniel.* Daniel and Revelation Committee Series. Vol. 2. Washington, D.C.: Biblical Research Institute, 1986.

Kelly, J.N.D. *Early Christian Creeds.* London: Longmans, 1950.

Kubo, Sakae. *God Meets Man: A Theology of the Sabbath and Second Advent.* Nashville: Southern Publishing, 1978.

Landa, Paul. "The Advent Hope in Early Christianity." In *The Advent Hope in Scripture and History.* Ed. V. Norskov Olsen. Hagerstown, Md.: Review and Herald, 1987. Pp. 65-94.

Lehmann, Richard. "Advent on Ice." *Ministry,* November 1984.

Miller, William. *Evidence From Scripture and History of the Second Coming of Christ About the Year 1843.* Boston: J. V. Himes, 1842; reprinted, Payson, Ariz.: Leaves of Autumn, 1985.

Moore, Arthur L. *The Parousia in the New Testament.* Supplements to Novum Testamentum. No. 13. Leiden: Brill, 1966.

Olsen, V. Norskov, ed. *The Advent Hope in Scripture and History.* Washington, D.C.: Review and Herald, 1987.

Pache, René. *The Return of Jesus Christ.* Trans. William S. LaSor. Chicago: Moody, 1955.

Pannenberg, Wolfhart. *What Is Man?* Philadelphia: Fortress, 1970.

Pease, Norval F. "The Second Advent in Seventh-day Adventist History and Theology." In *The Advent Hope in Scripture and History.* Ed. V. Norskov Olsen. Washington, D.C.: Review and Herald, 1987. Pp. 173-190.

Pelikan, Jaroslav. *The Christian Tradition: A History of the Development of Doctrine.* Vol. 4, *Reformation of Church and Dogma (1300-1700).* Chicago: University of Chicago Press, 1984.

Pidoux, Georges. *Le Dieu qui vient: espérance d'Israël.* Cahiers théologiques de l'actualité protestante, 17. Neuchâtel: Delachaux et Niestlé, 1947.

Rast, Thimoteus. "L'eschatologie." *Bilan de la théologie du XXIe siècle.* Ed. Robert Vander Gucht et Herbert Vorgrimler. Paris: Casterman, 1970. Vol. 2. Pp. 501-515.

Schwantes, Siegfried J. "'*Ereb Bōqer*' of Daniel 8:14 Re-examined." In *Symposium on Daniel.* Ed. Frank B. Holbrook. Washington, D.C.: Biblical Research Institute, 1986. Pp. 462-474.

Schweitzer, Albert. *The Mysticism of Paul the Apostle.* New York: Seabury, 1968.

Shea, William. *Selected Studies on Prophetic Interpretation.* Daniel and Revelation Committee Series. Vol. 1. Washington, D.C.: General Conference of Seventh-day Adventists, 1982.

Smith, Uriah. *The Prophecies of Daniel and the Revelation.* Washington, D.C.: Review and Herald, 1944. First published in 1867.

Torrance, Thomas F. *Les réformateurs et la fin des temps.* Cahiers théologiques, 35. Neuchâtel: Delachaux et Niestlé, 1955.

Vaucher, Alfred F. *Une célébrité oubliée: le P. Manuel de Lacunza y Diaz (1731-1801).* Collonges-sous-Salève, France: Fides, 1968.

The Millennium

Eric Claude Webster

Introduction

Only in Revelation 20 is there biblical reference to the period known as the 1,000 years, commonly called the millennium. Accepting the Apocalypse as an inspired biblical book, we must integrate the concept of the millennium into its general scheme of eschatology. Because some early Church Fathers developed a picture of the millennium that resulted in extreme views of earthliness, many have neglected this issue. In fact, the millennium has been rejected by many.

As described in Revelation 20:1-14, the millennium is a period of 1,000 years bounded by two resurrections; the first is that of the righteous at the second advent of Christ and the second is that of the wicked at the conclusion of the period. Satan is bound at the beginning of the millennium—his opportunity for deception comes to an end. All the righteous, living and resurrected, are given immortality and taken to heaven to live and reign with Christ for the duration of the millennium. The wicked are destroyed by the brightness of Christ's coming, leading to the depopulation of the earth. In this condition the earth becomes a "bottomless pit," to which Satan and his angels are confined for the 1,000 years.

In heaven the righteous reign with Christ and take part in the deliberative phase of the judgment upon the wicked. Upon the completion of this work Christ and the saints return to this earth accompanied by the New Jerusalem. With the descent of Christ and the city the wicked are raised, resulting in another opportunity for Satan to become active. He performs his last act of deception in persuading the wicked to attack the New Jerusalem.

At this time the final judgment of the wicked takes place, and all who have rejected God's mercy and grace face the tribunal. There is no advocate to plead mercy, and final retribution falls upon them. The fires that destroy Satan and his followers also destroy all vestiges of sin. Out of the dust and ashes of this judgment will emerge God's re-created world, the eternal home for the people of God.

I. A Biblical Exposition

A. Principles of Interpretation

The results of an exegesis of Revelation depend on the general hermeneutical principles followed. Thus, the difference between premillennialism and amillennialism is mostly a matter of interpretation.

A prominent and important hermeneutical principle in biblical interpretation is the Christocentric principle. This regards Christ as the key to the unlocking of prophetic Scripture in both the OT and NT. This principle is a safeguard against excessive literalism, such as that followed by dispensational premillennialists. This literalism has led dispensationalists to seek a literal fulfillment for all OT prophecies and to develop different dispensations that culminate in the kingdom dispensation during the millennium.

Another important hermeneutical principle is the unity in God's plan of salvation, in the OT and NT, between Israel and the church. This again differs from dispensationalist interpretation, which sees two distinct plans in salvation history. In contrast with dispensationalism, one essential Christocentric plan of salvation from Creation to the Second Advent should be seen as the foundation of the biblical view. Augmenting this concept is that of the basic unity of God's covenant through the ages.

An additional important hermeneutical principle is that Scripture is its own interpreter. This principle often leads to a symbolic and spiritual application of OT prophecies. Where literalism would call for these prophecies to be fulfilled in the future in literal Israel of the Middle East, the spiritual key applies them to the true people of God from all nations. This principle has been adopted by many Protestant interpreters since the Reformation.

B. The Setting of Revelation 20

The word "millennium" is derived from two Latin words, *mille,* meaning "one thousand," and *annus* meaning "year"; hence, "a thousand years." The concept comes from Revelation 20, where the phrase "a thousand years" is used six times (verses 2, 3, 4, 5, 6, 7). Only here in Scripture is the teaching of the millennium explicitly formulated.

The context of chapter 20 in the general theme of the book must be determined at the outset. This task is complicated by the fact that Revelation does not follow a straight-line time progression. As an alternative, a recapitulationist order has been proposed. Barr has defined "recapitulation" as the theory that holds "that the same message is retold several times in the apocalypse, with later cycles duplicating the meaning of earlier cycles" (43). This idea of "progressive parallelism" or "recapitulation" fits the prophecies of both Daniel and Revelation well, but the location of Revelation 20 in this scheme still needs to be determined.

The book of Revelation has a chiastic (inverted parallel) structure. In this scheme the prologue (1:1-10) and the epilogue (22:6-21) are counterparts, while the eight intervening visions are paired in chiastic or inverse order. The first half (1-14) deals with the historical era, while the second half pertains to an "eschatological-judgment" era, after the close of human probation. Section 7 (19:1–21:4) presents God's judgment finale, with the Second Advent, the millennium, and the white throne judgment. These three parts must not be separated. Thus, the period of 1,000 years cannot take place before the Second Coming.

Revelation 16:13 sees a triumvirate of the dragon, the beast, and the false prophet in opposition to God in the final days just before the Parousia. Two of these powers, the beast and the false prophet, are dealt with in Revelation 19:20, at the second advent of Christ. Revelation 20 follows logically by describing the fate of the third power, the dragon, at this same time. Revelation 20 completes the picture of Revelation 19:11-21 in depicting Christ's confrontation with these three powers. Revelation 20 should be seen, therefore, in chronological sequence with Revelation 19:11-21.

C. The Millennium in Revelation 20

1. Events at the Beginning of the Millennium

The events that take place at the beginning of the millennium are those that accompany the Second Coming, when the wicked are slain by the glory of Christ's presence and the righteous are taken to their heavenly reward. (See Second Coming I. E, G.) Three of these are specific to Revelation 20 and deserve to be considered anew.

a. The first resurrection. The resurrection of Revelation 20:4-6 should be seen as the literal resurrection of the righteous in conjunction with the second coming of Christ. This is the event of which Paul wrote in 1 Thessalonians 4:16-18. Paul affirmed that the dead in Christ would be raised; these include all of God's faithful people since the beginning of earth's history. John the Revelator describes them as "blessed and holy" because they believed in Christ, now participate in His heavenly reign, and will never see death, because the second death has no power over them (Rev. 20:6; see Resurrection I. A; Death I. F. 5).

This passage has a "first resurrection" and the one in which the "rest of the dead" come to life after the 1,000 years. Similarly, in John 5:29 the two resurrections are the "resurrection of life" and the "resurrection of judgment." Evidently, the "first resurrection" is the "resurrection of life."

b. Satan bound. In symbolic language Revelation 20:1-3 describes the binding of Satan. Four names are given to this being: the dragon, that old serpent, the devil, and Satan. This is undoubtedly the same being mentioned in Revelation 12:7-9 by the same names, the archenemy of God's people throughout the ages.

Since Satan and his angels are spiritual beings (as noted by Paul in Ephesians 6:11, 12), the "key" and the "chain" that bind him should likewise be considered as spiritual. They symbolize those circumstances that immobilize his powers at the beginning of the 1,000 years, making it impossible for him to deceive the nations.

Various NT texts indicate that progressive limitations have been put on Satan's work. Jesus spoke about binding the strong man (Matt. 12:29). He also "saw Satan fall like lightning from heaven" (Luke 10:18). Nearing His crucifixion, He affirmed, "Now is the judgment of this world, now shall the ruler of this world be cast out" (John 12:31). Together with Revelation 12:7-12, these passages indicate that the "casting out" of Satan is a progressive work, taking place in stages and reaching its climax at the second advent of Christ with the final and full binding of Satan. As he is "bound," with the pit shut and "sealed . . . over him," Satan must remain on this chaotic and empty earth until the end of the 1,000 years. "After that he must be loosed for a little while" (Rev. 20:3, 7) before his final destruction.

The devil is cast into "the pit" (RSV), "the bottomless pit" (KJV), or the "abyss" (NASB, NIV). The Greek word *abyssos,* "abyss," appears in other NT passages as a place for evil spirits (Luke 8:31) or the dwelling place of the dead (Rom. 10:7); it is also used in intertestamental Jewish literature for the place of punishment (1 Enoch 10:4-6; Jubilees 5:6-10). In Revelation 11:7 and 17:8 *abyssos* is the place from which the beast comes. The word used here is the same as that employed by the LXX in Genesis 1:2 to describe the chaotic situation of earth at Creation, when darkness was "upon the face of the deep." The earth reverts to chaos at the second advent of Christ and the beginning of the 1,000 years.

c. The earth desolated. Convulsions of nature accompany the destruction of the wicked at the Second Advent, bringing the earth into a state of chaos. When the angel pours out the seventh plague, there is a "great earthquake such as had never been since men were on the earth" (Rev. 16:18) and "every island fled away, and no mountains were to be found" (verse 20). Isaiah's apocalypse describes a similar condition: "The earth is utterly broken, the earth is rent asunder, the earth is violently shaken. The earth staggers like a drunken man, it sways like a hut" (Isa. 24:19, 20). Other aspects of this prophecy are parallel to Revelation: "On that day the Lord will punish the host of heaven, in heaven, and the kings of the earth, on the earth. They will be gathered together as prisoners in a pit; they will be shut up in a prison" (verses 21, 22; cf. Rev. 19:19-21). The world becomes the "pit" or "abyss" to which Satan and his angels are confined. Satan can exercise no creative or organizational power over the earth; it remains in a chaotic state for the entire millennium.

At the same time, the earth is depopulated. Jesus affirmed that those who were not prepared for the Second Coming would be destroyed "on the day when the Son of man is revealed," as had happened in the days of Noah and Lot (Luke 17:26-30). Paul confirmed the destruction of the wicked at the Parousia (2 Thess. 1:7, 8). While the wicked are destroyed, the righteous are removed from the earth. Paul made it clear that at the Second Advent the "dead in Christ" would "rise first"; then the living saints would be "caught up together with them in the clouds to meet the Lord in the air" (1 Thess. 4:16, 17). Thus would be fulfilled Jesus' promise: "In my Father's house are many rooms; if it were not so, would I have told you that I go to prepare a place for you? And when I go and prepare a place for you, I will come again and will take you to myself, that where I am you may be also" (John 14:2, 3). Neither wicked nor righteous remain

on this earth for Satan to tempt or harass.

2. Events During the Millennium

While Revelation 20:1-3 describes what happens at the beginning of the millennium, verses 4-6 speak of what happens during the 1,000 years. In verse 4 the revelator describes a judgment scene in which the righteous reign with Christ for 1,000 years. A closer look at the location of this judgment and the judgment itself is in order.

a. The location. The scene is set in heaven. In verses 4-6 nothing is said about the earth. In the book of Revelation the word "throne" is used 47 times. In all but three of these cases (2:13; 13:2; 16:10), the thrones are in heaven. This passage, likewise, refers to heaven. Instead of Christ's reigning with the saints on their earth, we have the saints reigning with Christ in His heaven.

The question of where the righteous will spend the millennium can be addressed by other passages in Revelation. While these do not refer to the 1,000 years, they do indicate where the saints will be immediately after the Second Coming. In the first half of Revelation 7, the saints are sealed; in the second half they are located before the throne of God, where they serve Him day and night within His temple (verse 15). There God Himself comforts them and provides for them so that they never have to suffer privation and persecution as they did on earth (verses 16, 17). The same throne of God—with its living beings, elders, and sea of glass—appears in Revelation 4:1-6. There is no doubt that this scene takes place in heaven. According to Revelation 21:22, there is no temple in the new esarth; thus the place of God's throne in Revelation 4 and 7 is in heaven.

Revelation 14:1-5 locates the 144,000 on Mount Zion, with the Lamb. As individuals redeemed "from the earth" they sing a new song (verse 3) before the throne, the living beings, and the elders. They are the same ones who were sealed in Revelation 7, who have been victorious over the beast of Revelation

13 and 14. Because what follows in verses 6-13 occurs before the appearance of the Son of man seated on a white cloud, one might think that the place referred to is on earth. "Mount Zion" appears only here in Revelation, and may be considered parallel to the city of Hebrews 12:22: "Mount Zion . . . the city of the living God, the heavenly Jerusalem." The scene of these verses is the result, shown first, before the events leading up to it. The earthly city of Jerusalem plays no significant role in Revelation. Certainly the city must have been destroyed before the book was written. In addition, John hears their song, as "the sound of many waters," from heaven (verse 2). The Zion referred to in Revelation 14 must be the heavenly Zion.

In Revelation 15:2-4 the victorious saints stand on the sea of glass with harps in hand and sing the Song of Moses and the Lamb. Immediately the temple of God is opened (verses 5-7), showing that the scene takes place in heaven.

The relations between Revelation 4; Revelation 7:9-17; 14:1-5; and 15:2-5 indicate that all refer to the same setting. The descriptions are of the redeemed before the throne of God in heaven. Each text contributes to the total picture. Revelation 4 emphasizes the throne and its surroundings. Revelation 7 places the throng of the redeemed before that throne. Revelation 14 describes the joy of the redeemed, the spotless ones, who play harps and sing a new song. In Revelation 15 we have the words of this new song.

The same setting is seen in Revelation 20:4. Those who were victorious, those who had not worshiped the beast nor received its mark are with Christ in heaven. Here they share in His reign and in His judgment.

b. The persons who judge. According to Revelation 20:4, judgment is committed to those who are seated on thrones, those who were "beheaded for their testimony to Jesus and for the word of God," who have come to life to reign "with Christ a thousand years." Immediately we are told that these are partici-

pants in the "first resurrection," over whom a blessing is pronounced. Three times it is made clear that the first resurrection is a prerequisite to their living and reigning with Christ.

The phrase "souls of those who had been beheaded" deserves special attention. The word *psychē*, "soul," has a broad range of meanings. These fall into four basic categories: (1) a living organism, (2) a person or personality, (3) the physical life of a human being, (4) the inner life of a person. The word is consistently used as a synonym for the Heb. *nepeš*, which has a similar range of meaning. Never is the word used in the Bible to refer to a disembodied soul. The word *psychē* occurs 103 times in the NT. In the KJV it is translated as "soul" 58 times, as "life" 40 times, as "mind" three times. In the RSV *psychē* is rendered "soul" only 40 times; in the NIV, only 25; and in the NEB, only 19 times. Newer translations often use personal pronouns or the word "life" rather than "soul." (See Man I. E; Death I. A. 4.)

If *psychē* in Revelation 20:4 is taken to mean "life" or "person," the revelator saw people in heaven who had been dead and who had participated in the resurrection at the Second Advent and were now living and reigning with Christ for 1,000 years. These are full persons, not disembodied spirits, enjoying full resurrection life.

While the RSV of Revelation 20:4 makes it appear that all those who were living and reigning with Christ were those who had been martyred and had come to life in the first resurrection, the Greek suggests two groups. The second is made up of those who had not worshiped the beast or its image and "had not received its mark on their foreheads or their hands."

c. The judgment. A careful look at the concept of judgment reveals a rich spectrum of events under this one heading. At least six judgments cover the period from the Incarnation to the close of the earth's history. There is first the judgment of Christ's life and death (John 12:31, 32). A second aspect of judgment is one's personal decision for or against Christ

(John 3:14-18). A third phase of judgment is the heavenly pre-Advent judgment depicted in Daniel 7:9-13. A fourth kind of judgment occurs at the Second Advent, when the wicked are destroyed by the brightness of His coming. The fifth aspect of judgment is the one depicted in Revelation 20:4, while the sixth and final is the "great white throne" judgment after the millennium (verses 11-14). (For the three major phases of the final judgment, see Judgment III. B.)

In this article we are specifically concerned with the phase of final judgment that takes place in heaven during the millennium. The fate of all has already been sealed at Christ's return. The dead in Christ have come to life in the first resurrection (Rev. 20:5, 6); they and the living saints have been "caught up together . . . in the clouds" and are living and reigning with the Lord (1 Thess. 4:16, 17; Rev. 20:4). Those who "do not obey the gospel of our Lord Jesus" have been destroyed (2 Thess. 1:7, 8; Luke 17:26-30). What, then, is the purpose of this judgment if rewards have already been given at the Second Coming?

The judgment given to the saints in Revelation 20:4 corresponds to the judgment Paul announced in 1 Corinthians 6:2, 3: "Do you not know that the saints will judge the world? . . . Do you not know that we are to judge angels?" During the millennium the saints participate in a deliberative judgment that reviews the cases of the lost of this earth and the fallen angels. This judgment is evidently necessary in view of the cosmic nature of the sin problem. The course of the rebellion of sin has been the object of concern and interest on the part of other worlds (Job 1; 2; Eph. 3:10). The whole interlude of sin must be handled in such a way that hearts and minds throughout God's universe are satisfied with its treatment and conclusion, with particular reference to God's character. It is especially important for the redeemed from earth to understand God's dealings with those who called for the rocks to fall on them and deliver them from the "face of him who is seated

on the throne" (Rev. 6:16). They must be totally satisfied that God was just in His decision regarding the lost.

d. Conditions on earth. While in heaven the saints reign and judge with Christ, the earth is desolate. The wicked are dead; Satan is bound to this earth (see I. C. 1. b, c). With no one to tempt or mislead, Satan is inoperative and powerless. His angels are in a contemplative and rebellious mood on a desolate and barren world.

The earth is devastated and in chaos, as it was at the beginning. The great earthquake of Revelation 16:18-20 has leveled all the cities. The words of Isaiah find their fulfillment: "The earth is utterly broken, the earth is rent asunder, the earth is violently shaken. The earth staggers like a drunken man, it sways like a hut; its transgression lies heavy upon it, and it falls, and will not rise again." At that time, God will punish "the host of the high ones" (KJV) and the kings of the earth, who are "gathered together as prisoners in a pit," and shall be "shut up in a prison" (Isa. 24:19-22).

3. Events at the End of the Millennium

The events that will take place at the end of the millennium are noted in Revelation 20:5, 7-10 and chapter 21. It is difficult to put them in exact chronological order since there is recapitulation in both chapters 20 and 21.

a. The Holy City descends. For a resurrection to occur, the Life-giver must be present. Thus one may assume that the first event after the millennium is the return of Christ to this earth. Given that He appears with the saints in the Holy City, one may also safely say that all come together from heaven to earth (Rev. 21:2). At this point, "the Lord will become king over all the earth" (Zech. 14:9; cf. Rev. 21:2, 3).

b. The second resurrection. Revelation 20:5 affirms that "the rest of the dead did not come to life until the thousand years were ended." The wicked thus return to life; this is the resurrection of judgment of John 5:29. It is also the same resurrection described in Revelation 20:13. This resurrection gives Satan a new opportunity to deceive (verse 8).

c. Satan loosed from his prison. At the second resurrection, Satan is "loosed from his prison" (verse 7) "for a little while" (verse 3). God does not unfasten a literal chain or open the door of a literal prison; rather, the resurrection of the wicked makes it again possible for Satan to have subjects with whom he can work.

Ever the master deceiver, Satan now goes about doing what he knows best. He sets out to "deceive the nations which are in the four quarters of the earth" (verse 8 [KJV]). The global extent of his deception should be noted. Gog and Magog are symbols of universal rebellion against the God of heaven (see Eze. 38:2). The number of the wicked of all the ages involved is likened to "the sand of the sea" (Rev. 20:8). Satan now inspires the wicked nations of the world to overthrow the City of God, which has descended from heaven (Rev. 21:2). The city is called "the camp of the saints and the beloved city" (Rev. 20:9). The hosts of evil march up to the city and surround it (verse 9). The fact that they are still hostile to God indicates how right was the divine decision to deprive them of the reward of the saints.

d. The judgment of the "great white throne." Revelation 20:11, 12 presents a picture of the great final assize. The one who judges is Christ; before Him, the wicked tremble and nature is convulsed. The revelator notes: "And I saw the dead, great and small, standing before the throne, and books were opened. Also another book was opened, which is the book of life. And the dead were judged by what was written in the books, by what they had done" (verse 12). Those who had been dead were judged by their actions recorded in "books." The description also notes the book of life, in which the names of the redeemed are inscribed, mentioned also in Revelation 3:5; 13:8; 17:8; 20:15. In this judgment there is no reference to grace, no mention of an advocate. Those who failed to make Christ their advocate face the stark reality of a judgment according to works, from which there is no escape.

e. The destruction of the wicked. After the final judgment before the "great white throne," at the end of the 1,000 years, the destruction of the wicked takes place. This destruction is introduced in Revelation 20:9: "Fire came down from heaven and consumed them." The thought is repeated in verses 14 and 15: "Then Death and Hades were thrown into the lake of fire. This is the second death, the lake of fire; and if any one's name was not found written in the book of life, he was thrown into the lake of fire." Throughout Revelation, the "second death" is seen as the terrible and inescapable end of the wicked (Rev. 2:11; 20:6; 21:8).

In Revelation 20:14, the second death is equated with the "lake of fire." In Revelation 19:20 and 20:10, the lake burns with sulfur. According to the third angel's message, those who receive the mark of the beast are "tormented with fire and sulphur in the presence of the holy angels and in the presence of the Lamb" (Rev. 14:10).

In parable and prophecy Jesus described the fires of God's retribution. In Matthew 13:40-42 we read: "Just as the weeds are gathered and burned with fire, so will it be at the close of the age. The Son of man will send his angels, and they will gather out of his kingdom all causes of sin and all evildoers, and throw them into the furnace of fire; there men will weep and gnash their teeth." In the sermon on the final judgment, Christ affirmed that those who had not done works of mercy would "go away into eternal punishment, but the righteous into eternal life" (Matt. 25:46). Matthew 3:12 pictures an "unquenchable fire."

In Revelation 20 there appears to be a discrepancy. In verse 9 the wicked are "consumed" (Gr. *katesthiō,* "eaten up"), pointing to total annihilation; in verses 14, 15 they are thrown into a lake of fire, which elsewhere is described as "eternal" or "unquenchable," suggesting eternal torment (Rev. 14:11).

Christ's statement in Matthew 10:28, regarding hell that destroys both body and soul, points to total destruction. Since human beings are not immortal, they are consumed by the last fire. (See Man II. C. 2, 3; Death I. G. 1; Judgment II. E.)

According to Revelation 20:10, the devil is thrown into the lake of fire together with the beast and the false prophet. This reiterates the idea of Revelation 19:20, where the beast and the false prophet are "thrown alive into the lake of fire that burns with sulphur." These two, symbols of anti-Christian forces in the end-times, are destroyed. With them, the devil, who incited them to persecute God's people, is also destroyed. In addition, death and Hades, the place of the dead, are specifically mentioned (Rev. 20:14) as being cast into the lake of fire, there to be totally destroyed.

This is the final destruction predicted already in the OT. Malachi 4:1 states, "For behold, the day comes, burning like an oven, when all the arrogant and all evildoers will be stubble; the day that comes shall burn them up, says the Lord of hosts, so that it will leave them neither root nor branch." Here the emphasis is on annihilation. The root—Satan—and the branches—his followers—will be no more.

For many, the matter of the duration of this punishment is a problem. The Greek phrase translated "for ever and ever" in Revelation 14:11 is *eis aiōnas aiōnōn*. An *aiōn* (age) refers to a continuous time period, whether short, long, or never-ending. Its meaning is derived in part from the noun to which it is attached; thus the adjective *aiōnios* means that something lasts as long as the noun it describes. Thus, the devil's eternal punishment must be limited to the finitude of the devil. He is a created being and does not possess inherent, natural immortality. The results of his punishment will be final and eternal. The lake of fire into which the devil, the beast, the false prophet, along with death and Hades, are cast will eventually fulfill its task. It brings the second death to all and comes to an end. Out of the ashes of this destruction God will create a new earth in which only the righteousness will dwell (2 Peter 3:13).

II. Theological Significance of the Millennium

To summarize what the Bible says, the Second Advent is climactic and not an introduction to an unprecedented period of evangelism on earth. The 1,000 years are a real period of time after the Second Advent when Satan will be bound and the saints will reign with Christ. During this time Satan will be confined to a desolate earth, and the reign of the saints is in heaven with Christ. From this general conclusion some theological lessons may be elaborated.

A. Object Lesson Revealing Nature of Sin

The stark reality of a desolate world following the Second Advent and its accompanying events will be in sharp contrast with the glory of the saints' reign with Christ in the New Jerusalem in heaven. As noted earlier, the earth reverts to its state of chaos prior to Creation, when the world "was without form and void" (Gen. 1:2). Satan and his cohorts are confined to this desolate planet with no living beings to tempt or mislead.

During the millennium the inhabitants of the universe will have time to reflect on the result of the application of Satan's principles. The tragic consequences of sin will be indelibly inscribed in the minds of all living beings. There will be no desire for sin to arise again.

B. Confirmation of God's Character

According to Revelation 20:4 a judgment will be carried on by the saints during the millennium. This judgment involves more than agreeing with Christ's judgments; the saints have opportunity to make their own independent judgments about earthly affairs and find that these agree with divine decisions already made.

During this interlude, before sinners are finally destroyed and before the new earth is brought forth, all beings of the universe—the redeemed, the angels, and those from unfallen worlds—will have an opportunity to evaluate God's dealings with humanity. Every opportunity will be given to clear away any lingering doubts about God's character. His dealings with every sinner and with Satan and his angels will become crystal-clear, and there will be universal agreement on the loving nature of God's character.

The saints will be deeply involved in this judgment with Christ. Since the saved are already in heaven, this judgment has reference to the eternal destiny of the lost. The saved will have an opportunity to complete their understanding and be satisfied concerning the fate of their friends, loved ones, and acquaintances. During the judging activity of the millennium humanity will see the tragedy of sin from the divine viewpoint. Full opportunity will be given for clarification, understanding, confirmation, and acceptance of human destiny.

C. The Changing of the Guard

The millennium has been compared to the changing of the guard. The old evil order, so long dominant on the earth, has finally given way to the new order. The millennium lies between the times. It will serve as a divine orientation between the tragedy of sin and the triumph of the new world. The "changing of the guard" will afford time for the saints, the inhabitants of the universe, and the angels to adjust their thinking from a sin-oriented world to a universe in which its ruinous effects exist no longer. Just as God in His wisdom has seen that there should be a period of time between the first coming of Christ and His second coming, so He has also seen that there should be a period of time between His second coming and the final restoration of this world.

D. A Getting-acquainted Period

As a part of the purpose for the millennium, the millennial period in heaven might provide an ideal setting needed by God's people from vastly different cultures and eras to become acquainted with one another.

This suggests that culture and individuality will not be obliterated in the resurrection. There will still be differences between individuals, and we will still be able to recognize those differences. Although the resurrection will result in glorious spiritual bodies (1 Cor. 15:44), they will be real and will be "like his glorious body" (Phil. 3:21). During the millennium the redeemed will have the opportunity of getting acquainted with each other and the heavenly beings. (See Man III. A-C.)

III. Historical Overview

Before we sketch the positions taken through the centuries by Christians on the millennium, a definition of terms related to the topic is appropriate. The overview will then follow a chronological sequence. (See Apocalyptic IV. C. 2; D. 3.)

A. Definition of Terms

1. Millenarianism or Millennialism

Although both *millenarianism* and *millennialism,* as well as their derivatives, are based on the word *millennium* (derived from the Latin), and technically should refer to a belief in a millennium, the term *millenerianism* often used in a different and much broader sense. *Millenarianism* may point to an expectation of the Second Coming and the end of all things. Specifically, it is employed in relation to different emphases on the end of the world by Christians in Europe in the Middle Ages. *Chiliasm* from the Greek is often used in the same broad sense.

2. Amillennialism

Amillennialism may take two forms. One considers a future millennial reign as an unnecessary addendum to eschatology, a pointless interim between the glorious Advent and the climactic judgment. The other places the millennium between the death of Christ and His second coming; during this time Satan is bound in the sense that he cannot prevent the preaching of the gospel to all nations! To a great extent, *amillennialists* view Revelation 20 as describing an unveiling of the reality of salvation in Christ as a backdrop to the reality of the suffering and martyrdom on this earth.

3. Premillennialism

Basically, this term refers to a belief in the second coming of Christ *before* the millennium. There are, however, at least two distinct types of *premillennialism.*

a. Dispensational premillennialism. For dispensationalists, the goal of history is a millennial reign of Christ on earth. Indispensable to this scheme is the literal fulfillment of OT prophecies to Israel as a nation. After the coming of Christ, the millennium will be a period of evangelism and testing, under the personal reign of Christ on earth.

b. Biblical premillennialism. This name refers to premillennialists who believe that the millennium will follow the Second Coming. However, the millennial kingdom will be in heaven, while on earth all is desolation. See Section I of this article.

4. Postmillennialism

Postmillennialism claims to have a positive view of the triumph of the gospel of Christ upon the earth. Its proponents expect the gospel to go forward with great power to defeat the forces of evil before the Second Advent. During the millennium the power of the gospel will be evident and the influence of Christianity will permeate nations and societies. This millennial kingdom will be set up on this earth as convincing evidence of the power and triumph of Christ. Once this evidence has been presented, Christ will return to set up His eternal kingdom.

B. *The Millennium in History*

1. Its Roots in Jewish Apocalyptic

It has been suggested that the millennium of Revelation 20 is expressed in symbolism borrowed from Jewish apocalyptic. While there may be no clear enunciation of a millennium in Jewish apocalyptic, the seeds of Jewish expectation are in the background of later Christian understandings.

The Secrets of Enoch, known also as Slavonic Enoch or 2 Enoch (late first century A.D.), suggests that one day of Creation corresponds to 1,000 years of the world's history (2 Enoch 32:2; 33:1, 2). With this work the "stage was set for speculation of a world-week of seven thousand years—six thousand of labor and toil from Creation to judgment, followed by a millennium of rest and blessedness before the gates of eternity will open" (PFOF 1:196). While this concept is not expressed in Revelation 20, it became common among Christians for centuries.

Fourth Ezra, from about A.D. 100, speaks of a 400-year Messianic reign, after which the Messiah dies and the earth returns to silence for seven days before the resurrection and the final judgment (4 Ezra 7:28-32). While originally Jewish, this book was early taken over by Christians.

2. The Early Church

While some early Christian writers understood clearly the biblical message of Revelation 20, most had difficulties. A survey of the Church Fathers shows some of the confusion.

In the *Epistle of Barnabas* (c. A.D. 100) we find reference to the notion that, as the earth was created in six days, so history would be completed in 6,000 years. The seventh-day rest after Creation represented the Second Coming and the destruction of the wicked (verse 15). This theory is repeated by later writers; among them were Hippolytus (d. c. 236), who went so far as to predict the date of the end of the world (*Commentary on Daniel* 2. 4-7), and Jerome

(c. 342-420; *Letter* 140 to Cyprian).

Papias, an early second-century Christian writer whose works have come down to us only in fragments, is one of the earliest witnesses to millenarianism. He appears to have understood the millennial kingdom as earthly and material. Church historian Eusebius (c. 260-c. 339) referred to his "strange teachings" on the 1,000 years when, after the resurrection, Christ would set up a material kingdom on earth (*Church History* 3. 39. 11, 12).

Justin Martyr (d. c. 165) was an ardent believer in the second coming of Christ and in a literal resurrection. After that resurrection there would be "a thousand years in Jerusalem, which will then be built, enlarged, and adorned" (*Dialogue With Trypho* 80). He quotes Isaiah 65:17-25 as applying to the "thousand years." Finally Justin makes specific reference to John's prophecy that the saints would "dwell a thousand years in Jerusalem," after which the "resurrection of judgment" would take place (*ibid.* 81).

Irenaeus (c. 130-c. 200) witnessed to the premillennial position by emphasizing a literal resurrection at the Second Advent. This was to be followed by "the times of the kingdom," to which he assigned no specific length. After this would come the judgment of the "great white throne" (*Against Heresies* 5. 35. 2). After Irenaeus, Methodius of Olympus affirmed that after the resurrection the saints would "celebrate with Christ the millennium of rest." After the 1,000 years, they would pass on "to greater and better things" (*Banquet of the Ten Virgins* 9. 5).

The heterodox writer Cerinthus (second century A.D.) is quoted by Eusebius as teaching that after the resurrection, the kingdom of Christ would take place on earth and that all flesh would once again serve lusts and pleasures. The period of 1,000 years would be spent in feasting and immorality. At the same time, animal sacrifices would be made (*Church History* 3. 28. 2-5).

Tertullian (c. 160-c. 230) was a great force for Christianity in Carthage. He firmly believed that the resurrection would take place at the second coming of Christ at the end of the world (*On the Resurrection of the Flesh* 22). He further affirmed that for 1,000 years after the Second Advent the saints would live on this earth and inhabit "the divinely built city of Jerusalem." After this period of rest, the saints would be changed in a moment and transported to the kingdom of heaven (*Against Marcion* 3. 25).

Lactantius, who wrote for the religious instruction of Emperor Constantine's son, put the 1,000 years after the destruction of the wicked and the resurrection of the saints. During the millennium the saints would "produce an infinite multitude," "preside over the living as judges," and "subject the remaining nations to slavery." His description of the peace of that period intertwines biblical ideas with quotations from the *Sibylline Oracles* and Latin poetry (*Divine Institutes* 24).

As can be seen, the biblical doctrine of the millennium was soon deformed. This brought the concept into disrepute. Jerome expressed his exasperation thus: "The saints will never have an earthly kingdom, but a heavenly. Then let the story of the thousand years cease" (*Commentary on Daniel* 7:17).

3. Augustine

When the early church was a persecuted minority, the millennial hope offered comfort and solace. When the church became recognized, dominant, and powerful, however, it was far easier to look upon the present age as the time of God's special blessing on the flourishing of the gospel. The way was thus prepared for Augustine's reasoned exposition of the role of the church in his *City of God* (A.D. 413).

In his interpretation of Revelation, Augustine was heavily dependent on the "Seven Rules" and the presuppositions of Tyconius, a fourth-century Donatist. Following the rules he had devised, Tyconius had made the first resurrection spiritual (happening at conversion) and the second literal (at the Second

Coming). The millennium became a 1,000-year reign of the saints on earth, already begun with Christ's first advent. Beyond that, Tyconius had shortened the 1,000 years to 350 (three and a half times) and affirmed that the church was the New Jerusalem of Revelation 21.

Following Tyconius, Augustine made the 1,000 years extend from the first advent to the second advent of Christ. Since Satan had been cast down (Rev. 12), the "kingdom of God" was moving on to victory in the present realm. The first resurrection of Revelation 20:6 became a spiritual resurrection of the soul at conversion rather than a literal resurrection at the Second Advent. The millennium of Revelation 20 was taking place on earth. Satan was bound so that he could not seduce the church. Augustine admitted having believed in a millennium after the Second Coming, but had then changed his mind, in part because of the extreme views of its advocates, who asserted that "those who then rise again shall enjoy the leisure of immoderate carnal banquets, furnished with an amount of meat and drink such as not only to shock the feeling of the temperate, but even to surpass the measure of credulity itself. Such assertions can be believed only by the carnal" (*City of God* 20. 7).

Augustine's position, that the Christian Era constituted the millennium, became dominant, ruling throughout the Middle Ages. It remained embedded in the theological framework of the Protestant Reformers and has served as the basis for much modern biblical interpretation.

4. Joachim of Floris and the Reformation

As a forerunner to the Protestant Reformation, Joachim of Floris (1130-1202) revived interest in prophetic interpretation. His *Exposition of the Apocalypse* is of particular interest for the topic of the millennium. In it Joachim challenged the prevailing Augustinian philosophical framework, which saw the church as dominant and the interest in historical realities as insignificant. He shifted the emphasis to God's revelation in history.

Joachim saw Revelation 20 as portraying the seventh period of the world or the third age of the Spirit. This period dated from the overthrow of antichrist and might be very short. Joachim did not completely depart from Augustine's position, for he did not equate the millennium with a full 1,000 historical years. He made room for an interim period between the fall of antichrist and the final kingdom, but he did not accept the chiliastic idea of a future kingdom of a 1,000 years. During this interim period Satan would be finally bound. "The Holy Spirit has already bound the devil in part, and He will bind him more fully in that day, . . . until the time is fulfilled which is signified by the thousand years, from the time of the Lord's resurrection to the time of his [Satan's] loosing" (*Exposition on the Apocalypse,* fol. 211 v).

While still clinging to an Augustinian type of view of the 1,000 years, Joachim spoke of the future binding of Satan and set in motion forces that would challenge the traditional position. Joachim provided the prologue to the development of the historical view of prophetic fulfillment that was to culminate in the Protestant Reformation. Thus he prefigured the new interest in premillennialism.

Others, even Roman Catholics, took issue with Augustine's view on the millennium. In the late sixteenth century, Francisco Ribera, a Spanish Jesuit scholar, placed the millennium between the binding of Satan at the death of Christ and the coming of the antichrist. However, he repudiated Augustine's view of the reign of the church on earth, considering rather that during this period, the saints reigned in heaven. Furthermore, the 1000 years could be "elastic, figurative," or at least "indefinite" (PFOF 2:492).

With the exception of Heinrich Bullinger, who was a premillennialist, most Protestant scholars of the sixteenth century held—with Augustine—that the millennium had begun with Christ's death and the binding of Satan. Only in the seventeenth century did Protestants begin to locate the millennium in the future. Thus Joseph Mede (1586-1638) wrote in the *Key of Revelation* that the millennium would begin with the judgment of antichrist—clearly understood to be the Roman Church—and would last 1,000 years. The New Jerusalem would be on this earth until the universal resurrection and judgment of the wicked. John Cotton, Puritan divine in New England (1584-1652) affirmed that the 1,000 years would begin after the destruction of antichrist and Rome, not with Constantine or Theodosius. At the same time, Cotton held that the first resurrection was to be a spiritual one. Later several British and German authors emphasized the future nature of the millennium. Nevertheless, some held erroneous positions, such as that maintained by Johann Bengel (1687-1752), who advocated two millenniums: the first on earth, with Satan bound, and the second in heaven, with the saints ruling.

5. The Rise of Postmillennialism

Daniel Whitby (1638-1726) was born in England and educated in Trinity College at Oxford. He became rector of St. Edmund's in Salisbury and was a voluminous writer. In his two-volume *Paraphrase and Commentary on the New Testament,* Whitby set forth his views on the 1,000 years of Revelation 20.

Whitby spiritualized the first resurrection as Augustine had done, but this event was still future. The "first resurrection" would be a great outpouring of the Holy Spirit, the national establishment of the Jews, the overthrow of the pope and the Turks. These events would mark the beginning of the millennium when the gospel would go forth with convincing power. Under the ministration of the Holy Spirit the church, with converted Jews and Gentiles, would march across the world and bring great light to the nations. During this time Satan would be bound and the victories of the gospel would lend credence to the promise of Christ to be with His disciples to the end of the world. Christ's second advent would take place only at the end of this glorious earthly millennium. After this golden age, the end would come and Christ would return to judge all and raise the dead.

Postmillennialism grew in popularity throughout the eighteenth and nineteenth centuries. It was a very optimistic view of the human situation and naturally tended to push Christ's second advent into the distant future. This particular form of millennialism was introduced to North America by Jonathan Edwards, the foremost theologian of the Great Awakening. This line of thought was also adopted by his illustrious grandson, Timothy Dwight (1752-1817), who became president of Yale and famous as a preacher, writer, and administrator. Postmillennialism became a mark of intellectual Christians of the eighteenth and nineteenth centuries in America and Europe. It provided a place for man to cooperate with God in the establishment of the millennium upon earth in the golden age ahead.

This particular teaching was still prevalent in North America in the middle of the nineteenth century and stood in opposition to the premillennial view of Adventists, not simply for setting a date for the second coming of Christ, but for suggesting that Christ would come suddenly at this time when the golden age still lay ahead of the church on earth. Early Adventist writer James White characterized this view: "The popular view of this subject is that the world is to be converted, and that all men will become holy. This happy state of things, it is said, will continue one thousand years, during which time Christ will reign with His people spiritually" (17).

Postmillennialism was in its heyday when Adventism was in its infancy. An influential book, *The Second Advent,* by David Brown, a Scottish Presbyterian minister, made its appearance in 1846 (revised in 1849). For many years this work was recognized as a standard work on the postmillennial position. Another important work advocating this view was the *Systematic Theology* of Charles Hodge (1871), a professor at Princeton. Other influential theologians at Princeton who advocated this view included W.G.T. Shedd, R. L. Dabney,

B. H. Smith, A. H. Strong, and B. B. Warfield (Boettner 10).

The latter part of the twentieth century has seen support for the postmillennial position evaporate. The stark realities of this century with its two world wars, continuing violence, and base inhumanity have dimmed the glory of this vision of the future. The controversy over the millennium is now mainly between amillennialists and premillennialists.

6. Amillennialism Revisited

As already described, Augustine first systematized the amillennial scheme of interpretation. His views were extremely influential and "became the traditional position in both Catholicism and Protestantism." To a great extent, Augustinian amillennialism is still predominant in "conservative Reformed and Presbyterian churches" (LaRondelle September 1982).

Amillennialism takes different forms. For example, nineteenth-century German theologian Theodor Kliefoth saw the 1,000 years as applying to an intermediate state. Rather than focusing on the church on earth between the two advents, his view concentrated on the preresurrection reign of the saints in heaven. Another example is the "end-historical" view of H. Bietenhard, who contended that the millennium was to be "the last period of the dominion of Christ over this age" and " 'only the final phase and full revelation' of the one messianic kingdom." At this time, "the church will be revealed as the millennial church, and Satan will be bound" (Berkouwer 299). Some amillennialists say that the 1,000 years of Revelation 20 correspond to the present time. Others find no particular significance in this time period.

7. The Revival of Premillennialism

With the advent of the nineteenth century, a revival of interest in the prophecies and the imminence of the coming of Christ began to sweep over England and America. Many people became involved in the prophetic re-

vival and proclaimed the premillennial coming of Christ, holding to the historical method of prophetic interpretation.

Henry Drummond sponsored a series of prophetic conferences at Albury Park from 1826 to 1830; these were marked by a premillennial, historical interpretation. Edward Irving added his weight to the growth of the premillennial movement.

Flowing out of further Bible conferences at Powerscourt House came two new interpretations: futurism and Darbyism. Futurism was really a revival of the prophetic system of the Spanish Jesuit Ribera, whose work in 1590 shifted the emphasis from the Papacy as the antichrist to a future individual person who would persecute the church for three and a half literal years. This view was revived in prophetic conferences throughout England and America and brought premillennialism to the fore again.

Another wing of premillennialism was spawned by J. N. Darby (1800-1882) of the Plymouth Brethren. He became a leading figure at the Powerscourt meetings. A prolific writer, he is known as the modern founder of dispensationalism. Darby supported the pretribulation rapture of the church, which has become characteristic of this system. He visited the United States six times between 1859 and 1874 and in this way dispensationalism took hold there. The prophetic and Bible conference movement in North America was the outgrowth of this interest and many Bible students became involved in conferences such as the ones at Niagara from 1883 to 1897. As time has continued, this group has become divided between those who accept the pretribulation secret rapture and those who believe the church will go through the tribulation. The latter group has become known as postribulationists.

Among the influential followers of Darby's pretribulation rapture was C. I. Scofield (1843-1921), who produced the influential *Scofield Reference Bible*. The latter has had great influence in propagating dispensational teachings. Premillennialism has been a very important aspect of dispensationalism, and the earthly millennium following Christ's return is featured prominently in its teachings. There are also differences in viewpoint among the interpreters in this school.

Today premillennialists are divided into two basic groups: historic premillennialists and dispensational premillennialists. Both locate the millennium between two literal resurrections; both believe that the kingdom will be inaugurated by the glorious Second Coming, shortly after a time of persecution of the believers. Both see the millennial kingdom as taking place on this earth. However, while historic premillennialists see the church as the true Israel of God, dispensational premillennialists expect that the OT prophecies about Israel will be fulfilled with the literal restoration of the nation and its temple in Jerusalem.

8. Adventist Understanding

Seventh-day Adventists have their roots in the Millerite Advent awakening message of the 1840s. William Miller adopted a premillennial view as opposed to the postmillennial view current in many circles at the time. Postmillennialism had a very optimistic view of the world and its golden age, which was soon to be inaugurated by the power of the gospel prior to Christ's second advent. William Miller diametrically opposed this view by his insistence on the imminence of the second coming of Christ, even suggesting the possible date of 1843.

While Miller was a premillennialist, he was not in harmony with all the proponents of this view. Both Miller and the literalists believed in a second coming of Christ prior to the millennium and in two resurrections separated by 1,000 years. Miller did not follow the literalists, however, in their insistence on the Jewish fulfillment of all the OT prophecies during the millennium.

The *First Report of the General Conference of Christians Expecting the Advent,* published in 1841, contained the following statements on the millennium:

"We are also agreed and firmly persuaded, that the popular theory of a thousand years, or more, of the spiritual and invisible reign of Christ *'in this present evil world,'* . . . is altogether unscriptural. . . .

"We are also agreed, that at the very commencement of the millennium the Lord will come in the glory of his Father and all the saints with him, and that the sinners then remaining alive and ungodly will be slain by the sword of the Lord, . . . instead of being all converted to the obedience of the gospel" (PFOF 4:563, 564).

Following the great disappointment of 1844 an important change took place in the Adventist interpretation of the millennium: "After the dissolution of the Millerite movement in 1844, its main successor became the Seventh-day Adventists, who continued their premillennialism with one new facet: the millennial kingdom or reign of the glorified saints would be *in heaven* and not on earth. Only *after* the millennium would the New Jerusalem—together with the saints—descend to the earth to be made new as its eternal abode" (LaRondelle September 1982).

James White, an early Adventist leader who had been associated with the Millerite movement, dealt with the millennium in his booklet *A Word to the Little Flock,* published in 1849. Among other things, he transcribed a letter from his wife Ellen: "I fully agree with you, that there will be two literal resurrections, one thousand years apart. I also agree with you that . . . the new earth . . . will not appear till after the wicked dead are raised, and destroyed, at the end of the thousand years." In two 1876 articles in the *Signs of the Times,* White refuted the temporal millennium and universal conversion teachings, asserting instead the biblical and literal understanding of the 1,000 years (ST Jan. 6, 13, 1876). In his book *Bible Adventism,* published around the same time, White clearly pointed out that the millennial kingdom would be in heaven: "The immortal subjects of the kingdom will ascend with their Lord to the eternal city, and reign with Him in the judgment of the wicked a thousand years, during which time the earth will be desolate" (84).

In 1881 Uriah Smith's *Daniel and the Revelation* (which has been reprinted a number of times) presented the millennium in much the same way as was done by Ellen and James White. *Our Day in the Light of Prophecy* (1917), by W. A. Spicer, followed the same lines, as did *Questions on Doctrine* (1957). In 1980 the church adopted the following statement as Fundamental Belief No. 26.

"The millennium is the thousand-year reign of Christ with His saints in heaven between the first and second resurrections. During this time the wicked dead will be judged; the earth will be utterly desolate, without living human inhabitants, but occupied by Satan and his angels. At its close Christ with His saints and the Holy City will descend from heaven to earth. The unrighteous dead will then be resurrected, and with Satan and his angels will surround the city; but fire from God will consume them and cleanse the earth. The universe will thus be freed of sin and sinners forever" (SDA Yearbook 1981, 8).

IV. Ellen G. White Comments

Interestingly, Ellen White makes a neat distinction between the word "millennium" and the phrase "thousand years." She applies the first to the erroneous, postmillenarian idea of a "temporal millennium"; the second, she uses to describe the biblical 1,000-year period, with the saints in heaven and the devil chained to this earth.

A. Millennium

Until she heard Miller preach in 1840, Ellen White had been taught that "a temporal millennium would take place prior to the coming of Christ in the clouds of heaven" (LS 21). When she heard that Christ would come in 1843 she was seized by a great "terror," for the "time seemed so short for the conversion and salvation of the world" (*ibid.* 20). After she accepted Miller's preaching, her understanding of the millennium contributed to her separation from the Methodist Church. At a class meeting Ellen spoke of her joyful hope in the Second Coming. "When the presiding elder addressed others in the class, he expressed great joy in anticipating the temporal millennium, when the earth should be filled with the knowledge of the Lord as the waters cover the sea. He longed to see this glorious period ushered in." After the meeting she and her brother Robert were "conscious of being treated with marked coldness by those who had formerly been kind and friendly" (*ibid.* 44). Some of her comments on the "temporal millennium" follow.

"Much of the preaching of the present day is of a character to lull the people into a spiritual sleep. The doctrine of the millennium is a soothing potion to the sinner who does not desire to cease from sin. And Satan is better pleased with the help which the shepherds of the flock give him when they present truth mingled with error, than with the help given by the boldest unbeliever" (ST July 4, 1900).

"The churches of our time are seeking worldly aggrandizement, and are as unwilling to see the light of the prophecies, and receive the evidences of their fulfillment which show that Christ is soon to come, as were the Jews in reference to His first appearing. They were looking for the temporal and triumphant reign of Messiah in Jerusalem. Professed Christians of our time are expecting the temporal prosperity of the church, in the conversion of the world, and the enjoyment of the temporal millennium" (Mar 11).

"Before the Lawgiver shall come to punish the disobedient, transgressors are warned to repent, and return to their allegiance; but with the majority these warnings will be in vain. Says the apostle Peter, 'there shall come in the last days scoffers, walking after their own lusts, and saying, Where is the promise of his coming? for since the fathers fell asleep, all things continue as they were from the beginning' (2 Peter 3:3, 4). Do we not hear these very words repeated, not merely by the openly ungodly, but by many who occupy the pulpits of our land? 'There is no cause for alarm,' they cry. 'Before Christ shall come, all the world is to be converted, and righteousness is to reign for a thousand years. Peace, peace! all things continue as they were from the beginning. Let none be disturbed by the exciting message of these alarmists.' But this doctrine of the millennium does not harmonize with the teachings of Christ and His apostles. Jesus asked the significant question, 'When the Son of man cometh, shall he find faith on the earth?' (Luke 18:8). And, as we have seen, He declares that the state of the world will be as in the days of Noah. Paul warns us that we may look for wickedness to increase as the end draws near: 'The Spirit speaketh expressly, that in the latter times some shall depart from the faith, giving heed to seducing spirits, and doctrines of devils' (1 Tim. 4:1). The apostle says that 'in the last days perilous times shall come' (2 Tim. 3:1). And he gives a startling list of sins that will be found among those who have a form of godliness" (PP 102, 103).

Ellen White chided the workers in God's cause for their lethargy. She wrote, "They move as listlessly as though a temporal millennium were allowed them in which to work for souls" (2T 335). In a *Review and Herald* article in 1885, she penned: "Here in this world we are to fit up for these great trials that are soon coming upon us. And yet some of us act as though we had a whole millennium before us in which to accomplish the work. But, says the text, 'Watch and pray; for ye know not when the time is'" (RH Aug. 18, 1885). In *Gospel Workers* she wrote, "Many have failed, signally failed, where they might have made a success. They have not felt the burden of the work; they have taken things as leisurely as if they had a temporal millennium in which to work for the salvation of souls" (GW 279).

B. The 1,000 Years

Most of Ellen White's passages on the 1,000 years of Revelation 20 describe the events taking place before, during, and after the millennium. The first one transcribed here, however, has to do with the positive results of accepting the biblical doctrine.

"Such were the blessed results experienced by those who accepted the advent message. They came from different denominations, and their denominational barriers were hurled to the ground; conflicting creeds were shivered to atoms; the unscriptural hope of a temporal millennium was abandoned, false views of the second advent were corrected, pride and conformity to the world were swept away; wrongs were made right; hearts were united in the sweetest fellowship, and love and joy reigned supreme. If this doctrine did this for the few who did receive it, it would have done the same for all if all had received it" (GC 379, 380).

1. Before the Millennium

"The revelator foretells the banishment of Satan and the condition of chaos and desolation to which the earth is to be reduced, and he declares that this condition will exist for a thousand years. After presenting the scenes of the Lord's second coming and the destruction of the wicked, the prophecy continues: 'I saw an angel come down from heaven, having the key of the bottomless pit and a great chain in his hand. And he laid hold on the dragon, that old serpent, which is the devil, and Satan, and bound him a thousand years, and cast him into the bottomless pit, and shut him up, and set a seal upon him, that he should deceive the nations no more, till the thousand years should be fulfilled: and after that he must be loosed a little season' (Rev. 20:1-3)" (*ibid.* 658).

"In the typical service the high priest, having made the atonement for Israel, came forth and blessed the congregation. So Christ, at the close of His work as a mediator, will appear, 'without sin unto salvation' (Heb. 9:28), to bless His waiting people with eternal life. As the priest, in removing the sins from the sanctuary, confessed them upon the head of the scapegoat, so Christ will place all these sins upon Satan, the originator and instigator of sin. The scapegoat, bearing the sins of Israel, was sent away 'unto a land not inhabited' (Lev. 16:22); so Satan, bearing the guilt of all the sins which he has caused God's people to commit, will be for a thousand years confined to the earth, which will then be desolate, without inhabitant, and he will at last suffer the full penalty of sin in the fires that shall destroy all the wicked. Thus the great plan of redemption will reach its accomplishment in the final eradication of sin, and the deliverance of all who have been willing to renounce evil" (*ibid.* 485, 486).

2. During the Millennium

"After the saints are changed to immortality and caught up together with Jesus, after they receive their harps, their robes, and their crowns, and enter the city, Jesus and the saints sit in judgment. The books are opened—the book of life and the book of death. The book of life contains the good deeds of the saints; and the book of death contains the evil deeds of the wicked. These books are compared with the statute book, the Bible, and according to that men are judged. The saints, in unison with Jesus, pass their judgment upon the wicked dead. 'Behold ye,' said the angel, 'the saints, in unison with Jesus, sit in judgment, and mete out to the wicked according to the deeds done in the body, and that which they must receive at the execution of the judgment is set off against their names.' This, I saw, was the work of the saints with Jesus through the one thousand years in the Holy City before it descends to the earth" (EW 52, 53).

"I heard another angel answer. . . . 'The saints will rest in the Holy City and reign as kings and priests one thousand years; then Jesus will descend with the saints upon the Mount of Olives, and the mount will part asunder and become a mighty plain for the Para-

dise of God to rest upon. The rest of the earth will not be cleansed until the end of the one thousand years, when the wicked dead are raised, and gather up around the city. The feet of the wicked will never desecrate the earth made new. Fire will come down from God out of heaven and devour them—burn them up root and branch. Satan is the root, and his children are the branches. The same fire that will devour the wicked will purify the earth' " (*ibid.* 51, 52).

"During the thousand years between the first and the second resurrection the judgment of the wicked takes place. The apostle Paul points to this judgment as an event that follows the second advent. 'Judge nothing before the time, until the Lord come, who both will bring to light the hidden things of darkness, and will make manifest the counsels of the hearts' (1 Cor. 4:5). Daniel declares that when the Ancient of Days came, 'judgment was given to the saints of the Most High' (Dan. 7:22). At this time the righteous reign as kings and priests unto God. John in the Revelation says: 'I saw thrones, and they sat upon them, and judgment was given unto them.' 'They shall be priests of God and of Christ, and shall reign with Him a thousand years' (Rev. 20:4, 6). It is at this time that, as foretold by Paul, 'the saints shall judge the world' (1 Cor. 6:2). In union with Christ they judge the wicked, comparing their acts with the statute book, the Bible, and deciding every case according to the deeds done in the body. Then the portion which the wicked must suffer is meted out, according to their works; and it is recorded against their names in the book of death" (GC 660, 661).

"The earth looked like a desolate wilderness. Cities and villages, shaken down by the earthquake, lay in heaps. Mountains had been moved out of their places, leaving large caverns. Ragged rocks, thrown out by the sea, or torn out of the earth itself, were scattered all over its surface. Large trees had been uprooted and were strewn over the land. Here is to be the home of Satan with his evil angels for a thousand years. Here he will be confined, to wander up and down over the broken surface of the earth and see the effects of his rebellion against God's law. For a thousand years he can enjoy the fruit of the curse which he has caused. Limited alone to the earth, he will not have the privilege of ranging to other planets, to tempt and annoy those who have not fallen. During this time, Satan suffers extremely. Since his fall his evil traits have been in constant exercise. But he is then to be deprived of his power, and left to reflect upon the part which he has acted since his fall, and to look forward with trembling and terror to the dreadful future, when he must suffer for all the evil that he has done and be punished for all the sins that he has caused to be committed" (EW 290).

3. After the Millennium

"At the close of the thousand years, Christ again returns to the earth. He is accompanied by the host of the redeemed, and attended by a retinue of angels. As He descends in terrific majesty, He bids the wicked dead arise to receive their doom. They come forth, a mighty host, numberless as the sands of the sea. What a contrast to those who were raised at the first resurrection! The righteous were clothed with immortal youth and beauty. The wicked bear the traces of disease and death" (FLB 355).

"At the end of one thousand years, Jesus, the king of glory, descends from the holy city, clothed with brightness like the lightning, upon the mount of olives—the same mount from whence He ascended after His resurrection. As His feet touch the mountain, it parts asunder, and becomes a very great plain, and is prepared for the reception of the holy city in which is the paradise of God, the garden of Eden, which was taken up after man's transgression. Now it descends with the city, more beautiful, and gloriously adorned than when removed from the earth. The city of God comes down and settles upon the mighty plain prepared for it. Then Jesus leaves the city surrounded by the redeemed host, and is escorted on His way by the angelic throng. In fearful majesty He calls forth the wicked dead. They are wakened from their long sleep. What a dreadful waking! They behold the Son of God in His stern majesty and resplendent glory. All, as soon as they behold Him, know that He is the crucified one who died to save them, whom they had despised and rejected. They are in number like the sand upon the seashore. At the first resurrection all come forth in immortal bloom, but at the second, the marks of the curse are visible upon all. All come up as they went down into their graves. Those who lived before the flood come forth with their giant-like stature, more than twice as tall as men now living upon the earth, and well proportioned. The generations after the flood were less in stature. There was a continual decrease through successive generations, down to the last that lived upon the earth. The contrast between the first wicked men who lived upon the earth, and those of the last generation, was very great. The first were of lofty height and well proportioned—the last came up as they went down, a dwarfed, feeble, deformed race. A mighty host of kings, warriors, statesmen and nobles, down to the most degraded, came up together upon the desolate earth. When they behold Jesus in His glory they are affrighted, and seek to hide from His terrible presence. They are overwhelmed with His exceeding glory, and with one accord are compelled to exclaim in anguish, 'Blessed is he who cometh in the name of the Lord' " (3SG 83-85).

"Consider the wondrous power of our God, and then call to mind His love for fallen man. He 'so loved the world, that he gave his only begotten Son, that whosoever believeth in him should not perish, but have everlasting life.' How can man, for whom God has done so much, for whom Christ has given his life, continue in his perversity? Can we wonder that at the close of the thousand years, all who have refused to accept him shall be destroyed with fire from heaven outside of the city of God? God declares that this shall be so. He says,

'Behold, the day of the Lord cometh, cruel both with wrath and fierce anger, to lay the land desolate: and he shall destroy the sinners thereof out of it. . . . And I will punish the world for their evil, and the wicked for their iniquity; and I will cause the arrogancy of the proud to cease, and will lay low the haughtiness of the terrible' " (GCB 1897, 80).

V. Literature

Badina, Joel. "Le Millénium d'Apocalypse 20:4-6: État de la question: proposition d'interprétation." M.Th. thesis, Faculté Adventiste de Théologie, 1983.

Barr, David L. "The Apocalypse as a Symbolic Transformation of the World." *Interpretation* 38 (January 1984): 39-50.

Berkouwer, G. C. *The Return of Christ.* Grand Rapids: Eerdmans, 1972.

Boettner, Loraine. *The Millennium.* Philadelphia: Presbyterian and Reformed Pub. Co., 1957.

Caird, G. B. *A Commentary on the Revelation of Saint John the Divine.* Peabody, Mass.: Hendrickson, 1987.

Clouse, Robert G., ed. *The Meaning of the Millennium: Four Views.* Downers Grove, Ill.: InterVarsity, 1977.

Daniélou, Jean. *The Theology of Jewish Christianity.* Translated and edited by John A Baker. A History of the Early Christian Doctrine Before the Council of Nicaea, 1. London: Barton, Longman and Todd, 1964.

Erickson, Millard J. *Contemporary Options in Eschatology: A Study of the Millennium.* Grand Rapids: Baker, 1977.

Feinberg, Charles L. *Millennialism: the Two Major Views: The Premillennial and Amillennial Systems of Biblical Interpretation Analyzed and Compared.* 3rd ed. Chicago: Moody, 1980.

Froom, LeRoy. *The Prophetic Faith of Our Fathers.* 4 vols. Washington, D.C.: Review and Herald, 1950-1954.

Gladson, Jerry. "The Significance of the Millennium." *Adventist Review,* Nov. 16, 1989.

———. "William Miller and the Triumph of Premillennialism," *Adventist Review,* Nov. 9, 1989.

Gullón, David P. "An Investigation of Dispensational Premillennialism: Analysis and Evaluation of the Eschatology of John F. Walvoord." Ph.D. dissertation, Andrews University, 1992.

Hoekema, Anthony A. *The Bible and the Future.* Grand Rapids: Eerdmans, 1979.

Ladd, George Eldon. *A Theology of the New Testament.* Rev. ed. Grand Rapids: Eerdmans, 1993.

———. *The Blessed Hope.* Grand Rapids: Eerdmans, 1956.

LaRondelle, Hans K. *The Israel of God in Prophecy.* Berrien Springs, Mich.: Andrews University Press, 1983.

———. "The Millennium: Its Old Testament Roots." *Ministry,* November 1982.

———. "The One Thousand Years of Revelation 20." *Ministry,* September 1982.

Mealy, J. Webb. *After the Thousand Years: Resurrection and Judgment in Revelation 20. Journal for the Study of the New Testament* Supplement Series, 70. Sheffield, England: JSOT, 1992.

Nichol, Francis D. *The Midnight Cry.* Washington, D.C.: Review and Herald, 1944.

———. *Reasons for Our Faith.* Washington, D.C.: Review and Herald, 1947.

Rice, Richard. "The Mission of the Church, Eschatology, and the Sabbath." *Journal of Adventist Education* 51 (February-March 1989): 17-30.

Ryrie, Charles C. *Dispensationalism Today.* Chicago: Moody, 1965.

Smith, Uriah. *Daniel and the Revelation.* Battle Creek, Mich.: Review and Herald, 1897. (Repeatedly reprinted since then.)

Strand, Kenneth A. *Interpreting the Book of Revelation.* Naples, Fla.: Ann Arbor, 1979.

———. "What the Millennium Means to Me." *Adventist Review,* Mar. 12, 1987.

Tenney, Merrill C. *Interpreting Revelation.* Grand Rapids: Eerdmans, 1959.

Torrance, T. F. *The Apocalypse Today.* Grand Rapids, Eerdmans, 1959.

White, James. *Bible Adventism.* Battle Creek, Mich.: Seventh-day Adventist Pub. Assn., 1870; reprinted Nashville: Southern Pub. Assn., 1972.

The New Earth and the Eternal Kingdom

Daegeuk Nam

Introduction

Expectations of divine rewards for those who do good on earth exist in almost all cultures and all peoples of the human race. The Bible presents an unequivocal teaching on this question. There will be a new earth, new in terms of both time and form, different from the present one. Upon that new earth will be established a new and eternal kingdom ruled by the King of kings. The subjects of that kingdom will be those rescued from sin by God's plan of salvation.

The establishment of this kingdom will fulfill the everlasting covenant of God with human beings. This eternal kingdom is an actual place; it is both the reward and final home of the redeemed. It is the ultimate objective of the gospel and salvation history. In it the divine promises to the world and the purpose of Christ's coming to this world will be accomplished.

I. Heaven in the Bible

The word "heaven(s)" in English versions of the Bible is commonly translated from the Hebrew *šāmayim* and the Greek *ouranos*. The meaning of both words is "that which is high or above."

The word "heaven(s)" in Scripture is used to refer to one of three major realms: (1) the atmospheric heavens immediately above us; (2) the astronomic or stellar heavens; and (3) the dwelling place of God. The atmospheric heavens refer to the space that immediately surrounds the earth, technically known as the troposphere, in which the birds fly (Gen. 1:20; Jer. 4:25). In this realm the rain and snow fall (Gen. 7:11; Deut. 11:11; Isa. 55:10) and the winds and clouds move (Ps. 78:26; 147:8). The astronomic or stellar heavens are the space where the sun, moon, and stars have their orbits (Gen. 1:14, 16, 17; 22:17; Isa. 13:10; Matt. 24:29).

At the dedication of the Temple, Solomon prayed to God: "O Lord, God of Israel, there is no God like thee, in heaven above or on earth beneath. . . . But will God indeed dwell on the earth? Behold, heaven and the highest heaven cannot contain thee; how much less this house which I have built!" (1 Kings 8:23-27; cf. 2 Chron. 2:6; 6:18). Nevertheless, the Scriptures clearly and repeatedly affirm that God dwells in heaven. He looks down from His holy habitation, from heaven, and blesses His people (Deut. 26:15; Ps. 53:2; Isa. 63:15). When His people pray toward the Temple, He hears in heaven, His dwelling place, and forgives them (1 Kings 8:30, 39, 43, 49). During the time of Hezekiah, "the priests and the Levites arose and blessed the people, and their voice was heard, and their prayer came to his holy habitation in heaven" (2 Chron. 30:27). The psalmist states, "The Lord is in his holy temple, the Lord's throne is in heaven" (Ps. 11:4); "The Lord has established his throne in the heavens, and his kingdom rules over all" (103:19). Jesus constantly referred to the "Father who is in heaven" (Matt. 5:16, 45; Mark 11:25). All these references indicate that "heaven" is the abode or habitation of God, which the apostle Paul designated as "the third heaven" or "Paradise" (2 Cor. 12:2, 3).

Not only does the word "heaven" stand for the place where God dwells, where His throne is, heaven is His throne (Isa. 66:1), the symbol of His authority. Thus "heaven" is used as a metonymy for God. Especially in postexilic Judaism this term came to be used as a circumlocution for the divine name "Yahweh" or as a synonym for "God," reflecting the Jews' reluctance to pronounce God's name. In the NT this phenomenon is found with some frequency. In the parable of the prodigal, the returning son said to his father: "I have sinned against heaven" (Luke 15:18, 21), meaning that he had sinned against God. Jesus used "heaven" as a synonym for God when He said, "He who swears by heaven, swears by the throne of God and by him who sits upon it" (Matt. 23:22). Here God is represented by His dwelling place.

In modern parlance, "heaven" is used in the same ways as in the Bible. In addition, however, "heaven" is often understood as the place where the redeemed will receive their reward immediately after death. While this use of the word "heaven" for the abode of the blessed is not biblical, the concept of a real place where the redeemed will live with God— often called a new earth—is indeed scriptural and will be explored in the following sections of this article.

II. The Dwelling Place of the Redeemed

The OT and NT speak repeatedly of the reward of the righteous. Thus Paul wrote to the Romans that God would give eternal life "to those who by patience in well-doing seek for glory and honor and immortality" (Rom. 2:7). However, before the Bible teachings on the topic are examined, the time when the righteous will live in this glorious place needs to be ascertained.

The Bible clearly teaches that at death human beings sleep an unconscious sleep (see Death I. C. 4). This state continues until the resurrection (see Resurrection I. A). The dead are no more until brought to life by the resurrection trumpet. Thus the rewards of all, righteous and wicked, are received only at their respective resurrections (see Second Coming I. G. 2; Millennium I. C. 1, 3). To imagine that the dead immediately receive their reward goes against the biblical teaching of the reward of the righteous, to be received at the Second Coming.

According to the Bible, the redeemed will spend the millennium in heaven (see Millennium I. C. 2). After that they, together with the heavenly city, will return to this earth, where they will live eternally. This earth made new is the topic of the rest of this article.

A. The Dwelling Place of the Redeemed in the OT

Among the promises given to Israel, several deal extensively with a renewed earth under the rulership of the promised Messiah. These promises describe a happy people in a beautiful land, where all things are peaceful and good. They describe what might have been if Israel had fulfilled its covenant obligations (see Deut. 28:1, 2, 13, 14). In reality, because of its apostasy and rebellion over the centuries, culminating in the rejection of Jesus as Messiah, Israel lost its right to the fulfillment of these conditional prophecies of glorious well-being. The Christian church has come to occupy the place of Israel, as a spiritual nation. The warnings and prophecies given to Israel are now applicable to the Christian church. (See Apocalyptic II. B. 1; Remnant/Three Angels I; 4BC 25-38.) Thus while the primary application of OT prophecies regarding a renewed earth was to a renewed land of Israel, the secondary application, made in the light of NT writings,

is to the earth made new expected by Christian believers.

Because of the conditional nature of these prophecies, not all details can be applied to the earth made new described in Revelation 21 and 22; however, there is little doubt that the OT view of the "new earth" is very similar to that given in the NT and can be safely applied to the eternal home of the redeemed. Several aspects of the OT teaching on the "new earth" must be considered.

1. A New Kingdom

Isaiah announces God's determination: "Behold, I create new heavens and a new earth; and the former things shall not be remembered or come into mind" (Isa. 65:17; cf. 42:9; 43:19; 66:22). In the original intention, Canaan was to be miraculously renewed. The "former things," the sad memories of captivity and domination, were to be forgotten. According to F. Delitzsch, "Jahve creates a new heaven and a new earth which so charm men by their glory, so thoroughly satisfy all desires, that no one recalls the former ones or wishes them back again" (2:464).

Not only would the heavens and earth be made new; the spirit in the dwellers of the new earth would be new. God would give them a new heart and a new spirit (Eze. 11:19; 18:31; 36:26) in place of their old and stony heart. On this new heart would be written the law of God's new covenant (Jer. 31:31-34).

2. A Messianic Kingdom

The King of the new earth would be the Messiah, the descendant of David (Isa. 11:1; cf. Jer. 33:17). He would sit on the Davidic throne and be empowered with the Spirit of Yahweh (Isa. 11:1-3). His kingdom, that is, His government and judgment, would be characterized by "righteousness" and "faithfulness" (verse 5).

The Messianic King is totally different from all earthly and temporal kings and rulers. The essential meanings of righteousness (ṣedeq) may be summarized as (1) loyalty or faithfulness to the community and (2) rightness, as in what is correct and according to law, here God's own law. When Yahweh judges the world "with righteousness" (Ps. 9:4, 8; Isa. 11:4, 5), He directs and sustains the world in the divine order, which is morally correct and right in nature. Righteousness includes the covenant relation that characterizes God's dealings with His people as always being for their good and corresponding to what He has promised. Righteousness and faithfulness are the foundation principles upon which God's reign in the renewed earth will be based.

Zechariah 12-14 describes the Messiah's triumphant intervention in human history. The day of the Lord, the last battle of all nations against Jerusalem, is described in 14:1-8, while verses 9-21 delineate the establishment of the Messianic kingdom: "And the Lord will become king over all the earth; on that day the Lord will be one and his name one" (verse 9). Here is proclaimed the absolute lordship and universal kingdom of the Messianic King.

3. Jerusalem the Capital

The capital of the "new earth" is Jerusalem. According to Zechariah 14, topographical changes, including the splitting of the Mount of Olives (verse 4), make possible the enlargement, fortification, and glorification of Jerusalem (verse 10). The city will be inhabited, the curse will be lifted, and "Jerusalem shall dwell in security" (verse 11).

The "mountain of the house of the Lord" would be established as "the highest of the mountains" (Isa. 2:2). The "Lord of hosts" would reign on Mount Zion (Isa. 24:23); He would rejoice in the city's inhabitants (Isa. 65:19). Because of the Lord's presence in the city, the "mountain" would be holy and the city, faithful (Zech. 8:3). In this holy city, where God "roars" from the temple and dwells, no strangers or unclean persons would enter (Isa. 52:1; Joel 3:16, 17), but all nations would come to Jerusalem, bringing with them their wealth (Isa. 60:11) and the desire to seek the presence of the Lord (Jer. 3:17).

4. A Worshiping Kingdom

The New Jerusalem would be the religious center of the kingdom. To Mount Zion would come "the nations" and "peoples" to learn of the Lord's ways, to walk in His paths (Isa. 2:2, 3; Micah 4:1). The remnant of Israel would return to worship at the Lord's holy mountain (Isa. 27:13). Those who loved the Lord and kept His Sabbaths would come to the "house of prayer for all peoples" (Isa. 56:6-8). Foreigners would be welcome (Isa. 66:20).

In these descriptions, worship of the Lord centers on three different festivals. Isaiah 66:23 affirms that the redeemed will come "from new moon to new moon, and from sabbath to sabbath." The construction of this verse may be interpreted in two ways. The redeemed will come on every new moon festival and on every Sabbath or they may come constantly, from one feast to another. Thus the redeemed would be worshiping daily at the throne of God. The first interpretation puts more emphasis on the particular days of worship, while the second stresses the perpetuity of worship. While the first interpretation is probably more in harmony with the meaning of the original language, the spiritual richness of the second interpretation need not be excluded.

Under the Mosaic law the new moon festival (Num. 10:10; 28:11-14) celebrated the beginning of the new month. The Sabbath was kept as a memorial of Creation (Gen. 2:2, 3; Ex. 20:8-11) and of Israel's liberation from Egypt (Deut. 5:12-15). Since there would be new heavens and earth in the new creation, mention of these two special days seems appropriate. Most significant is the idea that "all flesh," meaning everyone, would come to worship God as Creator, Saviour, and Redeemer, both regularly and unceasingly.

According to Zechariah 14:16, the redeemed would come to Jerusalem to celebrate the yearly feast of Tabernacles. This joyful harvest festival (Deut. 16:13-15) reminded the Jews of God's protection during their wilderness wandering (Lev. 23:43). It also pointed forward to the gathering of the saved and their celebration of salvation in the new earth. The feast spoke of the final joyful reunion and restoration of Israel.

5. A Holy Kingdom

In that future realm, the King in the midst of it would be holy (Isa. 12:6). Likewise, the city and the land would be holy (Zech. 2:12); the mountain would be holy (Isa. 27:13). The inhabitants of Jerusalem would be holy, cleansed from all filth (4:3, 4; 33:24); "the unclean shall not pass over" the way to that land (Isa. 35:8). "They shall be called The holy people, the redeemed of the Lord" (Isa. 62:12).

Holiness permeates the kingdom. The bells of the horses bear the inscription "Holy to the Lord." The pots in the house of the Lord are holy and the cooking pots are sacred (Zech. 14:20, 21). In former times Aaron's turban had been adorned with a gold plate engraved with the words "Holy to the Lord" (Ex. 28:36). Now the designation once reserved for the high priest can be applied to everyone and everything; public life, religious life, and private life are included.

6. A Joyful Kingdom

Not only would God's people "be glad and rejoice for ever" in God's creation; Yahweh Himself would "rejoice in Jerusalem and be glad" with His people. There would be no more "sound of weeping" or "cry of distress" (Isa. 65:17-19). The blind would see, the lame jump, the deaf hear, the dumb sing (Isa. 35:5, 6). The city's inhabitants would no longer be called "forsaken" or "desolate" (Isa. 62:5). Gloom and depression would be banished from the glorious New Jerusalem. This was in stark contrast with the situation in Jerusalem when Isaiah pronounced this prophecy. At that time the Assyrian armies had besieged the city and required a heavy tribute of Hezekiah (Isa. 36; 37). In addition Isaiah had prophesied that Babylonian armies would invade Jerusalem and carry off its treasures and people (Isa. 39:6, 7). Yet God was planning a glorious future for the city, which would be "a crown of beauty in the hand of the Lord" (see Isa. 52:9; 62:1-7). One reason for this joy would be the vindication and salvation of God's people (Isa. 62:1, 2). But the greatest source of joy would be the presence of the Lord among His people.

Through Isaiah God promised that the "offspring of the blessed of the Lord" (Isa. 65:23) would have a special relation with their Maker: "Before they call I will answer" (verse 24). The barrier of sin that had hindered communication with God (Isa. 59:2) would be removed. There would exist an intimate relationship and perfect communication between God and His people. No request would go unnoticed; no delay in response would exist. God would provide everything necessary for the people's well-being and happiness. The Lord would place His sanctuary in the midst of Israel for evermore (Eze. 37:28). As a symbol of the richness of this heavenly kingdom, Isaiah describes a banquet of good things (Isa. 25:6).

7. A Peaceable Kingdom

In this joyful kingdom, every kind of enmity and hostility will disappear. Harmony and peace will exist, not merely among humans, but also among animals (Isa. 11:6-9; 65:25). The wolf, formerly the lamb's major enemy, will be its guest. The formerly rapacious leopard will lie down with the kid in peaceful rest. The lion, king of beasts, in the past cruel and fierce, now shares his meal of straw with the calf and fatling he would have torn to pieces. The bear is at peace with the cow; their young lie down together with no sign of animosity. Undoubtedly the world has been restored to its unfallen situation, when all animals ate green plants (Gen. 1:30). More remarkable yet, a little child leads them without fear and in perfect safety (Isa. 11:6).

Isaiah 11:8 notes a further contrast. "The suckling child shall play over the hole of the asp, and the weaned child shall put his hand on the adder's den." The fundamental enmity between the serpent and human beings—"the first of all enmities, whereby man's relationship with all the animal world was really thrown out of joint" (Young 389)—will be wiped out. "The most helpless of human beings, the child that has just been weaned, will be unharmed by mankind's deadliest enemy" (ibid.). The serpent, representative of Satan, will become harmless. At the same time, God will destroy the ultimate enemy: death. "He will swallow up death for ever, and the Lord God will wipe away tears from all faces" (Isa. 25:8).

A summary of the peacefulness of that beautiful land is given in Isaiah 11:9 (cf. 65:25): "They shall not hurt or destroy in all my holy mountain; for the earth shall be full of the knowledge of the Lord as the waters cover the sea." There is no harm, no fear. There is no war or even preparation for war (Isa. 2:4; Hosea 2:18; Micah 4:3). There is only a peaceful fellowship of love among all creatures and all nations under the Messiah's government. The cause of this peace is "the knowledge of the Lord." Both theoretical and experiential, this knowledge of God will be so extensive as to fill the earth. The true knowledge of the Lord who is the "Prince of Peace" (Isa. 9:6), the one who makes and brings peace (John 14:27; 16:33; Rom. 5:1; Col. 1:20), the God of peace (1 Cor. 14:33) is the prerequisite for enjoying genuine peace and safety in the earth made new.

8. A Fruitful Kingdom

The Messianic kingdom was not to be a place of idleness. Its inhabitants would build houses and inhabit them (Isa. 65:21, 22). Not only would the redeemed build houses—undoubtedly including designing, constructing, furnishing, arranging, and even adorning them—they would also enjoy the satisfaction of living in the houses they had planned and built. There would be no creditors or victors to push them out of their rightful heritage.

The inhabitants of the land would plant and harvest; they would enjoy the work of their hands (Isa. 62:9; 65:22). The crops to be planted were the traditional ones of Canaan: vines and fig trees (Isa. 65:21; Micah 4:4) and

grain (Isa. 62:8, 9). The increased fertility of the land would go beyond the planted fields. Deserts would become productive (Isa. 43:19-21) and full of trees (Isa. 41:18, 19); the wilderness would "rejoice and blossom" (Isa. 35:1, 6, 7); the mountains would "drip sweet wine" and the hills would "flow with milk" (Joel 3:18; Amos 9:13).

The joyful work given to Adam and Eve in the garden, "to till it and keep it" (Gen. 2:15), would be restored. The inhabitants of the earth restored would "sit every man under his vine and under his fig tree" (Micah 4:4). Work there would be a comfort and source of delight.

9. A Permanent Kingdom

In Isaiah 65:23 God declares the permanence of His new creation and the people who will live there. As the new heavens and earth will remain forever, so will those who dwell there. Those who live in this Promised Land will have long life: Old men and women sit in the streets with the children playing around them (Zech. 8:4, 5). Infant mortality—a common problem in the ancient world—disappears; one who dies at 100 years is still a child (Isa. 65:20).

When applied to the purified and holy earth made new, the death element in Isaiah 65:20 and 66:24 does not fit, for death is banned from the abode of the redeemed (Rev. 21:4). Both verses refer to what might have been but never was.

B. The Dwelling Place of the Redeemed in the NT

1. In the Gospels

To a great extent, Jesus' teaching regarding the reward of the redeemed was a natural continuation of the OT teaching just explored. However, great emphasis is laid on "the kingdom," called either "kingdom of heaven" (32 times in Matthew, but none in Luke) or "kingdom of God" (32 times in Luke, four times in Matthew) by the Gospel writers. That the terms are equivalent is shown in their parallel use (Matt. 13:11 and Luke 8:10; Matt. 10:7 and Luke 9:2). While the kingdom at times appears to be a spiritual realm (see the parables of the kingdom in Matthew 13), undoubtedly it is also a physical place where God's people live. For example, one enters the kingdom (Matt. 5:20; 18:3; 19:23; Mark 9:47; Luke 18:25). The "kingdom of God" is a real place where Jesus will again eat and drink with His disciples (Mark 14:25; Luke 22:16, 18).

Throughout the Gospels, Jesus speaks of "heaven" not only as the dwelling place of God (Matt. 6:9) or the place from whence He had come (John 6:51), but as the place where the righteous will be rewarded: "Rejoice and be glad, for your reward is great in heaven" (Matt. 5:12; Luke 6:23). In speaking of this reward, Jesus uses the figure of the heavenly banquet, at which the saved Gentiles will sit "at table with Abraham, Isaac, and Jacob in the kingdom of heaven" (Matt. 8:11; cf. Luke 13:28; 14:15). The "messianic banquet" is an OT symbol (Isa. 25:6) that appears in the intertestamental literature (3 Enoch 48:10), and represents the fullness of satisfaction the redeemed—including the Gentiles—would enjoy. Jesus also promised that the "meek" would "inherit the earth" (Matt. 5:5).

"Eternal life," the opposite of eternal damnation, was prominent in Christ's teaching (Matt. 25:46). Those who had sacrificed family for His cause would receive "in the age to come eternal life" (Mark 10:30; Luke 18:30). It appears in that favorite of verses, "For God so loved the world that he gave his only Son, that whoever believes in him should not perish but have eternal life" (John 3:16). Although one may rightly contend that "eternal life" begins in the here and now, Jesus' use of the term points to "the age to come," to a time when the saved will participate in the glory of the heavenly kingdom.

In John 14:2, 3 Jesus equates heaven, the dwelling place of God, with the place where His disciples will be welcomed. Here He Himself will prepare them dwelling places so that they may live with Him.

2. In the Epistles

In the Pauline Epistles, no precise description is made of the place where the redeemed will live. There is, however, no doubt regarding their reward: "To those who by patience in well-doing seek for glory and honor and immortality, he will give eternal life" (Rom. 2:7). In fact, the "sufferings of this present time are not worth comparing with the glory that is to be revealed to us" (Rom. 8:18). Furthermore, the glorious reward is eternal. (Rom. 6:23; 2 Cor. 4:18; 2 Tim. 2:10). This eternal glory is the "hope laid up for you in heaven" (Col. 1:5), the "promised eternal inheritance" (Heb. 9:15).

While in 1 Corinthians 2:9 Paul is describing the greatness of God's plan of salvation, there is little doubt that the paean of praise would apply to Paul's understanding of the eternal glory awaiting God's children: "What no eye has seen, nor ear heard, nor the heart of man conceived, what God has prepared for those who love him." Paul himself was confident of being in this place, saved for God's "heavenly kingdom" (2 Tim. 4:18).

Peter echoes Paul's certainty regarding the "inheritance which is imperishable, undefiled, and unfading, kept in heaven" for the believers (1 Peter 1:4). His readers were to set their "hope fully upon the grace" that would be coming to them "at the revelation of Jesus Christ" (verse 13). In his Second Epistle the apostle climaxes his fiery description of the last day with the promise of "new heavens and a new earth in which righteousness dwells," obviously where the righteous will live (2 Peter 3:11-13).

3. In Revelation

The prophetic book of John contains a great deal of information regarding the new earth. From it we learn also about the millennium and the characteristics of those who inherit the new earth.

a. The millennium. A detailed study of the millennium appears in a separate article. Here

953

it is enough to point out that during this 1,000-year period the redeemed of the earth, both the righteous dead and those who were alive at the Second Coming, will be with the Lord in heaven (1 Thess. 4:16, 17). At His second advent Christ sends "out his angels with a loud trumpet call" to "gather his elect from the four winds" (Matt. 24:31). He then takes the redeemed to the "Father's house," which He has prepared for His own (John 14:2, 3). In the heavenly kingdom those who shared in the first resurrection are "priests of God and of Christ" and "reign with him a thousand years" (Rev. 20:4, 6).

b. Qualifications for entry into the new earth. In Revelation we find information on the characteristics of those who qualify to live on the earth made new and of those who have excluded themselves from it.

The inhabitants are overcomers, victors, conquerors. "To him who conquers I will grant to eat of the tree of life, which is in the paradise of God" (Rev. 2:7). The overcomer is not hurt by the second death (verse 11) and receives a new name (verse 17). The conquerors are dressed in white and walk with Christ (Rev. 3:5); in fact they share the throne with Christ (verse 21). Those who have been victors over the beast and its image stand beside the sea of glass, singing the song of Moses (Rev. 15:2, 3). After describing the atmosphere of the new earth, John quotes Christ's identification of its inhabitants: "He who conquers shall have this heritage, and I will be his God and he shall be my son" (Rev. 21:7).

All those who live in the new earth are written in the "Lamb's book of life" (verse 27). This book appears once in Paul (Phil. 4:3) and six times in Revelation. It is one of the books on which judgment is based (Rev. 20:12). In it are written the names of those who have given allegiance to Christ, who have no part with the beast (Rev. 13:8; 17:8). The conqueror's name is not blotted out of this book (Rev. 3:5). Closely related to the idea of being inscribed in the book of life is the concept expressed in Revelation 22:14: "Blessed are those who wash their robes, that they may have the right to the tree of life and that they may enter the city by the gates." In Revelation 7:14 more information on the washing of robes is given: "They have washed their robes and made them white in the blood of the Lamb." Elsewhere in the NT, believers are "justified" (Rom. 5:9), redeemed (Eph. 1:7), "brought near" (Eph. 2:13), and reconciled (Col. 1:20) by Christ's blood shed on Calvary. Hebrews indicates that God's people are purified (Heb. 9:14) and forgiven (verse 22) through the blood of Jesus. Being clothed in Christ's righteousness is the paramount qualification for entrance into the heavenly kingdom (cf. Jesus' parable of the wedding garment in Matthew 22:1-14).

The KJV and other versions, reflecting some ancient manuscripts, translate Revelation 22:14 differently: "Blessed are they that do his commandments." While the manuscript evidence favors the translation "wash their robes," and the modification of "washing robes" to "doing commandments" in the process of copying Greek manuscripts is easily understandable, one must accept that the two ideas are not mutually exclusive. Keeping the commandments is a sign of knowing, following (1 John 2:3-6), and loving the Master (John 14:15).

Those who specifically exclude themselves from the new earth and condemn themselves to the lake of fire are the cowardly, the faithless, the polluted, the murderers, the fornicators, the sorcerers, the idolaters, and the liars (Rev. 21:8). To these, Revelation 22:15 adds "dogs" (vile, shameless persons) and "every one who loves and practices falsehood." The basis for exclusion is given in Revelation 21:27: "But nothing unclean shall enter it."

The picture given in Revelation of who may and who may not enter the kingdom agrees with what is found elsewhere in the Bible. David describes the one who can dwell on God's "holy hill": "He who walks blamelessly, and does what is right, and speaks truth from his heart; who does not slander with his tongue, and does no evil to his friend, nor takes up a reproach against his neighbor" (Ps.

15:2, 3). Isaiah likewise identifies the one who can dwell "on the heights": "He who walks righteously and speaks uprightly; he who despises the gain of oppressions, who shakes his hands, lest they hold a bribe, who stops his ears from hearing of bloodshed, and shuts his eyes from looking upon evil" (Isa. 33:15). In one of his conditional prophecies of the glory that might have been Israel's, and which await their fulfillment in the earth made new, Isaiah affirmed that the "unclean" would be absent (Isa. 35:8). While expressed in a somewhat different way, the qualifications given by Jesus for entry into the kingdom of heaven are closely related to those in Revelation. One's righteousness should exceed "that of the scribes and Pharisees" (Matt. 5:20); words alone do not gain a person's access into the kingdom (Matt. 7:21); and a childlike spirit is requisite for entry (Matt. 18:3).

c. A description of the new earth. The last two chapters of Revelation contain a great deal of information on the new earth. Additional information can be gleaned from other sections of the book (Rev. 3:5, 12, 21; 14:3; 15:2-4).

According to the revelator, the new earth comes into being after the millennium, after the purification by fire of the earth we know today (Rev. 21:1). At that time the "holy city, New Jerusalem," comes "down out of heaven from God." It is safe to assume that this is the capital of God's kingdom, God's dwelling place. After its descent to earth, God makes His dwelling on the new earth, among the redeemed (verses 2, 3, 9).

The "New Jerusalem" (Rev. 3:12; 21:2), also called "the city of my God" (Rev. 3:12) and "the holy city" (Rev. 21:2, 10), is the "Mount Zion . . . the city of the living God, the heavenly Jerusalem" in Hebrews 12:22. The city is beautiful, "as a bride adorned for her husband" (Rev. 21:2). It is radiant, "like a most rare jewel, like a jasper, clear as crystal" (verse 11). At this point we recognize the limitations of our human understanding; we cannot comprehend that which we have not seen.

Yet in faith we accept that this city is lovely beyond compare.

The city is square and very large. The measurement of the city is given as 12,000 *stadia*. Whether that is one side or the perimeter is not clear. At 185 meters (202 yards) per *stadion,* the length of each side would be 2,220 kilometers, or approximately 1,380 miles. Even if the measure were that of the perimeter, as was often given in antiquity, a contour of 1,380 miles would make for a very large city. To further complicate the picture, "its length and breadth and height are equal" (Rev. 21:16). Many attempts have been made to explain these dimensions. Some have suggested that one must recognize them as "angel's" measures (verse 17), but this would not solve the puzzle. Others have posited that "equal" *(isos)* should be translated "proportionate." Yet others suggest that John meant that the perimeter of the base of the wall was equal to the perimeter of the crown of the wall. Ultimately, human understanding fails. As I. T. Beckwith states, "the Apocalypticist, regardless of architectural reality, is struggling to express by symbols the vastness, the perfect symmetry, and the splendor of the new Jerusalem" (760).

The wall of the city is built of jasper, measures 144 cubits, and has 12 gates—three on each side (Rev. 21:13, 17, 18). The Greek *iaspis* appears to refer to a translucent green stone, as described by first-century naturalist Pliny; however, here a transparent stone may be intended (as suggested by the translation "diamond" in *The Jerusalem Bible*). In any case, as in Revelation 4:3, "jasper" is used to describe shining brilliance. At 0.45 meters (18 inches) a cubit, the 144 cubits would be equivalent to some 65 meters (213 feet). This measure may represent the height or the thickness of the walls. Each of the 12 gates is a single pearl (Rev. 21:21) and remains open all the time, since there is no night (verse 25). Some have suggested that as pearls are formed only by suffering, salvation is made possible only by the anguish and death Christ suffered for us. Again the measurements and descriptions defy human comprehension.

The city is made of gold and its foundations are gemstones. The gold is described as pure and "transparent as glass" (verse 21), a most unusual combination to modern understanding, but which certainly suggests brilliance and light. The 12 stones of the foundations are listed in the RSV as jasper, sapphire, agate, emerald, onyx, carnelian, chrysolite, beryl, topaz, chrysoprase, jacinth, and amethyst (verses 19, 20). Of the names of these gemstones in Greek, seven correspond to LXX names of stones on the priest's breastplate (Ex. 28:17-20; 39:10-13). In the RSV translation of the same lists, nine are the same in Exodus and Revelation. What the symbolic relation between the two sets of gemstones may be is not clear. John's description attempts to portray the glory and beauty of the city he saw in vision.

"Through the middle of the street of the city" flows the "river of the water of life," issuing from the "throne of God and of the Lamb" (Rev. 22:1). The tree of life, with a trunk on each side of the river, produces each month one of 12 kinds of fruit; its leaves are "for the healing of the nations" (verse 2). The water of life quenches the physical and spiritual thirst of the redeemed (Rev. 21:6). The fruits of the tree "contain the vital element the human race has gone without since Adam and Eve had to leave Eden—the antidote for aging, burnout, and simple fatigue" (*Seventh-day Adventists Believe* 377; cf. Gen. 3:22).

John saw "no temple in the city, for its temple is the Lord God the Almighty and the Lamb" (Rev. 21:22). This is in contrast with Revelation 15:5, where a temple is clearly in view. With the sin problem solved, there is no longer any need for ceremonies to bring humanity and Deity into agreement. The need for a temple is past; the throne of God and the Lamb is open to all (Rev. 22:3).

Throughout the description, light is an important feature. The city itself is brilliant gold and gems, with the "glory of God" (Rev. 21:11). The water of the river of life is "bright as crystal" (Rev. 22:1). "There shall be no night there" (Rev. 21:25; 22:5). There is no need for sun or moon, for Christ and the Father provide all the illumination needed (Rev. 21:23).

d. Activities in the new earth. While Isaiah stresses the agricultural and even commercial pursuits of the renewed earth (Isa. 60:4-7), John writes about the worship and fellowship activities. Neither excludes the other.

According to Revelation, the principal activity of the redeemed is the worship of the Lamb. Free from "anything accursed" (Rev. 22:3), outside of the grasp of death (Rev. 21:4), in the close company of God, who dwells with them (verse 3), the redeemed prostrate themselves in joyous worship of the One who has made heaven possible. This agrees with the worship predicted in Isaiah 66:22, 23.

The Greek verb translated "worship" in Revelation 22:3 is *latreuō,* generally used in reference to service or worship in the house of God (cf. Matt. 4:10; Luke 2:37; Phil. 3:3; 2 Tim. 1:3; Heb. 8:5; 9:14; 13:10). It is also used in Revelation 7:15 to describe the worship and service of those who "have washed their robes and made them white in the blood of the Lamb" (verse 14).

Singing makes up an important part of heavenly worship. The 144,000 "sing a new song before the throne and before the four living creatures and before the elders"; this is a song of experience that only they can learn (Rev. 14:3). Those who conquer sing the Song of Moses and the Song of the Lamb; in it they praise God for His justice and holiness (Rev. 15:2-4).

Both during the millennium in heaven and later on the earth made new, the righteous share God's rule. They reign "with Christ" (Rev. 20:4) "for ever and ever" (Rev. 22:5). They do not assert their own authority but share in Christ's royal rule.

The new earth will be a place of ultimate fellowship, among the redeemed and of these with heavenly beings. God will dwell among His people; "they shall see his face, and his name shall be on their foreheads" (Rev. 22:3,

4). In close and sweet communion, ransomed sinners will learn to know God, with none of the past separation. In this relation, they will learn of God's ways (Micah 4:1, 2), of His power displayed in Creation and re-creation. Then they will be able to join the elders in singing: "Worthy art thou, our Lord and God, to receive glory and honor and power, for thou didst create all things, and by thy will they existed and were created" (Rev. 4:11). In addition, they will praise Christ's worthiness, "for thou wast slain and by thy blood didst ransom men for God from every tribe and tongue and people and nation, and hast made them a kingdom and priests to our God, and they shall reign on earth" (Rev. 5:9, 10).

III. The Significance of the Doctrine

The doctrine of the new earth and the eternal kingdom is of great importance, not simply because it involves the last things, but because it is related to the final stage of salvation history and the goal of redemption. It concerns God's purpose in Creation, His covenant and promises, and Christ's message and ministry. It also impacts our Christian life in this world.

A. Fulfillment of God's Purpose in Creation

When God created human beings in the beginning, His plan for them was to "be fruitful and multiply, and fill the earth and subdue it; and have dominion over" everything in the world (Gen. 1:28). His purpose in Creation was that human beings made in His image would lead a blissful eternal life and exercise kind dominion over the whole world and all its creatures (verses 26, 27). However, this original purpose was thwarted by the fall of Adam and Eve. But God's will in Creation could not be entirely frustrated and nullified. He announced the plan of redemption in order to redeem fallen humanity from death, which resulted from their sin (Gen. 3:15; Rom. 6:23; Eph. 2:1). Thus the course of the history of redemption is the story of the restoration of His creation from its present mortal state to God's originally intended state.

Therefore, the eternal kingdom that will be established on the new earth is the final fulfillment of the divine purpose of Creation. God has waited long for the establishment of His kingdom, in which His children will freely and fully enjoy all the blessings provided by His infinite wisdom. As Paul states, "creation itself will be set free from its bondage to decay and obtain the glorious liberty of the children of God" (Rom. 8:21). Not only has the whole creation been awaiting this development, but the human race as a whole groans inwardly as its members wait for the "adoption of sons, the redemption of our bodies" (verses 22, 23).

God will make the heavens and the earth new (Isa. 65:17), but this does not necessarily involve another creation *ex nihilo*. The terms employed in 2 Peter 3:7-13 imply renewal and restoration that will produce a purified universe out of the old. In Matthew 19:28 the term *palingenesia* signals the renewal of the world, not a totally new creation; the word is translated "new world" (RSV), "New Age" (TEV), or "regeneration" (KJV). Through this re-creation God the Creator ultimately will fulfill His original purpose for creating "the first heaven and the first earth" (Rev. 21:1). Peter calls the time when this will take place "the times of restitution of all things" (Acts 3:21, KJV; "restore," NIV).

B. Accomplishment of God's Covenant and Promises

The doctrine of the eternal kingdom also represents the accomplishment of the covenant and promises that God has made with His people throughout OT history. With all of its prophecies and promises, the whole Bible is focused upon a great eschatological event, i.e., the coming of the Messiah and His kingdom.

Many prophecies of the OT point to the end of time, when the Messiah will come to reign on the new earth. Many prophecies in the NT concern the second coming of Jesus Christ and the signs that precede it. These prophecies are grounded upon the fact that God is faithful and never fails to keep His promises. God is a God of recompense who will reveal to us the glorious reward that cannot be compared with the sufferings of this present time (Rom. 8:18).

Jesus counseled His followers, "When you give a feast, invite the poor, the maimed, the lame, the blind, and you will be blessed, because they cannot repay you," and He concluded His counsel with a guarantee: "You will be repaid at the resurrection of the just" (Luke 14:13, 14). Paul encourages us to be steadfast and immovable in our faith, because in the Lord our labor is not in vain (1 Cor. 15:58) and the present life is not the only one if we hope in Christ (verse 19). The "crown of righteousness" is laid up as a reward for "all who have loved his appearing" (2 Tim. 4:8), and the "crown of life" will be given to every person who is "faithful unto death" (Rev. 2:10). All these promises will be fully accomplished when the eternal kingdom is established.

C. Consummation of Christ's Message and Ministry

Another important aspect of the eternal kingdom is that it consummates the teaching and ministry of Jesus Christ. At the climax of his prologue to the ministry of Jesus, Mark sets forth this significant passage: "Jesus came into Galilee, preaching the gospel of God, and saying, 'The time is fulfilled, and the kingdom of God is at hand; repent, and believe in the gospel'" (Mark 1:14, 15). As G. R. Beasley-Murray notes, this passage is intended "to supply a summary of the gospel preached by Jesus, of which the teaching of Jesus in the body of the gospel can be viewed as exposition" (71), or as John Bright has stated: "Mark thus makes it plain that the burden of Jesus' preaching was to announce the Kingdom of God; that was the central thing with which he was concerned. A reading of the teachings of

Jesus as they are found in the Gospels only serves to bear this statement out. Everywhere the Kingdom of God is on his lips, and it is always a matter of desperate importance" (17).

The Synoptic Gospels make this clear in passages of a summary nature that indicate that the evangelists saw Jesus' primary purpose in terms of preaching the kingdom (Matt. 4:12-17, 23; 9:35; Mark 1:14, 15; Luke 4:43; 8:1; 9:2). Many sayings and parables of Jesus concern the coming of the kingdom of God. Some of them relate to the nature of the kingdom of God (Matt. 13:3-9, 31-33, 45-50). Some teach how one can enter the kingdom of God: One's righteousness must exceed that of the scribes and Pharisees (Matt. 5:20) and must do the will of the Father who is in heaven (Matt. 7:21). Others illustrate the importance of the kingdom of God: It would be better to mutilate oneself and enter maimed than not enter at all (Matt. 18:8, 9), and it is worthwhile to sacrifice any human relationship and earthly property for the kingdom of God (19:29).

Some sayings and parables of Jesus concern the kingdom of God in the present, while others concern the kingdom of God in the future. The former may be called "the kingdom of grace" and the latter "the kingdom of glory." From either point of view, "the kingdom of God" was the burden of Christ's teachings. Therefore, when the glorious kingdom of God finally does come to this earth to be established forever, it will be a grand consummation of Christ's message and ministry.

D. Spiritual Impact on the Christian Life

The doctrine of the new earth and the eternal kingdom is of great significance, not merely as an integral part of biblical teachings, but as an important factor that upholds the Christian's faith and offers practical benefits for the believer's spiritual life. It provides the believer with strength and courage to endure and overcome the temptations of this world. Moses chose rather "to share ill-treatment" with God's people than "to enjoy the fleeting pleasures of sin" (Heb. 11:25); he considered "abuse suffered for the Christ greater wealth than the treasures of Egypt," because "he looked to the reward" (verse 26). Jesus Himself "endured the cross, despising the shame," because He could see "the joy that was set before him" (Heb. 12:2). Paul renewed his courage by contemplating the future glory: "I consider that the sufferings of this present time are not worth comparing with the glory that is to be revealed to us" (Rom. 8:18). "So we do not lose heart. . . . For this slight momentary affliction is preparing for us an eternal weight of glory beyond all comparison" (2 Cor. 4:16, 17).

Belief in the doctrine of the eternal kingdom and its reward brings joy and hope to Christians. Paul says, "If the work which any man has built on the foundation survives, he will receive a reward" (1 Cor. 3:14). "We rejoice in our hope of sharing the glory of God" (Rom. 5:2). The believers may joyfully accept "the plundering" of their property, since they know that they have "a better possession and an abiding one" (Heb. 10:34). Peter encourages us, "Rejoice in so far as you share Christ's sufferings, that you may also rejoice and be glad when his glory is revealed" (1 Peter 4:13). Jesus also says, "Rejoice and be glad, for your reward is great in heaven" (Matt. 5:12).

Belief in the hereafter provides a more positive and constructive thrust for life in this world. The Christian who plans and prepares to live eternally will lead a sincere and honest life on earth. Those who will enter the eternal kingdom are those who have established the

kingdom of God in their hearts by accepting Jesus Christ as their Lord and King. When Jesus was asked by the Pharisees when the kingdom of God was going to come, He answered, "The kingdom of God is not coming with signs to be observed, . . . the kingdom of God is in the midst of you" (Luke 17:20, 21). The phrase "in the midst of you" *(entos hymōn)* may also be rendered as "within you" as in KJV, NIV, and TEV. Only those who have already experienced the "kingdom of grace" in the present life can inherit and enjoy the "kingdom of glory" in the afterlife.

Finally, the biblical truth about Paradise restored helps us understand God's true character and His original purpose and ideal in creating humanity. Sin has so marred and damaged this earth that the present world grossly misrepresents God's character and His original plan for this planet. The picture of the new heaven and new earth portrayed in Scripture reveals God's character more clearly. In other words, "in what God has planned for the redeemed—a world untouched by Satan's influence, a world in which God's purpose rules alone—we have a truer representation of His character" (*Seventh-day Adventists Believe* 382).

As Christians glimpse a clearer picture of the new heaven and the new earth, they are attracted to desire that better world. The more clearly one understands the nature of the eternal kingdom and God's will for the redeemed, the greater the meaning of the Lord's Prayer: "Thy kingdom come, thy will be done, on earth as it is in heaven" (Matt. 6:10).

IV. Historical Overview

In all cultures and ages, the concept of the rewards of righteous and wicked is closely related to the understanding of the state of the dead. Here we deal only with what has often been called the "abode of the redeemed," the place where God's people are recompensed after the final resurrection. Although frequently more emphasis is placed on the reward of the wicked than that of the righteous,

the eternal kingdom promised to the righteous has been through the ages an integral part of the Christian hope.

A. Ancient World

Ancient Mesopotamians thought that after death, human beings were doomed to exist as shades in the nether regions. Little could be done in life to assure any kind of blissful existence in the hereafter.

For the ancient Egyptians, death was a continuation of life as known on earth, with a fulfillment of the best one might expect. A person who succeeded in passing the judgment hall of Osiris entered paradise: the Fields of Aalu. There the pleasures of food, wine, and leisure were enjoyed. To ensure a happy passage, a long list of good deeds done and bad ones avoided—the Book of the Dead—routinely was placed in the tomb with the body.

The Greeks considered that at the end of life the soul was rewarded or punished. The judges pronounced sentence at the parting of the ways, one of which led to the abode of the blessed. No clear picture of the activities in such a place is available.

B. Judaism

Jewish pseudepigraphical writings of the intertestamental period follow the OT theme of a "new earth" (2 Baruch 32:6; 57:2). In 4 Ezra 8:52 we read, "It is for you that Paradise is opened, the tree of life is planted, the age to come is prepared, plenty is provided, a city is built, rest is appointed, goodness is established and wisdom perfected beforehand."

The second-century B.C. book of Jubilees notes, "The day of the new creation when the heaven and earth and all of their creatures shall be renewed according to the powers of heaven and according to the whole nature of earth, until the sanctuary of the Lord is created in Jerusalem upon Mount Zion" (1:29). Similar ideas appear in 1 Enoch: "On that day, I shall cause my Elect One to dwell among them, I shall transform heaven and make it a blessing of light forever. I shall (also) transform the earth and make it a blessing, and cause my Elect One to dwell in her. Then those who have committed sin and crime shall not set foot in her" (45:4, 5). According to 2 Enoch, the place prepared for the righteous, "who afflict their souls, and who avert their eyes from injustice, and who carry out righteous judgment" (9:1) "has an appearance of pleasantness that has

never been seen" (8:1). Every kind of ripe fruit, food, gardens, and fragrance (8:3) are there; and "the tree of life is in that place" (8:3; cf. Testament of Levi 18:11).

According to rabbinic Judaism, the righteous went to paradise, the Garden of Eden. The Messianic reign was to be political and physical Utopia; after it would be the world to come, when the righteous sit in glory and enjoy the splendor of the divine presence in a world of pure spiritual bliss (Babylonian Talmud *Berakoth* 17a, 34b). References to this world are tied to Isaiah 64:3, with the recognition that none but God can have a conception of the matter.

The "new earth" is commonly called 'ôlām ha-bā', the "world to come." This phrase is first used in 1 Enoch 71:15, dated in the second or first century B.C. The 'ôlām ha-bā' follows the age of the Messiah and begins with the last judgment. According to the Babylonian Talmud, a third-century-B.C. rabbi described the 'ôlām ha-bā' as follows: "In the future world there is no eating nor drinking nor propagation nor business nor jealousy nor hatred nor competition, but the righteous sit with their crowns on their heads feasting on the brightness of the divine presence" (*Berakoth* 17a).

Jews today accept the ancient teaching in varied degrees. The more secularized have little belief in the age to come. The orthodox still hold to the doctrine.

C. Islam

At the final judgment, those who have achieved sanctification, who know God and are close to Him, will reach *al-Jannah*, "the garden," luxuriant with tall shadowing trees. The delights prepared for the blessed are hardly imaginable. In that heavenly garden the righteous recline on couches, dressed in garments of silk, enjoying the best of food and drink (Qur'an 76:5-22). "Rivers of water unpolluted, and rivers of milk whereof the flavour changeth not, and rivers of wine delicious to the drinkers, and rivers of clear-run honey;

therein for them is every kind of fruit with pardon from their Lord" (Qur'an 47:15).

D. Eastern Religions

For Buddhists, as for Hindus, a person's fate after death is decided by one's karma. At death, souls pass over a bridge into the abode of the gods; the good pass easily into the celestial realm, the most important feature of which is light and splendor. Because this blissful state is impermanent, it is not worthy of one's desire. In popular thinking, however, those who do good look forward to going to a delightful place of abundance and happiness.

In Hinduism the dead pass by two fires, which burn the wicked but let the good pass by to bliss. *Rig-Veda* devotees implore deities to grant them immortality in the third heaven, the undecaying world. The blessed there enjoy eternal life, as a result of their past sacrifices and gifts made to the priests. In place of the frail human body they receive a blemishless and vigorous body.

E. Early Christianity

Early Christian teaching on the reward of the saved deviates little from the biblical position. The *Didache,* from the late first or early second century, instructs Christians to pray: "Remember, Lord, your Church, to save it from all evil and to make it perfect by your love. Make it holy, and gather it together from the four winds into your Kingdom which you have made ready for it. Let Grace come and let this world pass away" (10:5, 6).

Although purporting to have been written by Solomon, the *Odes of Solomon* represents a Christian hymnbook, from the first or second century A.D. They speak of the reward of the faithful: "Blessed, O Lord, are they who are planted in your land, and who have a place in your Paradise" (11:18). Further: "Indeed, there is much room in your Paradise. And there is nothing in it which is barren, but everything is filled with fruit" (verse 23).

In early Christian thinking, heaven was conceived as a place where the faithful enjoyed a life full of joy. Scenes from the catacombs in Rome depict the heavenly life as a banquet or a garden landscape. Funerary inscriptions place the dead as "refreshed and joyful among the stars," expressing not only a belief in a reward for the righteous but in a conscious state prior to the resurrection. In the second-century Gospel of Thomas, a brief description of Paradise appears: "For you have five trees in Paradise, which do not move in summer or in winter, and their leaves do not fall. He who knows them shall not taste death" (19).

For Gregory of Nazianzus (c. 329-390) the believer not only found release from the troubles of this life, but came to enjoy a full knowledge of God and nearness to the divine presence. In the poems of Ephraim the Syrian (fourth century), paradise had three divisions. Its one river flowed from under the throne in the garden, dividing itself into four streams.

In the East, complete salvation had to wait until the day of resurrection. In the West, Augustine taught that resurrection from the dead would enhance the joys of salvation already available to the departed soul, but was not indispensable to enjoyment of the presence of God. Some excerpts from the last chapter of *The City of God* show Augustine's beliefs regarding heaven. "Who can measure the happiness of heaven, where no evil can touch us, no good will be out of reach; where life is to be one long laud extolling God, who will be all in all." "The promised reward of virtue will be the best and the greatest of all possible prizes—the very Giver of virtue Himself." There "sin will have no power to tempt." Heaven will be "that ultimate Sabbath," foreshadowed on earth by the weekly Sabbath. This final Sabbath was to be the seventh age, following the sixth, in which Augustine placed himself. It would be a "kingdom without end, the real goal of our present life" (*City of God* 22. 30).

F. Roman Catholicism

Medieval monks contemplated the bliss of heaven and wrote poems about it. Bernard of

Cluny (twelfth century) composed one of the most familiar: "Jerusalem the Golden," still sung today. Others who wrote hymns about heaven were Peter Abélard (1079-1142) and Thomas à Kempis (1380-1471).

Benedict XII's fourteenth-century papal constitution *Benedictus Deus* affirms the existence of the beatific vision and its essence as an intuitive vision of God. Its direct concern was to ensure that for those who need no further purification, the beatific vision follows immediately upon death and endures continuously forever. This was affirmed in reaction to the teaching of John XXII, who had held that the joys of heaven would be experienced only after the resurrection of the body.

In modern Roman Catholic thinking on heaven there is emphasis on heaven as a state, although it is also a place, given that glorified bodies require a place in which to dwell. "This community of life and love with the Trinity, with the Virgin Mary, the angels and all the blessed is called 'heaven.' Heaven is the ultimate end and fulfillment of the deepest human longings, the state of supreme, definitive happiness" (*Catechism of the Catholic Church* 1024). "Heaven is not primarily a place but a personal relationship" (*The New Dictionary of Theology* 456). Ultimately the renewal of the world, together with the restoration of the body, constitutes the final completion of God's salvific plan.

The "Letter on Certain Questions Concerning Eschatology" issued by the Sacred Congregation for the Doctrine of the Faith (1979) is very reserved concerning details of doctrine on heaven. While affirming belief in the resurrection of the body, the survival of the "human self" after death, and "in the happiness of the just who will one day be with Christ," it warns against arbitrary imaginative representations since "neither Scripture nor theology provides sufficient light for a proper picture of life after death."

G. Protestantism

The Reformers appear to have taken heaven for granted. But from the little they wrote we learn of their firm belief in the reward of the redeemed. For example, Martin Luther describes the "celestial, spiritual body" of those who will be resurrected at the last day: "The entire body will be as pure and bright as the sun and as light as air, and, finally, so healthy, so blissful, and filled with such heavenly, eternal joy in God that it will never hunger, thirst, grow weary or decline" (*Luther's Works* 28:196). Likewise John Calvin affirmed the certainty of the resurrection and the eternal happiness of the redeemed. In his *Catechism* he wrote, "That blessedness will be the Kingdom of God, crammed with all brightness, joy, power, happiness—things far removed now from human sense, and which we now see only darkly, until that day comes on which the Lord will show His glory for us to see" (20. 9).

Protestant hymnody has proclaimed the certainty of the reward of the righteous. Isaac Watts (1674-1748) penned many hymns about heaven; of these, one of the best known reads as follows: "There is a land of pure delight,/ Where saints immortal reign;/Infinite day excludes the night/And pleasures banish pain." Nineteenth-century Protestant hymnody presents many songs extolling the beauties of heaven. Fanny Crosby wrote many of these, including "When My Life Work is Ended."

While Protestants generally believe in heaven as a place where the redeemed will spend eternity with God and the angelic hosts, there appears to have been no attempt to systematize a doctrine of heaven. The inroads of rationalism and secularization have resulted in an erosion of the clarity of the millennial hope. While expressing belief in the "symbols" of Christ's kingdom, Reinhold Niebuhr wrote: "It is unwise for Christians to claim any knowledge of either the furniture of heaven or the temperature of hell" (2:294).

H. Adventist Understanding

With the expectation of the Second Advent as a foundation of their doctrinal system,

Adventists constantly have affirmed their conviction of the reality of a new heaven and new earth following Christ's second coming. The redeemed will spend the millennium in heaven (see II. B. 3) before descending to this earth with the New Jerusalem. At that time the planet will be renewed by fire and re-created. The saints will then spend eternity with the Lord on this earth made new.

Ellen White's visions of the heavenly home and the renewed earth have contributed much to the realism with which the future of the blessed is viewed. In *Early Writings* she describes the glories of the heavenly city as she had seen them in vision in the 1840s (EW 39, 40).

Adventist art forms also extol the wonders of the earth made new. The artistic renderings of painters Harry Anderson and Russell Harlan have captured the imagination of generations of Adventist readers, young and old. Adventist songwriters since William Miller ("I'm Going Home") have expressed in music the glorious hope for a future of bliss. These include, to name a few, James White ("What Heavenly Music"), Annie R. Smith ("Long Upon the Mountains"), Frank Belden ("Joy By and By"), and Henry de Fluiter ("Over Yonder").

The last of the 27 fundamental beliefs of Seventh-day Adventists, adopted in 1980, presents a synthesis of the Adventist understanding of the new earth (*SDA Yearbook* 1981:8).

"On the new earth, in which righteousness dwells, God will provide an eternal home for the redeemed and a perfect environment for everlasting life, love, joy, and learning in His presence. For here God Himself will dwell with His people, and suffering and death will have passed away. The great controversy will be ended, and sin will be no more. All things, animate and inanimate, will declare that God is love; and He shall reign forever. Amen. (2 Peter 3:13; Isa. 35; 65:17-25; Matt. 5:5; Rev. 21:1-7; 22:1-5; 11:15.)"

V. Ellen G. White Comments

A. Heavenly Abode—Real Place

"A fear of making the future inheritance seem too material has led many to spiritualize away the very truths which lead us to look upon it as our home. Christ assured His disciples that He went to prepare mansions for them in the Father's house. Those who accept the teachings of God's word will not be wholly ignorant concerning the heavenly abode. And yet, 'eye hath not seen, nor ear heard, neither have entered into the heart of man, the things which God hath prepared for them that love Him' (1 Cor. 2:9). Human language is inadequate to describe the reward of the righteous. It will be known only to those who behold it. No finite mind can comprehend the glory of the Paradise of God" (GC 674, 675).

B. Privileges of the Redeemed

"Heaven is a good place. I long to be there and behold my lovely Jesus, who gave His life for me, and be changed into His glorious image. Oh, for language to express the glory of the bright world to come! I thirst for the living streams that make glad the city of our God.

"The Lord has given me a view of other worlds. Wings were given me, and an angel attended me from the city to a place that was bright and glorious. The grass of the place was living green, and the birds there warbled a sweet song. The inhabitants of the place were of all sizes; they were noble, majestic, and lovely. They bore the express image of Jesus, and their countenances beamed with holy joy, expressive of the freedom and happiness of the place. I asked one of them why they were so much more lovely than those on the earth. The reply was, 'We have lived in strict obedience to the commandments of God, and have not fallen by disobedience, like those on the earth.' . . . I begged of my attending angel to let me remain in that place. I could not bear the thought of coming back to this dark world again. Then the angel said, 'You must go back, and if you are faithful, you, with the 144,000, shall have the privilege of visiting all the worlds and viewing the handiwork of God'" (EW 39, 40).

C. No Night and No Weariness

"In the City of God 'there shall be no night.' None will need or desire repose. There will be no weariness in doing the will of God and offering praise to His name. We shall ever feel the freshness of the morning and shall ever be far from its close. 'And they need no candle, neither light of the sun; for the Lord God giveth them light' (Rev. 22:5). The light of the sun will be superseded by a radiance which is not painfully dazzling, yet which immeasurably surpasses the brightness of our noontide. The glory of God and the Lamb floods the Holy City with unfading light. The redeemed walk in the sunless glory of perpetual day" (GC 676).

D. Heaven as a School

"Heaven is a school; its field of study, the universe; its teacher, the Infinite One. A branch of this school was established in Eden; and, the plan of redemption accomplished, education will again be taken up in the Eden school.

"'Eye hath not seen, nor ear heard, neither have entered into the heart of man, the things which God hath prepared for them that love Him' (1 Cor. 2:9). Only through His word can a knowledge of these things be gained; and even this affords but a partial revelation.

"The prophet of Patmos thus describes the location of the school of the hereafter:

"'I saw a new heaven and a new earth: for the first heaven and the first earth were passed away. . . . And I John saw the Holy City, New Jerusalem, coming down from God out of heaven, prepared as a bride adorned for her husband' (Rev. 21:1, 2).

"'The city had no need of the sun, neither of the moon, to shine in it: for the glory of God did lighten it, and the Lamb is the light thereof' (Rev. 21:23).

"Between the school established in Eden at the beginning and the school of the hereafter there lies the whole compass of this world's history—the history of human transgression and suffering, of divine sacrifice, and of victory over death and sin. Not all the conditions of that first school of Eden will be found in the school of the future life. No tree of knowledge of good and evil will afford opportunity for temptation. No tempter is there, no possibility of wrong. Every character has withstood the testing of evil, and none are longer susceptible to its power" (Ed 301, 302).

E. Treasures of the Universe Opened

"All the treasures of the universe will be open to the study of God's children. With unutterable delight we shall enter into the joy and the wisdom of unfallen beings. We shall share the treasures gained through ages upon ages spent in contemplation of God's handiwork. And the years of eternity, as they roll, will continue to bring more glorious revelations. 'Exceeding abundantly above all that we ask or think' (Eph. 3:20) will be, forever and forever, the impartation of the gifts of God.

"'His servants shall serve Him' (Rev. 22:3). The life on earth is the beginning of the life in heaven; education on earth is an initiation into the principles of heaven; the lifework here is a training for the lifework there. What we now are, in character and holy service, is the sure foreshadowing of what we shall be" (Ed 307).

F. Higher Education in the Future Life

"Christ, the heavenly Teacher, will lead His people to the tree of life that grows on either side of the river of life, and He will explain to them the truths they could not in this life understand. In that future life His people will gain the higher education in its completeness. Those who enter the city of God will have the golden crowns placed upon their heads. That will be a joyful scene that none of us can afford to miss. We shall cast our crowns at the feet of Jesus, and again and again we will give Him the glory and praise His holy name. Angels will unite in the songs of triumph. Touching their golden harps, they will fill all heaven with rich music and songs to the Lamb" (MS 31, 1909 in 7BC 988).

G. Harmonious Social Life and Endless Increasing of Knowledge

"There the redeemed shall know, even as also they are known. The loves and sympathies which God Himself has planted in the soul shall there find truest and sweetest exercise. The pure communion with holy beings, the harmonious social life with the blessed angels and with the faithful ones of all ages who have washed their robes and made them white in the blood of the Lamb, the sacred ties that bind together 'the whole family in heaven and earth' (Eph. 3:15)—these help to constitute the happiness of the redeemed.

"There, immortal minds will contemplate with never-failing delight the wonders of creative power, the mysteries of redeeming love. There will be no cruel, deceiving foe to tempt to forgetfulness of God. Every faculty will be developed, every capacity increased. The acquirement of knowledge will not weary the mind or exhaust the energies. There the grandest enterprises may be carried forward, the loftiest aspirations reached, the highest ambitions realized; and still there will arise new heights to surmount, new wonders to admire, new truths to comprehend, fresh objects to call forth the powers of mind and soul and body.

"All the treasures of the universe will be open to the study of God's redeemed. Unfettered by mortality, they wing their tireless flight to worlds afar—worlds that thrilled with sorrow at the spectacle of human woe and rang with songs of gladness at the tidings of a ransomed soul. With unutterable delight the children of earth enter into the joy and the wisdom of unfallen beings. They share the treasures of knowledge and understanding gained through ages upon ages in contemplation of God's handiwork. With undimmed vision they gaze upon the glory of creation—suns and stars and systems, all in their appointed order circling the throne of Deity. Upon all things, from the least to the greatest, the Creator's name is written, and in all are the riches of His power displayed.

"And the years of eternity, as they roll, will bring richer and still more glorious revelations of God and of Christ. As knowledge is progressive, so will love, reverence, and happiness increase. The more men learn of God, the greater will be their admiration of His character. As Jesus opens before them the riches of redemption and the amazing achievements in the great controversy with Satan, the hearts of the ransomed thrill with more fervent devotion, and with more rapturous joy they sweep the harps of gold; and ten thousand times ten thousand and thousands of thousands of voices unite to swell the mighty chorus of praise.

"'And every creature which is in heaven, and on the earth, and under the earth, and such as are in the sea, and all that are in them, heard I saying, Blessing, and honor, and glory, and power, be unto Him that sitteth upon the throne, and unto the Lamb for ever and ever' (Rev. 5:13).

"The great controversy is ended. Sin and sinners are no more. The entire universe is clean. One pulse of harmony and gladness beats through the vast creation. From Him who created all, flow life and light and gladness, throughout the realms of illimitable space. From the minutest atom to the greatest world, all things, animate and inanimate, in their unshadowed beauty and perfect joy, declare that God is love" (GC 677, 678).

H. The Life in Garden and Field

"There, when the veil that darkens our vision shall be removed, and our eyes shall behold that world of beauty of which we now catch glimpses through the microscope; when we look on the glories of the heavens, now scanned afar through the telescope; when, the blight of sin removed, the whole earth shall appear in 'the beauty of the Lord our God,' what a field will be open to our study! There the student of science may read the records of creation and discern no reminders of the law of evil. He may listen to the music of nature's voices and detect no note of wailing or undertone of sorrow. In all created things he may trace one handwriting—in the vast universe behold 'God's name writ large,' and not in earth or sea or sky one sign of ill remaining.

"There the Eden life will be lived, the life in garden and field. 'They shall build houses, and inhabit them; and they shall plant vineyards, and eat the fruit of them. They shall not build, and another inhabit; they shall not plant, and another eat: for as the days of a tree are the days of my people, and mine elect shall long enjoy the work of their hands' (Isa. 65:21, 22).

"There shall be nothing to 'hurt nor destroy in all my holy mountain, saith the Lord' (Isa. 65:25). There man will be restored to his lost kingship, and the lower order of beings will again recognize his sway; the fierce will become gentle, and the timid trustful.

"There will be open to the student, history of infinite scope and of wealth inexpressible. Here, from the vantage ground of God's Word, the student is afforded a view of the vast field of history and may gain some knowledge of the principles that govern the course of human events. But his vision is still clouded, and his knowledge incomplete. Not until he stands in the light of eternity will he see all things clearly.

"Then will be opened before him the course of the great conflict that had its birth before time began, and that ends only when time shall cease. The history of the inception of sin; of fatal falsehood in its crooked working; of truth that, swerving not from its own straight lines, has met and conquered error—all will be made manifest. The veil that interposes between the visible and the invisible world will be drawn aside, and wonderful things will be revealed" (Ed 303, 304).

I. No Marriage and No Birth

"There are men today who express their belief that there will be marriages and births in the new earth, but those who believe the Scriptures cannot accept such doctrines. The doctrine that children will be born in the new earth is not a part of the 'sure word of prophecy.' The words of Christ are too plain to be misunderstood. They should forever settle the question of marriages and births in the new earth. Neither those who shall be raised from the dead, nor those who shall be translated without seeing death, will marry or be given in marriage. They will be as the angels of God, members of the royal family" (MM 99, 100).

J. Travel in the Future Life

"Many seem to have the idea that this world and the heavenly mansions constitute the universe of God. Not so. The redeemed throng will range from world to world, and much of their time will be employed in searching out the mysteries of redemption. And throughout the whole stretch of eternity, this subject will be continually opening to their minds. The privileges of those who overcome by the blood of the Lamb and the word of their testimony are beyond comprehension" (RH Mar. 9, 1886).

K. The Reward of Earnest Effort

" 'If any man's work abide, . . . he shall receive a reward' (1 Cor. 3:14). Glorious will be the reward bestowed when the faithful workers gather about the throne of God and of the Lamb. When John in his mortal state beheld the glory of God, he fell as one dead; he was not able to endure the sight. But when the children of God shall have put on immortality, they will 'see him as he is' (1 John 3:2). They will stand before the throne, accepted in the Beloved. All their sins have been blotted out, all their transgressions borne away. Now they can look upon the undimmed glory of the throne of God. They have been partakers with Christ in His sufferings, they have been workers together with Him in the plan of redemption, and they are partakers with Him in the joy of seeing souls saved in the kingdom of God, there to praise God through all eternity.

"My brother, my sister, I urge you to prepare for the coming of Christ in the clouds of heaven. Day by day cast the love of the world out of your hearts. Understand by experience what it means to have fellowship with Christ. Prepare for the judgment, that when Christ shall come, to be admired in all them that believe, you may be among those who will meet Him in peace. In that day the redeemed will shine forth in the glory of the Father and the Son. The angels, touching their golden harps, will welcome the King and His trophies of victory—those who have been washed and made white in the blood of the Lamb" (9T 285).

L. A Happy, United Family

"All will be a happy, united family, clothed with the garments of praise and thanksgiving— the robe of Christ's righteousness. All nature, in its surpassing loveliness, will offer to God a constant tribute of praise and adoration. The world will be bathed in the light of heaven. The years will move on in gladness. The light of the moon will be as the light of the sun, and the light of the sun will be sevenfold greater than it is now. Over the scene the morning stars will sing together, and the sons of God will shout for joy, while God and Christ will unite in proclaiming, 'There shall be no more sin, neither shall there be any more death' " (RH Nov. 26, 1903).

M. The Bright Home of the Saints

"Heaven was the subject of my contemplation—heaven, the much-longed-for heaven. I seemed to be there, where all was peace, where no stormy conflicts of earth could ever come. Heaven, a kingdom of righteousness where all the holy and pure and blessed are congregated—ten thousand times ten thousand and thousands of thousands—living and walking in happy, pure intimacy, praising God and the Lamb who sitteth on the throne! Their voices were in perfect harmony. They never do each other wrong. Princes of heaven, the potentates of this mighty realm, are rivals only in good, seeking the happiness and joy of each other. The greatest there is least in self-esteem, and the least is greatest in his gratitude and wealth of love.

"There are no dark errors to cloud the intellect. Truth and knowledge, clear, strong, and perfect, have chased every doubt away, and no gloom of doubt casts its baleful shadow upon its happy inhabitants. No voices of contention mar the sweet and perfect peace of heaven. Its inhabitants know no sorrow, no grief, no tears. All is in perfect harmony, in perfect order and perfect bliss. . . .

"Heaven, sweet heaven, the saints' eternal home, the abode for the toilers, where the weary who have borne the heavy burdens through life find rest, peace, and joy! They sowed in tears, they reap with joy and triumph. Heaven is a home where sympathy is alive in every heart, expressed in every look. Love reigns there. There are no jarring elements, no discord or contentions or war of words" (letter 30, 1882; 9MR 104, 105).

N. City of God for Commandment Keepers

"None who have had the light of truth will enter the city of God as commandment-breakers. His law lies at the foundation of His government in earth and in heaven. If they have knowingly trampled upon and despised His law on the earth, they will not be taken to heaven to do the same work there; there is no change of character when Christ comes. The character building is to go on during the hours of probation. Day by day their actions are registered in the books of heaven, and they will, in the great day of God, be rewarded as their works have been. It will then be seen who receives the blessing. 'Blessed are they that do his commandments, that they may have right to the tree of life, and may enter in through the gates into the city' " (RH Aug. 25, 1885).

O. The Eternal Abode of the Obedient

"The great plan of redemption results in fully bringing back the world into God's favor. All that was lost by sin is restored. Not only man but the earth is redeemed, to be the eternal abode of the obedient. For six thousand years Satan has struggled to maintain possession of the earth. Now God's original purpose in its creation is accomplished. 'The saints of the Most High shall take the kingdom, and possess the kingdom forever, even forever and ever' (Dan. 7:18)" (PP 342).

VI. Literature

Augustine. *The City of God.* Trans. G. G. Walsh; D. B. Zema; G. Monahan; D. J. Honan. Ed. V. J. Bourke. New York: Doubleday, 1958.

Beasley-Murray, G. R. *Jesus and the Kingdom of God.* Grand Rapids: Eerdmans, 1986.

Beckwith, Isbon T. *The Apocalypse of John.* Grand Rapids: Baker, 1919.

Berkhof, L. *The Kingdom of God.* Grand Rapids: Eerdmans, 1951.

Bright, John. *The Kingdom of God: The Biblical Concept and Its Meaning for the Church.* Nashville: Abingdon, 1953.

Catechism of the Catholic Church. St. Paul: Wanderer, 1994.

Delitzsch, Franz. *Biblical Commentary on the Prophecies of Isaiah.* 2 vols. New York: Funk and Wagnalls, 1872.

Froom, LeRoy Edwin. *The Conditionalist Faith of Our Fathers.* 2 vols. Washington, D.C.: Review and Herald, 1965-1966.

Komonchak, Joseph, Mary Collins, and Dermot Lane, eds. *The New Dictionary of Theology.* Wilmington, Del.: Michael Glazier, 1987.

Ladd, George Eldon. *Crucial Questions About the Kingdom of God.* Grand Rapids: Eerdmans, 1952.

———. *Jesus and the Kingdom: The Eschatology of Biblical Realism.* New York: Harper and Row, 1964.

———. *The Presence of the Future: The Eschatology of Biblical Realism.* Grand Rapids: Eerdmans, 1973.

Luther, M. *Luther's Works.* Ed. Hilton C. Oswald. Vol. 28, *Commentaries on 1 Corinthians 7 and 15.* Saint Louis: Concordia Pub. House, 1973.

Niebuhr, Reinhold. *The Nature and Destiny of Man.* 2 vols. New York: Scribner's, 1964.

Smith, Wilbur M. *The Biblical Doctrine of Heaven.* Chicago: Moody, 1980.

Strong, August Hopkins. *Systematic Theology.* Philadelphia: Judson, 1907.

Vos, Geerhardus. *The Teaching of Jesus Concerning the Kingdom of God and the Church.* Phillipsburg, N.J.: Presbyterian and Reformed, 1972.

Willis, Wendell, ed. *The Kingdom of God in 20th-Century Interpretation.* Peabody, Mass.: Hendrickson, 1987.

Young, Edward J. *The Book of Isaiah.* 3 vols. Grand Rapids: Eerdmans, 1964-1971.

The Great Controversy

Frank B. Holbrook

Introduction

Scattered across the pages of both the OT and NT lie many references and allusions to an unrelenting war between God and Satan, between good and evil on both cosmic and personal levels. Comparing these passages, we inlay their individual insights to form a mosaic window of truth through which we can perceive the total message of Scripture with greater clarity than otherwise.

The moral controversy, which has troubled the universe of God's creation, is closely linked to the plan of salvation. The latter provides not only deliverance for humanity from the enslavement of sin, but also a theodicy for the Godhead against Satan's accusations.

In the following study the biblical data have been arranged in chronological sequence in order to demonstrate more effectively the nature of the war, how it unfolded, its course through the centuries, the final struggle, which ends in Satan's defeat and God's triumph and vindication. The article concludes with a summary of some of the more important theological truths exhibited by this foundational teaching of Scripture.

I. The Controversy Foreseen
  A. The Divine Secret
    1. Grace Initiated the Plan
    2. Atoning Death of Christ
    3. Accepting the Provisions of Salvation
    4. Character Restoration
    5. The Eternal Rewards
  B. The Challenger
II. The Origin of the Controversy
  A. God and His Creation
  B. Heaven's Laws
  C. Issues in the Controversy
    1. Lucifer
    2. The Issues
    3. Whose Authority Is Best?
    4. The Fall of Lucifer From Heaven
    5. The Fall of Humanity
  D. Heaven's Added Dimension
  E. Heaven's Objectives
III. The Controversy on Earth—OT
  A. God's Initiative
    1. The Promise
    2. Sacrificial Rituals
    3. Prophetic Portrayals
    4. Preserving and Propagating Salvation Truths

  B. Satan's Counterattack
    1. Antediluvian Wickedness
    2. Development of Paganism and Idolatry
    3. Corrupting the True Religion
    4. Satanic Accusations
    5. Satan's "Almost" Success
IV. The Controversy on Earth—NT
  A. Overruling Providence
    1. Growing Centrality of Scripture
    2. The Dispersion (Diaspora, John 7:35)
    3. The Jewish Mission
  B. The First Advent of Christ
    1. Christ's Victory Prophetically Portrayed
    2. Christ's Victory Over Temptations
    3. Christ's Daily Victory Over the Demons
    4. Christ's Multiple Victories at the Cross
  C. Satanic Attacks on the Church
    1. Corrupting the Doctrines
    2. Persecuting the Church
  D. The Controversy in Microcosm
V. The Controversy Completed
  A. The Final Struggle
    1. Leopardlike Beast (Rev. 13:1-10)
    2. Two-horned Beast (Rev. 13:11-17)
  B. The Judgment-Hour Invitation
    1. Three Angels' Messages (Rev. 14:6-13)

I. The Controversy Foreseen

A. *The Divine Secret*

God created all intelligent beings as free moral agents with the ability to render loving allegiance to the Creator or to reject His authority. Several New Testament passages indicate God foresaw the defection that would take place among the angels and the insurrection that would follow. He foresaw that mankind would be deceived into joining the rebellion.

Before time began (as far as this earth is concerned)—at some point in eternity past—God, that is, Father, Son, and Holy Spirit, devised the plan of salvation to meet this foreseen crisis. The apostle Paul refers to that plan as "the mystery which was kept secret for long ages" (Rom. 16:25). This "secret," or "hidden wisdom," he asserts, "God decreed before the ages," before earth time began (1 Cor. 2:7).

The secret or mystery is "the mystery of the gospel," he explains elsewhere (Eph. 6:19). It is evident, then, that the rebellion, which eventually broke out among some of the created intelligences in the universe, did not take God by surprise. The Godhead had already devised a "rescue operation" for deceived human rebels—a plan that would also provide an effective weapon in putting down the rebellion permanently.

1. Grace Initiated the Plan

"Grace" is heaven's loving merciful attitude toward undeserving, rebellious, human sinners. On this basis God chose to save and transform all repentant sinners who would accept the provisions made for their salvation. The apostle observes that their deliverance would not be by virtue of some good works they might render, but would be by "virtue of his [God's] own purpose and the grace which he gave us in Christ Jesus ages ago [lit. "before times eternal"]" (2 Tim. 1:9).

2. Atoning Death of Christ

God determined that the atoning death of Jesus Christ would stand at the heart of the plan. The apostle Peter testified to this decision when he told the crowds attending the Feast of Pentecost in Jerusalem that Christ had been "delivered up according to the definite plan and foreknowledge of God" to die (Acts 2:23). Later he wrote to fellow Christians, "You know that you were ransomed . . . with the precious blood of Christ, like that of a lamb without blemish or spot. He was destined before the foundation of the world but was made manifest at the end of the times for your sake" (1 Peter 1:18-20).

In character God is both just and merciful, holy and gracious. No matter how much God loved rebellious human sinners, He would not be just if He simply excused the sinner. But before the entrance of sin and rebellion into the universe, God planned to extend grace (mercy) to repentant rebels by means of Jesus Christ, that is, by means of Christ's atoning death. The penal, substitutionary death of Christ would satisfy divine justice and would make it possible for forgiveness and reconciliation to be extended to penitent sinners (cf. Rom. 3:21-26).

3. Accepting the Provisions of Salvation

God—Father, Son, and Holy Spirit—chose to adopt into His "family" from Adam's sinful race all who would receive Christ as their Saviour and Lord and would enter into a bond of union with them. The apostle wrote, "Blessed be the God and Father of our Lord Jesus Christ, who has blessed us in Christ with every spiritual blessing . . . even as he chose us in him [Christ] before the foundation of the world. . . . He destined us in love to be his sons through Jesus Christ, according to the purpose of his will, to the praise of his glorious grace which he freely bestowed on us in the Beloved" (Eph. 1:3-6). None was predeter-

mined to be lost, but a plan was laid that, as the apostle John would later write, "to all who received him [Christ], who believed in his name, he gave power to become children of God" (John 1:12; see God IV. B.)

4. Character Restoration

The apostle Paul hints that God also made provision to restore penitent sinners from the internal ravages of sin. His task was to make known "the mystery hidden for ages and generations," particularly a certain aspect of "this mystery, which is Christ in you, the hope of glory" (Col. 1:26, 27). Since Christ indwells the believer (Gal. 2:20) by means of the Holy Spirit (John 14:16-18, 23; Rom. 8:9, 10), provision for an indwelling Christ probably refers to the transforming and restoring operations of the Holy Spirit in the lives of believers (see John 3:6-8; Rom. 8:14-16; see God VII. C. 5. c).

If this assessment of the Colossian passage is correct, the plan laid by God was designed to meet the two great needs of fallen humanity: (1) death, the penalty for sin, would be canceled by the atoning and penal substitutionary death of Christ; (2) the power of sin in the human heart would be displaced by the indwelling Christ through the operation of the Holy Spirit.

5. The Eternal Rewards

Two passages refer to the rewards determined by God for those who accept the plan of salvation. The apostle Paul speaks in Titus 1:2 of the believer's "hope of eternal life which God, who never lies, promised ages ago [lit. "before times eternal"]." Jesus' parable of the final judgment widens this promise of eternal life: "Then the King will say to those at his right hand, 'Come, O blessed of my Father, inherit the kingdom prepared [lit. "which has been prepared"] for you from the foundation of the world' " (Matt. 25:34). Since the inherited kingdom is the recreated and restored earth—a condition yet future (see Matt. 5:5; 2 Peter 3:13), the expression "which has been prepared" is an allusion to the decision

God made in eternity past in laying the plan of salvation.

In the same parable Jesus refers to the decision also determined in regard to impenitent rebels: "Depart from me, you cursed, into the eternal fire prepared [lit. "which has been prepared"] for the devil [*diabolos*] and his angels" (Matt. 25:41). Hence, in this heavenly council held before the creation of the world God announced the ultimate destiny of both the penitent and impenitent from the human race. We note in this statement that He never intended humans to be lost. The destruction determined was for "the devil and his angels."

This group of remarkable passages, which sketches the major provisions of the divine plan of salvation, identifies the "enemy" and instigator of the moral controversy that would convulse the universe for millennia: "the devil" and the angels who confederate with him. One reason for the Messiah's coming to earth was to announce the decisions which the Father, Son, and Holy Spirit had made for human salvation. "I will open my mouth in parables, I will utter what has been hidden since the foundation of the world" (Matt.

13:35; see Salvation II. A).

B. The Challenger

In the parable of the judgment (Matt. 25) Jesus designated the challenger to God's order as "the devil," one of several names and titles ascribed to this evil personality. He is also referred to as "Satan," and as "the tempter" (Matt. 4:1, 3, 10). In the book of Revelation he is identified as "the great dragon," the "ancient serpent"—an allusion to the mode he used to tempt Eve—and as "the deceiver of the whole world" (Rev. 12:9; cf. 20:2). He is also depicted as "the evil one" or "wicked one" (Matt. 13:19; see also KJV), and as "the accuser of our brethren" (Rev. 12:10).

Satan is viewed as the leader of the angels confederated with him (Matt. 25:41) under the title of Beelzebul, "the prince of demons" (Mark 3:22). At times the demons are designated spirits (Luke 9:39, 42), unclean spirits (Mark 7:25, 26), or "evil spirits" (Luke 8:2). Satan is also acknowledged in Scripture as "the prince of the power of the air" (Eph. 2:2), "the ruler of this world" (John 12:31; 14:30; 16:11), and "the god of this world" (2 Cor. 4:4; see Death I. B. 2. a-d).

II. The Origin of the Controversy

A. God and His Creation

Holy Scripture begins with the creation of the earth by God. "In the beginning God created the heavens and the earth" (Gen. 1:1). Although the Creation account implies the activity of all three, the Father, Son, and Holy Spirit (1:2, 26), the NT plainly describes God the Son as the active Creator who spoke the earth and its life-forms into existence (Heb. 1:1-3; John 1:1-3, 10, 14).

The apostle Paul goes even further, ascribing the existence of the total cosmos—populated by angels and other intelligent beings as well as humans—to the creative and sustaining power of God the Son. "For in him all things were created, in heaven and on earth,

visible and invisible, whether thrones or dominions or principalities or authorities—all things were created through him and for him. He is before all things, and in him all things hold together" (Col. 1:16, 17).

Thus, when in eternity past the Godhead laid an emergency plan to save the human family should they sin, He planned to be the active Saviour of the race, God the Son—who agreed to become incarnate and to die an atoning, substitutionary death to redeem the repentant. The Creator Himself would become humanity's Saviour. (See Creation II. C.)

B. Heaven's Laws

A wise God placed the created cosmos, animate and inanimate, under physical or natural law. Everything is subject to the laws designed for its place in the cosmos. No true science of the natural world could exist if the universe did not function in an orderly manner. Plants and animals grow and develop in their cycles in harmony with the laws governing their existence, just as suns and galaxies move in their ordained orbits. If physical law were to break down, the natural world would collapse in chaos.

Likewise, intelligent beings are subject to physical laws that order their lives. But the Creator also has placed them under governance of moral law. God determined that all created, intelligent beings would exist as free moral agents—endowed with the right of choice. This is inherent in the many biblical appeals to obey God and to turn away from sin and Satan (see Deut. 30:19, 20; Amos 5:14, 15; James 4:7). Since the divine character is described as one of infinite love (Ex. 34:5-7; 1 John 4:8), God requires only that the allegiance and service rendered to Him by all His intelligent subjects shall arise from a genuine, loving appreciation of His character.

Moral law expresses the will of the Creator and does not oppress. Divine love could design only just and good commands (cf. 1 John 5:3). Furthermore, obedience is not drudgery to one who loves the Lawgiver. Since "love does no wrong to a neighbor," the apostle Paul avers, "love is the fulfilling of the law" (Rom. 13:10). It follows, then, that the moral beings brought into existence by a Creator whose very nature is love, would have possessed loving hearts themselves and would have delighted to obey any commands or requests of God.

The Ten Commandments are an adaptation of heaven's moral law into 10 precepts for guidance of the human race. The dual principle of the moral law is stated in Jesus' summarization of the two tables of the Ten Commandments. The intent of the first table (first four precepts) is as follows: "You shall love the Lord your God with all your heart, and with all your soul, and with all your mind. This is the great and first commandment" (Matt. 22:37, 38). The intent of the last six precepts is summarized in a similar manner: "And a second is like it, You shall love your neighbor as yourself. On these two commandments depend all the law and the prophets" (Matt. 22:39, 40; cf. Rom. 13:8-10).

We may infer that love's twofold principle expresses God's will for all orders of the intelligent creation, just as it lies at the heart of biblical religion: The creature's whole duty is to render supreme love to his Creator and impartial love to his fellow beings. We may also infer that this twofold principle is adapted in precepts suitable to each order of intelligent creation just as the Decalogue is an adaptation to the conditions of human beings. Therefore, since angels do not marry (see Matt. 22:30), the fifth and seventh precepts would have little meaning for them. On the other hand, Satan is accused of both murder and lying, violations of the sixth and ninth precepts (John 8:44).

Although the Decalogue was not given in written form until God proclaimed it on Mount Sinai and wrote it on tables of stone (Ex. 20:2-17; Deut. 10:4), the records of Genesis reveal that the human family knew these precepts orally from the earliest times (see First Table: Genesis 2:1-3; 35:1-4; Second Table: Genesis 4:8-11; 12:11-19; 18:19; 19:1-10; 39:7-9; 44:8).The apostle Paul claims in one inclusive statement that the Ten Commandments were known orally in the period from Creation to Moses (Rom. 5:13, 14). The extreme wickedness attributed to the antediluvians rests upon their knowledge of God's will; but they chose to violate and ignore the divine guidelines for human behavior and happiness (Gen. 6:5).

The moral law, however, expressed to the different orders of created beings in specific precepts, is central to the controversy that arose in the universe. God's authority, government, and the imposition of His will (the moral law) upon the intelligent creation became the matter of contention, a polemic leading to a wrenching estrangement between God and a large portion of the angels as well as the newly created order of humanity.

C. Issues in the Controversy

To see more clearly the biblical perspective of the moral controversy that has embroiled the universe, we must understand the issues involved and how they came to be agitated among the angels.

1. Lucifer

Satan, the adversary of God, did not come from the creative hand of God the Son as an evil devil. On the contrary, the Creator brought him into existence as a wise and glorious angel. Two OT passages indirectly describe the origin, position, and moral fall of this mighty being (Isa. 14:4-21; Eze. 28:12-19). In their primary setting these prophecies are addressed to pagan kings of Tyre and Babylon who lived in the times of Ezekiel and Isaiah, respectively. Although liberal scholars reject this long-standing Christian interpretation, it seems evident from even a casual reading that some of the details stated could be true only of a personage greater than those Near Eastern rulers.

The riddle is resolved through a better understanding of the nature of biblical writings. Although Israel, in a sense, rejected God as their king when the people asked the prophet Samuel to establish a monarchy (1 Sam. 8:7; 12:12), in fact God continued to be recognized as the nation's theocratic ruler who reigned through His human representative on the national throne (see Isa. 41:21; Zeph. 3:15). Just as God stood behind the Davidic throne of Israel, so Satan stood behind the throne of these pagan kingdoms. Just as the Davidic kings were expected to reveal character traits and attributes of the true God, so these pagan princes mirrored characteristics of their demonic king.

Furthermore, just as in the Davidic psalms, from time to time a striking detail of the Messiah (the greater Son of David) is unveiled—although not true of David—so in these prophecies addressed to the kings of Tyre and Babylon, the veil drops away for a moment to expose the features of Satan. For an example of this kind of phenomenon, see the apostle Peter's argument that Psalm 16:8-11 refers to Christ and not to David, although David wrote the passage in the first person (Acts 2:25-36).

From a combination of these passages we learn that Satan's original name was "Lucifer" (Isa. 14:12, NKJV) or, literally, "Day Star" (RSV), and that as an angel, he stood in the immediate presence of God. "You were the anointed cherub who covers. . . . You were on the holy mountain of God; you walked in the midst of the stones of fire" (Eze. 28:14, NASB). Furthermore, Lucifer was created a sinless being. "You were blameless in your ways from the day you were created, until unrighteousness was found in you" (verse 15, NASB).

Then the prophets explain how this highly exalted angel began to cherish thoughts of self-importance. "Your heart was lifted up because of your beauty; you corrupted your wisdom by reason of your splendor" (verse 17, NASB). "You said in your heart, 'I will ascend to heaven; I will raise my throne above the stars of God, and I will sit on the mount of assembly in the recesses of the north. I will ascend above the heights of the clouds; I will make myself like the Most High'" (Isa. 14:13, 14, NASB). The apostle Paul confirms this prophetic description when he warns against ordaining a new convert, lest he "become conceited and fall under the same judgment as the devil" (1 Tim. 3:6, NIV).

These passages enable us to sense the seriousness of the controversy. It began among the highest order of God's created intelligences—the angels of heaven. And it began with a noble angel—the covering cherub—who stood in the presence of God.

The challenge originated in the throne room, as it were, of God Himself. (See Sin III. A.)

2. The Issues

It is not likely the rebellion appeared in full strength immediately. It would have taken time to develop. Nor would the conflict have arisen without an apparent rationale to justify it. However, in a perfect universe, which lacked nothing, it remains a mystery how a created, dependent being should aspire to the throne of the self-existent Creator—an impossibility in the very nature of things.

What were the issues? No single passage directly states the specific questions Lucifer raised as, blinded by pride, he endeavored to usurp the divine prerogatives. However, we may safely infer from several biblical passages the nature of the issues involved.

a. God's law. The apostle John provides the simplest definition of the nature of sin. "Everyone who sins breaks the law; in fact, sin is lawlessness" (1 John 3:4, NIV). It is evident from the Epistle itself that the apostle is speaking about the moral law, under which the Creator has placed the intelligent creation (cf. verse 15; 5:21).

But sin is more serious than simple lawlessness. The Scriptures equate the principles and precepts of the moral law (however adapted to the intelligent orders of Creation) with the Creator's personal will. The psalmist sings in a messianic passage, "I delight to do thy will, O my God; thy law is within my heart" (Ps. 40:8). Sin is thus viewed as a deliberate transgression or rebellion against the "will," or Person, of the Creator. When sinners knowingly transgress the moral law, they flaunt and spurn the Creator Himself.

When the Scriptures say, therefore, that "the devil [Satan] has sinned from the beginning" (1 John 3:8), we may rightly infer that Lucifer questioned the necessity for holy beings like the angels to be subject to God's moral commands. He would have considered the law of God as a restriction to angelic

liberty. The apostle's statement indicates that Lucifer eventually rejected divine authority, threw off the yoke of submission to his Creator's government, and openly chose to violate the commands of His expressed will.

b. God's character. Behind the expressed will of the Lawgiver is His character. By calling God's law into question, Lucifer called the Creator's character into question. If—as Lucifer apparently argued—the moral law as expressed to angels was unnecessary and restrictive to personal liberty, then the Creator must have had ulterior motives in subjecting intelligent creatures to its guidelines. Thus, he may have reasonably argued among the angels that the Creator's motives were bad. Perhaps God gained a sense of power by arbitrarily regimenting the creation under blind obedience.

Jesus' description of the archrebel is germane to this discussion, because He implies Lucifer's misrepresentation of the divine character. "He [the devil] was a murderer from the beginning, and has nothing to do with the truth, because there is no truth in him. When he lies, he speaks according to his own nature, for he is a liar and the father of lies" (John 8:44). Christ plainly accuses Lucifer of murder and lying, violations of the moral law. But whom did he kill or lie about in heaven before his expulsion?

Since both Jesus and the apostle John define "anger" and "hatred" as the heart roots of murder, the Master evidently is alluding to the strange feelings that Lucifer came to cherish and that prompted his actions. In the light of Jesus' statement we may infer that Lucifer, nursing an inward hatred toward the Deity, went about heaven misrepresenting God to the other angels. Only by subtle lying about the divine character and government could he ever have succeeded in persuading a large portion of the angels to cast their lot with him.

c. Autonomy of the creature. The first two issues concealed Lucifer's real desire: to be independent of his Creator. Since God is the source and sustainer of life, it follows that all created beings are dependent upon Him for their existence. The desire and attempt to be independent of God is the primary sin of the creature and is at the heart of the rebellion to challenge the divine government and to throw off the yoke of submission and obedience.

Lucifer—the first sinner—sought to be free from God's authority. Isaiah's prophecy reflects this: "You said in your heart, 'I will ascend to heaven; above the stars of God I will set my throne on high; I will sit on the mount of assembly in the far north; I will ascend above the heights of the clouds, I will make myself like the Most High'" (Isa. 14:13, 14). Five times Lucifer boasts what *"I"* (he) will do. Self became the center of his thoughts, expelling the natural attitude of self-sacrificing love that the Creator implanted within him at Creation. Lucifer desired to be his own god. This is the issue of autonomy. The rebelling creature says, "I don't need You, God; I am fully capable of running my own life."

d. Divine justice and mercy. Lucifer apparently thought he saw an internal conflict in the divine character. The Scriptures describe Satan as "the accuser of our brethren . . . , who accuses them day and night before our God" (Rev. 12:10; cf. Zech. 3:1-5). We may infer that Satan claims they, like himself, are transgressors of God's law, and he denies heaven's right to extend grace and forgiveness to them. The issue is How can the Creator be both just and merciful? If obedience to God's expressed will is so vital to the happiness of the intelligent creation, Lucifer would argue, then God can exercise justice only against sinners who violate it. It is unfair to show mercy to the violator. Justice and mercy are mutually exclusive attitudes, Lucifer would assert.

It will be seen at once that any issue pertaining to the exercise of the divine attributes of justice and mercy immediately calls into question the validity of the plan of salvation. At the time of Lucifer's rebellion the plan was unknown to the intelligent creation. It was a "secret" locked within the heart of God (cf. Rom. 16:25, 26; 1 Cor. 2:7).

This particular issue enables us to perceive how real a problem sin and rebellion pose to God. Divine love and compassion for the intelligences of His creating have not changed or abated. But how can a holy God extend mercy to the rebellious sinner—penitent though he or she may be—and yet be just and true to His own nature? Heaven's plan of salvation would supply the answer.

3. Whose Authority Is Best?

If we may judge by the situation on this planet, every intelligent being in God's created universe is subject to authority. Absolute freedom does not exist in the natural order or in human society. The question then is not how to escape authority, but rather under what authority will life be made the most meaningful—now and eternally?

The most useful spiritual authority in the universe would be one fostering the fullest development of the mental, physical, and spiritual powers of its subjects. Such an authority would be motivated by a genuine, loving concern for the governed, for only in an atmosphere of acceptance and appreciation could the governed develop to their full potential. This is the kind of authority that ruled the universe of God's creation.

But in the dawn of the Creation how could it be known whether the authority of God was really best? It was the only authority known. The created intelligences of the universe actually had only two options: (1) they could trust their Creator's word that His governance was best for the creation, or (2) they could submit to the rule of another authority and perhaps prove their Creator wrong.

Lucifer's questions and eventual insurrection forced the issues to a decision among the angels. Heaven's highest angel directly challenged the Creator. God's moral law and government were rejected, His character and motives questioned and besmirched. Satan asserted the so-called right of the creature to be independent and free from the Creator's control. Furthermore, the exercise of both justice and mercy on the part of God was challenged as incompatible with His essential holiness. God could not change the mind-set of Lucifer and associates, so they were expelled from heaven and their positions. Thus, the great moral controversy between God and Lucifer (Satan) began. These issues would be further developed in the arena of later human history.

In the ensuing centuries of this conflict on earth, two great truths regarding authority are being tested before the intelligent beings of God's universe: (1) A governing authority based on love is unselfish. It will always govern in the best interests of the governed. Laws, requirements, or restraints will always have the interest of the creation at heart, although at first that may not be perceived. (2) Any other authority, by the nature of things, will be an authority motivated by selfishness. Such an authority will ultimately exploit and ruin its subjects. It might promise much, might even permit its subjects apparent freedom, but ultimately its very nature will be ruinous to the best interests of its peoples.

4. The Fall of Lucifer From Heaven

Four passages speak directly to the expulsion of Lucifer and his fellow angels from heaven:

a. Luke 10:18. When the "seventy"—disciples Jesus trained to assist Him in addition to the twelve—returned after their first mission, they exclaimed, "Lord, even the demons are subject to us in your name!" (verse 17). Jesus replied, "I saw Satan fall like lightning from heaven." Literally, the phrasing reads, "I was seeing [Gk. imperfect tense] Satan . . . fall" (verse 18).

The Greek imperfect tense provides a moving panorama. Jesus, perhaps in vision, be-

held the original expulsion of Lucifer from heaven, the collapsing of his kingdom of darkness as it was being shaken by His ministry and that of His disciples, and the certainty of the devil's ultimate ruin which would be accomplished by His atoning death on the cross.

b. Revelation 12:7-9. "Now war arose in heaven, Michael and his angels fighting against the dragon; and the dragon and his angels fought, but they were defeated and there was no longer any place for them in heaven. And the great dragon was thrown down, that ancient serpent, who is called the Devil and Satan, the deceiver of the whole world—he was thrown down to the earth, and his angels were thrown down with him."

It is not unusual for a Bible writer to blend two distinct events as though they were one. For example, Matthew records Jesus' presentation of His second coming and the executive phase of the final judgment as a single event, although the latter takes place at the close of the Millennium—1,000 years later (Matt. 25:31, 32; Rev. 20:11-15). The apostle Peter also describes "the day of the Lord" as the Second Coming, extending it, however, to the re-creation of the earth (2 Peter 3:10-13).

It would appear that the expulsion of Satan and his angels described in Revelation 12 is a similar kind of blend, involving both the original expulsion from their positions in the heavenly courts and their later spiritual casting down of Satan at the cross, the latter being the primary emphasis of the passage.

The evidence that the passage includes Satan's original, physical expulsion lies in the reference to the personage of Michael, who with the angels loyal to God, is depicted as fighting against the challenger. Michael, whose name means "Who is like God?" and is referred to as "the archangel," ignored the claims of Satan on the body of Moses with a simple rebuke as he proceeded to resurrect the deceased patriarch (Jude 9). This confrontation between the Lifegiver and the devil indicates that Michael is no ordinary being.

Although he is described as "the" chief or head *(arch)* of the angels, Scripture indicates that *the leader* of the angels is a *divine* personage—not a created angel. When Joshua came into the presence of "the commander [Heb. *śar*] of the Lord's army [the heavenly host of angels]," he fell down and worshiped, and he obeyed the order: "Put off your shoes from your feet; for the place where you stand is holy" (Joshua 5:13-15). Since humans are forbidden to worship angels, the chief leader of the angels must be a divine Being (cf. Rev. 19:10; 22:8, 9).

In the book of Daniel, Michael is referred to three times (Dan. 10:13, 21; 12:1). In the latter passage He is described as "the great prince" who "stands" for "your people" (verse 1, Heb.). To "stand" for, or in behalf of, Israel describes a mediatorial role. Such a role is ascribed only to Jesus Christ (see 1 Tim. 2:5).

Because Michael, as a heavenly personage, appears to have resurrecting powers and authority, as well as mediatorial functions, many Christians believe He is God the Son, so described in His preexistent state, and that it was He, together with the angels loyal to God, who fought in this spiritual and moral war with Lucifer and his followers, finally expelling them from heaven and their former positions. They were "thrown down to the earth" (Rev. 12:9). Thus, the presence of Michael in the passage indicates that the original, physical expulsion of Satan is being blended with the later spiritual fall he experienced when at Christ's death, he was fully exposed to the universe as the enemy of all righteousness.

c. 2 Peter 2:4; Jude 6. Why didn't God destroy Lucifer and his followers at the outset of the conflict? These passages, which touch on the expulsion, begin to answer this question. "God did not spare the angels when they sinned, but cast them into hell *[tartarus]*

and committed them to pits of nether gloom to be kept until the judgment" (2 Peter 2:4). "And the angels that did not keep their own position but left their proper dwelling have been kept by him in eternal chains in the nether gloom until the judgment of the great day" (Jude 6).

The English word "hell" (2 Peter 2:4) is not in the Greek text. It appears in our common English Bibles as an interpretive translation of the Greek verb *tartaroō*, meaning literally, "to cast into Tartarus." Tartarus was thought by the pagan Greeks to be a subterranean place where punishment was meted out to its inmates. The verb occurs only once in the NT, but clearly the apostle Peter, as a Christian, did not endorse the pagan teaching. Using this verb with a Christian meaning, Peter simply meant this earth, into which Satan and his angels were cast (Rev. 12:9).

The parallel passage in Jude asserts in a similar manner that the fallen angels have been separated from the light of God's presence and are confined to the moral darkness of this world. "The pits of darkness," "the chains of darkness," and *Tartarus* itself are being used simply as figurative expressions indicating the restrictions and limits God has placed upon these supernatural beings. If these wicked angels were totally free to function as they chose, they would destroy humankind and this earth at once in their war against heaven.

The moral sphere in which Satan and the devils function is presented as the realm of darkness. They are "the world rulers of this present darkness" (Eph. 6:12). Satan's "kingdom" (Matt. 12:26) is "the dominion of darkness" (Col. 1:13), which wars against God and His people. Jesus acknowledged this when arrested in Gethsemane: "This is your hour," He said to those who came to arrest Him. Then He exposed the higher power who sought to destroy Him: "and the power [*exousia*, "authority"] of darkness" (Luke 22:53).

It will be noted that the activities of the

fallen angels are limited "until the judgment of the great day" (Jude 6), that is the final judgment. That fact prompts an important question: Why is a waiting period necessary? Furthermore, since the Father, Son, and Holy Spirit have determined the destruction of "the devil and his angels" (Matt. 25:41), and the atoning death of Christ was planned to bring about the condemnation of Satan and his destruction (John 12:31, 32; Heb. 2:14), we ask, Why is their execution delayed?

From the biblical data we may infer that the period of probation for the fallen angels manifests the character of God. In order to be fair to the intelligent Creation the Creator must give time for the principles of self-centeredness and transgression against His will to develop and mature so that all free moral beings may make their decisions about whom they will serve, with a full understanding of the issues. And so, as the apostle Paul said of himself and his associates, "we have become a spectacle [Gr. *theatron,* "theater"] to the world, to angels and to men" (1 Cor. 4:9)—just so the principles of sin and of righteousness, with all their enormous, overwhelming consequences, are being played out on the stage of this earth. The two principles are locked in mortal combat. And we, the watching creation, must choose which antagonist is right—to whom we will give our wholehearted allegiance. Here, being displayed before us are "things into which angels long to look" (1 Peter 1:12).

5. The Fall of Humanity

Like the angels, Adam and Eve were created free moral agents. The prohibition against eating the fruit from the tree of the knowledge of good and evil placed a simple test before them, providing an option to obey God because they loved Him or to disobey by asserting their own wills in opposition to His. When Satan confronted Eve through the guise of a serpent lying on one of the tree's branches (cf. Rev. 12:9), he intended to plant seeds of doubt

about God's integrity in her mind so that she would be deceived into disobeying Him. In response to Eve's admission that they could eat from all the trees but were not to touch or eat the fruit of this particular tree, Satan injected his poison with clever assertion and reasoning: "You shall not die. For God knows that when you eat of it your eyes will be opened, and you will be like God, knowing good and evil" (Gen. 3:4, 5).

Eve accepted Satan's lie and doubt, quickly forgetting what she knew about her Creator. She may have reasoned that if God's motives behind the prohibition were questionable, then the prohibition and death threat might not be true at all. With these supposed facts firmly embedded in her thinking, her final act was to assert her autonomy—to exercise her will and to disobey God's command. Eve clutched the fruit and ate it, later persuading Adam to eat it also (verse 6).

Satan deceived Eve into reasoning as she did, but Adam chose openly to violate the will of his Creator after Eve's decision (1 Tim. 2:14). He evidently accepted Eve's view of the matter and was reluctant to lose her as well. As the head of the race, however, Adam is held accountable for implicating the race in sin (Rom. 5:12-19).

When the fall of angels and the fall of Adam and Eve are compared, we see a marked similarity. Both sinning orders of the intelligent creation questioned (1) the Creator's character and (2) His commands. As a result, (3) they asserted their creaturely will against His expressed will. Sin—at its core—is the assertion of creaturely independence from God. The sinner refuses to be submissive to the divine authority, whether the rebellion is on a cosmic scale or within a single heart. Sin is the same for angels or persons: a determined stubbornness to submit to no god but self.

Humankind's fall affected the race in several ways. 1. Death became their lot (Gen. 3:19; Rom. 5:12). 2. The rulership of earth passed to Satan. For the time being God allows Satan to exercise limited control; he is described as "the god of this world" and its "ruler" (2 Cor. 4:4, 5; John 12:31). 3. The Fall resulted in depraving human nature; every aspect—intellect, emotions, will—was affected (cf. Jer. 17:9; Eph. 4:18). In sum, Adam's rebellion estranged the race from God. Humanity became God's "enemies" (Rom. 5:10) and "children of wrath" (Eph. 2:3), that is, under divine judgment. The characteristic quality of the sinner is a mindset opposed to the Creator's law and authority (Rom. 8:7; see Sin III. B. 1-4).

D. Heaven's Added Dimension

The Fall did not result in freedom and independence for the human race. Satan's moral conquest of Adam and Eve enabled him to establish this earth as a beachhead in his war against God. Fallen angels and fallen humanity were now in league in a corrupt confederation opposed to the authority of the Creator. Both had become evil through apostasy.

In His oral judgment on Satan (serpent), however, the Creator added a new dimension to the controversy by providing the means by which the fallen race could break from their sinful bond with Satan, if it chose to do so. God said to Satan, "I will put enmity between you and the woman, and between your seed and her seed" (Gen. 3:15).

The Hebrew word for "enmity" (ʾêbāh) carries the meaning of personal hostility or hatred between persons. Satan, in his war against the Creator, has developed an intense hostility toward his Maker and every aspect of His rule. On the other hand, the sinful human entertained no natural hatred toward Satan. In His decree (cited above) the Creator informed Satan that He would now place such an attitude within fallen humanity.

The Scriptures indicate that this new element is divine grace, that is, the operation of the Holy Spirit on the human heart. His presence and function would enable sinners to hate sin and to turn away from Satan's control. Jesus discussed this truth in His visit with Nicodemus: "Unless one is born of water and the Spirit, he cannot enter the kingdom of God.

That which is born of the flesh is flesh, and that which is born of the Spirit is spirit. Do not marvel that I said to you, 'You must be born anew.' The wind blows where it wills, and you hear the sound of it, but you do not know whence it comes or whither it goes; so it is with every one who is born of the Spirit" (John 3:5-8).

The Holy Spirit, working through the conscience (cf. Rom. 9:1), moves across the masses of humanity endeavoring to draw sinners to God. As He convicts and converts, He also engenders a hostility toward evil and a love for righteousness (cf. Amos 5:14, 15; Heb. 1:9). This essential function of the Holy Spirit—the creating of enmity against sin and unrighteousness—makes possible deliverance from enslavement to Satan.

E. Heaven's Objectives

With the fall of Adam and Eve, Satan gained what appeared to be a signal victory in the controversy. Humankind, as well as a multitude of angels, openly flouted the divine authority. The rebellion, begun in heaven, had spread to the order of human beings. Earth was now in revolt and estranged from heaven. Perhaps other orders would join the insurgents.

But the widening insurrection did not find God unprepared. The moral battle was now joined, and the plan of salvation—laid in eternity past—was put into operation. Reflecting on its major aspects (see I. A), we may discern its four-point objective:

1. To clear (vindicate) the character, law, and government of God from all charges.

2. To secure and reaffirm the loyalty of the unfallen intelligent creation.

3. To effect the salvation of all human sinners who would respond to Heaven's invitation to accept the Creator's gracious lordship.

4. To destroy Satan and his rebel angels and impenitent human sinners, and to erase the effects of sin by restoring the earth to its pristine condition and the universe to its original harmony.

III. The Controversy on Earth—OT

A. *God's Initiative*

In His judgment on Satan (serpent) in Eden, the Creator announced for the first time the coming of the Messiah—the Redeemer who by His atoning death would make possible the salvation of repentant sinners and the destruction of Satan and his evil host.

1. The Promise

"He shall bruise your head [a mortal blow to the serpent/Satan], and you shall bruise his heel [an allusion to the cross]" (Gen. 3:15). Just as a bud gradually unfolds, so this cryptic prediction slowly disclosed its meaning across the centuries as details were revealed in prophetic oracles. The followers of God were told that the promised Seed of the woman would descend through the line of Abraham (Gen. 12:3; 22:18; cf. Gal. 3:16), his great grandson Judah (Gen. 49:10); and through the latter's descendant, David (Ps. 89:20-37; Jer. 23:5, 6). The apostle Paul charged Timothy, "Remember Jesus Christ, risen from the dead, descended from David, as preached in my gospel" (2 Tim. 2:8).

2. Sacrificial Rituals

Evidently the sacrificial system was introduced immediately after the fall of Adam and Eve to keep alive in them and their descendants the hope of the promised Saviour (cf. Gen. 4:4; Heb. 11:4). The sacrifices also provided a symbolic means by which sin could be forgiven on the basis of the offerer's faith in God (Heb. 9:22) who would send the true Lamb to die an atoning death for human sin (cf. Heb. 10:4; John 1:29).

The simple patriarchal sacrifices (Gen. 8:20; Job 1:5) eventually were expanded into a fully developed sacrificial system with certified priests and a sanctuary (first, a tabernacle; later, a permanent temple). The biblical data indicate that the Hebrew sanctuary worship system (like the simpler patriarchal system that preceded it) was designed to teach by type and symbol "the gospel," or plan of salvation, as originally established by the Godhead. As the writer to the Hebrews observes, "we [Christians] also have had the gospel preached to us, just as they [the Israelites] did" (Heb. 4:2, NIV; see Sanctuary I).

3. Prophetic Portrayals

As the centuries rolled on, the rituals' dim foreshadowings of the Messianic Redeemer's atoning death and priestly ministry were enlarged by inspired, written portrayals (cf. 1 Peter 1:10, 11). For example, the place of His birth (Micah 5:2), the time of His appearing and death (Dan. 9:24-27), His teaching ministry (Isa. 42:1-7; 61:1-4), the substitutionary nature of His death (Isa. 53), and His priesthood (Ps. 110:1, 4) were specifically spelled out.

4. Preserving and Propagating Salvation Truths

At first God preserved on earth the knowledge of Himself through a line of faithful patriarchs and their families (cf. Gen. 5; 11:10-32). But as the human life span declined after the Flood and racial populations developed throughout the earth, God determined to form a nation from Abraham's descendants (Gen. 12:1, 2), who would function as His witness to the entire world.

At Mount Sinai God organized Abraham's descendants into a nation. He entrusted this chosen agency with the Scriptures—the written revelation of His will (Rom. 3:1, 2), the moral law in the form of the Ten Commandments, an enlarged sacrificial system of worship, and His promises (Rom. 9:4, 5). He entered into a covenant relationship with the nation in a renewal of the Abrahamic covenant, promising, "I will . . . be your God, and you shall be my people" (Lev. 26:12).

The Lord planted Israel in Palestine on the connecting bridge of three continents

(Europe, Africa, Asia). "I have set her [Jerusalem, the capital] in the center of the nations, with countries round about her," He told the prophet Ezekiel (Eze. 5:5). It was God's design that Israel should be a beacon of truth to draw the peoples of the world to Himself. "My house," He declared, "shall be called a house of prayer for all peoples" (Isa. 56:7). The Lord intended for the nations of earth to seek saving truth at His sanctuary, and that they would say to one another, "Come, let us go up to the mountain of the Lord, to the house of the God of Jacob; that he may teach us his ways and that we may walk in his paths" (Isa. 2:3).

B. Satan's Counterattack

In the NT Satan is designated "the spirit that is now at work in the sons of disobedience" (Eph. 2:2). Although he is rarely named in the OT, the wickedness that now appears everywhere in the OT is mute evidence of his presence and activity. He now carries on the conflict with Heaven by means of his new allies, sinful humanity.

1. Antediluvian Wickedness

Within the recorded life spans of the first 10 patriarchs (Gen. 5), the inhabitants of the earth became so wicked that the Creator intervened.

"The Lord saw that the wickedness of man was great in the earth, and that every imagination of the thoughts of his heart was only evil continually. . . . Now the earth was corrupt in God's sight, and the earth was filled with violence. And God saw the earth, and behold, it was corrupt; for all flesh had corrupted their way upon the earth" (Gen. 6:5-12).

The Lord checked this terrible condition by causing a universal flood to cleanse the earth of that long-lived race of bold rebels. He spared righteous Noah and his family (2 Peter 2:5) and entrusted them with His truths of grace and salvation (Heb. 11:7) for the growing populations of the earth.

2. Development of Paganism and Idolatry

In an early move in the war against heaven, Satan developed systems of counterfeit worship, that is, counterfeit religions, to oppose the worship of the true God and to cause humanity to forget the Creator. In broad terms we may describe these counterfeit religions under the rubric of "paganism." The apostle Paul describes how this occurred early after the Fall:

"Ever since the creation of the world his [God's] invisible nature, namely, his eternal power and deity, has been clearly perceived in the things that have been made. So they [the wicked who turned away from the Creator] are without excuse; for although they knew God they did not honor him as God or give thanks to him, but they became futile in their thinking and their senseless minds were darkened. Claiming to be wise, they became fools, and exchanged the glory of the immortal God for images resembling mortal man or birds or animals or reptiles. Therefore God gave them up in the lusts of their hearts to impurity, to the dishonoring of their bodies among themselves, because they exchanged the truth about God for a lie and worshiped and served the creature rather than the Creator, who is blessed for ever! Amen. . . . And since they did not see fit to acknowledge God, God gave them up to a base mind and to improper conduct" (Rom. 1:20-28).

In connection with developing idolatry, Satan perverted the typical, sacrificial rites God instituted after Eden. Both Testaments acknowledge that the devils or demons are the powers behind the pagan forms of sacrifice (Deut. 32:17, 18; 1 Cor. 10:14-22).

3. Corrupting the True Religion

In the period between the settling of the nation of Israel in Palestine (fifteenth century B.C.) and its collapse and deportation by Babylonian conquest (sixth century B.C.), Satan persistently sought to corrupt the true faith by seducing Israel into pagan idolatry (cf. Ps. 106:34-38). During this period Hebrew spiritual history was an up-and-down experience of national apostasy, revival, and repentance, only to succumb once more to the morally degrading influences of surrounding paganism.

At the ascension to the throne of Israel's fourth king, Rehoboam (c. 931 B.C.) the nation was divided politically into two segments, a northern kingdom of 10 tribes and a southern kingdom of two. Because of spiritual decay, the northern kingdom collapsed before the armies of Assyria in 722 B.C. and was subsequently deported to other Near Eastern countries (2 Kings 17:5, 6). Approximately a century and a half later God disciplined the southern kingdom of Judah in a similar manner by permitting the Babylonian conquest under Nebuchadnezzar. This severe discipline—a 70-year period of captivity accompanied by promises of restoration—forever cured Judah of the idolatry that had weakened and marred her allegiance to the true God (see 2 Chron. 36:11-21).

Satan had nearly succeeded in bringing the Hebrew nation to total ruin, but throughout its national history a faithful remnant always existed to give witness to the true God (e.g., see 1 Kings 19:18). In times of national greatness, such as under David and Solomon, the name of the true God was honored and heralded far beyond the borders of the kingdom (cf. 1 Kings 4:29-34; 10:1-13, 24). Later in Hebrew history, under the preaching of a reluctant Jonah, the Assyrian inhabitants of Nineveh were brought to repentance and an acknowledgement of the true God (Jonah 3:1-10). Even during the long years of the Babylonian captivity and the early years of the reign of Persia over the Near East, the true God was universally honored through the loyal witness of Daniel and his companions (Dan. 2:47; 3:28, 29; 6:25-27), Mordecai and Esther (Esther 8:17), Zerubbabel and Joshua (Ezra 1:1-5, 7-11), and Ezra (Ezra 7:11-16) and Nehemiah (Neh. 2:1-8).

4. Satanic Accusations

Although the activity of the devils is mentioned only briefly in the OT, two major texts mention Satan by name. These indicate another side of his activity in the controversy.

a. Job 1:6-12; 2:1-8. The experience of Job appears outside the Hebrew culture and apparently took place in patriarchal times. Expelled from his heavenly office, Satan usurped the dominion of the earth from Adam when the latter sinned. Thus, in the book of Job, Satan appears in heaven's councils as the ruler of this earth. "There was a day when the sons of God came to present themselves before the Lord, and Satan also came among them" (Job 1:6; cf. verse 7; 2:1).

With reference to the moral war between God and Satan, two main points stand out from Job's terrible experience of suffering: 1. Since in the Creator's wisdom, Satan and the fallen angels are permitted to live and mature the principles of self-centeredness and sin, the followers of God, just as others, may expect to suffer the attacks of these enemies of all good (within limits, 1 Cor. 10:13). 2. However, personal suffering is not necessarily the consequence of personal sinning; it may well be a direct attack from Satan, as in the case of Job.

b. Zechariah 3:1-10. The penitent Hebrew exiles returned from Babylonian captivity to Palestine under the political leadership of Zerubbabel and the spiritual oversight of the high priest, Joshua, probably in the spring of 536 B.C. They sought to rebuild the Temple and to reestablish the nation. But opposition from the surrounding pagan nations was nearly overwhelming. In vision the prophet Zechariah sees Joshua, the high priest, clothed in "filthy garments"—the former sins of the nation—standing before "the angel of the Lord" as he pleads for God's forgiveness and grace so that the nation might be reestablished.

Satan is depicted also as standing at his side accusing the nation (in the person of the high priest) of its former sins and protesting against God's willingness to extend forgiveness. But the angel of the Lord rebukes Satan, and the repentance of the priest (on behalf of the nation) is accepted. The filthy garments are removed, and he is clothed in the beautiful garments of his priesthood. Divine mercy prevails over Satan's accusations.

5. Satan's "Almost" Success

The Lord permitted the severe discipline of the Babylonian captivity. By this means He intended to save and purify a remnant of the nation who would return to their homeland to prepare the world for the advent of the Messiah (see Jer. 24). In fact fewer than 50,000 returned under Zerubbabel (Ezra 2:64, 65); no figures are given for the second recorded migration under Ezra in 457 B.C., but the data suggests a much smaller number (see Ezra 8). The greater proportion of the Jews chose to remain in lands outside Palestine where their captors had settled them.

Some years later, during the reign of the Persian king, Xerxes (the biblical Ahasuerus, 486-465 B.C.), the king's chief courtier, Haman the Agagite, schemed to destroy all the Jews in the empire on a single day (Esther 3:8-15). Through God's providence and the intervention of the Jewish queen Esther, the plot was averted. Satan's attempt to silence the Hebrew witness to the true God was foiled once more.

IV. The Controversy on Earth—NT

A. Overruling Providence

God's intended witness through the nation of Israel to prepare the world for the advent of the promised Redeemer appeared to have largely failed. However, God's "eternal purpose" (Eph. 3:11) knows no failure. In spite of confused human experience, God carries forward His design to accomplish the plan of salvation. We observe how heaven next advanced the cause of truth in its battle against Satan.

1. Growing Centrality of Scripture

No longer burdened with the cares of political autonomy, following the Babylonian captivity the reestablished nation of Judah was more open to the study of God's will as revealed in the sacred Scriptures. Approximately 80 years after the first exiles returned to Palestine, "Ezra the priest, the scribe of the law of the God of heaven" (Ezra. 7:11, 12) arrived with a commission from the Persian king, Artaxerxes I (verses 11-26). "For Ezra had set his heart to study the law of the Lord, and to do it, and to teach his statutes and ordinances in Israel" (verse 10). Together with Nehemiah, who later joined him as the king's appointed governor, Ezra led the nation in rededication to the true God through a kind of "back to the Bible" movement (cf. Neh. 8-10).

Although this initiative later became cumbered with the teachings of the rabbis, the possession of and access to God's Written Word was one of Judaism's prized privileges. The apostle Paul remarks, "What advantage has the Jew? . . . Much in every way. To begin with, the Jews are entrusted with the oracles of God" (Rom. 3:1, 2).

2. The Dispersion (Diaspora, John 7:35)

During the several centuries of the Intertestament Period, a widespread, voluntary dispersion of the Jews occurred in the Mediterranean world. Conservative estimates place the Jewish population in the Roman Empire (excepting Palestine) at four million with an additional three million in Palestine itself and another million in the lands of their former exile east of the Roman Empire. The phenomenon of the Diaspora led to two important developments among the Jewish populations outside Palestine: (1) the establishment of synagogues wherever 10 Jewish men could assemble, and (2) the translation of the Hebrew Bible into Greek

(LXX, third and second centuries B.C.).

3. The Jewish Mission

Between 50 B.C. and A.D. 70 a Jewish mission developed in the empire. Thousands of Gentiles crowded into the synagogues. Jewish emphasis on monotheism and the high ethical standards of the moral law attracted them. Many became proselytes to the Jewish faith, but the bulk hesitated to accept circumcision and other elements of Jewish practice. These attendees were designated by two technical expressions, "God fearers" (see Acts 10:1, 2; 13:16, 26) or "God worshipers" (see Acts 16:14; 18:7). Thus, when the apostle Paul or other Christian Jews were permitted to speak in a given synagogue (Acts 13:15), they addressed two major classes of serious worshipers: "Men of Israel [Jews], and you that fear God [Gentile "God fearers"]" (verse 16). Christianity's rapid growth in the empire was a result, in part, of this large Gentile group—already cultivated in spiritual truths by the Greek translation of the Scriptures—who found in Jesus of Nazareth the Messiah/Christ, the ultimate hope of the Jewish faith. In these and other ways God overruled Jewish failure and Gentile ignorance to prepare earth for its greatest event: the incarnation and ministry of God the Son (1 Tim. 3:16).

B. The First Advent of Christ

The Scriptures treat the first advent of Christ and related events as the climax of the great controversy. Satan is defeated and judged at the cross, the plan of salvation for sinful humanity is confirmed, atonement for sin made, and the moral law and character of God upheld. God is victorious. The "battles" that continue serve to expose in clearer detail the true nature of the rebellion and the fuller development of the principles in conflict. The NT depicts Satan's incessant attempts to hinder Christ's ministry, weaken His influence with the people, and to kill Him if possible.

1. Christ's Victory Prophetically Portrayed

In the multifaceted prophecy of Revelation 12 Satan's intense purpose to destroy Christ at the outset is symbolized. In vision the apostle sees "a woman clothed with the sun" (a symbol for God's people, cf. Isa. 54:5, 6; Jer. 6:2) about to give birth to the long-promised Saviour (verses 1, 2). In horror he watches as "a great red dragon, with seven heads and ten horns, and seven diadems upon his heads" takes position before the woman "that he might devour her child when she brought it forth" (verses 3, 4). The woman eventually gives birth to "a male child . . . who is to rule all the nations with a rod of iron" (a reference which identifies the "child" as the Christ, cf. Rev. 19:11-16). Before the dragon (Satan, Rev. 12:9) can seize the child, however, the child "[is] caught up to God and to his throne" (verse 5).

Thus, in broad strokes the symbolism alludes to Satan's attempt to destroy Christ at His birth (cf. Matt. 2:1-18). The prophecy does not specifically mention Christ's death under the procurator Pilate, but later alludes to its results. The vision is underscoring the fact that Christ's incarnation and entrance into the domain of Satan (this earth) resulted in His being a victor over the devil, and not his victim.

2. Christ's Victory Over Temptations

During His ministry, Jesus' first direct conflict with Satan occurred shortly after His inauguration at His baptism as the Messiah/Christ, the Anointed One (Matt. 3:13-17; Acts 10:38). During a 40-day fast, Christ sought by communion with His Father to prepare Himself for His brief, but intensive, mission. At this point Satan confronted the Saviour with three severe temptations designed to divert Him from His purpose (Matt. 4:1-11). All three had essentially the same thrust: to create doubt and distrust in the heavenly Father and His plan for the salvation of the world. At one point Satan brazenly asserted he would give Christ "the kingdoms of the world and the glory of them" (without the sufferings of Calvary, implied) "if you will fall down and worship me" (verses 8, 9). To each seductive test Christ countered with the witness of Scripture (cf. verses 4, 7, 10). Finally, Christ dismissed the insolent devil: "Begone, Satan!" (verse 10). Although Satan left, he repeatedly returned to tempt the Saviour throughout His earthly ministry (cf. Luke 4:13).

3. Christ's Daily Victory Over the Demons

The angels expelled from heaven with Lucifer (Satan) usually are designated in the NT as demons, devils, or unclean spirits. When Christ healed a demon-possessed person, it was common for the demon to acknowledge His true identity as the Son of God (cf. Mark 3:11, 12; Luke 4:33-35, 41). On one occasion the demons, speaking through two possessed men, questioned Christ's right to heal their victims: "And behold, they cried out, 'What have you to do with us, O Son of God? Have you come here to torment us before the time?'" (Matt. 8:29). The demons knew their destruction already was determined (cf. Matt. 25:41). Their failure to discourage Christ and to turn people from Him foreshadowed His victory and their ultimate doom.

4. Christ's Multiple Victories at the Cross

Christ foresaw that several goals of His mission would be accomplished by His death. "The hour has come for the Son of man to be glorified. Truly, truly, I say to you, unless a grain of wheat falls into the earth and dies, it remains alone; but if it dies, it bears much fruit" (John 12:23, 24). We list four of the most important "fruits" resulting from His death.

a. Judgment secured against Satan. One objective was the destruction of Satan (Heb. 2:14). Jesus explained to the Greeks how His death would accomplish this end. "Now is the

judgment [Gr. *krisis,* act of judging] of this world, now shall the ruler of this world [Satan] be cast out; and I, when I am lifted up from the earth [the cross], will draw all men to myself" (John 12:31, 32).

Demonic beings participated with humans in the Crucifixion. Jesus recognized this when He said to the rabble in Gethsemane, "This is your hour, and the power [Gr. *exousia,* "authority, domain"] of darkness" (Luke 22:53). This is a direct reference to Satan and his host of demons who had pursued Him throughout His ministry and now sought in one more desperate attempt to cause Him to sin or to withdraw from the divine plan. Although Christ was fully aware of Satan's part in His death, He declared, "He has no power over me"—literally, "he has nothing in me" (John 14:30).

At the cross this wicked adversary of God stood exposed and condemned in the eyes of loyal angels and inhabitants of unfallen worlds. The "judgment" at Calvary and the casting out of Satan (John 12:31) do not refer to the final, eschatological judgment at the end of the age (cf. Acts 17:31). Rather, this "judgment" refers to that passed on Satan at the time of Christ's death by the universe of loyal beings as well as by God. At the cross, Satan (including the other fallen angels) was seen clearly in his true light as a rebel and murderer. We may infer that any link of sympathy still existing in the minds of heavenly beings for Lucifer's cause was forever broken. Satan stood, as it were, before the bar of justice, condemned by his former peers.

b. Plan of salvation confirmed. Christ's atoning death, while it collapsed Satan's claims, at the same time confirmed God's plan of salvation. In vision (Rev. 12) the apostle John heard "a loud voice in heaven, saying, '*Now* the salvation and the power and the kingdom of our God and the authority of his Christ have come, for the accuser of our brethren has been thrown down, who accuses them day and night before God. . . . Rejoice then, O heaven and you that dwell therein! But woe to you, O earth and sea, for the devil has come down to you in great wrath, because he knows that his time is short!'" (verses 10-12).

When the Saviour died "for the sins of the whole world" (1 John 2:2), then—and not until then—could heaven proclaim, "Salvation has *just now* come" *(Gr. arti).* At Calvary the divine promise became a reality. The plan of salvation, God's kingdom of grace, and Christ's authority to grant eternal life to repentant sinners (John 17:2) now stood confirmed.

c. Atonement made for human sin. While the atoning death of Christ has cosmic significance in meeting the issues in the great controversy between God and Satan, it also has personal meaning for the individual sinner (cf. Gal. 2:20). Christ's death provided a substitutionary, penal atonement for all sinners (1 John 2:2). "For our sake he [God] made him [Christ] to be sin who knew no sin, so that in him we might become the righteousness of God" (2 Cor. 5:21).

Christ Himself was sinless, but according to the plan, humanity's sins were imputed to Him, and He died under divine judgment as our sin bearer. Here is the inexplicable love that draws repentant sinners to God (1 John 4:10). The Scriptures are abundant and clear regarding Christ's vicarious sacrifice in our behalf: "the Lord has laid on him the iniquity of us all"; "he shall bear their iniquities"; "He bore the sin of many" (Isa. 53:6, 11, 12). "He himself bore our sins in his body on the tree" (1 Peter 2:24); "For Christ also died for sins once for all, the righteous for the unrighteous" (1 Peter 3:18); "Christ redeemed us from the curse of the law, having become a curse for us—for it is written, 'Cursed be every one who hangs on a tree'" (Gal. 3:13). In this latter passage the apostle's point is plain. As sinners, the human family is under the curse/condemnation of God's law before the bar of heaven. But Christ voluntarily accepted the liability of our sins and bore the legal consequences in our stead. At Calvary He took God's judgment on sin upon Him-self. (See Christ II. A. 9; D.)

d. The moral law and character of God up-held. Originally Lucifer questioned the necessity of the moral law and impugned God's motives for requiring obedience to it. If the law could have been abolished or in some manner changed, then sin (the violation of its precepts, 1 John 3:4) would not have existed, and consequently Christ would not have needed to die to atone for human sin. However, the moral law itself was a reflection of the divine, unchangeable character and could not be altered.

To meet the challenge, the Godhead assumed Their own judgment on sin (i.e., death). By means of the Incarnation, God the Son (the Creator) took upon Himself our humanity so that His life—more than equal to all human, creaturely lives—when laid down would atone for the sins of all humanity. In this manner the death of Christ upheld the validity of the moral law (expressed to humans in the form of the Ten Commandments), and demonstrated that God could be both just and merciful in character. The apostle Paul explains the significance of the cross on these points: "God [the Father] presented him [Christ] as a sacrifice of atonement, through faith in his blood. He did this to demonstrate his justice, because in his forbearance he had left the sins committed beforehand unpunished [that is, moral sin in OT times could not really be atoned by animal blood, Heb. 10:4]—he did it to demonstrate his justice at the present time, so as to be just and the one who justifies those who have faith in Jesus" (Rom. 3:25, 26, NIV; cf. Heb. 9:15).

C. Satanic Attacks on the Church

Just as Satan corrupted the religious faith of Israel, so he sought to corrupt the faith of the Christian church. The apostle Paul warned, "Now the Spirit expressly says that in later times some will depart from the faith by giving heed to deceitful spirits and doctrines of demons" (1 Tim. 4:1).

1. Corrupting the Doctrines

In the presence of some church leaders the apostle Paul explained how apostasy would occur from within the Christian church. "I know that after my departure fierce wolves will come in among you, not sparing the flock; and from among your own selves will arise men speaking perverse things, to draw away the disciples after them. Therefore be alert" (Acts 20:29-31). The apostle Peter warned of the same danger: "There will be false teachers among you, who will secretly bring in destructive heresies" (2 Peter 2:1). About a quarter of a century later the apostle John would write, "You have heard that antichrist is coming, so now many antichrists have come. . . . They went out from us" (1 John 2:18, 19).

This satanic-influenced corruption of the Christian religion would eventually lead to divisions and unprecedented persecutions. The apostle Paul again forewarned of the results of the coming apostasy before Christ's second advent: "Now, brethren, concerning the coming of our Lord Jesus Christ and our gathering together to Him. . . . Let no one deceive you by any means; for *that Day will not come* unless the falling away [Gr. *apostasia*, "apostasy"] comes first, and the man of sin is revealed, the son of perdition, who opposes and exalts himself above all that is called God or that is worshiped, so that he sits as God in the temple of God, showing himself that he is God" (2 Thess. 2:1-4, NKJV).

The apostle is not speaking of a Jewish temple which some Christians mistakenly think will be rebuilt in Jerusalem in this modern era. Rather, he is describing the apostasy that would eventually develop within the Christian church and attempt to exercise divine authority over other believers. In the NT the church is commonly referred to as God's temple (cf. 1 Cor. 3:11, 16, 17; 2 Cor. 6:16; Eph. 2:19-22; 1 Peter 2:4, 5). This organized apostasy would remain within Christendom until Christ's second coming (2 Thess. 2:5-8). Christians have generally identified "the man of sin" (verses 3, 4, NKJV)

with the same entity that the apocalyptic prophecies of Daniel and Revelation describe as a little horn (Dan. 7:8) and as a leopardlike beast (Rev. 13:1-10), respectively.

2. Persecuting the Church

Satan first sought to stamp out the early church by persecuting it; the corrupting of beliefs came later. Jewish persecution began after Pentecost in Jerusalem with threats (Acts 4:21), but moved on to the arrest and beating of some of the apostles (Acts 5:40). The mob-stoning of Stephen (Acts 6:8-15; 7) led to a more ruthless and systematic attempt to put down the Christian faith by the energetic Saul of Tarsus (Acts 8:1-4; 1 Tim. 1:12, 13). Although Herod Agrippa I executed the apostle James a little later, and intended the same fate for the apostle Peter (Acts 12:1-4), initially the Roman government outside Palestine did not generally oppose the church. Roman authorities may have regarded Christianity as a variant of the Jewish faith, a licensed religion. Civil policy with regard to Christians began to change with the emperor Nero's charges subsequent to the burning of Rome in A.D. 64.

But the prophecies of Daniel and Revelation—and of Jesus Himself (Matt. 24:21, 22)—predicted far more extensive waves of persecution against the church than those carried out by either Jewish or Roman authorities. Note again the pivotal prophecy of Revelation 12: "And when the dragon [Satan, verse 9] saw that he had been thrown down to the earth, he pursued the woman [symbol of God's people] who had borne the male child. But the woman was given the two wings of the great eagle that she might fly from the serpent into the wilderness, to the place where she is to be nourished for a time, and times, and half a time. The serpent poured water like a river out of his mouth after the woman, to sweep her away with the flood. But the earth came to the help of the woman, and the earth opened its mouth and swallowed the river which the dragon poured from his mouth" (verses 13-16).

Earlier in this same prophecy is a similar statement: "And the woman fled into the wilderness, where she has a place prepared by God, in which to be nourished for one thousand two hundred and sixty days" (verse 6).

This period of time, during which Satan sought to destroy the church, occupied many centuries following Christ's ascension. It is mentioned seven times in the prophecies of Daniel and Revelation in connection with the persecuting careers of the little horn and leopardlike beast and appears in three different forms: (1) "time, two times, and half a time" equals 3½ prophetic years (Dan. 7:25; 12:7; Rev. 12:14); (2) "forty-two months" (Rev. 11:2; 13:5); and (3) "one thousand two hundred and sixty days" (Rev. 11:3; 12:6). The three forms—3½ years, 42 months, 1260 days—equal the same amount of time. According to historicist principles of apocalyptic interpretation a symbolic day is equivalent to a literal year. Consequently, the prophecies are dealing with a period of 1260 years of recurrent "war on the saints." (See Apocalyptic II. D.)

D. The Controversy in Microcosm

The doctrine of salvation (in Pauline terms, justification, sanctification, glorification) through faith in the merits of Christ and His transforming grace (see Salvation III) is also described in terms of the moral conflict between God and Satan. Adam's fall resulted in the depraving of his nature and that of his posterity (see II. C. 5). The enmity, or hostility, that God placed between Satan and the human family is brought about by the function of the Holy Spirit working through the conscience (see II. D). This condition creates within each individual a microcosm of the same moral controversy that is being fought on the cosmic level. Note the thrust of the following passages: "For the desires of the flesh [the human carnal nature with its bent to sin] are against the Spirit, and the desires of the Spirit are against the flesh; for these are opposed to each other, to prevent you from doing what you would" (Gal. 5:17). "To set the mind on the flesh is death, but to set the mind on the Spirit is life and peace. For the mind that is set on the flesh is hostile to God; it does not submit to God's law, indeed it cannot; and those who are in the flesh cannot please God" (Rom. 8:6-8). "Each person is tempted when he is lured and enticed by his own desire. Then desire when it has conceived gives birth to sin; and sin when it is full-grown brings forth death" (James 1:14, 15).

The apostle Paul recognized the dominant control his carnal nature exercised over him, and cried for deliverance. "Wretched man that I am! Who will deliver me from this body of death [his controlling carnality]?" He answers his own question with glad assurance: "Thanks be to God through Jesus Christ our Lord!" (Rom. 7:24, 25).

Although the NT has more to say about the individual's internal conflict than the OT, the latter is not silent. David prayed, "Create in me a clean heart, O God, and put a new and right spirit within me. Cast me not away from thy presence, and take not thy holy Spirit from me" (Ps. 51:10, 11).

And God promised the repentant exiles in Babylonian captivity: "A new heart I will give you, and a new spirit I will put within you; and I will take out of your flesh the heart of stone and give you a heart of flesh. And I will put my spirit within you, and cause you to walk in my statutes and be careful to observe my ordinances" (Eze. 36:26, 27).

In a similar manner the NT promises those who receive Christ as Saviour and Lord (John 1:12) the forgiveness of sin (1 John 1:9), sonship/daughtership in God's family (1 John 3:1, 2), a changed heart (John 3:5-8; 2 Cor. 5:17), and eternal life (1 John 5:11, 12). And in the new covenant commitment God promises to write His law in each mind (Heb. 8:10) so that the believer will delight to do the

Father's will from the heart (cf. Ps. 40:8). This whole transaction (becoming a follower of God) results in the believer's deliverance "from the dominion of darkness" (the realm of Satan's control) and a transference "to the kingdom of his [God's] beloved Son" (Col. 1:13).

But the acceptance of Christ as Saviour and Lord by the repentant sinner does not end the "war." In some respects the personal controversy is intensified. Satan is always seeking to gain "the advantage over us," declares the apostle, "for we are not ignorant of his designs" (2 Cor. 2:11). Consequently, the believer is encouraged to develop spiritual strength for the combat through a close bond of union with God: "Finally, be strong in the Lord and in the strength of his might. Put on the whole armor of God, that you may be able to stand against the wiles of the devil. For we are not contending against flesh and blood, but against principalities, . . . against the spiritual hosts of wickedness in the heavenly places. Therefore take the whole armor of God, that you may be able to withstand in the evil day, and having done all, to stand" (Eph. 6:10-13).

The other apostles give similar warnings: "Be sober, be watchful. Your adversary the devil prowls around like a roaring lion, seeking some one to devour. Resist him, firm in your faith" (1 Peter 5:8, 9). "Submit yourselves therefore to God. Resist the devil and he will flee from you" (James 4:7). Ultimately, the only safety for the believer lies in a daily consecration, dedication to God—a daily surrender of the will to the heavenly Father through the mediation of Christ. The apostle Paul admonishes believers, "Consider yourselves dead to sin and alive to God in Christ Jesus" (Rom. 6:11), or rather, as the construction in the original language indicates, "Keep on considering yourselves dead to sin, and keep on considering yourselves alive to God in Christ." The life of a believer can be rightfully described at times as a battle. Sometimes it may be termed "a battle and a march, a battle and a march." But the "battle"—after the cross—is against a defeated foe who can only employ delaying tactics.

V. The Controversy Completed

With the ending of the 1260 years, during which Satan intermittently but relentlessly persecuted the church (see IV. C. 2), Daniel's forecast of "the time of the end" began (Dan. 11:33-35; 12:4). The terminology indicates an era extending to the close of human probation. Near the termination of this period Satan launches his final attack against God's people. "Then the dragon was angry with the woman, and went off to make war on the rest of her offspring [the remnant of her seed," KJV], on those who keep the commandments of God and bear testimony to Jesus" (Rev. 12:17). How this last conflict will occur is sketched in Revelation 13 and 14.

A. The Final Struggle

The apocalyptic prophecy describes two earthly powers in particular that participate on Satan's side in the final struggle.

1. Leopardlike Beast (Rev. 13:1-10)

This NT composite symbol, containing body parts of the four beasts in Daniel's vision (Dan. 7), may be correctly identified with the religiopolitical power symbolized by the horn with the eyes and mouth of a man on Daniel's fourth beast (verse 8). Both are said to make war on God's people (verse 21; Rev. 13:7) for the same specified length of time, 1260 years (Dan. 7:25; Rev. 13:5). However, the NT's symbolic account adds important details.

First, the prophecy recalls the beast's apparent death at the close of the 1260-year period from "a mortal wound" to one of its heads (Rev. 13:3). This wounding is also described as a "captivity" and as a slaying "by the sword" (verses 10, 14). Second, the prophecy foresees a revival and resurgence of the beast's life and authority. "Its mortal wound was healed, and the whole earth followed the beast with wonder. Men worshiped . . . the beast saying, 'Who is like the beast, and who can fight against it?' . . . And all who dwell on earth will worship it" (verses 3, 4, 8). Thus, the leopardlike beast is prepared to carry out its role in "the time of the end."

2. Two-horned Beast (Rev. 13:11-17)

As the leopardlike beast is wounded and going into captivity (Rev. 13:3, 10), another animal appears. "Then I saw another beast which rose out of the earth; it had two horns like a lamb and it spoke like a dragon" (verse 11). The time of its rise (around the time of the wounding of the "first beast"), the place of its origin (from the earth, rather than the sea), and its lamblike horns serve as identifying marks for this power. Its speech—"like a dragon"—indicates its eventual, persecuting nature. In a later prophecy this same entity is designated "the false prophet" (Rev. 19:20).

In a few verses the prophecy describes how Satan will use these two powers to bring heavy oppression and persecution upon God's people. We summarize the biblical data:

a. The second beast (the two-horned beast), exercising all the authority of the first power, "makes the earth and its inhabitants worship the first beast" (Rev. 13:12).

b. The second beast, by means of unusual miracles, "deceives" the people and bids them to "make an image for the beast" (verses 13, 14)—also designated "the image of the beast" (verse 15).

c. The second beast is able "to give breath," or life, to "the image of the beast" (verse 15).

d. Thus empowered, the image of the beast causes "those who . . . [will] not worship," or obey it, "to be slain" (verse 15). Moreover, it causes all "to be marked on the

right hand or the forehead." A boycott on buying and selling is imposed upon those who refuse to accept "the mark, that is, the name of the beast or the number of its name" (verses 16, 17).

Even apart from the identification of the specific symbols and acts on the basis of historicist principles, the overall intent of the apocalyptic symbolism is clear. In his last struggle against God and His church, Satan attempts by economic boycott and death to overthrow the faith of believers in Christ, even to the destruction of their persons.

B. The Judgment-Hour Invitation

Whereas Revelation 12:17—13:18 describes Satan's final assault on God's people in "the time of the end," Revelation 14 describes God's countermoves to bring the moral conflict to an end. Two major actions on God's part occur during this period: (1) the proclaiming of Heaven's last worldwide warning and invitation to accept the gospel (Rev. 14:6-13); and (2) the first of three phases of the final judgment (verses 6, 7; Dan. 7:9, 10, 13, 14).

1. Three Angels' Messages (Rev. 14:6-13)

These "angels" fly in the era designated as "the time of the end," because their ministry takes place prior to the second coming of Christ (Rev. 14:14). Since only human beings are commissioned to proclaim the gospel (Matt. 28:18-20), we may regard them as symbols of Christians moving throughout the world to share the good news of salvation. The first proclaims the "eternal gospel," evidence in itself that he will continue to "fly" until the close of human probation. Since the other two angels, in their turn, join the first, the three pronouncements eventually form one final message: the eternal gospel with certain end-time emphases—the final judgment (Rev. 14:6, 7), the fall of "Babylon" (verse 8), and a severe warning against receiving "the mark of the beast" (verses 9-13). The three form a judgment-hour warning and God's last invitation of grace to humanity. (See Remnant/Three

Angels V. B-D.)

2. Final Judgment (Rev. 14:7)

In connection with the "eternal gospel," the first message announces the onset of the final judgment and appeals to earth's inhabitants to worship the Creator, the true God. "Fear God and give him glory, for the hour of his judgment has come; and worship him who made heaven and earth, the sea and the fountains of waters" (verse 7). Normally such an announcement would indicate the end of human probation and the cessation of gospel activity. But the prophecy represents the gospel spreading worldwide as the final judgment begins and continues in session. The paradox is only apparent. The first angel's announcement refers to the commencement of the final judgment in heaven during "the time of the end" prior to Christ's second coming, according to Daniel (Dan. 7:9, 10, 13, 14, 26, 27; see Judgment III. B. 1).

It is evident from Daniel's vision that it deals with the final judgment, because at its close "one like a son of man" (Christ) is awarded the eternal kingdom (verses 13, 14). Since this judgment takes place in heaven in the presence of the angels (verses 9, 10), it may be correctly described as a pre-Advent phase of the final judgment. When Christ returns the second time, He comes in the glory and majesty of His kingdom as "King of kings and Lord of lords" (Rev. 19:16). It may be inferred that Daniel's scene of the judgment is its initial phase that clears God of Satan's wrongful charges and condemns the fallen angel as an archrebel, for at Christ's return Satan is "arrested" and imprisoned in this chaotic earth until sentenced and destroyed at the close of the millennium (Rev. 20:1-3, 10). God's genuine followers are also attested in this phase of judgment (Dan. 7:22) and receive their reward in the eternal kingdom at Christ's return (verses 18, 27).

Christ's appointment "by God to be the judge of . . . the dead" as well as "of the living" (Acts 10:42) enables heaven to warn the *living* of their impending judgment (while offering them the gospel) and yet to commence and carry on the final judgment of the generations of the dead recorded in the book of life (cf. Ex. 32:32; Rev. 3:5). Thus, in "the time of the end," when the three angels' messages are going worldwide to every people group on earth and the pre-Advent phase of the final judgment is in session, Satan launches his last attack on the church (Rev. 12:17).

C. The Central Issues

God's followers, who choose to be loyal to Him during Satan's final clash, are symbolized in Revelation by the number 144,000 (Rev. 14:1-5). Actually, they are an innumerable population from all nations of earth (Rev. 7:9-17). These end-time believers are God's spiritual Israel (Rev. 14:1; James 1:1; 2:1; cf. Gal. 6:14-16) upon whom He will place His seal of ultimate approval and protection (Rev. 7:1-8; cf. 2 Tim. 2:19). They successfully resist Satan's attempts to turn them from their obedience to God's commandments and from their wholehearted worship of the Creator.

1. Obedience: The Ten Commandments

The believers facing Satan's onslaught are characterized as observers of the Ten Commandments. "Then the dragon was angry with the woman, and went to make war on the rest of her offspring, on those who keep the commandments of God" (Rev. 12:17). "Here is a call for the endurance of the saints, those who keep the commandments of God and the faith of Jesus" (Rev. 14:12).

Since the appeal of the first angel's message is to "fear God and give him glory" and to acknowledge Him as the Creator "who made heaven and earth, the sea and the fountains of water," it seems clear that their obedience to the Decalogue includes the observance of the seventh-day Sabbath, its fourth precept. The Sabbath is the Creator's own designed memorial of His creative power (Gen. 2:2, 3), and He commands its observance (Ex. 20:8-11).

But those whom God seals in the final crisis (Rev. 7:1-8) will not render mere mechanical obedience. They are described as having "[Christ's] name and his father's name written on their foreheads" (Rev. 14:1). In biblical usage, God's name stands for His character (Ex. 34:5-7). In covenant with God—with His law written in their hearts (Heb. 8:10)—these end-time believers reflect the character traits of their Creator and Redeemer as they render steadfast obedience.

2. Worship: God or Satan?

As at its beginning, so in this last conflict, the war between God and Satan is a religious war. Now the second beast commands earth's inhabitants to "worship the first beast" (Rev. 13:12); and "the image of the beast" causes mankind to "worship" itself under penalties of boycott and death, enforcing the first beast's mark and its name—its characteristics (verses 15-17).

The final crisis erupts when Satan (working through the two beast powers) demands worship and allegiance due only the Creator. God anticipates the crisis. Through the first and third angels' messages He announces both an invitation and a severe warning to the inhabitants of earth.

First angel: "Fear God and give him glory, for the hour of his judgment has come; and *worship* him who made heaven and earth, the sea and the fountains of water" (Rev. 14:7).

Third angel: "If any one *worships* the beast and its image, and receives a mark on his forehead or on his hand, he also shall drink the wine of God's wrath, poured unmixed into the cup of his anger, and he shall be tormented with fire and sulphur in the presence of the holy angels and in the presence of the Lamb" (verses 9, 10).

Since the messages extend worldwide (verse 6), the prophecy foresees a worldwide conflict. The last living generation of humanity will be required to choose between worshipful obedience to the "beast and its image" or worshipful obedience to God, the Creator. As decisions are made, the *living*—in a very real sense—decide their own destiny. We may infer that the pre-Advent judgment session moves to examine their lives and decisions. Human probation closes, and the solemn words are spoken: "Let the evildoer still do evil, and the filthy still be filthy, and the righteous still do right, and the holy still be holy," to which Christ adds His promise: "Behold, I am coming soon, bringing my recompense, to repay every one for what he has done" (Rev. 22:11, 12).

D. The Defeat and Destruction of Satan

Revelation depicts the return of Christ under two different symbols: (1) as a heavenly farmer who comes to reap the harvest of His redeemed people, alluding also to the reaping and destruction of the impenitent (Rev. 14:14-20); and (2) as a heavenly warrior advancing with His forces to conquer His enemies. The latter figuratively portrays God's ultimate victory over Satan in the moral controversy (Rev. 19:11-21).

1. Satan Imprisoned

Seated on a white horse and followed by "the armies of heaven," Christ, as "King of kings and Lord of lords," is represented as engaging in battle with the religious and political confederation which has been fighting against Him in the person of His people near the close of the time of the end (verse 19). "And the beast was captured, and with it the false prophet who in its presence had worked the signs by which he deceived those who had received the mark of the beast and those who worshiped its image [a different symbol for the two-horned beast, Rev. 13:11-17]" (verse 20). Proleptically, these entities are destroyed in the final fires (verse 20).

Satan himself is arrested and imprisoned for a thousand years, a period commonly referred to as the millennium. (See Millennium I. C.)

"Then I saw an angel coming down from heaven, holding in his hand the key of the bottomless pit and a great chain. And he seized the dragon, that ancient serpent, who is the Devil and Satan, and bound him for a thousand years, and threw him into the pit, and shut it and sealed it over him, that he should deceive the nations no more, till the thousand years were ended. After that he must be loosed for a little while" (Rev. 20:1-3).

2. The Millennium

As He promised, Christ takes His followers—the redeemed of all the ages—to heaven (John 14:1-3; Matt. 24:30, 31; 1 Thess. 4:16-18). There they reign with Him (Rev. 20:6). During their reign the redeemed participate in the second phase of the final judgment (verse 4). The apostle Paul also mentions this judgment, which, like the initial pre-Advent phase, takes place in heaven. "Do you not know that the saints will judge the world? . . . Do you not know that we are to judge angels?" (1 Cor. 6:2, 3). We may infer that such a "review" of lost humans and angels will allow the redeemed to understand as fully as possible the nature of sin and Satan and the response that a just and loving God made to the challenge. (See Judgment III. B. 2.)

At the close of the millennium the prophet sees the Holy City, the New Jerusalem, descend from heaven to earth, together with Christ and the redeemed (Rev. 21:2, 10). Christ resurrects the wicked dead (John 5:28, 29; Rev. 20:5). The presence of all humanity (the redeemed within the city; the lost without) immediately looses Satan. Still true to his nature, he deceives and persuades the armies of the lost to attack the Holy City. This constitutes Satan's dying struggle, as it were, to fight against God and His people (Rev. 20:7-10).

3. Final Judgment: Executive Phase

As the attack is about to begin, God intervenes. All humanity is summoned to the judgment bar of God (verses 11-15). The dead, who stand (after their resurrection) before the throne in this passage (verse 12), are the great hosts of the lost who "did not come to life until the thousand years were ended" (verse 5). Although the executive phase of the final judgment involves the total human family (righteous and unrighteous) as well as the fallen angels (cf. Matt. 25:32-46), in some respects it centers on the lost. We may infer that as they stand before the bar of judgment, they are caused to understand the issues in the great rebellion as well as why they chose to reject God's grace and salvation so freely offered during probationary time.

In the executive aspect of the final judgment (which takes place on earth) the sentences determined in the first two phases are pronounced and carried out. The impenitent—angelic and human—are punished and destroyed. They come under the sentence of "the second death" from which there is no resurrection (Rev. 20:10, 14, 15). Jesus summed up the finality of the executive judgment as it pertains to the saved, lost, and Satan and his angels: "Then the King will say to those at his right hand, 'Come, O blessed of my Father, inherit the kingdom prepared for you from the foundation of the world.' . . . Then he will say to those at his left hand, 'Depart from me, you cursed, into the eternal fire prepared for the devil and his angels.' . . . And they will go away into eternal punishment, but the righteous into eternal life" (Matt. 25:34-46).

In the NT the English translations "forever," "for ever and ever," and "everlasting/eternal" are renderings for the Greek noun *aiōn* and its adjective *aiōnios* respectively (see Rev. 14:11; 20:10; Matt. 25:41, 46). Their basic idea is one of *duration,* a period of uninterrupted time. The *length* of time may or may not be endless, but derives from the *nature* of the object or person described by these terms. God "alone" has inherent immortality (1 Tim. 6:15, 16), and He will bestow immortality upon the redeemed at Christ's return (1 Cor. 15:51-57). Thus, when Scripture speaks of the eternal God or of the redeemed entering into eternal life, it speaks of "endlessness," because God's nature is immortal, and He has bestowed that condition upon the redeemed. On the other hand neither Satan and his angels nor wicked human beings are immortal by nature. Both classes will be punished according to their sinful deeds and will then perish. The "wages of sin is death" (Rom. 6:23), the "second death" (Rev. 20:14, 15; 21:8).

In the execution of the fallen angels and impenitent humanity the earth itself is purified by the fires (2 Peter 3:11-13). Created anew, it is awarded to the redeemed as their eternal home (Rev. 21:1, 5; Matt. 5:5). In this restoration of Paradise God chooses to dwell with the saved (Rev. 21:3, 4; see New Earth II).

At last, the war, which began in heaven (Rev. 12:7), is ended. The great moral controversy, which troubled the universe for so long, is finished. The breach in the relationship between heaven and earth is healed. The divine purpose, "to unite all things in him [Christ], things in heaven and things on earth," now is accomplished (Eph. 1:10).

VI. Some Theological Implications

A. Moral Harmony Secured

The biblical record of the cosmic controversy indicates that God endowed the various orders of intelligent beings with the freedom of choice. They could choose to give God their allegiance or they could rebel. Consequently, the moral harmony of the divine government always lay at risk.

The Creator did not introduce rebellion, but He permitted it to arise. In spite of the enormous tide of suffering and pain that transgression of the divine will has brought, both to humanity and to God, the long centuries of the conflict ultimately will bring about the moral security of the universe. Out of this terrible experience all orders of intelligent beings—loyal and fallen—will freely reject the principles of sin and acknowledge the rightness and goodness of the Creator. At the executive judgment, God says, "every knee shall bow to me, and every tongue shall give praise to God" (Rom. 14:11).

B. Worldview

An understanding of the cosmic conflict provides the Christian with a worldview of history that is both rational and coherent. Behind the rise and fall of nations and the play and counterplay of human interests lies the unseen struggle between the Godhead, together with the hosts of loyal angels, and Satan with his host of fallen angels— a struggle that directly impacts all human activity (cf. Dan. 10:1-3, 12, 13). Although Satan is described as "the god of this world" (2 Cor. 4:4), the Creator "does according to his will . . . among the inhabitants of the earth" (Dan. 4:35) to carry out His "eternal purpose" (Eph. 3:11).

Unlike the ancient concept of time as circular and repetitious, the scriptural worldview of time is linear. The divine hand, although countered by satanic activity, nevertheless is deliberately moving human history to its consummation: the second coming of Christ, the eradication of Satan and all the forces of evil, and the establishment of God's eternal kingdom.

Such a worldview brings hope to the believer. While solutions to cure the multiple woes of society can only ameliorate life on a planet dominated by sin, the Christian— as part of the web of human society—seeks to function as "salt" and "light" in the community, as Christ did (Matt. 5:13, 14; Acts 10:38).

C. Human Suffering

The cosmic controversy sheds light on the problem of human suffering. It provides the biblical basis for reconciling the Christian belief of a good God (as revealed in Jesus Christ) with an evil world. In the first place, it becomes evident that God is not responsible for evil. The Creator brought into existence sinless angels and human beings, some of whom—exercising their free will—chose to rebel against a good and just Creator. As a result they have filled the earth with the terrible consequences of transgression.

Because of the nature of Satan's challenges and the fall of Adam and Eve, the righteous as well as the unrighteous suffer the effects of sin's reign. Both classes experience disease, crime, war, natural disasters, etc. Both die. However, the believer is the recipient of God's saving grace and sustaining promises (Eph. 2:8-10; 1 Cor. 10:13; 1 Peter 4:12, 13) and is steadied by the "blessed hope" of Christ's return (Titus 2:13) and the end of the controversy. The blame for human suffering does not lie at the throne of God; rather, it issues from the rebellion and activity of Satan and his angels and depraved humanity.

D. Character of God

The course of the controversy has disclosed depths of the divine character heretofore unknown to any of the created orders. Neither angel nor man can grasp the enormity of the cost of the self-sacrificing Godhead to devise and carry out the plan of salvation. The incarnation of God the Son and His atoning death testify to the lavishness of divine grace and love (2 Tim. 1:9; John 3:16, 17). The conflict has also revealed God's attributes of justice and fairness. Sin is atoned, not winked at (Rom. 3:23-26). The plan completed fully justifies the ascriptions made to God: "Great and wonderful are thy deeds, O Lord God the Almighty! Just and true are thy ways, O King of the ages!" (Rev. 15:3).

E. Believer Preparedness

Revelation's description of Satan's attack against the church in the last phase of the cosmic controversy (Rev. 12:17–14:20) is intended to awaken believers to their peril. The parable of the 10 virgins portrays a sleeping church, only partially prepared for the Lord's return (Matt. 25:1-13). However, just as God has a special message for the world in the "time of the end"—the three angels' messages (Rev. 14:6-14)—so also He has a special message for His followers, symbolized by "the church in Laodicea" (Rev. 3:14-22).

"You are lukewarm" and nauseous to Me, Christ declares, because you say "I am rich, . . . and I need nothing," but in reality "you are . . . poor, blind, and naked" (verses 16, 17). Christ offers to rectify their abject condition. He stands at the door of their hearts, offering to enter and provide them with gold, clothing, and eyesalve (verses 18-20). Under this symbolism Christ is calling the last stage of His church (as individuals) to surrender fully to His Lordship. When Christ rules in the life, the believer is enriched by His faith and love (cf. Gal. 5:6), clothed and accepted in His righteousness (Gal. 3:27), and given accurate insight into His will by the healing salve of the Holy Spirit (John 16:13).

Believers who heed the Laodicean message to "be zealous and repent" (Rev. 3:19) arouse from their stupor. In the strength of the Lord they repent and put away their known sins, and they resist the temptations that struggle for the mastery. They join the ranks of those proclaiming the three angels' messages. Holding fast to God by a strong faith, they stand loyal and true to God under immense pressures of the worldwide enforcement of the mark and worship of the beast and its image, even at the cost of life itself.

The prophetic vignette assures an end-time, victorious people of God in whose "mouth no lie . . . [is] found, for they are spotless" (Rev. 14:5), having "washed their robes and made them white in the blood of the Lamb"

(Rev. 7:14). They stand before God, as conquerors over Satan's most vicious onslaught, to sing the triumphant song of their experience (Rev. 14:2, 3; 15:2-4).

VII. Historical Overview

Although the existence of Satan and the forces of evil were understood by the earliest Christians, in the succeeding centuries Christian understanding of the moral conflict between God and Satan became less clear, being impacted by other beliefs. A few of these perspectives as they appeared across the centuries are highlighted below.

A. Ante-Nicene and Post-Nicene Fathers

1. Origen (185-254)

Considered the greatest of the early Greek church theologians, Origen, in an early work, summarized the general Christian belief about Satan: "Regarding the devil and his angels, and the opposing influences, the teaching of the Church has laid down that these beings exist indeed; but what they are, or how they exist, it has not explained with sufficient clearness. This opinion, however, is held by most, that the devil was an angel, and that, having become an apostate, he induced as many of the angels as possible to fall away with himself, and these up to the present time are called his angels" (*De principiis*, preface, 6 [ANF 4:239, 240]).

Origen is sometimes designated as "the first Christian universalist." He speculated that "the goodness of God, through His Christ, may recall all His creatures to one end, even His enemies being conquered and subdued." By the expression "subdued" he meant "subjection" in the sense of belonging to Christ. "For the name 'subjection,' by which we are subject to Christ, indicates that the salvation which proceeds from Him belongs to His subjects" (*ibid.* 1. 6. 1-3 [ANF 4:260]).

Carried to its logical conclusion, Origen's restoration theory included Satan and his demons. Although in a few later statements Origen appears to deny salvation to Satan, Augustine, and others, even in modern times, charge him with this belief (Schaff; Gonzáles).

2. Augustine of Hippo (354-430)

Near the close of his life, Augustine—the chief of the Latin Fathers—developed an extensive reply to the pagans who blamed the Christian religion and the resulting abolition of pagan worship for the sack of Rome by the barbarian Goths (A.D. 410). Over a period of 13 years (413-426) he wrote a work consisting of 22 books, known in English as "The City of God" (*De Civitate Dei*). The first 10 books Augustine dedicated to refuting the charges, but in the last 12 he developed a philosophy of history, the first of its kind by a Christian.

Employing the figures of two cities—the heavenly (composed of God, His angels, and people) and the earthly (composed of the devil, his angels, and wicked humanity), Augustine traced their origin, progress—commingled and entangled as they are in this present world—and ultimate destinies (*City of God* 11. 1 [NPNF-1 2:205]). The tracking is done through biblical history from the fall of the angels to the final punishment of the lost and the bliss of the saved as Augustine interprets the several events and persons selected. The experience of Cain and Abel illustrates "the hatred that subsists between the two cities, that of God and that of men" (*ibid.* 15. 5 [NPNF-1 2:287]).

The origin, or "foundations," of the two cities issued from "the difference that arose among the angels," leading to a separation of the good and bad (*ibid.* 11. 1 [NPNF-1 2:205]). Although the devil and his angels were expelled from heaven, their fall was not because

God created them wicked by nature. "He caused the devil (good by God's creation, wicked by his own will) to be cast down from his high position" (*ibid.* 11. 17 [NPNF-1 2:214]). Augustine held that God foreknew the fall of Satan and humanity, arguing, however, that "God would never have created any, I do not say angel, but even man, whose future wickedness He foreknew, unless He had equally known to what uses in behalf of the good He could turn him, thus embellishing the course of the ages, as it were, an exquisite poem set off with antitheses" (*ibid.* 11. 18 [NPNF-1 2:215]).

Augustine interpreted the 1,000 years and the binding of Satan (Rev. 20:1-3) as symbolic of the Christian Era. He says the angel "bridled and restrained his power" (*ibid.* 20. 7 [NPNF-1 2:427]). "Now the devil was thus bound not only when the Church began . . . , but is now and shall be bound till the end of the world" (*ibid.* 20. 8 [NPNF-1 2:428]). He argued that the binding prevents the devil from exercising "his whole power." Otherwise, during this long period "many persons, such as God would not wish to expose to such temptation, would have their faith overthrown, or would be prevented from believing; and that this might not happen, he is bound" (*ibid.*).

Moreover, the church "even now is the kingdom of Christ. . . . Even now His saints reign with Him." The seats and judges mentioned in the vision (Rev. 20:4) are interpreted to mean "the seats of the rulers and to the rulers themselves by whom the church is now governed" (*ibid.* 20. 9 [NPNF-1 2:430]).

At the end of the world the devil will be loosed and will "rage with the whole force of himself and his angels for three years and six months" (*ibid.* 20. 8 [NPNF-1 2:428]). Their attack on "the camp of the saints and the beloved city" (verse 9) is interpreted as the last persecution of the worldwide church by all its enemies (*ibid.* 20. 11 [NPNF-1 2:432]).

"When the two cities, the one of God, the other of the devil, shall have reached their proper ends through Jesus Christ our Lord,

the Judge of the quick and dead" (*ibid.* 21. 1 [NPNF-1 2:452]), "the bodies of the damned, whether men or devils" will suffer the torments of an eternally burning lake of fire (*ibid.* 21. 10, 23 [NPNF-1 2:462, 469]). Thus, the earthly city meets its ultimate destiny.

B. Reformation and Post-Reformation Eras

1. John Calvin (1509-1564)

As a second-generation Reformer, John Calvin is noted for his systematizing of the doctrines of the reformed faith. Calvin denied the humanist notion that the devils were nothing more than "bad affections or perturbations suggested by our carnal nature." He asserted their reality as personal beings, their doom to eternal punishment being one evidence of their existence (*Institutes* 1. 14. 19). However, he did not think it useful to inquire into the nature of Satan's fall. "Some murmur because the Scripture does not . . . give a distinct and regular exposition of Satan's fall, its cause, mode, date and nature. But as these things are of no consequence to us, it was better, if not entirely to pass them in silence, at least only to touch lightly upon them" (*ibid.* 1. 14. 16).

Satan's present malicious nature was "not from creation, but from depravation." At one time the devils "were the angels of God, but by revolting they both ruined themselves and became the instruments of perdition to others" (*ibid.*).

Calvin recognized a cosmic conflict between Satan and God, but argued that God restricts Satan, and at times He forces him to do His will.

"With regard to the strife and war which Satan is said to wage with God, it must be understood with this qualification, that Satan cannot possibly do anything against the will and consent of God. . . . Moreover, though we say that Satan resists God, and does work at variance with His works, we at the same time maintain that this contrariety and opposition depend on the permission of God. . . . But as God holds him bound and fettered by the curb of his power, he executes those things only for which permission has been given him, and thus, however unwilling, obeys his Creator, being forced, whenever he is required, to do Him service" (*ibid.* 1. 14. 17).

Guided by his predestinarian views, Calvin allowed that God employed Satan and the devils in "exercising believers," but denied they could be "vanquished." On the other hand, God "gives over to his [Satan's] sway the impious and unbelieving, whom he designs not to number among his flock" (*ibid.* 1. 14. 18).

2. John Milton (1608-1674)

In 1667, some 100 years after Calvin's death, John Milton, the English poet, published an extended poem, *Paradise Lost,* enlarging it a few years later. The poem, a mixture of biblical data, human lore, and the poet's imagination, ascribes man's fall and loss of Paradise to Satan's deceptions. Milton phrases the origin and ongoing animosity of the devil in terms of a "war." The cause for his hatred is attributed to pride and ambition to place himself above his peers by making himself equal to God:

Th' infernal Serpent; he it was, whose guile
Stirr'd up with Envy and Revenge, deceiv'd
The Mother of Mankinde, what time his
   Pride
Had cast him out from Heav'n, with all his
   Host
Of Rebel Angels, by whose aid aspiring
To set himself in Glory above his Peers,
He trusted to have equal'd the most High,
If he oppos'd; and with ambitious aim
Against the Throne and Monarchy of God
Rais'd impious War in Heav'n and Battle
   proud
With vain attempt. Him the Almighty Power
Hurl'd headlong flaming from th'Ethereal
   Sky
With hideous ruin and combustion down
To bottomless perdition, there to dwell
In Adamantine Chains and penal Fire,

Who durst defy th'Omnipotent to Arms.
Nine times the Space that measures Day
   and Night
To mortal men, he with his horrid crew
Lay vanquisht, rolling in the fiery Gulfe
Confounded though immortal: But his doom
Reserv'd him to more wrath. (1. 34-54).

Milton follows the Bible's account only in part. His belief that Satan is immortal means the war will cease, but Satan's existence in torment is endless.

C. Modern Era

The discovery of the Dead Sea scrolls (1947) popularized the hypothesis that Jewish interest in Satan, as reflected in the OT and more so in the intertestamental literature (Apocrypha, Pseudepigrapha), developed from Persian dualism. It argues that the conflict between the good Ahura Mazda and the evil Angra Mainyu (Zoroastrianism) provides the underlying basis for Jewish understanding of a cosmic controversy between God and Satan. However, important differences exist, and the alleged parallels are questioned (LaSor 1202; Fuller 4:341).

The more common view among intellectuals and liberal scholars simply denies the existence of a personal devil and evil angels. One humanist approach presses the premise that "competing versions of Christianity" developed the notion of Satan from ancient combat myths. "More than any other factor, the struggle about heresy produced the story of Satan's original rebellion. . . . What was seen as Satan's opposition to Christ in the present was projected backward into the story of his origin." "If Satan had not already existed, the church would have had to invent him" (Forsyth 310, 311, 317). On the other hand, the well-known Christian apologist, C. S. Lewis, argued for the existence of Satan. "This Dark Power was created by God, and was good when he was created, and went wrong. Christianity agrees with Dualism that this universe is at war. But it does not think this is a war between independent powers. It thinks it is a civil war, a rebellion, and that we are living in part of the universe occupied by the rebel" (Lewis 50, 51).

In general, liberal NT scholars question the authenticity of various aspects of the recorded Gospels, especially Jesus' sayings and miracles. After applying the literary canons of the higher critical method, Joachim Jeremias, the respected German professor, concedes, "Thus even when strict critical standards have been applied to the miracle stories, a demonstrably historical nucleus remains" (Jeremias 92). In that accepted "nucleus" are the exorcisms of the devils performed by Jesus and His disciples, or "battles" with Satan, as he describes them. Commenting on Jesus' response to His disciples' success (Luke 10:18), he observes: "Thus the *logion* means 'I watched Satan cast headlong from heaven like lightning.' The casting of Satan out of the heavenly world presupposes an earlier battle in heaven, like that described in Revelation 12:7-9. Jesus' visionary cry of joy leaps over the interval of time before the final crisis and sees in the exorcisms performed by the disciples the dawn of the annihilation of Satan. This stage has already been reached: the evil spirits are powerless, Satan is being destroyed (Luke 10:18), paradise is opening up (verse 19), the names of the redeemed stand in the book of life (verse 20).

"There is no analogy to these statements in contemporary Judaism; neither the synagogue nor Qumran knows anything of a vanquishing of Satan that is already beginning in the present" (Jeremias 95).

Evangelical scholars hold to the reality of a personal devil and evil angels. Satan is understood to have been "a high angelic creature" who rebelled against the Creator. A distinction is made in the fallen angels: one class is free to "roam the heavenlies" and earth with Satan, while a second class is "incarcerated in Tartarus." Satan caused the moral fall of humankind. Although limited as a creature, he is permitted to carry out his evil activities. In time he will be removed from the heavenlies and earth and confined in "the abyss for a thousand years." At their close Satan will make one last attack against God, but will meet his final doom in the lake of fire (Rev. 20:1-10). "This will be the one place where evil angels and unsaved men will be kept and quarantined so that the rest of God's sinless universe will not be corrupted in the eternal state" (Unger 972, 973).

To provide a more adequate theodicy in view of the upsurge of evil and violence in contemporary society, a recent evangelical scholar has proposed a thoroughgoing "warfare worldview." Reacting against the classical-philosophical Christian approach to evil ("This view at the very least [holds] that all things, even bad things, have a specific divine purpose for their existence"), he calls attention to the cosmic conflict between the Creator and created beings (fallen angels and humankind) who have willed to rebel against Him and to cause what havoc they can in this world. "While the sovereign God can and will strive to bring some good out of the horrifying demonic event (Rom. 8:28), the evil event itself exists only because free beings who are against God have willed it" (Boyd 35, 291, 292).

D. Seventh-day Adventist Understanding

A worldview featuring a great cosmic controversy between God and Satan is a hallmark of Adventist thought. A brief survey of Bible and church history, written from this perspective, was first presented in 1858 to Sabbatarian Adventists by Ellen G. White under the title *Spiritual Gifts: The Great Controversy Between Christ and His Angels, and Satan and His Angels* (17-219). Beginning with the fall of Satan, the account sketched the conflict through Christ's first advent, the early church, the medieval ages, and the sixteenth-century Reformation. The last half focused on events foretold in Revelation, extending to the new earth. White's lifetime writing on this theme developed the well-known Conflict of the Ages Series, in which the first four volumes trace the outworkings of the controversy from Genesis to Revelation. The fifth volume, bearing the shortened title of the original work, *The Great Controversy Between Christ and Satan,* directs the reader to the conflict in the Christian dispensation so as "to shed a light on the fast-approaching struggle of the future" (GC xi).

In 1980 the General Conference of Seventh-day Adventists included in its revised and enlarged "Fundamental Beliefs," paragraph 8, entitled "The Great Controversy."

"All humanity is now involved in a great controversy between Christ and Satan regarding the character of God, His law, and His sovereignty over the universe. This conflict originated in heaven when a created being, endowed with freedom of choice, in self-exaltation became Satan, God's adversary, and led into rebellion a portion of the angels. He introduced the spirit of rebellion into this world when he led Adam and Eve into sin. This human sin resulted in the distortion of the image of God in humanity, the disordering of the created world, and its eventual devastation at the time of the worldwide flood. Observed by the whole creation, this world became the arena of the universal conflict, out of which the God of love will ultimately be vindicated. To assist His people in this controversy, Christ sends the Holy Spirit and the loyal angels to guide, protect, and sustain them in the way of salvation. (Rev. 12:4-9; Isa. 14:12-14; Eze. 28:12-18; Gen. 3; Rom. 1:19-32; 5:12-21; 8:19-22; Gen. 6-8; 2 Peter 3:6; 1 Cor. 4:9; Heb. 1:14.)"

Pioneer Sabbatarian Adventists and their later writers developed their understanding of the cosmic struggle largely from their studies of the Hebrew sanctuary system and the prophecies of Daniel and Revelation. Examining the sanctuary ritual, they agreed with Millerite Owen Crosier (Crosier 43) that the scapegoat (Heb. *Azāzel*), which figured in the Day of Atonement rites (Lev. 16:8, 20-22), was "a type of *Satan,*" and that the goat's banishment to the wilderness foreshadowed Satan's binding and imprisonment in the bottomless pit, according to Revelation 20. Thus, the Sabbathkeepers early grasped the truth that God would bring an *end* to the controversy. Satan, the originator of sin, would be punished for his rebellion and destroyed (4SP 266, 267; Gilbert 205).

The prophetic books of Daniel and Revelation gave the emerging church its broadest understanding of the movements involved in the cosmic controversy as it transpired on earth. "They looked upon prophecy as the inspired portrayal of the age-old conflict between good and evil; and, back of that, of the personalized war between Christ and Satan for the winning of the human race. Prophecy was to them the inerrant depiction of the great controversy between truth and error throughout the centuries" (PFOF 4:1054).

The 1887 edition of *The Bible-Reading Gazette* in book form contained 162 Bible readings in a question-and-Bible-answer format, two of which dealt with Satan and his work (Nos. 90, 138). The studies mixed both prophecy and general biblical statements and provided the basis for later editions of *Bible Readings for the Home Circle,* a denominational standard work, presenting the topic under the titles "Origin of Evil," "Origin, History, and Destiny of Satan," and "Satan's Warfare Against the Church" (see 1935, 1947 editions). Approaching the conflict more from the prophetic side was J. H. Waggoner's *From Eden to Eden.* In 1905 S. N. Haskell presented a study on Revelation 12 entitled "The Great Controversy" in his book *The Story of the Seer of Patmos* (209-223). Today the Scripture segment embracing Revelation 11:19 to 14:20 is still referred to as the "Great Controversy" vision, since it summarizes Satan's origin, war against Christ and His people in the Christian Era, and final attack (Maxwell 2:60, chart).

Satan's last "war" (Rev. 12:17) was of paramount interest to early Sabbathkeeping Adventists. Having participated in the sounding of the first and second angels' messages, they searched for the meaning of the third and last one (14:9-14). As Protestants, employing historicist principles of prophetic interpretation, the pioneers of the movement were familiar with the identifications of the little horn (Dan. 7:8, 21, 25) and the seven-headed leopardlike beast (Rev. 13:1-10) with the Roman Papacy, and its medieval era of "war on the saints" (1260 years) extending from A.D. 538 to 1798.

In the nineteenth century they identified the two-horned beast (13:11-17) as the United States of America, its lamblike horns—symbols of its power—as republicanism and Protestantism. The "mark of the beast" was identified as the papal change of the Sabbath to Sunday, and the "image of the beast" as a church-state union that would enforce Sunday observance under the penalty of boycott and death (see Remnant/Three Angels VI. H. 3; cf. PFOF 4:941-1173; Damsteegt 192-220).

From these studies Seventh-day Adventists concluded that Satan's last battle would center on the issue of obedience to God's moral law of the Ten Commandments, especially the Sabbath precept. Inasmuch as the message of the third angel (Rev. 14:9-13) bears a severe, worldwide warning against the reception of the mark, and against the worship of the beast and image, decisions in that ultimate conflict will be matters of life and death. With some refinements this view of the closing "battle" of the cosmic war became standard Adventist understanding.

In recent times Seventh-day Adventists have come to see Revelation's reference to the battle of Armageddon (Rev. 16:12-16) as an integral part of the theological unit of Revelation 12-19. Consequently, the vision is not limited to a great, end-time political clash of the nations, a belief that came to be entertained after the initial pioneer years—and shared by other Christian groups. Rather, "Armageddon is presented as the climactic battle of the great controversy between the forces of good and evil, which started in heaven and will end on earth (Rev. 12:7-9, 12). Armageddon is characterized

as 'the battle on the great day of God the Almighty' (Rev. 16:14). It coincides therefore with the universal judgment day of God" (LaRondelle 7:374).

The Adventist grasp of the broad aspects of the cosmic conflict has led to a keen awareness of that same conflict on the personal level.

If believers are to come under severe satanic deception and temptation, especially in the end-time, they need to evidence a commitment to Christ that controls everyday decisions and ways of living. In this setting the biblical theme of preparation for the coming kingdom takes on special significance. As Paul wrote to Titus: "For the grace of God has appeared for the salvation of all men, training us to renounce irreligion and worldly passions, and to live sober, upright, and godly lives in this world, awaiting our blessed hope, the appearing of the glory of our great God and Savior Jesus Christ" (Titus 2:11-13).

For this reason Christians should have a deep and genuine interest in practicing the ways of God in everyday life, for a life in harmony with Christian principles, both those explicit in the Scriptures and in God's laws of nature, is appropriate for people preparing to meet the returning Christ. On occasion, some have misapplied this penchant to emphasize Christian living to the diminishing of the central gospel truth of Christ's justifying power. Among Adventists, this tendency came to be theologically balanced in the revival of justification by faith begun with a meeting of the General Conference in 1888. At first resisted by many, including major leaders of the church, righteousness by faith is today a core element in a balanced biblical theology.

This practical emphasis on a way of life is an outgrowth of a deep-seated conviction that the Seventh-day Adventist movement functions in a role similar to that of Elijah and John the Baptist: to prepare a people for Christ's return (1SG 30, 31). John appealed to the people to repent of their sins and to "bear fruit" that befitted genuine repentance (Matt.

3:2, 8). In view of the tremendous pressures Satan will exert against end-time believers, when life itself will be at risk (Rev. 13), only those whose characters are in harmony with God will receive His seal of approval and stand true.

"What are you doing, brethren, in the great work of preparation? Those who are uniting with the world are receiving the worldly mold and preparing for the mark of the beast. Those who are distrustful of self, who are humbling themselves before God and purifying their souls by obeying the truth—these are receiving the heavenly mold and preparing for the seal of God in their foreheads. When the decree goes forth and the stamp is impressed, their character will remain pure and spotless for eternity" (5T 216).

Summary. Adventist understanding of the cosmic controversy has provided the church with a rational, integrated worldview. Every biblical teaching has its place and significance within its theological scope. The concept provides a "window" on the Sovereign Creator-God—His character, law, and government. It exposes the mystery of sin—what

it is, how it began, and why it continues. In response to humanity's plight, God's grace is seen as lavished on sinners through a plan of salvation—pictured in broad strokes in the Hebrew sanctuary types and foretold by prophecy; accomplished by the death, resurrection, and priestly mediation of the incarnate God the Son; and committed to the church for carrying to the world's populations through the enabling of the Holy Spirit.

The far-reaching consequences of the controversy require a final judgment that maintains the integrity of creaturely choice and at the same time results in a united decision that rejects Satan's assertions and accusations in favor of God, the true moral governor of the universe. The ruin wrought by the reign of sin makes necessary the return of Christ, the resurrection of the dead, the destruction of Satan—the fallen angels and impenitent human beings—and the re-creation of the earth as the eternal home of the redeemed. Thus, divine Providence overrules in the terrible loss of this cosmic controversy to secure the eternal harmony and happiness of the intelligent creation.

VIII. Ellen G. White Comments

A. An Appeal to Understand

"The Bible is its own expositor. . . . The student should learn to view the word as a whole, and to see the relation of its parts. He should gain a knowledge of its grand central theme, of God's original purpose for the world, of the rise of the great controversy, and of the work of redemption. He should understand the nature of the two principles that are contending for supremacy, and should learn to trace their working through the records of history and prophecy, to the great consummation. He should see how this controversy enters into every phase of human experience; how in every act of life he himself reveals the one or the other of the two

antagonistic motives; and how, whether he will or not, he is even now deciding upon which side of the controversy he will be found" (Ed 190).

B. The Controversy Foreseen

"The plan for our redemption was not an afterthought, a plan formulated after the fall of Adam. . . . From the beginning, God and Christ knew of the apostasy of Satan, and of the fall of man through the deceptive power of the apostate. God did not ordain that sin should exist, but He foresaw its existence, and made provision to meet the terrible emergency" (DA 22).

"The Godhead was stirred with pity for the race, and the Father, the Son, and the Holy

Spirit gave Themselves to the working out of the plan of redemption" (CH 222).

"In the councils of heaven, before the world was created, the Father and the Son covenanted together that if man proved disloyal to God, Christ, one with the Father, would take the place of the transgressor, and suffer the penalty of justice that must fall upon him" (MS 145, 1897; 6BC 1070).

C. The Origin of the Controversy

1. The Moral Law: Foundation of the Divine Government

"Everything in nature, from the mote in the sunbeam to the worlds on high, is under law. And upon obedience to these laws the order and harmony of the natural world depend. So there are great principles of righteousness to control the life of all intelligent beings, and upon conformity to these principles the well-being of the universe depends. Before this earth was called into being, God's law existed. Angels are governed by its principles, and in order for earth to be in harmony with heaven, man also must obey the divine statutes" (MB 48).

"The law of love being the foundation of the government of God, the happiness of all created beings depended upon their perfect accord with its great principles of righteousness. God desires from all His creatures the service of love—homage that springs from an intelligent appreciation of His character. He takes no pleasure in a forced allegiance, and to all He grants freedom of will, that they may render Him voluntary service" (GC 493).

2. Why Lucifer Not Destroyed at Onset of the Controversy

"Even when it was decided that he could no longer remain in heaven, Infinite Wisdom did not destroy Satan. Since the service of love can alone be acceptable to God, the allegiance of His creatures must rest upon a con-

viction of His justice and benevolence. The inhabitants of heaven and of other worlds, being unprepared to comprehend the nature or consequences of sin, could not then have seen the justice and mercy of God in the destruction of Satan. Had he been immediately blotted from existence, they would have served God from fear rather than from love. The influence of the deceiver would not have been fully destroyed, nor would the spirit of rebellion have been utterly eradicated. Evil must be permitted to come to maturity. For the good of the entire universe through ceaseless ages Satan must more fully develop his principles, that his charges against the divine government might be seen in their true light by all created beings, that the justice and mercy of God and the immutability of His law might forever be placed beyond all question" (GC 498, 499).

3. The Fall of Humanity: Pattern Similar to Satan's Fall

"There was nothing poisonous in the fruit itself, and the sin was not merely in yielding to appetite. It was distrust of God's goodness, disbelief of His Word, and rejection of His authority, that made our first parents transgressors, and that brought into the world a knowledge of evil" (Ed 25).

D. The Controversy on Earth—OT

1. Satan Usurps Control of Earth

"After tempting man to sin, Satan claimed the earth as his, and styled himself the prince of this world. Having conformed to his own nature the father and mother of our race, he thought to establish here his empire. He declared that men had chosen him as their sovereign. Through his control of men, he held dominion over the world" (DA 114, 115).

2. Obedience to Moral Law: Underlies Prosperity

"In the creation it was His [God's] purpose

that the earth be inhabited by beings whose existence should be a blessing to themselves and to one another, and an honor to their Creator."

"God has revealed in His law the principles that underlie all true prosperity both of nations and of individuals. "This is your wisdom and your understanding," Moses declared to the Israelites of the law of God. "It is not a vain thing for you; because it is your life" (Deut. 4:6; 32:47). The blessings thus assured to Israel are, on the same conditions and in the same degree, assured to every nation and every individual under the broad heavens" (Ed 174).

3. Satan Subverts Israelite Obedience

"Satan was determined to keep his hold on the land of Canaan, and when it was made the habitation of the children of Israel, and the law of God was made the law of the land, he hated Israel with a cruel and malignant hatred and plotted their destruction. Through the agency of evil spirits strange gods were introduced; and because of transgression, the chosen people were finally scattered from the Land of Promise" (PP 688, 689).

E. The Controversy
on Earth—NT

1. The Need to Reveal God's True Character to Humanity

"The earth was dark through misapprehension of God. That the gloomy shadows might be lightened, that the world might be brought back to God, Satan's deceptive power was to be broken. This could not be done by force. The exercise of force is contrary to the principles of God's government; He desires only the service of love; and love cannot be commanded; it cannot be won by force or authority. Only by love is love awakened. To know God is to love Him; His character must be manifested in contrast to the character of Satan. This work only one Being in all the universe could do. Only He who knew the height

and depth of the love of God could make it known. Upon the world's dark night the Sun of Righteousness must rise, 'with healing in his wings' (Mal. 4:2)" (DA 22).

2. Satan's True Character Also Disclosed at the Cross

"Satan . . . prompted the world's rejection of Christ. . . . The pent-up fires of envy and malice, hatred and revenge, burst forth on Calvary against the Son of God, while all heaven gazed upon the scene in silent horror" (GC 501).

"Not until the death of Christ was the character of Satan clearly revealed to the angels or to the unfallen worlds. The archapostate had so clothed himself with deception that even holy beings had not understood his principles. They had not clearly seen the nature of his rebellion" (DA 758).

"Satan saw that his disguise was torn away. His administration was laid open before the unfallen angels and before the heavenly universe. He had revealed himself as a murderer. By shedding the blood of the Son of God, he had uprooted himself from the sympathies of the heavenly beings. . . . The last link of sympathy between Satan and the heavenly world was broken" (ibid. 761).

3. The Cross: Divine Justice and Mercy Displayed

"God did not change His law, but He sacrificed Himself, in Christ, for man's redemption. 'God was in Christ, reconciling the world unto himself' (2 Cor. 5:19)" (ibid. 762).

"God had manifested His abhorrence of the principles of rebellion. All heaven saw His justice revealed, both in the condemnation of Satan and in the redemption of man. Lucifer had declared that if the law of God was changeless, and its penalty could not be remitted, every transgressor must be forever debarred from the Creator's favor. He had claimed that the sinful race were placed beyond redemption and were therefore his rightful prey. But the death of Christ was an argument in man's behalf that could not be overthrown. The penalty of the law fell upon Him who was equal with God, and man was free to accept the righteousness of Christ and by a life of penitence and humiliation to triumph, as the Son of God had triumphed, over the power of Satan. Thus God is just and yet the justifier of all who believe in Jesus" (GC 502, 503).

4. The Controversy in Microcosm

"Many look on this conflict between Christ and Satan as having no special bearing on their own life; and for them it has little interest. But within the domain of every human heart this controversy is repeated. Never does one leave the ranks of evil for the service of God without encountering the assaults of Satan. The enticements which Christ resisted were those that we find so difficult to withstand" (DA 116).

"Satan assailed Christ with his fiercest and most subtle temptations, but he was repulsed in every conflict. Those battles were fought in our behalf; those victories make it possible for us to conquer. Christ will give strength to all who seek it. No man without his own consent can be overcome by Satan. The tempter has no power to control the will or to force the soul to sin. He may distress, but he cannot contaminate. He can cause agony, but not defilement. The fact that Christ has conquered should inspire His followers with courage to fight manfully the battle against sin and Satan" (GC 510).

"The law requires righteousness—a righteous life, a perfect character; and this man has not to give. He cannot meet the claims of God's holy law. But Christ, coming to the earth as man, lived a holy life, and developed a perfect character. These He offers as a free gift to all who will receive them. His life stands for the life of men. Thus they have remission of sins that are past, through the forbearance of God. More than this, Christ imbues men with the attributes of God. He builds up the human character after the similitude of the divine character, a goodly fabric of spiritual strength and beauty. Thus the very righteousness of the law is fulfilled in the believer in Christ. God can 'be just, and the justifier of him which believeth in Jesus' (Rom. 3:26)" (DA 762).

F. The Controversy Completed

1. The Nature of the Last Conflict Over God's Law

"From the very beginning of the great controversy in heaven it has been Satan's purpose to overthrow the law of God. It was to accomplish this that he entered upon his rebellion against the Creator, and though he was cast out of heaven he has continued the same warfare upon the earth. To deceive men, and thus lead them to transgress God's law, is the object which he has steadfastly pursued. Whether this be accomplished by casting aside the law altogether, or by rejecting one of its precepts, the result will be ultimately the same. He that offends 'in one point,' manifests contempt for the whole law; his influence and example are on the side of transgression; he becomes 'guilty of all' (James 2:10).

"In seeking to cast contempt upon the divine statutes, Satan has perverted the doctrines of the Bible, and errors have thus become incorporated into the faith of thousands who profess to believe the Scriptures. The last great conflict between truth and error is but the final struggle of the long-standing controversy concerning the law of God. Upon this battle we are now entering—a battle between the laws of men and the precepts of Jehovah, between the religion of the Bible and the religion of fable and tradition" (GC 582).

2. The Sabbath: Test of Loyalty

"But not one is made to suffer the wrath of God until the truth has been brought home to his mind and conscience, and has been rejected. . . . Everyone is to have sufficient light to make his decision intelligently.

"The Sabbath will be the great test of loyalty, for it is the point of truth especially controverted. When the final test shall be brought to bear upon men, then the line of distinction will be drawn between those who serve God and those who serve Him not. While the observance of the false sabbath in compliance with the law of the state, contrary to the fourth commandment, will be an avowal of allegiance to a power that is in opposition to God, the keeping of the true Sabbath, in obedience to God's law, is an evidence of loyalty to the Creator. While one class, by accepting the sign of submission to earthly powers, receive the mark of the beast, the other choosing the token of allegiance to divine authority, receive the seal of God" (GC 605).

"Now is the time to prepare. The seal of God will never be placed upon the forehead of an impure man or woman. It will never be placed upon the forehead of the ambitious, world-loving man or woman. It will never be placed upon the forehead of men or women of false tongues or deceitful hearts. All who receive the seal must be without spot before God—candidates for heaven" (5T 216).

G. Some Theological Implications

1. Vindication of God's Character

"The plan of redemption had a yet broader and deeper purpose than the salvation of man. It was not for this alone that Christ came to the earth; it was not merely that the inhabitants of this little world might regard the law of God as it should be regarded; but it was to vindicate the character of God before the universe. To this result of His great sacrifice—its influence upon the intelligences of other worlds, as well as upon man—the Saviour looked forward when just before His crucifixion He said: 'Now is the judgment of this world: now shall the prince of this world be cast out. And I, if I be lifted up from the earth, will draw all men unto me' (John 12:31, 32). The act of Christ in dying for the salvation of man would not only make heaven accessible to men, but

before all the universe it would justify God and His Son in their dealing with the rebellion of Satan. It would establish the perpetuity of the law of God and would reveal the nature and the results of sin" (PP 68, 69).

2. The Rebellion: A Lesson to the Universe

"Satan's rebellion was to be a lesson to the universe through all coming ages, a perpetual testimony to the nature and terrible results of sin. The working out of Satan's rule, its effects upon both men and angels, would show what must be the fruit of setting aside the divine authority. It would testify that with the existence of God's government and His law is bound up the well-being of all the creatures He has made. Thus the history of this terrible experiment of rebellion was to be a perpetual safeguard to all holy intelligences, to prevent them from being deceived as to the nature of transgression, to save them from committing sin and suffering its punishments" (GC 499).

3. A Tested Creation: Forever Loyal

"The whole universe will have become witnesses to the nature and results of sin. And its utter extermination, which in the beginning would have brought fear to angels and dishonor to God, will now vindicate His love and establish His honor before the universe of beings who delight to do His will, and in whose heart is His law. Never will evil again be manifest. Says the word of God: 'Affliction shall not rise up the second time' (Nahum 1:9). The law of God, which Satan has reproached as the yoke of bondage, will be honored as the law of liberty. A tested and proved creation will never again be turned from allegiance to Him whose character has been fully manifested before them as fathomless love and infinite wisdom" (ibid. 504).

4. Divine Justice

"A life of rebellion against God has unfitted them [the wicked] for heaven. Its purity, holiness, and peace would be torture to them; the glory of God would be a consuming fire. They would long to flee from that holy place. They would welcome destruction, that they might be hidden from the face of Him who died to redeem them. The destiny of the wicked is fixed by their own choice. Their exclusion from heaven is voluntary with themselves, and just and merciful on the part of God" (*ibid.* 543).

IX. Literature

Augustine. *The City of God.* Trans. Marcus Dods. *Nicene and Post-Nicene Fathers of the Christian Church.* Ed. Philip Schaff. Grand Rapids: Eerdmans, 1979. Vol. 2.

Bauer, Walter. *A Greek-English Lexicon of the New Testament.* Trans. William F. Arndt and F. Wilbur Gingrich. Chicago: University of Chicago Press, 1957.

Bible-Reading Gazette, The. Battle Creek, Mich.: Review and Herald, 1887.

Bible Readings for the Home Circle. Washington, D.C.: Review and Herald, 1914, 1935, rev. 1947.

Boyd, Gregory A. *God at War: The Bible and Spiritual Conflict.* Downers Grove, Ill: InterVarsity Press, 1997.

Calvin, John. *Institutes of the Christian Religion.* Trans. Henry Beveridge. Grand Rapids: Eerdmans (one-vol. ed.), 1989, 1997.

Crosier, O.R.L. "The Law of Moses." *The Day-Star Extra,* Feb. 7, 1846.

Damsteegt, P. Gerard. *Foundations of the Seventh-day Adventist Message and Mission.* Berrien Springs, Mich.: Andrews University Press, 1977.

Daniells, Arthur G. *Christ Our Righteousness.* Washington, D.C.: Review and Herald, 1941.

Forsyth, Neil. *The Old Enemy: Satan and the Combat Myth.* Princeton, N.J.: Princeton University Press, 1987.

Froom, LeRoy E. *The Prophetic Faith of Our Fathers,* Washington, D.C.: Review and Herald, 1946-1954. 4 vols.

Fuller, Daniel P. "Satan." *International Standard Bible Encyclopedia,* fully rev. Geoffrey W. Bromiley, ed. Grand Rapids: Eerdmans, 1988. Vol. 4.

Gilbert, F. C. *Messiah in His Sanctuary.* Washington, D.C.: Review and Herald, 1937.

González, Justo L. *A History of Christian Thought.* Nashville/New York: Abingdon Press, 1970. Vol. 1.

Haskell, Stephen N. *The Story of the Seer of Patmos.* Washington, D.C.: Review and Herald, 1905.

Holbrook, Frank B. *The Atoning Priesthood of Jesus Christ.* Berrien Springs, Mich: Adventist Theological Society Publications, 1996.

Jeremias, Joachim. *New Testament Theology.* New York: Charles Scribner's Sons, 1971.

LaSor, William S. "Zoroastrianism." *Evangelical Dictionary of Theology.* Ed. Walter A. Elwell. Grand Rapids: Baker Book House, 1984.

LaRondelle, Hans K. "Armageddon: Sixth and Seventh Plagues." *Symposium on Revelation.* Daniel and Revelation Committee Series. Ed. Frank B. Holbrook. Silver Spring, Md.: Biblical Research Institute, 1992. 2: 373-390.

Lewis, C. S. *Mere Christianity.* New York: Macmillan, 1952.

Maxwell, C. Mervyn. *God Cares.* Boise, Idaho: Pacific Press, 1985. Vol. 2.

Milton, John. *Paradise Lost and Paradise Regained.* Ed. Christopher Ricks. The Signet Classic Poetry Series. New York: Penquin Books U.S.A., Inc., 1968.

Origen. *De Principiis. Ante-Nicene Fathers.* Ed. Alexander Roberts, James Donaldson. Grand Rapids: Eerdmans, 1979. Vol. 4.

Schaff, Philip. *History of the Christian Church.* Grand Rapids: Eerdmans, 1959 reprint. Vol. 2.

Seventh-day Adventists Believe . . . Washington, D.C.: Ministerial Association, General

Conference of Seventh-day Adventists, 1988.

Unger, Merrill F. "Satan." *Evangelical Dictionary of Theology.* Ed. Walter A. Elwell. Grand Rapids: Baker Book House, 1984.

Van Alstine, G. A. "Dispersion." *The International Standard Bible Encyclopedia,* fully rev. Ed. Geoffrey W. Bromiley. Grand Rapids: Eerdmans, 1979. Vol. 1.

Waggoner, J. H. *Eden to Eden.* Oakland, Calif.: Pacific Press, 1890.

General Index

GENERAL INDEX

Image of God, 206-208, 235, 236, 423, 424
  dignity and uniqueness of the human being, 235
  emotions, 424
  freedom of choice, 424
  in Creation, 752
  includes a physical likeness, 424
  man's function, 208
  moral maturity, 209
  moral nature, 208
  rational powers, 424
  resemblance, 208
  similitude between God and humanity, 113
Images of the gods, 424
Imago Dei, 677
Immanence
  God exists within the world, 117
  in the Incarnation, 118
  in the Sabbath, 118
  in the sanctuary, 118
Immortality, 225
  belongs to God alone, 318
  conditional, 229
  of the soul, 350, 351, 365
Immutability
  characteristic of God's being, 109
  conditional, 217
Impassibility, 109
Impurity
  associated with the sphere of death, 383
Incarnation, 161, 162
  deeper revelation of God's plural nature, 125
Incest, 696
Inerrancy
  of the Bible, 52
Infant baptism, 587, 589, 591
  accepted, 589
  Barth, Karl, 591
  Council of Carthage, 589
  Cullmann, Oscar, 591
  Jeremias, Joachim, 591
  marriage, 743
  Origen, 589
  Tertullian, 589
  World Council of Churches, 591
Infant mortality, 952
Inheritance, 953
Insemination
  artificial, 739, 741
Inspiration, 34
  activity of the Holy Spirit, 34
  definition, 33
  effects of, 40
  extent of, 39
  human and divine activity involved, 34
  human factor, 35, 40
  kinds of, 34
  modes of, 37-39
  primary locus, 39
Integrity, 712
Intemperance, 689
Interpretation of Scripture
  book-by-book approach, 79
  "grand central theme" perspective, 80
  of biblical apocalyptic, 791
  practical application of, 86
  specific guidelines for, 68
  task of the entire church, 59
  thematic/topical study, 79
  verse-by-verse exposition, 79
Interpretation of the apocalyptic
  futurism, 796
  historico-critical perspective, 796
  idealism, 797
  respect the cosmic range, 796
  see also Apocalyptic
Interpretations
  contemporary theological, 918
  ecclesiological, 865
  of modern prophecy, 808-810

Interpreter
  be spiritual, 67
  futurist and preterist, 805, 806
  pay close attention to grammar and syntax, 78
  pre-Reformation, 880
  under the control of the Bible, 67
Intimacy, 696
Investigative judgment, 397, 398
  according to Revelation, 399
  between 1798 and the Second Advent, 835
  Ellen White, 853
  in heaven, 402
  in the Most Holy Place, 844
  judge of, 840
  only professed people of God, 841
  place of the, 842
  purpose of the, 844
  timing of the, 833
  timing according to Revelation, 833
  timing according to Daniel, 834
  timing in the typology of the earthly sanctuary, 839
  see also Judgment
Irenaeus of Gaul, 519
  doctrine of God, 141
  free will, 259
  judgment, 849
  Lord's Supper, 600
  millennium, 937
  prophecy, 803
  resurrection, 366
  rule of faith, 88
  salvation, 300
  Second Coming, 915
  state of the dead, 338
  tithes, 663
  Word of God, 46, 47
Irving, Edward, 917
Israel
  a people or nation, 858
  a religious congregation, 858
  and the church, 543
  as remnant, 858, 860
  assembly that worships Yahweh, 859
  chosen and redeemed, 859
  role of, 858
  rejected, 544
Israelite sanctuary, 381
Islam, 960

Jeremias, Joachim, 1000
Jerome
  prophecy, 803
Jerusalem
  capital of the "new earth," 950
  New, 950-954
Jerusalem Council
  highest authority, 579
Jesus
  an example, 170
  and the Decalogue, 468-470
  appealed to the Scriptures, 36
  as God, 167
  as healer, 763-768
  as Lord, 290
  as perfect steward, 658
  came to heal, 171
  could have sinned, 165
  divine self-consciousness, 168
  fulfillment of the OT sacrificial system, 176
  glorified state of, 361
  God's perfect steward, 658
  His work and mission, 169
  human nature, 164
  kingdom, 169
  ministry of healing, 550
  mission and work, 169
  names and titles, 165
  on the Sabbath, 502

  only true priestly mediator, 390
  political Messiahship, 165
  Saviour, 169
  separated from the Father, 177
  sinless character, 164
  supreme example, 687
  testimony of, 632, 870, 878, 883, 888
  truly human, 163
  truly divine, truly human, 168
  two natures, 168
  see also Christ
Jesus seminar, 198
Jewish mission, 985
Jewelry, 707, 708
Jews
  Sabbathkeepers, 525
Joachim of Fiore, 804, 938
  of Floris and the millennium, 938
Johnsson, W. G., 708
Josephus, Flavius, 444
  Sabbath, 517
Jubilees
  book of, 404, 515
Judgment, 333, 396, 849
  according to works, 289, 828, 848, 850
  Adventist teachings on, 853
  allegorized, 849
  and grace, 819-828, 850
  and the believer, 848
  and the Christian life, 848
  cosmic qualities of, 842
  divine, 816-849
  double in Aquinas, 850
  during the millennium, 931, 932, 937
  eternal destiny of the lost, 935
  final, 464, 815, 992, 994
  for ancient Israel, 824
  for the Canaanites, 821
  for the nations, 823
  from the Age of the Enlightenment to the present, 850
  from the early church to the Age of the Enlightenment, 849
  in Daniel, 396-398, 834-840
  in evangelical theology, 853
  in liberal theology, 850-853
  in OT history, 819, 828
  investigative, 397-402, 833-844, 853
  judge in, 840
  Judgment and grace, 824
  language in the NT, 817
  language in the OT, 816
  last, 830-833
  leads to the cleansing of the universe, 400
  liberal theology, 850
  millennial, 846, 854
  nature of, 833-836
  of God, 896, 899-901
  of the "great white throne," 933
  postmillennial, 846, 847
  pre-Advent investigative, 833-835, 874
  punitive and remedial, 820
  purpose of, 844, 845
  retributive, 829, 830
  serves to vindicate God Himself, 400
  six judgments, 931
  specific language, 816
  starting point of, 897
  terminology of, 816-818
  timing of, 834
  used as incentive to morality, 850
  vindicates God's people, 400
Julian-Gregorian Calendar, 536
Justice of God, 258
Justification, 278-284
  a right relationship with God, 280
  acquittal, 280
  biblical meaning, 180
  by faith, 286
  divine forgiveness, 281

1016

GENERAL INDEX

eschatological life and new creation, 283
exchange of lordships, 283
forensic background, 278
grants assurance, 291
ground of, 284, 285
in the OT, 279
in the teaching of Jesus, 279
reality of righteousness, 284
reception of, 286
reckoning of righteousness, 280
terminology, 278
Justifying the ungodly, 281
Justin Martyr, 519
resurrection, 366

Kellogg, John Harvey, 9, 12, 17
Kenoticism, 194
Kingdom, 169
central theme, 170
consummates the teaching and ministry of
Jesus, 958
entry into the, 954
future, 901
holy, 951
of God, 542, 900
of heaven, 542
spiritual, 901
Knowledge
of God, 106, 170
of good and evil, 214
Koch, K., 829
Krima, 818
Krinō, 817
Krisis, 817
Kritēs, 819
Kubo, Sakae, 363, 919
Küng, Hans
church, 574

Lactantius
judgment, 849
millennium, 937
Lacunza, Manuel, 917
Ladd, G. E., 867
resurrection, 370
Lamparter, H., 844
Lampstand, 378
Language, analogical
reveals to us aspects of God's being, 113
Laodicea
Council of, 520
Laodicean message, 996
LaRondelle, Hans K., 941
Last Supper, see Lord's Supper
Latter rain, 631
Laver, 378
Law
and Christian obedience, 483
and grace, 482
and character of God, 460
and covenant, 479-482
and gospel, 484, 485, 490
and final judgment, 464
and freedom, 472-475
and the cross, 484, 485
ceremonial, 458, 468, 484, 824
civil, 86, 458
dietary, 824
difficult texts, 475-477
in contemporary Christianity, 488, 489
in Galatians, 474, 475, 490
in John's writings, 477-479
moral, 459, 462, 973
of retribution, 174
oral, 503
prior to Sinai, 465, 466
respect for, 701
standard by which God judges, 398
Lawlessness, 239
mystery of, 868

Laws
kinds in Bible, 458
of nature, 776
sacrificial/ceremonial, 86, 458, 468, 484, 824
Lawsuit
covenant, 825
Laying on of hands
imparting of the Spirit, 556
Legalism, 483
Leopardlike beast of Rev. 13, 990
Lessing, G. E., 50
Leviathan, 273
Leviathan and Rahab
symbols of God's enemies, 321
Levitical
code, 773
ministry of intercession and reconciliation,
187
Lewis, C. S., 999
Liberalism
Protestant, 572, 573
Liberation theology, 196, 197, 264
Life
and death, 316, 329
and health, 669
eternal, 189, 289, 353, 354, 953
human,703
Lamb's book of, 954
spiritual, 401
Life-breath
energizing power from God, 316
Lifestyle
and Scripture, 717
Christian, 678-681, 693, 716
Light
on the first day of Creation, 430
Linnemann, Eta, 92
Lisbon earthquake, 906
Literalism, 928
Literary analysis, 74
Literary criticism of Genesis, 447
Literary helpers
Ellen White used, 636
Literary structure, 76
Little flock, 864
Little horn power, 834, 835
does not contaminate the sanctuary, 395
Locke, John, 339, 572
Lombard, Peter, 743
Lord's day, 507
the Sabbath, 439
Lord's Supper, 601
a basis for unity, 557
Adventist practice of, 603, 604
early centuries, 600
emblems of, 599, 600
fellowship of, 562
foot washing, 558
frequency of celebration, 599
historical overview, 600
in early centuries, 600, 601
in 1 Corinthians, 596, 597
in the New Testament, 595
in the Synoptics, 595
Luther, 570
meaning and purpose, 606
medieval interpretations, 601
new "exodus," 557
ordained rite, 557
origin of, 595, 596
practice of, 599
Reformers' beliefs on, 602, 603
Second Coming, 557
Synoptic reports, 595, 596
the church, 569
theological significance of, 597-600
unleavened bread and unfermented wine,
599
who may participate, 599
Loud cry, 879

Love
and divine judgment, 851
as an imperative, 685
impact of on obedience, 684-686
key to perfection, 299
of Christ, 175
of God and, 175
supreme fruit of, 684
ultimate basis for repentance, 294
Lucifer, 974, 975, 977, 997, 998
and Calvin as prophetic interpreters, 805
expulsion from heaven, 977
on Second Advent, 916
misrepresenting God, 975
rejected divine authority, 975
wise and glorious angel, 974
see also Satan
Lücke, F., 807
Luther, Martin, 48, 145, 304
baptism, 590
Christ as priest, 403
church, 880
Creation, 445, 446
doctrine of Christ, 193
doctrine of God, 145
foot washing, 594
heaven, 962
immortality of the soul, 224
interpreting Scripture, 89
judgment, 850
Lord's Supper, 602
marriage, 744
nature of Christ, 193
on immortality, 339
on sin, 261, 487
original sin, 261
resurrection, 367
Sabbath, 522
salvation, 304
Scripture, 48, 61
Second Coming, 916
soul, 339
Lyell, Charles, 448
Lytron, 250

Maccabean revolt, 514
Magic and healing, 759
Maier, G., 95
Man
image of God, 207
moral maturity, 209
new, 292
Management and labor, 700
Maranatha Volunteers International, 16, 899
Marital
influences, 748
relations, 748
Mark of the beast, 878, 879
Marriage
a common faith, 746
aberrant practices in, 736
aberrations, 736
Adventist understandings, 745
and family, 690
as a symbol, 726
celebration of, 725
Christian, 690, 691, 725-734
early Christian, 743
guiding principles of, 728, 729
ideal, 735, 736
in the Bible, 725
instituted in Eden, 725
institution of, 725
Judaism, 742
Luther and Calvin on, 744
not in heaven, 966
principle of endogamy, 728
principle of exclusivity, 729
principle of interdependence, 728
principle of monogamy, 728

1017

principle of permanence, 728
principle of privacy, 729
principle of unity, 728
reasons for, 726, 727
regulated in Mosaic law, 725
sacredness of, 694
sanctity of, 748
source of personal fulfillment, 223
triangle, 690
Marriage and family
historical perspective, 742
in early Christianity, 743
Judaism, 742
Middle Ages, 743
Martyr, Justin
doctrine of God, 141
Lord's Supper, 600
millennium, 937
prophecy, 802
Second Coming, 915
soul not immortal, 224
Masoretic text, 68
Masturbation, 698
Maxwell, C. M., 835
Mede, Joseph
millennium, 939
Mediate imputation, 262
Medical work, 9, 17
Medieval church, 337
Melchizedec, 390
Memphite theology, 443
Mennonite teaching, 917
Messiah, 540
Jesus as, 165
political Messiahship, 165
Messianic
kingdom, 949
prophecy, 391
Methodius, 803
Mexia, Ramos, 225
Michael, 977, 978
divine personage, 978
the archangel, 977-979
Millenarianism
millennialism, 935
Millennial judgment, 854
judges of, 846
purpose of, 846
recipients of, 846
timing of, 846
Millennium, 928, 935, 994
Adventist understanding, 941
chiasm in the book of Revelation, 928
Christian Era, 938
conditions on earth, 932
cosmic struggle climaxed, 929, 934
during, 930
early church, 936
Ellen G. White, 942
events at the beginning of, 929
events at the end of the, 932
final judgment, 994
first resurrection, 929
historical overview, 935
in heaven, 930
in Jewish apocalyptic, 936
interpretative principles, 928
judgment, 930
patristic concepts of, 937
purposes of millennial reign, 935
roots in Jewish, 936
Satan bound, 929
theological significance of, 934
time to reflect, 934
Miller, William, 2-4
Christ's coming, 882
churches, 883
Daniel 8:14, 404
judgment, 884
millennium, 941

Millerite movement, 2, 3, 918
Milton, John, 339
Paradise Lost, 999
Satan, 999
Minneapolis General Conference session, 10
Miracle workers
counterfeit, 619
Miracles and healings, 612
Miracles, 438
among Seventh-day Adventists, 644
Mishnah
Sabbath, 515
Mission
message, 551
of the church, 549
ships, 10, 14
Mission and message, 441
Missionary Commission, 584
Missionary work, 9, 10, 12, 13
Modalism
Sabellian, 143
Models
normative, 687
Modesty, 707
Moltmann, Jürgen, 918
resurrection, 369
Monarchian theories, 142
Monarchianism
dynamic, 142
modalistic, 142
Monism, 212
Monotheism, 687
Montanism, 638
assessment of, 638
view on spiritual gifts, 638
Montanists opposed, 639
Moon
new, 950
Moore, A. L., 912
Moral law, 459, 462
central to the controversy, 973
will of the Creator, 973
Moral laws' purposes, 463, 464
Morris, Leon, 848
Mothers and wives, 731, 732
Mourning for the dead, 323
Music, 712

Natural
catastrophies, 254
death, 258
disaster, 27
laws, 762
theology, 29
Nature, 451, 776, 777
ambivalent picture of good and evil, 27
shows divine glory, wisdom, 27
Neoorthodoxy, 264, 573
Neoplatonism, 140, 224
Nepeš, 212
Nestorius, 191
New birth, 683
from the Holy Spirit, 135
New covenant, 388
actualization of the covenant at Sinai, 277
superior to the old, 388
with the church, 866
New earth, 439, 947
activities, 956
after the millennium, 955
characteristics of, 949-956
doctrine, impact on life, 958
fruitful kingdom, 952
future inheritance of God's people, 220
holy kingdom, 950
home of redeemed, 948, 949, 952
joyful kingdom, 951
Messianic kingdom, 949
new kingdom, 949
OT teaching on, 949

peaceable kingdom, 951
permanent kingdom, 952, 953
principal activity of the redeemed, 956
theological significance, 957
worshiping kingdom, 950
New Exodus, 388
New Jerusalem, 950
and millennium, 953, 954
measurement of the city, 955
religious center of the kingdom, 950
wall of the city, 955
New man
in God's likeness, 292
New moon festival, 950
New school theology, 263
Newman, A. H., 638
Newness of life
Christian's ethical walk, 295
Newton, Isaac, 446, 806
Nicea, Council of, 143, 190, 915
Nickelsburg, George W. E., 365
Niebuhr, H. R., 699, 962
original sin, 264
Night, 432
Nisdaq, 395
Noncanonical prophet, 628
Nonnatural conception, 741
Normative models, 687
Norms of behavior, 680
Nuclear family, 738
Nurturing, 691
Nutrition, 689

Oakes, Rachel, 4, 526
Obedience
primacy of faith, 277
October 22, 1844, 3
Offerings
daily burnt, 385
Oikonomia, 653
Old covenant
polemical context, 277
Omniscience, 118
God's embracing everything in His knowledge, 114
One hundred forty-four thousand, 870, 871, 992
Oneness
characteristic of the church, 562
Oral prophecy
examples, 623
illustrated by the sanctuary singers, 624
Oral law, 503
Ordinances
baptism, 558, 582
foot washing, 582
Lord's Supper, 558, 582
Organization
early church, 552
indispensable, 578
Origen
doctrine of God, 142
foot washing, 594
hermeneutics, 88
judgment, 849
prophecy, 803
resurrection, 367
salvation, 301
Satan, 997
Second Coming, 915
sinful condition, 259
souls, 259, 338
Origin of sin, 240
in Satan, 240
prehuman and angelic, 240
Original sin, 215, 256, 260, 265, 301
Ornamentation, 708
Outpouring of God's Spirit, 137, 631
Owen, John, 404
Owusu-Antwi, B., 838

overcoming, 216
penalty for, 257
pervasive reality, 214
predisposition to, 216
rebellion, 174, 975
"systemic" in our life, 216
transmission of, 256
universal extent of, 255
unpardonable, 282
Singleness, 698
Sinlessness of Christ, 164, 165
Situationism, 675
Smith, Uriah, 8
Smith, William "Strata," 448
Social
gospel, 264
justice, 701
responsibility, 701
Socrates, 341
Sodomy, 697
Sola scriptura, 60
by Scripture alone, 42
Luther, 48
Son of God, 166
Son of man, 899, 900
Sons of the prophets, 625
Soul, 362
in the Bible, 213
no existence without physical life, 317
Soul and spirit, 328
in Bible, 213, 219
Source criticism, 91
Sources
canonical writers used, 636
Ellen White's use of, 635
Spear, Samuel, 150
Special resurrection, 360
Special revelation, 30-32, 373
Species
fixity of, 421
Speech, 713
Spener, P. J., 882
Spinoza, B., 49, 447
Spirit(s), 362
gifts of, 552
of just men made perfect, 328
place in the hermeneutical spiral, 67
Spirit of prophecy, see Gift of prophecy,
Testimony of Jesus
Spiritism, 325, 326
Spiritual death, 258
Spiritual life
cleansed from sin, 401
Spiritual gifts, 637
ability to distinguish between spirits, 616
acts of mercy, 616
conditions must be met before the reception, 618
contributing, 616
counterfeit, 618-620
definition of terms, 613
exhorting, 616
faith, 616
for the completion of the mission, 617
general Christian view, 639
given by the Holy Spirit, 614
giving aid, 616
healing, 612, 616
historical overview, 637
identified, 614
in the NT, 611-613
in the OT, 613-620
knowledge, 612, 615
languages, 616
lists of, 615
originate with the Father and the Son, 614
permanence of, 617
prophecy, 611
Protestantism, 640
purpose of, 617

ranked, 615
Roman Catholicism, 639
service, 616
teaching, 616
to build up the church, 610
tongues, 616, 617
wisdom, 613, 615
working miracles, 616
see also Gifts
Spousal relationships, 732, 733
Špt, 816
Standards
health-preserving, 688
of apparel, 719
of personal responsibility, 706
of physical dimension, 688
of spiritual dimension, 686
of recreation, 719
social dimension, 690
Stars, 432
State of the dead, 322
Steward
a manager, 651
majordomo, 652
Stewardship, 718
Creation basis of, 653
Christian, 703-706
definition of, 651, 652
department organized, 667
development among Adventists, 665
example of biblical, 653-657
God as owner, 653
grateful and responsible use of all God's gifts, 651
in apostolic church, 659, 660
in the medieval system of giving, 664
in Christ's parables, 658
informs the whole of Christian teaching and doctrines, 651
limits of, 654, 655
of body, 668
of children, 670
of community, 671
of divine grace, 660
of health, 774, 778
of life, 661, 669, 703
of nature, 704
of time, 705
of talents, 662, 670
of the environment, 662, 667, 668
of wealth and property, 555, 556, 659, 704
origin in Creation, 653
Reformation, 664
rooted in the whole of Scripture, 652
Sabbath, stewardship of time, 655, 669
service to God the Creator, 441
source of mandate, 660
Storrs, George, 4, 225
Stott, John
resurrection, 369
Strand, K. A., 870
Stress, 689
Structuralism, 93
Submission of wives
introduced in the world by sin, 210
Subordinationism, 148, 149
Substitution, 177
Suffering
of Christ, 173
physical, 254
Sun, 431, 432
darkening of the, 906
Sunday worship, 517-519, 522
Supralapsarianism, 305
Symbolism, 85, 798, 799
Synchronic approach, 93
Systematic benevolence, 702

Ta hagia in Hebrews, 412-416
designates the sanctuary as a whole, 389

Tabernacle
earthly, 187
Tabernacles
Feast of, 950
Table, 378
Tabnît, 381
Talents and abilities, 670
Tāmîd
work of the priest in the holy place, 394
Tartarus, 978
Television and radio, 13, 14, 710
Ten Commandments, 459, 460, 466-468
adaptation of heaven's moral law, 973
from Creation to Moses, 973
Tertullian, 663
judgment, 849
millennium, 937
Montanism, 639
prophecy, 804
resurrection, 366
Sabbath, 520
salvation, 301
souls, 338
Testimony of Jesus, 870, 878, 883, 888
is the spirit of prophecy, 632
Testing the prophetic gift
by their fruits, 629
fulfilled predictions, 629
to the law and the testimony, 629
Texts, difficult, 903
Thanksgivings
reference to the Second Advent, 899
Theocracy, 864
Theater, 711, 719
Theology, 20
federal, 262
feminist, 197
liberation, 196, 197, 264
memphite, 443
natural, 29
new school, 263
of health, 755-757, 779
philosophical, 29
Theophany, 431, 433
Thiele, Edwin, 73, 74
This generation, 872-879, 904, 905
Third angel's message, 877, 886
Three Angels Broadcasting Network, 16
Three angels' messages, 991
a work of rebuilding and restoration, 399
Adventist understanding, 883-891
Babylon, fallen, 875, 876
death decree, 878
end-time setting, 873
God's end-time message, 872
judgment theme, 874, 875
heaven's final appeal, 872
last message of grace, 575
mark of the beast, 877-879
prior to the second coming of Christ, 991
symbolic of Christian religious movements, 872
worship of Creator, 874
wrath of God, 877
Time
precious gift of God, 670
value, 655
Time of the end
in Daniel, 871, 872
will begin at a fixed time, 871
Time periods, 795, 796
Tithes and offerings, 655, 656, 705
Abraham paid, 655
early church, 663
Israelites were commanded, 655
Tithing, 9
medieval, merged with civil taxes, 664
beginning among Adventists, 666
Jewish practices, 662, 663
not practiced in postapostolic church, 663

Selective Scriptural Index